Philosophy and Choice

SELECTED READINGS FROM AROUND THE WORLD

Philosophy and Choice

SELECTED READINGS FROM AROUND THE WORLD

Second Edition

Kit R. Christensen

BEMIDJI STATE UNIVERSITY

Boston   Burr Ridge, IL   Dubuque, IA   Madison, WI   New York
San Francisco   St. Louis   Bangkok   Bogotá   Caracas   Kuala Lumpur
Lisbon   London   Madrid   Mexico City   Milan   Montreal   New Delhi
Santiago   Seoul   Singapore   Sydney   Taipei   Toronto

McGraw-Hill Higher Education

*A Division of The **McGraw-Hill** Companies*

Library of Congress Cataloging-in-Publication Data

Philosophy and choice : selected readings from around the world /
[edited by] Kit R. Christensen.—2nd ed.
    p. cm.
  ISBN 0-7674-2027-6
  1. Philosophy.   I. Christensen, Kit Richard.
BD21 .P4685 2001
100—dc21
                                           2001030296

1 2 3 4 5 6 7 8 9 0 BAH/BAH 0 9 8 7 6 5 4 3 2 1

Sponsoring editor, Ken King; production editor, Linda Ward; manuscript editor, Judith Brown; design manager, Violeta Diaz; text designer, Laurie Anderson; cover designer, Roy Neuhaus; cover photo, © Mike Mazzaschi/Stock, Boston; manufacturing manager, Danielle Javier. The text was set in 10/12 Minion by Thompson Type and printed on 45# Chromatone Matte by Banta Book Group.

Acknowledgments and copyrights continue at the back of the book on pages 655–657, which constitute an extension of the copyright page.

www.mhhe.com

Preface

In this second edition of *Philosophy and Choice,* I have pursued the same goals that oriented the first edition: (1) to provide an anthology of readings that would offer a wide-ranging yet coherent first encounter with the *academic discipline* of philosophy, helping students see how it compares with other academic disciplines, where and why it emerged historically, and why it continues to be a worthwhile area of study; (2) to demonstrate the nature, application, limits, and personal relevance of philosophy as a distinctive type of *intellectual activity,* broadly construed as the reason-bound critical analysis of belief and its justifications; (3) to illuminate the reciprocal influence of philosophical discourse and the *social contexts* within which it has appeared. Implicit in these goals is the notion that studying philosophical issues in a systematic way gives students tools for living their own lives thoughtfully and responsibly. They can use the methods of philosophy to think through issues and then *choose* the ideas and beliefs that will become part of their worldviews.

For a long time it has been apparent to me that in order to fully achieve these goals, I also should not let students finish an "Introduction to Philosophy" course thinking that philosophy is exclusively a Western cultural phenomenon. In contrast to most introductory textbooks currently used in North America, then, this anthology includes historically diverse writings by men and women working within some of the Asian, African, Latin American, and native North American cultural traditions, as well as readings from classical and recent Western sources. My intention is to present students with a global, multicultural, and gender-sensitive picture of philosophical inquiry and the range of issues it can productively confront. More books with this emphasis have become available in recent years, which I take as evidence of healthy growth and a true enrichment of our discipline, and I am happy to offer this new edition as a contribution to the continuation of that trend. At the same time, as far as I can tell, this book is still distinguishable from these other textbooks because, first, to a greater extent I have used whole essays or book chapters as readings wherever feasible, rather than snippets from longer works. This way, students can better see how philosophical writing in different times and places has been done. Second, once again I place a much greater emphasis on value issues, as reflected not only in the questions before and after each reading but also in the choice of readings themselves and their organization. For example, in addition to the conventionally categorized writings on both moral and political philosophy, I include a section on "Knowledge and Responsibility" in Part II (Epistemology) and an extensive list of readings in aesthetics (Part VI). In emphasizing value issues, one of my goals, as already indicated, is to help students see the connection between topics in philosophy and the choices they have the opportunity—and the responsibility—to make in their own lives.

Although not all of the authors exhibit the same philosophical methodology, the wide variety of philosophical issues dealt with throughout the book still can be approached critically by the reader in all cases. For this reason I have stayed with the approach I used in the previous edition: I offer in the introduction a summary of the principles of good reasoning (logic) and guidelines for accurate interpretation and evaluation of attempts at persuasive writing. Also in the introduction is a section titled "Five Steps for Successful Reading," to further help students make the most of their encounter with these diverse readings. Before each reading, a short biographical introduction provides the social and historical context rather than simply summing up beforehand the main philosophical points. Also preceding each reading are "Questions for Critical Reading" and "Terms to Note," the latter feature comprising a nonexhaustive, variably sized (though always fairly short) list of terms used by that particular author. Terms likely to be unfamiliar to students are defined to make smoother the reading of that essay or excerpt. After each reading, "Discussion Questions" are aimed primarily at getting students to reflect on their own agreements and disagreements, or at least their similarity or difference of perspective, with the conclusions and standpoint of the author. Although I have not included a common feature of many introductory textbooks—a "selected bibliography" following each selection—I identify some general reference sources for each of the six parts of the book in the Instructor's Manual.

For the most part, changes in the second edition are a response to the many helpful comments and criticisms by philosophy instructors who reviewed and used the book in their classes. I have reorganized the table of contents to clarify the philosophical topics that each reading addresses. Also, I have included seven new readings that I think will enhance the diversity of perspectives for students to evaluate, and thus their opportunities to engage in informed choice of what to believe regarding significant life issues. In Part I, I added an essay by Tsenay Serequeberhan on African philosophy; in Part III, there are now selections from the ancient Indian Cārvāka school of materialism, Walter Stace on free will, and Martin Buber from *I and Thou*; in Part IV, I included an essay on Native American environmental ethics by Donald Grinde and Bruce Johansen; and in Part V, there is now an essay by Lucas Introna on the need for privacy in the computer age, and a piece by Noam Chomsky on the media and democracy.

Acknowledgments

A book project of this sort is always a group project, and once again I owe thanks to many people whose diligent efforts have been indispensable in the production of this edition of the anthology. Ken King, Lynn Rabin Bauer, Linda Ward, Judith Brown, Marty Granahan, and the other staff at Mayfield Publishing Company are all great to work with, and I am very appreciative of their professional expertise, editorial and otherwise, as well as their consistent enthusiasm, good spirits, and guidance. Again, I also want to thank all my philosophy colleagues everywhere who responded to the first edition with their many ideas on how to make this a better book; I found their advice crucial during the revision process: Theodore Haber, Edinboro University; Hugh C. Hunt, Kennesaw State University; William M. Hutchins, Appalachian State University; Brian D. Skelly, University of Hartford; and June M. Whitler, Eastern Kentucky University. Finally, I want to acknowledge all the students over the years who let me know directly or indirectly, intentionally or unintentionally, that an introductory philosophy textbook like this one was and still is needed. They are the ones who originally prompted this effort, and I am hopeful that this new edition will serve them well.

Contents

What Is Philosophy?

Bᴇᴄᴀᴜꜱᴇ ʏᴏᴜ ᴅᴇᴄɪᴅᴇᴅ to take a philosophy course, you probably have some general notions about what philosophy is. Coaches talk about a "philosophy" of defensive strategy; CEOs write about their "philosophies" of management; a friend may tell you she is being "philosophical" in the face of a personal setback. What is meant when we talk about philosophy as an academic discipline is something different, however. Philosophy in this more formal sense can be defined as *the systematic, reflective, critical, primarily reason-bound inquiry into the basic assumptions and guiding beliefs that people use to make sense of any dimension of their lives.* As a subject of study, philosophy has its own history and its own place in human intellectual life; it is distinguished both by its subject matter and its methodology.

Even if they rarely spell them out, most people have some grounding beliefs about what is most important to them, how they know what they think they know, what is real, and how they think we ought to treat one another. These concerns are also the stuff of rigorous analysis, speculation, and debate among philosophers. The subject matter of philosophy thus is distinctive because of its breadth, since it can be an inquiry into any of the basic assumptions and beliefs that people use to make sense of their experiences. Its boundaries are determined solely by the philosopher's own interests and curiosity.

What has counted as a worthwhile philosophical topic has changed over the centuries, however. Sometimes the changes have been due to changes in society, and sometimes they have been due to the development of alternative investigative techniques that are more productive in answering certain kinds of questions. For example, in the not-too-distant past, explanations of planetary motion, disease, and urban population growth were assumed to be within the purview of philosophical speculation. Today, these subjects are usually assigned to the separate academic disciplines of astronomy, medicine, and sociology, respectively. However, as you will see, the boundaries of philosophy in relation to other disciplines still can be quite permeable. Some of the readings in this text address the similarities and differences between philosophy and what are now called the sciences, and some of the authors themselves were trained as scientists rather than as philosophers.

The Methods of Philosophy

Although the range of issues investigated by philosophers is virtually unlimited, philosophical inquiry—or the critical analysis of beliefs and their justifications—is not meaningfully practiced in just any old way. To critically analyze a belief means to evaluate its plausibility and reasonableness and thus determine whether the reasons offered for it are adequate. This assumes a situation in which someone is trying to communicate persuasively, that is, to convince a listener or reader to accept the belief in question. Because not all communication is meant to be persuasive, naturally, critical analysis is not always relevant in our interactions with others or in our attempts at self-understanding and, in fact, can get in the way of mutual understanding and personal insight in some circumstances. But when it comes time to decide whether to adopt a particular belief over another, philosophers generally have agreed that principles of correct reasoning are needed to provide an intellectual common ground for assessing the alternatives. These "rules," in effect, guide our rational thinking in everyday life more thoroughly than many people realize, in much the same way that rules of grammar guide our use of a language, whether we are aware of it or not. Similarly, as we can be more or less grammatically correct, or fluent, and subsequently more or less successful in communicating with others in that language, so also we can reason well or badly and thus be more or less persuasive to a reasonable audience.

For at least a few thousand years the study of these rules of reasoning has constituted a subfield within the discipline of philosophy, called logic. Although there has been plenty of debate among logicians regarding other issues, two distinct kinds of rational, sequential thought are almost universally recognized. These two "logics" are referred to as deduction and induction, and they are different enough to require different standards of evaluation even though they both involve deciding to accept some belief, statement, or judgment as true *because of* some other beliefs, statements, or judgments one also accepts as true.

Logical analysis tries to determine whether the assertions offered as reasons for accepting a primary assertion justify that acceptance in the way the speaker or writer intended. All these assertions together constitute an argument. An argument, as normally defined by philosophers, is not merely some sort of dispute but, more technically, a set of two or more statements, one of which (the conclusion) is to be believed because the other statement or statements (the premise or premises) provide adequate reason for such belief. Determining whether a strong enough relationship exists between premises and conclusions in arguments is essential to effective critical analysis, and this is where distinguishing between deductive and inductive argumentation becomes crucial.

Deductive Argumentation

When people use deductive reasoning to justify their claims, they try to show that if the premises they offer are accepted, then the particular conclusion they want to "prove" necessarily follows. In other words, from a rational standpoint, it would be impossible for that conclusion not to be the case if the premises are true. Consider this example of a deductive argument:

Premise: People must be 18 in order to vote in the upcoming election.
Premise: By that time, Joe will be only 17.
Conclusion: Therefore, he won't be able to vote in the election.

If we accept as true both of the premises as stated, we cannot deny the conclusion without being logically inconsistent. Since logical consistency is one of the foundational principles of correct reasoning, we are rationally compelled to recognize that this argument exemplifies what we call a valid deductive inference. As assumed by most philosophers, validity is attributed only to a deductive argument, in which the conclusion follows necessarily, unavoidably from the premises.

When the conclusion does not follow necessarily from the premises, even though it is intended to, the argument is invalid. For example:

Premise: In the election four years from now, people will have to be at least 18 in order to vote.
Premise: Joan is 17 now.
Conclusion: Therefore, she won't be old enough to vote in that election.

A second condition is required for a deductive argument to be rationally persuasive. Not only does it need to be valid rather than invalid, but also all of its premises have to be true. Consider this argument:

Premise: All herbivores are mammals.
Premise: An iguana is an herbivore.
Conclusion: Therefore, an iguana is a mammal.

If we were to accept as true the two premises in this case, we would have to admit that the conclusion should also be true because it does follow necessarily from those premises. But an iguana is a reptile, not a mammal, so something must be wrong other than the relationship between the premises and conclusion, because it is a valid inference. Obviously, the problem is that the first premise is false, and once we realize this we can reject the argument on that basis alone. A deductive argument that is valid and has all true premises is called a sound argument; an argument that fails to meet one or both of these criteria is called an unsound argument.

Inductive Argumentation

When using inductive reasoning to argue a point, the speaker or writer claims only that the conclusion probably rather than necessarily follows from the premises. In other words, in an inductive argument the premises are intended to provide sufficient reasons for accepting the conclusion as true, even though strictly speaking there would be no logical inconsistency in denying it. For example, here is an argument that entails a rationally compelling inductive inference:

Premise: The sun always has risen in the east in the past.
Conclusion: Therefore, it will rise in the east tomorrow.

If we accept this premise, the evidence it provides in favor of the conclusion is strong enough that it would be unreasonable not to accept it. But this conclusion does not necessarily follow because one could come up with a logically possible scenario, no matter how unlikely or unbelievable, in which tomorrow the sun would not rise in the east. In evaluating inductive argumentation then, the relationship between premises and conclusion need not be one of ironclad necessity, just one of sufficient probability.

When the premises give a high enough degree of probability, or likelihood, for the truth of the conclusion, usually the inference expressed is called a strong inductive argument. On the other hand, in a weak inductive argument the evidence offered does not provide enough support for rationally accepting the likelihood of the conclusion, as in this case:

Premise: Chili peppers upset his stomach.
Premise: They also upset his sister's stomach and his uncle's stomach.
Conclusion: Chili peppers must be inedible for humans.

Even assuming a lack of knowledge regarding the diversity of human diet, and recognizing that there might be a slight connection between the premises and conclusion, it is still obvious that this inductive inference is weak and not persuasive to a reasonable person. At the very least, making a general claim about what is inedible for all people based on the unpleasant but nonlethal experience of three family members is an extreme example of a standard type of inductive fallacy logicians label a hasty generalization.

In the two previous examples of induction, the truth of the premises is not in question, but it is an issue in many other inductive arguments. Here is an example:

Premise: The death penalty is more effective than long-term imprisonment as a deterrent for murder.
Conclusion: Thus, more extensive use of the death penalty in the United States will lower the murder rate.

As formulated, and lacking other information regarding what makes murder rates go up or down in the United States, the conclusion does follow probably from the premise. But whether the premise itself is true remains controversial for many people who have studied the capital punishment debate. The evidence gathered by extensive research on the matter has not been conclusive, and yet the plausibility of the conclusion depends on the truth of that premise. This illustrates both that our assessments of arguments have to be tentative when we don't have enough relevant knowledge to tell whether the reasons used to support a claim are good ones and that it is appropriate for us to remain unconvinced by any line of reasoning relying on questionable premises. So an inductive argument also has to meet two criteria to be considered a good argument: (1) We have to decide whether it is strong, while realizing that inductive strength is a matter of degrees and thus often more difficult to determine than deductive validity, and (2) its premises have to be true. When both of these conditions are present, it is often called a cogent argument (though the terminology varies among logicians), and when either condition is absent, it is an uncogent argument.

Value Judgments

The instances of deductive and inductive argumentation discussed so far are made up of all factual statements, that is, true or false claims about actual states of affairs.

But in many of the readings in this text, you will also find value judgments as premises and conclusions in arguments. After all, many of our most important beliefs in life are not so much about how things are but about how they ought to be or not, or about what is desirable and undesirable, or good and bad; and we are compelled regularly, willingly or not, to justify them to ourselves and others. Here are two examples:

1. Self-destructive behavior is wrong because such behavior harms the community to which one belongs, and such harm is always wrong.
2. The stronger the emotional response on the part of the audience, the better the piece of music performed. The audience had a stronger emotional response to the second song in the set than to the first song, so the second song was better than the first.

The first argument is a justification of a moral belief, while the second argument is a defense of an aesthetic belief. Both are deductively valid, and both include factual statements and value statements that may need further argumentation. Also, in the first argument the conclusion is asserted first rather than last, with two premises following "because" in one long sentence; and in the second argument the conclusion (following "so") is combined with the second premise in a longer sentence.

In everyday life as well as in philosophical writing, attempts at rational persuasion are often presented informally, and we must pay careful attention to what is being said in order to evaluate it. It isn't always obvious which assertion is intended as the conclusion and which other assertions are being used as premises, especially when arguments are embedded in larger pieces of spoken or written discourse. The listener or reader can sometimes identify premises and conclusions by indicator words such as "because," "since," "so," and "therefore." Indicator words and phrases can also help us decide whether an argument is inductive or deductive. For example, "necessarily," "certainly," "absolutely," or "it has to be the case that" usually signal deductive arguments, and "probably," "likely," "quite possibly," or "it is reasonable to believe that" usually signal inductive arguments. In any case, even without memorizing the whole list of formal logical rules the way you might memorize all the formal grammar rules in a language, to critically analyze beliefs and to apply the standards of correct reasoning briefly summarized here requires at the very least a rational sensitivity to inferential thinking and how it can go astray.

Other Guidelines for Philosophical Analysis

In addition to using the rules of formal logic, philosophers typically follow at least three other guidelines that are related to their overall goals. First, an argument presented to persuade someone to accept a belief always must be made with honesty and integrity. It should not rely on fallacious inferences, verbal obscurity, attitudes of self-righteousness and bluster, or other tricks of persuasion to cover up the fact that it isn't rationally convincing. Further, if the logical implications of a belief are not acceptable to the philosopher, the honorable thing to do is to give it up or to appropriately modify it rather than to ignore or gloss over the inconsistency. The aim in philosophical analysis is not to win the argument, after all, but to use argumentation as a vehicle for deciding which belief option is the most reasonable, defensible, and closest to the truth of the matter.

Second, a position must be given a fair hearing and be adequately understood before it is rejected. We often tend to discount immediately an opinion that is different from our own or argued from an unfamiliar perspective. When analyzing a philosophical argument, however, you should start by giving the writer or speaker the benefit of the doubt. Assume that he or she is rational, sane, and making a good faith effort to communicate a relevant insight, regardless of how complex or imprecisely formulated its defense. Reading or listening sympathetically usually results in a more accurate critical assessment of the claims made. You may even find that as you come to better understand the author's perspective, you can identify reasons in support of the conclusions beyond those already presented.

Third, as noted earlier, critical analysis has its limits, and not all beliefs and assertions are worth arguing about. If, for example, a loved one is trying to describe to you how he or she is feeling, or a friend remarks on how beautiful the sunset was last evening, you almost certainly would be missing the point if you subjected such conversation to rigorous rational critique. Knowing just where those limits are in any particular case is not always easy, but if motivated by a spirit of mutual respect, intellectual diplomacy, and attentiveness to what is at stake, we will be more likely to deal with that situation in a productive and beneficial manner.

How to Read Philosophy

All the readings in this text include attempts at persuasiveness and inferential reasoning that are carried out in a variety of ways. As you will discover, reading philosophy is different from reading newspapers or popular novels. You cannot speed-read or skim philosophical writing, for example, and adequately make sense out of what is said and decide whether it is plausible.

In reading philosophy you must also be aware that philosophers generally operate with some unstated assumptions or implied premises as they develop their answers to philosophical questions. All writers have an audience in mind with whom they share a worldview, and they take for granted some common factual beliefs and shared values. However, what may be common knowledge to a writer in one context may be completely unfamiliar to readers from a different period of history or a different culture. For example, Confucius in ancient China and Plato in ancient Greece were addressing their contemporaries in their writings, not readers from the twenty-first century. Conversely, we make certain assumptions about our world that Confucius and Plato undoubtedly would have found very strange.

As you read the selections in this book, also keep in mind that not all the authors use the methods of academic philosophy, even though they all address widely recognized philosophical issues. Even though some of the voices are from different disciplines, or are not from any academic discipline at all, you can still read them from a philosophical point of view.

Five Steps for Successful Reading

Because so many different perspectives and discourse styles are represented in this text, a consistent approach is recommended for a more successful reading of each of the selections.

Step 1. Identify the specific philosophical issues addressed in the reading. The writings are organized into general categories and subcategories (such as "Metaphysics" and "Right and Wrong Conduct"), but each author has a unique agenda regarding one or more of these.

Step 2. For each philosophical question or controversy in the essay or excerpt, *identify the answer (or answers) explicitly or implicitly offered by the author.* In addition, look for possible answers formulated and subsequently rejected by the author in favor of other conclusions.

Step 3. For each position taken on an issue, try to *identify the reasons given to justify it.* This is fairly easy if authors make one or two obvious claims in defense of a position, but it is more difficult if they use long and complex lines of reasoning, entailing arguments within arguments. Especially in complex arguments, you will need to look for hidden premises and unstated assumptions and be willing to read creatively in an attempt to grasp the intended meaning of particular passages. You also may find it useful to remember the guideline of giving an argument a fair hearing and trying hard to understand it before you reject it.

Step 4. Once you have figured out the specific issue being addressed, the answers being offered, and the reasons given for those answers, the next step is to *decide whether the reasons are convincing.* To evaluate these reasons, you must determine whether the logical inferences they entail are good ones and whether the various kinds of human experience and grounding beliefs they rely on should be considered as evidence in their favor.

Step 5. Finally, since a recurring theme in this text will be how authors' social and historical contexts influence the reader's comprehension of what is said, try to answer the following question after the critical analysis of each selection: *How would somebody with a background different from the author's respond to the author's conclusions?* In other words, would it make any significant difference in the persuasiveness of an author's claims if the reader lived in a different historical period or culture, in different economic conditions, or was of the other sex? If yes, then why? If not, why not?

How the Five Steps Work

To see how this recipe for reading works, let's apply it first to a short passage (the eighth chapter) of the ancient Chinese classic the *Dao De Jing,* generally thought to be authored by Laozi, and the primary literary text associated with the philosophical and spiritual tradition of Daoism.[1]

> The best (man) is like water.
> Water is good; it benefits all things and does not
> compete with them.
> It dwells in (lowly) places that all disdain.
> This is why it is so near to Tao.
> [The best man] in his dwelling loves the earth.
> In his heart, he loves what is profound.

---

1. See reading 46 of this anthology for this passage, along with other excerpts from the translation of the *Dao De Jing* by Wing-Tsit Chan. He uses the Wade-Giles system of transliteration, rendering the title as *Tao Te Ching,* by Lao Tzu. I have used the currently more accepted Pinyin system.

In his associations, he loves humanity.
In his words, he loves faithfulness.
In government, he loves order.
In handling affairs, he loves competence.
In his activities, he loves timeliness.
It is because he does not compete that he is
without reproach.

Step 1. The primary question addressed in the reading has to do with what kind of moral character the individual should try to achieve—that is, what would the morally ideal person be like? When read in conjunction with other passages in the work, it becomes clear that although this question is relevant for all individuals, it is directed especially at political rulers, so that a secondary issue is the character of a good ruler.

Step 2. The answer (or conclusion) to both the primary and secondary questions is not a single, simple statement, but a complex description of character traits as manifested in different aspects of daily life (lines 6–13) and unified by the analogy with water in line 1. What is meant in this context by "profound," "humanity," "order," and other terms, and their connection to the image of water, may take more investigation.

Step 3. The justification for this composite answer also involves a couple of different claims: Lines 2–5 point out that water is not only a powerful natural element (an implied assumption) and an essential good for all living things, but it is also a yielding element that flows to the point of least resistance even while being ultimately unstoppable. The Tao (the Way) is the natural order of the universe—the naturally harmonious, underlying flow and rhythm of life itself—and thus water exhibits the nature of the Tao more obviously than does, say, a solid object. By analogy, the more a person possesses such character traits as simplicity, humility, nonaggressive persistence, allowing things to happen naturally rather than forcing them to happen, the more that person is in harmony with the Tao, and subsequently the more he or she benefits others and is a better person, morally speaking. Further, line 14 asserts that the person who lives this way will not suffer reproach from others (typically considered a good outcome).

Step 4. Is the position on the best moral character one that you find persuasive? The author makes both fact and value claims, in the complex conclusion and among its supporting reasons, that have to be assessed. For example, is noncompetition always good? Would political leaders with this kind of character have improved the lives of Chinese people back then, or would they be better for us today? Is the Tao real?

Step 5. Imagine how a contemporary European American corporate executive, or a trade unionist, might respond to this writing. What would be the basis of agreement or disagreement? Does gender have any influence in the reader's acceptance of this account of moral character? If so, is that because males and females experience social relations differently?

Next, let us take a passage from the *Meditations*, written by the seventeenth-century French philosopher René Descartes, and use the same five steps to analyze it.[2]

---

2. See reading 12 for this paragraph from "Meditation II," translated by Elizabeth S. Haldane and G. R. T. Ross.

But what am I? . . . Can I affirm that I possess the least of all those things which I have just said pertain to the nature of body? I pause to consider, I revolve all these things in my mind, and I find none of which I can say that it pertains to me. . . . Let us pass to the attributes of soul and see if there is any one which is in me? What of nutrition or walking [the first mentioned]? But if it is so that I have no body it is also true that I can neither walk nor take nourishment. Another attribute is sensation. But one cannot feel without body, and besides I have thought I perceived many things during sleep that I recognised in my waking moments as not having been experienced at all. What of thinking? I find here that thought is an attribute that belongs to me; it alone cannot be separated from me. I am, I exist, that is certain. But how often? Just when I think; for it might possibly be the case if I ceased entirely to think, that I should likewise cease altogether to exist. I do not now admit anything which is not necessarily true: to speak accurately I am not more than a thing which thinks, that is to say a mind or a soul, or an understanding, or a reason, which are terms whose significance was formerly unknown to me. I am, however, a real thing and really exist; but what thing? I have answered: a thing which thinks.

Step 1. The central issue in this passage is the essential nature of the human person, yet Descartes is trying to answer that question not by focusing on humans generally, but by reflecting on what he can assert about himself with absolute certainty (that is, what is "necessarily true" and what thus logically cannot be otherwise).

Step 2. Earlier in the *Meditations,* Descartes had established with certainty that he exists, at least when he is thinking; now he concludes that what he is, essentially, is "a thing which thinks." Also, this thinking thing must be nonphysical.

Step 3. For Descartes, the metaphysical question of the nature of the self is inseparable from the epistemological question of how we can acquire certain knowledge about the self (mere probabilistic, inductive judgments were seldom good enough for him). He handles this latter question by excluding from the concept of his own self any property that is not logically necessary to it, and then also assumes that the essence of any conceivable thing is the sum of its logically necessary properties (that is, those attributes without which it cannot be clearly conceived). Since each of the properties he associates with the "nature of body" can be conceived of as at least *possibly* not part of his self, whether or not they really are so, he reasons that nothing of the body is essential to the self. On the other hand, at least in the present moment when he is thinking about all of this, it is logically impossible for him to conceive of himself as *not thinking* (though he can't yet say *for sure* that he will be thinking two minutes hence, or that he was thinking two minutes earlier), and thus the attribute of thought itself is essential to the concept of his self.

Step 4. Whether or not you are convinced by Descartes's conclusions, and find them useful for understanding human nature generally, will depend on a number of factors beyond your immediate assessment of the deductive inferences he employs. Is the set of logically necessary properties the most insightful way to characterize the essence of something? Is his conceptual split between body and mind defensible? Is something important missing from his account in this passage (maybe to be discovered by reading the preceding parts of the *Meditations,* as well as what follows)? If he is correct, are social relations then inessential for human nature?

Step 5. In traditional Native American thought, it is rather common to deny the dualistic assumption that the individual person has both a bodily aspect and a qualitatively distinct, separate mental/spiritual aspect: It is argued instead that there is no essential distinction between the two. How would you resolve this disagreement? How should we assess Descartes's position in light of the gender colorings that body and mind/soul have often been given throughout recorded history (for example, that mind is superior and associated with the male, while body is inferior and associated with the female)?

Organization of the Topics

The readings in Part I present a number of perspectives on the role of philosophy in human life. In addition to being interesting examples of philosophical inquiry, they also show the kinds of real-world contexts to which philosophers have responded over the centuries. The selections in the remaining parts of the book are grouped according to the categories typically used at least in the European and Asian academic traditions, and yet they reflect the types of intellectual problems confronted in one way or another by people in every society in recorded history. Each part is divided into sections representing fairly typical divisions of topics within the general category. The questions explored in Parts II–VI are the following:

- How do we know what we think we know? Part II: Epistemology (with sections on truth and objectivity, ways of knowing, and knowledge and responsibility)
- What is real, and what is the nature of reality? Part III: Metaphysics (with sections on the nature of the universe, the nature of the human person, and the existence of divine beings)
- How should people treat one another? Part IV: Morality (with sections on ethical judgment and human nature, moral character, and right and wrong conduct)
- Who makes decisions for the group, what do they decide, and for what ends? Part V: Political Philosophy (with sections on individuals and communities, social power and group conflict, and principles of government)
- What is aesthetically valuable and why? Part VI: Aesthetics (with sections on the nature of art and aesthetic experience and the evaluation of art)

The readings represent a plurality of voices from a variety of geographical, historical, and cultural locations. Because a single book cannot contain a comprehensive treatment of all important human thought around the globe and throughout history, what is included here is a first taste of the diversity of responses to different dimensions of human experience. Because the majority of those who will use this text live in North America, there are more samples from the European cultural tradition (itself very diverse) to shed light on the origins of many of the concepts and values many of us take for granted. Even though the number of samples from other cultural standpoints is smaller, they should be enough for readers to make some productive comparisons and enrich their own worldview in the process.

In addition to illustrating the diversity of philosophical issues and modes of inquiry, each selection in this anthology meets at least one of the following criteria:

1. In the specific intellectual tradition of which it is a part, it has been historically influential as a piece of philosophical discourse.
2. It is representative of an academically acknowledged philosophical trend or systematically articulated worldview, past or present, in some part of the world.
3. It can be readily compared to theoretical viewpoints, positions, and historically recurring concerns in other traditions.

The Point of It All

In this volume of readings you will find a variety of possible answers, or belief options, for many of the most basic questions of human existence. The answers to these questions have mattered to many different people throughout history and around the world. As you reflect on the various readings, you may find that the answers matter to you more than you would have expected and that some seem more plausible than others within the context of your own life.

By seeing some of the different ways that philosophy is actually done, you can learn to employ similar approaches to the critical analysis of other written and spoken discourse. In addition, and more importantly, you can use the methods of philosophy in the ongoing process of constructing a workable, coherent, defensible worldview for yourself. Even though our belief systems are strongly influenced by our social environments, in the end all of us are individually responsible for what we believe. If we take that responsibility seriously, we need to make a sincere effort to explore the choices of belief that are available. In fact, it can be argued that any meaningful education is fundamentally a matter of discovering and assessing relevant belief options, and thus we are all essentially responsible for our own education.

Do not expect, however, that after using this book you will have identified a fixed and final set of correct answers to life's basic questions. The search for those answers should be a lifelong endeavor, and these readings represent only some of the choices that various committed inquirers have found useful. Rational consistency, deeper understanding, and personal progress require flexibility in how we think about and value different aspects of our world. Beliefs about matters of significance should be largely open ended, allowing for further growth. If nothing else, philosophical inquiry can offer us a means for proceeding along this developmental path with intellectual modesty, vigilance, and integrity.

PART I   # Philosophical Inquiry:
         # How and Why?

In one way or another all of the authors of the seven selections in Part I are reflecting philosophically on the nature of philosophy itself. The variety of conclusions they reach about how philosophy is appropriately practiced, its value to human life, and its limitations illustrates both the commonality and the diversity of opinion expressed on this singular form of inquiry throughout recorded history. Comparisons and contrasts can be drawn readily between the different writings; for example, compare Socrates' characterization of the philosophical life in ancient Athens to Russell's early twentieth-century account of the benefits of philosophical reflection in his own society, where he noticed a strong bias in favor of the "practical."

Note, too, how each writer locates philosophical activity within a real-life context inescapably bounded by social and personal circumstances. In the excerpt from Tuana's book, for example, she shows how connotations of masculinity and femininity have infused philosophical categories and reinforced a male-dominant worldview. On the other hand, Boethius's philosophical conclusions were a response to a predicament resulting in large part from the wealth and political power he formerly possessed.

Because of the nature of the discipline, philosophers might be able to distance themselves from the conventions and prejudices of their time more easily than some other people, but their thinking too is influenced by the social environments in which they live. Our understanding of philosophy thus will be incomplete if we ignore the effects of personal fortune or misfortune on philosophers themselves as members of communities with their own histories, traditions, and organization of social relations, including those based on economic class, gender, and ethnic affiliation.

1. Plato (429–347 B.C.E.)
"The Apology"

The Greek philosopher Plato is considered one of the most influential writers in all of Western intellectual history, and the impact of his theories regarding reality, knowledge, and values still is felt today. Although he most often developed his own philosophical positions using a format of fictional dialogue, in "The Apology" his approach and agenda are different. He presents an account, generally thought to be factually accurate though stylistically embellished, of the public trial of his friend and teacher Socrates (469–399 B.C.E.).

At the time of his trial in 399 B.C.E., Socrates had been a lifelong resident of the city-state of Athens. Even though he never wrote down any of his views, he was widely known for his devotion to philosophical inquiry especially aimed at deciding how a person ought to live. He also had a well-deserved reputation for skillfully engaging his fellow citizens in rational dialogue and exposing the inadequacy of their opinions, regardless of their social status. As a result, Socrates had acquired many friends and followers over the years, as well as many enemies, some of whom eventually brought charges against him to the Athenian Assembly. During that period of limited political democracy, the Assembly was made up of all the adult males in the city who met certain property and residency qualifications. The official indictment contained two related accusations: that Socrates rejected conventional religious doctrines and that he corrupted the youth with his teachings.

Plato's narrative describes Socrates' response to these charges before the roughly 500 Assembly members who made up the jury in this case, where a simple majority vote would decide the verdict. The essay consists of three distinct speeches: first, Socrates' actual defense; next, his response to the guilty verdict, which had been decided by a vote of 281 to 220; and then a final address upon his being condemned to death.

QUESTIONS FOR CRITICAL READING

1. What are the two charges against Socrates, and what arguments does he use to refute each one?
2. Socrates' method of rational analysis often included his claim to be ignorant of the matters he discussed with others. How is his use of this stance of ignorance (whether real or pretended) illustrated in the essay, and what are its outcomes?
3. What does Socrates mean by referring to himself as a "gadfly," and why is this a good or bad thing to be?
4. What is the divine "voice," or "spiritual sign," to which Socrates refers, and how does he use it to justify his actions?

TERMS TO NOTE

apology: In this context, a verbal defense.
atheism: The belief that no divine supernatural beings really exist.
oracle: A sacred place of prophecy and divination, where a god or goddess speaking through a priest or priestess provided what were usually enigmatic answers to human questions. The term also has been used to refer to the divine answer itself, as well as to the priest or priestess who acted as the medium. The oracle at Delphi was the most famous oracle in Greece during Plato's time, and the god appealed to there was Apollo.
Presidents' Hall: The reference here is to the Prytaneum, a public building in ancient Athens that served as a place of hospitality for honored citizens and dignitaries from other states.

Part I

Before the Verdict

I. I do not know, men of Athens, what you have felt in listening to my accusers, but they almost made even me forget myself, they spoke so plausibly. And yet, I may say, they have not spoken one word of truth. And of all the lies they told, I wondered most at their saying that you ought to be on your guard against being misled by me, as I was a great speaker. To feel no shame when they knew that they would be refuted immediately by my own action, when I show you that I am not a great speaker at all,—that did seem to me the height of their audacity; unless perhaps they mean by a great speaker a man who speaks the truth. If that is their meaning, I should agree that I am an orator, though not like them. For they, as I have told you, have said little or nothing that is true; from me you will hear the whole truth. Not, I assure you, that you will get fine arguments like theirs, men of Athens, decked out in splendid phrases, no, but plain speech set forth in any words that come to hand. I believe what I have to say is true, and I ask that none of you should look for anything else. Indeed, gentlemen, it would hardly suit my age to come before you like a boy, with a made-up speech. And yet, I do ask one thing of you, and I ask it very earnestly: if you find I speak in my defence just as I have been accustomed to speak over the bankers' tables in the market-place,—as many of you have heard me, there and elsewhere; do not be surprised at it, and do not interrupt. For this is how the matter stands. This is the first time I have ever been in a lawsuit, and I am seventy years old,—so I am really an entire stranger to the language of this place. Now, just as you would have forgiven me, I am sure, had I been actually a foreigner, if I had spoken in the tongue and manner to which I had been born, so I think I have a right to ask you now to let my way of speaking pass—be it good or bad—and to give your minds to this question and this only, whether what I say is right or not. That is the virtue of the judge, as truth is the virtue of the orator.

II. Now in making my defence, men of Athens, it will be well for me to deal first with the first false accusations and my first accusers, and afterwards with those that followed. For I have had many accusers who have come before you now for many years, and have not said one word of truth, and I fear them more than Anytus and his supporters, though they are formidable too. But the others, gentlemen, are still more to be feared, I mean the men who took most of you in hand when you were boys, and have gone on persuading you ever since, and accusing me—quite falsely—telling you that there is a man called Socrates, a philosopher, who speculates about the things in the sky, and has searched into the secrets of the earth, and makes the worse appear the better reason. These men, Athenians, the men who have spread this tale abroad, they are the

accusers that I fear: for the listeners think that those who study such matters must be atheists as well. Besides, these accusers of mine are many, and they have been at this work for many years, and that, too, when you were at an age at which you would be most ready to believe them, for you were young, some of you mere striplings, and judgment has really gone by default, since there was no one to make the defence. And what is most troublesome of all, it is impossible even to find out their names, unless there be a comedian among them. As for those who have tried to persuade you through envy and prejudice, some, it is true, convincing others because they were convinced themselves,— these are the hardest to deal with of all. It is not possible to call up any of them here and cross-examine them: one is compelled, as it were, to fight with shadows in making one's defence, and hold an inquiry where there is nobody to reply. So I would have you understand with me that my accusers have been, as I say, of two kinds: those who have just brought this charge against me, and others of longer standing, of whom I am speaking now; and I ask you to realise that I must defend myself against the latter first of all, for they were the first whom you heard attack me, and at much greater length than these who followed them. And now, I presume, I must make my defence, men of Athens, and try in the short time I have before me to remove from your minds this calumny which has had so long to grow. I could wish for that result, and for some success in my defence, if it would be good for you and me. But I think it a difficult task, and I am not unaware of its nature. However, let the result be what God wills; I must obey the law, and make my defence.

III. Let us begin from the beginning and see what the accusation is that gave birth to the prejudice on which Meletus relied when he brought this charge. Now, what did they say to raise this prejudice? I must treat them as though they were prosecutors and read their affidavit: "Socrates, we say, is a trouble to the State. He is guilty of inquiring into the things beneath the earth, and the things of the firmament, he makes the worse appear the better reason, and he teaches others so." That is the sort of thing they say: you saw it yourselves in the comedy of Aristophanes,—a character called Socrates carried about in a basket, saying that he walked on air, and talking a great deal more nonsense about matters of which I do not understand one word, great or small. And I do not say this in contempt of such knowledge, if any one is clever at those things. May Meletus never bring so grave a charge against me! But in truth, gentlemen, I have nothing to do with these subjects. I call you yourselves,—most of you,—to witness: I ask you to instruct and tell each other,—those of you who have ever heard me speak, and many of you have,—tell each other, I say, if any of you have ever heard one word from me, small or great, upon such themes; and you will realise from this that the other tales people tell about me are of the same character.

IV. There is, in fact, no truth in them at all, nor yet in what you may have heard from others, that I try to make money by my teaching. Now here again, I think it would be a great thing if one could teach men as Gorgias of Leontini can, and Prodicus of Keos, and Hippias of Elis. They can all go to every one of our cities, and take hold of the young men,—who are able, as it is, to associate free of charge with any of their fellow-citizens they may choose,—and they can persuade them to leave this society for theirs and pay them money and be very grateful to them too. Why, there is another philosopher here from Paros; he is in town, I know: for I happened to meet a friend of mine who has spent more money on sophists than all the rest put together,—Callias the son of Hipponicus. Now I put a question to him,—he has two sons of his own,—"Callias," I said, "if your two sons were only colts or bullocks we could have hired a trainer for them to make them beautiful and good, and all that they should be; and our trainer would have been, I take it, a horseman or a farmer. But now that they are human beings, have you any trainer in your mind for them? Is there any one who understands what a man and a citizen ought to be? I am sure you have thought of it, because you have sons of your own. Is there any one," I said, "or not?" "Oh yes," said he, "certainly there is." "Who is he?" I asked, "and where does he come from and how much does he charge?" "Euenus," he answered, "from Paros; five minas a head." And I thought Euenus the happiest of men if he really has that power and can teach for such a moderate fee. Now I should have been set up and given myself great airs if I had possessed that knowledge; but I do not possess it, Athenians.

V. Some of you will say perhaps:—"But, Socrates, what can your calling be? What has given rise to these calumnies? Surely, if you had done nothing more than any other man, there would not have been all this talk, had you never acted differently from other people. You must tell us what it is, that we may not be left to make our own theories about you."

That seems to me a fair question, and I will try to show you myself what it can be that has given me my name and produced the calumny. Listen to me then. Some of you may think I am in jest, but I assure you I will only tell the truth. The truth is, men of Athens, that I have won my name because of a kind of wisdom, nothing more nor less. What can this wisdom be? The wisdom, perhaps, that is proper to man. It may really be that I am wise in that wisdom: the men I have just named may have a wisdom greater than man's,—or else I know not what to call it. Certainly I do not possess it myself; whoever says I do lies, and speaks to calumniate me. And pray, gentlemen, do not interrupt me: not even if you think I boast. The words that I say will not be my own; I will refer you to a speaker whom you must respect. The witness I will bring you of my wisdom,—if such it really is,—and of its nature, is the god whose dwelling is at Delphi. Now you knew Chairephon, I think. He was my friend from boyhood, and the friend of your democracy; he went with you into exile, and came back with you.[1] And you know, I think, the kind of man Chairephon was—how eager in everything he undertook. Well, he made a pilgrimage to Delphi, and had the audacity to ask this question from the oracle: and now I beg you, gentlemen, do not interrupt me in what I am about to say. He actually asked if there was any man wiser than I. And the priestess answered, No. I have his brother here to give evidence of this, for Chairephon himself is dead.

VI. Now see why I tell you this. I am going to show you how the calumny arose. When I heard the answer, I asked myself: What can the god mean? What can he be hinting? For certainly I have never thought myself wise in anything, great or small. What can he mean then, when he asserts that I am the wisest of men? He cannot lie of course: that would be impossible for him.

---

1. In 404 B.C. after the submission to Sparta, the democratic government of Athens was overthrown. A body of thirty oligarchs, appointed at first provisionally, got practically the whole power into their hands and acted with great injustice and cruelty. The leading democrats of those who escaped judicial murder went into exile, but in a year's time effected a re-entry, partly by force of arms, and established the democracy again.

And for a long while I was at a loss to think what he could mean. At last, after much thought, I started on some such course of search as this. I betook myself to one of the men who seemed wise, thinking that there, if anywhere, I should refute the utterance, and could say to the oracle: "This man is wiser than I, and you said I was the wisest." Now when I looked into the man—there is no need to give his name—it was one of our citizens, men of Athens, with whom I had an experience of this kind—when we talked together I thought, "This man seems wise to many men, and above all to himself, but he is not so;" and then I tried to show him that he thought he was wise, but he was not. Then he got angry with me, and so did many who heard us, but I went away and thought to myself, "Well, at any rate I am wiser than this man: probably neither of us knows anything of beauty or of good, but he thinks he knows something when he knows nothing, and I, if I know nothing, at least never suppose that I do. So it looks as though I really were a little wiser than he, just in so far as I do not imagine myself to know things about which I know nothing at all." After that I went to another man who seemed to be wiser still, and I had exactly the same experience: and then he got angry with me too, and so did many more.

VII. Thus I went round them all, one after the other, aware of what was happening and sorry for it, and afraid that they were getting to hate me: but still I felt I must put the word of the god first and foremost, and that I must go through all who seemed to have any knowledge in order to find out what the oracle meant. And by the Dog, men of Athens,—for I must tell you the truth,—this was what I experienced. As I went on with the quest the god had imposed on me, it seemed to me that those who had the highest reputation were very nearly the most deficient of all, and that others who were thought inferior came nearer being men of understanding. I must show you, you see, that my wanderings were a kind of labour of Hercules to prove to myself that the oracle was right. After I had tried the statesmen I went to the poets,—tragedians, writers of lyrics, and all,—thinking that there I should take myself in the act and find I really was more ignorant than they. So I took up the poems of theirs on which they seemed to have spent most pains, and asked them what they meant, hoping to learn something from them too. Now I am really ashamed to tell

you the truth; but tell it I must. On the whole, almost all the bystanders could have spoken better about the poems than the men who made them. So here again I soon perceived that what the poets make is not made by wisdom, but by a kind of gift and inspiration, as with the prophets and the seers: they, too, utter many glorious sayings, but they understand nothing of what they say. The poets seemed to me in much the same state; and besides, I noticed that on account of their poetry they thought themselves the wisest of men in other matters too, which they were not. So I left them also, thinking that I had just the same advantage over them as over the politicians.

VIII. Finally I turned to the men who work with their hands. I was conscious I knew nothing that could be called anything; and I was quite sure I should find that they knew a great many wonderful things. And in this I was not disappointed; they did know things that I did not, and in this they were wiser than I. But then, gentlemen, the skilled artisans in their turn seemed to me to have just the same failing as the poets. Because of his skill in his own craft every one of them thought that he was the wisest of men in the highest matters too, and this error of theirs obscured the wisdom they possessed. So that I asked myself, on behalf of the oracle, whether I would rather be as I am, without their wisdom and without their ignorance, or like them in both. And I answered for myself and for the oracle that it was better for me to be as I am.

IX. It was this inquiry, men of Athens, that gave rise to so much enmity against me, and that of the worst and bitterest kind: a succession of calumnies followed, and I received the surname of the Wise. For those who meet me think me wise wherever I refute others; but, sirs, the truth may be that God alone has wisdom, and by that oracle he may have meant just this, that human wisdom is of little or no account. It seems as though he had not been speaking of Socrates the individual; but had merely used my name for an illustration, as if to say: "He, O men, is the wisest of you all, who has learnt, like Socrates, that his wisdom is worth nothing." Such has been my search and my inquiry ever since up to this day, in obedience to the god, whenever I found any one—fellow-citizen or foreigner—who might be considered wise: and if he did not seem so to me I have borne God witness, and pointed out to him that he was not wise at all. And through this incessant work I have had no leisure for any public action worth mentioning, nor yet for my private affairs, but I live in extreme poverty because of this service of mine to God.

X. And besides this, the young men who follow me, those who have most leisure,—sons of our wealthiest citizens,—they take a keen delight themselves in hearing people questioned, and they often copy me and try their hand at examining others on their own account; and, I imagine, they find no lack of men who think they know something but know little or nothing at all. Now those whom they examine get angry—not with themselves, but with me—and say that there is a man called Socrates, an utter scoundrel, who is ruining the young. And when any one asks them what he does or what he teaches, they have really nothing whatever to say, but so as not to seem at a loss they take up the accusations that lie ready to hand against all philosophers, and say that he speaks of the things in the heavens and beneath the earth and teaches men not to believe in the gods and to make the worse appear the better reason. The truth, I imagine, they would not care to say, namely, that they have been convicted of claiming knowledge when they have none to claim. And being, as I think they are, ambitious, energetic, and numerous, well-organised and using great powers of persuasion, they have gone on calumniating me with singular persistence and vigour till your ears are full of it all. After them Meletus attacked me and Anytus and Lycon,—Meletus on behalf of the poets, Anytus for the artisans and the statesmen, Lycon for the orators,—so that, as I said at first, I should be greatly surprised if in the short time before me I could remove the prejudice that has grown to be so great. There, men of Athens, that is the truth;—I have not hidden one thing from you, great or small; I have not kept back one word. Yet I am fairly sure that I have roused hostility by so doing, which is in itself a proof that what I say is true, and that the calumnies against me are of this nature, and the reasons those I have given. And if you look into the matter,—now or afterwards,—you will find it to be so.

XI. Well, that is a sufficient defence in answer to my first accusers. Now I must try to defend myself against Meletus,—the good man and the patriot, as he calls himself,—and the rest who followed. These are my second accusers, and let us take up their affidavit

in its turn. It runs somewhat as follows: Meletus asserts that Socrates is guilty of corrupting the young and not believing in the gods in whom the city believes, but in some strange divinities. That is the sort of charge, and let us take it point by point. He does really say that I am guilty of corrupting the young. But I answer, men of Athens, that Meletus is guilty of an unseemly jest, bringing men to trial on a frivolous charge, pretending that he cares intensely about matters on which he has never spent a thought. That this is so I will try to prove.

XII. Come here, Meletus, and tell me: you really think it of importance that our young men should be as good as possible? "I do indeed." Well, will you tell the court who it is that makes them better? It is plain that you must know since you have given the matter thought. You have found, so you say, the man who corrupts them in me; you have accused me and brought me to trial before these judges: go on and point out to them who it is that makes them better. See, Meletus, you are silent and have not a word to say: and now, are you not ashamed? Is not this proof enough of what I say, that you have never thought of it at all? Yet once more, my friend, I ask you, who is it makes them better? "The laws." No, my good fellow, that is not what I ask: I ask what *man* makes them better, and he, of course, must know the laws already. "Well, then, Socrates, I say these judges are the men." Really, Meletus, can these men really teach our youth and make them better? "Most certainly they can." All of them, do you mean, or only some? "All of them." Splendid! Splendid! What a wealth of benefactors! And what of the audience? Can they do so or not? "Yes, they can do so too." And what about the Councillors? "Yes, the Councillors too." Well, Meletus, what of the Assembly and those who sit there? They do not corrupt our young men, I suppose? All of them too, you would say, make them better? "Yes, all of them too." Then it really seems that all the Athenians except me can make men good, and that I alone corrupt them. Is that what you mean? "That is exactly what I mean." What a dreadful fate to be cursed with! But answer me: have you the same opinion in the case of horses? Do you think that those who make them better consist of all mankind, with the exception of one single individual who ruins them? Or, on the contrary, that there is only one man who can do them good, or very, very few, the men, namely, who understand them? And that most people, if they use horses and have to do with them, ruin them? Is it not so, Meletus, with horses and all other animals too? Of course it is, whether you and Anytus admit it or not. It would be well, and more than well, with our youth if there was only one man to corrupt them and all the others did them good. However, Meletus, you show us clearly enough that you have never considered our young men: you have made it quite plain that you care nothing about them, that you have never given a thought to the cause for which you have brought me here.

XIII. But tell us now, Meletus, I entreat you, is it better to live in an evil city or a good? Answer us, my friend: it is not a hard question after all. Do not bad men do evil to their nearest neighbours and good men good? "Yes, of course." Well, is there any man who would rather be injured than aided by his fellows? Answer me, my good man. Indeed the law says you must. Is there any one who wishes to be harmed? "Certainly not." Well, you accuse me, we know, of corrupting the youth and making them worse: do you suppose that I do it intentionally or unintentionally? "Intentionally, I have no doubt." Really and truly, Meletus? Is a man of your years so much wiser than a man of mine that you can understand that bad men always do some evil, and good men some good to those who come nearest to them, while I have sunk to such a depth of folly that I am ignorant of it and do not know that if I make one of my fellows wicked I run the risk of getting harm from him,—and I bring about this terrible state of things intentionally, so you say? I do not believe you, Meletus, nor can any one else, I think. Either I do not corrupt them at all, or if I do, it is done unintentionally, so that in either case you are wrong. And if I do it unintentionally, it is not legal to bring me here for such involuntary errors; you ought to have taken me apart and taught me and reproved me in private; for it is evident that when I learn the truth I shall cease to do what I have done in ignorance. But you shrank from meeting me and teaching me,—you did not choose to do that: you brought me here where those should be brought who need punishment, not those who need instruction.

XIV. Well, men of Athens, it has been plain for some time that Meletus, as I say, has never spent a thought on these matters,—not one, great or small.

Nevertheless, you must tell us, Meletus, how you think I corrupt the youth. No doubt, as you say in the indictment, by teaching them not to believe in the gods in whom our city believes but in some new divinities. Is not that how you say I ruin them? "Certainly, I do say so, as strongly as I can." Then, in the name of those gods of whom we speak, explain yourself more clearly to me and to the court. I have not been able to discover whether you say I teach belief in divinities of some kind, in which case I do after all believe in gods, and am not an utter atheist, and so far I am not guilty; only they are not the gods in which the city believes, they are quite different, and that is your charge against me. Or perhaps you mean to say that I do not believe in gods of any kind, and that I teach others so. "Yes, that is what I say; you do not believe in them at all." Meletus, Meletus, you astound me. What makes you say so? Then I do not even believe that the sun and the moon are gods as other men believe? "Most certainly, gentlemen of the court, most certainly; for he says the sun is stone and the moon earth." My dear Meletus, do you imagine you are attacking Anaxagoras? Or do you think so little of the jury, do you fancy them so illiterate as not to know that the books of Anaxagoras, the philosopher of Clazomenæ, are full of all these theories? The young men, we are to suppose, learn them all from me, when they can buy them in the theatre for tenpence at the most and laugh at Socrates if he should pretend that they were his, especially when they are so extraordinary. Now tell me in heaven's name, is this really what you think?—that I believe in no god at all? "In none at all." I cannot believe you, Meletus, I cannot think you can believe yourself. Men of Athens, I think this man an audacious scoundrel, I consider he has framed this indictment in a spirit of sheer insolence, aggression, and arrogance. One would think he was speaking in riddles, to try "whether the wise Socrates will discover that I am jesting and contradicting myself, or whether I shall deceive him and all who hear me." For he surely contradicts himself in his own indictment, almost as if he said: "Socrates is guilty of not believing in gods but believing in them." Such words can only be in jest.

XV. Look at the matter with me, gentlemen of the court, and see how it appears to me. And you must answer us, Meletus, and you sirs, I ask you, as I asked you at first, not to interrupt me if I put the questions in my usual way. Now is there any man, Meletus, who believes that human things exist, but not human beings? Let him answer, sirs, but do not allow him only to interrupt. Is there any one who does not believe in horses but does believe in their trappings? Or who does not believe in flute-players but does believe in flutes? There cannot be, my worthy man; for if you will not answer, I must tell you myself and tell the court as well. But answer this at least: is there any one who believes in things divine and disbelieves in divinities? "No, there is not." How kind of you to answer at last, under pressure from the court! Well, you admit that I believe in things divine, and that I teach others so. They may be new or they may be old, but at the least, according to your own admission, I do believe in things that are divine, and you have sworn to this in your deposition. And if I believe in things divine I must believe in divinities as well. Is that not so? Indeed it is; for since you will not answer I must assume that you assent. And do we not believe that divinities are gods, or the sons of gods? You admit this? "Yes, certainly." Well, now if I believe in divinities, as you grant I do, and if divinities are gods of some kind, then this is what I meant when I said you were speaking in riddles and jesting with us, saying that I do not believe in gods and yet again that I do, since I believe in divinities. Again if these divinities are the bastards of the gods, with nymphs and other women for their mothers, as people say they are,—what man is there who could believe in sons of gods and not in gods? It would be as absurd as to believe in the offspring of horses and of asses, and not believe in horses and asses too. No, Meletus, it can only be that you were testing me when you drew up that charge, or else it was because you could find nothing to accuse me of with any truth. There is no possible way by which you could persuade any man of the least intelligence to doubt that he who believes in things divine and godlike must believe in divinities and gods, while he who disbelieves the one must disbelieve the other.

XVI. However, men of Athens, I do not think much defence is needed to show that I am innocent of the charge Meletus has made; I think I have now said enough; but what I told you before, namely, that there is deep and widespread enmity against me, that, you must remember, is perfectly true. And this is what will overthrow me, if I am overthrown, not Meletus nor yet Anytus, but the prejudices and envy of the majority, forces that have overthrown many a good man ere now, and will, I imagine, overthrow many more; there is little fear that it will end with me. But maybe some of you will say to me: "And are you not ashamed of a practice that has brought you to the verge of death?" But I have a good answer to give him. "You are not right, my friend," so I would say, "if you think that a man of any worth at all, however slight, ought to reckon up the chances of life and death, and not consider one thing and one alone, and that is whether what he does is right or wrong, a good man's deed or a craven's." According to you, the sons of the gods who died at Troy would have been foolish creatures, and the son of Thetis above all, who thought so lightly of danger compared with the least disgrace, that, when he was resolved to kill Hector and when his mother, goddess as she was, spoke to him, to this effect, if I remember right: "My son, if you avenge the slaughter of your friend Patroclus, and kill Hector, you will die yourself:—

'After the fall of Hector, death is waiting for you;'"—

those were her words. But he, when he heard, thought scorn of death and danger: he was far more afraid to live a coward's life and leave his friend unavenged. "Come death then!" he answered, "when I have punished the murderer, that I may not live on here in shame,—

'Here by my longships lying, a burden for earth to bear!'"

Do you think that that man cared for death or danger? Hear the truth, men of Athens! The post that a man has taken up because he thought it right himself or because his captain put him there, that post, I believe, he ought to hold in face of every danger, caring no whit for death or any other peril in comparison with disgrace.

XVII. So it would be a strange part for me to have played, men of Athens, if I had done as I did under the leaders you chose for me, at Potidæa and Amphipolis and Delium, standing my ground like any one else where they had posted me and facing death, and yet, when God, as I thought and believed, had set me to live the life of philosophy, making inquiry into myself and into others, I were to fear death now, or anything else whatever, and desert my post. It would be very strange; and then, in truth, one would have reason to bring me before the court, because I did not believe in the gods, since I disobeyed the oracle and was afraid of death, and thought I was wise where I was not. For to fear death, sirs, is simply to think we are wise when we are not so: it is to think we know what we know not. No one knows whether death is not the greatest of all goods that can come to man; and yet men fear it as though they knew it was the greatest of all ills. And is not this the folly that should be blamed, the folly of thinking we know what we do not know? Here, again, sirs, it may be that I am different from other men, and if I could call myself wiser than any one in any point, it would be for this, that as I have no real knowledge about the world of Death, so I never fancy that I have. But I do know that it is evil and base to do wrong and disobey the higher will, be it God's or man's. And so for the sake of evils, which I know right well are evils, I will never fear and never fly from things which are, it may be, good. Therefore, though you should acquit me now and refuse to listen to Anytus when he says that either I ought never to have been brought here at all, or else, now that I have been, it is impossible not to sentence me to death, assuring you that if I am set at liberty, your sons will at once put into practice all that I have taught them, and all become entirely corrupt—if, in face of this, you should say to me, "Socrates, for this once we will not listen to Anytus; we will set you free, but on this condition, that you spend your time no longer in this search, and follow wisdom no more. If you are found doing it again you will be put to death." If, I repeat, you were to set me free on that condition, I would answer you: Men of Athens, I thank you and I am grateful to you, but I must obey God rather than you, and, while I have life and strength, I will never cease to follow wisdom, and urge you forward, explaining to every man of you I meet, speaking as I have always spoken, saying, "See here, my friend, you are an Athenian, a citizen of the greatest city in the world, the most famous for wisdom and for power; and are you not ashamed to care for money and money-making and fame and reputation, and not care at all, not make one effort, for truth and understanding and the welfare of your soul?" And should he protest, and assert he cares, I will not let

him go at once and send him away free: no! I will question him and examine him, and put him to the proof, and if it seems to me that he has not attained to virtue, and yet asserts he has, I will reproach him for holding cheapest what is worth most, and dearer what is worth less. This I will do for old and young,—for every man I meet,—foreigner and citizen,—but most for my citizens, since you are nearer to me by blood. It is God's bidding, you must understand that; and I myself believe no greater blessing has ever come to you or to your city than this service of mine to God. I have gone about doing one thing and one thing only,— exhorting all of you, young and old, not to care for your bodies or for money above or beyond your souls and their welfare, telling you that virtue does not come from wealth, but wealth from virtue, even as all other goods, public or private, that man can need. If it is by these words that I corrupt our youth, then these words do harm; but if any one asserts that I say anything else, there is nothing in what he says. In face of this I would say, "Men of Athens, listen to Anytus or not, acquit me or acquit me not, but remember that I will do nothing else, not if I were to die a hundred deaths."

XVIII. No! do not interrupt me, Athenians; keep the promise I asked you to give,—not to interrupt what I had to say, but to hear it to the end. I believe it will do you good. I am about to say something else for which you might shout me down, only I beg you not to do so. You must understand that if you put me to death when I am the kind of man I say I am, you will not injure me so much as your own selves. Meletus or Anytus could not injure me; they have not the power. I do not believe it is permitted that a good man should be injured by a bad. He could be put to death, perhaps, or exiled, or disfranchised, and it may be Meletus thinks, and others think, that these are terrible evils, but I do not believe they are. I think it far worse to do what he is doing now,—trying to put a man to death without a cause. So it comes about, men of Athens, that I am far from making my defence for my own sake, as might be thought: I make it for yours, that you may not lose God's gift by condemning me. For if you put me to death you will not easily find another of my like; one, I might say,—even if it sounds a little absurd,—who clings to the city at God's command, as a gadfly clings to a horse; and the horse is tall and thorough-bred, but lazy from his growth, and he needs to be stirred up. And God, I think, has set me here as something of the kind,—to stir you up and urge you, and prick each one of you and never cease, sitting close to you all day long. You will not easily find another man like that; and, sirs, if you listen to me you will not take my life. But probably you have been annoyed, as drowsy sleepers are when suddenly awakened, and you will turn on me and listen to Anytus, and be glad to put me to death; and then you will spend the rest of your life in sleep, unless God, in his goodness, sends you another man like me. That I am what I say I am, given by God to the city, you may realise from this: it is not the way of a mere man to leave all his own affairs uncared for and all his property neglected during so many years, and go about your business all his life, coming to each individual man, as I have come, as though I were his father or his elder brother, and bidding him think of righteousness. If I had got any profit by this, if I had taken payment for these words, there would have been some explanation for what I did; but you can see for yourselves that my accusers—audacious in everything else— have yet not had the audacity to bring witnesses to assert that I have ever taken payment from any man, or ever asked for it. The witness I could bring myself in my own poverty, would be enough, I think, to prove I speak the truth.

XIX. It may perhaps seem strange that while I have gone about in private to give this counsel, and have been so busy over it, yet I have not found it in my heart to come forward publicly before your democracy and advise the State. The reason is one you have heard me give before, at many times and in many places; and it is this: I have a divine and supernatural sign that comes to me. Meletus referred to it scoffingly in his indictment, but, in truth, it has been with me from boyhood, a kind of voice that comes to me; and, when it comes, it always holds me back from what I may intend to do; it never urges me forward. It is this which has stopped me from taking part in public affairs; and it did well, I think, to stop me. For you may be sure, men of Athens, if I had attempted to enter public life, I should have perished long ago, without any good to you or to myself. Do not be angry with me if I tell you the truth. No man will ever be safe who stands up boldly against you, or against any other democracy, and forbids the many sins and crimes that are com-

mitted in the State; the man who is to fight for justice— if he is to keep his life at all—must work in private, not in public.

XX. I will give you a remarkable proof of this, a proof not in words, but in what you value—deeds. Listen, and I will tell you something that happened to me, and you may realise from it that I will never consent to injustice at any man's command for fear of death, but would die on the spot rather than give way. What I have to tell you may seem an arrogant tale and a commonplace of the courts, but it is true.

You know, men of Athens, that I have never held any other office in the State, but I did serve on the Council. And it happened that my tribe, Antiochis, had the Presidency at the time you decided to try the ten generals who had not taken up the dead after the fight at sea.[2] You decided to try them in one body, contrary to law, as you all felt afterwards. On that occasion I was the only one of the Presidents who opposed you, and told you not to break the law; and I gave my vote against it; and when the orators were ready to impeach and arrest me, and you encouraged them and hooted me, I thought then that I ought to take all risks on the side of law and justice, rather than side with you, when your decisions were unjust, through fear of imprisonment or death. That while the city was still under the democracy. When the oligarchy came into power, the Thirty, in their turn, summoned me with four others to the Rotunda, and commanded us to fetch Leon of Salamis from that island, in order to put him to death: the sort of commands they often gave to many others, anxious as they were to incriminate all they could. And on that occasion I showed, not by words only, that for death, to put it bluntly, I did not care one straw,—but I did care, and to the full, about doing what was wicked and unjust. I was not terrified then into doing wrong by that government in all its power: when we left the Rotunda, the other four went off to Salamis and brought Leon back, but I went

---

2. This was after the sea-fight of Arginusæ, 406 B.C., one of the last Athenian successes in the Peloponnesian war. In spite of the success, twenty-five ships were lost. Their crews were not saved, and it was felt that the generals—eight in number—must have been careless in the matter. The popular indignation was extreme; the case was tried in the Assembly, and the generals were sentenced to death in a body. This was contrary to recognised law, as each should have been tried separately.

home. And probably I should have been put to death for it if the government had not been overthrown soon afterwards. Many people will confirm me in what I say.

XXI. Do you believe now that I should have lived so long as this, if I had taken part in public affairs and done what I could for justice like an upright man, putting it, as I was bound to put it, first and foremost? Far from it, men of Athens. Not I, nor any other man on earth. And all through my life you will find that this has been my character,—in public, if ever I had any public work to do, and the same in private,— never yielding to any man against right and justice, though he were one of those whom my calumniators call my scholars. But I have never been any one's teacher. Only, if any man, young or old, has ever heard me at my work and wished to listen, I have never grudged him my permission; I have not talked with him if he would pay me, and refused him if he would not; I am ready for questions from rich and poor alike, and equally ready to question them should they care to answer me and hear what I have to say. And for that, if any one is the better or any one the worse, I ought not to be held responsible; I never promised instruction, I never taught, and if any man says he has ever learnt or heard one word from me in private other than all the world could hear, I tell you he does not speak the truth.

XXII. What then can it be that makes some men delight in my company? You have heard my answer, sirs. I told you the whole truth when I said their delight lay in hearing men examined who thought that they were wise but were not so; and certainly it is not unpleasant. And I, as I believe, have been commanded to do this by God, speaking in oracles and in dreams, in every way by which divine grace has ever spoken to man at all and told him what to do. That, men of Athens, is the truth, and easy to verify. For if it were really the case that I corrupt our young men and have corrupted them, then surely, now that they are older, if they have come to understand that I ever meant to do them harm when they were young, some of them ought to come forward here and now, to accuse and punish me, or if they did not care to come themselves, some who are near to them—their fathers, or their brothers, or others of their kin,—ought to remember and punish it now, if it be true that those who are dear

to them have suffered any harm from me. In fact, there are many of them here at this very moment; I can see them for myself; there is Crito, my contemporary, who belongs to the same deme as I, the father of Critobulus there; and here is Lusanias of Sphettos, the father of Æschines, who is beside him; and Antiphon of Kephisia, the father of Epigenes; and others too whose brothers have spent their time with me, Nicostratus, the son of Theozotides, brother of Theodotus. Theodotus is dead; so it cannot be his entreaty that has stopped his brother. And Paralus is here, the son of Demodocus, whose brother Theages was; and Adeimantus, the son of Ariston, whose brother Plato I see, and Aiantodorus with his brother Apollodorus too. And I could tell you of many more, one of whom at least Meletus should have called as a witness in his attack; or, if he forgot then, let him call one now, and I will stand aside, and he can speak if he has anything to say. But, gentlemen, you will find precisely the reverse; you will find them all prepared to stand by me, the man who has done the harm, the man who has injured their nearest and dearest, as Meletus and Anytus say. Those, perhaps, who are ruined themselves might have some reason for supporting me, but those who are uncorrupted,—men of advancing years, their relatives,—what other reason could they have for their support except the right and worthy reason that they know Meletus is lying and I am speaking the truth?

XXIII. There, gentlemen, that is on the whole what I had to say in my defence, with something more, perhaps, to the same effect. Now there may be a man among you who will feel annoyed if he remembers his own conduct when undergoing a trial far less serious than this of mine; how he prayed and supplicated the judges with floods of tears, and brought his little children into court to rouse as much pity as possible, and others of his family and many of his friends; but I, it would appear, will not do anything of the kind, and that in the face, as it might seem, of the utmost danger. Such a man, it may be, observing this, will harden himself against me; this one fact will enrage him and he will give his vote in anger. If this is so with any of you,—I do not say it is, but if it is,—I think it would be reasonable for me to say, "I too, my good man, have kindred of my own, I too was not born, as Homer says, 'from stock or stone,' but from men, so that I have kinsfolk and sons also, three sons,—the eldest of them is already a stripling, the other two are children. And yet I do not intend to bring one of them here, or entreat you to acquit me." And why is it that I will not do anything of the kind? Not from pride, men of Athens, nor from disrespect for you: nor is it because I am at peace about death; it is for the sake of my honour and yours and the honour of the city. I do not think it fitting that I should do such things, a man of my years, and with the name I bear; it may be true or false, but at any rate it is believed that Socrates is in some way different from most other men. And if those among you who bear a name for wisdom or courage or any other virtue were to act like this, it would be disgraceful. I have seen it often in others, when they came under trial, men of some repute, but who behaved in a most extraordinary way, thinking, apparently, that it would be a fearful thing for them to die; as though they would be immortal if you did not put them to death. Such men, I think, bring disgrace upon the city, and any stranger might suppose that the Athenians who bore the highest name for virtue, who had been chosen out expressly for office and reward, were no whit better than women. We must not behave so, men of Athens, those of us who are thought to be of any worth at all, and you must not allow it, should we try: you must make it plain, and quite plain, that you will be more ready to condemn the man who acts these pitiful scenes before you and makes the city absurd, than him who holds his peace.

XXIV. Even putting honour aside, gentlemen, it does not seem to me right to supplicate a judge and gain acquittal so: we ought rather to instruct him and convince him. The judge does not sit here to grant justice as a favour, but to try the case; he has sworn, not that he will favour those he chooses, but that he will judge according to the law. So we should not teach you to break your oath, and you should not let yourselves be taught. Neither of us would reverence the gods if we did that. Therefore you must not expect me, men of Athens, to act towards you in a way which I do not think seemly or right or reverent—more especially when I am under trial for impiety, and have Meletus here to face. For plainly, were I to win you over by my entreaties, and have you do violence to your oath, plainly I should be teaching you not to believe in the gods, and my own speech would accuse me unmistakably of unbelief. But it is far from being so; for I believe, men of Athens, as not one of my accusers believes, and I leave it to you and to God to decide my case as may be best for me and you.

Part II

After the Verdict and Before the Sentence

XXV. There are many reasons, men of Athens, why I feel no distress at what has now occurred, I mean your condemnation of me. It is not unexpected; on the contrary, I am surprised at the number of votes on either side. I did not think it would be so close. I thought the majority would be great; but in fact, so it appears, if only thirty votes had gone otherwise, I should have been acquitted. Against Meletus, as it is, I appear to have won, and not only so, but it is clear to every one that if Anytus and Lycon had not come forward to accuse me, he would have been fined a thousand drachmas, for he would not have obtained a fifth part of the votes.

XXVI. The penalty he fixes for me is, I understand, death. Very good. And what am I going to fix in my turn, men of Athens? It must be, must it not, what I deserve? Well, then, what do I deserve to receive or pay because I chose not to sit quiet all my life, and turned aside from what most men care for,—money-making and household affairs, leadership in war and public speaking, and all the offices and associations and factions of the State,—thinking myself, as a matter of fact, too upright to be safe if I went into that life? So I held aloof from it all; I should have been of no use there to you or to myself, but I set about going in private to each individual man and doing him the greatest of all services—as I assert—trying to persuade every one of you not to think of what he had but rather of what he was, and how he might grow wise and good, nor consider what the city had, but what the city was, and so with everything else in the world. What, then, do I deserve for this? A reward, men of Athens, if I am really to consider my deserts, and a reward, moreover, that would suit me. And what reward would suit a poor man who has been a public benefactor, and who is bound to refrain from work because of his services in exhorting you? There could be nothing so suitable, men of Athens, as a place at the table in the Presidents' Hall; far more suitable than if any of you had won a horse-race at Olympia or a chariot race. The Olympian victor brings you fancied happiness, but I bring you real: he does not need maintenance, but I do. If I am to fix what I deserve in all fairness, then this is what I fix:—a place at the table in the Presidents' Hall.

XXVII. Perhaps when I say this you will feel that I am speaking much as I spoke about entreaties for pity, that is to say, in a spirit of pride; but it is not so, Athenians. This is how it is: I am convinced that I have never done wrong to any man intentionally, but I cannot convince you; we have only had a little time to talk together. Had it been the custom with you, as with other nations, to spend not one day but many on a trial for life and death, I believe you would have been convinced; but, as matters are, it is not easy to remove a great prejudice in a little time.

Well, with this conviction of mine that I have never wronged any man, I am far from meaning to wrong myself by saying that I deserve any harm, or assigning myself anything whatever of the kind. What should I be afraid of? Of suffering what Meletus has assigned, when I say that I do not know, after all, whether it is not good? And to escape it I am to choose what I know quite well is bad? And what punishment should I fix? Imprisonment? Why should I live in prison, slave to the Eleven[3] of the day? Or should I say a fine, with imprisonment until I pay it? But then there is just the difficulty I mentioned a moment ago: I have no money to pay a fine. Or am I to say exile? You might, I know, choose that for my punishment. My love of life would indeed be great if I were so blind as not to see that you, my own fellow-citizens, have not been able to endure my ways and words, you have found them too trying and too heavy to bear, so that you want to get rid of them now. And if that is so, will strangers put up with them? Far from it, men of Athens. And it would be a grand life for a man of my years to go into exile and wander about from one city to another. For well I know that wherever I went the young men would listen to my talk as they listen here; and if I drove them away, they would drive me out themselves and persuade their elders to side with them, and if I

let them come, their fathers and kindred would banish me on their account.

XXVIII. Perhaps some one will say: "But, Socrates, cannot you leave us and live in peace and quietness?" Now that is just what it is hardest to make you, some of you, believe. If I were to say that this would be to disobey God, and therefore I cannot hold my peace, you would not believe me; you would say I was using my irony. And if I say again that it is in fact the greatest of all goods for a man to talk about virtue every day, and the other matters on which you have heard me speaking and making inquiry into myself and others: if I say that the life without inquiry is no life for man— you would believe that even less. Yet it is so, even as I tell you—only it is not easy to get it believed. Moreover, I am not accustomed to think myself deserving of punishment. However, if I had had any money I should have fixed a price that I could pay, for that would not have harmed me at all; but as it is, since I have no money—unless perhaps you would consent to fix only so much as I could afford to pay? Perhaps I might be able to pay one mina silver; and I will fix the fine at that. But Plato here, gentlemen, and Crito, and Critobulus, and Apollodorus, beg me to say thirty minas, and they tell me they will guarantee it. So I will fix it at this sum, and these men, on whom you can rely, will be sureties for the amount.

Part III

After the Sentence of Death

XXIX. You have hastened matters a little, men of Athens, but for that little gain you will be called the murderers of Socrates the Wise by all who want to find fault with the city. For those who wish to reproach you will insist that I am wise, though I may not be so. Had you but waited a little longer, you would have found this happen of itself: for you can see how old I am, far on in life, with death at hand. In this I am not speaking to all of you, but only to those who have sentenced me to death. And to them I will say one thing more. It may be, gentlemen, that you imagine I have been convicted for lack of arguments by which I could have convinced you, had I thought it right to say and do anything in order to escape punishment. Far from it. No; convicted I have been, for lack of—not arguments,

---

3. The Eleven formed a board consisting of a secretary and ten members appointed by lot every year. They had charge of the prisons and superintended executions.

but audacity and impudence, and readiness to say what would have been a delight for you to hear, lamenting and bewailing my position, saying and doing all kinds of things unworthy of myself, as I consider, but such as you have grown accustomed to hear from others. I did not think it right then to behave through fear unlike a free-born man, and I do not repent now of my defence; I would far rather die after that defence than live upon your terms. As in war, so in a court of justice, not I nor any man should scheme to escape death by any and every means. Many a time in battle it is plain the soldier could avoid death if he flung away his arms and turned to supplicate his pursuers, and there are many such devices in every hour of danger for escaping death, if we are prepared to say and do anything whatever. But, sirs, it may be that the difficulty is not to flee from death, but from guilt. Guilt is swifter than death. And so it is that I, who am slow and old, have been caught by the slower-paced, and my accusers, who are clever and quick, by the quick-footed, by wickedness. And now I am to go away, under sentence of death from you: but on them truth has passed sentence of unrighteousness and injustice. I abide by the decision, and so must they. Perhaps indeed, it had to be just so: and I think it is very well.

XXX. And now that that is over I desire to prophesy to you, you who have condemned me. For now I have come to the time when men can prophesy—when they are to die. I say to you, you who have killed me, punishment will fall on you immediately after my death, far heavier for you to bear—I call God to witness!—than your punishment of me. For you have done this thinking to escape the need of giving any account of your lives: but exactly the contrary will come to pass, and so I tell you. Those who will call you to account will be more numerous,—I have kept them back till now, and you have not noticed them,—and they will be the harder to bear inasmuch as they are younger, and you will be troubled all the more. For if you think that by putting men to death you can stop every one from blaming you for living as you should not live, I tell you you are mistaken; that way of escape is neither feasible nor noble; the noblest way, and the easiest, is not to maim others, but to fit ourselves for righteousness. That is the prophecy I give to you who have condemned me, and so I leave you.

XXXI. But with those who have acquitted me I should be glad to talk about this matter, until the Archons are at leisure and I go to the place where I am to die. So I will ask you, gentlemen, to stay with me for the time. There is no reason why we should not talk together while we can, and tell each other our dreams. I would like to show you, as my friends, what can be the meaning of this that has befallen me. A wonderful thing, my judges,—for I may call you judges, and not call you amiss,—a wonderful thing has happened to me. The warning that comes to me, my spiritual sign, has always in all my former life been most incessant, and has opposed me in most trifling matters, whenever I was about to act amiss; and now there has befallen me, as you see yourselves, what might really be thought, as it is thought, the greatest of all evils. And yet, when I left my home in the morning, the signal from God was not against me, nor when I came up here into the court, nor in my speech, whatever I was about to say; and yet at other times it has often stopped me in the very middle of what I was saying; but never once in this matter has it opposed me in any word or deed. What do I suppose to be the reason? I will tell you. This that has befallen me is surely good, and it cannot possibly be that we are right in our opinion, those of us who hold that death is an evil. A great proof of this has come to me: it cannot but be that the well-known signal would have stopped me, unless what I was going to meet was good.

XXXII. Let us look at it in this way too, and we shall find much hope that it is so. Death must be one of two things: either it is to have no consciousness at all of anything whatever, or else, as some say, it is a kind of change and migration of the soul from this world to another. Now if there is no consciousness at all, and it is like sleep when the sleeper does not dream, I say there would be a wonderful gain in death. For I am sure if any man were to take that night in which he slept so deeply that he saw no dreams, and put beside it all the other nights and days of his whole life, and compare them, and say how many of them all were better spent or happier than that one night,—I am sure that not the ordinary man alone, but the King of Persia himself, would find them few to count. If death is of this nature I would consider it a gain; for the whole of time would seem no longer than one single night. But if it is a journey to another land, if what some say is true and all the dead are really there, if this is so, my judges, what greater good could there be? If a man were to go to the House of Death, and leave all these self-styled judges to find the true judges there, who, so it is said, give justice in that world,—Minos and Rhadamanthus, Æacus and Triptolemus, and all the sons of the gods who have done justly in this life,—would that journey be ill to take? Or to meet Orpheus and Musæus, Hesiod and Homer, what would you give for that, any of you? I would give a hundred deaths if it is true. And for me especially it would be a wonderful life there, if I met Palamedes, and Ajax, the son of Telamon, or any of the men of old who died by an unjust decree: to compare my experience with theirs would be full of pleasure, surely. And best of all, to go on still with the men of that world as with the men of this, inquiring and questioning and learning who is wise among them, and who may think he is, but is not. How much would one give, my judges, to question the hero who led the host at Troy, or Odysseus, or Sisyphus, or any of the countless men and women I could name? To talk with them there, and live with them, and question them, would be happiness unspeakable. Certainly there they will not put one to death for that; they are far happier in all things than we of this world, and they are immortal for evermore,—if what some say is true.

XXXIII. And you too, my judges, must think of death with hope, and remember this at least is true, that no evil can come to a good man in life or death, and that he is not forgotten of God; what has come to me now has not come by chance, but it is clear to me that it was better for me to die and be quit of trouble. That is why the signal never came to turn me back,

and I cannot say that I am altogether angry with my accusers and those who have condemned me. Yet it was not with that intention that they condemned and accused me; they meant to do me harm, and they are to be blamed for that. This much, however, I will ask of them. When my sons come of age, sirs, will you reprove them and trouble them as I troubled you, if you think they care for money or anything else more than righteousness? And if they seem to be something when they are really nothing, reproach them as I reproached you for not seeking what they need, and for thinking they are somewhat when they are worth nothing. And if you do this, we shall have received justice at your hands, my sons and I.

But now it is time for us to go, I to death, and you to life; and which of us goes to the better state is known to none but God.

DISCUSSION QUESTIONS

1. What does Socrates mean by "wisdom," and what does it have to do with a truly moral life, in his estimation?
2. Compare the jury trial Socrates faced with the current trial system in the United States, or another country. What are the pros and cons of each?
3. Do you find Socrates' argument against the fear of death convincing? Why or why not?
4. The Socratic method of philosophizing, as it has come to be known, involves rational dialogue primarily based on a question-and-answer format, in which the questioner assumes a stance of ignorance. How might this method be used in our everyday lives on issues that matter to us?

2. Boethius (c. 480–524)
From *The Consolation of Philosophy*

Ancius Manlius Severinus Boethius was a Roman philosopher and statesman whose extensive writings provided a bridge between classical, pre-Christian Greek systems of thought (especially those of Plato and Aristotle) and early medieval, Christianized Latin philosophy. He came from a wealthy patrician family and, for several years, enjoyed a successful and honorable political career serving under Theodoric, the Ostrogoth king in northern Italy. However, the course of political events led to his being charged with treason, whereafter he was stripped of his wealth, imprisoned, and finally executed.

Today Boethius is most remembered for *The Consolation of Philosophy*, which he wrote while in prison. Apparently it was a way of coming to grips with his dramatic reversal of fortune and impending unjust death. The recurrent theme is that only a life of reason devoted to truth can lead to the knowledge of what is ultimately valuable in life and thus enable a person to rise above the inevitable miseries to which all mortals are subject. Boethius presents his thoughts in the form of a dialogue that takes place in a vision, a stylistic device employed regularly in subsequent medieval literature. In his present state of despair, he thinks that only poetry can give him comfort, but Philosophy personified as a woman then appears to him. She proceeds to show him why wisdom grounded in reason is the only reliable means to achieve true happiness. The text is composed of five "books," each one made up of alternating prose passages and poems. Book III is reprinted here.

QUESTIONS FOR CRITICAL READING

1. By the end of the reading, how has the Muse of Philosophy defined the "highest good," and "happiness," and how are they related?
2. How does Philosophy characterize "God," and what arguments does she use to link God to both the good and happiness?
3. What is the significance of the concept of "unity"?
4. What are the "false goods" of mortal life, and how does Philosophy evaluate them?

TERMS TO NOTE

virtue: In general, excellence of character, though not always in an exclusively moralistic sense. Particular virtues (for example, temperance, courage, and integrity) are more specific positively valued personality traits, in this context associated with our "higher nature."

vice: As the opposite of virtue, deficiency or corruption of character. Specific vices (for example, intemperance, cowardice, and untrustworthiness) are negatively valued personality traits or predispositions, associated with our "lower nature."

simple: That which is unitary and without parts.

Prose 1

Philosophy promises to lead Boethius to true happiness.

When her song was finished, its sweetness left me wondering and alert, eager to hear more. After a while I said, "You are the perfect comforter for weak spirits. I feel greatly refreshed by the strength of your ideas and the sweetness of your music; in fact, I think I may now be equal to the attacks of Fortune. And those remedies you spoke of earlier as being rather harsh— I not only do not fear them, I am quite eager to hear them."

Philosophy answered, "I knew it when I saw you so engrossed, so attentive to what I was saying. I waited for you to achieve this state of mind, or, to put it more truly, I led you to it. You will find what I have yet to say bitter to the taste, but, once you have digested it, it will seem sweet. Even though you say that you want to hear more, your eagerness would be even greater if you knew where I am about to lead you."

"Where?" said I.

"To true happiness, to the goal your mind has dreamed of. But your vision has been so clouded by false images you have not been able to reach it."[1]

"Tell me then," I said. "Show me quickly what true happiness is."

"I will gladly, for your sake. But first I must try to make something else clear, something you know much more about. When you have understood that, you may turn your attention in the opposite direction and then you will be able to recognize the nature of true blessedness.

Poem 1

"The man who wants to sow a fertile field must first clear the ground of brush, then cut out the ferns and brambles with his sharp hook, so that the new grain may grow abundantly.[2]

---

1. Cf. Plato, *Republic* 515c.
2. The text uses Ceres, goddess of harvest, for grain. Notus, in the paragraph following, is the south wind.

"Honey is sweeter to the taste if the mouth has first tried bitter flavors. Stars shine more brightly after Notus has stopped his rainy blasts. Only after Hesperus has driven away the darkness does the day drive forward his splendid horses.

"Just so, by first recognizing false goods, you begin to escape the burden of their influence; then afterwards true goods may gain possession of your spirit."

Prose 2

Philosophy defines the supreme good and the perfect happiness to which all men naturally aspire. She then lists the kinds of false goods which men mistake for the true good.

Philosophy looked away for a moment, as though withdrawn into the sacred chamber of her mind; then she began to speak: "Mortal men laboriously pursue many different interests along many different paths, but all strive to reach the same goal of happiness. Now the good is defined as that which, once it is attained, relieves man of all further desires. This is the supreme good and contains within itself all other lesser goods. If it lacked anything at all, it could not be the highest good, because something would be missing, and this could still be desired. Clearly, then, perfect happiness is the perfect state in which all goods are possessed. And, as I said, all men try by various means to attain this state of happiness; for there is naturally implanted in the minds of men the desire for the true good, even though foolish error draws them toward false goods.

"Some men, believing that the highest good is to have everything, exert themselves to become very rich. Others think that the highest good is to be found in the highest honors, and so they try to gain the esteem of their fellow citizens by acquiring various honors. Still others equate the highest good with the greatest personal power. Such men want to be rulers, or at least to associate themselves closely with those in power. Then there are those for whom fame seems the highest good and they labor to spread the glory of their names either in war or in practicing the arts of peace. Others measure the good in terms of gaiety and enjoyment; they think that the greatest happiness is found in pleasure. Finally, there are those who interchange the causes and results of these false goods: some desire riches in order to get power and pleasure; some desire power in order to get money or fame.

"Toward such false goods, and others like them, men direct their actions and desires; they want nobility and popularity, for example, because these seem to bring fame; or they want a wife and children because they regard them as sources of pleasure. With regard to friendship, the most sacred kind belongs to the goods of virtue, not of Fortune; all other kinds of friendship are sought out of a desire for power or pleasure. At this point it is a simple matter to evaluate the goods of the body in relation to those we have already discussed: size and strength seem to give power; beauty and speed bring fame; health gives pleasure. All this shows clearly that all men seek happiness; for whatever anyone desires beyond all else, he regards as the highest good. And, since we have defined the highest good as happiness, everyone thinks that the condition which he wants more than anything else must constitute happiness.

"You see here practically the whole range of human happiness: riches, honor, power, fame, and pleasure. Epicurus, who considered only these possibilities, held pleasure to be the highest good of them all, since the rest seem to bring joy to the soul.[3]

"But let me return now to the goals men set for themselves. In spite of its hazy memory, the human soul seeks to return to its true good; but, like the drunken man who cannot find his way home, the soul no longer knows what its good is. Should we consider those men mistaken who try to have everything? Not at all, for nothing can so surely make a man happy as being in full possession of all good things, sufficient in himself and needing no one else. Nor are they mistaken who think that the best men are most worthy of honor, for nothing which nearly all men aspire to achieve can be despised as vile. Power, too, must be considered a good thing, for it would be ridiculous to regard as trivial an asset which can accomplish more than anything else. And what of fame; should we be scornful of it? Surely we must admit that great excellence always carries with it great fame. Finally, it goes

---

3. Epicurus, *Fragmenta* 348. Cf. St. Augustine, *De civitate Dei* XIX. 1.

without saying that happiness excludes sadness and anguish, that it implies freedom from grief and misery, since even in small things we desire whatever brings delight and enjoyment.

"These, then, are the things which men desire to have: riches, high rank, administrative authority, glory and pleasure, because they believe that these things will give them a good standard of living, honor, power, fame and joy. And whatever men strive for in so many ways must be the good. It is easy to show how strong and natural this striving is because, in spite of the variety and difference of opinion, still all men agree in loving and pursuing the goal of good.

Poem 2

"Now I will show you in graceful song, accompanied by pliant strings, how mighty Nature guides the reins of all things; how she providently governs the immense world by her laws; how she controls all things, binding them with unbreakable bonds.

"The Carthaginian lions endure their fair chains, are fed by hand, and fear the beatings they get from their masters; but if blood should smear their fierce mouths, their sluggish spirits revive, and with a roar they revert to their original nature. They shake off their chains and turn their mad fury on their masters, tearing them with bloody teeth.

"When the chattering bird, who sings in the high branches, is shut up in a narrow cage, she is not changed by the lavish care of the person who feeds her with sweet drink and tasty food. If she can escape from the cramped cage and see the cool shade of the wood, she will scatter the artificial food and fly with yearning to the trees where she will make the forest ring with her sweet voice.

"A treetop bent down by heavy pressure will bow its head to the ground; but if the pressure is released, the tree looks back to heaven again. Phoebus sets at night beneath the Hesperian waves, but returning again along his secret path he drives his chariot to the place where it always rises.

"Thus all things seek again their proper courses, and rejoice when they return to them. The only stable order in things is that which connects the beginning to the end and keeps itself on a steady course.

Prose 3

Nature inclines men toward the true good, but error deceives them with partial goods. Specifically, riches can never be wholly satisfying.

"You, too, who are creatures of earth, dream of your origin. However weak the vision of your dream may be, you have some vague idea of that goal of true happiness toward which you gaze. Nature leads you toward true good, but manifold error turns you away from it. Consider for a moment whether the things men think can give them happiness really bring them to the goal which nature planned for them. If money, or honor, or other goods of that kind really provide something which seems completely and perfectly good, then I too will admit that men can be happy by possessing them. But, if they not only cannot deliver what they promise, but are found to be gravely flawed in themselves, it is obvious that they have only the false appearance of happiness.

"First, then, since you recently were very rich, let me ask whether or not you were ever worried in spite of your abundant wealth."

"Yes," I answered, "I cannot recall a time when my mind was entirely free from worry."

"And wasn't it because you wanted something you did not have, or had something you did not want?"

"That is true," I answered.

"You wanted this, or didn't want that?"

"Yes."

"Then doesn't everyone lack something that he wants?"

"Yes, he does," I replied.

"And isn't the man who lacks something less than wholly self-sufficient?"

"That is true."

"And even you at the peak of your wealth felt this insufficiency?"

"Of course," I agreed.

"Then wealth cannot give a man everything and make him entirely self-sufficient, even though this is what money seems to promise. But I think it most important to observe that there is nothing in the nature of wealth to prevent its being taken from those who have it."

"That is quite true," I said.

"And why shouldn't you agree, since every day those who are powerful enough snatch it from those who are weaker. In fact, most lawsuits are concerned with efforts to recover money taken by violence or fraud."

I agreed that this was the case.

"Therefore, a man needs the help of others to protect his money."

"Of course."

"But he wouldn't need it, if he had no money to lose."

"There is no doubt about that."

"Well then, the situation is upside down; for riches, which are supposed to make men self-sufficient, actually make them dependent on the help of others.

"And now let us see whether riches really drive away need. Don't the wealthy become hungry and thirsty; don't they feel cold in the winter? You may argue that they have the means to satisfy their hunger and thirst, and to protect themselves against the cold. Nevertheless, the needs remain, and riches can only minimize them. For if needs are always present and making demands which must be met by spending money, clearly there will always be some need which is unsatisfied. And here I do not press the point that, although nature makes very modest demands, avarice is never satisfied. My present point is simply this: if riches cannot eliminate need, but on the contrary create new demands, what makes you suppose that they can provide satisfaction?

Poem 3

"Though the rich man has a flowing torrent of gold, his avarice can never be fully satisfied. He may decorate his neck with oriental pearls, and plow his fertile lands with a hundred oxen, but biting care will not leave him during life, and when he dies his wealth cannot go with him.

Prose 4

Honor is not the true good, nor is it the way to true happiness.

"But you may say that high public office makes the man who receives it honorable and worthy of reverence. Do you think that such offices have the power to make those who hold them virtuous and to free them from their vices? On the contrary, public honors usually reveal wickedness rather than correct it, and so we often complain that these honors are given to the worst men. Catullus, for example, called Nonius an ulcer, though he occupied high office.[4] You can see, then, the disgrace that comes to evil men who receive honors. Their unworthiness would be less obvious without the publicity of public recognition. In your own case, could any threats of danger have persuaded you to share public office with Decoratus, once you had found him to be a scoundrel and a spy?[5] We cannot judge men worthy of respect on account of the honors given them, if we find them unworthy of the honors they have received.

"But, if you found a man distinguished by his wisdom, could you think him unworthy of honor, or of the wisdom which is his?"

"Certainly not," I answered.

"For virtue has its own honor, and this honor is transferred to those who possess virtue. Since popular acclaim cannot accomplish this, clearly it does not have the beauty which is characteristic of true honor. More attention should be paid to this point, for if public contempt makes men abject, public acclaim makes wicked men even more despised since it cannot make them worthy of honor and it exposes them to the world. But public rank itself does not escape untouched, for unworthy men tarnish the offices which they hold by infecting them with their own disease.

"And, to prove further that true honor cannot be attained through these specious dignities, think what would happen if a man who had been many times consul should go to some uncivilized foreign coun-

---

4. See Catullus LII. 2.
5. Decoratus, a contemporary public official, was Quaestor about the year 508.

tries. Would the honors which he held at home make him worthy of respect in those places? But, if veneration were a natural part of public honors, it would certainly be given in every nation, just as fire always gives heat wherever it is found in the world. But because popular respect is not a natural consequence of public office, but merely something which depends on untrustworthy public opinion, it vanishes when a man finds himself among those who do not regard his position in his home country as a special dignity.

"What I have said so far has to do with the attitudes of foreigners. Do you think that popular acclaim lasts forever among the citizens in the place where it had its origin? The office of praetor once had great power; now it is an empty name and a heavy burden on the treasury of the Senate. The man who in earlier times was responsible for food supply and distribution was counted a great man; now there is no office lower in public esteem. For, as I said before, whatever does not have its own honor in itself, but depends on public whim, is sometimes valued highly, sometimes not at all. Therefore, if public honors cannot make those who have them worthy of reverence, and if, in addition, they are often tainted by the touch of wicked men, and if their value deteriorates with the passage of time, and if they are contemptible in the eyes of foreigners, what desirable beauty do they have in themselves or give to others?

Poem 4

"Although proud Nero in his raging lust adorned himself in Tyrian purple and white pearls, he was hated by all his subjects. But this wicked man once assigned the tainted seats of consulship to venerable men. Who, then, can consider those men blessed who receive their honors from evil men?

Prose 5

Power is not a guarantee of happiness.

"Can royal power, or familiarity with kings, make a man truly powerful? Perhaps, you may say, as long as his happy situation endures. But both the past and the present are full of examples of kings who have fallen from happiness to misery. How wonderful is power which is found incapable even of preserving itself! And even though political power is a cause of happiness, is it not also a cause of misery when it diminishes? Although some human empires extend very widely, there are always some nations which cannot be brought under control; and at the point where power, which makes rulers happy, ends, there the impotence, which makes them miserable, begins. For this reason, rulers have always more misery than happiness. A famous tyrant, who knew the dangers of his position, symbolized the fears of kingship by hanging a drawn sword over the head of a member of his court.[6]

"What, then, is the nature of this power which cannot rid a man of gnawing anxieties nor save him from fear? Those who brag of their power want to live in security, but cannot. Do you consider a person powerful whom you see unable to have what he wants? Do you think a person mighty who is always surrounded by bodyguards, who is more afraid than those whom he intimidates, who puts himself in the hands of his servants in order to seem powerful?

"And what shall I say about the followers of men in power, when the power they attach themselves to is obviously so weak? They can be destroyed by the fall of their leader, or even by his whim while he is still in power. Nero forced his friend and teacher, Seneca, to choose his own manner of execution; Antoninus had Papinianus cut down by the swords of the soldiers, even though he had long been a power among the courtiers.[7] Both of these unfortunate men wanted to give up their power; indeed, Seneca tried to give his wealth to Nero and retire.[8] But both were destroyed by their very greatness and neither could have what he wanted.

---

6. Dionysius the Elder promised to give the flatterer Damocles a taste of the life of a ruler. He placed him in luxurious surroundings and then suspended a sword above his neck. Cf. Cicero, *Tusculan Disputations* V. 21.

7. Papinianus, the Roman jurist, was executed in A.D. 212 after a brilliant career, for disapproving of the emperor's brother.

8. See above p. 8, n. 8. In A.D. 62, when Seneca was 70, his relations with Nero were severely strained. The philosopher attempted to retire and give his wealth to Nero, but the emperor refused it. See Tacitus, *Annales* XIV. 54.

"What, then, is the value of power which frightens those who have it, endangers those who want it, and irrevocably traps those who have it? Are those true friends whom we acquire by fortune rather than virtue? Misfortune will make an enemy of the man whom good fortune made a friend. And what scoundrel is more deadly than one who has been a friend?

Poem 5

"The man who wishes to be powerful must check his desires; he must not permit himself to be overcome by lust, or submit to its foul reins. For even though your rule extends so far that India trembles before you and Ultima Thule[9] serves you, if you cannot withstand black care, and live without wretched moaning, you have no power.

Prose 6

True happiness is not found in fame.

"As for glory, how deceptive it often is, and how shameful! The tragic playwright justly cries: 'Oh Fame, Fame, how many lives of worthless men you have exalted!'[10] For many men have achieved a great name based on the false opinion of the masses; and what is more disgraceful than that? Those who are falsely praised must blush when they hear the applause. And, even if the praise is merited, what does it matter to the wise man who measures his virtue by the truth of his conscience, not by popular esteem. And if it seems a good thing to have widened one's fame, it follows that it must seem a bad thing not to have done so. But since, as I explained earlier, there will always be some countries to which a man's fame does not extend, it follows that the person you think famous will be unknown in some other part of the world.

"In this discussion of fame, I do not think mere popularity even worth mentioning since it does not rest on good judgment, nor has it any lasting life.

Moreover, everyone knows that to be called noble is a stupid and worthless thing. If it has anything to do with fame, the fame belongs to others; for nobility appears to be a kind of praise which is really merited by parents. If praise makes a person famous, then those who receive praise are famous; therefore, the praise of others (in this case, of your parents) will not make you famous if you have no fame of your own. In my opinion, therefore, if there is anything to be said for nobility, it lies only in the necessity imposed on the nobility to carry on the virtues of their ancestors.

Poem 6

"The whole race of men on this earth springs from one stock. There is one Father of all things; One alone provides for all. He gave Phoebus his rays, the moon its horns. To the earth He gave men, to the sky the stars. He clothed with bodies the souls He brought from heaven.

"Thus, all men come from noble origin. Why then boast of your ancestors? If you consider your beginning, and God your Maker, no one is base unless he deserts his birthright and makes himself a slave to vice.

Prose 7

Bodily pleasure cannot make men happy.

"What now shall I say about bodily pleasures? The appetite for them is full of worry, and the fulfillment full of remorse. What dreadful disease and intolerable sorrow, the fruits of wickedness, they bring to the bodies of those who enjoy them! What pleasure there may be in these appetites I do not know, but they end in misery as anyone knows who is willing to recall his own lusts. If they can produce happiness, then there is no reason why beasts should not be called happy, since their whole life is devoted to the fulfillment of bodily needs. The pleasure one finds in his wife and children ought to be a most wholesome thing, but the man who protested that he found his sons to be his torturers spoke what may too often be true. How terrible such a condition can be you must learn from me, since you have never experienced it at first hand, nor do you

---

9. Ultima Thule was, to the ancients, the northernmost region of the earth.
10. Euripides, *Andromache* 319f.

now suffer from it. In this matter I commend the opinion of Euripides who said that the childless man is happy by his misfortune.[11]

Poem 7

"It is the nature of all bodily pleasure to punish those who enjoy it. Like the bee after its honey is given, it flies away, leaving its lingering sting in the hearts it has struck.

Prose 8

Philosophy concludes that these limited goods are transitory and cannot bring happiness. On the contrary, they are often positively harmful.

"There is no doubt, therefore, that these are the wrong roads to happiness; they cannot take anyone to the destination which they promise. Let me briefly show you the evils within them. If you try to accumulate money, you must deprive someone else of it. If you want to cover yourself with honors, you will become indebted to those who can bestow them; and, by wishing to outdo others in honor, you will humiliate yourself by begging.

"If you want power, you risk the danger of your subjects' treachery. If you seek fame, you will become involved in difficulties and lose your security. If you seek a life of pleasure—but who would not spurn and avoid subjection to so vile and fragile a thing as his body? Indeed, those who boast of bodily goods are relying on weak and uncertain possessions. For you are not bigger than an elephant, nor stronger than a bull, nor as quick as a tiger.

"Fix your gaze on the extent, the stability, the swift motion of the heavens, and stop admiring base things. The heavens are not more remarkable in these qualities than in the reason by which they are governed. The beauty of your person passes swiftly away; it is more fleeting than spring flowers. And if, as Aristotle says, men had the eyes of Lynceus and could see

through stone walls, would they not find the superficially beautiful body of Alcibiades to be most vile upon seeing his entrails?[12] It is not your nature which makes you seem fair but the weak eyes of those who look at you. You may esteem your bodily qualities as highly as you like as long as you admit that these things you admire so much can be destroyed by the trifling heat of a three-day fever.

"All these arguments can be summed up in the truth that these limited goods, which cannot achieve what they promise, and are not perfect in embracing all that is good, are not man's path to happiness, nor can they make him happy in themselves.

Poem 8

"Alas, what ignorance drives miserable men along crooked paths! You do not look for gold in the green trees, nor for jewels hanging on the vine; you do not set your nets in the high mountains when you want a fish for dinner; nor, if you want to hunt deer, do you seek them along the Tyrenean seas. On the contrary, men are skilled in knowing the hidden caves in the sea, and in knowing where white pearls and scarlet dye are found; they know what beaches are rich in various kinds of fish.

"But, when it comes to the location of the good which they desire, they are blind and ignorant. They dig the earth in search of the good which soars above the star-filled heavens. What can I say to show what fools they are? Let them pursue their riches and honors and, when they have painfully accumulated their false goods, then they may come to recognize the true.

Prose 9

Philosophy completes her discussion of false happiness and its causes. She then takes up the subject of true happiness and the supreme good.

11. *Ibid.* 420.

12. This seems to be from a lost work of Aristotle. Lynceus was an Argonaut whose sight was so sharp that he could distinguish objects more than nine miles away. Alcibiades was a noble Athenian youth noted for his beauty and talent, but also for his arrogance and political dishonesty.

"Up to this point," said Philosophy, "I have shown clearly enough the nature of false happiness, and, if you have understood it, I can now go on to speak of true happiness."

"I understand well enough," I answered, "that sufficiency is not attained by riches, nor power by ruling others, nor honor by public recognition, nor fame by public acclaim, nor joy by pleasures."

"But have you understood the reasons why this is so?"

"I think I have a vague idea," I said, "but I wish you would show me more plainly."

"The reasons are clear enough. What nature has made simple and indivisible, human error has divided and changed from true and perfect to false and imperfect. Would you say that one who lacks nothing stands in need of power?"

"Of course not."

"You are quite right; for whoever is deficient in any way needs outside help."

"That is true," I said.

"Therefore, sufficiency and power have one and the same nature."

"That seems to be true."

"And would you say that a thing which is perfectly self-sufficient and completely powerful should be scorned, or is it, on the contrary, worthy of honor?"

"Undoubtedly it is most worthy of honor."

"Then we may add reverence to sufficiency and power, and conclude that all three are really one."

"That is true."

"Next, would you think such a thing obscure and base, or rather, famous and renowned? Now think for a moment whether that which is conceded to be self-sufficient, all powerful, and worthy of great reverence can stand in need of any fame which it cannot give to itself, and therefore seem in some way defective."

"I confess that being what it is it must also be famous."

"It follows, then, that fame cannot be separated from the other three."

"That is true."

"Therefore, that which is self-sufficient, which can do everything by its own power, which is honored and famous, is not this also most pleasant and joyful?"

"I cannot imagine how anyone possessing all these attributes could be sad; and so, if the argument thus far is sound, I must confess that this thing must also be joyful."

"Then," Philosophy went on, "it must be granted that, although the names of sufficiency, power, fame, reverence, and joy are different, in substance all are one and the same thing."

"That must be granted," I agreed.

"Human depravity, then, has broken into fragments that which is by nature one and simple; men try to grasp part of a thing which has no parts and so get neither the part, which does not exist, nor the whole, which they do not seek."

"How is this?" I asked.

"The man who seeks wealth in order to avoid poverty is not interested in power; he would rather be obscure and weak and will even deprive himself of many natural pleasures so that he won't lose the money he has collected. But such a man does not even acquire sufficiency; he is powerless, plagued by trouble, held in contempt, and hidden in obscurity. Similarly, the man who seeks only power wastes his money, scorns pleasures and honors that carry with them no power, and thinks nothing of fame. But see how much he is missing: sometimes he is without the necessities of life, he is plagued by anxieties, and when he cannot overcome them he loses that which he wants most—he ceases to be powerful. Honors, fame, and pleasure can be shown to be equally defective; for each is connected with the others, and whoever seeks one without the others cannot get even the one he wants."

"What happens when someone tries to get them all at the same time?" I asked.

"He, indeed, reaches for the height of happiness, but can he find it in these things which, as I have shown, cannot deliver what they promise?"

"Of course not," I said.

"Happiness, then, is by no means to be sought in these things which are commonly thought to offer the parts of what is sought for."

"Nothing can be truer than this," I agreed.

"Now you have grasped the nature of false happiness and its causes. Now turn your mind's eye in the opposite direction and there you will see the true happiness which I promised to show you."

"But this is clear even to a blind man," I said, "and you revealed it a little while ago when you tried to explain the causes of false happiness. For, unless I am mistaken, true and perfect happiness is that which makes a man self-sufficient, powerful, worthy of reverence and renown, and joyful. And, to show that I have understood you, I acknowledge that whatever can truly provide any one of these must be true and perfect happiness, since all are one and the same."

"O, my scholar," Philosophy answered, "your observation is a happy one if you add just one thing."

"What is that?" I asked.

"Do you imagine that there is any mortal and frail thing which can bring about a condition of this kind?"

"Not at all," I said, "but I think you have proved that beyond any need for further discussion."

"Then these false causes of happiness are mere appearances of the true good and merely seem to give certain imperfect goods to mortal men; but they cannot give true and perfect good."

"I agree," I said.

"Now then, since you know what true happiness is, and the things that falsely seem to offer it, you must now learn where to look for true happiness."

"This," I answered, "is what I have eagerly looked forward to."

"But since, as Plato says in his *Timaeus*,[13] we ought to implore divine help even in small things, what do you think is called for now if we are to gain access to the throne of the highest good?"

"We must invoke the Father of all things without whose aid no beginning can be properly made."

"You are right," said Philosophy, and she began to sing this song:

Poem 9[14]

"Oh God, Maker of heaven and earth, Who govern the world with eternal reason, at your command time passes from the beginning. You place all things in motion, though You are yourself without change. No external causes impelled You to make this work from chaotic matter. Rather it was the form of the highest good, existing within You without envy, which caused You to fashion all things according to the eternal exemplar. You who are most beautiful produce the beautiful world from your divine mind and, forming it in your image, You order the perfect parts in a perfect whole.

"You bind the elements in harmony so that cold and heat, dry and wet are joined, and the purer fire does not fly up through the air, nor the earth sink beneath the weight of water.

"You release the world-soul throughout the harmonious parts of the universe as your surrogate, threefold in its operations, to give motion to all things.[15] That soul, thus divided, pursues its revolving course in two circles, and, returning to itself, embraces the profound mind and transforms heaven to its own image.

"In like manner You create souls and lesser living forms and, adapting them to their high flight in swift chariots, You scatter them through the earth and sky. And when they have turned again toward You, by your gracious law, You call them back like leaping flames.

"Grant, Oh Father, that my mind may rise to Thy sacred throne. Let it see the fountain of good; let it find light, so that the clear light of my soul may fix itself in Thee. Burn off the fogs and clouds of earth and shine through in Thy splendor. For Thou art the serenity, the tranquil peace of virtuous men. The sight of Thee is beginning and end; one guide, leader, path, and goal.

Prose 10

Philosophy teaches Boethius that the supreme good and highest happiness are found in God and are God.

"Since you have seen the forms of imperfect and perfect good, I think it is now time to show where this

---

13. *Timaeus* 27c.
14. This remarkable philosophical poem is an epitome of the first part of Plato's *Timaeus*. The poem was widely used and commented on in the Middle Ages.

15. A difficult and ambiguous sentence. The text is: "Tu triplicis medium naturae cuncta moventem / connectens animam per consona membra resolvis" (II. 13–14). I have rendered *triplicis naturae* as modifying *animam*, "the world-soul . . . threefold in its operations," because this is the reading of Boethius' early medieval commentators. The idea that nature itself is threefold, "the soul of threefold nature," is also supported by historical evidence. Given the relation between the world-soul and nature, the difference between these readings is not crucial to Boethius' statement here.

perfection of happiness resides. First, we must ask whether a good of the kind you defined a short while ago can exist at all, so that we may not be deceived by an empty shadow of thought and thus be prevented from reaching the truth of our problem. Now, no one can deny that something exists which is a kind of fountain of all goodness; for everything which is found to be imperfect shows its imperfection by the lack of some perfection. It follows that if something is found to be imperfect in its kind, there must necessarily be something of that same kind which is perfect. For without a standard of perfection we cannot judge anything to be imperfect. Nature did not have its origins in the defective and incomplete but in the integral and absolute; it fell from such beginnings to its present meanness and weakness.

"But if, as I have just pointed out, there is a certain imperfect happiness in transitory goods, no one can doubt that there is a perfect and enduring happiness."

"That is firmly and truly established," I said.

"Now consider where this perfect happiness has its dwelling place. It is the common conception of the human mind that God, the ruler of all things, is good. For, since nothing can be thought of better than God, who can doubt that He is the good, other than whom nothing is better. And that God is good is demonstrated by reason in such a way as to convince us that He is the perfect good. If He were not, He could not be the ruler of all things; for there would be something better than He, something possessing perfect good, which would seem to be older and greater than He. For all perfect things have been shown to come before less perfect ones. And so, if we are to avoid progression *ad infinitum,* we must agree that the most high God is full of the highest and most perfect good. But we have already established that perfect good is true happiness; therefore it follows that true happiness has its dwelling in the most high God."

"I agree," I said. "Your argument cannot be contradicted."

"But observe," Philosophy continued, "how you may prove scrupulously and inviolably what I have just said, namely, that the most high God is full of the highest good."

"How?" I asked.

"By avoiding the notion that the Father of all things has received from others the highest good with which He is filled, or that He has it naturally in such a way that He and the happiness which He has may be said to differ in essence. For, if you should suppose that He receives it from someone else, you could think that the one who gives it is greater than the one who receives it; but we worthily confess that God is the most excellent of all beings. And if He has this happiness by nature, but differs from it, then someone else who can will have to explain how these diverse things are joined together, since we are speaking of God the Creator of all things. Finally, that which is different from anything cannot be the thing from which it differs; therefore, that which according to its nature differs from the highest good cannot be the highest good. But it is blasphemous to think this about One other than whom, as we know, nothing is greater. And surely there can be nothing better by nature than its source; therefore, I may conclude with certainty that whatever is the source of all things must be, in its substance, the highest good."

"I agree."

"And do you also agree that the highest good is happiness?"

"Yes."

"Then," said Philosophy, "you must agree that God is happiness."

"I found your earlier arguments unassailable, and I see that this conclusion follows from them."

"Then consider whether the same conclusion is not even more firmly established by this, that there cannot exist two highest goods which differ from one another. Clearly, when two goods differ, one cannot be the other; therefore, neither can be perfect since it lacks the other. But that which is not perfect certainly cannot be the highest good; therefore, those things which are the highest good cannot be diverse. But I have proved that happiness and God are the highest good; therefore, that must be the highest happiness which is the highest divinity."

"I can think of nothing truer, or more reasonable, or worthier of God," I said.

"From this conclusion, then, I will give you a kind of corollary, just as the geometricians infer from their demonstrated propositions things which they call deductions. Since men become happy by acquiring happiness, and since happiness is divinity itself, it follows that men become happy by acquiring divinity. For as men become just by acquiring integrity, and wise by acquiring wisdom, so they must in a similar way become gods by acquiring divinity. Thus everyone who is happy is a god and, although it is true that God is one by nature, still there may be many gods by participation."

"This is a beautiful and precious idea," I said, "whether you call it a corollary or a deduction."

"And there is nothing more beautiful," Philosophy went on, "than the truth which reason persuades us to add to this."

"What is that?" I asked.

"Since happiness seems composed of many things, would you say that all these are joined together in happiness, as a variety of parts in one body, or does one of the parts constitute the essence of happiness with all the rest complementing it?"

"I wish you would explain this point by recalling what is involved."

Philosophy then continued. "Do we not agree that happiness is good?"

"Indeed, it is the highest good," I replied.

"Then we must add this good to all the others; for happiness is considered the fullest sufficiency, the greatest power, honor, fame, and pleasure. Now are all these to be regarded as good in the sense that they are members or parts of happiness, or are they simply related to the good as to their crown?"

"I understand the problem now and am eager to have your answer."

"Here then is the solution. If all these goods were constituent parts of happiness, each would differ from the others; for it is the nature of parts to be different things constituting one body. But I have proved that all these goods are one and the same thing; therefore they cannot be parts. Otherwise, happiness would seem to be constituted of one part, which is a contradiction in terms."

"There is no doubt about that," I said, "but you have not yet given me the solution."

"Clearly, all the rest must be related to the good. For riches are sought because they are thought good, power because it is believed to be good, and the same is true of honor, fame, and pleasure. Therefore, the good is the cause and sum of all that is sought for; for if a thing has in it neither the substance nor the appearance of good, it is not sought or desired by men.

On the other hand, things which are not truly good, but only seem to be, are sought after as if they were good. It follows, then, that goodness is rightly considered the sum, pivot, and cause of all that men desire. The most important object of desire is that for the sake of which something else is sought as a means; as, for example, if a person wishes to ride horseback in order to improve his health, he desires the effect of health more than the exercise of riding.

"Since, therefore, all things are sought on account of the good, it is the good itself, not the other things, which is desired by everyone. But, as we agreed earlier, all those other things are sought for the sake of happiness; therefore, happiness alone is the object of men's desires. It follows clearly from this that the good and happiness are one and the same thing."

"I cannot see how any one could disagree."

"But we have also proved that God and true happiness are one and the same."

"That is so."

"We can, therefore, safely conclude that the essence of God is to be found in the good, and nowhere else."

Poem 10[16]

"Come, all you who are trapped and bound by the foul chains of that deceiving lust which occupies earthbound souls. Here you will find rest from your labors, a haven of steady quiet, a refuge from misery.

"Nothing that the river Tagus with its golden shores can give, nor the Hermus with its jeweled banks, the Indus of the torrid zone, gleaming with green and white stones, none of these can clear man's vision. Instead, they hide blind souls in their shadows.

"Whatever pleases and excites your mind here, Earth has prepared in her deep caves. The shining light which rules and animates the heavens avoids the dark ruins of the soul. Whoever can see this light will discount even the bright rays of Phoebus."

---

16. With the discussions of the nature of the Good in this poem and the following prose section, compare Boethius' treatment of the same subject in his theological treatise *Quomodo substantiae*, Loeb Classical Library, pp. 38ff.

Prose 11

Philosophy shows that God is One and that He is the goal toward which all things tend.

"I must agree, since your entire argument is established by sound reasons."

"Then," Philosophy continued, "how highly would you value it, if you could know what the absolute good is?"

"Such knowledge would be of infinite value," I said, "if I were also able to know God who is the absolute good."

"Well, I will show you this with certainty, if the conclusions we have arrived at so far are correct."

"They are indeed," I said.

"I have already proved that the things which most people want are not the true and perfect good since they differ from one another; and, since one or the other is always missing, they cannot provide full and perfect good. But I have also shown that they become the true good when they are gathered together as it were into a single form and operation, so that sufficiency becomes the same as power, honor, fame, and pleasure. And I have further shown that unless they are all one and the same, there is no reason to consider them desirable."

"You have proved this beyond doubt."

"Therefore, if these partial goods cannot be truly good if they are different, but are good if they become one, then clearly they become good by acquiring unity."

"This seems to be true," I said.

"But, if you also grant that every good is good by participating in the perfect good, then you should concede by a similar line of reasoning that the good and the one are the same. For things are of the same essence if their effects are of the same nature."

"I cannot deny that."

"And do you also understand that everything that is remains and subsists in being as long as it is one; but that when it ceases to be one it dies and corrupts?"

"How is this?"

"In the case of animals, when body and spirit are joined together in one being and remain so, that being is called a living thing; but when this unity is dissolved by the separation of body and soul, the being dies and is no longer a living animal. Even the body seems to be human as long as it remains one form in the union of its members; but, if this unity is broken by the separation and scattering of the body's members, it ceases to be what it was before. If we go on to examine other things we will see that each has its being as long as it is one, but when it begins to lose that oneness, it dies."

"On further consideration, I see that this is so."

"Is there anything, then, which acting naturally, gives up its desire to live and chooses to die and decay?"

"When I consider animals whose natures give them some choice, I know of none which gives up the will to live and of its own accord seeks death as long as it is free of external pressure. For every living being acts to preserve its life and to avoid death and injury. But, about plants and trees and inanimate objects, I simply do not know."

"You should not be in doubt about them, since you observe that trees and plants take root in suitable places and, to the extent made possible by their natures, do not wither and die. Some grow in the fields, some in the mountains, some in marshland, some in rocky places, some flourish in the sterile sands; but if any of these should be transplanted to some other place, they would die. Nature gives all things what they need and takes care that they live as long as they can. Why do all plants get their nourishment from roots, like a mouth drinking from the ground, and build up rugged bark over the pith? Why is the soft substance on the inside, while on the outside is the firm wood, and covering all is the bark, a rugged defender against harm, protecting the plant against storms? Note, too, how diligent nature is in propagating every species by multiplying the seed. Everyone knows that these natural processes are designed for the permanent preservation of the species as well as for the present life of individual plants.

"Even things believed to be inanimate do what is proper to their natures in much the same way. Why does lightness cause flames to rise and weight cause earth to settle, if not that these phenomena are appropriate to the things concerned? In addition, each thing is kept in being by that which is naturally proper to it, just as each thing is corrupted by that which is naturally opposed to it. Hard things, such as stones, resist fragmentation by the tough cohesion of their parts; but fluid things, such as air and water, are easily parted, but then quickly flow together again; fire, however, cannot be cut at all. We are not concerned here with the voluntary motions of the intelligent soul, but only of those natural operations of which we are unconscious, such as, for example, digestion of food and breathing during sleep. Indeed, even in living beings, the desire to live comes not from the wishes of the will but from the principles of nature. For often the will is driven by powerful causes to seek death, though nature draws back from it. On the other hand, the work of generation, by which alone the continuation of mortal things is achieved, is sometimes restrained by the will, even though nature always desires it. Thus, this love for the self clearly comes from natural instinct and not from voluntary activity. Providence gave to his creatures this great urge for survival so that they would desire to live as long as they naturally could. Therefore you cannot possibly doubt that everything which exists naturally desires to continue in existence and to avoid harm."

"I now see clearly," I said, "what up to now seemed uncertain."

"Furthermore," Philosophy went on, "whatever seeks to exist and endure also desires to be one; for without unity existence itself cannot be sustained."

"That is true," I said.

"Then all things desire unity."

I agreed.

"But I have already shown that unity is the same as goodness."

"True," I said.

"Therefore, all things desire the good, so that we can define the good as that which is desired by all."

"That is perfectly correct," I agreed. "For either there is no one thing to which all other things are related, and therefore they wander without direction or goal, or, if there is something toward which all things hasten, it is the highest of all goods."

"I am greatly pleased with you, my pupil, for you have found the key to truth. And you also see clearly what a while ago you said you did not understand."

"What is that?" I asked.

"The end, or goal, of all things. For surely it is that which is desired by all; and, since we have identified

that as the good, we must conclude that the good is the end toward which all things tend.

Poem 11

"The man who searches deeply for the truth, and wishes to avoid being deceived by false leads, must turn the light of his inner vision upon himself. He must guide his soaring thoughts back again and teach his spirit that it possesses hidden among its own treasures whatever it seeks outside itself.

"Then all that was hidden by the dark cloud of error will shine more clearly than Phoebus; for the body, with its burden of forgetfulness, cannot drive all light from his mind. The seed of truth grows deep within and is roused to life by the breath of learning. For how can you answer questions truly unless the spark of truth glows deep in your heart? If Plato's Muse speaks truly, whatever is learned is a recollection of something forgotten."[17]

Prose 12

Philosophy shows that God rules the universe by his goodness and that all created things obey him.

"I agree fully with Plato," I said, "for this is the second time I have been reminded of these truths. I forgot them first under the oppressive influence of my body, then later when I was depressed by grief."

Philosophy replied, "If you consider carefully the conclusions you have so far granted, you will quickly remember something else which you said a while ago that you did not know."

"What is that?"

"The way the world is governed," she said.

"I do remember confessing my ignorance about that," I answered, "and, even though I can now anticipate your answer, I want to hear it plainly from you."

---

17. Plato's theories of reminiscence may be found in *Phaedo* 72–76.

"Earlier in our discussion," Philosophy said, "you affirmed without any doubt that the world is ruled by God."[18]

"I still have no doubt about it, and never will, for these reasons: this world could never have achieved its unity of form from such different and contrary parts unless there were One who could bring together such diverse things. And, once this union was effected, the very diversity of discordant and opposed natures would have ripped it apart and destroyed it, if there were not One who could sustain what He had made. Nor could the stable order of nature continue, nor its motions be so regular in place, time, causality, space and quality, unless there were One who could govern this variety of change while remaining immutable Himself. This power, whatever it may be, by which created things are sustained and kept in motion, I call by the name which all men use, God."[19]

Philosophy answered, "Since this is your conviction, I think it will be easy to restore your happiness and bring you back safely to your own country. Now let us return to our task. Have we not already shown that sufficiency is among the attributes of happiness, and are we not agreed that God is absolute happiness?"

"That is right," I said.

"Then He needs no outside help in ruling the world; otherwise, if He were in need of anything He would not be completely self-sufficient."

"That is necessarily true," I said.

"Therefore He disposes all things by himself alone."

"I agree."

"Moreover, I have proved that God is absolute good."

"I remember that," I said.

"Then if He, whom we have agreed to be the good, rules all things by himself, He must dispose everything according to the good. He is, in a manner of speaking, the wheel and rudder by which the vessel of the world is kept stable and undamaged."

"I fully agree," I said, "and I saw in advance, though somewhat vaguely, that this is what you would say."

"I don't doubt it," Philosophy replied, "for I think that you are now looking more sharply for the truth. But what I am now going to tell you is equally clear."

"What is that?" I asked.

"Since God is rightly believed to govern all things with the rudder of goodness, and since all these things naturally move toward the good, as I said earlier, can you doubt that they willingly accept His rule and submit freely to His pleasure as subjects who are agreeable and obedient to their leader?"

"This must be so," I answered, "for no rule could be called happy if it were a bondage of willing slaves rather than one designed for the welfare of compliant citizens."

"Then there is nothing which, by following nature, strives to oppose God?"

"Nothing," I agreed.

"And, if anything should try to oppose Him, could it be at all successful against the One we have rightly shown to be the supreme power of happiness?"

"It would have no chance whatever," I said.

"Then there is nothing which has either the desire or the power to oppose this highest good?"

"Nothing."

"Then it is the supreme good which rules all things firmly and disposes all sweetly."

"I am delighted," I said, "not only by your powerful argument and its conclusion, but even more by the words you have used. And I am at last ashamed of the folly that so profoundly depressed me."

"You have read in the fables of the poets how giants made war on heaven; but this benign power overthrew them as they deserved. But now let us set our arguments against each other and perhaps from their opposition some special truth will emerge."

"As you wish," I said.

"No one can doubt that God is almighty," Philosophy began.

"Certainly not, unless he is mad," I answered.

"But nothing is impossible for one who is almighty."

"Nothing."

"Then can God do evil?"

"No, of course not."

"Then evil is nothing, since God, who can do all things, cannot do evil."

"You are playing with me," I said, "by weaving a labyrinthine argument from which I cannot escape.

---

18. See Book I, Prose 6 and Book III, Poem 9.
19. Compare Boethius' treatment of creation in the theological treatise *De fide Catholica*, Loeb Classical Library, pp. 56ff.

You seem to begin where you ended and to end where you began. Are you perhaps making a marvelous circle of the divine simplicity? A little while ago you began with happiness, declared it to be the highest good, and located its dwelling in almighty God. You said that God himself is the highest good and perfect happiness. From this you inferred that no one could be happy unless he too were a god. Then you went on to say that the very form of the good is the essence of God and of happiness; and you said further that unity is identical with the good which is sought by everything in nature. You also affirmed that God rules the universe by the exercise of His goodness, that all things willingly obey Him, and that there is no evil in nature. And you proved all this without outside assumptions and used only internal proofs which draw their force from one another."

Philosophy answered, "I have not mocked you at all. With the help of God whose aid we invoked we have reached the most important point of all. For it is the nature of the divine essence neither to pass to things outside itself nor to take any external thing to itself. As Parmenides puts it, the divine essence is 'in body like a sphere, perfectly rounded on all sides';[20] it rotates the moving orb of the universe while it remains unmoved itself. You ought not to be surprised that I have sought no outside proofs, but have used only those within the scope of our subject, since you have learned, on Plato's authority, that the language we use ought to be related to the subject of our discourse.[21]

Poem 12

"Happy is he who can look into the shining spring of good; happy is he who can break the heavy chains of earth.

"Long ago the Thracian poet, Orpheus, mourned for his dead wife. With his sorrowful music he made the woodland dance and the rivers stand still. He made the fearful deer lie down bravely with the fierce lions; the rabbit no longer feared the dog quieted by his song.

---

20. Parmenides, *Fragment* VIII. 43.
21. *Timaeus* 29b.

"But as the sorrow within his breast burned more fiercely, that music which calmed all nature could not console its maker. Finding the gods unbending, he went to the regions of hell. There he sang sweet songs to the music of his harp, songs drawn from the noble fountains of his goddess mother, songs inspired by his powerless grief and the love which doubled his grief.

"Hell is moved to pity when, with his melodious prayer, he begs the favor of those shades. The three-headed guardian of the gate is paralyzed by that new song; and the Furies, avengers of crimes who torture guilty souls with fear, are touched and weep in pity. Ixion's head is not tormented by the swift wheel, and Tantalus, long maddened by his thirst, ignores the waters he now might drink. The vulture is filled by the melody and ignores the liver of Tityus.

"At last, the judge of souls, moved by pity, declares, 'We are conquered. We return to this man his wife, his companion, purchased by his song. But our gift is bound by the condition that he must not look back until he has left hell.' But who can give lovers a law? Love is a stronger law unto itself. As they approached the edge of night, Orpheus looked back at Eurydice, lost her, and died.

"This fable applies to all of you who seek to raise your minds to sovereign day. For whoever is conquered and turns his eyes to the pit of hell, looking into the inferno, loses all the excellence he has gained."

DISCUSSION QUESTIONS

1. How does Boethius view the relationship between "matter" and "spirit," and how is this view related to his understanding of chaos and order in the universe? How does this compare with our contemporary understanding of these concepts?
2. Concerning the essential nature of things and their origins, Boethius claims that the less perfect always comes from the more perfect, not the other way around. What are some examples that would support or weaken his position?
3. Do you think God is essential for providing the consolation that Boethius finds? Can philosophy provide consolation without God?
4. Who are some more recent examples of people achieving life-changing philosophical (or spiritual) insight while in prison?

3. Sarvepalli Radhakrishnan (1888–1975)
"The Spirit of Indian Philosophy"

The written tradition of philosophical thought in India goes back at least to 2500 B.C.E., but no exact documentation of the chronology of philosophical writings exists for much of that history. According to Sarvepalli Radhakrishnan, this is primarily because ancient Indian thinkers were more concerned with what was written than who wrote it and when. Little is known for sure about many of the most influential philosophers, especially in the earlier periods, and yet their often anonymously authored theories have continued to be the subject of commentary, critique, and further development up to the present day.

While the dominant philosophical systems that have evolved over the millenia in India have been greatly diverse, they also have much in common, and this selection emphasizes the commonalities. Also, Radhakrishnan wrote this in the 1950s, not long after India achieved its political independence from Britain, when questions of cultural identity and value in the face of Western supremacist ideology were very much on the minds of most Indian intellectuals. Thus, not only does the author identify the common threads running through almost all Indian philosophy throughout its vast history, but he also shows that no one who believes in the importance of philosophical inquiry for discovering the true meaning of human life can justifiably ignore the contributions of the Indian tradition to that universal quest. In his various roles as internationally respected philosopher, diplomat, and political leader, Radhakrishnan has done much to convince people in Eastern and Western societies of the truth of that claim.

QUESTIONS FOR CRITICAL READING

1. What are the seven points made by the author to summarize the "distinct spirit of Indian philosophy"?
2. What are the four aspects of the "fundamental unity of perspective in the practical realm" (the fourth referring to the Hindu tradition exclusively)?
3. What does Radhakrishnan mean when he claims that a "world perspective" in philosophy is needed in the contemporary world (that is, at the time of this writing)? Is his assertion any more or less relevant today? Why?
4. What explicit and implicit value judgments does the author make in his discussion?

TERMS TO NOTE

idealism: In this context, the metaphysical position that reality is fundamentally spiritual or mental in nature.

materialism: In this context, the metaphysical position that reality is fundamentally physical/material in nature.

monism: The metaphysical position that all of reality is essentially one or unitary, or that it is composed of only one type of substance or being (in which case a person could be either an idealist monist or a materialist monist).

dualism: The metaphysical position that both material and spiritual/mental things exist and are qualitatively distinct. Deciding whether the material or the spiritual is more fundamental to reality, or causally primary, makes a person either a materialist dualist or an idealist dualist.

Vedas: The Sanskrit word *veda* literally means a text containing knowledge, and the four Vedas, *Ṛg Veda* (the oldest known text in India), *Yajur Veda, Sāma Veda,* and the *Atharva Veda,* constitute the foundational writings in the Indian intellectual tradition, often treated as sacred texts.

Upanishads: From the Sanskrit words *upa* (near), *ni* (down), *sad* (to sit), in reference to students sitting down near a teacher to learn the truth. These texts make up the concluding sections of the Vedas and go back at least as far as the eighth century B.C.E. They are also often considered the most thoroughly philosophical parts of the Vedic writings.

Indian philosophy, it has been noted, is extremely complex. Through the ages the Indian philosophical mind has probed deeply into many aspects of human experience and the external world. Although some methods, such as the experimental method of modern science, have been relatively less prominent than others, not only the problems of Indian philosophy but also the methods used and the conclusions reached in the pursuit of truth have certainly been as far-reaching in their extent, variety, and depth as those of other philosophical traditions. The six basic systems and the many subsystems of Hinduism, the four chief schools of Buddhism, the two schools of Jainism, and the materialism of the Cārvāka are evidence enough of the diversity of views in Indian philosophy. The variety of the Indian perspective is unquestionable. Accordingly, it is very difficult to cite any specific doctrines or methods as characteristic of Indian philosophy as a whole and applicable to all the multitudinous systems and subsystems developed through nearly four millenniums of Indian philosophical speculation.

Nevertheless, in certain respects there is what might be called a distinct spirit of Indian philosophy. This is exemplified by certain attitudes which are fairly characteristic of the Indian philosophical mind or which stand as points of view that have been emphasized characteristically by Indians in their philosophies.

(1) The chief mark of Indian philosophy in general is its concentration upon the spiritual. Both in life and in philosophy the spiritual motive is predominant in India. Except for the relatively minor materialistic school of the Cārvāka and related doctrines, philosophy in India conceives man to be spiritual in nature, interested primarily in his spiritual destiny, and relates him in one way or another to a universe which is also spiritual in essential character. Neither man nor the universe is looked upon as physical in essence, and material welfare is never recognized as the goal of human life, except by the Cārvāka. Philosophy and religion are intimately related because philosophy itself is regarded as a spiritual adventure, and also because the motivation both in philosophy and in religion concerns the spiritual way of life in the here-and-now and the eventual spiritual salvation of man in relation to the universe. Practically all of Indian philosophy, from its beginning in the Vedas to the present day, has striven to bring about a socio-spiritual reform in the country, and philosophical literature has taken many forms, mythological, popular, or technical, as the cir-

cumstances required, in order to promote such spiritual life. The problems of religion have always given depth and power and purpose to the Indian philosophical mind and spirit.

(2) Another characteristic view of Indian philosophy is the belief in the intimate relationship of philosophy and life. This attitude of the practical application of philosophy to life is found in every school of Indian philosophy. While natural abundance and material prosperity paved the way for the rise of philosophical speculation, philosophy has never been considered a mere intellectual exercise. The close relationship between theory and practice, doctrine and life, has always been outstanding in Indian thought. Every Indian system seeks the truth, not as academic "knowledge for its own sake," but to learn the truth which shall make men free. This is not, as it has been called, the modern pragmatic attitude. It is much larger and much deeper than that. It is not the view that truth is measured in terms of the practical, but rather that the truth is the only sound guide for practice, that truth alone has efficacy as a guide for man in his search for salvation. Every major system of Indian philosophy takes its beginning from the practical and tragic problems of life and searches for the truth in order to solve the problem of man's distress in the world in which he finds himself. There has been no teaching which remained a mere word of mouth or dogma of schools. Every doctrine has been turned into a passionate conviction, stirring the heart of man and quickening his breath, and completely transforming his personal nature. In India, philosophy is for life; it is to be lived. It is not enough to *know* the truth; the truth must be *lived*. The goal of the Indian is not to know the ultimate truth but to *realize* it, to become one with it.

Another aspect of the intimate inseparability of theory and practice, philosophy and life, in Indian philosophy is to be found in the universally prevalent demand for moral purification as an imperative preliminary for the would-be student of philosophy or searcher after truth. Śaṁkara's classic statement of this demand calls for a knowledge of the distinction between the eternal and the noneternal, that is, a questioning tendency in the inquirer; the subjugation of all desire for the fruits of action either in this life or in a hereafter, a renunciation of all petty desire, personal motive, and practical interest; tranquillity, self-control, renunciation, patience, peace of mind, and faith; and a desire for release (*mokṣa*) as the supreme goal of life.

(3) Indian philosophy is characterized by the introspective attitude and the introspective approach to reality. Philosophy is thought of as *ātmavidyā*, knowledge of the self. Philosophy can start either with the external world or with the internal world of man's inner nature, the self of man. In its pursuit of the truth, Indian philosophy has always been strongly dominated by concern with the inner life and self of man rather than the external world of physical nature. Physical science, though developed extensively in the Golden Age of Indian culture, was never considered the road to ultimate truth; truth is to be sought and found within. The subjective, then, rather than the objective, becomes the focus of interest in Indian philosophy, and, therefore, psychology and ethics are considered more important as aspects or branches of philosophy than the sciences which study physical nature. This is not to say that the Indian mind has not studied the physical world; in fact, on the contrary, India's achievements in the realm of positive science were at one time truly outstanding, especially in the mathematical sciences such as algebra, astronomy, and geometry, and in the applications of these basic sciences to numerous phases of human activity. Zoology, botany, medicine, and related sciences have also been extremely prominent in Indian thought. Be this as it may, the Indian, from time immemorial, has felt that the inner spirit of man is the most significant clue to his reality and to that of the universe, more significant by far than the physical or the external.

(4) This introspective interest is highly conducive to idealism, of course, and consequently most Indian philosophy is idealistic in one form or another. The tendency of Indian philosophy, especially Hinduism, has been in the direction of monistic idealism. Almost all Indian philosophy believes that reality is *ultimately* one and *ultimately* spiritual. Some systems have seemed to espouse dualism or pluralism, but even these have been deeply permeated by a strong monistic character. If we concentrate our attention upon the underlying spirit of Indian philosophy rather than its variety of opinions, we shall find that this spirit is embodied in the tendency to interpret life and reality in

the way of monistic idealism. This rather unusual attitude is attributable to the nonrigidity of the Indian mind and to the fact that the attitude of monistic idealism is so plastic and dynamic that it takes many forms and expresses itself even in seemingly conflicting doctrines. These are not conflicting doctrines in fact, however, but merely different expressions of an underlying conviction which provides basic unity to Indian philosophy as a whole.

Materialism undoubtedly had its day in India, and, according to sporadic records and constant and determined efforts on the part of other systems to denounce it, the doctrine apparently enjoyed widespread acceptance at one time. Nevertheless, materialism could not hold its own; its adherents have been few in number, and its positive influence has been negligible. Indian philosophy has not been oblivious to materialism; rather, it has known it, has overcome it, and has accepted idealism as the only tenable view, whatever specific form that idealism might take.

(5) Indian philosophy makes unquestioned and extensive use of reason, but intuition is accepted as the only method through which the ultimate can be known. Reason, intellectual knowledge, is not enough. Reason is not useless or fallacious, but it is insufficient. To know reality one must have an actual experience of it. One does not merely *know* the truth in Indian philosophy; one *realizes* it. The word which most aptly describes philosophy in India is *darśana*, which comes from the verbal root *dṛś*, meaning "to see." "To see" is to have a direct intuitive experience of the object, or, rather, to realize it in the sense of becoming one with it. No complete knowledge is possible as long as there is the relationship of the subject on one hand and the object on the other. Later developments in Indian philosophy, from the time of the beginning of the systems, have all depended in large part upon reason for the systematic formulation of doctrines and systems, for rational demonstration or justification, and in polemical conflicts of system against system. Nevertheless, all the systems, except the Cārvāka, agree that there is a higher way of knowing reality, beyond the reach of reason, namely, the direct perception or experience of the ultimate reality, which cannot be known by reason in any of its forms. Reason can demonstrate the truth, but reason cannot discover or reach the truth. While reason may be the method of philosophy in its more

intellectualistic sense, intuition is the only method of comprehending the ultimate. Indian philosophy is thus characterized by an ultimate dependence upon intuition, along with the recognition of the efficacy of reason and intellect when applied in their limited capacity and with their proper function.

(6) Another characteristic of Indian philosophy, one which is closely related to the preceding one, is its so-called acceptance of authority. Although the systems of Indian philosophy vary in the degree to which they are specifically related to the ancient *śruti,* not one of the systems—orthodox or unorthodox, except the Cārvāka—openly stands in violation of the accepted intuitive insights of its ancient seers, whether it be the Hindu seers of the Upaniṣads, the intuitive experience of the Buddha, or the similarly intuitive wisdom of Mahāvīra, the founder of Jainism, as we have it today. Indian philosophers have always been conscious of tradition and, as has been indicated before, the great system-builders of later periods claimed to be merely commentators, explaining the traditional wisdom of the past. While the specific doctrines of the past may be changed by interpretation, the general spirit and frequently the basic concepts are retained from age to age. Reverence for authority does not militate against progress, but it does lend a unity of spirit by providing a continuity of thought which has rendered philosophy especially significant in Indian life and solidly unified against any philosophical attitude contradicting its basic characteristics of spirituality, inwardness, intuition, and the strong belief that the truth is to be lived, not merely known.

The charge of indulging in an exaggerated respect for authority may be legitimately leveled against some of Indian philosophy, but this respect for the past is rooted in the deep conviction that those who really know reality are those who have *realized* the truth and that it is to them that we must turn ultimately, beyond all our power of reasoning, if we are to attain any comprehension of the truth which they saw and realized. As has been said, India has produced a great variety of philosophical doctrines and systems. This has been true despite universal reverence for and acceptance of the authority of the ancient seers as the true discoverers of wisdom. The variety of the systems, even in their basic conceptions, looked at in the light of the prevalent acceptance of authority, reveals the

fact that this reverence has not made Indian philosophy a dogmatic religious creed, as is often alleged, but rather a single tone or trend of thought on basic issues. How completely free from traditional bias the systems are is seen, for example, by the fact that the original Sāṃkhya says nothing about the possible existence of God, although it is emphatic in its doctrine of the theoretical undemonstrability of his existence; the Vaiśeṣika and the Yoga, especially the latter, admit the existence of God, but do not consider him to be the creator of the universe; the Mīmāṃsā speaks of God but denies his importance and efficacy in the moral ordering of the world. To emphasize the point further, reference should be made also to the early Buddhist systems, which reject God, and to the Cārvākas, who deny God without qualification.

(7) Finally, there is the over-all synthetic tradition which is essential to the spirit and method of Indian philosophy. This is as old as the *Ṛg Veda,* where the seers realized that true religion comprehends all religions, so that "God is one but men call him by many names." Indian philosophy is clearly characterized by the synthetic approach to the various aspects of experience and reality. Religion and philosophy, knowledge and conduct, intuition and reason, man and nature, God and man, noumenon and phenomena, are all brought into harmony by the synthesizing tendency of the Indian mind. The Hindu is prone to believe even that all the six systems, as well as their varieties of subsystems, are in harmony with one another, in fact, that they complement one another in the total vision, which is one. As contrasted with Western philosophy, with its analytic approach to reality and experience, Indian philosophy is fundamentally synthetic. The basic texts of Indian philosophy treat not only one phase of experience and reality, but of the full content of the philosophic sphere. Metaphysics, epistemology, ethics, religion, psychology, facts, and value are not cut off one from the other but are treated in their natural unity as aspects of one life and experience or of a single comprehensive reality.

It is this synthetic vision of Indian philosophy which has made possible the intellectual and religious tolerance which has become so pronounced in Indian thought and in the Indian mind throughout the ages. Recent squabbles between religious communities, bred of new political factionalism, are not outgrowths of the Indian mind but, instead, are antagonistic to its unique genius for adaptability and tolerance, which takes all groups and all communities into its one truth and one life.

In addition to these general characteristics of Indian philosophy from the intellectual or theoretical point of view, there is also a fundamental unity of perspective in the practical realm. This has several aspects. In the first place, there is the fact, mentioned earlier, that all philosophies in India—Hindu, Buddhist, Jaina, and Cārvāka—have a practical motivation, stemming from man's practical problems of life, his limitations and suffering, and culminating in every case except the Cārvāka in a consideration of his ultimate liberation. In every case, including the Cārvāka, the motivation is practical rather than theoretical, for the Cārvāka is interested, not in theory for its own sake, but in living a life of pleasure since it believes the world is conducive to that type of life and justifies no other. The goal of life in Hinduism, Buddhism, and Jainism is essentially the same. *Mokṣa* (liberation) is the ultimate objective for Hinduism and Jainism, and *nirvāṇa* is the goal in Buddhism. The precise meanings of liberation vary among the different schools, even among those within the framework of Buddhism and Hinduism, but the essential meaning of both *mokṣa* and *nirvāṇa* is emancipation or liberation from turmoil and suffering and freedom from rebirth. In some instances, the goal seems to be negative, consisting essentially of freedom from pain and freedom from rebirth, but in reality it is the positive achievement of a richer and fuller life and the attainment of infinite bliss. The spirit re-achieves its original purity, sometimes by becoming identical with the Absolute, sometimes by a life of communion with God, sometimes simply by the eternal existence of the pure spirit in its individuality, but in all cases free from the limitations and entanglements of life.

The several schools and systems of Indian philosophy are of one mind not only with reference to the goal of life, but also with reference to the good life on earth. The essential spirit of the philosophy of life of Hinduism, Buddhism, and Jainism is that of non-attachment. This is an attitude of mind with which the individual fulfills his part in life and lives a "normal" everyday existence in company with his fellow men, without being entangled in or emotionally disturbed

by the results of his actions. He attains a mental and spiritual superiority to worldly values and is never enslaved by them. This is not negativism or escapism, for one takes part in everyday activities in accordance with his place in society. However, it is living and acting without any sense of attachment to the things of this world and without any selfishness whatsoever.

Hinduism, Buddhism, and Jainism, in all their branches, also accept the underlying doctrines of *karma* and rebirth. All of these schools believe that man must be morally and spiritually perfected before he can attain salvation. They also believe that justice is the law of the moral life exactly as cause-and-effect is the law of the natural world. What one sows one must reap. Since justice and moral and spiritual perfection are not achievable in one life, all these systems believe in rebirth, so as to provide the opportunity for moral progress and eventual perfection. Throughout Indian philosophy, from the earliest Vedas to the latest developments, the moral order of the universe has been an accepted doctrine of all Indian thinkers except the Cārvākas. *Karma* and rebirth are the instrumentalities by which the moral order of the universe is worked out in the life of man.

There is a further common element which unifies all schools of Hindu philosophy in the practical realm, although the heterodox schools, the Cārvāka, Buddhism, and Jainism, do not conform to this pattern. The way of life accepted by all schools of Hinduism, regardless of metaphysical and epistemological variations, includes the fourfold division of society, the four stages of life, and the four basic values which man seeks. In Hinduism, society is divided into four groups (*varṇa*, frequently translated as castes) determined generally according to occupational ability, namely, the priest-teacher (*brāhmin*),[1] the king or political and military leader (*kṣatriya*), the merchant (*vaiśya*), and the laborer (*śūdra*). The first three of these are called the twice-born, that is, they are religiously initiated Hindus, whereas the *śūdras* are not so accepted. The lives of the twice-born are to consist of the four

---

1. *Brāhmin* is used throughout this volume in preference to *brāhmaṇa* to designate this group because the latter term also refers to a group of early Indian texts, and thus may lead to confusion. Technically speaking, however, "*brāhmin*" is not a correct Sanskrit term, although it is used rather widely.

stages of the student (*brahmacārin*), the householder (*gṛhastha*), the forest-dweller (*vānaprastha*), and the wandering monk (*sannyāsin* or *saṁnyāsin*). In this social scheme, one does not enter the life of asceticism until after he has fulfilled his obligations to his fellow man as a student and as a householder, but in the later stages of life one is to concentrate more and more upon the spiritual and upon his search for liberation. The goals of life which are accepted by all Hindus are righteousness or obedience to the moral law (*dharma*), wealth or material welfare (*artha*), pleasure (*kāma*), and emancipation (*mokṣa*). *Dharma* prevails throughout life, that is, neither pleasure nor wealth is to be obtained through violation of the rules of morality. *Mokṣa* is the ultimate goal to which all men should aspire. This social philosophy is accepted without question by all Hindus. It is presented in the literature of the Dharmaśāstras, but is not found in any elaboration or with any philosophical justification in the basic technical philosophical texts. This common ideal life of all Hindus provides a spirit of unity to the social and moral life of the country, although Buddhists and Jainas, who are greatly in the minority, do not follow the same specific pattern of life.

The Value of the Study of Indian Philosophy

The study of Indian philosophy is important historically, philosophically, and even politically. The Indian philosophical tradition is man's oldest as well as the longest continuous development of speculation about the nature of reality and man's place therein. It began with the ancient Vedas, which are probably the earliest documents of the human mind that have come down to us, and has continued age after age in progressive philosophical advance in the effort to understand life and reality. But it is not as a piece of antiquarian investigation that we of today should study Indian philosophy. Despite the tendency to respect and revere the greatness of the past, Indian thinkers of all ages have been deeply and profoundly concerned with the ultimate truth which is timeless. Nor should we study Indian philosophy as a merely provincial or geographical approach to reality. Despite charges by some Western critics who would accuse Indian philosophy of neglecting scientific method, Indian thinkers have not been anti-empirical and have not neglected nature in

their study of reality; nor, in their study of man, have they been excessively restricted to those characteristics which may be peculiar to man in India. India's concentrated study of the inner nature of man is, in the end, a study of man universal.

The teachings of Indian philosophers from the days of the Vedas till today have been landmarks of human thought. Not all ideas and not all systems of Indian philosophy are deeply significant, but the heights and depths reached by Indian thinkers and seers are indications and examples of the profound powers of the human mind. Indian thought is neither merely ancient speculation nor merely provincial Indian thinking. It is man's mind and soul at their best in philosophy and religion.

Philosophically, the study of Indian philosophy is important in the search for the truth. Philosophy must include all insights and all experiences in its purview, and Indian philosophy has much to contribute. The major problems of Indian philosophy are the problems faced by thinking man ever since he first began to speculate about life and reality, but Indian philosophy also has special problems, different emphases, unique approaches and methods, and unique solutions—all of which are India's contributions to the total picture of the truth which is the substance of philosophy. The need of philosophy today is for a world perspective which will include the philosophical insights of all the world's great traditions. The goal is not a single philosophy which would annihilate differences of perspective, but there must be agreement on basic perspectives and ultimate values. Such a world philosophy should certainly incorporate the spiritual insights of the seers of ancient India and of the thinkers who have guided the many centuries of Indian philosophical speculation.

It is politically important, too, that Indian philosophy should be studied by the West. The current appeal for "one world" is too often thought of merely in the realm of politics. Political unity is impossible without philosophical understanding. Political insights, agreements, and differences are on the secondary level of man's thinking. Social and political conditions in the several areas of the world depend, in the final analysis, upon the philosophical and spiritual thought and ideals of the peoples of the world. It is to philosophy, then, that man must turn in his hope to bring the peoples of the world together in greater mutual understanding and in the intellectual and spiritual harmony without which a unified world will be impossible in any sphere, political or otherwise. The future of civilization depends upon the return of spiritual awareness to the hearts and minds of men. To this purpose the contribution of Indian philosophy, with its agelong spiritual emphasis, is inestimable and indispensable.

DISCUSSION QUESTIONS

1. Radhakrishnan maintains that philosophy is crucial for achieving harmony among the peoples of the world. Do you agree? Why or why not?
2. What is the difference between the "analytic" and the "synthetic" approach to philosophical inquiry, and why might one be preferable to the other?
3. What is the difference between "intuition" and "reason," and do they really lead to different kinds of "knowledge"?
4. Radhakrishnan indicates that the conservative and progressive elements in Indian philosophy are fairly well reconciled because of the fundamental sense of continuity with the past. How does this compare with the influence of tradition and changes in ideas in Western history?
5. How does the Indian philosophical view of the ultimate goal of life for humans, as characterized by Radhakrishnan, compare with the view presented by Boethius?

4. Nancy Tuana
From *Woman and the History of Philosophy*

Nancy Tuana is an American philosopher who has been actively involved in the development of feminist theory in recent years, primarily within the Western, English-speaking academic world. One important dimension of feminist analysis has been to illuminate the ways social construction of gender and customary relations between men and women affect how all of us understand our lives. Because this applies just as much to the intellectuals in a society as to anybody else, in *Woman and the History of Philosophy,* Tuana provides a feminist critique of the history of Western philosophy along these lines.

She shows how explicit and implicit assumptions about the male and masculinity, and the female and femininity, have shaped influential philosophies in more than just a peripheral way. In her analysis she also exposes the traditional claim of gender neutrality in philosophy as the product of socially reinforced illusion and self-deception, as well as an obstacle to the development of a more open, insightful, and nonsexist approach to philosophical practice. This selection is from the epilogue of her book; here she summarizes her investigations, pointing out the value of reading philosophical texts self-consciously as a woman or man and indicating theoretical directions that can be taken toward positively transforming the discipline.

QUESTIONS FOR CRITICAL READING

1. With regard to philosophical theory, what does Tuana mean by claiming that gender has remained "a basic metaphysical category"?
2. Identify the different facets of the feminist critique of traditional Western conceptions of rationality and knowledge.
3. According to Tuana, how can we go about "turning the philosophy of dualisms 'inside out'"?
4. How have assumptions about gender differences influenced moral and political theory, in Tuana's estimation?

TERMS TO NOTE

androcentrism: A male-centered approach to the understanding and evaluation of experience. What is associated with maleness is normal and appropriately dominant; anything else, especially that which is female, is then deficient or abnormal and appropriately subordinate by comparison.

canon: In this context, the conventionally accepted list of "great works" in Western philosophical history.

gender essentialism: The belief that there exists one set of traits essentially defining the feminine and another set of traits essentially defining the masculine.

liberalism: In this context, the political perspective that emphasizes equal rights among all citizens and advocates equal opportunity to pursue individual self-interest.

Reading as a woman we discover that there are indeed many changes to be made. Such a strategy of reading illustrates the falsity of the supposition that either readers or discourse is gender-neutral. We find woven throughout the philosophical canon a system of gender assumptions. In the course of writing these chapters, I have endeavored to highlight the patterns of these beliefs. I have argued that philosophers from diverse time periods, writing from competing philosophical traditions, perpetuate a strikingly similar conception of woman—as inferior to man, less capable of reason, less capable of moral agency, as functioning primarily within the private realm of family. My intention has not been simply to display the sexism of certain canonical philosophers, but rather to expose the fact that assumptions concerning gender differences are often a fundamental component of a philosophical system. Furthermore, I have argued that these assumptions are so intricately woven into the theoretical structure of a philosopher's thought that removing them requires far more than simple revisions of the system.

This conception of woman, along with the tenet that readers and texts can be (and should be) gender-neutral, arises out of a long and complex tradition of understanding the world in terms of dualisms, that is, in terms of pairs of traits which are seen as oppositional and in which one term of the polarity is privileged over the other. Aristotle, for example, tells us that the Pythagoreans accepted ten such principles: "limit and unlimited, odd and even, one and plurality, right and left, male and female, resting and moving, straight and curved, light and darkness, good and bad, square and oblong." (*Metaphysics* 986a 23–25.) Others have included mind and body, form and matter, reason and emotion, objectivity and subjectivity, public and private, culture and nature. The history of such

dualisms is not static, nor is it always consistent, but throughout this changing history, gender remains a basic metaphysical category.

It is this latter point, that gender is a basic metaphysical category, that is highlighted by the strategy of reading philosophy as a woman. We not only become sensitive to the definitions of woman as inferior to man or her exclusion from the realm of the political, we also perceive the ways in which reason and morality have been defined as masculine. We become aware that the gender of the reader of the texts of philosophy is not irrelevant. It is a fact that enters into the context of our encounters with the texts of philosophy. If, as entreated by Descartes, I attempt to eradicate all the influences of my body, if I attempt to proceed as a disinterested reader, as a genderless, thinking being, I will be quickly stymied by the fact that the texts of philosophy too often contain the depiction of woman as incapable of the type of cognitive ability required to be a Cartesian reader. I, a woman, cannot ignore my body when I am told that the female body precludes or impedes my ability to be rational, to be moral, to participate within the realm of politics. Reading as a woman, being embodied readers, undermines the image of the reader, as well as the text, as genderless.

An understanding of the gender assumptions underpinning philosophy provides the reader with a place, a standpoint, although a continually shifting one, from which to read such gendered structures. We cannot stand "outside the texts" to critique them, but we can use this understanding of the language of gender to move through the texts differently than we did in the past. The value of embodied reading is well expressed by Carol H. Cantrell in her essay "Analogy as Destiny: Cartesian Man and the Woman Reader":

> For a woman reader, the presence of a language of dualisms within the texts she reads means that she is represented in those texts at critical moments of suppression and valuation. Paradoxically, this language, which has in so many destructive ways shaped her experience and her sense of herself, can be turned inside out, so to speak, and used to track what has been denigrated and what has been lost. Though she cannot jump out of her culture's discourses or her own skin any more than the "man of reason"

can, she can use her understanding of the language of gender as a lever to move her self into a new relationship to that language.[1]

This alternative approach to the texts of philosophy provides a basis for resisting the definitions of woman (and of man) and for acknowledging and recovering those experiences and abilities that have previously been denigrated because of their association with the feminine.

One of the first steps in turning the philosophy of dualisms "inside out" is to give voice to that which remains silent and unspoken. Luce Irigaray in her book *The Speculum of the Other Woman* offers a model of this approach to reading.[2] Sensitive to the movements of gender in the texts of Descartes, Freud, Hegel, Kant, Lacan, and Plato, Irigaray carefully delineates the systematic exclusion of the feminine in their theories. For example, in her essay "Plato's *Hystera*," Irigaray offers a very different reading of the Platonic cave metaphor of the ascent to wisdom. She carefully discloses the ways in which Plato's discourse was constructed as a masculine discourse between men. Demonstrating in this way the systematic exclusion of the feminine from the myth of the cave, Irigaray argues that far from being absent, the feminine actually plays a vital function in the masculine economy of the cave by providing the silent matrix which reflects the masculine—what Irigaray calls "the memoryless mirror of representation."[3] Thus, the task of the woman reader, according to Irigaray, is to subvert the dualisms of masculine discourse by unveiling the feminine which has been concealed by the discourse of men.[4] According to Andrea Nye, Irigaray's method "clears the way for a new kind of feminist thinking. Once the simple presence/absence of phallic logic is abandoned, the feminine can appear as a value in its own right opening the way . . . for a real, not sham, sexual difference in which both sexes are valorized."[5]

In adopting such a strategy, indeed in accepting my challenge to read philosophy as a woman, it is tempting to simply reverse the valorization of traits identified as masculine and privilege those seen as feminine. But simply reversing the dualism only perpetuates it. If, for example, a feminist attempts to develop a theory of rationality that privileges the emotional over the rational, her or his "success" in such an endeavor is suspect. It is doubtful that a theorist could in fact achieve an empowerment of the feminine using the very dichotomy which defines the female as inferior. As long as the rationality of male thought remains the standard by which feminine virtues are judged, they will always be found wanting. To subvert the standard itself requires undermining the very dualisms simple reversal perpetuates. The focus on the dualisms thus must aim at dislocating the boundaries between the polarities.

Reading as a woman makes us aware of the hidden fact of the androcentrism of the traditional discourses of philosophy. But as we become aware of the presuppositions of masculine discourse in the texts of the philosophers, we in turn become aware of the ways in which gender assumptions are inextricably intertwined with others such as race, class, and sexuality. Our location as a reader is neither fixed nor unitary, but rather multiple and dispersed. In our focus on gender we cannot neglect the other sites of polarization—white/nonwhite, rich/poor, heterosexual/homosexual—for the exchange among these various divisions is continual.

My analysis in this book makes clear the depth of the challenge feminism poses for philosophy. A canonical philosopher's views about women cannot simply be dismissed as not being integral to his central philosophical doctrines. Philosophers' gender assumptions often affect the central categories of their system—their conceptions of rationality, their construals of the nature of morality, their visions of the public realm. Feminist critiques thus pose a serious challenge to mainstream Western philosophy, requiring a careful reevaluation of its basic concepts.

Feminist critiques like that contained within this book unveil the severity of the problems posed to women by the central categories of Western philosophy. We cannot, for example, expect that all people will be seen as equally rational when the philosophical definitions of rationality privilege traits viewed as masculine. Feminist theorists have argued that Western conceptions of objectivity and the corresponding separation of knower from the known are a part of this emphasis of masculine traits.[6] A gender-neutral conception of rationality will thus require changes throughout the philosophical system.

One central concern of feminist critiques of rationality is to question the denigration of the emotions and the perception of the body as an impediment to knowledge. Seeing knowledge as grounded in experience, theorists such as Nancy Hartsock, Sara Ruddick, and Hilary Rose argue that the activities assigned to women, understood through the categories of feminist theory, provide a starting point for developing claims to knowledge that are potentially more comprehensive and less distorted than those of privileged men.[7] They believe that women's sensuous, relational, and contextual perspective allows them to understand aspects of nature and social life not available to those men who are cut off from such activities. Thus women's experiences provide a basis for developing an alternative epistemology that unifies manual, mental, and emotional activity. For example, Sara Ruddick develops a theory of what she calls "maternal thinking." Ruddick argues that the "agents of maternal practice, acting in response to the demands of their children, acquire a conceptual scheme—a vocabulary and logic of connections—through which they order and express the facts and values of their practice. In judgments and self-reflection, they refine and concretize this scheme. Intellectual activities are distinguishable but not separable from disciplines of feeling. There is a unity of reflection, judgment, and emotion."[8] Similarly, Patricia Hill Collins sketches an alternative epistemology based on the standpoint of black women's experiences. Collins discusses two features of this standpoint.

> First, Black women's political and economic status provides them with a distinctive set of experiences that offers a different view of material reality than that available to other groups. The unpaid and paid work that Black women perform, the types of communities in which they live, and the kinds of relationships they have with others suggest that African-American women, as a group, experience a different world than those who are not Black and not female. Second, these experiences stimulate a distinctive Black female consciousness concerning that material reality.[9]

Collins argues that in articulating this standpoint, Black women often employ an alternative epistemology that reflects these experiences as well as embracing Afrocentric values. Collins delineates four central features of this epistemology: concrete experience as a criterion of meaning; the use of dialogue in assessing knowledge claims; the ethic of caring; and the ethic of personal accountability.[10]

Many of the alternative epistemologies developed by feminists attempt to develop a conception of rationality that involves a "unity" of emotion and reason. But the lesson learned from careful attention to the history of philosophy is that this blending cannot be simply additive, but must be transformative. As can be seen from my analysis of Rousseau, it is not sufficient for feminists simply to attempt to construct a theory of rationality that includes both masculine and feminine traits. As long as masculine traits are ranked as superior to feminine traits, such theories would modify but not correct the gender bias. Feminists must carefully undercut the subtle ranking of masculine over feminine traits.

Part of the process of questioning this ranking has involved critiques of dualistic thought. Feminists have argued that all knowledge involves values and politics. Feminist science criticism, for example, is aimed at demonstrating the ways in which factors such as the social and political identity of a scientist, including her or his gender experiences, are part of the practice of science.[11] This dissolution of the boundary between science and values or politics has in turn opened the way to a revised conception of the knowing subject. Rather than the disinterested, disembodied Cartesian knower, feminists are offering a conception of the knowing subject as situated, as engaged, and as a part of a community. For example, Lynn Harkinson Nelson has argued that "who knows" is not individuals, but communities. Accepting the view of theorists such as Hartsock, Rose, and Ruddick that our experiences as women are epistemologically significant, Nelson reminds us of the necessity of interpersonal relationships and of a public conceptual scheme for knowing. Nelson argues that our experiences of the world arise out of a conceptual scheme, a system of theories about the world that we inherit when we learn to speak and act within society, and which we continue to learn and refine throughout our lives. Nelson concludes that "what constitutes evidence for a claim is not determined by individuals, but by the standards a community accepts concomitantly with constructing, adopting, and refining theories. Those standards constrain what it is possible for an individual to believe as well as the theorizing we engage in together."[12] Feminist critiques of dualistic thinking offer radically transformed notions of the basic epistemological categories, including objectivity, the knowing subjects, and truth.

Feminists are working on similar transformations of moral theories. The critiques parallel those of rationality. Feminists argue that the basic categories of moral theory lead to a definition of moral competence as masculine; that is, the moral agent is perceived as male. Thus traditional ethical theory is seen as insufficient to address the concerns and experiences of women. Rather than attempt to argue that women are capable of full moral agency as traditionally defined, feminist ethicists are working to reconstruct moral theory. Traditional moral theory is criticized for positing a conception of people as disinterested, independent individuals, who are both free and equals, and of a moral agent as impartial.[13] Many feminist theorists argue instead for a model of moral thinking based on relationships, with moral actions arising out of responsibilities and affiliations rather than duties or rights.

Currently the most influential of these alternative models of morality is what has been labeled an "ethics of care." Advanced in large part by the work of Carol Gilligan, Nel Noddings, and Sara Ruddick, an ethics of care replaces the autonomous moral agent who uses reason to understand and apply a set of universal moral rules with the member of a community who responds to others in a caring way that aims to prevent harm and to sustain relationships.[14] Many of the care theorists believe that the experience of rearing a child provides the basis of an alternative moral sensibility, and that the mother-child relationship can provide a new model for moral relationships.[15] It is believed that such transformations of ethical theory will both acknowledge the experiences of women and include issues of special concern to women, both of which are neglected in traditional ethical theory.

As with feminist research in epistemology, current work in feminist ethics is both exciting and promising. Still, it is important that we keep the lessons of history clearly before us. Feminists have identified the ways in which women are excluded from moral agency when morality is defined in terms of traits perceived as masculine. As I noted in my discussion of Kant, when the characteristics used to define the moral individual are seen as masculine, a woman must overcome or control her feminine qualities and become like a man in order to act morally. This will lead to the belief that it is more difficult for a woman to be moral than for a man. But it is easier to miss the ways in which a moral theory that includes attributes perceived as feminine in addition to those accepted as masculine can nevertheless exclude women.

What we learn from a careful study of Hume's moral theory is, first of all, that it is not sufficient to simply infuse traditional moral theory with traits seen as feminine. As mentioned before, it will not be sufficient to simply "mix in" qualities viewed as feminine. Those traits perceived as masculine are ranked higher and seen as more valuable than those accepted as feminine. Thus to simply add in so-called "feminine components" will not erase such ranking. Feminists who are concerned to correct the omission of the "feminine" must also develop a moral theory which rejects the ways in which masculine traits are privileged over feminine traits. Some theorists believe that this can be accomplished while retaining the distinction between feminine and masculine; others believe that the distinction itself will have to be eradicated. I believe it is premature to come to a conclusion concerning this debate. The distinction between feminine and masculine and its various theoretical permutations must be examined carefully and critically in order to determine whether it should be retained, revised, or rejected.

A second lesson that we learn from Hume is that moral theory does not exist in a vacuum. Despite the potential gender neutrality of Hume's moral theory, his acceptance of an Aristotelian view of woman's natural inferiority led him to conclude that women would be less likely to act morally than men. So even if feminists are successful in advancing and finding acceptance for a moral theory that does not privilege masculine traits, as long as socially held beliefs about women's inferiority persist, we must not think that such a moral theory will be sufficient to eradicate the perception that woman is less capable of moral action than man. We cannot limit our critiques simply to moral theory or to theories of rationality. We must also transform the gaze from outside the garden walls that defines woman as inferior. Feminist theorists must never forget that our political action goes hand in hand with our theorizing.

In addition, in developing theories which include or are modeled on women's experiences and which address issues, whether in ethics or in science, associated with women that had been previously neglected, it is important to explicitly undermine the assumption that such experiences are limited to women or that women's concern for such issues is innate or inevitable. Given the gender essentialism that persists in contemporary scientific, religious, and commonsense views, such theories run the risk of reinforcing such stereotypes unless the theory is carefully and consciously designed to subvert them. One important component of this transformation is to recognize that the experiences and concerns of women, like those of men, are plural and diverse.[16]

Feminist criticisms of the public/private dichotomy are similarly complex. In identifying the ways in which various political theorists have excluded women or limited their participation in the state, one comes to the realization that this exclusion is not easily rectified. First of all, one must counter the persistent and powerful prejudice of woman's inferiority. As I have shown, theorists as diverse as Hegel and Locke were moved by the force of this prejudice to conclude that women are to be limited to the private realm of family. Second, as with theories of rationality and morality, feminist investigations of androcentric biases in political theory are showing that the political realm is constructed as masculine. The institutions of the political realm are, in the words of Wendy Brown, "saturated with highly problematic, often dangerous, ideals and practices of manhood."[17] Concepts such as freedom, political power, and property are defined in terms of masculinity.

As feminist critiques of versions of liberal feminism make clear, discrimination on the basis of gender will not be eradicated by simply attempting to include women within the public realm. As long as the values and activities of the private realm continue to be denigrated and as long as the prejudice of woman's inferiority goes unquestioned, so-called "equal opportunity" will be neither. Nor can we simply reverse the values and attempt to inscribe politics with "female virtues." Some of the characteristics that feminists offer as female virtues, such as a sense of community and empathy, are important and should be taken seriously in attempting to reconstruct society. But in recognizing that the feminine, as well as the masculine, is socially constructed, and in fact often constructed in reaction to the masculine, we have every reason to think that it too will be far too limited to universalize as characteristic of humanity. In the process of developing alternative political theories, feminists may decide to embrace traits constructed as feminine, but we must do so carefully. First of all, even the most positive of the so-called "female virtues," such as caring, are traditionally envisioned as involving negative aspects such as a failure to acknowledge one's own needs, being overprotective, and a fear of autonomy. As Wendy Brown cautions, the fact that

> we like some of the sensibilities women have developed pursuant to the role they have been assigned historically is a good reason to explore the political potential of these sensibilities but does not mean we can develop them into an idealized and mobile value *system* that abstracts from the context in which the sensibilities were formed and eschews their less lovely aspects. Similarly, while the traditional work of women as mothers and managers of emotional life provides rich material for rethinking political relations, this experience cannot simply replace political relations.[18]

Second, in investigating the feminine it is crucial that differences between women arising from differences such as race, class, and culture not be erased. As Elizabeth Spelman reminds us, the concept of womanhood is not the same for all women and thus we cannot conclude that the sexism that all women experience is the same. "We have to understand what one's oppression 'as a woman' means in each case. The sexism most Black women have experienced has not typically included being put on a pedestal. Moreover, we cannot describe what it is to be subject to several forms of oppression, say, sexism and racism and classism, by adding together their separate accounts. For example, we surely cannot produce an accurate picture of Latina women's lives simply by combining an account of Anglo women's lives and one of Latino men's lives."[19]

The feminist challenge to philosophy is onerous. It goes far beyond the definitions of womanhood contained within specific philosophical accounts to reveal and question the gender bias woven into the concepts central to philosophy. I have discussed three of these—rationality, morality, and political agency—revealing the complexities of the impact of gender assumptions upon the construction and definition of these concepts. But my account only brushes the surface of the ways in which gender assumptions are woven into the fabric of philosophy. There are many more concepts needing similar analysis; there are patterns of bias not revealed in my account. Although I have provided a method for reading philosophy and identified a series of common assumptions, there is much more to be done. My challenge to you is to take the tools I have offered you, refine them, and use them to reread the entirety of the philosophical canon—this time with a focus on gender.

In this endeavor we must work together, for there are many changes to be made.

Epilogue

1. *Hypatia: A Journal of Feminist Philosophy* 5, 2 (1990): 11–12.

2. Luce Irigaray, *The Speculum of the Other Woman,* trans. Gillian Gill (Ithaca: Cornell University Press, 1985).

3. Ibid., p. 345.

4. Although some readers of Irigaray have objected to a perceived essentialism within her writings, Diana Fuss persuasively argues that despite the fact that Irigaray "reopens the question of essence and woman's access to it . . . essentialism represents not a trap she falls into but rather a key strategy she puts into play, not a dangerous oversight but rather a lever of displacement." *Essentially Speaking: Feminism, Nature & Difference* (New York: Routledge, 1989), p. 72.

5. *Feminist Theory and the Philosophies of Man* (London: Croom Helm, 1988), p. 151.

6. See, for example, Susan Bordo, *The Flight to Objectivity* (Albany: State University of New York Press, 1987); Elizabeth Fee, "Is Feminism a Threat to Objectivity?" *International Journal of Women's Studies* 4, 4 (1980); Sandra Harding, *The Science Question in Feminism* (Ithaca: Cornell University Press, 1986); Evelyn Fox Keller, *Reflections on Gender and Science* (New Haven: Yale University Press, 1985); Nancy Tuana, *Feminism & Science* (Bloomington: Indiana University Press, 1988).

7. Nancy Hartsock, *Money, Sex, and Power: Toward a Feminist Historical Materialism* (New York: Longman, 1983); Hilary Rose, "Hand, Brain and Heart: A Feminist Episte-

mology for the Natural Sciences," *Signs: Journal of Women in Culture and Society* 9, 1 (1983): 73–90, and "Beyond Masculinist Realities: A Feminist Epistemology for the Sciences," in *Feminist Approaches to Science,* ed. Ruth Bleier (New York: Pergamon Press, 1988); Sara Ruddick, *Maternal Thinking: Toward a Politics of Peace* (Boston: Beacon Press, 1989).

8. Sara Ruddick, "Maternal Thinking," in *Mothering: Essays in Feminist Theory,* ed. Joyce Trebilcot (Savage, MD: Rowman and Littlefield, 1983), p. 214.

9. Patricia Hill Collins, "The Social Construction of Black Feminist Thought," in *Black Women in America: Social Science Perspectives,* ed. Micheline R. Malson, Elisabeth Mudimbe-Boyi, Jean F. O'Barr, and Mary Wyer (Chicago: University of Chicago Press, 1990), pp. 299–300.

10. Her analysis is developed in depth in *Black Feminist Thought* (Winchester, MA: Unwin Hyman, 1990).

11. See, for example, debates between "man, the hunter" and "woman, the gatherer" theories of human evolution. For example, see Ruth Hubbard, "Have Only Men Evolved?" in *Biological Woman—the Convenient Myth,* ed. R. Hubbard, M. Henifin, and B. Fried (Cambridge: Schenkman, 1982); and Sarah Blaffer Hrdy, *The Woman That Never Evolved* (Cambridge: Harvard University Press, 1981).

12. Lynn Harkinson Nelson, *Who Knows: From Quine to a Feminist Empiricism* (Philadelphia: Temple University Press, 1990).

13. See, for example, Seyla Benhabib, "The Generalized and the Concrete Other: The Kohlberg-Gilligan Controversy and Feminist Theory," in *Feminism as Critique: On the Politics of Gender,* ed. Seyla Benhabib and Drucilla Cornell (Minneapolis: University of Minnesota Press, 1987); and Virginia Held, "Non-Contractual Society," in *Science, Morality and Feminist Theory,* ed. Marsha Hanen and Kai Nielsen (Calgary: University of Calgary Press, 1987).

14. Carol Gilligan, *In a Different Voice: Psychological Theory and Women's Development* (Cambridge: Harvard University Press, 1982); Nel Noddings, *Caring: A Feminine Approach to Ethics and Moral Education* (Berkeley: University of California Press, 1984); Ruddick, *Maternal Thinking.*

15. For the former point see the writings of Sara Ruddick, for the latter see Virginia Held, "Feminism and Moral Theory," in *Women and Moral Theory,* ed. Eva Feder Kittay and Diana T. Meyers (Savage, MD: Rowman and Littlefield, 1987).

16. Gilligan's study, for example, has been criticized for being based on a study of female students at Harvard and thus arising out of a nonrepresentative sample. Also ethical theories like those of Ruddick which emphasize the mother-child relationship are being criticized for not recognizing the diversity of experiences of this relationship as well as being criticized by women who are not mothers as not representing their experiences.

17. Wendy Brown, *Manhood and Politics: A Feminist Reading in Political Theory* (Totowa, NJ: Rowman & Littlefield, 1988), p. 12.

18. Ibid., p. 190.

19. Elizabeth Spelman, *Inessential Woman: Problems of Exclusion in Feminist Thought* (Boston: Beacon Press, 1988), p. 14.

DISCUSSION QUESTIONS

1. In what ways is our culture today still affected by traditional mind/body dualism, as well as the superiority/inferiority, male/female connotations that have gone along with it? What should philosophers do about this, if anything?

2. What is the difference between a gender-neutral philosophy and a nonsexist philosophy?

3. According to Tuana, in our philosophical reading and writing our gender assumptions interweave with our assumptions about race, culture, class, and sexuality. What are some examples that would confirm or weaken her claims?

4. Using the perspective Tuana provides, what kinds of gender colorings can you find in the previous three selections?

5. Leopoldo Zea (b. 1912)
"The Actual Function of Philosophy in Latin America"

Leopoldo Zea is a Mexican philosopher who has become known over the last fifty years for his work on the possibilities of a distinctive Latin American philosophy. Although he wrote this essay in the 1940s, partially in response to the European crisis caused by the successes of fascism, the issues it raised then resonate today with many intellectuals in Spanish-speaking America. The central question has to do with Latin American cultural identity, originally in relation to European culture, and more recently in relation to Anglo North American culture as well.

Specifically with respect to academic philosophy, Zea argues that, in the first place, formally educated Latin Americans are more or less cut off from the indigenous systems of thought in their part of the world. Secondly, although trained in the European intellectual tradition, they are at the same time distanced from it in a unique way. He does believe that philosophical inquiry by its very nature deals with the universal issues that have always confronted humanity, but he also believes that philosophers respond to those issues, appropriately, from a standpoint informed by their own cultural and geographical circumstances. In effect, what appears to be a predicament for Latin American philosophers turns out to be an opportunity, in Zea's estimation, to contribute to increased human understanding and a better world by explicitly utilizing their own culturally unique experience and the philosophical perspectives it makes possible.

QUESTIONS FOR CRITICAL READING

1. What is the value of philosophy, according to Zea?

2. What are the "tasks" Zea recommends for a possible Latin American philosophy?

3. Ultimately, if a distinctive Latin American philosophy is created, how will it happen, in Zea's view?

4. How does Zea characterize the relationship between Latin American culture and European culture, and how is it different from the relationship between Asian culture and European culture, and Anglo-American culture and European culture?

5. What is the "human essence" according to Zea, and what is the balance necessary for its "safekeeping"?

1

Some years ago, a young Mexican teacher published a book that caused much sensation. This young teacher was Samuel Ramos and the book was *El perfil del hombre y la cultura en México*. This book was the first attempt at interpreting Mexican culture. In it Mexican culture became the subject of philosophical interpretation. Philosophy came down from the world of ideal entities to a world of concrete entities like Mexico, a symbol of men who live and die in their cities and farms. This daring attempt was derogatorily termed *literature.* Philosophy could not be anything other than a clever game of words taken from an alien culture. These words of course lacked meaning: the meaning they had for that alien culture.

Years later another teacher, this time the Argentinian Francisco Romero, emphasized Ibero-America's need to begin thinking about its own issues, and the need to delve into the history of its culture in order to take from it the issues needed for the development of a new type of philosophical concern. This time, however, Romero's call was based on a series of cultural phenomena that he identified in an essay entitled "Sobre la filosofía en Iberoamerica." In this article he showed how the interest in philosophical issues in Latin America was increasing on a daily basis. The public at large now follows and asks with interest for works of a philosophical character and nature. This has resulted in numerous publications—books, journals, newspaper articles, etc.—and also in the creation of institutes and centers for philosophical studies where philosophy is practiced. This interest in philosophy stands in sharp contrast with periods when such an activity was confined to a few misunderstood men. Their activity did not transcend literary or academic circles. Today, we have reached the level that Romero calls "the period of philosophical normalcy," that is, a period in which the practice of philosophy is seen as a function of culture just as is the case with any other activity of a cultural nature. The philosopher ceases to be an eccentric whom nobody cares to understand and becomes a member of his country's culture. There is what one may call a "philosophical environment," that is, a public opinion that judges philosophical production, thus forcing it to address the issues that concern those who are part of this so-called "public opinion."

Now, there is one particular issue that concerns not only a few men in our continent, but the Latin American man in general. This issue concerns the possibility or impossibility of Latin American culture, and, as an aspect of the same issue, the possibility or impossibility of Latin American philosophy. Latin American philosophy can exist if there is a Latin American culture from which this philosophy may take its issues. The existence of Latin American philosophy depends on whether or not there is Latin American culture. However, the formulation and attempt to solve this problem, apart from the affirmative or negative character of the answer, are already Latin American philosophy, since they are an attempt to answer affirmatively or negatively a Latin American question. Hence, the works of Ramos, Romero, and others on this issue, whatever their conclusions, are already Latin American philosophy.

The issue involved in the possibility of Latin American culture is one demanded by our time and the historical circumstances in which we find ourselves. The Latin American man had not thought much about this issue before because it did not worry him. A Latin American culture, a culture proper to the Latin American man, was considered to be an irrelevant issue; Latin America lived comfortably under the shadow of European culture. However, the latter culture has been shaken (or is in crisis) today, and it seems to have disappeared from the entire European continent. The Latin American man who had lived so comfortably found that the culture that supported him fails him, that he has no future, and that the ideas in which he believed have become useless artifacts, without sense, lacking value even for their own authors. The man who had lived with so much confidence under a tree he had not planted now finds himself in the open when the planter cuts down the tree and throws it into the fire as useless. The man now has to plant his own cultural tree, create his own ideas. But a culture does not emerge miraculously; the seed of that culture must be taken from somewhere, it must belong to someone. Now—and this is the issue that concerns the Latin American man—where is he going to find that seed? That is, what ideas is he going to develop? To what ideas is he going to give his faith? Will he continue to believe and develop the ideas inherited from Europe? Or is there a group of ideas and issues to be developed that are proper to the Latin American circumstance? Or rather, will he have to invent those ideas? In a word, the problem of the existence, or lack of existence, of ideas that are proper to America, as well as the problem of the acceptance or rejection of ideas belonging to European culture that is now in crisis, comes to the fore. Specifically, the problem of the relationship between Latin America and European culture, and the problem of the possibility for a genuinely Latin American ideology.

2

In light of what has been said it is clear that one of the primary issues involved in Latin American philosophy concerns the relations between Latin America and European culture. Now, the first thing that needs to be asked has to do with the type of relations that Latin America has with that culture. There are some who have compared this relationship to that between Asia and European culture. It is said that Latin America, just as Asia, has assimilated only technology from Europe. But if this is so, what would belong to Latin American culture? For the Asian man, what he has adopted from European culture is regarded as something superimposed that he has had to assimilate owing to the change in his own circumstance caused in turn by European intervention. However, what he has adopted from European culture is not properly the culture, that is, a life-style, a world view, but only its instruments, its technology. Asians know that they have inherited an age-old culture that has been transmitted from generation to generation; they know that they have their own culture. Their view of the world is practically the opposite of the European. From Europeans they have only adopted their technology, and only because they have been forced to do so by the intervention of Europeans and their technology in a circumstance that is properly Asian. Our present day shows what Asians can do with their own world view while using European technology. Asians have little concern for the future of European culture, and they will try to destroy it if they feel that it gets in their way or continues to intervene in what they regard as their own culture.

Now, can we Latin Americans think in a similar way about European culture? To think so is to believe that we have our own culture, but that this culture has not perhaps reached full expression yet because Europe has prevented it. In light of this, one could think that this is a good time to achieve cultural liberation. If that were the case, the crisis of European culture would not concern us. More than a problem, such a crisis would be a solution. But this is not the case: we are deeply concerned about the crisis of European culture; we experience it as our own crisis.

This is due to the fact that our relationship with European culture as Latin Americans is different from that of the Asians. We do not feel, as Asians do, the heirs of our own autochthonous culture. There was, yes, an indigenous culture—Aztec, Maya, Inca, etc.—but this culture does not represent, for us contemporary Latin Americans, the same thing that ancient Oriental culture represents for contemporary Asians. While Asians continue to view the world as their ancestors did, we Latin Americans do not view the world as the Aztecs or the Mayans did. If we did, we would have the same devotion for pre-Columbian temples and divinities that an Oriental has for his very ancient gods and temples. A Mayan temple is as alien and meaningless to us as a Hindu temple.

What belongs to us, what is properly Latin American, is not to be found in pre-Columbian culture. Is it to be found in European culture? Now, something strange happens to us in relation to European culture: we use it but we do not consider it ours; we feel *imitators* of it. Our way of thinking, our world view, is similar to the European. European culture has a meaning for us that we do not find in pre-Columbian culture. Still, we do not feel it to be our own. We feel as bastards who profit from goods to which they have no right. We feel as if we were wearing someone else's clothes: they are too big for our size. We assimilate their ideas but cannot live up to them. We feel that we should realize the ideals of European culture, but we also feel incapable of carrying out the task: we are content with admiring them and thinking that they are not made for us. This is the knot of our problem: we do not feel heirs of an autochthonous culture, because that culture has no meaning for us; and that which has meaning for us, like the European, does not feel as our own. There is something that makes us lean toward European culture while at the same time resists becoming part of that culture. Our view of the world is European but we perceive the achievements of that culture as alien. And when we try to realize its ideals in Latin America we feel as imitators.

What is properly ours, what is Latin American, makes us lean toward Europe and at the same time resists being Europe. Latin America leans toward Europe as a son to his father, but at the same time it resists becoming like his own father. This resistance is noticeable in that, despite leaning toward European culture, Latin America still feels like an imitator when it seeks to achieve what that culture does. It does not feel that it is realizing what is proper to it but only what Europe alone can achieve. That is why we feel inhibited by and inferior to Europeans. The malaise resides in that we perceive what is Latin American, that is, what is ours, as something inferior. The Latin American man's resistance to being like a European is felt as an incapacity. We think as Europeans, but we do not feel that this is enough; we also want to achieve the same things that Europe achieves. The malaise is that we want to adjust the Latin American circumstance to a conception of the world inherited from Europe, rather than adjusting that conception of the world to the Latin American circumstance. Hence the divorce between ideas and reality. We need the ideas of European culture, but when we bring them into our circumstance we find them to be too big because we do not dare to fit them to this circumstance. We find them big and are afraid to cut them down; we prefer to endure the ridicule of wearing an oversize suit. Indeed, until recently the Latin American man wanted to forget what he is for the sake of becoming another European. This is similar to the case of a son who wants to forget being a son in order to be his own father: the result has to be a gross imitation. This is what the Latin American man feels: that he has tried to imitate rather than to realize his own personality.

Alfonso Reyes portrays the Latin American man's resistance to being Latin American with great humor. The Latin American man felt "in addition to the misfortune of being human and modern, the very specific misfortune of being Latin American; that is, having been born and having roots in a land that was not the center of civilization, but rather a branch of it."[1] To be a Latin American was until very recently a great misfortune, because this did not allow us to be European. Today it is just the opposite: the inability to become European, in spite of our great efforts, allows us to have a personality; it allows us to learn, in this moment of crisis for European culture, that there is something of our own that can give us support. What this something is should be one of the issues that a Latin American philosophy must investigate.

3

Latin America is the daughter of European culture; it is the product of one of its major crises. The discovery of America[2] was not a matter of chance, but rather the product of necessity. Europe needed America: in every European mind there was the idea of America, the idea of a promised land. A land where the European man could place his ideas, since he could no longer continue to place them in the highest places. He could no longer place them in the heavens. Owing to the emergence of a new physics, the heavens were no longer the home of ideals but rather became something unlimited, a mechanical and therefore dead infinity. The idea of an ideal world came down from heaven and landed in America. Hence the European man came out in search of the land and he found it.

The European needed to rid himself of a world view of which he was tired. He needed to get rid of his past and begin a new life. He needed to build a new history, one that would be well planned and calculated, without excess or wanting. What the European was afraid of openly proposing in his own land, he took for granted in this land called America. America became the pretext for criticizing Europe. What he wanted Europe to be became imaginarily fulfilled in America. Fantastic cities and governments that corresponded to the ideals of the modern man were imagined in America. America was presented as the idea of what Europe should be. America became Europe's utopia. It became the ideal world that the old Western world was to follow to rebuild itself. In a word, America was the ideal creation of Europe.

America was born to history as a land of projects, as a land of the future, but of projects and a future that were not its own. Such projects and such future were Europe's. The European man who put his feet in this America—becoming part of the Latin American circumstance and giving rise to the Latin American man—has been unable to see what is properly American. He has only seen what Europe wanted America to be. When he did not find what European imagination had placed in the American continent, he was disappointed, and this produced the uprooting of the Latin American man from his own circumstance. The Latin American man feels European by origin, but he feels inferior to the European man by reason of his circumstance. He feels inadequate because he regards himself as superior to his circumstance, but inferior to the culture he comes from. He feels contempt for things Latin American, and resentment toward Europe.

Rather than attempting to achieve what is proper to Latin America, the Latin American man labors to achieve the European utopia and thus stumbles, as it could be expected, into a Latin American reality that resists being anything other than what it is: Latin America. This gives rise to the feeling of inferiority about which we already have spoken. The Latin American man considers his reality to be inferior to what he believes to be his destiny. In Anglo-Saxon America this feeling expresses itself in the desire to achieve what Europe has achieved in order to satisfy its own needs. North America has strived to become a second Europe, a magnified copy of it. Original creation does not matter, what matters is to achieve the European models in a big way and with the greatest perfection. Everything is reduced to numbers: so many dollars or so many meters. In the end, the only thing that is sought with this is to hide a feeling of inferiority. The North American tries to show that he is as capable as the European. And the way to show it is by doing the same things that Europeans have done, on a bigger scale and with greater technical perfection. But this only demonstrates technical, not cultural ability, because cultural ability is demonstrated in the solution one gives to the problems of man's existence, and not in the technical imitation of solutions that other men found for their own problems.

The Latin American man, however, feels inferior not only to the European, but also to the North American man. Not only does he no longer try to hide his feeling of inferiority, but he also exhibits it through self-denigration. The only thing that he has tried to do so far is to live comfortably under the shadow of ideas he knows are not his own. To him, ideas do not matter as much as the way to benefit from them. That is why our politics have turned into bureaucracy. Politics is no longer an end but an instrument to get a job in the bureaucracy. Banners and ideals do not matter anymore; what matters is how these banners and ideals can help us get the job we want. Hence the miraculous and quick change of banners; whence also that we al-

ways plan and project but we never achieve definitive results. We are continually experimenting and projecting with always-changing ideologies. There is no single national plan because there is no sense of nation. And there is no sense of nation for the same reason that there is no sense of what is Latin American. He who feels inferior as Latin American also feels inferior as a national, that is, as a member of one of the Latin American nations. This is not to say that the fanatic nationalist who talks about a Mexican, Argentinian, Chilean, or any other Latin American nation's culture, to the exclusion of anything that smacks of foreign, has any better sense of what a nation is. No, in the end he would only try to eliminate what makes him feel inferior. This is the case of those who say that this is the appropriate time to eliminate everything European from our culture.

This position is wrong because, whether we want it or not, we are the children of European culture. From Europe we have received our cultural framework, what could be called our structure: language, religion, customs; in a word, our conception of life and world is European. To become disengaged from it would be to become disengaged from the heart of our personality. We can no more deny that culture than we can deny our parents. And just as we have a personality that makes us distinct from our parents without having to deny them, we should also be able to have a cultural personality without having to deny the culture of which we are children. To be aware of our true relations with European culture eliminates our sense of inferiority and gives us instead a *sense of responsibility*. This is the feeling that animates the Latin American man today. He feels that he has "come of age," and, as any other man who reaches maturity, he acknowledges that he has a past that he does not need to deny, just as no one is ashamed of having had a childhood. The Latin American man knows himself to be the heir of Western culture and now demands a place in it. The place that he demands is that of collaborator. As a son of that culture he no longer wants to live off it but to work for it. Alfonso Reyes, speaking on behalf of a Latin America that feels responsible, demanded from Europe "the right of universal citizenship that we have already conquered," because already "we have come of age."[3] Latin America is at a point in its history when it must realize its cultural mission. To determine this mission constitutes another issue that what we have called Latin American philosophy has to develop.

4

Once we know our cultural relations with Europe, another task for this possible Latin American philosophy would be to continue to develop the philosophical issues of that culture, but most especially the issues that European philosophy regards as universal. That is, issues whose level of abstraction allows them to be valid at any time and at any place. Among such issues are those of being, knowledge, space, time, God, life, death, etc. A Latin American philosophy can collaborate with Western culture by attempting to resolve the problems posed by the issues that European philosophy has not been able to resolve, or to which it has failed to find a satisfactory solution. Now, it could be said—particularly by those who are interested in building up a philosophy with a Latin American character—that this cannot be of interest to a philosophy concerned with what is properly Latin American. This is not true, however, because both the issues that we have called universal and the issues that are peculiar to the Latin American circumstance are very closely linked. When we discuss the former we need also to discuss the latter. The abstract issues will have to be seen from the Latin American man's own circumstance. Each man will see in such issues what is closest to his own circumstance. He will look at these issues from the standpoint of his own interests, and those interests will be determined by his way of life, his abilities and inabilities, in a word, by his own circumstance. In the case of Latin America, his contribution to the philosophy of such issues will be permeated by the Latin American circumstance. Hence, when we address abstract issues, we shall formulate them as issues of our own. Even though being, God, etc., are issues appropriate for every man, the solution to them will be given from a Latin American standpoint. We may not say what these issues mean for every man, but we can say what they mean for us Latin Americans. Being, God, death, etc., would be what these abstractions mean for us.

It should not be forgotten that all European philosophy has worked on these issues on the assumption that their solutions would be universal. However, the product has been an aggregate of philosophies very different from each other. Despite their universalistic goals, the product has been a Greek philosophy, a Christian philosophy, a French philosophy, a British philosophy, and a German philosophy. Likewise, independently of our attempts to realize a Latin American philosophy and despite our efforts to provide universal solutions, our solutions will bear the mark of our own circumstance.

Another type of issue to be addressed by our possible Latin American philosophy is related to our own circumstance. That is, our possible philosophy must try to resolve the problems posed by our circumstance. This point of view is as legitimate and valid a philosophical issue as the one we have just discussed. As Latin Americans we have a series of problems that arise only in the context of our circumstance and that therefore only we can resolve. The posing of such problems does in no way diminish the philosophical character of our philosophy, because philosophy attempts to solve the problems that man encounters during his existence. Hence the problems encountered by the Latin American man are the problems of the circumstance in which he lives.

Among such issues is that of our history. History is part of man's circumstance: it gives him a configuration and a profile, thus making him capable of some endeavors and incapable of others. Hence we must take our history into account, because it is there that we can find the source of our abilities and inabilities. We cannot continue to ignore our past and our experiences, because without knowing them we cannot claim to be mature. Maturity, age, is experience. He who ignores his history lacks experience, and he who lacks experience cannot be a mature, responsible man.

With respect to the history of our philosophy, one might think that nothing could be found in it other than bad copies of European philosophical systems. In effect, that is what one will find if one is looking for Latin American philosophical systems that have the same value as European ones. But this is a shortsighted attempt: we must approach the history of our philosophy from a different standpoint. This standpoint is provided by our denials, our inability to do much be-sides bad copies of European models. It is pertinent to ask the reason why we do not have our own philoso-phy: perhaps the very answer will be a Latin American philosophy. This may show us a way of thinking that is our own and that perhaps has not needed to ex-press itself through the formulae used by European philosophy.

It is also pertinent to ask why our philosophy is a *bad copy* of European philosophy. Because being a bad copy may very well be part of our Latin American philosophy. To be a bad copy does not necessarily mean to be bad, but simply different. Perhaps our feel-ing of inferiority has made us consider bad anything that is our own just because it is not like, or equal to, its model. To acknowledge that we cannot create the same European philosophical systems is not to ac-knowledge that we are inferior to the authors of those philosophies, but simply that we are different. On the basis of this assumption we will not view our philoso-phers' production as an aggregate of bad copies of European philosophy, but as Latin American interpre-tations of that philosophy. The Latin American ele-ment will be present in spite of our philosophers' attempts at objectivity. It will be present despite our thinkers' attempt to depersonalize it.

5

Philosophy in its universal character has been con-cerned with one of the problems that has agitated men the most at all times: the problem of the relations be-tween man and society. This problem has been posed as political, asking about the forms of organization of these relations, that is, the organization of human in-teraction. Since the institution in charge of such rela-tions is the State, philosophy has asked by whom it should be established and who should govern. The State must take care to maintain the balance between individual and society; it must take care to avoid both anarchy and totalitarianism. Now, in order to achieve this balance a moral justification is necessary. Philos-ophy attempts to offer such a justification. Hence, every metaphysical abstraction ultimately leads to ethics and politics. Every metaphysical idea provides the

foundation for a concrete fact, the justification for any proposed type of political organization.

There is a multitude of philosophical examples in which metaphysical abstractions have provided the basis for a political construct. One example is found in Plato's philosophy, whose theory of ideas provides the basis and the justification for *The Republic*. In Saint Augustine's *The City of God* we find another ex-ample: the Christian community, the Church, is sup-ported by a metaphysical being that in this case is God. The *Utopias* of the Renaissance constitute yet other examples where rationalism justifies the forms of gov-ernment that have given birth to our present democ-racy. One thinker has said that the French Revolu-tion finds its justification in Descartes's *Discourse on Method*. The Marxist revision of Hegel's dialectics has given way to such forms of government as commu-nism. Even totalitarianism has sought metaphysical justification in the ideas of Nietzsche, Sorel, and Pa-reto. Many other examples from the history of philos-ophy can be cited where metaphysical abstraction provides the basis for social and political practices.

What we have just discussed underlines how theory and practice must go together. It is necessary that man's material acts be justified by ideas, because this is what makes him different from animals. But our times are characterized by a schism between ideas and reality. European culture is in crisis because of this schism. Man is now lacking a moral theory to jus-tify his acts and hence has been unable to resolve the problems of human interaction. All that he has achieved is the fall into the extremes of anarchy and totalitarianism.

The various crises of Western culture have been produced by a lack of ideas to justify human acts, man's existence. When some ideas have no longer jus-tified this existence, it has been necessary to search for other sets of ideas. The history of Western culture is the history of the crises that man has endured when the harmony that should exist between ideas and re-ality has been broken. Western culture has gone from crisis to crisis, finding salvation sometimes in ideas, sometimes in God, other times in reason, up to the present time when it no longer has ideas, God, or rea-son. Culture is now asking for new foundations of support. But this is, from our point of view, practically impossible. However, this point of view belongs to men who are in a situation of crisis, and this could not be otherwise, since we would not be in a situation of crisis if the problem seemed to us to have an easy solution. The fact that we are in a crisis, and that we do not have the much-wanted solution, still does not mean that the solution does not exist. Men who like us have been in situations of crisis before have had a similar pessimism; however, a solution has always been found. We do not know which values will replace those that we see sinking, but what we do know for certain is that such values will emerge, and it is our task as Latin Americans to contribute to this process.

From this we can infer yet another goal for a possible Latin American philosophy. The Western culture of which we are children and heirs needs new values on which to rest. These new values will have to be derived from new human experiences, that is, from the experiences that result from men being in the new circumstances of today. Because of its particular situation, Latin America can contribute to culture with the novelty of untapped experiences. That is why it is necessary that it tell its truth to the world. But it must be a truth without pretensions, a sincere truth. Latin America should not pretend to be the director of Western culture; what it must aspire to do is to produce culture purely and simply. And that can be accomplished by attempting to resolve the problems that are posed to the Latin American man by his own Latin American perspective.

Latin America and Europe will find themselves in a similar situation after the crisis. Both will have to resolve the same problem: what will be the new way of life that they will have to adopt to deal with the new circumstances? Both will have to continue ahead with the interrupted task of universal culture. But the difference is that Latin America will no longer be under the shadow of Europe's accomplishments, because there is neither a shadow nor a place of support at this point. On the contrary, Latin America finds itself at a vantage point in time—which may not last long—but that must be used to initiate the task that belongs to it as an adult member of Western culture.

A Latin American philosophy must begin the task of searching for the values that will provide the basis for a future type of culture. And this task will be carried out with the purpose of safekeeping the human

essence: that which makes a man a man. Now, man is essentially an individual who is at the same time engaged in interaction with others, and hence it is necessary to maintain a balance between these two components of his essence. This is the balance that has been upset to the point of leading man to extremes: individualism to the point of anarchy, and social existence to the point of massification. Hence it is imperative to find values that make social interaction possible without detriment to individuality.

This task, which is universal and not simply Latin American, will be the supreme goal of our possible philosophy. This philosophy of ours cannot be limited to purely Latin American problems, that is, the problems of Latin America's circumstance. It must be concerned with the larger circumstance called humanity, of which we are also a part. It is not enough to attempt to reach a Latin American truth, but we must also attempt to reach a truth that is valid for all men, even if this truth may not in fact be accomplished. What is Latin American cannot be regarded as an end in itself, but as a boundary of a larger goal. Hence the reason why every attempt to make a Latin American philosophy, guided by the sole purpose of being Latin American, is destined to fail. One must attempt to do purely and simply philosophy, because what is Latin American will arise by itself. Simply by being Latin American, philosophers will create a Latin American philosophy in spite of their own efforts at depersonalization. Any attempt to the contrary will be anything but philosophy.

When we attempt to resolve the problems of man in any spatiotemporal situation whatever, we will necessarily have to start with ourselves because we are men; we will have to start with our own circumstances, our limitations, and our being Latin Americans, just as the Greeks started with their own circumstance called Greece. But, just like them, we cannot limit ourselves to stay in our own circumstances. If we do that it will be in spite of ourselves, and we will produce Latin American philosophy, just as the Greeks produced Greek philosophy in spite of themselves.

It is only on the basis of these assumptions that we will accomplish our mission within universal culture, and collaborate with it fully aware of our abilities, and be aware also of our capacities as members of the cultural community called humanity, as well as of our limits as children of a circumstance that is our own and to which we owe our personality: Latin America.

Notes

1. Alfonso Reyes, "Notas sobre la inteligencia americana," *Sur,* no. 24 (September 1936).

2. Zea consistently uses "America" and "Americanos" to refer to Latin America and its inhabitants. I use "Latin America" and "Latin Americans" respectively to render these terms throughout the paper, except in the present case, because here Zea is referring to the period of discovery, when there was no distinction between Anglo-Saxon and Latin America.—TRANS.

3. Reyes, "Notas."

DISCUSSION QUESTIONS

1. Zea alludes to the demoralizing effect the events surrounding World War II had on many European intellectuals and how that affected Latin American cultural life. How is the relationship between the various cultures of the Americas and the culture of Europe different today?

2. How might people who more actively participate in indigenous cultural traditions in Latin America respond to Zea's conclusions in this selection?

3. The implication of Zea's position is that attempts at nationalistic or exclusivistic cultural philosophies are misguided. Do you agree or disagree? Why?

4. What are the similarities and differences between Zea's conclusions regarding the contributions of Latin American philosophy and Radhakrishnan's view of the contributions of Indian philosophy?

6. Bertrand Russell (1872–1970)
On the Value of Philosophy

Throughout the twentieth century, Bertrand Russell was considered one of the most influential philosophers in the English-speaking academic world. He was one of the originators of what came to be known as analytic philosophy, still the predominant orientation among Anglo-American professional philosophers today. Although it had its antecedents in pre-twentieth-century Western thought, this analytic approach to philosophical reflection has been distinguished by its almost exclusive focus on the logical analysis, critique, and clarification of concepts, definitions, and propositions as they are found both in everyday language use and in the more formal discourse of mathematics and science. Russell's interest in philosophical analysis of this sort led to significant contributions in the development of the philosophy of mathematics and the philosophy of science in the first two decades of the twentieth century. Throughout his life he published many writings, often arguing for controversial and unconventional positions on social, political, and ethical topics as well. He was part of the traditional titled class in Britain, but his aristocratic lineage was not enough to keep him from losing his appointment at Cambridge University in 1916 because of his political views, primarily his opposition to Britain's participation in World War I.

The selection presented here is the last chapter of *The Problems of Philosophy* (1912), which was written for a popular audience and dealt mainly with issues in epistemology and metaphysics. As Russell saw it, in light of the successes of science and the increased emphasis on taking care of human material needs in the contemporary world, it becomes all the more important to show why the study of philosophy still can be valuable for anyone.

QUESTIONS FOR CRITICAL READING

1. What are the human goods that can be achieved by philosophy, according to Russell?

2. Compare and contrast the outlook on life of the "practical man" and the "instinctive man," as Russell characterizes each.

3. What does Russell mean by asserting that doubt can be "liberating"?

4. What is the nature of "true philosophic contemplation," and why is it at odds with the ancient adage "Man is the measure of all things," in Russell's view?

Having now come to the end of our brief and very incomplete review of the problems of philosophy, it will be well to consider, in conclusion, what is the value of philosophy and why it ought to be studied. It is the more necessary to consider this question, in view of the fact that many men, under the influence of science or of practical affairs, are inclined to doubt whether philosophy is anything better than innocent but useless trifling, hair-splitting distinctions, and controversies on matters concerning which knowledge is impossible.

This view of philosophy appears to result, partly from a wrong conception of the ends of life, partly from a wrong conception of the kind of goods which philosophy strives to achieve. Physical science, through the medium of inventions, is useful to innumerable people who are wholly ignorant of it; thus the study of physical science is to be recommended, not only, or primarily, because of the effect on the student, but rather because of the effect on mankind in general. Thus utility does not belong to philosophy. If the study of philosophy has any value at all for others than students of philosophy, it must be only indirectly, through its effects upon the lives of those who study it. It is in these effects, therefore, if anywhere, that the value of philosophy must be primarily sought.

But further, if we are not to fail in our endeavour to determine the value of philosophy, we must first free our minds from the prejudices of what are wrongly called 'practical' men. The 'practical' man, as this word is often used, is one who recognizes only material needs, who realizes that men must have food for the body, but is oblivious of the necessity of providing food for the mind. If all men were well off, if poverty and disease had been reduced to their lowest possible point, there would still remain much to be done to produce a valuable society; and even in the existing world the goods of the mind are at least as important as the goods of the body. It is exclusively among the goods of the mind that the value of philosophy is to be found; and only those who are not indifferent to these goods can be persuaded that the study of philosophy is not a waste of time.

Philosophy, like all other studies, aims primarily at knowledge. The knowledge it aims at is the kind of knowledge which gives unity and system to the body of the sciences, and the kind which results from a critical examination of the grounds of our convictions, prejudices, and beliefs. But it cannot be maintained that philosophy has had any very great measure of success in its attempts to provide definite answers to its questions. If you ask a mathematician, a mineralogist, a historian, or any other man of learning, what definite body of truths has been ascertained by his science, his answer will last as long as you are willing to listen. But if you put the same question to a philosopher, he will, if he is candid, have to confess that his study has not achieved positive results such as have been achieved by other sciences. It is true that this is partly accounted for by the fact that, as soon as definite knowledge concerning any subject becomes possible, this subject ceases to be called philosophy, and becomes a separate science. The whole study of the heavens, which now belongs to astronomy, was once included in philosophy; Newton's great work was called 'the mathematical principles of natural philosophy.' Similarly, the study of the human mind, which was a part of philosophy, has now been separated from philosophy and has become the science of psychology. Thus, to a great extent, the uncertainty of philosophy is more apparent than real: those questions which are already capable of definite answers are placed in the sciences, while those only to which, at present, no definite answer can be given, remain to form the residue which is called philosophy.

This is, however, only a part of the truth concerning the uncertainty of philosophy. There are many questions—and among them those that are of the profoundest interest to our spiritual life—which, so far as we can see, must remain insoluble to the human intellect unless its powers become of quite a different order from what they are now. Has the universe any unity of plan or purpose, or is it a fortuitous concourse of atoms? Is consciousness a permanent part of the universe, giving hope of indefinite growth in wisdom, or is it a transitory accident on a small planet on which life must ultimately become impossible? Are good and evil of importance to the universe or only to man? Such questions are asked by philosophy, and variously answered by various philosophers. But it would seem that, whether answers be otherwise discoverable or not, the answers suggested by philosophy are none of them demonstrably true. Yet, however slight may be the hope of discovering an answer, it is part of the business of philosophy to continue the consideration of such questions, to make us aware of their importance, to examine all the approaches to them, and to keep alive that speculative interest in the universe which is apt to be killed by confining ourselves to definitely ascertainable knowledge.

Many philosophers, it is true, have held that philosophy could establish the truth of certain answers to such fundamental questions. They have supposed that what is of most importance in religious beliefs could be proved by strict demonstration to be true. In order to judge such attempts, it is necessary to take a survey of human knowledge, and to form an opinion as to its methods and its limitations. On such a subject it would be unwise to pronounce dogmatically; but if the investigations of our previous chapters have not led us astray, we shall be compelled to renounce the hope of finding philosophical proofs of religious beliefs. We cannot, therefore, include as part of the value of philosophy any definite set of answers to such questions. Hence, once more, the value of philosophy must not depend upon any supposed body of definitely ascertainable knowledge to be acquired by those who study it.

The value of philosophy is, in fact, to be sought largely in its very uncertainty. The man who has no tincture of philosophy goes through life imprisoned in the prejudices derived from common sense, from the habitual beliefs of his age or his nation, and from convictions which have grown up in his mind without the co-operation or consent of his deliberate reason. To such a man the world tends to become definite, finite, obvious; common objects rouse no questions, and unfamiliar possibilities are contemptuously rejected. As soon as we begin to philosophize, on the contrary, we find, as we saw in our opening chapters, that even the most everyday things lead to problems to which only very incomplete answers can be given. Philosophy, though unable to tell us with certainty what is the true answer to the doubts which it raises, is able to suggest many possibilities which enlarge our thoughts and free them from the tyranny of custom. Thus, while diminishing our feeling of certainty as to what things are, it greatly increases our knowledge as to what they may be; it removes the somewhat arrogant dogmatism of those who have never travelled into the region of lib-

erating doubt, and it keeps alive our sense of wonder by showing familiar things in an unfamiliar aspect.

Apart from its utility in showing unsuspected possibilities, philosophy has a value—perhaps its chief value—through the greatness of the objects which it contemplates, and the freedom from narrow and personal aims resulting from this contemplation. The life of the instinctive man is shut up within the circle of his private interests: family and friends may be included, but the outer world is not regarded except as it may help or hinder what comes within the circle of instinctive wishes. In such a life there is something feverish and confined, in comparison with which the philosophic life is calm and free. The private world of instinctive interests is a small one, set in the midst of a great and powerful world which must, sooner or later, lay our private world in ruins. Unless we can so enlarge our interests as to include the whole outer world, we remain like a garrison in a beleaguered fortress, knowing that the enemy prevents escape and that ultimate surrender is inevitable. In such a life there is no peace, but a constant strife between the insistence of desire and the powerlessness of will. In one way or another, if our life is to be great and free, we must escape this prison and this strife.

One way of escape is by philosophic contemplation. Philosophic contemplation does not, in its widest survey, divide the universe into two hostile camps—friends and foes, helpful and hostile, good and bad—it views the whole impartially. Philosophic contemplation, when it is unalloyed, does not aim at proving that the rest of the universe is akin to man. All acquisition of knowledge is an enlargement of the Self, but this enlargement is best attained when it is not directly sought. It is obtained when the desire for knowledge is alone operative, by a study which does not wish in advance that its objects should have this or that character, but adapts the Self to the characters which it finds in its objects. This enlargement of Self is not obtained when, taking the Self as it is, we try to show that the world is so similar to this Self that knowledge of it is possible without any admission of what seems alien. The desire to prove this is a form of self-assertion and, like all self-assertion, it is an obstacle to the growth of Self which it desires, and of which the Self knows that it is capable. Self-assertion, in philosophic speculation as elsewhere, views the world as a means to its own ends; thus it makes the world of less account than Self, and the Self sets bounds to the greatness of its goods. In contemplation, on the contrary, we start from the not-Self, and through its greatness the boundaries of Self are enlarged; through the infinity of the universe the mind which contemplates it achieves some share in infinity.

For this reason greatness of soul is not fostered by those philosophies which assimilate the universe to Man. Knowledge is a form of union of Self and not-Self; like all union, it is impaired by dominion, and therefore by any attempt to force the universe into conformity with what we find in ourselves. There is a widespread philosophical tendency towards the view which tells us that Man is the measure of all things, that truth is man-made, that space and time and the world of universals are properties of the mind, and that, if there be anything not created by the mind, it is unknowable and of no account for us. This view, if our previous discussions were correct, is untrue; but in addition to being untrue, it has the effect of robbing philosophic contemplation of all that gives it value, since it fetters contemplation to Self. What it calls knowledge is not a union with the not-Self, but a set of prejudices, habits, and desires, making an impenetrable veil between us and the world beyond. The man who finds pleasure in such a theory of knowledge is like the man who never leaves the domestic circle for fear his word might not be law.

The true philosophic contemplation, on the contrary, finds its satisfaction in every enlargement of the not-Self, in everything that magnifies the objects contemplated, and thereby the subject contemplating. Everything, in contemplation, that is personal or private, everything that depends upon habit, self-interest, or desire, distorts the object, and hence impairs the union which the intellect seeks. By thus making a barrier between subject and object, such personal and private things become a prison to the intellect. The free intellect will see as God might see, without a *here* and *now*, without hopes and fears, without the trammels of customary beliefs and traditional prejudices, calmly, dispassionately, in the sole and exclusive desire of knowledge—knowledge as impersonal, as purely contemplative, as it is possible for man to attain. Hence also the free intellect will value more the abstract and universal knowledge into which the accidents of private history do not enter, than the knowledge brought by the senses, and dependent, as such knowledge must be, upon an exclusive and personal point of view and a body whose sense-organs distort as much as they reveal.

The mind which has become accustomed to the freedom and impartiality of philosophic contemplation will preserve something of the same freedom and impartiality in the world of action and emotion. It will view its purposes and desires as parts of the whole, with the absence of insistence that results from seeing them as infinitesimal fragments in a world of which all the rest is unaffected by any one man's deeds. The impartiality which, in contemplation, is the unalloyed desire for truth, is the very same quality of mind which, in action, is justice, and in emotion is that universal love which can be given to all, and not only to those who are judged useful or admirable. Thus contemplation enlarges not only the objects of our thoughts, but also the objects of our actions and our affections: it makes us citizens of the universe, not only of one walled city at war with all the rest. In this citizenship of the universe consists man's true freedom, and his liberation from the thraldom of narrow hopes and fears.

Thus, to sum up our discussion of the value of philosophy; Philosophy is to be studied, not for the sake of any definite answers to its questions, since no definite answers can, as a rule, be known to be true, but rather for the sake of the questions themselves; because these questions enlarge our conception of what is possible, enrich our intellectual imagination and diminish the dogmatic assurance which closes the mind against speculation; but above all because, through the greatness of the universe which philosophy contemplates, the mind also is rendered great, and becomes capable of that union with the universe which constitutes its highest good.

DISCUSSION QUESTIONS

1. Do you agree with Russell's claim that the "goods of the mind are at least as important as the goods of the body"? Why or why not?
2. What are some examples of the difference between the philosophical treatment of a specific factual question and how one of the sciences would approach that question?

3. What kind of "freedom" is Russell talking about in this selection? Are there other kinds of freedom that would be more or less valuable?

4. Russell in effect argues that "true philosophic contemplation" can achieve decontextualized knowledge and understanding. To what extent is this really possible, or desirable? How would Tuana respond to his position?

7. Tsenay Serequeberhan (contemporary)
"African Philosophy: The Point in Question"

Tsenay Serequeberhan is a philosopher from Eritrea, who received his doctorate from Boston College and who most recently has been on the philosophy faculty at Simmons College in Boston. His work has focused primarily on the history, nature, and possible future directions of African philosophy and as such represents an important, and for many scholars quite controversial, development in academic philosophy within the last few decades. Thus far, most questions associated with the study of African philosophy have presupposed various comparisons and contrasts with the European philosophical tradition, and as the author makes clear, problems of cultural, regional, and political identity are inescapable in this domain of inquiry.

This essay, "African Philosophy: The Point in Question," is Serequeberhan's own contribution to an anthology he edited of writings by a number of contemporary African philosophers, published in 1991. All of the authors included in this anthology in one way or another address issues surrounding the nature and appropriate goals of African philosophy, and Serequeberhan's lead article provides a helpful overview of the range of their concerns and disagreements, as well as some of his own conclusions on the subject.

QUESTIONS FOR CRITICAL READING

1. According to Serequeberhan, what are the two "forms of estranged existence" to be found in contemporary African society, and what is their relationship to each other?

2. In Serequeberhan's account, what is the "basic question" that confronts the peoples of Africa today and provides the foundation for reflective inquiry by African philosophers?

3. How does the author characterize the task of the contemporary African philosopher?

4. What are the five main trends in African philosophy identified in this essay, and which one does the author align himself with most clearly?

TERMS TO NOTE

de facto: A Latin phrase meaning "in fact," often contrasted with *de jure,* meaning "in principle."

Eurocentrism: Understanding and evaluating experience presupposing as universally true the dominant intellectual norms and assumptions associated with the general European (and European American) cultural worldview. From such a standpoint, non-European perspectives and beliefs are thus false or deficient insofar as they are different.

hermeneutical: Having to do with the interpretation of discourse.

interiority: In this context, referring to the internal domain of human subjectivity.

metaphilosophical: Having to do with the conditions under which philosophical inquiry is carried out, or the underlying assumptions regarding appropriate philosophical methods or goals.

transcendental: In this context, that which obtains universally, beyond all contingency, context, or localized experience.

Any discourse on philosophy is necessarily implicated in an already presupposed conception of philosophy. As Martin Heidegger and Hans-Georg Gadamer tell us, reading or interpreting a text (compiling an anthology!) means being already involved with it. What needs doing then, is not to try to avoid this unavoidable "circle" of interpretation/philosophy, but to engage it fully. In other words, to bring to the fore—as much as possible—the operative prejudgments at work in one's philosophical engagement.

In what follows, I will present a broadly historical, political, existential discussion of the question of African philosophy. My purpose will be to expose and legitimate my own prejudgments in terms of the historicopolitical horizon within and out of which African philosophy originates as a discourse. In doing so, I will stake out a critical position in the debate on and also within African philosophy.

I

The closing years of the nineteenth century witnessed the consummation of European imperial ambitions in the complete dismemberment and colonization—except for the kingdom of Abyssinia—of Africa.[1] Colonial conquest and the imposition of violent European rule on the partially destroyed and suppressed indigenous societies and the insertion of Africa into the modern European capitalist world as a dependent appendage to it effected decisive breaks and distortions in the previous patterns of life prevalent on the continent at large.[2] As Basil Davidson points out:

> The colonial period, in *European mythology,* was supposed to have effected that particular transition [from pre-colonial to modern society]. Generally however, it did nothing of the kind. Historically . . . the colonial period was a hiatus, a standstill, an interlude when African history was stopped or was forced to become, for that period, a part of European history.[3]

African historical existence was suppressed and Africa was forced to become the negative underbelly of European history. What is paradoxical in all of this is the fact that Europe undertook the domination of Africa and the world not in the explicit and cynical recognition of its imperial interests but in the delusion that it was spreading civilization. In the poetic words of Rudyard Kipling:

> Take up the White Man's burden
>   Send forth the best ye breed
> Go bind your sons to exile
>   To serve your captives need;

> To wait in heavy harness
>   On fluttered folk and wild
> Your new-caught, sullen peoples,
>   Half devil and half child.[4]

This first stanza of Kipling's *The White Man's Burden* depicts concisely the European conception of itself and of the non-European. This conception unhesitatingly sees itself as the proper embodiment of human existence *as such* and goes on to impose itself on the non-European, who is viewed as "half devil and half child." This conception was not an isolated image concocted by Kipling. Rather, it is an accurate articulation of European colonial consciousness, which was amply represented not only in the popular literature of the day but also in the enduring conceptions and speculations of modern European thought.[5]

In the name of the universality of values, European colonialism violently universalized its own singular particularity and annihilated the historicality of the colonized. In this context, Western philosophy—in the guise of a disinterested, universalistic, transcendental, speculative discourse—served the indispensable function of being the ultimate *veracious buttress* of European conquest. This service, furthermore, was rendered in the name of "Man" and the emancipation of "Man." In the words of Immanuel Kant, European modernity saw itself as "man's release from his self-incurred tutelage."[6]

James Schmidt has pointed out that "the question of enlightenment" in modern European thought was a politically oriented struggle against superstitious beliefs (as distinct from established Christian doctrine) aimed at the "release" of "Man" from darkness and ignorance through the employment of Reason.[7] As Antonio Gramsci correctly observes, this orientation of modern European thought "presupposes a single culture, a single religion, a single global 'conformism,'"[8] that is, a singular globalized cultural totality.

It is important to notice that such a homogenizing globalization of the historical, political, and cultural horizon of European modernity inevitably sees the "world" as nothing more than a homogenate replica of Europe. Given this orientation, the *subjugation* of the non-European world—"half devil and half child"— by Europe, understood as the historical embodiment of Reason, has to necessarily be seen as the *emancipation* of "Man" on a global scale. Thus, victorious over superstition and the darkness of ignorance, Europe spreads the light of Reason!

In this manner, colonial "European mythology" found, in the speculative discourse of Western philosophy, its highest pinnacle and ultimate justification. For, as Enrique Dussel has correctly observed, Western philosophy has always been the "philosophy of the center" which designates the periphery and frames it as such.[9] Let us now take a quick glance at some choice samplings of the philosophical underpinnings of this colonial "European mythology."

Hume and Kant held the view that Africans, in virtue of their blackness, are precluded from the realm of reason and civilization. As Hume puts it, "I am apt to suspect the negroes, and in general all the other species of men (for there are four or five different kinds) to be naturally inferior to whites. There never was a civilized nation of any complexion than white." Kant, in agreement with Hume, asserts that "[s]o fundamental is the difference between the two races of men, and it appears to be as great in regard to mental capacities as in color."[10] Making a subtle observation on the intellectual capacities of a black person, Kant astutely remarks that "this fellow was quite black from head to foot, a clear proof that what he said was stupid."[11] In the same vein, but now reflecting on history, Kant asserts that "if one adds episodes from the national histories of other peoples insofar as they are known from the history of the *enlightened* nations, one will discover a regular progress in the constitution of states on our continent (which will probably *give law,* eventually, to all *the others*)."[12]

Expressing the same "enlightened" view in the *Philosophy of History,* after describing the Negro as beyond the pale of humanity proper, Hegel categorically affirms that Africa "is no historical part of the world; it has no movement or development to exhibit. Historical movements in it—that is in its northern part—belong to the Asiatic or European World."[13] As Lucius Outlaw points out:

This orientation to Africa so poignantly expressed by Hegel was widely shared by many of its earliest European visitors (explorers, missionaries, seekers after wealth and fame, colonizers, etc.), whose travelogues and "reports" served to validate the worst characterization as the European *invention* of Africa and Africans

out of the racism and ethnocentrism infecting Europe's project in its encounter with Africa as a different and black other.[14]

In the *Philosophy of Right,* Hegel systematically presents this same perspective as the unfolding of Reason in its world-historical process of self-institution. What the "explorer" and the "colonizer" express as a crude Eurocentric racism, Hegel and modern European philosophy articulate as the universality of Reason, the trademark of Europe. In fact, for Hegel, the possibility of "ethical life" in the context of modernity is predicated on the necessity of colonial expansion.[15]

In like manner, the Marxist critique of idealist philosophy and European capitalism sees the possibility of the actualization of its critical project as directly linked to the colonial globalization of Europe. Marx and Engels—the self-proclaimed radical critics of nineteenth-century European capitalism—articulate this same Eurocentrism as an integral part of their philosophicohistorical position. For both, the colonial Europeanization of the globe was a prerequisite for the possibility of true human freedom, that is, communism.[16]

The very hope for the possibility of human emancipation anticipated and articulated out of European history—the Marxist project—is itself predicated on the subjugation and obliteration of non-European histories and cultures. As Marx points out, commenting on the world-historical role of European colonialist expansion:

England has to fulfill a double mission in India: one destructive, the other regenerating—the annihilation of old Asiatic [African] society, and the laying of the material foundations of Western society in Asia [Africa].[17]

In the same vein, but more forcefully, Engels states that:

Then there is also the case of the conquest and brutal destruction of economic resources. . . . Nowadays such a case usually has the opposite effect, at least among great peoples [nineteenth-century colonialist Europe!]: in the long run the vanquished [the African, the Asiatic, the non-European] often gains more economically, politically and morally than the victor.[18]

It is important to note that, behind and beyond the differing Eurocentric views of the above thinkers—and the modern tradition of Western philosophy as a whole—lies the *singular* and grounding metaphysical belief that European humanity is properly speaking isomorphic with the humanity of the human *as such.* Beyond all differences and disputes this is the common thread that constitutes the unity of the tradition. Philosophy, furthermore, is the privileged discourse singularly rooted in European/human existence *as such,* which articulates and discloses the *essence* of the *real.* Thus, European cultural-historical prejudgments are passed off as transcendental wisdom!

European colonialism established the material and cultural conditions in which this self-aggrandizing and grounding metaphysical delusion could be institutionally embodied and incarnated in the consciousness of the colonized. Simultaneously, this same delusionary metaphysical belief also provided the evidence—in its material instantiations and inculcation in the consciousness of the colonized—for its own "veracity." The very fact of conquest was taken as metaphysical proof of the unhistoricality—the lack of humanness—of the colonized. In Hegal's words, the "civilized [European] nation is conscious that the rights of *barbarians* are unequal to its own and treats their autonomy as only a formality."[19]

As Edward Said correctly points out, the result of colonialism in the colonized world was "a widely varied group of little Europes throughout Asia, Africa and the Americas."[20] The "little Europes" constituted on the African continent required the replication of European institutions and forms of life and the simultaneous depreciation and suppression—as barbaric, savage, nonhuman—of African institutions and culture. They also required the systematic inculturation of urbanized Africans, whose very formation as a section of the dominated society was predicated on the rupture of African historical existence in the face of European violence.[21] Thus, the Europeanized sections of colonized Africa were physically and culturally disinherited. The non-Europeanized sections, on the other hand, were forced to submit to a petrification of their indigenous cultural and historical existence.

This is not to suggest that the urbanized and—at various levels—Europeanized African consciously and in these very terms endorses the European metaphysi-

cal prejudices cited above. Nor is it to argue that indigenous cultures were completely obliterated by colonial conquest. Rather, it is to indicate and strongly emphasize the fact that the Europeanized African's internalized negative disposition toward his own indigenousness and his estrangement from African cultures and traditions has deep roots and finds its ultimate "veracious" justification in the delusionary metaphysical belief articulated in and out of the tradition of Western philosophy. On the other hand, the cultural-historical stagnation of the indigenous non-Europeanized African is itself the result of European conquest, which ironically is used to justify this same conquest.[22]

Encased between these two contradictory and complementary forms of estranged existence, one finds contemporary Africa. The estranging dialectic of these two broad segments of society consitutes the existential crisis of the continent. In a paradoxical and distorted manner, these two segments of African society, mimic and replicate the estranged and estranging violent dialectic of the colonizer and the colonized described so well by Albert Memmi. But in this case the roles of colonizer and colonized are played by the native, cast on both sides of this antagonistic relation, by reference to the culture of the former colonial power. Power or empowerment is thus a function of European culture which manifests itself in and legitimates the power of the neocolonial elites of postcolonial Africa.

As Davidson points out, the African anticolonial struggle did not only expel the physical presence of colonialism but it also put in "question the smoothly borrowed assumptions of the social hybrids [Europeanized Africans] about the opposition of 'European civilization' to 'African barbarism.'"[23] Indeed, beyond the political and historical combat to expel colonialism, contemporary Africa finds itself confronted and hindered, at every turn, by that which this combat has put in *question* without fundamentally eradicating.

Present-day African realities are thus constituted partly by the ossified remnants of European colonialism/neocolonialism—as embodied at every level in the institutional forms of contemporary Africa and in the conscious self-awareness of Europeanized Africans—and by the varied forms of struggle aimed at actualizing the possibility of an autonomous and free Africa in the context of the modern world. The hope, in other words, is of actualizing the real but unactualized possibilities of the African anticolonial struggle.

It is in and out of this overall historical-political-existential *horizon* that the discourse of African philosophy carves out and secures a space in which, and out of which, it can articulate itself as a viable and pertinent undertaking. African philosophy is thus a reflective supplement to the concrete efforts under way on the continent. As is evinced by the papers collected in this volume and in the field at large, in *differing* ways, the concerns of African philosophy and the efforts of African philosophers hover around this central point: the historical-political-existential crisis of an Africa saddled with a broken and ambiguous heritage.

In the poetic words of Aimé Césaire, "more and more the old negritude is turning into a corpse."[24] But the new "negritude" is yet to be born and in and out of this historical interlude—this absence, this lack, this impasse—African philosophy finds its problems and concerns. Whether these problems are expressed in explicit political terms or as questions regarding science and its importation, this impasse, this felt need, today calls forth and motivates the varied struggles on the African continent and simultaneously engenders and makes possible the further elaboration and development of African philosophical questioning.

As Theophilus Okere puts it:

[W]hether it is a Plato from Greek antiquity, a Hegel from modern philosophy, or a contemporary philosopher like Heidegger himself, the conclusion is the same, namely, that their thought is inscribed and their problematic dictated by the non-philosophy which is their own cultural background, especially by their religious beliefs and myths.[25]

The basic and most fundamental fact in Africa today is the misery the continent is immersed in and the varied struggles—in different arenas—to overcome this wretched condition. In response to this grim reality, this somber "nonphilosophy," philosophical reflection has become relevant in the present African situation.

To be sure, African thinkers can also reflect on their traditional "religious beliefs and myths." But if African thinkers are really to engage actual problems, then it is clear that African philosophy has to—at some level or other—be connected with the contemporary struggles and concerns facing the continent and its diverse peoples. For it is not the "beliefs and myths" of the peoples of Africa—in their intricate magnificence—that are mindboggling, but the concrete misery and political insanity of the contemporary African situation.

It is necessary to note that Placide Tempels's book, *Bantu Philosophy,* published in 1945—which provoked and served as both the positive (ethnophilosophy) and negative (professional philosophy) point of departure for the contemporary exchanges in African philosophy—was not a book innocent of politics.[26] The basic intent of Tempels's work was to explore and appropriate by subversion the lived world outlook of the Bantu in the service of Belgian colonialism, that is, the European "civilizing mission" in the Congo. In fact, Tempels's work is an exemplary effort aimed at the expropriation of the interiority of the subjugated in the service of colonialism.

Bantu Philosophy articulates the need to expose and appropriate the intellectual productions of the Bantu/African in order to better anchor the European colonialist project in the consciousness of the colonized. For Tempels, one had to recognize the humanity of the colonized in order to better colonize and Christianize them! But is not colonialism itself predicated on the absence of humanity—as Western philosophy affirms—in the "savage," who thus needs to be colonized in order to be "humanized"?

The fruitful ambivalence of Tempels's position, from the perspective of the colonized, is rather obvious. Inadvertently and in the service of colonialism, Tempels was forced to admit—against the grain of the then established "knowledge"—that the Bantu/African is not a mere beast devoid of consciousness, but a human being whose conscious awareness of existence is grounded on certain foundational notions. Thus, the positive response to Tempels's work (ethnophilosophy) is an attempt to capitalize on this ambivalence—the recognition of the humanity of the colonized. The negative response to his work (professional philosophy) on the other hand is a scientist attempt to expose and guard against the colonialist ambivalences utilized to placate, minimize, and bypass the obdurate political-cultural resistance of the colonized.

In either case, these philosophical responses are inherently political precisely because they are provoked by the politics of colonialism in the realm of philosophy. At this point, it is necessary to note that Tempels's singular effort in philosophy can best be understood for what it is only if it is seen as the practical and de facto implementation of the grounding metaphysical prejudice embodied in the Western tradition of philosophy as a whole. As was indicated earlier, this is the delusionary metaphysical belief that European existence is isomorphic with human existence *as such*. As V. Y. Mudimbe has observed, the colonizing and the missionary/evangelic "work" of Europe in Africa has always been and cannot help but be (two sides, spiritual and earthly, of) a single project of domination.[27]

Viewed in this light, the political imperative of African philosophy is rather clear. For, as E. Wamba-Dia-Wamba has observed, "[i]n today's Africa, to think is increasingly to think *for* or *against* imperialism."[28] That is to say, "to think for or against" the Eurocentric metaphysics of Western philosophy and the perpetual subordination—at all levels—of Africa.

II

The period of world history that begins with the end of the Second World War has been for Africa not a period of relative calm and peace, but rather a period of accelerated war and political turmoil. To be sure, these conflicts have not been futile. By the end of the 1960s, most of Africa had achieved the status of political independence, and the early 1970s witnessed the end of Portuguese colonialism, the oldest European colonial empire in Africa.

To this day, however, armed political conflicts rage on—in the midst of famine and "natural" calamities—in both independent and nonindependent Africa. Grim as this picture may be, it is important to remember that it constitutes the African people's varied and differing struggles to define and establish their freedom. But what are the people of Africa trying to free themselves from and what are they trying to establish?

This is the basic question, as we noted earlier—formulated in a variety of ways—out of which the differing concerns of African philosophers are articulated and which constitutes the basic concern of African philosophy. As Okere correctly observes, the discourse of African philosophy is located within the

"movement in both artistic and intellectual life to establish a certain [African] identity."[29] It is an effort, on the plane of theoretical struggle, to explore reflectively and supplement theoretically the concrete emancipatory efforts—at various levels and in differing arenas—concretely under way on the continent. It is a concrete engagement with "Africa in metamorphosis."[30]

In being so, it institutes itself in the context of and by concretely engaging the contemporary problems and questions pertinent to the African situation. Furthermore, this is not a question of "choosing" or "preferring" one set of questions as opposed to another, as if one could choose what needs to be thought! It is, rather, a question of being *open* to that which *needs* to be *thought* in contemporary Africa. As Okanda Okolo puts it, this is the hermeneutical situation of the "formerly colonized, the oppressed, that of the underdeveloped, struggling for more justice and equality."[31]

For philosophers, as Marcien Towa has observed, are

beings of flesh and bones who belong to a continent, to a particular culture and a specific period. And for a particular philosopher, to really philosophize is necessarily to examine in a critical and methodic manner the essential problems of his milieu and of his period.[32]

In the differing formulations of the papers presented in this collection—and in the varied works of African philosophy at large—there is a dispute as to how these "essential problems" might best be engaged. This dispute, however, is grounded on a shared understanding that it is the present-day African situation as it arises out of the ambiguous and broken heritage of the African past that calls for thinking. Thus, these "essential problems" are the lived concerns, the questions and issues, embedded in a concrete existential-historical-political *horizon,* that evoke questioning, that is, the discourse of African philosophy.

As Heidegger points out, philosophy or "meditative thought," does not just happen; rather, it is interior to and arises out of the region/horizon that is originatively its own.[33] In each case, and for philosophical reflection *as such*, it is the lived life concerns of a culture and of a tradition, as they are disclosed by questions posed from within a concrete situation, that serve as the bedrock on which and out of which philosophical reflection is established. Or, as Okolo puts it, "hermeneutics [philosophy] exists *only* in particular traditions."[34]

Thus, the fact that African philosophers have been concerned with and have made the problems of their own, that is, Africa's own lived historicality and broken heritage/tradition, the focal point of their reflections is as it should be. For ultimately, whether we are aware of it or not, it is out of a lived heritage or tradition that we speak; and even when we deny this, it is a particular tradition (scientism?) that *speaks* and utilizes our voice.

III

Given what has been said thus far, what then is the point in question in the question of African philosophy? In the history of philosophy and presently, ethnic qualifiers have been and are still operative with regard to designating specific philosophical perspectives. Jewish, Arabic/Islamic, Medieval/Christian, European, German, Greek, Oriental, American, and so forth— all these ethnic, religious, continental qualifiers designate the specificity of a philosophical perspective in terms of the background culture or tradition within which and out of which a particular philosophical discourse is articulated. The latest addition to this list of ethnic qualifiers in philosophy is "Contemporary French Philosophy," which Vincent Descombes describes as "coincident with the sum of the discourses elaborated in France and considered by the public of today as philosophical."[35]

In short, what has to be noted is that the designation "African philosophy" has behind it a long list of precedents and thus needs no justification. And yet, the justification of this label or conversely the attempt to reduce it to an external, merely geographic[36] designation has been a basic preoccupation of much of the literature to date.

To be sure, African philosophy does present problems for the established tradition of Western philosophy. Okere convincingly argues that the possibility of African philosophy as a legitimate field of discourse presupposes the weakening, if not the demise, of the absolutist and Eurocentric paradigm of thought dominant in Western philosophy thus far. Indeed, it is no accident that the discussion of African philosophy is taking place in the context of the increasing contemporary importance of hermeneutics, deconstruction, and, in general, context-oriented modes of doing philosophy in the discipline at large. The "historicity and relativity of truth—and this always means truth as we can and do attain it—is one of the main insights of the hermeneutical revolution in philosophy,"[37] which is substantiated and in turn substantiates the efforts embedded in African philosophy.

In this regard, African philosophy is an added questioning voice in the varied current discourses of contemporary philosophy. For as Outlaw pointedly observes, at a deeper philosophical level the methodological "issues involved" in the question of African philosophy "are only immediately concerned" with philosophy as an intellectual discipline.

> The deeper issue is one with much higher stakes: it [the question of African philosophy] is a struggle over the meaning of "man" and "civilized human," and all that goes with this in the context of the political economy of the capitalized and Europeanized Western world.[38]

On the other hand, for Lansana Keita, Kwasi Wiredu, Peter O. Bodunrin, and Paulin J. Hountondji, the concerns of African philosophy are centered on questions of methodology focused on the role that philosophy can play as the "handmaid" of science in the context of Africa.[39] In order to better understand how these (scientistic?) concerns are superimposed on the substantive politico-philosophic questions articulated thus far in our discussion by Okere, Outlaw, Wamba, Towa, and Okolo, it is necessary to begin by taking a quick glance at the diversified literature that presently constitutes African philosophy.

Thus far, African philosophy has been an exploratory metaphilosophical discourse that simultaneously harbors and is articulated out of substantive philosophical positions and concerns. Following Henry Odera Oruka, one can classify African philosophy into four basic trends: ethnophilosophy, philosophic sagacity, nationalistic-ideological philosophy, and professional philosophy.[40] In his more recent work, without substantially changing this order of classification, Oruka recognizes an added hermeneutical-historical trend in African philosophical thought. This orientation is, broadly speaking, basically concerned with interpretatively engaging and thinking through the concrete politico-historical actuality of the present African situation and its future possibilities.[41]

Oruka's classificatory schema has pedagogic merit insofar as it presents a concise overview of the field at large. But this merit is offset by the fact that this ordering gives the false impression that these trends are somehow independent of each other. Thus, while utilizing Oruka's schema, we will supplement it with V. Y. Mudimbe's and Kwame Gyekye's more accurate conceptions.

For Mudimbe, the works of African philosophy can be viewed as extending on a continuum. On one extreme of this continuum, one would place all those efforts aimed at documenting the philosophies of African peoples. On the other extreme, one would place the work of those who have insisted that African philosophy is basically the work of Africans trained in the Eastern tradition of philosophy.[42] This schema has the merit of placing these seemingly contradictory perspectives on the same spectrum and presenting them as differing refractions originating from the same source, that is, "Africa in metamorphosis." In like manner, for Gyekye,

> a distinction must be made between traditional African philosophy and modern African philosophy: The latter, to be African, and have a basis in African culture and experience, must have a connection with the former, the traditional.[43]

In other words, the literature of African philosophy is a body of texts produced by Africans (and non-Africans) directed at philosophically engaging African problems and/or documenting the philosophies of African peoples. The hesitation expressed by the conjunction/disjunction in the previous sentence is the hesitation on which the question of African philosophy hangs and on which the methodological and politico-philosophical issues indicated above are focused. As Oruka points out:

> Early writers on the subject of African philosophy such as Fr. P. Tempels, J. Mbiti, Alexis Kagame and to a lesser extent Prof. W. Abraham, have all fallen into the pitfall of considering African philosophy to be a philosophy only in the unique and debased sense. By saying this

I am not saying something new. It has been said before; and we now have various philosophical articles that point out the danger of this pitfall.[44]

By the "unique and debased sense" of philosophy Oruka means the effort to document the philosophies and worldviews of African peoples—that is, ethnophilosophy. The "various philosophical articles" he refers to are the works of Hountondji, Wiredu, Bodunrin, and himself, which he collectively designates as the school of professional philosophy. On Mudimbe's schema, these two trends—ethnophilosophy and professional philosophy—would constitute the two extremes of the continuum of African philosophy. In like manner, for Gyekye, these two trends represent the "traditional" and the "modern" aspects of African philosophy.

Without in any way sharing Oruka's prejudice, let us now look at how this confrontation is articulated, for it is the polemic out of which the discourse on and in African philosophy is constituted in its inception.

Ethnophilosophy

This orientation is basically aimed at systematizing and documenting the differing worldviews of African peoples, which are viewed—by the proponents of this trend—as properly constituting African philosophy. For the proponents of this trend, African philosophy is incarnated in the mythical/religious conceptions, worldviews, and lived ritual practices of ethnic Africans, which can and should be documented by Europeans and Africans with a Western education.

The basic direction and motivation of this orientation is to expose the "mentality" of the African to the European missionary or to those engaged with the task of "civilizing"/colonizing and/or modernizing the African. This is, at least in its inception, the motivation of this current as documented in Tempels's work, *Bantu Philosophy.*

The disclosing of the "mentality" of the African for modernizing purposes is still viewed—by the African followers of Tempels—as the basic task of African philosophy. Without making a clear distinction between philosophy and religion, John S. Mbiti puts it thus:

> These religions [and the philosophy they embody] are a reality which calls for academic scrutiny and which must be reckoned with in

modern fields of life like economics, politics, education and Christian or Muslim work. To ignore these traditional beliefs and practices can only lead to a lack of understanding African behaviour and problems.[45]

While lacking Tempels's colonialist orientation, Mbiti's aim is to expose the interiority of the African to the subversive gaze of the Christian, Muslim, or modernizing Europeanized African. The basic aim is to document the

philosophical understanding of African peoples concerning different issues of life. Philosophy of one kind or another is behind the thinking and acting of every people, and a study of traditional religions brings us into those areas of African life where, through word and action, we may be able to discern the philosophy behind.[46]

Thus, the designation "ethnophilosophy" (coined by Hountondji); that is, philosophy deriving from the ethnological study of ethnic Africans. In its own positive self-designation, this perspective calls itself "cultural philosophy" or African philosophy without qualifications.[47]

The basic criticism that has been directed against this orientation is that philosophy is not equal to the worldviews and or religious conceptions of ethnic peoples. African philosophy, if it is to be philosophy properly speaking, must be capable of being subsumed under a common notion of philosophy understood as the critical self-reflection of a culture engaged in by specific individuals in that culture. Politically, it has been criticized as part of the European colonialist discourse aimed at disarming and subjugating the African. Indeed, this is the explicit intent of Tempels's work. His *Bantu Philosophy* is aimed at the "colonizer of good will," who, according to Tempels, needs to know the Bantu/African in order to better "civilize" and convert him to the "true" faith.

In a more charitable tone, Outlaw and Oruka observe that in its inception Tempels's work served— even if inadvertently—a positive function. It challenged the then common notion that the African was completely sterile in intellectual and moral-spiritual productions of his own.[48] But even in this edifying role, the singular development of this current can have no further function than to abstractly assert the existence of a static African culture and civilization predating the colonial conquest. As Frantz Fanon remarks, commenting on similar edifying quests for the African past:

Let us be clearly understood. I am convinced that it would be of the greatest interest to be able to have contact with a Negro literature or architecture of the third century before Christ. I should be very happy to know that a correspondence had flourished between some Negro philosopher and Plato. But I can absolutely not see how this fact would change anything in the lives of the eight-year-old children who labor in the cane fields of Martinique or Guadeloupe [or, for that matter, any part of contemporary Africa].[49]

In other words, documenting the traditional philosophies and worldviews of African peoples is fruitful only when undertaken within the context of and out of an engagement with the concrete and actual problems facing the peoples of Africa.

Philosophic Sagacity

Philosophic sagacity, the position advocated by Oruka, is an attempt to carve out a middle ground between the opposing positions of ethnophilosophy and professional philosophy. For Oruka, in spite of the fact that Africa has predominantly nonliterate cultures, it has had in the past and has presently indigenous wise men sages/philosophers who critically engage the established tradition and culture of their respective ethnic groups and/or societies. In contrast to ethnophilosophy, these sages inhabit a critical space within their cultural milieu, which allows them to reflect on it instead of merely being the trusted preservers of tradition. In view of this fact, the task of a modern African philosopher is to dialogically extract the philosophical wisdom embodied in these sages. Thus the designation philosophic sagacity.[50]

Oruka has been criticized for failing to recognize the facticity of the interpretative situation in which the modern African philosopher finds himself when engaged in dialogue with an African sage. These dialogues and interviews are indeed works of African philosophy. But they are the joint products of the sage and the modern African philosopher, whose questions elicit the responses and thus direct the sage in the articulation of his wisdom. Oruka's strong claim of uncovering "authentic African philosophy," in some primordial "uncontaminated" form, is thus made questionable—for the claim of philosophic sagacity is that beyond the collective myths (ethnophilosophy) of African peoples, the African past and present has traditional (non-Western educated) sages/philosophers in critical dialogue with their respective traditions.

National-Ideological Philosophy

This trend is embodied in the assorted manifestos, pamphlets and political works produced by the African liberation struggle. The writings of Nkrumah, Toure, Nyerere, Fanon, Senghor, Césaire, and Cabral, and the national liberation literature as a whole, harbor differing politico-philosophical conceptions that articulate the emancipatory possibilities opened up by the African anticolonial struggle. A critical interpretative engagement with these texts is thus a properly philosophical and historical task, since the critical examination and exploration of these texts promises the possibility of developing an African philosophical discourse on politics.

More importantly, as Wamba correctly observes, this discourse—which is the theoretical offshoot of the African anticolonial struggle—has to be taken as the grounding point of departure of African philosophical engagement. In this respect, Wamba points to the work of Amilcar Cabral, who represents the zenith of this politico-philosophical undertaking.[51]

But beyond particular thinkers and their contributions, the political and philosophic output of the African anticolonial struggle as a whole has to be understood as the originative grounding that is—implicitly or explicitly—presupposed by contemporary African intellectual work *as such*. To explore and examine the emancipatory possibilities embedded in this lived political and historical presupposition of contemporary African intellectual production is thus a properly philosophical task.

Professional Philosophy

This fourth trend is the self-designation of Odera H. Oruka, Kwasi Wiredu, Paulin J. Hountondji, and Peter O. Bodunrin. They call themselves a "school" in view

of the fact that they share certain basic positions and assumptions.[52] Except for Oruka, they all share the view that a philosophical tradition in Africa is only presently—in their joint efforts—beginning to develop. They all share in the criticism of ethnophilosophy and see philosophy in Africa as the "handmaid" of science and (uncritical) modernization.

To be sure, the above enumeration of trends in African philosophy is partial and incomplete. As we noted above, Oruka himself recognizes an added hermeneutical trend in African philosophy. Furthermore, precisely because the discourse of African philosophy is still in the process of self-constitution, such categorizations cannot but be tentative. Presently, Hountondji is compiling what promises to be an exhaustive bibliographical documentation of African philosophical writings.[53] It is only after such preliminary work has been done that a definitive conceptualization of the various constitutive elements of African philosophy can be achieved.

In accordance with Mudimbe's and Gyekye's conceptions, the above enumerated trends, along with the hermeneutical perspective in African philosophy, can be seen as constituting a continuum differentiated by various ways of articulating the same fundamental concern—thus the documentation of the traditional myths and religions of Africa—ethnophilosophy; the dialogical appropriation of the wisdom of African sages—philosophic sagacity; the critical encounter and examination of the politico-philosophical texts produced by the African liberation struggle—nationalist-ideological philosophy; and the historically and hermeneutically sensitive dialogue with these texts, in and out of the context of the concrete concerns of contemporary Africa—all this and more is the legitimate task of the modern African philosopher.

IV

As we noted earlier in this paper, African philosophy—the very fact of the existence of such a discourse—threatens the stability of the philosophical prejudices that sanctioned and justified European expansion and the obliteration of African historical existence. As Outlaw puts it, in "light of the European incursion into Africa, the emergence of 'African philosophy' poses deconstructive (and reconstructive) challenges."[54] Let us conclude then by looking at the "deconstructive and reconstructive" challenges of African philosophy.

The "deconstructive challenge" of African philosophy is directed at the Eurocentric residues inherited from colonialism. Educational, political, juridical, and cultural institutions have been taken over by the independent states of Africa, but the basic parameters within which they function, the cultural codes inscribed within them, and the Eurocentric principles and attitudes that inform these institutions remain unthought and unchanged. The "deconstructive" orientation of African philosophy is thus aimed at the unmasking of these Eurocentric residues in modern Africa that still sanction—in the guise of science and enlightenment—the continued political subordination and intellectual domination of Africa. This subordination—which is concretely embedded in the institutional structures left over from colonialism and the internalized conscious self-awareness of Europeanized Africans—is ultimately grounded on the delusions of the Western metaphysical tradition.

Conversely, and in conjunction with the above, the "reconstructive challenge" of African philosophy is aimed at critically revitalizing—in the context of the modern world—the historico-cultural possibilities of the broken African heritage. It is an indigenizing theoretical-practical project. Borrowing the words of Ngúgí wa Thiong'o, one can describe it as an effort to "[d]ecolonize the mind,"[55] or in the words of Amilcar Cabral as an effort to "return to the source."[56]

The discourse of African philosophy is thus directly and historically linked to the demise of European hegemony (colonialism and neocolonialism) and is aimed at fulfilling/completing this demise. It is a reflective and critical effort to rethink the African situation beyond the confines of Eurocentric concepts and categories. In this indigenized context, furthermore, questions of "class struggle" (the "universal" concern of Marxist theory!) and the empowerment of the oppressed can fruitfully be posed and engaged.

It should be noted that, insofar as Marxist theory is itself a European cultural-historical product, it is only through an indigenizing appropriation that elements of this theory can be positively utilized in the African situation. In other words, as Cabral emphatically asserts, "we have our own class struggles" in Africa.[57] These "class struggles" are not replicas, nor extensions, of the "global" European "class struggle." Rather, these "class struggles" have their own politico-historical-cultural specificity, inscribed within the confines and the dynamic that structures the vitality of the diverse cultural totalities that constitute contemporary Africa.

The concrete resurrection of Africa, beyond the tutelage of Europe, requires—in all spheres of life—a rethinking of the contemporary state of affairs in terms that are conducive and congenial to the emancipation and growth of Africa and its diverse peoples. This then is the task of the African philosopher.

In the insightful words of Frantz Fanon,

> culture is the whole body of efforts made by a people in the sphere of thought [philosophy!] to describe, justify, and praise the actions through which that people has created itself and keeps itself in existence.[58]

Africa has been for some time now in the process of recovering and establishing its own cultural-historical existence after almost a century of colonial rule. In order to be properly undertaken, this recovery requires a rethinking of much that we have inherited—consciously and subliminally—from the colonial past. It also requires the revitalization of the broken and suppressed indigenous African heritage. Africa, in other words, needs to rid itself of the cultural, historical, political, economic, and existential indigence created by colonialism and perpetuated by neocolonialism and *mistaken* for the true indigenousness of the formerly colonized African. In this respect, the tasks of the African philosopher acquire historical and political importance in the contemporary situation of the continent.

Seen in this light, African philosophy is a vital part of what Cabral has called the overall historical process of "re-Africanization."[59] As part of the cultural-intellectual production of a people—a continent—the efforts of the African philosopher are interior to the "efforts made by a people in the sphere of thought" to constitute and "keep itself in existence." For in the last quarter of the twentieth century, the very existence of Africa, the historicalness and concrete indigenous particularity of cultural, political, and economic life is at stake.

This then is the point in question around which the questioning of African philosophy and the questions of African philosophers revolve. As Fanon has observed: "Each generation must, out of relative obscurity, discover its mission, fulfil it, or betray it."[60] But, to discover and explore the yet to *Be,* this is the task of thinking!

Thinking, furthermore, is always interior to the lived possibilities and limits of a "generation" or a historicalness within which and out of which a "mission" can be envisioned and traced out. Thus, to "fulfil" or "betray" is to *affirm* or *deny* the inherent and lived possibilities of our own most historicalness. For "our paths, I say, the political as well as the cultural paths, aren't ready traced on any map . . . they remain to be discovered."[61]

Notes

All emphasis throughout the text is in the original unless otherwise indicated.

1. Addis Hiwet, *Ethiopia, From Autocracy to Revolution* (Review of African Political Economy, 1975), chapter one. As Hiwet explains, modern Ethiopia (minus colonized Eritrea) came into existence at the end of the nineteenth century as the result of the expansionist developments of the Abyssinian kingdom, in collusion and contention with imperial Europe, engaged in the colonial scramble for Africa. Thus, modern Ethiopia established itself by the colonial subjugation of the Oromo and Somali territories that today constitute the southern, south-eastern and the south-western parts of its territory.

2. Basil Davidson, *Africa in Modern History* (Penguin Books, 1985), part two, section four.

3. Basil Davidson and Antonio Bronda. *Cross Roads in Africa* (Spokesman Press, 1980), p. 47, emphasis added.

4. T. S. Eliot, *A Choice of Kipling's Verse* (Anchor Books, 1962), p. 143.

5. In this regard, see the *Critical Inquiry* issue entitled, "'Race' Writing and Difference," vol. 12, no. 1, Autumn 1985; Edward W. Said, "Representing the Colonized: Anthropology's Interlocutors," *Critical Inquiry,* vol. 15, no. 2, Winter 1989; Richard H. Popkin, "The Philosophical Basis of Eighteenth-Century Racism," in *Studies in Eighteenth-Century Culture,* vol. 3 (Case Western Reserve University Press, 1973), Harold E. Pagliano, ed.; Cornel West, *Prophesy Deliverance!* (Westminister Press, 1982), chapter 2; Dona Richards, "The Ideology of European Dominance," *Présence Africaine,* no. 111, 3rd quarterly, 1979.

6. *Kant on History,* Lewis White Beck, ed. (Bobbs-Merrill, 1963), p. 3.

7. James Schmidt, "The Question of Enlightenment," *Journal of the History of Ideas,* vol. 50, no. 2, April–June 1989.

8. Antonio Gramsci, *Quaderni Del Carcere,* vol. 2, edizione critica dell'Instituto Gramsci, a cura di Valentino Gerratana (Torino: Giulio Einaudi, 1975), p. 1484, my own translation.

9. Enrique Dussel, *Philosophy of Liberation* (Orbis Books, 1985), pp. 1–8.

10. As quoted by Richard H. Popkin, "Hume's Racism," *The Philosophical Forum,* vol. 9, nos. 2–3, Winter–Spring 1977–1978; for Hume's remark, see p. 213; for Kant's remark, see p. 218.

11. Ibid., p. 218.

12. *Kant on History,* Lewis White Beck, ed., p. 24, emphasis added.

13. Georg Wilhelm Friedrich Hegel, *The Philosophy of History* (Dover Publications, 1956), p. 99.

14. Lucius Outlaw, "African 'Philosophy': Deconstructive and Reconstructive Challenges," *Contemporary Philosophy: A New Survey,* vol. 5, African Philosophy, Guttorm Floistad, ed. (Martinus Nijhoff Publishers, 1987), p. 18.

15. For a systematic elaboration of this point, see my paper "The Idea of Colonialism in Hegel's *Philosophy of Right,*" *International Philosophical Quarterly,* vol. 29, no. 3, issue no. 115, September 1989.

16. In this regard, see my paper "Karl Marx and African Emancipatory Thought," forthcoming, *Parxis International.*

17. Karl Marx, "The Future Results of British Rule in India" (written in 1853), in Karl Marx and Frederick Engels, *On Colonialism* (International Publishers, 1972), p. 82.

18. Frederick Engels, "Letters to Joseph Bloch" (written in 1890), *The Marx-Engels Reader,* second edition, R. C. Tucker, ed. (Norton, 1978), p. 762.

19. *Hegel's Philosophy of Right,* T. M. Knox, trans. (Oxford University Press, 1973), p. 219, paragraph #351, emphasis added.

20. Edward W. Said, *The Question of Palestine* (Vintage Books, 1980), p. 78.

21. Frantz Fanon, *Black Skin, White Masks* (Grove Press, 1967), passim. For an insightful description of the dilemma created by this situation in the consciousness of the colonized and Europeanized African, see the novel by Cheikh Hamidou Kane, *Ambiguous Adventure* (Collier Books, 1969), passim and specifically p. 140. For an interesting—even if slightly Eurocentric—cinematographic rendering of this dilemma, see Pier Paolo Pasolini's *Notes for an African Orestes* (1970 production).

22. Albert Memmi, *The Colonizer and the Colonized* (Beacon Press, 1965), part two, the section entitled the "Mythical Portrait of the Colonized." In the same text, see also the discussion of the "Nero complex," p. 52.

23. Basil Davidson, *Africa in Modern History,* p. 44.

24. Aimé Césaire, *Return to My Native Land* (Penguin Books, 1969), p. 88.

25. Theophilus Okere, *African Philosophy A Historico-Hermeneutical Investigation of the Conditions of Its Possibility* (University Press of America, 1983), p. xiv.

26. Placide Tempels, *Bantu Philosophy* (*Présence Africaine*, 1969), see especially chapter 7.

27. V. Y. Mudimbe, "African Gnosis: Philosophy and the Order of Knowledge," *African Studies Review,* vol. 28, no. 2–3, June–September 1985, p. 154.

28. E. Wamba-Dia-Wamba, "Philosophy in Africa: Challenges of the African Philosopher," *Mawazo,* vol. 5, no. 2, December 1983. [Also included in this volume on p. 244.]

29. Okere, *African Philosophy,* p. vii.

30. Ibid., p. 121.

31. Okonda Okolo, "Tradition et destin: Horizons d'une hermeneutique philosophique africaine," *Présence Africaine,* no. 114, 2nd quarterly 1980, p. 25. Also included in this volume, translated by Kango Lare-Lantone, p. 208.

32. Marcien Towa, "Conditions d'affirmation d'une pensee philosophique africaine moderne," *Présence Africaine,* nos. 117–18, 1st and 2nd quarterlies 1981, p. 348. Also included in this volume, translated by Aster Gashaw, pp. 194–195.

33. For a detailed discussion of this point, see my paper "Heidegger and Gadamer: Thinking as 'Meditative' and as 'Effective-Historical Consciousness,'" *Man and World,* vol. 20, no. 1, 1987. *Passim.*

34. Okolo, "Tradition et destin," p. 21, emphasis added. [Also included in this volume, p. 204.]

35. Vincent Descombes, *Modern French Philosophy* (Cambridge University Press, 1980), p. 1.

36. Paulin J. Hountondji, *African Philosophy: Myth and Reality* (Indiana University Press, 1983), p. 66. [Also included in this volume, p. 123.]

37. Okere, *African Philosophy,* p. 124.

38. Outlaw, "African 'Philosophy': Deconstructive and Reconstructive Challenges," p. 11.

39. In this respect, see Olabiyi Yai, "Theory and Practice in African Philosophy: The Poverty of Speculative Philosophy," *Second Order,* vol. 6, no. 2, July 1977.

40. Henry Odera Oruka, "Four Trends in Current African Philosophy," *Philosophy in the Present Situation of Africa,* Alwin Diemer, ed. (Franz Steiner Verlag Wiesbaden, 1981).

41. Henry Odera Oruka, "African Philosophy: A Brief Personal History and Current Debate," *Contemporary Philosophy: A New Survey,* vol. 5, African Philosophy, Guttorm Floistad, ed. (Martinus Nijhoff Publishers, 1987), pp. 72–74.

42. V. Y. Mudimbe, "African Philosophy as an Ideological Practice: The Case of French-Speaking Africa," *African Studies Review,* vol. 26, no. 3–4, September–December 1983.

43. Kwame Gyekye, *An Essay On African Philosophical Thought* (Cambridge University Press, 1987), pp. 11–12.

44. Henry Odera Oruka, "The Fundamental Principles in the Question of 'African Philosophy,'" *Second Order,* vol. 4, no. 2, 1975, p. 49.

45. John S. Mbiti, *African Religions and Philosophy* (Heinemann, 1988), p. 1.

46. Ibid.

47. K. C. Anyanwu, "Cultural Philosophy as a Philosophy of Integration and Tolerance," *International Philosophical Quarterly,* vol. 25, no. 3, issue no. 99, September 1985. See also Anyanwu and E. A. Ruch, *African Philosophy* (Catholic Book Agency, 1981), especially the introduction, entitled "Is There an African Philosophy?"

48. Outlaw, "African 'Philosophy': Deconstructive and Reconstructive Challenges," pp. 19–20; Oruka, "African Philosophy: A Brief Personal History and Current Debate," p. 46.

49. Fanon, *Black Skin, White Masks,* p. 230.

50. Henry Odera Oruka, "Sagacity in African Philosophy," *International Philosophical Quarterly,* vol. 23, no. 4, issue no. 92, December 1983. [Also included in this volume, pp. 47–62.]

51. Wamba, "Philosophy in Africa: Challenges of the African Philosopher," p. 88. Also included in this volume, p. 237.

52. Oruka, "Four Trends in Current African Philosophy," p. 7, no. 15.

53. In this regard, see Kwame Anthony Appiah's report, *Sapina,* vol. 2, no. 1, January–April 1989, p. 54.

54. Outlaw, "African 'Philosophy': Deconstructive and Reconstructive Challenges," p. 11.

55. Ngũgĩ wa Thiong'o, *Decolonising The Mind* (Heinemann, 1987).

56. Amilcar Cabral, *Return to the Source: Selected Speeches* (Monthly Review Press, 1973), p. 63.

57. Amilcar Cabral, *Revolution in Guinea: Selected Texts* (Monthly Review Press, 1969), p. 68.

58. Frantz Fanon, *The Wretched of the Earth* (Grove Press, 1963), p. 233.

59. Cabral, *Revolution in Guinea,* p. 76.

60. Fanon, *Wretched of the Earth,* p. 206.

61. Aimé Césaire, *Letter to Maurice Thorez,* English translation by *Présence Africaine* (*Présence Africaine,* 1957), pp. 6–7.

DISCUSSION QUESTIONS

1. Which of the five trends of African philosophy identified by Serequeberhan do you think will be the most productive or significant in the coming years?

2. Do you agree with the author's position on what should be the main task of African philosophers in contemporary circumstances?

3. What common ground can you identify between Serequeberhan's account of the impact of Eurocentrism on native African peoples, and Tuana's account of the impact of androcentrism on women?

4. How would you compare and contrast Serequeberhan's conclusions regarding the nature and goals of contemporary African philosophy with Zea's conclusions about Latin American philosophy?

PART II · Epistemology

Epistemology is the traditional area of study in academic philosophy that focuses on the nature and possible grounds of human knowledge. We all think we "know" at least some things, for example, our own name, the score from yesterday's ball game, that twice two is four, and so on. But philosophers around the world have always recognized that questions about how we know, why we think we know, as well as what we really can know in the first place are often not easily resolved. There are even those philosophers, referred to as epistemological skeptics, who have argued in various ways that humans don't know anything and are incapable of knowing anything. The word "epistemology" itself comes from one of the ancient Greek words for knowledge, *episteme,* and *logos* (here, as "explanation"). Although it has not always been treated everywhere as a separate branch of systematic inquiry, its subject matter reflects concerns that tend to appear in every cultural environment where the differences between knowledge and ignorance, truth and falsehood, and justified versus unjustified belief are considered significant.

Readings 8 through 11 focus primarily on the nature of truth and how we justify our claims to truth. Specific theories of truth come to different conclusions, especially regarding the question of justification; but they tend to agree that conceptually truth is inseparable from its opposite, falsehood, and that both truth and falsehood are not things in themselves but properties of beliefs, statements, propositions, or judgments. These readings also address related issues concerning what is meant by the objective as opposed to the subjective justification of beliefs, as well as the question of our motivation for choosing what to believe.

Readings 12 through 17 describe and evaluate different approaches to acquiring knowledge and some of the different kinds of knowledge that might be acquired. Age-old controversies regarding the role of reason and experience as sources of knowledge are dealt with, as are the different contributions of science, common sense, and mystical insight. The influence of social context on the quest for and valuing of knowledge also comes up explicitly or implicitly in the readings.

Readings 18 through 21 focus even more extensively and directly on some of the value questions surrounding knowledge acquisition and its motivations. Whether we are obligated to become knowledgeable in some areas, or to believe this or that, and whether we are responsible for putting our knowledge to good use are issues of central concern, especially when the impact of a person's knowledge on other people is taken into account.

8. Satischandra Chatterjee (1893–c. 1970)
Indian and Western Theories of Truth

During his professional career Satischandra Chatterjee was best known in India as a proponent of Nyāya philosophy (or Nyāya-Vaishesika), one of the six "orthodox" systems in traditional Hinduism. As is the case with the other philosophical systems, Nyāya thought ultimately aims at contributing to human spiritual liberation from mortal life, but its distinction lies in its primary emphasis on the principles of inference and their relation to the conditions of knowledge. According to Chatterjee, the Sanskrit term *Nyāya* literally means "methodical study," and this focus on logical and evidential standards (or "methods") for distinguishing between true and false beliefs was motivated by the conviction that rational knowledge of the things in our world was a necessary means for achieving spiritual goals. As such, the epistemological analyses of Nyāya are carried out within a frame of reference constituted by theological and metaphysical elements as well.

In this selection Chatterjee focuses more specifically on the nature of truth itself and how we can best determine whether our beliefs are true. He compares and contrasts some theories of truth in the Indian tradition with some of the main alternative accounts of truth in Western philosophical history and then shows how a Nyāya account of truth offers a synthesis of the best elements of these other approaches.

QUESTIONS FOR CRITICAL READING

1. How does Chatterjee define "knowledge" here?
2. What are the theories of the "intrinsic validity of knowledge" and the "extrinsic validity of knowledge"?
3. What are the "correspondence," the "coherence," and the "pragmatic" theories of truth in Western philosophy?
4. In Chatterjee's view, how does the Nyāya theory of truth combine elements of the correspondence, coherence, and pragmatic theories?
5. According to Chatterjee, how is the knowledge of self-consciousness different from our other kinds of knowledge?

TERMS TO NOTE

objectivity: Refers to that which exists, or that which is so, independently of what any particular individual thinks is the case or wants to be so.

subjectivity: Refers to someone's perception or personal belief that something is so.

realism: In general, the position that there is a world of objects and/or facts that actually exists independently of our thought.

coherence: The attribute of being internally consistent, noncontradictory, or harmonious.

a priori: A Latin term referring to that which is accepted independent of, or prior to, experiential verification; to be contrasted with *a posteriori*, which refers to acceptance of beliefs, assertions, or principles based on experience or evidence.

Here we propose to examine the Indian theories of truth, as explained above, in the light of parallel Western theories. With regard to truth there are two main questions, namely, how truth is constituted, and how truth is known. The first question relates to the nature of truth and the answers to it give us the definitions of truth. The second question refers to the ascertainment of truth and the answers to it gives us the tests or criteria of truth.

With regard to these two questions there seem to be two possible answers. Thus it may be said that truth is a self-evident character of all knowledge. Every knowledge is true and known to be true by its very nature. Knowledge does not depend on any external conditions either to be made true or to be known as true. This is the theory of the intrinsic validity (*svataḥ prāmāṇya*) of knowledge as advocated by the Sāṅkhya, Mīmāṁsā and Advaita Vedānta systems of Indian Philosophy. According to the last two schools, the truth of knowledge consists just in its being uncontradicted (*abādhita*). The absence of contradiction, however, is not a positive but a negative condition of truth. Knowledge is both made true and known to be true by its own internal conditions. It is only falsehood that is externally conditioned. So truth is self-evident, while falsity requires to be evidenced by external grounds. The Sāṅkhya goes further than this. It maintains that both truth and falsehood are internally conditioned and immediately known, *i.e.* are self-evident.

There is no exact parallel to the above theory of truth in Western philosophy. It is true that in modern European philosophy knowledge, in the strict sense, is always taken to mean true belief. But truth or validity is not regarded as intrinsic to all knowledge, independently of all external conditions. It is in the writings of Professor L. A. Reid, a modern realist who owns no allegiance to the current schools of realism, that we find some approach to the view that truth is organic to knowledge. But even Reid makes it conditional on knowledge efficiently fulfilling its function, namely, the apprehension of reality as it is. He thinks that truth is nothing else but knowledge doing its job. Thus he says: "Truth is, indeed, simply, . . . the quality of knowledge perfectly fulfilling its functions." Again he observes: "If knowledge were not transitive, if we were not in direct contact, joined with reality, then all our tests, coherence, correspondence, and the rest, would be worthless."[1] Here truth is admitted to be a natural function of knowledge, but not as inherent and self-evident in all knowledge. In the theory of intuitionism, we find a close approach to the view of self-evident validity. To the question 'How do we know that a belief is true or valid?' intuitionism has a simple answer to give, namely, that we know it immediately to be such. As Hobhouse puts the matter: "Intuitionism has a royal way of cutting this, and indeed most other knots: for it has but to appeal to a perceived necessity, to a clear idea, to the inconceivability of the opposite, all of which may be known by simply attending to our own judgment, and its task is done."[2] Among intuitionists, Lossky has made an elaborate attempt to show that truth and falsity are known through an immediate consciousness of their objectivity and subjectivity re-

spectively. For him, truth is the objective and falsity the subjective appearance of the object. But how do we know that the one is objective and the other is subjective? The answer given by Lossky as also by Lipps is that we have "an immediate consciousness of subjectivity" and "an immediate consciousness of objectivity." To quote Lossky's own words: "It is in this consciousness of objectivity and subjectivity, and not . . . in the laws of identity, contradiction, and excluded middle, that our thought has a real and immediate guide in its search for truth."[3]

It should be remarked here that the above theories of self-evident truth or intrinsic validity give us a rather jejune and untenable solution of the logical problem of truth. They leave no room for the facts of doubt and falsehood in the sphere of knowledge. But any theory of truth which fails to explain its correlate, namely, falsehood, becomes so far inadequate. Further, it makes a confusion between psychological belief and logical certainty. Psychologically a wrong belief may be as firm as a right one. But this does not mean that there is no distinction between the two. Subjective certitude, as such, cannot be accepted as a test of truth. It is true that the theory of intrinsic validity does not appeal to any test of truth other than the truth itself. It assumes that the truth of knowledge is self-evident, and that we cannot think of the opposite. In fact, however, there is no such self-evident truth. It is only in the case of the self that we can speak of self-evidence in this sense. The self is a self-manifesting reality. It is manifest even in any doubt or denial of its reality. Hence self-evidence belongs really to the self only. It is on the analogy of the self that we speak of the self-evidence of any other truth. A truth is self-evident in so far as it has the evidence of the self or is evident like the self. But as we have just said, there is no such self-evident truth other than the self itself. In the case of any other truth, we can always think of the opposite in a sensible way. That 'two and two make five' is not as nonsensical as 'abracadabra.' Even if the opposite of a certain belief be inconceivable, it does not follow that the belief is infallible. What was once inconceivable is now not only conceivable but perfectly true. Hence we

---

1. L. A. Reid, *Knowledge and Truth*, pp. 185, 199, 204.
2. Hobhouse, *Theory of Knowledge*, p. 488.

3. Lossky, *The Intuitive Basis of Knowledge*, pp. 227–29.

cannot say that self-evident validity is intrinsic to all knowledge.

The second answer to the question 'How is truth constituted and known?' leads us to the theory of extrinsic validity (*paratah prāmāṇya*). According to this, the truth of any knowledge is both constituted and known by certain external conditions. As a general rule, the validity of knowledge is due to something that is not inherent in it. So also the knowledge of validity depends on certain extraneous tests. Validity is thus assigned to one knowledge on the ground of some other knowledge. This is the theory of extrinsic validity as advocated by the Nyāya and the Buddha systems. In Western philosophy, the correspondence, the coherence and the pragmatist theories of truth all come under the doctrine of extrinsic validity. In each of them the truth of knowledge is made to depend on certain external conditions other than the knowledge itself. According to almost all realists, old and new, it is correspondence to facts that constitutes both the nature and the test of truth.[4] Of course, some realists differ from this general position and hold a different view of the matter. Thus Alexander[5] makes coherence the ground of truth. But in speaking of coherence as determined by reality, he accepts indirectly the theory of correspondence. Reid,[6] on the other hand, treats correspondence to the given only as a test of truth. Russell[7] defines truth in terms of correspondence and accepts coherence as a test of some truths, while others are said to be self-evident. In the philosophy of objective idealism,[8] coherence in the sense of the systematic unity of all experiences is made both the ground and the test of truth. The truth consists in the coherence of all experiences as one self-maintaining and all-inclusive system. It is in this sense that Bosanquet[9] says that "the truth is the whole and it is its own criterion. Truth can only be tested by more of itself." Hence any particular knowledge is true in so far as it is consistent with the whole system of experience. On this view, the

truth of human knowledge becomes relative, since coherence as the ideal of the completed system of experience is humanly unattainable. For pragmatism,[10] truth is both constituted and known by practical utility. The truth of knowledge consists in its capacity to produce practically useful consequences. So also the method of ascertaining truth is just to follow the practical consequences of a belief and see if they have any practical value. With this brief statement of the realistic, the idealistic and the pragmatist theories of truth, we proceed to examine the Buddhist and the Nyāya theories of extrinsic validity.

From what we have said before it is clear that the Buddhists adopt the pragmatist theory of truth and reality. For them, practical efficiency is the test of both truth and reality. The real is what possesses practical efficiency (*arthakriyā*) and the true is the useful and so practically efficient (*arthakriyāsāmarthya*). But the pragmatic conception of truth is embarrassed by serious difficulties. The Nyāya criticism of the Buddha conception of *pramāṇa* has brought out some of these difficulties. Here we may note that to reduce the true to the useful is to make it almost meaningless. It is by no means the case that truth is only a matter of practical utility. The atomic and the electron theories of matter make very little difference in our practical life. Similarly, the different theories of truth involve no great difference in their practical consequences. But in the absence of any other test than that of practical utility we cannot say which one is true and which is false. Further, there are certain beliefs which are admittedly wrong but which are otherwise useful for certain purposes of life. But no one would claim any truth for a wrong belief on account of its practical utility. Hence the Buddhist and the pragmatist theories of truth cannot be accepted as sound and satisfactory.

The Nyāya theory of truth, it will be seen, combines the correspondence, the coherence and the pragmatist theories with certain modifications. According to it, the truth of knowledge consists in its correspondence with objective facts, while coherence and practical utility are the tests of truth in such cases in which we

---

4. *Vide The New Realism* and *Essays in Critical Realism.*
5. *Space, Time and Deity,* Vol. II, pp. 251 f.
6. *Knowledge and Truth,* Chap. VIII.
7. *The Problems of Philosophy,* Chaps. XII, XIII; *Our Knowledge of the External World,* p. 58; *The Analysis of Mind,* p. 165.
8. *Vide* Joachim, *The Nature of Truth,* Chap. III.
9. *Logic,* Vol. II, pp. 265–67.

10. James, *Pragmatism,* Lect. VI; Perry, *Present Philosophical Tendencies,* Pts. IV and V.

require a test. It defines the truth of all knowledge as a correspondence of relations (*tadvati tatprakāraka*). To know a thing is to judge it as having such-and-such a character. This knowledge of the thing will be true if the thing has really such-and-such a character; if not, it will be false. The Nyāya view of correspondence is thus different from the new realistic idea of structural correspondence or identity of contents.[11] That knowledge corresponds to some object does not, for the Naiyāyika, mean that the contents of the object bodily enter into consciousness and become its contents. When, for example, I know a table, the table as a physical existent does not figure in my consciousness. This means only that I *judge* something as having the attribute of 'tableness' which really belongs to it. There is a subjective cognition of a physical object. The one corresponds to the other, because it *determines* the object as it is, and does not itself become what it is. If it so became the object itself, there would be nothing left on the subjective side that might correspond to the physical object. Nor again does the Nyāya follow the critical realist's idea of correspondence between character-complexes, referred to the object by the knowing mind, and the characters actually belonging to the object. When we know anything we do not first apprehend a certain logical essence or a character-complex and then refer it to the thing known. Our knowledge is in direct contact with the object. In knowing the object we judge it as having a relation to certain characters or attributes. Our knowledge will be true if there is correspondence between the relation asserted in knowledge, and that existing among facts. Thus my knowledge of a conch shell as white is true because there is a real relation between the two corresponding to the relation affirmed by me. On the other hand, the perception of silver in a shell is false because it asserts a relation between the two, which does not correspond to a real relation between them.[12]

While truth consists in correspondence, the criterion of truth is, for the Nyāya, coherence in a broad sense (*saṁvāda*). But coherence does not here mean anything of the kind that objective idealism means by it. The Nyāya coherence is a practical test and means the harmony between cognitive and conative experiences (*pravṛttisāmarthya*) or between different kinds of knowledge (*tajjātīyatva*). That there is truth in the sense of correspondence cannot, as a general rule, be known directly by intuition. We know it indirectly from the fact that the knowledge in question coheres with other experiences of the same object as also with the general system of our knowledge. Thus the perception of water is known to be valid when different ways of reaction or experiment give us experience of the same water. It is this kind of coherence that Alexander accepts as a test of truth when he says: "If truth is tested by reference to other propositions, the test is not one of correspondence to reality but of whether the proposition tested is consistent or not with other propositions."[13] Hobhouse[14] also means the same thing by 'consilience' as a measure of validity. According to him, validity belongs to judgments as forming a consilient system. Of course, he admits that such validity is relative and not absolute, since the ideal of a complete system of consilient judgments is unattainable. The Nyāya idea of *saṁvāda* or coherence may be better explained as a combination of Reid's methods of correspondence and coherence. If we take the judgment 'that is the light of a ship,' we can test its truth by what Reid calls the correspondence method "of approaching the light and seeing a ship." This is exactly what the Nyāya means by *pravṛttisāmarthya* or successful activity. Or, we can employ, so says Reid, the cheaper coherence method "of comparing this knowledge with other kinds of knowledge and see if it is consistent with them."[15] In this we have the Nyāya method of testing one knowledge by reference to some other valid knowledge (*tajjātīyatva*). But the Nyāya goes further than this and accepts practical utility also as a test of truth. Thus the validity of the perception of water may be known from correspondence and coherence in the above sense. But it may be further known from the satisfaction of our practical needs or the fulfilment of our practical purposes in relation to water, such as

---

11. *Cf.* Chapter III, Sec. 3, above.
12. *Cf.* "Smith's judgment that it is the light of a ship is true just because 'it,' the light, is in fact so related to a real ship. Jones' judgment (that it is the light of a star), on the other hand, is false, because this thought is not an apprehension of the existing present complex fact, light-belonging-to-ship."—Reid, *Knowledge and Truth*, pp. 209–10.

13. *Space, Time and Deity*, Vol. II, p. 252.
14. *The Theory of Knowledge*, pp. 499–500.
15. *Knowledge and Truth*, pp. 203–4, 211–12.

drinking, bathing, washing, etc. But the Nyāya never admits the pragmatist contention that the truth of any knowledge is constituted by its utility or serviceableness. Knowledge is made true by its correspondence to some reality or objective fact. It is true not because it is useful, but it is useful because it is already true. Hence truth consists in correspondence and is tested by coherence and practical efficiency.

But from the standpoint of the modern Nyāya, all truths do not require to be tested. Some truths are known as such without any test or confirmation. These are manifestly necessary and so self-evident truths. Here the Nyāya view has some affinity with Russell's theory of truth.[16] In both, truth is defined by correspondence to fact, but in different ways. Although truth is thus externally conditioned, some truths are admitted by both to be self-evident. For the Nyāya, however, such truths are only necessary truths or what Russell calls *a priori* principles. Of the different kinds of knowledge by acquaintance—sensation, memory, introspection, etc.—which are admitted by Russell to have self-evident truth, it is only introspection or self-consciousness (*anuvyavasāya*) that is admitted by the Nyāya as having self-evident validity. The validity of self-consciousness is self-evident because there is a necessary relation between consciousness and its contents. When I become conscious of a desire for food, I find that my consciousness is necessarily related to the desire, it is the desire itself as it becomes explicit.[17] Here I not only know something, but know that I am knowing it, *i.e.* the truth of my knowledge is self-evident.

The different theories of truth discussed above may be shown to supplement one another and be reconciled as complementary aspects of a comprehensive theory. The first requisite of such a theory is the independent existence of a world of objects. If there were no such world, there would be no ground for the distinction between truth and falsehood. Some of our beliefs are true or false according as they are or are not borne out by independent objects or facts. It is because

there are certain independent objects, to which our beliefs may or may not conform, that we distinguish between truth and error. Hence we say that truth consists in the correspondence of our knowledge with independent objects or facts. The difficulty on this view, it is generally remarked, is that if the objects are independent of knowledge, we cannot know whether our knowledge corresponds with them or not. How can we know what is outside and beyond knowledge, and see that true knowledge agrees with it? The reply to this is that in the case of external objects, physical things and other minds, we cannot straightway know the correspondence between our knowledge and its objects. Still, we cannot deny the reality of these external objects. But for the independent existence of other things and minds we cannot explain the order and uniformity of our experiences and the similarity of the experiences that different individuals may have under similar circumstances. That some of our experiences represent the real qualities of things may then be known from the fact that they are given in the same way to different persons, or to the same persons through different senses. As Professor Price has shown, "sense-data cohere together in families, and families are coincident with physical occupants."[18] On the other hand, some of our experiences are not taken to represent the qualities of things, because they do not cohere with other experiences of the same individual or of different individuals. The first kind of experiences is considered to be true and objective, while the second is judged to be false and subjective. Similarly, our knowledge of other minds is true when it correctly represents the contents of those minds. It will be false, if what we impute to them forms no part of their actual contents. This shows that it is correspondence to facts that constitutes the nature of truth, although we cannot directly *know* such correspondence in the case of physical things and other minds. To know this we have to consider if one knowledge coheres with others or the whole body of human knowledge, and also consider if we can successfully act on our knowledge. What is true works, although whatever works is not true. Thus we know the correspondence of knowledge with facts from its coherence and

16. *The Problems of Philosophy*, Chaps. XI, XII, XIII.
17. *Cf.* C. Hartshorne's article in *The Monist* (Vol. XLIV, No. 2, p. 171): "Must this (feeling) not be admitted to present an obvious dual aspect of being at once subjective and yet a content or object of consciousness, at once a mode and a datum of awareness?"

18. *Cf. Perception*, p. 302.

pragmatic value. But to know that a certain knowledge corresponds with facts is to *know* its truth. It does not constitute its truth. The knowledge becomes true if, and only if, it corresponds with facts. We know or test its truth when we find that it is coherent with other parts of our knowledge and our practical activities. So truth is constituted by correspondence with facts and is tested by coherence and practical activity.

The Vedānta view of truth as uncontradicted experience logically implies the coherence theory of truth. That some experience is uncontradicted means that it is different from the contradicted. But to be different from the contradicted means to belong to the body of coherent knowledge. We do not and cannot rightly judge an experience to be uncontradicted unless we relate it to other experiences and find that it is congruous with them. A dream experience is wrongly judged by the dreamer to be uncontradicted and true, because he cannot relate it to his waking experiences. It cannot be said that a dream experience is true for the time being and becomes false afterwards. What is once true is always true. A dream experience may sometimes be *judged* to be true, but it is really false for all time. And its falsity appears from its incoherence with waking experience. Hence we are to say that an experience is really uncontradicted when it is related to other experiences and is found to be coherent with them.

It may be urged against the above view that truth consists in correspondence and is tested by coherence, that it either assumes the truth of the testing knowledge, or must go on testing knowledge *ad infinitum*. If knowledge is true when it corresponds with facts, and if the correspondence cannot be directly known, then the truth of every knowledge must be tested by its coherence with others. This, however, means that there can be no end of the process of proving knowledge and, therefore, no final proof of any knowledge. To solve this difficulty we must admit that there is at least one case in which knowledge is, by itself, known to be true. We have such a case in self-consciousness. While the truth of all other knowledge is to be tested by coherence, the truth of self-consciousness is self-evident and requires no extraneous test. The self is a self-manifesting reality. Hence the contents of our mind or the self are manifested by themselves. They are at once existent facts and contents of consciousness. To become conscious of the contents of one's mind is just to make them explicit. What we are here conscious of are not outside or beyond consciousness. Mental contents not only *are*, but are conscious of themselves. The state of knowledge and the object of knowledge being identical, we cannot strictly speak of a correspondence of the one with the other. Or, if we speak of a correspondence between them, we are to say that it is directly known and so need not be known or tested in any other way. When we feel pain, or know something, or resolve to do anything, we may be conscious of feeling it, or knowing it, or resolving to do it. What we are here conscious of as objects are the objects themselves as they become explicit or conscious of themselves. Similarly, necessary truths and *a priori* principles like the laws of thought, logical and mathematical truths seem to have self-evident validity. The reason for this is that these truths are or express the forms and contents of our own consciousness. They are inherent in or arise out of the nature of our own thought and consciousness, and in knowing them consciousness knows itself, *i.e.* its own forms. They are at once modes and objects of consciousness. In any judgment or knowledge of them, the content and object of consciousness are the same and directly known to be the same. Such knowledge is, therefore, not only true, but also known to be true by itself. Hence we admit that the truth of self-consciousness is self-evident, while all other truths are evidenced by external tests like coherence and pragmatic utility or verification.

DISCUSSION QUESTIONS

1. How do deductive reasoning and inductive reasoning contribute to the acquisition of knowledge? Use examples.

2. What are the problems with the correspondence, coherence, and pragmatic theories of truth, if each is taken by itself?

3. Most philosophers these days characterize knowledge as "justified true belief." What would be some examples of unjustified true belief, justified false belief, and unjustified false belief?

4. How would the Nyāya theory of truth illustrate the "spirit of Indian philosophy" as described by Radhakrishnan?

9. Friedrich Nietzsche (1844–1900)
"On Truth and Lie in an Extra-Moral Sense"

Although Friedrich Nietzsche's writing career was finished by early 1889 when he finally succumbed to a degenerative disease that cost him his mental competence, he is to this day one of the most controversial thinkers in Western philosophy. His works have been interpreted, labeled, and used by others in widely divergent, often contrary ways. As yet there is no final consensus among academicians regarding the real meaning (if there is such a thing) and significance of what he wrote, other than its intentionally provocative character and enduring fascination for many.

In the twentieth century he was associated with Nazism because of that movement's selective use of his writings to justify its goals. However, in his own time, Nietzsche was critical of the racist nationalism and expansionism that already had its adherents in his native Germany and eventually found expression in Nazi ideology. For quite different reasons he often has been categorized as an existentialist thinker, referring to the philosophical and literary movement of the nineteenth and twentieth centuries that emphasized the problem of meaningful existence for the self-defining human individual. But this label is not altogether consistent with a recurrent theme of biological determinism in his works. More recently he has been seen as one of the first postmodernist theorists, which is to identify him with an academic approach to the critical interpretation of modern Western intellectual history that stresses its cultural imperialism and illusory pretense of enlightenment and progress. Once again, his rather premodern acceptance of domination/subordination relations between people as natural and inevitable is difficult to reconcile with this interpretation.

Nietzsche seemed to be less interested in systematic theory-construction than most other philosophers in his day, often presenting his views in an aphoristic, poetical, or simply polemical style. The selection reprinted here was written in 1873 and taken from a large collection of often fragmentary writings published posthumously. As was typical of his approach to philosophical questions, in this piece Nietzsche is reflecting not only on the nature of ideas such as "knowledge" and "truth" but also on their value for human beings.

QUESTIONS FOR CRITICAL READING

1. According to Nietzsche, what is the significance of the human intellect when seen from the vantage point of natural history?
2. What is "truth," and how does Nietzsche explain its value for humans?
3. Why is deception generally undesirable to humans, in Nietzsche's view?
4. How does Nietzsche explain the origin of "concepts"?

TERMS TO NOTE

metaphor: A word, phrase, or image to be understood not in its literal or immediate sense, but applied as a figure of speech to something else thought to be similar.

metonym: From the Greek *metōnymiā* (literally, "change of name"), a term used figuratively to stand for something else of which it is literally only one aspect, or to which it is normally related anyway. Example: "man's history" for "human history."

anthropomorphism: The attribution of human qualities to that which is nonhuman.

illusion: Something that seems to be so to the perceiver but in actuality is not so, or at least is very different from how it seems; a misleading or false appearance, or the belief based on such appearance.

qualitas occulta: Latin for "hidden quality."

In some remote corner of the universe, poured out and glittering in innumerable solar systems, there once was a star on which clever animals invented knowledge. That was the haughtiest and most mendacious minute of "world history"—yet only a minute. After nature had drawn a few breaths the star grew cold, and the clever animals had to die.

One might invent such a fable and still not have illustrated sufficiently how wretched, how shadowy and flighty, how aimless and arbitrary, the human intellect appears in nature. There have been eternities when it did not exist; and when it is done for again, nothing will have happened. For this intellect has no further mission that would lead beyond human life. It is human, rather, and only its owner and producer gives it such importance, as if the world pivoted around it. But if we could communicate with the mosquito, then we would learn that it floats through the air with the same self-importance, feeling within itself the flying center of the world. There is nothing in nature so despicable or insignificant that it cannot immediately be blown up like a bag by a slight breath of this power of knowledge; and just as every porter wants an admirer, the proudest human being, the philosopher, thinks that he sees the eyes of the universe telescopically focused from all sides on his actions and thoughts.

It is strange that this should be the effect of the intellect, for after all it was given only as an aid to the most unfortunate, most delicate, most evanescent beings in order to hold them for a minute in existence, from which otherwise, without this gift, they would have every reason to flee as quickly as Lessing's son. That haughtiness which goes with knowledge and feeling, which shrouds the eyes and senses of man in a blinding fog, therefore deceives him about the value of existence by carrying in itself the most flattering evaluation of knowledge itself. Its most universal effect is deception; but even its most particular effects have something of the same character.

The intellect, as a means for the preservation of the individual, unfolds its chief powers in simulation; for this is the means by which the weaker, less robust individuals preserve themselves, since they are denied the chance of waging the struggle for existence with horns or the fangs of beasts of prey. In man this art of simulation reaches its peak: here deception, flattery, lying and cheating, talking behind the back, posing, living in borrowed splendor, being masked, the disguise of convention, acting a role before others and before oneself—in short, the constant fluttering

around the single flame of vanity is so much the rule and the law that almost nothing is more incomprehensible than how an honest and pure urge for truth could make its appearance among men. They are deeply immersed in illusions and dream images; their eye glides only over the surface of things and sees "forms"; their feeling nowhere leads into truth, but contents itself with the reception of stimuli, playing, as it were, a game of blindman's buff on the backs of things. Moreover, man permits himself to be lied to at night, his life long, when he dreams, and his moral sense never even tries to prevent this—although men have been said to have overcome snoring by sheer will power.

What, indeed, does man know of himself! Can he even once perceive himself completely, laid out as if in an illuminated glass case? Does not nature keep much the most from him, even about his body, to spellbind and confine him in a proud, deceptive consciousness, far from the coils of the intestines, the quick current of the blood stream, and the involved tremors of the fibers? She threw away the key; and woe to the calamitous curiosity which might peer just once through a crack in the chamber of consciousness and look down, and sense that man rests upon the merciless, the greedy, the insatiable, the murderous, in the indifference of his ignorance—hanging in dreams, as it were, upon the back of a tiger. In view of this, whence in all the world comes the urge for truth?

Insofar as the individual wants to preserve himself against other individuals, in a natural state of affairs he employs the intellect mostly for simulation alone. But because man, out of need and boredom, wants to exist socially, herd-fashion, he requires a peace pact and he endeavors to banish at least the very crudest *bellum omnium contra omnes*[1] from his world. This peace pact brings with it something that looks like the first step toward the attainment of this enigmatic urge for truth. For now that is fixed which henceforth shall be "truth"; that is, a regularly valid and obligatory designation of things is invented, and this linguistic legislation also furnishes the first laws of truth: for it is here that the contrast between truth and lie first originates. The liar uses the valid designations, the words,

---

1. "War of all against all."

to make the unreal appear as real; he says, for example, "I am rich," when the word "poor" would be the correct designation of his situation. He abuses the fixed conventions by arbitrary changes or even by reversals of the names. When he does this in a self-serving way damaging to others, then society will no longer trust him but exclude him. Thereby men do not flee from being deceived as much as from being damaged by deception: what they hate at this stage is basically not the deception but the bad, hostile consequences of certain kinds of deceptions. In a similarly limited way man wants the truth: he desires the agreeable life-preserving consequences of truth, but he is indifferent to pure knowledge, which has no consequences; he is even hostile to possibly damaging and destructive truths. And, moreover, what about these conventions of language? Are they really the products of knowledge, of the sense of truth? Do the designations and the things coincide? Is language the adequate expression of all realities?

Only through forgetfulness can man ever achieve the illusion of possessing a "truth" in the sense just designated. If he does not wish to be satisfied with truth in the form of a tautology—that is, with empty shells—then he will forever buy illusions for truths. What is a word? The image of a nerve stimulus in sounds. But to infer from the nerve stimulus, a cause outside us, that is already the result of a false and unjustified application of the principle of reason. . . . The different languages, set side by side, show that what matters with words is never the truth, never an adequate expression; else there would not be so many languages. The "thing in itself" (for that is what pure truth, without consequences, would be) is quite incomprehensible to the creators of language and not at all worth aiming for. One designates only the relations of things to man, and to express them one calls on the boldest metaphors. A nerve stimulus, first transposed into an image—first metaphor. The image, in turn, imitated by a sound—second metaphor. . . .

Let us still give special consideration to the formation of concepts. Every word immediately becomes a concept, inasmuch as it is not intended to serve as a reminder of the unique and wholly individualized original experience to which it owes its birth, but must at the same time fit innumerable, more or less similar cases—which means, strictly speaking, never equal—in other words, a lot of unequal cases. Every concept originates through our equating what is unequal. No leaf ever wholly equals another, and the concept "leaf" is formed through an arbitrary abstraction from these individual differences, through forgetting the distinctions; and now it gives rise to the idea that in nature there might be something besides the leaves which would be "leaf"—some kind of original form after which all leaves have been woven, marked, copied, colored, curled, and painted, but by unskilled hands, so that no copy turned out to be a correct, reliable, and faithful image of the original form. We call a person "honest." Why did he act so honestly today? we ask. Our answer usually sounds like this: because of his honesty. Honesty! That is to say again: the leaf is the cause of the leaves. After all, we know nothing of an essence-like quality named "honesty"; we know only numerous individualized, and thus unequal actions, which we equate by omitting the unequal and by then calling them honest actions. In the end, we distill from them a *qualitas occulta* with the name of "honesty". . . .

What, then, is truth? A mobile army of metaphors, metonyms, and anthropomorphisms—in short, a sum of human relations, which have been enhanced, transposed, and embellished poetically and rhetorically, and which after long use seem firm, canonical, and obligatory to a people: truths are illusions about which one has forgotten that this is what they are; metaphors which are worn out and without sensuous power; coins which have lost their pictures and now matter only as metal, no longer as coins.

We still do not know where the urge for truth comes from; for as yet we have heard only of the obligation imposed by society that it should exist: to be truthful means using the customary metaphors—in moral terms: the obligation to lie according to a fixed convention, to lie herd-like in a style obligatory for all. . . .

DISCUSSION QUESTIONS

1. Nietzsche seems to be rejecting the special status of the human species in the universe and even on this planet. Do you agree with him? Why or why not?

2. Do you agree with Nietzsche's account of the evolutionary role of the human intellect? Why or why not?

3. If truth is just a function of linguistic convention, how do we explain what happens when some individuals in a society discover that conventional beliefs are false? Is there room in Nietzsche's account for objective truth?

4. How would Nietzsche's perspective on the philosophical interest in truth compare with Russell's argument for the value of philosophical inquiry?

10. Charles Sanders Peirce (1839–1914)
"The Fixation of Belief"

Charles Sanders Peirce grew up in Cambridge, Massachusetts. His father was a Harvard professor of mathematics and astronomy, and the younger Peirce studied physical science, mathematics, and philosophy, also at Harvard, but never was able to secure a permanent academic position anywhere. Peirce worked instead as a scientist with the U.S. Coast and Geodetic Survey for thirty years, after which he retired to a life of philosophical study, writing, occasional lecturing, and poverty. In spite of such obstacles, he became one of the most influential theorists associated with the American school of thought known as pragmatism. The pragmatists argue that the verification or falsification, and even the intelligibility, of our belief options on almost any subject are to be found in the application of those beliefs within a real-life context of goal-oriented, practical activity. Pragmatists also were some of the first in the Western intellectual tradition to systematically treat knowledge as at least in part a social product. This functional approach to epistemological issues was a response both to the perceived successes of scientific methodology in the nineteenth and early twentieth centuries and to the increasing impatience on the part of many intellectuals with the chronic unverifiability of the results of traditional philosophical speculation.

In this 1877 essay Peirce is engaging as much in psychological and historical description as in philosophical analysis. He focuses on the methods by which we acquire and maintain our beliefs, what our motivations are in doing so, and what happens when we are faced with a diversity of belief on topics we consider significant for our lives.

QUESTIONS FOR CRITICAL READING

1. What is the state of doubt, what is the state of belief, and what are their differences, according to Peirce?

2. What is the "method of tenacity," and what impact does the "social impulse" have on it?

3. What is the "method of authority," and how is it related to the social impulse?

4. What is the "*a priori* method," and why is Peirce critical of it?

5. What is the "method of science," and why does Peirce think it is superior to the other methods of "fixing belief"?

TERMS TO NOTE

ratiocination: The process of rational thought.
metaphysical: Having to do with what ultimately exists and its essential nature; in this context, it refers somewhat disparagingly to philosophical speculation about various aspects of reality that cannot be proved by factual evidence.

I

Few persons care to study logic, because everybody conceives himself to be proficient enough in the art of reasoning already. But I observe that this satisfaction is limited to one's own ratiocination, and does not extend to that of other men.

We come to the full possession of our power of drawing inferences the last of all our faculties, for it is not so much a natural gift as a long and difficult art. . . .

II

The object of reasoning is to find out, from the consideration of what we already know, something else which we do not know. Consequently, reasoning is good if it be such as to give a true conclusion from true premises, and not otherwise. Thus, the question of validity is purely one of fact and not of thinking. A being the premises and B being the conclusion, the question is, whether these facts are really so related that if A is, B is. If so, the inference is valid; if not, not. It is not in the least the question whether, when the premises are accepted by the mind, we feel an impulse to accept the conclusion also. It is true that we do generally reason correctly by nature. But that is an accident; the true conclusion would remain true if we had no impulse to accept it; and the false one would remain false, though we could not resist the tendency to believe in it.

We are, doubtless, in the main logical animals, but we are not perfectly so. Most of us, for example, are naturally more sanguine and hopeful than logic would justify. We seem to be so constituted that in the absence of any facts to go upon we are happy and self-satisfied; so that the effect of experience is continually to counteract our hopes and aspirations. Yet a lifetime of the application of this corrective does not usually eradicate our sanguine disposition. Where hope is unchecked by any experience, it is likely that our optimism is extravagant. Logicality in regard to practical matters is the most useful quality an animal can possess, and might, therefore, result from the action of natural selection; but outside of these it is probably of more advantage to the animal to have his mind filled with pleasing and encouraging visions, independently of their truth; and thus, upon unpractical subjects, natural selection might occasion a fallacious tendency of thought.

That which determines us, from given premises, to draw one inference rather than another is some habit of mind, whether it be constitutional or acquired. The habit is good or otherwise, according as it produces true conclusions from true premises or not; and an inference is regarded as valid or not, without reference to the truth or falsity of its conclusion specially, but according as the habit which determines it is such as to produce true conclusions in general or not. The particular habit of mind which governs this or that inference may be formulated in a proposition whose truth depends on the validity of the inferences which the habit determines; and such a formula is called a *guiding principle* of inference. Suppose, for example, that we observe that a rotating disk of copper quickly comes to rest when placed between the poles of a magnet, and we infer that this will happen with every disk of copper. The guiding principle is that what is true of one piece of copper is true of another. Such a guiding principle with regard to copper would be much safer than with regard to many other substances—brass, for example.

A book might be written to signalize all the most important of these guiding principles of reasoning. It would probably be, we must confess, of no service to a person whose thought is directed wholly to practical subjects, and whose activity moves along thoroughly beaten paths. The problems which present themselves to such a mind are matters of routine which he has learned once for all to handle in learning his business. But let a man venture into an unfamiliar field, or where his results are not continually checked by experience, and all history shows that the most masculine intellect will ofttimes lose his orientation and waste his efforts in directions which bring him no nearer to his goal, or even carry him entirely astray. He is like a ship on the open sea, with no one on board who understands the rules of navigation. And in such a case some general study of the guiding principles of reasoning would be sure to be found useful.

The subject could hardly be treated, however, without being first limited; since almost any fact may serve as a guiding principle. But it so happens that there exists a division among facts, such that in one class are all those which are absolutely essential as guiding principles, while in the other are all those which have any other interest as objects of research. This division is between those which are necessarily taken for granted in asking whether a certain conclusion follows from certain premises, and those which are not implied in that question. A moment's thought will show that a variety of facts are already assumed when the logical question is first asked. It is implied, for instance, that there are such states of mind as doubt and belief—that a passage from one to the other is possible, the object of thought remaining the same, and that this transition is subject to some rules which all minds are alike bound by. As these are facts which we must already know before we can have any clear conception of reasoning at all, it cannot be supposed to be any longer of much interest to inquire into their truth or falsity. On the other hand, it is easy to believe that those rules of reasoning which are deduced from the very idea of the process are the ones which are the most essential; and, indeed, that so long as it conforms to these it will, at least, not lead to false conclusions from true premises. In point of fact, the importance of what may be deduced from the assumptions involved in the logical question turns out to be greater than might be supposed, and this for reasons which it is difficult to exhibit at the outset. The only one which I shall here mention is that conceptions which are really products of logical reflections, without being readily seen to be so, mingle with our ordinary thoughts, and are frequently the causes of great confusion. This is the case, for example, with the conception of quality. A quality as such is never an object of observation. We can see that a thing is blue or green, but the quality of being blue and the quality of being green are not things which we see; they are products of logical reflections. The truth is that common sense, or thought as it first emerges above the level of the narrowly practical, is deeply imbued with that bad logical quality to which the epithet *metaphysical* is commonly applied; and nothing can clear it up but a severe course of logic.

III

We generally know when we wish to ask a question and when we wish to pronounce a judgment, for there is a dissimilarity between the sensation of doubting and that of believing.

But this is not all which distinguishes doubt from belief. There is a practical difference. Our beliefs guide our desires and shape our actions. The Assassins, or followers of the Old Man of the Mountain, used to rush into death at his least command, because they believed that obedience to him would insure everlasting felicity. Had they doubted this, they would not have acted as they did. So it is with every belief, according to its degree. The feeling of believing is a more or less sure indication of there being established in our nature some habit which will determine our actions. Doubt never has such an effect.

Nor must we overlook a third point of difference. Doubt is an uneasy and dissatisfied state from which we struggle to free ourselves and pass into the state of belief; while the latter is a calm and satisfactory state which we do not wish to avoid, or to change to a belief in anything else. On the contrary, we cling tenaciously, not merely to believing, but to believing just what we do believe.

Thus, both doubt and belief have positive effects upon us, though very different ones. Belief does not make us act at once, but puts us into such a condition that we shall behave in a certain way, when the occasion arises. Doubt has not the least effect of this sort, but stimulates us to action until it is destroyed. This reminds us of the irritation of a nerve and the reflex action produced thereby; while for the analogue of belief, in the nervous system, we must look to what are called nervous associations—for example, to that habit of the nerves in consequence of which the smell of a peach will make the mouth water.

IV

The irritation of doubt causes a struggle to attain a state of belief. I shall term this struggle *inquiry*, though it must be admitted that this is sometimes not a very apt designation.

The irritation of doubt is the only immediate motive for the struggle to attain belief. It is certainly best for us that our beliefs should be such as may truly guide our actions so as to satisfy our desires; and this reflection will make us reject any belief which does not seem to have been so formed as to insure this result. But it will only do so by creating a doubt in the place of that belief. With the doubt, therefore, the struggle begins, and with the cessation of doubt it ends. Hence, the sole object of inquiry is the settlement of opinion. We may fancy that this is not enough for us, and that we seek not merely an opinion, but a true opinion. But put this fancy to the test, and it proves groundless; for as soon as a firm belief is reached we are entirely satisfied, whether the belief be false or true. And it is clear that nothing out of the sphere of our knowledge can be our object, for nothing which does not affect the mind can be a motive for a mental effort. The most that can be maintained is that we seek for a belief that we shall *think* to be true. But we think each one of our beliefs to be true, and, indeed, it is mere tautology to say so.

That the settlement of opinion is the sole end of inquiry is a very important proposition. It sweeps away, at once, various vague and erroneous conceptions of proof. A few of these may be noticed here.

1. Some philosophers have imagined that to start an inquiry it was only necessary to utter or question or set it down on paper, and have even recommended us to begin our studies with questioning everything! But the mere putting of a proposition into the interrogative form does not stimulate the mind to any struggle after belief. There must be a real and living doubt, and without all this, discussion is idle.

2. It is a very common idea that a demonstration must rest on some ultimate and absolutely indubitable propositions. These, according to one school, are first principles of a general nature; according to another, are first sensations. But, in point of fact, an inquiry, to have that completely satisfactory result called demonstration, has only to start with propositions perfectly free from all actual doubt. If the premises are not in fact doubted at all, they cannot be more satisfactory than they are.

3. Some people seem to love to argue a point after all the world is fully convinced of it. But no further advance can be made. When doubt ceases, mental action on the subject comes to an end; and, if it did go on, it would be without a purpose, except that of self-criticism.

V

If the settlement of opinion is the sole object of inquiry, and if belief is of the nature of a habit, why should we not attain the desired end, by taking any answer to a question, which we may fancy, and constantly reiterating it to ourselves, dwelling on all which may conduce to that belief, and learning to turn with contempt and hatred from anything which might disturb it? This simple and direct method is really pursued by many men. I remember once being entreated not to read a certain newspaper lest it might change my opinion upon free-trade. "Lest I might be entrapped by its fallacies and misstatements" was the form of expression. "You are not," my friend said, "a special student of political economy. You might, therefore, easily be deceived by fallacious arguments upon the subject. You might, then, if you read this paper, be led to believe in protection. But you admit that free-trade is the true doctrine; and you do not wish to believe what is not true." I have often known this system to be deliberately adopted. Still oftener, the instinctive dislike of an undecided state of mind, exaggerated into a vague dread of doubt, makes men cling spasmodically to the views they already take. The man feels that if he only holds to his belief without wavering, it will be entirely satisfactory. Nor can it be denied that a steady and immovable faith yields great peace of mind. It may, indeed, give rise to inconveniences, as if a man should resolutely continue to believe that fire would not burn him, or that he would be eternally damned if he received his *ingesta* otherwise than through a stomach-pump. But then the man who adopts this method will not allow that its inconveniences are greater than its advantages. He will say, "I hold steadfastly to the truth and the truth is always wholesome." And in many cases it may very well be that the pleasure he derives from his calm faith overbalances any inconveniences resulting from its deceptive character. Thus, if it be true that death is annihilation, then the man who believes that he will certainly go straight to heaven when he dies, provided he have fulfilled certain simple observances in this life, has a cheap pleasure which will not be followed by the least disappointment. A similar consideration seems to have weight with many persons in religious topics, for we frequently hear it said, "Oh, I could not believe so-and-so, because I should be wretched if I did." When an ostrich buries its head in the sand as danger approaches, it very likely takes the happiest course. It hides the danger, and then calmly says there is no danger; and, if it feels perfectly sure there is none, why should it raise its head to see? A man may go through life, systematically keeping out of view all that might cause a change in his opinions, and if he only succeeds—basing his method, as he does, on two fundamental psychological laws—I do not see what can be said against his doing so. It would be an egotistical impertinence to object that his procedure is irrational, for that only amounts to saying that his method of settling belief is not ours. He does not propose to himself to be rational, and indeed, will often talk with scorn of man's weak and illusive reason. So let him think as he pleases.

But this method of fixing belief, which may be called the method of tenacity, will be unable to hold its ground in practice. The social impulse is against it. The man who adopts it will find that other men think differently from him, and it will be apt to occur to him in some saner moment that their opinions are quite as good as his own, and this will shake his confidence in his belief. This conception, that another man's thought or sentiment may be equivalent to one's own, is a distinctly new step, and a highly important one. It arises from an impulse too strong in man to be suppressed, without danger of destroying the human species. Unless we make ourselves hermits, we shall necessarily influence each other's opinions; so that the problem becomes how to fix belief, not in the individual merely, but in the community.

Let the will of the state act, then, instead of that of the individual. Let an institution be created which shall have for its object to keep correct doctrines before the attention of the people, to reiterate them perpetually, and to teach them to the young; having at the same time power to prevent contrary doctrines from being taught, advocated, or expressed. Let all possible causes of a change of mind be removed from men's apprehensions. Let them be kept ignorant, lest they should learn of some reason to think otherwise than they do. Let their passions be enlisted, so that they may regard private and unusual opinions with hatred and horror. Then, let all men who reject the established belief be terrified into silence. Let the people turn out and tar-and-feather such men, or let inquisitions be made into the manner of thinking of suspected persons, and, when they are found guilty of forbidden beliefs, let them be subjected to some signal punishment. When complete agreement could not otherwise

be reached, a general massacre of all who have not thought in a certain way has proved a very effective means of settling opinion in a country. If the power to do this be wanting, let a list of opinions be drawn up, to which no man of the least independence of thought can assent, and let the faithful be required to accept all these propositions, in order to segregate them as radically as possible from the influence of the rest of the world.

This method has, from the earliest times, been one of the chief means of upholding correct theological and political doctrines, and of preserving their universal or catholic character. In Rome, especially, it has been practiced from the days of Numa Pompilius to those of Pius Nonus. This is the most perfect example in history; but wherever there is a priesthood—and no religion has been without one—this method has been more or less made use of. Wherever there is aristocracy, or a guild, or any association of a class of men whose interests depend or are supposed to depend on certain propositions, there will be inevitably found some traces of this natural product of social feeling. Cruelties always accompany this system; and when it is consistently carried out, they become atrocities of the most horrible kind in the eyes of any rational man. Nor should this occasion surprise, for the officer of a society does not feel justified in surrendering the interests of that society for the sake of mercy, as he might his own private interests. It is natural, therefore, that sympathy and fellowship should thus produce a most ruthless power.

In judging this method of fixing belief, which may be called the method of authority, we must, in the first place, allow its immeasurable mental and moral superiority to the method of tenacity. Its success is proportionally greater; and in fact it has over and over again worked the most majestic results. The mere structures of stone which it has caused to be put together—in Siam, for example, in Egypt, and in Europe—have many of them a sublimity hardly more than rivaled by the greatest works of nature. And, except the geological epochs, there are no periods of time so vast as those which are measured by some of these organized faiths. If we scrutinize the matter closely, we shall find that there has not been one of their creeds which has remained always the same; yet the change is so slow as to be imperceptible during one person's life, so that individual belief remains sensibly fixed. For the mass of mankind, then, there is perhaps no better method than this. If it is their highest impulse to be intellectual slaves, then slaves they ought to remain.

But no institution can undertake to regulate opinions upon every subject. Only the most important ones can be attended to, and on the rest men's minds must be left to the action of natural causes. This imperfection will be no source of weakness so long as men are in such a state of culture that one opinion does not influence another—that is, so long as they cannot put two and two together. But in the most priest-ridden states some individuals will be found who are raised above that condition. These men possess a wider sort of social feeling; they see that men in other countries and in other ages have held to very different doctrines from those which they themselves have been brought up to believe; and they cannot help seeing that it is the mere accident of their having been taught as they have, and of their having been surrounded with the manners and associations they have, that has caused them to believe as they do and not far differently. And their candor cannot resist the reflection that there is no reason to rate their own views at a higher value than those of other nations and other centuries; and this gives rise to doubts in their minds.

They will further perceive that such doubts as these must exist in their minds with reference to every belief which seems to be determined by the caprice either of themselves or of those who originated the popular opinions. The willful adherence to a belief, and the arbitrary forcing of it upon others, must, therefore, both be given up and a new method of settling opinions must be adopted, which shall not only produce an impulse to believe, but shall also decide what proposition it is which is to be believed. Let the action of natural preferences be unimpeded, then, and under their influence let men conversing together and regarding matters in different lights, gradually develop beliefs in harmony with natural causes. This method resembles that by which conceptions of art have been brought to maturity. The most perfect example of it is to be found in the history of metaphysical philosophy. Systems of this sort have not usually rested upon observed facts, at least not in any great degree. They have been chiefly adopted because their fundamental propositions seemed "agreeable to reason." This is an apt

expression; it does not mean that which agrees with experience, but that which we find ourselves inclined to believe. Plato, for example, finds it agreeable to reason that the distances of the celestial spheres from one another should be proportional to the different lengths of strings which produce harmonious chords. Many philosophers have been led to their main conclusions by considerations like this; but this is the lowest and least developed form which the method takes, for it is clear that another man might find Kepler's [earlier] theory, that the celestial spheres are proportional to the inscribed and circumscribed spheres of the different regular solids, more agreeable to *his* reason. But the shock of opinions will soon lead men to rest on preferences of a far more universal nature. Take, for example, the doctrine that man only acts selfishly—that is, from the consideration that acting in one way will afford him more pleasure than acting in another. This rests on no fact in the world, but it has had a wide acceptance as being the only reasonable theory.

This method is far more intellectual and respectable from the point of view of reason than either of the others which we have noticed. But its failure has been the most manifest. It makes of inquiry something similar to the development of taste; but taste, unfortunately, is always more or less a matter of fashion, and accordingly, metaphysicians have never come to any fixed agreement, but the pendulum has swung backward and forward between a more material and a more spiritual philosophy, from the earliest times to the latest. And so from this, which has been called the *a priori* method, we are driven, in Lord Bacon's phrase, to a true induction. We have examined into this *a priori* method as something which promised to deliver our opinions from their accidental and capricious element. But development, while it is a process which eliminates the effect of some casual circumstances, only magnifies that of others. This method, therefore, does not differ in a very essential way from that of authority. The government may not have lifted its finger to influence my convictions; I may have been left outwardly quite free to choose, we will say, between monogamy and polygamy, and appealing to my conscience only, I may have concluded that the latter practice is in itself licentious. But when I come to see that the chief obstacle to the spread of Christianity among a people of as high culture as the Hindoos has been a conviction of the immorality of our way of treating women, I cannot help seeing that, though governments do not interfere, sentiments in their development will be very greatly determined by accidental causes. Now, there are some people, among whom I must suppose that my reader is to be found, who, when they see that any belief of theirs is determined by any circumstance extraneous to the facts, will from that moment not merely admit in words that that belief is doubtful, but will experience a real doubt of it, so that it ceases in some degree at least to be a belief.

To satisfy our doubts, therefore, it is necessary that a method should be found by which our beliefs may be caused by nothing human, but by some external permanency—by something upon which our thinking has no effect. Some mystics imagine that they have such a method in a private inspiration from on high. But that is only a form of the method of tenacity, in which the conception of truth as something public is not yet developed. Our external permanency would not be external, in our sense, if it was restricted in its influence to one individual. It must be something which affects, or might affect, every man. And, though these affections are necessarily as various as are individual conditions, yet the method must be such that the ultimate conclusion of every man shall be the same, or would be the same if inquiry were sufficiently persisted in. Such is the method of science. Its fundamental hypothesis, restated in more familiar language, is this: There are real things, whose characters are entirely independent of our opinions about them; those realities affect our senses according to regular laws, and, though our sensations are as different as our relations to the objects, yet, by taking advantage of the laws of perception, we can ascertain by reasoning how things really are, and any man, if he have sufficient experience and reason enough about it, will be led to the one true conclusion. The new conception here involved is that of reality. It may be asked how I know that there are any realities. If this hypothesis is the sole support of my method of inquiry, my method of inquiry must not be used to support my hypothesis. The reply is this: (1) If investigation cannot be regarded as proving that there are real things, it at least does not lead to a contrary conclusion; but the method and the conception on which it is based remain ever in har-

mony. No doubts of the method, therefore, necessarily arise from its practice, as is the case with all the others. (2) The feeling which gives rise to any method of fixing belief is a dissatisfaction at two repugnant propositions. But here already is a vague concession that there is some *one* thing to which a proposition should conform. Nobody, therefore, can really doubt that there are realities, or, if he did, doubt would not be a source of dissatisfaction. The hypothesis, therefore, is one which every mind admits. So that the social impulse does not cause men to doubt it. (3) Everybody uses the scientific method about a great many things, and only ceases to use it when he does not know how to apply it. (4) Experience of the method has not led us to doubt it, but, on the contrary, scientific investigation has had the most wonderful triumphs in the way of settling opinion. These afford the explanation of my not doubting the method or the hypothesis which it supposes; and not having any doubt, nor believing that anybody else whom I could influence has, it would be the merest babble for me to say more about it. If there be anybody with a living doubt upon the subject, let him consider it.

To describe the method of scientific investigation is the object of this series of papers. At present I have only room to notice some points of contrast between it and other methods of fixing belief.

This is the only one of the four methods which presents any distinction of a right and a wrong way. If I adopt the method of tenacity and shut myself out from all influences, whatever I think necessary to doing this is necessary according to that method. So with the method of authority: the state may try to put down heresy by means which, from a scientific point of view, seems very ill-calculated to accomplish its purposes; but the only test *on that method* is what the state thinks, so that it cannot pursue the method wrongly. So with the *a priori* method. The very essence of it is to think as one is inclined to think. All metaphysicians will be sure to do that, however they may be inclined to judge each other to be perversely wrong. The Hegelian system recognizes every natural tendency of thought as logical, although it is certain to be abolished by countertendencies. Hegel thinks there is a regular system in the succession of these tendencies, in consequence of which, after drifting one way and the other for a long time, opinion will at last go right. And it is true that metaphysicians get the right ideas at last; Hegel's system of Nature represents tolerably the science of his day; and one may be sure that whatever scientific investigation has put out of doubt will presently receive *a priori* demonstration on the part of the metaphysicians. But with the scientific method the case is different. I may start with known and observed facts to proceed to the unknown; and yet the rules which I follow in doing so may not be such as investigation would approve. The test of whether I am truly following the method is not an immediate appeal to my feelings and purposes, but, on the contrary, itself involves the application of the method. Hence it is that bad reasoning as well as good reasoning is possible; and this fact is the foundation of the practical side of logic.

It is not to be supposed that the first three methods of settling opinion present no advantage whatever over the scientific method. On the contrary, each has some peculiar convenience of its own. The *a priori* method is distinguished for its comfortable conclusions. It is the nature of the process to adopt whatever belief we are inclined to, and there are certain flatteries to one's vanities which we all believe by nature, until we are awakened from our pleasing dream by rough facts. The method of authority will always govern the mass of mankind; and those who wield the various forms of organized force in the state will never be convinced that dangerous reasoning ought not to be suppressed in some way. If liberty of speech is to be untrammeled from the grosser forms of constraint, then uniformity of opinion will be secured by a moral terrorism to which the respectability of society will give its thorough approval. Following the method of authority is the path of peace. Certain non-conformities are permitted; certain others (considered unsafe) are forbidden. These are different in different countries and in different ages; but, wherever you are let it be known that you seriously hold a tabooed belief, and you may be perfectly sure of being treated with a cruelty no less brutal but more refined than hunting you like a wolf. Thus, the greatest intellectual benefactors of mankind have never dared, and dare not now, to utter the whole of their thought; and thus a shade of *prima facie* doubt is cast upon every proposition which is considered essential to the security of society. Singularly enough, the persecution does not all come from without; but a

man torments himself and is oftentimes most distressed at finding himself believing propositions which he has been brought up to regard with aversion. The peaceful and sympathetic man will, therefore, find it hard to resist the temptation to submit his opinions to authority. But most of all I admire the method of tenacity for its strength, simplicity, and directness. Men who pursue it are distinguished for their decision of character, which becomes very easy with such a mental rule. They do not waste time in trying to make up their minds to what they want, but, fastening like lightning upon whatever alternative comes first, they hold to it to the end, whatever happens, without an instant's irresolution. This is one of the splendid qualities which generally accompany brilliant, unlasting success. It is impossible not to envy the man who can dismiss reason, although we know how it must turn out at last.

Such are the advantages which the other methods of settling opinions have over scientific investigation. A man should consider well of them; and then he should consider that, after all, he wishes his opinions to coincide with the fact, and that there is no reason why the results of those first three methods should do so. To bring about this effect is the prerogative of the method of science. Upon such considerations he has to make his choice—a choice which is far more than the adoption of any intellectual opinion, which is one of the ruling decisions of his life, to which when once made he is bound to adhere. The force of habit will sometimes cause a man to hold on to old beliefs after he is in a condition to see that they have no sound basis. But reflection upon the state of the case will overcome these habits, and he ought to allow reflection full weight. People sometimes shrink from doing this, having an idea that beliefs are wholesome which they cannot help feeling rest on nothing. But let such persons suppose an analogous though different case from their own. Let them ask themselves what they would say to a reformed Mussulman who should hesitate to give up his old notions in regard to the relations of the sexes; or to a reformed Catholic who should still shrink from the Bible. Would they not say that these persons ought to consider the matter fully, and clearly understand the new doctrine, and then ought to embrace it in its entirety? But, above all, let it be considered that what is more wholesome than any particular belief is integrity of belief; and that to avoid looking into the support of any belief from a fear that it may turn out rotten is quite as immoral as it is disadvantageous. The person who confesses that there is such a thing as truth, which is distinguished from falsehood simply by this, that if acted on it should, on full consideration, carry us to the point we aim at and not astray, and then, though convinced of this, dares not know the truth and seeks to avoid it, is in a sorry state of mind, indeed.

Yes, the other methods do have their merits: a clear logical conscience does cost something—just as any virtue, just as all that we cherish, costs us dear. But, we should not desire it to be otherwise. The genius of a man's logical method should be loved and reverenced as his bride, whom he has chosen from all the world. He need not condemn the others; on the contrary, he may honor them deeply, and in doing so he only honors her the more. But she is the one that he has chosen, and he knows that he was right in making that choice. And having made it, he will work and fight for her, and will not complain that there are blows to take,

hoping that there may be as many and as hard to give, and will strive to be the worthy knight and champion of her from the blaze of whose splendors he draws his inspiration and his courage.

DISCUSSION QUESTIONS

1. Do you agree with Peirce's claim that for humans the truth or falsehood of a belief isn't as important as whether it can be held to securely? Why or why not? What are some examples that would verify or falsify his position?

2. How would you apply Peirce's analysis of the methods of "settling opinion" to people who belong to various kinds of cults?

3. As Peirce characterizes it, can the method of science help us settle our moral beliefs? Why or why not?

4. Is the method of authority ever a justified practice in human social life? Why or why not?

5. How would the concept of objectivity, as applied to our beliefs, fit into Peirce's account?

11. Mao Zedong (1893–1976)
"On Practice"

Mao Zedong (the Wade-Giles spelling of his name is Mao Tse Tung) was one of the original founders of the Chinese Communist Party in 1921, and for most of the rest of his life, he was its primary leader. After the Communist Party took over the government in 1949 and established the People's Republic of China, Mao became even more influential as a world leader of the communist movement. His extensive writings on revolutionary strategy, political organization, and economic policy always stressed both the practical necessity of socialist transformation in societies victimized by capitalist imperialism and the peasants' essential role in those mostly agrarian societies for the success of such radical change. In this way Mao modified some of the earlier revolutionary principles of Marx, Engels, and Lenin to fit the circumstances in China. In so doing he provided an attractive theoretical basis for a number of national liberation and anti-imperialist movements in the twentieth century.

Because of Mao's lifelong participation in political events, military conflicts, and attempts at radical socio-economic change, he was never very interested in academic philosophy and science for their own sake. As he makes clear in this essay, traditional philosophical problems, including epistemological issues, only have importance for humans insofar as they are understood and resolved in the context of concrete, practical activity. Written in 1937 during a time of civil war and Japanese invasion, "On Practice" is one of Mao's few efforts to address directly the long-standing philosophical debates surrounding the nature, functions, and criteria of knowledge and truth. Even here, however, he frames his conclusions in terms of the actual demands of specific social conditions.

QUESTIONS FOR CRITICAL READING

1. What is "social practice," according to Mao, and how is knowledge dependent on it?
2. How does Mao characterize "perceptual knowledge"?
3. What does Mao mean by "rational knowledge," and how is it related to perceptual knowledge?
4. What does Mao mean by "revolutionary practice," and how is it related to rational knowledge?
5. How does Mao distinguish the proper use of the dialectical materialist theory of knowledge from both "Rightist opportunism" and "Leftist adventurism"?

TERMS TO NOTE

class: In this context, an economic grouping of people defined not primarily in terms of income, but in terms of (a) their location in the social division of labor and (b) the extent of their ownership and control of the means of production relative to the other classes in that society.

proletariat: In a capitalist economy, the class of wage laborers who have little or no ownership or control of the means of production and yet are the primary producers of goods and services—the "working class."

Marxism: Named after the nineteenth-century German philosopher Karl Marx (see Part V, reading 59), the historicist theory that attempts to explain social life in terms of technological development and conflict between classes. It points to the future possibility of a classless, egalitarian society with no central government (a communist society).

dialectical materialism: A phrase first used by the Russian Marxist G. V. Plekhanov in 1891; since the early twentieth century it has been used to designate the Marxist-Leninist philosophy of the natural world generally and of human social life as part of nature. "Materialism" refers to the natural processes of human and nonhuman life. "Dialectical" refers to the developmental character of change, which occurs not in a merely linear fashion, but through the synthesizing interaction of and conflict between different elements.

On the Relation between Knowledge and Practice—Between Knowing and Doing

There used to be a group of doctrinaires in the Chinese Communist Party who, disregarding the experience of the Chinese revolution and denying the truth that "Marxism is not a dogma but a guide to action", for a long time bluffed people with words and phrases torn out of their context from Marxist works. There was also a group of empiricists who, for a long time clinging to their own fragmentary experience, could neither understand the importance of theory for revolutionary practice nor see the whole of the revolutionary situation, and thus worked blindly, though industriously. The Chinese revolution in 1931–4 was greatly damaged by the incorrect ideas of these two groups of comrades, particularly by those of the doctrinaires who, wearing the cloak of Marxism, misled large numbers of comrades. This article was written to expose from the viewpoint of Marxist theory of knowledge such subjectivist mistakes in the Party as doctrinairism and empiricism, especially doctrinairism. As its stress is laid on exposing doctrinaire subjectivism which belittles practice, this article is entitled "On Practice". These views were originally presented in a lecture at the Anti-Japanese Military and Political College in Yenan.

Pre-Marxist materialism could not understand the dependence of knowledge upon social practice, namely, the dependence of knowledge upon production and class struggle, because it examined the problem of knowledge apart from man's social nature, apart from his historical development.

To begin with, the Marxist regards man's productive activity as the most fundamental practical activity, as the determinant of all other activities. In his cognition man, depending mainly upon activity in material production, gradually understands nature's phenomena, nature's characteristics, nature's laws, and the relations between himself and nature; and through productive activity he also gradually acquires knowledge in varying degrees about certain human interrelations. None of such knowledge can be obtained apart from productive activity. In a classless society every person, as a member of society, joins in effort with the other members, enters into certain relations of production with them, and engages in productive activity to solve the problem of material life. In the various kinds of class society, on the other hand, members of society of all classes also enter, in different ways, into certain relations of production and engage in productive activity to solve the problem of material life. This is the primary source from which human knowledge develops.

Man's social practice is not confined to productive activity; there are many other forms of activity—class struggle, political life, scientific and artistic activity; in short, man in society participates in all spheres of practical social life. Thus in his cognition man, besides knowing things through material life, knows in varying degrees the various kinds of human interrelations through political life and cultural life (both of which are closely connected with material life). Among these the various forms of class struggle exert a particularly profound influence on the development of man's knowledge. In a class society everyone lives within the status of a particular class and every mode of thought is invariably stamped with the brand of a class.

The Marxist holds that productive activity in human society develops step by step from a lower to a higher level, and consequently man's knowledge, whether of nature or of society, also develops step by step from a lower to a higher level, that is, from the superficial to the deep and from the one-sided to the many-sided. For a very long period in history man was confined to a merely one-sided understanding of social history because, on the one hand, the biased views of the exploiting classes constantly distorted social history and, on the other, small-scale production limited man's outlook. It was only when the modern proletariat emerged along with the big forces of production (large-scale industry) that man could acquire a comprehensive, historical understanding of the development of social history and turn his knowledge of society into science, the science of Marxism.

The Marxist holds that man's social practice alone is the criterion of the truth of his knowledge of the external world. In reality, man's knowledge becomes verified only when, in the process of social practice (in the process of material production, of class struggle, and of scientific experiment), he achieves the anticipated results. If man wants to achieve success in his work, that is, to achieve the anticipated results, he must make his thoughts correspond to the laws of the objective world surrounding him; if they do not correspond, he will fail in practice. If he fails he will derive lessons from his failure, alter his ideas, so as to make them correspond to the laws of the objective world, and thus turn failure into success; this is what is meant by "failure is the mother of success", and "a fall into the pit, a gain in your wit".

The theory of knowledge of dialectical materialism raises practice to the first place, holds that human knowledge cannot be separated the least bit from practice, and repudiates all incorrect theories which deny the importance of practice or separate knowledge from practice. Thus Lenin said, "Practice is higher than (theoretical) knowledge because it has not only the virtue of universality, but also the virtue of immediate reality".[1]

Marxist philosophy, i.e. dialectical materialism, has two most outstanding characteristics: one is its class nature, its open declaration that dialectical materialism is in the service of the proletariat; the other is its practicality, its emphasis on the dependence of theory on practice, emphasis on practice as the foundation of theory which in turn serves practice. In judging the trueness of one's knowledge or theory, one cannot depend upon one's subjective feelings about it, but upon its objective result in social practice. Only social practice can be the criterion of truth. The viewpoint of practice is the first and basic viewpoint in the theory of knowledge of dialectical materialism.[2]

But how after all does human knowledge arise from practice and in turn serve practice? This becomes clear after a glance at the process of development of knowledge.

In fact man, in the process of practice, sees at the beginning only the phenomena of various things, their separate aspects, their external relations. For instance, a number of visitors come to Yenan on a tour of observation: in the first day or two, they see the topography, the streets and the houses of Yenan; meet a number of people; attend banquets, evening parties and mass meetings; hear various kinds of talk; and read various documents—all these being the phenomena of things, the separate aspects of things, the external relations between such things. This is called the perceptual stage of knowledge, namely, the stage of perceptions and impressions. That is, various things in

Yenan affect the sense organs of the members of the observation group, give rise to their perceptions, and leave on their minds many impressions, together with an idea of the general external relations between these impressions: this is the first stage of knowledge. At this stage, man cannot as yet form profound concepts or draw conclusions that conform with logic.

As social practice continues, things that give rise to man's perceptions and impressions in the course of his practice are repeated many times; then a sudden change (a leap) takes place in the process of knowledge in man's mind, resulting in concepts. Concepts as such no longer represent the phenomena of things, their separate aspects, or their external relations, but embrace their essence, their totality and their internal relations. Conception and perception are not only quantitatively but also qualitatively different. Proceeding farther and employing the method of judgment and inference, we can then draw conclusions that conform with logic. What is described in the *Tale of the Three Kingdoms* as "knitting the brows one hits upon a stratagem", or in our workaday language as "let me think it over", refers precisely to the procedure of man's manipulation of concepts in his mind to form judgments and inferences. This is the second stage of knowledge.

When our visitors, the members of the observation group, have collected various kinds of data and, furthermore, "thought them over", they can come to the following judgment: "the Communist Party's policy of the Anti-Japanese National United Front is thorough, sincere and honest". Having made this judgment, they can, if they are honest about unity for national salvation, go a step farther and draw the following conclusion: "the Anti-Japanese National United Front can succeed". In the whole process of man's knowledge of a thing, conception, judgment and inference constitute the more important stage, the stage of rational knowledge. The real task of knowledge is to arrive at thought through perception, at a gradual understanding of the internal contradictions of objective things, their laws and the internal relations of various processes, that is, at logical knowledge. To repeat, the reason why logical knowledge is different from perceptual knowledge is that perceptual knowledge concerns the separate aspects, the phenomena, the external relations of things; whereas logical knowledge takes a big

stride forward to reach the wholeness, the essence and the internal relations of things, discloses the internal contradictions of the surrounding world, and is therefore capable of grasping the development of the surrounding world in its totality, in the internal relations between all its aspects.

Such a dialectical-materialist theory of the process of development of knowledge, based on practice and proceeding from the superficial to the deep, was not put forward by anybody before the rise of Marxism. Marxist materialism for the first time correctly solved the problem of the process of development of knowledge, pointing out both materialistically and dialectically the deepening process of knowledge, the process of how perceptual knowledge turns into logical knowledge through the complex and regularly recurrent practices of production and class struggle of man in society. Lenin said: "The abstract concept of matter, of a law of nature, of economic value or any other scientific (*i.e.* correct and basic, not false or superficial) abstraction reflects nature more deeply, truly and fully."[3] Marxism-Leninism holds that the characteristics of the two stages of the process of knowledge are that, at the lower stage, knowledge appears in perceptual form, while at the higher stage it appears in logical form; but both stages belong to a single process of knowledge. Perception and reason are different in nature, but not separate from each other; they are united on the basis of practice.

Our practice proves that things perceived cannot be readily understood by us and that only things understood can be more profoundly perceived. Perception only solves the problem of phenomena; reason alone solves the problem of essence. Such problems can never be solved apart from practice. Anyone who wants to know a thing has no way of doing so except by coming into contact with it, *i.e.* by living (practising) in its surroundings.

In feudal society it was impossible to know beforehand the laws of capitalist society, because, with capitalism not yet on the scene, the corresponding practice did not exist. Marxism could only be the product of capitalist society. In the age of free, competitive capitalism, Marx could not have known specifically beforehand some of the special laws pertaining to the era of imperialism, because imperialism—the last stage of capitalism—had not yet emerged and the corresponding practice did not exist; only Lenin and Stalin could take up this task.

Apart from their genius, the reason why Marx, Engels, Lenin and Stalin could work out their theories is mainly their personal participation in the practice of the contemporary class struggle and scientific experimentation; without this no amount of genius could bring success. The saying "a scholar does not step outside his gate, yet knows all the happenings under the sun" was mere empty talk in the technologically undeveloped old times; and although this saying can be realised in the present age of technological development, yet the people with real first-hand knowledge are those engaged in practice, and only when they have obtained "knowledge" through their practice, and when their knowledge, through the medium of writing and technology, reaches the hands of the "scholar", can the "scholar" know indirectly "the happenings under the sun".

If a man wants to know certain things or certain kinds of things directly, it is only through personal participation in the practical struggle to change reality, to change those things or those kinds of things, that he can come into contact with the phenomena of those things or those kinds of things; and it is only during the practical struggle to change reality, in which he personally participates, that he can disclose the essence of those things or those kinds of things and understand them. This is the path to knowledge along which everyone actually travels, only some people, distorting things deliberately, argue to the contrary. The most ridiculous person in the world is the "wiseacre" who, having gained some half-baked knowledge by hearsay, proclaims himself "the world's number one"; this merely shows that he has not taken a proper measure of himself. The question of knowledge is one of science, and there must not be the least bit of insincerity or conceit; what is required is decidedly the reverse— a sincere and modest attitude. If you want to gain knowledge you must participate in the practice of changing reality. If you want to know the taste of a pear you must change the pear by eating it yourself. If you want to know the composition and properties of atoms you must make experiments in physics and chemistry to change the state of atoms. If you want to know the theory and methods of revolution, you must

participate in revolution. All genuine knowledge originates in direct experience. But man cannot have direct experience in everything; as a matter of fact, most of our knowledge comes from indirect experience, *e.g.* all knowledge of ancient times and foreign lands. To the ancients and foreigners, such knowledge comes from direct experience; if, as the direct experience of the ancients and foreigners, such knowledge fulfils the condition of "scientific abstraction" mentioned by Lenin, and scientifically reflects objective things, then it is reliable, otherwise it is not. Hence a man's knowledge consists of two parts and nothing else, of direct experience and indirect experience. And what is indirect experience to me is nevertheless direct experience to other people. Consequently, taking knowledge in its totality, any kind of knowledge is inseparable from direct experience.

The source of all knowledge lies in the perception through man's physical sense organs of the objective world surrounding him; if a person denies such perception, denies direct experience, and denies personal participation in the practice of changing reality, then he is not a materialist. That is why the "wiseacres" are ridiculous. The Chinese have an old saying: "How can one obtain tiger cubs without entering the tiger's lair?" This saying is true of man's practice as well as of the theory of knowledge. There can be no knowledge apart from practice.

To make clear the dialectical-materialist process of knowledge arising from the practice of changing reality—the gradually deepening process of knowledge—a few concrete examples are further given below:

In its knowledge of capitalist society in the first period of its practice—the period of machine-smashing and spontaneous struggle—the proletariat, as yet in the stage of perceptual knowledge, only knew the separate aspects and external relations of the various phenomena of capitalism. At that time the proletariat was what we call a "class in itself". But when this class reached the second period of its practice (the period of conscious, organised, economic struggle and political struggle), when through its practice, through its experiences gained in long-term struggles, and through its education in Marxist theory, which is a summing-up of these experiences by Marx and Engels according to scientific method, it came to understand the essence of capitalist society, the relations of exploitation between social classes, and its own historical task, and then became a "class for itself".

Similarly with the Chinese people's knowledge of imperialism. The first stage was one of superficial, perceptual knowledge, as shown in the indiscriminate anti-foreign struggles of the Movement of the T'aip'ing Heavenly Kingdom, the Boxer Movement, etc. It was only in the second stage that the Chinese people arrived at rational knowledge, when they saw the internal and external contradictions of imperialism, as well as the essence of the oppression and exploitation of China's broad masses by imperialism in alliance with China's compradors and feudal class; such knowledge began only about the time of the May 4 Movement of 1919.

Let us also look at war. If those who direct a war lack war experience, then in the initial stage they will not understand the profound laws for directing a particular war (*e.g.* our Agrarian Revolutionary War of the past ten years). In the initial stage they merely undergo the experience of a good deal of fighting, and what is more, suffer many defeats. But from such experience (of battles won and especially of battles lost), they are able to understand the inner thread of the whole war, namely, the laws governing that particular war, to understand strategy and tactics, and consequently they are able to direct the war with confidence. At such a time, if an inexperienced person takes over the command, he, too, cannot understand the true laws of war until after he has suffered a number of defeats (after he has gained experience).

We often hear the remark made by a comrade when he has not the courage to accept an assignment: "I have no confidence." Why has he no confidence? Because he has no systematic understanding of the nature and conditions of the work, or because he has had little or even no contact with this kind of work; hence the laws governing it are beyond him. After a detailed analysis of the nature and conditions of the work, he will feel more confident and become willing to do it. If, after doing the work for some time, this person has gained experience in it, and if moreover he is willing to look at things with an open mind and does not consider problems subjectively, one-sidedly and su-

perficially, he will be able to draw conclusions as to how to proceed with his work and his confidence will be greatly enhanced. Only those are bound to stumble who look at problems subjectively, one-sidedly and superficially and, on arriving at a place, issue orders or directives in a self-complacent manner without considering the circumstances, without viewing things in their totality (their history and their present situation as a whole), and without coming into contact with the essence of things (their qualities and the internal relations between one thing and another).

Thus the first step in the process of knowledge is contact with the things of the external world; this belongs to the stage of perception. The second step is a synthesis of the data of perception by making a rearrangement or a reconstruction; this belongs to the stage of conception, judgment and inference. It is only when the perceptual data are extremely rich (not fragmentary or incomplete) and are in correspondence to reality (not illusory) that we can, on the basis of such data, form valid concepts and carry out correct reasoning.

Here two important points must be emphasised. The first, a point which has been mentioned before, but should be repeated here, is the question of the dependence of rational knowledge upon perceptual knowledge. The person is an idealist who thinks that rational knowledge need not be derived from perceptual knowledge. In the history of philosophy there is the so-called "rationalist" school which admits only the validity of reason, but not the validity of experience, regarding reason alone as reliable and perceptual experience as unreliable; the mistake of this school consists in turning things upside down. The rational is reliable precisely because it has its source in the perceptual, otherwise it would be like water without a source or a tree without roots, something subjective, spontaneous and unreliable. As to the sequence in the process of knowledge, perceptual experience comes first; we emphasise the significance of social practice in the process of knowledge precisely because social practice alone can give rise to man's knowledge and start him on the acquisition of perceptual experience from the objective world surrounding him. For a person who shuts his eyes, stops his ears and totally cuts himself off from the objective world, there can be no knowledge to speak of. Knowledge starts with experience—this is the materialism of the theory of knowledge.

The second point is that knowledge has yet to be deepened, the perceptual stage of knowledge has yet to be developed to the rational stage—this is the dialectics of the theory of knowledge.[4] It would be a repetition of the mistake of "empiricism" in history to hold that knowledge can stop at the lower stage of perception and that perceptual knowledge alone is reliable while rational knowledge is not. This theory errs in failing to recognise that, although the data of perception reflect certain real things of the objective world (I am not speaking here of idealist empiricism which limits experience to so-called introspection), yet they are merely fragmentary and superficial, reflecting things incompletely instead of representing their essence. To reflect a thing fully in its totality, to reflect its essence and its inherent laws, it is necessary, through thinking, to build up a system of concepts and theories by subjecting the abundant perceptual data to a process of remodelling and reconstructing—discarding the crude and selecting the refined, eliminating the false and retaining the true, proceeding from one point to another, and going through the outside into the inside; it is necessary to leap from perceptual knowledge to rational knowledge. Knowledge which is such a reconstruction does not become emptier or less reliable; on the contrary, whatever has been scientifically reconstructed on the basis of practice in the process of knowledge is something which, as Lenin said, reflects objective things more deeply, more truly, more fully. As against this, the vulgar plodders, respecting experience yet despising theory, cannot take a comprehensive view of the entire objective process, lack clear direction and long-range perspective, and are self-complacent with occasional successes and peep-hole views. Were those persons to direct a revolution, they would lead it up a blind alley.

The dialectical-materialist theory of knowledge is that rational knowledge depends upon perceptual knowledge and perceptual knowledge has yet to be developed into rational knowledge. Neither "rationalism" nor "empiricism" in philosophy recognises the historical or dialectical nature of knowledge, and although each contains an aspect of truth (here I am referring to materialist rationalism and empiricism, not to idealist rationalism and empiricism), both are erroneous in the theory of knowledge as a whole. The dialectical-materialist process of knowledge from the perceptual to the rational applies to a minor process of knowledge (*e.g.* knowing a single thing or task) as well as to a major one (*e.g.* knowing a whole society or a revolution).

But the process of knowledge does not end here. The statement that the dialectical-materialist process of knowledge stops at rational knowledge, covers only half the problem. And so far as Marxist philosophy is concerned, it covers only the half that is not particularly important. What Marxist philosophy regards as the most important problem does not lie in understanding the laws of the objective world and thereby becoming capable of explaining it, but in actively changing the world by applying the knowledge of its objective laws. From the Marxist viewpoint, theory is important, and its importance is fully shown in Lenin's statement: "Without a revolutionary theory there can be no revolutionary movement."[5] But Marxism emphasises the importance of theory precisely and only because it can guide action. If we have a correct theory, but merely prate about it, pigeon-hole it, and do not put it into practice, then that theory, however good, has no significance.

Knowledge starts with practice, reaches the theoretical plane via practice, and then has to return to practice. The active function of knowledge not only manifests itself in the active leap from perceptual knowledge to rational knowledge, but also—and this is the more important—in the leap from rational knowledge to revolutionary practice. The knowledge which enables us to grasp the laws of the world must be redirected to the practice of changing the world, that is, it must again be applied in the practice of production, in the practice of the revolutionary class struggle and revolutionary national struggle, as well as in the practice of scientific experimentation. This is the process of testing and developing theory, the continuation of the whole process of knowledge.

The problem of whether theory corresponds to objective reality is not entirely solved in the process of knowledge from the perceptual to the rational as described before, nor can it be completely solved in this way. The only way of solving it completely is to re-direct rational knowledge to social practice, to apply theory to practice and see whether it can achieve the anticipated results. Many theories of natural science are considered true, not only because they were so considered when natural scientists originated them, but also because they have been verified in subsequent scientific practice. Similarly, Marxism-Leninism is considered true not only because it was so considered when Marx, Engels, Lenin and Stalin scientifically formulated it but also because it has been verified in the subsequent practice of revolutionary class struggle and revolutionary national struggle. Dialectical materialism is a universal truth because it is impossible for anyone to get away from it in his practice. The history of human knowledge tells us that the truth of many theories is incomplete and that this incompleteness is remedied only through the test of practice. Many theories are incorrect, and it is through the test of practice that their incorrectness will be rectified. This is the reason why practice is called the criterion of truth and why "the standpoint of life, of practice, should be first and fundamental in the theory of knowledge".[6] Stalin well said: "Theory becomes aimless if it is not connected with revolutionary practice, just as practice gropes in the dark if its path is not illumined by revolutionary theory."[7]

When we get to this point, is the process of knowledge completed? Our answer is: it is and yet it is not. When man in society devotes himself to the practice of changing a certain objective process at a certain stage of its development (whether changing a natural or social process), he can, by the reflection of the objective process in his thought and by the functioning of his own subjective activity, advance his knowledge from the perceptual to the rational and bring forth ideas, theories, plans or programmes which on the whole correspond to the laws of that objective process; he then puts these ideas, theories, plans or programmes into practice in the same objective process; and the process of knowledge as regards this concrete process can be considered as completed if, through the practice in that objective process, he can realise his preconceived aim, viz. if he can turn or on the whole turn these preconceived ideas, theories, plans or programmes into facts. For example, in the process of

changing nature, such as in the realisation of an engineering plan, the verification of a scientific hypothesis, the production of a utensil or instrument, the reaping of a crop; or in the process of changing society, such as in the victory of a strike, the victory of a war, the fulfilment of an educational plan—all these can be considered as the realisation of preconceived aims. But generally speaking, whether in the practice of changing nature or of changing society, people's original ideas, theories, plans or programmes are seldom realised without any change whatever. This is because people engaged in changing reality often suffer from many limitations: they are limited not only by the scientific and technological conditions, but also by the degree of development and revelation of the objective process itself (by the fact that the aspects and essence of the objective process have not yet been fully disclosed). In such a situation, ideas, theories, plans or programmes are often altered partially and sometimes even wholly along with the discovery of unforeseen circumstances during practice. That is to say, it does happen that the original ideas, theories, plans or programmes fail partially or wholly to correspond to reality and are partially or entirely incorrect. In many instances, failures have to be repeated several times before erroneous knowledge can be rectified and made to correspond to the laws of the objective process, so that subjective things can be transformed into objective things, viz. the anticipated results can be achieved in practice. But in any case, at such a point, the process of man's knowledge of a certain objective process at a certain stage of its development is regarded as completed.

As regards man's process of knowledge, however, there can be no end to it. As any process, whether in the natural or social world, advances and develops through its internal contradictions and struggles, man's process of knowledge must also advance and develop accordingly. In terms of social movement, not only must a true revolutionary leader be adept at correcting his ideas, theories, plans or programmes when they are found to be erroneous, as we have seen, but he must also, when a certain objective process has already advanced and changed from one stage of development to another, be adept at making himself and all his fellow revolutionaries advance and revise their subjective ideas accordingly, that is to say, he must propose new revolutionary tasks and new working programmes corresponding to the changes in the new situation. Situations change very rapidly in a revolutionary period; if the knowledge of revolutionaries does not change rapidly in accordance with the changed situation, they cannot lead the revolution towards victory.

It often happens, however, that ideas lag behind actual events; this is because man's knowledge is limited by a great many social conditions. We oppose the die-hards in the revolutionary ranks whose ideas, failing to advance with the changing objective circumstances, manifest themselves historically as Right opportunism. These people do not see that the struggles arising from contradictions have already pushed the objective process forward, while their knowledge has stopped at the old stage. This characterises the ideas of all die-hards. With their ideas divorced from social practice, they cannot serve to guide the chariot-wheels of society; they can only trail behind the chariot grumbling that it goes too fast, and endeavour to drag it back and make it go in the opposite direction.

We also oppose the phrase-mongering of the "Leftists". Their ideas are ahead of a given stage of development of the objective process: some of them regard their fantasies as truth; others, straining to realise at present an ideal which can only be realised in the future, divorce themselves from the practice of the majority of the people at the moment and from the realities of the day and show themselves as adventurist in their actions. Idealism and mechanistic materialism, opportunism and adventurism, are all characterised by a breach between the subjective and the objective, by the separation of knowledge from practice. The Marxist-Leninist theory of knowledge, which is distinguished by its emphasis on social practice as the criterion of scientific truth, cannot but resolutely oppose these incorrect ideologies. The Marxist recognises that in the absolute, total process of the development of the universe, the development of each concrete process is relative; hence, in the great stream of absolute truth, man's knowledge of the concrete process at each given stage of development is only relatively true. The sum total of innumerable relative truths is the absolute truth.[8]

The development of the objective process is one full of contradictions and struggles. The development of the process of man's knowledge is also one full of contradictions and struggles. All the dialectical movements of the objective world can sooner or later be reflected in man's knowledge. As the process of emergence, development and disappearance in social practice is infinite, the process of emergence, development and disappearance in human knowledge is also infinite. As the practice directed towards changing objective reality on the basis of definite ideas, theories, plans or programmes develops farther ahead each time, man's knowledge of objective reality likewise becomes deeper each time. The process of change in the objective world will never end, nor will man's knowledge of truth through practice. Marxism-Leninism has in no way summed up all knowledge of truth, but is ceaselessly opening up, through practice, the road to the knowledge of truth. Our conclusion is for the concrete and historical unity of the subjective and the objective, of theory and practice, and of knowing and doing, and against all incorrect ideologies, whether Right or "Left", which depart from concrete history. With society developed to its present stage, it is upon the shoulders of the proletariat and its party that, from historical necessity, the responsibility for correctly understanding and changing the world has fallen. This process of the practice of changing the world, determined on the basis of scientific knowledge, has already reached a historic moment in the world and in China, a moment of such importance as human history has never before witnessed, *i.e.* a moment for completely dispelling the darkness in the world and in China and bringing about such a world of light as never existed before.

The struggle of the proletariat and revolutionary people in changing the world consists in achieving the following tasks: to remould the objective world as well as their own subjective world—to remould their faculty of knowing as well as the relations between the subjective world and the objective world. Such a remoulding has already been effected in one part of the globe, namely, the Soviet Union. The people there are still expediting this remoulding process. The people of China and the rest of the world are either passing, or will pass, through such a remoulding process. And the objective world which is to be remoulded includes the opponents of remoulding, who must undergo a stage of compulsory remoulding before they can pass to a stage of conscious remoulding. When the whole of mankind consciously remoulds itself and changes the world, the era of world communism will dawn.

To discover truth through practice, and through practice to verify and develop truth. To start from perceptual knowledge and actively develop it into rational knowledge, and then, starting from rational knowledge, actively direct revolutionary practice so as to remould the subjective and the objective world. Practice, knowledge, more practice, more knowledge; the cyclical repetition of this pattern to infinity, and with each cycle, the elevation of the content of practice and knowledge to a higher level. Such is the whole of the dialectical materialist theory of knowledge, and such is the dialectical materialist theory of the unity of knowing and doing.   *July 1937.*

Notes

1. V. I. Lenin, *Philosophical Notebooks*, Russian edition, Moscow 1947, p. 185.

2. *Cf.* Karl Marx, *Theses on Feuerbach*, published as an Appendix in Frederick Engels's *Ludwig Feuerbach and the End of Classical German Philosophy*; and V. I. Lenin, *Materialism and Empirio-Criticism*, Chapter III, Section 6.

3. V. I. Lenin, *loc. cit.*, p. 146.

4. *Cf.* Lenin, *loc. cit.*, p. 146: "For the sake of knowing, one must start to know, to study, on the basis of experience and rise from experience to general knowledge."

5. V. I. Lenin, *What Is To Be Done?*

6. V. I. Lenin, *Materialism and Empirio-Criticism*, Chapter II, Section 6.

7. Joseph Stalin, *Foundations of Leninism*.

8. *Cf.* V. I. Lenin, *Materialism and Empirio-Criticism*, Chapter II, Section 5.

DISCUSSION QUESTIONS

1. How is Mao's account of the determination of truth and falsehood similar to or different from the "pragmatic theory of truth"?

2. Mao assumes that all knowledge about the world, and all inquiry, is influenced by class interests in one way or another. What are some examples that would strengthen or weaken this assumption?

3. How can Mao's views on the unity of "knowing and doing," "theory and practice," and the "subjective and objective" be applied to activities of scientists as well as political leaders today?

12. René Descartes (1596–1650)
The Quest for Rational Certainty

One of the most influential philosophers in modern history, René Descartes was born, raised, and formally educated in France. At 22, after receiving his university degrees, he decided to travel around Europe for several years (coincidentally during the time of the Thirty Years War) to learn what he could about the practical world. He eventually settled down in the Netherlands, where he lived and wrote for most of the rest of his life. During an extended visit to the Swedish court, Descartes caught pneumonia and died in 1650.

Descartes lived during a period of European history that included not only the carnage and chaos of war but also dramatic intellectual change, to which he significantly contributed. Many intellectuals were increasingly dissatisfied with the medieval approaches to knowledge and inquiry, especially about the natural world. These approaches—often referred to as scholasticism—had

dominated for centuries, and many modern thinkers sought new foundations for philosophy and the sciences. Descartes was influenced by the groundbreaking ideas of the so-called natural philosophers, such as Copernicus, Kepler, and Galileo, and their application of mathematics to questions of astronomy, physics, and mechanics. Descartes too was committed to discovering new methods for acquiring certain, or at least reliable, knowledge about as much of reality as possible.

This reading consists of the first two chapters of Descartes's most famous philosophical work, *Meditations on First Philosophy*. Here he attempts to establish just what he can know with logical certainty about himself and the world around him, while relying on nothing more than his own reason operating independently of experience. His conclusions in this investigation constitute not only a paradigm case of modern metaphysical dualism but also a historically influential version of what has become known as the rationalist position in the epistemological debate about the sources of human knowledge.

QUESTIONS FOR CRITICAL READING

1. In "Meditation I," what are the steps Descartes follows in systematically doubting all of his beliefs, and what is the point of this procedure?
2. What does Descartes mean by referring to an "evil genius," and what role does it play in his investigation?
3. In "Meditation II," what is the first undoubtable truth Descartes arrives at, and what reasoning does he use to get there?
4. What does Descartes conclude about his own essential nature, and what does this imply about the relationship between mind and body?
5. What are Descartes's conclusions regarding the piece of wax?

TERMS TO NOTE

indubitable: That which is undoubtable; for Descartes, synonymous with "certain" in its strict logical sense.

extension: In this context, the property of taking up space.

composite: Having distinct parts; the opposite of "simple."

chimera: Here, a figurative term referring to an idea or image of something unreal or fantastic.

Meditation I.

Of the things which may be brought within the sphere of the doubtful.

It is now some years since I detected how many were the false beliefs that I had from my earliest youth admitted as true, and how doubtful was everything I had since constructed on this basis; and from that time I was convinced that I must once for all seriously undertake to rid myself of all the opinions which I had formerly accepted, and commence to build anew from the foundation, if I wanted to establish any firm and permanent structure in the sciences. But as this enter-

prise appeared to be a very great one, I waited until I had attained an age so mature that I could not hope that at any later date I should be better fitted to execute my design. This reason caused me to delay so long that I should feel that I was doing wrong were I to occupy in deliberation the time that yet remains to me for action. To-day, then, since very opportunely for the plan I have in view I have delivered my mind from every care [and am happily agitated by no passions] and since I have procured for myself an assured leisure in a peaceable retirement, I shall at last seriously and freely address myself to the general upheaval of all my former opinions.

Now for this object it is not necessary that I should show that all of these are false—I shall perhaps never arrive at this end. But inasmuch as reason already persuades me that I ought no less carefully to withhold my assent from matters which are not entirely certain and indubitable than from those which appear to me manifestly to be false, if I am able to find in each one some reason to doubt, this will suffice to justify my rejecting the whole. And for that end it will not be requisite that I should examine each in particular, which would be an endless undertaking; for owing to the fact that the destruction of the foundations of necessity brings with it the downfall of the rest of the edifice, I shall only in the first place attack those principles upon which all my former opinions rested.

All that up to the present time I have accepted as most true and certain I have learned either from the senses or through the senses; but it is sometimes proved to me that these senses are deceptive, and it is wiser not to trust entirely to any thing by which we have once been deceived.

But it may be that although the senses sometimes deceive us concerning things which are hardly perceptible, or very far away, there are yet many others to be met with as to which we cannot reasonably have any doubt, although we recognise them by their means. For example, there is the fact that I am here, seated by the fire, attired in a dressing gown, having this paper in my hands and other similar matters. And how could I deny that these hands and this body are mine, were it not perhaps that I compare myself to certain persons, devoid of sense, whose cerebella are so troubled and clouded by the violent vapours of black bile, that they constantly assure us that they think they are kings when they are really quite poor, or that they are clothed in purple when they are really without covering, or who imagine that they have an earthenware head or are nothing but pumpkins or are made of glass. But they are mad, and I should not be any the less insane were I to follow examples so extravagant.

At the same time I must remember that I am a man, and that consequently I am in the habit of sleeping, and in my dreams representing to myself the same things or sometimes even less probable things, than do those who are insane in their waking moments. How often has it happened to me that in the night I dreamt that I found myself in this particular place, that I was dressed and seated near the fire, whilst in reality I was lying undressed in bed! At this moment it does indeed seem to me that it is with eyes awake that I am looking at this paper; that this head which I move is not asleep, that it is deliberately and of set purpose that I extend my hand and perceive it; what happens in sleep does not appear so clear nor so distinct as does all this. But in thinking over this I remind myself that on many occasions I have in sleep been deceived by similar illusions, and in dwelling carefully on this reflection I see so manifestly that there are no certain indications by which we may clearly distinguish wakefulness from sleep that I am lost in astonishment. And my astonishment is such that it is almost capable of persuading me that I now dream.

Now let us assume that we are asleep and that all these particulars, e.g. that we open our eyes, shake our head, extend our hands, and so on, are but false delusions; and let us reflect that possibly neither our hands nor our whole body are such as they appear to us to be. At the same time we must at least confess that the things which are represented to us in sleep are like painted representations which can only have been formed as the counterparts of something real and true, and that in this way those general things at least, i.e. eyes, a head, hands, and a whole body, are not imaginary things, but things really existent. For, as a matter of fact, painters, even when they study with the greatest skill to represent sirens and satyrs by forms the most strange and extraordinary, cannot give them natures which are entirely new, but merely make a certain medley of the members of different animals; or if their imagination is extravagant enough to invent something so novel that nothing similar has ever be-

fore been seen, and that then their work represents a thing purely fictitious and absolutely false, it is certain all the same that the colours of which this is composed are necessarily real. And for the same reason, although these general things, to wit, [a body], eyes, a head, hands, and such like, may be imaginary, we are bound at the same time to confess that there are at least some other objects yet more simple and more universal, which are real and true; and of these just in the same way as with certain real colours, all these images of things which dwell in our thoughts, whether true and real or false and fantastic, are formed.

To such a class of things pertains corporeal nature in general, and its extension, the figure of extended things, their quantity or magnitude and number, as also the place in which they are, the time which measures their duration, and so on.

That is possibly why our reasoning is not unjust when we conclude from this that Physics, Astronomy, Medicine and all other sciences which have as their end the consideration of composite things, are very dubious and uncertain; but that Arithmetic, Geometry and other sciences of that kind which only treat of things that are very simple and very general, without taking great trouble to ascertain whether they are actually existent or not, contain some measure of certainty and an element of the indubitable. For whether I am awake or asleep, two and three together always form five, and the square can never have more than four sides, and it does not seem possible that truths so clear and apparent can be suspected of any falsity [or uncertainty].

Nevertheless I have long had fixed in my mind the belief that an all-powerful God existed by whom I have been created such as I am. But how do I know that He has not brought it to pass that there is no earth, no heaven, no extended body, no magnitude, no place, and that nevertheless [I possess the perceptions of all these things and that] they seem to me to exist just exactly as I now see them? And, besides, as I sometimes imagine that others deceive themselves in the things which they think they know best, how do I know that I am not deceived every time that I add two and three, or count the sides of a square, or judge of things yet simpler, if anything simpler can be imagined? But possibly God has not desired that I should be thus deceived, for He is said to be supremely good.

If, however, it is contrary to His goodness to have made me such that I constantly deceive myself, it would also appear to be contrary to His goodness to permit me to be sometimes deceived, and nevertheless I cannot doubt that He does permit this.

There may indeed be those who would prefer to deny the existence of a God so powerful, rather than believe that all other things are uncertain. But let us not oppose them for the present, and grant that all that is here said of a God is a fable; nevertheless in whatever way they suppose that I have arrived at the state of being that I have reached—whether they attribute it to fate or to accident, or make out that it is by a continual succession of antecedents, or by some other method—since to err and deceive oneself is a defect, it is clear that the greater will be the probability of my being so imperfect as to deceive myself ever, as is the Author to whom they assign my origin the less powerful. To these reasons I have certainly nothing to reply, but at the end I feel constrained to confess that there is nothing in all that I formerly believed to be true, of which I cannot in some measure doubt, and that not merely through want of thought or through levity, but for reasons which are very powerful and maturely considered; so that henceforth I ought not the less carefully to refrain from giving credence to these opinions than to that which is manifestly false, if I desire to arrive at any certainty [in the sciences].

But it is not sufficient to have made these remarks, we must also be careful to keep them in mind. For these ancient and commonly held opinions still revert frequently to my mind, long and familiar custom having given them the right to occupy my mind against my inclination and rendered them almost masters of my belief; nor will I ever lose the habit of deferring to them or of placing my confidence in them, so long as I consider them as they really are, i.e. opinions in some measure doubtful, as I have just shown, and at the same time highly probable, so that there is much more reason to believe in than to deny them. That is why I consider that I shall not be acting amiss, if, taking of set purpose a contrary belief, I allow myself to be deceived, and for a certain time pretend that all these opinions are entirely false and imaginary, until at last, having thus balanced my former prejudices with my latter [so that they cannot divert my opinions more to one side than to the other], my judgment will no longer be dominated by bad usage or turned away from the right knowledge of the truth. For I am assured that there can be neither peril nor error in this course, and that I cannot at present yield too much to distrust, since I am not considering the question of action, but only of knowledge.

I shall then suppose, not that God who is supremely good and the fountain of truth, but some evil genius not less powerful than deceitful, has employed his whole energies in deceiving me; I shall consider that the heavens, the earth, colours, figures, sound, and all other external things are nought but the illusions and dreams of which this genius has availed himself in order to lay traps for my credulity; I shall consider myself as having no hands, no eyes, no flesh, no blood, nor any senses, yet falsely believing myself to possess all these things; I shall remain obstinately attached to this idea, and if by this means it is not in my power to arrive at the knowledge of any truth, I may at least do what is in my power [i.e. suspend my judgment], and with firm purpose avoid giving credence to any false thing, or being imposed upon by this arch deceiver, however powerful and deceptive he may be. But this task is a laborious one, and insensibly a certain lassitude leads me into the course of my ordinary life. And just as a captive who in sleep enjoys an imaginary liberty, when he begins to suspect that his liberty is but a dream, fears to awaken, and conspires with these agreeable illusions that the deception may be prolonged, so insensibly of my own accord I fall back into my former opinions, and I dread awakening from this slumber, lest the laborious wakefulness which would follow the tranquillity of this repose should have to be spent not in daylight, but in the excessive darkness of the difficulties which have just been discussed.

Meditation II.

Of the Nature of the Human Mind; and that it is more easily known than the Body.

The Meditation of yesterday filled my mind with so many doubts that it is no longer in my power to forget them. And yet I do not see in what manner I can resolve them; and, just as if I had all of a sudden fallen into very deep water, I am so disconcerted that I can neither make certain of setting my feet on the bottom, nor can I swim and so support myself on the surface. I shall nevertheless make an effort and follow anew the same path as that on which I yesterday entered, i.e. I shall proceed by setting aside all that in which the least doubt could be supposed to exist, just as if I had discovered that it was absolutely false; and I shall ever follow in this road until I have met with something which is certain, or at least, if I can do nothing else, until I have learned for certain that there is nothing in the world that is certain. Archimedes, in order that he might draw the terrestrial globe out of its place, and transport it elsewhere, demanded only that one point should be fixed and immoveable; in the same way I shall have the right to conceive high hopes if I am happy enough to discover one thing only which is certain and indubitable.

I suppose, then, that all the things that I see are false; I persuade myself that nothing has ever existed of all that my fallacious memory represents to me. I consider that I possess no senses; I imagine that body, figure, extension, movement and place are but the fictions of my mind. What, then, can be esteemed as true? Perhaps nothing at all, unless that there is nothing in the world that is certain.

But how can I know there is not something different from those things that I have just considered, of which one cannot have the slightest doubt? Is there not some God, or some other being by whatever name we call it, who puts these reflections into my mind? That is not necessary, for is it not possible that I am capable of producing them myself? I myself, am I not at least something? But I have already denied that I had senses and body. Yet I hesitate, for what follows from that? Am I so dependent on body and senses that I cannot exist without these? But I was persuaded that there was nothing in all the world, that there was no heaven, no earth, that there were no minds, nor any bodies: was I not then likewise persuaded that I did not exist? Not at all; of a surety I myself did exist since I persuaded myself of something [or merely because I thought of something]. But there is some deceiver or other, very powerful and very cunning, who ever employs his ingenuity in deceiving me. Then without doubt I exist also if he deceives me, and let him deceive me as much as he will, he can never cause me to be nothing so long as I think that I am something. So that after having reflected well and carefully examined all things, we must come to the definite conclusion that this proposition: I am, I exist, is necessarily true each time that I pronounce it, or that I mentally conceive it.

But I do not yet know clearly enough what I am, I who am certain that I am; and hence I must be careful to see that I do not imprudently take some other object in place of myself, and thus that I do not go astray in respect of this knowledge that I hold to be the most certain and most evident of all that I have formerly learned. That is why I shall now consider anew what I believed myself to be before I embarked upon these last reflections; and of my former opinions I shall withdraw all that might even in a small degree be invalidated by the reasons which I have just brought forward, in order that there may be nothing at all left beyond what is absolutely certain and indubitable.

What then did I formerly believe myself to be? Undoubtedly I believed myself to be a man. But what is a man? Shall I say a reasonable animal? Certainly not; for then I should have to inquire what an animal is, and what is reasonable; and thus from a single question I should insensibly fall into an infinitude of others more difficult; and I should not wish to waste the little time and leisure remaining to me in trying to unravel subtleties like these. But I shall rather stop here to consider the thoughts which of themselves spring up in my mind, and which were not inspired by anything beyond my own nature alone when I applied myself to the consideration of my being. In the first place, then, I considered myself as having a face, hands, arms, and all that system of members composed of bones and flesh as seen in a corpse which I designated by the name of body. In addition to this I considered that I was nourished, that I walked, that I felt, and that I thought, and I referred all these actions to the soul: but I did not stop to consider what the soul was, or if I did stop, I imagined that it was something extremely rare and subtle like a wind, a flame, or an ether, which was spread throughout my grosser parts. As to body I had no manner of doubt about its nature, but thought I had a very clear knowledge of it; and if I had desired to explain it according to the notions that I had then formed of it, I should have described it thus: By the body I understand all that which can be defined by a certain figure: something which can be confined in a certain place, and which can fill a given space in such a way that every other body will be excluded from it; which can be perceived either by touch, or by sight, or by hearing, or by taste, or by smell: which can be moved in many ways not, in truth, by itself, but by something which is foreign to it, by which it is touched [and from which it receives impressions]: for to have the power of self-movement, as also of feeling or of thinking, I did not consider to appertain to the nature of body: on the contrary, I was rather astonished to find that faculties similar to them existed in some bodies.

But what am I, now that I suppose that there is a certain genius which is extremely powerful, and, if I may say so, malicious, who employs all his powers in deceiving me? Can I affirm that I possess the least of all those things which I have just said pertain to the nature of body? I pause to consider, I revolve all these things in my mind, and I find none of which I can say that it pertains to me. It would be tedious to stop to enumerate them. Let us pass to the attributes of soul and see if there is any one which is in me? What of nutrition or walking [the first mentioned]? But if it is so that I have no body it is also true that I can neither walk nor take nourishment. Another attribute is sensation. But one cannot feel without body, and besides I have thought I perceived many things during sleep that I recognised in my waking moments as not having been experienced at all. What of thinking? I find here that thought is an attribute that belongs to me; it alone cannot be separated from me. I am, I exist, that is certain. But how often? Just when I think; for it might possibly be the case if I ceased entirely to think, that I should likewise cease altogether to exist. I do not now admit anything which is not necessarily true: to speak accurately I am not more than a thing which thinks, that is to say a mind or a soul, or an understanding, or a reason, which are terms whose significance was formerly unknown to me. I am, however, a real thing and really exist; but what thing? I have answered: a thing which thinks.

And what more? I shall exercise my imagination [in order to see if I am not something more]. I am not a collection of members which we call the human body: I am not a subtle air distributed through these members, I am not a wind, a fire, a vapour, a breath, nor anything at all which I can imagine or conceive; be-

cause I have assumed that all these were nothing. Without changing that supposition I find that I only leave myself certain of the fact that I am somewhat. But perhaps it is true that these same things which I supposed were non-existent because they are unknown to me, are really not different from the self which I know. I am not sure about this, I shall not dispute about it now; I can only give judgment on things that are known to me. I know that I exist, and I inquire what I am, I whom I know to exist. But it is very certain that the knowledge of my existence taken in its precise significance does not depend on things whose existence is not yet known to me; consequently it does not depend on those which I can feign in imagination. And indeed the very term *feign* in imagination[1] proves to me my error, for I really do this if I image myself a something, since to imagine is nothing else than to contemplate the figure or image of a corporeal thing. But I already know for certain that I am, and that it may be that all these images, and, speaking generally, all things that relate to the nature of body are nothing but dreams [and chimeras]. For this reason I see clearly that I have as little reason to say, 'I shall stimulate my imagination in order to know more distinctly what I am,' than if I were to say, 'I am now awake, and I perceive somewhat that is real and true: but because I do not yet perceive it distinctly enough, I shall go to sleep of express purpose, so that my dreams may represent the perception with greatest truth and evidence.' And, thus, I know for certain that nothing of all that I can understand by means of my imagination belongs to this knowledge which I have of myself, and that it is necessary to recall the mind from this mode of thought with the utmost diligence in order that it may be able to know its own nature with perfect distinctness.

But what then am I? A thing which thinks. What is a thing which thinks? It is a thing which doubts, understands, [conceives], affirms, denies, wills, refuses, which also imagines and feels.

Certainly it is no small matter if all these things pertain to my nature. But why should they not so pertain? Am I not that being who now doubts nearly

---

1. Or 'form an image' (effingo).

everything, who nevertheless understands certain things, who affirms that one only is true, who denies all the others, who desires to know more, is averse from being deceived, who imagines many things, sometimes indeed despite his will, and who perceives many likewise, as by the intervention of the bodily organs? Is there nothing in all this which is as true as it is certain that I exist, even though I should always sleep and though he who has given me being employed all his ingenuity in deceiving me? Is there likewise any one of these attributes which can be distinguished from my thought, or which might be said to be separated from myself? For it is so evident of itself that it is I who doubts, who understands, and who desires, that there is no reason here to add anything to explain it. And I have certainly the power of imagining likewise; for although it may happen (as I formerly supposed) that none of the things which I imagine are true, nevertheless this power of imagining does not cease to be really in use, and it forms part of my thought. Finally, I am the same who feels, that is to say, who perceives certain things, as by the organs of sense, since in truth I see light, I hear noise, I feel heat. But it will be said that these phenomena are false and that I am dreaming. Let it be so; still it is at least quite certain that it seems to me that I see light, that I hear noise and that I feel heat. That cannot be false; properly speaking it is what is in me called feeling[2]; and used in this precise sense that is no other thing than thinking.

From this time I begin to know what I am with a little more clearness and distinction than before; but nevertheless it still seems to me, and I cannot prevent myself from thinking, that corporeal things, whose images are framed by thought, which are tested by the senses, are much more distinctly known than that obscure part of me which does not come under the imagination. Although really it is very strange to say that I know and understand more distinctly these things whose existence seems to me dubious, which are unknown to me, and which do not belong to me, than others of the truth of which I am convinced, which are known to me and which pertain to my real nature, in

a word, than myself. But I see clearly how the case stands: my mind loves to wander, and cannot yet suffer itself to be retained within the just limits of truth. Very good, let us once more give it the freest rein, so that, when afterwards we seize the proper occasion for pulling up, it may the more easily be regulated and controlled.

Let us begin by considering the commonest matters, those which we believe to be the most distinctly comprehended, to wit, the bodies which we touch and see; not indeed bodies in general, for these general ideas are usually a little more confused, but let us consider one body in particular. Let us take, for example, this piece of wax: it has been taken quite freshly from the hive, and it has not yet lost the sweetness of the honey which it contains; it still retains somewhat of the odour of the flowers from which it has been culled; its colour, its figure, its size are apparent; it is hard, cold, easily handled, and if you strike it with the finger, it will emit a sound. Finally all the things which are requisite to cause us distinctly to recognise a body, are met with in it. But notice that while I speak and approach the fire what remained of the taste is exhaled, the smell evaporates, the colour alters, the figure is destroyed, the size increases, it becomes liquid, it heats, scarcely can one handle it, and when one strikes it, no sound is emitted. Does the same wax remain after this change? We must confess that it remains; none would judge otherwise. What then did I know so distinctly in this piece of wax? It could certainly be nothing of all that the senses brought to my notice, since all these things which fall under taste, smell, sight, touch, and hearing, are found to be changed, and yet the same wax remains.

Perhaps it was what I now think, viz. that this wax was not that sweetness of honey, nor that agreeable scent of flowers, nor that particular whiteness, nor that figure, nor that sound, but simply a body which a little while before appeared to me as perceptible under these forms, and which is now perceptible under others. But what, precisely, is it that I imagine when I form such conceptions? Let us attentively consider this, and, abstracting from all that does not belong to the wax, let us see what remains. Certainly nothing remains excepting a certain extended thing which is flexible and movable. But what is the meaning of flexible and

---

2. Sentire.

movable? Is it not that I imagine that this piece of wax being round is capable of becoming square and of passing from a square to a triangular figure? No, certainly it is not that, since I imagine it admits of an infinitude of similar changes, and I nevertheless do not know how to compass the infinitude by my imagination, and consequently this conception which I have of the wax is not brought about by the faculty of imagination. What now is this extension? Is it not also unknown? For it becomes greater when the wax is melted, greater when it is boiled, and greater still when the heat increases; and I should not conceive [clearly] according to truth what wax is, if I did not think that even this piece that we are considering is capable of receiving more variations in extension than I have ever imagined. We must then grant that I could not even understand through the imagination what this piece of wax is, and that it is my mind[3] alone which perceives it. I say this piece of wax in particular, for as to wax in general it is yet clearer. But what is this piece of wax which cannot be understood excepting by the [understanding or] mind? It is certainly the same that I see, touch, imagine, and finally it is the same which I have always believed it to be from the beginning. But what must particularly be observed is that its perception is neither an act of vision, nor of touch, nor of imagination, and has never been such although it may have appeared formerly to be so, but only an intuition[4] of the mind, which may be imperfect and confused as it was formerly, or clear and distinct as it is at present, according as my attention is more or less directed to the elements which are found in it, and of which it is composed.

Yet in the meantime I am greatly astonished when I consider [the great feebleness of mind] and its proneness to fall [insensibly] into error; for although without giving expression to my thoughts I consider all this in my own mind, words often impede me and I am almost deceived by the terms of ordinary language. For we say that we see the same wax, if it is present, and not that we simply judge that it is the same from its having the same colour and figure. From

this I should conclude that I knew the wax by means of vision and not simply by the intuition of the mind; unless by chance I remember that, when looking from a window and saying I see men who pass in the street, I really do not see them, but infer that what I see is men, just as I say that I see wax. And yet what do I see from the window but hats and coats which may cover automatic machines? Yet I judge these to be men. And similarly solely by the faculty of judgment which rests in my mind, I comprehend that which I believed I saw with my eyes.

A man who makes it his aim to raise his knowledge above the common should be ashamed to derive the occasion for doubting from the forms of speech invented by the vulgar; I prefer to pass on and consider whether I had a more evident and perfect conception of what the wax was when I first perceived it, and when I believed I knew it by means of the external senses or at least by the common sense[5] as it is called, that is to say by the imaginative faculty, or whether my present conception is clearer now that I have most carefully examined what it is, and in what way it can be known. It would certainly be absurd to doubt as to this. For what was there in this first perception which was distinct? What was there which might not as well have been perceived by any of the animals? But when I distinguish the wax from its external forms, and when, just as if I had taken from it its vestments, I consider it quite naked, it is certain that although some error may still be found in my judgment, I can nevertheless not perceive it thus without a human mind.

But finally what shall I say of this mind, that is, of myself, for up to this point I do not admit in myself anything but mind? What then, I who seem to perceive this piece of wax so distinctly, do I not know myself, not only with much more truth and certainty, but also with much more distinctness and clearness? For if I judge that the wax is or exists from the fact that I see it, it certainly follows much more clearly that I am or that I exist myself from the fact that I see it. For it may be that what I see is not really wax, it may also be that I do not possess eyes with which to see anything; but it cannot be that when I see, or (for I no longer take

---

3. entendement F., mens L.
4. inspectio.

5. sensus communis.

account of the distinction) when I think I see, that I myself who think am nought. So if I judge that the wax exists from the fact that I touch it, the same thing will follow, to wit, that I am; and if I judge that my imagination, or some other cause, whatever it is, persuades me that the wax exists, I shall still conclude the same. And what I have here remarked of wax may be applied to all other things which are external to me [and which are met with outside of me]. And further, if the [notion or] perception of wax has seemed to me clearer and more distinct, not only after the sight or the touch, but also after many other causes have rendered it quite manifest to me, with how much more [evidence] and distinctness must it be said that I now know myself, since all the reasons which contribute to the knowledge of wax, or any other body whatever, are yet better proofs of the nature of my mind! And there are so many other things in the mind itself which may contribute to the elucidation of its nature, that those which depend on body such as these just mentioned, hardly merit being taken into account.

But finally here I am, having insensibly reverted to the point I desired, for, since it is now manifest to me that even bodies are not properly speaking known by the senses or by the faculty of imagination, but by the understanding only, and since they are not known

from the fact that they are seen or touched, but only because they are understood, I see clearly that there is nothing which is easier for me to know than my mind. But because it is difficult to rid oneself so promptly of an opinion to which one was accustomed for so long, it will be well that I should halt a little at this point, so that by the length of my meditation I may more deeply imprint on my memory this new knowledge.

DISCUSSION QUESTIONS

1. Descartes's thought experiment assumes that he can start out in his philosophical inquiry with no preconceptions or assumptions about himself or his surrounding world. Does he really pull this off, and is this possible for anybody? Why or why not?

2. Do you agree with Descartes's conclusions about the essence of the self? Why or why not?

3. Concerning our knowledge about ourselves, physical phenomena, and divine beings, can we really do without sensory experience? Give examples to show how this is or is not possible.

4. Can we adequately explain the natural world solely on the basis of the laws of mechanics, algebra, and geometry, as Descartes implies? Why or why not?

13. John Locke (1632–1704)
Experience as the Basis of Knowledge

John Locke was an English philosopher and physician who was active in the political and scientific affairs of his time, largely through his association with the first Earl of Shaftesbury. Locke's significance for subsequent Western history is the result of both his political writings and his epistemological work. He wrote *Second Treatise of Government* (published anonymously for political reasons in 1689) during the height of the parliamentary struggles with the English monarchy that culminated in the revolution of 1688. In that essay he advocated a constitutional state based on the consent of the citizenry, as well as the right of a people to overthrow its government and establish a new one if circum-

stances warranted it. These ideas, very radical at the time, strongly influenced many of those involved in the effort to establish democratic republics in France and America toward the end of the next century.

On the other hand, the reading here is from Locke's major work in epistemology, *An Essay Concerning Human Understanding* (published under his own name, also in 1689). In it he carries out what seems to us today as much an exercise in descriptive psychology as a systematic philosophical analysis of how humans acquire knowledge. Locke argues that the foundation of all knowledge is experience and that reason by itself can generate nothing without experiential material upon which to operate. His extensive investigations attempting to verify this empiricist position and draw out its implications made him one of its most famous philosophical representatives of the modern age as well as one of the most influential critics of rationalism.

QUESTIONS FOR CRITICAL READING

1. According to Locke, what are the two sources of all our ideas, which of the two is primary, and what does all this have to do with knowledge?
2. How does Locke deal with the question of whether or not the soul is always perceiving something?
3. How do Locke's observations about children provide evidence for his conclusions?
4. What is the difference between a "simple idea" and a "complex idea"?

———

1. Every man being conscious to himself that he thinks; and that which his mind is applied about whilst thinking being the *ideas* that are there, it is past doubt that men have in their minds several ideas,—such as are those expressed by the words *whiteness, hardness, sweetness, thinking, motion, man, elephant, army, drunkenness,* and others: it is in the first place then to be inquired, *How he comes by them?*

I know it is a received doctrine, that men have native ideas, and original characters, stamped upon their minds in their very first being. This opinion I have at large examined already; and, I suppose what I have said in the foregoing Book will be much more easily admitted, when I have shown whence the understanding may get all the ideas it has; and by what ways and degrees they may come into the mind;—for which I shall appeal to every one's own observation and experience.

2. Let us then suppose the mind to be, as we say, white paper, void of all characters, without any ideas:—How comes it to be furnished? Whence comes it by that vast store which the busy and boundless fancy of man has painted on it with an almost endless variety? Whence has it all the *materials* of reason and knowledge? To this I answer, in one word, from EXPERIENCE. In that all our knowledge is founded; and

from that it ultimately derives itself. Our observation employed either, about external sensible objects, or about the internal operations of our minds perceived and reflected on by ourselves, is that which supplies our understandings with all the *materials* of thinking. These two are the fountains of knowledge, from whence all the ideas we have, or can naturally have, do spring.

3. First, our Senses, conversant about particular sensible objects, do convey into the mind several distinct perceptions of things, according to those various ways wherein those objects do affect them. And thus we come by those *ideas* we have of *yellow, white, heat, cold, soft, hard, bitter, sweet,* and all those which we call sensible qualities; which when I say the senses convey into the mind, I mean, they from external objects convey into the mind what produces there those perceptions. This great source of most of the ideas we have, depending wholly upon our senses, and derived by them to the understanding, I call SENSATION.

4. Secondly, the other fountain from which experience furnisheth the understanding with ideas is,—the perception of the operations of our own mind within us, as it is employed about the ideas it has got;—which operations, when the soul comes to reflect on and consider, do furnish the understanding with another set of ideas, which could not be had from things without. And such are *perception, thinking, doubting, believing, reasoning, knowing, willing,* and all the different actings of our own minds;—which we being conscious of, and observing in ourselves, do from these receive into our understandings as distinct ideas as we do from bodies affecting our senses. This source of ideas every man has wholly in himself; and though it be not sense, as having nothing to do with external objects, yet it is very like it, and might properly enough be called *internal sense.* But as I call the other Sensation, so I call this REFLECTION, the ideas it affords being such only as the mind gets by reflecting on its own operations within itself. By reflection then, in the following part of this discourse, I would be understood to mean, that notice which the mind takes of its own operations, and the manner of them, by reason whereof there come to be ideas of these operations in the understanding. These two, I say, viz. external material things, as the objects of SENSATION, and the op-

erations of our own minds within, as the objects of REFLECTION, are to me the only originals from whence all our ideas take their beginnings. The term *operations* here I use in a large sense, as comprehending not barely the actions of the mind about its ideas, but some sort of passions arising sometimes from them, such as is the satisfaction or uneasiness arising from any thought.

5. The understanding seems to me not to have the least glimmering of any ideas which it doth not receive from one of these two. *External objects* furnish the mind with the ideas of sensible qualities, which are all those different perceptions they produce in us; and *the mind* furnishes the understanding with ideas of its own operations.

These, when we have taken a full survey of them, and their several modes, [combinations, and relations,] we shall find to contain all our whole stock of ideas; and that we have nothing in our minds which did not come in one of these two ways. Let any one examine his own thoughts, and thoroughly search into his understanding; and then let him tell me, whether all the original ideas he has there, are any other than of the objects of his senses, or of the operations of his mind, considered as objects of his reflection. And how great a mass of knowledge soever he imagines to be lodged there, he will, upon taking a strict view, see that he has not any idea in his mind but what one of these two have imprinted;—though perhaps, with infinite variety compounded and enlarged by the understanding, as we shall see hereafter.

6. He that attentively considers the state of a child, at his first coming into the world, will have little reason to think him stored with plenty of ideas, that are to be the matter of his future knowledge. It is *by degrees* he comes to be furnished with them. And though the ideas of obvious and familiar qualities imprint themselves before the memory begins to keep a register of time or order, yet it is often so late before some unusual qualities come in the way, that there are few men that cannot recollect the beginning of their acquaintance with them. And if it were worth while, no doubt a child might be so ordered as to have but a very few, even of the ordinary ideas, till he were grown up to a man. But all that are born into the world, being surrounded with bodies that perpetually and diversely affect them, variety of ideas, whether care be taken of it

or not, are imprinted on the minds of children. Light and colours are busy at hand everywhere, when the eye is but open; sounds and some tangible qualities fail not to solicit their proper senses, and force an entrance to the mind;—but yet, I think, it will be granted easily, that if a child were kept in a place where he never saw any other but black and white till he were a man, he would have no more ideas of scarlet or green, than he that from his childhood never tasted an oyster, or a pine-apple, has of those particular relishes.

7. Men then come to be furnished with fewer or more simple ideas from without, according as the objects they converse with afford greater or less variety; and from the operations of their minds within, according as they more or less reflect on them. For, though he that contemplates the operations of his mind, cannot but have plain and clear ideas of them; yet, unless he turn his thoughts that way, and considers them *attentively,* he will no more have clear and distinct ideas of all the operations of his mind, and all that may be observed therein, than he will have all the particular ideas of any landscape, or of the parts and motions of a clock, who will not turn his eyes to it, and with attention heed all the parts of it. The picture, or clock may be so placed, that they may come in his way every day; but yet he will have but a confused idea of all the parts they are made up of, till he applies himself with attention, to consider them each in particular.

8. And hence we see the reason why it is pretty late before most children get ideas of the operations of their own minds; and some have not any very clear or perfect ideas of the greatest part of them all their lives. Because, though they pass there continually, yet, like floating visions, they make not deep impressions enough to leave in their mind clear, distinct, lasting ideas, till the understanding turns inward upon itself, reflects on its own operations, and makes them the objects of its own contemplation. Children [when they come first into it, are surrounded with a world of new things, which, by a constant solicitation of their senses, draw the mind constantly to them; forward to take notice of new, and apt to be delighted with the variety of changing objects. Thus the first years are usually employed and diverted in looking abroad. Men's business in them is to acquaint themselves with what is to be found without;] and so growing up in a constant

attention to outward sensations, seldom make any considerable reflection on what passes within them, till they come to be of riper years; and some scarce ever at all.

9. To ask, at what *time* a man has first any ideas, is to ask, when he begins to perceive;—*having ideas,* and *perception,* being the same thing. I know it is an opinion, that the soul always thinks, and that it has the actual perception of ideas in itself constantly, as long as it exists; and that actual thinking is as inseparable from the soul as actual extension is from the body; which if true, to inquire after the beginning of a man's ideas is the same as to inquire after the beginning of his soul. For, by this account, soul and its ideas, as body and its extension, will begin to exist both at the same time.

10. But whether the soul be supposed to exist antecedent to, or coeval with, or some time after the first rudiments of organization, or the beginnings of life in the body, I leave to be disputed by those who have better thought of that matter. I confess myself to have one of those dull souls, that doth not perceive itself always to contemplate ideas; nor can conceive it any more necessary for the soul always to think, than for the body always to move: the perception of ideas being (as I conceive) to the soul, what motion is to the body; not its essence, but one of its operations. And therefore, though thinking be supposed never so much the proper action of the soul, yet it is not necessary to suppose that it should be always thinking, always in action. That, perhaps, is the privilege of the infinite Author and Preserver of all things, who 'never slumbers nor sleeps'; but is not competent to any finite being, at least not to the soul of man. We know certainly, by experience, that we *sometimes* think; and thence draw this infallible consequence,—that there is something in us that has a power to think. But whether that substance *perpetually* thinks or no, we can be no further assured than experience informs us. For, to say that actual thinking is essential to the soul, and inseparable from it, is to beg what is in question, and not to prove it by reason;—which is necessary to be done, if it be not a self-evident proposition. But whether this, 'That the soul always thinks,' be a self-evident proposition, that everybody assents to at first hearing, I appeal to mankind. [It is doubted whether I thought at

all last night or no. The question being about a matter of fact, it is begging it to bring, as a proof for it, an hypothesis, which is the very thing in dispute: by which way one may prove anything, and it is but supposing that all watches, whilst the balance beats, think, and it is sufficiently proved, and past doubt, that my watch thought all last night. But he that would not deceive himself, ought to build his hypothesis on matter of fact, and make it out by sensible experience, and not presume on matter of fact, because of his hypothesis, that is, because he supposes it to be so; which way of proving amounts to this, that I must necessarily think all last night, because another supposes I always think, though I myself cannot perceive that I always do so.

But men in love with their opinions may not only suppose what is in question, but allege wrong matter of fact. How else could any one make it an inference of mine, that a thing is not, because we are not sensible of it in our sleep? I do not say there is no *soul* in a man, because he is not sensible of it in his sleep; but I do say, he cannot *think* at any time, waking or sleeping, without being sensible of it. Our being sensible of it is not necessary to anything but to our thoughts; and to them it is; and to them it always will be necessary, till we can think without being conscious of it.] . . .

20. I see no reason, therefore, to believe that the soul thinks before the senses have furnished it with ideas to think on; and as those are increased and retained, so it comes, by exercise, to improve its faculty of thinking in the several parts of it; as well as, afterwards, by compounding those ideas, and reflecting on its own operations, it increases its stock, as well as facility in remembering, imagining, reasoning, and other modes of thinking.

21. He that will suffer himself to be informed by observation and experience, and not make his own hypothesis the rule of nature, will find few signs of a soul accustomed to much thinking in a new-born child, and much fewer of any reasoning at all. And yet it is hard to imagine that the rational soul should think so much, and not reason at all. And he that will consider that infants newly come into the world spend the greatest part of their time in sleep, and are seldom awake but when either hunger calls for the teat, or

some pain (the most importunate of all sensations), or some other violent impression on the body, forces the mind to perceive and attend to it;—he, I say, who considers this, will perhaps find reason to imagine that a *fœtus* in the mother's womb differs not much from the state of a vegetable, but passes the greatest part of its time without perception or thought; doing very little but sleep in a place where it needs not seek for food, and is surrounded with liquor, always equally soft, and near of the same temper; where the eyes have no light, and the ears so shut up are not very susceptible of sounds; and where there is little or no variety, or change of objects, to move the senses.

22. Follow a child from its birth, and observe the alterations that time makes, and you shall find, as the mind by the senses comes more and more to be furnished with ideas, it comes to be more and more awake; thinks more, the more it has matter to think on. After some time it begins to know the objects which, being most familiar with it, have made lasting impressions. Thus it comes by degrees to know the persons it daily converses with, and distinguishes them from strangers; which are instances and effects of its coming to retain and distinguish the ideas the senses convey to it. And so we may observe how the mind, *by degrees,* improves in these; and *advances* to the exercise of those other faculties of enlarging, compounding, and abstracting its ideas, and of reasoning about them, and reflecting upon all these; of which I shall have occasion to speak more hereafter.

23. If it shall be demanded then, *when* a man *begins* to have any ideas, I think the true answer is,—*when he first has any sensation.* For, since there appear not to be any ideas in the mind before the senses have conveyed any in, I conceive that ideas in the understanding are coeval with *sensation; which is such an impression or motion made in some part of the body, as [produces some perception]* in the understanding. [It is about these impressions made on our senses by outward objects that the mind seems *first* to employ itself, in such operations as we call perception, remembering, consideration, reasoning, &c.]

24. [In time the mind comes to reflect on its own operations about the ideas got by sensation, and thereby stores itself with a new set of ideas, which I call ideas of reflection. These are the impressions that

are made on our senses by outward objects that are extrinsical to the mind; and its own operations, proceeding from powers intrinsical and proper to itself, which, when reflected on by itself, become also objects of its contemplation—are, as I have said, the original of all knowledge.] Thus the first capacity of human intellect is,—that the mind is fitted to receive the impressions made on it; either through the senses by outward objects, or by its own operations when it reflects on them. This is the first step a man makes towards the discovery of anything, and the groundwork whereon to build all those notions which ever he shall have naturally in this world. All those sublime thoughts which tower above the clouds, and reach as high as heaven itself, take their rise and footing here: in all that great extent wherein the mind wanders, in those remote speculations it may seem to be elevated with, it stirs not one jot beyond those ideas which *sense* or *reflection* have offered for its contemplation.

25. In this part the understanding is merely passive; and whether or no it will have these beginnings, and as it were materials of knowledge, is not in its own power. For the objects of our senses do, many of them, obtrude their particular ideas upon our minds whether we will or not; and the operations of our minds will not let us be without, at least, some obscure notions of them. No man can be wholly ignorant of what he does when he thinks. These simple ideas, when offered to the mind, the understanding can no more refuse to have, nor alter when they are imprinted, nor blot them out and make new ones itself, than a mirror can refuse, alter, or obliterate the images or ideas which the objects set before it do therein produce. As the bodies that surround us do diversely affect our organs, the mind is forced to receive the impressions; and cannot avoid the perception of those ideas that are annexed to them. . . .

Of Simple Ideas.

1. The better to understand the nature, manner, and extent of our knowledge, one thing is carefully to be observed concerning the ideas we have; and that is, that some of them are *simple* and some *complex.*

Though the qualities that affect our senses are, in the things themselves, so united and blended, that there is no separation, no distance between them; yet it is plain, the ideas they produce in the mind enter by the senses simple and unmixed. For, though the sight and touch often take in from the same object, at the same time, different ideas;—as a man sees at once motion and colour; the hand feels softness and warmth in the same piece of wax: yet the simple ideas thus united in the same subject, are as perfectly distinct as those that come in by different senses. The coldness and hardness which a man feels in a piece of ice being as distinct ideas in the mind as the smell and whiteness of a lily; or as the taste of sugar, and smell of a rose. And there is nothing can be plainer to a man than the clear and distinct perception he has of those simple ideas; which, being each in itself uncompounded, contains in it nothing but *one uniform appearance, or conception in the mind,* and is not distinguishable into different ideas.

2. These simple ideas, the materials of all our knowledge, are suggested and furnished to the mind only by those two ways above mentioned, viz. sensation and reflection. When the understanding is once stored with these simple ideas, it has the power to repeat, compare, and unite them, even to an almost infinite variety, and so can make at pleasure new complex ideas. But it is not in the power of the most exalted wit, or enlarged understanding, by any quickness or variety of thought, to *invent* or *frame* one new simple idea in the mind, not taken in by the ways before mentioned: nor can any force of the understanding *destroy* those that are there. The dominion of man, in this little world of his own understanding being muchwhat the same as it is in the great world of visible things; wherein his power, however managed by art and skill, reaches no farther than to compound and divide the materials that are made to his hand; but can do nothing towards the making the least particle of new matter, or destroying one atom of what is already in being. The same inability will every one find in himself, who shall go about to fashion in his understanding one simple idea, not received in by his senses from external objects, or by reflection from the operations of his own mind about them. I would have any one try to fancy any taste which had never affected his palate; or frame the idea of a scent he had never smelt: and when he can do this, I will also conclude that a blind man hath ideas of colours, and a deaf man true distinct notions of sounds.

3. This is the reason why—though we cannot believe it impossible to God to make a creature with other organs, and more ways to convey into the understanding the notice of corporeal things than those five, as they are usually counted, which he has given to man—yet I think it is not possible for any *man* to imagine any other qualities in bodies, howsoever constituted, whereby they can be taken notice of, besides sounds, tastes, smells, visible and tangible qualities. And had mankind been made but with four senses, the qualities then which are the objects of the fifth sense had been as far from our notice, imagination, and conception, as now any belonging to a sixth, seventh, or eighth sense can possibly be;—which, whether yet some other creatures, in some other parts of this vast and stupendous universe, may not have, will be a great presumption to deny. He that will not set himself proudly at the top of all things, but will consider the immensity of this fabric, and the great variety that is to be found in this little and inconsiderable part of it which he has to do with, may be apt to think that, in other mansions of it, there may be other and different intelligent beings, of whose faculties he has as little knowledge or apprehension as a worm shut up in one drawer of a cabinet hath of the senses or understanding of a man; such variety and excellency being suitable to the wisdom and power of the Maker. I have here followed the common opinion of man's having but five senses; though, perhaps, there may be justly counted more;—but either supposition serves equally to my present purpose.

DISCUSSION QUESTIONS

1. Do you agree with Locke that prior to experience the mind is devoid of all ideas and knowledge (what he calls a "white paper")? Why or why not? When does experience start?

2. In your view, are there any other sources of ideas besides sensation and reflection? Explain.

3. Is there knowledge that can be gained from dream states, or only from waking states? Explain.

4. How would you compare Locke's and Descartes's accounts of "sensation" and its role in the acquisition of knowledge?

14. Ernest Nagel (1901–1985)
Scientific and Commonsense Knowledge

For more than a hundred years the philosophy of science has been one of the most attractive subdisciplines in which to specialize for Western professional philosophers, and during his career Ernest Nagel was one of the major figures in the field. He received his Ph.D. from Columbia University in 1931 and was a member of the philosophy faculty there from 1930 to 1970.

The next selection is the introduction to *The Structure of Science*, a widely acclaimed book published in 1960. The three themes of the book are the nature of scientific explanation, the logical structure of scientific concepts, and the evaluation of knowledge-claims in the different sciences. In this introductory chapter Nagel describes the similarities and differences between "common-sense knowledge" and "scientific knowledge" with the aim of neutralizing a number of commonly held misconceptions of both. Whether we like it or not, directly or indirectly most people in the contemporary world are significantly affected by at least some of the conclusions generated in scientific study, and yet for laypersons it is often not apparent just how the practice of science leads to what is accepted as knowledge. Nagel tries to clarify the "how" of scientific inquiry, as well as the "What for?" while showing the utility of both common sense and science for human life.

QUESTIONS FOR CRITICAL READING

1. What are the similarities between common sense and science, as identified by Nagel?
2. According to Nagel, what are some of the common misuses of the terms "science" and "scientific"?
3. Identify the six differences between common sense and science in Nagel's account.
4. How does Nagel define "scientific explanation"?

TERMS TO NOTE

hypothesis: Here, an explanation of an event offered for subsequent verification or falsification.

proposition: In this context, the formal meaning of what is expressed by a statement about some actual or possible state of affairs.

prima facie: A Latin phrase meaning "at first sight."

———

Long before the beginnings of modern civilization, men acquired vast funds of information about their environment. They learned to recognize substances which nourished their bodies. They discovered the uses of fire and developed skills for transforming raw materials into shelters, clothing, and utensils. They invented arts of tilling the soil, communicating, and governing themselves. Some of them discovered that objects are moved more easily when placed on carts with wheels, that the sizes of fields are more reliably compared when standard schemes of measurement are employed, and that the seasons of the year as well as many phenomena of the heavens succeed each other with a certain regularity. John Locke's quip at Aristotle—that God was not so sparing to men as to make them merely two-legged creatures, leaving it to Aristotle to make them rational—seems obviously applicable to modern science. The acquisition of reliable knowledge concerning many aspects of the world certainly did not wait upon the advent of modern science and the self-conscious use of its methods. Indeed, in this respect, many men in every generation repeat in their own lives the history of the race: they manage to secure for themselves skills and competent information, without benefit of training in the sciences and without the calculated adoption of scientific modes of procedure.

If so much in the way of knowledge can be achieved by the shrewd exercise of native gifts and "common-sense" methods, what special excellence do the sciences possess, and what do their elaborate intellectual and physical tools contribute to the acquisition of knowledge? The question requires a careful answer if a definite meaning is to be associated with the word 'science.'

The word and its linguistic variants are certainly not always employed with discrimination, and they are frequently used merely to confer an honorific distinction on something or other. Many men take pride in being "scientific" in their beliefs and in living in an "age of science." However, quite often the sole discoverable ground for their pride is a conviction that, unlike their ancestors or their neighbors, they are in possession of some alleged final truth. It is in this spirit that currently accepted theories in physics or biology are sometimes described as scientific, while all previously held but no longer accredited theories in those domains are firmly refused that label. Similarly, types of practice that are highly successful under prevailing physical and social conditions, such as certain techniques of farming or industry, are occasionally contrasted with the allegedly "unscientific" practices of other times and places. Perhaps an extreme form of the tendency to rob the term 'scientific' of all definite content is illustrated by the earnest use that advertisers sometimes make of such phrases as 'scientific haircutting,' 'scientific rug cleaning,' and even 'scientific astrology.' It will be clear, however, that in none of the above examples is a readily identifiable and differentiating characteristic of beliefs or practices associated with the word. It would certainly be ill-advised to adopt the suggestion, implicit in the first example, to limit the application of the adjective 'scientific' to beliefs that are indefeasibly true—if only because infallible guaranties of truth are lacking in most if not all areas of inquiry, so that the adoption of such a suggestion would in effect deprive the adjective of any proper use.

The words 'science' and 'scientific' are nevertheless not quite so empty of a determinate content as their frequently debased uses might indicate. For in fact the words are labels either for an identifiable, continuing enterprise of inquiry or for its intellectual products, and they are often employed to signify traits that distinguish those products from other things. In the present chapter we shall therefore survey briefly some of the ways in which "prescientific" or "common-sense" knowledge differs from the intellectual products of modern science. To be sure, no sharp line separates beliefs generally subsumed under the familiar but vague rubric of "common sense" from those cognitive claims recognized as "scientific." Nevertheless, as in the case of other words whose fields of intended application have notoriously hazy boundaries (such as the term 'democracy'), absence of precise dividing lines is not incompatible with the presence of at least a core of firm meaning for each of these words. In their more sober uses, at any rate, these words do in fact connote important and recognizable differences. It is these differences that we must attempt to identify, even if we are compelled to sharpen some of them for the sake of expository emphasis and clarity.

1. No one seriously disputes that many of the existing special sciences have grown out of the practical concerns of daily living: geometry out of problems of measuring and surveying fields, mechanics out of problems raised by the architectural and military arts, biology out of problems of human health and animal husbandry, chemistry out of problems raised by metallurgical and dyeing industries, economics out of problems of household and political management, and so on. To be sure, there have been other stimuli to the development of the sciences than those provided by problems of the practical arts; nevertheless, these latter have had, and still continue to have, important roles in the history of scientific inquiry. In any case, commentators on the nature of science who have been impressed by the historical continuity of common-sense convictions and scientific conclusions have sometimes proposed to differentiate between them by the formula that the sciences are simply "organized" or "classified" common sense.

It is undoubtedly the case that the sciences are organized bodies of knowledge and that in all of them a classification of their materials into significant types or kinds (as in biology, the classification of living things into species) is an indispensable task. It is clear, nonetheless, that the proposed formula does not adequately express the characteristic differences between science and common sense. A lecturer's notes on his travels in Africa may be very well organized for the purposes of communicating information interestingly and efficiently, without thereby converting that information into what has historically been called a science.

A librarian's card catalogue represents an invaluable classification of books, but no one with a sense for the historical association of the word would say that the catalogue is a science. The obvious difficulty is that the proposed formula does not specify what *kind* of organization or classification is characteristic of the sciences.

Let us therefore turn to this question. A marked feature of much information acquired in the course of ordinary experience is that, although this information may be accurate enough within certain limits, it is seldom accompanied by any explanation of why the facts are as alleged. Thus societies which have discovered the uses of the wheel usually know nothing of frictional forces, nor of any reasons why goods loaded on vehicles with wheels are easier to move than goods dragged on the ground. Many peoples have learned the advisability of manuring their agricultural fields, but only a few have concerned themselves with the reasons for so acting. The medicinal properties of herbs like the foxglove have been recognized for centuries, though usually no account was given of the grounds for their beneficent virtues. Moreover, when "common sense" does attempt to give explanations for its facts—as when the value of the foxglove as a cardiac stimulant is explained in terms of the similarity in shape of the flower and the human heart—the explanations are frequently without critical tests of their relevance to the facts. Common sense is often eligible to receive the well-known advice Lord Mansfield gave to a newly appointed governor of a colony who was unversed in the law: "There is no difficulty in deciding a case—only hear both sides patiently, then consider what you think justice requires, and decide accordingly; but never give your reasons, for your judgment will probably be right, but your reasons will certainly be wrong."

It is the desire for explanations which are at once systematic and controllable by factual evidence that generates science; and it is the organization and classification of knowledge on the basis of explanatory principles that is the distinctive goal of the sciences. More specifically, the sciences seek to discover and to formulate in general terms the conditions under which events of various sorts occur, the statements of such determining conditions being the explanations of the corresponding happenings. This goal can be achieved only by distinguishing or isolating certain properties in the subject matter studied and by ascertaining the repeatable patterns of dependence in which these properties stand to one another. In consequence, when the inquiry is successful, propositions that hitherto appeared to be quite unrelated are exhibited as linked to each other in determinate ways by virtue of their place in a system of explanations. In some cases, indeed, the inquiry can be carried to remarkable lengths. Patterns of relations may be discovered that are pervasive in vast ranges of fact, so that with the help of a small number of explanatory principles an indefinitely large number of propositions about these facts can be shown to constitute a logically unified body of knowledge. The unification sometimes takes the form of a deductive system, as in the case of demonstrative geometry or the science of mechanics. Thus a few principles, such as those formulated by Newton, suffice to show that propositions concerning the moon's motion, the behavior of the tides, the paths of projectiles, and the rise of liquids in thin tubes are intimately related, and that all these propositions can be rigorously deduced from those principles conjoined with various special assumptions of fact. In this way a systematic explanation is achieved for the diverse phenomena which the logically derived propositions report.

Not all the existing sciences present the highly integrated form of systematic explanation which the science of mechanics exhibits, though for many of the sciences—in domains of social inquiry as well as in the various divisions of natural science—the idea of such a rigorous logical systematization continues to function as an ideal. But even in those branches of departmentalized inquiry in which this ideal is not generally pursued, as in much historical research, the goal of finding explanations for facts is usually always present. Men seek to know why the thirteen American colonies rebelled from England while Canada did not, why the ancient Greeks were able to repel the Persians but succumbed to the Roman armies, or why urban and commercial activity developed in medieval Europe in the tenth century and not before. To explain, to establish some relation of dependence between propositions superficially unrelated, to exhibit systematically connections between apparently miscellaneous items of information are distinctive marks of scientific inquiry.

2. A number of further differences between common sense and scientific knowledge are almost direct consequences of the systematic character of the latter. A well-recognized feature of common sense is that, though the knowledge it claims may be accurate, it seldom is aware of the limits within which its beliefs are valid or its practices successful. A community, acting on the rule that spreading manure preserves the fertility of the soil, may in many cases continue its mode of agriculture successfully. However, it may continue to follow the rule blindly, in spite of the manifest deterioration of the soil, and it may therefore be helpless in the face of a critical problem of food supply. On the other hand, when the reasons for the efficacy of manure as a fertilizer are understood, so that the rule is connected with principles of biology and soil chemistry, the rule comes to be recognized as only of restricted validity, since the efficiency of manure is seen to depend on the persistence of conditions of which common sense is usually unaware. Few who know them are capable of withholding admiration for the sturdy independence of those farmers who, without much formal education, are equipped with an almost endless variety of skills and sound information in matters affecting their immediate environment. Nevertheless, the traditional resourcefulness of the farmer is narrowly circumscribed: he often becomes ineffective when some break occurs in the continuity of his daily round of living, for his skills are usually products of tradition and routine habit and are not informed by an understanding of the reasons for their successful operation. More generally, common-sense knowledge is most adequate in situations in which a certain number of factors remain practically unchanged. But since it is normally not recognized that this adequacy does depend on the constancy of such factors—indeed, the very existence of the pertinent factors may not be recognized—common-sense knowledge suffers from a serious incompleteness. It is the aim of systematic science to remove this incompleteness, even if it is an aim which frequently is only partially realized.

The sciences thus introduce refinements into ordinary conceptions by the very process of exhibiting the systematic connections of propositions about matters of common knowledge. Not only are familiar practices thereby shown to be explicable in terms of principles formulating relations between items in wide areas of fact; those principles also provide clues for altering and correcting habitual modes of behavior, so as to make them more effective in familiar contexts and more adaptable to novel ones. This is not to say, however, that common beliefs are necessarily mistaken, or even that they are inherently more subject to change under the pressure of experience than are the propositions of science. Indeed, the age-long and warranted stability of common-sense convictions, such as that oaks do not develop overnight from acorns or that water solidifies on sufficient cooling, compares favorably with the relatively short life span of many theories of science. The essential point to be observed is that, since common sense shows little interest in systematically explaining the facts it notes, the range of valid application of its beliefs, though in fact narrowly circumscribed, is not of serious concern to it.

3. The ease with which the plain man as well as the man of affairs entertains incompatible and even inconsistent beliefs has often been the subject for ironic commentary. Thus, men will sometimes argue for sharply increasing the quantity of money and also demand a stable currency; they will insist upon the repayment of foreign debts and also take steps to prevent the importation of foreign goods; and they will make inconsistent judgments on the effects of the foods they consume, on the size of bodies they see, on the temperature of liquids, and the violence of noises. Such conflicting judgments are often the result of an almost exclusive preoccupation with the immediate consequences and qualities of observed events. Much that passes as common-sense knowledge certainly is about the effects familiar things have upon matters that men happen to value; the relations of events to one another, independent of their incidence upon specific human concerns, are not systematically noticed and explored.

The occurrence of conflicts between judgments is one of the stimuli to the development of science. By introducing a systematic explanation of facts, by ascertaining the conditions and consequences of events, by exhibiting the logical relations of propositions to one another, the sciences strike at the sources of such conflicts. Indeed, a large number of extraordinarily able minds have traced out the logical consequences of basic principles in various sciences; and an even larger number of investigators have repeatedly checked such consequences with other propositions obtained as a result of critical observation and experiment. There is no iron-clad guaranty that, in spite of this care, serious inconsistencies in these sciences have been eliminated. On the contrary, mutually incompatible assumptions sometimes serve as the bases for inquiries in different branches of the same science. For example, in certain parts of physics atoms were at one time assumed to be perfectly elastic bodies, although in other branches of physical science perfect elasticity was not ascribed to atoms. However, such inconsistencies are sometimes only apparent ones, the impression of inconsistency arising from a failure to note that different assumptions are being employed for the solution of quite different classes of problems. Moreover, even when the inconsistencies are genuine, they are often only temporary, since incompatible assumptions may be employed only because a logically coherent theory is not yet available to do the complex job for which those assumptions were originally introduced. In any event, the flagrant inconsistencies that so frequently mark common beliefs are notably absent from those sciences in which the pursuit of unified systems of explanation has made considerable headway.

4. As has already been noted, many everyday beliefs have survived centuries of experience, in contradistinction to the relatively short life span that is so often the fate of conclusions advanced in various branches of modern science. One partial reason for this circumstance merits attention. Consider some instance of common-sense beliefs, such as that water solidifies when it is sufficiently cooled; and let us ask what is signified by the terms 'water' and 'sufficiently' in that assertion. It is a familiar fact that the word 'water,' when used by those unacquainted with modern science, generally has no clear-cut meaning. It is then frequently employed as a name for a variety of liquids despite important physicochemical differences between them, but is frequently rejected as a label for other liquids even though these latter liquids do not differ among themselves in their essential physicochemical characteristics to a greater extent than do the former fluids. Thus, the word may perhaps be used to designate the liquids falling from the sky as rain, emerging from the ground in springs, flowing in rivers and roadside ditches, and constituting the seas and oceans; but the word may be employed less frequently if at all for liquids pressed out of fruits, contained in soups and other beverages, or evacuated through the pores of the human skin. Similarly, the word 'sufficiently' when used to characterize a cooling process may sometimes signify a difference as great as that between the maximum temperature on a midsummer day and the minimum temperature of a day in midwinter; at other times, the word may signify a difference no greater than that between the noon and the twilight temperatures on a day in winter. In short, in its common-sense use for characterizing temperature changes, the word 'sufficiently' is not associated with a precise specification of their extent.

If this example can be taken as typical, the language in which common-sense knowledge is formulated and transmitted may exhibit two important kinds of indeterminacy. In the first place, the terms of ordinary speech may be quite vague, in the sense that the class of things designated by a term is not sharply and clearly demarcated from (and may in fact overlap to a considerable extent with) the class of things not so designated. Accordingly, the range of presumed validity for statements employing such terms has no determinate limits. In the second place, the terms of ordinary speech may lack a relevant degree of specificity, in the sense that the broad distinctions signified by the terms do not suffice to characterize more narrowly drawn but important differences between the things denoted by the terms. Accordingly, relations of dependence between occurrences are not formulated in a precisely determinate manner by statements containing such terms.

As a consequence of these features of ordinary speech, experimental control of common-sense beliefs is frequently difficult, since the distinction between confirming and contradicting evidence for such beliefs cannot be easily drawn. Thus, the belief that "in general" water solidifies when sufficiently cooled may answer the needs of men whose interest in the phenomenon of freezing is circumscribed by their concern to achieve the routine objectives of their daily lives, despite the fact that the language employed in codifying this belief is vague and lacks specificity. Such men may therefore see no reason for modifying their belief, even if they should note that ocean water fails to freeze although its temperature is sensibly the same as that of well water when the latter begins to solidify, or that some liquids must be cooled to a greater extent than others before changing into the solid state. If pressed to justify their belief in the face of such facts, these men may perhaps arbitrarily exclude the oceans from the class of things they denominate as water; or, alternatively, they may express renewed confidence in their belief, irrespective of the extent of cooling that may be required, on the ground that liquids classified as water do indeed solidify when cooled.

In their quest for systematic explanations, on the other hand, the sciences must mitigate the indicated indeterminacy of ordinary language by refashioning it. For example, physical chemistry is not content with the loosely formulated generalization that water solidifies if it is sufficiently cooled, for the aim of that discipline is to explain, among other things, why drinking water and milk freeze at certain temperatures although at those temperatures ocean water does not. To achieve this aim, physical chemistry must therefore introduce clear distinctions between various kinds of water and between various amounts of cooling. Several devices reduce the vagueness and increase the specificity of linguistic expressions. Counting and measuring are for many purposes the most effective of these techniques, and are perhaps the most familiar ones. Poets may sing of the infinity of stars which stud the visible heavens, but the astronomer will want to specify their exact number. The artisan in metals may be content with knowing that iron is harder than lead, but the physicist who wishes to explain this fact will require a precise measure of the difference in hardness. Accordingly, an obvious but important consequence of the precision thus introduced is that statements become capable of more thorough and critical testing by experience. Prescientific beliefs are frequently incapable of being put to definite experiential tests, simply because those beliefs may be vaguely compatible with an indeterminate class of unanalyzed facts. Scientific statements, because they are required to be in agreement with more closely specified materials of observation, face greater risks of being refuted by such data.

This difference between common and scientific knowledge is roughly analogous to differences in standards of excellence which may be set up for handling firearms. Most men would qualify as expert shots if the standard of expertness were the ability to hit the side of a barn from a distance of a hundred feet. But only a much smaller number of individuals could meet the more rigorous requirement of consistently centering their shots upon a three-inch target at twice that distance. Similarly, a prediction that the sun will be eclipsed during the autumn months is more likely to be fulfilled than a prediction that the eclipse will occur at a specific moment on a given day in the fall of the year. The first prediction will be confirmed should the eclipse take place during any one of something like a hundred days; the second prediction will be refuted if the eclipse does not occur within something like a small fraction of a minute from the time given. The latter prediction could be false without the former being so, but not conversely; and the latter prediction must therefore satisfy more rigorous standards of experiential control than are assumed for the former.

This greater determinacy of scientific language helps to make clear why so many common-sense beliefs have a stability, often lasting for many centuries, that few theories of science possess. It is more difficult to devise a theory that remains unshaken by repeated confrontation with the outcome of painstaking experimental observation, when the standards are high for the agreement that must obtain between such experimental data and the predictions derived from the theory, than when such standards are lax and the admissible experimental evidence is not required to be established by carefully controlled procedures. The more advanced sciences do in fact specify almost invariably the extent to which predictions based on a theory may deviate from the results of experiment without invalidating the theory. The limits of such permissible deviations are usually quite narrow, so that discrepancies between theory and experiment which common sense would ordinarily regard as insignificant are often judged to be fatal to the adequacy of the theory.

On the other hand, although the greater determinacy of scientific statements exposes them to greater risks of being found in error than are faced by the less precisely stated common-sense beliefs, the former have an important advantage over the latter. They have a greater capacity for incorporation into comprehensive but clearly articulated systems of explanation. When such systems are adequately confirmed by experimental data, they codify frequently unsuspected relations of dependence between many varieties of experimentally identifiable but distinct kinds of fact. In consequence, confirmatory evidence for statements belonging to such a system can often be accumulated more rapidly and in larger quantities than for statements (such as those expressing common-sense beliefs) not belonging to such a system. This is so because evidence for statements in such a system may be obtainable by observations of an extensive class of events, many of which may not be explicitly mentioned by those statements but which are nevertheless relevant sources of evidence for the statements in question, in view of the relations of dependence asserted by the system to hold between the events in that class. For example, the data of spectroscopic analysis are employed in modern physics to test assumptions concerning the chemical structure of various substances; and experiments on thermal properties of solids are used to support theories of light. In brief, by increasing the determinacy of statements and incorporating them into logically integrated systems of explanation, modern science sharpens the discriminating powers of its testing procedure and augments the sources of relevant evidence for its conclusions.

5. It has already been mentioned in passing that, while common-sense knowledge is largely concerned with the impact of events upon matters of special value to men, theoretical science is in general not so provincial. The quest for systematic explanations requires that inquiry be directed to the relations of dependence between things irrespective of their bearing upon human values. Thus, to take an extreme case, astrology is concerned with the relative positions of stars and planets in order to determine the import of such conjunctions for the destinies of men; in contrast, astronomy studies the relative positions and motions of celestial bodies without reference to the fortunes of human beings. Similarly, breeders of horses and of other animals have acquired much skill and knowledge relating to the problem of developing breeds that will implement certain human purposes; theoretical biologists, on the other hand, are only incidentally concerned

with such problems, and are interested in analyzing among other things the mechanisms of heredity and in obtaining laws of genetic development.

One important consequence of this difference in orientation between theoretical and common-sense knowledge, however, is that theoretical science deliberately neglects the immediate values of things, so that the statements of science often appear to be only tenuously relevant to the familiar events and qualities of daily life. To many people, for example, an unbridgeable chasm seems to separate electromagnetic theory, which provides a systematic account of optical phenomena, and the brilliant colors one may see at sunset; and the chemistry of colloids, which contributes to an understanding of the organization of living bodies, appears to be an equally impossible distance from the manifold traits of personality exhibited by human beings.

It must certainly be admitted that scientific statements make use of highly abstract concepts, whose pertinence to the familiar qualities which things manifest in their customary settings is by no means obvious. Nevertheless, the relevance of such statements to matters encountered in the ordinary business of life is also indisputable. It is well to bear in mind that the unusually abstract character of scientific notions, as well as their alleged "remoteness" from the traits of things found in customary experience, are inevitable concomitants of the quest for systematic and comprehensive explanations. Such explanations can be constructed only if the familiar qualities and relations of things, in terms of which individual objects and events are usually identified and differentiated, can be shown to depend for their occurrence on the presence of certain other pervasive relational or structural properties that characterize in various ways an extensive class of objects and processes. Accordingly, to achieve generality of explanation for qualitatively diverse things, those structural properties must be formulated without reference to, and in abstraction from, the individualizing qualities and relations of familiar experience. It is for the sake of achieving such generality that, for example, the temperature of bodies is defined in physics not in terms of directly felt differences in warmth, but in terms of certain abstractly formulated relations characterizing an extensive class of reversible thermal cycles.

However, although abstractness in formulation is an undoubted feature in scientific knowledge, it would be an obvious error to suppose that common-sense knowledge does not involve the use of abstract conceptions. Everyone who believes that man is a mortal creature certainly employs the abstract notions of humanity and mortality. The conceptions of science do not differ from those of common sense merely in being abstract. They differ in being formulations of pervasive structural properties, abstracted from familiar traits manifested by limited classes of things usually only under highly specialized conditions, related to matters open to direct observation only by way of complex logical and experimental procedures, and articulated with a view to developing systematic explanations for extensive ranges of diverse phenomena.

6. Implicit in the contrasts between modern science and common sense already noted is the important difference that derives from the deliberate policy of science to expose its cognitive claims to the repeated challenge of critically probative observational data, procured under carefully controlled conditions. As we had occasion to mention previously, however, this does not mean that common-sense beliefs are invariably erroneous or that they have no foundations in empirically verifiable fact. It does mean that common-sense beliefs are not subjected, as a matter of established principle, to systematic scrutiny in the light of data secured for the sake of determining the accuracy of those beliefs and the range of their validity. It also means that evidence admitted as competent in science must be obtained by procedures instituted with a view to eliminating known sources of error; and it means, furthermore, that the weight of the available evidence for any hypothesis proposed as an answer to the problem under inquiry is assessed with the help of canons of evaluation whose authority is itself based on the performance of those canons in an extensive class of inquiries. Accordingly, the quest for explanation in science is not simply a search for any *prima facie* plausible "first principles" that might account in a vague way for the familiar "facts" of conventional experience. On the contrary, it is a quest for explanatory hypotheses that are genuinely testable, because they are required to have logical consequences precise enough not to be compatible with almost every conceivable state of affairs. The hypotheses sought must therefore be subject to the possibility of rejection, which will depend on the outcome of critical procedures, integral to the scientific quest, for determining what the actual facts are.

The difference just described can be expressed by the dictum that the conclusions of science, unlike common-sense beliefs, are the products of scientific method. However, this brief formula should not be misconstrued. It must not be understood to assert, for example, that the practice of scientific method consists in following prescribed rules for making experimental discoveries or for finding satisfactory explanations for matters of established fact. There are no rules of discovery and invention in science, any more than there are such rules in the arts. Nor must the formula be construed as maintaining that the practice of scientific method consists in the use in all inquiries of some special set of techniques (such as the techniques of measurement employed in physical science), irrespective of the subject matter or the problem under investigation. Such an interpretation of the dictum is a caricature of its intent; and in any event the dictum on that interpretation is preposterous. Nor, finally, should the formula be read as claiming that the practice of scientific method effectively eliminates every form of personal bias or source of error which might otherwise impair the outcome of the inquiry, and more generally that it assures the truth of every conclusion reached by inquiries employing the method. But no such assurances can in fact be given; and no antecedently fixed set of rules can serve as automatic safeguards against unsuspected prejudices and other causes of error that might adversely affect the course of an investigation.

The practice of scientific method is the persistent critique of arguments, in the light of tried canons for judging the reliability of the procedures by which evidential data are obtained, and for assessing the probative force of the evidence on which conclusions are based. As estimated by standards prescribed by those canons, a given hypothesis may be strongly supported by stated evidence. But this fact does not guarantee the truth of the hypothesis, even if the evidential statements are admitted to be true—unless, contrary to standards usually assumed for observational data in the empirical sciences, the degree of support is that which the premises of a valid deductive argument give to its conclusion. Accordingly, the difference between the cognitive claims of science and common sense, which stems from the fact that the former are the products of scientific method, does not connote that the former are invariably true. It does imply that, while common-sense beliefs are usually accepted without a critical evaluation of the evidence available, the evidence for the conclusions of science conforms to standards such that a significant proportion of conclusions supported by similarly structured evidence remains in good agreement with additional factual data when fresh data are obtained.

Further discussion of these considerations must be postponed. However, one brief addendum is required at this point. If the conclusions of science are the products of inquiries conducted in accordance with a definite policy for obtaining and assessing evidence, the rationale for confidence in those conclusions as warranted must be based on the merits of that policy. It must be admitted that the canons for assessing evidence which define the policy have, at best, been explicitly codified only in part, and operate in the main only as intellectual habits manifested by competent investigators in the conduct of their inquiries. But despite this fact the historical record of what has been achieved by this policy in the way of dependable and systematically ordered knowledge leaves little room for serious doubt concerning the superiority of the policy over alternatives to it.

This brief survey of features that distinguish in a general way the cognitive claims and the logical method of modern science suggests a variety of questions for detailed study. The conclusions of science are the fruits of an institutionalized system of inquiry which plays an increasingly important role in the lives of men. Accordingly, the organization of that social institution, the circumstances and stages of its development and influence, and the consequences of its expansion have been repeatedly explored by sociologists, economists, historians, and moralists. However, if the nature of the scientific enterprise and its place in contemporary society are to be properly understood, the types and the articulation of scientific statements, as well as the logic by which scientific conclusions are established, also require careful analysis. This is a task—a major if not exclusive task—that the philosophy of science undertakes to execute. Three broad areas for such an analysis are in fact suggested by the survey just concluded: the logical patterns exhibited by explanations in the sciences; the construction of scientific concepts; and the validation of scientific conclusions. The chapters that follow deal largely though not exclusively with problems concerning the structure of scientific explanations.

DISCUSSION QUESTIONS

1. How does Nagel's characterization of scientific practice compare to the popular stereotypes of scientists?
2. Do you agree with Nagel's descriptions of "common-sense knowledge"? Why or why not?
3. What is knowledge in Nagel's account, and does it have anything to do with the certainty of belief?
4. In comparing Peirce's nineteenth-century account of "the method of science" with Nagel's twentieth-century account of the same, do you think there has or has not been a general change over time in the philosophical view of science and its goals? Explain.

15. John (Fire) Lame Deer (c. 1895–1976)
On Vision Seeking

John Lame Deer was born near the end of the nineteenth century on the Rosebud Reservation in western South Dakota. He was of the Lakota nation and became a respected *wičaśa wakan,* usually translated as "medicine man"/"medicine woman" or "holy man"/ "holy woman." The selection is from a book in which

Lame Deer describes to coauthor Richard Erdoes many of his beliefs and observations about the nature of reality, morality, spirituality, and the interaction between traditional Lakota culture and the now-dominant European American culture.

Lame Deer also talks about acquiring special kinds of knowledge through what is often called a vision quest—especially the knowledge necessary for individuals to fulfill their purpose in life or actualize special potentialities they possess. The extent to which the individual is successful in acquiring such knowledge depends not primarily on reason, or sense experience, or the confirmation of experimental hypotheses, though none of these epistemological means are necessarily excluded either. In Lame Deer's account what is required is courage, a ceremonial preparation of the person so he or she will be receptive to the vision, and a proper relationship with the rest of the living world of which the individual is inescapably a part.

QUESTIONS FOR CRITICAL READING

1. What knowledge does Lame Deer acquire in his vision, and what sort of power is associated with it?
2. What are the purposes of the various objects Lame Deer takes with him into the vision pit?
3. How does Lame Deer characterize a *wićaśa wakan,* and what is that person's role in the community?
4. According to Lame Deer, what does Wakan Tanka expect of all individual living things?

TERMS TO NOTE

Sioux: The conventional American English term for one of the American Indian peoples inhabiting the plains of the northern United States and southern Canada; originally a French derivation of a disparaging Ojibwe term meaning "enemy." The people traditionally referred to themselves as Lakota, Dakota, or Nakota, depending on region.

"All my relations": English translation of the Lakota term *Metakuyeayasi* (or *Mitakuye Oyasin*). Often used in prayer and ceremony, it is an expression of the belief that the speaker is spiritually related to everything in the universe, not only to all other humans.

I was all alone on the hilltop. I sat there in the vision pit, a hole dug into the hill, my arms hugging my knees as I watched old man Chest, the medicine man who had brought me there, disappear far down in the valley. He was just a moving black dot among the pines, and soon he was gone altogether.

Now I was all by myself, left on the hilltop for four days and nights without food or water until he came back for me. You know, we Indians are not like some white folks—a man and a wife, two children, and one baby sitter who watches the TV set while the parents are out visiting somewhere.

Indian children are never alone. They are always surrounded by grandparents, uncles, cousins, relatives of all kinds, who fondle the kids, sing to them, tell them stories. If the parents go someplace, the kids go along.

But here I was, crouched in my vision pit, left alone by myself for the first time in my life. I was sixteen then, still had my boy's name and, let me tell you, I was scared. I was shivering and not only from the cold. The nearest human being was many miles away, and four days and nights is a long, long time. Of course, when it was all over, I would no longer be a boy, but a man. I would have had my vision. I would be given a man's name.

Sioux men are not afraid to endure hunger, thirst and loneliness, and I was only ninety-six hours away from being a man. The thought was comforting. Comforting, too, was the warmth of the star blanket which old man Chest had wrapped around me to cover my nakedness. My grandmother had made it especially for this, my first *hanblechia*, my first vision-seeking. It was a beautifully designed quilt, white with a large morning star made of many pieces of brightly colored cloth. That star was so big it covered most of the blanket. If Wakan Tanka, the Great Spirit, would give me the vision and the power, I would become a medicine man and perform many ceremonies wrapped in that quilt. I am an old man now and many times a grandfather, but I still have that star blanket my grandmother made for me. I treasure it; some day I shall be buried in it.

The medicine man had also left a peace pipe with me, together with a bag of *kinnickinnick*—our kind of tobacco made of red willow bark. This pipe was even more of a friend to me than my star blanket. To us the pipe is like an open Bible. White people need a church house, a preacher and a pipe organ to get into a praying mood. There are so many things to distract you: who else is in the church, whether the other people notice that you have come, the pictures on the wall, the sermon, how much money you should give and did you bring it with you. We think you can't have a vision that way.

For us Indians there is just the pipe, the earth we sit on and the open sky. The spirit is everywhere. Sometimes it shows itself through an animal, a bird or some trees and hills. Sometimes it speaks from the Badlands, a stone, or even from the water. That smoke from the peace pipe, it goes straight up to the spirit world. But this is a two-way thing. Power flows down to us through that smoke, through the pipe stem. You feel that power as you hold your pipe; it moves from the pipe right into your body. It makes your hair stand up. That pipe is not just a thing; it is alive. Smoking this pipe would make me feel good and help me to get rid of my fears.

As I ran my fingers along its bowl of smooth red pipestone, red like the blood of my people, I no longer felt scared. That pipe had belonged to my father and to his father before him. It would someday pass to my son and, through him, to my grandchildren. As long as we had the pipe there would be a Sioux nation. As I fingered the pipe, touched it, felt its smoothness that came from long use, I sensed that my forefathers who had once smoked this pipe were with me on the hill, right in the vision pit. I was no longer alone.

Besides the pipe the medicine man had also given me a gourd. In it were forty small squares of flesh which my grandmother had cut from her arm with a razor blade. I had seen her do it. Blood had been streaming down from her shoulder to her elbow as she carefully put down each piece of skin on a handkerchief, anxious not to lose a single one. It would have made those anthropologists mad. Imagine, performing such an ancient ceremony with a razor blade instead of a flint knife! To me it did not matter. Someone dear to me had undergone pain, given me something of herself, part of her body, to help me pray and make me stronghearted. How could I be afraid with so many people—living and dead—helping me?

One thing still worried me. I wanted to become a medicine man, a *yuwipi*, a healer carrying on the an-

cient ways of the Sioux nation. But you cannot learn to be a medicine man like a white man going to medical school. An old holy man can teach you about herbs and the right ways to perform a ceremony where everything must be in its proper place, where every move, every word has its own, special meaning. These things you can learn—like spelling, like training a horse. But by themselves these things mean nothing. Without the vision and the power this learning will do no good. It would not make me a medicine man.

What if I failed, if I had no vision? Or if I dreamed of the Thunder Beings, or lightning struck the hill? That would make me at once into a *heyoka*, a contrary-wise, an upside-down man, a clown. "You'll know it, if you get the power," my Uncle Chest had told me. "If you are not given it, you won't lie about it, you won't pretend. That would kill you, or kill somebody close to you, somebody you love."

Night was coming on. I was still lightheaded and dizzy from my first sweat bath in which I had purified myself before going up the hill. I had never been in a sweat lodge before. I had sat in the little beehive-shaped hut made of bent willow branches and covered with blankets to keep the heat in. Old Chest and three other medicine men had been in the lodge with me. I had my back against the wall, edging as far away as I could from the red-hot stones glowing in the center. As Chest poured water over the rocks, hissing white steam enveloped me and filled my lungs. I thought the heat would kill me, burn the eyelids off my face! But right in the middle of all this swirling steam I heard Chest singing. So it couldn't be all that bad. I did not cry out "All my relatives!"—which would have made him open the flap of the sweat lodge to let in some cool air—and I was proud of this. I heard him praying for me: "Oh, holy rocks, we receive your white breath, the steam. It is the breath of life. Let this young boy inhale it. Make him strong."

The sweat bath had prepared me for my vision-seeking. Even now, an hour later, my skin still tingled. But it seemed to have made my brains empty. Maybe that was good, plenty of room for new insights.

Darkness had fallen upon the hill. I knew that *han-hepi-wi* had risen, the night sun, which is what we call the moon. Huddled in my narrow cave, I did not see it. Blackness was wrapped around me like a velvet cloth. It seemed to cut me off from the outside world, even from my own body. It made me listen to the voices within me. I thought of my forefathers who had crouched on this hill before me, because the medicine men in my family had chosen this spot for a place of meditation and vision-seeking ever since the day they had crossed the Missouri to hunt for buffalo in the White River country some two hundred years ago. I thought that I could sense their presence right through the earth I was leaning against. I could feel them entering my body, feel them stirring in my mind and heart.

Sounds came to me through the darkness: the cries of the wind, the whisper of the trees, the voices of nature, animal sounds, the hooting of an owl. Suddenly I felt an overwhelming presence. Down there with me in my cramped hole was a big bird. The pit was only as wide as myself, and I was a skinny boy, but that huge bird was flying around me as if he had the whole sky to himself. I could hear his cries, sometimes near and sometimes far, far away. I felt feathers or a wing touching my back and head. This feeling was so overwhelming that it was just too much for me. I trembled and my bones turned to ice. I grasped the rattle with the forty pieces of my grandmother's flesh. It also had many little stones in it, tiny fossils picked up from an ant heap. Ants collect them. Nobody knows why. These little stones are supposed to have a power in them. I shook the rattle and it made a soothing sound, like rain falling on rock. It was talking to me, but it did not calm my fears. I took the sacred pipe in my other hand and began to sing and pray: "Tunkashila, grandfather spirit, help me." But this did not help. I don't know what got into me, but I was no longer myself. I started to cry. Crying, even my voice was different. I sounded like an older man, I couldn't even recognize this strange voice. I used long-ago words in my prayer, words no longer used nowadays. I tried to wipe away my tears, but they wouldn't stop. In the end I just pulled that quilt over me, rolled myself up in it. Still I felt the bird wings touching me.

Slowly I perceived that a voice was trying to tell me something. It was a bird cry, but I tell you, I began to understand some of it. That happens sometimes. I know a lady who had a butterfly sitting on her shoulder. That butterfly told her things. This made her become a great medicine woman.

I heard a human voice too, strange and high-pitched, a voice which could not come from an ordinary, living being. All at once I was way up there with the birds. The hill with the vision pit was way above everything. I could look down even on the stars, and the moon was close to my left side. It seemed as though the earth and the stars were moving below me. A voice said, "You are sacrificing yourself here to be a medicine man. In time you will be one. You will teach other medicine men. We are the fowl people, the winged ones, the eagles and the owls. We are a nation and you shall be our brother. You will never kill or harm any one of us. You are going to understand us whenever you come to seek a vision here on this hill. You will learn about herbs and roots, and you will heal people. You will ask them for nothing in return. A man's life is short. Make yours a worthy one."

I felt that these voices were good, and slowly my fear left me. I had lost all sense of time. I did not know whether it was day or night. I was asleep, yet wide awake. Then I saw a shape before me. It rose from the darkness and the swirling fog which penetrated my earth hole. I saw that this was my great-grandfather, Tahca Ushte, Lame Deer, old man chief of the Minneconjou. I could see the blood dripping from my great-grandfather's chest where a white soldier had shot him. I understood that my great-grandfather wished me to take his name. This made me glad beyond words.

We Sioux believe that there is something within us that controls us, something like a second person almost. We call it *nagi*, what other people might call soul, spirit or essence. One can't see it, feel it or taste it, but that time on the hill—and only that once—I knew it was there inside of me. Then I felt the power surge through me like a flood. I cannot describe it, but it filled all of me. Now I knew for sure that I would become a *wičaśa wakan*, a medicine man. Again I wept, this time with happiness.

I didn't know how long I had been up there on that hill—one minute or a lifetime. I felt a hand on my shoulder gently shaking me. It was old man Chest, who had come for me. He told me that I had been in the vision pit four days and four nights and that it was time to come down. He would give me something to eat and water to drink and then I was to tell him everything that had happened to me during my *hanblechia*. He would interpret my visions for me. He told me that the vision pit had changed me in a way that I would not be able to understand at that time. He told me also that I was no longer a boy, that I was a man now. I was Lame Deer. . . .

I am a medicine man—a *wićaśa wakan.* "Medicine man"—that's a white man's word like squaw, papoose, Sioux, tomahawk—words that don't exist in the Indian language. I wish there were better words to make clear what "medicine man" stands for, but I can't find any, and you can't either, so I guess medicine man will have to do. But it doesn't convey the many different meanings that come to an Indian's mind when you say "medicine man."

We have different names for different men doing different things for which you have only that one puny name. First, we distinguish the healer—*pejuta wićaśa*—the man of herbs. He does not cure with the herbs alone; he must also have the *wakan* power to heal. Then we have the *yuwipi,* the tied-one, the man who uses the power of the rawhide and the stones to find and to cure. We also speak of the *waayatan*—the man of vision who can foretell events which will happen in the future, who has been given the power to see ahead. Things that have come true according to such a man's prediction are called *wakinyanpi.* This word also means the winged-ones, those who fly through the air, because the power to foretell the future comes from them.

Then there is the *wapiya*—the conjurer—what you might call a witch doctor. If he is a good man he does the *waanazin*—the shooting at the disease, the drawing up and sucking out of your body evil things which have been put into a person by a bad spirit, such as a particular kind of gopher that will shoot sharp blades of grass and tiny bits of porcupine quills from his hole in the ground into your body, causing it to break out in boils.

If such a conjurer is bad, he himself will put a sickness into you which only he can cure—for a price. There are some fakers among this group of men. They give a little medicine to a soldier boy which is supposed to protect him from harm, make him bulletproof and ensure his coming home safely. If he comes back in one piece, they collect. If he doesn't—well, that's just too bad.

Another kind of medicine man is the *heyoka*—the sacred clown—who uses his thunder power to cure some people. If you want to stretch the word out like a big blanket to cover everybody, even a peyote roadman could squeeze underneath it and qualify as a medicine man. But the more I think about it, the more I believe that the only real medicine man is the *wićaśa wakan*—the holy man. Such a one can cure, prophesy, talk to the herbs, command the stones, conduct the sun dance or even change the weather, but all this is of no great importance to him. These are merely stages he has passed through. The *wićaśa wakan* has gone beyond all this. He has the *wakanya wowanyanke*—the great vision. Sitting Bull was such a man. When he had his sun-dance vision at Medicine Deer Rock he saw many blue-coated soldiers fall backward into the Indian camp and he heard a voice telling him, "I give you these, because they have no ears." Sitting Bull knew then that the Indians would win the next battle. He did not fight himself, he commanded no men, he did not do anything except let his wisdom and power work for his people.

The *wićaśa wakan* wants to be by himself. He wants to be away from the crowd, from everyday matters. He likes to meditate, leaning against a tree or rock, feeling the earth move beneath him, feeling the weight of that big flaming sky upon him. That way he can figure things out. Closing his eyes, he sees many things clearly. What you see with your eyes shut is what counts.

The *wićaśa wakan* loves the silence, wrapping it around himself like a blanket—a loud silence with a voice like thunder which tells him of many things. Such a man likes to be in a place where there is no sound but the humming of insects. He sits facing the west, asking for help. He talks to the plants and they answer him. He listens to the voices of the *wama kaśkan*—all those who move upon the earth, the animals. He is as one with them. From all living beings something flows into him all the time, and something flows from him. I don't know where or what, but it's there. I know.

This kind of medicine man is neither good nor bad. He lives—and that's it, that's enough. White people pay a preacher to be "good," to behave himself in public, to wear a collar, to keep away from a certain kind of women. But nobody pays an Indian medicine man to be good, to behave himself and act respectable. The *wićaśa wakan* just acts like himself. He has been given the freedom—the freedom of a tree or a bird. That freedom can be beautiful or ugly; it doesn't matter much.

Medicine men—the herb healers as well as our holy men—all have their own personal ways of acting according to their visions. The Great Spirit wants people to be different. He makes a person love a particular animal, tree or herb. He makes people feel drawn to certain favorite spots on this earth where they experience a special sense of well-being, saying to themselves, "That's a spot which makes me happy, where I belong." The Great Spirit is one, yet he is many. He is part of the sun and the sun is a part of him. He can be in a thunderbird or in an animal or plant.

A human being, too, is many things. Whatever makes up the air, the earth, the herbs, the stones is also part of our bodies. We must learn to be different, to feel and taste the manifold things that are us. The animals and plants are taught by Wakan Tanka what to do. They are not alike. Birds are different from each other. Some build nests and some don't. Some animals live in holes, others in caves, others in bushes. Some get along without any kind of home.

Even animals of the same kind—two deer, two owls—will behave differently from each other. Even your daughter's little pet hamsters, they all have their own ways. I have studied many plants. The leaves of one plant, on the same stem—none is exactly alike. On all the earth there is not one leaf that is exactly like another. The Great Spirit likes it that way. He only sketches out the path of life roughly for all the creatures on earth, shows them where to go, where to arrive at, but leaves them to find their own way to get there. He wants them to act independently according to their nature, to the urges in each of them.

If Wakan Tanka likes the plants, the animals, even little mice and bugs, to do this, how much more will he abhor people being alike, doing the same thing, getting up at the same time, putting on the same kind of store-bought clothes, riding the same subway, working in the same office at the same job with their eyes on the same clock and, worst of all, thinking alike

all the time. All creatures exist for a purpose. Even an ant knows what that purpose is—not with its brain, but somehow it knows. Only human beings have come to a point where they no longer know why they exist. They don't use their brains and they have forgotten the secret knowledge of their bodies, their senses, or their dreams. They don't use the knowledge the spirit has put into every one of them; they are not even aware of this, and so they stumble along blindly on the road to nowhere—a paved highway which they themselves bulldoze and make smooth so that they can get faster to the big, empty hole which they'll find at the end, waiting to swallow them up. It's a quick, comfortable superhighway, but I know where it leads to. I have seen it. I've been there in my vision and it makes me shudder to think about it.

I believe that being a medicine man, more than anything else, is a state of mind, a way of looking at and understanding this earth, a sense of what it is all about. Am I a *wićaśa wakan*? I guess so.

DISCUSSION QUESTIONS

1. "Knowledge is power" has become a cliché in Western society. How would its meaning be similar or different in the Lakota worldview that Lame Deer describes?

2. Do you agree with Lame Deer's contrast between the typical Native American and European American approaches to spiritual experience and insight? Why or why not?

3. In what ways would the knowledge achieved in the vision-seeking Lame Deer describes be compatible or incompatible with the scientific knowledge described by Nagel?

4. Compare the visions of Boethius (Part I, reading 2) and Lame Deer. How are they similar or different?

16. D. T. Suzuki (1870–1966)
"The Meaning of Satori"

Daisetz Teitaro Suzuki was a Japanese philosopher who probably did more than any other individual in the twentieth century to acquaint the English-speaking world with Zen Buddhism. Although

he was an internationally respected scholar of Chinese and Sanskrit Buddhist texts, and was well versed in European philosophies as well, his lifelong interest was not primarily academia but the practice of Zen as a way of life. Thus he became well known in Western society, where he traveled extensively, not only as a theoretician of Zen but also as a spiritual guide and living example of that particular spiritual path. He was a gifted expositor of Zen thought, especially for Western audiences not familiar with Asian religious traditions or cultural perspectives.

The selection is from a collection of Suzuki's articles and recorded talks from the 1950s, edited and published by Christmas Humphreys on behalf of the Buddhist Society of London. As the title of this essay implies, the focus is on *satori,* the Japanese term for the experience of enlightenment, which is the central aim in all schools of Buddhism. The Sanskrit term *Buddha* itself means "the enlightened one" and was originally a title bestowed by his followers on Siddhartha Gautama (563–483 B.C.E.). Over time Buddhism evolved into at least two distinct traditions, the *Hinayana* ("Lesser Vehicle"), also called *Theravada* ("Doctrine of the Elders"), and the *Mahayana* ("Greater Vehicle"). Zen (or *Chan* in Chinese) developed as one of the Mahayana schools in China during the sixth and seventh centuries C.E. and later spread to Japan. It emphasized somewhat less a tradition of sacred writings and cosmological speculation regarding the real and unreal, focusing more on the here and now of everyday life in the striving for Buddhahood.

QUESTIONS FOR CRITICAL READING

1. What is the difference between *prajna* and *vijnana?*
2. What is *satori,* and why is it considered valuable?
3. How does one prepare oneself to experience satori? Can training alone bring about this achievement?
4. Is satori something we can share with, or prove to, others?

TERMS TO NOTE

bifurcation: Synonymous with "dichotomy"; making a distinction between this and that, or "A and not-A."

sui generis: A Latin phrase meaning something is "self-caused" or "of its own kind."

asceticism: The practice of physical self-denial, usually for spiritual reasons.

Satori is a Japanese term, *wu* in Chinese. The Sanskrit *bodhi* and *buddha* come from the same root, *bud,* "to be aware of", "to wake". *Buddha* is thus "the awakened one", "the enlightened one", while *bodhi* is "enlightenment". "Buddhism" means the teaching of the enlightened one, that is to say, Buddhism is the doctrine of enlightenment. What Buddha teaches, therefore, is the realisation of bodhi, which is satori. Satori is the centre of all Buddhist teachings. Some may think satori is characteristic of Mahayana Buddhism, but it is not so. Earlier Buddhists also talk about this, the realization of *bodhi;* and as long as they talk about *bodhi* at all they must be said to base their doctrine on the experience of satori.

We have to distinguish between *prajna* and *vijnana.* We can divide knowledge into two categories: intuitive knowledge which is *prajna* whereas discursive knowledge is *vijnana.* To distinguish further: *prajna* grasps reality in its oneness, in its totality; *vijnana* analyses it into subject and object. Here is a flower; we can take this flower as representing the universe itself. We talk about the petals, pollen, stamen and stalk; that is physical analysis. Or we can analyse it chemically into so much hydrogen, oxygen, etc. Chemists analyse a flower, enumerate all its elements and say that the aggregate of all those elements makes up the flower. But they have not exhausted the flower; they have simply analysed it. That is the *vijnana* way of understanding a flower. The *prajna* way is to understand it just as it is without analysis or chopping it into pieces. It is to grasp it in its oneness, in its totality, in its suchness (*sono mame*) in Japanese.

We are generally attracted to analytical knowledge or discriminative understanding, and we divide reality into several pieces. We dissect it and by dissecting it we kill reality. When we have finished our analysis we have murdered reality, and this dead reality we think is our understanding of it. When we see reality dead, after analysing it, we say that we understand it, but what we understand is not reality itself but its corpse after it has been mutilated by our intellect and senses. We fail to see that this result of dissection is not reality itself, and when we take this analysis as a basis of our understanding it is inevitable that we go astray, far away from the truth. Because in this way we shall never reach the final solution of the problem of reality.

Prajna grasps this reality in its oneness, in its totality, in its suchness. *Prajna* does not divide reality into any form of dichotomy; it does not dissect it either metaphysically or physically or chemically. The dividing of reality is the function of *vijnana* which is very useful in a practical way, but *prajna* is different.

Vijnana can never reach infinity. When we write the numbers 1, 2, 3, etc., we never come to an end, for the series goes on to infinity. By adding together all those individual numbers we try to reach the total of the numbers, but as numbers are endless this totality can never be reached. *Prajna,* on the other hand, intuits the whole totality instead of moving through 1, 2, 3 to infinity; it grasps things as a whole. It does not appeal to discrimination; it grasps reality from inside, as it were. Discursive *vijnana* tries to grasp reality objectively, that is, by addition objectively one after another. But this objective method can never reach its end because things are infinite, and we can never exhaust them objectively. Subjectively, however, we turn that position upside down and get to the inside. By looking at this flower objectively we can never reach its essence or life, but when we turn that position inside out, enter into the flower, and become the flower itself, we live through the process of growth: I am the shoot, I am the stem, I am the bud, and finally I am the flower and the flower is me. That is the *prajna* way of comprehending the flower.

In Japan there is a seventeen syllable poem called *haiku,* and one composed by a modern woman-poet reads in literal translation:

Oh, Morning Glory!
Bucket taken captive,
I beg for water.

The following was the incident that led her to compose it. One early morning the poet came outdoors to draw water from the well, and saw the morning glory winding round the bamboo pole attached to the bucket. The morning glory in full bloom looks its best in the early morning after a dewy night. It is bright, refreshing, vivifying; it reflects heavenly glory not yet tarnished by things earthly. She was so struck with its untainted beauty that she remained silent for a little while; she was so absorbed in the flower that she lost the power of speech. It took a few seconds at least

before she could exclaim: "Oh, Morning Glory!" Physically, the interval was a space of a second or two or perhaps more; but metaphysically, it was eternity as beauty itself is. Psychologically, the poet was the unconscious itself in which there was no dichotomisation of any kind.

The poet was the morning glory and the morning glory was the poet. There was self-identity of flower and poet. It was only when she became conscious of herself seeing the flower that she cried: "Oh, Morning Glory!" When she said that, consciousness revived in her. But she did not like to disturb the flower, because although it is not difficult to unwind the flower from the bamboo pole she feared that to touch the flower with human hands would be the desecration of the beauty. So she went to a neighbour and asked for water.

When you analyse that poem you can picture to yourself how she stood before the flower, losing herself. There was then no flower, no human poet; just a "something" which was neither flower nor poet. But when she recovered her consciousness, there was the flower, there was herself. There was an object which was designated as morning glory and there was one who spoke—a bifurcation of subject-object. Before the bifurcation there was nothing to which she could give expression, she herself was non-existent. When she uttered, "Oh, Morning Glory!" the flower was created and along with it herself, but before that bifurcation, that dualisation of subject and object, there was nothing. And yet there was a "something" which could divide itself into subject-object, and this "something" which had not yet divided itself, not become subject to bifurcation, to discriminative understanding (i.e. before *vijnana* asserted itself)—this is *prajna.* For *prajna* is subject and at the same time object; it divides itself into subject-object and also stands by itself, but that standing by itself is not to be understood on the level of duality. Standing by itself, being absolute in its complete totality or oneness—that is the moment which the poet realised, and that is satori. Satori consists in not staying in that oneness, not remaining with itself, but in awakening from it and being just about to divide itself into subject and object. Satori is the staying in oneness and yet rising from it and dividing itself into subject-object. First, there is "something" which has not divided itself into subject-object; this is oneness as it is. Then this "something," becoming conscious of itself, divides itself into flower and poet. The becoming conscious is the dividing. Poet now sees flower and flower sees poet, there is mutual seeing. When this seeing each other, not just from one side alone but from the other side as well when this kind of seeing actually takes place, there is a state of satori.

When I talk like this it takes time. There is something which has not divided itself but which then becomes conscious of itself, and this leads to an utterance, and so on. But in actual satori there is no time interval, hence no consciousness of the bifurcation. The oneness dividing itself into subject-object and yet retaining its oneness at the very moment that there is the awakening of a consciousness—this is satori.

From the human point of view we talk of *prajna* and *vijnana* as the integral understanding and the discriminative understanding of reality respectively. We speak of these things in order to satisfy our human understanding. Animals and plants do not divide themselves; they just live and act, but humans have awakened this consciousness. By the awakening of consciousness we become conscious of this and that, and this universe of infinite diversity arises. Because of this awakening we discriminate, and because of discrimination we talk of *prajna* and *vijnana* and make these distinctions, which is characteristic of human beings. To satisfy this demand we talk about having satori, or the awakening of this self-identity consciousness.

When the poet saw the flower, that very moment before she spoke even a word there was an intuitive apprehension of something which eludes our ordinary intuition. This *sui generis* intuition is what I would call *prajna*-intuition. The moment grasped by *prajna*-intuition is satori. That is what made Buddha the Enlightened one. Thus, to attain satori, *prajna*-intuition is to be awakened.

That is more or less a metaphysical explanation of satori, but psychologically satori may be said to take place this way. Our consciousness contains all things; but there must be at least two things whereby consciousness is possible. Consciousness takes place when

two things stand opposing one another. In our ordinary life, consciousness is kept too busy with all things going on in it and has not time to reflect within itself. Consciousness has thus no opportunity to become conscious of itself. It is so deeply involved in action, it is in fact action itself. Satori never takes place as long as consciousness is kept turning outwardly, as it were. Satori is born of self-consciousness. Consciousness must be made to look within itself before it is awakened to satori.

To get satori, all things which crowd into our daily-life consciousness must be wiped off clean. This is the function of *samadhi*, which Indian philosophers emphasize so much. "Entering into *samadhi*" is to attain uniformity of consciousness, i.e., to wipe consciousness clean, though practically speaking, this wiping clean is something almost impossible. But we must try to do it in order to attain this state of uniformity, which, according to early Buddhist thinkers, is a perfect state of mental equilibrium, for here there are no passions, no intellectual functions, but only a perfectly balanced state of indifference. When this takes place it is known as *samadhi*, or entering into the fourth stage of *dhyana* or *jhana*, as described in most early Buddhist sutras. This is not, however, a state of satori. *Samadhi* is not enough, which is no more than the unification of consciousness. There must be an awakening from this state of unification or uniformity. The awakening is becoming aware of consciousness in its own activities. When consciousness starts to move, begins to divide itself into subject-object and says: I am sorry, or glad, or I hear, and so on—this very moment as it moves on is caught up in satori. But as soon as you say "I have caught it" it is no more there. Therefore, satori is not something you can take hold of and show to others, saying, "See, it is here!"

Consciousness is something which never ceases to be active though we may be quite unconscious of it, and what we call perfect uniformity is not a state of sheer quietness, that is, of death. As consciousness thus goes on unceasingly, no one can stop it for inspection. Satori must take place while consciousness is going through stages or instant points of becoming. Satori is realised along with the becoming, which knows no stoppage. Satori is no particular experience like other experiences of our daily life. Particular experiences are experiences of particular events while the satori experience is the one that runs through all experiences. It is for this reason that satori cannot be singled out of other experiences and pronounced, "See, here is my satori!" It is always elusive and alluring. It can never be separated from our everyday life, it is for ever there, inevitably there. Becoming, not only in its each particularisable moment but through its never-terminating totality is the body of satori.

The nature of human understanding and reasoning is to divide reality into the dichotomy of this and that, of "A" and "not-A" and then to take reality so divided as really reality. We do not seem to understand reality in any other way. This being so, as long as we are depending on "the understanding," there will be no grasping of reality, no intuitive taking hold of reality, and satori is no other than this intuitive taking hold of reality. There is no reality beside becoming, becoming is reality and reality is becoming. Therefore, the satori intuition of reality consists in identifying oneself with becoming, to take becoming as it goes on becoming. We are not to cut becoming into pieces, and, picking up each separate piece which drops from "becoming," to say to people, "Here is reality." While making this announcement we will find that becoming is no more there; reality is flown away into the realm of the irrevocable past.

This is illustrated by a Zen story. A woodman went to the mountains and saw a strange animal on the other side of the tree which he was cutting. He thought: "I might kill that animal." The animal then spoke to the woodman and said: "Are you going to kill me?" Having his mind read, the woodman got angry and wondered what to do. The animal said: "Now you are thinking what to do with me." Whatever thought the woodman had, the animal intuited, and told him so. Finally, the woodman said: "I will stop thinking about the animal and go on cutting wood." While he was so engaged the top of the axe flew off and killed the animal.

This illustrates that when you are not thinking of it there is satori. When you try to realise satori, the more

you struggle the farther it is away. You cannot help pursuing satori, but so long as you make that special effort satori will never be gained. But you cannot forget about it altogether. If you expect satori to come to you of its own accord, you will not get it.

To realise satori is very difficult, as the Buddha found. When he wished to be liberated from the bondage of birth and death he began to study philosophy, but this did not avail him, so he turned to asceticism. This made him so weak that he could not move, so he took milk and decided to go on with his search for liberation. Reasoning did not do any good and pursuing moral perfection did not help him either. Yet the urge to solve this problem was still there. He could go no farther, yet he could not retreat, so he had to stay where he was, but even that would not do. This state of spiritual crisis means that you cannot go on, nor retreat, nor stay where you are. When this dilemma is genuine, there prevails a state of consciousness ready for satori. When we really come to this stage (but we frequently think that what is not real is real), when we find ourselves at this critical moment, something is sure to rise from the depths of reality, from the depths of our own being. When this comes up there is satori. Then you understand all things and are at peace with the world as well as with yourself.

DISCUSSION QUESTIONS

1. If you experienced satori, how would it alter your understanding of the world and how you lived your life?

2. Some philosophers claim that there is no meaningful content, and thus no knowledge to be acquired, in mystical experience. Do you agree? Why or why not?

3. How would you compare and contrast the satori experience described by Suzuki with the vision experience described by Lame Deer?

4. Who are some Western philosophers or artists (poets, musicians, or others) who advocate seeking the kind of experience Suzuki describes? Explain.

17. Uma Narayan

"The Project of Feminist Epistemology: Perspectives from a Nonwestern Feminist"

Uma Narayan, an Indian philosopher, was working in the United States at the time she wrote this essay in the mid-1980s. The article was generated by Narayan's participation in a seminar at Rutgers University in New Jersey in 1985 that focused on a feminist challenge to the standard philosophical and scientific approaches to epistemological issues in modern Western society.

For understanding the scope and variety of controversy in contemporary epistemology, the value of Narayan's analysis is twofold. In the first place she provides the reader with an overview of the "enterprise of feminist epistemology," and secondly she compares and contrasts the concerns of Western and non-Western feminism in this domain. In the process she also points out the dangers of ethnocentrism—the attitude that one's own cultural norms are universally applicable—to which Western feminism especially has been vulnerable. In the last few decades, more philosophers worldwide have started to take more seriously the fact that humans do employ different ways of knowing in order to achieve different kinds of knowledge, which are valued differently depending on one's personal and social circumstances. Narayan's emphasis on the significance and interconnection of both gender and cultural affiliation illustrates this increasingly influential trend.

QUESTIONS FOR CRITICAL READING

1. In Narayan's account, what is feminism generally, and what are the major themes of feminist epistemology in particular?
2. What are the political problems for non-Western feminists, as identified by Narayan, in their pursuit of a feminist epistemological critique of the distinctive cultural worlds they inhabit?
3. How does Narayan critique the Western feminist focus on the problems of "positivism"?
4. What does Narayan mean by the "epistemic privilege of oppressed groups," and what are the differences between the Western and non-Western feminist perspectives on this issue?

TERMS TO NOTE

incommensurable: Not able to be measured, evaluated, or explained by the same standards, criteria, or principles.

positivism: In this context, a nineteenth- and twentieth-century theoretical perspective that rejects the meaningfulness of assertions that are not in principle subject to factual verification through evidence or objective observation. For many this implied the meaninglessness of spiritual, metaphysical, and value claims, or at least their reduction to the status of merely relativistic, subjective self-expressions.

intentional: Here, a technical philosophical term referring to the characteristic of being "about something," for example, a belief is always about something, so beliefs are intentional.

reification: Treating concepts or ideas as real, independently existing entities.

A fundamental thesis of feminist epistemology is that our location in the world as women makes it possible for us to perceive and understand different aspects of both the world and human activities in ways that challenge the male bias of existing perspectives. Feminist epistemology is a particular manifestation of the general insight that the nature of women's experiences as individuals and as social beings, our contributions to work, culture, knowledge, and our history and political interests have been systematically ignored or misrepresented by mainstream discourses in different areas.

Women have been often excluded from prestigious areas of human activity (for example, politics or science) and this has often made these activities seem clearly "male." In areas where women were not excluded (for example, subsistence work), their contribution has been misrepresented as secondary and inferior to that of men. Feminist epistemology sees mainstream theories about various human enterprises, including mainstream theories about human knowledge, as one-dimensional and deeply flawed because of the exclusion and misrepresentation of women's contributions.

Feminist epistemology suggests that integrating women's contribution into the domain of science and knowledge will not constitute a mere adding of details; it will not merely widen the canvas but result in a shift of perspective enabling us to see a very different picture. The inclusion of women's perspective will not merely amount to women participating in greater numbers in the existing practice of science and knowledge, but it will change the very nature of these activities and their self-understanding.

It would be misleading to suggest that feminist epistemology is a homogenous and cohesive enterprise. Its practitioners differ both philosophically and politically in a number of significant ways (Harding 1986). But an important theme on its agenda has been to undermine the abstract, rationalistic, and universal image of the scientific enterprise by using several different strategies. It has studied, for instance, how contingent historical factors have colored both scientific theories and practices and provided the (often sexist) metaphors in which scientists have conceptualized their activity (Bordo 1986; Keller 1985; Harding and O'Barr 1987). It has tried to reintegrate values and emotions into our account of our cognitive activities, arguing for both the inevitability of their presence and the importance of the contributions they are capable of making to our knowledge (Gilligan 1982; Jaggar and Tronto essays in this volume). It has also attacked various sets of dualisms characteristic of western philosophical thinking—reason versus emotion, culture versus nature, universal versus particular—in which the first of each set is identified with science, rationality, and the masculine and the second is relegated to the nonscientific, the nonrational, and the feminine (Harding and Hintikka 1983; Lloyd 1984; Wilshire essay in this volume).

At the most general level, feminist epistemology resembles the efforts of many oppressed groups to re-

claim for themselves the value of their own experience. The writing of novels that focused on working-class life in England or the lives of black people in the United States shares a motivation similar to that of feminist epistemology—to depict an experience different from the norm and to assert the value of this difference.

In a similar manner, feminist epistemology also resembles attempts by third-world writers and historians to document the wealth and complexity of local economic and social structures that existed prior to colonialism. These attempts are useful for their ability to restore to colonized peoples a sense of the richness of their own history and culture. These projects also mitigate the tendency of intellectuals in former colonies who are westernized through their education to think that anything western is necessarily better and more "progressive." In some cases, such studies help to preserve the knowledge of many local arts, crafts, lore, and techniques that were part of the former way of life before they are lost not only to practice but even to memory.

These enterprises are analogous to feminist epistemology's project of restoring to women a sense of the richness of their history, to mitigate our tendency to see the stereotypically "masculine" as better or more progressive, and to preserve for posterity the contents of "feminine" areas of knowledge and expertise—medical lore, knowledge associated with the practices of childbirth and child rearing, traditionally feminine crafts, and so on. Feminist epistemology, like these other enterprises, must attempt to balance the assertion of the value of a different culture or experience against the dangers of romanticizing it to the extent that the limitations and oppressions it confers on its subjects are ignored.

My essay will attempt to examine some dangers of approaching feminist theorizing and epistemological values in a noncontextual and nonpragmatic way, which could convert important feminist insights and theses into feminist epistemological dogmas. I will use my perspective as a nonwestern, Indian feminist to examine critically the predominantly Anglo-American project of feminist epistemology and to reflect on what such a project might signify for women in nonwestern cultures in general and for nonwestern feminists in particular. I will suggest that different cultural contexts and political agendas may cast a very different light on both the "idols" and the "enemies" of knowledge as they have characteristically been typed in western feminist epistemology.

In keeping with my respect for contexts, I would like to stress that I do not see nonwestern feminists as a homogenous group and that none of the concerns I express as a nonwestern feminist may be pertinent to or shared by *all* nonwestern feminists, although I do think they will make sense to many.

In the first section, I will show that the enterprise of feminist epistemology poses some political problems for nonwestern feminists that it does not pose, in the same way, for western feminists. In the second section, I will explore some problems that nonwestern feminists may have with feminist epistemology's critical focus on positivism. In the third section, I will examine some political implications of feminist epistemology's thesis of the "epistemic privilege" of oppressed groups for nonwestern feminists. And in the last section, I will discuss the claim that oppressed groups gain epistemic advantages by inhabiting a larger number of contexts, arguing that such situations may not always confer advantages and may sometimes create painful problems.

Nonwestern Feminist Politics and Feminist Epistemology

Some themes of feminist epistemology may be problematic for nonwestern feminists in ways that they are not problematic for western feminists. Feminism has a much narrower base in most nonwestern countries. It is primarily of significance to some urban, educated, middle-class, and hence relatively westernized women, like myself. Although feminist groups in these countries do try to extend the scope of feminist concerns to other groups (for example, by fighting for childcare, women's health issues, and equal wages issues through trade union structures), some major preoccupations of western feminism—its critique of marriage, the family, compulsory heterosexuality—presently engage the attention of mainly small groups of middle-class feminists.

These feminists must think and function within the context of a powerful tradition that, although it systematically oppresses women, also contains within itself a discourse that confers a high value on women's place in the general scheme of things. Not only are the roles of wife and mother highly praised, but women also are seen as the cornerstones of the spiritual well-being of their husbands and children, admired for their supposedly higher moral, religious, and spiritual qualities, and so on. In cultures that have a pervasive religious component, like the Hindu culture with which I am familiar, everything seems assigned a place and value as long as it keeps to its place. Confronted with a powerful traditional discourse that values woman's place as long as she keeps to the place prescribed, it may be politically counterproductive for nonwestern feminists to echo uncritically the themes of western feminist epistemology that seek to restore the value, cognitive and otherwise, of "women's experience."

The danger is that, even if the nonwestern feminist talks about the value of women's experience in terms totally different from those of the traditional discourse, the difference is likely to be drowned out by the louder and more powerful voice of the traditional discourse, which will then claim that "what those feminists say" vindicates its view that the roles and experiences it assigns to women have value and that women should stick to those roles.

I do not intend to suggest that this is not a danger for western feminism or to imply that there is no tension for western feminists between being critical of the experiences that their societies have provided for women and finding things to value in them nevertheless. But I am suggesting that perhaps there is less at risk for western feminists in trying to strike this balance. I am inclined to think that in nonwestern countries feminists must still stress the negative sides of the female experience within that culture and that the time for a more sympathetic evaluation is not quite ripe.

But the issue is not simple and seems even less so when another point is considered. The imperative we experience as feminists to be critical of how our culture and traditions oppress women conflicts with our desire as members of once colonized cultures to affirm the value of the same culture and traditions.

There are seldom any easy resolutions to these sorts of tensions. As an Indian feminist currently living in the United States, I often find myself torn between the desire to communicate with honesty the miseries and oppressions that I think my own culture confers on its women and the fear that this communication is going to reinforce, however unconsciously, western prejudices about the "superiority" of western culture. I have often felt compelled to interrupt my communication, say on the problems of the Indian system of arranged marriages, to remind my western friends that the experiences of women under their system of "romantic love" seem no more enviable. Perhaps we should all attempt to cultivate the methodological habit of trying to understand the complexities of the oppression involved in different historical and cultural settings while eschewing, at least for now, the temptation to make comparisons across such settings, given the dangers of attempting to compare what may well be incommensurable in any neat terms.

The Nonprimacy of Positivism as a Problematic Perspective

As a nonwestern feminist, I also have some reservations about the way in which feminist epistemology seems to have picked positivism as its main target of attack. The choice of positivism as the main target is reasonable because it has been a dominant and influential western position and it most clearly embodies some flaws that feminist epistemology seeks to remedy.

But this focus on positivism should not blind us to the facts that it is not our only enemy and that nonpositivist frameworks are not, by virtue of that bare qualification, any more worthy of our tolerance. Most traditional frameworks that nonwestern feminists regard as oppressive to women are not positivist, and it would be wrong to see feminist epistemology's critique of positivism given the same political importance for nonwestern feminists that it has for western feminists. Traditions like my own, where the influence of religion is pervasive, are suffused through and through with values. We must fight not frameworks that assert the separation of fact and value but frameworks that are pervaded by values to which we, as feminists, find ourselves opposed. Positivism in epistemology flourished at the same time as liberalism in western political theory. Positivism's view of values as

individual and subjective related to liberalism's political emphasis on individual rights that were supposed to protect an individual's freedom to live according to the values she espoused.

Nonwestern feminists may find themselves in a curious bind when confronting the interrelations between positivism and political liberalism. As colonized people, we are well aware of the facts that many political concepts of liberalism are both suspicious and confused and that the practice of liberalism in the colonies was marked by brutalities unaccounted for by its theory. However, as feminists, we often find some of its concepts, such as individual rights, very useful in our attempts to fight problems rooted in our traditional cultures.

Nonwestern feminists will no doubt be sensitive to the fact that positivism is not our only enemy. Western feminists too must learn not to uncritically claim any nonpositivist framework as an ally; despite commonalities, there are apt to be many differences. A temperate look at positions we espouse as allies is necessary since "the enemy of my enemy is my friend" is a principle likely to be as misleading in epistemology as it is in the domain of Realpolitik.

The critical theorists of the Frankfurt School will serve well to illustrate this point. Begun as a group of young intellectuals in the post–World War I Weimar Republic, the members were significantly influenced by Marxism, and their interests ranged from aesthetics to political theory to epistemology. Jürgen Habermas, the most eminent critical theorist today, has in his works attacked positivism and the claim of scientific theories to be value neutral or "disinterested." He has attempted to show the constitutive role played by human interests in different domains of human knowledge. He is interested, as are feminists, in the role that knowledge plays in the reproduction of social relations of domination. But, as feminist epistemology is critical of all perspectives that place a lopsided stress on reason, it must also necessarily be critical of the rationalist underpinnings of critical theory.

Such rationalist foundations are visible, for example, in Habermas's "rational reconstruction" of what he calls "an ideal speech situation," supposedly characterized by "pure intersubjectivity," that is, by the absence of any barriers to communication. That Habermas's "ideal speech situation" is a creature of reason is clear from its admitted character as a "rationally reconstructed ideal" and its symmetrical distribution of chances for all of its participants to choose and apply speech acts.

This seems to involve a stress on formal and procedural equality among speakers that ignores substantive differences imposed by class, race, or gender that may affect a speaker's knowledge of the facts or the capacity to assert herself or command the attention of others. Women in academia often can testify to the fact that, despite not being forcibly restrained from speaking in public forums, they have to overcome much conditioning in order to learn to assert themselves. They can also testify as to how, especially in male-dominated disciplines, their speech is often ignored or treated with condescension by male colleagues.

Habermas either ignores the existence of such substantive differences among speakers or else assumes they do not exist. In the latter case, if one assumes that the speakers in the ideal speech situation are not significantly different from each other, then there may not be much of significance for them to speak about. Often it is precisely our differences that make dialogue imperative. If the ideal speakers of the ideal speech situation are unmarked by differences, there may be nothing for them to surmount on their way to a "rational consensus." If there are such differences between the speakers, then Habermas provides nothing that will rule out the sorts of problems I have mentioned.

Another rationalist facet of critical theory is revealed in Habermas's assumption that justifiable agreement and genuine knowledge arise only out of "rational consensus." This seems to overlook the possibility of agreement and knowledge based on sympathy or solidarity. Sympathy or solidarity may very well promote the uncovering of truth, especially in situations when people who divulge information are rendering themselves vulnerable in the process. For instance, women are more likely to talk about experiences of sexual harassment to other women because they would expect similar experiences to have made them more sympathetic and understanding. Therefore, feminists should be cautious about assuming that they necessarily have much in common with a frame-work simply because it is nonpositivist. Nonwestern feminists may be more alert to this error because many problems they confront arise in nonpositivist contexts.

The Political Uses of "Epistemic Privilege"

Important strands in feminist epistemology hold the view that our concrete embodiments as members of a specific class, race, and gender as well as our concrete historical situations necessarily play significant roles in our perspective on the world; moreover, no point of view is "neutral" because no one exists unembedded in the world. Knowledge is seen as gained not by solitary individuals but by socially constituted members of groups that emerge and change through history.

Feminists have also argued that groups living under various forms of oppression are more likely to have a critical perspective on their situation and that this critical view is both generated and partly constituted by critical emotional responses that subjects experience vis-à-vis their life situations. This perspective in feminist epistemology rejects the "Dumb View" of emotions and favors an intentional conception that emphasizes the cognitive aspect of emotions. It is critical of the traditional view of the emotions as wholly and always impediments to knowledge and argues that many emotions often help rather than hinder our understanding of a person or situation (see Jaggar essay in this volume).

Bringing together these views on the role of the emotions in knowledge, the possibility of critical insights being generated by oppression, and the contextual nature of knowledge may suggest some answers to serious and interesting political questions. I will consider what these epistemic positions entail regarding the possibility of understanding and political cooperation between oppressed groups and sympathetic members of a dominant group—say, between white people and people of color over issues of race or between men and women over issues of gender.

These considerations are also relevant to questions of understanding and cooperation between western and nonwestern feminists. Western feminists, despite their critical understanding of their own culture, often tend to be more a part of it than they realize. If they fail to see the contexts of their theories and assume that their perspective has universal validity for all feminists, they tend to participate in the dominance that western culture has exercised over nonwestern cultures.

Our position must explain and justify our dual need to criticize members of a dominant group (say men or white people or western feminists) for their lack of attention to or concern with problems that affect an oppressed group (say, women or people of color or nonwestern feminists, respectively), as well as for our frequent hostility toward those who express interest, even sympathetic interest, in issues that concern groups of which they are not a part.

Both attitudes are often warranted. On the one hand, one cannot but be angry at those who minimize, ignore, or dismiss the pain and conflict that racism and sexism inflict on their victims. On the other hand, living in a state of siege also necessarily makes us suspicious of expressions of concern and support from those who do not live these oppressions. We are suspicious of the motives of our sympathizers or the extent of their sincerity, and we worry, often with good reason, that they may claim that their interest provides a warrant for them to speak for us, as dominant groups throughout history have spoken for the dominated.

This is all the more threatening to groups aware of how recently they have acquired the power to articulate their own points of view. Nonwestern feminists are especially aware of this because they have a double struggle in trying to find their own voice: they have to learn to articulate their differences, not only from their own traditional contexts but also from western feminism.

Politically, we face interesting questions whose answers hinge on the nature and extent of the communication that we think possible between different groups. Should we try to share our perspectives and insights with those who have not lived our oppressions and accept that they may fully come to share them? Or should we seek only the affirmation of those like ourselves, who share common features of oppression, and rule out the possibility of those who have not lived these oppressions ever acquiring a genuine understanding of them?

I argue that it would be a mistake to move from the thesis that knowledge is constructed by human subjects who are socially constituted to the conclusion that those who are differently located socially can never attain *some* understanding of our experience or *some* sympathy with our cause. In that case, we would be committed to not just a perspectival view of knowledge but a relativistic one. Relativism, as I am using it, implies that a person could have knowledge of only the sorts of things she had experienced personally and that she would be totally unable to communicate any of the contents of her knowledge to someone who did not have the same sorts of experiences. Not only does this seem clearly false and perhaps even absurd, but it is probably a good idea not to have any a priori views that would imply either that all our knowledge is always capable of being communicated to every other person or that would imply that some of our knowledge is necessarily incapable of being communicated to some class of persons.

"Nonanalytic" and "nonrational" forms of discourse, like fiction or poetry, may be better able than other forms to convey the complex life experiences of one group to members of another. One can also hope that being part of one oppressed group may enable an individual to have a more sympathetic understanding of issues relating to another kind of oppression—that, for instance, being a woman may sensitize one to issues of race and class even if one is a woman privileged in those respects.

Again, this should not be reduced to some kind of metaphysical presumption. Historical circumstances have sometimes conspired, say, to making working-class men more chauvinistic in some of their attitudes than other men. Sometimes one sort of suffering may simply harden individuals to other sorts or leave them without energy to take any interest in the problems of other groups. But we can at least try to foster such sensitivity by focusing on parallels, not identities, between different sorts of oppressions.

Our commitment to the contextual nature of knowledge does not require us to claim that those who do not inhabit these contexts can never have any knowledge of them. But this commitment does permit us to argue that it is *easier* and *more likely* for the oppressed to have critical insights into the conditions of their own oppression than it is for those who live outside these structures. Those who actually *live* the oppressions of class, race, or gender have faced the issues that such oppressions generate in a variety of different situations. The insights and emotional responses engendered by these situations are a legacy with which they confront any new issue or situation.

Those who display sympathy as outsiders often fail both to understand fully the emotional complexities of living as a member of an oppressed group and to carry what they have learned and understood about one situation to the way they perceive another. It is a commonplace that even sympathetic men will often fail to perceive subtle instances of sexist behavior or discourse.

Sympathetic individuals who are not members of an oppressed group should keep in mind the possibility of this sort of failure regarding their understanding of issues relating to an oppression they do not share. They should realize that nothing they may do, from participating in demonstrations to changing their lifestyles, can make them one of the oppressed. For instance, men who share household and child-rearing responsibilities with women are mistaken if they think that this act of choice, often buttressed by the gratitude and admiration of others, is anything like the woman's experience of being forcibly socialized into these tasks and of having others perceive this as her natural function in the scheme of things.

The view that we can understand much about the perspectives of those whose oppression we do not share allows us the space to criticize dominant groups for their blindness to the facts of oppression. The view that such an understanding, despite great effort and interest, is likely to be incomplete or limited, provides us with the ground for denying total parity to members of a dominant group in their ability to understand our situation.

Sympathetic members of a dominant group need not necessarily defer to our views on any particular issue because that may reduce itself to another subtle form of condescension, but at least they must keep in mind the very real difficulties and possibility of failure to fully understand our concerns. This and the very important need for dominated groups to control the means of discourse about their own situations are important reasons for taking seriously the claim that oppressed groups have an "epistemic advantage."

The Dark Side of "Double Vision"

I think that one of the most interesting insights of feminist epistemology is the view that oppressed groups, whether women, the poor, or racial minorities, may derive an "epistemic advantage" from having knowledge of the practices of both their own contexts and those of their oppressors. The practices of the dominant groups (for instance, men) govern a society; the dominated group (for instance, women) must acquire some fluency with these practices in order to survive in that society.

There is no similar pressure on members of the dominant group to acquire knowledge of the practices of the dominated groups. For instance, colonized people had to learn the language and culture of their colonizers. The colonizers seldom found it necessary to have more than a sketchy acquaintance with the language and culture of the "natives." Thus, the oppressed are seen as having an "epistemic advantage" because they can operate with two sets of practices and in two different contexts. This advantage is thought to lead to critical insights because each framework provides a critical perspective on the other.

I would like to balance this account with a few comments about the "dark side," the disadvantages, of being able to or of having to inhabit two mutually incompatible frameworks that provide differing perspectives on social reality. I suspect that nonwestern feminists, given the often complex and troublesome interrelationships between the contexts they must inhabit, are less likely to express unqualified enthusiasm about the benefits of straddling a multiplicity of contexts. Mere access to two different and incompatible contexts is not a guarantee that a critical stance on the part of an individual will result. There are many ways in which she may deal with the situation.

First, the person may be tempted to dichotomize her life and reserve the framework of a different context for each part. The middle class of nonwestern countries supplies numerous examples of people who are very westernized in public life but who return to a very traditional lifestyle in the realm of the family. Women may choose to live their public lives in a "male" mode, displaying characteristics of aggressiveness, competition, and so on, while continuing to play dependent and compliant roles in their private lives. The pressures of jumping between two different lifestyles may be mitigated by justifications of how each pattern of behavior is appropriate to its particular context and of how it enables them to "get the best of both worlds."

Second, the individual may try to reject the practices of her own context and try to be as much as possible like members of the dominant group. Westernized intellectuals in the nonwestern world often may almost lose knowledge of their own cultures and practices and be ashamed of the little that they do still know. Women may try both to acquire stereotypically male characteristics, like aggressiveness, and to expunge stereotypically female characteristics, like emotionality. Or the individual could try to reject entirely the framework of the dominant group and assert the virtues of her own despite the risks of being marginalized from the power structures of the society; consider, for example, women who seek a certain sort of security in traditionally defined roles.

The choice to inhabit two contexts critically is an alternative to these choices and, I would argue, a more useful one. But the presence of alternative contexts does not by itself guarantee that one of the other choices will not be made. Moreover, the decision to inhabit two contexts critically, although it may lead to an "epistemic advantage," is likely to exact a certain price. It may lead to a sense of totally lacking roots or any space where one is at home in a relaxed manner.

This sense of alienation may be minimized if the critical straddling of two contexts is part of an ongoing critical politics, due to the support of others and a deeper understanding of what is going on. When it is not so rooted, it may generate ambivalence, uncertainty, despair, and even madness, rather than more positive critical emotions and attitudes. However such a person determines her locus, there may be a sense of being an outsider in both contexts and a sense of clumsiness or lack of fluency in both sets of practices. Consider this simple linguistic example: most people who learn two different languages that are associated with two very different cultures seldom acquire both with equal fluency; they may find themselves devoid of vocabulary in one language for certain contexts of

life or be unable to match real objects with terms they have acquired in their vocabulary. For instance, people from my sort of background would know words in Indian languages for some spices, fruits, and vegetables that they do not know in English. Similarly, they might be unable to discuss "technical" subjects like economics or biology in their own languages because they learned about these subjects and acquired their technical vocabularies only in English.

The relation between the two contexts the individual inhabits may not be simple or straightforward. The individual subject is seldom in a position to carry out a perfect "dialectical synthesis" that preserves all the advantages of both contexts and transcends all their problems. There may be a number of different "syntheses," each of which avoids a different subset of the problems and preserves a different subset of the benefits.

No solution may be perfect or even palatable to the agent confronted with a choice. For example, some Indian feminists may find some western modes of dress (say trousers) either more comfortable or more their "style" than some local modes of dress. However, they may find that wearing the local mode of dress is less socially troublesome, alienates them less from more traditional people they want to work with, and so on. Either choice is bound to leave them partly frustrated in their desires.

Feminist theory must be temperate in the use it makes of this doctrine of "double vision"—the claim that oppressed groups have an epistemic advantage and access to greater critical conceptual space. Certain types and contexts of oppression certainly may bear out the truth of this claim. Others certainly do not seem to do so; and even if they do provide space for critical insights, they may also rule out the possibility of actions subversive of the oppressive state of affairs.

Certain kinds of oppressive contexts, such as the contexts in which women of my grandmother's background lived, rendered their subjects entirely devoid of skills required to function as independent entities in the culture. Girls were married off barely past puberty, trained for nothing beyond household tasks and the rearing of children, and passed from economic dependency on their fathers to economic dependency on their husbands to economic dependency on their sons in old age. Their criticisms of their lot were articulated, if at all, in terms that precluded a desire for any radical change. They saw themselves sometimes as personally unfortunate, but they did not locate the causes of their misery in larger social arrangements.

I conclude by stressing that the important insight incorporated in the doctrine of "double vision" should not be reified into a metaphysics that serves as a substitute for concrete social analysis. Furthermore, the alternative to "buying" into an oppressive social system need not be a celebration of exclusion and the mechanisms of marginalization. The thesis that oppression may bestow an epistemic advantage should not tempt us in the direction of idealizing or romanticizing oppression and blind us to its real material and psychic deprivations.

Note

I would like to acknowledge the enormous amount of help that Alison Jaggar and Susan Bordo have given me with this essay. Alison has been influential all the way from suggesting the nature of the project to suggesting changes that cleared up minor flaws in writing. Susan's careful reading has suggested valuable changes in the structure of the paper, and she has also been very helpful with references. I would like to thank them both for the insightful nature of their comments and the graciousness with which they made them. I would like to thank Dilys Page for her painstaking reading and comments on the first draft of this paper. I would also like to thank Radhika Balasubramanian, Sue Cataldi, Mary Geer, Mary Gibson, Rhoda Linton, Josie Rodriguez-Hewitt, and Joyce Tigner for sharing their work with me, for taking an interest in my work, and for providing me with a community of women who sustain me in many, many ways.

References

Bordo, S. 1986. "The Cartesian Masculinization of Thought." *Signs* 11:439–456.

Gilligan, C. 1982. *In A Different Voice: Psychological Theory and Women's Development.* Cambridge, Mass.: Harvard University Press.

Harding, S. 1986. *The Science Question in Feminism.* Ithaca, N.Y.: Cornell University Press.

Harding, S., and M. Hintikka. 1983. *Discovering Reality: Feminist Perspectives on Epistemology, Metaphysics, Methodology, and Philosophy of Science.* Dordrecht: Reidel.

Harding, S., and J. O'Barr, eds. 1987. *Sex and Scientific Inquiry.* Chicago: University of Chicago Press.

Keller, E. F. 1985. *Reflections on Gender and Science.* New Haven, Conn.: Yale University Press.

Lloyd, G. 1984. *The Man of Reason.* Minneapolis: University of Minnesota Press.

DISCUSSION QUESTIONS

1. In your experience do males and females acquire knowledge about the world around them in different ways, and if so, how?

2. What is the relationship between culture, language, thought, and knowledge, and why might this relationship have political implications from a feminist standpoint?

3. Why would you agree or disagree with Narayan's account of "double vision"?

4. What are the similarities and differences between colonialism and patriarchy (male-dominant society) in terms of their effects on the social conditioning of women and men?

18. William Clifford (1845–1879)
"The Ethics of Belief"

William Clifford was a British philosopher and mathematician who held academic positions at Cambridge and University College in London, before his career was cut short by tuberculosis in 1879. In addition to his mathematical work, he wrote on a variety of epistemological and metaphysical topics, especially in science and religion. Much of this work remained un-published until after his death. In modern intellectual history, he is most often remembered for his explicit formulation of the position that we have a moral duty to believe only that which is sufficiently justified by the evidence. As you have seen already in the other readings, philosophers typically assume that beliefs need adequate justification in order for reasonable people to accept them. But Clifford translated this epistemological expectation into an ethical responsibility and in so doing noticeably altered the terms of the debate.

With the rise of the scientific worldview in eighteenth- and nineteenth-century Western culture, and the challenge to traditional belief systems (religious and otherwise) that it generated, Clifford's conclusions were valuable because they directly addressed the social consequences of what we accept as knowledge. That issue still informs today the often uneasy relationship between science, technological innovation, religion, and morality. In this selection, from his essay "The Ethics of Belief," Clifford develops and defends the still controversial view that it matters *morally* not only what we believe but also how we arrive at our beliefs.

QUESTIONS FOR CRITICAL READING

1. What are the two illustrations of unjustified belief used by Clifford, and how does he evaluate them?
2. According to Clifford, why is the truth of a belief by itself insufficient for its being justified?
3. How does Clifford defend his position that it is always morally wrong "to believe anything upon insufficient evidence"?
4. Why does Clifford think it is socially harmful to make oneself "credulous"?

TERMS TO NOTE

Providence: A term for God in the Western religious traditions, connoting especially the characteristics of benevolence and caretaking.

in foro conscientiae: Literally "in the forum of conscience"; in other words, what conscience discovers to be right.

I. The Duty of Inquiry

A shipowner was about to send to sea an emigrant-ship. He knew that she was old, and not over-well built at the first; that she had seen many seas and climes, and often had needed repairs. Doubts had been suggested to him that possibly she was not seaworthy. These doubts preyed upon his mind, and made him unhappy; he thought that perhaps he ought to have her thoroughly overhauled and refitted, even though this should put him to great expense. Before the ship sailed, however, he succeeded in overcoming these melancholy reflections. He said to himself that she had gone safely through so many voyages and weathered so many storms that it was idle to suppose she would not come safely home from this trip also. He would put his trust in Providence, which could hardly fail to protect all these unhappy families that were leaving their fatherland to seek for better times elsewhere. He would dismiss from his mind all ungenerous suspicions about the honesty of builders and contractors. In such ways he acquired a sincere and comfortable conviction that his vessel was thoroughly safe and seaworthy; he watched her departure with a light heart, and benevolent wishes for the success of the exiles in their strange new home that was to be; and he got his insurance-money when she went down in mid-ocean and told no tales.

What shall we say of him? Surely this, that he was verily guilty of the death of those men. It is admitted that he did sincerely believe in the soundness of his ship; but the sincerity of his conviction can in no wise help him, because *he had no right to believe on such evidence as was before him.* He had acquired his belief not by honestly earning it in patient investigation, but by stifling his doubts. And although in the end he may have felt so sure about it that he could not think otherwise, yet inasmuch as he had knowingly and willingly worked himself into that frame of mind, he must be held responsible for it.

Let us alter the case a little, and suppose that the ship was not unsound after all; that she made her voyage safely, and many others after it. Will that diminish the guilt of her owner? Not one jot. When an action is once done, it is right or wrong for ever; no accidental failure of its good or evil fruits can possibly alter that. The man would not have been innocent, he would only have been not found out. The question of right or wrong has to do with the origin of his belief, not the matter of it; not what it was, but how he got it; not whether it turned out to be true or false, but whether he had a right to believe on such evidence as was before him.

There was once an island in which some of the inhabitants professed a religion teaching neither the doctrine of original sin nor that of eternal punishment. A suspicion got abroad that the professors of this religion had made use of unfair means to get their doctrines taught to children. They were accused of wresting the laws of their country in such a way as to remove children from the care of their natural and legal guardians; and even of stealing them away and keeping them concealed from their friends and relations. A certain number of men formed themselves into a society for the purpose of agitating the public about this matter. They published grave accusations against individual citizens of the highest position and character, and did all in their power to injure these citizens in the exercise of their professions. So great was the noise they made, that a Commission was appointed to investigate the facts; but after the Commission had carefully inquired into all the evidence that could be got, it appeared that the accused were innocent. Not only had they been accused on insufficient evidence, but the evidence of their innocence was such as the agitators might easily have obtained, if they had attempted a fair inquiry. After these disclosures the inhabitants of that country looked upon the members of the agitating society, not only as persons whose judgment was to be distrusted, but also as no longer to be counted honourable men. For although they had sincerely and conscientiously believed in the charges they had made, yet *they had no right to believe on such evidence as was before them.* Their sincere convictions, instead of being honestly earned by patient inquiring, were stolen by listening to the voice of prejudice and passion.

Let us vary this case also, and suppose, other things remaining as before, that a still more accurate investigation proved the accused to have been really guilty. Would this make any difference in the guilt of the accusers? Clearly not; the question is not whether their belief was true or false, but whether they entertained it on wrong grounds. They would no doubt say, 'Now you see that we were right after all; next time perhaps you will believe us.' And they might be believed, but they would not thereby become honourable men. They would not be innocent, they would only be not found out. Every one of them, if he chose to examine himself *in foro conscientiæ,* would know that he had acquired and nourished a belief, when he had no right to believe on such evidence as was before him; and

therein he would know that he had done a wrong thing.

It may be said, however, that in both of these supposed cases it is not the belief which is judged to be wrong, but the action following upon it. The shipowner might say, 'I am perfectly certain that my ship is sound, but still I feel it my duty to have her examined, before trusting the lives of so many people to her.' And it might be said to the agitator, 'However convinced you were of the justice of your cause and the truth of your convictions, you ought not to have made a public attack upon any man's character until you had examined the evidence on both sides with the utmost patience and care.'

In the first place, let us admit that, so far as it goes, this view of the case is right and necessary; right, because even when a man's belief is so fixed that he cannot think otherwise, he still has a choice in regard to the action suggested by it, and so cannot escape the duty of investigating on the ground of the strength of his convictions; and necessary, because those who are not yet capable of controlling their feelings and thoughts must have a plain rule dealing with overt acts.

But this being premised as necessary, it becomes clear that it is not sufficient, and that our previous judgment is required to supplement it. For it is not possible so to sever the belief from the action it suggests as to condemn the one without condemning the other. No man holding a strong belief on one side of a question, or even wishing to hold a belief on one side, can investigate it with such fairness and completeness as if he were really in doubt and unbiased; so that the existence of a belief not founded on fair inquiry unfits a man for the performance of this necessary duty.

Nor is that truly a belief at all which has not some influence upon the actions of him who holds it. He who truly believes that which prompts him to an action has looked upon the action to lust after it, he has committed it already in his heart. If a belief is not realized immediately in open deeds, it is stored up for the guidance of the future. It goes to make a part of that aggregate of beliefs which is the link between sensation and action at every moment of all our lives, and which is so organized and compacted together that no part of it can be isolated from the rest, but every new addition modifies the structure of the whole. No real belief, however trifling and fragmentary it may seem, is ever truly insignificant; it prepares us to receive more of its like, confirms those which resembled it before, and weakens others; and so gradually it lays a stealthy train in our inmost thoughts, which may some day explode into overt action, and leave its stamp upon our character for ever.

And no one man's beliefs is in any case a private matter which concerns himself alone. Our lives are guided by that general conception of the course of things which has been created by society for social purposes. Our words, our phrases, our forms and processes and modes of thought, are common property, fashioned and perfected from age to age; an heirloom which every succeeding generation inherits as a precious deposit and a sacred trust to be handed on to the next one, not unchanged but enlarged and purified, with some clear marks of its proper handiwork. Into this, for good or ill, is woven every belief of every man who has speech of his fellows. An awful privilege, and an awful responsibility, that we should help to create the world in which posterity will live.

In the two supposed cases which have been considered, it has been judged wrong to believe on insufficient evidence, or to nourish belief by suppressing doubts and avoiding investigation. The reason of this judgment is not far to seek: it is that in both these cases the belief held by one man was of great importance to other men. But forasmuch as no belief held by one man, however seemingly trivial the belief, and however obscure the believer, is ever actually insignificant or without its effect on the fate of mankind, we have no choice but to extend our judgment to all cases of belief whatever. Belief, that sacred faculty which prompts the decisions of our will, and knits into harmonious working all the compacted energies of our being, is ours not for ourselves, but for humanity. It is rightly used on truths which have been established by long experience and waiting toil, and which have stood in the fierce light of free and fearless questioning. Then it helps to bind men together, and to strengthen and direct their common action. It is desecrated when given to unproved and unquestioned statements, for the solace and private pleasure of the believer; to add a tinsel splendour to the plain straight road of our life and display a bright mirage beyond it; or even to drown the common sorrows of our kind by a self-deception which allows them not only to cast down, but also to degrade us. Whoso would deserve well of his fellows in this matter will guard the purity of his belief with a very fanaticism of jealous care, lest at any time it should rest on an unworthy object, and catch a stain which can never be wiped away.

It is not only the leader of men, statesman, philosopher, or poet, that owes this bounden duty to mankind. Every rustic who delivers in the village alehouse his slow, infrequent sentences, may help to kill or keep alive the fatal superstitions which clog his race. Every hard-worked wife of an artisan may transmit to her children beliefs which shall knit society together, or rend it in pieces. No simplicity of mind, no obscurity of station, can escape the universal duty of questioning all that we believe.

It is true that this duty is a hard one, and the doubt which comes out of it is often a very bitter thing. It leaves us bare and powerless where we thought that we were safe and strong. To know all about anything is to know how to deal with it under all circumstances. We feel much happier and more secure when we think we know precisely what to do, no matter what happens, than when we have lost our way and do not know where to turn. And if we have supposed ourselves to know all about anything, and to be capable of doing what is fit in regard to it, we naturally do not like to find that we are really ignorant and powerless, that we have to begin again at the beginning, and try to learn what the thing is and how it is to be dealt with—if indeed anything can be learnt about it. It is the sense of power attached to a sense of knowledge that makes men desirous of believing, and afraid of doubting.

This sense of power is the highest and best of pleasures when the belief on which it is founded is a true belief, and has been fairly earned by investigation. For then we may justly feel that it is common property, and holds good for others as well as for ourselves. Then we may be glad, not that *I* have learned secrets by which I am safer and stronger, but that *we men* have got mastery over more of the world; and we shall be strong, not for ourselves, but in the name of Man and in his strength. But if the belief has been accepted on insufficient evidence, the pleasure is a stolen one. Not only does it deceive ourselves by giving us a sense of power which we do not really possess, but it is sinful, because it is stolen in defiance of our duty to mankind.

That duty is to guard ourselves from such beliefs as from a pestilence, which may shortly master our own body and then spread to the rest of the town. What would be thought of one who, for the sake of a sweet fruit, should deliberately run the risk of bringing a plague upon his family and his neighbours?

And, as in other such cases, it is not the risk only which has to be considered; for a bad action is always bad at the time when it is done, no matter what happens afterwards. Every time we let ourselves believe for unworthy reasons, we weaken our powers of self-control, of doubting, of judicially and fairly weighing evidence. We all suffer severely enough from the maintenance and support of false beliefs and the fatally wrong actions which they lead to, and the evil born when one such belief is entertained is great and wide. But a greater and wider evil arises when the credulous character is maintained and supported, when a habit of believing for unworthy reasons is fostered and made permanent. If I steal money from any person, there may be no harm done by the mere transfer of possession; he may not feel the loss, or it may prevent him from using the money badly. But I cannot help doing this great wrong towards Man, that I make myself dishonest. What hurts society is not that it should lose its property, but that it should become a den of thieves; for then it must cease to be society. This is why we ought not to do evil that good may come; for at any rate this great evil has come, that we have done evil and are made wicked thereby. In like manner, if I let myself believe anything on insufficient evidence, there may be no great harm done by the mere belief; it may be true after all, or I may never have occasion to exhibit it in outward acts. But I cannot help doing this great wrong towards Man, that I make myself credulous. The danger to society is not merely that it should believe wrong things, though that is great enough; but that it should become credulous, and lose the habit of testing things and inquiring into them; for then it must sink back into savagery.

The harm which is done by credulity in a man is not confined for the fostering of a credulous character in others, and consequent support of false beliefs. Habitual want of care about what I believe leads to habitual want of care in others about the truth of what is told to me. Men speak the truth to one another when each reveres the truth in his own mind and in the other's

mind; but how shall my friend revere the truth in my mind when I myself am careless about it, when I believe things because I want to believe them, and because they are comforting and pleasant? Will he not learn to cry, 'Peace,' to me, when there is no peace? By such a course I shall surround myself with a thick atmosphere of falsehood and fraud, and in that I must live. It may matter little to me, in my cloudcastle of sweet illusions and darling lies; but it matters much to Man that I have made my neighbours ready to deceive. The credulous man is father to the liar and the cheat; he lives in the bosom of this his family, and it is no marvel if he should become even as they are. So closely are our duties knit together, that whoso shall keep the whole law, and yet offend in one point, he is guilty of all.

To sum up: it is wrong always, everywhere, and for anyone, to believe anything upon insufficient evidence. If a man, holding a belief which he was taught in childhood or persuaded of afterwards, keeps down and pushes away any doubts which arise about it in his mind, purposely avoids the reading of books and the company of men that call in question or discuss it, and regards as impious these questions which cannot easily be asked without disturbing it—the life of that man is one long sin against mankind.

If this judgment seems harsh when applied to those simple souls who have never known better, who have been brought up from the cradle with a horror of doubt, and taught that their eternal welfare depends on *what* they believe, then it leads to the very serious question, *Who hath made Israel to sin?*

It may be permitted me to fortify this judgment with the sentence of Milton[1]—

'A man may be a heretic in the truth; and if he believe things only because his pastor says so, or the assembly so determine, without knowing other reason, though his belief be true, yet the very truth he holds becomes his heresy.'

And with this famous aphorism of Coleridge[2]—

'He who begins by loving Christianity better than Truth, will proceed by loving his own sect or Church better than Christianity, and end in loving himself better than all.'

---

1. *Areopagitica.*
2. *Aids to Reflection.*

Inquiry into the evidence of a doctrine is not to be made once for all, and then taken as finally settled. It is never lawful to stifle a doubt; for either it can be honestly answered by means of the inquiry already made, or else it proves that the inquiry was not complete.

'But,' says one, 'I am a busy man; I have no time for the long course of study which would be necessary to make me in any degree a competent judge of certain questions, or even able to understand the nature of the arguments.' Then he should have no time to believe.

DISCUSSION QUESTIONS

1. Why would you agree or disagree with Clifford's claim that all of our beliefs directly or indirectly have an impact on other people? Should this matter morally?

2. What are some other situations in which we might hold people morally or legally responsible for their beliefs, their knowledge, or their ignorance (say, in business, government, or scientific research)?

3. Is Clifford's position that we have no right to insufficiently justified beliefs compatible with the principle of freedom of thought? Why or why not?

4. What are the similarities and differences between Clifford's analysis and Peirce's account of the "fixation of belief"?

19. William James (1842–1910)
"The Will to Believe"

Although the only academic degree he ever earned was in medicine, by the time of his death in 1910 William James (older brother of the novelist Henry James) was famous internationally as a philosopher and psychologist. At Harvard University he first taught courses in anatomy and physiology, then became professor of psychology, and finally, professor of philosophy as well. His teaching and writing career illustrates the easy interchange between different academic disciplines that still was possible in the United States around the turn of the twentieth century. In fact, many consider his major work to have been the voluminous *The Principles of Psychology* (1890), which included a critical summary of almost all of the work that had been done in that field at the time.

James was recognized in Europe and North America as another of the most influential American pragmatists, and thus, like Peirce, he emphasized the goal-oriented character of human experience and belief acquisition. He sometimes described his epistemological approach as a "radical empiricism," which focused not only on the active rather than passive nature of experiential life but also on its diversity and irreducibility among distinct individuals.

The reading is from an essay published in 1897 as part of a collection of his writings intended for wider public consumption. Its affirmation of individual choice and a motivational role for emotion in the development of our beliefs was in part a response to the various deterministic theories of cognition and conduct that were widely accepted during the late nineteenth and early twentieth centuries. It also includes a direct response to Clifford's position on the ethics of belief (see the previous reading). In arguing against Clifford, James demonstrates his pragmatist orientation to questions about knowledge and truth, as well as his concern to defend the legitimacy of human belief "in things unseen."

QUESTIONS FOR CRITICAL READING

1. What is the difference between a "live" and a "dead" hypothesis, according to James?

2. What does James mean by an "option," and what are the seven different kinds of options he identifies?

3. How does James criticize Clifford's position on the duty of belief, and what alternative "thesis" does he defend?

4. What is the difference between the "empiricist" and the "absolutist" way of "believing in truth," according to James?

5. What does James mean by distinguishing between the demand to "know the truth" and the demand to "avoid error"?

6. How does James characterize the "religious hypothesis," and how is it different from the "naturalistic hypothesis"?

TERMS TO NOTE

enfant terrible: A French phrase literally meaning "terrible child"; here, it refers to an overly precocious, rebellious newcomer to an enterprise—a young upstart who loudly challenges convention.
pathos: The expression of feeling or emotion, especially of tenderness and melancholy.
pyrrhonist: An extreme skeptic; one who denies that humans can know anything for sure. Derived from the name of Pyrrho, an ancient Greek philosopher from Elis.
sacerdotal: Having to do with the priesthood.
Grenzbegriff: A limiting concept.
Mephistopheles: The devil in the story of Faust.
omniscience: The attribute of being all knowing.

In the recently published Life by Leslie Stephen of his brother, Fitz-James, there is an account of a school to which the latter went when he was a boy. The teacher, a certain Mr. Guest, used to converse with his pupils in this wise: "Gurney, what is the difference between justification and sanctification?—Stephen, prove the omnipotence of God!" etc. In the midst of our Harvard freethinking and indifference we are prone to imagine that here at your good old orthodox College conversation continues to be somewhat upon this order; and to show you that we at Harvard have not lost all interest in these vital subjects, I have brought with me to-night something like a sermon on justification by faith to read to you,—I mean an essay in justification *of* faith, a defence of our right to adopt a believing attitude in religious matters, in spite of the fact that our merely logical intellect may not have been coerced. 'The Will to Believe,' accordingly, is the title of my paper.

I have long defended to my own students the lawfulness of voluntarily adopted faith; but as soon as they have got well imbued with the logical spirit, they have as a rule refused to admit my contention to be lawful philosophically, even though in point of fact they were personally all the time chock-full of some faith or other themselves. I am all the while, however, so profoundly convinced that my own position is correct, that your invitation has seemed to me a good occasion to make my statements more clear. Perhaps your minds will be more open than those with which I have hitherto had to deal. I will be as little technical as I can, though I must begin by setting up some technical distinctions that will help us in the end.

I

Let us give the name of *hypothesis* to anything that may be proposed to our belief; and just as the electricians speak of live and dead wires, let us speak of any hypothesis as either *live* or *dead.* A live hypothesis is one which appeals as a real possibility to him to whom it is proposed. If I ask you to believe in the Mahdi, the notion makes no electric connection with your nature,—it refuses to scintillate with any credibility at all. As an hypothesis it is completely dead. To an Arab, however (even if he be not one of the Mahdi's followers), the hypothesis is among the mind's possibilities: it is alive. This shows that deadness and liveness in an hypothesis are not intrinsic properties, but relations to the individual thinker. They are measured by his willingness to act. The maximum of liveness in an hypothesis means willingness to act irrevocably. Practically, that means belief; but there is some believing tendency wherever there is willingness to act at all.

Next, let us call the decision between two hypotheses an *option.* Options may be of several kinds. They may be—1, *living* or *dead;* 2, *forced* or *avoidable;* 3, *momentous* or *trivial;* and for our purposes we may call an option a *genuine* option when it is of the forced, living, and momentous kind.

1. A living option is one in which both hypotheses are live ones. If I say to you: "Be a theosophist or be a Mohammedan," it is probably a dead option, because for you neither hypothesis is likely to be alive. But if I say: "Be an agnostic or be a Christian," it is otherwise: trained as you are, each hypothesis makes some appeal, however small, to your belief.

2. Next, if I say to you: "Choose between going out with your umbrella or without it," I do not offer you a genuine option, for it is not forced. You can easily

avoid it by not going out at all. Similarly, if I say, "Either love me or hate me," "Either call my theory true or call it false," your option is avoidable. You may remain indifferent to me, neither loving nor hating, and you may decline to offer any judgment as to my theory. But if I say, "Either accept this truth or go without it," I put on you a forced option, for there is no standing place outside of the alternative. Every dilemma based on a complete logical disjunction, with no possibility of not choosing, is an option of this forced kind.

3. Finally, if I were Dr. Nansen and proposed to you to join my North Pole expedition, your option would be momentous; for this would probably be your only similar opportunity, and your choice now would either exclude you from the North Pole sort of immortality altogether or put at least the chance of it into your hands. He who refuses to embrace a unique opportunity loses the prize as surely as if he tried and failed. *Per contra,* the option is trivial when the opportunity is not unique, when the stake is insignificant, or when the decision is reversible if it later prove unwise. Such trivial options abound in the scientific life. A chemist finds an hypothesis live enough to spend a year in its verification: he believes in it to that extent. But if his experiments prove inconclusive either way, he is quit for his loss of time, no vital harm being done.

It will facilitate our discussion if we keep all these distinctions well in mind.

II

The next matter to consider is the actual psychology of human opinion. When we look at certain facts, it seems as if our passional and volitional nature lay at the root of all our convictions. When we look at others, it seems as if they could do nothing when the intellect had once said its say. Let us take the latter facts up first.

Does it not seem preposterous on the very face of it to talk of our opinions being modifiable at will? Can our will either help or hinder our intellect in its perceptions of truth? Can we, by just willing it, believe that Abraham Lincoln's existence is a myth, and that the portraits of him in McClure's Magazine are all of

some one else? Can we, by any effort of our will, or by any strength of wish that it were true, believe ourselves well and about when we are roaring with rheumatism in bed, or feel certain that the sum of the two one-dollar bills in our pocket must be a hundred dollars? We can *say* any of these things, but we are absolutely impotent to believe them; and of just such things is the whole fabric of the truths that we do believe in made up,—matters of fact, immediate or remote, as Hume said, and relations between ideas, which are either there or not there for us if we see them so, and which if not there cannot be put there by any action of our own.

In Pascal's Thoughts there is a celebrated passage known in literature as Pascal's wager. In it he tries to force us into Christianity by reasoning as if our concern with truth resembled our concern with the stakes in a game of chance. Translated freely his words are these: You must either believe or not believe that God is—which will you do? Your human reason cannot say. A game is going on between you and the nature of things which at the day of judgment will bring out either heads or tails. Weigh what your gains and your losses would be if you should stake all you have on heads, or God's existence: if you win in such case, you gain eternal beatitude; if you lose, you lose nothing at all. If there were an infinity of chances, and only one for God in this wager, still you ought to stake your all on God; for though you surely risk a finite loss by this procedure, any finite loss is reasonable, even a certain one is reasonable, if there is but the possibility of infinite gain. Go, then, and take holy water, and have masses said; belief will come and stupefy your scruples,—*Cela vous fera croire et vous abêtira.* Why should you not? At bottom, what have you to lose?

You probably feel that when religious faith expresses itself thus, in the language of the gaming-table, it is put to its last trumps. Surely Pascal's own personal belief in masses and holy water had far other springs; and this celebrated page of his is but an argument for others, a last desperate snatch at a weapon against the hardness of the unbelieving heart. We feel that a faith in masses and holy water adopted wilfully after such a mechanical calculation would lack the inner soul of faith's reality; and if we were ourselves in the place of the Deity, we should probably take particular pleasure in cutting off believers of this pattern from their infinite reward. It is evident that unless there be some pre-existing tendency to believe in masses and holy water, the option offered to the will by Pascal is not a living option. Certainly no Turk ever took to masses and holy water on its account; and even to us Protestants these means of salvation seem such foregone impossibilities that Pascal's logic, invoked for them specifically, leaves us unmoved. As well might the Mahdi write to us, saying, "I am the Expected One whom God has created in his effulgence. You shall be infinitely happy if you confess me; otherwise you shall be cut off from the light of the sun. Weigh, then, your infinite gain if I am genuine against your finite sacrifice if I am not!" His logic would be that of Pascal; but he would vainly use it on us, for the hypothesis he offers us is dead. No tendency to act on it exists in us to any degree.

The talk of believing by our volition seems, then, from one point of view, simply silly. From another point of view it is worse than silly, it is vile. When one turns to the magnificent edifice of the physical sciences, and sees how it was reared; what thousands of disinterested moral lives of men lie buried in its mere foundations; what patience and postponement, what choking down of preference, what submission to the icy laws of outer fact are wrought into its very stones and mortar; how absolutely impersonal it stands in its vast augustness,—then how besotted and contemptible seems every little sentimentalist who comes blowing his voluntary smoke-wreaths, and pretending to decide things from out of his private dream! Can we wonder if those bred in the rugged and manly school of science should feel like spewing such subjectivism out of their mouths? The whole system of loyalties which grow up in the schools of science go dead against its toleration; so that it is only natural that those who have caught the scientific fever should pass over to the opposite extreme, and write sometimes as if the incorruptibly truthful intellect ought positively to prefer bitterness and unacceptableness to the heart in its cup.

It fortifies my soul to know
That, though I perish, Truth is so—

sings Clough, while Huxley exclaims: "My only consolation lies in the reflection that, however bad our posterity may become, so far as they hold by the plain rule of not pretending to believe what they have no reason to believe, because it may be to their advantage so to pretend [the word 'pretend' is surely here redundant], they will not have reached the lowest depth of immorality." And that delicious *enfant terrible* Clifford writes: "Belief is desecrated when given to unproved and unquestioned statements for the solace and private pleasure of the believer.... Whoso would deserve well of his fellows in this matter will guard the purity of his belief with a very fanaticism of jealous care, lest at any time it should rest on an unworthy object, and catch a stain which can never be wiped away.... If [a] belief has been accepted on insufficient evidence [even though the belief be true, as Clifford on the same page explains] the pleasure is a stolen one.... It is sinful because it is stolen in defiance of our duty to mankind. That duty is to guard ourselves from such beliefs as from a pestilence which may shortly master our own body and then spread to the rest of the town.... It is wrong always, everywhere, and for every one, to believe anything upon insufficient evidence."

III

All this strikes one as healthy, even when expressed, as by Clifford, with somewhat too much of robustious pathos in the voice. Free-will and simple wishing do seem, in the matter of our credences, to be only fifth wheels to the coach. Yet if any one should thereupon assume that intellectual insight is what remains after wish and will and sentimental preference have taken wing, or that pure reason is what then settles our opinions, he would fly quite as directly in the teeth of the facts.

It is only our already dead hypotheses that our willing nature is unable to bring to life again. But what has made them dead for us is for the most part a previous action of our willing nature of an antagonistic kind. When I say 'willing nature,' I do not mean only such deliberate volitions as may have set up habits of belief that we cannot now escape from,—I mean all such factors of belief as fear and hope, prejudice and passion, imitation and partisanship, the circumpressure of our caste and set. As a matter of fact we find ourselves believing, we hardly know how or why. Mr. Balfour gives the name of 'authority' to all those influences, born of the intellectual climate, that make hypotheses possible or impossible for us, alive or dead. Here in this room, we all of us believe in molecules and the conservation of energy, in democracy and necessary progress, in Protestant Christianity and the duty of fighting for 'the doctrine of the immortal Monroe,' all for no reasons worthy of the name. We see into these matters with no more inner clearness, and probably with much less, than any disbeliever in them might possess. His unconventionality would probably have some grounds to show for its conclusions; but for us, not insight, but the *prestige* of the opinions, is what makes the spark shoot from them and light up our sleeping magazines of faith. Our reason is quite satisfied, in nine hundred and ninety-nine cases out of every thousand of us, if it can find a few arguments that will do to recite in case our credulity is criticised by some one else. Our faith is faith in some one else's faith, and in the greatest matters this is most the case. Our belief in truth itself, for instance, that there is a truth, and that our minds and it are made for each other,—what is it but a passionate affirmation of desire, in which our social system backs us up? We want to have a truth; we want to believe that our experiments and studies and discussions must put us in a continually better and better position towards it; and on this line we agree to fight out our thinking lives. But if a pyrrhonistic sceptic asks us *how we know* all this, can our logic find a reply? No! certainly it cannot. It is just one volition against another,—we willing to go in for life upon a trust or assumption which he, for his part, does not care to make.[1]

As a rule we disbelieve all facts and theories for which we have no use. Clifford's cosmic emotions find no use for Christian feelings. Huxley belabors the bishops because there is no use for sacerdotalism in his scheme of life. Newman, on the contrary, goes over to Romanism, and finds all sorts of reasons good for staying there, because a priestly system is for him an organic need and delight. Why do so few 'scientists' even look at the evidence for telepathy, so called? Because they think, as a leading biologist, now dead,

once said to me, that even if such a thing were true, scientists ought to band together to keep it suppressed and concealed. It would undo the uniformity of Nature and all sorts of other things without which scientists cannot carry on their pursuits. But if this very man had been shown something which as a scientist he might *do* with telepathy, he might not only have examined the evidence, but even have found it good enough. This very law which the logicians would impose upon us—if I may give the name of logicians to those who would rule out our willing nature here—is based on nothing but their own natural wish to exclude all elements for which they, in their professional quality of logicians, can find no use.

Evidently, then, our non-intellectual nature does influence our convictions. There are passional tendencies and volitions which run before and others which come after belief, and it is only the latter that are too late for the fair; and they are not too late when the previous passional work has been already in their own direction. Pascal's argument, instead of being powerless, then seems a regular clincher, and is the last stroke needed to make our faith in masses and holy water complete. The state of things is evidently far from simple; and pure insight and logic, whatever they might do ideally, are not the only things that really do produce our creeds.

IV

Our next duty, having recognized this mixed-up state of affairs, is to ask whether it be simply reprehensible and pathological, or whether, on the contrary, we must treat it as a normal element in making up our minds. The thesis I defend is, briefly stated, this: *Our passional nature not only lawfully may, but must, decide an option between propositions, whenever it is a genuine option that cannot by its nature be decided on intellectual grounds; for to say, under such circumstances, "Do not decide, but leave the question open," is itself a passional decision,—just like deciding yes or no,—and is attended with the same risk of losing the truth.* The thesis thus abstractly expressed will, I trust, soon become quite clear. But I must first indulge in a bit more of preliminary work.

1. Compare the admirable page 310 in S. H. Hodgson's *Time and Space* (London, 1865).

V

It will be observed that for the purposes of this discussion we are on 'dogmatic' ground,—ground, I mean, which leaves systematic philosophical scepticism altogether out of account. The postulate that there is truth, and that it is the destiny of our minds to attain it, we are deliberately resolving to make, though the sceptic will not make it. We part company with him, therefore, absolutely, at this point. But the faith that truth exists, and that our minds can find it, may be held in two ways. We may talk of the *empiricist* way and of the *absolutist* way of believing in truth. The absolutists in this matter say that we not only can attain to knowing truth, but we can *know when* we have attained to knowing it; while the empiricists think that although we may attain it, we cannot infallibly know when. To *know* is one thing, and to know for certain *that* we know is another. One may hold to the first being possible without the second; hence the empiricists and the absolutists, although neither of them is a sceptic in the usual philosophic sense of the term, show very different degrees of dogmatism in their lives.

If we look at the history of opinions, we see that the empiricist tendency has largely prevailed in science, while in philosophy the absolutist tendency has had everything its own way. The characteristic sort of happiness, indeed, which philosophies yield has mainly consisted in the conviction felt by each successive school or system that by it bottom-certitude had been attained. "Other philosophies are collections of opinions, mostly false; *my* philosophy gives standing-ground forever."—who does not recognize in this the key-note of every system worthy of the name? A system, to be a system at all, must come as a *closed* system, reversible in this or that detail, perchance, but in its essential features never!

Scholastic orthodoxy, to which one must always go when one wishes to find perfectly clear statement, has beautifully elaborated this absolutist conviction in a doctrine which it calls that of 'objective evidence.' If, for example, I am unable to doubt that I now exist before you, that two is less than three, or that if all men are mortal then I am mortal too, it is because these things illumine my intellect irresistibly. The final

ground of this objective evidence possessed by certain propositions is the *adaequatio intellectûs nostri cum rê.* The certitude it brings involves an *aptitudinem ad extorquendum certum assensum* on the part of the truth envisaged, and on the side of the subject a *quietem in cognitione,* when once the object is mentally received, that leaves no possibility of doubt behind; and in the whole transaction nothing operates but the *entitas ipsa* of the object and the *entitas ipsa* of the mind. We slouchy modern thinkers dislike to talk in Latin,—indeed, we dislike to talk in set terms at all; but at bottom our own state of mind is very much like this whenever we uncritically abandon ourselves: You believe in objective evidence, and I do. Of some things we feel that we are certain: we know, and we know that we do know. There is something that gives a click inside of us, a bell that strikes twelve, when the hands of our mental clock have swept the dial and meet over the meridian hour. The greatest empiricists among us are only empiricists on reflection: when left to their instincts, they dogmatize like infallible popes. When the Cliffords tell us how sinful it is to be Christians on such 'insufficient evidence,' insufficiency is really the last thing they have in mind. For them the evidence is absolutely sufficient, only it makes the other way. They believe so completely in an anti-christian order of the universe that there is no living option: Christianity is a dead hypothesis from the start.

VI

But now, since we are all such absolutists by instinct, what in our quality of students of philosophy ought we to do about the fact? Shall we espouse and indorse it? Or shall we treat it as a weakness of our nature from which we must free ourselves, if we can?

I sincerely believe that the latter course is the only one we can follow as reflective men. Objective evidence and certitude are doubtless very fine ideals to play with, but where on this moonlit and dream-visited planet are they found? I am, therefore, myself a complete empiricist so far as my theory of human knowledge goes. I live, to be sure, by the practical faith that we must go on experiencing and thinking over our experience, for only thus can our opinions grow more true; but to hold any one of them—I absolutely do not care which—as if it never could be reinterpretable or corrigible, I believe to be a tremendously mistaken attitude, and I think that the whole history of philosophy will bear me out. There is but one indefectibly certain truth, and that is the truth that pyrrhonistic scepticism itself leaves standing,—the truth that the present phenomenon of consciousness exists. That, however, is the bare starting-point of knowledge, the mere admission of a stuff to be philosophized about. The various philosophies are but so many attempts at expressing what this stuff really is. And if we repair to our libraries what disagreement do we discover! Where is a certainly true answer found? Apart from abstract propositions of comparison (such as two and two are the same as four), propositions which tell us nothing by themselves about concrete reality, we find no proposition ever regarded by any one as evidently certain that has not either been called a falsehood, or at least had its truth sincerely questioned by some one else. The transcending of the axioms of geometry, not in play but in earnest, by certain of our contemporaries (as Zöllner and Charles H. Hinton), and the rejection of the whole Aristotelian logic by the Hegelians, are striking instances in point.

No concrete test of what is really true has ever been agreed upon. Some make the criterion external to the moment of perception, putting it either in revelation, the *consensus gentium,* the instincts of the heart, or the systematized experience of the race. Others make the perceptive moment its own test,—Descartes, for instance, with his clear and distinct ideas guaranteed by the veracity of God; Reid with his 'common-sense;' and Kant with his forms of synthetic judgment *a priori.* The inconceivability of the opposite; the capacity to be verified by sense; the possession of complete organic unity or self-relation, realized when a thing is its own other,—are standards which, in turn, have been used. The much lauded objective evidence is never triumphantly there; it is a mere aspiration or *Grenzbegriff,* marking the infinitely remote ideal of our thinking life. To claim that certain truths now possess it, is simply to say that when you think them true and they *are* true, then their evidence is objective, otherwise it is not. But practically one's conviction that the evidence one goes by is of the real objective brand, is only one more subjective opinion added to the lot. For what a contradictory array of opinions have objective evidence and absolute certitude been claimed! The world is rational through and through,—its existence is an ultimate brute fact; there is a personal God,—a personal God is inconceivable; there is an extramental physical world immediately known,—the mind can only know its own ideas; a moral imperative exists,—obligation is only the resultant of desires; a permanent spiritual principle is in every one,—there are only shifting states of mind; there is an endless chain of causes,—there is an absolute first cause; an eternal necessity,—a freedom; a purpose,—no purpose; a primal One,—a primal Many; a universal continuity,—an essential discontinuity in things; an infinity,—no infinity. There is this,—there is that; there is indeed nothing which some one has not thought absolutely true, while his neighbor deemed it absolutely false; and not an absolutist among them seems ever to have considered that the trouble may all the time be essential, and that the intellect, even with truth directly in its grasp, may have no infallible signal for knowing whether it be truth or no. When, indeed, one remembers that the most striking practical application to life of the doctrine of objective certitude has been the conscientious labors of the Holy Office of the Inquisition, one feels less tempted than ever to lend the doctrine a respectful ear.

But please observe, now, that when as empiricists we give up the doctrine of objective certitude, we do not thereby give up the quest or hope of truth itself. We still pin our faith on its existence, and still believe that we gain an ever better position towards it by systematically continuing to roll up experiences and think. Our great difference from the scholastic lies in the way we face. The strength of his system lies in the principles, the origin, the *terminus a quo* of his thought; for us the strength is in the outcome, the upshot, the *terminus ad quem.* Not where it comes from but what it leads to is to decide. It matters not to an empiricist from what quarter an hypothesis may come to him: he may have acquired it by fair means or by foul; passion may have whispered or accident suggested it; but if the total drift of thinking continues to confirm it, that is what he means by its being true.

VII

One more point, small but important, and our preliminaries are done. There are two ways of looking at our duty in the matter of opinion,—ways entirely different, and yet ways about whose difference the theory of knowledge seems hitherto to have shown very little concern. *We must know the truth;* and *we must avoid error,*—these are our first and great commandments as would-be knowers; but they are not two ways of stating an identical commandment, they are two separable laws. Although it may indeed happen that when we believe the truth *A,* we escape as an incidental consequence from believing the falsehood *B,* it hardly ever happens that by merely disbelieving *B* we necessarily believe *A.* We may in escaping *B* fall into believing other falsehoods, *C* or *D,* just as bad as *B;* or we may escape *B* by not believing anything at all, not even *A.*

Believe truth! Shun error!—these, we see, are two materially different laws; and by choosing between them we may end by coloring differently our whole intellectual life. We may regard the chase for truth as paramount, and the avoidance of error as secondary; or we may, on the other hand, treat the avoidance of error as more imperative, and let truth take its chance. Clifford, in the instructive passage which I have quoted, exhorts us to the latter course. Believe nothing, he tells us, keep your mind in suspense forever, rather than by closing it on insufficient evidence incur the awful risk of believing lies. You, on the other hand, may think that the risk of being in error is a very small matter when compared with the blessings of real knowledge, and be ready to be duped many times in your investigation rather than postpone indefinitely the chance of guessing true. I myself find it impossible to go with Clifford. We must remember that these feelings of our duty about either truth or error are in any case only expressions of our passional life. Biologically considered, our minds are as ready to grind out falsehood as veracity, and he who says, "Better go without belief forever than believe a lie!" merely shows his own preponderant private horror of becoming a dupe. He may be critical of many of his desires and fears, but this fear he slavishly obeys. He cannot imagine any one questioning its binding force. For my own part, I have also a horror of being duped; but I can believe that

worse things than being duped may happen to a man in this world: so Clifford's exhortation has to my ears a thoroughly fantastic sound. It is like a general informing his soldiers that it is better to keep out of battle forever than to risk a single wound. Not so are victories either over enemies or over nature gained. Our errors are surely not such awfully solemn things. In a world where we are so certain to incur them in spite of all our caution, a certain lightness of heart seems healthier than this excessive nervousness on their behalf. At any rate, it seems the fittest thing for the empiricist philosopher.

VIII

And now, after all this introduction, let us go straight at our question. I have said, and now repeat it, that not only as a matter of fact do we find our passional nature influencing us in our opinions, but that there are some options between opinions in which this influence must be regarded both as an inevitable and as a lawful determinant of our choice.

I fear here that some of you my hearers will begin to scent danger, and lend an inhospitable ear. Two first steps of passion you have indeed had to admit as necessary,—we must think so as to avoid dupery, and we must think so as to gain truth; but the surest path to those ideal consummations, you will probably consider, is from now onwards to take no further passional step.

Well, of course, I agree as far as the facts will allow. Wherever the option between losing truth and gaining it is not momentous, we can throw the chance of *gaining truth* away, and at any rate save ourselves from any chance of *believing falsehood,* by not making up our minds at all till objective evidence has come. In scientific questions, this is almost always the case; and even in human affairs in general, the need of acting is seldom so urgent that a false belief to act on is better than no belief at all. Law courts, indeed, have to decide on the best evidence attainable for the moment, because a judge's duty is to make law as well as to ascertain it, and (as a learned judge once said to me) few cases are worth spending much time over: the great thing is to have them decided on *any* acceptable principle, and got out of the way. But in our dealings with objective nature we obviously are recorders, not makers, of the truth; and decisions for the mere sake of deciding promptly and getting on to the next business would be wholly out of place. Throughout the breadth of physical nature facts are what they are quite independently of us, and seldom is there any such hurry about them that the risks of being duped by believing a premature theory need be faced. The questions here are always trivial options, the hypotheses are hardly living (at any rate not living for us spectators), the choice between believing truth or falsehood is seldom forced. The attitude of sceptical balance is therefore the absolutely wise one if we would escape mistakes. What difference, indeed, does it make to most of us whether we have or have not a theory of the Röntgen rays, whether we believe or not in mind-stuff, or have a conviction about the causality of conscious states? It makes no difference. Such options are not forced on us. On every account it is better not to make them, but still keep weighing reasons *pro et contra* with an indifferent hand.

I speak, of course, here of the purely judging mind. For purposes of discovery such indifference is to be less highly recommended, and science would be far less advanced than she is if the passionate desires of individuals to get their own faiths confirmed had been kept out of the game. See for example the sagacity which Spencer and Weismann now display. On the other hand, if you want an absolute duffer in an investigation, you must, after all, take the man who has no interest whatever in its results: he is the warranted incapable, the positive fool. The most useful investigator, because the most sensitive observer, is always he whose eager interest in one side of the question is balanced by an equally keen nervousness lest he become deceived.[2] Science has organized this nervousness into a regular *technique,* her so-called method of verification; and she has fallen so deeply in love with the method that one may even say she has ceased to care for truth by itself at all. It is only truth as technically verified that interests her. The truth of truths might come in merely affirmative form, and she would decline to

touch it. Such truth as that, she might repeat with Clifford, would be stolen in defiance of her duty to mankind. Human passions, however, are stronger than technical rules. "Le cœur a ses raisons," as Pascal says, "que la raison ne connaît pas;" and however indifferent to all but the bare rules of the game the umpire, the abstract intellect, may be, the concrete players who furnish him the materials to judge of are usually, each one of them, in love with some pet 'live hypothesis' of his own. Let us agree, however, that wherever there is no forced option, the dispassionately judicial intellect with no pet hypothesis, saving us, as it does, from dupery at any rate, ought to be our ideal.

The question next arises: Are there not somewhere forced options in our speculative questions, and can we (as men who may be interested at least as much in positively gaining truth as in merely escaping dupery) always wait with impunity till the coercive evidence shall have arrived? It seems *a priori* improbable that the truth should be so nicely adjusted to our needs and powers as that. In the great boarding-house of nature, the cakes and the butter and the syrup seldom come out so even and leave the plates so clean. Indeed, we should view them with scientific suspicion if they did.

IX

Moral questions immediately present themselves as questions whose solution cannot wait for sensible proof. A moral question is a question not of what sensibly exists, but of what is good, or would be good if it did exist. Science can tell us what exists; but to compare the *worths,* both of what exists and of what does not exist, we must consult not science, but what Pascal calls our heart. Science herself consults her heart when she lays it down that the infinite ascertainment of fact and correction of false belief are the supreme goods for man. Challenge the statement, and science can only repeat it oracularly, or else prove it by showing that such ascertainment and correction bring man all sorts of other goods which man's heart in turn declares. The question of having moral beliefs at all or not having them is decided by our will. Are our moral preferences true or false, or are they only odd biological phenomena, making things good or bad for *us,* but in themselves indifferent? How can your pure intellect

---

2. Compare Wilfrid Ward's essay, "The Wish to Believe," in his *Witnesses to the Unseen* (New York: Macmillan & Co., 1893).

decide? If your heart does not *want* a world of moral reality, your head will assuredly never make you believe in one. Mephistophelian scepticism, indeed, will satisfy the head's play-instincts much better than any rigorous idealism can. Some men (even at the student age) are so naturally cool-hearted that the moralistic hypothesis never has for them any pungent life, and in their supercilious presence the hot young moralist always feels strangely ill at ease. The appearance of knowingness is on their side, of *naïveté* and gullibility on his. Yet, in the inarticulate heart of him, he clings to it that he is not a dupe, and that there is a realm in which (as Emerson says) all their wit and intellectual superiority is no better than the cunning of a fox. Moral scepticism can no more be refuted or proved by logic than intellectual scepticism can. When we stick to it that there *is* truth (be it of either kind), we do so with our whole nature, and resolve to stand or fall by the results. The sceptic with his whole nature adopts the doubting attitude; but which of us is the wiser, Omniscience only knows.

Turn now from these wide questions of good to a certain class of questions of fact, questions concerning personal relations, states of mind between one man and another. *Do you like me or not?*—for example. Whether you do or not depends, in countless instances, on whether I meet you half-way, am willing to assume that you must like me, and show you trust and expectation. The previous faith on my part in your liking's existence is in such cases what makes your liking come. But if I stand aloof, and refuse to budge an inch until I have objective evidence, until you shall have done something apt, as the absolutists say, *ad extorquendum assensum meum,* ten to one your liking never comes. How many women's hearts are vanquished by the mere sanguine insistence of some man that they *must* love him! he will not consent to the hypothesis that they cannot. The desire for a certain kind of truth here brings about that special truth's existence; and so it is in innumerable cases of other sorts. Who gains promotions, boons, appointments, but the man in whose life they are seen to play the part of live hypotheses, who discounts them, sacrifices other things for their sake before they have come, and takes risks for them in advance? His faith acts on the powers above him as a claim, and creates its own verification.

A social organism of any sort whatever, large or small, is what it is because each member proceeds to his own duty with a trust that the other members will simultaneously do theirs. Wherever a desired result is achieved by the co-operation of many independent persons, its existence as a fact is a pure consequence of the precursive faith in one another of those immediately concerned. A government, an army, a commercial system, a ship, a college, an athletic team, all exist on this condition, without which not only is nothing achieved, but nothing is even attempted. A whole train of passengers (individually brave enough) will be looted by a few highwaymen, simply because the latter can count on one another, while each passenger fears that if he makes a movement of resistance, he will be shot before any one else backs him up. If we believed that the whole carfull would rise at once with us, we should each severally rise, and train-robbing would never even be attempted. There are, then, cases where a fact cannot come at all unless a preliminary faith exists in its coming. *And where faith in a fact can help create the fact,* that would be an insane logic which should say that faith running ahead of scientific evidence is the 'lowest kind of immorality' into which a thinking being can fall. Yet such is the logic by which our scientific absolutists pretend to regulate our lives!

X

In truths dependent on our personal action, then, faith based on desire is certainly a lawful and possibly an indispensable thing.

But now, it will be said, these are all childish human cases, and have nothing to do with great cosmical matters, like the question of religious faith. Let us then pass on to that. Religions differ so much in their accidents that in discussing the religious question we must make it very generic and broad. What then do we now mean by the religious hypothesis? Science says things are; morality says some things are better than other things; and religion says essentially two things.

First, she says that the best things are the more eternal things, the overlapping things, the things in the universe that throw the last stone, so to speak, and say the final word. "Perfection is eternal,"—this phrase of Charles Secrétan seems a good way of putting this first affirmation of religion, an affirmation which obviously cannot yet be verified scientifically at all.

The second affirmation of religion is that we are better off even now if we believe her first affirmation to be true.

Now, let us consider what the logical elements of this situation are *in case the religious hypothesis in both its branches be really true.* (Of course, we must admit that possibility at the outset. If we are to discuss the question at all, it must involve a living option. If for any of you religion be a hypothesis that cannot, by any living possibility be true, then you need go no farther. I speak to the 'saving remnant' alone.) So proceeding, we see, first, that religion offers itself as a *momentous* option. We are supposed to gain, even now, by our belief, and to lose by our non-belief, a certain vital good. Secondly, religion is a *forced* option, so far as that good goes. We cannot escape the issue by remaining sceptical and waiting for more light, because, although we do avoid error in that way *if religion be untrue,* we lose the good, *if it be true,* just as certainly as if we positively chose to disbelieve. It is as if a man should hesitate indefinitely to ask a certain woman to marry him because he was not perfectly sure that she would prove an angel after he brought her home. Would he not cut himself off from that particular angel-possibility as decisively as if he went and married some one else? Scepticism, then, is not avoidance of option; it is option of a certain particular kind of risk. *Better risk loss of truth than chance of error,*—that is your faith-vetoer's exact position. He is actively playing his stake as much as the believer is; he is backing the field against the religious hypothesis, just as the believer is backing the religious hypothesis against the field. To preach scepticism to us as a duty until 'sufficient evidence' for religion be found, is tantamount therefore to telling us, when in presence of the religious hypothesis, that to yield to our fear of its being error is wiser and better than to yield to our hope that it may be true. It is not intellect against all passions, then; it is only intellect with one passion laying down its law. And by what, forsooth, is the supreme wisdom of this passion warranted? Dupery for dupery, what proof is there that dupery through hope is so much worse than dupery through fear? I, for one, can see no proof; and I simply refuse obedience to the scientist's command to imitate his kind of option, in a case where my own stake is important enough to give me the right to choose my own form of risk. If religion be true and the evidence for it be still insufficient, I do not wish, by putting your extinguisher upon my nature (which feels to me as if it had after all some business in this matter), to forfeit my sole chance in life of getting upon the winning side,—that chance depending, of course, on my willingness to run the risk of acting as if my passional need of taking the world religiously might be prophetic and right.

All this is on the supposition that it really may be prophetic and right, and that, even to us who are discussing the matter, religion is a live hypothesis which may be true. Now, to most of us religion comes in a still further way that makes a veto on our active faith even more illogical. The more perfect and more eternal aspect of the universe is represented in our religions as having personal form. The universe is no longer a mere *It* to us, but a *Thou,* if we are religious; and any relation that may be possible from person to person might be possible here. For instance, although in one sense we are passive portions of the universe, in another we show a curious autonomy, as if we were small active centres on our own account. We feel, too, as if the appeal of religion to us were made to our own active good-will, as if evidence might be forever withheld from us unless we met the hypothesis half-way. To take a trivial illustration: just as a man who in a company of gentlemen made no advances, asked a warrant for every concession, and believed no one's word without proof, would cut himself off by such churlishness from all the social rewards that a more trusting spirit would earn,—so here, one who should shut himself up in snarling logicality and try to make the gods extort his recognition willy-nilly, or not get it at all, might cut himself off forever from his only opportunity of making the gods' acquaintance. This feeling, forced on us we know not whence, that by obstinately believing that there are gods (although not to do so would be so easy both for our logic and our life) we are doing the universe the deepest service we can, seems part of the living essence of the religious hypothesis. If the hypothesis *were* true in all its parts, including this one, then pure intellectualism, with its veto on our making willing advances, would be an absurdity; and some participation of our sympathetic nature would be logically required. I, therefore, for one, cannot see my way to accepting the agnostic rules for truth-seeking, or wilfully agree to keep my willing nature out of the game. I cannot do so for this plain reason, that *a rule of thinking which would absolutely prevent me from acknowledging certain kinds of truth if those kinds of truth were really there, would be an irrational rule.* That for me is the long and short of the formal logic of the situation, no matter what the kinds of truth might materially be.

I confess I do not see how this logic can be escaped. But sad experience makes me fear that some of you may still shrink from radically saying with me, *in abstracto,* that we have the right to believe at our own risk any hypothesis that is live enough to tempt our will. I suspect, however, that if this is so, it is because you have got away from the abstract logical point of view altogether, and are thinking (perhaps without realizing it) of some particular religious hypothesis which for you is dead. The freedom to 'believe what we will' you apply to the case of some patent superstition; and the faith you think of is the faith defined by the schoolboy when he said, "Faith is when you believe something that you know ain't true." I can only repeat that this is misapprehension. *In concreto,* the freedom to believe can only cover living options which the intellect of the individual cannot by itself resolve; and living options never seem absurdities to him who has them to consider. When I look at the religious question as it really puts itself to concrete men, and when I think of all the possibilities which both practically and theoretically it involves, then this command that we shall put a stopper on our heart, instincts, and courage, and *wait*—acting of course meanwhile more or less as if religion were *not* true[3]—till doomsday, or till such time as our

intellect and senses working together may have raked in evidence enough,—this command, I say, seems to me the queerest idol ever manufactured in the philosophic cave. Were we scholastic absolutists, there might be more excuse. If we had an infallible intellect with its objective certitudes, we might feel ourselves disloyal to such a perfect organ of knowledge in not trusting to it exclusively, in not waiting for its releasing word. But if we are empiricists, if we believe that no bell in us tolls to let us know for certain when truth is in our grasp, then it seems a piece of idle fantasticality to preach so solemnly our duty of waiting for the bell. Indeed we *may* wait if we will,—I hope you do not think that I am denying that,—but if we do so, we do so at our peril as much as if we believed. In either case we *act,* taking our life in our hands. No one of us ought to issue vetoes to the other, nor should we bandy words of abuse. We ought, on the contrary, delicately and profoundly to respect one another's mental freedom: then only shall we bring about the intellectual republic; then only shall we have that spirit of inner tolerance without which all our outer tolerance is soulless, and which is empiricism's glory; then only shall we live and let live, in speculative as well as in practical things.

I began by a reference to Fitz-James Stephen; let me end by a quotation from him. "What do you think of yourself? What do you think of the world? . . . These are questions with which all must deal as it seems good to them. They are riddles of the Sphinx, and in some way or other we must deal with them. . . . In all important transactions of life we have to take a leap in the dark. . . . If we decide to leave the riddles unanswered, that is a choice; if we waver in our answer, that, too, is a choice: but whatever choice we make, we make it at our peril. If a man chooses to turn his back altogether on God and the future, no one can prevent him; no one can show beyond reasonable doubt that he is mistaken. If a man thinks otherwise and acts as he thinks, I do not see that any one can prove that *he* is mistaken. Each must act as he thinks best; and if he is wrong, so much the worse for him. We stand on a mountain pass in the midst of whirling snow and blinding mist, through which we get glimpses now and then of paths which may be deceptive. If we stand still we shall be frozen to death. If we take the wrong road we shall be dashed to pieces. We do not certainly know

---

3. Since belief is measured by action, he who forbids us to believe religion to be true, necessarily also forbids us to act as we should if we did believe it to be true. The whole defence of religious faith hinges upon action. If the action required or inspired by the religious hypothesis is in no way different from that dictated by the naturalistic hypothesis, then religious faith is a pure superfluity, better pruned away, and controversy about its legitimacy is a piece of idle trifling, unworthy of serious minds. I myself believe, of course, that the religious hypothesis gives to the world an expression which specifically determines our reactions, and makes them in a large part unlike what they might be on a purely naturalistic scheme of belief.

whether there is any right one. What must we do? 'Be strong and of a good courage.' Act for the best, hope for the best, and take what comes. . . . If death ends all, we cannot meet death better."[4]

DISCUSSION QUESTIONS

1. Do you agree with James's account of scientific inquiry and its outcomes? Why or why not?

---

4. *Liberty, Equality, Fraternity,* p. 353, 2d edition (London, 1874).

2. In James's view, are we ever unjustified in believing something if it is important to us? Explain. What is a "mistaken belief," for him?
3. Does James's analysis adequately provide for a way to avoid epistemological relativism (roughly, the view that what is true or false is merely what anybody thinks it is)? Why or why not?
4. How might the differences between Clifford's and James's positions be resolved, if at all?

20. Lorraine Code (b. 1937)
"Experience, Knowledge and Responsibility"

Lorraine Code is a Canadian philosopher who has taught at different universities in Ontario. Her published research has been in the areas of epistemology, philosophy of language, and feminist philosophy. She also has done work on the status of women specifically in Canada. The selection was originally published in the late 1980s as part of an English-language collection of writings by feminist thinkers working in United Kingdom countries (mainly Britain).

In her essay Code too is dealing with some recurrent themes that emerge in the "enterprise of feminist epistemology" (as Narayan calls it), but her special focus is on the connection between moral and epistemological concerns. In this respect her analysis is similar to Clifford's, though she argues for the personal development of the *intellectual virtue* of "epistemic responsibility," while he argued that all capable persons have a *moral duty* to follow in the choice of belief. A particularly important aspect of this virtue of "knowing well" is the ability to "listen attentively" to first-person accounts of real-life experience, and in Code's estimation this dimension of knowing has been too often overlooked in traditional Western epistemology.

QUESTIONS FOR CRITICAL READING

1. What does Code mean by "epistemic responsibility," and what illustrations does she use to show when it is and is not achieved?
2. In Code's view what kind of relationship ought to be maintained between a "feminist theory of knowledge" and "malestream" epistemology?
3. What does Code mean by "continuity with experience," and how does she argue for developing epistemological theory that maintains it?
4. How does Code critique Carol Gilligan's work on women's responses to moral dilemmas? (See also Part IV, reading 52.)

TERMS TO NOTE

cognitive: Having to do with the ability to know, perceive, or recognize something as being so.

ontological: Here, relating to the essential being of something or someone.

imperative: Here, a rationally binding principle of voluntary activity.

fallibilist: Susceptibility to error; acknowledging that something is incapable of being true beyond all possible doubt.

Kantian: Referring to the philosophical theories of Immanuel Kant (1724–1804). (For example, see Part IV, reading 51.)

akrasia: A Greek term traditionally meaning weakness of will or lack of self-control.

Introduction

Two central, interconnected tasks that face feminist philosophers working in theory of knowledge are that of finding appropriate ways of knowing women's experiences and the structures that shape them; and that of developing theoretical accounts of knowledge which retain continuity with those experiences. To perform the first task adequately, it is necessary, among other things, to break out of stereotyped perceptions of woman's 'nature' which work, persistently, to constrain possibilities of knowing well. In this connection, I shall argue that ways of knowing can be judged 'appropriate' partly on the basis of responsibility manifested by cognitive agents in making knowledge claims, and in acting upon assumptions that they know. Adequate performance of the second task requires a shift in perspective about the purpose of 'the epistemological project'. It involves moving away from theoretical positions which advocate a purity in knowledge that would leave experience behind in a search for an epistemic ideal of unrealisable clarity.

To perform these tasks successfully it will be useful, too, to eschew any idea that ethics and epistemology are separate and distinct areas of enquiry. This could provide scope both for the view that knowing well is good for its own sake—a moral *and* an epistemological point—and for a recognition of the extent to which the explanatory capacities of moral theories and of policies based upon them depend upon their having a basis in responsible knowledge of human experience. Hence, in the elaboration of feminist epistemological concerns that I shall present here, epistemic responsibility will figure as a central intellectual virtue, with the potential to play a regulatory role in cognitive activity analogous to the role moral virtues can play in moral activity.

Certain preliminary points need to be made before proceeding to a more detailed discussion of these tasks. First, in naming the task of coming to know women's experiences as one of the two central tasks I shall discuss, I mean to indicate from the outset that the notion of women's experience (in the singular) is an artificial construct. While it may often be expedient, in the course of the discussion, to use the term in the singular, it should always be read with a sensitivity to the fact that there is no such singular entity. To assume that there could be would be to mask crucial differences between and among women, and hence to break that continuity with experiences that it is important to maintain.

Secondly, it needs to be made clear that the point of this exploration is neither to provide a female-experience-based nor a responsibility-based epistemology, designed to *supplant* traditional epistemological modes, though running parallel to them in structure and content. Nor is it simply to *add* an account of female experiences and of the workings of epistemic responsibility to 'traditional' epistemological theories, leaving their presuppositions and structures otherwise intact. While it is by no means clear what theory of knowledge might look like when attention is directed towards maintaining continuity with experience(s) and clarifying the implications of epistemic responsibility, it seems to be highly probable that it must differ markedly, both in its aims and in its conclusions, from traditional epistemological enterprises. Some of these differences will become apparent in the discussion that follows; but my purpose is much more to offer an exploration, from a feminist perspective, of certain epistemological problems, and to give some indication of the directions one might take in trying to solve them, than it is to present a fully articulated feminist theory of knowledge.

These points reflect my conviction that, while feminist epistemological practice may indeed reject and/or seek to render problematic much of traditional 'malestream' epistemology, it can most fruitfully do so by remaining in dialogue with that tradition. In genuine dialogue, as contrasted both with polite conversation and with adversarial confrontation, both of the participants are changed.[1] So the process I envisage does not involve simply turning away from the malestream tradition in order to celebrate 'the feminine', however that might be understood. Rather, it involves engaging with that tradition, trying to see what can be learned from reading it 'against the grain' so that different of its facets are highlighted, and its gaps and exclusions understood and elaborated.[2]

But engagement with the *philosophical* tradition alone will not enable feminists to perform these tasks successfully. Disciplinary boundaries constitute some of the most intractable exclusionary structures impeding possibilities of insight and illumination. It is becoming a well-established aspect of feminist practice to move back and forth across such boundaries with the aims both of demonstrating their artificiality, and of tapping sources of understanding that fall outside the scope of traditional disciplinary orthodoxy. Hence feminist epistemological practice engaged in from a philosophical perspective is continuous with the epistemological concerns of feminists working in such traditionally disparate areas as sociology, anthropology, history and political theory. Feminists have much to learn from each other.

With respect to the practical effects that such learning might have, it should be mentioned that in commenting upon the *artificiality* of a conception of women's experience (in the singular), and upon the artificiality of disciplinary boundaries, my point is not to equate goodness with 'naturalness'. Rather, it is to draw attention to a connection between artificiality and contingency. What has been labelled or created by human beings out of contingent circumstances can likewise be labelled and understood differently by them, or altered when its flaws are revealed. Suspending such artificial constructs may reveal other possibilities, perhaps more creative ones, just as reading traditional texts, theories and presuppositions against the grain may reveal other perspectives on seemingly entrenched ideas.

Stereotypes and Responsibility

Stereotyped perceptions of women's nature, and actions based upon them, count amongst the most intransigent of constructs that shape women's experiences and make it difficult for women to move 'beyond domination'.[3] Manifestations of such perceptions are perhaps best known as they come across in anthropological, psychological and sociological studies and the (often unquestioned) assumptions about gender differences in terms of which such studies are conducted. But it is clear from a closer perusal of some of these studies that their implications are as much ontological, in their structuring effects upon women's possibilities of being, and epistemological, in their constraints upon responsible knowing, as they are practical. Indeed, such studies often work as self-fulfilling prophecies, leading people to *be* much as stereotype-governed research takes them to be.[4] It is because of these consequences that a principal requirement of epistemically responsible knowing centres about the need to become aware of the extent to which stereotypes govern perception and shape alleged

knowledge (both one's own, and those of other members of one's epistemic community). It is part of responsible epistemic practice to work towards freeing cognitive activity from such constraining influences: this is an indispensable first step in the project of developing an epistemological approach that can maintain continuity with experience.

The point is not, however, that if stereotypes are stripped away, then experience will present itself 'pure' and untainted. Experience is always mediated by the location of experiencing subjects within a certain time, place, culture and environment, and it is always shaped as much by unconscious considerations and motivations. It is, arguably, also shaped by the gender of the experiencer. But stereotypes constitute a particular sort of knower-adopted overlay upon these structures, of whose effects one can become aware, and which one can work to rethink and restructure. It is especially for this reason that it makes sense to illustrate something of what is involved in epistemic responsibility by looking at some of the epistemological and political effects of stereotypes.

I have spelled out the features and implications of epistemic responsibility more extensively elsewhere.[5] My belief in its importance stems from my view that the Kantian conception of the creative synthesis of the imagination is one of the most important innovations in the history of philosophy, and that to think of knowledge as arising out of that synthesis is to take human cognition to be an active process of *taking* and *structuring* experience. Such activity is constrained by the (often fluid) nature of human cognitive equipment, and by the (also fluid) nature of reality. But within these constraints there is considerable freedom in making sense of the world. To take an example particularly relevant to this context, one is free to know, conduct one's life, and interact with other people on the basis of the alleged knowledge, that women are deficient in reason by comparison with an alleged masculine norm. Certainly it is possible to 'make sense' of many aspects of the world on these terms, and to construct a view of human relations and possibilities which depends upon this alleged 'knowledge'. Yet feminists are showing how serious a bias is at the basis of such knowledge claims, and how they provide the cognitive basis for devastatingly oppressive practices. And many other analogous examples can be cited from a wide variety of contexts. They show why imperatives are required to limit the kinds of sense that can responsibly be made of experience; and I take the notion of *epistemic responsibility* to stand for a cluster of considerations that work to constitute such imperatives.

Evidence for such responsibility is to be found in intellectual virtue, and in the recognition of a normative force that attaches to 'realism'. By the former, I mean a certain kind of orientation to the world and to one's knowledge-seeking self as part of the world. An intellectually virtuous person would value knowing and understanding how things 'really' are, to the extent that this is possible, renouncing both the temptation to live with partial explanations when fuller ones are attainable, and the temptation to live in fantasy or illusion. Such a person would consider it better to *know,* despite the comfortable complacency that a life indiscriminately governed by fantasy and illusion might offer. And this connects directly to the idea that 'realism' has normative force. In terms of this idea, the value of understanding how things are, to the best possible extent, is greater than, and supersedes, any value that might be taken to attach to consistent adherence to established theory or received opinion about how things might be. To achieve the 'right' perceptions implied by such an approach requires honesty and humility, the courage not to pretend to know what one does not know, the wisdom not to ignore its relevance, and the humility not to yield to temptations to suppress facts damaging to a cherished theoretical stance.

Now it seems to be beyond dispute that claims to know based in stereotypical perceptions and conceptions fail in just this respect. In their extreme crudity as epistemological tools, stereotypes violate the requirements of epistemic responsibility, opting, in its place, for what one might term both epistemic indolence and epistemic imperialism. The former is manifested in a stereotype-user's conviction that s/he knows what s/he is talking about and is absolved from any need to attempt to know better. This encourages a kind of intellectual *akrasia,* an entrenched reluctance to enquire further lest one face the necessity of having to 'reconsider a range of treasured beliefs'.[6] The latter is manifested in a belief that a stereotyped person or situation is summed up, that

the putative knower has labelled it for what it is, and has thus claimed it as part of his/her stock of cognitive possessions.

From the minimal concern with knowing well that is apparent in such epistemic postures, it is clear that these are epistemically irresponsible ways of claiming to know. Here there is none of the humility, openness and concern with the normative force of realism that marks responsible cognitive endeavour. In fact, stereotypes close off possibilities of understanding; and this feature of their functioning is attributable, in part at least, to their resemblance, at once, to products of hasty generalisations, and to illegitimate appeals to authority. Both in its manner of selecting accidental characteristics of people and stretching them to sum up all people of that sort (be they women, blacks or men), and in its posing as a finished product, not open to amendment, the use of a stereotype has all the reprehensible features of pronouncements based upon hasty generalisations. Yet it is unlikely to have been derived by the overly simple (empiricist) process of simple enumeration by which hasty generalisations, in the main, are formed. Stereotypes are just as much the products of accumulated cultural lore, acquired as part of an acculturation process, and, as such, both deepseated and tenacious. To allow them to pass for knowledge is to grant that cultural tradition undue authority and to abandon the critical perspective characteristic of responsible knowing.

Yet having said this, it is perhaps paradoxical to observe that something very like stereotypes is in fact needed if knowledge, or language, are to be possible at all. Categories and classifications, derived both from cultural traditions and from generalisations based on particular experiences, are part of the essential stuff of which both language and knowledge are made. So it is part of this epistemological task to devise responsible ways to distinguish open, potentially 'fallibilist' categories and classificatory devices from rigid, dogmatism-evincing stereotypes. It is as much part of responsible knowing to become mindful of the possibilities of acting according to stereotypes oneself, and of succumbing to stereotyped self-perceptions, as it is to avoid stereotyping others.

With special reference to stereotypes of women, feminists in several disciplines have documented the way in which actions and attitudes shaped by such stereotypes structure the ways in which women are perceived and know, and come thereby to know themselves. Much of this documentation is philosophically pertinent just because it shows, precisely with reference to people's experience of themselves as participants in the world, that how one comes to know oneself through 'received' doctrine has profound effects upon one's possibilities of being. In a complex process of reciprocal structuring and restructuring, what a person comes to believe that she (or he) *is* affects what that person can know, and to a large extent, structures what s/he is. In short, a stereotype is an unjust tyrant whose effects are both ontological and ethical. Two examples of such documentation are worth citing here to show something of what I mean.[7]

Margaret Rossiter's historical study of *Women Scientists in America: Struggles and Strategies to 1940* (1982) takes as one of its central themes a demonstration of the tyranny of stereotypes as they work to construct women's lives and to confine them both within certain possibilities for using their qualifications, and within certain modes of self-awareness which reinforce the stereotypes. Rossiter shows, for example, that if women can bring themselves to 'know', even within their professional lives, that it is more appropriate to seek employment compatible with what it is (stereotypically) to be a woman (the 'helpmate' role of a research assistant is an obvious example), then they make themselves less threatening to social structures, and hence more employable. In this mode, one simply buys into the 'complementarity' thesis and engages gratefully in mediocre work allegedly more suited to one's own different (=inferior) female capacities. One's possibilities of knowing both one's own experiences and 'the world' responsibly are thereby diminished.

A somewhat different manifestation of the feminine stereotype is evident in the case of Christine English who was found guilty not of murder but of manslaughter, in the 1981 killing of her lover. She successfully pleaded diminished responsibility as a result of severe premenstrual tension. Initial feminist enthusiasm for the decision in this case arose out of belief that doctors and lawyers had in fact granted reality to women's experiences of menstrual and premenstrual sufferings, long dismissed (on a common reading of the stereotype) as 'all in her mind'. But in a subtler way the decision contributes to a re-entrenchment of the

very stereotype it appears to challenge. For the stereotype of female hysteria, emotional immaturity and irrationality might readily, now, be reinstated, on the basis of the expertise of highly accredited authorities.[8] Despite their rigidity, on the basis of which one is rightly critical of their usage, stereotypes also have a curious elasticity which enables them to stretch and shift so as to accommodate (and condemn) quite contradictory ways of behaving.

To return, then, to the complex interrelation between the avoidance of stereotypes, and epistemic responsibility, ordinarily I would take some version of the ancient Greek injunction 'Know thyself' to be one of the imperatives that responsible knowers would try to follow. I think one can work towards observing this injunction even while acknowledging that 'selves' are not fixed and are never fully conscious entities, and that claims to self-knowledge are not absolutely privileged by contrast with other people's claims to know one. Selves are constructed and reconstructed out of narratives, perspectives, experiences and events; and out of first-, second- and third-person accounts. But even within these acknowledgements there is a place for some version of self-knowledge, however provisionally it may need to be construed.

But when it comes to knowing oneself responsibly in defiance of stereotypes, the examples just cited indicate that this is an even more convoluted requirement than it seems to be, even with the ephemerality of 'selves' taken into account. Particularly in cases such as that of the scientific helpmate, *not* knowing oneself may be conducive to survival. On the other hand, to undermine a stereotype strengthened by evidence from the English case, the most responsible approach would seem indeed to be to know oneself as well as possible, to work to acquire a just perception of one's own capacities and incapacities, starting from the well-justified assumption that the authority of the experts is as fallible as any other human posture. Plainly there are no straightforward or universal solutions to the puzzles posed by efforts to know women's experiences, or to challenge structures that systematically distort them.

Experience and Knowledge

In Carol Gilligan's work on the responses of female moral agents to Lawrence Kohlberg's tests for measuring levels of moral maturity, it is the clash between the moral experiences of those female subjects and the requirements of the Kohlberg theory that leads her to conclude that women speak in a *different* (moral) voice (Gilligan, 1982). In fact, within the terms of the present discussion, one might take it to be Gilligan's (implicit) working hypothesis that the epistemological assumptions of Kohlberg's work preclude the possibility of accounting for women's experiences within the theoretical conclusions he draws.

Very much in keeping with traditional Kantian morality, Kohlberg assumes that moral maturity is characterised by a capacity for the autonomous endorsement of universalisable moral principles. The worthiness of such principles will be apparent from their applicability, with impartiality and following the dictates of duty alone, across all situations where moral judgement is required. Epistemologically speaking, it is tacitly assumed, although the question itself is not raised, that situations requiring moral judgement will be *known* in just the same way by all moral agents.[9] But it is a serious oversimplification to take for granted that perceptions are always unproblematically 'right'. Indeed, the moral quality of an action is dependent upon the cognition in which it is based, and this cognition is itself a proper object of evaluation.

Now Kohlberg's female and male subjects differ from one another as much in their *apprehensions* of the situations upon which they are called to pronounce as they do in their moral judgements. This cognitive asymmetry evidenced in their disparate responses seems to inspire much of Gilligan's dissatisfaction with the way those responses have been read so as to reinforce traditional stereotypes of the rational and morally mature male, and the irrational and morally immature female. Rather than considering an equally plausible interpretation to the effect that the complexity of female responses to Kohlberg's tests (statistically speaking) might be read as evidence of a finely tuned moral sense and a high level of moral sophistication, readers of these responses have tended automatically to favour the conclusion that female respondents are too much immersed in particularity to achieve the principled impartiality characteristic of mature moral being. It can at least be suggested that there has been a failure to maintain a responsible degree of openness on the part of these readers, too easy a willingness to

structure their readings so as to confirm entrenched stereotypes and theoretical presuppositions.

In claiming that Gilligan's work lends itself to this kind of epistemological interpretation, I do not mean either to suggest that there *are* intrinsically incommensurable 'masculine' and 'feminine' ways of knowing, or that such statistical differences as emerge from female and male responses are essentially and/or 'naturally' female and male. Gilligan herself argues that although the moral voices she discerns have traditionally been differentiated along gender lines, this is a matter of historical contingency rather than biological necessity.[10] It is partially consequent, she suggests, upon the ways in which gender has been constituted in mother-dominated Western child-rearing practices.[11] Both voices, she maintains, are at least in principle accessible to women and to men.

None the less, a distinctive mode of moral discourse is discernible in Gilligan's work, especially in women's responses to her abortion study. This mode is markedly different from the kinds of deliberation commonly conducted within the rubric either of a Kantian or of a utilitarian approach to moral questions. While it is difficult to specify exactly how it differs, and quite inappropriate to see it either as arising out of, or as constituting a rival moral *theory,* certain of its features can be sketched out.

Both in the perceptions of relevance they reflect, and in their manner of apprehending and structuring situations, the responses Gilligan records are characterisable by what might be described as an analogue of practical reasoning (*phronimos*).[12] This is manifested in a kind of reflective posture, a thoughtfulness, which contrasts markedly with the Kantian-derived concentration upon achieving a principled moral stance that carries over into Kohlberg's work. But this is not the standard utilitarian contrast. The concern at its core is not so much with the consequences as with the *implications* both of motives and of actions, as much for other people, with whom one recognises a complex network of affinities and connections, as for oneself.

The possibility of discerning these implications seems to involve attempting to position oneself reflectively within a situation, in relation to various of its aspects, so as to achieve a stance which will allow one to take account of as many of these implications as possible, while not destroying one's capacity to act. To do this well one needs to cultivate an attitude perhaps best described, borrowing Annette Kuhn's useful and evocative phrase, as one of 'passionate detachment' (Kuhn, 1982, ch. 1). It is rather like the attitude a good therapist brings to a client: a kind of 'objective' sympathy, a mode of participation without intervention, of compassion without passion, which, at its best, succeeds at once in being involved and maintaining an appropriate distance. It is a matter of positioning and repositioning oneself within a situation until the best course of action comes to suggest itself; but always at points within the situation, for there is no removed, God's-eye vantage point. Whether such a mode of moral response is 'naturally' or contingently female remains an open question.

It is an advantage of Gilligan's methodological approach that she makes it possible for this moral voice to be heard, not as affording evidence of stereotypically muddled female thinking, but as worthy of a hearing equivalently thoughtful to that accorded to products of male deliberation. There is an evident *concern*, in her work, to maintain contact with, and derive insights from, accounts which not only arise out of experience and are firmly grounded in it, but which stay in touch with that experience in drawing their conclusions. This contrasts with methods of epistemological and moral theory construction which aim to transcend experience, to move beyond it, allegedly towards greater clarity and accuracy but at the expense, I believe, of the insight and understanding that a maintained continuity with experience can afford.

Gilligan listens to people's stories (to *women's* stories) as they recount their experiences; and her aim seems to be the laudable one of listening responsively, and so, I would maintain, responsibly, to these stories.[13] For responsiveness seems to be a necessary component of any approach that purports to retain continuity with experience: it signals an appropriate receptiveness and humility towards that recounted experience, from which one moves only cautiously in the direction of interpretation. Such caution is enjoined in recognition of the fact that subjective factors are bound to structure any interpretation, and it is important to be cognisant of them, to the extent that one can. By no means the least significant of such factors is in the fact that a subject's account of her/his own experiences is as much structured by unconscious and semiconscious forces as it is by conscious ones; and this is true, too, of any interpretation. Listening to, responding to and interpreting stories are acquired capacities. One has to put some effort into learning how to exercise them well. The need for *responsibility* in their exercise is particularly clear when one considers that there can be no uniquely True story, nor is there any uniquely right interpretation. But some are clearly better, or worse, than others, at least for now, and one can learn to recognise which ones.

In elaborating the potential value of Gilligan's methodological approach through these considerations, I do not mean to suggest that she herself shows a sensitivity to all of them. But the story-listening techniques she uses could be adapted and amplified so as to be more tentative, more qualified and nuanced in their interpretative moves. And even within the limitations of her own use of the approach, one sees some indication of how both epistemological and moral thinking might begin to move away from a preoccupation with transcending experience, not bothering about *who* the knowing subject, or the acting subject, really is.[14] Extrapolating from what Gilligan has done, it is possible to make sense of how it is that actual, historically situated, gendered epistemological and moral subjects know and respond to actual, complex experiences.

Clearly if any conclusions, however tentative and provisional, are to be derived from the process of telling and listening to stories, then the subject matter, the theme, of these stories must be specified, at least roughly. It is unlikely that randomly collected stories could be of much use in providing solutions—even tentative ones—to specific theoretical problems. So the investigator who would use such an approach must take a good deal of care to select stories both open enough *and* theoretically specified enough to elicit a range of responses which will neither predetermine possible conclusions, nor offer no possibility of discerning a common thread. If Gilligan is indeed committed to the view that this 'different' moral voice is accessible equally to women and to men, then I think one must have serious reservations about her use of a study of women's responses to abortion as a means of making it audible. She makes too little of an epistemological constraint that is built into the structure of the investigation.[15]

Leaving open the question as to whether there are essentially 'feminine' and 'masculine' ways of knowing, it is none the less reasonable to maintain that there is a range of experiences which could not be known in ways similar enough, from knower to knower, to produce 'common' knowledge in differently gendered subjects. Experiences which depend upon natural biological differences, in areas of sexuality, parenthood, and some aspects of physical and emotional being, must be different for women and for men to the extent that it would be impossible for them to know them in anything like 'the same' way.[16] Hence it cannot make sense to imply that conclusions about moral maturity *per se* could be drawn from biologically specific experiences available only to women, particularly if one grants the point that the quality of moral action is dependent upon, and a direct reflection of, the cognitive activity in which it is based. The abortion study could only work to generate a universally relevant new perspective on moral maturity if one could assume, with respect to the questions that arise within it, that women and men count as a group who have to make this kind of decision *as equals.* But to make such an assumption is to ignore the crucial practical respects in which women and men are not equally implicated in and affected by decisions about abortion. It is to gloss over the unequal impact upon women's and men's lives, at least within current social structures, of child-bearing and rearing. Hence it creates an intolerable discontinuity between experience and theory.[17]

On the other hand, stories must be specified sufficiently to provide experiential accounts of a *certain kind* of situation, if any substantive conclusions at all are to be drawn from them. And there is good reason to think that it is imperative to hear stories drawn from undervalued aspects of women's experiences, in view of the age-old imbalance in the standard selection of examples from stereotypically masculine experience. So the question arises as to what Gilligan's primary purpose is. If it is to make the 'different' voice audible as one in which both women and men can speak, then the abortion study does not serve her well. In advocating that a necessarily female kind of experience, and hence of knowledge and moral judgement, be allowed to generate an alternative standard of moral maturity she creates a structure for judging moral

practice in which male knowledge, and hence male moral judgement, must equally necessarily be Other.

If, however, it is Gilligan's purpose to develop a specifically female morality, then perhaps the abortion stories are well chosen after all. But such a project would, I think, be of doubtful worth in the long run. Any celebration of specifically 'feminine' modes which would aim to revalue them, yet leave them intact, would be in danger of obscuring the constraints commonly attendant upon their manifestation. If 'connectedness', for example, were selected as a primary value, it would be important to keep in mind that, at least in the past, women's concentration upon 'connection' within the domestic sphere has limited their capacity to contest exploitation, and has contributed to their powerlessness and oppression. So if the project is to open the way for the development of an ethics of care and responsibility which could be juxtaposed *against* an ethics of rights and justice, the most likely consequences would be to reinstate and reinforce precisely those stereotypes Gilligan sets out to undermine. It would be but a short step towards the contention that the former—the caring morality—is female morality, attuned to women's softer, more emotional, and lesser concerns; the latter—the rights and justice morality—is male morality, appropriate to men's more serious moral endeavours.

Gilligan would, I think, be better advised to choose themes for her stories which might enable male and female responses to be more nearly commensurable. Then her readers could more readily entertain the possibility that her work contributes to a long-needed challenge to the tyranny of feminine *and* masculine stereotypes.

Conclusion

My discussion has centred on the question of how people and situations are known; and I have made a particular plea in favour of taking seriously a certain kind of story—first-person accounts of experiences. Such stories provide access to a kind of knowledge not ordinarily regarded as appropriate for epistemological consideration. Indeed, this is one of the gaps that shows up when one reads standard, 'malestream' epistemology against the grain, and wonders what has become of the *people* whose knowledge it allegedly analyses and explains. I have suggested that reflection upon epistemological and moral matters which is responsibly attuned to such narratives might be able to retain a kind of contact with human lives that is often lost in formalistic and abstract theoretical structures. Moreover, the subtlety and variety of narrative of this kind is such as to highlight the crudity of stereotypes, and their ineffectuality as putative cognitive devices. Responsible knowing simply has no place for them.[18]

The rejection of stereotypes as cognitive tools does not force one to fall back upon a belief in pure, unmediated experiences. Indeed, it would be a complete mistake to believe that stories, narratives, somehow provide unmediated access to experiences. Stories, even first-person stories, are not necessarily *truer* either than stereotypes or than standard philosophical analyses. Nor is there any kind of reliable criterion for determining their truth. Rather, the main point is that stories convey something about cognitive and moral experiences, in their manifold manifestations, which slip through the formalist nets of moral principles and duties, or standards of evidence and justification. The modest proposal urged here is that perhaps, by taking stories into account, theorists will be better able to repair some of the rifts in continuity that are so glaringly evident between moral theory and moral experiences, and theory of knowledge and cognitive experiences.

It is unlikely that this project could ever result in a seamless, invisible mending of these rifts. Theoretical structures and patterns that emerge from responsible reflection upon experience will more likely be piecemeal, comprised of interpretations of stories, and interpretations of interpretations. The point is not to generate a neat, comprehensive theoretical structure, but to learn how to let experience shape and reshape theory. In a word, the aim is to *understand* rather than to find methods of justification, verification and control. So the price to be paid in terms of loss of certainty, clarity and precision is, admittedly, high. The position is a vertiginous one, and understanding is fleeting. But the certainty, clarity and precision claimed for dominant theoretical structures is as illusory as the truth claimed for stereotypes. And the vertigo will not be the source of dismay that it may at first sight seem to be, if cognitive activity does, in fact, be-

gin to move towards thoughtful, responsible practice. Such practice can generate theoretical accounts of knowledge which stand a good chance of retaining contact with women's experiences without, carelessly and dismissively, simply slotting them into stereotyped categories.[19]

Notes

1. In her article, 'A Paradigm of Philosophy: The Adversary Method', Janice Moulton (1983) shows how adversarial argumentation, which is characteristic of most present-day philosophical discourse, is minimally productive of understanding, insight or change.

2. Some of the most significant of these gaps and exclusions are made clear in Lloyd (1984), where it is argued that reason itself is defined by exclusion of character-traits traditionally associated with femaleness.

3. Here I cite the title of Carol Gould's book, *Beyond Domination* (1983). Stereotyped perception of women's nature is, of course, continuous with stereotyping of any sort and shares its reprehensibly dogmatic, unthinking character. Nor could one argue that only women are stereotyped and hence, by implication, that it is only men who stereotype. Women are prone to stereotyping each other, anti-feminists to stereotyping feminists, and vice versa. It is the stereotyping of women that concerns me here, whether by men or by other women. But epistemologically speaking, the use of stereotypes is always a crude and irresponsible way of not bothering to know, yet posing as though one does.

4. Classic feminist discussions of such practices are found in Hubbard (1983), Weisstein (1972) and Rubin (1975).

5. See Code (1983a, 1983b and 1984). The theory is still more fully elaborated in my *Epistemic Responsibility* (forthcoming). In the account given here, I borrow from the discussion of this idea that appears in Code (1983b).

6. This is Amélie Rorty's phrase in Rorty (1983).

7. For the sake of clarity, these examples are taken from patriarchal structures, where stereotypes are imposed upon women from the vantage point of male experience and alleged expertise. In coming to a philosophical understanding of the problem of stereotypes as such, one would have to take account of the facts, already mentioned, that women, too, stereotype other women; and that people are prone, also, to stereotype themselves. So the problem is more complex than these examples might suggest. But I think its solution would follow the same lines for its various manifestations, all of which, I think, are evidence of irresponsible cognitive practice.

8. I discuss these examples more fully in my 'The Tyranny of Stereotypes', in Storrie (ed.), (forthcoming).

9. Hence Lawrence Blum (1979) argues that there are two aspects to any occasion of moral judgement: the appre-

hension of a situation, and the action(s) based upon that apprehension.

10. Cf. Gilligan (1982) p. 2. But it should be noted, as Debra Nails (1983) points out, that the book is 'characterized by generalizations about the sexes, offered as descriptions of differences', hence that it has 'the power to exaggerate existing differences' (p. 662).

11. In this connection, Gilligan draws upon the work of Nancy Chodorow (1978).

12. Gilligan is not a philosopher, and would be unlikely to characterise them in this way. But it seems to be a potentially fruitful way of understanding something of what is at issue.

13. That she is not always successful in achieving this aim does not detract from its commendability as a guiding methodological principle. Gilligan seems often to interpret too swiftly, and it has been suggested that she quotes too selectively, and unjustifiably out of context (cf. Nails, 1983, esp. pp. 640–52). But the aim itself could be pursued somewhat differently, and its worthiness become more clearly apparent.

14. The use of narrative partially to effect this move is analogous to Alasdair MacIntyre's advocacy of the importance of narrative in understanding moral judgements and actions within the context of a life (see MacIntyre, 1981).

15. These reservations are also expressed in Code (1983b).

16. This is not to suggest that all women and all men would know these situations and aspects of their being in the same (stereotypical) way—only that the lines of difference would be differently drawn in terms of their common starting points within one sex, and between the sexes.

17. I am indebted in my formulation of this point to Jean Grimshaw's discussion of philosophical writings on the ethics of abortion in her *Feminist Philosophers* (1986), pp. 31–3.

18. I discuss the epistemological value of story-telling in greater detail in my 'Stories People Tell' in the *New Mexico Law Review* (forthcoming).

19. Work on this paper was made possible by a Strategic Grant from the Social Sciences and Humanities Research Council of Canada, and by a Visiting Fellowship at the Humanities Research Centre at the Australian National University in Canberra.

References

Blum, Lawrence (1979), *Friendship, Altruism and Morality* (London: Routledge & Kegan Paul).

Chodorow, Nancy (1978), *The Reproduction of Mothering: Psychoanalysis and the Sociology of Gender* (Berkeley: University of California Press).

Code, Lorraine (1983a), 'Father and Son: A Case Study in Epistemic Responsibility', *The Monist*, vol. 66, pp. 268–82.

Code, Lorraine (1983b), 'Responsibility and the Epistemic Community: Woman's Place', *Social Research*, vol. 50, no. 3, pp. 537–55.

Code, Lorraine (1984), 'Toward a "Responsibilist" Epistemology', *Philosophy and Phenomenological Research*, vol. 45, no. 1, pp. 29–50.

Code, Lorraine (forthcoming), *Epistemic Responsibility* (Hanover, New Hampshire: University Press of New England).

Code, Lorraine (forthcoming), 'Stories People Tell', *New Mexico Law Review*.

Code, Lorraine (forthcoming), 'The Tyranny of Stereotypes', in Kathleen Storrie (ed.), *Women, Isolation and Bonding: The Ecology of Gender* (Toronto: Methuen).

Gilligan, Carol (1982), *In a Different Voice: Psychological Theory and Women's Development* (Cambridge, Mass: Harvard University Press).

Gould, Carol C. (ed.) (1983), *Beyond Domination: New Perspectives on Women and Philosophy* (Totowa, NJ: Littlefield Adams).

Grimshaw, Jean (1986), *Feminist Philosophers: Women's Perspectives on Philosophical Traditions* (Brighton: Wheatsheaf).

Harding, Sandra, and Hintikka, Merrill B. (eds) (1983), *Discovering Reality: Feminist Perspectives on Epistemology, Metaphysics, Methodology, and Philosophy of Science* (Dordrecht: Reidel).

Hubbard, Ruth (1983), 'Have Only Men Evolved?' in S. Harding and M. Hintikka (eds), pp. 45–69.

Kuhn, Annette (1982), *Women's Pictures: Feminism and Cinema* (London: Routledge & Kegan Paul).

Lloyd, Genevieve (1984), *The Man of Reason: 'Male' and 'Female' in Western Philosophy* (London: Methuen).

MacIntyre, Alasdair (1981), *After Virtue: A Study in Moral Theory* (London: Duckworth).

Moulton, Janice (1983), 'A Paradigm of Philosophy: The Adversary Method', in S. Harding and M. Hintikka (eds), pp. 149–64.

Nails, Debra (1983), 'Social Scientific Sexisms: Gilligan's Mismeasure of Man', *Social Research*, vol. 50, no. 3, pp. 643–64.

Rorty, Amélie (1983), 'Akratic Believers', *The American Philosophical Quarterly*, vol. 20, no. 2, pp. 174–83.

Rossiter, Margaret (1982), *Women Scientists in America: Struggles and Strategies to 1940* (Baltimore: Johns Hopkins University Press).

Rubin, Gayle (1975), 'The Traffic in Women: Notes on the Political Economy of Sex', in Rayna Rapp Reiter (ed.), *Toward an Anthropology of Women* (New York: Monthly Review Press), pp. 157–210.

Weisstein, Naomi (1972), 'Psychology Constructs the Female', in Vivian Gornick and Barbara K. Moran (eds), *Women in Sexist Society* (New York: Signet Books), pp. 207–24.

DISCUSSION QUESTIONS

1. Using Code's criteria and your personal experience, what are some ways that we can be "epistemically irresponsible" in our daily lives?

2. Code's position seems to imply a rejection of epistemological relativism. Why would you agree or disagree with her on this point?

3. Many philosophers have argued that evaluating knowledge-claims by focusing on the person who makes such claims is to fall prey to a logical fallacy traditionally known as the *ad hominem* fallacy. Is the person claiming to know something always irrelevant in assessing the claim? Why or why not?

4. What are some similarities and differences between Code's analysis and Narayan's views on the project of feminist epistemology?

21. Thomas Jefferson (1743–1826)
On Education and Citizenship

One of the most influential political leaders in early U.S. history, Thomas Jefferson played a pivotal role in the colonies' fight for independence from Great Britain. Born in Virginia, he eventually trained as a lawyer and spent most of his adult life in political office at one level or another. He served as governor of Virginia, member of Congress, minister to France, secretary of state, vice president, and president for two terms (1801–1809). The Declaration of Independence, written in 1776 and adopted by the Continental Congress on July 4 of that year, remains his most famous work.

Since the late seventeenth century, various other intellectuals in Europe and the American colonies (including Locke, as mentioned in reading 13) had advocated the philosophical views expressed in much of Jefferson's political writing. Monarchy, and the so-called natural authority over people as subjects that traditionally was assumed to go with it, was increasingly rejected during this era, especially by the educated middle classes. Critics often argued instead for the establishment of a republic, where legally equal citizens in effect governed themselves through their elected representatives, and every citizen's "natural liberty" was recognized as foundational. Such ideas, which were radical at the time, provided theoretical support for the revolutions that occurred, first in the American colonies (1776) and then in France (1789), as well as for the language of their respective constitutions.

The reading is from two separate writings by Jefferson. The first selection is from *Notes on the State of Virginia* (1784–1785), and the second is part of a letter he wrote to John Adams in 1813. In both selections the central theme is the nature and purpose of an effective public (that is, state-supported) education system, which stems from the need for an adequately educated citizenry. In Jefferson's view knowledgeable citizens were essential to maintaining social order, protecting personal rights, and keeping the government as uncorrupted as possible. Thus, not only for moral reasons but also for political reasons, Jefferson shows that it is not only *how* we know and *what* we know that is at issue but also *why* we should know.

QUESTIONS FOR CRITICAL READING

1. In the system of public education Jefferson advocates, what is to be the focus of instruction in the "schools of the hundreds," and what social benefits are expected to result from it?

2. According to Jefferson, what subject matter should be taught in the grammar schools and then in the universities, and how does he justify these different curricula?

3. What is the connection among proper education, responsible citizenship, and good government, in Jefferson's view?

4. What is the difference between a "natural" and an "artificial" aristocracy, and why does Jefferson think good public education for all will encourage the development of the one and diminish the harmful influences of the other?

TERM TO NOTE

republicanism: The principles of a republican form of government, ultimately based on government by consent of the governed; the doctrine of the self-government of a people.

Many of the laws which were in force during the monarchy being relative merely to that form of government, or inculcating principles inconsistent with republicanism, the first assembly which met after the establishment of the commonwealth, appointed a committee to revise the whole code, to reduce it into proper form and volume, and report it to the assembly. This work has been executed by three gentlemen, and reported; but probably will not be taken up till a restoration of peace shall leave to the legislature leisure to go through such a work.

The plan of the revisal was this. The common law of England, by which is meant that part of the English law which was anterior to the date of the oldest statutes extant, is made the basis of the work. It was thought dangerous to attempt to reduce it to a text: it was therefore left to be collected from the usual monuments of it. Necessary alterations in that, and so much of the whole body of the British statutes, and of acts of assembly, as were thought proper to be retained, were digested into 126 new acts, in which simplicity of style was aimed at, as far as was safe. . . .

Another object of the revisal is, to diffuse knowledge more generally through the mass of the people. This bill proposes to lay off every county into small districts of five or six miles square, called hundreds and in each of them to establish a school for teaching, reading, writing, and arithmetic. The tutor to be supported by the hundred, and every person in it entitled to send their children three years gratis, and as much longer as they please, paying for it. These schools to be under a visitor who is annually to chuse the boy of best genius in the school, of those whose parents are too poor to give them further education, and to send him forward to one of the grammar schools, of which twenty are proposed to be erected in different parts of the country, for teaching Greek, Latin, geography, and the higher branches of numerical arithmetic. Of the boys thus sent in any one year, trial is to be made at the grammar schools one or two years, and the best genius of the whole selected, and continued six years, and the residue dismissed. By this means twenty of the best geniuses will be raked from the rubbish annually, and be instructed, at the public expence, so far as the grammar schools go. At the end of six years instruction, one half are to be discontinued (from among

whom the grammar schools will probably be supplied with future masters); and the other half, who are to be chosen for the superiority of their parts and disposition, are to be sent and continued three years in the study of such sciences as they shall chuse, at William and Mary college, the plan of which is proposed to be enlarged, as will be hereafter explained, and extended to all the useful sciences. The ultimate result of the whole scheme of education would be the teaching all the children of the State reading, writing, and common arithmetic; turning out ten annually, of superior genius, well taught in Greek, Latin, geography, and the higher branches of arithmetic; turning out ten others annually, of still superior parts, who, to those branches of learning, shall have added such of the sciences as their genius shall have led them to; the furnishing to the wealthier part of the people convenient schools at which their children may be educated at their own expence.—The general objects of this law are to provide an education adapted to the years, to the capacity, and the condition of every one, and directed to their freedom and happiness. Specific details were not proper for the law. These must be the business of the visitors entrusted with its execution. The first stage of this education being the schools of the hundreds, wherein the great mass of the people will receive their instruction, the principal foundations of future order will be laid here. Instead, therefore, of putting the Bible and Testament into the hands of the children at an age when their judgments are not sufficiently matured for religious inquiries, their memories may here be stored with the most useful facts from Grecian, Roman, European, and American history. The first elements of morality too may be instilled into their minds; such as, when further developed as their judgments advance in strength, may teach them how to work out their own greatest happiness, by shewing them that it does not depend on the condition of life in which chance has placed them, but is always the result of a good conscience, good health, occupation, and freedom in all just pursuits.—Those whom either the wealth of their parents or the adoption of the state shall destine to higher degrees of learning, will go on to the grammar schools, which constitute the next stage, there to be instructed in the languages. The learning Greek and Latin, I am told, is going into disuse in Europe. I know not what their manners and occupations may call for: but it would be very ill-judged in us to follow their example in this instance. There is a certain period of life, say from eight to fifteen or sixteen years of age, when the mind like the body is not yet firm enough for laborious and close operations. If applied to such, it falls an early victim to premature exertion; exhibiting, indeed, at first, in these young and tender subjects, the flattering appearance of their being men while they are yet children, but ending in reducing them to be children when they should be men. The memory is then most susceptible and tenacious of impressions; and the learning of languages being chiefly a work of memory, it seems precisely fitted to the powers of this period, which is long enough too for acquiring the most useful languages, ancient and modern. I do not pretend that language is science. It is only an instrument for the attainment of science. But that time is not lost which is employed in providing tools for future operation: more especially as in this case the books put into the hands of the youth for this purpose may be such as will at the same time impress their minds with useful facts and good principles. If this period be suffered to pass in idleness, the mind becomes lethargic and impotent, as would the body it inhabits if unexercised during the same time. The sympathy between body and mind during their rise, progress and decline, is too strict and obvious to endanger our being misled while we reason from the one to the other.—As soon as they are of sufficient age, it is supposed they will be sent on from the grammar schools to the university, which constitutes our third and last stage, there to study those sciences which may be adapted to their views.—By that part of our plan which prescribes the selection of the youths of genius from among the classes of the poor, we hope to avail the state of those talents which nature has sown as liberally among the poor as the rich, but which perish without use, if not sought for and cultivated.—But of all the views of this law none is more important, none more legitimate, than that of rendering the people the safe, as they are the ultimate, guardians of their own liberty. For this purpose the reading in the first stage, where *they* will receive their whole education, is proposed, as has been said, to be chiefly historical. History, by apprising them of the past, will enable them to judge of the future; it will avail them of the experience of other times and other nations; it will qualify them as judges of the actions and designs of men; it will enable them to know ambition under every disguise it may assume; and knowing it, to defeat its views. In every government on earth is some trace of human weakness, some germ of corruption and degeneracy, which cunning will discover, and wickedness insensibly open, cultivate and improve. Every government degenerates when trusted to the rulers of the people alone. The people themselves therefore are its only safe depositories. And to render even them safe, their minds must be improved to a certain degree. This indeed is not all that is necessary, though it be essentially necessary. An amendment of our constitution must here come in aid of the public education. The influence over government must be shared among all the people. If every individual which composes their mass participates of the ultimate authority, the government will be safe; because the corrupting the whole mass will exceed any private resources of wealth; and public ones cannot be provided but by levies on the people. In this case every man would have to pay his own price. The government of Great Britain has been corrupted, because but one man in ten has a right to vote for members of parliament. The sellers of the government, therefore, get nine-tenths of their price clear. It has been thought that corruption is restrained by confining the right of suffrage to a few of the wealthier of the people: but it would be more effectually restrained by an extension of that right to such numbers as would bid defiance to the means of corruption.

From a Letter to John Adams

For I agree with you that there is a natural aristocracy among men. The grounds of this are virtue and talents. Formerly, bodily powers gave place among the aristoi. But since the invention of gunpowder has armed the weak as well as the strong with missile death, bodily strength, like beauty, good humor, politeness and other accomplishments, has become but an auxiliary ground for distinction. There is also an artificial aristocracy, founded on wealth and birth, without either virtue or talents; for with these it would belong to the first class. The natural aristocracy I consider as the most precious gift of nature, for the instruction, the trusts, and government of society. And indeed, it would have been inconsistent in creation to have formed man for the social state, and not to have provided virtue and wisdom enough to manage the concerns of the society. May we not even say, that that form of government is the best, which provides the most effectually for a pure selection of these natural aristoi into the offices of government? The artificial aristocracy is a mischievous ingredient in government, and provision should be made to prevent its ascendency. On the question, what is the best provision, you and I differ; but we differ as rational friends, using the free exercise of our own reason, and mutually indulging its errors. You think it best to put the pseudo-aristoi into a separate chamber of legislation, where they may be hindered from doing mischief by their co-ordinate branches, and where, also, they may be a protection to wealth against the Agrarian and plundering enterprises of the majority of the people. I think that to give them power in order to prevent them from doing mischief, is arming them for it, and increasing instead of remedying the evil. For if the co-ordinate branches can arrest their action, so may they that of the co-ordinates. Mischief may be done negatively as well as positively. Of this, a cabal in the Senate of the United States has furnished many proofs. Nor do I believe them necessary to protect the wealthy; because enough of these will find their way into every branch of the legislation, to protect themselves. From fifteen to twenty legislatures of our own, in action for thirty years past, have proved that no fears of an equalization of property are to be apprehended from them. I think the best remedy is exactly that provided by all our constitutions, to leave to the citizens the free election and separation of the aristoi from the pseudo-aristoi, of the wheat from the chaff. In general they will elect the really good and wise. In some instances, wealth may corrupt, and birth blind them; but not in sufficient degree to endanger the society.

It is probable that our difference of opinion may, in some measure, be produced by a difference of character in those among whom we live. From what I have seen of Massachusetts and Connecticut myself, and still more from what I have heard, and the character given of the former by yourself, who know them so much better, there seems to be in those two States a traditionary reverence for certain families, which has rendered the offices of the government nearly heredi-

tary in those families. I presume that from an early period of your history, members of those families happening to possess virtue and talents, have honestly exercised them for the good of the people, and by their services have endeared their names to them. In coupling Connecticut with you, I mean it politically only, not morally. For having made the Bible the common law of their land, they seemed to have modeled their morality on the story of Jacob and Laban. But although this hereditary succession to office with you, may, in some degree, be founded in real family merit, yet in a much higher degree, it has proceeded from your strict alliance of Church and State. These families are canonised in the eyes of the people on common principles, "you tickle me, and I will tickle you." In Virginia we have nothing of this. Our clergy, before the revolution, having been secured against rivalship by fixed salaries, did not give themselves the trouble of acquiring influence over the people. Of wealth, there were great accumulations in particular families, handed down from generation to generation, under the English law of entails. But the only object of ambition for the wealthy was a seat in the King's Council. All their court then was paid to the crown and its creatures; and they Philipised in all collisions between the King and the people. Hence they were unpopular; and that unpopularity continues attached to their names. A Randolph, a Carter, or a Burwell must have great personal superiority over a common competitor to be elected by the people even at this day. At the first session of our legislature after the Declaration of Independence, we passed a law abolishing entails. And this was followed by one abolishing the privilege of primogeniture, and dividing the lands of intestates equally among all their children, or other representatives. These laws, drawn by myself, laid the ax to the foot of pseudo-aristocracy. And had another which I prepared been adopted by the legislature, our work would have been complete. It was a bill for the more general diffusion of learning. This proposed to divide every county into wards of five or six miles square, like your townships; to establish in each ward a free school for reading, writing and common arithmetic; to provide for the annual selection of the best subjects from these schools, who might receive, at the public expense, a higher degree of education at a district school; and from these district schools to select a certain number of the most promising subjects, to be completed at an University, where all the useful sciences should be taught. Worth and genius would thus have been sought out from every condition of life, and completely prepared by education for defeating the competition of wealth and birth for public trusts. My proposition had, for a further object, to impart to these wards those portions of self-government for which they are best qualified, by confiding to them the care of their poor, their roads, police, elections, the nomination of jurors, administration of justice in small cases, elementary exercises of militia; in short, to have made them little republics, with a warden at the head of each, for all those concerns which, being under their eye, they would better manage than the larger republics of the county or State. A general call of ward meetings by their wardens on the same day through the State, would at any time produce the genuine sense of the people on any required point, and would enable the State to act in mass, as your people have so often done, and with so much effect by their town meetings. The law for religious freedom, which made a part of this system, having put down the aristocracy of the clergy, and restored to the citizen the freedom of the mind, and those of entails and descents nurturing an equality of condition among them, this on education would have raised the mass of the people to the high ground of moral respectability necessary to their own safety, and to orderly government; and would have completed the great object of qualifying them to select the veritable aristoi, for the trusts of government, to the exclusion of the pseudalists; and the same Theognis who has furnished the epigraphs of your two letters, assures us that "Ουδεμιαν πω, Κυον,' αγαθοι πολιν ωλεσαν ανδοες." Although this law has not yet been acted on but in a small and inefficient degree, it is still considered as before the legislature, with other bills of the revised code, not yet taken up, and I have great hope that some patriotic spirit will, at a favorable moment, call it up, and make it the keystone of the arch of our government.

With respect to aristocracy, we should further consider, that before the establishment of the American States, nothing was known to history but the man of the old world, crowded within limits either small or overcharged, and steeped in the vices which that situation generates. A government adapted to such men would be one thing; but a very different one, that for the man of these States. Here every one may have land to labor for himself, if he chooses; or, preferring the exercise of any other industry, may exact for it such compensation as not only to afford a comfortable subsistence, but wherewith to provide for a cessation from labor in old age. Every one, by his property, or by his satisfactory situation, is interested in the support of law and order. And such men may safely and advantageously reserve to themselves a wholesome control over their public affairs, and a degree of freedom, which, in the hands of the *canaille* of the cities of Europe, would be instantly perverted to the demolition and destruction of everything public and private. The history of the last twenty-five years of France, and of the last forty years in America, nay of its last two hundred years, proves the truth of both parts of this observation.

But even in Europe a change has sensibly taken place in the mind of man. Science had liberated the ideas of those who read and reflect, and the American example had kindled feelings of right in the people. An insurrection has consequently begun, of science, talents, and courage, against rank and birth, which have fallen into contempt. It has failed in its first effort, because the mobs of the cities, the instrument used for its accomplishment, debased by ignorance, poverty and vice, could not be restrained to rational action. But the world will recover from the panic of this first catastrophe. Science is progressive, and talents and enterprise on the alert. Resort may be had to the people of the country, a more governable power from their principles and subordination; and rank, and birth, and tinsel-aristocracy will finally shrink into insignificance, even there. This, however, we have no right to meddle with. It suffices for us, if the moral and physical condition of our own citizens qualifies them to select the able and good for the direction of their government, with a recurrence of elections at such short periods as will enable them to displace an unfaithful servant, before the mischief he meditates may be irremediable.

I have thus stated my opinion on a point on which we differ, not with a view to controversy, for we are both too old to change opinions which are the result of a long life of inquiry and reflection; but on the suggestions of a former letter of yours, that we ought not to die before we have explained ourselves to each other. We acted in perfect harmony, through a long and perilous contest for our liberty and independence. A constitution has been acquired, which, though neither of us thinks perfect, yet both consider as competent to render our fellow citizens the happiest and the securest on whom the sun has ever shone. If we do not think exactly alike as to its imperfections, it matters little to our country, which, after devoting to it long lives of disinterested labor, we have delivered over to our successors in life, who will be able to take care of it and of themselves.

Of the pamphlet on aristocracy which has been sent to you, or who may be its author, I have heard nothing but through your letter. If the person you suspect, it may be known from the quaint, mystical, and hyperbolical ideas, involved in affected, new-fangled and pedantic terms which stamp his writings. Whatever it be, I hope your quiet is not to be affected at this day by the rudeness or intemperance of scribblers; but that you may continue in tranquillity to live and to rejoice in the prosperity of our country, until it shall be your own wish to take your seat among the aristoi who have gone before you. Ever and affectionately yours.

DISCUSSION QUESTIONS

1. Why would you agree or disagree with Jefferson that the goal of state-supported education should be the maximization of the freedom and happiness of all citizens?

2. What kinds of knowledge did Jefferson seem to think were most important for citizens to acquire? How would his outlook on this differ from the dominant views on relevant knowledge today?

3. In contemporary technologically advanced societies people often complain about information overload and its social consequences. How might Jefferson respond to this problem if he were around today?

4. Do you agree with Jefferson that a "pseudo-aristocracy" based on wealth and birth is a bad thing for society? Why or why not?

PART III Metaphysics

At the most general level, metaphysics is the traditional branch of philosophy that inquires into the nature of reality. All people everywhere capable of thinking about such things in the first place have some beliefs about what is real or not, as well as about the nature of things that exist. But often these beliefs are so taken for granted and deeply embedded in our own worldviews that critical evaluation is difficult. And yet, because people in different times and places have varied quite a bit in their views on the existence and essence of things, philosophers have always tried to determine which accounts of reality are the most plausible.

As the empirical sciences evolved over the last few centuries, the continued legitimacy of metaphysics as a distinct field of systematic inquiry has been questioned, especially in Western intellectual circles. After all, it has been argued, factual questions about what exists, its nature, and the relations between real entities or events have been more productively addressed by science than by philosophy, so why bother anymore with unresolvable speculative argument? As some of the readings in Part III will illustrate, however, the boundaries between philosophy and science remain fairly permeable, and scientists themselves unavoidably operate with fundamental (often unstated) metaphysical assumptions without which their research cannot coherently proceed.

Readings 22 through 25 focus on cosmology—that is, on different accounts of the origin, structure, and makeup of the universe as the totality of all that exists. Included are varying answers to the ancient (and continuing) question of whether reality as a whole is fundamentally physical in nature (the materialist view) or fundamentally mental and/or spiritual (the idealist view).

Readings 26 through 32 address traditional issues concerning the metaphysical status of a human individual. For example, the materialist and idealist positions appear here as competing answers to the so-called mind-body problem—that is, the problem of whether we are bodies only, minds/spirits only, or some combination of both. Different perspectives on the nature of the self and personal identity over time are represented as well, as are divergent views on whether human nature is in some sense free or causally determined by forces beyond its control.

Problems usually considered the domain of what has been called, at least in the Western tradition, philosophy of religion are the focus of readings 33 through 40. In this group of readings religious beliefs and interpretations of experience are critically analyzed, especially those beliefs having to do with the existence of a Supreme Being. Whether such a being exists, what characteristics it possesses, and what its relationship might be to the rest of reality (including us) are all metaphysical questions and have been dealt with in many different cultural contexts using both rational and nonrational means of justification.

22. Plato (429–347 B.C.E.)
The Intellectual World and the Visible World

Plato was born into a wealthy and powerful family in Athens, so as he grew up he was expected to pursue a political career. After Socrates' trial and execution, however, Plato decided against these plans and instead devoted his life to philosophical study. His disillusionment with politics generally and Athenian democracy in particular did not lead to indifference but rather to extensive reflection on the nature and possibility of a truly good society. In his estimation this meant discovering both the organizational principles of good government and the moral virtues without which a *polis* (a distinct politically organized community) could never be secure, healthy, or just. Plato traveled to other kingdoms in the Mediterranean world of his day and observed them critically. Eventually he founded a school he called the Academy outside Athens, where he spent his remaining years teaching and writing. He always nourished the hope that a systematic program of philosophical training could influence those who would become political rulers, so that they could more successfully approximate his social ideals in practice.

This selection is from *The Republic,* usually considered Plato's major work in political and moral philosophy. In it, however, he goes to some lengths to show why the political wisdom of the ideal ruler is directly related to a knowledge of metaphysical truth. He recommends that a properly educated ruler not only know the difference between what is more real and less real but also know and love the essences of things ultimately constituting reality. In this part of *The Republic* Plato provides a version of the metaphysics for which he is most remembered, his so-called theory of the Forms. "Forms" are pure essences actually existing beyond the perceivable world, and he explains their place and function in the universe by his image of the divided line and his allegory of the cave. The text was written as a fictional dialogue between Socrates and several other characters (long after the historical Socrates' death), and the views Socrates espouses in the literary role as protagonist are really those of Plato's.

QUESTIONS FOR CRITICAL READING

1. What comparisons does Plato make between the sun and the "Form of Good"?
2. In the divided line analogy (or simile), what are the four levels of reality Plato identifies, and what are the four epistemological states of the soul corresponding to them?
3. In the allegory of the cave, what are the different levels of reality and corresponding mental states?
4. According to Plato, what is likely to happen when the person who has acquired knowledge of the "intellectual world" becomes involved in everyday human affairs within the "visible world"?

TERM TO NOTE

dialectic: In this context, the formal process of the logical analysis of concepts, in which the goal is rational discovery of the essences of things; different from the concept of dialectics described in Part II, reading 11 (Mao).

Are you aware, that whenever a person makes an end of looking at objects, upon which the light of day is shedding colour, and looks instead at objects coloured by the light of the moon and stars, his eyes grow dim and appear almost blind, as if they were not the seat of distinct vision?

I am fully aware of it.

But whenever the same person looks at objects on which the sun is shining, these very eyes, I believe, see clearly, and are evidently the seat of distinct vision?

Unquestionably it is so.

Just in the same way understand the condition of the soul to be as follows. Whenever it has fastened upon an object, over which truth and real existence are shining, it seizes that object by an act of reason, and knows it, and thus proves itself to be possessed of reason: but whenever it has fixed upon objects that are blent with darkness,—the world of birth and death,—then it rests in *opinion,* and its sight grows dim, as its opinions shift backwards and forwards, and it has the appearance of being destitute of reason.

True, it has.

Now, this power, which supplies the objects of real knowledge with the truth that is in them, and which renders to him who knows them the faculty of knowing them, you must consider to be the essential Form of Good, and you must regard it as the origin of science, and of truth, so far as the latter comes within the range of knowledge: and though knowledge and truth are both very beautiful things, you will be right in looking upon good as something distinct from them, and even more beautiful. And just as, in the analogous case, it is right to regard light and vision as resembling the sun, but wrong to identify them with the sun; so, in the case of science and truth, it is right to regard both of them as resembling good, but wrong to identify either of them with good; because, on the contrary, the quality of the good ought to have a still higher value set upon it.

That implies an inexpressible beauty, if it not only is the source of science and truth, but also surpasses them in beauty; for, I presume, you do not mean by it pleasure.

Hush! I exclaimed, not a word of that. But you had better examine the illustration further, as follows.

Shew me how.

I think you will admit that the sun ministers to visible objects, not only the faculty of being seen, but also their vitality, growth, and nutriment, though it is not itself equivalent to vitality.

Of course it is not.

Then admit that, in like manner, the objects of knowledge not only derive from the good the gift of being known, but are further endowed by it with a real and essential existence; though the good, far from being identical with real existence, actually transcends it in dignity and power.

Hereupon Glaucon exclaimed with a very amusing air, Good heavens! what a miraculous superiority!

Well, I said, you are the person to blame, because you compel me to state my opinions on the subject.

Nay, let me entreat you not to stop, till you have at all events gone over again your similitude of the sun, if you are leaving anything out.

Well, to say the truth, I am leaving out a great deal.

Then pray do not omit even a trifle.

I fancy I shall leave much unsaid; however, if I can help it under the circumstances, I will not intentionally make any omission.

Pray do not.

Now understand that, according to us, there are two powers reigning, one over an intellectual, and the other over a visible region and class of objects;—if I were to use the term 'firmament' you might think I was playing on the word. Well then, are you in possession of these as two kinds,—one visible, the other intellectual?

Yes, I am.

Suppose you take a line divided into two unequal parts,—one to represent the visible class of objects, the other the intellectual,—and divide each part again into two segments on the same scale. Then, if you make the lengths of the segments represent degrees of distinctness or indistinctness, one of the two segments of the part which stands for the visible world will represent all images:—meaning by images, first of all, shadows; and, in the next place, reflections in water, and in close-grained, smooth, bright substances, and everything of the kind, if you understand me.

Yes, I do understand.

Let the other segment stand for the real objects corresponding to these images,—namely, the animals about us, and the whole world of nature and of art.

Very good.

Would you also consent to say that, with reference to this class, there is, in point of truth and untruthfulness, the same distinction between the copy and the original, that there is between what is matter of opinion and what is matter of knowledge?

Certainly I should.

Then let us proceed to consider how we must divide that part of the whole line which represents the intellectual world.

How must we do it?

Thus: one segment of it will represent what the soul is compelled to investigate by the aid of the segments of the other part, which it employs as images, starting from hypotheses, and travelling not to a first principle, but to a conclusion. The other segment will represent the objects of the soul, as it makes its way from an hypothesis to a first principle which is not hypothetical, unaided by those images which the former division employs, and shaping its journey by the sole help of real essential forms.

I have not understood your description so well as I could wish.

Then we will try again. You will understand me more easily when I have made some previous observations. I think you know that the students of subjects like geometry and calculation, assume by way of materials, in each investigation, all odd and even numbers, figures, three kinds of angles, and other similar data. These things they are supposed to know, and having adopted them as hypotheses, they decline to give any account of them, either to themselves or to others, on the assumption that they are self-evident; and, making these their starting point, they proceed to travel through the remainder of the subject, and arrive at last, with perfect unanimity, at that which they have proposed as the object of investigation.

I am perfectly aware of the fact, he replied.

Then you also know that they summon to their aid visible forms, and discourse about them, though their thoughts are busy not with these forms, but with their originals, and though they discourse not with a view to the particular square and diameter which they draw, but with a view to the absolute square and the absolute diameter, and so on. For while they employ by way of images those figures and diagrams aforesaid, which again have their shadows and images in water, they are really endeavouring to behold those abstractions which a person can only see with the eye of thought.

True.

This, then, was the class of things which I called intellectual; but I said that the soul is constrained to employ hypotheses while engaged in the investigation of them,—not travelling to a first principle, (because it is unable to step out of, and mount above, its hypotheses,) but using, as images, just the copies that are presented by things below,—which copies, as compared with the originals, are vulgarly esteemed distinct and valued accordingly.

I understand you to be speaking of the subject-matter of the various branches of geometry and the kindred arts.

Again, by the second segment of the intellectual world understand me to mean all that the mere reasoning process apprehends by the force of dialectic, when it avails itself of hypotheses not as first principles, but as genuine hypotheses, that is to say, as stepping-stones and impulses, whereby it may force its way up to something that is not hypothetical, and arrive at the first principle of every thing, and seize it in its grasp; which done, it turns round, and takes hold of that which takes hold of this first principle, till at last it comes down to a conclusion, calling in the aid of no sensible object whatever, but simply employing abstract, self-subsisting forms, and terminating in the same.

I do not understand you so well as I could wish, for I believe you to be describing an arduous task; but at any rate I understand that you wish to declare distinctly, that the field of real existence and pure intellect, as contemplated by the science of dialectic, is more certain than the field investigated by what are called the arts, in which hypotheses constitute first principles, which the students are compelled, it is true, to contemplate with the mind and not with the senses; but, at the same time, as they do not come back, in the course of inquiry, to a first principle, but push on from hypothetical premises, you think that they do not exercise pure reason on the questions that engage them, although taken in connexion with a first principle these questions come within the domain of the pure reason. And I believe you apply the term understanding, not pure reason, to the mental habit of such people as geometricians,—regarding understanding as something intermediate between opinion and pure reason.

You have taken in my meaning most satisfactorily; and I beg you will accept these four mental states, as corresponding to the four segments,—namely pure reason corresponding to the highest, understanding to the second, belief to the third, and conjecture to the last; and pray arrange them in gradation, and believe them to partake of distinctness in a degree corresponding to the truth of their respective objects.

I understand you, said he. I quite agree with you, and will arrange them as you desire. . . .

Now then, I proceeded to say, go on to compare our natural condition, so far as education and ignorance are concerned, to a state of things like the following. Imagine a number of men living in an underground cavernous chamber, with an entrance open to the light, extending along the entire length of the cavern, in which they have been confined, from their childhood, with their legs and necks so shackled, that they are obliged to sit still and look straight forwards, because their chains render it impossible for them to turn their heads round: and imagine a bright fire burning some way off, above and behind them, and an elevated roadway passing between the fire and the prisoners, with a low wall built along it, like the screens which conjurors put up in front of their audience, and above which they exhibit their wonders.

I have it, he replied.

Also figure to yourself a number of persons walking behind this wall, and carrying with them statues of men, and images of other animals, wrought in wood and stone and all kinds of materials, together with various other articles, which overtop the wall; and, as you might expect, let some of the passers-by be talking, and others silent.

You are describing a strange scene, and strange prisoners.

They resemble us, I replied. For let me ask you, in the first place, whether persons so confined could have seen anything of themselves or of each other, beyond the shadows thrown by the fire upon the part of the cavern facing them?

Certainly not, if you suppose them to have been compelled all their lifetime to keep their heads unmoved.

And is not their knowledge of the things carried past them equally limited?

Unquestionably it is.

And if they were able to converse with one another, do you not think that they would be in the habit of giving names to the objects which they saw before them?

Doubtless they would.

Again: if their prison-house returned an echo from the part facing them, whenever one of the passers-by opened his lips, to what, let me ask you, could they refer the voice, if not to the shadow which was passing?

Unquestionably they would refer it to that.

Then surely such persons would hold the shadows of those manufactured articles to be the only realities.

Without a doubt they would.

Now consider what would happen if the course of nature brought them a release from their fetters, and a remedy for their foolishness, in the following manner. Let us suppose that one of them has been released, and compelled suddenly to stand up, and turn his neck round and walk with open eyes towards the light; and let us suppose that he goes through all these actions with pain, and that the dazzling splendour renders him incapable of discerning those objects of which he used formerly to see the shadows. What answer should you expect him to make, if some one were to tell him that in those days he was watching foolish phantoms, but that now he is somewhat nearer to reality, and is turned towards things more real, and sees more correctly; above all, if he were to point out to him the several objects that are passing by, and question him, and compel him to answer what they are? Should you not expect him to be puzzled, and to regard his old visions as truer than the objects now forced upon his notice?

Yes, much truer.

And if he were further compelled to gaze at the light itself, would not his eyes, think you, be distressed, and would he not shrink and turn away to the things which he could see distinctly, and consider them to be really clearer than the things pointed out to him?

Just so.

And if some one were to drag him violently up the rough and steep ascent from the cavern, and refuse to let him go till he had drawn him out into the light of the sun, would he not, think you, be vexed and indignant at such treatment, and on reaching the light, would he not find his eyes so dazzled by the glare as to be incapable of making out so much as one of the objects that are now called true?

Yes, he would find it so at first.

Hence, I suppose, habit will be necessary to enable him to perceive objects in that upper world. At first he will be most successful in distinguishing shadows; then he will discern the reflections of men and other things in water, and afterwards the realities; and after this he will raise his eyes to encounter the light of the moon and stars, finding it less difficult to study the heavenly bodies and the heaven itself by night, than the sun and the sun's light by day.

Doubtless.

Last of all, I imagine, he will be able to observe and contemplate the nature of the sun, not as it *appears* in water or on alien ground, but as it *is* in itself in its own territory.

Of course.

His next step will be to draw the conclusion, that the sun is the author of the seasons and the years, and the guardian of all things in the visible world, and in a manner the cause of all those things which he and his companions used to see.

Obviously, this will be his next step.

What then? When he recalls to mind his first habitation, and the wisdom of the place, and his old fellow-prisoners, do you not think he will congratulate himself on the change, and pity them?

Assuredly he will.

And if it was their practice in those days to receive honour and commendations one from another, and to give prizes to him who had the keenest eye for a passing object, and who remembered best all that used to precede and follow and accompany it, and from these data divined most ably what was going to come next, do you fancy that he will covet these prizes, and envy those who receive honour and exercise authority among them? Do you not rather imagine that he will feel what Homer describes, and wish extremely

'To drudge on the lands of a master,
Under a portionless wight,'

and be ready to go through anything, rather than entertain those opinions, and live in that fashion?

For my own part, he replied, I am quite of that opinion. I believe he would consent to go through anything rather than live in that way.

And now consider what would happen if such a man were to descend again and seat himself on his old seat? Coming so suddenly out of the sun, would he not find his eyes blinded with the gloom of the place?

Certainly, he would.

And if he were forced to deliver his opinion again, touching the shadows aforesaid, and to enter the lists against those who had always been prisoners, while his sight continued dim, and his eyes unsteady,—and if this process of initiation lasted a considerable time,—would he not be made a laughingstock, and would it not be said of him, that he had gone up only to come back again with his eyesight destroyed, and that it was not worth while even to attempt the ascent? And if any one endeavoured to set them free and carry them to the light, would they not go so far as to put him to death, if they could only manage to get him into their power?

Yes, that they would.

Now this imaginary case, my dear Glaucon, you must apply in all its parts to our former statements, by comparing the region which the eye reveals, to the prison-house, and the light of the fire therein to the power of the sun: and if, by the upward ascent and the contemplation of the upper world, you understand the mounting of the soul into the intellectual region, you will hit the tendency of my own surmises, since you desire to be told what they are; though, indeed, God only knows whether they are correct. But, be that as it may, the view which I take of the subject is to the following effect. In the world of knowledge, the essential Form of Good is the limit of our inquiries, and can barely be perceived; but, when perceived, we cannot help concluding that it is in every case the source of all that is bright and beautiful,—in the visible world giving birth to light and its master, and in the intellectual world dispensing, immediately and with full authority, truth and reason;—and that whosoever would act wisely, either in private or in public, must set this Form of Good before his eyes.

To the best of my power, said he, I quite agree with you.

That being the case, I continued, pray agree with me on another point, and do not be surprised, that those who have climbed so high are unwilling to take a part in the affairs of men, because their souls are ever loath to desert that upper region. For how could it be otherwise, if the preceding simile is indeed a correct representation of their case?

True, it could scarcely be otherwise.

Well: do you think it a marvellous thing, that a person, who has just quitted the contemplation of divine objects for the study of human infirmities, should betray awkwardness, and appear very ridiculous, when with his sight still dazed, and before he has become sufficiently habituated to the darkness that reigns around, he finds himself compelled to contend in courts of law, or elsewhere, about the shadows of justice, or images which throw the shadows, and to enter the lists in questions involving the arbitrary suppositions entertained by those who have never yet had a glimpse of the essential features of justice?

No, it is anything but marvellous.

Right: for a sensible man will recollect that the eyes may be confused in two distinct ways and from two distinct causes,—that is to say, by sudden transitions either from light to darkness, or from darkness to light. And, believing the same idea to be applicable to the soul, whenever such a person sees a case in which the mind is perplexed and unable to distinguish objects, he will not laugh irrationally, but he will examine whether it has just quitted a brighter life, and has been blinded by the novelty of darkness, or whether it has come from the depths of ignorance into a more brilliant life, and has been dazzled by the unusual splendour; and not till then will he congratulate the one upon its life and condition, and compassionate the other; and if he chooses to laugh at it, such laughter will be less ridiculous than that which is raised at the expense of the soul that has descended from the light of a higher region.

You speak with great judgment.

Hence, if this be true, we cannot avoid adopting the belief, that the real nature of education is at variance with the account given of it by certain of its professors, who pretend, I believe, to infuse into the mind a knowledge of which it was destitute, just as sight might be instilled into blinded eyes.

True; such are their pretensions.

Whereas, our present argument shews us that there is a faculty residing in the soul of each person, and an instrument enabling each of us to learn; and that, just as we might suppose it to be impossible to turn the eye round from darkness to light without turning the whole body, so must this faculty, or this instrument, be wheeled round, in company with the entire soul, from the perishing world, until it be enabled to endure the contemplation of the real world and the brightest part thereof, which, according to us, is the Form of Good. Am I not right?

You are. . . .

DISCUSSION QUESTIONS

1. Do you agree with Plato's account of reality as composed of a visible and an intellectual world (and thus a version of idealist dualism)? Why or why not?

2. Plato believed that the general and abstract was more real than the particular and concrete. How would you defend or refute his position?

3. Given Plato's account of "the Forms" in this dialogue, how would he explain change in the universe, and would he view it as good or bad?

4. How does Plato's metaphysical dualism compare to that of Descartes's?

23. George Berkeley (1685–1753)
All Reality Is Mental

George Berkeley was an Irish philosopher whose most influential writings were completed before he had turned 30, while he was a fellow of Trinity College in Dublin. After that period he traveled widely in Europe and visited the American colonies as well, most notably spending four years in Rhode Island while he worked on starting a college on the island of Bermuda. Eventually failing at this, he became a bishop in the Anglican Church of Ireland in 1734 and primarily pursued his ecclesiastical duties thereafter.

Berkeley's philosophical work clearly illustrates the relationship between metaphysics and epistemology— that is, what we are justified in believing about reality must depend on what we can know about it. As an epistemologist he is considered one of the most important advocates of empiricism in the Western intellectual tradition, but his arguments for a strictly experience-based account of knowledge led to the metaphysical conclusions for which he became even more famous. His claim that everyday physical objects only exist when somebody perceives them generated quite a controversy among his contemporaries and still perplexes thinkers today. In part this is because his theory seems so unconvincing and contrary to our intuitions and yet is so difficult to refute once we accept his epistemological starting point. Actually, he believed his position served to support everyday common sense and, even more, to defend against the religious skepticism (and "free thinking") he thought was encouraged by the assumption that physical things exist independently of some mind perceiving them.

In this excerpt from *A Treatise Concerning the Principles of Human Knowledge*, Berkeley lays out both his empiricist views and the metaphysics resulting from them—that all that exists in reality are ideas and minds that perceive those ideas. In the process he also gives us an example of how a conception of God has been used as an explanatory principle in a number of philosophical systems in Western intellectual history. The theory of "abstract ideas" and the account of "primary and secondary qualities" he also criticizes here are those of fellow empiricist John Locke.

QUESTIONS FOR CRITICAL READING

1. What is an idea, how does it exist, and what are the different types of ideas we can perceive, in Berkeley's theory?
2. How does Berkeley reason to the conclusion that "unthinking things" only exist insofar as they are perceived by a mind, and how does this lead to his version of what is usually called idealist monism (that all of reality is only mental/spiritual in nature, and there is no separate material substance)?
3. According to Berkeley, why can't we have an idea of a mind, and how can we know minds exist?
4. What is the role of God in Berkeley's theory?

TERMS TO NOTE

substance: In this context, more or less synonymous with "substratum," or something in which properties inhere; more generally, a type of being, existing thing, or "stuff" of which reality is made (for example, "mental substance" or "material substance").

accident: Here, a traditional philosophical term for a property, aspect, or relation of a substance.

_____

It is evident to anyone who takes a survey of the *objects* of human knowledge that they are either ideas actually imprinted on the senses, or else such as are perceived by attending to the passions and operations of the mind, or lastly, ideas formed by help of memory and imagination—either compounding, dividing, or barely representing those originally perceived in the aforesaid ways. By sight I have the ideas of light and colors, with their several degrees and variations. By touch I perceive, for example, hard and soft, heat and cold, motion and resistance, and of all these more and less either as to quantity or degree. Smelling furnishes me with odors, the palate with tastes, and hearing conveys sounds to the mind in all their variety of tone and composition. And as several of these are observed to accompany each other, they come to be marked by one name, and so to be reputed as one thing. Thus, for example, a certain color, taste, smell, figure, and consistence having been observed to go together, are accounted one distinct thing signified by the name "*apple*"; other collections of ideas constitute a stone, a tree, a book, and the like sensible things—which as they are pleasing or disagreeable excite the passions of love, hatred, joy, grief, and so forth.

2. But, besides all that endless variety of ideas or objects of knowledge, there is likewise something which knows or perceives them and exercises divers operations, as willing, imagining, remembering, about them. This perceiving, active being is what I call *mind, spirit, soul,* or *myself.* By which words I do not denote any one of my ideas, but a thing entirely distinct from them, wherein they exist or, which is the same thing, whereby they are perceived—for the existence of an idea consists in being perceived.

3. That neither our thoughts, nor passions, nor ideas formed by the imagination exist without the mind is what everybody will allow. And it seems no less evident that the various sensations or ideas imprinted on the sense, however blended or combined together (that is, whatever objects they compose), cannot exist otherwise than in a mind perceiving them.— I think an intuitive knowledge may be obtained of this by anyone that shall attend to what is meant by the term *exist* when applied to sensible things. The table I write on I say exists, that is, I see and feel it; and if I were out of my study I should say it existed—meaning thereby that if I was in my study I might perceive it, or that some other spirit actually does perceive it. There was an odor, that is, it was smelled, there was a sound, that is to say, it was heard; a color or figure, and it was

perceived by sight or touch. This is all that I can understand by these and the like expressions. For as to what is said of the absolute existence of unthinking things without any relation to their being perceived, that seems perfectly unintelligible. Their *esse* is *percipi,* nor is it possible they should have any existence out of the minds or thinking things which perceive them.

4. It is indeed an opinion strangely prevailing amongst men that houses, mountains, rivers, and, in a word, all sensible objects have an existence, natural or real, distinct from their being perceived by the understanding. But with how great an assurance and acquiescence soever this principle may be entertained in the world, yet whoever shall find in his heart to call it in question may, if I mistake not, perceive it to involve a manifest contradiction. For what are the forementioned objects but the things we perceive by sense? And what do we perceive besides our own ideas or sensations? And is it not plainly repugnant that any one of these, or any combination of them, should exist unperceived?

5. If we thoroughly examine this tenet it will, perhaps, be found at bottom to depend on the doctrine of *abstract ideas.* For can there be a nicer strain of abstraction than to distinguish the existence of sensible objects from their being perceived, so as to conceive them existing unperceived? Light and colors, heat and cold, extension and figures—in a word, the things we see and feel—what are they but so many sensations, notions, ideas, or impressions on the sense? And is it possible to separate, even in thought, any of these from perception? For my part, I might as easily divide a thing from itself. I may, indeed, divide in my thoughts, or conceive apart from each other, those things which, perhaps, I never perceived by sense so divided. Thus I imagine the trunk of a human body without the limbs, or conceive the smell of a rose without thinking on the rose itself. So far, I will not deny, I can abstract—if that may properly be called *abstraction* which extends only to the conceiving separately such objects as it is possible may really exist or be actually perceived asunder. But my conceiving or imagining power does not extend beyond the possibility of real existence or perception. Hence, as it is impossible for me to see or feel anything without an actual sensation of that thing, so is it impossible for me to conceive in my thoughts any sensible thing or object distinct from the sensation or perception of it.

6. Some truths there are so near and obvious to the mind that a man need only open his eyes to see them. Such I take this important one to be, to wit, that all the choir of heaven and furniture of the earth, in a word, all those bodies which compose the mighty frame of the world, have not any subsistence without a mind—that their *being* is to be perceived or known, that, consequently, so long as they are not actually perceived by me or do not exist in my mind or that of any other created spirit, they must either have no existence at all or else subsist in the mind of some eternal spirit—it being perfectly unintelligible, and involving all the absurdity of abstraction, to attribute to any single part of them an existence independent of a spirit. [To be convinced of which, the reader need only reflect, and try to separate in his own thoughts, the *being* of a sensible thing from its *being perceived.*]

7. From what has been said it follows there is not any other substance than *Spirit,* or that which perceives. But, for the fuller proof of this point, let it be considered the sensible qualities are color, figure, motion, smell, taste, and such like—that is, the ideas perceived by sense. Now, for an idea to exist in an unperceiving thing is a manifest contradiction, for to have an idea is all one as to perceive; that, therefore, wherein color, figure, and the like qualities exist must perceive them; hence it is clear there can be no unthinking substance or *substratum* of those ideas.

8. But, say you, though the ideas themselves do not exist without the mind, yet there may be things like them, whereof they are copies or resemblances, which things exist without the mind in an unthinking substance. I answer, an idea can be like nothing but an idea; a color or figure can be like nothing but another color or figure. If we look but ever so little into our thoughts, we shall find it impossible for us to conceive a likeness except only between our ideas. Again, I ask whether those supposed originals or external things, of which our ideas are the pictures or representations, be themselves perceivable or no? If they are, then they are ideas and we have gained our point; but if you say they are not, I appeal to anyone whether it be sense to assert a color is like something which is invisible; hard or soft, like something which is intangible; and so of the rest.

9. Some there are who make a distinction betwixt *primary* and *secondary* qualities. By the former they mean extension, figure, motion, rest, solidity or impenetrability, and number; by the latter they denote all other sensible qualities, as colors, sounds, tastes, and so forth. The ideas we have of these they acknowledge not to be the resemblances of anything existing without the mind, or unperceived, but they will have our ideas of the primary qualities to be patterns or images of things which exist without the mind, in an unthinking substance which they call "matter." By "matter," therefore, we are to understand an inert, senseless substance, in which extension, figure, and motion do actually subsist. But it is evident from what we have already shown that extension, figure, and motion are only ideas existing in the mind, and that an idea can be like nothing but another idea, and that consequently neither they nor their archetypes can exist in an unperceiving substance. Hence it is plain that the very notion of what is called *matter* or *corporeal substance* involves a contradiction in it.

10. They who assert that figure, motion, and the rest of the primary or original qualities do exist without the mind in unthinking substances do at the same time acknowledge that colors, sounds, heat, cold, and suchlike secondary qualities do not—which they tell us are sensations existing in the mind alone, that depend on and are occasioned by the different size, texture, and motion of the minute particles of matter. This they take for an undoubted truth which they can demonstrate beyond all exception. Now, if it be certain that those original qualities are inseparably united with the other sensible qualities, and not, even in thought, capable of being abstracted from them, it plainly follows that they exist only in the mind. But I desire anyone to reflect and try whether he can, by any abstraction of thought, conceive the extension and motion of a body without all other sensible qualities. For my own part, I see evidently that it is not in my power to frame an idea of a body extended and moved, but I must withal give it some color or other sensible quality which is acknowledged to exist only in the mind. In short, extension, figure, and motion, abstracted from all other qualities, are inconceivable. Where therefore the other sensible qualities are, there must these be also, to wit, in the mind and nowhere else.

11. Again, *great* and *small,* *swift* and *slow* are allowed to exist nowhere without the mind, being entirely relative, and changing as the frame or position of the organs of sense varies. The extension, therefore, which exists without the mind is neither great nor small, the motion neither swift nor slow; that is, they are nothing at all. But, say you, they are extension in general, and motion in general: thus we see how much the tenet of extended movable substances existing without the mind depends on that strange doctrine of *abstract ideas.* And here I cannot but remark how nearly the vague and indeterminate description of matter or corporeal substance, which the modern philosophers are run into by their own principles, resembles that antiquated and so much ridiculed notion of *materia prima,* to be met with in Aristotle and his followers. Without extension, solidity cannot be conceived; since, therefore, it has been shown that extension exists not in an unthinking substance, the same must also be true of solidity.

12. That number is entirely the creature of the mind, even though the other qualities be allowed to exist without, will be evident to whoever considers that the same thing bears a different denomination of number as the mind views it with different respects. Thus the same extension is one, or three, or thirty-six, according as the mind considers it with reference to a yard, a foot, or an inch. Number is so visibly relative and dependent on men's understanding that it is strange to think how anyone should give it an absolute existence without the mind. We say one book, one page, one line; all these are equally units, though some contain several of the others. And in each instance it is plain the unit relates to some particular combination of ideas arbitrarily put together by the mind.

13. Unity I know some will have to be a simple or uncompounded idea accompanying all other ideas into the mind. That I have any such idea answering the word *unity* I do not find; and if I had, methinks I could not miss finding it; on the contrary, it should be the most familiar to my understanding, since it is said to accompany all other ideas and to be perceived by all the ways of sensation and reflection. To say no more, it is an *abstract idea.*

14. I shall further add that, after the same manner as modern philosophers prove certain sensible qualities to have no existence in matter, or without the

mind, the same thing may be likewise proved of all other sensible qualities whatsoever. Thus, for instance, it is said that heat and cold are affections only of the mind, and not at all patterns of real beings existing in the corporeal substances which excite them, for that the same body which appears cold to one hand seems warm to another. Now, why may we not as well argue that figure and extension are not patterns or resemblances of qualities existing in matter, because to the same eye at different stations, or eyes of a different texture at the same station, they appear various and cannot, therefore, be the images of anything settled and determinate without the mind? Again, it is proved that sweetness is not really in the sapid thing, because, the thing remaining unaltered, the sweetness is changed into bitter, as in case of a fever or otherwise vitiated palate. Is it not as reasonable to say that motion is not without the mind, since if the succession of ideas in the mind become swifter, the motion, it is acknowledged, shall appear slower [without any alteration in any external object?]

15. In short, let anyone consider those arguments which are thought manifestly to prove that colors and taste exist only in the mind, and he shall find they may with equal force be brought to prove the same thing of extension, figure, and motion. Though it must be confessed this method of arguing does not so much prove that there is no extension or color in an outward object as that we do not know by sense which is the true extension or color of the object. But the arguments foregoing plainly show it to be impossible that any color or extension at all, or other sensible quality whatsoever, should exist in an unthinking subject without the mind, or, in truth, that there should be any such thing as an outward object.

16. But let us examine a little the received opinion.—It is said extension is a mode or accident of matter, and that matter is the *substratum* that supports it. Now I desire that you would explain what is meant by matter's *supporting* extension. Say you, I have no idea of matter and, therefore, cannot explain it. I answer, though you have no positive, yet, if you have any meaning at all, you must at least have a relative idea of matter; though you know not what it is, yet you must be supposed to know what relation it bears to accidents, and what is meant by its supporting them. It is evident "support" cannot here be taken in its usual or literal sense—as when we say that pillars support a building; in what sense therefore must it be taken?

17. If we inquire into what the most accurate philosophers declare themselves to mean by *material substance,* we shall find them acknowledge they have no other meaning annexed to those sounds but the idea of being in general together with the relative notion of its supporting accidents. The general idea of being appears to me the most abstract and incomprehensible of all other; and as for its supporting accidents, this, as we have just now observed, cannot be understood in the common sense of those words; it must, therefore, be taken in some other sense, but what that is they do not explain. So that when I consider the two parts or branches which make the signification of the words *material substance,* I am convinced there is no distinct meaning annexed to them. But why should we trouble ourselves any further in discussing this material *substratum* or support of figure and motion and other sensible qualities? Does it not suppose they have an existence without the mind? And is not this a direct repugnance and altogether inconceivable?

18. But, though it were possible that solid, figured, movable substances may exist without the mind, corresponding to the ideas we have of bodies, yet how is it possible for us to know this? Either we must know it by sense or by reason. As for our senses, by them we have the knowledge only of our sensations, ideas, or those things that are immediately perceived by sense, call them what you will; but they do not inform us that things exist without the mind, or unperceived, like to those which are perceived. This the materialists themselves acknowledge. It remains therefore that if we have any knowledge at all of external things, it must be by reason, inferring their existence from what is immediately perceived by sense. But what reason can induce us to believe the existence of bodies without the mind, from what we perceive, since the very patrons of matter themselves do not pretend there is any necessary connection betwixt them and our ideas? I say it is granted on all hands (and what happens in dreams, frenzies, and the like, puts it beyond dispute) that it is possible we might be affected with all the ideas we have now, though no bodies existed without resembling them. Hence it is evident the supposition of external bodies is not necessary for the producing our ideas; since it is granted they are produced some-

times, and might possibly be produced always in the same order we see them in at present, without their concurrence.

19. But though we might possibly have all our sensations without them, yet perhaps it may be thought easier to conceive and explain the manner of their production by supposing external bodies in their likeness rather than otherwise; and so it might be at least probable there are such things as bodies that excite their ideas in our minds. But neither can this be said, for, though we give the materialists their external bodies, they by their own confession are never the nearer knowing how our ideas are produced, since they own themselves unable to comprehend in what manner body can act upon spirit, or how it is possible it should imprint any idea in the mind. Hence it is evident the production of ideas or sensations in our minds can be no reason why we should suppose matter or corporeal substances, since that is acknowledged to remain equally inexplicable with or without this supposition. If therefore it were possible for bodies to exist without the mind, yet to hold they do so must needs be a very precarious opinion, since it is to suppose, without any reason at all, that God has created innumerable beings that are entirely useless and serve to no manner of purpose.

20. In short, if there were external bodies, it is impossible we should ever come to know it; and if there were not, we might have the very same reasons to think there were that we have now. Suppose—what no one can deny possible—an intelligence without the help of external bodies, to be affected with the same train of sensations or ideas that you are, imprinted in the same order and with like vividness in his mind. I ask whether that intelligence has not all the reason to believe the existence of corporeal substances, represented by his ideas and exciting them in his mind, that you can possibly have for believing the same thing? Of this there can be no question—which one consideration is enough to make any reasonable person suspect the strength of whatever arguments he may think himself to have for the existence of bodies without the mind.

21. Were it necessary to add any further proof against the existence of matter after what has been said, I could instance several of those errors and difficulties (not to mention impieties) which have sprung from that tenet. It has occasioned numberless controversies and disputes in philosophy, and not a few of far greater moment in religion. But I shall not enter into the detail of them in this place as well because I think arguments *a posteriori* are unnecessary for confirming what has been, if I mistake not, sufficiently demonstrated *a priori*, as because I shall hereafter find occasion to speak somewhat of them.

22. I am afraid I have given cause to think me needlessly prolix in handling this subject. For to what purpose is it to dilate on that which may be demonstrated with the utmost evidence in a line or two to anyone that is capable of the least reflection? It is but looking into your own thoughts, and so trying whether you can conceive it possible for a sound, or figure, or motion, or color to exist without the mind or unperceived. This easy trial may make you see that what you contend for is a downright contradiction. Insomuch that I am content to put the whole upon this issue: if you can but conceive it possible for one extended movable substance, or, in general, for any one idea, or anything like an idea, to exist otherwise than in a mind perceiving it, I shall readily give up the cause. And, as for all that compages of external bodies which you contend for, I shall grant you its existence, though you cannot either give me any reason why you believe it exists, or assign any use to it when it is supposed to exist. I say the bare possibility of your opinion's being true shall pass for an argument that it is so.

23. But, say you, surely there is nothing easier than to imagine trees, for instance, in a park, or books existing in a closet, and nobody by to perceive them. I answer you may so, there is no difficulty in it; but what is all this, I beseech you, more than framing in your mind certain ideas which you call books and trees, and at the same time omitting to frame the idea of anyone that may perceive them? But do not you yourself perceive or think of them all the while? This therefore is nothing to the purpose; it only shows you have the power of imagining or forming ideas in your mind; but it does not show that you can conceive it possible the objects of your thought may exist without the mind. To make out this, it is necessary that you conceive them existing unconceived or unthought of, which is a manifest repugnancy. When we do our utmost to conceive the existence of external bodies, we

are all the while only contemplating our own ideas. But the mind, taking no notice of itself, is deluded to think it can and does conceive bodies existing unthought of or without the mind, though at the same time they are apprehended by or exist in itself. A little attention will discover to anyone the truth and evidence of what is here said, and make it unnecessary to insist on any other proofs against the existence of *material substance*.

24. It is very obvious, upon the least inquiry into our own thoughts, to know whether it be possible for us to understand what is meant by the *absolute existence of sensible objects in themselves, or without the mind*. To me it is evident those words mark out either a direct contradiction or else nothing at all. And to convince others of this, I know no readier or fairer way than to entreat they would calmly attend to their own thoughts; and if by this attention the emptiness or repugnance of those expressions does appear, surely nothing more is requisite for their conviction. It is on this, therefore, that I insist, to wit, that "the absolute existence of unthinking things" are words without a meaning, or which include a contradiction. This is what I repeat and inculcate, and earnestly recommend to the attentive thoughts of the reader.

25. All our ideas, sensations, or the things which we perceive, by whatsoever names they may be distinguished, are visibly inactive—there is nothing of power or agency included in them. So that one idea or object of thought cannot produce or make any alteration in another. To be satisfied of the truth of this, there is nothing else requisite but a bare observation of our ideas. For since they and every part of them exist only in the mind, it follows that there is nothing in them but what is perceived; but whoever shall attend to his ideas, whether of sense or reflection, will not perceive in them any power or activity; there is, therefore, no such thing contained in them. A little attention will discover to us that the very being of an idea implies passiveness and inertness in it, insomuch that it is impossible for an idea to do anything or, strictly speaking, to be the cause of anything; neither can it be the resemblance or pattern of any active being, as is evident from sect. 8. Whence it plainly follows that extension, figure, and motion cannot be the cause of our sensations. To say, therefore, that these are the effects of powers resulting from the configura-

tion, number, motion, and size of corpuscles must certainly be false.

26. We perceive a continual succession of ideas, some are anew excited, others are changed or totally disappear. There is, therefore, some cause of these ideas, whereon they depend and which produces and changes them. That this cause cannot be any quality or idea or combination of ideas is clear from the preceding section. It must therefore be a substance; but it has been shown that there is no corporeal or material substance: it remains, therefore, that the cause of ideas is an incorporeal, active substance or spirit.

27. A spirit is one simple, undivided, active being—as it perceives ideas it is called the *understanding*, and as it produces or otherwise operates about them it is called the *will*. Hence there can be no *idea* formed of a soul or spirit; for all ideas whatever, being passive and inert (*vide* sect. 25), they cannot represent unto us, by way of image or likeness, that which acts. A little attention will make it plain to anyone that to have an idea which shall be like that active principle of motion and change of ideas is absolutely impossible. Such is the nature of *spirit*, or that which acts, that it cannot be of itself perceived, but only by the effects which it produces. If any man shall doubt of the truth of what is here delivered, let him but reflect and try if he can frame the idea of any power or active being, and whether he has ideas of two principal powers marked by the names *will* and *understanding*, distinct from each other as well as from a third idea of substance or being in general, with a relative notion of its supporting or being the subject of the aforesaid powers—which is signified by the name *soul* or *spirit*. This is what some hold; but, so far as I can see, the words *will, soul, spirit* do not stand for different ideas or, in truth, for any idea at all, but for something which is very different from ideas, and which, being an agent, cannot be like unto, or represented by, any idea whatsoever. [Though it must be owned at the same time that we have some notion of soul, spirit, and the operations of the mind, such as willing, loving, hating—in as much as we know or understand the meaning of those words.]

28. I find I can excite ideas in my mind at pleasure, and vary and shift the scene as oft as I think fit. It is no more than willing, and straightway this or that idea arises in my fancy; and by the same power it is

obliterated and makes way for another. This making and unmaking of ideas does very properly denominate the mind active. Thus much is certain and grounded on experience; but when we talk of unthinking agents or of exciting ideas exclusive of volition, we only amuse ourselves with words.

29. But, whatever power I may have over my own thoughts, I find the ideas actually perceived by sense have not a like dependence on my will. When in broad daylight I open my eyes, it is not in my power to choose whether I shall see or no, or to determine what particular objects shall present themselves to my view; and so likewise as to the hearing and other senses; the ideas imprinted on them are not creatures of my will. There is therefore some *other* will or spirit that produces them.

30. The ideas of sense are more strong, lively, and distinct than those of the imagination; they have likewise a steadiness, order, and coherence, and are not excited at random, as those which are the effects of human wills often are, but in a regular train or series, the admirable connection whereof sufficiently testifies the wisdom and benevolence of its Author. Now the set rules or established methods wherein the mind we depend on excites in us the ideas of sense are called the *laws of nature;* and these we learn by experience, which teaches us that such and such ideas are attended with such and such other ideas in the ordinary course of things.

31. This gives us a sort of foresight which enables us to regulate our actions for the benefit of life. And without this we should be eternally at a loss; we could not know how to act anything that might procure us the least pleasure or remove the least pain of sense. That food nourishes, sleep refreshes, and fire warms us; that to sow in the seedtime is the way to reap in the harvest; and in general that to obtain such or such ends, such or such means are conducive—all this we know, not by discovering any necessary connection between our ideas, but only by the observation of the settled laws of nature, without which we should be all in uncertainty and confusion, and a grown man no more know how to manage himself in the affairs of life than an infant just born.

32. And yet this consistent, uniform working which so evidently displays the goodness and wisdom of that Governing Spirit whose Will constitutes the laws of nature, is so far from leading our thoughts to Him that it rather sends them awandering after second causes. For when we perceive certain ideas of sense constantly followed by other ideas, and we know this is not of our own doing, we forthwith attribute power and agency to the ideas themselves and make one the cause of another, than which nothing can be more absurd and unintelligible. Thus, for example, having observed that when we perceive by sight a certain round, luminous figure, we at the same time perceive by touch the idea or sensation called heat, we do from thence conclude the sun to be the cause of heat. And in like manner perceiving the motion and collision of bodies to be attended with sound, we are inclined to think the latter an effect of the former.

33. The ideas imprinted on the senses by the Author of Nature are called *real things;* and those excited in the imagination, being less regular, vivid, and constant, are more properly termed *ideas* or *images of things* which they copy and represent. But then our sensations, be they never so vivid and distinct, are nevertheless ideas, that is, they exist in the mind, or are perceived by it, as truly as the ideas of its own framing. The ideas of sense are allowed to have more reality in them, that is, to be more strong, orderly, and coherent than the creatures of the mind; but this is no argument that they exist without the mind. They are also less dependent on the spirit, or thinking substance which perceives them, in that they are excited by the will of another and more powerful spirit; yet still they are *ideas;* and certainly no idea, whether faint or strong, can exist otherwise than in a mind perceiving it.

DISCUSSION QUESTIONS

1. How would you go about trying to refute Berkeley's claim that physical things don't exist unless they are perceived, if you had to?
2. How might Berkeley's theory hold up if God wasn't a part of it? Explain.
3. What are some examples that would strengthen or weaken the plausibility of Berkeley's views concerning our relations with other persons?
4. How would you compare Berkeley's idealist monism with the idealist monism that Radhakrishnan attributes generally to traditional Indian philosophy?

24. Cārvāka
Materialism

In the traditional categorization of ancient Indian philosophies, the Cārvāka school of thought has been treated as one of the three main "heterodox systems" (along with Buddhism and Jainism), in contrast to the six "orthodox systems" of Hinduism. It also stands out as the only one based on a materialist monist metaphysics, regarding both reality as a whole and the human person. Named after its presumed founder, Cārvāka, it reached the height of its intellectual influence in India around the sixth century B.C.E. Its adherents explicitly challenged the religious doctrines of the Vedic tradition in particular and, generally, all "other-worldly," idealist beliefs about life after death, the soul, the existence of divine beings, and what makes life worth living.

The following selections are translated from the Sanskrit and found in Radhakrishnan's and Moore's anthology, *A Sourcebook in Indian Philosophy* (see reading 3). Because the main text associated with the Cārvāka system, the *Brhaspati Sutra* (authored by Brhaspati, also known as Vacaspati, around 600 B.C.E.), has not survived, these writings are by later scholars attempting to sum up Cārvāka doctrines accurately while remaining quite critical of them. The first selection is a chapter from a fourteenth century C.E. work by Madhava Acarya, the *Sarvadarśanasaṁgraha;* the second is a chapter from the *Sarvasiddhāntasaṁgraha* by Sankara (788–820 C.E.); the third is a brief section of an ancient drama entitled *Prabodha-Candrodaya* (*The Rise of the Moon of Intellect*).

QUESTIONS FOR CRITICAL READING

1. According to the Cārvāka doctrine of materialism, what are the basic elements out of which all existing things are made?
2. How is the relation between body and soul explained in the Cārvāka system?
3. In this version of materialism, what is the relationship between perception and reality?
4. How are heaven and hell characterized in Cārvāka thought, and what does this have to do with the appropriate goals of human life?

TERMS TO NOTE

Śāstra (or *shastra*): An important or influential discourse.
Lokāyata: Naturalism, referring to the belief that nothing exists beyond, or other than, "this world."
pandit: A Hindu scholar.

Sarvadarśanasaṁgraha

The efforts of Cārvāka are indeed hard to be eradicated, for the majority of living beings hold by the current refrain—

> While life is yours, live joyously;
> None can escape Death's searching eye:
> When once this frame of ours they burn,
> How shall it e'er again return?

The mass of men, in accordance with the Śāstras of policy and enjoyment, considering wealth and desire the only ends of man and denying the existence of any object belonging to a future world, are found to follow only the doctrine of Cārvāka. Hence another name for that school is Lokāyata,—a name well accordant with the thing signified.

In this school the four elements, earth, &c., are the original principles; from these alone, when transformed into the body, intelligence is produced, just as the inebriating power is developed from the mixing of certain ingredients; and when these are destroyed, intelligence at once perishes also. They quote the *śruti* [Vedic text] for this [*Bṛhadāraṇyaka Upaniṣad* II.iv.12]: "Springing forth from these elements, itself solid knowledge, it is destroyed when they are destroyed,—after death no intelligence remains." Therefore the soul is only the body distinguished by the attribute of intelligence, since there is no evidence for any self distinct from the body, as such cannot be proved, since this school holds that perception is the only source of knowledge and does not allow inference, &c.

The only end of man is enjoyment produced by sensual pleasures. Nor may you say that such cannot be called the end of man as they are always mixed with some kind of pain, because it is our wisdom to enjoy the pure pleasure as far as we can, and to avoid the pain which inevitably accompanies it; just as the man who desires fish takes the fish with their scales and bones, and having taken as many as he wants, desists; or just as the man who desires rice, takes the rice, straw and all, and having taken as much as he wants, desists. It is not therefore for us, through a fear of pain, to reject the pleasure which our nature instinctively recognises as congenial. Men do not refrain from sowing rice, because forsooth there are wild animals to devour it; nor do they refuse to set the cooking-pots on the fire, because forsooth there are beggars to pester us for a share of the contents. If any one were so timid as to forsake a visible pleasure, he would indeed be foolish like a beast, as has been said by the poet—

> The pleasure which arises to men from contact with sensible objects,
> Is to be relinquished as accompanied by pain,—such is the reasoning of fools;
> The berries of paddy, rich with the finest white grains,
> What man, seeking his true interest, would fling away because covered with husk and dust?

If you object that, if there be no such thing as happiness in a future world, then how should men of experienced wisdom engage in the *Agnihotra*[1] and other sacrifices, which can only be performed with great expenditure of money and bodily fatigue, your objection cannot be accepted as any proof to the contrary, since the *Agnihotra*, &c., are only useful as means of livelihood, for the Veda is tainted by the three faults of untruth, self-contradiction, and tautology; then again the impostors who call themselves Vaidic [or Vedic] pandits are mutually destructive, as the authority of the *jñāna-kāṇḍa* (section on knowledge) is overthrown by those who maintain that of the *karma-kāṇḍa* (section on action), while those who maintain the authority of the *jñāna-kāṇḍa* reject that of the *karma-kāṇḍa*; and lastly, the three Vedas themselves are only the incoherent rhapsodies of knaves, and to this effect runs the popular saying—

> The *Agnihotra*, the three Vedas, the ascetic's three staves, and smearing oneself with ashes,—
> Bṛhaspati says these are but means of livelihood for those who have no manliness nor sense.

Hence it follows that there is no other hell than mundane pain produced by purely mundane causes, as thorns, &c.; the only Supreme is the earthly monarch whose existence is proved by all the world's eyesight; and the only liberation is the dissolution of the body. By holding the doctrine that the soul is identical with the body, such phrases as "I am thin," "I am black," &c., are at once intelligible, as the attributes of thinness, &c., and self-consciousness will reside in the same subject (the body); and the use of the phrase "my body" is metaphorical like "the head of Rāhu" [Rāhu being really *all head*].

All this has been thus summed up—

> In this school there are four elements, earth, water, fire, and air;
> And from these four elements alone is intelligence produced,—
> Just like the intoxicating power from *kiṇva*,[2] &c., mixed together;
> Since in "I am fat," "I am lean," these attributes abide in the same subjects,
> And since fatness, &c., reside only in the body, it alone is the soul and no other,
> And such phrases as "my body" are only significant metaphorically.

"Be it so," says the opponent; "your wish would be gained if inference, &c., had no force of proof; but then they have this force; else, if they had not, then how, on perceiving smoke, should the thoughts of the ingelligent immediately proceed to fire; or why, on hearing another say, 'There are fruits on the bank of the river,' do those who desire fruit proceed at once to the shore?"

All this, however, is only the inflation of the world of fancy.

Those who maintain the authority of inference accept the sign or middle term as the causer of knowledge, which middle term must be found in the minor and be itself invariably connected with the major. Now this invariable connection must be a relation destitute of

---

1. Sacrificial offering to fire.

2. An intoxicating herb.

any condition accepted or disputed; and this connection does not possess its power of causing inference by virtue of its existence, as the eye, &c., are the cause of perception, but by virtue of its being known. What then is the means of this connection's being known?

We will first show that it is not perception. Now perception is held to be of two kinds, external and internal [i.e., as produced by the external senses, or by the inner sense, mind]. The former is not the required means; for although it is possible that the actual contact of the senses and the object will produce the knowledge of the particular object thus brought in contact, yet as there can never be such contact in the case of the past or the future, the universal proposition which was to embrace the invariable connection of the middle and major terms in every case becomes impossible to be known. Nor may you maintain that this knowledge of the universal proposition has the general class as its object, because, if so, there might arise a doubt as to the existence of the invariable connection in this particular case [as, for instance, in this particular smoke as implying fire].

Nor is internal perception the means, since you cannot establish that the mind has any power to act independently towards an external object, since all allow that it is dependent on the external senses, as has been said by one of the logicians, "The eye, &c., have their objects as described; but mind externally is dependent on the others."

Nor can inference be the means of the knowledge of the universal proposition, since in the case of this inference we should also require another inference to establish it, and so on, and hence would arise the fallacy of an *ad infinitum* retrogression.

Nor can testimony be the means thereof, since we may either allege in reply, in accordance with the Vaiśeṣika doctrine of Kaṇāda, that this is included in the topic of inference; or else we may hold that this fresh proof of testimony is unable to leap over the old barrier that stopped the progress of inference, since it depends itself on the recognition of a sign in the form of the language used in the child's presence by the old man; and, moreover, there is no more reason for our believing on another's word that smoke and fire are invariably connected than for our receiving the *ipse dixit* of Manu, &c. [which, of course, we Cārvākas reject].

And again, if testimony were to be accepted as the only means of the knowledge of the universal proposition, then in the case of a man to whom the fact of the invariable connection between the middle and major terms had not been pointed out by another person, there could be no inference of one thing [as fire] on seeing another thing [as smoke]; hence, on your own showing, the whole topic of inference for oneself would have to end in mere idle words.

Then again, comparison, &c., must be utterly rejected as the means of the knowledge of the universal proposition, since it is impossible that they can produce the knowledge of the unconditioned connection [i.e., the universal proposition], because their end is to produce the knowledge of quite another connection, viz., the relation of a name to something so named.

Again, this same absence of a condition, which has been given as the definition of an invariable connection [i.e., a universal proposition], can itself never be known; since it is impossible to establish that all conditions must be objects of perception; and therefore, although the absence of perceptible things may be itself perceptible, the absence of non-perceptible things must be itself non-perceptible; and thus, since we must here too have recourse to inference, &c., we cannot leap over the obstacle which has already been planted to bar them. Again, we must accept as the definition of the condition, "it is that which is reciprocal or equipollent in extension with the major term though not constantly accompanying the middle." These three distinguishing clauses, "not constantly accompanying the middle term," "constantly accompanying the major term," and "being constantly accompanied by it" [i.e., reciprocal], are needed in the full definition to stop respectively three such fallacious conditions, in the argument to prove the non-eternity of sound, as "being produced," "the nature of a jar," and "the not causing audition"; wherefore the definition holds,—and again it is established by the *śloka* of the great doctor begining "*samāsama.*"[3]

But since the knowledge of the condition must here precede the knowledge of the condition's absence, it is

---

3. This refers to an obscure *śloka* of Udayanācārya, "where a reciprocal and a non-reciprocal universal connection (i.e., universal propositions which severally do and do not distribute their predicates) relate to the same argument (as e.g., to prove the existence of smoke), there that non-reciprocating term of the second will be a fallacious middle, which is not invariably accompanied by the other reciprocal of the first."

only when there is the knowledge of the condition, that the knowledge of the universality of the proposition is possible, i.e., a knowledge in the form of such a connection between the middle term and major term as is distinguished by the absence of any such condition; and, on the other hand, the knowledge of the condition depends upon the knowledge of the invariable connection. Thus we fasten on our opponents as with adamantine glue the thunderbolt-like fallacy of reasoning in a circle. Hence by the impossibility of knowing the universality of a proposition it becomes impossible to establish inference, &c.

The step which the mind takes from the knowledge of smoke, &c., to the knowledge of fire, &c., can be accounted for by its being based on a former perception or by its being an error; and that in some cases this step is justified by the result is accidental just like the coincidence of effects observed in the employment of gems, charms, drugs, &c.

From this it follows that fate, &c., do not exist, since these can only be proved by inference. But an opponent will say, if you thus do not allow adṛṣṭa,[4] the various phenomena of the world become destitute of any cause. But we cannot accept this objection as valid, since these phenomena can all be produced spontaneously from the inherent nature of things. Thus it has been said—

> The fire is hot, the water cold, refreshing cool the breeze of morn;
> By whom came this variety? from their own nature was it born.
> And all this has been also said by Bṛhaspati—
> There is no heaven, no final liberation, nor any soul in another world,
> Nor do the actions of the four castes, orders, &c., produce any real effect.
> The Agnihotra, the three Vedas, the ascetic's three staves, and smearing oneself with ashes,
> Were made by Nature as the livelihood of those destitute of knowledge and manliness.
> If a beast slain in the Fyotiṣṭoma rite[5] will itself go to heaven,
> Why then does not the sacrificer forthwith offer his own father?

> If the Śrāddha[6] produces gratification to beings who are dead,
> Then here, too, in the case of travellers when they start, it is needless to give provisions for the journey.
> If beings in heaven are gratified by our offering the Śrāddha here,
> Then why not give the food down below to those who are standing on the housetop?
> While life remains let a man live happily, let him feed on ghee[7] even though he runs in debt;
> When once the body becomes ashes, how can it ever return again?
> If he who departs from the body goes to another world,
> How is it that he comes not back again, restless for love of his kindred?
> Hence it is only as a means of livelihood that brāhmins have established here
> All these ceremonies for the dead—there is no other fruit anywhere.
> The three authors of the Vedas were buffoons, knaves, and demons.
> All the well-known formulas of the pandits, jarpharī, turpharī, &c.[8]
> And all the obscene rites for the queen commanded in the Aśvamedha,[9]
> These were invented by buffoons, and so all the various kinds of presents to the priests,
> While the eating of flesh was similarly commanded by night-prowling demons.

Hence in kindness to the mass of living beings must we fly for refuge to the doctrine of Cārvāka. Such is the pleasant consummation.

Sarvasiddhāntasaṁgraha

1. According to the Lokāyatika doctrine the four elements alone are the ultimate principles—earth, water, fire and air; there is none other.

2. Only the perceived exists; the unperceivable does not exist, by reason of its never having been perceived; even the believers in the invisible never say that the invisible has been perceived.

---

4. The unseen force.
5. A Vedic sacrifice.

6. Oblations to the dead.
7. Clarified butter.
8. See Ṛg Veda x.106.
9. A Vedic sacrificial ritual: the "horse sacrifice."

3. If the rarely perceived be taken for the unperceived, how can they call it the unperceived? How can the ever-unperceived, like things such as the horns of a hare, be an existent?

4. Others should not here postulate [the existence of] merit and demerit from happiness and misery. A person is happy or miserable through [the laws of] nature; there is no other cause.

5. Who paints the peacocks, or who makes the cuckoos sing? There exists here no cause excepting nature.

6. The soul is but the body characterised by the attributes signified in the expressions, "I am stout," "I am youthful," "I am grown up," "I am old," etc. It is not something other than that [body].

7. The consciousness that is found in the modifications of non-intelligent elements [i.e., in organisms formed out of matter] is produced in the manner of the red colour out of the combination of betel, areca-nut and lime.

8. There is no world other than this; there is no heaven and no hell; the realm of Śiva and like regions are invented by stupid impostors of other schools of thought.

9. The enjoyment of heaven lies in eating delicious food, keeping company of young women, using fine clothes, perfumes, garlands, sandal paste, etc.

10. The pain of hell lies in the troubles that arise from enemies, weapons, diseases; while liberation (*mokṣa*) is death which is the cessation of life-breath.

11. The wise therefore ought not to take pains on account of that [i.e., liberation]; it is only the fool who wears himself out by penances, fasts, etc.

12. Chastity and other such ordinances are laid down by clever weaklings. Gifts of gold and land, the pleasure of invitations to dinner, are devised by indigent people with stomachs lean with hunger.

13. The construction of temples, houses for water-supply, tanks, wells, resting places, and the like, is praised only by travellers, not by others.

14. The *Agnihotra* ritual, the three Vedas, the triple staff,[10] the ash-smearing, are the ways of gaining a livelihood for those who are lacking in intellect and energy,—so thinks Bṛhaspati.

15. The wise should enjoy the pleasures of this world through the proper visible means of agriculture, keeping cattle, trade, political administration, etc.

Prabodha-Candrodaya

PASSION: (*Smiling.*) Uncivilized ignorant fools, who imagine that spirit is something different from body, and reaps the reward of actions in a future state; we might as well expect to find excellent fruit drops from trees growing in the air. But assuming the existence of what is the mere creature of their own imagination, they deceive the people. They falsely affirm the existence of that which does not exist; and by their frequent disputations endeavour to bring reproach upon the *nāstikas*[11] who maintain the words of truth. Who has seen the soul existing in a state separate from the body? Does not life result from the ultimate configuration of matter? Consider this attentively. They not only deceive themselves, but likewise deceive the world. On what grounds do they establish distinctions among beings formed with bodies possessing the same parts and organs, as a mouth, etc.? Why do they affirm that this woman belongs to one person, and this thing to another; these are distinctions which I do not know. Those who enquire whether slaying animals, indulgence at pleasure in the tender passions, or taking what belongs to another, be lawful or unlawful, do not act conformably to the principal end of life. (*Meditating proudly.*) The *Śāstra*[12] whose doctrines are obvious to all, and which is founded on the evidence of the senses; which admits only the elements of earth, water, fire, air; which maintains that sustenance and love are the objects of human existence; which asserts that matter possesses intelligence; which denies the existence of separate spirits, and affirms that death is blessedness, was written by Vācaspati,[13] a believer in this system; he delivered it to a materialist, who taught it to his disciples, and these disciples instructed their followers. Thus it has become widely diffused in the world.

(A MATERIALIST and one of his pupils enter.)

---

10. A triple staff carried by a priest.

11. Unbelievers in the Vedas.
12. That is, the *Cārvāka-śāstra*.
13. The same as Bṛhaspati.

MATERIALIST: My son, you know that Legislation [the law of punishment by fear of which alone are men influenced in their conduct] is the only Science, and that it comprises everything else. The three Vedas are a cheat. Behold if Heaven be obtained through the officiating priest, sacrificial rites, and the destruction of the substances employed, why is not abundance of excellent fruit obtained from the ashes of a tree which has been burnt up by the fire of the forest. If the victims slain in sacrifices ascend to heaven, why are not parents offered up in sacrifice by their children? If funeral oblations nourish the deceased, why is not the flame of an extinguished taper renovated by pouring on oil?

PUPIL: Venerable tutor, if to gratify the appetites be the principal end of life, why do these men renounce sensual pleasures, and submit to pain arising from the severest mortifications?

MATERIALIST: These fools are deceived by the lying Śāstras, and are fed with the allurements of hope. But can begging, fasting, penance, exposure to the burning heat of the sun, which emaciate the body, be compared with the ravishing embraces of women with large eyes, whose prominent breasts are compressed with one's arms?

PUPIL: Do these pilgrims indeed torture themselves in order to remove the happiness which is mingled with this miserable existence?

MATERIALIST: (Smiling.) You ignorant boy, such are the fooleries of these unenlightened men. They conceive that you ought to throw away the pleasures of life, because they are mixed with pain; but what prudent man will throw away unpeeled rice which incloses excellent grain because it is covered with the husk?

PASSION: These opinions which are supposed to be verified by futurity, merely gratify the ear. (Looking with joy.) Materialist, you are my beloved friend.

MATERIALIST: (Looks at the great King Passion and advances towards him.) May thou be victorious. Materialist salutes thee.

PASSION: My friend, you are welcome, sit down here.

MATERIALIST: (Sitting down.) Vice [Kali, the name of the present or sinful age] prostrates himself at your feet.

PASSION: The felicity of Vice, I hope, is unimpaired.

MATERIALIST: By your bounty all are happy. Having accomplished what he was ordered to perform, he now desires to touch your feet; for blessed is he who after destroying the enemies of his Lord beholds his gracious face with exceeding joy, and prostrates himself at his lotus foot.

PASSION: What exploits have been performed by Vice?

MATERIALIST: He has caused the most virtuous men to forsake the road commanded in the Vedas, and to follow their own inclinations. This achievement, however, belongs neither to Vice nor myself; for it was your Majesty who inspired us with courage. The people who are doomed to inferior duties, and who were created last[14] have renounced the three Vedas; who then are Quiet, Mortification and others?[15] Besides, those who read the Vedas do it merely for the sake of subsistence. The teacher Bṛhaspati has declared that the performance of sacrifice, reading the Vedas, penances, and rubbing the body with ashes, are the means by which ignorant, weak men contrive to support themselves. . . .

DISCUSSION QUESTIONS

1. Do you agree with the Cārvāka account of the relation between body and soul? Why or why not?

2. Cārvāka thinkers apparently were quite critical of the social status and economic benefits accruing to the Hindu priesthood, the kind of criticism sometimes directed at the clergy in other organized religions in more recent times as well. Do you agree with such criticism? Why or why not?

3. How would you criticize or defend the position that all of reality is only material in nature?

4. Concerning the relationship between perception and reality, how would you compare Cārvāka doctrine and Berkeley's theory?

---

14. The military, husbandry, and the servile classes.
15. These are characters in the play.

25. Thomas W. Overholt (b. 1935) and J. Baird Callicott (b. 1941)
On the Ojibwa Worldview

At the time *Clothed-in-Fur and Other Tales* was published in 1982, Thomas Overholt and J. Baird Callicott were members of the philosophy faculty at the University of Wisconsin-Stevens Point. The book focuses on the traditional belief system of the Ojibwa ("Chippewa" is the conventional English term; they often call themselves Anishanabe), an indigenous North American people of the western Great Lakes region. Overholt and Callicott present different aspects of an Ojibwa worldview primarily by means of a compilation of traditional stories, or narratives, that had already been gathered from various Ojibwa communities and translated by anthropologists. Apart from this collection of narratives, these two philosophers then provide an interpretation of them using explicitly philosophical categories, and it is from this interpretive analysis that the reading was selected.

Although none of the actual narratives are included in the selection, the authors constantly make specific reference to them, so it may seem a little disjointed as you read. However, if you focus on what they say about the metaphysical assumptions grounding the Ojibwa worldview, you will discover a good deal of philosophical material with which to work and several metaphysical belief options to evaluate. Maybe you will also be motivated to seek out the narratives themselves for further study.

QUESTIONS FOR CRITICAL READING

1. According to Overholt and Callicott, what is "ethnometaphysics," and how do the authors recommend applying it in the reading of narratives from a different culture?
2. In the Ojibwa worldview described here, what is a "person," and how is this similar to and different from the dominant Western concept of "person"?
3. What is the relationship between the physical and the spiritual, and is one of these dimensions more fundamental than the other to the nature of reality itself in the Ojibwa worldview? What does this have to do with the understanding of life and death?

4. According to Overholt and Callicott, what kind of reality does dream experience possess from an Ojibwa perspective, what is its function in a person's life, and how would this be different from a typical Western account of dreams?

TERMS TO NOTE

manitou: In traditional Ojibwa belief, a nonhuman spirit-being, typically considered to have greater powers than physical living things (human and nonhuman).

ethnography: A descriptive rather than critical/analytical study of a culture.

shaman: In many indigenous cultures, a person having a special function in the community because he or she is thought to possess extraordinary powers of knowledge, healing, and relating to the unseen spiritual world.

The Elements of the World View

Some two decades ago the distinguished anthropologist, A. Irving Hallowell, published an essay which provides both a substantial impetus and a rationale for the present volume. In it he wrote,

> Human beings in whatever culture are provided with cognitive orientation in a cosmos; there is "order" and "reason" rather than chaos. There are basic premises and principles implied, even if these do not happen to be consciously formulated and articulated by the people themselves. We are confronted with the philosophical implications of their thought, the nature of the world of being as they conceive it. If we pursue the problem deeply enough we come face to face with a relatively unexplored territory—ethno-metaphysics (1960, p. 20).

Ethnometaphysics may be understood as a subdiscipline of philosophy (related to metaphysics as ethnohistory is to history) concerned with the exploration and analysis of the conceptual structures of different cultures. One of its implicit assumptions is that all peoples do not cognitively organize human experience in the same way and thus that there exists a variety of "world views," perhaps as many as there are distinct cultures. This book focuses on the world view of the Ojibwa, a group of American Indians living in the woodland country of the western Great Lakes, and the metaphysical underpinnings on which it is based.

Let us state our approach to ethnometaphysics directly and concretely. Everyone, we suppose, likes a good story, and if our own reactions and those of our students are any indication, Ojibwa narratives like the ones included here are good stories, holding one's attention and arousing the imagination. But reading them is not without its difficulties for those who grew up in a very different cultural tradition. Consider the following: In one of the tales (4) a woman marries a man and later discovers him to be a beaver. The two live together for years in a beaver lodge, raising successive generations of beaver offspring, and while these animals are periodically hunted and slain by humans, the dead individuals always return to life and receive offerings in the bargain. Finally, the woman returns to her human relatives, bringing with her specific instructions on how to hunt beavers. It seems safe to assume that many readers will find such plots somewhat strange, if not altogether unintelligible, and be at a loss about what to make of them.

Faced with such a problem of understanding, a reader may be tempted either to give up on the narratives altogether, or to resort to the more familiar elements of his or her own culture's world view to interpret them. Neither of these options seems satisfactory, and the latter has a special pitfall: given the great differences that exist between the Western reader's reality and that in which the stories are embedded, there will be an almost irresistible inclination toward cultural chauvinism and an almost inevitable evaluation of them as children's "fairytales" or, worse, the childlike fantasies of superstitious adults. Our concern is to find an approach suitable for beginning to understand these narratives in their own terms.

Two possibilities come to mind. Since these stories arise in a particular cultural context and by necessity share its world view, one approach would be to provide the reader with some knowledge of that world view as a preparation for comprehending them in their own terms. Thus, we might provide extensive background information about the culture prior to a presentation of the narratives. Victor Barnouw's (1977) collection of Wisconsin Chippewa texts is one example of a study which proceeds in this fashion, and it is a perfectly viable option. On the other hand, one could examine the narratives first, posing certain philosophical questions, which would lead one beyond one's own culturally-conditioned world view. One would thus construct one's own tentative picture of the world view assumed in the texts. This construction could then be supplemented and tried against the ethnographic material available on the group that produced them. We have chosen the latter strategy, feeling that it has the clear advantages of encouraging active involvement by the reader in an interpretation of the stories and of being capable of generalization. When next the reader encounters tales from a culture alien to him or her, he or she will have had some experience in dealing constructively with such material.

It may be worth mentioning that we began this project after having for another reason read both a good number of Ojibwa narratives and many ethnographic and historical studies of that group. It is clear to us that both these kinds of material are of great importance for an understanding of the Ojibwa, and our decision to emphasize the narratives is not intended to depreciate the ethnography and ethnohistory. We have adopted our strategy because of our hunch that most readers will probably start with the stories (they have a certain inherent appeal), and may never get to the often rather imposing and technical ethnography. We hope our readers will acquire some sense of how to appreciate such stories in their own integrity, and therefore understand them better. We also find the approach to be particularly appropriate to our concern with Ojibwa ethnometaphysics, since philosophical studies traditionally begin with primary sources. . . .

When one who has been nurtured in the technologically-oriented European-American cultural tradition reads a collection of Indian myths like the one presented here, he or she will inevitably encounter ideas and occurrences which from his or her perspective seem quite strange. Some of these will be on the level of everyday life and will represent little more than differences in taste (e.g., the idea that a dried beaver tail could be considered a delicacy, 18), but others will have more far-reaching significance. In what follows we propose to identify a number of these "strange" ideas which are essential to a systematic understanding of the Ojibwa world view.

Power

Perhaps one of the most striking features of these stories is that so many of the characters, creatures, and objects in them are pictured as performing actions which from a Western point of view we would consider quite extraordinary. From the canoe of the wicked old man of the first narrative, which moves under its own power when struck by its owner's paddle, to the unusual method of luring and killing moose employed by Nanabushu in the last, we are confronted with a variety of occurrences without analogue in our world of everyday experience. These aptitudes and capacities of the various actors may conveniently be designated as manifestations of "power," and they occur in every one of the myths here assembled.

We must not, of course, take the term "actors" in too narrow a sense, since it is clear that not only humans can be wielders of power, but manitous, animals, plants, and material objects as well. We notice, however, that when manifested in non-human subjects, the latter tend to be pictured as displaying "social" characteristics like volition (the animals determine to set out on an expedition to release the captive birds of summer, 15), speech (trees tell a man which direction he should travel, 2), emotion (beavers are said to be "very fond of the people," 4), rationality (animals plot elaborate strategies in response to clearly-defined problems, 15), generosity (Nanabushu's hosts always offer him food, 21), and existence within a family or community (the beaver and moose, 3, 4, 7).

Power is not manifested in any one way exclusively. Most often in these tales its exercise involves a metamorphosis, either of the actor himself or of some other person or object which he is pictured as transforming. Sometimes it takes the form of knowledge about future events (1A, 6) or of the ability to bestow a blessing (9, 11). Some men have a special capacity for hunting a particular species, like the bear (2, 5), while for their part animals have the power to withhold or give them-

selves to the men who hunt them (3, 4, 5). The source of the power is not often specified. Presumably, extraordinary power is a defining characteristic of the manitous, though even there, power is unevenly distributed: Nanabushu, himself a manitou, is sometimes pictured as being blessed by a being more powerful than himself (18, 22). As for men, the stories indicate that any special powers they may acquire tend to come as the result of fasting, dreaming, or the obtaining of certain medicines (2, 10, 11, 17).

That every one of these tales makes mention of the exercise of some (to us) unusual power suggests that such powers are conceived of by the Ojibwa as a regular part of the world of everyday experience. Indeed, in some respects it might be said that the quality of life depends on the balancing of these powers. If, for example, either animals or humans act inappropriately, both will suffer, the former from a poverty of offering goods or perhaps from a failure to return to life (or to do so with a whole and healthy body) after being killed in the hunt, the latter for want of food (3, 4, 7). It is evident, of course, that some have more power than others. The tales display what has been referred to as a "hierarchy of power," sometimes simply assuming it (the Great Sturgeon is obviously more powerful than the man he blesses and rescues, 1B; fear of more powerful beings motivates humans to make offerings, 9; the woman who had sexual intercourse with the snakes had greater-than-human powers, 1A), but sometimes raising it to the level of conscious reflection (while debating whether the stump is in fact really Nanabushu, one of the manitous expresses his doubts that such is the case on the grounds that "He is without the power of being a manitou to that extent," 19; see also Nanabushu's acknowledgement that Great Fisher is an older and more powerful manitou than he, 20). In the story of "Little-image" (10) both the man and the bear dream and have power, but in their contest that of the former proves greater than that of the latter. Within the same animal species certain individuals, sometimes white in color, may be singled out as being especially powerful (sturgeon, 6; lynx, 19).

Perhaps we should view as another aspect of this hierarchy of power the notion that one cannot use powers which are inappropriate. Mashos (1B) is unable to use heated stones to make himself a path through the snow, and the "bungling host" episodes

(21) are a classic example of this notion, since the actions so productive of food when undertaken by one with the proper capabilities produce only pain and humiliation when copied by Nanabushu. As if this lesson could possibly be lost upon the attentive listener to such stories, the narrator of the squirrel episode explicitly calls Nanabushu a fool for always imitating others (21C).

There is much about this conception of power which has a familiar ring. Indeed, the word "power" serves precisely because the commonest connotation which the term has in Western culture—the ability to act—seems so appropriate to our analysis of this aspect of the narratives. The plural, "powers," even refers frequently to a special capacity for such action, as in the phrase, "powers of persuasion." It is true that for us the term may have a decided mechanical and/or quantitative aspect (cf. its use in the language of physics, optics, electricity, and mathematics) and imply the existence of certain causal sequences. Still, though they stand outside the world view of Western science, these narratives do sometimes give the impression that power is associated with recognizable causal sequences (cf. below on reciprocity and hunting rules).

But for all that, a fundamental difference remains. This is perhaps most noticeable in the non-mechanical ways in which this power is exercised. Canoes and awls move of their own volition (1B, 16), animals act like humans (14, 15), and all sorts of things change their outward forms in the most surprising ways. Objects and entities in the physical environment may not always be what they seem. Appearances can be deceptive, for power resides not in a tangible outward form, but rather in some intangible inner essence. One might say that in these narratives power has a certain spiritual quality.

Metamorphosis

Let us take up more explicitly the matter of metamorphosis. In these tales changes in bodily form and appearance are a characteristic way in which power becomes manifest. These metamorphoses are striking not only in number, they occur in most of the stories assembled here, but also in their variety and in the apparent fluidity which exists between what seem to be distinct categories. So, for example, beings which we would consider to be "alive" can change into ob-

jects to us inanimate: Nanabushu turns himself into a stump, 19 ("Little-Image's" burying himself in the ice may be another somewhat attenuated example of a manitou changing into an object, 10); animals can do the same (a fisher into a constellation, 15), as can men (the youth in 3 seems to turn himself into a ball; at the very least he transforms himself into such a minute figure that he can conceal himself within a ball). And of course the reverse is also true: chips of ice may become sturgeons and moccasins dried beaver tails (18), a piece of dried fish may become a grouse (5) and metal a serpent (8, cf. also 1A, 16). Frequently humans change into animals, and while the transformation sometimes seems to be considered permanent (the brother-become-wolf of 1B; the rejected wives who become wolf, raven, porcupine, and jay, 3; the boy-robin, 12), the ability to alternate between the two forms at will is presupposed for the beaver and bear (3, 4), the woodpecker and mallard "hosts" (21B, D), and the woman (bird) and man (butterfly, duck, squirrel) who are the chief actors in 2. Among the manitous, the Thunders are able to assume either a human or a bird form (2).

The circumstances under which such transformations are said to take place are similarly varied. Abandoned by his human protector, the infant brother is apparently befriended by wolves and becomes one of them (1B). While pursuing his fleeing wife, a young man encounters obstacles which he is able to overcome only by taking the form of a butterfly, then a duck, and finally a squirrel (2). In one case the metamorphosis is an unwanted and unfortunate consequence of over-fasting (12), while in another it is a useful part of a strategy for revenge (19). In the "bungling host" episodes (21) it is an act preliminary to the exercise of the special power of a particular species. Beyond this, however, there are two circumstances which are recurring in these tales: sometimes transformations take place in order to establish and maintain a marriage relationship between an animal and a human (2, 3, 4), while in others the metamorphosis occurs as part of an actor's escape from a dangerous situation (1A, 3, 15).

It should be noted that the general setting for most of these tales, and thus the context in which the transformations take place, is the mythic world, the world at the time of its "origins," in which the order of things is not yet firmly fixed. It is a world in which the duration of the seasons has not yet been determined (15); the wolf, raven, porcupine, jay, kingfisher, and painted turtle have not yet attained their final forms (3, 19); and a manitou can undertake to fundamentally reverse a previous situation, so that now people will eat bears and bears will fear people, and not vice versa (10). Because the changes they bring about result in the world assuming the form in which later humans experienced it, the characters of the myths sometimes appear in the role of transformers and culture heroes (cf. also 11). And here, as was the case with "power," one finds oneself in a world in which the inner subjective dimension of experience is more fixed and permanent than the physical.

As Hallowell has shown, when one stands puzzling before this phenomenon of metamorphosis one is primed for the recognition that the notion of "person" is one of the basic categories of Ojibwa metaphysics. The "person" category is, however, somewhat more inclusive in Ojibwa thought than it is in European, encompassing both human and "other-than-human" persons. The latter term is favored by Hallowell over such alternatives as "supernatural beings" which mistakenly imply that the Ojibwa distinguished between an orderly "natural" world and some realm which transcended it. It of course follows from the fact that the category "person" is not limited to humans that what one might term "society" is cosmic in scope.

One notices in reading these narratives that the bodily form of the actors is sometimes ambiguous. The young woman who fasted, for example, beheld a "man" standing before her and inviting her to accompany him (4). The text says that "she went along with him who was in the form of a human being" and became his wife. Only after some intervening description of her new life are we told that "the woman knew that she had married a beaver." Conversely, even while in his sturgeon form the boy-turned-fish is referred to as a "human being" (6). Human form as such appears not to be a defining characteristic of beings belonging to the category "person." More central to the definition of "person" is the ability and willingness of such beings to enter into social relationships. One might note parenthetically that the European tradition has also looked upon such ability as an important characteristic of personhood, so much so that there are de-

bates over the extent to which the unborn and the comatose are fully persons. The difference, of course, is that the European tradition resolutely limits the category to humans. The Ojibwa narratives, on the other hand, mirror a series of complex interrelationships among a variety of kinds of persons: spirits and men (10, 13, 17), spirits and animals (15), spirits and spirits (20), men and men (1), men and animals (2, 4, 7), men and "inanimate" objects (1). We notice also that animals are said to possess what we would normally consider to be human qualities: they can speak (5) and plot complicated strategies (15), and they have human emotions (3). Nanabushu is a prime example of the fact that the same is also true of the spirit beings: he talks and plots, and is stubborn, short-sighted and disobedient. The fact that the spirit beings "pity" men and grant them blessings will be discussed below.

The impression of a broader than human social world is strengthened by the frequency with which the characters of the myths undergo metamorphosis, though the narratives are not terribly explicit about how all of this is possible. Scholarly discussions like that of Jenness (who reports that the Parry Island Ojibwa whom he studied thought of all objects in the world as made up of three parts, body, soul, and shadow; thus in theory anything can appear to be animate, and a part of one's self can wander free of the body) may be of some help. What is important for our purposes, however, is that the narratives simply assume that this is the way reality is, a fact that the attentive reader is likely to find both obvious and puzzling.

The Situation of Blessing

In the stories power is often pictured as flowing from one "person" to another, the more powerful of the two assuming the posture of a bestower of blessings. We therefore need to turn our attention to the characteristics of what we might call the "situation of blessing." We may say first of all that upon receipt of a blessing an individual's circumstances are altered (or at least potentially so) for the better. The harassed son-in-law, for example, was aided when his life was in danger by beings who had "blessed" or "pitied" him in the past (a sturgeon, a gull, and a cedar, 1B). The recipient of a blessing may be given food and/or the ability to successfully acquire additional supplies of that precious commodity (4, 5, 10, 18, 22), or may obtain the promise of a long life (11, 13; cf. 10).

A second characteristic of the situation of blessing is the already-mentioned fact that the movement of the action is from the more to the less powerful actor. Such action can, of course, involve the relative power of humans, as in the case of the "grandmothers" who "pitied" the fleeing brothers and Mashos' daughter, who subsequently became the protector and wife of the elder of them (1A, B). Usually, however, blessing flows from other-than-human persons (that is, from beings like Great Sturgeon, Great Gull, cedar, beaver, bear, Thunderbirds, cliff-dwelling spirits, and Nanabushu) to humans. Because of his relative powerlessness over against the powers in the world around him, man's situation is inherently "pitiable," and the act of blessing can be seen as motivated by "pity": thus, the small boy who was continually flogged by his old father was rescued, provided for, and blessed by a bear who had "come to take pity upon him" (5).

Though the bestowal of blessing is often a more or less spontaneous occurrence, it is a third characteristic of the situation of blessing that it can be, and frequently is, created (or at least facilitated) by humans. Our tales specify one way in which this is accomplished, namely the fast. After a ten-day fast, the boy was rewarded with long life and a game for the amusement of his people (11), the woman who fasted gained both a beaver-husband and knowledge of the proper relationship between beavers and the men who hunt them, which she was ultimately able to carry back to her human relatives (4), and the man and children in the story of "Little-Image" (10) fasted to gain long life and the specific powers needed to be successful in their contest with the bears. Offerings appear to be another way of effecting the proper situation for the giving of blessing, as the cliff-spirits' response to the gifts of tobacco, ribbon, and other goods indicates (17). In the tales which deal with the hunting of animals by humans, offerings seem to perform the function of maintaining the continuing effectiveness of the blessing (4, 7). More will be said on this subject below. The unwilling transformation of the fasting youth into a robin illustrates another aspect of this matter, the danger inherent in over-exploiting the situation created (12).

Our tales make it clear that the modes by which the fact of the blessing most frequently comes to consciousness are dreams and other encounters with guardian spirits (like the youth's encounters with Sturgeon and Gull, 1B). Thus the situation of blessing highlights again the fact that for the Ojibwa it is the spiritual rather than the material aspects of experience which deserve to be considered the more fundamentally real.

Finally, we notice that in two of the episodes involving Nanabushu (18, 22) over-confidence in the blessing one has received, taking it for granted, so to speak, is explicitly frowned upon. In the former the contrast is explicit between Pilferer, who follows all the manitou's instructions perfectly but does not aggressively assert his claim to the blessing ("perhaps . . . we shall yet be blessed"), and Nanabushu, who is disobedient but still confidently claims the blessing ("I have been blessed . . . By no means a mere morsel have I seen."). Only after coming up empty-handed does Nanabushu display the requisite obedience and reticence ("Yes, but it is uncertain how it will turn out; for according as I was told so I did."). One wonders whether such an attitude is bad in itself (the harassed youth of 1B seems the picture of confidence), or whether it is so only in conjunction with the kind of foolish disobedience to the terms of the blessing for which Nanabushu is famous. To this matter of obedience we now turn.

Disobedience and Its Consequences

Early in this collection of myths (2), we encounter the story of ten brothers, the youngest of whom acquires a wife under what seem to us somewhat unusual circumstances. Motivated by jealousy, the eldest brother shoots and severely wounds the woman. When the husband finds her, she instructs him to place her in a small, isolated lodge and not return to her for ten days, but after eight days he "became extremely anxious to see his wife" and went to the lodge. As he approached, however, he "saw a large bird rising from the place and flying away." Presently it alighted on a tree and addressed him saying, " 'You are to be pitied, for too soon have you come to look for me.' And then off it went flying away." Similar episodes occur in other tales: a young moose is warned by his father not to run away from the hunters, but he does so and is mutilated and humiliated as a result (7); otter ignores fisher's instructions and laughs when the old lady farts, with the result that she withholds her food from the traveling band of animal-people (15); and Nanabushu is constantly getting in trouble because he ignores the instructions of his benefactors (18, 20, 22; the first of these episodes shows us that partial obedience is not good enough). In all, this theme of obedience occurs in twelve of the tales in our collection (in addition to those already mentioned see 1A, 3, 11, 12, 17, 19).

What we notice is that the giving of instructions is the predominant context for speaking about obedience. Often the instructions are disobeyed and the offender suffers negative consequences, as in the case of Clothed-in-Fur, who kept losing "wives" because he failed to obey their instructions (3; cf. the mother's fate in 1A). In one instance, that of the boy who was transformed into a robin (12), instructions are obeyed and disaster results, but here the instructions themselves are clearly out of harmony with the values of the culture: greed is frowned upon, but the father has urged upon his son a greedy over-fasting; though he had already "dreamed of everything," he was urged by his father to seek yet more power. In the other cases where instructions are obeyed positive rewards follow: Pilferer and, belatedly, Nanabushu receive a gift of sturgeons to tide them over the starvation months of late winter (18), and after one failure to do so, Nanabushu, with the urging and assistance of his wife, conserves the power given him by Big Skunk and is able to kill moose (22). In these stories the rewarded obedience seems intended to contrast sharply with punished disobedience, and the same is probably also true about the short episode in another myth (7), which depicts the moose calves singing exuberantly and wishing for more snow. That they heed their father's instructions not to do so sets them in stark contrast to the actions of the arrogant young moose, who is the central character of that story. This impression is confirmed by explicit statements within the stories themselves. Thus when Big Skunk heard the sound of power being wasted, he said, "'How stupid of Nanabushu to bring disaster upon his children by not paying heed!'" (22).

Reciprocity, Life, and Death

Closely related to the elements already discussed are the notions of reciprocity and of the fluid line that exists between life and death. We encounter these conceptions chiefly in stories which deal with the relationship between men and animals. Toward the end of the tale about Clothed-in-Fur we learn that the beavers are willing to give themselves to humans for food, but only if the humans live up to a certain set of obligations centering around the giving of offerings and the proper treatment of the bones of the dead beavers (3; similarly, 4 and 7). Similar reciprocal relationships exist between humans and manitous (12, 14).

What is the nature of the requirements on the parties in the human-animal relationship? Two things seem to be required of humans. First of all, they must make appropriate offerings to the animals, who are said to be "happy" with the material goods given them (utensils, clothing, earrings, and the like) and wealthy because of their accumulation (4, 7). The beaver are said to like tobacco (4), and several times the pipe, acting under its own power, is pictured as playing the role of mediator between humans and animals (3, 7; similarly, between men and the cliff spirits, 17). The second requirement is that they have the proper attitude toward the animals they intend to hunt. Several things are involved here, for one the caution against crediting one's own hunting ability too highly. In the story of Clothed-in-Fur the people initially recognize the physical difficulties involved in successfully hunting the beaver and make the proper offerings (send a pipe); as a result, they hunt successfully. But then one of them notices the low water level around the beavers' lodge and reports this to the others. Confident that the taking of beavers will now be easy, that is, within their own unaugmented abilities to accomplish, they fail to make the offering and are unsuccessful in their hunt. The prohibition against thinking disparaging thoughts about the one upon whom you depend is another aspect of the required proper attitude. "'Never speak you ill of a beaver!'," said the woman to her own people after returning from years as the beaver's wife (4), for "'should you speak ill of (a beaver), you will not (be able to) kill one.'" We notice that the emotions attributed to the beaver here are quite "human" in character. The beavers love those who love them, but tend to reciprocate in kind against those who do not. Similarly with respect to the cliff-manitous from whom the people received "every kind of medicine there was," there was a prohibition against speaking "nonsense upon a cliff or upon the water" (17). Finally, we infer that a continual, appreciative remembrance of the gifts received from a benefactor also constitutes part of the proper attitude (10).

For their part, when the men fulfill their obligations faithfully, the animals will give themselves willingly to the hunters to be killed. It is perhaps not too much to suggest that they must do so, since the coming of the pipe into the animals' dwelling seems to have a certain compelling effect (3, 7). In these stories the pipe is refused only when it is known that the humans are guilty of a prior infraction. The apparent harshness of this requirement is mitigated by the notion that the death of animals killed under the proper circumstances is not final; rather, they will come back to life to enjoy the offerings they receive (3, 4, 7; while not dealing directly with hunting rules, 5 also demonstrates the willingness of animals to give themselves to humans, and 14 illustrates the fluidity of the line between life and death). The specific mechanism for facilitating this rebirth often involves special treatment of the bones. And just as humans must not be overconfident in their own abilities, the father's admonishing of the young moose regarding his arrogant attitude toward humans shows that the reverse is also true (7).

The last section of the story about Clothed-in-Fur (3) illustrates some of these points nicely. Clothed-in-Fur learns that it is all right for him to kill and eat his beaver relatives, as long as he preserves the bones intact and gathers them up for deposit in a watercourse. If the bones are broken, the revived individual will be deformed. Now other men appear on the scene. At first they make the proper offerings and the beaver allow themselves to be killed, but eventually they neglect the offerings and the beaver withhold themselves. This state of affairs continues for some time until the beaver again decide, somewhat reluctantly, to accept the offering pipes that the humans have been sending. The beaver wife seems to express at least part of the reason for this reluctance to reestablish the relationship with the humans when she says, "'The people surely ill-use us.'" But to what does she refer? The answer may be suggested in a conversation which follows. The next day the people come again with their hunting dogs which, as usual, the beavers shoo away. But of one old dog they ask, "'On what do they by whom we are killed feed you?'" When the dog replies,

"'Your livers,'" the beavers are satisfied and again allow themselves to be killed. The implication is that since they are fed on livers, they are not being given the beavers' bones to eat and the men are therefore not disrespectfully ill-using the beavers.

If men keep the rules, the deaths of the animals are not final. For practical life in the world this means that the instinct toward self-preservation, certainly observable in nature, need not be the most powerful factor influencing animal actions. There is a hint of ambiguity in the story of the young moose (7), for in the father's warnings there is a sense of foreboding, as if one should avoid meeting men whenever possible. Yet when the offering pipe is sent, the father submits and advises the others of his family to do likewise. Could it be that to be shot by a man met by chance (from whom, that is, one had not received a pipe in advance) would be dangerous because one would not know if he had kept the rules and therefore whether one would be able to return to life whole?

Dreams

Finally, the reader will recognize from these narratives that dreams play a much different role in traditional Ojibwa culture than in contemporary Western civilization. Above all, they reveal that dreams are an important means by which an individual gains power. For example, the man who was pursuing his wife called upon the power of a dream he had had in his youth to transform himself into a butterfly and (by implication, also) a duck and a squirrel, and thereby he overcame some of the obstacles that stood in his path (2). Later his dream power enabled him to win a contest and regain her. In the story of "Little-Image" (10) the outcome of a contest for high stakes between humans and bears turned on the power gained in dreams, their importance being mirrored by the narrator's statement that the human children were fasting in hopes of dreaming "of what shall give them life." Here we see as well that objects from the dream may be worn on one's person to symbolize the power gained. In accordance with Ojibwa values over-fasting and -dreaming are represented as a kind of greed for power, and are shown to have disastrous results (12). It also appears that dreams function as a means of obtaining knowledge, in one case specifically about the future (19).

The latter point is of special importance. It seems to be commonly understood in Western culture that dreams are related to waking life and may even convey knowledge. On a superficial level they seem to reflect waking experiences and express emotions, like desire and fear. It is also known that at a deeper level they may reveal something of the structure and dynamics of the unconscious, though typically the assistance of a professional psychotherapist is required to bring this information to the level of conscious awareness. But in both cases the knowledge gained is essentially subjective. It is *reflective* of worldly experience, not a category of such experience.

In traditional Ojibwa culture, however, an individual's memories of both dreaming and waking experiences were much more fully integrated, both being considered a part of actual past history. Hallowell reports the case of a young faster who, visited in a dream by the Great Eagle, saw his body become covered with feathers until he could spread his "wings" and fly off after the great bird. Now just as we do, the Ojibwa could and did differentiate between dreams and waking life, and the bulk of their experience centered on the latter. And yet, Hallowell says, "in later life the boy will recall that in his dream fast he himself became transformed into a bird" (1966/1976, p. 468; cf. 1955, p. 178). Though he may never undergo such a transformation again, that one occasion on which he did is considered to be as much a part of his actual past history as any waking experience. The story of "Hero" (13) also illustrates this close interrelation between dreaming and waking experiences: mauled by a bear and on the brink of death, he owed his life both to the motivation and encouragement provided by his visionary experience and to certain concrete, this-worldly actions. It is, therefore, clear that dream experiences were considered to be as direct, straight-forward, and tangible as those of one's waking life. They were assumed to affect the future in very palpable ways, most importantly in fixing an individual's fate, which was in fact the expected result of the puberty fasting-dreaming experience.

Dreams provide an important means of coming into direct contact with other-than-human persons, and the "good life," as we shall see, depends heavily upon a proper relationship with such persons.

Dreams, therefore, had a crucial role to play, for "whereas social relations with human beings belong to the sphere of waking life, the most intimate social interaction with other-than-human persons is experienced chiefly, but not exclusively, by the self in dream" (Hallowell, 1966/1976, p. 456). Dreams provide knowledge of these persons and of the nature of their relationship to the dreamer (1), a knowledge which supplements and is supplemented by that gained in the myths. The dream visitors are not strangers, "but . . . well-known living entities of the Ojibwa world . . . [relations with whom] could not be interpreted as other than [actual] experiences of the self" (Hallowell, 1966/1976, p. 461).

There is another thing worth pointing out about dreams. Not only were they a prime source of knowledge about matters important to the Ojibwa people, they were also "a positive factor in the operation of their aboriginal sociocultural system" (Hallowell, 1966/1976, p. 453). Hallowell in fact considers that from the standpoint of the Ojibwa world view the boys' puberty dream fast was "a necessary institution." This is true in the first place because in the puberty dreams the very existence of other-than-human persons, so important in the individual's relationship to the surrounding world, was experientially validated. In the second place, the life of the hunter was not an easy one. The quest for game was a rigorous and often dangerous enterprise, and the animals were never completely predictable. Dreams in which one learned the direction of one's life and was given the power to pursue it engendered self-confidence in meeting these "vicissitudes." Finally, living in a society which lacked formal legal controls over behavior (e.g., police and the courts), the dream experience "reinforced a type of personality structure that, functioning primarily with emphasis upon inner control rather than outward coercion, was a necessary psychological component in the operation of the Ojibwa sociocultural system" (Hallowell, 1966/1976, pp. 470-1).

World View and "Reality"

To identify the elements just discussed as central to the world view of the people who told these stories, is to designate rather precisely the problem which a person of another culture may have when reading them: these things do not at all reflect our everyday experience of the world from the Western point of view. Europeans and Euro-Americans are children of another culture, forever looking into the starry northern sky and thinking, "dipper." It is, therefore, important for us to grasp the fact that for a traditional Ojibwa, schooled in a different way of perceiving, the stories do reflect the way in which the world is experienced.

As we have said, these stories and hundreds of others like them were important in the transmission and reinforcement of the traditional Ojibwa world view: the repeated tellings of such stories during winter evenings reiterated this understanding of the world and gave it the stamp of social approval. At the same time, other cultural institutions served to confirm the world view which they contained. When the conjurer began his performance, the spirits entered and shook his specially-constructed lodge and carried on an audible dialogue with him and with members of the audience gathered outside. Thus the existence and personality characteristics, so to speak, of these spirits was a widely known and verified fact. Of perhaps even greater importance was the period of fasting at puberty. The goal of the individual who undertook the fast was a dream in which he would be visited and blessed by some other-than-human person and his destiny determined. Such dreams were an experientially real occasion of social interaction with such persons, and although a secrecy taboo has meant that actual accounts of individual dreams are rare, enough is known about their content to indicate that a sensation of being transformed in order to accompany the dream visitor on a journey to another land was a fairly common feature.

References to both conjuring (14) and dreams (2, 10, 12, 19) occur in the narratives printed above. Another narrative from the Jones collection, not reproduced here, tells of a council of manitous which followed a contest of majic powers between two particularly powerful shamans. Among its decrees the council ordained that the manitous were to bless the human people and teach them how to live only after they had fasted, and that Snapping Turtle was to be a leader in the giving of knowledge and conjuring. And so just as conjuring and dreaming, practices which in

the traditional culture were wide-spread, provided experiential confirmation of the world view of the narratives, the reverse is also true.

We might also note in passing certain "historical" incidents which served to confirm the validity of the world view. Hallowell tells the story of a hunter, who, when his first shot failed to kill a bear, was attacked by the angered beast. Unable to reload his rifle, he tried to hold off the attack by thrusting its stock in the bear's chest as he rose up on his hind legs in front of him. Then he remembered his father had told him that if one spoke to a bear, it would understand what was said. And so he said to the bear, "If you want to live, go away!" The bear dropped onto all fours and departed, thereby "proving" that he was capable of understanding and rational deliberation. True to his part of the bargain, the man did not fire at him again. One of our narratives tells of a man, mauled by a bear, who had a vision of Nanabushu in which he was promised that he would recover and live a long life (13; cf. also 11). This man was barely able to crawl home, and though by the time he arrived his wounds were festering, he did, we are told, recover and live to an old age. Certainly occurrences such as these were widely known and tended to confirm belief in the reality described by the narratives. . . .

Sam Gill (1977, p. 7) relates an anecdote about a Papago elder who rose to speak in a public meeting and before getting to the specific topic of his address spent fifteen minutes summarizing his people's mythology. Apparently for this man "knowledge has meaning and value only when placed within a particular view of the world." The intent of this volume has been to discuss the nature and importance of world views in general and to present and interpret that of the Ojibwa Indians in particular, and a brief summary of the latter would seem an appropriate way to conclude this commentary on the texts.

The Ojibwa perception of objects in the world begins, very much as in the Western tradition, with a distinction between one's self and objects other than the self, and divides the latter category into living things on the one hand and nonliving things on the other. People, animals, plants, and at least some things Westerners would classify as material objects, such as certain shells and stones, are all understood to be living things. "Persons," one basic metaphysical category, is a class which includes both human and other-than-human beings. With respect to the latter, the manitous; dream visitors and guardian spirits; the sun, moon, and winds; Thunderbirds; the "bosses" of animal species; and certain stones, animals, and trees are examples of the variety of entities which may be found in this class.

As we have seen in our examination of the myths, it is the presupposition that such other-than-human persons exist as essentially spiritual entities and have certain characteristics (the power of metamorphosis, an instability of outer form, speech, volition, social relationships, and the like) which shapes the Ojibwa perception of their world as a kind of drama in which actors of unequal power relate to each other through patterns of blessing and reciprocal obligation. Though those who were "socialized" in a vastly different cultural context will of necessity find many of the elements of this world view strange, it may perhaps be true nevertheless that the very attempt by the Ojibwa to comprehend the world as a complex and interrelated whole will seem more sound and intelligible, as non-Indians become increasingly aware of the intricate pattern of interrelationships which exist within ecological systems and the dependence of humans upon these communities for their survival.

This commentary has not, of course, exhausted these narratives. We have only scratched the surface of the complex figure of Nanabushu, who is a trickster, a creator, and culture hero, and many of the narratives and separate themes in them are worthy of extensive individual treatment. Much less does it claim to establish a pattern for the interpretation of all Ojibwa narratives. What this commentary has tried to illustrate is that such narratives do contain rather easily-recognizable indications of the world view of the people who transmitted them. An alert reading of them should enable one to isolate metaphysical principles which form the basic assumptions of the traditional Ojibwa world view and formulate a notion of the nature of the human condition and certain principles of ethics consistent with it. That the insights obtained through such a reading can be refined and vastly enriched by reference to ethnographic and other literature should be evident to all. But we hope it is also clear that even prior to such investigations a start may be made toward understanding an Ojibwa world view in its own terms.

DISCUSSION QUESTIONS

1. Is the Ojibwa metaphysics described here essentially dualistic? Why or why not?
2. Do you think we should treat nonhuman living things as "persons"? Why or why not?
3. According to Overholt and Callicott, there is a very fluid boundary between life and death in Ojibwa metaphysics. What examples or evidence can you think of that would strengthen or weaken such a perspective?
4. What similarities and differences are there between the role of dream experience in the Ojibwa worldview and the other accounts of "visions" already encountered in this anthology?

26. Risieri Frondizi (1910–1983)
From *The Nature of the Self: A Functional Interpretation*

Risieri Frondizi was an Argentinian philosopher whose major influences were European. He was especially influenced by the German philosophical theories of the first half of the twentieth century that emphasized questions of human nature, fundamental values, and the meaning of life. He is best known in the English-speaking world for his book, *The Nature of the Self*, which was published in 1953. It reflects this Continental influence but in an expanded way. In it he appropriates for his own purposes ideas both from other European philosophers and from the German Gestalt psychologists (Köhler, Koffka, Lewin, and others).

In this selection of excerpts from his book, Frondizi argues for a conception of the individual human self as a dynamic, complex, but organically unified phenomenon, which he labels a "Gestalt." His frame of reference for the development of his position is the long-standing metaphysical debate in Western philosophy regarding both the existence and the essential nature of the self. He believed his Gestalt conception could resolve this debate by providing a kind of synthesis of the old opposing views. In large part it would be based on a more directly experiential approach to understanding what is "there" in the first place when we refer to the self, how the self might change over time, and if so, whether or not it is still the same self.

QUESTIONS FOR CRITICAL READING

1. How does Frondizi characterize the "substantialist" and "atomist" accounts of the self, and what are the problems with each?
2. What does Frondizi mean by referring to the twofold nature of the "complexity and heterogeneity" of the self as an "integrated structure"?
3. In Frondizi's estimation, why is the self more like a symphony than a painting, and what does this have to do with "psychological time"?
4. According to Frondizi, how does the Gestalt conception of the self resolve three central issues in the traditional substantialist-atomist debate?

TERMS TO NOTE

Gestalt: A German term literally meaning "form" or "configuration"; used here to designate a dynamic "organized structure."

transversal: Extending or lying across something; in this context, it refers more to a cross section.

immutable: That which is unchangeable, where its opposite is "mutable," or changeable.

immanence: The state of dwelling within something, or being part of it, as opposed to the state of transcendence, which is being separate from or external to something.

4. The structural unity of the self

When we considered the applicability of the category of substance to the self, we noticed that none of the three classic characteristics of this concept—immutability, simplicity, and independence—belonged to the self. We obtained a similarly negative result from the consideration of the atomistic conception. In the first

place, the supposed psychic atom is a poorly defined unit which, when one attempts to fix it with any precision, vanishes into thin air, becoming a mere arbitrary instant in an uninterrupted process. In the second place, the aggregation of atoms, which can have only a relationship of juxtaposition one to another, looks like a grotesque caricature of the real organic unity of the self. Let us now see if the category which we have called Gestalt or structure is any more successful.[1]

It seems unquestionable that the psychic life is not chaotic, that each state or experience is connected to all the rest. This connection, however, is not of experience to experience, like the links of a chain, for if this were so there would be a fixed order of connections and in order to get to one link we should necessarily have to go by way of the preceding ones. But in the same way that Köhler showed that there is no constant relation between stimulus and response, it would be easy to show that in like manner there is no constant relation between one experience and another. No laboratory experiment is needed to prove this, for our daily experiences supply all the material we require—the sound and sight of the sea is exhilarating one day and depressing the next; the same piece of music arouses in us different reactions according to the situation in which we hear it; our arrival at the same port and in the same ship can start altogether different trains of reflection in us, depending on whether we have arrived to stay for the rest of our life or only for a short vacation; the memory of a disagreement with a friend, which irritated us so much when it happened,

---

1. An exposition of the Gestalt theory of the Ego may be found in Koffka's work, *Principles of Gestalt Psychology,* especially pp. 319–42. If one compares Koffka's theory with the one which I am here proposing, he will see that although I have taken the concept of structure from the Gestalttheorie I am not subscribing to the theory of the German psychologist. In the first place, Koffka defines psychology as the science of behavior (*ibid.,* p. 25)—though not in Watson's sense of the word—and faces the problem of the self or Ego as a problem of *segregation* from its field (pp. 319–33). The procedure that I am following is just the reverse: my problem is that of the *integration.* This fundamental difference in our points of departure and the philosophical attitude which I have adopted (which obliges me to transcend the limits of experimental psychology, a thing which Koffka never does since he has adopted a strictly scientific attitude) allow me more freedom in my thesis. What is more, in my opinion the categories of function, process, and intentionality are just as important as that of structure in the interpretation of the self.

may now provoke only an indifferent smile. The relations of experiences to each other resemble the relations between stimuli and responses in the fact that they arise within a given context.

These undeniable data of the psychic life are founded on the fact that the self is not a sum of experiences or an aggregate of parts in juxtaposition but a structure—in the sense defined above; whatever happens to one of its elements affects the whole, and the whole in turn exerts an influence upon each element. It is because the whole reacts as a structural unity and not as a mechanism that a stimulus can provoke consequences in an altogether different field from the one in which it has arisen. Thus, a strictly intellectual problem can give rise to emotional torment, and a fact of an emotional sort can have far-reaching volitional consequences. The self is not departmentalized—like modern bureaucracy—but constitutes an organic unity with intimate, complex, and varied interrelations.

The self presents itself, then, as an organized whole, an integrated structure, and experiences are related to one another not through but within the whole. For that reason, when the structure is modified the nature of the experiences and of the relationships between them are also modified. The interdependence of the different experiential groups shows that the self is a structure which is organized and "makes sense" and that each member occupies its proper place within the structure.

This does not mean, of course, that the structure which constitutes the self cannot be analyzed and broken down, theoretically, into less complex structures. It does mean, however, that we are in fact dealing with a unity that is formed upon substructures and the intimate and complex interrelation of these substructures.[2]

And here we notice another characteristic of the concept of structure which is directly applicable to the self: the members of a structure are heterogeneous in contrast with the homogeneity of the parts of a non-structural unity. Let us state, first of all, that the structure which constitutes the self, being a very complex structure, is made up not of "simple members" but of

substructures; it is consequently to the heterogeneity of these substructures that we are referring. It must also be kept in mind that the substructures are not of an abstract nature, like concepts, and that we are not trying to reconstruct a reality by juxtaposing abstractions such as the so-called "faculties of the soul."

The complexity and heterogeneity of the structure are twofold: on the one hand there is the complexity which we may call transversal; on the other there is the horizontal or, better, the temporal complexity. In actuality the self embraces the combination of both complexes, which do not and cannot exist in separation.

If we make a cross section at a given moment in our life, we find that we have a slice of a process that is made up of bundles of three different kinds of experience: the intellectual, the emotive, and the volitive. This shows that not even in the briefest moment of our life is it possible to catch ourselves concentrated upon a single type of experience. To prove this statement it is necessary to show that every experiential situation, however elemental it may be—provided that it is real—is made up of intellectual, emotive, and volitive elements.

Let us begin with the emotive elements. Every perception or representation is accompanied by an emotive reaction. What happens is that the reaction, in general, is very weak and passes unnoticed. Let us leave out of consideration those special perceptions which produce a pleasure or pain which is so intense that no one would dare deny the existence of the relation: the taste of something sweet or savory, on the one hand, or a deep burn or cut, on the other. Let us, rather, consider the perceptions of color, which are generally held to possess a weaker affective tonality. We are walking in the country just as the sun is about to go down behind the horizon. Without being in anguish, we feel a certain sadness in our spirit. Suddenly we realize that we are still wearing a pair of dark glasses. We take them off, and at once a glow of happiness surges through our spirit. With the change of the color of the landscape there is a change in affective tonality. This is a phenomenon known not only to psychologists but also to housewives, who change the color of the wallpaper because it is "sad" or remove heavy curtains so that happiness may come in with the sunlight. The common expressions of "sad color" and

---

2. By substructure I mean any of the structural parts that constitute the total Gestalt that makes up the self.

"gay color" have been coined to express the bonds of affective tonality which tend to be attached to visual perceptions. We have been concerned solely with perceptions of color, but what we have discovered could be applied equally well to the other forms of visual perception, as well as to auditory and other kinds of perceptions.

For reasons of clarity we have restricted our attention to the affective tonality which accompanies perceptions, but in all of the examples cited there are also volitional elements. When we noticed that the sadness of the landscape was due in part to the dark tint of our spectacles, we ceased to use them for the rest of that day; similarly, on the following day, if the intensity of the sunlight irritated us, we should decide to put them on again. The housewife does the same thing in the cases alluded to, and we repeat the process daily when we draw nearer to that which arouses in us a certain pleasure and draw away from that which displeases us.

We have referred to the volitive act which has its origin in an emotive state, but the order can be just the reverse. A resolution that we make—or the lack of resolution, which is also a case of volition—may have an agreeable or disagreeable effect upon us, according to the circumstances. We are never left in a state of absolute indifference. Perceptions and images, too, are accompanied by a volitional state, though at times only in its most elemental forms. An object attracts our attention, and we direct our gaze toward it. We approach, we withdraw, we choose between two or more alternatives. Total volitional indifference toward something we perceive or imagine seems to be as impossible as total emotive indifference.

In order to prove that the three different states are always present in each cross section of our psychic life, we now have only to show that "intellectual" experiences (perceptions, images, and the like) cannot be absent when we undergo emotional and volitional experiences. But is it possible that we can be afraid or happy without having any sort of perception or images? It does not seem possible. An image is present in the case of a person who is frightened by phantoms as well as in the case of a person who sees a real danger approaching him. And what has been said with respect to fear or happiness can be applied to the other emotive states. In the same way that there is no perception or image that is not accompanied by an emotive to-

nality, it seems impossible that there could be an emotion simultaneous with a complete absence of an image.

The same thing happens with regard to volition, for we do not make resolutions out of thin air—a resolution presupposes a definite situation. And this situation must occur in a perceptive, imaginative, or conceptual form. There is, therefore, no volitional experience that is unaccompanied by an intellectual one.

So far we have arrived only at an idea of the "transversal" structure of our psychic life. This is inadequate, of course, for our life is a process, and any cross section implies its paralyzation. Nevertheless, such an approach is very useful, for the "longitudinal" structure cannot be understood if one does not first have a transversal idea of each of the bundles that make it up.

Atomism was unable to comprehend either the transversal substructure of our self or the substructure which we might call longitudinal. Under the misconception that a whole is constituted necessarily by the sum or mechanical aggregate of the parts, it ignored the complex inner relationships which make it impossible to explain the structure of the self by the application of the physical principle of causality.

The atomists should not be blamed too much for their failure to perceive the structure that goes through time, its development and evolution. Their error in this case is due to their conception of time as an empty and indifferent form which may be filled by either one content or another, without making any difference. Psychological time, however, is not empty, and it is impossible to separate its content from its form. It cannot be disintegrated into the supposed instants which constitute it, for each psychological "moment" is a structure with unity of meaning. And, what is more, the "present" conceived of by the atomists is arbitrary. It aspires to be a fragment without extension. But for the present to make real sense it must contain the past and the future.

The gradual change of structure through time can be seen both by observing the development of the process itself and by comparing cross sections made at different points in the process. If one makes such a comparison, one will notice not only that the experiences vary but also that the type of structure does. At one moment the emotive is predominant and the intellectual and volitional are secondary; at another the intellectual is predominant, etc. The only thing that remains is the presence of a structure made up of three types of experiences.

This diversity and opposition among the elements which constitute the self should not lead us to forget the unity which characterizes every structure. The self is no exception. Its multiplicity does not exclude its unity or vice versa. And this is not the abstract unity of a concept which points to what is common; it is a concrete unity, of "flesh and blood" as Unamuno would say, for there is nothing more real and concrete than our self. Diversity underlies the structure but is in turn lost within it, for the elements uphold each other mutually in an intimate sort of interweaving in which it is impossible to distinguish warp from woof. This is not because the three types of substructure have equivalent strength and no one of them dominates the other two—as in the theory of the so-called balance of power—but because they vary constantly. At a given moment one element stands forth as the figure and the others form the ground; after a while there is a change of roles. These changes are explained by the fact that the self is a dynamic structure and thus resembles a symphony rather than a painting.

We should perhaps stress the point that the changes undergone by the self are not due exclusively to a different distribution of the members, for the members themselves are of a dynamic nature. Moreover, the self is constituted not only of members but also of the *tensions* produced by the reciprocal play of influences. The breakdown of the equilibrium of tensions is what generally produces the most important changes.

It now appears obvious that the relations between the experiences are not fixed, for each experience as it is incorporated into the structure modifies its former state. This member in turn undergoes the influence of the whole, which is another characteristic of a Gestalt easy to find in the self. Thus, the perceptions which we have at this moment depend upon our former state. The new experience immediately acquires the coloration given it both by the basic structure of the self and by the particular situation in which it finds itself at that moment. If we are happy and in pleasant company, for example, the color of the spectacles we happen to be wearing has very little effect upon the emotive state of our spirit. This is not because visual perception ceases to have emotional tonality but be-

cause a greater affective tone—the happiness which results from a different cause—completely overshadows it. What is more, the stable nature of the self colors the transitory state. There are people who give the impression of seeing the world in the rosiest colors, whatever the tint of the spectacles they wear, and there are others who see clouds in the clearest sky.

This is the influence of the whole upon the member which is incorporated, but there is also an influence of the member upon the whole. We must not forget that a structure is not suspended in thin air but rests solely upon the members which constitute it. A symphonic orchestra is something more than the sum of the musicians that go to form it, but it cannot exist without the musicians. A self without the experiential structures that go to make it up would be the same as an orchestra without musicians, that is, a pure fantasy, the fantasy of a spiritual entity that would be unable to love, hate, decide, want, perceive, etc., and would pretend to be immutable substance. Such a concept would be immutable without doubt, but it would have the immutability of nothingness.

In the same way that the total suppression of the experiential structures would mean the suppression of the self, any change or alteration of a member has repercussions on the whole structure. By this I do not mean a man lacking in emotional life, for example, for it is obvious that he would not be a man but a mere caricature, or projection on a plane of two dimensions, of a three-dimensional reality. I am referring to the alteration of a structural subcomplex. Abulia, for example, is a disease of the will, but the changes which it provokes are not limited to the volitional—it has immediate repercussions in the emotive and intellectual spheres and consequently in the total structure. Its intellectual repercussions are easily seen, for the person suffering from abulia is unable to concentrate his attention, and thus his intellectual processes break down completely. And the emotional sphere is impaired too, for the sufferer is unable, by an act of the will, to get rid of the emotion which has taken control of him, so he lets himself be so possessed by this emotion that it changes his whole personality.

Of the characteristics of the structure that are applicable to the self we have only to consider now the first and most important, that is, the fact that the structure possesses qualities not possessed by the members that make it up. At this stage in our inquiry it seems a waste of time to insist that this is one of the characteristics of the self. Let us consider only the most obvious reasons. The self has a permanence—in the sense of constant presence—and a stability that the experiences and experiential groups do not have. Experiences are totally unstable; transiency is their characteristic. The self, on the other hand, remains stable in the face of the coming and going of experiences. If experiences do not have stability, even less can they have permanence, which is the fundamental characteristic of the self. And this is not all. The structure of the self is such that the members that make it up cannot exist in separation from it. There is no experience that does not belong to a particular self. The self depends, then, upon the experiences, but it is not equivalent to their sum. It is a structural quality.

When we state that the self is a structure, we do not maintain that everything that happens to us automatically occupies the position in the totality that belongs to it, as if it were a matter of a sort of "pre-established harmony." There are facts that have no major significance for us, that come in like so much dead matter—even though, under certain circumstances, the accumulation of such matter can acquire significance.[3]

The use of an interpretative category does not mean that all the facts are organized in accord with the category; only those are which have significance. Thus, when the scientist states that natural phenomena are related by causality, he does not claim that all, but only certain, facts are connected to others by the relation of cause and effect. In addition to this relation there are many others, such as that of proximity in time and in space, etc., but they are not so important as causality for the comprehension and explanation of reality. The same thing happens with regard to structure—it is a concept that, in my opinion, better than any other reveals the intimate nature of the self, but it is not applicable to everything that happens to the self.

That the self has a structural unity is proved not only by the reasons given so far but also by certain

very concrete experiments, of which I shall cite only one, the experiment carried out by Arnheim, one of Wertheimer's pupils at the University of Berlin.[4] Arnheim asked his subjects to match different aspects or expressions of certain well-known personages. Sometimes the experiment involved deciding to which person—Leonardo, Michelangelo, or Raphael—a page of manuscript belonged; sometimes it involved matching up persons, whose pictures were shown, with their handwriting, a characteristic page of their works, or descriptions of the ways in which they were wont to behave. The percentage of correct answers was so high that it would be absurd to attribute them to mere chance.

The experiment proves that the different aspects of a personality and all its forms of expression proceed from a unified structure and they are therefore harmonious among themselves. This fact was already pointed out by Johann K. Lavater in his work, published in four volumes in 1775–78, entitled *Physiognomische Fragmente zur Beförderung der Menschenkenntnis und Menschenliebe*.

It is clear that not all the aspects of a personality are equally important; otherwise we need to know only one feature to grasp the whole structure. Besides, the relation among the different features is very complex and therefore the "axis" of a personality is not easy to discover.

Every day we come across examples of definite personal structure. Among criminals, for example, a certain individual is capable of killing a child but is incapable of stealing a brief case from a careless person on a streetcar. He has a certain professional pride which derives from his "personal style." The police know it. When a crime is committed, the police analyze its characteristics and look for the probable criminal within a file arranged according to the personal style of each criminal.

In the same way, a person knowing the people who run a political party, a business company, or a nation can tell who is the author of a certain platform, policy,

---

3. The slamming of a door, for example, is a trivial fact that has little meaning. Nevertheless, if we should listen for a period of ten hours or so to such slamming at a fairly rapid rate, it could very well give rise to a profound psychological disturbance in us and in this way affect the totality of our self.

4. Referred to by Koffka, *Principles of Gestalt Psychology*, p. 678. See also G. W. Allport, *Personality. A Psychological Interpretation* (London, 1949), pp. 476–81; G. W. Allport and P. E. Vernon, *Studies in Expressive Movement* (New York, 1933), *passim;* and P. E. Vernon's article in *Psychol. Bull.*, 33 (1936), 149–77.

or decree. The style reveals the author and identifies him. On the same level of comparison, a careful study discloses the affinities that exist between a predilection for a certain type of music and an inclination toward a particular kind of painting or poetry. It would seem that the arts were organized in certain structural unities that correspond to certain psychological structures.

Sometimes the structure appears to be fragmentary, and it is difficult to determine in a concrete case. This difficulty, in the majority of cases, is due to the fact that the structure is not well defined and presents contours which are hard to discern; this is the situation of the so-called "man without personality." His typical structure is actually characterized by its very vagueness.

In cases in which the structure seems to be fragmentary—as, for example, a man who is "revolutionary" in politics and "reactionary" in science or vice versa—one should not judge too hastily. In the first place, concepts like "revolutionary" and "reactionary" are very ambiguous, and the two terms may mean completely different things in science and politics. In the second place, one should not underestimate the different motives that interfere with an attitude, however scientific this attitude may seem: personal situations, resentments, sympathies, etc. These difficulties do not invalidate the doctrine but rather emphasize the complexity of the self and serve as a warning that one must be very careful not to fall into simplistic interpretations.

5. Problems solved by the structural conception[5]

A. Permanence and Mutability of the Self.   At the beginning of this chapter we saw that both substantialism and atomism were unable to give an adequate picture of the self because they could not comprehend how its permanence and continuity could be compatible with the changes that it undergoes. Substantialism emphasized the permanence and atomism the mutability.

The structural conception that we are here proposing allows us to see that the two characteristics are not only compatible but also complementary. The historical survey of past thought on the subject, which occupied the first part of this book, showed us that substantialism could not understand the changing nature of the self because it held fast to an irreducible and immutable nucleus and that Hume's atomism, in its effort to destroy the doctrine of a substantial nucleus, confused it with the very real permanence and continuity of the self.

If we free ourselves of the limitations of both historical positions and observe reality just as it presents itself, we shall see that the permanence and continuity of the self are based upon its structural character, for it is a dynamic structure made up not only of the elements which we can isolate in a cross section of our life but also of the substructures that form the complex longitudinal bundles that constitute the self. And change occurs each time a new element is taken in, which alters but does not destroy the structure.

In this way the constant alteration of the self insures its stability. It is undeniable that a new experience modifies, or can modify, the structure of the self. The loss of a child or a friend, a war, a religious experience, etc. can produce such an inner commotion that they may alter the total structure. From that time on we are not the same person as before. We act in a different way, we see life in a different perspective, and it may be that not only the future but also the past is colored by the new attitude. But it is just this experience causing us to change which gives endurance to the self. From now on we shall be the man who has lost his son or his friend or who had this or that religious experience. Other children that we may have or the new friends which we may take into our hearts may cover up but can never completely obliterate the existence of an experience that at one time shook us deeply and persists in the structure of our spirit despite all that may happen to us in the future.

What happens on a large scale in the case of experiences that are profoundly moving happens on a smaller scale in all the other experiences of our life. Each new experience alters the structure or substructure to which it is connected, and thus it is incorporated "definitively," so to speak. Whatever happens afterward may alter the meaning of the experience within the whole—increasing it or diminishing it—but it can never erase the experience completely.

---

5. What follows should be regarded as an illustration of the doctrine of the self as a functional Gestalt.

An analogy of a physical sort, even though inadequate to characterize our psychic life, may perhaps make clear the meaning of what I am trying to put across. The self resembles, in this respect, a mixture of colors. If we add to the mixture a new color—for example, blue—the mixture will be altered to a degree that will depend upon the quantity and shade of blue added and upon the combination of colors that were there before. This quantity of blue which produces a change in the former mixture is incorporated definitively into the whole, and however many more colors we add we shall never be able completely to counteract its presence.

The nature of the whole and the influence of the element incorporated into it are controlled, in the case of the analogy, by certain stable physical laws in which quantity plays an important role. This is not the case with psychic structures, in which quantity gives way to equality. Psychic structures obey certain principles, carefully studied by the Gestalt psychologists in the case of visual perception, which also exist in all the other orders of life and in the constitution of the total structure of the self. These general principles governing the organization of our total personality are what the most psychologically acute educators use as the basis for their choice of one type of experience rather than another in their endeavor to devise a system of corrective education for an aberrant personality.

Every self has a center or axis around which its structure is organized. When the personality has already developed, this axis is what gives direction and organization to our life, not only in that new experiences do not succeed in dislodging it from its route but also in that it chooses the type of experience that it finds to be in tune with it. But it is not a nucleus immutable in itself or fixed in relation to the rest of the structure. In the first place it undergoes an evolution which we can consider normal. The axis that predominates changes at the different stages of our life. In our earliest childhood the predominant experiential substructure is that related to alimentation, later it is play, and so on through life.

What is more, the center undergoes sudden displacements caused by new experiences that shake and modify the total structure. This is the case with the soldier who, according to war records, after devoting his life to the acquisition or intensification of his capacity for destruction and after exercising this capacity for years at the cost of many lives, suddenly discovers "the truth," "finds himself," decides that "we are all brothers." The center of his personality is completely displaced. His technical capacity as a killer, in which he formerly took pride—and centered his whole personality—is now a source of humiliation and shame. His personality must retrace its steps and choose another route.

These changes are due to many varied and complex reasons. Usually they have a long period of germination, as it were, in the world of the subconscious and burst forth full blown at a propitious moment. I recall the case of an American pilot who fought for several years in the Pacific; all of a sudden "the truth was revealed to him" while he was reading, more or less by chance, certain passages in the Bible. At other times the change comes about because of the intensification of the means of destruction; the explosion of the atomic bomb produced a psychological shock in many of those who had launched 200-pound bombs under the same flag. Most commonly it comes about because of the shock of contrast; the soldier, in the midst of hatred, destruction, and death, comes across people who are devoting their lives to healing, in a spirit of disinterested love, the physical and moral wounds that other men cause. These external situations usually act as the immediate cause for the eruption of subterranean currents; at other times they stir up for the first time currents that burst forth later on, if a propitious situation presents itself. . . .

B. Immanence and Transcendence of the Self. Another apparent paradox—similar to that of permanence and mutability—which is resolved by the structural conception is that of the immanence and transcendence of the self. For both atomism and substantialism, immanence and transcendence are incompatible. Either the self is equivalent to the totality of experiences—and in this sense is immanent to them—or it is something that transcends the experiences. Atomism holds the first position and substantialism the second.

According to the theory that I am proposing, the self is immanent and transcends experiences at the same time, though admittedly the terms have different meanings from those attributed to them both by atomism and by substantialism. The self is immanent because it is, indeed, equivalent to the totality of experiences; but this totality, in turn, should be interpreted not as the sum or aggregate of the experiences but as a structure that has properties that cannot be found in its parts. According to this interpretation of the concept of totality, the self transcends the experiences and becomes a structural quality, in the sense in which Ehrenfels used this expression. Nevertheless, this is not the transcendence defended by the substantialists when they affirm the existence of a being that supports states or experiences. Mine is a transcendence that not only does not exclude immanence but actually takes it for granted.

Let us look at the problem from another point of view. The relation between the self and its experiences is so intimate that every experience reveals some aspect of the self; what is more, every experience forms part of the self. In this sense, the self seems to be represented in each one of the experiences, to be nothing but them. No experience, however, is able to reveal to us the self in its entirety. Not even the sum of all the experiences can do that. The self is able to transcend its autobiography; hence the possibility of a true repentance, a conversion, a new life. In the first instance the self seems to be immanent; in the second it is seen to be something that transcends its experiences.

The problem is clarified considerably if one turns his attention to those two propositions which Hume, and many others after him, considered to be incompatible: *a*) that the self is nothing apart from its experiences; *b*) that the self cannot be reduced to its experiences. I, of course, affirm that both propositions are true. When Hume maintained that the self should be reduced to a bundle of perceptions because it could not exist without them, he let himself be misled by the substantialist prejudice in favor of the so-called independence of the self. But the self, though not independent of the perceptions, is not reducible to the mere sum of them.

The paradox of the immanence and transcendence of the self, just like the paradox which we examined before, has arisen as a consequence of the way in which substantialists stated the problem of the self, a statement that the atomists accepted without realizing its consequences. The problem, as stated, presupposes a metaphysics and a logic which our conception rejects. First, it conceives of real existence as substance,

independent and immutable; and second, it interprets the principles of identity and of noncontradiction in a very rigid way. My concept, on the other hand, gives a very dynamic interpretation to both principles, to the point of seeing in contradiction much of the essence of the real. What is more, I believe that there is nothing independent and immutable. I can hardly believe, therefore, in the independence and immutability of the self, the stuff of which is relationship and the essence of which is creative process.

C. Unity and Multiplicity. A variant of the preceding paradoxes is that of unity and multiplicity. When atomism took over the analysis of the self, its unity was destroyed forever and the self was turned into a great mosaic of loose pieces. Each perception became a reality in itself, independent, separable, sharply delimited. With this conception of the elements it proved impossible to rewin the lost unity. Atomists maintained, therefore, the plurality of the self, even though they sighed from time to time for the unity that they themselves had destroyed. When atomists—and men like William James who criticized atomism without being able to free themselves from the source of its confusion—ask what unites the different parts constituting the self, one must simply answer that the self never ceased to constitute a unity. Atomism's difficulties in reaching the unity of the self are merely a consequence of the arbitrary way in which it was dismembered. First they build a wall; then they complain they cannot see beyond the wall.

Substantialism, on the other hand, takes as its point of departure the postulate of unity and relegates multiplicity to accidents. The self is only one, although many different things happen to it.

With the importance that these "happenings" have for us—the self is made up of what it does—the whole statement of the problem collapses; the self is one or multiple according to how one looks at it. It is one if one focuses on the whole; it is multiple if one focuses on the members that constitute it. The self is the unity of the multiplicity of its experiences.

The unity of the self is not like the pseudo unity of a concept that is arrived at by abstraction. Its unity is quite concrete and is arrived at by a process of integration. It is a unity that does not abolish but preserves the differences in the members that make it up. That the self has members does not mean that it can be divided, as one divides a generic concept into the different species that it contains. The self is indivisible, though this does not keep us from distinguishing the different members that constitute it. The self has no existence apart from its members, nor do the members, if separated from the totality of the self, have existence.

DISCUSSION QUESTIONS

1. Do you think Frondizi adequately accounts for personal identity over time? Why or why not?

2. How might Frondizi's theory be applied further in the explanation of various kinds of mental illness?

3. Is Frondizi's Gestalt conception of the self compatible with a belief that the self lives on after physical death? Why or why not?

4. How would Frondizi explain the role of social relations in the development of the self and the content of personal identity? Why would you agree or disagree with him?

27. Kwame Gyekye
"The Concept of a Person"

Kwame Gyekye was raised in the Akan culture of western Africa and has spent a number of years as professor of philosophy at the University of Ghana. Given the growing interest in African philosophy in the English-speaking academic world in recent decades, Gyekye's efforts at systematic interpretation and analysis of traditional Akan thought have contributed significantly to the continuation of this trend.

This reading is the sixth chapter of his 1987 book, *An Essay on African Philosophical Thought: The Akan Conceptual Scheme.* The book covers a wide range of philosophical topics—from value questions and epistemological issues to religious and metaphysical concerns—as they are treated from the standpoint of an Akan worldview. In this excerpt Gyekye focuses on traditional Akan beliefs regarding the metaphysical status of the human person, especially the nature of and interrelations among an individual's body, soul, and spirit. An important part of his investigation is an ongoing comparison and contrast between the Akan responses to these issues and traditional positions argued for in Western philosophy.

QUESTIONS FOR CRITICAL READING

1. How does Gyekye argue for his conception of *ōkra* as "soul," and how does he critique alternative positions on this issue?

2. How does Gyekye argue for his conception of *sunsum* as immaterial "spirit," and how does he critique alternative accounts?

3. According to Gyekye, what is the relationship between *ōkra* and *sunsum,* and how does he critique alternative positions on this issue?

4. How does Gyekye argue for his "dualistic" and "interactionist" positions on the relation between the individual body (*honam*) and soul?

5. What is the relationship between the soul and God, in the Akan worldview presented here, and what does this have to do with personal immortality?

6. How does Gyekye compare and contrast the Akan views on the body, soul, and spirit with different Western philosophical and psychological theories?

TERMS TO NOTE

antemundane: That which is before the existence of the physical world.

reductio ad absurdum: A Latin phrase meaning "reduction to absurdity"; it refers to the refutation or undermining of a conclusion by showing that its logical implications are absurd or contradictory.

ontology: Sometimes used as a synonym for metaphysics; sometimes used more specifically to designate inquiry into what types of things actually exist and their "way of being."

What is a person? Is a person just the bag of flesh and bones that we see with our eyes, or is there something additional to the body that we do not see? A conception of the nature of a human being in Akan philosophy is the subject of this chapter.

6.1. Ōkra (soul)

We are given to understand from a number of often quoted, though mistaken, anthropological accounts that the Akan people consider a human being to be constituted of three elements: *ōkra, sunsum,* and *honam* (or *nipadua:* body).

The *ōkra* is said to be that which constitutes the innermost self, the essence, of the individual person. *Ōkra* is the individual's life, for which reason it is usually referred to as *ōkrateasefo,* that is, the living soul, a seeming tautology that yet is significant. The expression is intended to emphasize that *ōkra* is identical with life. The *ōkra* is the embodiment and transmitter of the individual's destiny (fate: *nkrabea*). It is explained as a spark of the Supreme Being (Onyame) in man. It is thus described as divine and as having an antemundane existence with the Supreme Being. The presence of this divine essence in a human being may have been the basis of the Akan proverb, "All men are the children of God; no one is a child of the earth" (*nnipa nyinaa yē Onyame mma, obiara nnyē asase ba*). So conceived, the *ōkra* can be considered as the equivalent of the concept of the soul in other metaphysical systems. Hence, it is correct to translate *ōkra* into English as soul.

Wiredu, however, thinks that this translation "is quite definitely wrong." He, for his part, would translate the *ōkra* as "*that whose presence in the body means life and whose absence means death* and which also receives the individual's destiny from God." Surely the (here) italicized part of the quotation accurately captures the Akan conception of the soul—*ōkrateasefo,* the living soul—whose departure means death. This

is indeed the primary definition of the soul in practically all metaphysical systems. I do not think, however, that the concept of destiny is an essential feature of the Akan definition of the soul, even though the concept of the soul is an essential feature of the Akan conception of destiny. . . .

Wiredu's reason for thinking that it is wrong to translate *ōkra* as soul is mainly that whereas "the soul is supposed in Western philosophy to be a purely immaterial entity that somehow inhabits the body, the *ōkra,* by contrast, is quasi-physical." He adds, however, that "It is not of course supposed to be straightforwardly physical as it is believed not to be fully subject to spatial constraints. Nor is it perceivable to the naked eye. Nevertheless, in some ways it seems to be credited with paraphysical properties." Wiredu's characterizations of the *ōkra* as "quasi-physical" and having "paraphysical" properties are completely wrong. He acknowledges that "highly developed medicine men" or people with extrasensory (or medicinally heightened) perception in Akan communities are said to be capable of seeing and communicating with the *ōkra.* It must be noted, however, that these phenomena do not take place in the ordinary spatial world; otherwise anyone would be able to see or communicate with the *ōkra* (soul). This must mean that what those with special abilities see or communicate with is something nonspatial. Thus, the fact that the *ōkra* can be seen by such people does not make it physical or quasi-physical (whatever that expression means), since this act or mode of seeing is not at the physical or spatial level.

I understand the term "quasi-physical" to mean "seemingly physical," "almost physical." Such description of the *ōkra* (soul) in Akan thought runs counter to the belief of most Akan people in disembodied survival or life after death. For a crucial aspect of Akan metaphysics is the existence of the world of spirits (*asamando*), a world inhabited by the departed souls of the ancestors. The conception or interpretation of the *ōkra* as a quasi-physical object having paraphysical properties would mean the total or "near total" (whatever that might mean) extinction of the *ōkra* (soul) upon the death of the person. And if this were the case, it would be senseless to talk of departed souls continuing to exist in the world of spirits (*asamando*).

In attempting further to distinguish the Akan *ōkra* from the Western soul, Wiredu writes:

> The *ōkra* is postulated in Akan thought to account for the fact of life and of destiny *but not of thought.* The soul, on the other hand, seems in much Western philosophy to be intended to account, not just for life *but also for thought.* Indeed, in Cartesian philosophy, the sole purpose of introducing the soul is to account for the phenomenon of *thinking.*

Wiredu, I believe, is here taking "thought" in the ratiocinative or cognitive sense, its normal meaning in English. But his position is undercut by his reference to the concept of *thought* in Cartesian philosophy. For it is agreed by scholars of Descartes that by *thought* (or thinking: *cogitatio*) Descartes means much more than what is normally connoted by the English word. Thus, Bernard Williams writes:

> It is an important point that in Descartes' usage the Latin verb *cogitare* and the French verb *penser* and the related nouns *cogitatio* and *pensée*, have a wider significance than the English *think* and *thought.* In English such terms are specially connected with ratiocinative or *cognitive* processes. For Descartes, however, *cogitatio* or *pensée* is any sort of conscious state or activity whatsoever; it can as well be a sensation (at least, in its purely psychological aspect) or an act of will, as judgment or belief or intellectual questioning.

Thus, what Descartes means by mind or thought is *consciousness.* Despite his reference to Descartes, I think Wiredu uses "thought" in the narrow sense, that is, of ratiocination or cognition. "Thought" in the narrow sense is of course a function or an act of consciousness. Any living human being must have consciousness. This being the case, consciousness, which is equivalent to the soul or mind in Descartes, can be a translation of *ōkra.* On this showing, it cannot be true, as Wiredu thinks, that "when we come to Descartes, the difference between the *ōkra* and the soul becomes radical and complete." My analysis, if correct, implies the opposite. I argue below (section 6.3) that thought (*adwen*) in the narrow sense is in Akan phi-

losophy an activity of the *sunsum*, which I interpret as a part of the soul (*ōkra*). Having raised some objections to Wiredu's interpretation of what he calls the Akan concept of mind, I return to my own analysis of the Akan concept of the person.

The conception of the *ōkra* as constituting the individual's life, the life force, is linked very closely with another concept, *honhom. Honhom* means "breath"; it is the noun form of *home,* to breathe. When a person is dead, it is said "His breath is gone" (*ne honhom kō*) or "His soul has withdrawn from his body" (*ne 'kra afi ne ho*). These two sentences, one with *honhom* as subject and the other with *ōkra,* do, in fact, say the same thing; they express the same thought, the death-of-the-person. The departure of the soul from the body means the death of the person, and so does the cessation of breath. Yet this does not mean that the *honhom* (breath) is identical with the *ōkra* (soul). It is the *ōkra* that "causes" the breathing. Thus, the *honhom* is the tangible manifestation or evidence of the presence of the *ōkra.* [In some dialects of the Akan language, however, *honhom* has come to be used interchangeably with *sunsum* ("spirit"), so that the phrase *honhom bōne* has come to mean the same thing as *sunsum bōne,* that is, evil spirit. The identification of the *honhom* with the *sunsum* seems to me to be a recent idea, and may have resulted from the translation of the Bible into the various Akan dialects; *honhom* must have been used to translate the Greek *pneuma* (breath, spirit).] The clarification of the concepts of *ōkra, honhom, sunsum* and others bearing on the Akan conception of the nature of a person is the concern of this chapter.

6.2. Sunsum *(spirit)*

Sunsum is another of the constituent elements of the person. It has usually been rendered in English as "spirit." It has already been observed that *sunsum* is used both generically to refer to all unperceivable, mystical beings and forces in Akan ontology, and specifically to refer to the activating principle in the person. It appears from the anthropological accounts that even when it is used specifically, "spirit" (*sunsum*) is not identical with soul (*ōkra*), as they do not refer to the same thing. However, the anthropological accounts of the *sunsum* involve some conceptual blunders, as I shall show. As for the *mind*—when it is not identified with the soul—it may be rendered also by *sunsum*, judging from the functions that are attributed by the Akan thinkers to the latter.

On the surface it might appear that "spirit" is not an appropriate rendition for *sunsum,* but after clearing away misconceptions engendered by some anthropological writings, I shall show that it is appropriate but that it requires clarification. Anthropologists and sociologists have held (1) that the *sunsum* derives from the father, (2) that it is not divine, and (3) that it perishes with the disintegration of the *honam,* that is, the material component of a person. It seems to me, however, that all these characterizations of the *sunsum* are incorrect.

Let us first take up the third characterization, namely, as something that perishes with the body. Now, if the *sunsum* perishes along with the body, a physical object, then it follows that the *sunsum* also is something physical or material. Danquah's philosophical analysis concludes that "*sunsum* is, in fact, the matter or the physical basis of the ultimate ideal of which *ōkra* (soul) is the form and the spiritual or mental basis." Elsewhere he speaks of an "interaction of the material mechanism (*sunsum*) with the soul," and assimilates the *sunsum* to the "sensible form" of Aristotle's metaphysics of substance and the *ōkra* to the "intelligible form." One might conclude from these statements that Danquah also conceived the *sunsum* as material, although some of his other statements would seem to contradict this conclusion. The relation between the *honam* (body) and the *sunsum* (supposedly bodily), however, is left unexplained. Thus, philosophical, sociological, and anthropological accounts of the nature of the person give the impression of a tripartite conception of a human being in Akan philosophy:

Ōkra (soul)	immaterial
Sunsum ("spirit")	material (?)
Honam (body)	material

As we shall see, however, this account or analysis of a person, particularly the characterization of the *sunsum* ("spirit") as something material, is not satisfactory. I must admit, however, that the real nature of the *sunsum* presents perhaps the greatest difficulty in the Akan metaphysics of a person and has been a source of confusion for many. The difficulty, however, is not insoluble.

The functions or activities attributed to the *sunsum* indicate that it is neither material nor mortal nor derived from the father. Busia says that the *sunsum* "is what moulds the child's personality and disposition. It is that which determines his character and individuality." Danquah says: "But we now know the notion which corresponds to the Akan '*sunsum*' namely, not 'spirit' as such, but personality which covers the relation of the 'body' to the 'soul' (*Ōkra*)." That the *sunsum* constitutes or rather determines the personality and character of a person is stated by Danquah several times. Rattray observed that the *sunsum* is the basis of character and personality. Eva Meyerowitz also considered the *sunsum* as personality. My own researches indicate that the views of Busia and Danquah regarding the connection between *sunsum* and personality are correct, but that they failed to see the logical implications of their views. There are indeed sentences in the Akan language in which *sunsum* refers to a person's personality and traits. Thus, for "He has a strong personality" the Akans would say, "His *sunsum* is 'heavy' or 'weighty'" (*ne sunsum yē duru*). When a man is generous they would say that he has a good *sunsum* (*ōwō sunsum pa*). When a man has an impressive or imposing personality they would say that he has an overshadowing *sunsum* (*ne sunsum hyē me so*). In fact sometimes in describing a dignified person they would simply say, "He has *spirit*" (*ōwō sunsum*), that is, he has a commanding presence. And a man may be said to have a "gentle" *sunsum,* a "forceful" *sunsum,* a "submissive" or "weak" *sunsum.* Thus, the concept of the *sunsum* corresponds in many ways to what is meant by personality, as was observed by earlier investigators.

It is now clear that in Akan conceptions the *sunsum* ("spirit") is the basis of a man's personality, and, in the words of Busia, "his ego." Personality, of course, is a word that has been variously defined by psychologists. But I believe that whatever else that concept may mean, it certainly involves the idea of a set of characteristics as evidenced in a person's behavior—thoughts, feelings, actions, etc. (The sentences given above demonstrate that it refers to more than a person's physical appearance.) Thus, if the *sunsum* is that which constitutes the basis of an individual's personality, it cannot be a physical thing, for qualities like courage, jealousy, gentleness, forcefulness, and dignity are psychological, not sensible or physical. The conception of personality as the function of the *sunsum* makes a material conception of the latter logically impossible. (Some Western philosophers and theologians in fact identify personality with the soul.) On the basis of the characteristics of *sunsum,* Parrinder describes it as the "personality-soul," perhaps using the term for the first time.

As noted, certain statements of Danquah suggest a physicalistic interpretation of the *sunsum.* On the other hand, he also maintains that "it is the *sunsum* that 'experiences,'" and that it is through the *sunsum* that "the *ōkra* or soul manifests itself in the world of experience." Elsewhere he says of the *sunsum:* "It is the bearer of conscious experience, the unconscious or subliminal self remaining over as the *ōkra* or soul." It is not clear what Danquah means by the "bearer" of experience. Perhaps what he means is that the *sunsum* is the subject of experience—that which experiences. Experience is the awareness of something. Since a purely material thing, such as wood or a dead body, cannot experience anything, it follows that the *sunsum, qua* subject of experience, cannot be material. If, as Danquah thought, it is the *sunsum* that makes it possible for the destiny (*nkrabea*) of the soul to be "realized" or "carried out" on earth, then, like the *ōkra* (soul), an aspect of whose functions it performs, the *sunsum* also must be spiritual and immaterial. Danquah's position on the concept of the *sunsum,* then, is ambivalent, as is Busia's. Busia says that one part of a person is "the personality that comes indirectly from the Supreme Being." By "personality" Busia must, on his own showing, be referring to the *sunsum,* which must, according to my analysis, derive directly from the Supreme Being, and not from the father. (What derives from the father is the *ntoro,* to be explained directly.) It must, therefore, be divine and immortal, contrary to what he and others thought. That *sunsum* cannot derive from the child's father is proved also by the fact that trees, plants, and other natural objects also contain *sunsum,* as we saw in the previous chapter.

The explanation given by most Akans of the phenomenon of dreaming also indicates, it seems to me, that *sunsum* must be immaterial. In Akan thought, as in Freud's, dreams are not somatic but psychical phenomena. It is held that in a dream it is the person's

sunsum that is the "actor." As an informant told Rattray decades ago, "When you sleep your 'Kra (soul) does not leave you, as your *sunsum* may." In sleep the *sunsum* is said to be released from the fetters of the body. As it were, it fashions for itself a new world of forms with the materials of its waking experience. Thus, although one is deeply asleep, yet one may "see" oneself standing atop a mountain or driving a car or fighting with someone or pursuing a desire like sexual intercourse; also, during sleep (that is, in dreams) a person's *sunsum* may talk with other *sunsum.* The actor in any of these "actions" is thought to be the *sunsum,* which thus can leave the body and return to it. The idea of the psychical part of a person leaving the body in sleep appears to be widespread in Africa. The Azande, for instance, maintain "that in sleep the soul is released from the body and can roam about at will and meet other spirits and have other adventures, though they admit something mysterious about its experiences. . . . During sleep a man's soul wanders everywhere."

The idea that some part of the soul leaves the body in sleep is not completely absent from the history of Western thought, even though, as Parrinder says, "the notion of a wandering soul is [are] foreign to the modern European mind." The idea occurs, for instance, in Plato. In the *Republic* Plato refers to "the wild beast in us" that in pursuit of desires and pleasures bestirs itself "in *dreams* when the *gentler part of the soul* slumbers and the control of reason is withdrawn; then the wild beast in us, full-fed with meat and drink, becomes rampant and shakes off sleep to go in quest of what will gratify its own instincts." The context is a discussion of tyranny. But Plato prefaces his discussion with remarks on the *psychological* foundation of the tyrannical man, and says that desire (Greek: *epithumia*) is the basis of his behavior.

It is not surprising that both scholars of Plato and modern psychologists have noted the relevance of the above passage to the analysis of the nature of the human psyche. On this passage the classical scholar James Adam wrote: "The theory is that in dreams the part of the soul concerned is not asleep, but awake and goes out to seek the object of its desire." The classicist Paul Shorey observed that "The Freudians have at least discovered Plato's anticipation of their main thesis." The relevance of the Platonic passage to Freud has been noted also by other scholars of Plato such as Renford Bambrough and Thomas Gould, and by psychologists. Valentine, a psychologist, observed: "The germ of several aspects of the Freudian view of dreams, including the characteristic doctrine of the censor, was to be found in Plato."

It is clear that the passage in Plato indicates a link between dreams and (the gratification of) desires. In Akan psychology the *sunsum* appears not only as unconscious but also as that which pursues and experiences desires. (In Akan dreams are also considered predictive.) But the really interesting part of Plato's thesis for our purposes relates to *the idea of some part of the human soul leaving the body in dreams.* "The wild beast in us" in Plato's passage is not necessarily equivalent to the Akan *sunsum,* but one may say that just as Plato's "wild beast" (which, like the *sunsum,* experiences dreams) is a *part* of the soul and thus not a physical object, so is *sunsum.*

It might be supposed that if the *sunsum* can engage in activity, such as traveling through space or occupying a physical location—like standing on the top of a mountain—then it can hardly be said not to be a physical object. The problem here is obviously complex. Let us assume, for the moment, that the *sunsum* is a physical object. One question that would immediately arise is: How can a purely physical object leave the person when he or she is asleep? Dreaming is of course different from imagining or thinking. The latter occurs during waking life, whereas the former occurs only during sleep: *wōnda a wōnso dae,* that is, "Unless you are asleep you do not dream" is a well-known Akan saying. The fact that dreaming occurs only in sleep makes it a unique sort of mental activity and its subject, namely *sunsum,* a different sort of subject. A purely physical object cannot be in two places at the same time: A body lying in bed cannot at the same time be on the top of a mountain. Whatever is on the top of the mountain, then, must be something nonphysical, nonbodily, and yet somehow connected to a physical thing—in this case, the body. This argument constitutes a *reductio ad absurdum* of the view that *sunsum* can be a physical object.

But, then, how can the *sunsum,* qua nonphysical, extrasensory object, travel in physical space and have a physical location? This question must be answered within the broad context of the African belief in the activities of the supernatural (spiritual) beings in the physical world. The spiritual beings are said to be insensible and intangible, but they are also said to make themselves felt in the physical world. They can thus interact with the physical world. But from this it cannot be inferred that they are physical or quasi-physical or have permanent physical properties. It means that a spiritual being can, when it so desires, take on physical properties. That is, even though a spiritual being is nonspatial in essence, it can, by the sheer operation of its power, assume spatial properties. Debrunner speaks of "temporary 'materializations,' i.e., as spirits having taken on the body of a person which afterwards suddenly vanish." Mbiti observed that "Spirits are invisible, but may make themselves visible to human beings." We should view the "physical" activities of the *sunsum* in dreaming from the standpoint of the activities of the spiritual beings in the physical world. As a microcosm of the world spirit, the *sunsum* can also interact with the external world. So much then for the defense of the psychical, nonphysical nature of *sunsum,* the subject of experiences in dreaming.

As the basis of personality, as the coperformer of some of the functions of the *ōkra* (soul)—undoubtedly held as a spiritual entity—and as the subject of the psychical activity of dreaming, the *sunsum* must be something spiritual (immaterial). This is the reason for my earlier assertion that "spirit" might not be an inappropriate translation for *sunsum.* On my analysis, then, we have the following picture:

Ōkra (soul) ⎫	immaterial (spiritual)
Sunsum ("spirit") ⎭	
Honam (body)	material (physical)

In their conception of the nature of the person the Akans distinguish the *ntoro* and the *mogya* (blood). In contrast to the *sunsum* and *ōkra,* which definitely are of divine origin, the *ntoro* and the *mogya* are endowed by human beings. The *ntoro* is held as coming from the father of the child. It has been confused with *sunsum.* Thus, Busia says that the two terms are synonymous, and hence renders *ntoro* as "spirit." He writes: "*Ntoro* is the generic term of which *sunsum* is a specific instance." Rattray also translated *ntoro* by "spirit," though he thought it corresponded with the semen. He said elsewhere that the *ntoro* is "passed into the woman by a male during the act of coition." One of my discussants stated that *ntoro* is derived from the father's semen, but the *sunsum,* he said, comes from the Supreme Being. The *ntoro* appears to be the basis of inherited characteristics and may therefore be simply translated as "sperm-transmitted characteristic," even though spiritual as well as physiological qualities are attributed to it. Both *ntoro* and *mogya* (blood, which is believed to be transmitted by the mother) are genetic factors responsible for inherited characteristics, on the basis of which the Akan thinkers have created proverbs such as:

> The crab does not give birth to a bird.
> The offspring of an antelope cannot possibly
>   resemble a deer's offspring.
> The antelope does not leap for its offspring to
>   crawl.

The introduction of inherited characteristics into the constitution of a person introduces an element of complexity into the Akan concept of the person.

6.3. *Relation of* ōkra *and* sunsum

Having shown that the *sunsum* is in fact something spiritual (and for this reason I shall henceforth translate *sunsum* as "spirit"), we must examine whether the expressions *sunsum* and *ōkra* are identical in terms of their referent. In the course of my field research some discussants stated that the *sunsum, ōkra,* and *honhom* (breath) are identical; they denote the same object; it is one and the same object that goes under three names. I have already shown that although there is a close link between *ōkra* and *honhom,* the two cannot be identified; likewise the identification of *honhom* and *sunsum* is incorrect. What about the *sunsum* and *ōkra*? Are they identical?

The relation between the *sunsum* and *ōkra* is a difficult knot to untie. The anthropologist Rattray, perhaps the most perceptive and analytical researcher into the Ashanti culture, wrote: "It is very difficult sometimes to distinguish between the *'kra* and the next kind of soul, the *sunsum,* and sometimes the words seem synonymous, but I cannot help thinking this is a loose use of the terms." Rattray was, I think, more inclined to believe that the two terms are not identical. Such a supposition, in my view, would be correct, for to say that the two are identical would logically mean that

whatever can be asserted of one can or must be asserted of the other. Yet there are some things the Akans say of the *sunsum* which are not said of the *ōkra,* and vice versa; the attributes or predicates of the two are different. The Akans say:

A (1) "His *'kra* is sad" (*ne 'kra di awerēhow*); never, "His *sunsum* is sad."
  (2) "His *'kra* is worried or disturbed" (*ne 'kra teetee*).
  (3) "His *'kra* has run away" (*ne 'kra adwane*), to denote someone who is scared to death.
  (4) "His *'kra* is good" (*ne 'kra ye*), referring to a person who is lucky or fortunate. [The negative of this statement is "His *'kra* is not good." If you used *sunsum* in lieu of *'kra,* and made the statement "His *sunsum* is not good" (*ne sunsum nnyē*), the meaning would be quite different; it would mean that his *sunsum* is evil, that is to say, he is an evil spirit, a witch.]
  (5) "His *'kra* has withdrawn from his body" (*ne 'kra afi ne ho*).
  (6) "But for his *'kra* that followed him, he would have died" (*ne 'kra dii n'akyi, anka owui*).
  (7) "His *'kra* is happy" (*ne 'kra aniagye*).

In all such statements the attributions are made to the *ōkra* (soul), never to the *sunsum.* On the other hand, the Akans say:

B (1) "He has *sunsum*" (*ōwō sunsum*), an expression they use when they want to refer to someone as dignified and as having a commanding presence. Here they never say, "He has *ōkra,*" soul, for it is believed that it is the nature of the *sunsum* (not the *ōkra*) that differs from person to person; hence they speak of "gentle *sunsum,*" "forceful *sunsum,*" "weak or strong *sunsum,*" etc.
  (2) "His *sunsum* is heavy or weighty" (*ne sunsum yē duru*), that is, he has a strong personality.
  (3) "His *sunsum* overshadows mine" (*ne sunsum hyē me so*).
  (4) "Someone's *sunsum* is bigger or greater than another's" (*obi sunsum so kyēn obi deē*). To

say "someone's *'kra* is greater than another's" would be meaningless.

(5) "He has a good *sunsum*" (*ōwō sunsum pa*), that is, he is a generous person.

In all such statements the attributions are made to the *sunsum* (spirit), never to the *ōkra* (soul). Rattray also pointed out correctly that "an Ashanti would never talk of washing his *sunsum*." It is the *ōkra* that is washed (*okraguare*). In the terminology of the modern linguist, sentences containing *ōkra* and *sunsum* differ, according to my analysis, not only in their surface structures but also in their deep structures.

It is pretty clear from this semantic analysis that *ōkra* and *sunsum* are not intersubstitutable in predications. Intersubstitution of the terms, as we saw above, leads either to nonsense as in B(4) or to change of meaning as in A(4) and B(1). Semantic analysis suggests a nonidentity relation between *sunsum* and *ōkra*. One might reject this conclusion by treating these distinctions as merely idiomatic and not, therefore, as evidence for considering *ōkra* and *sunsum* as distinct. Let us call this the "idiomatic thesis." In the English language, for instance, it is idiomatic to say "He's a sad soul" rather than "He's a sad spirit," without implying that soul and spirit are distinct. But in English the substitution of one for the other of the two terms—even if unidiomatic—will not lead to nonsense and would not change the *meaning;* in Akan it would.

The "idiomatic thesis" has been advanced by a former student of mine in an undergraduate "Long Essay" written under my supervision. He denied that any ontological distinctions can be made from the fact that attributions in some statements in Akan are made to the *ōkra*, whereas in others they are made to the *sunsum*. He wrote:

> If the Akans use *ōkra* instead of *sunsum,* or the latter instead of the former in expressions such as those given above, they do so not because of their belief in the distinction between the *ōkra* and the *sunsum*, but merely as a matter of *locution*. The Akans do not say, *ne sunsum ye* simply because such expression is not *idiomatic*. In many instances the two terms are used interchangeably.

He went on to say that "the words *sunsum* and *ōkra* refer to one and the same thing, the soul, the spiritual substance of a human being. Therefore any attribute predicated of the *ōkra* can be predicated of the *sunsum*." My student's point is that the use of the terms *ōkra* and *sunsum* in different statements is a matter of usage and that no ontological distinction between *ōkra* and *sunsum* can be made on the basis of sentences in the Akan language. Sentences containing *ōkra* and *sunsum* differ in their surface structures but not, according to my student, in their deep structures (that is, meanings). Language, he would say, at any rate in the present context, is therefore a misleading guide to metaphysics. This view is plausible and ought not to be rejected cavalierly; it is the view of some of my discussants and others. This is not to say, however, that that view is not irrefutable. My refutation of it is grounded on, and strengthened by, what the Akans say regarding the nature and functions of *ōkra* and *sunsum*. That is, the distinction between *ōkra* and *sunsum* is not based solely on semantic grounds. It may be the easiest way out of an interpretative labyrinth to identify *ōkra* and *sunsum*, but I do not think it is the most satisfactory way out. There are, I believe, other considerations for rejecting the "identity theory."

First, most Akans agree that in dreaming it is the *sunsum*, not the *ōkra*, that leaves the body. The departure of the *ōkra* (soul) from the body means the death of the person, whereas the *sunsum* can leave the body, as in dreaming, without causing the death of the person. Second, moral predicates are generally applied to the *sunsum*. Rattray wrote: "Perhaps the *sunsum* is the more volatile part of the whole *'kra*," and "... but the *'kra* is not volatile in life, as the *sunsum* undoubtedly is." Moreover, the *ōkra* and *sunsum* appear to be different in terms of their functions or activities. The *ōkra*, as mentioned before, is the principle of life of a person and the embodiment and transmitter of his or her destiny (*nkrabea*). Personality and character dispositions of a person are the function of the *sunsum*. The *sunsum* appears to be the source of dynamism of a person, the *active* part or force of the human psychological system; its energy is the ground for its interaction with the external world. It is said to have extrasensory powers; it is that which thinks, desires, feels, etc. It is in no way identical with the brain, which is a physical organ. Rather it acts upon the brain (*amene, hon*). In short, people believe that it is upon the *sunsum* that one's health, worldly power, position, influence, success, etc. would depend. The attributes and activities of the *sunsum* are therefore not ascribable to the *ɔkra*. Lystad was wrong when he stated: "In many respects the *sunsum* or spirit is so identical with the *ɔkra* or soul in its functions that it is difficult to distinguish between them."

Now, given *x* and *y*, if whatever is asserted of *x* can be asserted of *y*, then *x* can be said to be identical with *y*. If there is at least one characteristic that *x* has but *y* does not, then *x* and *y* are not identical. On this showing, insofar as things asserted of the *ɔkra* are not assertable of the *sunsum*, the two cannot logically be identified. However, although they are logically distinct, they are not *ontologically* distinct. That is to say, they are not independent existents held together in an accidental way by an external bond. They are a unity in duality, a duality in unity. The distinction is not a relation between two separate entities. The *sunsum* may, more accurately, be characterized as a *part*—the active part—of the *ɔkra* (soul).

I once thought that the *sunsum* might be characterized as a state, an epiphenomenon, of the *ɔkra*. I now think that characterization is wrong, for it would subvert the entitative nature of *sunsum*. The fact that we can speak of the inherence of the *sunsum* in natural objects as their activating principle means that in some contexts reference can be made to the *sunsum* independently of the *ɔkra*. This, however, is not so in the context of the human psyche: In man *sunsum* is part of the *ɔkra* (soul). Plato held a tripartite conception of the human soul, deriving that conception from his view of the functions said to be performed by the various parts of the soul. So did Freud. There is nothing inappropriate or illogical or irrational for some Akan thinkers to hold and argue for a bipartite conception of the human soul. Neither a tripartite nor a bipartite conception of the soul subverts its *ontic unity*. As already stated, the *ɔkra* and *sunsum* are constitutive of a spiritual unity, which survives after death. Therefore the soul (that is, *ɔkra* plus *sunsum*) does not lose its individuality after death. It survives individually. Beliefs in reincarnation (which I do not intend to explore now) and in the existence of the ancestors in the world

of spirits (*asamando*) undoubtedly presuppose—and would be logically impossible without—the survival of each individual soul.

6.4. Relation of ɔkra (soul) and honam (body)

Understanding the *sunsum* and *ɔkra* to constitute a spiritual unity, one may say that Akan philosophy maintains a dualistic, not a tripartite, conception of the person: A person is made up of two principal entities or substances, one spiritual (immaterial: *ɔkra*) and the other material (*honam*: body).

But Akans sometimes speak as if the relation between the soul (that is, *ɔkra* plus *sunsum*) and the body is so close that they comprise an indissoluble or indivisible unity, and that, consequently, a person is a homogeneous entity. The basis for this observation is the assertion by some discussants that "*ɔkra* is blood" (*mogya*), or "*ɔkra* is in the blood." They mean by this, I think, that there is some connection between the soul and the blood, and that ordinarily the former is integrated or fused with the latter. I think the supposition here is that the blood is the physical or rather physiological "medium" for the soul. However difficult it is to understand this doctrine, it serves as a basis for a theory of the unity of soul and body. But Akan thinkers cannot strictly or unreservedly maintain such a theory, for it logically involves the impossibility of the doctrine of disembodied survival or life after death, which they tenaciously and firmly hold. The doctrine of the indivisible unity of soul and body is a doctrine that eliminates the notion of life after death, inasmuch as both soul and body are held to disintegrate together. The doctrine that the souls of the dead have some form of existence or life therefore cannot be maintained together with a doctrine of the indivisible unity of soul and body. The former doctrine implies an independent existence for the soul. I think their postulation of some kind of connection between the soul and blood is a response to the legitimate, and indeed fundamental, question as to how an entity (that is, the soul), supposed to be immaterial and separate, can "enter" the body. Though their response certainly bristles with difficulties and may be regarded as inadequate, like most theses on the soul, Akan thinkers had sufficient awareness to focus philosophical attention also on the intractable question regarding the beginnings of the connection of the soul to the body, of the immaterial to the material. Other philosophies attempt to demonstrate that man consists of soul and body, but they do not, to my knowledge, speculate on the manner of the soul's "entry" into the body.

In the Akan conception, the soul is held to be a spiritual entity (substance). It is not a bundle of qualities or perceptions, as it is held to be in some Western systems. The basis of this assertion is the Akan belief in disembodied survival. A bundle theory of substance implies the elimination of the notion of substance, for if a substance is held to be a bundle or collection of qualities or perceptions, when the qualities or perceptions are removed, nothing would be left. That is, there would then be no substance, that is, a substratum or an "owner" of those qualities. Thus, if the soul is held to be a bundle of perceptions, as it is in the writings of David Hume, it would be impossible to talk of disembodied survival in the form of a soul or self since the bundle itself is an abstraction. One Akan maxim, expressed epigrammatically, is that "when a man dies he is not (really) dead" (*onipa wu a na onwui*). What is implied by this is that there is something in a human being that is eternal, indestructible, and that continues to exist in the world of spirits (*asamando*). An Akan motif expresses the following thought: "Could God die, I will die" (*Onyame bewu na m'awu*). In Akan metaphysics, . . . God is held to be eternal, immortal (*Ōdomankoma*). The above saying therefore means that since God will not die, a person, that is, his or her 'kra (soul), conceived as an indwelling spark of God, will not die either. That is, the soul of man is immortal. The attributes of immortality make sense if, and only if, the soul is held to be a substance, an entity, and not a bundle of qualities or perceptions (experiences).

But where in a human being is this spiritual substance located? Descartes thought that the soul was in the pineal gland. The Akans also seem to hold that the soul is lodged in the head, although they do not specify exactly where. But "although it is in the head you cannot see it with your natural eyes," as they would put it, since it is immaterial. That the soul is "in the head (*ti*)" may be inferred from the following expressions: When they want to say that a person is lucky or fortunate they say: "His head is well (good)" (*ne ti ye*), or

"His soul is well (good)" (*ne 'kra ye*). From such expressions one may infer some connection between the head and the soul. And although they cannot point to a specific part of the head as the "residence" of the soul, it may be conjectured that it is in the region of the brain which, as observed earlier, receives its energy from the *sunsum* (spirit), a part of the soul. That is, the soul acts on the brain in a specific locality, but it is itself not actually localized.

The Akan conception of a person, in my analysis, is dualistic, not tripartite, although the spiritual component of a person is highly complex. Such dualistic conception does not necessarily imply a belief in a causal relation or interaction between the two parts, the soul and body. For instance, some dualistic philosophers in the West maintain a doctrine of psychophysical parallelism, which completely denies interaction between soul and body. Other dualists advance a doctrine of epiphenomenalism, which, while not completely rejecting causal interaction, holds that the causality goes in one direction only, namely, from the body to the soul; such a doctrine, too, is thus not interactionist. Akan thinkers, however, are thoroughly interactionist on the relation between soul and body. They hold that not only does the body have a causal influence on the soul but also that the soul has a causal influence on the body (*honam*). What happens to the soul takes effect or reflects on the condition of the body. Thus, writing on Akan culture, Busia stated:

> They (that is, Akans) believed also that spiritual uncleanness was an element of ill-health and that the cleansing of the soul was necessary for health. When, for example, a patient was made to stand on a broom while being treated, it was to symbolize this cleansing. The broom sweeps filth away from the home and keeps it healthy; so the soul must be swept of filth to keep the body healthy.

Similarly, what happens to the body reflects on the conditions of the soul. It is the actual bodily or physical behavior of a person that gives an idea of the condition of the soul. Thus, if the physical behavior of a man suggests that he is happy they would say, "His soul is happy" (*ne 'kra aniagye*); if unhappy or morose they would say, "His soul is sorrowful" (*ne 'kra di awerēhow*). When the soul is enfeebled or injured by evil spirits, ill health results; the poor conditions of the body affect the condition of the soul. The condition of the soul depends upon the condition of the body. The belief in psychophysical causal interaction is the whole basis of spiritual or psychical healing in Akan communities. There are certain diseases that are believed to be "spiritual diseases" (sunsum yare) and cannot be healed by the application of physical therapy. In such diseases attention must be paid to both physiological and spiritual aspects of the person. Unless the soul is healed, the body will not respond to physical treatment. The removal of a disease of the soul is the activity of the diviners or the traditional healers (adunsifo).

6.5. Akan psychology and Freud

There are some similarities between the functions and activities of the sunsum of Akan psychology and the ego of Freud. An essential task of the ego is to engage in intercourse with the external world. Like the sunsum, it directs the business of everyday living; it is the executive of the personality and the representative of the id in the external world. An aspect of the sunsum is or may be similar to the ego. The sunsum is not always conscious, and a person does not always know what the sunsum wants. It is the sunsum with which the Akan diviner (ōkōmfo), believed to possess extrasensory abilities, communicates. It tells the diviner what it really wants without the person knowing or being aware of what he or she wants: Thus, the sunsum may be unconscious. Freud said: "And it is indeed the case that large portions of the ego and super-ego can remain unconscious and are normally unconscious. That is to say, the individual knows nothing of their contents and it requires an expenditure of effort to make them conscious." It is, I suppose, for these reasons that some scholars have not hesitated to identify the sunsum with the ego of Freud, and having done so to go on to identify the ōkra with the id.

There are, however, dissimilarities as well. First, in Freud the id is the original system of the psyche, the matrix within which the ego and the superego become differentiated. In the Akan conceptions both the ōkra and sunsum at once constitute the original system of the psyche. Unlike the id, the ōkra is not the only entity present at birth. Second, in Freud the ego and the superego are formed or developed later. In Akan the sunsum is not formed later; it is a constitutive part of the original psychical structure, the ōkra, soul. At birth the child possesses a sunsum as well as an ōkra. Freud thought in fact that the mental structure of the person was pretty well formed by the end of the fifth year of life. Third, the superego is the moral dimension of personality; it represents the claims of morality. In the Akan system moral attributes are generally ascribed to the sunsum. Thus, the sunsum of the Akan seems to perform aspects of the functions of both the ego and the superego.

6.6. Conclusion

The Akan conception of the person, on my analysis, is both dualistic and interactionist. It seems to me that an interactionist psychophysical dualism is a realistic doctrine. Even apart from the prospects for disembodied survival that this doctrine holds out—prospects that profoundly affect the moral orientation of some people—it has had significant pragmatic consequences in Akan communities, as evidenced in the application of psychophysical therapies. There are countless testimonies of people who have been subjected to physical treatment for months or years in modern hospitals without being cured, but who have been healed by traditional healers applying both physical and psychical (spiritual) methods. In such cases the diseases are believed not to be purely physical, affecting only the body (honam). They are believed rather to have been inflicted on the sunsum through mystical or spiritual powers, and in time the body also gets affected. When Western-trained doctors pay attention only to the physical aspects of such diseases, they almost invariably fail to heal them. The fact that traditional healers, operating at both the physical and psychical levels, cope successfully with such diseases does seem to suggest a close relationship between the body and the soul.

From the point of view of the Akan metaphysics of the person and of the world in general, all this seems to imply that a human being is not just an assemblage of flesh and bone, that he or she is a complex being who cannot completely be explained by the same laws of physics used to explain inanimate things, and that our world cannot simply be reduced to physics.

1. Do you agree with Gyekye's dualism and inter-actionism regarding the physical and/or non-physical nature of the human person, or the so-called mind-body problem? Why or why not?

2. Can one believe in "disembodied survival" of the person and at the same time be an atheist? Why or why not?

3. How would you compare and contrast Gyekye's idealist dualism with the metaphysical position of the Cārvāka theory?

4. Gyekye is often arguing for or against an interpretation of conventional Akan words and beliefs. How would this be similar to or different from the analyses and methodology of an anthropologist?

28. Gilbert Ryle (1900–1976)
A Critique of Mind-Body Dualism

Gilbert Ryle was an English philosopher whose most notable writings were produced during the middle of the twentieth century. He is associated with an influential trend in English-speaking analytic philosophy of that period, usually called philosophical (or logical) behaviorism. Like their counterparts in psychology, philosophical behaviorists maintained that mental phenomena were best understood and explained in terms of observable behavior. But they were concerned primarily with semantic issues, that is, with the meaning and logic of "mentalistic" language and how that ought to be understood as signifying observable actions or at least behavioral predispositions. Ryle would claim, for example, that saying someone is "brilliant," "vain," or "puzzled" is really just saying that person behaves, or is predisposed to behave, in certain observable ways under certain identifiable circumstances.

This selection is the first chapter of *The Concept of Mind* (1949), generally considered Ryle's most influential work and certainly one of the more often cited books since its publication in the subfield of metaphysics known as philosophy of mind. His critique in this chapter of the then-dominant dualistic approach to the human person, traceable to Descartes (hence, "Cartesian dualism"), challenges the conceptual framework within which the debate on the mind-body problem functions. Ryle implies that this long-standing philosophical problem is really the result of conceptual and linguistic confusion, and it would either resolve itself or be quite differently reconstituted once it was formulated in a more semantically accurate manner.

QUESTIONS FOR CRITICAL READING

1. What are the main features of what Ryle calls "the dogma of the Ghost in the Machine"?

2. How does Ryle demonstrate that the "official doctrine" of mind-body dualism is based on a "category-mistake" and thereby false?

3. How does Ryle explain the origin of this category-mistake in the theories of Descartes?

4. What does Ryle mean by claiming that idealism and materialism both are "answers to an improper question"?

TERMS TO NOTE

myth: In the introduction to *The Concept of Mind*, Ryle defines "myth" for his purposes as "the presentation of facts belonging to one category in the idioms appropriate to another" (p. 8). The term thus is not simply synonymous with "falsehood."

corollary: An inference resulting from something else already proved.

Descartes' Myth

(1) The Official Doctrine.

There is a doctrine about the nature and place of minds which is so prevalent among theorists and even among laymen that it deserves to be described as the official theory. Most philosophers, psychologists and religious teachers subscribe, with minor reservations, to its main articles and, although they admit certain theoretical difficulties in it, they tend to assume that these can be overcome without serious modifications being made to the architecture of the theory. It will be argued here that the central principles of the doctrine are unsound and conflict with the whole body of what we know about minds when we are not speculating about them.

The official doctrine, which hails chiefly from Descartes, is something like this. With the doubtful exceptions of idiots and infants in arms every human being has both a body and a mind. Some would prefer to say that every human being is both a body and a mind. His body and his mind are ordinarily harnessed together, but after the death of the body his mind may continue to exist and function.

Human bodies are in space and are subject to the mechanical laws which govern all other bodies in space. Bodily processes and states can be inspected by external observers. So a man's bodily life is as much a public affair as are the lives of animals and reptiles and even as the careers of trees, crystals and planets.

But minds are not in space, nor are their operations subject to mechanical laws. The workings of one mind are not witnessable by other observers; its career is private. Only I can take direct cognisance of the states and processes of my own mind. A person therefore lives through two collateral histories, one consisting of what happens in and to his body, the other consisting of what happens in and to his mind. The first is public, the second private. The events in the first history are events in the physical world, those in the second are events in the mental world.

It has been disputed whether a person does or can directly monitor all or only some of the episodes of his own private history; but, according to the official doctrine, of at least some of these episodes he has direct and unchallengeable cognisance. In consciousness, self-consciousness and introspection he is directly and authentically apprised of the present states and operations of his mind. He may have great or small uncertainties about concurrent and adjacent episodes in the physical world, but he can have none about at least part of what is momentarily occupying his mind.

It is customary to express this bifurcation of his two lives and of his two worlds by saying that the things and events which belong to the physical world, includ-

ing his own body, are external, while the workings of his own mind are internal. This antithesis of outer and inner is of course meant to be construed as a metaphor, since minds, not being in space, could not be described as being spatially inside anything else, or as having things going on spatially inside themselves. But relapses from this good intention are common and theorists are found speculating how stimuli, the physical sources of which are yards or miles outside a person's skin, can generate mental responses inside his skull, or how decisions framed inside his cranium can set going movements of his extremities.

Even when 'inner' and 'outer' are construed as metaphors, the problem how a person's mind and body influence one another is notoriously charged with theoretical difficulties. What the mind wills, the legs, arms and the tongue execute; what affects the ear and the eye has something to do with what the mind perceives; grimaces and smiles betray the mind's moods and bodily castigations lead, it is hoped, to moral improvement. But the actual transactions between the episodes of the private history and those of the public history remain mysterious, since by definition they can belong to neither series. They could not be reported among the happenings described in a person's autobiography of his inner life, but nor could they be reported among those described in some one else's biography of that person's overt career. They can be inspected neither by introspection nor by laboratory experiment. They are theoretical shuttlecocks which are forever being bandied from the physiologist back to the psychologist and from the psychologist back to the physiologist.

Underlying this partly metaphorical representation of the bifurcation of a person's two lives there is a seemingly more profound and philosophical assumption. It is assumed that there are two different kinds of existence or status. What exists or happens may have the status of physical existence, or it may have the status of mental existence. Somewhat as the faces of coins are either heads or tails, or somewhat as living creatures are either male or female, so, it is supposed, some existing is physical existing, other existing is mental existing. It is a necessary feature of what has physical existence that it is in space and time; it is a necessary feature of what has mental existence that it is in time but not in space. What has physical existence is composed of matter, or else is a function of matter; what has mental existence consists of consciousness, or else is a function of consciousness.

There is thus a polar opposition between mind and matter, an opposition which is often brought out as follows. Material objects are situated in a common field, known as 'space', and what happens to one body in one part of space is mechanically connected with what happens to other bodies in other parts of space. But mental happenings occur in insulated fields, known as 'minds', and there is, apart maybe from telepathy, no direct causal connection between what happens in one mind and what happens in another. Only through the medium of the public physical world can the mind of one person make a difference to the mind of another. The mind is its own place and in his inner life each of us lives the life of a ghostly Robinson Crusoe. People can see, hear and jolt one another's bodies, but they are irremediably blind and deaf to the workings of one another's minds and inoperative upon them.

What sort of knowledge can be secured of the workings of a mind? On the one side, according to the official theory, a person has direct knowledge of the best imaginable kind of the workings of his own mind. Mental states and processes are (or are normally) conscious states and processes, and the consciousness which irradiates them can engender no illusions and leaves the door open for no doubts. A person's present thinkings, feelings and willings, his perceivings, rememberings and imaginings are intrinsically 'phosphorescent'; their existence and their nature are inevitably betrayed to their owner. The inner life is a stream of consciousness of such a sort that it would be absurd to suggest that the mind whose life is that stream might be unaware of what is passing down it.

True, the evidence adduced recently by Freud seems to show that there exist channels tributary to this stream, which run hidden from their owner. People are actuated by impulses the existence of which they vigorously disavow; some of their thoughts differ from the thoughts which they acknowledge; and some of the actions which they think they will to perform they do not really will. They are thoroughly gulled by some of their own hypocrisies and they successfully ignore facts about their mental lives which on the official theory ought to be patent to them. Holders of the official

theory tend, however, to maintain that anyhow in normal circumstances a person must be directly and authentically seized of the present state and workings of his own mind.

Besides being currently supplied with these alleged immediate data of consciousness, a person is also generally supposed to be able to exercise from time to time a special kind of perception, namely inner perception, or introspection. He can take a (non-optical) 'look' at what is passing in his mind. Not only can he view and scrutinize a flower through his sense of sight and listen to and discriminate the notes of a bell through his sense of hearing; he can also reflectively or introspectively watch, without any bodily organ of sense, the current episodes of his inner life. This self-observation is also commonly supposed to be immune from illusion, confusion or doubt. A mind's reports of its own affairs have a certainty superior to the best that is possessed by its reports of matters in the physical world. Sense-perceptions can, but consciousness and introspection cannot, be mistaken or confused.

On the other side, one person has no direct access of any sort to the events of the inner life of another. He cannot do better than make problematic inferences from the observed behaviour of the other person's body to the states of mind which, by analogy from his own conduct, he supposes to be signalised by that behaviour. Direct access to the workings of a mind is the privilege of that mind itself; in default of such privileged access, the workings of one mind are inevitably occult to everyone else. For the supposed arguments from bodily movements similar to their own to mental workings similar to their own would lack any possibility of observational corroboration. Not unnaturally, therefore, an adherent of the official theory finds it difficult to resist this consequence of his premises, that he has no good reason to believe that there do exist minds other than his own. Even if he prefers to believe that to other human bodies there are harnessed minds not unlike his own, he cannot claim to be able to discover their individual characteristics, or the particular things that they undergo and do. Absolute solitude is on this showing the ineluctable destiny of the soul. Only our bodies can meet.

As a necessary corollary of this general scheme there is implicitly prescribed a special way of construing our ordinary concepts of mental powers and operations. The verbs, nouns and adjectives, with which in ordinary life we describe the wits, characters and higher-grade performances of the people with whom we have do, are required to be construed as signifying special episodes in their secret histories, or else as signifying tendencies for such episodes to occur. When someone is described as knowing, believing or guessing something, as hoping, dreading, intending or shirking something, as designing this or being amused at that, these verbs are supposed to denote the occurrence of specific modifications in his (to us) occult stream of consciousness. Only his own privileged access to this stream in direct awareness and introspection could provide authentic testimony that these mental-conduct verbs were correctly or incorrectly applied. The onlooker, be he teacher, critic, biographer or friend, can never assure himself that his comments have any vestige of truth. Yet it was just because we do in fact all know how to make such comments, make them with general correctness and correct them when they turn out to be confused or mistaken, that philosophers found it necessary to construct their theories of the nature and place of minds. Finding mental-conduct concepts being regularly and effectively used, they properly sought to fix their logical geography. But the logical geography officially recommended would entail that there could be no regular or effective use of these mental-conduct concepts in our descriptions of, and prescriptions for, other people's minds.

(2) The Absurdity of the Official Doctrine.

Such in outline is the official theory. I shall often speak of it, with deliberate abusiveness, as 'the dogma of the Ghost in the Machine'. I hope to prove that it is entirely false, and false not in detail but in principle. It is not merely an assemblage of particular mistakes. It is one big mistake and a mistake of a special kind. It is, namely, a category-mistake. It represents the facts of mental life as if they belonged to one logical type or category (or range of types or categories), when they actually belong to another. The dogma is therefore a philosopher's myth. In attempting to explode the myth I shall probably be taken to be denying well-known facts about the mental life of human beings, and my plea that I aim at doing nothing more than rectify the logic of mental-conduct concepts will probably be disallowed as mere subterfuge.

I must first indicate what is meant by the phrase 'Category-mistake'. This I do in a series of illustrations.

A foreigner visiting Oxford or Cambridge for the first time is shown a number of colleges, libraries, playing fields, museums, scientific departments and administrative offices. He then asks 'But where is the University? I have seen where the members of the Colleges live, where the Registrar works, where the scientists experiment and the rest. But I have not yet seen the University in which reside and work the members of your University.' It has then to be explained to him that the University is not another collateral institution, some ulterior counterpart to the colleges, laboratories and offices which he has seen. The University is just the way in which all that he has already seen is organized. When they are seen and when their coordination is understood, the University has been seen. His mistake lay in his innocent assumption that it was correct to speak of Christ Church, the Bodleian Library, the Ashmolean Museum *and* the University, to speak, that is, as if 'the University' stood for an extra member of the class of which these other units are members. He was mistakenly allocating the University to the same category as that to which the other institutions belong.

The same mistake would be made by a child witnessing the march-past of a division, who, having had pointed out to him such and such battalions, batteries, squadrons, etc., asked when the division was going to appear. He would be supposing that a division was a counterpart to the units already seen, partly similar to them and partly unlike them. He would be shown his mistake by being told that in watching the battalions, batteries and squadrons marching past he had been watching the division marching past. The march-past was not a parade of battalions, batteries, squadrons *and* a division; it was a parade of the battalions, batteries and squadrons *of* a division.

One more illustration. A foreigner watching his first game of cricket learns what are the functions of the bowlers, the batsmen, the fielders, the umpires and the scorers. He then says 'But there is no one left on the field to contribute the famous element of team-spirit. I see who does the bowling, the batting and the wicket-keeping; but I do not see whose role it is to exercise *esprit de corps.*' Once more, it would have to be explained that he was looking for the wrong type of thing. Team-spirit is not another cricketing-operation supplementary to all of the other special tasks. It is, roughly, the keenness with which each of the special tasks is performed, and performing a task keenly is not performing two tasks. Certainly exhibiting team-spirit is not the same thing as bowling or catching, but nor is it a third thing such that we can say that the bowler first bowls *and* then exhibits team-spirit or that a fielder is at a given moment *either* catching *or* displaying *esprit de corps*.

These illustrations of category-mistakes have a common feature which must be noticed. The mistakes were made by people who did not know how to wield the concepts *University, division* and *team-spirit*. Their puzzles arose from inability to use certain items in the English vocabulary.

The theoretically interesting category-mistakes are those made by people who are perfectly competent to apply concepts, at least in the situations with which they are familiar, but are still liable in their abstract thinking to allocate those concepts to logical types to which they do not belong. An instance of a mistake of this sort would be the following story. A student of politics has learned the main differences between the British, the French and the American Constitutions, and has learned also the differences and connections between the Cabinet, Parliament, the various Ministries, the Judicature and the Church of England. But he still becomes embarrassed when asked questions about the connections between the Church of England, the Home Office and the British Constitution. For while the Church and the Home Office are institutions, the British Constitution is not another institution in the same sense of that noun. So interinstitutional relations which can be asserted or denied to hold between the Church and the Home Office cannot be asserted or denied to hold between either of them and the British Constitution. 'The British Constitution' is not a term of the same logical type as 'the Home Office' and 'the Church of England'. In a partially similar way, John Doe may be a relative, a friend, an enemy or a stranger to Richard Roe; but he cannot be any of these things to the Average Taxpayer. He knows how to talk sense in certain sorts of discussions about the Average Taxpayer, but he is baffled to say why he could not come across him in the street as he can come across Richard Roe.

It is pertinent to our main subject to notice that, so long as the student of politics continues to think of the British Constitution as a counterpart to the other institutions, he will tend to describe it as a mysteriously occult institution; and so long as John Doe continues to think of the Average Taxpayer as a fellow-citizen, he will tend to think of him as an elusive insubstantial man, a ghost who is everywhere yet nowhere.

My destructive purpose is to show that a family of radical category-mistakes is the source of the double-life theory. The representation of a person as a ghost mysteriously ensconced in a machine derives from this argument. Because, as is true, a person's thinking, feeling and purposive doing cannot be described solely in the idioms of physics, chemistry and physiology, therefore they must be described in counterpart idioms. As the human body is a complex organised unit, so the human mind must be another complex organised unit, though one made of a different sort of stuff and with a different sort of structure. Or, again, as the human body, like any other parcel of matter, is a field of causes and effects, so the mind must be another field of causes and effects, though not (Heaven be praised) mechanical causes and effects.

(3) The Origin of the Category-mistake.

One of the chief intellectual origins of what I have yet to prove to be the Cartesian category-mistake seems to be this. When Galileo showed that his methods of scientific discovery were competent to provide a mechanical theory which should cover every occupant of space, Descartes found in himself two conflicting motives. As a man of scientific genius he could not but endorse the claims of mechanics, yet as a religious and moral man he could not accept, as Hobbes accepted, the discouraging rider to those claims, namely that human nature differs only in degree of complexity from clockwork. The mental could not be just a variety of the mechanical.

He and subsequent philosophers naturally but erroneously availed themselves of the following escape-route. Since mental-conduct words are not to be construed as signifying the occurrence of mechanical processes, they must be construed as signifying the occurrence of non-mechanical processes; since mechanical laws explain movements in space as the effects of other movements in space, other laws must explain some of the non-spatial workings of minds as the effects of other non-spatial workings of minds. The difference between the human behaviours which we describe as intelligent and those which we describe as unintelligent must be a difference in their causation; so, while some movements of human tongues and limbs are the effects of mechanical causes, others must be the effects of non-mechanical causes, i.e. some issue from movements of particles of matter, others from workings of the mind.

The differences between the physical and the mental were thus represented as differences inside the common framework of the categories of 'thing', 'stuff', 'attribute', 'state', 'process', 'change', 'cause' and 'effect'. Minds are things, but different sorts of things from bodies; mental processes are causes and effects, but different sorts of causes and effects from bodily movements. And so on. Somewhat as the foreigner expected the University to be an extra edifice, rather like a college but also considerably different, so the repudiators of mechanism represented minds as extra centres of causal processes, rather like machines but also considerably different from them. Their theory was a paramechanical hypothesis.

That this assumption was at the heart of the doctrine is shown by the fact that there was from the beginning felt to be a major theoretical difficulty in explaining how minds can influence and be influenced by bodies. How can a mental process, such as willing, cause spatial movements like the movements of the tongue? How can a physical change in the optic nerve have among its effects a mind's perception of a flash of light? This notorious crux by itself shows the logical mould into which Descartes pressed his theory of the mind. It was the self-same mould into which he and Galileo set their mechanics. Still unwittingly adhering to the grammar of mechanics, he tried to avert disaster by describing minds in what was merely an obverse vocabulary. The workings of minds had to be described by the mere negatives of the specific descriptions given to bodies; they are not in space, they are not motions, they are not modifications of matter, they are not accessible to public observation. Minds are not bits of clockwork, they are just bits of not-clockwork.

As thus represented, minds are not merely ghosts harnessed to machines, they are themselves just spectral machines. Though the human body is an engine, it is not quite an ordinary engine, since some of its workings are governed by another engine inside it—this interior governor-engine being one of a very special sort. It is invisible, inaudible and it has no size or weight. It cannot be taken to bits and the laws it obeys are not those known to ordinary engineers. Nothing is known of how it governs the bodily engine.

A second major crux points the same moral. Since, according to the doctrine, minds belong to the same category as bodies and since bodies are rigidly governed by mechanical laws, it seemed to many theorists to follow that minds must be similarly governed by rigid non-mechanical laws. The physical world is a deterministic system, so the mental world must be a deterministic system. Bodies cannot help the modifications that they undergo, so minds cannot help pursuing the careers fixed for them. *Responsibility, choice, merit* and *demerit* are therefore inapplicable concepts—unless the compromise solution is adopted of saying that the laws governing mental processes, unlike those governing physical processes, have the congenial attribute of being only rather rigid. The problem of the Freedom of the Will was the problem how to reconcile the hypothesis that minds are to be described in terms drawn from the categories of mechanics with the knowledge that higher-grade human conduct is not of a piece with the behaviour of machines.

It is an historical curiosity that it was not noticed that the entire argument was broken-backed. Theorists correctly assumed that any sane man could already recognise the differences between, say, rational and non-rational utterances or between purposive and automatic behaviour. Else there would have been nothing requiring to be salved from mechanism. Yet the explanation given presupposed that one person could in principle never recognise the difference between the rational and the irrational utterances issuing from other human bodies, since he could never get access to the postulated immaterial causes of some of their utterances. Save for the doubtful exception of himself, he could never tell the difference between a man and a Robot. It would have to be conceded, for example, that, for all that we can tell, the inner lives of persons who are classed as idiots or lunatics are as rational as those of anyone else. Perhaps only their overt behaviour is disappointing; that is to say, perhaps 'idiots' are not really idiotic, or 'lunatics' lunatic. Perhaps, too, some of those who are classed as sane are really idiots. According to the theory, external observers could never know how the overt behaviour of others is correlated with their mental powers and processes and so they could never know or even plausibly conjecture whether their applications of mental-conduct concepts to these other people were correct or incorrect. It would then be hazardous or impossible for a man to claim sanity or logical consistency even for himself, since he would be debarred from comparing his own performances with those of others. In short, our characterisations of persons and their performances as intelligent, prudent and virtuous or as stupid, hypocritical and cowardly could never have been made, so the problem of providing a special causal hypothesis to serve as the basis of such diagnoses would never have arisen. The question, 'How do persons differ from machines?' arose just because everyone already knew how to apply mental-conduct concepts before the new causal hypothesis was introduced. This causal hypothesis could not therefore be the source of the criteria used in those applications. Nor, of course, has the causal hypothesis in any degree improved our handling of those criteria. We still distinguish good from bad arithmetic, politic from impolitic conduct and fertile from infertile imaginations in the ways in which Descartes himself distinguished them before and after he speculated how the applicability of these criteria was compatible with the principle of mechanical causation.

He had mistaken the logic of his problem. Instead of asking by what criteria intelligent behaviour is actually distinguished from non-intelligent behaviour, he asked 'Given that the principle of mechanical causation does not tell us the difference, what other causal principle will tell it us?' He realised that the problem was not one of mechanics and assumed that it must therefore be one of some counterpart to mechanics. Not unnaturally psychology is often cast for just this role.

When two terms belong to the same category, it is proper to construct conjunctive propositions embodying them. Thus a purchaser may say that he bought a left-hand glove and a right-hand glove, but not that he bought a left-hand glove, a right-hand glove and a pair of gloves. 'She came home in a flood of tears and a sedan-chair' is a well-known joke based on the absurdity of conjoining terms of different types. It would have been equally ridiculous to construct the disjunction 'She came home either in a flood of tears or else in a sedan-chair'. Now the dogma of the Ghost in the Machine does just this. It maintains that there exist both bodies and minds; that there occur physical processes and mental processes; that there are mechanical causes of corporeal movements and mental causes of corporeal movements. I shall argue that these and other analogous conjunctions are absurd; but, it must be noticed, the argument will not show that either of the illegitimately conjoined propositions is absurd in itself. I am not, for example, denying that there occur mental processes. Doing long division is a mental process and so is making a joke. But I am saying that the phrase 'there occur mental processes' does not mean the same sort of thing as 'there occur physical processes', and, therefore, that it makes no sense to conjoin or disjoin the two.

If my argument is successful, there will follow some interesting consequences. First, the hallowed contrast between Mind and Matter will be dissipated, but dissipated not by either of the equally hallowed absorptions of Mind by Matter or of Matter by Mind, but in quite a different way. For the seeming contrast of the two will be shown to be as illegitimate as would be the contrast of 'she came home in a flood of tears' and 'she came home in a sedan-chair'. The belief that there is a polar opposition between Mind and Matter is the belief that they are terms of the same logical type.

It will also follow that both Idealism and Materialism are answers to an improper question. The 'reduction' of the material world to mental states and processes, as well as the 'reduction' of mental states and processes to physical states and processes, presuppose the legitimacy of the disjunction 'Either there exist minds or there exist bodies (but not both)'. It would be like saying, 'Either she bought a left-hand and a right-hand glove or she bought a pair of gloves (but not both)'.

It is perfectly proper to say, in one logical tone of voice, that there exist minds and to say, in another logical tone of voice, that there exist bodies. But these expressions do not indicate two different species of existence, for 'existence' is not a generic word like 'coloured' or 'sexed'. They indicate two different senses of 'exist', somewhat as 'rising' has different senses in 'the tide is rising', 'hopes are rising', and 'the average age of death is rising'. A man would be thought to be making a poor joke who said that three things are now rising, namely the tide, hopes and the average age of death. It would be just as good or bad a joke to say that there exist prime numbers and Wednesdays and public opinions and navies; or that there exist both minds and bodies. In the succeeding chapters I try to prove that the official theory does rest on a batch of category-mistakes by showing that logically absurd corollaries follow from it. The exhibition of these absurdities will have the constructive effect of bringing out part of the correct logic of mental-conduct concepts.

(4) Historical Note.

It would not be true to say that the official theory derives solely from Descartes' theories, or even from a more widespread anxiety about the implications of seventeenth century mechanics. Scholastic and Reformation theology had schooled the intellects of the scientists as well as of the laymen, philosophers and clerics of that age. Stoic-Augustinian theories of the will were embedded in the Calvinist doctrines of sin and grace; Platonic and Aristotelian theories of the intellect shaped the orthodox doctrines of the immortality of the soul. Descartes was reformulating already prevalent theological doctrines of the soul in the new syntax of Galileo. The theologian's privacy of conscience became the philosopher's privacy of consciousness, and what had been the bogy of Predestination reappeared as the bogy of Determinism.

It would also not be true to say that the two-worlds myth did no theoretical good. Myths often do a lot of theoretical good, while they are still new. One benefit bestowed by the para-mechanical myth was that it partly superannuated the then prevalent para-political myth. Minds and their Faculties had previously been described by analogies with political superiors and political subordinates. The idioms used were those of ruling, obeying, collaborating and rebelling. They survived and still survive in many ethical and some epistemological discussions. As, in physics, the new myth of occult Forces was a scientific improvement on the old myth of Final Causes, so, in anthropological and psychological theory, the new myth of hidden operations, impulses and agencies was an improvement on the old myth of dictations, deferences and disobediences.

DISCUSSION QUESTIONS

1. Do you agree with Ryle's critique of Descartes, based on your reading of the latter's second "Meditation"? Why or why not?
2. Although Ryle is critical of materialism in some respects too, how might one develop a materialist (or "physicalist") account of the human person that is compatible with his position?
3. What are the similarities and differences between human mental activity and a computer? How do you think Ryle would deal with this comparison?
4. How would you compare Ryle's position on the mind-body problem with Gyekye's position? Who do you find more convincing? Why?

29. Sri Aurobindo (1872–1950)
"The Reincarnating Soul"

~≈ The author was born Arabinda Ghose, and as he became one of the most well known mystics and philosophers in India during the first half of the twentieth century, he was given the name Sri Aurobindo. (*Sri* is an honorific title literally meaning "exalted" in Sanskrit.) Even today, decades after his death, he has many followers in many countries around the world, including the United States. He was trained in the Hindu tradition, and his writing and teaching was affiliated with the Vedānta school of thought (see Terms to Note). As was the case with most modern Vedānta philosophers, he re-

lied on the standard competing commentaries and interpretations of the Vedānta system composed many centuries earlier, but he developed his own more synthetic version of their significance for human spiritual life.

The selection reprinted here is the second in a series of essays, all originally published between 1915 and 1921 and collected in book form in 1952 under the title *The Problem of Rebirth*. As the title of this essay indicates, Sri Aurobindo's focus is on the doctrine of reincarnation, one of the essential beliefs in both Hinduism and

Buddhism. "Reincarnation" means being reborn into a new body after the death of one's previous body and is sometimes also called transmigration of the soul (a version of which Plato apparently accepted as well). So our present life is not our first, nor will it be our last in most cases. However, this is generally thought to be an undesirable state of affairs, and the ultimate goal of spiritual liberation in both Hinduism and Buddhism is to eventually no longer be reborn. In this essay Sri Aurobindo assumes this frame of reference and addresses more specifically the issue of which aspect of our nonphysical selves gets reincarnated.

QUESTIONS FOR CRITICAL READING

1. How does Sri Aurobindo critique the "vulgar conception" of reincarnation?
2. What is the difference between the Buddhist and Vedantist positions on what it is that is reincarnated after physical death, and what side does Sri Aurobindo take on this issue?
3. According to Sri Aurobindo, what is the "Self," and how is it related to the body?
4. How does Sri Aurobindo explain the nature of the individual's "personality," and how is it related to the mind?

TERMS TO NOTE

Vedānta: One of the six orthodox schools of Hinduism and the most philosophically influential. Originally it was the name given to a body of writings that appeared between 500 and 200 B.C.E., which focused on the religious and philosophical ideas of the Upanishads.

karma: A Sanskrit term meaning "action"; in Hindu and Buddhist thought, it is a lawlike principle of the consequences of our actions; so right and wrong actions inescapably lead to good or bad consequences, which we experience either in this life or some future life.

Human thought in the generality of men is no more than a rough and crude acceptance of unexamined ideas; it is a sleepy sentry and allows anything to pass the gates which seems to it decently garbed or wears a plausible appearance or can mumble anything that resembles some familiar password. Especially is this so in subtle matters, those remote from the concrete facts of our physical life and environment. Even men who will reason carefully and acutely in ordinary matters and there consider vigilance against error an intellectual or a practical duty, are yet content with the most careless stumbling when they get upon higher and more difficult ground. Where precision and subtle thinking are most needed, there they are most impatient of it and averse to the labour demanded of them. Men can manage fine thought about palpable things, but to think subtly about the subtle is too great a strain on the grossness of our intellects; so we are content with making a dab at the truth, like the painter who threw his brush at his picture when he could not get the effect that he desired. We mistake the smudge that results for the perfect form of a verity.

It is not surprising then that men should be content to think crudely about such a matter as rebirth. Those who accept it, take it usually ready-made, either as a cut and dried theory or a crude dogma. The soul is reborn in a new body,—that vague and almost meaningless assertion is for them sufficient. But what is the soul and what can possibly be meant by the rebirth of a soul? Well, it means reincarnation; the soul, whatever that may be, had got out of one case of flesh and is now getting into another case of flesh. It sounds simple,—let us say, like the Djinn of the Arabian tale expanding out of and again compressing himself into his bottle or perhaps as a pillow is lugged out of one pillow-case and thrust into another. Or the soul fashions itself a body in the mother's womb and then occupies it, or else, let us say, puts off one robe of flesh and then puts on another. But what is it that thus "leaves" one body and "enters" into another? Is it another, a psychic body and subtle form, that enters into the gross corporeal form,—the Purusha perhaps of the ancient image, no bigger than a man's thumb, or is it something in itself formless and impalpable that incarnates in the sense of becoming or assuming to the senses a palpable shape of bone and flesh?

In the ordinary, the vulgar conception there is no birth of a soul at all, but only the birth of a new body into the world occupied by an old personality unchanged from that which once left some now discarded physical frame. It is John Robinson who has gone out of the form of flesh he once occupied; it is John Robinson who tomorrow or some centuries hence will reincarnate in another form of flesh and resume the course of his terrestrial experiences with another name and in another environment. Achilles, let us say, is reborn as Alexander, the son of Philip, a Macedonian, conqueror not of Hector but of Darius, with a wider scope, with larger destinies; but it is still Achilles, it is the same personality that is reborn, only the bodily circumstances are different. It is this survival of the identical personality that attracts the European mind today in the theory of reincarnation. For it is the extinction or dissolution of the personality, of this mental, nervous and physical composite which I call myself that is hard to bear for the man enamoured of life, and it is the promise of its survival and physical reappearance that is the great lure. The one objection that really stands in the way of its acceptance is the obvious non-survival of memory. Memory is the man, says the modern psychologist, and what is the use of the survival of my personality, if I do not remember my past, if I am not aware of being the same person still and always? What is the utility? Where is the enjoyment?

The old Indian thinkers,—I am not speaking of the popular belief which was crude enough and thought not at all about the matter,—the old Buddhistic and Vedantist thinkers surveyed the whole field from a very different standpoint. They were not attached to the survival of the personality; they did not give to that survival the high name of immortality; they saw that personality being what it is, a constantly changing composite, the survival of an identical personality was a non-sense, a contradiction in terms. They perceived indeed that there is a continuity and they sought to discover what determines this continuity and whether the sense of identity which enters into it is an illusion or the representation of a fact, of a real truth, and, if the latter, then what that truth may be. The Buddhist denied any real identity. There is, he said, no self, no person; there is simply a continuous stream of energy in action like the continuous flowing of a river or the continuous burning of a flame. It is this continuity which creates in the mind the false sense of identity. I am not now the same person that I was a year ago, not even the same person that I was a moment ago, any more than the water flowing past yonder ghaut is the

same water that flowed past it a few seconds ago; it is the persistence of the flow in the same channel that preserves the false appearance of identity. Obviously, then, there is no soul that reincarnates, but only Karma that persists in flowing continuously down the same apparently uninterrupted channel. It is Karma that incarnates; Karma creates the form of a constantly changing mentality and physical bodies that are, we may presume, the result of that changing composite of ideas and sensations which I call myself. The identical "I" is not, never was, never will be. Practically, so long as the error of personality persists, this does not make much difference and I can say in the language of ignorance that I am reborn in a new body; practically, I have to proceed on the basis of that error. But there is this important point gained that it is all an error and an error which can cease; the composite can be broken up for good without any fresh formation, the flame can be extinguished, the channel which called itself a river destroyed. And then there is non-being, there is cessation, there is the release of the error from itself.

The Vedantist comes to a different conclusion; he admits an identical, a self, a persistent immutable reality,—but other than my personality, other than this composite which I call myself. In the Katha Upanishad the question is raised in a very instructive fashion, quite apposite to the subject we have in hand. Nachiketas, sent by his father to the world of Death, thus questions Yama, the lord of that world: Of the man who has gone forward, who has passed away from us, some say that he is and others "this he is not"; which then is right? What is the truth of the great passage? Such is the form of the question and at first sight it seems simply to raise the problem of immortality in the European sense of the word, the survival of the identical personality. But that is not what Nachiketas asks. He has already taken as the second of three boons offered to him by Yama the knowledge of the sacred Flame by which man crosses over hunger and thirst, leaves sorrow and fear far behind him and dwells in heaven securely rejoicing. Immortality in that sense he takes for granted as, already standing in that farther world, he must surely do. The knowledge he asks for involves the deeper, finer problem, of which Yama affirms that even the gods debated this of old and it is not easy to know, for subtle is the law of it; something survives that appears to be the same person, that descends into hell, that ascends into heaven, that returns upon the earth with a new body, but is it really the same person that thus survives? Can we really say of the man "He still is", or must we not rather say "This he no longer is"? Yama too in his answer speaks not at all of the survival of death, and he only gives a verse or two to a bare description of that constant rebirth which all serious thinkers admitted as a universally acknowledged truth. What he speaks of is the Self, the real Man, the Lord of all these changing appearances; without the knowledge of that Self the survival of the personality is not immortal life but a constant passing from death to death; he only who goes beyond personality to the real Person becomes the Immortal. Till then a man seems indeed to be born again and again by the force of his knowledge and works, name succeeds to name, form gives place to form, but there is no immortality.

Such then is the real question put and answered so divergently by the Buddhist and the Vedantin. There is a constant re-forming of personality in new bodies, but this personality is a mutable creation of force at its work streaming forward in Time and never for a moment the same, and the ego-sense that makes us cling to the life of the body and believe readily that it is the same idea and form, that it is John Robinson who is reborn as Sidi Hossain, is a creation of the mentality. Achilles was not reborn as Alexander but the stream of force in its works which created the momentarily changing mind and body of Achilles flowed on and created the momentarily changing mind and body of Alexander. Still, said the ancient Vedanta, there is yet something beyond this force in action, Master of it, one who makes it create for him new names and forms, and that is the Self, the Purusha, the Man, the Real Person. The ego-sense is only its distorted image reflected in the flowing stream of embodied mentality.

Is it then the Self that incarnates and reincarnates? But the Self is imperishable, immutable, unborn, undying. The Self is not born and does not exist in the body; rather the body is born and exists in the Self. For the Self is one everywhere,—in all bodies, we say, but really it is not confined and parcelled out in different bodies except as the all-constituting ether seems to be formed into different objects and is in a sense in them. Rather all these bodies are in the Self; but that also is a figment of space-conception, and rather these bodies are only symbols and figures of itself created by it in its own consciousness. Even what we call the individual soul is greater than its body and not less, more subtle than it and therefore not confined by its grossness. At death it does not leave its form, but casts it off, so that a great departing Soul can say of this death in vigorous phrase, "I have spat out the body."

What then is it that we feel to inhabit the physical frame? What is it that the Soul draws out from the body when it casts off this partial physical robe which enveloped not it, but part of its members? What is it whose issuing out gives this wrench, this swift struggle and pain of parting, creates this sense of violent divorce? The answer does not help us much. It is the subtle or psychical frame which is tied to the physical by the heart-strings, by the cords of life-force, of nervous energy which have been woven into every physical fibre. This the Lord of the body draws out and the violent snapping or the rapid or tardy loosening of the life-cords, the exit of the connecting force constitutes the pain of death and its difficulty.

Let us then change the form of the question and ask rather what it is that reflects and accepts the mutable personality, since the Self is immutable? We have, in fact, an immutable Self, a real Person, lord of this ever-changing personality which, again, assumes ever-changing bodies, but the real Self knows itself always as above the mutation, watches and enjoys it, but is not involved in it. Through what does it enjoy the changes and feel them to be its own, even while knowing itself to be unaffected by them? The mind and ego-sense are only inferior instruments; there must be some more essential form of itself which the Real Man puts forth, puts in front of itself, as it were, and at the back of the changings to support and mirror them without being actually changed by them. This more essential form is the mental being or mental person which the Upanishads speak of as the mental leader of the life and body, *mano-mayaḥ prāṇa-śarīra-neta*. It is that which maintains the ego-sense as a function in the mind and enables us to have the firm conception of continuous identity in Time as opposed to the timeless identity of the Self.

The changing personality is not this mental person; it is a composite of various stuff of Nature, a formation of Prakriti and is not at all the Purusha. And it is a very complex composite with many layers; there is a layer of physical, a layer of nervous, a layer of mental, even final stratum of supramental personality; and within these layers themselves there are strata within each stratum. The analysis of the successive couches of the earth is a simple matter compared with the analysis of this wonderful creation we call the personality. The mental being in resuming bodily life forms a new personality for its new terrestrial existence; it takes material from the common matter-stuff, life-stuff, mind-stuff of the physical world and during earthly life it is constantly absorbing fresh material, throwing out what is used up, changing its bodily, nervous and mental tissues. But this is all surface work; behind is the foundation of past experience held back from the physical memory so that the superficial consciousness may not be troubled or interfered with by the conscious burden of the past, but may concentrate on the work immediately in hand. Still that foundation of past experience is the bed-rock of personality; and it is more than that. It is our real fund on which we can always draw even apart from our present superficial commerce with our surroundings. That commerce adds to our gain, modifies the foundation for a subsequent existence.

Moreover, all this is, again, on the surface. It is only a small part of ourselves which lives and acts in the energies of our earthly existence. As behind the physical universe there are worlds of which ours is only a last result, so also within us there are worlds of our self-existence which throw out this external form of our being. The subconscient, the super-conscient are oceans from which and to which this river flows. Therefore to speak of ourselves as a soul reincarnating

is to give altogether too simple an appearance to the miracle of our existence; it puts into too ready and too gross a formula the magic of the supreme Magician. There is not a definite psychic entity getting into a new case of flesh; there is a metempsychosis, a reinsouling, a rebirth of a new psychic personality as well as a birth of a new body. And behind is the Person, the unchanging entity, the Master who manipulates this complex material, the Artificer of this wondrous artifice.

This is the starting-point from which we have to proceed in considering the problem of rebirth. To view ourselves as such and such a personality getting into a new case of flesh is to stumble about in the ignorance, to confirm the error of the material mind and the senses. The body is a convenience, the personality is a constant formation for whose development action and experience are the instruments; but the Self by whose will and for whose delight all this is, is other than the body, other than the action and experience, other than the personality which they develop. To ignore it is to ignore the whole secret of our being.

DISCUSSION QUESTIONS

1. Do you agree with Sri Aurobindo's views on reincarnation and immortality? Why or why not?
2. How might a materialist argue against Sri Aurobindo's position on the reality of the physical and nonphysical aspects of a person?
3. Do you think the force of karma is real? Why or why not? What are the moral implications of this principle?
4. How would you compare Sri Aurobindo's account of "personality" and personal identity with Frondizi's characterization of the "self"?

30. B. F. Skinner (1904–1990)
The Denial of Free Will

Burrhus Frederic Skinner was an American psychologist who was born in Pennsylvania, received his Ph.D. in psychology from Harvard University in 1931, and spent his academic career at the University of Minnesota, Indiana University, and then Harvard. His is the most well known name associated with the field of behavioral psychology in the twentieth century, and to the

end of his life he argued for the scientific focus on observable behavior and against psychologists' attempts to study unobservable inner mental states. He also advocated the application of the behaviorists' findings to a wide range of social situations in which the control of people's actions was important, and his research on what became known as behavior modification had a major impact in the fields of education, corrections, and commercial enterprise in the United States.

Although most of Skinner's writing was in the form of straightforward scientific prose, this selection is from a novel titled *Walden Two* that he wrote at the end of World War II. It was admittedly an exercise in utopian speculation, in which he described a successful, peaceful community of self-actualizing individuals organized on the basis of a "science of behavior." The title was in acknowledgment of the original *Walden* written by Henry David Thoreau in 1854. The three characters here are Frazier, in effect the founder and director of the Walden Two community, and two of his guests, the philosopher Castle and the psychologist (and narrator) Burris.

At this point in the story these three are discussing human freedom and the control of behavior, and thus they bring up a perennial philosophical issue regarding human nature: Are we as individuals free, or are we causally determined by forces beyond our control to think and act as we do? This "problem of free will" (or the "free will versus determinism debate") has been treated as a metaphysical problem historically, but it also has significant moral and legal implications. After all, if every choice you make really is caused by other factors independent of your will and thus could not have been otherwise in those circumstances, you don't *freely* choose, and so you are not personally responsible for that choice. Skinner's own position on this issue is based on his behaviorist principles, of course, and is articulated in this context by Frazier.

QUESTIONS FOR CRITICAL READING

1. When Frazier denies that freedom exists for the human individual, how is he defining "freedom," and how is it different from the "feeling of freedom"?

2. What does Frazier mean by arguing that all our choices of action are "lawful," and how does Castle try to refute him?

3. What is the difference between "positive reinforcement" and "negative reinforcement," and how does Frazier use this distinction to explain most of the violence and war in human history?

4. How should the "science of behavior" be applied to large-scale social planning in the contemporary world, according to Frazier, and what would be its goals?

"Mr. Castle," said Frazier very earnestly, "let me ask you a question. I warn you, it will be the most terrifying question of your life. *What would you do if you found yourself in possession of an effective science of behavior?* Suppose you suddenly found it possible to control the behavior of men as you wished. What would you do?"

"That's an assumption?"

"Take it as one if you like. *I* take it as a fact. And apparently you accept it as a fact too. I can hardly be as despotic as you claim unless I hold the key to an extensive practical control."

"What would I do?" said Castle thoughtfully. "I think I would dump your science of behavior in the ocean."

"And deny men all the help you could otherwise give them?"

"And give them the freedom they would otherwise lose forever!"

"How could you give them freedom?"

"By refusing to control them!"

"But you would only be leaving the control in other hands."

"Whose?"

"The charlatan, the demagogue, the salesman, the ward heeler, the bully, the cheat, the educator, the priest—all who are now in possession of the techniques of behavioral engineering."

"A pretty good share of the control would remain in the hands of the individual himself."

"That's an assumption, too, and it's your only hope. It's your only possible chance to avoid the implications of a science of behavior. If man is free, then a technology of behavior is impossible. But I'm asking you to consider the other case."

"Then my answer is that your assumption is contrary to fact and any further consideration idle."

"And your accusations—?"

"—were in terms of intention, not of possible achievement."

Frazier sighed dramatically.

"It's a little late to be proving that a behavioral technology is well advanced. How can you deny it? Many of its methods and techniques are really as old as the hills. Look at their frightful misuse in the hands of the Nazis! And what about the techniques of the psychological clinic? What about education? Or religion? Or practical politics? Or advertising and salesmanship? Bring them all together and you have a sort of rule-of-thumb technology of vast power. No, Mr. Castle, the science is there for the asking. But its techniques and methods are in the wrong hands—they are used for personal aggrandizement in a competitive world or, in the case of the psychologist and educator, for futilely corrective purposes. My question is, have you the courage to take up and wield the science of behavior for the good of mankind? You answer that you would dump it in the ocean!"

"I'd want to take it out of the hands of the politicians and advertisers and salesmen, too."

"And the psychologists and educators? You see, Mr. Castle, you can't have that kind of cake. The fact is, we not only *can* control human behavior, we *must*. But who's to do it, and what's to be done?"

"So long as a trace of personal freedom survives, I'll stick to my position," said Castle, very much out of countenance.

"Isn't it time we talked about freedom?" I said. "We parted a day or so ago on an agreement to let the question of freedom ring. It's time to answer, don't you think?"

"My answer is simple enough," said Frazier. "I deny that freedom exists at all. I must deny it—or my program would be absurd. You can't have a science about a subject matter which hops capriciously about. Perhaps we can never *prove* that man isn't free; it's an assumption. But the increasing success of a science of behavior makes it more and more plausible."

"On the contrary, a simple personal experience makes it untenable," said Castle. "The experience of freedom. I *know* that I'm free."

"It must be quite consoling," said Frazier.

"And what's more—you do, too," said Castle hotly. "When you deny your own freedom for the sake of playing with a science of behavior, you're acting in plain bad faith. That's the only way I can explain it."

He tried to recover himself and shrugged his shoulders. "At least you'll grant that you *feel* free."

"The 'feeling of freedom' should deceive no one," said Frazier. "Give me a concrete case."

"Well, right now," Castle said. He picked up a book of matches. "I'm free to hold or drop these matches."

"You will, of course, do one or the other," said Frazier. "Linguistically or logically there seem to be two possibilities, but I submit that there's only one in fact. The determining forces may be subtle but they are inexorable. I suggest that as an orderly person you will probably hold—ah! you drop them! Well, you see, that's all part of your behavior with respect to me. You couldn't resist the temptation to prove me wrong. It was all lawful. You had no choice. The deciding factor entered rather late, and naturally you couldn't foresee the result when you first held them up. There was no strong likelihood that you would act in either direction, and so you said you were free."

"That's entirely too glib," said Castle. "It's easy to argue lawfulness after the fact. But let's see you predict what I will do in advance. Then I'll agree there's law."

"I didn't say that behavior is always predictable, any more than the weather is always predictable. There are often too many factors to be taken into account. We can't measure them all accurately, and we couldn't perform the mathematical operations needed to make a prediction if we had the measurements. The legality is usually an assumption—but none the less important in judging the issue at hand."

"Take a case where there's no choice, then," said Castle. "Certainly a man in jail isn't free in the sense in which I am free now."

"Good! That's an excellent start. Let us classify the kinds of determiners of human behavior. One class, as you suggest, is physical restraint—handcuffs, iron bars, forcible coercion. These are ways in which we shape human behavior according to our wishes. They're crude, and they sacrifice the affection of the controllee, but they often work. Now, what other ways are there of limiting freedom?"

Frazier had adopted a professorial tone and Castle refused to answer.

"The threat of force would be one," I said.

"Right. And here again we shan't encourage any loyalty on the part of the controllee. He has perhaps a shade more of the feeling of freedom, since he can always 'choose to act and accept the consequences,' but he doesn't feel exactly free. He knows his behavior is being coerced. Now what else?"

I had no answer.

"Force or the threat of force—I see no other possibility," said Castle after a moment.

"Precisely," said Frazier.

"But certainly a large part of my behavior has no connection with force at all. There's my freedom!" said Castle.

"I wasn't agreeing that there was no other possibility—merely that *you* could see no other. Not being a good behaviorist—or a good Christian, for that matter—you have no feeling for a tremendous power of a different sort."

"What's that?"

"I shall have to be technical," said Frazier. "But only for a moment. It's what the science of behavior calls 'reinforcement theory.' The things that can happen to us fall into three classes. To some things we are indifferent. Other things we like—we want them to happen, and we take steps to make them happen again. Still other things we don't like—we don't want them to happen and we take steps to get rid of them or keep them from happening again.

"*Now,*" Frazier continued earnestly, "if it's in our power to create any of the situations which a person likes or to remove any situation he doesn't like, we can control his behavior. When he behaves as we want him to behave, we simply create a situation he likes, or remove one he doesn't like. As a result, the probability that he will behave that way again goes up, which is what we want. Technically it's called 'positive reinforcement.'

"The old school made the amazing mistake of supposing that the reverse was true, that by removing a situation a person likes or setting up one he doesn't like—in other words by punishing him—it was possible to *reduce* the probability that he would behave in a given way again. That simply doesn't hold. It has been established beyond question. What is emerging at this critical stage in the evolution of society is a behavioral and cultural technology based on positive reinforcement alone. We are gradually discovering—at an untold cost in human suffering—that in the long run punishment doesn't reduce the probability that an act will occur. We have been so preoccupied with the contrary that we always take 'force' to mean punishment. We don't say we're using force when we send shiploads of food into a starving country, though we're displaying quite as much *power* as if we were sending troops and guns."

"I'm certainly not an advocate of force," said Castle. "But I can't agree that it's not effective."

"It's *temporarily* effective, that's the worst of it. That explains several thousand years of bloodshed. Even nature has been fooled. We 'instinctively' punish a person who doesn't behave as we like—we spank him if he's a child or strike him if he's a man. A nice distinction! The immediate effect of the blow teaches us to strike again. Retribution and revenge are the most natural things on earth. But in the long run the man we strike is no less likely to repeat his act."

"But he won't repeat it if we hit him hard enough," said Castle.

"He'll still *tend* to repeat it. He'll *want* to repeat it. We haven't really altered his potential behavior at all. That's the pity of it. If he doesn't repeat it in our presence, he will in the presence of someone else. Or it will be repeated in the disguise of a neurotic symptom. If we hit hard enough, we clear a little place for ourselves in the wilderness of civilization, but we make the rest of the wilderness still more terrible.

"Now, early forms of government are naturally based on punishment. It's the obvious technique when the physically strong control the weak. But we're in the throes of a great change to positive reinforcement—from a competitive society in which one man's reward is another man's punishment, to a cooperative society in which no one gains at the expense of anyone else.

"The change is slow and painful because the immediate, temporary effect of punishment overshadows the eventual advantage of positive reinforcement. We've all seen countless instances of the temporary effect of force, but clear evidence of the effect of not using force is rare. That's why I insist that Jesus, who was apparently the first to discover the power of refusing to punish, must have hit upon the principle by accident. He certainly had none of the experimental evidence which is available to us today, and I can't conceive that it was possible, no matter what the man's genius, to have discovered the principle from casual observation."

"A touch of revelation, perhaps?" said Castle.

"No, accident. Jesus discovered one principle because it had immediate consequences, and he got another thrown in for good measure."

I began to see light.

"You mean the principle of 'love your enemies'?" I said.

"Exactly! To 'do good to those who despitefully use you' has two unrelated consequences. You gain the peace of mind we talked about the other day. Let the stronger man push you around—at least you avoid the torture of your own rage. *That's* the immediate consequence. What an astonishing discovery it must have been to find that in the long run you could *control the stronger man* in the same way!"

"It's generous of you to give so much credit to your early colleague," said Castle, "but why are we still in the throes of so much misery? Twenty centuries should have been enough for one piece of behavioral engineering."

"The conditions which made the principle difficult to discover made it difficult to teach. The history of the Christian Church doesn't reveal many cases of doing good to one's enemies. To inoffensive heathens, perhaps, but not enemies. One must look outside the field of organized religion to find the principle in practice at all. Church governments are devotees of *power*, both temporal and bogus."

"But what has all this got to do with freedom?" I said hastily.

Frazier took time to reorganize his behavior. He looked steadily toward the window, against which the rain was beating heavily.

"Now that we *know* how positive reinforcement works and why negative doesn't," he said at last, "we can be more deliberate, and hence more successful, in our cultural design. We can achieve a sort of control under which the controlled, though they are following a code much more scrupulously than was ever the case under the old system, nevertheless *feel free*. They are doing what they want to do, not what they are forced to do. That's the source of the tremendous power of positive reinforcement—there's no restraint and no revolt. By a careful cultural design, we control not the

final behavior, but the *inclination* to behave—the motives, the desires, the wishes.

"The curious thing is that in that case the *question of freedom never arises*. Mr. Castle was free to drop the matchbook in the sense that nothing was preventing him. If it had been securely bound to his hand he wouldn't have been free. Nor would he have been quite free if I'd covered him with a gun and threatened to shoot him if he let it fall. The question of freedom arises when there is restraint—either physical or psychological.

"But restraint is only one sort of control, and absence of restraint isn't freedom. It's not control that's lacking when one feels 'free,' but the objectionable control of force. Mr. Castle felt free to hold or drop the matches in the sense that he felt no restraint—no threat of punishment in taking either course of action. He neglected to examine his positive reasons for holding or letting go, in spite of the fact that these were more compelling in this instance than any threat of force.

"We have no vocabulary of freedom in dealing with what we want to do," Frazier went on. "The question never arises. When men strike for freedom, they strike against jails and the police, or the threat of them—against oppression. They never strike against forces which make them want to act the way they do. Yet, it seems to be understood that governments will operate only through force or the threat of force, and that all other principles of control will be left to education, religion, and commerce. If this continues to be the case, we may as well give up. A government can never create a free people with the techniques now allotted to it.

"The question is: Can men live in freedom and peace? And the answer is: Yes, if we can build a social structure which will satisfy the needs of everyone and in which everyone will want to observe the supporting code. But so far this has been achieved only in Walden Two. Your ruthless accusations to the contrary, Mr. Castle, this is the freest place on earth. And it is free precisely because we make no use of force or the threat of force. Every bit of our research, from the nursery through the psychological management of our adult membership, is directed toward that end—to exploit every alternative to forcible control. By skillful planning, by a wise choice of techniques we *increase* the feeling of freedom.

"It's not planning which infringes upon freedom, but planning which uses force. A sense of freedom was practically unknown in the planned society of Nazi Germany, because the planners made a fantastic use of force and the threat of force.

"No, Mr. Castle, when a science of behavior has once been achieved, there's no alternative to a planned society. We can't leave mankind to an accidental or biased control. But by using the principle of positive reinforcement—carefully avoiding force or the threat of force—we can preserve a personal sense of freedom."

Frazier threw himself back upon the bed and stared at the ceiling.

"But you haven't denied that you are in complete control," said Castle. "You are still the long-range dictator."

"As you will," said Frazier, waving his hands loosely in the air and then cupping them behind his head. "In fact, I'm inclined to agree. When you have once grasped the principle of positive reinforcement, you can enjoy a sense of unlimited power. It's enough to satisfy the thirstiest tyrant."

"There you are, then," said Castle. "That's my case."

"But it's a limited sort of despotism," Frazier went on. "And I don't think anyone should worry about it.

The despot must wield his power for the good of others. If he takes any step which reduces the sum total of human happiness, his power is reduced by a like amount. What better check against a malevolent despotism could you ask for?"

DISCUSSION QUESTIONS

1. Do you agree with Frazier's position that even though we feel free, all of our choices are determined by causal factors beyond our immediate control? Why or why not?

2. On this issue of free will versus determinism, how would psychologists and philosophers approach it differently, and what kind of common ground might they have as well?

3. Skinner published *Walden Two* originally in 1948 and was optimistic at that time about the possibilities of large-scale social planning using "reinforcement theory" to dramatically improve human society. Do you think his vision of a happy, peaceful, cooperative social world with minimal restraints imposed on the individual is still relevant today, or possible? Why or why not?

4. Do you agree with Skinner's critique of punishment and the threat of force as means of controlling others? Why or why not?

31. Walter T. Stace (1886–1967)
The Compatibility of Free Will and Determinism

Walter Stace was born and raised in Britain but moved to the United States in 1932, where for many years he was a member of the philosophy faculty at Princeton University in New Jersey. His extensive writing on a number of traditional philosophical issues had a significant impact in the English-speaking academic world, especially during the middle decades of the twentieth century.

The following selection is from the eleventh chapter of Stace's 1952 book, *Religion and the Modern Mind,* and provides his account of the "problem of free will." Here he accepts the general scientific view that because all (or most) natural events are caused and thus in principle

predictable, and human choices are natural events, all (or most) human choices are caused and thus in principle predictable too. However, he argues that this deterministic account of human choice does not after all rule out the belief in free will, that in fact they are compatible. His own conclusions amount to a version of what is sometimes called "compatibilism," in contrast to the "incompatibilist" stance on the relation between determinism and free will. The position Stace takes on this issue also is sometimes referred to as "soft determinism," as opposed to the "hard determinism" that typically denies both free will and personal moral responsibility for actions.

QUESTIONS FOR CRITICAL READING

1. According to Stace, what is the relationship between free will and morality?

2. How does Stace explain the "problem of free will" as being for the most part a mere verbal dispute?

3. How does Stace argue against the definition of free will as "indeterminism," and what definition does he argue for instead?

4. If determinism is compatible with both free will and moral responsibility, as Stace argues, how does he justify punishment?

The . . . problem which the rise of scientific naturalism has created for the modern mind concerns the foundations of morality. The old religious foundations have largely crumbled away, and it may well be thought that the edifice built upon them by generations of men is in danger of collapse. A total collapse of moral behavior is, as I pointed out before, very unlikely. For a society in which this occurred could not survive. Nevertheless the danger to moral standards inherent in the virtual disappearance of their old religious foundations is not illusory.

I shall first discuss the problem of free will, for it is certain that if there is no free will there can be no morality. Morality is concerned with what men ought and ought not to do. But if a man has no freedom to choose what he will do, if whatever he does is done under compulsion, then it does not make sense to tell him that he ought not to have done what he did and that he ought to do something different. All moral precepts would in such case be meaningless. Also if he acts always under compulsion, how can he be held morally responsible for his actions? How can he, for example, be punished for what he could not help doing?

It is to be observed that those learned professors of philosophy or psychology who deny the existence of free will do so only in their professional moments and in their studies and lecture rooms. For when it comes to doing anything practical, even of the most trivial kind, they invariably behave as if they and others were free. They inquire from you at dinner whether you will choose this dish or that dish. They will ask a child why he told a lie, and will punish him for not having chosen the way of truthfulness. All of which is inconsistent with a disbelief in free will. This should cause us to suspect that the problem is not a real one; and this, I believe, is the case. The dispute is merely verbal, and is due to nothing but a confusion about the meanings of words. It is what is now fashionably called a semantic problem.

How does a verbal dispute arise? Let us consider a case which, although it is absurd in the sense that no one would ever make the mistake which is involved in it, yet illustrates the principle which we shall have to use in the solution of the problem. Suppose that someone believed that the word "man" means a certain sort of five-legged animal; in short that "five-legged animal" is the correct *definition* of man. He might then look around the world, and rightly observing that there are no five-legged animals in it, he might proceed to deny the existence of men. This preposterous conclusion would have been reached because he was using an incorrect definition of "man." All you would have to do to show him his mistake would be to give him the correct definition; or at least to show him that his definition was wrong. Both the problem and its solution would, of course, be entirely verbal. The problem of free will, and its solution, I shall maintain, is verbal in exactly the same way. The problem has been created by the fact that learned men, especially philosophers, have assumed an incorrect definition of free will, and then finding that there is nothing in the world which answers to their definition, have denied its existence. As far as logic is concerned, their conclusion is just as absurd as that of the man who denies the existence of men. The only difference is that the mistake in the latter case is obvious and crude, while the mistake which the deniers of free will have made is rather subtle and difficult to detect.

Throughout the modern period, until quite recently, it was assumed, both by the philosophers who denied free will and by those who defended it, that *determinism is inconsistent with free will.* If a man's actions were wholly determined by chains of causes stretching back into the remote past, so that they could be predicted beforehand by a mind which knew all the causes, it was assumed that they could not in that case be free. This implies that a certain definition of actions done from free will was assumed, namely that they are actions *not* wholly determined by causes or predictable beforehand. Let us shorten this by saying that free will was defined as meaning indeterminism. This is the incorrect definition which has led to the denial of free will. As soon as we see what the true definition is we shall find that the question whether the world is deterministic, as Newtonian science implied, or in a measure indeterministic, as current physics teaches, is wholly irrelevant to the problem.

Of course there is a sense in which one can define a word arbitrarily in any way one pleases. But a definition may nevertheless be called correct or incorrect. It is correct if it accords with a *common usage* of the word defined. It is incorrect if it does not. And if you give an incorrect definition, absurd and untrue results are likely to follow. For instance, there is nothing to prevent you from arbitrarily defining a man as a five-legged animal, but this is incorrect in the sense that it does not accord with the ordinary meaning of the word. Also it has the absurd result of leading to a denial of the existence of men. This shows that *common usage is the criterion for deciding whether a definition is correct or not.* And this is the principle which I shall apply to free will. I shall show that indeterminism is not what is meant by the phrase "free will" *as it is commonly used.* And I shall attempt to discover the correct definition by inquiring how the phrase is used in ordinary conversation.

Here are a few samples of how the phrase might be used in ordinary conversation. It will be noticed that they include cases in which the question whether a man acted with free will is asked in order to determine whether he was morally and legally responsible for his acts.

JONES: I once went without food for a week.

SMITH: Did you do that of your own free will?

JONES: No. I did it because I was lost in a desert and could find no food.

But suppose that the man who had fasted was Mahatma Gandhi. The conversation might then have gone:

GANDHI: I once fasted for a week.

SMITH: Did you do that of your own free will?

GANDHI: Yes. I did it because I wanted to compel the British Government to give India its independence.

Take another case. Suppose that I had stolen some bread, but that I was as truthful as George Washington. Then, if I were charged with the crime in court, some exchange of the following sort might take place:

JUDGE: Did you steal the bread of your own free will?

STACE: Yes. I stole it because I was hungry.

Or in different circumstances the conversation might run:

JUDGE: Did you steal of your own free will?

STACE: No. I stole because my employer threatened to beat me if I did not.

At a recent murder trial in Trenton some of the accused had signed confessions, but afterwards asserted that they had done so under police duress. The following exchange might have occurred:

JUDGE: Did you sign this confession of your own free will?

PRISONER: No. I signed it because the police beat me up.

Now suppose that a philosopher had been a member of the jury. We could imagine this conversation taking place in the jury room.

FOREMAN OF THE JURY: The prisoner says he signed the confession because he was beaten, and not of his own free will.

PHILOSOPHER: This is quite irrelevant to the case. There is no such thing as free will.

FOREMAN: Do you mean to say that it makes no difference whether he signed because his conscience made him want to tell the truth or because he was beaten?

PHILOSOPHER: None at all. Whether he was caused to sign by a beating or by some desire of his own—the desire to tell the truth, for example—in either case his signing was causally determined, and therefore in neither case did he act of his own free will. Since there is no such thing as free will, the question whether he signed of his own free will ought not to be discussed by us.

The foreman and the rest of the jury would rightly conclude that the philosopher must be making some mistake. What sort of a mistake could it be? There is only one possible answer. The philosopher must be using the phrase "free will" in some peculiar way of his own which is not the way in which men usually use it when they wish to determine a question of moral responsibility. That is, he must be using an incorrect definition of it as implying action not determined by causes.

Suppose a man left his office at noon, and were questioned about it. Then we might hear this:

JONES: Did you go out of your own free will?

SMITH: Yes. I went out to get my lunch.

But we might hear:

JONES: Did you leave your office of your own free will?

SMITH: No. I was forcibly removed by the police.

We have now collected a number of cases of actions which, in the ordinary usage of the English language, would be called cases in which people have acted of their own free will. We should also say in all these cases that they *chose* to act as they did. We should also say that they could have acted otherwise, if they had chosen. For instance, Mahatma Gandhi was not compelled to fast; he chose to do so. He could have eaten if he had wanted to. When Smith went out to get his lunch, he chose to do so. He could have stayed and done some more work, if he had wanted to. We have also collected a number of cases of the opposite kind. They are cases in which men were not able to exercise their free will. They had no choice. They were compelled to do as they did. The man in the desert did not fast of his own free will. He had no choice in the matter. He was compelled to fast because there was nothing for him to eat. And so with the other cases. It ought to be quite easy, by an inspection of these cases, to tell what we ordinarily mean when we say that a man did or did not exercise free will. We ought therefore to be able to extract from them the proper definition of the term. Let us put the cases in a table:

Free Acts	Unfree Acts
Gandhi fasting because he wanted to free India.	The man fasting in the desert because there was no food.
Stealing bread because one is hungry.	Stealing because one's employer threatened to beat one.
Signing a confession because one wanted to tell the truth.	Signing because the police beat one.
Leaving the office because one wanted one's lunch.	Leaving because forcibly removed.

It is obvious that to find the correct definition of free acts we must discover what characteristic is common to all the acts in the left-hand column, and is, at the same time, absent from all the acts in the right-hand column. This characteristic which all free acts have, and which no unfree acts have, will be the defining characteristic of free will.

Is being uncaused, or not being determined by causes, the characteristic of which we are in search? It cannot be, because although it is true that all the acts in the right-hand column have causes, such as the beating by the police or the absence of food in the desert, so also do the acts in the left-hand column. Mr. Gandhi's fasting was caused by his desire to free India, the man leaving his office by his hunger, and so on. Moreover there is no reason to doubt that these causes of the free acts were in turn caused by prior conditions, and that these were again the results of causes, and so on back indefinitely into the past. Any physiologist can tell us the causes of hunger. What caused Mr. Gandhi's tremendously powerful desire to free India is no doubt more difficult to discover. But it must have had causes. Some of them may have lain in peculiarities of his glands or brain, others in his past experiences, others in his heredity, others in his education. Defenders of free will have usually tended to deny such facts. But to do so is plainly a case of special pleading, which is unsupported by any scrap of evidence.

The only reasonable view is that all human actions, both those which are freely done and those which are not, are either wholly determined by causes, or at least as much determined as other events in nature. It may be true, as the physicists tell us, that nature is not as deterministic as was once thought. But whatever degree of determinism prevails in the world, human actions appear to be as much determined as anything else. And if this is so, it cannot be the case that what distinguishes actions freely chosen from those which are not free is that the latter are determined by causes while the former are not. Therefore, being uncaused or being undetermined by causes, must be an incorrect definition of free will.

What, then, is the difference between acts which are freely done and those which are not? What is the characteristic which is present to all the acts in the left-hand column and absent from all those in the right-hand column? Is it not obvious that, although both sets of actions have causes, the causes of those in the left-hand column are *of a different kind* from the causes of those in the right-hand column? The free acts are all caused by desires, or motives, or by some sort of internal psychological states of the agent's mind. The unfree acts, on the other hand, are all caused by physical forces or physical conditions, outside the agent. Police arrest means physical force exerted from the outside; the absence of food in the desert is a physical condition of the outside world. We may therefore frame the following rough definitions. *Acts freely done are those whose immediate causes are psychological states in the agent. Acts not freely done are those whose immediate causes are states of affairs external to the agent.*

It is plain that if we define free will in this way, then free will certainly exists, and the philosopher's denial of its existence is seen to be what it is—nonsense. For it is obvious that all those actions of men which we should ordinarily attribute to the exercise of their free will, or of which we should say that they freely chose to do them, are in fact actions which have been caused by their own desires, wishes, thoughts, emotions, impulses, or other psychological states.

In applying our definition we shall find that it usually works well, but that there are some puzzling cases which it does not seem exactly to fit. These puzzles can always be solved by paying careful attention to the ways in which words are used, and remembering that they are not always used consistently. I have space for only one example. Suppose that a thug threatens to shoot you unless you give him your wallet, and suppose that you do so. Do you, in giving him your wallet, do so of your own free will or not? If we apply our definition, we find that you acted freely, since the immediate cause of the action was not an actual outside force but the fear of death, which is a psychological cause. Most people, however, would say that you did not act of your own free will but under compulsion. Does this show that our definition is wrong? I do not think so. Aristotle, who gave a solution of the problem of free will substantially the same as ours (though he did not use the term "free will") admitted that there are what he called "mixed" or borderline cases in which it is difficult to know whether we ought to call the acts free or compelled. In the case under discussion, though no actual force was used, the gun at your forehead so nearly approximated to actual force that we tend to say the case was one of compulsion. It is a borderline case.

Here is what may seem like another kind of puzzle. According to our view an action may be free though it could have been predicted beforehand with certainty. But suppose you told a lie, and it was certain beforehand that you would tell it. How could one then say, "You could have told the truth"? The answer is that it is perfectly true that you could have told the truth *if you had wanted to*. In fact you would have done so, for in that case the causes producing your action, namely your desires, would have been different, and would therefore have produced different effects. It is a delusion that predictability and free will are incompatible. This agrees with common sense. For if, knowing your character, I predict that you will act honorably, no one would say when you do act honorably, that this shows you did not do so of your own free will.

Since free will is a condition of moral responsibility, we must be sure that our theory of free will gives a sufficient basis for it. To be held morally responsible for one's actions means that one may be justly punished or rewarded, blamed or praised, for them. But it is not just to punish a man for what he cannot help doing. How can it be just to punish him for an action which it was certain beforehand that he would do? We have not attempted to decide whether, as a matter of fact, all events, including human actions, are completely determined. For that question is irrelevant to the problem of free will. But if we assume for the purposes of argument that complete determinism is true, but that we are nevertheless free, it may then be asked whether such a deterministic free will is compatible with moral responsibility. For it may seem unjust to punish a man for an action which it could have been predicted with certainty beforehand that he would do.

But that determinism is incompatible with moral responsibility is as much a delusion as that it is incompatible with free will. You do not excuse a man for doing a wrong act because, knowing his character, you felt certain beforehand that he would do it. Nor do you deprive a man of a reward or prize because, knowing his goodness or his capabilities, you felt certain beforehand that he would win it.

Volumes have been written on the justification of punishment. But so far as it affects the question of free will, the essential principles involved are quite simple. The punishment of a man for doing a wrong act is justified, either on the ground that it will correct his own character, or that it will deter other people from doing similar acts. The instrument of punishment has been in the past, and no doubt still is, often unwisely used; so that it may often have done more harm than good. But that is not relevant to our present problem. Punishment, if and when it is justified, is justified only on one or both of the grounds just mentioned. The question then is how, if we assume determinism, punishment can correct character or deter people from evil actions.

Suppose that your child develops a habit of telling lies. You give him a mild beating. Why? Because you believe that his personality is such that the usual motives for telling the truth do not cause him to do so. You therefore supply the missing cause, or motive, in the shape of pain and the fear of future pain if he repeats his untruthful behavior. And you hope that a few treatments of this kind will condition him to the habit of truth-telling, so that he will come to tell the truth without the infliction of pain. You assume that his actions are determined by causes, but that the usual causes of truth-telling do not in him produce their usual effects. You therefore supply him with an artificially injected motive, pain and fear, which you think will in the future cause him to speak truthfully.

The principle is exactly the same where you hope, by punishing one man, to deter others from wrong actions. You believe that the fear of punishment will cause those who might otherwise do evil to do well.

We act on the same principle with non-human, and even with inanimate, things, if they do not behave in the way we think they ought to behave. The rose bushes in the garden produce only small and poor blooms, whereas we want large and rich ones. We supply a cause which will produce large blooms, namely fertilizer. Our automobile does not go properly. We supply a cause which will make it go better, namely oil in the works. The punishment for the man, the fertilizer for the plant, and the oil for the car, are all justified by the same principle and in the same way. The only difference is that different kinds of things require different kinds of causes to make them do what they should. Pain may be the appropriate remedy to apply, in certain cases, to human beings, and oil to the machine. It is, of course, of no use to inject motor oil into the boy or to beat the machine.

Thus we see that moral responsibility is not only consistent with determinism, but requires it. The assumption on which punishment is based is that human behavior is causally determined. If pain could not be a cause of truth-telling there would be no justification at all for punishing lies. If human actions and volitions were uncaused, it would be useless either to punish or reward, or indeed to do anything else to correct people's bad behavior. For nothing that you could do would in any way influence them. Thus moral responsibility would entirely disappear. If there were no determinism of human beings at all, their actions would be completely unpredictable and capricious, and therefore irresponsible. And this is in itself a strong argument against the common view of philosophers that free will means being undetermined by causes.

DISCUSSION QUESTIONS

1. Do you agree with Stace's account of the free will versus determinism debate as not involving a "real" problem, but only a "semantic" one? Why or why not?

2. Do you agree with Stace's definition of acts "freely done" and "not freely done," and his rejection of free will as "indeterminism"? Why or why not?

3. How would you criticize or defend the version of compatibilism Stace advocates here?

4. How would you compare the views of Stace and Skinner on the justification of punishment?

32. Jean-Paul Sartre (1905–1980)
Existentialism and Freedom

Jean-Paul Sartre was a French philosopher, novelist, and playwright who became the most internationally famous existentialist thinker in the twentieth century. Existentialism is a philosophical and literary movement that started in nineteenth-century continental Europe and reached the height of its influence on both the academic world and popular culture in the 1950s. As opposed to the systematic, purely rational, and abstract orientation to the study of humanity that has characterized Western philosophy at least since Plato, existentialist writers have focused more directly on the unique, flesh-and-blood existence of the human individual. They have been especially interested in illuminating how a person copes with, and makes meaningful, his or her own existence as a conscious individual, rather than how that person manifests allegedly universal properties of the "human essence" as such. Not surprisingly then, existentialist thought always has utilized in-depth psychological description as much as rational argumentation in its exploration of human reality; so it quite easily has found expression in literary art and even therapeutic strategies over the years, as much as in philosophical study itself.

The rise of existentialism is often thought to be an outcome of a number of changes occurring in Western society over the last few centuries. In the view of many analysts, the Industrial Revolution and the advances of capitalism that radically restructured social relations, the many-sided challenges to the traditional Judeo-Christian worldview, the rise of the bureaucratic nation-state, and the bewildering human slaughter of two world wars with the threat of worse to come have all contributed to this interest in the individual's "search for meaning" in Western intellectual culture. And in one way or another, all existentialist writers have pointed out how, in such circumstances, all conscious human individuals inescapably create their own "meaning" and are fundamentally responsible for whatever significance their own lives are thought to possess.

The essay reprinted here, "Existentialism Is a Humanism," was published in 1946 and originally presented as a public lecture by Sartre. It is probably the summary of existentialism for which he is best known (a fact about which he apparently was dismayed later on). He covers a lot of ground, dealing with political and moral issues as well as with metaphysical concerns regarding the human person. But the background and foreground of his discussion remain basically the same. In the case of the former, he is responding to the horror and devastation experienced by Europeans generally and the French particularly during the recently ended war. In the case of the latter, he always stresses the inseparable themes of human freedom and responsibility, arguing that even though we often can't choose our circumstances, we always choose our response to those circumstances and thus in this sense really are who we individually choose to be.

QUESTIONS FOR CRITICAL READING

1. What does Sartre mean by, and how does he argue for, the existentialist tenet that "existence precedes essence"? What does this have to do with humanism?

2. According to Sartre, what do existentialists mean by claiming that "man is in anguish"?

3. What does Sartre mean by "abandonment," and his claim that all humans are "condemned to be free"?

4. What are the moral implications of the existentialist account of the human condition, in Sartre's estimation?

5. How does Sartre argue against determinism?

TERMS TO NOTE

quietism: A stance of intentional passivity and non-participation in worldly affairs, focusing instead on one's "inner life."

bourgeois: A French term originally meaning "shop-keeper"; in this context, it refers to that which is a product of, or influenced by, modern capitalist society and its dominant values (for example, there is a "bourgeois culture," "bourgeois philosophy," the "bourgeois family," and so on).

naturalism: Very generally, the philosophical theory that says the knowable universe is entirely made up of natural objects and their interrelations—that is, natural rather than supernatural (or otherworldly) phenomena, which are bound by the laws of nature.

collaborator: In this context, a French citizen who worked with, helped, or actively supported the Nazi occupation forces in France during World War II.

My purpose here is to offer a defence of existentialism against several reproaches that have been laid against it.

First, it has been reproached as an invitation to people to dwell in quietism of despair. For if every way to a solution is barred, one would have to regard any action in this world as entirely ineffective, and one would arrive finally at a contemplative philosophy. Moreover, since contemplation is a luxury, this would be only another bourgeois philosophy. This is, especially, the reproach made by the Communists.

From another quarter we are reproached for having underlined all that is ignominious in the human situation, for depicting what is mean, sordid or base to the neglect of certain things that possess charm and beauty and belong to the brighter side of human nature: for example, according to the Catholic critic, Mlle. Mercier, we forget how an infant smiles. Both from this side and from the other we are also reproached for leaving out of account the solidarity of mankind and considering man in isolation. And this, say the Communists, is because we base our doctrine upon pure subjectivity—upon the Cartesian "I think": which is the moment in which solitary man attains to himself; a position from which it is impossible to regain solidarity with other men who exist outside of the self. The *ego* cannot reach them through the *cogito*.

From the Christian side, we are reproached as people who deny the reality and seriousness of human affairs. For since we ignore the commandments of God and all values prescribed as eternal, nothing remains but what is strictly voluntary. Everyone can do what he likes, and will be incapable, from such a point of view, of condemning either the point of view or the action of anyone else.

It is to these various reproaches that I shall endeavor to reply today; that is why I have entitled this brief exposition "Existentialism is a Humanism." Many may be surprised at the mention of humanism in this connection, but we shall try to see in what sense we understand it. In any case, we can begin by saying that existentialism, in our sense of the word, is a doctrine that does render human life possible; a doctrine, also, which affirms that every truth and every action imply both an environment and a human subjectivity. The essential charge laid against us is, of course, that of over-emphasis upon the evil side of human life. I have lately been told of a lady who, whenever she lets slip a vulgar expression in a moment of nervousness, excuses herself by exclaiming, "I believe I am becoming an existentialist." So it appears that ugliness is being identified with existentialism. That is why some people say we are "naturalistic," and if we are, it is strange to see how much we scandalize and horrify them, for no one seems to be much frightened or humiliated nowadays by what is properly called naturalism. Those who can quite well keep down a novel by Zola such as *La Terre* are sickened as soon as they read an existentialist novel. Those who appeal to the wisdom of the people—which is a sad wisdom—find ours sadder still. And yet, what could be more disillusioned than such sayings as "Charity begins at home" or "Promote a rogue and he'll sue you for damage, knock him down and he'll do you homage"? We all know how many common sayings can be quoted to this effect, and they all mean much the same—that you must not oppose the powers-that-be; that you must not fight against superior force; must not meddle in matters that are above your station. Or that any action not in accordance with some tradition is mere romanticism; or that any undertaking which has not the support of proven experience is foredoomed to frustration; and that since experience has shown men to be invariably inclined to evil, there must be firm rules to restrain them, otherwise we shall have anarchy. It is, however, the people who are forever mouthing these dismal proverbs and, whenever they are told of some more or less repulsive action, say "How like human nature!"— it is these very people, always harping upon realism, who complain that existentialism is too gloomy a view of things. Indeed their excessive protests make me suspect that what is annoying them is not so much our pessimism, but, much more likely, our optimism. For at bottom, what is alarming in the doctrine that I am about to try to explain to you is—is it not?—that it confronts man with a possibility of choice. To verify this, let us review the whole question upon the strictly philosophic level. What, then, is this that we call existentialism?

Most of those who are making use of this word would be highly confused if required to explain its meaning. For since it has become fashionable, people cheerfully declare that this musician or that painter is "existentialist." A columnist in *Clartés* signs himself "The Existentialist," and, indeed, the word is now so loosely applied to so many things that it no longer means anything at all. It would appear that, for the lack of any novel doctrine such as that of surrealism, all those who are eager to join in the latest scandal or movement now seize upon this philosophy in which, however, they can find nothing to their purpose. For in truth this is of all teachings the least scandalous and the most austere: it is intended strictly for technicians and philosophers. All the same, it can easily be defined.

The question is only complicated because there are two kinds of existentialists. There are, on the one hand, the Christians, amongst whom I shall name Jaspers and Gabriel Marcel, both professed Catholics; and on the other the existential atheists, amongst whom we must place Heidegger as well as the French existentialists and myself. What they have in common is simply the fact that they believe that *existence* comes before *essence*—or, if you will, that we must begin from the subjective. What exactly do we mean by that?

If one considers an article of manufacture—as, for example, a book or a paper-knife—one sees that it has been made by an artisan who had a conception of it; and he has paid attention, equally, to the conception

of a paper-knife and to the pre-existent technique of production which is a part of that conception and is, at bottom, a formula. Thus the paper-knife is at the same time an article producible in a certain manner and one which, on the other hand, serves a definite purpose, for one cannot suppose that a man would produce a paper-knife without knowing what it was for. Let us say, then, of the paper-knife that its essence—that is to say the sum of the formulae and the qualities which made its production and its definition possible—precedes its existence. The presence of such-and-such a paper-knife or book is thus determined before my eyes. Here, then, we are viewing the world from a technical standpoint, and we can say that production precedes existence.

When we think of God as the creator, we are thinking of him, most of the time, as a supernal artisan. Whatever doctrine we may be considering, whether it be a doctrine like that of Descartes, or of Leibnitz himself, we always imply that the will follows, more or less, from the understanding or at least accompanies it, so that when God creates he knows precisely what he is creating. Thus, the conception of man in the mind of God is comparable to that of the paper-knife in the mind of the artisan: God makes man according to a procedure and a conception, exactly as the artisan manufactures a paper-knife, following a definition and a formula. Thus each individual man is the realization of a certain conception which dwells in the divine understanding. In the philosophic atheism of the eighteenth century, the notion of God is suppressed, but not, for all that, the idea that essence is prior to existence; something of that idea we still find everywhere, in Diderot, in Voltaire and even in Kant. Man possesses a human nature; that "human nature," which is the conception of human being, is found in every man; which means that each man is a particular example of a universal conception, the conception of Man. In Kant, this universality goes so far that the wild man of the woods, man in the state of nature and the bourgeois are all contained in the same definition and have the same fundamental qualities. Here again, the essence of man precedes that historic existence which we confront in experience.

Atheistic existentialism, of which I am a representative, declares with greater consistency that if God does not exist there is at least one being whose existence comes before its essence, a being which exists before it can be defined by any conception of it. That being is man or, as Heidegger has it, the human reality. What do we mean by saying that existence precedes essence? We mean that man first of all exists, encounters himself, surges up in the world—and defines himself afterwards. If man as the existentialist sees him is not definable, it is because to begin with he is nothing. He will not be anything until later, and then he will be what he makes of himself. Thus, there is no human nature, because there is no God to have a conception of it. Man simply is. Not that he is simply what he conceives himself to be, but he is what he wills, and as he conceives himself after already existing—as he wills to be after that leap towards existence. Man is nothing else but that which he makes of himself. That is the first principle of existentialism. And this is what people call its "subjectivity," using the word as a reproach against us. But what do we mean to say by this, but that man is of a greater dignity than a stone or a table? For we mean to say that man primarily exists—that man is, before all else, something which propels itself towards a future and is aware that it is doing so. Man is, indeed, a project which possesses a subjective life, instead of being a kind of moss, or a fungus or a cauliflower. Before that projection of the self nothing exists; not even in the heaven of intelligence: man will only attain existence when he is what he purposes to be. Not, however, what he may wish to be. For what we usually understand by wishing or willing is a conscious decision taken—much more often than not—after we have made ourselves what we are. I may wish to join a party, to write a book or to marry—but in such a case what is usually called my will is probably a manifestation of a prior and more spontaneous decision. If, however, it is true that existence is prior to essence, man is responsible for what he is. Thus, the first effect of existentialism is that it puts every man in possession of himself as he is, and places the entire responsibility for his existence squarely upon his own shoulders. And, when we say that man is responsible for himself, we do not mean that he is responsible only for his own individuality, but that he is responsible for all men. The word "subjectivism" is to be understood in two senses, and our adversaries play upon only one of them. Subjectivism means, on the one hand, the freedom of the individual subject and, on the other, that

man cannot pass beyond human subjectivity. It is the latter which is the deeper meaning of existentialism. When we say that man chooses himself, we do mean that every one of us must choose himself; but by that we also mean that in choosing for himself he chooses for all men. For in effect, of all the actions a man may take in order to create himself as he wills to be, there is not one which is not creative, at the same time, of an image of man such as he believes he ought to be. To choose between this or that is at the same time to affirm the value of that which is chosen; for we are unable ever to choose the worse. What we choose is always the better; and nothing can be better for us unless it is better for all. If, moreover, existence precedes essence and we will to exist at the same time as we fashion our image, that image is valid for all and for the entire epoch in which we find ourselves. Our responsibility is thus much greater than we had supposed, for it concerns mankind as a whole. If I am a worker, for instance, I may choose to join a Christian rather than a Communist trade union. And if, by that membership, I choose to signify that resignation is, after all, the attitude that best becomes a man, that man's kingdom is not upon this earth, I do not commit myself alone to that view. Resignation is my will for everyone, and my action is, in consequence, a commitment on behalf of all mankind. Or if, to take a more personal case, I decide to marry and to have children, even though this decision proceeds simply from my situation, from my passion or my desire, I am thereby committing not only myself, but humanity as a whole, to the practice of monogamy. I am thus responsible for myself and for all men, and I am creating a certain image of man as I would have him to be. In fashioning myself I fashion man.

This may enable us to understand what is meant by such terms—perhaps a little grandiloquent—as anguish, abandonment and despair. As you will soon see, it is very simple. First, what do we mean by anguish? The existentialist frankly states that man is in anguish. His meaning is as follows—When a man commits himself to anything, fully realizing that he is not only choosing what he will be, but is thereby at the same time a legislator deciding for the whole of mankind—in such a moment a man cannot escape from the sense of complete and profound responsibility. There are many, indeed, who show no such anxiety. But we affirm that they are merely disguising their anguish or are in flight from it. Certainly, many people think that in what they are doing they commit no one but themselves to anything: and if you ask them, "What would happen if everyone did so?" they shrug their shoulders and reply, "Everyone does not do so." But in truth, one ought always to ask oneself what would happen if everyone did as one is doing; nor can one escape from that disturbing thought except by a kind of self-deception. The man who lies in self-excuse, by saying "Everyone will not do it" must be ill at ease in his conscience, for the act of lying implies the universal value which it denies. By its very disguise his anguish reveals itself. This is the anguish that Kierkegaard called "the anguish of Abraham." You know the story: An angel commanded Abraham to sacrifice his son: and obedience was obligatory, if it really was an angel who had appeared and said, "Thou, Abraham, shalt sacrifice thy son." But anyone in such a case would wonder, first, whether it was indeed an angel and secondly, whether I am really Abraham. Where are the proofs? A certain mad woman who suffered from hallucinations said that people were telephoning to her, and giving her orders. The doctor asked, "But who is it that speaks to you?" She replied: "He says it is God." And what, indeed, could prove to her that it was God? If an angel appears to me, what is the proof that it is an angel; or, if I hear voices, who can prove that they proceed from heaven and not from hell, or from my own subconsciousness or some pathological condition? Who can prove that they are really addressed to me?

Who, then, can prove that I am the proper person to impose, by my own choice, my conception of man upon mankind? I shall never find any proof whatever; there will be no sign to convince me of it. If a voice speaks to me, it is still I myself who must decide whether the voice is or is not that of an angel. If I regard a certain course of action as good, it is only I who choose to say that it is good and not bad. There is nothing to show that I am Abraham: nevertheless I also am obliged at every instant to perform actions which are examples. Everything happens to every man as though the whole human race had its eyes fixed upon what he is doing and regulated its conduct accordingly. So every man ought to say, "Am I really a man who has the right to act in such a manner that humanity regulates itself by what I do." If a man does not say that, he is dissembling his anguish. Clearly, the anguish with which we are concerned here is not one that could lead to quietism or inaction. It is anguish pure and simple, of the kind well known to all those who have borne responsibilities. When, for instance, a military leader takes upon himself the responsibility for an attack and sends a number of men to their death, he chooses to do it and at bottom he alone chooses. No doubt he acts under a higher command, but its orders, which are more general, require interpretation by him and upon that interpretation depends the life of ten, fourteen or twenty men. In making the decision, he cannot but feel a certain anguish. All leaders know that anguish. It does not prevent their acting, on the contrary it is the very condition of their action, for the action presupposes that there is a plurality of possibilities, and in choosing one of these, they realize that it has value only because it is chosen. Now it is anguish of that kind which existentialism describes, and moreover, as we shall see, makes explicit through direct responsibility towards other men who are concerned. Far from being a screen which could separate us from action, it is a condition of action itself.

And when we speak of "abandonment"—a favorite word of Heidegger—we only mean to say that God does not exist, and that it is necessary to draw the consequences of his absence right to the end. The existentialist is strongly opposed to a certain type of secular moralism which seeks to suppress God at the least possible expense. Towards 1880, when the French professors endeavored to formulate a secular morality, they said something like this:—God is a useless and costly hypothesis, so we will do without it. However, if we are to have morality, a society and a law-abiding world, it is essential that certain values should be taken seriously; they must have an *à priori* existence ascribed to them. It must be considered obligatory *à priori* to be honest, not to lie, not to beat one's wife, to bring up children and so forth; so we are going to do a little work on this subject, which will enable us to show that these values exist all the same, inscribed in an intelligible heaven although, of course, there is no God. In other words—and this is, I believe, the purport of all that we in France call radicalism—nothing will be changed if God does not exist; we shall rediscover the same norms of honesty, progress and humanity, and we shall have disposed of God as an out-of-date hypothesis which will die away quietly of itself. The existentialist, on the contrary, finds it extremely embarrassing that God does not exist, for there disappears with Him all possibility of finding values in an intelligible heaven. There can no longer be any good *à priori,* since there is no infinite and perfect consciousness to think it. It is nowhere written that "the good" exists, that one must be honest or must not lie, since we are now upon the plane where there are only men. Dostoevsky once wrote "If God did not exist, everything would be permitted"; and that, for existentialism, is the starting point. Everything is indeed permitted if God does not exist, and man is in consequence forlorn, for he cannot find anything to depend upon either within or outside himself. He discovers forthwith, that he is without excuse. For if indeed existence precedes essence, one will never be able to explain one's action by reference to a given and specific human nature; in other words, there is no determinism—man is free, man *is* freedom. Nor, on the other hand, if God does not exist, are we provided with any values or commands that could legitimize our behavior. Thus we have neither behind us, nor before us in a luminous realm of values, any means of justification or excuse. We are left alone, without excuse. That is what I mean when I say that man is condemned to be free. Condemned, because he did not create himself, yet is nevertheless at liberty, and from the moment that he is thrown into this world he is responsible for everything he does. The existentialist does not believe in the power of passion. He will never regard a grand passion as a destructive torrent upon which a man is swept into certain actions as by fate, and which, therefore, is an excuse for them. He thinks that man is responsible for his passion. Neither will an existentialist think that a man can find help through some sign being vouchsafed upon earth for his orientation: for he thinks that the man himself interprets the sign as he chooses. He thinks that every man, without any support or help whatever, is condemned at every instant to invent man. As Ponge has written in a very fine article, "Man is the future of man." That is exactly true. Only, if one took this to mean that the future is laid up in Heaven, that God knows what it is, it would be false, for then it would no longer even be

a future. If, however, it means that, whatever man may now appear to be, there is a future to be fashioned, a virgin future that awaits him—then it is a true saying. But in the present one is forsaken.

As an example by which you may the better understand this state of abandonment, I will refer to the case of a pupil of mine, who sought me out in the following circumstances. His father was quarrelling with his mother and was also inclined to be a "collaborator"; his elder brother had been killed in the German offensive of 1940 and this young man, with a sentiment somewhat primitive but generous, burned to avenge him. His mother was living alone with him, deeply afflicted by the semi-treason of his father and by the death of her eldest son, and her one consolation was in this young man. But he, at this moment, had the choice between going to England to join the Free French Forces or of staying near his mother and helping her to live. He fully realized that this woman lived only for him and that his disappearance—or perhaps his death—would plunge her into despair. He also realized that, concretely and in fact, every action he performed on his mother's behalf would be sure of effect in the sense of aiding her to live, whereas anything he did in order to go and fight would be an ambiguous action which might vanish like water into sand and serve no purpose. For instance, to set out for England he would have to wait indefinitely in a Spanish camp on the way through Spain; or, on arriving in England or in Algiers he might be put into an office to fill up forms. Consequently, he found himself confronted by two very different modes of action; the one concrete, immediate, but directed towards only one individual; and the other an action addressed to an end infinitely greater, a national collectivity, but for that very reason ambiguous—and it might be frustrated on the way. At the same time, he was hesitating between two kinds of morality; on the one side the morality of sympathy, of personal devotion and, on the other side, a morality of wider scope but of more debatable validity. He had to choose between those two. What could help him to choose? Could the Christian doctrine? No. Christian doctrine says: Act with charity, love your neighbour, deny yourself for others, choose the way which is hardest, and so forth. But which is the harder road? To whom does one owe the more brotherly love, the patriot or the mother? Which is the more useful aim, the general one of fighting in and for the whole community, or the precise aim of helping one particular person to live? Who can give an answer to that *à priori?* No one. Nor is it given in any ethical scripture. The Kantian ethic says, Never regard another as a means, but always as an end. Very well; if I remain with my mother, I shall be regarding her as the end and not as a means: but by the same token I am in danger of treating as means those who are fighting on my behalf; and the converse is also true, that if I go to the aid of the combatants I shall be treating them as the end at the risk of treating my mother as a means.

If values are uncertain, if they are still too abstract to determine the particular, concrete case under consideration, nothing remains but to trust in our instincts. That is what this young man tried to do; and when I saw him he said, "In the end, it is feeling that counts; the direction in which it is really pushing me is the one I ought to choose. If I feel that I love my mother enough to sacrifice everything else for her— my will to be avenged, all my longings for action and adventure—then I stay with her. If, on the contrary, I feel that my love for her is not enough, I go." But how does one estimate the strength of a feeling? The value of his feeling for his mother was determined precisely by the fact that he was standing by her. I may say that I love a certain friend enough to sacrifice such or such a sum of money for him, but I cannot prove that unless I have done it. I may say, "I love my mother enough to remain with her," if actually I have remained with her. I can only estimate the strength of this affection if I have performed an action by which it is defined and ratified. But if I then appeal to this affection to justify my action, I find myself drawn into a vicious circle.

Moreover, as Gide has very well said, a sentiment which is play-acting and one which is vital are two things that are hardly distinguishable one from another. To decide that I love my mother by staying beside her, and to play a comedy the upshot of which is that I do so—these are nearly the same thing. In other words, feeling is formed by the deeds that one does; therefore I cannot consult it as a guide to action. And that is to say that I can neither seek within myself for an authentic impulse to action, nor can I expect, from some ethic, formulae that will enable me to act. You

may say that the youth did, at least, go to a professor to ask for advice. But if you seek counsel—from a priest, for example—you have selected that priest; and at bottom you already knew, more or less, what he would advise. In other words, to choose an adviser is nevertheless to commit oneself by that choice. If you are a Christian, you will say, Consult a priest; but there are collaborationists, priests who are resisters and priests who wait for the tide to turn: which will you choose? Had this young man chosen a priest of the resistance, or one of the collaboration, he would have decided beforehand the kind of advice he was to receive. Similarly, in coming to me, he knew what advice I should give him, and I had but one reply to make. You are free, therefore choose—that is to say, invent. No rule of general morality can show you what you ought to do: no signs are vouchsafed in this world. The Catholics will reply, "Oh, but they are!" Very well; still, it is I myself, in every case, who have to interpret the signs. While I was imprisoned, I made the acquaintance of a somewhat remarkable man, a Jesuit, who had become a member of that order in the following manner. In his life he had suffered a succession of rather severe setbacks. His father had died when he was a child, leaving him in poverty, and he had been awarded a free scholarship in a religious institution, where he had been made continually to feel that he was accepted for charity's sake, and, in consequence, he had been denied several of those distinctions and honours which gratify children. Later, about the age of eighteen, he came to grief in a sentimental affair; and finally, at twenty-two—this was a trifle in itself, but it was the last drop that overflowed his cup—he failed in his military examination. This young man, then, could regard himself as a total failure: it was a sign— but a sign of what? He might have taken refuge in bitterness or despair. But he took it—very cleverly for him—as a sign that he was not intended for secular successes, and that only the attainments of religion, those of sanctity and of faith, were accessible to him. He interpreted his record as a message from God, and became a member of the Order. Who can doubt but that this decision as to the meaning of the sign was his, and his alone? One could have drawn quite different conclusions from such a series of reverses—as, for example, that he had better become a carpenter or a revolutionary. For the decipherment of the sign, however, he bears the entire responsibility. That is what "abandonment" implies, that we ourselves decide our being. And with this abandonment goes anguish.

As for "despair," the meaning of this expression is extremely simple. It merely means that we limit ourselves to a reliance upon that which is within our wills, or within the sum of the probabilities which render our action feasible. Whenever one wills anything, there are always these elements of probability. If I am counting upon a visit from a friend, who may be coming by train or by tram, I presuppose that the train will arrive at the appointed time, or that the tram will not be derailed. I remain in the realm of possibilities; but one does not rely upon any possibilities beyond those that are strictly concerned in one's action. Beyond the point at which the possibilities under consideration cease to affect my action, I ought to disinterest myself. For there is no God and no prevenient design, which can adapt the world and all its possibilities to my will. When Descartes said, "Conquer yourself rather than the world," what he meant was, at bottom, the same—that we should act without hope.

Marxists, to whom I have said this, have answered: "Your action is limited, obviously, by your death; but you can rely upon the help of others. That is, you can count both upon what the others are doing to help you elsewhere, as in China and in Russia, and upon what they will do later, after your death, to take up your action and carry it forward to its final accomplishment which will be the revolution. Moreover you must rely upon this; not to do so is immoral." To this I rejoin, first, that I shall always count upon my comrades-in-arms in the struggle, in so far as they are committed, as I am, to a definite, common cause; and in the unity of a party or a group which I can more or less control—that is, in which I am enrolled as a militant and whose movements at every moment are known to me. In that respect, to rely upon the unity and the will of the party is exactly like my reckoning that the train will run to time or that the tram will not be derailed. But I cannot count upon men whom I do not know, I cannot base my confidence upon human goodness or upon man's interest in the good of society, seeing that man is free and that there is no human nature which I can take as foundational. I do not know where the Russian revolution will lead. I can admire it and take it as an example in so far as it is evident, today, that the proletariat plays a part in Russia which it has attained in no other nation. But I cannot affirm that this will necessarily lead to the triumph of the proletariat: I must confine myself to what I can see. Nor can I be sure that comrades-in-arms will take up my work after my death and carry it to the maximum perfection, seeing that those men are free agents and will freely decide, tomorrow, what man is then to be. Tomorrow, after my death, some men may decide to establish Fascism, and the others may be so cowardly or so slack as to let them do so. If so, Fascism will then be the truth of man, and so much the worse for us. In reality, things will be such as men have decided they shall be. Does that mean that I should abandon myself to quietism? No. First I ought to commit myself and then act my commitment, according to the time-honored formula that "one need not hope in order to undertake one's work." Nor does this mean that I should not belong to a party, but only that I should be without illusion and that I should do what I can. For instance, if I ask myself "Will the social ideal as such, ever become a reality?" I cannot tell, I only know that whatever may be in my power to make it so, I shall do; beyond that, I can count upon nothing.

Quietism is the attitude of people who say, "let others do what I cannot do." The doctrine I am presenting before you is precisely the opposite of this, since it declares that there is no reality except in action. It goes further, indeed, and adds, "Man is nothing else but what he purposes, he exists only in so far as he realizes himself, he is therefore nothing else but the sum of his actions, nothing else but what his life is." Hence we can well understand why some people are horrified by our teaching. For many have but one resource to sustain them in their misery, and that is to think, "Circumstances have been against me, I was worthy to be something much better than I have been. I admit I have never had a great love or a great friendship; but that is because I never met a man or a woman who were worthy of it; if I have not written any very good books, it is because I had not the leisure to do so; or, if I have had no children to whom I could devote myself it is because I did not find the man I could have lived with. So there remains within me a wide range of abilities, inclinations and potentialities, unused but perfectly viable, which endow me with a worthiness that could never be inferred from the mere history of my actions." But in reality and for the existentialist, there is no love apart from the deeds of love; no potentiality of love other than that which is manifested in loving; there is no genius other than that which is expressed in works of art. The genius of Proust is the totality of the works of Proust; the genius of Racine is the series of his tragedies, outside of which there is nothing. Why should we attribute to Racine the capacity to write yet another tragedy when that is precisely what he did not write? In life, a man commits himself, draws his own portrait and there is nothing but that portrait. No doubt this thought may seem comfortless to one who has not made a success of his life. On the other hand, it puts everyone in a position to understand that reality alone is reliable; that dreams, expectations and hopes serve to define a man only as deceptive dreams, abortive hopes, expectations unfulfilled; that is to say, they define him negatively, not positively. Nevertheless, when one says, "You are nothing else but what you live," it does not imply that an artist is to be judged solely by his works of art, for a thousand other things contribute no less to his definition as a man. What we mean to say is that a man is no other than a series of undertakings, that he is the sum, the organization, the set of relations that constitute these undertakings.

In the light of all this, what people reproach us with is not, after all, our pessimism, but the sternness of our optimism. If people condemn our works of fiction, in which we describe characters that are base, weak, cowardly and sometimes even frankly evil, it is not only because those characters are base, weak, cowardly or evil. For suppose that, like Zola, we showed that the behavior of these characters was caused by their heredity, or by the action of their environment upon them, or by determining factors, psychic or organic. People would be reassured, they would say, "You see, that is what we are like, no one can do anything about it." But the existentialist, when he portrays a coward, shows him as responsible for his cowardice. He is not like that on account of a cowardly heart or lungs or cerebrum, he has not become like that through his physiological organism; he is like that because he has made himself into a coward by his actions. There is no such thing as a cowardly temperament. There are nervous temperaments; there is what is called impoverished blood, and there are also rich temperaments. But the man whose blood is poor is not a coward for all that, for what produces cowardice is the act of giving up or giving way; and a temperament is not an action. A coward is defined by the deed that he has done. What people feel obscurely, and with horror, is that the coward as we present him is guilty of being a coward. What people would prefer would be to be born either a coward or a hero. One of the charges most often laid against the *Chemins de la Liberté* is something like this—"But, after all, these people being so base, how can you make them into heroes?" That objection is really rather comic, for it implies that people are born heroes: and that is, at bottom, what such people would like to think. If you are born cowards, you can be quite content; you can do nothing about it and you will be cowards all your lives whatever you do; and if you are born heroes you can again be quite content; you will be heroes all your lives eating and drinking heroically. Whereas the existentialist says that the coward makes himself cowardly, the hero makes himself heroic; and that there is always a possibility for the coward to give up cowardice and for the hero to stop being a hero. What counts is the total commitment, and it is not by a particular case or particular action that you are committed altogether.

We have now, I think, dealt with a certain number of the reproaches against existentialism. You have seen that it cannot be regarded as a philosophy of quietism since it defines man by his action; nor as a pessimistic description of man, for no doctrine is more optimistic, the destiny of man is placed within himself. Nor is it an attempt to discourage man from action since it tells him that there is no hope except in his action, and that the one thing which permits him to have life is the deed. Upon this level therefore, what we are considering is an ethic of action and self-commitment. However, we are still reproached, upon these few data, for confining man within his individual subjectivity. There again people badly misunderstand us.

Our point of departure is, indeed, the subjectivity of the individual, and that for strictly philosophic reasons. It is not because we are bourgeois, but because we seek to base our teaching upon the truth, and not upon a collection of fine theories, full of hope but lacking real foundations. And at the point of departure there cannot be any other truth than this, *I think, therefore I am*, which is the absolute truth of consciousness as it attains to itself. Every theory which begins with man, outside of this moment of self-attainment, is a theory which thereby suppresses the truth, for outside of the Cartesian *cogito,* all objects are no more than probable, and any doctrine of probabilities which is not attached to a truth will crumble into nothing. In order to define the probable one must possess the true. Before there can be any truth whatever, then, there must be an absolute truth, and there is such a truth which is simple, easily attained and within the reach of everybody; it consists in one's immediate sense of one's self.

In the second place, this theory alone is compatible with the dignity of man, it is the only one which does not make man into an object. All kinds of materialism lead one to treat every man including oneself as an object—that is, as a set of pre-determined reactions, in no way different from the patterns of qualities and phenomena which constitute a table, or a chair or a stone. Our aim is precisely to establish the human kingdom as a pattern of values in distinction from the material world. But the subjectivity which we thus postulate as the standard of truth is no narrowly individual subjectivism, for as we have demonstrated, it is not only one's own self that one discovers in the *cogito,* but those of others too. Contrary to the philosophy of Descartes, contrary to that of Kant, when we say "I think" we are attaining to ourselves in the presence of the other, and we are just as certain of the other as we are of ourselves. Thus the man who discovers himself directly in the *cogito* also discovers all the others, and discovers them as the condition of his own existence. He recognizes that he cannot be anything (in the sense in which one says one is spiritual, or that one is wicked or jealous) unless others recognize him as such. I cannot obtain any truth whatsoever about myself, except through the mediation of another. The other is indispensable to my existence, and equally so to any knowledge I can have of myself. Under these conditions, the intimate discovery of myself is at the same time the revelation of the other as a freedom which confronts mine, and which cannot think or will without doing so either for or against me. Thus, at once, we find ourselves in a world which is, let us say, that of "intersubjectivity." It is in this world that man has to decide what he is and what others are.

Furthermore, although it is impossible to find in each and every man a universal essence that can be called human nature, there is nevertheless a human universality of *condition.* It is not by chance that the thinkers of today are so much more ready to speak of the condition than of the nature of man. By his condition they understand, with more or less clarity, all the *limitations* which *à priori* define man's fundamental situation in the universe. His historical situations are variable: man may be born a slave in a pagan society, or may be a feudal baron, or a proletarian. But what never vary are the necessities of being in the world, of having to labor and to die there. These limitations are neither subjective nor objective, or rather there is both a subjective and an objective aspect of them. Objective, because we meet with them everywhere and they are everywhere recognizable: and subjective because they are *lived* and are nothing if man does not live them—if, that is to say, he does not freely determine himself and his existence in relation to them. And, diverse though man's purposes may be, at least none of them is wholly foreign to me, since every human purpose presents itself as an attempt either to surpass these limitations, or to widen them, or else to deny or to accommodate oneself to them. Consequently every purpose, however individual it may be, is of universal value. Every purpose, even that of a Chinese, an Indian or a Negro, can be understood by a European. To say it can be understood, means that the European of 1945 may be striving out of a certain situation towards the same limitations in the same way, and that he may reconceive in himself the purpose of the Chinese, of the Indian or the African. In every purpose there is universality, in this sense that every purpose is comprehensible to every man. Not that this or that purpose defines man for ever, but that it may be entertained again and again. There is always some way of understanding an idiot, a child, a primitive man or a foreigner if one has sufficient information. In this sense we may say that there is a human universality, but it is not something given; it is being perpetually made. I make this universality in choosing myself; I also make it by understanding the purpose of any other man, of whatever epoch. This absoluteness of the act of choice does not alter the relativity of each epoch.

What is at the very heart and center of existentialism, is the absolute character of the free commitment, by which every man realizes himself in realizing a type of humanity—a commitment always understandable, to no matter whom in no matter what epoch—and its bearing upon the relativity of the cultural pattern which may result from such absolute commitment. One must observe equally the relativity of Cartesianism and the absolute character of the Cartesian commitment. In this sense you may say, if you like, that every one of us makes the absolute by breathing, by eating, by sleeping or by behaving in any fashion whatsoever. There is no difference between free being—being as self-committal, as existence choosing its essence—and absolute being. And there is no difference whatever between being as an absolute, temporarily localized—that is, localized in history—and universally intelligible being.

This does not completely refute the charge of subjectivism. Indeed that objection appears in several other forms, of which the first is as follows. People say to us, "Then it does not matter what you do," and they say this in various ways. First they tax us with anarchy; then they say, "You cannot judge others, for there is no reason for preferring one purpose to another"; finally, they may say, "Everything being merely voluntary in this choice of yours, you give away with one hand what you pretend to gain with the other." These three are not very serious objections. As to the first, to say that it does not matter what you choose is not correct. In one sense choice is possible, but what is not possible is not to choose. I can always choose, but I must know that if I do not choose, that is still a choice. This, although it may appear merely formal, is of great importance as a limit to fantasy and caprice. For, when I confront a real situation—for example, that I am a sexual being, able to have relations with a being of the other sex and able to have children—I am obliged to choose my attitude to it, and in every respect I bear the responsibility of the choice which, in committing myself, also commits the whole of humanity. Even if my choice is determined by no *à priori* value whatever, it can have nothing to do with caprice: and if anyone thinks that this is only Gide's theory of the *acte gratuit* over again, he has failed to see the enormous difference between this theory and that of Gide. Gide does not know what a situation is, his "act" is one of pure caprice. In our view, on the contrary, man finds himself in an organized situation in which he is himself involved: his choice involves mankind in its entirety, and he cannot avoid choosing. Either he must remain single, or he must marry without having children, or he must marry and have children. In any case, and whichever he may choose, it is impossible for him, in respect of this situation, not to take complete responsibility. Doubtless he chooses without reference to any pre-established values, but it is unjust to tax him with caprice. Rather let us say that the moral choice is comparable to the construction of a work of art.

But here I must at once digress to make it quite clear that we are not propounding an aesthetic morality, for our adversaries are disingenuous enough to reproach us even with that. I mention the work of art only by way of comparison. That being understood, does anyone reproach an artist, when he paints a picture, for not following rules established *à priori*? Does one ever ask what is the picture that he ought to paint? As everyone knows, there is no pre-defined picture for him to make; the artist applies himself to the composition of a picture, and the picture that ought to be made is precisely that which he will have made. As everyone knows, there are no aesthetic values *à priori*, but there are values which will appear in due course in the coherence of the picture, in the relation between the will to create and the finished work. No one can tell what the painting of tomorrow will be like; one cannot judge a painting until it is done. What has that to do with morality? We are in the same creative situation. We never speak of a work of art as irresponsible; when we are discussing a canvas by Picasso, we understand very well that the composition became what it is at the time when he was painting it, and that his works are part and parcel of his entire life.

It is the same upon the plane of morality. There is this in common between art and morality, that in both we have to do with creation and invention. We cannot decide *à priori* what it is that should be done. I think it was made sufficiently clear to you in the case of that student who came to see me, that to whatever ethical system he might appeal, the Kantian or any other, he could find no sort of guidance whatever; he was obliged to invent the law for himself. Certainly we cannot say that this man, in choosing to remain with his mother—that is, in taking sentiment, personal devotion and concrete charity as his moral foundations—would be making an irresponsible choice, nor could we do so if he preferred the sacrifice of going away to England. Man makes himself; he is not found ready-made; he makes himself by the choice of his morality, and he cannot but choose a morality, such is the pressure of circumstances upon him. We define man only in relation to his commitments; it is therefore absurd to reproach us for irresponsibility in our choice.

In the second place, people say to us, "You are unable to judge others." This is true in one sense and false in another. It is true in this sense, that whenever a man chooses his purpose and his commitment in all clearness and in all sincerity, whatever that purpose may be, it is impossible for him to prefer another. It is true in the sense that we do not believe in progress. Progress implies amelioration; but man is always the same, facing a situation which is always changing, and choice remains always a choice in the situation. The moral problem has not changed since the time when it was a choice between slavery and anti-slavery—from the time of the war of Secession, for example, until the present moment when one chooses between the M.R.P. [*Mouvement Rèpublicain Populaire*] and the Communists.

We can judge, nevertheless, for, as I have said, one chooses in view of others, and in view of others one chooses himself. One can judge, first—and perhaps this is not a judgment of value, but it is a logical judgment—that in certain cases choice is founded upon an error, and in others upon the truth. One can judge a man by saying that he deceives himself. Since we have defined the situation of man as one of free choice, without excuse and without help, any man who takes refuge behind the excuse of his passions, or by inventing some deterministic doctrine, is a self-deceiver. One may object: "But why should he not choose to deceive himself?" I reply that it is not for me to judge him morally, but I define his self-deception as an error. Here one cannot avoid pronouncing a judgment of truth. The self-deception is evidently a falsehood, because it is a dissimulation of man's complete liberty of commitment. Upon this same level, I say that it is also a self-deception if I choose to declare that certain values are incumbent upon me; I am in contradiction with myself if I will these values and at the same time say that they impose themselves upon me. If anyone says to me, "And what if I wish to deceive myself?" I answer, "There is no reason why you should not, but I declare that you are doing so, and that the attitude of strict consistency alone is that of good faith." Furthermore, I can pronounce a moral judgment. For I declare that freedom, in respect of concrete

circumstances, can have no other end and aim but itself; and when once a man has seen that values depend upon himself, in that state of forsakenness he can will only one thing, and that is freedom as the foundation of all values. That does not mean that he wills it in the abstract: it simply means that the actions of men of good faith have, as their ultimate significance, the quest of freedom itself as such. A man who belongs to some communist or revolutionary society wills certain concrete ends, which imply the will to freedom, but that freedom is willed in community. We will freedom for freedom's sake, in and through particular circumstances. And in thus willing freedom, we discover that it depends entirely upon the freedom of others and that the freedom of others depends upon our own. Obviously, freedom as the definition of a man does not depend upon others, but as soon as there is a commitment, I am obliged to will the liberty of others at the same time as my own. I cannot make liberty my aim unless I make that of others equally my aim. Consequently, when I recognize, as entirely authentic, that man is a being whose existence precedes his essence, and that he is a free being who cannot, in any circumstances, but will his freedom, at the same time I realize that I cannot not will the freedom of others. Thus, in the name of that will to freedom which is implied in freedom itself, I can form judgments upon those who seek to hide from themselves the wholly voluntary nature of their existence and its complete freedom. Those who hide from this total freedom, in a guise of solemnity or with deterministic excuses, I shall call cowards. Others, who try to show that their existence is necessary, when it is merely an accident of the appearance of the human race on earth—I shall call scum. But neither cowards nor scum can be identified except upon the plane of strict authenticity. Thus, although the content of morality is variable, a certain form of this morality is universal. Kant declared that freedom is a will both to itself and to the freedom of others. Agreed: but he thinks that the formal and the universal suffice for the constitution of a morality. We think, on the contrary, that principles that are too abstract break down when we come to defining action. To take once again the case of that student; by what authority, in the name of what golden rule of morality, do you think he could have decided, in perfect peace of mind, either to abandon his mother or to remain with her? There are no means of judging. The content is always concrete, and therefore unpredictable; it has always to be invented. The one thing that counts, is to know whether the invention is made in the name of freedom.

Let us, for example, examine the two following cases, and you will see how far they are similar in spite of their difference. Let us take *The Mill on the Floss.* We find here a certain young woman, Maggie Tulliver, who is an incarnation of the value of passion and is aware of it. She is in love with a young man, Stephen, who is engaged to another, an insignificant young woman. This Maggie Tulliver, instead of heedlessly seeking her own happiness, chooses in the name of human solidarity to sacrifice herself and to give up the man she loves. On the other hand, La Sanseverina in Stendhal's *Chartreuse de Parme*, believing that it is passion which endows man with his real value, would have declared that a grand passion justifies its sacrifices, and must be preferred to the banality of such conjugal love as would unite Stephen to the little goose he was engaged to marry. It is the latter that she would have chosen to sacrifice in realizing her own happiness, and, as Stendhal shows, she would also sacrifice herself upon the plane of passion if life made that demand upon her. Here we are facing two clearly opposed moralities; but I claim that they are equivalent, seeing that in both cases the overruling aim is freedom. You can imagine two attitudes exactly similar in effect, in that one girl might prefer, in resignation, to give up her lover while the other preferred, in fulfillment of sexual desire, to ignore the prior engagement of the man she loved; and, externally, these two cases might appear the same as the two we have just cited, while being in fact entirely different. The attitude of La Sanseverina is much nearer to that of Maggie Tulliver than to one of careless greed. Thus, you see, the second objection is at once true and false. One can choose anything, but only if it is upon the plane of free commitment.

The third objection, stated by saying, "You take with one hand what you give with the other," means, at bottom, "your values are not serious, since you choose them yourselves." To that I can only say that I am very sorry that it should be so; but if I have excluded God the Father, there must be somebody to invent values. We have to take things as they are. And moreover, to say that we invent values means neither more nor less than this; that there is no sense in life *à priori*. Life is nothing until it is lived; but it is yours to make sense of, and the value of it is nothing else but the sense that you choose. Therefore, you can see that there is a possibility of creating a human community. I have been reproached for suggesting that existentialism is a form of humanism: people have said to me, "But you have written in your *Nausée* that the humanists are wrong, you have even ridiculed a certain type of humanism, why do you now go back upon that?" In reality, the word humanism has two very different meanings. One may understand by humanism a theory which upholds man as the end-in-itself and as the supreme value. Humanism in this sense appears, for instance, in Cocteau's story *Round the World in 80 Hours,* in which one of the characters declares, because he is flying over mountains in an airplane, "Man is magnificent!" This signifies that although I, personally, have not built airplanes I have the benefit of those particular inventions and that I personally, being a man, can consider myself responsible for, and honored by, achievements that are peculiar to some men. It is to assume that we can ascribe value to man according to the most distinguished deeds of certain men. That kind of humanism is absurd, for only the dog or the horse would be in a position to pronounce a general judgment upon man and declare that he is magnificent, which they have never been such fools as to do—at least, not as far as I know. But neither is it admissible that a man should pronounce judgment upon Man. Existentialism dispenses with any judgment of this sort: an existentialist will never take man as the end, since man is still to be determined. And we have no right to believe that humanity is something to which we could set up a cult, after the manner of Auguste Comte. The cult of humanity ends in Comtian humanism, shut-in upon itself, and—this must be said—in Fascism. We do not want a humanism like that.

But there is another sense of the word, of which the fundamental meaning is this: Man is all the time outside of himself: it is in projecting and losing himself beyond himself that he makes man to exist; and, on the other hand, it is by pursuing transcendent aims that he himself is able to exist. Since man is thus self-surpassing, and can grasp objects only in relation to his self-surpassing, he is himself the heart and center of his transcendence. There is no other universe except the human universe, the universe of human subjectivity. This relation of transcendence as constitutive of man (not in the sense that God is transcendent, but in the sense of self-surpassing) with subjectivity (in such a sense that man is not shut up in himself but forever present in a human universe)—it is this that we call existential humanism. This is humanism, because we remind man that there is no legislator but himself; that he himself, thus abandoned, must decide for himself; also because we show that it is not by turning back upon himself, but always by seeking, beyond himself, an aim which is one of liberation or of some particular realization, that man can realize himself as truly human.

You can see from these few reflections that nothing could be more unjust than the objections people raise against us. Existentialism is nothing else but an attempt to draw the full conclusions from a consistently atheistic position. Its intention is not in the least that of plunging men into despair. And if by despair one means—as the Christians do—any attitude of unbelief, the despair of the existentialists is something different. Existentialism is not atheist in the sense that it would exhaust itself in demonstrations of the non-existence of God. It declares, rather, that even if God existed that would make no difference from its point of view. Not that we believe God does exist, but we think that the real problem is not that of His existence; what man needs is to find himself again and to understand that nothing can save him from himself, not even a valid proof of the existence of God. In this sense existentialism is optimistic. It is a doctrine of action, and it is only by self-deception, by confusing their own despair with ours that Christians can describe us as without hope.

DISCUSSION QUESTIONS

1. Do you agree with the existentialist claims that we are what we choose to be and that there is no fixed "human nature"? Why or why not?
2. How are existentialist ideas relevant for a believer in some traditional set of religious doctrines?
3. How would you compare Skinner's perspective on human freedom with Sartre's?
4. Do you think the existentialist approach to understanding individual human life can adequately account for childhood experience? Why or why not?

33. God and Human Striving in the *Bhagavad-Gītā*

The *Bhagavad-Gītā* (literally, the "Song of God"), probably the single most important written text in Hindu religious life, is thought to have been composed between the fifth and second centuries B.C.E. The authorship of this religious classic is not certain, but traditionally it has been attributed to a sage named Vyāsa. The Gītā is part of a much longer work called the *Mahābhārata,* one of the two great epic poems of classical Hindu literature. Thus it has not been considered scripture, as the Vedas and Upanishads are treated, but an elaboration of the principles and worldview found in those sacred writings.

For the most part the Gītā is a conversation between Arjuna and Krishna. Arjuna is one of the five Pandava brothers, all of whom are about to go into battle with their armies against the Kauravas, their cousins and rivals for the kingdom. Krishna has agreed to be Arjuna's charioteer. In the process of discussing the ultimate pointlessness of human striving after the things of this mortal world, which often include conflict, violence, and suffering, Krishna reveals himself to Arjuna as an incarnation of God. The excerpts reprinted here are sections from the text that deal more specifically with the nature of the Godhead in Hindu thought, how humans can come to know and achieve union with this Supreme Being, and why they should do so. The format of alternating prose and verse passages is the creation of the translators, not the original organization of the Sanskrit text.

QUESTIONS FOR CRITICAL READING

1. What is Prakriti, and how is it related to Krishna?
2. What is Brahman, and how is it related to Krishna?

3. What is Atman, and how is it related to Brahman?

4. What are the different paths to achieving union with God, and what does this goal have to do with reincarnation and karma?

5. What does Krishna mean by "attachment," and why must it be renounced if spiritual salvation eventually is to be achieved? What is the role of the "ego" in all this?

TERMS TO NOTE

om: A term connoting the absolute supremacy of Brahman; used throughout the Vedas in hymns of praise and prayer and as an invocation in ceremony and meditation.

gunas: The three forces of which Prakriti is composed; they are "sattwa" (the pure, refined, or essential), "rajas" (the active or passionate), and "tamas" (the dense, resistant, or sluggish), and all physical and psychical things contain various combinations of all three.

Maya: Another term for Prakriti.

deity: A divine being; a god or goddess.

yoga: From a Sanskrit word meaning "union," it refers to a discipline or systematic practice that has as its goal the experience of spiritual oneness.

VII. Knowledge and Experience

SRI KRISHNA:

Devote your whole mind to me, and practise yoga. Take me for your only refuge. I will tell you how, by doing this, you can know me in my total reality, without any shadow of doubt. I will give you all this knowledge, and direct spiritual experience, besides. When a man has that, nothing else in this world remains to be known.

Who cares to seek
For that perfect freedom?
One man, perhaps,
In many thousands.
Then tell me how many

Of those who seek freedom
Shall know the total
Truth of my being?
Perhaps one only.

My Prakriti is of eightfold composition: earth, water, fire, air, ether, mind, intellect and ego. You must understand that behind this, and distinct from it, is That which is the principle of consciousness in all beings, and the source of life in all. It sustains the universe.

Know this my Prakriti
United with me:
The womb of all beings.
I am the birth of this cosmos:
Its dissolution also.
I am He who causes:
No other beside me.
Upon me, these worlds are held
Like pearls strung on a thread.

I am the essence of the waters,
The shining of the sun and the moon:
OM in all the Vedas,
The word that is God.
It is I who resound in the ether
And am potent in man.
I am the sacred smell of the earth,
The light of the fire,
Life of all lives,
Austerity of ascetics.

Know me, eternal seed
Of everything that grows:
The intelligence of those who understand,
The vigour of the active.
In the strong, I am strength
Unhindered by lust
And the objects of craving:
I am all that a man may desire
Without transgressing
The law of his nature.

You must know that whatever belongs to the states of sattwa, rajas and tamas, proceeds from me. They are contained in me, but I am not in them. The entire world is deluded by the moods and mental states which are the expression of these three gunas. That is why the world fails to recognize me as I really am. I stand apart from them all, supreme and deathless.

> How hard to break through
> Is this, my Maya,
> Made of the gunas!
> But he who takes refuge
> Within me only
> Shall pass beyond Maya:
> He, and no other.

> The evil-doers
> Turn not toward me:
> These are deluded,
> Sunk low among mortals.
> Their judgment is lost
> In the maze of Maya,
> Until the heart
> Is human no longer:
> Changed within
> To the heart of a devil.

Among those who are purified by their good deeds, there are four kinds of men who worship me: the world-weary, the seeker for knowledge, the seeker for happiness and the man of spiritual discrimination. The man of discrimination is the highest of these. He is continually united with me. He devotes himself to me always, and to no other. For I am very dear to that man, and he is dear to me.

> Certainly, all these are noble:
> But the man of discrimination
> I see as my very Self.
> For he alone loves me
> Because I am myself:
> The last and only goal
> Of his devoted heart.

> Through many a long life
> His discrimination ripens:
> He makes me his refuge,
> Knows that Brahman is all.
> How rare are such great ones!

Men whose discrimination has been blunted by worldly desires, establish this or that ritual or cult and resort to various deities, according to the impulse of their inborn natures. But it does not matter what deity a devotee chooses to worship. If he has faith, I make his faith unwavering. Endowed with the faith I give him, he worships that deity, and gets from it everything he prays for. In reality, I alone am the giver.

But these men of small understanding only pray for what is transient and perishable. The worshippers of the devas will go to the devas. So, also, my devotees will come to me.

> Thus think the ignorant: that I, the unmanifest,
> Am become man. They do not know my nature
> That is one with Brahman, changeless,
>   superhuman.

> Veiled in my Maya, I am not shown to many.
> How shall this world, bewildered by delusion,
> Recognize me, who am not born and change
>   not?

I know all beings, Arjuna: past, present and to come. But no one knows me.

All living creatures are led astray as soon as they are born, by the delusion that this relative world is real. This delusion arises from their own desire and hatred. But the doers of good deeds, whose bad karma is exhausted, are freed from this delusion about the relative world. They hold firmly to their vows, and worship me.

Men take refuge in me, to escape from their fear of old age and death. Thus they come to know Brahman, and the entire nature of the Atman, and the creative energy which is in Brahman. Knowing me, they understand the nature of the relative world and the individual man, and of God who presides over all action. Even at the hour of death, they continue to know me thus. In that hour, their whole consciousness is made one with mine.

VIII. The Way To Eternal Brahman

ARJUNA:

Tell me, Krishna, what Brahman is. What is the Atman, and what is the creative energy of Brahman? Explain the nature of this relative world, and of the individual man.

Who is God who presides over action in this body, and how does He dwell here? How are you revealed at the hour of death to those whose consciousness is united with you?

SRI KRISHNA:

Brahman is that which is immutable, and independent of any cause but Itself. When we consider Brahman as lodged within the individual being, we call Him the Atman. The creative energy of Brahman is that which causes all existences to come into being.

The nature of the relative world is mutability. The nature of the individual man is his consciousness of ego. I alone am God who presides over action, here in this body.

At the hour of death, when a man leaves his body, he must depart with his consciousness absorbed in me. Then he will be united with me. Be certain of that. Whatever a man remembers at the last, when he is leaving the body, will be realized by him in the hereafter; because that will be what his mind has most constantly dwelt on, during this life.

Therefore you must remember me at all times, and do your duty. If your mind and heart are set upon me constantly, you will come to me. Never doubt this.

Make a habit of practising meditation, and do not let your mind be distracted. In this way you will come finally to the Lord, who is the light-giver, the highest of the high.

> He is all-knowing God, lord of the emperors,
> Ageless, subtler far than mind's inmost subtlety,
> Universal sustainer,
> Shining sunlike, self-luminous.
>
> What fashion His form has, who shall conceive
>   of it?
> He dwells beyond delusion, the dark of Maya.
> On Him let man meditate
> Always, for then at the last hour
> Of going hence from his body he will be strong
> In the strength of this yoga, faithfully followed:
> The mind is firm, and the heart
> So full, it hardly holds its love.
>
> Thus he will take his leave: and now, with the
>   life-force
> Indrawn utterly, held fast between the
>   eyebrows,
> He goes forth to find his Lord,
> That light-giver, who is greatest.

Now I will tell you briefly about the nature of Him who is called the deathless by those seers who truly understand the Vedas. Devotees enter into Him when the bonds of their desire are broken. To reach this goal, they practise control of the passions.

When a man leaves his body and departs,[1] he must close all the doors of the senses. Let him hold the mind firmly within the shrine of the heart, and fix the life-force between the eyebrows. Then let him take refuge in steady concentration, uttering the sacred syllable OM and meditating upon me. Such a man reaches the highest goal. When a yogi has meditated upon me unceasingly for many years, with an undistracted mind, I am easy of access to him, because he is always absorbed in me.

Great souls who find me have found the highest perfection. They are no longer reborn into this condition of transience and pain.

All the worlds, and even the heavenly realm of Brahma,[2] are subject to the laws of rebirth. But, for the man who comes to me, there is no returning.

> There is day, also, and night in the universe:
> The wise know this, declaring the day of
>   Brahma
> A thousand ages in span
> And the night a thousand ages.
>
> Day dawns, and all those lives that lay hidden
>   asleep
> Come forth and show themselves, mortally
>   manifest:
> Night falls, and all are dissolved
> Into the sleeping germ of life.
>
> Thus they are seen, O Prince, and appear
>   unceasingly,
> Dissolving with the dark, and with day
>   returning

---

1. According to yoga technique, the yogi must employ a special method of leaving the body at death. First, the vital force is drawn up the sushumna, the central spinal passage, and gathered in the brain, 'between the eyebrows.' The yogi then leaves the body through an aperture in the centre of the brain, called the sahashrara.

2. Brahma (not to be confused with Brahman) is God in the aspect of creator—one of the Hindu Trinity, with Vishnu, the preserver, and Shiva, the dissolver.

According to Hindu mythology, the worlds are variously classified as three, seven or fourteen. The Brahma-Loka (realm of Brahma) is said to be the highest.

Back to the new birth, new death:
All helpless. They do what they must.

But behind the manifest and the unmanifest, there is another Existence, which is eternal and changeless. This is not dissolved in the general cosmic dissolution. It has been called the unmanifest, the imperishable. To reach it is said to be the greatest of all achievements. It is my highest state of being. Those who reach It are not reborn. That highest state of being can only be achieved through devotion to Him in whom all creatures exist, and by whom this universe is pervaded.

I show you two paths.[3]
Let a yogi choose either
When he leaves this body:
The path that leads back to birth,
The path of no return.

There is the path of light,
Of fire and day,
The path of the moon's bright fortnight
And the six months' journey
Of the sun to the north:
The knower of Brahman
Who takes this path
Goes to Brahman:
He does not return.

There is the path of night and smoke,
The path of the moon's dark fortnight
And the six months' journey
Of the sun to the south:
The yogi who takes this path
Will reach the lunar light:*
This path leads back
To human birth, at last.

These two paths, the bright and the dark, may be said to have existed in this world of change from a time without any beginning. By the one, a man goes to the place of no return. By the other, he comes back

to human birth. No yogi who knows these two paths is ever misled. Therefore, Arjuna, you must be steadfast in yoga, always.

The scriptures declare that merit can be acquired by studying the Vedas, performing ritualistic sacrifices, practising austerities and giving alms. But the yogi who has understood this teaching of mine will gain more than any who do these things. He will reach that universal source, which is the uttermost abode of God. . . .

XII. The Yoga of Devotion

ARJUNA:

Some worship you with steadfast love. Others worship God the unmanifest and changeless. Which kind of devotee has the greater understanding of yoga?

SRI KRISHNA:

Those whose minds are fixed on me in steadfast love, worshipping me with absolute faith. I consider them to have the greater understanding of yoga.

As for those others, the devotees of God the unmanifest, indefinable and changeless, they worship that which is omnipresent, constant, eternal, beyond thought's compass, never to be moved. They hold all the senses in check. They are tranquil-minded, and devoted to the welfare of humanity. They see the Atman in every creature. They also will certainly come to me.

But the devotees of the unmanifest have a harder task, because the unmanifest is very difficult for embodied souls to realize.

Quickly I come
To those who offer me
Every action,
Worship me only,
Their dearest delight,
With devotion undaunted.

Because they love me
These are my bondsmen
And I shall save them
From mortal sorrow
And all the waves
Of Life's deathly ocean.

---

3. The 'path of no return' is called in the Upanishads the Deva Yana, 'the path of the bright ones,' who are liberated from rebirth. The path that leads back to birth is the Pitri Yana, the 'path of the fathers,' who reach the 'lunar light' (a paradise subject to the laws of time) and must ultimately be reborn.
* Fire, light, smoke, night, etc., probably represent stages of the soul's experience after death. Thus, light may symbolize knowledge; and smoke, ignorance.

Be absorbed in me,
Lodge your mind in me:
Thus you shall dwell in me,
Do not doubt it,
Here and hereafter.

If you cannot become absorbed in me, then try to reach me by repeated concentration. If you lack the strength to concentrate, then devote yourself to works which will please me. For, by working for my sake only, you will achieve perfection. If you cannot even do this, then surrender yourself to me altogether. Control the lusts of your heart, and renounce the fruits of every action.

Concentration which is practised with discernment is certainly better than the mechanical repetition of a ritual or a prayer. Absorption in God—to live with Him and be one with Him always—is even better than concentration. But renunciation brings instant peace to the spirit.

A man should not hate any living creature. Let him be friendly and compassionate to all. He must free himself from the delusion of 'I' and 'mine.' He must accept pleasure and pain with equal tranquillity. He must be forgiving, ever-contented, self-controlled, united constantly with me in his meditation. His resolve must be unshakable. He must be dedicated to me in intellect and in mind. Such a devotee is dear to me.

He neither molests his fellow men, nor allows himself to become disturbed by the world. He is no longer swayed by joy and envy, anxiety and fear. Therefore he is dear to me.

He is pure, and independent of the body's desire. He is able to deal with the unexpected: prepared for everything, unperturbed by anything. He is neither vain nor anxious about the results of his actions. Such a devotee is dear to me.

He does not desire or rejoice in what is pleasant. He does not dread what is unpleasant, or grieve over it. He remains unmoved by good or evil fortune. Such a devotee is dear to me.

His attitude is the same toward friend and foe. He is indifferent to honour and insult, heat and cold, pleasure and pain. He is free from attachment. He values praise and blame equally. He can control his speech. He is content with whatever he gets. His home

is everywhere and nowhere. His mind is fixed upon me, and his heart is full of devotion. He is dear to me.

This true wisdom I have taught will lead you to immortality. The faithful practise it with devotion, taking me for their highest aim. To me they surrender heart and mind. They are exceedingly dear to me.

XIII. The Field and Its Knower

ARJUNA:

And now, Krishna, I wish to learn about Prakriti and Brahman, the Field and the Knower of the Field. What is knowledge? What is it that has to be known?

SRI KRISHNA:

This body is called the Field, because a man sows seeds of action in it, and reaps their fruits. Wise men say that the Knower of the Field is he who watches what takes place within this body.

Recognize me as the Knower of the Field in every body. I regard discrimination between Field and Knower as the highest kind of knowledge.

Now listen, and I will tell you briefly what the Field is; its nature, modifications and origin. I will tell you also who the Knower is, and what are his powers.

The sages have expressed these truths variously, in many hymns, and in aphorisms on the nature of Brahman, subtly reasoned and convincing in their arguments.

Briefly I name them:
First, Prakriti
Which is the cosmos
In cause unseen
And visible feature;
Intellect, ego;
Earth, water and ether,
Air and fire;
Man's ten organs
Of knowing and doing,
Man's mind also;
The five sense-objects—
Sound in its essence,
Essence of aspect,
Essence of odour,
Of touch and of tasting;

Hate and desire,
And pain and pleasure;
Consciousness, lastly,
And resolution;
These, with their sum
Which is blent in the body:
These make the Field
With its limits and changes.

Therefore I tell you:
Be humble, be harmless,
Have no pretension,
Be upright, forbearing,
Serve your teacher
In true obedience,
Keeping the mind
And the body in cleanness,
Tranquil, steadfast,
Master of ego,
Standing apart
From the things of the senses,
Free from self;
Aware of the weakness
In mortal nature,
Its bondage to birth,
Age, suffering, dying;
To nothing be slave,
Nor desire possession
Of man-child or wife,
Of home or of household;
Calmly encounter
The painful, the pleasant;
Adore me only
With heart undistracted;
Turn all your thought
Toward solitude, spurning
The noise of the crowd,
Its fruitless commotion;
Strive without ceasing
To know the Atman,
Seek this knowledge
And comprehend clearly
Why you should seek it:
Such, it is said,
Are the roots of true wisdom:
Ignorance, merely,
Is all that denies them.

Now I shall describe That which has to be known, in order that its knower may gain immortality. That Brahman is beginningless, transcendent, eternal. He is said to be equally beyond what is, and what is not.

Everywhere are His hands, eyes, feet; His heads and
His faces:
This whole world is His ear; He exists, encompass-
ing all things;
Doing the tasks of each sense, yet Himself devoid of
the senses:
Standing apart, He sustains: He is free from the
gunas but feels them.
He is within and without: He lives in the live and
the lifeless:
Subtle beyond mind's grasp; so near us, so utterly
distant:
Undivided, He seems to divide into objects and
creatures;
Sending creation forth from Himself, He upholds
and withdraws it;
Light of all lights, He abides beyond our ignorant
darkness;
Knowledge, the one thing real we may study or
know, the heart's dweller.

Now I have told you briefly what the Field is, what knowledge is, and what is that one Reality which must be known. When my devotee knows these things, he becomes fit to reach union with me.

You must understand that both Prakriti and Brahman are without beginning. All evolution and all the gunas proceed from Prakriti. From Prakriti the evolution of body and senses is said to originate. The sense of individuality in us is said to cause our experience of pleasure and pain. The individual self, which is Brahman mistakenly identified with Prakriti, experiences the gunas which proceed from Prakriti. It is born of pure or impure parents, according to that kind of guna to which it is most attached.

The supreme Brahman in this body is also known as the Witness. It makes all our actions possible, and, as it were, sanctions them, experiencing all our experiences. It is the infinite Being, the supreme Atman. He who has experienced Brahman directly and known it to be other than Prakriti and the gunas, will not be reborn, no matter how he has lived his life.

Some, whose hearts are purified, realize the Atman within themselves through contemplation. Some realize the Atman philosophically, by meditating upon its independence of Prakriti. Others realize it by following the yoga of right action. Others, who do not know these paths, worship God as their teachers have taught them. If these faithfully practise what they have learned, they also will pass beyond death's power.

Know this, O Prince:
Of things created
All are come forth
From the seeming union
Of Field and Knower,
Prakriti with Brahman.

Who sees his Lord
Within every creature,
Deathlessly dwelling
Amidst the mortal:
That man sees truly.

Thus ever aware
Of the Omnipresent
Always about him,
He offers no outrage
To his own Atman,
Hides the face of God
Beneath ego no longer:
Therefore he reaches
That bliss which is highest.

Who sees all action
Ever performed
Alone by Prakriti,
That man sees truly:
The Atman is actless.
Who sees the separate
Lives of all creatures
United in Brahman
Brought forth from Brahman,
Himself finds Brahman.

Not subject to change
Is the infinite Atman,

Without beginning,
Beyond the gunas:
Therefore, O Prince,
Though It dwells in the body,
It acts not, nor feels
The fruits of our action.

For, like the ether,
Pervading all things,
Too subtle for taint,
This Atman also
Inhabits all bodies
But never is tainted.

By the single sun
This whole world is illumined:
By its one Knower
The Field is illumined.

Who thus perceives
With the eye of wisdom
In what manner the Field
Is distinct from its Knower,
How men are made free
From the toils of Prakriti:
His aim is accomplished,
He enters the Highest.

DISCUSSION QUESTIONS

1. Krishna shows Arjuna that he is the incarnation (in Hindu thought, one of many throughout the millenia) of the Supreme Being ("the Supreme Godhead," Brahman, or Vishnu). How is this version of the divine becoming human similar to and different from the version at the heart of Christian doctrine?
2. How far can rational analysis take us in understanding and evaluating the plausibility of the mystical claims made here?
3. Do you agree with the goal of renouncing all personal attachment to the things of this world? Why or why not?
4. Is the "manifest world" ultimately a delusion? Why or why not?

34. Martin Buber (1878–1965)
God as the Eternal You

Martin Buber was born in Vienna and studied philosophy and art history at the universities of Vienna, Berlin, Leipzig, and Zurich. By the time he was appointed professor of Jewish religion and ethics at Frankfurt-am-Main University in 1924, he had not only been active in the Zionist movement for many years but also was well known in Europe for his philosophical and journalistic writing. In 1933 Buber left his professorship, and in 1938 he emigrated to Palestine, as did many other German Jews who were fleeing Nazi persecution. In Jerusalem he served as professor of sociology of religion at Hebrew University from 1938 to 1951 and was one of the leaders of the Yihud movement, which aimed at the improvement of Arab-Jewish relations and the eventual creation of a binational state. He continued to write on a wide range of religious and cultural topics, remaining politically active as well for most of the rest of his life. He died in Jerusalem.

The following selections are from Buber's most widely read work, *I and Thou,* published in Berlin in 1922. It was this book more than any of his other writings that established his international reputation as a religious existentialist. It is usually interpreted as exhibiting the influence of Hasidism—a type of Jewish mysticism that emerged as an important religious force, especially in Eastern Europe during the eighteenth and nineteenth centuries. The original German title is *Ich und Du,* and in the translation by Walter Kaufmann printed here, "*Du*" is more appropriately rendered in the text itself (though not in the title) as "You" rather than the "Thou" found in earlier translations, given the latter's more archaic, formal, and distant flavor for a contemporary English-language audience. This issue of how best to translate a single German term into English may seem minor, but in fact, in this case it is very important in light of Buber's understanding of the "I-You" relation and its distinction from all "I-It" relations. "*Du*" implies an intimacy or informality (as opposed to the formal, polite "*Sie*"), which Buber clearly emphasizes in his characterization not only of authentic human interaction but also of a truly meaningful encounter with God.

QUESTIONS FOR CRITICAL READING

1. According to Buber, what are the two basic words of human life, and how are they different from each other?
2. How does Buber characterize the "eternal You," and how is it related to all other "Yous"?
3. What does Buber mean by arguing that one cannot truly *seek* God, and what does this have to do with "revelation"?
4. How does Buber describe the three spheres making up the "world of relation"?

TERMS TO NOTE

mysterium tremendum: A Latin phrase translatable as "awesome mystery."
noetic: In this context, having to do with intellectual understanding.

The world is twofold for man in accordance with his twofold attitude.

The attitude of man is twofold in accordance with the two basic words he can speak.

The basic words are not single words but word pairs.

One basic word is the word pair I-You.

The other basic word is the word pair I-It; but this basic word is not changed when He or She takes the place of It.

Thus the I of man is also twofold.

For the I of the basic word I-You is different from that in the basic word I-It.

*

Basic words do not state something that might exist outside them; by being spoken they establish a mode of existence.

Basic words are spoken with one's being.

When one says You, the I of the word pair I-You is said, too.

When one says It, the I of the word pair I-It is said, too.

The basic word I-You can only be spoken with one's whole being.

The basic word I-It can never be spoken with one's whole being.

*

There is no I as such but only the I of the basic word I-You and the I of the basic word I-It.

When a man says I, he means one or the other. The I he means is present when he says I. And when he says You or It, the I of one or the other basic word is also present.

Being I and saying I are the same. Saying I and saying one of the two basic words are the same.

Whoever speaks one of the basic words enters into the word and stands in it.

*

The life of a human being does not exist merely in the sphere of goal-directed verbs. It does not consist merely of activities that have something for their object.

I perceive something. I feel something. I imagine something. I want something. I sense something. I think something. The life of a human being does not consist merely of all this and its like.

All this and its like is the basis of the realm of It.

But the realm of You has another basis.

Whoever says You does not have something for his object. For wherever there is something there is also another something; every It borders on other Its; It is only by virtue of bordering on others. But where You is said there is no something. You has no borders.

Whoever says You does not have something; he has nothing. But he stands in relation.

*

We are told that man experiences his world. What does this mean?

Man goes over the surfaces of things and experiences them. He brings back from them some knowledge of their condition—an experience. He experiences what there is to things.

But it is not experiences alone that bring the world to man.

For what they bring to him is only a world that consists of It and It and It, of He and He and She and She and It.

I experience something.

All this is not changed by adding "inner" experiences to the "external" ones, in line with the non-eternal distinction that is born of mankind's craving to take the edge off the mystery of death. Inner things like external things, things among things!

I experience something.

And all this is not changed by adding "mysterious" experiences to "manifest" ones, self-confident in the wisdom that recognizes a secret compartment in things, reserved for the initiated, and holds the key. O mysteriousness without mystery, O piling up of information! It, it, it!

*

Those who experience do not participate in the world. For the experience is "in them" and not between them and the world.

The world does not participate in experience. It allows itself to be experienced, but it is not concerned, for it contributes nothing, and nothing happens to it.

*

The world as experience belongs to the basic word I-It.

The basic word I-You establishes the world of relation.

. . .

Extended, the lines of relationships intersect in the eternal You.

Every single You is a glimpse of that. Through every single You the basic word addresses the eternal You. The mediatorship of the You of all beings accounts for the fullness of our relationships to them—and for the lack of fulfillment. The innate You is actualized each time without ever being perfected. It attains perfection solely in the immediate relationship to the You that in accordance with its nature cannot become an It.

Men have addressed their eternal You by many names. When they sang of what they had thus named, they still meant You: the first myths were hymns of praise. Then the names entered into the It-language; men felt impelled more and more to think of and to talk about their eternal You as an It. But all names of God remain hallowed—because they have been used not only to speak *of* God but also to speak *to* him.

Some would deny any legitimate use of the word God because it has been misused so much. Certainly it is the most burdened of all human words. Precisely for that reason it is the most imperishable and unavoidable. And how much weight has all erroneous talk about God's nature and works (although there never has been nor can be any such talk that is not erroneous) compared with the one truth that all men who have addressed God really meant him? For whoever pronounces the word God and really means You, addresses, no matter what his delusion, the true You of his life that cannot be restricted by any other and to whom he stands in a relationship that includes all others.

But whoever abhors the name and fancies that he is godless—when he addresses with his whole devoted being the You of his life that cannot be restricted by any other, he addresses God. . . .

Every actual relationship to another being in the world is exclusive. Its You is freed and steps forth to confront us in its uniqueness. It fills the firmament—not as if there were nothing else, but everything else lives in *its* light. As long as the presence of the relationship endures, this world-wideness cannot be infringed. But as soon as a You becomes an It, the world-wideness of the relationship appears as an injustice against the world, and its exclusiveness as an exclusion of the universe.

In the relation to God, unconditional exclusiveness and unconditional inclusiveness are one. For those who enter into the absolute relationship, nothing particular retains any importance—neither things nor beings, neither earth nor heaven—but everything is included in the relationship. For entering into the pure relationship does not involve ignoring everything but seeing everything in the You, not renouncing the world but placing it upon its proper ground. Looking away from the world is no help toward God; staring at the world is no help either; but whoever beholds the world in him stands in his presence. "World here, God there"—that is It-talk; and "God in the world"—that, too, is It-talk; but leaving out nothing, leaving nothing behind, to comprehend all—all the world—in com-

prehending the You, giving the world its due and truth, to have nothing besides God but to grasp everything in him, that is the perfect relationship.

One does not find God if one remains in the world; one does not find God if one leaves the world. Whoever goes forth to his You with his whole being and carries to it all the being of the world, finds him whom one cannot seek.

Of course, God is "the wholly other"; but he is also the wholly same: the wholly present. Of course, he is the *mysterium tremendum* that appears and overwhelms; but he is also the mystery of the obvious that is closer to me than my own I.

When you fathom the life of things and of conditionality, you reach the indissoluble; when you dispute the life of things and of conditionality, you wind up before the nothing; when you consecrate life you encounter the living God.

*

The You-sense of the man who in his relationships to all individual Yous experiences the disappointment of the change into It, aspires beyond all of them and yet not all the way toward his eternal You. Not the way one seeks something: in truth, there is no God-seeking because there is nothing where one could not find him. How foolish and hopeless must one be to leave one's way of life to seek God: even if one gained all the wisdom of solitude and all the power of concentration, one would miss him. It is rather as if a man went his way and merely wished that it might be *the* way; his aspiration finds expression in the strength of his wish. Every encounter is a way station that grants him a view of fulfillment; in each he thus fails to share, and yet also does share, in the one because he is ready. Ready, not seeking, he goes his way; this gives him the serenity toward all things and the touch that helps them. But once he has found, his heart does not turn away from them although he now encounters everything in the one. He blesses all the cells that have sheltered him as well as all those where he will still put up. For this finding is not an end of the way but only its eternal center.

It is a finding without seeking; a discovery of what is most original and the origin. The You-sense that cannot be satiated until it finds the infinite You sensed its presence from the beginning; this presence merely had to become wholly actual for it out of the actuality of the consecrated life of the world.

It is not as if God could be inferred from anything—say, from nature as its cause, or from history as its helmsman, or perhaps from the subject as the self that thinks itself through it. It is not as if something else were "given" and this were then deduced from it. This is what confronts us immediately and first and always, and legitimately it can only be addressed, not asserted.

. . .

Every actual relationship in the world is exclusive; the other breaks into it to avenge its exclusion. Solely in the relation to God are unconditional exclusiveness and unconditional inclusiveness one in which the universe is comprehended.

Every actual relationship in the world rests upon individuation: that is its delight, for only thus is mutual recognition of those who are different granted—and that is its boundary, for thus is perfect recognition and being recognized denied. But in the perfect relationship my You embraces my self without being it; my limited recognition is merged into a boundless being-recognized.

Every actual relationship in the world alternates between actuality and latency; every individual You must disappear into the chrysalis of the It in order to grow wings again. In the pure relationship, however, latency is merely actuality drawing a deep breath during which the You remains present. The eternal You is You by its very nature; only *our* nature forces us to draw it into the It-world and It-speech.

*

The It-world coheres in space and time.

The You-world does not cohere in either.

It coheres in the center in which the extended lines of relationships intersect: in the eternal You.

In the great privilege of the pure relationship the privileges of the It-world are annulled. By virtue of it the You-world is continuous: the isolated moments of relationships join for a world life of association. By virtue of it the You-world has the power to give form: the spirit can permeate the It-world and change it. By virtue of it we are not abandoned to the alienation of the world and the deactualization of the I, nor are we overpowered by phantoms. Return signifies the recognition of the center, turning back to it again. In this

essential deed man's buried power to relate is resurrected, the wave of all relational spheres surges up in a living flood and renews our world.

Perhaps not only ours. Dimly we apprehend this double movement—that turning away from the primal ground by virtue of which the universe preserves itself in its becoming, and that turning toward the primal ground by virtue of which the universe redeems itself in being—as the metacosmic primal form of duality that inheres in the world as a whole in its relation to that which is not world, and whose human form is the duality of attitudes, of basic words, and of the two aspects of the world. Both movements are unfolded fatefully in time and enclosed, as by grace, in the timeless creation that, incomprehensibly, is at once release and preservation, at once bond and liberation. Our knowledge of duality is reduced to silence by the paradox of the primal mystery.

*

Three are the spheres in which the world of relation is built.

The first: life with nature, where the relation sticks to the threshold of language.

The second: life with men, where it enters language.

The third: life with spiritual beings, where it lacks but creates language.

In every sphere, in every relational act, through everything that becomes present to us, we gaze toward the train of the eternal You; in each we perceive a breath of it; in every You we address the eternal You, in every sphere according to its manner. All spheres are included in it, while it is included in none.

Through all of them shines the one presence.

But we can take each out of the presence.

Out of life with nature we can take the "physical" world, that of consistency; out of life with men, the "psychical" world, that of affectability; out of life with spiritual beings, the "noetic" world, that of validity. Now they have been deprived of their transparency and thus of sense; each has become usable and murky, and remains murky even if we endow it with shining names: cosmos, eros, logos. For in truth there is a cosmos for man only when the universe becomes a home for him with a holy hearth where he sacrifices; and there is eros for him only when beings become for him images of the eternal, and community with them becomes revelation; and there is logos for him only when he addresses the mystery with works and service of the spirit.

The demanding silence of forms, the loving speech of human beings, the eloquent muteness of creatures—all of these are gateways into the presence of the world.

But when the perfect encounter is to occur, the gates are unified into the one gate of actual life, and you no longer know through which one you have entered.

. . .

What is it that is eternal: the primal phenomenon, present in the here and now, of what we call revelation? It is man's emerging from the moment of the supreme encounter, being no longer the same as he was when entering into it. The moment of encounter is not a "living experience" that stirs in the receptive soul and blissfully rounds itself out: something happens to man. At times it is like feeling a breath and at times like a wrestling match; no matter: something happens. The man who steps out of the essential act of pure relation has something More in his being, something new has grown there of which he did not know before and for whose origin he lacks any suitable words. Wherever the scientific world orientation in its legitimate desire for a causal chain without gaps may place the origin of what is new here: for us, being concerned with the actual contemplation of the actual, no subconscious and no other psychic apparatus will do. Actually, we receive what we did not have before, in such a manner that we know: it has been given to us. In the language of the Bible: "Those who wait for God will receive strength in exchange." In the language of Nietzsche who is still faithful to actuality in his report: "One accepts, one does not ask who gives."

Man receives, and what he receives is not a "content" but a presence, a presence as strength. This presence and strength includes three elements that are not separate but may nevertheless be contemplated as three. First, the whole abundance of actual reciprocity, of being admitted, of being associated while one is altogether unable to indicate what that is like with which one is associated, nor does association make life any easier for us—it makes life heavier but heavy with meaning. And this is second: the inexpressible confirmation of meaning. It is guaranteed. Nothing, nothing can henceforth be meaningless. The question about the meaning of life has vanished. But if it were still

there, it would not require an answer. You do not know how to point to or define the meaning, you lack any formula or image for it, and yet it is more certain for you than the sensations of your senses. What could it intend with us, what does it desire from us, being revealed and surreptitious? It does not wish to be interpreted by us—for that we lack the ability—only to be done by us. This comes third: it is not the meaning of "another life" but that of this our life, not that of a "beyond" but of this our world, and it wants to be demonstrated by us in this life and this world. The meaning can be received but not experienced; it cannot be experienced, but it can be done; and this is what it intends with us. The guarantee does not wish to remain shut up within me, it wants to be born into the world by me. But even as the meaning itself cannot be transferred or expressed as a universally valid and generally acceptable piece of knowledge, putting it to the proof in action cannot be handed on as a valid ought; it is not prescribed, not inscribed on a table that could be put up over everybody's head. The meaning we receive can be put to the proof in action only by each person in the uniqueness of his being and in the uniqueness of his life. No prescription can lead us to the encounter, and none leads from it. Only the acceptance of the presence is required to come to it or, in a new sense, to go from it. As we have nothing but a You on our lips when we enter the encounter, it is with this on our lips that we are released from it into the world.

That before which we live, that in which we live, that out of which and into which we live, the mystery—has remained what it was. It has become present for us, and through its presence it has made itself known to us as salvation; we have "known" it, but we have no knowledge of it that might diminish or extenuate its mysteriousness. We have come close to God, but no closer to an unriddling, unveiling of being. We have felt salvation but no "solution." We cannot go to others with what we have received, saying: This is what needs to be known, this is what needs to be done. We can only go and put to the proof in action. And even this is not what we "ought to" do: rather we can—we cannot do otherwise.

This is the eternal revelation which is present in the here and now. I neither know of nor believe in any revelation that is not the same in its primal phenomenon. I do not believe in God's naming himself or in

God's defining himself before man. The word of revelation is: I am there as whoever I am there. That which reveals is that which reveals. That which has being is there, nothing more. The eternal source of strength flows, the eternal touch is waiting, the eternal voice sounds, nothing more.

DISCUSSION QUESTIONS

1. Do you agree with Buber's account of the differences between the "It-world" and the "You-world"? Why or why not?

2. What are the similarities and differences between Buber's characterization of God and that of the religious tradition with which you are most familiar?

3. Do you agree with Buber's explanation of the role of language in spiritual experience, thought, and/or "encounters"? Why or why not?

4. How would you compare the account of a Supreme Being offered in the selections from the *Bhagavad-Gītā* with Buber's account? Which do you find more attractive and/or convincing?

35. Anselm (1033–1109)
The Ontological Argument for God

Saint Anselm was born and grew up in Italy. He became a Benedictine monk and eventually served as archbishop of Canterbury in England. He wrote extensively during his career and today is still considered an important representative of Christian philosophical thought in the European Middle Ages. He became known especially for his efforts at what traditionally has been called natural theology (or natural religion)—that is, the justification of religious beliefs by reason and evidence, means that are natural to any intellectually functional human being. This approach contrasts with what has been called revealed theology (or revealed religion)—the justification of religious belief by nonrational or subjective means, for example, an appeal to faith, religious authority, or personal experience unprovable to others.

This selection from Anselm's book *Proslogion* is his most famous exercise in natural theology, a so-called ontological argument for the existence of the God of Christianity. Many other religious philosophers in the Western tradition also have put forth versions of the ontological argument for God, and as a type of rational argument its inferential pattern is generally the same in all of them. They start with a characterization of the nature or being of God, in effect, a partial definition of God, and then reason deductively to the conclusion that a being so defined must necessarily exist. Actually, Anselm gives a couple of related deductive arguments based on claims about God's nature, and in evaluating them, you should keep in mind the criteria of both validity and soundness.

QUESTIONS FOR CRITICAL READING

1. What is Anselm's first argument showing that God must exist, and on what conception of God is he relying?

2. Based on the same conception, what is Anselm's second argument for God's existence?

3. What is Anselm's point in distinguishing between two ways of conceiving of something?

Chapter II.

Truly there is a God, although the fool hath said in his heart, There is no God.

And so, Lord, do thou, who dost give understanding to faith, give me, so far as thou knowest it to be profitable, to understand that thou art as we believe; and that thou art that which we believe. And, indeed, we believe that thou art a being than which nothing greater can be conceived. Or is there no such nature, since the fool hath said in his heart, there is no God? (Psalms xiv. 1). But, at any rate, this very fool, when he hears of this being of which I speak—a being than which nothing greater can be conceived—understands what he hears, and what he understands is in his understanding; although he does not understand it to exist.

For, it is one thing for an object to be in the understanding, and another to understand that the object exists. When a painter first conceives of what he will afterwards perform, he has it in his understanding, but he does not yet understand it to be, because he has not yet performed it. But after he has made the painting, he both has it in his understanding and he understands that it exists, because he has made it.

Hence, even the fool is convinced that something exists in the understanding, at least, than which nothing greater can be conceived. For, when he hears of this, he understands it. And whatever is understood, exists in the understanding. And assuredly that, than which nothing greater can be conceived, cannot exist in the understanding alone. For, suppose it exists in the understanding alone: then it can be conceived to exist in reality; which is greater.

Therefore, if that, than which nothing greater can be conceived, exists in the understanding alone, the very being, than which nothing greater can be conceived, is one, than which a greater can be conceived. But obviously this is impossible. Hence, there is no doubt that there exists a being, than which nothing greater can be conceived, and it exists both in the understanding and in reality.

Chapter III.

God cannot be conceived not to exist.—God is that, than which nothing greater can be conceived.—That which can be conceived not to exist is not God.

And it assuredly exists so truly, that it cannot be conceived not to exist. For, it is possible to conceive of a being which cannot be conceived not to exist; and this is greater than one which can be conceived not to exist. Hence, if that, than which nothing greater can be conceived, can be conceived not to exist, it is not that, than which nothing greater can be conceived. But this is an irreconcilable contradiction. There is, then, so truly a being than which nothing greater can be conceived to exist, that it cannot even be conceived not to exist; and this being thou art, O Lord, our God.

So truly, therefore, dost thou exist, O Lord, my God, that thou canst not be conceived not to exist; and rightly. For, if a mind could conceive of a being

better than thee, the creature would rise above the Creator; and this is most absurd. And, indeed, whatever else there is, except thee alone, can be conceived not to exist. To thee alone, therefore, it belongs to exist more truly than all other beings, and hence in a higher degree than all others. For, whatever else exists does not exist so truly, and hence in a less degree it belongs to it to exist. Why, then, has the fool said in his heart, there is no God (Psalms xiv. 1), since it is so evident, to a rational mind, that thou dost exist in the highest degree of all? Why, except that he is dull and a fool?

Chapter IV.

How the fool has said in his heart what cannot be conceived.—A thing may be conceived in two ways: (1) when the word signifying it is conceived; (2) when the thing itself is understood. As far as the word goes, God can be conceived not to exist; in reality he cannot.

But how has the fool said in his heart what he could not conceive; or how is it that he could not conceive what he said in his heart? since it is the same to say in the heart, and to conceive.

But, if really, nay, since really, he both conceived, because he said in his heart; and did not say in his heart, because he could not conceive; there is more than one way in which a thing is said in the heart or conceived. For, in one sense, an object is conceived, when the word signifying it is conceived; and in another, when the very entity, which the object is, is understood.

In the former sense, then, God can be conceived not to exist; but in the latter, not at all. For no one who understands what fire and water are can conceive fire to be water, in accordance with the nature of the facts themselves, although this is possible according to the words. So, then, no one who understands what God is can conceive that God does not exist; although he says these words in his heart, either without any, or with some foreign, signification. For, God is that than which a greater cannot be conceived. And he who thoroughly understands this, assuredly understands that this being so truly exists, that not even in concept can it be non-existent. Therefore, he who understands that God so exists, cannot conceive that he does not exist.

I thank thee, gracious Lord, I thank thee; because what I formerly believed by thy bounty, I now so understand by thine illumination, that if I were unwilling to believe that thou dost exist, I should not be able not to understand this to be true.

DISCUSSION QUESTIONS

1. How would you defend or refute Anselm's arguments for God's existence?

2. Are Anselm's arguments more a matter of what we can logically say about God, or about whether there really is such a being? Explain.

3. Why do you think it might have been important to give a rational proof of God's existence in eleventh- and twelfth-century Christianized England?

4. If someone didn't already believe there was a Supreme Being, would rational arguments alone be sufficient to change his or her mind? Why or why not?

36. Thomas Aquinas (1225–1274)
The Cosmological Argument for God

Saint Thomas Aquinas was an Italian Christian philosopher who belonged to the Dominican order and spent the majority of his career as a writer and teacher in Paris. He is generally considered the most influential of all medieval European thinkers, and even today "Thomism" is still alive as a major school of thought in the Roman Catholic tradition. More than anyone else, he revived the interest in studying Aristotle among philosophers and theologians in medieval Europe, and his own philosophical system was in many ways a Christianized Aristotelianism. He also offered an influential view on the proper relationship between philosophy and theology, historically a major problem for Christian intellectuals who accepted the common view of faith as being both spiritually essential and essentially nonrational. For Aquinas, philosophy should proceed solely within the limits of human reason, taking rational inquiry as far as it can go in the discovery of truth. Theology, on the other hand, starts out assuming faith-based belief is informed by divine revelation and then reasons to the implications of this "revealed truth" for human life. As such, philosophy and theology, reason and faith, are compatible and complementary means of establishing beliefs, in his account.

In this brief selection from *Summa Theologica,* his best-known work in Christian philosophy, Aquinas shows on rational grounds why God must exist. His approach usually is called a cosmological argument, or first cause argument, for God's existence, and though another

exercise in natural theology, it is quite different from that of Anselm. Cosmological arguments, which have many versions in the Western tradition, generally have the following structure: They start with the observable existence of some phenomenon in the world and then reason to the conclusion that the only way to explain adequately that thing's existence is to assert that God is its original cause. This then is an experience-based (or *a posteriori*) argument rather than an experience-independent (or *a priori*) argument deriving solely from the logical analysis of a concept.

QUESTIONS FOR CRITICAL READING

1. What are the five distinct arguments for the existence of God offered by Aquinas?

2. What are the two objections to God's existence, and how does Aquinas attempt to refute both of them?

3. What conception of God's nature is Aquinas working with in his arguments?

TERMS TO NOTE

efficient cause: An archaic technical term (traceable to Aristotle) for our everyday notion of causality; that which acts on something else and brings about an effect.

possibility: Refers to the capability of being otherwise.

omnipotence: The attribute of being all powerful.

Third Article

Whether God Exists?

We proceed thus to the Third Article:—

Objection 1. It seems that God does not exist; because if one of two contraries be infinite, the other would be altogether destroyed. But the name *God* means that He is infinite goodness. If, therefore, God existed, there would be no evil discoverable; but there is evil in the world. Therefore God does not exist.

Obj. 2. Further, it is superfluous to suppose that what can be accounted for by a few principles has been produced by many. But it seems that everything we see in the world can be accounted for by other principles, supposing God did not exist. For all natural things can be reduced to one principle, which is nature; and all voluntary things can be reduced to one principle, which is human reason, or will. Therefore there is no need to suppose God's existence.

On the contrary, It is said in the person of God: *I am Who am* (Exod. iii, 14).

I answer that, The existence of God can be proved in five ways.

The first and more manifest way is the argument from motion. It is certain, and evident to our senses, that in the world some things are in motion. Now whatever is moved is moved by another, for nothing can be moved except it is in potentiality to that towards which it is moved; whereas a thing moves inasmuch as it is in act. For motion is nothing else than the reduction of something from potentiality to actuality. But nothing can be reduced from potentiality to actuality, except by something in a state of actuality. Thus that which is actually hot, as fire, makes wood, which is potentially hot, to be actually hot, and thereby moves and changes it. Now it is not possible that the same thing should be at once in actuality and potentiality in the same respect, but only in different respects. For what is actually hot cannot simultaneously be potentially hot; but it is simultaneously potentially cold. It is therefore impossible that in the same respect and in the same way a thing should be both mover and moved, *i.e.,* that it should move itself. Therefore, whatever is moved must be moved by another. If that by which it is moved be itself moved, then this also must needs be moved by another, and that by another again.

But this cannot go on to infinity, because then there would be no first mover, and, consequently, no other mover, seeing that subsequent movers move only inasmuch as they are moved by the first mover; as the staff moves only because it is moved by the hand. Therefore it is necessary to arrive at a first mover, moved by no other; and this everyone understands to be God.

The second way is from the nature of efficient cause. In the world of sensible things we find there is an order of efficient causes. There is no case known (neither is it, indeed, possible) in which a thing is found to be the efficient cause of itself; for so it would be prior to itself, which is impossible. Now in efficient causes it is not possible to go on to infinity, because in all efficient causes following in order, the first is the cause of the intermediate cause, and the intermediate is the cause of the ultimate cause, whether the intermediate cause be several, or one only. Now to take away the cause is to take away the effect. Therefore, if there be no first cause among efficient causes, there will be no ultimate, nor any intermediate, cause. But if in efficient causes it is possible to go on to infinity, there will be no first efficient cause, neither will there be an ultimate effect, nor any intermediate efficient causes; all of which is plainly false. Therefore it is necessary to admit a first efficient cause, to which everyone gives the name of God.

The third way is taken from possibility and necessity, and runs thus. We find in nature things that are possible to be and not to be, since they are found to be generated, and to be corrupted, and consequently, it is possible for them to be and not to be. But it is impossible for these always to exist, for that which can not-be at some time is not. Therefore, if everything can not-be, then at one time there was nothing in existence. Now if this were true, even now there would be nothing in existence, because that which does not exist begins to exist only through something already existing. Therefore, if at one time nothing was in existence, it would have been impossible for anything to have begun to exist; and thus even now nothing would be in existence—which is absurd. Therefore, not all beings are merely possible, but there must exist something the existence of which is necessary. But every necessary thing either has its necessity caused by another, or not. Now it is impossible to go on to infinity in necessary things which have their necessity caused by another, as has been already proved in regard to efficient causes. Therefore we cannot but admit the existence of some being having of itself its own necessity, and not receiving it from another, but rather causing in others their necessity. This all men speak of as God.

The fourth way is taken from the gradation to be found in things. Among beings there are some more and some less good, true, noble, and the like. But *more* and *less* are predicated of different things according as they resemble in their different ways something which is the maximum, as a thing is said to be hotter according as it more nearly resembles that which is hottest; so that there is something which is truest, something best, something noblest, and, consequently, something which is most being, for those things that are greatest in truth are greatest in being, as it is written in *Metaph.* ii.[1] Now the maximum in any genus is the cause of all in that genus, as fire, which is the maximum of heat, is the cause of all hot things, as is said in the same book.[2] Therefore there must also be something which is to all beings the cause of their being, goodness, and every other perfection; and this we call God.

The fifth way is taken from the governance of the world. We see that things which lack knowledge, such as natural bodies, act for an end, and this is evident from their acting always, or nearly always, in the same way, so as to obtain the best result. Hence it is plain that they achieve their end not fortuitously, but designedly. Now whatever lacks knowledge cannot move towards an end, unless it be directed by some being endowed with knowledge and intelligence; as the ar-

row is directed by the archer. Therefore some intelligent being exists by whom all natural things are directed to their end: and this being we call God.

Reply Obj. 1. As Augustine says: *Since God is the highest good, He would not allow any evil to exist in His works, unless His omnipotence and goodness were such as to bring good even out of evil.*[3] This is part of the infinite goodness of God, that He should allow evil to exist, and out of it produce good.

Reply Obj. 2. Since nature works for a determinate end under the direction of a higher agent, whatever is done by nature must be traced back to God as to its first cause. So likewise whatever is done voluntarily must be traced back to some higher cause other than human reason and will, since these can change and fail; for all things that are changeable and capable of defect must be traced back to an immovable and self-necessary first principle, as has been shown.

DISCUSSION QUESTIONS

1. What are the differences in logical structure between Anselm's ontological and Aquinas's cosmological arguments for God's existence? Which approach is more convincing to you, if you had to choose? Why?
2. How consistent are Aquinas's arguments with what we now know about the natural world? From a scientific standpoint, are some of his arguments weaker than others? Explain.
3. How would Aquinas's conception of God be similar to or different from the nature of God described in the passages from the *Bhagavad-Gītā*?

---

1. *Metaph.* Ia, I (993b 30).
2. *Ibid.* (993b 25).

3. *Enchir.,* XI (PL 40, 236).

37. David Hume (1711–1776)
From *Dialogues Concerning Natural Religion*

David Hume, a Scottish philosopher born and educated in Edinburgh, is considered one of the major figures of that "modern period" in Western thought that continues to inform much of what philosophers do to-

day. He is viewed typically as the third of the three primary British empiricists (besides Locke and Berkeley), and he probably contributed more than anybody in the eighteenth century to the rejection of metaphysical speculation by so many philosophers of the nineteenth and twentieth centuries. He wrote on a variety of philosophical and historical topics, including morality, politics, and religion, as well as epistemology and metaphysics. In all his works he consistently exhibited the skepticism for which he became famous (and infamous to many) in his time and our own.

This selection is from Hume's best-known work on the philosophy of religion. At his request it was not published until 1779, after his death, presumably to protect himself from the social consequences of its skeptical approach to mainstream Christian doctrine. As the title indicates, he wrote this in dialogue form, with the characters Demea, Cleanthes, and Philo representing different positions on the justification of religious belief. The whole thing is narrated by a young student named Pamphilus, and Hume's own views are expressed most often by Philo. Two major issues are addressed:

1. The plausibility of another type of rational argument for God's existence, often called the teleological argument because of the perceived purposefulness of the physical universe (including the biological world) on which it is based. It also has been called an argument from analogy for reasons that will be seen.

2. The so-called problem of evil—that is, the problem of explaining how the apparent existence of evil in the world is consistent with the alleged existence of an all-powerful, perfectly good God. As dealt with in the Western religious and philosophical traditions, this problem requires for its rational solution both (a) an explanation of "moral evil"—the harm and suffering inflicted by humans themselves, such as murder or rape—and (b) an explanation of "natural evil"—the harm and suffering caused by natural forces beyond human control, such as blizzards or earthquakes.

QUESTIONS FOR CRITICAL READING

1. What is the analogical argument Cleanthes puts forth for God's existence?

2. How does Philo refute Cleanthes' argument from analogy?

3. Why is Demea critical of Cleanthes' approach to establishing religious belief?

4. What is the traditional "problem of evil" as Philo formulates it, and what are its implications regarding our knowledge of God's nature and intentions?

5. What are the views of Cleanthes and Demea on human suffering?

TERMS TO NOTE

analogy: A comparison drawn between two things perceived to be similar in some respects; an analogical argument is a type of inductive inference based on such a comparison.

syllogism: A form of deductive argument involving two premises and a conclusion.

sophism: A deceptive or misleading, though skillful, argument.

final cause: The natural goal or purpose of something; a type of causality traceable to the theories of Aristotle and utilized widely in Western philosophy into the eighteenth century. It has been for the most part discarded as an explanatory concept given the advances in natural science.

design: In this context, it refers to that which is planned.

animalcule: A very tiny animal, too small to be seen by the naked eye.

Part II

I must own, Cleanthes, said Demea, that nothing can more surprise me, than the light, in which you have, all along, put this argument. By the whole tenor of your discourse, one would imagine that you were maintaining the being of a God, against the cavils of atheists and infidels; and were necessitated to become a champion for that fundamental principle of all religion. But this, I hope, is not by any means a question among us. No man; no man, at least, of common sense, I am persuaded, ever entertained a serious doubt with regard to a truth, so certain and self-evident. The question is not concerning the *being*, but the *nature* of God. This, I affirm, from the infirmities of human understanding, to be altogether incomprehensible and unknown to us. The essence of that supreme mind, his attributes, the manner of his existence, the very nature of his duration; these and every particular, which regards so divine a being, are mysterious to men. Finite, weak, and blind creatures, we ought to humble ourselves in his august presence, and, conscious of our frailties, adore in silence his infinite perfections, which eye hath not seen, ear hath not heard, neither hath it entered into the heart of man to conceive them. They are covered in a deep cloud from human curiosity: it is profaneness to attempt penetrating through these sacred obscurities: and next to the impiety of denying his existence, is the temerity of prying into his nature and essence, decrees and attributes.

But lest you should think, that my *piety* has here got the better of my *philosophy,* I shall support my opinion, if it needs any support, by a very great authority. I might cite all the divines almost, from the foundation of Christianity, who have ever treated of this or any other theological subject: but I shall confine myself, at present, to one equally celebrated for piety and philosophy. It is Father Malebranche, who, I remember, thus expresses himself.[1] 'One ought not so much (says he) to call God a spirit, in order to express positively what he is, as in order to signify that he is not matter. He is a Being infinitely perfect: of this we cannot doubt. But in the same manner as we ought not to imagine, even supposing him corporeal, that he is clothed with a human body, as the Anthropomorphites asserted, under color that that figure was the most perfect of any; so neither ought we to imagine, that the spirit of God has human ideas, or bears *any* resemblance to our spirit; under color that we know nothing more perfect than a human mind. We ought rather to believe, that as he comprehends the perfections of matter without being material. . . . he comprehends also the perfections of created spirits, without being spirit, in the manner we conceive spirit: that his true name is, *He that is,* or, in other words, Being without restriction, All Being, the Being infinite and universal.'

After so great an authority, Demea, replied Philo, as that which you have produced, and a thousand more, which you might produce, it would appear ridiculous in me to add my sentiment, or express my approbation of your doctrine. But surely, where reasonable men treat these subjects, the question can never be concerning the being, but only the nature of the Deity. The former truth, as you well observe, is unquestionable and self-evident. Nothing exists without a cause; and the original cause of this universe (whatever it be) we call God; and piously ascribe to him every species of perfection. Whoever scruples this fundamental truth, deserves every punishment, which can be inflicted among philosophers, to wit, the greatest ridicule, contempt and disapprobation. But as all perfection is entirely relative, we ought never to imagine, that we comprehend the attributes of this divine Being, or to suppose, that his perfections have any analogy or likeness to the perfections of a human creature. Wisdom, thought, design, knowledge; these we justly ascribe to him; because these words are honorable among men, and we have no other language or other conceptions, by which we can express our adoration of him. But let us beware, lest we think, that our ideas any wise correspond to his perfections, or that his attributes have any resemblance to these qualities among men. He is infinitely superior to our limited view and comprehension; and is more the object of worship in the temple, than of disputation in the schools.

In reality, Cleanthes, continued he, there is no need of having recourse to that affected scepticism, so displeasing to you, in order to come at this determination. Our ideas reach no farther than our experience: we have no experience of divine attributes and operations: I need not conclude my syllogism: you can draw the inference yourself. And it is a pleasure to me (and I hope to you too) that just reasoning and sound piety here concur in the same conclusion, and both of them establish the adorably mysterious and incomprehensible nature of the Supreme Being.

Not to lose any time in circumlocutions, said Cleanthes, addressing himself to Demea, much less in replying to the pious declamations of Philo; I shall briefly explain how I conceive this matter. Look round the world: contemplate the whole and every part of it: you will find it to be nothing but one great machine, subdivided into an infinite number of lesser machines, which again admit of subdivisions, to a degree beyond what human senses and faculties can trace and explain. All these various machines, and even their most minute parts, are adjusted to each other with an ac-

---

1. Recherche de la Vérité, liv. 3, chap. 9.

curacy, which ravishes into admiration all men, who have ever contemplated them. The curious adapting of means to ends, throughout all nature, resembles exactly, though it much exceeds, the productions of human contrivance; of human design, thought, wisdom, and intelligence. Since therefore the effects resemble each other, we are led to infer, by all the rules of analogy, that the causes also resemble; and that the Author of Nature is somewhat similar to the mind of men; though possessed of much larger faculties, proportioned to the grandeur of the work, which he has executed. By this argument *a posteriori,* and by this argument alone, do we prove at once the existence of a Deity, and his similarity to human mind and intelligence.

I shall be so free, Cleanthes, said Demea, as to tell you, that from the beginning, I could not approve of your conclusion concerning the similarity of the Deity to men; still less can I approve of the mediums, by which you endeavor to establish it. What! No demonstration of the being of a God! No abstract arguments! No proofs *a priori!* Are these, which have hitherto been so much insisted on by philosophers, all fallacy, all sophism? Can we reach no farther in this subject than experience and probability? I will not say, that this is betraying the cause of a deity: but surely, by this affected candor, you give advantage to atheists, which they never could obtain, by the mere dint of argument and reasoning.

What I chiefly scruple in this subject, said Philo, is not so much, that all religious arguments are by Cleanthes reduced to experience, as that they appear not to be even the most certain and irrefragable of that inferior kind. That a stone will fall, that fire will burn, that the earth has solidity, we have observed a thousand and a thousand times; and when any new instance of this nature is presented, we draw without hesitation the accustomed inference. The exact similarity of the cases gives us a perfect assurance of a similar event; and a stronger evidence is never desired nor sought after. But wherever you depart, in the least, from the similarity of the cases, you diminish proportionably the evidence; and may at last bring it to a very weak *analogy,* which is confessedly liable to error and uncertainty. After having experienced the circulation of the blood in human creatures, we make no doubt that it takes place in Titius and Maevius: but from its circulation in frogs and fishes, it is only a presump-

tion, though a strong one, from analogy, that it takes place in men and other animals. The analogical reasoning is much weaker, when we infer the circulation of the sap in vegetables from our experience, that the blood circulates in animals; and those, who hastily followed that imperfect analogy, are found, by more accurate experiments, to have been mistaken.

If we see a house, Cleanthes, we conclude, with the greatest certainty, that it had an architect or builder; because this is precisely that species of effect, which we have experienced to proceed from that species of cause. But surely you will not affirm, that the universe bears such a resemblance to a house, that we can with the same certainty infer a similar cause, or that the analogy is here entire and perfect. The dissimilitude is so striking, that the utmost you can here pretend to is a guess, a conjecture, a presumption concerning a similar cause; and how that pretension will be received in the world, I leave you to consider.

It would surely be very ill received, replied Cleanthes; and I should be deservedly blamed and detested, did I allow, that the proofs of a Deity amounted to no more than a guess or conjecture. But is the whole adjustment of means to ends in a house and in the universe so slight a resemblance? The economy of final causes? The order, proportion, and arrangement of every part? Steps of a stair are plainly contrived, that human legs may use them in mounting; and this inference is certain and infallible. Human legs are also contrived for walking and mounting; and this inference, I allow, is not altogether so certain, because of the dissimilarity which you remark; but does it, therefore, deserve the name only of presumption or conjecture?

Good God! cried Demea, interrupting him, where are we? Zealous defenders of religion allow, that the proofs of a Deity fall short of perfect evidence! And you, Philo, on whose assistance I depended, in proving the adorable mysteriousness of the Divine Nature, do you assent to all these extravagant opinions of Cleanthes? For what other name can I give them? Or why spare my censure, when such principles are advanced, supported by such an authority, before so young a man as Pamphilus?

You seem not to apprehend, replied Philo, that I argue with Cleanthes in his own way; and by showing him the dangerous consequences of his tenets, hope at last to reduce him to our opinion. But what sticks most with you, I observe, is the representation which

Cleanthes has made of the argument *a posteriori;* and finding, that that argument is likely to escape your hold and vanish into air, you think it so disguised, that you can scarcely believe it to be set in its true light. Now, however much I may dissent, in other respects, from the dangerous principles of Cleanthes, I must allow, that he has fairly represented that argument; and I shall endeavor so to state the matter to you, that you will entertain no farther scruples with regard to it.

Were a man to abstract from everything which he knows or has seen, he would be altogether incapable, merely from his own ideas, to determine what kind of scene the universe must be, or to give the preference to one state or situation of things above another. For as nothing which he clearly conceives, could be esteemed impossible or implying a contradiction, every chimera of his fancy would be upon an equal footing; nor could he assign any just reason, why he adheres to one idea or system, and rejects the others, which are equally possible.

Again; after he opens his eyes, and contemplates the world, as it really is, it would be impossible for him, at first, to assign the cause of any one event; much less, of the whole of things or of the universe. He might set his fancy a rambling; and she might bring him in an infinite variety of reports and representations. These would all be possible; but being all equally possible, he would never, of himself, give a satisfactory account for his preferring one of them to the rest. Experience alone can point out to him the true cause of any phenomenon.

Now, according to this method of reasoning, Demea, it follows (and is, indeed, tacitly allowed by Cleanthes himself) that order, arrangement, or the adjustment of final causes is not, of itself, any proof of design; but only so far as it has been experienced to proceed from that principle. For aught we can know *a priori,* matter may contain the source or spring of order originally, within itself, as well as mind does; and there is no more difficulty in conceiving, that the several elements, from an internal unknown cause, may fall into the most exquisite arrangement, than to conceive that their ideas, in the great, universal mind, from a like internal, unknown cause, fall into that arrangement. The equal possibility of both these suppositions is allowed. But by experience we find (according to Cleanthes), that there is a difference be-

tween them. Throw several pieces of steel together, without shape or form; they will never arrange themselves so as to compose a watch: stone, and mortar, and wood, without an architect, never erect a house. But the ideas in a human mind, we see, by an unknown, inexplicable economy, arrange themselves so as to form the plan of a watch or house. Experience, therefore, proves, that there is an original principle of order in mind, not in matter. From similar effects we infer similar causes. The adjustment of means to ends is alike in the universe, as in a machine of human contrivance. The causes, therefore, must be resembling.

I was from the beginning scandalized, I must own, with this resemblance, which is asserted, between the Deity and human creatures; and must conceive it to imply such a degradation of the Supreme Being as no sound theist could endure. With your assistance, therefore, Demea, I shall endeavor to defend what you justly called the adorable mysteriousness of the Divine Nature, and shall refute this reasoning of Cleanthes, provided he allows, that I have made a fair representation of it.

When Cleanthes had assented, Philo, after a short pause, proceeded in the following manner.

That all inferences, Cleanthes, concerning fact, are founded on experience, and that all experimental reasonings are founded on the supposition, that similar causes prove similar effects, and similar effects similar causes; I shall not, at present, much dispute with you. But observe, I entreat you, with what extreme caution all just reasoners proceed in the transferring of experiments to similar cases. Unless the cases be exactly similar, they repose no perfect confidence in applying their past observation to any particular phenomenon. Every alteration of circumstances occasions a doubt concerning the event; and it requires new experiments to prove certainly, that the new circumstances are of no moment or importance. A change in bulk, situation, arrangement, age, disposition of the air, or surrounding bodies; any of these particulars may be attended with the most unexpected consequences: and unless the objects be quite familiar to us, it is the highest temerity to expect with assurance, after any of these changes, an event similar to that which before fell under our observation. The slow and deliberate steps of philosophers, here, if anywhere, are distinguished from the precipitate march of the vulgar, who, hurried on by the smallest similitudes, are incapable of all discernment or consideration.

But can you think, Cleanthes, that your usual phlegm and philosophy have been preserved in so wide a step as you have taken, when you compared to the universe, houses, ships, furniture, machines; and from their similiarity in some circumstances inferred a similarity in their causes? Thought, design, intelligence, such as we discover in men and other animals, is no more than one of the springs and principles of the universe, as well as heat or cold, attraction or repulsion, and a hundred others, which fall under daily observation. It is an active cause, by which some particular parts of nature, we find, produce alterations on other parts. But can a conclusion, with any propriety, be transferred from parts to the whole? Does not the great disproportion bar all comparison and inference? From observing the growth of a hair, can we learn anything concerning the generation of a man? Would the manner of a leaf's blowing, even though perfectly known, afford us any instruction concerning the vegetation of a tree?

But allowing that we were to take the *operations* of one part of nature upon another for the foundation of our judgment concerning the *origin* of the whole (which never can be admitted), yet why select so minute, so weak, so bounded a principle as the reason and design of animals is found to be upon this planet? What peculiar privilege has this little agitation of the brain which we call *thought,* that we must thus make it the model of the whole universe? Our partiality in our own favor does indeed present it on all occasions; but sound philosophy ought carefully to guard against so natural an illusion.

So far from admitting, continued Philo, that the operations of a part can afford us any just conclusion concerning the origin of the whole, I will not allow any one part to form a rule for another part, if the latter be very remote from the former. Is there any reasonable ground to conclude, that the inhabitants of other planets possess thought, intelligence, reason, or anything similar to these faculties in men? When Nature has so extremely diversified her manner of operation in this small globe; can we imagine, that she incessantly copies herself throughout so immense a universe? And if thought, as we may well suppose, be confined merely to this narrow corner, and has even there so limited a sphere of action; with what propriety can we assign it for the original cause of all things? The narrow views of a peasant, who makes his domestic economy the rule for the government of kingdoms, is in comparison a pardonable sophism.

But were we ever so much assured, that a thought and reason, resembling the human, were to be found throughout the whole universe, and were its activity elsewhere vastly greater and more commanding than it appears in this globe; yet I cannot see, why the operations of a world, constituted, arranged, adjusted, can with any propriety be extended to a world, which is in its embryo state, and is advancing towards that constitution and arrangement. By observation, we know somewhat of the economy, action, and nourishment of a finished animal; but we must transfer with great caution that observation to the growth of a fetus in the womb, and still more, to the formation of an animalcule in the loins of its male parent. Nature, we find, even from our limited experience, possesses an infinite number of springs and principles, which incessantly discover themselves on every change of her position and situation. And what new and unknown principles would actuate her in so new and unknown a situation as that of the formation of a universe, we cannot, without the utmost temerity, pretend to determine.

A very small part of this great system, during a very short time, is very imperfectly discovered to us: and do we thence pronounce decisively concerning the origin of the whole?

Admirable conclusion! Stone, wood, brick, iron, brass, have not, at this time, in this minute globe of earth, an order or arrangement without human art and contrivance: therefore the universe could not originally attain its order and arrangement, without something similar to human art. But is a part of nature a rule for another part very wide of the former? Is it a rule for the whole? Is a very small part a rule for the universe? Is nature in one situation, a certain rule for nature in another situation, vastly different from the former?

And can you blame me, Cleanthes, if I here imitate the prudent reserve of Simonides, who, according to the noted story, being asked by Hiero, *What God was?* desired a day to think of it, and then two days more;

and after that manner continually prolonged the term, without ever bringing in his definition or description? Could you even blame me, if I had answered at first *that I did not know,* and was sensible that this subject lay vastly beyond the reach of my faculties? You might cry out sceptic and rallier as much as you pleased: but having found, in so many other subjects, much more familiar, the imperfections and even contradictions of human reason, I never should expect any success from its feeble conjectures, in a subject, so sublime, and so remote from the sphere of our observation. When two species of objects have always been observed to be conjoined together, I can infer, by custom, the existence of one wherever I see the existence of the other: and this I call an argument from experience. But how this argument can have place, where the objects, as in the present case, are single, individual, without parallel, or specific resemblance, may be difficult to explain. And will any man tell me with a serious countenance, that an orderly universe must arise from some thought and art, like the human; because we have experience of it? To ascertain this reasoning, it were requisite, that we had experience of the origin of worlds; and it is not sufficient surely, that we have seen ships and cities arise from human art and contrivance. . . .

Philo was proceeding in this vehement manner, somewhat between jest and earnest, as it appeared to me; when he observed some signs of impatience in Cleanthes, and then immediately stopped short. What I had to suggest, said Cleanthes, is only that you would not abuse terms, or make use of popular expressions to subvert philosophical reasonings. You know, that the vulgar often distinguish reason from experience, even where the question relates only to matter of fact and existence; though it is found, where that reason is properly analyzed, that it is nothing but a species of experience. To prove by experience the origin of the universe from mind is not more contrary to common speech than to prove the motion of the earth from the same principle. And a caviler might raise all the same objections to the Copernican system, which you have urged against my reasonings. Have you other earths, might he say, which you have seen to move? Have. . . .

Yes! cried Philo, interrupting him, we have other earths. Is not the moon another earth, which we see to turn round its center? Is not Venus another earth, where we observe the same phenomenon? Are not the revolutions of the sun also a confirmation, from analogy, of the same theory? All the planets, are they not earths, which revolve about the sun? Are not the satellites moons, which move round Jupiter and Saturn, and along with these primary planets, round the sun? These analogies and resemblances, with others, which I have not mentioned, are the sole proofs of the Copernican system: and to you it belongs to consider, whether you have any analogies of the same kind to support your theory.

In reality, Cleanthes, continued he, the modern system of astronomy is now so much received by all inquirers, and has become so essential a part even of our earliest education, that we are not commonly very scrupulous in examining the reasons upon which it is founded. It is now become a matter of mere curiosity to study the first writers on that subject, who had the full force of prejudice to encounter, and were obliged to turn their arguments on every side, in order to render them popular and convincing. But if we peruse Galileo's famous Dialogues concerning the system of the world, we shall find, that that great genius, one of the sublimest that ever existed, first bent all his endeavors to prove, that there was no foundation for the distinction commonly made between elementary and celestial substances. The schools, proceeding from the illusions of sense, had carried this distinction very far; and had established the latter substances to be ingenerable, incorruptible, unalterable, impassable; and had assigned all the opposite qualities to the former. But Galileo, beginning with the moon, proved its similarity in every particular to the earth; its convex figure, its natural darkness when not illuminated, its density, its distinction into solid and liquid, the variations of its phases, the mutual illuminations of the earth and moon, their mutual eclipses, the inequalities of the lunar surface, etc. After many instances of this kind, with regard to all the planets, men plainly saw, that these bodies became proper objects of experience; and that the similarity of their nature enabled us to extend the same arguments and phenomena from one to the other.

In this cautious proceeding of the astronomers, you may read your own condemnation, Cleanthes; or rather may see, that the subject in which you are engaged exceeds all human reason and inquiry. Can you pretend to show any such similarity between the fabric of a house, and the generation of a universe? Have you ever seen nature in any such situation as resembles the first arrangement of the elements? Have worlds ever been formed under your eye? and have you had leisure to observe the whole progress of the phenomenon, from the first appearance of order to its final consummation? If you have, then cite your experience, and deliver your theory. . . .

Part X

It is my opinion, I own, replied Demea, that each man feels, in a manner, the truth of religion within his own breast; and from a consciousness of his imbecility and misery, rather than from any reasoning, is led to seek protection from that Being, on whom he and all nature is dependent. So anxious or so tedious are even the best scenes of life, that futurity is still the object of all our hopes and fears. We incessantly look forward, and endeavor, by prayers, adoration, and sacrifice, to appease those unknown powers, whom we find, by experience, so able to afflict and oppress us. Wretched creatures that we are! what resource for us amidst the innumerable ills of life, did not religion suggest some methods of atonement, and appease those terrors, with which we are incessantly agitated and tormented?

I am indeed persuaded, said Philo, that the best and indeed the only method of bringing everyone to a due sense of religion, is by just representations of the misery and wickedness of men. And for that purpose a talent of eloquence and strong imagery is more requisite than that of reasoning and argument. For is it necessary to prove, what everyone feels within himself? 'Tis only necessary to make us feel it, if possible, more intimately and sensibly.

The people, indeed, replied Demea, are sufficiently convinced of this great and melancholy truth. The miseries of life, the unhappiness of men, the general corruptions of our nature, the unsatisfactory enjoyment of pleasures, riches, honors; these phrases have become almost proverbial in all languages. And who can doubt of what all men declare from their own immediate feeling and experience?

In this point, said Philo, the learned are perfectly agreed with the vulgar; and in all letters, sacred and profane, the topic of human misery has been insisted on with the most pathetic eloquence that sorrow and melancholy could inspire. The poets, who speak from sentiment, without a system, and whose testimony has therefore the more authority, abound in images of this nature. From Homer down to Dr. Young, the whole inspired tribe have ever been sensible, that no other representation of things would suit the feeling and observation of each individual.

As to authorities, replied Demea, you need not seek them. Look round this library of Cleanthes. I shall venture to affirm, that, except authors of particular sciences, such as chemistry or botany, who have no occasion to treat of human life, there scarce is one of those innumerable writers, from whom the sense of human misery has not, in some passage or other, extorted a complaint and confession of it. At least, the chance is entirely on that side; and no one author has ever, so far as I can recollect, been so extravagant as to deny it.

There you must excuse me, said Philo: Leibnitz has denied it; and is perhaps the first,[2] who ventured upon so bold and paradoxical an opinion; at least, the first, who made it essential to his philosophical system.

And by being the first, replied Demea, might he not have been sensible of his error? For is this a subject, in which philosophers can propose to make discoveries, especially in so late an age? And can any man hope by a simple denial (for the subject scarcely admits of reasoning) to bear down the united testimony of mankind, founded on sense and consciousness?

And why should man, added he, pretend to an exemption from the lot of all other animals? The whole earth, believe me, Philo, is cursed and polluted. A perpetual war is kindled amongst all living creatures. Necessity, hunger, want, stimulate the strong and courageous: fear, anxiety, terror, agitate the weak and infirm. The first entrance into life gives anguish to the new-born infant and to its wretched parent: weakness, impotence, distress, attend each stage of that life: and 'tis at last finished in agony and horror.

---

2. That sentiment had been maintained by Dr. King and some few others, before Leibnitz, though by none of so great fame as that German philosopher.

Observe too, says Philo, the curious artifices of nature, in order to embitter the life of every living being. The stronger prey upon the weaker, and keep them in perpetual terror and anxiety. The weaker too, in their turn, often prey upon the stronger, and vex and molest them without relaxation. Consider that innumerable race of insects, which either are bred on the body of each animal, or flying about infix their stings in him. These insects have others still less than themselves, which torment them. And thus on each hand, before and behind, above and below, every animal is surrounded with enemies, which incessantly seek his misery and destruction.

Man alone, said Demea, seems to be, in part, an exception to this rule. For by combination in society, he can easily master lions, tigers, and bears, whose greater strength and agility naturally enable them to prey upon him.

On the contrary, it is here chiefly, cried Philo, that the uniform and equal maxims of nature are most apparent. Man, it is true, can, by combination, surmount all his *real* enemies, and become master of the whole animal creation: but does he not immediately raise up to himself *imaginary* enemies, the demons of his fancy, who haunt him with superstitious terrors, and blast every enjoyment of life? His pleasure, as he imagines, becomes, in their eyes, a crime: his food and repose give them umbrage and offense: his very sleep and dreams furnish new materials to anxious fear: and even death, his refuge from every other ill, presents only the dread of endless and innumerable woes. Nor does the wolf molest more the timid flock, than superstition does the anxious breast of wretched mortals.

Besides, consider, Demea; this very society, by which we surmount those wild beasts, our natural enemies; what new enemies does it not raise to us? What woe and misery does it not occasion? Man is the greatest enemy of man. Oppression, injustice, contempt, contumely, violence, sedition, war, calumny, treachery, fraud; by these they mutually torment each other: and they would soon dissolve that society which they had formed, were it not for the dread of still greater ills, which must attend their separation.

But though these external insults, said Demea, from animals, from men, from all the elements, which assault us, form a frightful catalogue of woes, they are nothing in comparison of those, which arise within ourselves, from the distempered condition of our mind and body. How many lie under the lingering torment of diseases? Hear the pathetic enumeration of the great poet.

> Intestine stone and ulcer, colic-pangs,
> Demoniac frenzy, moping melancholy,
> And moon-struck madness, pining atrophy,
> Marasmus and wide-wasting pestilence.
> Dire was the tossing, deep the groans: Despair
> Tended the sick, busiest from couch to couch.
> And over them triumphant Death his dart
> Shook, but delay'd to strike, tho' oft invok'd
> With vows, as their chief good and final hope.[3]

The disorders of the mind, continued Demea, though more secret, are not perhaps less dismal and vexatious. Remorse, shame, anguish, rage, disappointment, anxiety, fear, dejection, despair; who has ever passed through life without cruel inroads from these tormentors? How many have scarcely ever felt any better sensations? Labor and poverty, so abhorred by everyone, are the certain lot of the far greater number; and those few privileged persons, who enjoy ease and opulence, never reach contentment or true felicity. All the goods of life united would not make a very happy man: but all the ills united would make a wretch indeed; and anyone of them almost (and who can be free from everyone), nay often the absence of one good (and who can possess all), is sufficient to render life ineligible.

Were a stranger to drop, on a sudden, into this world, I would show him, as a specimen of its ills, an hospital full of diseases, a prison crowded with malefactors and debtors, a field of battle strewed with carcasses, a fleet floundering in the ocean, a nation languishing under tyranny, famine, or pestilence. To turn the gay side of life to him, and give him a notion of its pleasures; whither should I conduct him? to a ball, to an opera, to court? He might justly think, that I was only showing him a diversity of distress and sorrow.

---

3. Milton: Paradise Lost, XI.

There is no evading such striking instances, said Philo, but by apologies, which still farther aggravate the charge. Why have all men, I ask, in all ages, complained incessantly of the miseries of life? . . . They have no just reason, says one: these complaints proceed only from their discontented, repining, anxious disposition. . . . And can there possibly, I reply, be a more certain foundation of misery, than such a wretched temper?

But if they were really as unhappy as they pretend, says my antagonist, why do they remain in life? . . .

Not satisfied with life, afraid of death.

This is the secret chain, say I, that holds us. We are terrified, not bribed to the continuance of our existence.

It is only a false delicacy, he may insist, which a few refined spirits indulge, and which has spread these complaints among the whole race of mankind. . . . And what is this delicacy, I ask, which you blame? Is it anything but a greater sensibility to all the pleasures and pains of life? and if the man of a delicate, refined temper, by being so much more alive than the rest of the world, is only so much more unhappy; what judgment must we form in general of human life?

Let men remain at rest, says our adversary; and they will be easy. They are willing artificers of their own misery. . . . No! reply I; an anxious languor follows their repose: disappointment, vexation, trouble, their activity and ambition.

I can observe something like what you mention in some others, replied Cleanthes: but I confess, I feel little or nothing of it in myself, and hope that it is not so common as you represent it.

If you feel not human misery yourself, cried Demea, I congratulate you on so happy a singularity. Others, seemingly the most prosperous, have not been ashamed to vent their complaints in the most melancholy strains. Let us attend to the great, the fortunate Emperor, Charles V, when, tired with human grandeur, he resigned all his extensive dominions into the hands of his son. In the last harangue, which he made on that memorable occasion, he publicly avowed, *that the greatest prosperities which he had ever enjoyed, had been mixed with so many adversities, that he might truly say he had never enjoyed any satisfaction or content-*

ment. But did the retired life, in which he sought for shelter, afford him any greater happiness? If we may credit his son's account, his repentance commenced the very day of his resignation.

Cicero's fortune, from small beginnings, rose to the greatest luster and renown; yet what pathetic complaints of the ills of life do his familiar letters, as well as philosophical discourses, contain? And suitably to his own experience, he introduces Cato, the great, the fortunate Cato, protesting in his old age, that, had he a new life in his offer, he would reject the present.

Ask yourself, ask any of your acquaintance, whether they would live over again the last ten or twenty years of their lives. No! but the next twenty, they say, will be better:

And from the dregs of life, hope to receive
What the first sprightly running could not give.[4]

Thus at last they find (such is the greatest of human misery; it reconciles even contradictions) that they complain, at once, of the shortness of life, and of its vanity and sorrow.

And is it possible, Cleanthes, said Philo, that after all these reflections, and infinitely more, which might be suggested, you can still persevere in your anthropomorphism, and assert the moral attributes of the Deity, his justice, benevolence, mercy, and rectitude, to be of the same nature with these virtues in human creatures? His power we allow infinite: whatever he wills is executed: but neither man nor any other animal is happy: therefore he does not will their happiness. His wisdom is infinite: he is never mistaken in choosing the means to any end: but the course of nature tends not to human or animal felicity: therefore it is not established for that purpose. Through the whole compass of human knowledge, there are no inferences more certain and infallible than these. In what respect, then, do his benevolence and mercy resemble the benevolence and mercy of men?

Epicurus's old questions are yet unanswered.

Is he willing to prevent evil, but not able? then is he impotent. Is he able, but not willing? then is he malevolent. Is he both able and willing? whence then is evil?

---

4. Dryden: Aurungzebe, Act IV., sc. i.

You ascribe, Cleanthes, (and I believe justly) a purpose and intention to nature. But what, I beseech you, is the object of that curious artifice and machinery, which she has displayed in all animals? The preservation alone of individuals and propagation of the species. It seems enough for her purpose, if such a rank be barely upheld in the universe, without any care or concern for the happiness of the members that compose it. No resource for this purpose: no machinery, in order merely to give pleasure or ease: no fund of pure joy and contentment: no indulgence without some want or necessity accompanying it. At least, the few phenomena of this nature are overbalanced by opposite phenomena of still greater importance.

Our sense of music, harmony, and indeed beauty of all kinds, gives satisfaction, without being absolutely necessary to the preservation and propagation of the species. But what racking pains, on the other hand, arise from gouts, gravels, megrims, toothaches, rheumatisms; where the injury to the animal-machinery is either small or incurable? Mirth, laughter, play, frolic, seem gratuitous satisfactions, which have no farther tendency: spleen, melancholy, discontent, superstition, are pains of the same nature. How then does the divine benevolence display itself, in the sense of you anthropomorphites? None but we mystics, as you were pleased to call us, can account for this strange mixture of phenomena, by deriving it from attributes, infinitely perfect, but incomprehensible.

And have you at last, said Cleanthes smiling, betrayed your intentions, Philo? Your long agreement with Demea did indeed a little surprise me; but I find you were all the while erecting a concealed battery against me. And I must confess, that you have now fallen upon a subject, worthy of your noble spirit of opposition and controversy. If you can make out the present point, and prove mankind to be unhappy or corrupted, there is an end at once of all religion. For to what purpose establish the natural attributes of the Deity, while the moral are still doubtful and uncertain?

You take umbrage very easily, replied Demea, at opinions the most innocent, and the most generally received even amongst the religious and devout themselves: and nothing can be more surprising than to find a topic like this, concerning the wickedness and misery of man, charged with no less than atheism and profaneness. Have not all pious divines and preachers, who have indulged their rhetoric on so fertile a subject: have they not easily, I say, given a solution of any difficulties, which may attend it? This world is but a point in comparison of the universe; this life but a moment in comparison of eternity. The present evil phenomena, therefore, are rectified in other regions, and in some future period of existence. And the eyes of men, being then opened to larger views of things, see the whole connection of general laws; and trace, with adoration, the benevolence and rectitude of the Deity, through all the mazes and intricacies of his providence.

No! replied Cleanthes, No! These arbitrary suppositions can never be admitted, contrary to matter of fact, visible and uncontroverted. Whence can any cause be known but from its known effects? Whence can any hypothesis be proved but from the apparent phenomena? To establish one hypothesis upon another, is building entirely in the air; and the utmost we ever attain, by these conjectures and fictions, is to ascertain the bare possibility of our opinion; but never can we, upon such terms, establish its reality.

The only method of supporting divine benevolence (and it is what I willingly embrace) is to deny absolutely the misery and wickedness of man. Your representations are exaggerated: your melancholy views mostly fictitious: your inferences contrary to fact and experience. Health is more common than sickness: pleasure than pain: happiness than misery. And for one vexation, which we meet with, we attain, upon computation, a hundred enjoyments.

Admitting your position, replied Philo, which yet is extremely doubtful, you must, at the same time, allow, that, if pain be less frequent than pleasure, it is infinitely more violent and durable. One hour of it is often able to outweigh a day, a week, a month of our common insipid enjoyments. And how many days, weeks, and months are passed by several in the most acute torments? Pleasure, scarcely in one instance, is ever able to reach ecstasy and rapture: and in no one instance can it continue for any time at its highest pitch and altitude. The spirits evaporate; the nerves relax; the fabric is disordered; and the enjoyment quickly degenerates into fatigue and uneasiness. But pain often, good God, how often! rises to torture and agony; and the longer it continues, it becomes still more genuine agony and torture. Patience is exhausted; courage languishes; melancholy seizes us; and nothing terminates our misery but the removal of its cause, or another event, which is the sole cure of all evil, but which, from our natural folly, we regard with still greater horror and consternation.

But not to insist upon these topics, continued Philo, though most obvious, certain, and important; I must use the freedom to admonish you, Cleanthes, that you have put this controversy upon a most dangerous issue, and are unawares introducing a total scepticism, into the most essential articles of natural and revealed theology. What! no method of fixing a just foundation for religion, unless we allow the happiness of human life, and maintain a continued existence even in this world, with all our present pains, infirmities, vexations, and follies, to be eligible and desirable! But this is contrary to everyone's feeling and experience: it is contrary to an authority so established as nothing can subvert: no decisive proofs can ever be produced against this authority; nor is it possible for you to compute, estimate, and compare all the pains and all the pleasures in the lives of all men and of all animals: and thus by your resting the whole system of religion on a point, which, from its very nature, must forever be uncertain, you tacitly confess, that that system is equally uncertain.

But allowing you, what never will be believed; at least, what you never possibly can prove, that animal, or at least, human happiness, in this life, exceeds its misery; you have yet done nothing: for this is not, by any means, what we expect from infinite power, infinite wisdom, and infinite goodness. Why is there any misery at all in the world? Not by chance surely. From some cause then. Is it from the intention of the Deity? But he is perfectly benevolent. Is it contrary to his intention? But he is almighty. Nothing can shake the solidity of this reasoning, so short, so clear, so decisive; except we assert, that these subjects exceed all human capacity, and that our common measures of truth and falsehood are not applicable to them; a topic, which I have all along insisted on, but which you have, from the beginning, rejected with scorn and indignation.

But I will be contented to retire still from this intrenchment: for I deny that you can ever force me in

it: I will allow, that pain or misery in man is *compatible* with infinite power and goodness in the Deity, even in your sense of these attributes: what are you advanced by all these concessions? A mere possible compatibility is not sufficient. You must *prove* these pure, unmixed, and uncontrollable attributes from the present mixed and confused phenomena, and from these alone. A hopeful undertaking! Were the phenomena ever so pure and unmixed, yet being finite, they would be insufficient for that purpose. How much more, where they are also so jarring and discordant!

Here, Cleanthes, I find myself at ease in my argument. Here I triumph. Formerly, when we argued concerning the natural attributes of intelligence and design, I needed all my sceptical and metaphysical subtilty to elude your grasp. In many views of the universe, and of its parts, particularly the latter, the beauty and fitness of final causes strikes us with such irresistible force, that all objections appear (what I believe they really are) mere cavils and sophisms; nor can we then imagine how it was ever possible for us to repose any weight on them. But there is no view of human life or of the condition of mankind, from which, without the greatest violence, we can infer the moral attributes, or learn that infinite benevolence, conjoined with infinite power and infinite wisdom, which we must discover by the eyes of faith alone. It is your turn now to tug the laboring oar, and to support your philosophical subtilties against the dictates of plain reason and experience.

DISCUSSION QUESTIONS

1. Do you agree with Philo's criticism of the tendency to anthropomorphize God? Why or why not?

2. What is the relationship between reason, skepticism, and faith that emerges in these excerpts?

3. Do you think theists can provide an adequate rational account of either moral or natural evil? Why or why not?

4. How would Hume's character Philo critique Aquinas's and Anselm's rational arguments for God's existence? Would his evaluation of the account of God in the *Bhagavad-Gītā* be any different? Why or why not?

38. Ludwig Feuerbach (1804–1872)
From *The Essence of Christianity*

Ludwig Feuerbach was a German philosopher who lived during a time of dramatic social and intellectual change in Europe and who, in his own way, contributed significantly to that change. He developed a version of materialism, radically new at the time, that placed fundamental value on the flesh-and-blood conscious human being and that individual's essential interrelations with others. His materialism then provided the standpoint from which he engaged in his influential "transformative critique" of both the dominant idealist philosophy of the day—that of G. W. F. Hegel (1770–1831)—and doctrinal religious belief, especially that of Christianity. Instead of an outright rejection of the Hegelian system, he "brought it down to earth" and materialized it; instead of a categorical denial of religious claims, he showed how they were really just inverted, alienated expressions of human self-understanding.

Feuerbach's open atheism and systematic reduction of "religious truth" to a very this-worldly "anthropological truth" were shocking and offensive to conventional academic and popular sensibilities during the 1840s but also were the inspiration for a whole generation of anti-establishment intellectuals. In the twentieth century as well, his influence has been felt in Marxism and existentialism, in the Freudian analysis of religion, and in contemporary social psychology. In his later years Feuerbach's materialist investigations led him to a study of the effect of diet on psychological life, and he is thought to be the original source of the saying "You are what you eat."

This selection is from his most famous, and for many still his most provocative, work. Published in 1841, the English translation is the original 1854 version by Mary Ann Evans (more familiar to most readers by her pseudonym George Eliot). As the title implies, Feuerbach is most interested in exposing what he considers to be both the true humanistic essence and the false religious essence of Christianity, but in this particular excerpt he focuses on "religious consciousness" in general and the human history of belief in divine beings. As radical as this writing was at the time, it also illustrates the increasingly dominant worldview among nineteenth-century Western intellectuals that assumed an inevitable "progress" in human society toward increased rationality, knowledge, and problem-solving capability and the subsequent outgrowing of traditional fears, prejudices, and "superstitions" of which religion is the most obvious expression.

QUESTIONS FOR CRITICAL READING

1. How does Feuerbach explain the historical development of religion, and in what sense is this development progressive?
2. What is the "essence of religion," in Feuerbach's view, and why does he think modern philosophical justifications of religious doctrine actually undermine it?
3. What does Feuerbach mean by claiming that "the predicate is the *truth* of the subject"?
4. How does Feuerbach explain the typical religious belief in the superiority and/or perfection of divine beings and the corresponding inferiority, imperfection, and sinfulness of human individuals?

TERMS TO NOTE

nihilism: In this context, the philosophical denial of the reality and value of the objective world.

pantheism: The belief that there is no distinction between the Divine Creator and the Creation; that God is an impersonal being that is one with the universe.

tautology: As most often used, it refers to an assertion that is necessarily true because it contains a redundancy in its meaning, for example, "God is God" or "God is perfect because God has no imperfection"; often logicians refer to any necessarily true statement or proposition as a tautology.

---

2. The Essence of Religion Considered Generally.

What we have hitherto been maintaining generally, even with regard to sensational impressions, of the relation between subject and object, applies especially to the relation between the subject and the religious object.

In the perceptions of the senses consciousness of the object is distinguishable from consciousness of self; but in religion, consciousness of the object and self-consciousness coincide. The object of the senses is out of man, the religious object is within him, and therefore as little forsakes him as his self-consciousness or his conscience; it is the intimate, the closest object. "God," says Augustine, for example, "is nearer, more related to us, and therefore more easily known by us, than sensible, corporeal things."[1] The object of the senses is in itself indifferent—independent of the disposition or of the judgment; but the object of religion is a selected object; the most excellent, the first, the supreme being; it essentially presupposes a critical judgment, a discrimination between the divine and the nondivine, between that which is worthy of adoration and that which is not worthy.[2] And here may be applied, without any limitation, the proposition: the object of any subject is nothing else than the subject's own nature taken objectively. Such as are a man's thoughts and dispositions, such is his God; so much worth as a man has, so much and no more has his God. Consciousness of God is self-consciousness, knowledge of God is self-knowledge. By his God thou knowest the man, and by the man his God; the two are identical. Whatever is God to a man, that is his heart and soul; and conversely, God is the manifested inward nature, the expressed self of a man,—religion the solemn unveiling of a man's hidden treasures, the revelation of his intimate thoughts, the open confession of his love-secrets.

But when religion—consciousness of God—is designated as the self-consciousness of man, this is not to be understood as affirming that the religious man is directly aware of this identity; for, on the contrary, ignorance of it is fundamental to the peculiar nature of religion. To preclude this misconception, it is better to say, religion is man's earliest and also indirect form of self-knowledge. Hence, religion everywhere precedes philosophy, as in the history of the race, so also in that of the individual. Man first of all sees his nature as if *out of* himself, before he finds it in himself. His own nature is in the first instance contemplated by him as that of another being. Religion is the childlike condition of humanity; but the child sees his nature—man—out of himself; in childhood a man is an object to himself, under the form of another man. Hence the historical progress of religion consists in this: that what by an earlier religion was regarded as objective, is now recognised as subjective; that is, what was formerly contemplated and worshipped as God is now perceived to be something *human*. What was at first religion becomes at a later period idolatry; man is seen to have adored his own nature. Man has given objectivity to himself, but has not recognised the object as his own nature: a later religion takes this forward step; every advance in religion is therefore a deeper self-knowledge. But every particular religion, while it pronounces its predecessors idolatrous, excepts itself—and necessarily so, otherwise it would no longer be religion—from the fate, the common nature of all religions: it imputes only to other religions what is the fault, if fault it be, of religion in general. Because it has a different object, a different tenor, because it has transcended the ideas of preceding religions, it erroneously supposes itself exalted above the necessary eternal laws which constitute the essence of religion—it fancies its object, its ideas, to be superhuman. But the essence of religion, thus hidden from the religious, is evident to the thinker, by whom religion is viewed objectively, which it cannot be by its votaries. And it is our task to show that the antithesis of divine and human is altogether illusory, that it is nothing else than the antithesis between the human nature in general and the human individual; that, consequently, the object and contents of the Christian religion are altogether human.

Religion, at least the Christian, is the relation of man to himself, or more correctly to his own nature (*i.e.*, his subjective nature);[3] but a relation to it, viewed as a nature apart from his own. The divine being is nothing else than the human being, or, rather, the human nature purified, freed from the limits of the

---

1. De Genesi ad litteram, l. v. c. 16.
2. "Unusquisque vestrum non cogitat, *prius* se debere Deum *nosse*, quam *colere*."—M. Minucii Felicis Octavianus, c. 24.

3. The meaning of this parenthetic limitation will be clear in the sequel.

individual man, made objective—*i.e.,* contemplated and revered as another, a distinct being. All the attributes of the divine nature are, therefore, attributes of the human nature.[4]

In relation to the attributes, the predicates, of the Divine Being, this is admitted without hesitation, but by no means in relation to the subject of these predicates. The negation of the subject is held to be irreligion, nay, atheism; though not so the negation of the predicates. But that which has no predicates or qualities, has no effect upon me; that which has no effect upon me has no existence for me. To deny all the qualities of a being is equivalent to denying the being himself. A being without qualities is one which cannot become an object to the mind, and such a being is virtually non-existent. Where man deprives God of all qualities, God is no longer anything more to him than a negative being. To the truly religious man, God is not a being without qualities, because to him he is a positive, real being. The theory that God cannot be defined, and consequently cannot be known by man, is therefore the offspring of recent times, a product of modern unbelief.

As reason is and can be pronounced finite only where man regards sensual enjoyment, or religious emotion, or aesthetic contemplation, or moral sentiment, as the absolute, the true; so the proposition that God is unknowable or undefinable, can only be enunciated and become fixed as a dogma, where this object has no longer any interest for the intellect; where the real, the positive, alone has any hold on man, where the real alone has for him the significance of the essential, of the absolute, divine object, but where at the same time, in contradiction with this purely worldly tendency, there yet exist some old remains of religiousness. On the ground that God is unknowable, man excuses himself to what is yet remaining of his religious conscience for his forgetfulness of God, his ab-

sorption in the world: he denies God practically by his conduct,—the world has possession of all his thoughts and inclinations,—but he does not deny him theoretically, he does not attack his existence; he lets that rest. But this existence does not affect or incommode him; it is a merely negative existence, an existence without existence, a self-contradictory existence,—a state of being which, as to its effects, is not distinguishable from non-being. The denial of determinate, positive predicates concerning the divine nature is nothing else than a denial of religion, with, however, an appearance of religion in its favour, so that it is not recognised as a denial; it is simply a subtle, disguised atheism. The alleged religious horror of limiting God by positive predicates is only the irreligious wish to know nothing more of God, to banish God from the mind. Dread of limitation is dread of existence. All real existence, *i.e.,* all existence which is truly such, is qualitative, determinative existence. He who earnestly believes in the Divine existence is not shocked at the attributing even of gross sensuous qualities to God. He who dreads an existence that may give offence, who shrinks from the grossness of a positive predicate, may as well renounce existence altogether. A God who is injured by determinate qualities has not the courage and the strength to exist. Qualities are the fire, the vital breath, the oxygen, the salt of existence. An existence in general, an existence without qualities, is an insipidity, an absurdity. But there can be no more in God than is supplied by religion. Only where man loses his taste for religion, and thus religion itself becomes insipid, does the existence of God become an insipid existence—an existence without qualities.

There is, however, a still milder way of denying the divine predicates than the direct one just described. It is admitted that the predicates of the divine nature are finite, and, more particularly, human qualities, but their rejection is rejected; they are even taken under protection, because it is necessary to man to have a definite conception of God, and since he is man he can form no other than a human conception of him. In relation to God, it is said, these predicates are certainly without any objective validity; but to me, if he is to exist for me, he cannot appear otherwise than as he does appear to me, namely, as a being with attributes analogous to the human. But this distinction between what God is in himself, and what he is for me destroys

---

4. "Les perfections de Dieu sont celles de nos âmes, mais il les possede sans bornes—il y a en nous quelque puissance, quelque connaissance, quelque bonté, mais elles sont toutes entières en Dieu."—Leibnitz (Théod. Preface). "Nihil in anima esse putemus eximium, quod non etiam divinæ naturæ proprium sit—Quidquid a Deo alienum extra definitionem animæ."—St. Gregorius Nyss. "Est ergo, ut videtur, disciplinarum omnium pulcherrima et maxima se ipsum nosse; si quis enim se ipsum norit, Deum cognoscet."—Clemens Alex. (Pæd. l. iii. c. 1).

the peace of religion, and is besides in itself an unfounded and untenable distinction. I cannot know whether God is something else in himself or for himself than he is for me; what he is to me is to me all that he is. For me, there lies in these predicates under which he exists for me, what he is in himself, his very nature; he is for me what he can alone ever be for me. The religious man finds perfect satisfaction in that which God is in relation to himself; of any other relation he knows nothing, for God is to him what he can alone be to man. In the distinction above stated, man takes a point of view above himself, *i.e.,* above his nature, the absolute measure of his being; but this transcendentalism is only an illusion; for I can make the distinction between the object as it is in itself, and the object as it is for me, only where an object can really appear otherwise to me, not where it appears to me such as the absolute measure of my nature determines it to appear—such as it must appear to me. It is true that I may have a merely subjective conception, *i.e.,* one which does not arise out of the general constitution of my species; but if my conception is determined by the constitution of my species, the distinction between what an object is in itself, and what it is for me ceases; for this conception is itself an absolute one. The measure of the species is the absolute measure, law, and criterion of man. And, indeed, religion has the conviction that its conceptions, its predicates of God, are such as every man ought to have, and must have, if he would have the true ones—that they are the conceptions necessary to human nature; nay, further, that they are objectively true, representing God as he is. To every religion the gods of *other* religions are only notions concerning God, but its own conception of God is to it God himself, the true God—God such as he is in himself. Religion is satisfied only with a complete Deity, a God without reservation; it will not have a mere phantasm of God; it demands God himself. Religion gives up its own existence when it gives up the nature of God; it is no longer a truth when it renounces the possession of the true God. Scepticism is the arch-enemy of religion; but the distinction between object and conception—between God as he is in himself, and God as he is for me—is a sceptical distinction, and therefore an irreligious one.

That which is to man the self-existent, the highest being, to which he can conceive nothing higher—that

is to him the Divine Being. How then should he inquire concerning this being, what he is in himself? If God were an object to the bird, he would be a winged being: the bird knows nothing higher, nothing more blissful, than the winged condition. How ludicrous would it be if this bird pronounced: To me God appears as a bird, but what he is in himself I know not. To the bird the highest nature is the bird-nature; take from him the conception of this, and you take from him the conception of the highest being. How, then, could he ask whether God in himself were winged? To ask whether God is in himself what he is for me, is to ask whether God is God, is to lift oneself above one's God, to rise up against him.

Wherever, therefore, this idea, that the religious predicates are only anthropomorphisms, has taken possession of a man, there has doubt, has unbelief, obtained the mastery of faith. And it is only the inconsequence of faint-heartedness and intellectual imbecility which does not proceed from this idea to the formal negation of the predicates, and from thence to the negation of the subject to which they relate. If thou doubtest the objective truth of the predicates, thou must also doubt the objective truth of the subject whose predicates they are. If thy predicates are anthropomorphisms, the subject of them is an anthropomorphism too. If love, goodness, personality, &c., are human attributes, so also is the subject which thou presupposest, the existence of God, the belief that there is a God, an anthropomorphism—a presupposition purely human. Whence knowest thou that the belief in a God at all is not a limitation of man's mode of conception? Higher beings—and thou supposest such—are perhaps so blest in themselves, so at unity with themselves, that they are not hung in suspense between themselves and a yet higher being. To know God and not oneself to be God, to know blessedness and not oneself to enjoy it, is a state of disunity, of unhappiness. Higher beings know nothing of this unhappiness; they have no conception of that which they are not.

Thou believest in love as a divine attribute because thou thyself lovest; thou believest that God is a wise, benevolent being because thou knowest nothing better in thyself than benevolence and wisdom; and thou believest that God exists, that therefore he is a subject—whatever exists is a subject, whether it be defined as substance, person, essence, or otherwise—because thou thyself existest, art thyself a subject. Thou knowest no higher human good than to love, than to be good and wise; and even so thou knowest no higher happiness than to exist, to be a subject; for the consciousness of all reality, of all bliss, is for thee bound up in the consciousness of being a subject, of existing. God is an existence, a subject to thee, for the same reason that he is to thee a wise, a blessed, a personal being. The distinction between the divine predicates and the divine subject is only this, that to thee the subject, the existence, does not appear an anthropomorphism, because the conception of it is necessarily involved in thy own existence as a subject, whereas the predicates do appear anthropomorphisms, because their necessity—the necessity that God should be conscious, wise, good, &c.,—is not an immediate necessity, identical with the being of man, but is evolved by his self-consciousness, by the activity of his thought. I am a subject, I exist, whether I be wise or unwise, good or bad. To exist is to man the first datum; it constitutes the very idea of the subject; it is presupposed by the predicates. Hence man relinquishes the predicates, but the existence of God is to him a settled, irrefragable, absolutely certain, objective truth. But, nevertheless, this distinction is merely an apparent one. The necessity of the subject lies only in the necessity of the predicate. Thou art a subject only in so far as thou art a human subject; the certainty and reality of thy existence lie only in the certainty and reality of thy human attributes. What the subject is lies only in the predicate; the predicate is the *truth* of the subject—the subject only the personified, existing predicate, the predicate conceived as existing. Subject and predicate are distinguished only as existence and essence. The negation of the predicates is therefore the negation of the subject. What remains of the human subject when abstracted from the human attributes? Even in the language of common life the divine predicates—Providence, Omniscience, Omnipotence—are put for the divine subject.

The certainty of the existence of God, of which it has been said that it is as certain, nay, more certain to man than his own existence, depends only on the certainty of the qualities of God—it is in itself no immediate certainty. To the Christian the existence of the Christian God only is a certainty; to the heathen that of the heathen God only. The heathen did not doubt the existence of Jupiter, because he took no offence at the nature of Jupiter, because he could conceive of God under no other qualities, because to him these qualities were a certainty, a divine reality. The reality of the predicate is the sole guarantee of existence.

Whatever man conceives to be true, he immediately conceives to be real (that is, to have an objective existence), because, originally, only the real is true to him—true in opposition to what is merely conceived, dreamed, imagined. The idea of being, of existence, is the original idea of truth; or, originally, man makes truth dependent on existence, subsequently, existence dependent on truth. Now God is the nature of man regarded as absolute truth,—the truth of man; but God, or, what is the same thing, religion, is as various as are the conditions under which man conceives this his nature, regards it as the highest being. These conditions, then, under which man conceives God, are to him the truth, and for that reason they are also the highest existence, or rather they are existence itself; for only the emphatic, the highest existence, is existence, and deserves this name. Therefore, God is an existent, real being, on the very same ground that he is a particular, definite being; for the qualities of God are nothing else than the essential qualities of man himself, and a particular man is what he is, has his existence, his reality, only in his particular conditions. Take away from the Greek the quality of being Greek, and you take away his existence. On this ground it is true that for a definite positive religion—that is, relatively—the certainty of the existence of God is *immediate;* for just as involuntarily, as necessarily, as the Greek was a Greek, so necessarily were his gods Greek beings, so necessarily were they real, existent beings. Religion is that conception of the nature of the world and of man which is essential to, *i.e.,* identical with, a man's nature. But man does not stand above this his necessary conception; on the contrary, it stands above him; it animates, determines, governs him. The necessity of a proof, of a middle term to unite qualities with existence, the possibility of a doubt, is abolished. Only that which is apart from my own being is capable of being doubted by me. How then can I doubt of God, who is my being? To doubt of God is to doubt of myself. Only when God is thought of abstractly, when his predicates are the result of philosophic abstraction, arises the distinction or separation between subject and predicate, existence and nature—arises the fiction that the existence or the subject is something else than the predicate, something immediate, indubitable, in distinction from the predicate, which is held to be doubtful. But this is only a fiction. A God who has abstract predicates has also an abstract existence. Existence, being, varies with varying qualities.

The identity of the subject and predicate is clearly evidenced by the progressive development of religion, which is identical with the progressive development of human culture. So long as man is in a mere state of nature, so long is his god a mere nature-god—a personification of some natural force. Where man inhabits houses, he also encloses his gods in temples. The temple is only a manifestation of the value which man attaches to beautiful buildings. Temples in honour of religion are in truth temples in honour of architecture. With the emerging of man from a state of savagery and wildness to one of culture, with the distinction between what is fitting for man and what is not fitting, arises simultaneously the distinction between that which is fitting and that which is not fitting for God. God is the idea of majesty, of the highest dignity: the religious sentiment is the sentiment of supreme fitness. The later more cultured artists of Greece were the first to embody in the statues of the gods the ideas of dignity, of spiritual grandeur, of imperturbable repose and serenity. But why were these qualities in their view attributes, predicates of God? Because they were in themselves regarded by the Greeks as divinities. Why did those artists exclude all disgusting and low passions? Because they perceived them to be unbecoming, unworthy, unhuman, and consequently ungodlike. The Homeric gods eat and drink;—that implies eating and drinking is a divine pleasure. Physical strength is an attribute of the Homeric gods: Zeus is the strongest of the gods. Why? Because physical strength, in and by itself, was regarded as something glorious, divine. To the ancient Germans the highest virtues were those of the warrior; therefore their supreme god was the god of war, Odin,—war, "the original or oldest law." Not the attribute of the divinity, but the divineness or deity of the attribute, is the first true Divine Being. Thus what theology and philosophy have held to be God, the Absolute, the Infinite, is not God; but that which they have held not to be God is

God: namely, the attribute, the quality, whatever has reality. Hence he alone is the true atheist to whom the predicates of the Divine Being,—for example, love, wisdom, justice,—are nothing; not he to whom merely the subject of these predicates is nothing. And in no wise is the negation of the subject necessarily also a negation of the predicates considered in themselves. These have an intrinsic, independent reality; they force their recognition upon man by their very nature; they are self-evident truths to him; they prove, they attest themselves. It does not follow that goodness, justice, wisdom, are chimæras because the existence of God is a chimæra, nor truths because this is a truth. The idea of God is dependent on the idea of justice, of benevolence; a God who is not benevolent, not just, not wise, is no God; but the converse does not hold. The fact is not that a quality is divine because God has it, but that God has it because it is in itself divine: because without it God would be a defective being. Justice, wisdom, in general every quality which constitutes the divinity of God, is determined and known by itself independently, but the idea of God is determined by the qualities which have thus been previously judged to be worthy of the divine nature; only in the case in which I identify God and justice, in which I think of God immediately as the reality of the idea of justice, is the idea of God self-determined. But if God as a subject is the determined, while the quality, the predicate, is the determining, then in truth the rank of the godhead is due not to the subject, but to the predicate.

Not until several, and those contradictory, attributes are united in one being, and this being is conceived as personal—the personality being thus brought into especial prominence—not until then is the origin of religion lost sight of, is it forgotten that what the activity of the reflective power has converted into a predicate distinguishable or separable from the subject, was originally the true subject. Thus the Greeks and Romans deified accidents as substances; virtues, states of mind, passions, as independent beings. Man, especially the religious man, is to himself the measure of all things, of all reality. Whatever strongly impresses a man, whatever produces an unusual effect on his mind, if it be only a peculiar, inexplicable sound or note, he personifies as a divine being. Religion embraces all the objects of the world: everything existing has been an object of religious reverence; in the nature and consciousness of religion there is nothing else than what lies in the nature of man and in his consciousness of himself and of the world. Religion has no material exclusively its own. In Rome even the passions of fear and terror had their temples. The Christians also made mental phenomena into independent beings, their own feelings into qualities of things, the passions which governed them into powers which governed the world, in short, predicates of their own nature, whether recognised as such or not, into independent subjective existences. Devils, cobolds, witches, ghosts, angels, were sacred truths as long as the religious spirit held undivided sway over mankind.

In order to banish from the mind the identity of the divine and human predicates, and the consequent identity of the divine and human nature, recourse is had to the idea that God, as the absolute, real Being, has an infinite fulness of various predicates, of which we here know only a part, and those such as are analogous to our own; while the rest, by virtue of which God must thus have quite a different nature from the human or that which is analogous to the human, we shall only know in the future—that is, after death. But an infinite plenitude or multitude of predicates which are really different, so different that the one does not immediately involve the other, is realised only in an infinite plenitude or multitude of different beings or individuals. Thus the human nature presents an infinite abundance of different predicates, and for that very reason it presents an infinite abundance of different individuals. Each new man is a new predicate, a new phasis of humanity. As many as are the men, so many are the powers, the properties of humanity. It is true that there are the same elements in every individual, but under such various conditions and modifications that they appear new and peculiar. The mystery of the inexhaustible fulness of the divine predicates is therefore nothing else than the mystery of human nature considered as an infinitely varied, infinitely modifiable, but, consequently, phenomenal being. Only in the realm of the senses, only in space and time, does there exist a being of really infinite qualities or predicates. Where there are really different predicates there are different times. One man is a distinguished musician, a distinguished author, a distinguished physician; but he cannot compose music, write books, and

perform cures in the same moment of time. Time, and not the Hegelian dialectic, is the medium of uniting opposites, contradictories, in one and the same subject. But distinguished and detached from the nature of man, and combined with the idea of God, the infinite fulness of various predicates is a conception without reality, a mere phantasy, a conception derived from the sensible world, but without the essential conditions, without the truth of sensible existence, a conception which stands in direct contradiction with the Divine Being considered as a spiritual, *i.e.*, an abstract, simple, single being; for the predicates of God are precisely of this character, that one involves all the others, because there is no real difference between them. If, therefore, in the present predicates I have not the future, in the present God not the future God, then the future God is not the present, but they are two distinct beings.[5] But this distinction is in contradiction with the unity and simplicity of the theological God. Why is a given predicate a predicate of God? Because it is divine in its nature, *i.e.*, because it expresses no limitation, no defect. Why are other predicates applied to him? Because, however various in themselves, they agree in this, that they all alike express perfection, unlimitedness. Hence I can conceive innumerable predicates of God, because they must all agree with the abstract idea of the Godhead, and must have in common that which constitutes every single predicate a divine attribute. Thus it is in the system of Spinoza. He speaks of an infinite number of attributes of the divine substance, but he specifies none except Thought and Extension. Why? Because it is a matter of indifference to know them; nay, Because they are in themselves indifferent, superfluous; for with all these innumerable predicates, I yet always mean to say the same thing as when I speak of Thought and Extension. Why is Thought an attribute of substance? Because, according to Spinoza, it is capable of being conceived by itself, because it expresses something indivisible, perfect, infinite. Why Extension or Matter? For the

---

5. For religious faith there is no other distinction between the present and future God than that the former is an object of faith, of conception, of imagination, while the latter is to be an object of immediate, that is, personal, sensible perception. In this life and in the next he is the same God; but in the one he is incomprehensible, in the other comprehensible.

same reason. Thus, substance can have an indefinite number of predicates, because it is not their specific definition, their difference, but their identity, their equivalence, which makes them attributes of substance. Or rather, substance has innumerable predicates only because (how strange!) it has properly no predicate; that is, no definite, real predicate. The indefinite unity which is the product of thought, completes itself by the indefinite multiplicity which is the product of the imagination. Because the predicate is not *multum,* it is *multa.* In truth, the positive predicates are Thought and Extension. In these two infinitely more is said than in the nameless innumerable predicates; for they express something definite—in them I have something. But substance is too indifferent, too apathetic to be *something;* that is, to have qualities and passions; that it may not be something, it is rather nothing.

Now, when it is shown that what the subject is lies entirely in the attributes of the subject; that is, that the predicate is the true subject; it is also proved that if the divine predicates are attributes of the human nature, the subject of those predicates is also of the human nature. But the divine predicates are partly general, partly personal. The general predicates are the metaphysical, but these serve only as external points of support to religion; they are not the characteristic definitions of religion. It is the personal predicates alone which constitute the essence of religion—in which the Divine Being is the object of religion. Such are, for example, that God is a Person, that he is the moral Lawgiver, the Father of mankind, the Holy One, the Just, the Good, the Merciful. It is, however, at once clear, or it will at least be clear in the sequel, with regard to these and other definitions, that, especially as applied to a personality, they are purely human definitions, and that consequently man in religion—in his relation to God—is in relation to his own nature; for to the religious sentiment these predicates are not mere conceptions, mere images, which man forms of God, to be distinguished from that which God is in himself, but truths, facts, realities. Religion knows nothing of anthropomorphisms; to it they are not anthropomorphisms. It is the very essence of religion, that to it these definitions express the nature of God. They are pronounced to be images only by the understanding, which reflects on religion, and which while

defending them yet before its own tribunal denies them. But to the religious sentiment God is a real Father, real Love and Mercy; for to it he is a real, living, personal being, and therefore his attributes are also living and personal. Nay, the definitions which are the most sufficing to the religious sentiment are precisely those which give the most offence to the understanding, and which in the process of reflection on religion it denies. Religion is essentially emotion; hence, objectively also, emotion is to it necessarily of a divine nature. Even anger appears to it an emotion not unworthy of God, provided only there be a religious motive at the foundation of this anger.

But here it is also essential to observe, and this phenomenon is an extremely remarkable one, characterising the very core of religion, that in proportion as the divine subject is in reality human, the greater is the apparent difference between God and man; that is, the more, by reflection on religion, by theology, is the identity of the divine and human denied, and the human, considered as such, is depreciated.[6] The reason of this is, that as what is positive in the conception of the divine being can only be human, the conception of man, as an object of consciousness, can only be negative. To enrich God, man must become poor; that God may be all, man must be nothing. But he desires to be nothing in himself, because what he takes from himself is not lost to him, since it is preserved in God. Man has his being in God; why then should he have it in himself? Where is the necessity of positing the same thing twice, of having it twice? What man withdraws from himself, what he renounces in himself, he only enjoys in an incomparably higher and fuller measure in God.

The monks made a vow of chastity to God; they mortified the sexual passion in themselves, but therefore they had in heaven, in the Virgin Mary, the image of woman—an image of love. They could the more easily dispense with real woman in proportion as an ideal woman was an object of love to them. The greater the importance they attached to the denial of

6. Inter creatorem et creaturam non potest tanta similitudo notari, quin inter eos major sit dissimilitudo notanda.—Later. Conc. can. 2. (Summa Omn. Conc. Carranza. Antw. 1559. p. 326.) The last distinction between man and God, between the finite and infinite nature, to which the religious speculative imagination soars, is the distinction between Something and Nothing, Ens and Non-Ens; for only in Nothing is all community with other beings abolished.

sensuality, the greater the importance of the heavenly virgin for them: she was to them in the place of Christ, in the stead of God. The more the sensual tendencies are renounced, the more sensual is the God to whom they are sacrificed. For whatever is made an offering to God has an especial value attached to it; in it God is supposed to have especial pleasure. That which is the highest in the estimation of man is naturally the highest in the estimation of his God; what pleases man pleases God also. The Hebrews did not offer to Jehovah unclean, ill-conditioned animals; on the contrary, those which they most highly prized, which they themselves ate, were also the food of God (*Cibus Dei,* Lev. iii. 2). Wherever, therefore, the denial of the sensual delights is made a special offering, a sacrifice well-pleasing to God, there the highest value is attached to the senses, and the sensuality which has been renounced is unconsciously restored, in the fact that God takes the place of the material delights which have been renounced. The nun weds herself to God; she has a heavenly bridegroom, the monk a heavenly bride. But the heavenly virgin is only a sensible presentation of a general truth, having relation to the essence of religion. Man denies as to himself only what he attributes to God. Religion abstracts from man, from the world; but it can only abstract from the limitations, from the phenomena; in short, from the negative, not from the essence, the positive, of the world and humanity: hence, in the very abstraction and negation it must recover that from which it abstracts, or believes itself to abstract. And thus, in reality, whatever religion consciously denies—always supposing that what is denied by it is something essential, true, and consequently incapable of being ultimately denied—it unconsciously restores in God. Thus, in religion man denies his reason; of himself he knows nothing of God, his thoughts are only worldly, earthly; he can only believe what God reveals to him. But on this account the thoughts of God are human, earthly thoughts: like man, he has plans in his mind, he accommodates himself to circumstances and grades of intelligence, like a tutor with his pupils; he calculates closely the effect of his gifts and revelations; he observes man in all his doings; he knows all things, even the most earthly, the commonest, the most trivial. In brief, man in relation to God denies his own knowledge, his own thoughts, that he may place them in God. Man gives up his

personality; but in return, God, the Almighty, infinite, unlimited being, is a person; he denies human dignity, the human *ego;* but in return God is to him a selfish, egotistical being, who in all things seeks only himself, his own honour, his own ends; he represents God as simply seeking the satisfaction of his own selfishness, while yet he frowns on that of every other being; his God is the very luxury of egoism.[7] Religion further denies goodness as a quality of human nature; man is wicked, corrupt, incapable of good; but, on the other hand, God is only good—the Good Being. Man's nature demands as an object goodness, personified as God; but is it not hereby declared that goodness is an essential tendency of man? If my heart is wicked, my understanding perverted, how can I perceive and feel the holy to be holy, the good to be good? Could I perceive the beauty of a fine picture if my mind were aesthetically an absolute piece of perversion? Though I may not be a painter, though I may not have the power of producing what is beautiful myself, I must yet have aesthetic feeling, aesthetic comprehension, since I perceive the beauty that is presented to me externally. Either goodness does not exist at all for man, or, if it does exist, therein is revealed to the individual man the holiness and goodness of human nature. That which is absolutely opposed to my nature, to which I am united by no bond of sympathy, is not even conceivable or perceptible by me. The holy is in opposition to me only as regards the modifications of my personality, but as regards my fundamental nature it is in unity with me. The holy is a reproach to my sinfulness; in it I recognise myself as a sinner; but in so doing, while I blame myself, I acknowledge what I am not, but ought to be, and what, for that very reason, I, according to my destination, can be; for an "ought" which has no corresponding capability does not affect me, is a ludicrous chimæra without any true relation to my mental constitution. But when I acknowledge goodness as my destination, as my law, I acknowledge it, whether consciously or unconsciously, as my own nature. Another nature than my own, one

---

7. Gloriam suam plus amat Deus quam omnes creaturas. "God can only love himself, can only think of himself, can only work for himself. In creating man, God seeks his own ends, his own glory," &c.—Vide P. Bayle, Ein Beitrag zur Geschichte der Philos. u. Menschh., pp. 104–107.

different in quality, cannot touch me. I can perceive sin as sin, only when I perceive it to be a contradiction of myself with myself—that is, of my personality with my fundamental nature. As a contradiction of the absolute, considered as another being, the feeling of sin is inexplicable, unmeaning.

The distinction between Augustinianism and Pelagianism consists only in this, that the former expresses after the manner of religion what the latter expresses after the manner of Rationalism. Both say the same thing, both vindicate the goodness of man; but Pelagianism does it directly, in a rationalistic and moral form; Augustinianism indirectly, in a mystical, that is, a religious form.[8] For that which is given to man's God is in truth given to man himself; what a man declares concerning God, he in truth declares concerning himself. Augustinianism would be a truth, and a truth opposed to Pelagianism, only if man had the devil for his God, and, with the consciousness that he was the devil, honoured, reverenced, and worshipped him as the highest being. But so long as man adores a good being as his God, so long does he contemplate in God the goodness of his own nature.

As with the doctrine of the radical corruption of human nature, so is it with the identical doctrine, that man can do nothing good, *i.e.*, in truth, nothing of himself—by his own strength. For the denial of human strength and spontaneous moral activity to be true, the moral activity of God must also be denied; and we must say, with the Oriental nihilist or pantheist: the Divine being is absolutely without will or action, indifferent, knowing nothing of the discrimination between evil and good. But he who defines God as an active being, and not only so, but as morally active and morally critical,—as a being who loves, works, and rewards good, punishes, rejects, and condemns evil,—he who thus defines God only in appearance denies human activity, in fact, making it the highest, the most real activity. He who makes God act humanly, declares human activity to be divine; he says: A god who is not active, and not morally or humanly active, is no god; and thus he makes the idea of the Godhead dependent on the idea of activity, that is, of human activity, for a higher he knows not.

Man—this is the mystery of religion—projects his being into objectivity,[9] and then again makes himself an object to this projected image of himself thus converted into a subject; he thinks of himself is an object to himself, but as the object of an object, of another being than himself. Thus here. Man is an object to God. That man is good or evil is not indifferent to God; no! He has a lively, profound interest in man's being good; he wills that man should be good, happy—for without goodness there is no happiness. Thus the religious man virtually retracts the nothingness of human activity, by making his dispositions and actions an object to God, by making man the end of God—for that which is an object to the mind is an end in action; by making the divine activity a means of human salvation. God acts, that man may be good and happy. Thus man, while he is apparently humiliated to the lowest degree, is in truth exalted to the highest. Thus, in and through God, man has in view himself alone. It is true that man places the aim of his action in God, but God has no other aim of action than the moral and eternal salvation of man: thus man has in fact no other aim than himself. The divine activity is not distinct from the human.

How could the divine activity work on me as its object, nay, work in me, if it were essentially different from me; how could it have a human aim, the aim of ameliorating and blessing man, if it were not itself human? Does not the purpose determine the nature of the act? When man makes his moral improvement an

---

8. Pelagianism denies God, religion—isti tantam tribuunt potestatem voluntati, ut pietati auferant orationem. (Augustin de Nat. et Grat. cont. Pelagium, c. 58.) It has only the Creator, *i.e.*, Nature, as a basis, not the Saviour, the true God of the religious sentiment—in a word, it denies God; but, as a consequence of this, it elevates man into a God, since it makes him a being not needing God, self-sufficing, independent. (See on this subject Luther against Erasmus and Augustine, l. c. c. 33.) Augustinianism denies man; but, as a consequence of this, it reduces God to the level of man, even to the ignominy of the cross, for the sake of man. The former puts man in the place of God, the latter puts God in the place of man; both lead to the same result—the distinction is only apparent, a pious illusion. Augustinianism is only an inverted Pelagianism; what to the latter is a subject, is to the former an object.

9. The religious, the original mode in which man becomes objective to himself, is (as is clearly enough explained in this work) to be distinguished from the mode in which this occurs in reflection and speculation; the latter is voluntary, the former involuntary, necessary—as necessary as art, as speech. With the progress of time, it is true, theology coincides with religion.

aim to himself, he has divine resolutions, divine projects; but also, when God seeks the salvation of man, he has human ends and a human mode of activity corresponding to these ends. Thus in God man has only his own activity as an object. But for the very reason that he regards his own activity as objective, goodness only as an object, he necessarily receives the impulse, the motive not from himself, but from this object. He contemplates his nature as external to himself, and this nature as goodness; thus it is self-evident, it is mere tautology to say that the impulse to good comes only from thence where he places the good.

God is the highest subjectivity of man abstracted from himself; hence man can do nothing of himself, all goodness comes from God. The more subjective God is, the more completely does man divest himself of his subjectivity, because God is, *per se,* his relinquished self, the possession of which he however again vindicates to himself. As the action of the arteries drives the blood into the extremities, and the action of the veins brings it back again, as life in general consists in a perpetual systole and diastole; so is it in religion. In the religious systole man propels his own nature from himself, he throws himself outward; in the religious diastole he receives the rejected nature into his heart again. God alone is the being who acts of himself,—this is the force of repulsion in religion; God is the being who acts in me, with me, through me, upon me, for me, is the principle of my salvation, of my good dispositions and actions, consequently my own good principle and nature,—this is the force of attraction in religion.

The course of religious development which has been generally indicated consists specifically in this, that man abstracts more and more from God, and attributes more and more to himself. This is especially apparent in the belief in revelation. That which to a later age or a cultured people is given by nature or reason, is to an earlier age, or to a yet uncultured people, given by God. Every tendency of man, however natural—even the impulse to cleanliness, was conceived by the Israelites as a positive divine ordinance. From this example we again see that God is lowered, is conceived more entirely on the type of ordinary humanity, in proportion as man detracts from himself. How can the self-humiliation of man go further than when he disclaims the capability of fulfilling sponta-

neously the requirements of common decency?[10] The Christian religion, on the other hand, distinguished the impulses and passions of man according to their quality, their character; it represented only good emotions, good dispositions, good thoughts, as revelations, operations—that is, as dispositions, feelings, thoughts,—of God; for what God reveals is a quality of God himself: that of which the heart is full overflows the lips; as is the effect such is the cause; as the revelation, such the being who reveals himself. A God who reveals himself in good dispositions is a God whose essential attribute is only moral perfection. The Christian religion distinguishes inward moral purity from external physical purity; the Israelites identified the two.[11] In relation to the Israelitish religion, the Christian religion is one of criticism and freedom. The Israelite trusted himself to do nothing except what was commanded by God; he was without will even in external things; the authority of religion extended itself even to his food. The Christian religion, on the other hand, in all these external things made man dependent on himself, *i.e.,* placed in man what the Israelite placed out of himself in God. Israel is the most complete presentation of Positivism in religion. In relation to the Israelite, the Christian is an *esprit fort,* a freethinker. Thus do things change. What yesterday was still religion is no longer such to-day; and what to-day is atheism, tomorrow will be religion.

DISCUSSION QUESTIONS

1. Do you agree with Feuerbach's account of the "essence of religion," especially Christianity, and his arguments for the true nature of divine beings? Why or why not?
2. What are some religious, or spiritual, traditions that may not fit Feuerbach's analyses here?
3. Feuerbach's perspective on religion has been criticized as too ethnocentric. Why might this be so, and how much would it undermine his conclusions? Explain.
4. Do you think, as Feuerbach did, that humans generally will eventually outgrow their belief in supernatural beings? Why or why not?

---

10. Deut. xxiii. 12, 13.
11. See, for example, Gen. xxxv. 2; Levit. xi. 44; xx. 26; and the Commentary of Le Clerc on these passages.

39. Carol Christ (b. 1944)

"Why Women Need the Goddess: Phenomenological, Psychological, and Political Reflections"

Carol Christ is an American theologian who over the past three decades has been actively involved in the feminist movement in the United States to rethink the place of religious belief and experience in human life. Responding primarily to the Christian and Jewish traditions, Christ and many other religious theorists have pointed out the variety of ways in which the male has been glorified and the female devalued in the religious worldview—for example, in conceptions of God, "his" Creation, and "his" expectations of "man." They also have explored the possibilities of a transformed religious life that would be nonsexist and affirming of women's experiences as valued participants in the Creation. Opinions have varied regarding whether this requires leaving behind Christian and Jewish doctrine and practice entirely or reforming those religions from within.

In this selection Christ seems to be moving in the direction of the former option, as she reflects on the nature and consequences of women's intentional use of Goddess symbolism in place of the traditional symbolism of "God the Father." Maintaining that most members of any culture need symbol, myth, and ritual to help make sense of their connection to the greater reality beyond their immediate perceptible experience, the task as she sees it is not simply to refute religious belief but also to reconstruct it on a new foundation so it becomes healthier and more empowering for all its adherents. This essay originally appeared in the journal *Heresies* in 1978 and has been reprinted widely since then.

QUESTIONS FOR CRITICAL READING

1. From the standpoint of women, according to Christ, what are the problems with patriarchal religion?
2. What is the political and psychological role of religious symbolism in human life, and how can women bring about a healthy change in such symbolism, in Christ's view?
3. What are the four aspects of Goddess symbolism Christ describes and advocates using?

4. How does the evaluation of personal will differ in patriarchal God-centered doctrine and the Goddess-centered approach described by Christ?

TERMS TO NOTE

phenomenological: In this context, a pretheoretical, descriptive approach to inquiry that as much as possible lets the subjects under study speak for themselves.

paradigm: An exemplary model.

trinitarian: Traditionally, that which has to do with the Holy Trinity of Christian doctrine, that is, the union of Father, Son, and Holy Spirit in one Divine Being.

misogynist: Expressing hostility toward women.

iconography: The illustration of a subject by means of visual images such as painted figures.

patriarchal: Referring to male-dominant social relations as well as their cultural or psychological products.

At the close of Ntosake Shange's stupendously successful Broadway play "For Colored Girls Who Have Considered Suicide When the Rainbow Is Enuf," a tall beautiful black woman rises from despair to cry out, "I found God in myself and I loved her fiercely."[1] Her discovery is echoed by women around the country who meet spontaneously in small groups on full moons, solstices, and equinoxes to celebrate the Goddess as symbol of life and death powers and waxing and waning energies in the universe and in themselves.[2]

> It is the night of the full moon. Nine women
> stand in a circle, on a rocky hill above the city.
> The western sky is rosy with the setting sun;
> in the east the moon's face begins to peer above

the horizon. . . . The woman pours out a cup of wine onto the earth, refills it and raises it high. "Hail, Tana, Mother of mothers!" she cries. "Awaken from your long sleep, and return to your children again!"[3]

What are the political and psychological effects of this fierce new love of the divine in themselves for women whose spiritual experience has been focused by the male God of Judaism and Christianity? Is the spiritual dimension of feminism a passing diversion, an escape from difficult but necessary political work? Or does the emergence of the symbol of Goddess among women have significant political and psychological ramifications for the feminist movement?

To answer this question, we must first understand the importance of religious symbols and rituals in human life and consider the effect of male symbolism of God on women. According to anthropologist Clifford Geertz, religious symbols shape a cultural ethos, defining the deepest values of a society and the persons in it. "Religion," Geertz writes "is a system of symbols which act to produce powerful, pervasive, and longlasting moods and motivations"[4] in the people of a given culture. A "mood" for Geertz is a psychological attitude such as awe, trust, and respect, while a "motivation" is the *social* and *political* trajectory created by a mood that transforms mythos into ethos, symbol system into social and political reality. Symbols have both psychological and political effects, because they create the inner conditions (deep-seated attitudes and feelings) that lead people to feel comfortable with or to accept social and political arrangements that correspond to the symbol system.

Because religion has such a compelling hold on the deep psyches of so many people, feminists cannot afford to leave it in the hands of the fathers. Even people who no longer "believe in God" or participate in the institutional structure of patriarchal religion still may not be free of the power of the symbolism of God the Father. A symbol's effect does not depend on rational assent, for a symbol also functions on levels of the psyche other than the rational. Religion fulfills deep psychic needs by providing symbols and rituals that enable people to cope with limit situations[5] in human life (death, evil, suffering) and to pass through life's

important transitions (birth, sexuality, death). Even people who consider themselves completely secularized will often find themselves sitting in a church or synagogue when a friend or relative gets married, or when a parent or friend has died. The symbols associated with these important rituals cannot fail to affect the deep or unconscious structures of the mind of even a person who has rejected these symbolisms on a conscious level—especially if the person is under stress. The reason for the continuing effect of religious symbols is that the mind abhors a vacuum. Symbol systems cannot simply be rejected, they must be replaced. Where there is not any replacement, the mind will revert to familiar structures at times of crisis, bafflement, or defeat.

Religions centered on the worship of a male God create "moods" and "motivations" that keep women in a state of psychological dependence on men and male authority, while at the same [time] legitimating the *political* and *social* authority of fathers and sons in the institutions of society.

Religious symbol systems focused around exclusively male images of divinity create the impression that female power can never be fully legitimate or wholly beneficent. This message need never be explicitly stated (as, for example, it is in the story of Eve) for its effect to be felt. A woman completely ignorant of the myths of female evil in biblical religion nonetheless acknowledges the anomaly of female power when she prays exclusively to a male God. She may see herself as like God (created in the image of God) only by denying her own sexual identity and affirming God's transcendence of sexual identity. But she can never have the experience that is freely available to every man and boy in her culture, of having her full sexual identity affirmed as being in the image and likeness of God. In Geertz' terms, her "mood" is one of trust in male power as salvific and distrust of female power in herself and other women as inferior or dangerous. Such a powerful, pervasive, and longlasting "mood" cannot fail to become a "motivation" that translates into social and political reality.

In *Beyond God the Father,* feminist theologian Mary Daly detailed the psychological and political ramifications of father religion for women. "If God in 'his' heaven is a father ruling his people," she wrote, "then it is the 'nature' of things and according to divine plan and the order of the universe that society be male dominated. Within this context, a *mystification of roles* takes place: The husband dominating his wife represents God 'himself.' The images and values of a given society have been projected into the realm of dogmas and 'Articles of Faith,' and these in turn justify the social structures which have given rise to them and which sustain their plausibility."[6]

Philosopher Simone de Beauvoir was well aware of the function of patriarchal religion as legitimater of male power. As she wrote, "Man enjoys the great advantage of having a god endorse the code he writes; and since man exercises a sovereign authority over women it is especially fortunate that this authority has been vested in him by the Supreme Being. For the Jew, Mohammedans, and Christians, among others, man is Master by divine right; the fear of God will therefore repress any impulse to revolt in the downtrodden female."[7]

This brief discussion of the psychological and political effects of God religion puts us in an excellent position to begin to understand the significance of the symbol of Goddess for women. In discussing the meaning of the Goddess, my method will first be phenomenological. I will isolate a meaning of the symbol of the Goddess as it has emerged in the lives of contemporary women. I will then discuss its psychological and political significance by contrasting the "moods" and "motivations" engendered by Goddess symbols with those engendered by Christian symbolism. I will also correlate Goddess symbolism with themes that have emerged in the women's movement, in order to show how Goddess symbolism undergirds and legitimates the concerns of the women's movement, much as God symbolism in Christianity undergirded the interests of men in patriarchy. I will discuss four aspects of Goddess symbolism here: the Goddess as affirmation of female power, the female body, the female will, and women's bonds and heritage. There are, of course, many other meanings of the Goddess that I will not discuss here.

The sources for the symbol of the Goddess in contemporary spirituality are traditions of Goddess worship and modern women's experience. The ancient Mediterranean, pre-Christian European, native Amer-

ican, Mesoamerican, Hindu, African, and other traditions are rich sources for Goddess symbolism. But these traditions are filtered through modern women's experiences. Traditions of Goddesses, subordination to Gods, for example, are ignored. Ancient traditions are tapped selectively and eclecticly, but they are not considered authoritative for modern consciousness. The Goddess symbol has emerged spontaneously in the dreams, fantasies, and thoughts of many women around the country in the past several years. Kirsten Grimstad and Susan Rennie reported that they were surprised to discover widespread interest in spirituality, including the Goddess, among feminists around the country in the summer of 1974.[8] *WomanSpirit* magazine, which published its first issue in 1974 and has contributors from across the United States, has expressed the grass roots nature of the women's spirituality movement. In 1976, a journal, *Lady Unique,* devoted to the Goddess emerged. In 1975, the first women's spirituality conference was held in Boston and attended by 1,800 women. In 1978, a University of Santa Cruz course on the Goddess drew over 500 people. Sources for this essay are these manifestations of the Goddess in modern women's experiences as reported in *WomanSpirit, Lady Unique,* and elsewhere, and as expressed in conversations I have had with women who have been thinking about the Goddess and women's spirituality.

The simplest and most basic meaning of the symbol of Goddess is the acknowledgement of the legitimacy of female power as a beneficent and independent power. A woman who echoes Ntosake Shange's dramatic statement, "I found God in myself and I loved her fiercely," is saying "Female power is strong and creative." She is saying that the divine principle, the saving and sustaining power, is in herself, that she will no longer look to men or male figures as saviors. The strength and independence of female power can be intuited by contemplating ancient and modern images of the Goddess. This meaning of the symbol of Goddess is simple and obvious, and yet it is difficult for many to comprehend. It stands in sharp contrast to the paradigms of female dependence on males that have been predominant in Western religion and culture. The internationally acclaimed novelist Monique Wittig captured the novelty and flavor of the affirmation of female power when she wrote, in her mythic work *Les Guerilleres,*

> There was a time when you were not a slave, remember that. You walked alone, full of laughter, you bathed bare-bellied. You say you have lost all recollection of it, remember . . . you say there are no words to describe it, you say it does not exist. But remember. Make an effort to remember. Or, failing that, invent.[9]

While Wittig does not speak directly of the Goddess here, she captures the "mood" of joyous celebration of female freedom and independence that is created in women who define their identities through the symbol of Goddess. Artist Mary Beth Edelson expressed the political "motivations" inspired by the Goddess when she wrote,

> The ascending archetypal symbols of the feminine unfold today in the psyche of modern Every woman. They encompass the multiple forms of the Great Goddess. Reaching across the centuries we take the hands of our Ancient Sisters. The Great Goddess alive and well is rising to announce to the patriarchs that their 5,000 years are up—Hallelujah! Here we come.[10]

The affirmation of female power contained in the Goddess symbol has both psychological and political consequences. Psychologically, it means the defeat of the view engendered by patriarchy that women's power is inferior and dangerous. This new "mood" of affirmation of female power also leads to new "motivations"; it supports and undergirds women's trust in their own power and the power of other women in family and society.

If the simplest meaning of the Goddess symbol is an affirmation of the legitimacy and beneficience of female power, then a question immediately arises, "Is the Goddess simply female power writ large, and if so, why bother with the symbol of Goddess at all? Or does the symbol refer to a Goddess 'out there' who is not reducible to a human potential?" The many women who have rediscovered the power of Goddess would give three answers to this question: (1) The Goddess is divine female, a personification who can be invoked in prayer and ritual; (2) the Goddess is symbol of the life, death, and rebirth energy in nature and culture, in personal and communal life and (3) the Goddess is symbol of the affirmation of the legitimacy and beauty of female power (made possible by the new becoming of women in the women's liberation movement). If one were to ask these women which answer is the "correct" one, different responses would be given. Some would assert that the Goddess definitely is *not* "out there," that the symbol of a divinity "out there" is part of the legacy of patriarchal oppression, which brings with it the authoritarianism, hierarchicalism, and dogmatic rigidity associated with biblical monotheistic religions. They might assert that the Goddess symbol reflects the sacred power within women and nature, suggesting the connectedness between women's cycles of menstruation, birth, and menopause, and the life and death cycles of the universe. Others seem quite comfortable with the notion of Goddess as a divine female protector and creator and would find their experience of Goddess limited by the assertion that she is not *also* out there as well as within themselves and in all natural processes. When asked what the symbol of Goddess means, feminist priestess Starhawk replied, "It all depends on how I feel. When I feel weak, she is someone who can help and protect me. When I feel strong, she is the symbol of my own power. At other times I feel her as the natural energy in my body and the world."[11] How are we to evaluate such a statement? Theologians might call these the words of a sloppy thinker. But my deepest intuition tells me they contain a wisdom that Western theological thought has lost.

To theologians, these differing views of the "meaning" of the symbol of Goddess might seem to threaten a replay of the trinitarian controversies. Is there, perhaps, a way of doing theology, which would not lead immediately into dogmatic controversy, which would not require theologians to say definitively that one understanding is true and the others are false? Could people's relation to a common symbol be made primary and varying interpretations be acknowledged? The diversity of explications of the meaning of the Goddess symbol suggests that symbols have a richer significance than any explications of their meaning can express, a point literary critics have long insisted on. This phenomenological fact suggests that theologians may need to give more than lip service to a theory of symbol in which the symbol is viewed as the primary fact and the meanings are viewed as secondary. It also suggests that a *thea*logy[12] of the Goddess would be very different from the *theo*logy we have known in the West. But to spell out this notion of the primacy of *symbol* in thealogy in contrast to the primacy of the *explanation* in theology would be the topic of another paper. Let me simply state that women, who have been deprived of a female religious symbol system for centuries, are therefore in an excellent position to recognize the power and primacy of symbols. I believe women must develop a theory of symbol and thealogy congruent with their experience at the same time as they "remember and invent" new symbol systems.

A second important implication of the Goddess symbol for women is the affirmation of the female body and the life cycle expressed in it. Because of women's unique position as menstruants, birthgivers, and those who have traditionally cared for the young and the dying, women's connection to the body, nature, and this world has been obvious. Women were denigrated because they seemed more carnal, fleshy, and earthy than the culture-creating males.[13] The misogynist anti*body* tradition in Western thought is symbolized in the myth of Eve who is traditionally viewed as a sexual temptress, the epitome of women's carnal nature. This tradition reaches its nadir in the *Malleus Maleficarum (The Hammer of Evil-Doing Women),* which states, "All witchcraft stems from carnal lust, which in women is insatiable."[14] The Virgin Mary, the positive female image in Christianity does not contradict Christian denigration of the female body and its powers. The Virgin Mary is revered because she, in her perpetual virginity, transcends the carnal sexuality attributed to most women.

The denigration of the female body is expressed in cultural and religious taboos surrounding menstruation, childbirth, and menopause in women. While menstruation taboos may have originated in a perception of the awesome powers of the female body,[15] they degenerated into a simple perception that there is something "wrong" with female bodily functions. Menstruating women were forbidden to enter the sanctuary in ancient Hebrew and premodern Christian communities. Although only Orthodox Jews still enforce religious taboos against menstruant women, few women in our culture grow up affirming their menstruation as a connection to sacred power. Most women learn that menstruation is a curse and grow up believing that the bloody facts of menstruation are best hidden away. Feminists challenge this attitude to the female body. Judy Chicago's art piece "Menstruation Bathroom" broke these menstrual taboos. In a sterile white bathroom, she exhibited boxes of Tampax and Kotex on an open shelf, and the wastepaper basket was overflowing with bloody tampons and sanitary napkins.[16] Many women who viewed the piece felt relieved to have their "dirty secret" out in the open.

The denigration of the female body and its powers is further expressed in Western culture's attitudes toward childbirth.[17] Religious iconography does not celebrate the birthgiver, and there is no theology or ritual that enables a woman to celebrate the process of birth as a spiritual experience. Indeed, Jewish and Christian traditions also had blood taboos concerning the woman who had recently given birth. While these religious taboos are rarely enforced today (again, only by Orthodox Jews), they have secular equivalents. Giving birth is treated as a disease requiring hospitalization, and the woman is viewed as a passive object, anesthetized to ensure her acquiescence to the will of the doctor. The women's liberation movement has challenged these cultural attitudes, and many feminists have joined with advocates of natural childbirth and home birth in emphasizing the need for women to control and take pride in their bodies, including the birth process.

Western culture also gives little dignity to the postmenopausal or aging woman. It is no secret that our culture is based on a denial of aging and death, and that women suffer more severely from this denial than men. Women are placed on a pedestal and considered powerful when they are young and beautiful, but they are said to lose this power as they age. As feminists have pointed out, the "power" of the young woman is illusory, since beauty standards are defined by men, and since few women are considered (or consider themselves) beautiful for more than a few years of their lives. Some men are viewed as wise and authoritative in age, but old women are pitied and shunned. Religious iconography supports this cultural attitude toward aging women. The purity and virginity of Mary and the female saints is often expressed in the iconographic convention of perpetual youth. Moreover, religious mythology associates aging women with evil in the symbol of the wicked old witch. Feminists have challenged cultural myths of aging women and have urged women to reject patriarchal beauty standards and to celebrate the distinctive beauty of women of all ages.

The symbol of Goddess aids the process of naming and reclaiming the female body and its cycles and processes. In the ancient world and among modern women, the Goddess symbol represents the birth, death, and rebirth processes of the natural and human worlds. The female body is viewed as the direct incarnation of waxing and waning, life and death, cycles in the universe. This is sometimes expressed through the symbolic connection between the twenty-eight-day cycles of menstruation and the twenty-eight-day cycles of the moon. Moreover, the Goddess is celebrated in the triple aspect of youth, maturity, and age, or maiden, mother, and crone. The potentiality of the young girl is celebrated in the nymph or maiden aspect of the Goddess. The Goddess as mother is sometimes depicted giving birth, and giving birth is viewed as a symbol for all the creative, life-giving powers of the universe.[18] The life-giving powers of the Goddess in her creative aspect are not limited to physical birth, for the Goddess is also seen as the creator of all the arts of civilization, including healing, writing, and the giving of just law. Women in the middle of life who are not physical mothers may give birth to poems, songs, and books, or nurture other women, men, and children. They too are incarnations of the Goddess in her creative, life-giving aspect. At the end of life, women incarnate the crone aspect of the Goddess. The wise old woman, the woman who knows from experience what life is about, the woman whose closeness to her own death gives her a distance and perspective on the problems of life, is celebrated as the third aspect of the Goddess. Thus, women learn to value youth, creativity, and wisdom in themselves and other women.

The possibilities of reclaiming the female body and its cycles have been expressed in a number of Goddess-centered rituals. Hallie Mountainwing and Barby My Own created a summer solstice ritual to celebrate menstruation and birth. The women simulated a birth canal and birthed each other into their circle. They raised power by placing their hands on each other's bellies and chanting together. Finally they marked

each other's faces with rich, dark menstrual blood saying, "This is the blood that promises renewal. This is the blood that promises sustenance. This is the blood that promises life."[19] From hidden dirty secret to symbol of the life power of the Goddess, women's blood has come full circle. Other women have created rituals that celebrate the crone aspect of the Goddess Z. Budapest believes that the crone aspect of the Goddess is predominant in the fall, especially at Halloween, an ancient holiday. On this day, the wisdom of the old woman is celebrated, and it is also recognized that the old must die so that the new can be born.

The "mood" created by the symbol of the Goddess in triple aspect is one of positive, joyful affirmation of the female body and its cycles and acceptance of aging and death as well as life. The "motivations" are to overcome menstrual taboos, to return the birth process to the hands of women, and to change cultural attitudes about age and death. Changing cultural attitudes toward the female body could go a long way toward overcoming the spirit-flesh, mind-body dualisms of Western culture, since, as Ruether has pointed out, the denigration of the female body is at the heart of these dualisms. The Goddess as symbol of the revaluation of the body and nature thus also undergirds the human potential and ecology movements. The "mood" is one of affirmation, awe, and respect for the body and nature, and the "motivation" is to respect the teachings of the body and the rights of all living beings.

A third important implication of the Goddess symbol for women is the positive valuation of will in a Goddess-centered ritual, especially in Goddess-centered ritual magic and spellcasting in womanspirit and feminist witchcraft circles. The basic notion behind ritual magic and spellcasting is energy as power. Here the Goddess is a center or focus of power and energy; she is the personification of the energy that flows between beings in the natural and human worlds. In Goddess circles, energy is raised by chanting or dancing. According to Starhawk, "Witches conceive of psychic energy as having form and substance that can be perceived and directed by those with a trained awareness. The power generated within the circle is built into a cone form, and at its peak is released—to the Goddess, to reenergize the members of the coven, or to do a specific work such as healing."[20] In ritual magic, the energy raised is directed by willpower. Women who celebrate in Goddess circles believe they can achieve their wills in the world.

The emphasis on the will is important for women, because women traditionally have been taught to devalue their wills, to believe that they cannot achieve their will through their own power, and even to suspect that the assertion of will is evil.

. . .

Patriarchal religion has enforced the view that female initiative and will are evil through the juxtaposition of Eve and Mary. Eve caused the fall by asserting her will against the command of God, while Mary began the new age with her response to God's initiative, "Let it be done to me according to thy word" (Luke 1:38). Even for men, patriarchal religion values the passive will subordinate to divine initiative. The classical doctrines of sin and grace view sin as the prideful assertion of will and grace as the obedient subordination of the human will to the divine initiative or order. While this view of will might be questioned from a human perspective, Valerie Saiving has argued that it has particularly deleterious consequences for women in Western culture. According to Saiving, Western culture encourages males in the assertion of will, and thus it may make some sense to view the male form of sin as an excess of will. But since culture discourages females in the assertion of will, the traditional doctrines of sin and grace encourage women to remain in their form of sin, which is self-negation or insufficient assertion of will.[21] One possible reason the will is denigrated in a patriarchal religious framework is that both human and divine will are often pictured as arbitrary, self-initiated, and exercised without regard for other wills.

In a Goddess-centered context, in contrast, the will is valued. *A woman is encouraged to know her will, to believe that her will is valid, and to believe that her will can be achieved in the world,* three powers traditionally denied to her in patriarchy. In a Goddess-centered framework, a woman's will is not subordinated to the Lord God as king and ruler, nor to men as his representatives. Thus a woman is not reduced to waiting and acquiescing in the wills of others as she is in patriarchy. But neither does she adopt the egocentric form of will that pursues self-interest without regard for the interests of others.

The Goddess-centered context provides a different understanding of the will than that available in the traditional patriarchal religious framework. In the Goddess framework, will can be achieved only when it is exercised in harmony with the energies and wills of other beings. Wise women, for example, raise a cone of healing energy at the full moon or solstice when the lunar or solar energies are at their high points with respect to the earth. This discipline encourages them to recognize that not all times are propitious for the achieving of every will. Similarly, they know that spring is a time for new beginnings in work and love, summer a time for producing external manifestations of inner potentialities, and fall or winter times for stripping down to the inner core and extending roots. Such awareness of waxing and waning processes in the universe discourages arbitrary ego-centered assertion of will, while at the same time encouraging the assertion of individual will in cooperation with natural energies and the energies created by the wills of others. Wise women also have a tradition that whatever is sent out will be returned and this reminds them to assert their wills in cooperative and healing rather than egocentric and destructive ways. This view of will allows women to begin to recognize, claim, and assert their wills without adopting the worst characteristics of the patriarchal understanding and use of will. In the Goddess-centered framework, the "mood" is one of positive affirmation of personal will in the context of the energies of other wills or beings. The "motivation" is for women to know and assert their wills in cooperation with other wills and energies. This of course does not mean that women always assert their wills in positive and life-affirming ways. Women's capacity for evil is, of course, as great as men's. My purpose is simply to contrast the differing attitudes toward the exercise of will *per se,* and the female will in particular, in Goddess-centered religion and in the Christian God-centered religion.

The fourth and final aspect of Goddess symbolism that I will discuss here is the significance of the Goddess for a revaluation of woman's bonds and heritage. As Virginia Woolf has said, "Chloe liked Olivia," a statement about a woman's relation to another woman, is a sentence that rarely occurs in fiction. Men have written the stories, and they have written about women almost exclusively in their relations to men.[22] The celebrations of women's bonds to each other, as mothers and daughters, as colleagues and coworkers, as sisters, friends, and lovers, is beginning to occur in the new literature and culture created by women in the women's movement. While I believe that the revaluing of each of these bonds is important, I will focus on the mother-daughter bond, in part because I believe it may be the key to the others.

Adrienne Rich has pointed out that the mother-daughter bond, perhaps the most important of woman's bonds, "resonant with charges . . . the flow of energy between two biologically alike bodies, one of which has lain in amniotic bliss inside the other, one of which has labored to give birth to the other,"[23] is rarely celebrated in patriarchal religion and culture. Christianity celebrates the father's relation to the son and the mother's relation to the son, but the story of mother and daughter is missing. So, too, in patriarchal literature and psychology the mothers and the daughters rarely exist. Volumes have been written about the oedipal complex, but little has been written about the girl's relation to her mother. Moreover, as de Beauvoir has noted, the mother-daughter relation is distorted in patriarchy because the mother must give her daughter over to men in a male-defined culture in which women are viewed as inferior. The mother must socialize her daughter to become subordinate to men, and if her daughter challenges patriarchal norms, the mother is likely to defend the patriarchal structures against her own daughter.[24]

These patterns are changing in the new culture created by women in which the bonds of women to women are beginning to be celebrated. Holly Near has written several songs that celebrate women's bonds and women's heritage. In one of her finest songs she writes of an "old-time woman" who is "waiting to die." A young woman feels for the life that has passed the old woman by and begins to cry, but the old woman looks her in the eye and says, "If I had not suffered, you wouldn't be wearing those jeans/Being an old-time woman ain't as bad as it seems."[25] This song, which Near has said was inspired by her grandmother, expresses and celebrates a bond and a heritage passed down from one woman to another. In another of Near's songs, she sings of "a hiking-boot mother who's seeing the world/For the first time with her own

little girl." In this song, the mother tells the drifter who has been traveling with her to pack up and travel alone if he thinks "traveling three is a drag" because "I've got a little one who loves me as much as you need me/ And darling, that's loving enough."[26] This song is significant because the mother places her relationship to her daughter above her relationship to a man, something women rarely do in patriarchy.[27]

Almost the only story of mothers and daughters that has been transmitted in Western culture is the myth of Demeter and Persephone that was the basis of religious rites celebrated by women only, the Thesmophoria, and later formed the basis of the Eleusian mysteries, which were open to all who spoke Greek. In this story, the daughter, Persephone, is raped away from her mother, Demeter, by the God of the underworld. Unwilling to accept this state of affairs, Demeter rages and withholds fertility from the earth until her daughter is returned to her. What is important for women in this story is that a mother fights for her daughter and for her relation to her daughter. This is completely different from the mother's relation to her daughter in patriarchy. The "mood" created by the story of Demeter and Persephone is one of celebration of the mother-daughter bond, and the "motivation" is for mothers and daughters to affirm the heritage passed on from mother to daughter and to reject the patriarchal pattern where the primary loyalties of mother and daughter must be to men.

The symbol of Goddess has much to offer women who are struggling to be rid of the "powerful, pervasive, and long-lasting moods and motivations" of devaluation of female power, denigration of the female body, distrust of female will, and denial of the women's bonds and heritage that have been engendered by patriarchal religion. As women struggle to create a new culture in which women's power, bodies, will, and bonds are celebrated, it seems natural that the Goddess would reemerge as symbol of the new-found beauty, strength, and power of women.

Notes

1. From the original cast album, Buddah Records, 1976.
2. See Susan Rennie and Kristen Grimstad, "Spiritual Explorations Cross-Country," *Quest,* 1975, *I* (4), 1975, 49–51; and *WomanSpirit* magazine.
3. See Starhawk, "Witchcraft and Women's Culture," in this volume.

4. "Religion as a Cultural System," in William L. Lessa and Evon V. Vogt, eds., *Reader in Comparative Religion,* 2nd ed. (New York: Harper & Row, 1972), p. 206.

5. Geertz, p. 210.

6. Boston: Beacon Press, 1974, p. 13, italics added.

7. *The Second Sex,* trans. H. M. Parshleys (New York: Alfred A. Knopf, 1953).

8. See Grimstad and Rennie.

9. *Les Guerilleres,* trans. David LeVay (New York: Avon Books, 1971), p. 89. Also quoted in Morgan MacFarland, "Witchcraft: The Art of Remembering," *Quest,* 1975, I (4), 41.

10. "Speaking for Myself," *Lady Unique,* 1976, I, 56.

11. Personal communication.

12. A term coined by Naomi Goldenberg to refer to reflection on the meaning of the symbol of Goddess.

13. This theory of the origins of the Western dualism is stated by Rosemary Ruether in *New Woman: New Earth* (New York: Seabury Press, 1975), and elsewhere.

14. Heinrich Kramer and Jacob Sprenger (New York: Dover, 1971), p. 47.

15. See Rita M. Gross, "Menstruation and Childbirth as Ritual and Religious Experience in the Religion of the Australian Aborigines," in *The Journal of the American Academy of Religion,* 1977, 45 (4), Supplement 1147–1181.

16. *Through the Flower* (New York: Doubleday & Company, 1975), plate 4, pp. 106–107.

17. See Adrienne Rich, *Of Woman Born* (New York: Bantam Books, 1977), chaps. 6 and 7.

18. See James Mellaart, *Earliest Civilizations of the Near East* (New York: McGraw-Hill, 1965), p. 92.

19. Barby My Own, "Ursa Major: Menstrual Moon Celebration," in Anne Kent Rush, ed., *Moon, Moon* (Berkeley, Calif., and New York: Moon Books and Random House, 1976), pp. 374–387.

20. Starhawk, in this volume.

21. "The Human Situation: A Feminine View," in *Journal of Religion,* 1960, *40,* 100–112, and reprinted in this volume.

22. *A Room of One's Own* (New York: Harcourt Brace Jovanovich, 1928), p. 86.

23. Rich, p. 226.

24. De Beauvoir, pp. 448–449.

25. "Old Time Woman," lyrics by Jeffrey Langley and Holly Near, from *Holly Near: A Live Album,* Redwood Records, 1974.

26. "Started Out Fine," by Holly Near from *Holly Near: A Live Album.*

27. Rich, p. 223.

DISCUSSION QUESTIONS

1. Do you agree with Christ's critique of traditional Western religion? Why or why not? How are gender relations changing in organized religion, if at all?

2. What is the connection between "Goddess-centered" spirituality and ecological attitudes toward the earth?

3. Can people in society eventually live without religious symbolism altogether? Why or why not?

4. How might the natural theology/revealed theology distinction be applied in the evaluation of Christ's perspective?

5. Can the traditional Western religions make room for Goddess symbolism, or must a separate set of beliefs and practices be created to accommodate it? Explain.

40. Vine Deloria Jr. (b. 1933)
From *God Is Red*

Vine Deloria is a Dakota (Sioux) philosopher and lawyer who was raised in South Dakota and has become one of the most well-known Native American writers in the United States over the last thirty-five years. His published works have covered issues in North American history as well as a wide range of topics in many of the standard subfields of philosophy, even though at least one American publisher told him that (to paraphrase) "Indians don't write books on philosophy." The recurring themes in Deloria's work have to do with the elucidation and defense of different dimensions of a Native American worldview and the critique of the dominant European worldview along with its theoretical and practical outcomes.

This selection is the fifth chapter from the 1992 revised edition of *God Is Red.* For both mainstream academic and popular American audiences, Deloria's book remains as controversial and provocative a work now as it was when the original version came out in 1972, at a time when Native American political activism was starting to receive more widespread public attention. Its systematic analysis of the values of Western civilization, religious and otherwise, and their historically destructive consequences for other human societies and the rest of the planet offered a serious challenge to the ethnocentric complacency of many European Americans. More specifically, in this chapter Deloria is critically comparing and contrasting what he takes to be the Christian perspective and the perspective of "Indian tribal religions" on the divine Creation of the universe, the nature of the Creator, and the proper place of humans in that Creation.

QUESTIONS FOR CRITICAL READING

1. According to Deloria, what is the difference between Indian tribal religions and Christianity regarding their respective accounts of the Creation as occurring in space and time? What are the consequences of this difference for deciding the question of "doctrinal truth"?

2. According to Deloria, what are the differences in the conceptions and images of the Creator found in Indian tribal religions and Christianity?

3. Concerning the relationship between humanity and the rest of nature, how do the two religious traditions differ, in Deloria's estimation, and what are the ecological consequences of these differences?

4. How is the understanding of human sinfulness and alienation different in these two religious traditions?

5. How compatible with contemporary science are the two religious belief systems, according to Deloria?

TERM TO NOTE

stewardship: The condition of being responsible for the care of someone else's property.

———

Indian tribal religions and Christianity differ considerably on numerous theological points, but a very major distinction that can be made between the two types of thinking concerns the idea of creation. Christianity has traditionally appeared to place its major emphasis on creation as a specific event while the Indian tribal religions could be said to consider creation as an eco-

system present in a definable place. In this distinction we have again the fundamental problem of whether we consider the reality of our experience as capable of being described in terms of space or time—as "what happened here" or "what happened then."

Both religions can be said to agree on the role and activity of a creator. Outside of that specific thing, there would appear to be little that the two views share. Tribal religions appear to be thereafter confronted with the question of the interrelationship of all things. Christians see creation as the beginning event of a linear time sequence in which a divine plan is worked out, the conclusion of the sequence being an act of destruction bringing the world to an end. The beginning and end of time are of no apparent concern for many tribal religions.

The act of creation is a singularly important event for the Christian. It describes the sequence in which the tangible features of human existence are brought into being, and although some sermons have made much of the element of light that appears in the creation account of Genesis and the prologue of St. John's Gospel, the similarity of the two books and their use of light do not appear to be of crucial importance in the doctrine of creation. For the Christian it would appear that the importance of the creation event is that it sets the scene for an understanding of the entrance of sin into the world.

Intimately tied with the actual creation event in the Christian theological scheme is the appearance of the first people, Adam and Eve. They are made after the image of God. It is important that this point be recognized, as it has affected popular conceptions held by Christians and seems to have some relevance to central theological doctrines. As the Genesis story relates that the first people were made after God's image, Christians, although not necessarily their Hebrew predecessors and Jewish contemporaries, have popularly conceived God as having a human form. That is to say, God looks like a man. Paintings represent Him generally as an old man, deriving perhaps from the old Hebrew conception of the "Ancient of Days."

The first distinction between Indian tribal religions and Christianity would appear to be in the manner in which deity is popularly conceived. The overwhelming majority of American Indian tribal religions refused to represent deity anthropomorphically.[1] To be sure, many tribes used the term *grandfather* when praying to God, but there was no effort to use that concept as the basis for a theological doctrine by which a series of complex relationships and related doctrines could be developed. While there was an acknowledgment that the Great Spirit has some resemblance to the role of a grandfather in the tribal society, there was no great demand to have a "personal relationship" with the Great Spirit in the same manner as popular Christianity has emphasized personal relationships with God.[2]

The difference between conceiving God as an anthropomorphic being and as an undefinable presence carries over into the distinction in the views of creation. Closely following the creation of the world in Christian theology comes the disobedience of man, Adam, in eating the forbidden fruit growing on a tree in the Garden of Eden. In this act as recorded in Genesis, humankind "fell" from God's grace and was driven out of the garden by the angry God. The major thesis of the Christian religion is thus contained in its creation story, because it is for the redemption of man that the atonement of Jesus of Nazareth is considered to make sense.

With the fall of Adam the rest of nature also falls out of grace with God, Adam being a surrogate for the whole of creation. This particular point has been a very difficult problem for Christian theologians. While it adequately explains the entrance of evil into the world, just how it could occur in a universe conceived as perfect has been difficult for theologians to answer. St. Augustine preferred to think that God Himself had taken the form of the snake that, in the story, talked Eve into eating the forbidden fruit.[3] St. Augustine's solution has not generally been accepted, even though it appears to explain the logical sequence.

Perhaps of more importance are two aspects of the Christian doctrine of creation bearing directly on us today. One aspect is that the natural world is thereafter considered as corrupted, and it becomes theoretically beyond redemption. Many Christian theologians have attempted to avoid this conclusion, but it appears to have been a central doctrine of the Christian religion during most of the Christian era. No less a thinker than Paul Tillich attempted to reconstruct the doctrine into more satisfying terms that would be acceptable to the modern world. In a rather complex analysis in his *Systematic Theology,* Tillich wrestled with the problem.

> Christianity must reject the idealistic separation of an innocent nature from guilty man. Such a rejection has become comparatively easy in our period because of the insights gained about the growth of man and his relation to nature within and outside himself. First, it can be shown that in the development of man there is no absolute discontinuity between animal bondage and human freedom. There are leaps between different stages, but there is also a slow and continuous transformation. It is impossible to say at which point in the process of natural evolution animal nature is replaced by the nature which, in our present experience we know as human, a nature which is qualitatively different from animal nature.[4]

> And, as there are analogies to human freedom in nature, so there are also analogies to human good and evil in all parts of the universe. It is worthy of note that Isaiah prophesied peace in nature for the new eon, thereby showing that he would not call nature "innocent." Nor would the writer who, in Genesis, chapter 3, tells about the curse over the land declare nature innocent. Nor would Paul do so in Romans, chapter 8, when he speaks about the bondage to futility which is the fate of nature. Certainly, all these expressions are poeticmythical. They could not be otherwise, since only poetic empathy opens the inner life of nature. Nevertheless, they are realistic in substance and certainly more realistic than the moral utopianism which confronts immoral man with innocent nature. Just as, within man, nature participates in the good and evil he does, so nature, outside man, shows analogies to man's good and evil doing. Man reaches into nature, as nature reaches into man. They participate in each other and cannot be separated from each other. This makes it possible and necessary to use the term "fallen world" and to apply the concept of existence (in contrast to essence) to the universe as well as man.[5]

Like many other Christian thinkers, Tillich cannot break the relationship between humans and the natural world in which both share a corrupt nature. Even his dependence on evolution appears to be but a temporary nod to the reflections of science, because he stands ready to label the nature of people corrupt at whatever point in the evolutionary process a human being comparable in psychological processes to ourselves emerges.

Indian tribal religions also held a fundamental relationship between human beings and the rest of nature, but the conception was radically different. For many Indian tribal religions the whole of creation was good, and because the creation event did not include a "fall," the meaning of creation was that all parts of it functioned together to sustain it. Young Chief, a Cayuse, refused to sign the Treaty of Walla Walla because he felt the rest of the creation was not represented in the transaction.

> I wonder if the ground has anything to say? I wonder if the ground is listening to what is said? I wonder if the ground would come alive and what is on it? Though I hear what the ground says. The ground says, It is the Great Spirit that placed me here. The Great Spirit tells me to take care of the Indians, to feed them aright. The Great Spirit appointed the roots to feed the Indians on. The water says the same thing. The Great Spirit directs me, Feed the Indians well. The grass says the same thing, Feed the Indians well. The ground, water and grass say, the Great Spirit has given us our names. We have these names and hold these names. The ground says, The Great Spirit placed me here to produce all that grows on me, trees and fruit. The same way the ground says, It was from me man was made. The Great Spirit, in placing men on earth, desired them to take good care of the ground and to do each other no harm.[6]

The similarity between Young Chief's conception of creation and the Genesis story is striking, but when one understands that the Genesis story is merely the starting place for theological doctrines of a rather abstract nature while Young Chief's beliefs are the practical articulations of his understanding of the relationship between the various entities of the creation, the difference becomes apparent. In the Indian tribal religions, man and the rest of creation are cooperative and respectful of the task set for them by the Great Spirit. In the Christian religion both are doomed from shortly after the creation event until the end of the world.

The second aspect of the Christian doctrine of creation that concerns us today is the idea that man receives domination over the rest of creation. Harvey Cox, a popular Protestant theologian, articulates rather precisely the attitude derived from this idea of Genesis: "Just after his creation man is given the crucial responsibility of naming the animals. He is their master and commander. It is his task to subdue the earth."[7] It is this attitude that has been adopted wholeheartedly by Western peoples in their economic exploitation of the earth. The creation becomes a mere object when this view is carried to its logical conclusion—a directly opposite result from that of the Indian religions.

Whether or not Christians wanted to carry their doctrine of human dominance as far as it has been carried, the fact remains that the modern world is just now beginning to identify the Christian religion's failure to show adequate concern for the planet as a major factor in our present ecological crisis. Among the earliest scholars to recognize the Christian responsibility for our present situation of ecological chaos was Lynn White, Jr., who gave a presentation titled "The Historical Roots of Our Ecological Crisis" in 1967 before the American Association for the Advancement of Science. White presented the same previously discussed criticism of Christian theology, emphasizing the tendency of the Christian religion to downgrade the natural world and its life forms in favor of the supernatural world of the Christian postjudgment world of eternal life.[8] But he was extremely kind for a man who had his intellectual arguments honed so fine that he could have gone for the jugular vein had he wanted. White proposed that St. Francis be made the ecological saint, elevating Francis to a pedestal he did not deserve.

A number of Christians appear to be taking up White's thesis, and one frequently hears arguments that St. Francis represents the true Christian tradition. The Franciscan tradition is not a major theme of either Christian or Western thought, however, and it would appear as if advocating St. Francis as a patron of the Christian attitude toward creation is not only historically late but uncertain. White's thesis proved unbearable to Dr. René Dubos, of New York City Rockefeller University, who gave a presentation in 1969 at the Smithsonian Institution in Washington, D.C., on "A Theology of the Earth." In it Dubos disclaimed White's charge against Christianity. Dubos contended that other societies had also created ecological disasters. He felt that Christianity was therefore not to be held accountable for the shortcomings of Westerners. He buttressed his thesis by references to St. Francis and, more particularly, to St. Benedict, founder of the Benedictine Order. Dubos found that the Benedictine work rules, which at that time included draining swamps and filling in lowlands, were more suitable for modern man than St. Francis' ideas of nature worship.[9]

Dubos' valiant defense of Christian thought lacks a number of substantial considerations. While other societies did create ecological disasters, Dubos would be hard put to find in the theologies of many other religions either a command to subdue the earth or the doctrine that the creation had "fallen" and shared responsibility for a man's direct violation of divine commands. There is also little evidence that destroying wetlands is ecologically sound, a fact the Bush administration ignores as it proposes to weaken federal law against tampering with the wetlands.

Further indications of Dubos's miscalculation of Christian sincerity—and evidence, perhaps, that Christians have not yet understood the complexity of the ecological crisis—were evidenced by the liturgy of the earth created by the National Cathedral in Washington, D.C. The confession used in this liturgy exemplifies the extent to which even concerned Christians have misunderstood the seriousness of the ecological problem.

> Lord God, we say here in Your presence and before each other that we, both individually and collectively, have not been good stewards of Your earth. We have fouled the air, spoiled the water, poisoned the land, and by these acts have gravely hurt each other. We know now that this has and will cost us, and for these and all other sins we are truly sorry. Give us, we pray, the strength and guidance to undo what we have done and grant us inspiration for a new style of living.[10]

Even in this attempt to bring religious sensitivity to the problem of ecological destruction, one can see the shallow understanding of the basis of the religious attitude that has been largely responsible for the crisis. No effort is made to begin a new theory of the meaning of creation. Indeed, the popular attitude of *stewardship* is invoked, as if it had no relationship to the cause of the ecological crisis whatsoever. Perhaps the best summary of the attitude inherent in the liturgy is, "Please, God, help us cut the cost, and we'll try to find a new life-style that won't be quite as destructive." The response is inadequate because it has not reached any fundamental problem; it is only a patch job over a serious theological problem. But at least in this liturgy we humans are bad and nature is good—a marked advance over earlier conceptions.

It would be difficult to find an Indian counterpart to this proposed liturgy. In the first place, traditional religions do not have the point-counterpoint recitation of beliefs that we find in the Near Eastern traditions. Singers and individual medicine people sing specific songs that compose the ceremony. While there is the expression of humility as humans stand before the higher spiritual powers, the Indian tradition lacks the admission of individual and corporate guilt which Near Eastern religions make the central part of their doctrines. The phrase "all my relatives" is frequently invoked by Indians performing ceremonies and this phrase is used to invite all other forms of life to participate as well as to inform them that the ceremony is being done on their behalf.

There is another, more serious problem involved in the Christian doctrine of creation. For most of the history of the Christian religion, people have been taught that the description of the event of creation as recorded in Genesis is historical fact. Although many Christian theologians have recognized that at best the Genesis account is mythological, it would be fair to conclude on the basis of what is known of the Christian religion that many Christian theologians and a substantial portion of the populace take the Genesis account as historical fact.

This issue has been a particularly difficult problem in the last century in America. The 1925 Scopes trial in Tennessee is perhaps the most publicized of the incidents marking the conflict between literal believers of Genesis and those who regard it symbolically, either as an analogy or as a mythological representation of a greater spiritual reality. Because people in a number of states, most prominently California, have petitioned their state legislatures to require the Genesis account of creation in the school curriculum indicates that the desire of many Christians is to believe in spite of the evidence, not because of it.[11]

Indian tribal religions have not had this problem. The tribes confront and interact with a particular land along with its life forms. The task or role of the tribal religions is to relate the community of people to each and every facet of creation as they have experienced it. Dr. Charles Eastman, the famous Sioux physician, relates a story in which the Indian viewpoint of the historicity of creation legends is illustrated:

> A missionary once undertook to instruct a group of Indians in the truths of his holy religion. He told them of the creation of the earth in six days, and of the fall of our first parents by eating an apple.

The courteous savages listened attentively, and, after thanking him, one related in his turn a very ancient tradition concerning the origin of maize. But the missionary plainly showed his disgust and disbelief, indignantly saying:

> "What I delivered to you were sacred truths, but this that you tell me is mere fable and falsehood!"
>
> "My Brother," gravely replied the offended Indian, "it seems that you have not been well grounded in the rules of civility. You saw that we, who practice these rules, believed your stories; why, then, do you refuse to credit ours?"[12]

The difference in approach goes back to the basic consideration discussed earlier. If a religion is tied to a sense of time, then everything forming a part of it must have some validity because it occurs within the temporal scheme. Christians are thus stuck within the assertion that the account of Genesis is an actual historical recording of the proceedings whether or not some of the theologians consent to such an interpretation.

Most important, perhaps, is that the major Christian theologian, the apostle Paul, made the historicity of the Genesis account the most important aspect of his theory of redemption. Paul's theory has formed a major part of the Christian teachings, and while some of the Christian sects would not agree with everything Paul wrote, he is not an insignificant figure in Christian history. Paul writes in Romans:

> Sin, you see, was in the world long before the Law, though I suppose, technically speaking, it was not 'sin' where there was no law to define it. Nevertheless death, the complement of sin, held sway over mankind from Adam to Moses, even over those whose sin was quite unlike Adam's.
>
> Adam, the first man, corresponds in some degree to the Man who was to come. But the gift of God through Christ is a very different matter from the 'account rendered' through the sin of Adam. For while as a result of one man's sin death by natural consequence became the common lot of men, it was by the generosity of God, the free giving of the grace of the One Man Jesus Christ, that the love of God overflowed for the benefit of all men.
>
> We see, then, that as one act of sin exposed the whole race of men to God's judgment and condemnation, so one Act of Perfect Righteousness presents all men freely acquitted in the sight of God. One man's disobedience placed all men under the threat of condemnation, but one Man's obedience has the power to present all men righteous before God.[13]

It would appear that if the Genesis account of Adam's disobedience is not a historical event (that is, an event that can be located at some specific time and place on the planet), subsequent explanations of the meaning of the death of Jesus of Nazareth are without validity. We have no need to question the historical existence of Jesus of Nazareth, although that particular conflict has also consumed considerable energy in the past. But we cannot project from the historical reality of Jesus as a man existing in Palestine during the time of Augustus and his successors to affirm the historical existence of a man called Adam in a garden someplace in Asia Minor. Without the historical existence of Adam, we are powerless to explain the death of Jesus as a religious event of cosmic or historic significance.

At best we can conclude that the Christian doctrine of creation has serious shortcomings. It is too often considered not only as a historical event but also as the event that determined all other facts of our existence. It is bad enough to consider Genesis as a historical account in view of what we know today of the nature of our world. But when we consider that the Genesis account places nature and nonhuman life systems in a polarity with us, tinged with evil and without hope of redemption except at the last judgment, the whole idea appears intolerable.

There are, to be sure, numerous accounts from the various tribal religious traditions relating how an animal, bird, or reptile participated in a creation event. We have already seen how some Indian people regarded such stories and the lack of belief in the historical nature of the event. Within the tribal accounts is contained, perhaps, an even greater problem, the problem of origins of peoples and religions, which we shall take up in chapter 8. At no point, however, does any tribal religion insist that its particular version of the creation is an absolute historical recording of the creation event or that the story necessarily leads to conclusions about humankind's good or evil nature. At best the tribal stories recount how the people experience the creative process which continues today.

The relationships that serve to form the unity of nature are of vastly more importance to most tribal religions. The Indian is confronted with a bountiful earth in which all things and experiences have a role to play. The task of the tribal religion, if such a religion can be said to have a task, is to determine the proper relationship that the people of the tribe must have with other living things and to develop the self-discipline within the tribal community so that man acts harmoniously with other creatures. The world that he experiences is dominated by the presence of power, the manifestation of life energies, the whole life-flow of a creation. Recognition that human beings hold an important place in such a creation is tempered by the thought that they are dependent on everything in creation for their existence. There is not, therefore, that determined cause that Harvey Cox projects to subdue Earth and its living things. Instead the awareness of the meaning of life comes from observing how the various living things appear to mesh to provide a whole tapestry.

Each form of life has its own purposes, and there is no form of life that does not have a unique quality to its existence. Shooter, a Sioux Indian, explained the view held by many tribal religions in terms of individuality as follows:

> Animals and plants are taught by Wakan Tanka what they are to do. Wakan Tanka teaches the birds to make nests, yet the nests of all birds are not alike. Wakan Tanka gives them merely the outline. Some make better nests than others.
>
> In the same way some animals are satisfied with very rough dwellings, while others make attractive places in which to live. Some animals also take better care of their young than others. The forest is the home of many birds and other animals, and the water is the home of fish and reptiles. All birds, even those of the same species, are not alike, and it is the same with animals, or human beings. The reason Wakan Tanka does not make two birds, or animals, or human beings exactly alike is because each is placed here by Wakan Tanka to be an independent individuality and to rely upon itself.[14]

To recognize or admit differences, even among the species of life, does not require then that human beings create forces to forge to gain a sense of unity or homogeneity. To exist in a creation means that living is more than tolerance for other life forms—it is recognition that in differences there is the strength of creation and that this strength is a deliberate desire of the creator.

Tribal religions find a great affinity among species of living creatures, and it is at this point that the fellowship of life is a strong part of the Indian way. The Hopi, for example, revere not only the lands on which they live but the animals with which they have a particular relationship. The dance for rain, which involves the use of reptiles in its ceremonies, holds a great fascination for whites, primarily because they have traditionally considered reptiles, particularly snakes, as their mortal enemy. In this attitude and its ensuing fascination, we may illustrate, perhaps, the alienation between the various life forms that Christian peoples read into the story in Genesis. This alienation is not present in tribal religions.

Behind the apparent kinship between animals, reptiles, birds, and human beings in the Indian way stands a great conception shared by a great majority of the tribes. Other living things are not regarded as insensitive species. Rather they are "people" in the same manner as the various tribes of human beings are people. The reason why the Hopi use live reptiles in their ceremony goes back to one of their folk heroes who lived with the snake people for a while and learned from them the secret of making rain for the crops.[15] It was a ceremony freely given by the snake people to the Hopi. In the same manner the Plains Indians considered the buffalo as a distinct people, the Northwest Coast Indians regarded the salmon as a people. Equality is thus not simply a human attribute but a recognition of the creatureness of all creation.

Very important in some of the tribal religions is the idea that humans can change into animals and birds and that other species can change into human beings. In this way species can communicate and learn from each other. Some of these tribal ideas have been classified as *witchcraft* by anthropologists, primarily because such phenomena occurring within the Western tradition would naturally be interpreted as evil and satanic. What Westerners miss is the rather logical implication of the unity of life. If all living things share a creator and a creation, is it not logical to suppose that all have the ability to relate to every part of the creation? How Westerners can believe in evolution and not see the logical consequences of this doctrine in the religious life of people is incomprehensible for many Indians. Recent studies with the dolphin and other animals may indicate that Westerners are beginning to shed superstitions and consider the possibility of having communication with other life forms.

But many tribal religions go even farther. The manifestation of power is simply not limited to mobile life forms. For some tribes the idea extends to plants, rocks, and natural features that Westerners consider inanimate. Walking Buffalo, a Stoney Indian from Canada, explained the nature of the unity of creation and the possibility of communicating with any aspect of creation when he remarked:

Did you know that trees talk? Well they do.
They talk to each other, and they'll talk to you if
you listen. Trouble is, white people don't listen.
They never learned to listen to the Indians, so
I don't suppose they'll listen to other voices
in nature. But I have learned a lot from trees;
sometimes about the weather, sometimes about
animals, sometimes about the Great Spirit.[16]

Again we must return to the Christian idea of the complete alienation of nature and the world from human beings as a result of Adam's immediate postcreation act in determining the Western and Christian attitude toward nature. Some theologians have felt that man's alienation from nature is a natural result of his coming to a sense of self-consciousness, and people dealing with psychological problems seem to have a tendency to emphasize the sense in which humans are alienated from nature by promulgating theories of childhood fears based on the unfolding of natural growth processes. Even Western poets have been articulating the Western fears of "I, a stranger and afraid, in a world I never made."[17]

By and large there was no fear of nature in the Indian view of the world. Chief Luther Standing Bear remarked on the "wildness" of nature in his autobiography as follows:

We did not think of the great open plains, the
beautiful rolling hills, and winding streams
with tangled growth as "wild." Only to the
white men was nature a "wilderness" and only
to him was the land "infested" with "wild" animals and "savage" people. To us it was tame.
Earth was bountiful and we were surrounded
with the blessings of the Great Mystery. Not
until the hairy man from the east came and
with brutal frenzy heaped injustices upon us
and the families that we loved was it "wild" for
us. When the very animals of the forest began
fleeing from his approach, then it was that for
us the "Wild West" began.[18]

In some sense, part of the alienation of human beings from nature is caused by the action of humans against nature and not as the result of some obscure and corrupted relationship that came into being as a result of the human's inability to relate to the creator. It is doubtful if Western Christians can change their understanding of creation at this point in their existence. Their religion is firmly grounded in their escape from a fallen nature, and it is highly unlikely to suppose at this late date that they can find a reconciliation with nature while maintaining the remainder of their theological understanding of salvation.

We have one final aspect to cover with respect to the creation. Whether it be considered as a specific event or as a tenet of faith that need not be explained, certain empirical data exists today that was unavailable to humankind when tribal religions and Christianity originated. Modern science has in large part pierced the veil of nature. We are becoming increasingly aware of some of the basic processes of the universe to a much greater degree than was ever possible. With the explosion of the atomic bomb, humankind moved far beyond the speculations of earlier science and philosophy. It may be yet too soon to conclude that our science can determine everything about the universe. Yet the possibility of almost instantaneous destruction through misuse of science should indicate that we are close to describing in an approximate manner how the universe works.

Our further question, therefore, should concern how religious statements are to be made which are either broad enough or specific enough to parallel what we are discovering in nature through scientific experiments. Christian theology has traditionally fluctuated between the philosophical views of Plato and Aristotle. Occasionally some theologian will go to the ideas of Kant or Descartes to find a usable system to explain religious ideas in a scientific manner. Some theologians have gone so far as Alfred North Whitehead's view of the universe to find a way to describe religious ideas by the same basic form of articulation as followed in scientific circles and created *process theology.*

Which religious atmosphere, Christian or Indian, would appear to be more compatible with contemporary scientific ideas? The question may appear absurd, but it has the highest relevance for a number of reasons. First, we must determine on what basis religious ideas are considered to be mere superstitions and on what basis religious ideas are said to be either valid or possible in the world in which we live. Indian dances for rain, for example, were said to be mere superstitions; songs to make corn grow were said to be even more absurd. Today people can make plants grow with music, and the information on the power of sound vibrations is coming into its own. The principles used by Indian tribal religions have tremendous parallels with contemporary scientific experiments. This can be either coincidental, which is very difficult to prove, or it can mean that the Indian tribal religions have been dealing at least partially with a fairly accurate conception of reality, which is difficult to argue convincingly to the scientific mind.

The second reason for determining compatibility of religion and science is to lay the groundwork for bringing our view of the world back to a unified whole, if at all possible. The competition between ministers and psychoanalysts, for example, to determine the sense of spiritual or psychological infirmity in effect promotes two distinct views of reality. Karl Heim relates in his incisive book, *Christian Faith and Natural Science,* as follows:

> In cases of physiologically conditioned depression, in which the religious responses are often involved, modern medicine applies with great success the electric shock treatment, passing an electric current through leads placed in contact with the patient's temples. These are often people who in their state of depression also despaired of their spiritual salvation, who were a prey in other words to what has been called in theological literature "certainty of damnation." And lo and behold! What the minister of religion had tried in vain to achieve with comforting exhortations and encouraging words from the Bible and the Catechism has now been accomplished by the electric current! The depression has gone and the patient not only faces his life with new courage but is filled with a joyful belief in God's forgiveness and in his own eternal salvation.[19]

It would thus appear that unless some new effort in the field of religion is made to provide a more realistic understanding of the universe, there may be no solution to people's problems except manipulation by artificial means—the *1984* solution, that we all dread.

The Indian tribal religions would probably suggest that the unity of life is manifested in the existence of the tribal community, for it is only in the tribal community that any Indian religions have relevance. James Jeans, in his book *Physics and Philosophy,* suggests that a profound view of nature lies in the concept of community:

> Space and time are inhabited by distinct individuals, but when we pass beyond space and time, from the world of phenomena

towards reality, individuality is replaced by community.

> When we pass beyond space and time, they [separate individuals] may perhaps form ingredients of a single continuous stream of life.[20]

The parallel with conceptions of the basic unity of existence held by American Indian tribal religions is striking. If the nature of the world is a "single continuous stream of life," there is no reason to reject the idea that one can learn to hear the trees talk. It would be strange if they did not have the power to communicate.

R. G. Collingwood, in *The Idea of Nature,* attempts to sketch out Alexander's cosmology as it applies to a whole continuum of life:

> In the physical world before the emergence of life, there are already various orders of being, each consisting of a pattern composed of elements belonging to the order next below it: point-instants form a pattern which is the electron having physical qualities, electrons form an atom having higher chemical qualities of a new and higher order, molecules like those of air form wave-patterns having sonority and so on.
>
> Living organisms in their turn are patterns whose elements are bits of matter. In themselves these bits of matter are inorganic; it is only the whole pattern which they compose that is alive, and its life is the time-aspect or rhythmic process of its material parts.[21]

We apparently have order and orders. We have time, but a time that is not a universal value, only a time internal to the complex relationships themselves. Above all, we have no disruption of the unity of the creation, only a variation on a general theme. If there is anything to the similarity of things, it is that a sense of alienation does not exist at a significant level.

We even have the startling statement of Whitehead about the nature of God: "Not only does God [primordial nature] arrange the eternal objects; he also makes them available for use by other actual entities. This is God's function as the principle of concretion."[22] Again we are dealing with a complexity of relationships in which no particular object is given primacy over any other object or entity. Energy or spirit and the manifestation of purposeful order seem to characterize both modern scientific speculations and Indian beliefs.

What is important is not an attempt to show that either Indian tribal religions or Christianity prefigured contemporary science, modern concern for ecological sanity, or a startlingly new idea of what the universe might eventually be. Rather we should find what religious ideas can credibly encompass the broadest field of both our thoughts and actions. We must show that religious ideas are at least not tied to any particular view of man, nature, or the relationship of man and nature that is clearly in conflict with what we know. In this sense, American Indian tribal religions certainly appear to be more at home in the modern world than Christian ideas and Westerners' traditional religious concepts.

Notes

1. Frederick Webb Hodge, *Handbook of American Indians North of Mexico,* vol. II (Lanham, Md.: Rowman & Littlefield, 1965), 366.

Something more needs to be said about anthropomorphic images. Medicine men report the existence of spiritual beings that have or take on human forms. Thus Black Elk and other Sioux mystics report that they have sat with the Six Grandfathers and counseled with them. Much more thought needs to be given to the question of whether the Indians had "gods" in the same sense as Near Eastern peoples. Was the mysterious power—*wakan tanka* in the Dakota language—the same as the spiritual power that provided life and was superior to any specific personifications of itself? If so, the ultimate representation of this sacred universe—and other sacred Indian universes—was without a deity in the Near Eastern sense.

2. For example, see Joseph Epes Brown, *The Sacred Pipe* (Norman: University of Oklahoma Press, 1953, 3–6) for Black Elk's discussion of this relationship.

3. In *The Confessions* by St. Augustine (London: Burns & Oates, 1954), the solution to the problem of evil seems to be completing the circle and suggesting that the deity himself is the tempter. Carl Jung also folds back the problem of good and evil to make a complete circle or circuit. The Plains Indian concept is considerably more complex and seems to involve the related question of the structure of conscious life—the difference between probable future events and the realization of existing possibilities. It is too complicated to deal with here except to note that there is a considerable difference between the two traditions.

4. Paul Tillich, *Systematic Theology,* vol. II (Chicago: University of Chicago Press, 1957), 41–42.

5. Ibid.

In all of North American Indian traditions there is, of course, no sense of "animal bondage" but rather relationships with the specific peoples of creation; hence, creation is ultimately good and humans are a part of it.

6. T. C. McLuhan, *Touch the Earth* (New York: Outerbridge & Dienstfrey, 1971), 8.

7. Harvey Cox, *The Secular City* (New York: Macmillan, 1965), 20.

8. Lynne White, Jr., "The Historical Roots of Our Ecological Crisis," paper. American Association for the Advancement of Science, 1967.

9. Rene Dubos' address is published as a small booklet by the Smithsonian Institution, Washington, D.C. It is singularly instructive, however, to note that filling in marshes and wetlands destroys habitat for a significant number of species and moves the planet toward ecological unbalance. Thus, White's thesis holds even when applied to what Christians believe is their most benign behavior.

10. Quoted in an article by Louis Cassels in the Religion Section, *The Denver Post* (March 7, 1970).

11. The Creation Science Research Center in San Diego has been extremely active in submitting textbooks to the State Board of Education which allege to give equal treatment to both Darwin and Genesis. There has apparently been some talk by people who support the center of forcing acceptance of their textbooks through court action. (Reported in *The Denver Post* Religion Section, August 12, 1972.)

12. Charles Eastman, *The Soul of the Indian* (Boston: Houghton Mifflin, 1911), 119–20.

13. Romans 5:13–19.

14. *Touch the Earth,* 18.

15. The ceremony is briefly described in *Book of the Hopi* by Frank Waters and Oswald White Bear Fredericks (Viking Press, 1963).

16. *Touch the Earth,* 23.

17. A. E. Houseman, *A Shropshire Lad* (New York: Grosset & Dunlap, 1932).

18. Luther Standing Bear, *Land of the Spotted Eagle* (Boston: Houghton Mifflin, 1933).

19. Karl Heim, *Christian Faith and Natural Science* (New York: Harper Torchbooks, 1957), 15.

20. James Jeans, *Physics and Philosophy,* Ann Arbor Papers (Ann Arbor: University of Michigan Press, 1958), 204.

21. R. G. Collingwood, *The Idea of Nature* (London: Oxford University Press, 1945), 160.

22. A. H. Johnson, *Whitehead's Theory of Reality* (New York: Dover Publications, 1962), 60–61.

DISCUSSION QUESTIONS

1. Which of the two religious accounts of creation makes the most sense to you? Why?

2. Based on Deloria's account, which characterization of the Supreme Being—the Christian or the traditional Native American—seems most plausible to you? Why?

3. Which of the two religious worldviews presented in Deloria's account can better address contemporary environmental problems? Why?

4. How are these two religious traditions different regarding their treatment of other religious or spiritual traditions? Which approach seems more reasonable to you? Why?

PART IV Morality

For the most part human beings spend their lives in communities, and so the quality of their social relations is always one of their primary concerns. As a result, all identifiable societies that have endured for any length of time, and for which there is any empirical record, develop standards of morality that determine how community members ought to treat each other. However, as customary and well entrenched as a culture's moral code often is, everyone does not always agree on how people ought to conduct themselves. Thus, very early in human history there appeared philosophical attempts to articulate defensible accounts of what constitutes "the moral life," not only for one's immediate social group but also for all others with whom one might interact. Further, increased contact between different cultures over the centuries has made it more difficult to assume either that the moral codes operating in our own society provide the only relevant belief options or that there is a universal, fixed set of discoverable moral truths existing independently of all cultural variations and historical circumstances.

The systematic rational inquiry into the issues surrounding moral decision making has been one of the major subfields of philosophy, and as such it is called ethics. In other words, ethics is the philosophical study of the possible criteria of right and wrong conduct, goods to pursue and evils to avoid, and the values and concepts upon which those criteria are based. As noted earlier, whether or not we are always aware of it, we conduct our daily lives with a more or less coherent set of moral beliefs and values that guide us in our conscious behavior and interactions with others. Whether those beliefs are justified is what interests ethicists, not only for theoretical reasons but also because such beliefs are translated into actions that affect our social environment.

Readings 41 through 45 deal with some of the preliminary issues that should be addressed before we can justifiably argue that something is morally right or wrong, good or bad. For example, what natural capabilities for moral goodness or evil humans are thought to possess will determine what we can say plausibly about what they ought to do or not do. Also, it must be decided before ethical analysis proceeds very far whether any answer to a moral problem is going to be considered as correct as any other, and thus what is morally right or wrong is whatever someone thinks it is. The alternative is to decide that some moral conclusions are better than others so that what is morally right or wrong in particular cases would be so, regardless of what some people think.

In readings 46 through 49, various answers are given to the perennial question of what it takes to be a morally good or bad person. The focus is on what kinds of virtues ought to be inculcated, and which vices avoided, in the moral development of the human individual. Issues regarding moral character traditionally have been an important part of ethics because what kind of person we become has a lot to do with how we treat others.

The last group of readings, 50 through 54, all address more directly the standards of ethically justified conduct that might be recommended both to moral agents themselves as they decide what to do in real-life circumstances and to those in a position to morally evaluate the actions of others. According to many philosophers, it makes sense to use moral standards in the evaluation of our own or someone else's actions when (a) the actors have choices, (b) their values influence their choices, (c) some question of obligation is relevant, and (d) some overarching ethical principle is appealed to in deciding our obligation in a specific situation. To avoid confusion, also keep in mind that most philosophers use the terms "ethical" and "moral" interchangeably.

41. Ruth Benedict (1887–1948)
Ethical Relativism

Ruth Benedict was an American anthropologist who was born in New York City and eventually spent most of her academic career as a member of the anthropology faculty at Columbia University. Through her fieldwork and theoretical writing, especially in the 1930s and 1940s, Benedict is generally considered one of the major influences in the development of cultural (or social) anthropology as a social science in the twentieth century.

The reading consists of excerpts from "Anthropology and the Abnormal," a 1934 journal article in which Benedict makes the case that social standards of so-called normal and abnormal behavior, attitudes, and emotional predispositions have always varied widely among different cultural groups around the world. Although she argues primarily for this *factual* conclusion, based on empirical research and aimed more at questions concerning the plausibility of cross-cultural assessments of mental health and illness, her claims strongly imply the *normative* conclusion as well, that moral good and evil are also solely a function of culture-specific beliefs. In other words, based on the obvious fact of cultural and historical diversity of moral standards among humans, Benedict seems to affirm the value judgment that moral truth also is culturally and historically diverse. So a specific practice might be treated as immoral in one society and morally right in a different society, and we have no adequate grounds for deciding which of the two cultural beliefs is more justified than its opposite. Even though Benedict's actual position is more ambiguously spelled out in the reading, to the extent that she advocates this moral conclusion, she is putting forth a version (still fairly common these days among social scientists) of what is usually called ethical relativism.

QUESTIONS FOR CRITICAL READING

1. How does Benedict define and explain the categories of "normality" and "abnormality" in human cultural life?
2. How does Benedict define morality and the immoral, and what is their connection to the normal and abnormal?
3. What is Benedict's position on the universality of ethical standards, and how does she argue for her position?
4. How does Benedict characterize an "unstable individual," and what does this have to do with morality?

Modern social anthropology has become more and more a study of the varieties and common elements of cultural environment and the consequences of these in human behavior. For such a study of diverse social orders primitive peoples fortunately provide a laboratory not yet entirely vitiated by the spread of a standardized worldwide civilization. Dyaks and Hopis, Fijians and Yakuts are significant for psychological and sociological study because only among these simpler peoples has there been sufficient isolation to give opportunity for the development of localized social forms. In the higher cultures the standardization of custom and belief over a couple of continents has given a false sense of the inevitability of the particular forms that have gained currency, and we need to turn to a wider survey in order to check the conclusions we hastily base upon this near-universality of familiar customs. Most of the simpler cultures did not gain the wide currency of the one which, out of our experience, we identify with human nature, but this was for various historical reasons, and certainly not for any that gives us as its carriers a monopoly of social good or of social sanity. Modern civilization, from this point of view, becomes not a necessary pinnacle of human achievement but one entry in a long series of possible adjustments.

These adjustments, whether they are in mannerisms like the ways of showing anger, or joy, or grief in any society, or in major human drives like those of sex, prove to be far more variable than experience in any one culture would suggest. In certain fields, such as that of religion or of formal marriage arrangements, these wide limits of variability are well known and can be fairly described. In others it is not yet possible to give a generalized account, but that does not absolve us of the task of indicating the significance of the work that has been done and of the problems that have arisen.

One of these problems relates to the customary modern normal-abnormal categories and our conclusions regarding them. In how far are such categories culturally determined, or in how far can we with assurance regard them as absolute? In how far can we regard inability to function socially as diagnostic of abnormality, or in how far is it necessary to regard this as a function of the culture?

As a matter of fact, one of the most striking facts that emerge from a study of widely varying cultures is the ease with which our abnormals function in other cultures. It does not matter what kind of "abnormality" we choose for illustration, those which indicate extreme instability, or those which are more in the nature of character traits like sadism or delusions of grandeur or of persecution, there are well-described cultures in which these abnormals function at ease and with honor, and apparently without danger or difficulty to the society. . . .

No one civilization can possibly utilize in its mores the whole potential range of human behavior. Just as there are great numbers of possible phonetic articulations, and the possibility of language depends on a selection and standardization of a few of these in order that speech communication may be possible at all, so the possibility of organized behavior of every sort, from the fashions of local dress and houses to the dicta of a people's ethics and religion, depends upon a similar selection among the possible behavior traits. In the field of recognized economic obligations or sex tabus this selection is as nonrational and subconscious a process as it is in the field of phonetics. It is a process which goes on in the group for long periods of time and is historically conditioned by innumerable accidents of isolation or of contact of peoples. In any comprehensive study of psychology, the selection that different cultures have made in the course of history within the great circumference of potential behavior is of great significance.

Every society, beginning with some slight inclination in one direction or another, carries its preference farther and farther, integrating itself more and more completely upon its chosen basis, and discarding those types of behavior that are uncongenial. Most of those organizations of personality that seem to us most incontrovertibly abnormal have been used by different civilizations in the very foundations of their institutional life. Conversely the most valued traits of our normal individuals have been looked on in differently organized cultures as aberrant. Normality, in short, within a very wide range, is culturally defined. It is primarily a term for the socially elaborated segment of human behavior in any culture; and abnormality, a term for the segment that that particular civilization does not use. The very eyes with which we see the problem are conditioned by the long traditional habits of our own society.

It is a point that has been made more often in relation to ethics than in relation to psychiatry. We do not any longer make the mistake of deriving the morality of our own locality and decade directly from the inevitable constitution of human nature. We do not elevate it to the dignity of a first principle. We recognize that morality differs in every society, and is a convenient term for socially approved habits. Mankind has always preferred to say, "It is morally good," rather than "It is habitual," and the fact of this preference is matter enough for a critical science of ethics. But historically the two phrases are synonymous.

The concept of the normal is properly a variant of the concept of the good. It is that which society has approved. A normal action is one which falls well within the limits of expected behavior for a particular society. Its variability among different peoples is essentially a function of the variability of the behavior patterns that different societies have created for themselves, and can never be wholly divorced from a consideration of culturally institutionalized types of behavior.

Each culture is a more or less elaborate working-out of the potentialities of the segment it has chosen. In so far as a civilization is well integrated and consistent within itself, it will tend to carry farther and farther, according to its nature, its initial impulse toward a particular type of action, and from the point of view of any other culture those elaborations will include more and more extreme and aberrant traits.

Each of these traits, in proportion as it reinforces the chosen behavior patterns of that culture, is for that culture normal. Those individuals to whom it is congenial either congenitally, or as the result of childhood sets, are accorded prestige in that culture, and are not visited with the social contempt or disapproval which their traits would call down upon them in a society that was differently organized. On the other hand, those individuals whose characteristics are not congenial to the selected type of human behavior in that community are the deviants, no matter how valued their personality traits may be in a contrasted civilization.

The Dobuan who is not easily susceptible to fear of treachery, who enjoys work and likes to be helpful, is their neurotic and regarded as silly. On the Northwest Coast the person who finds it difficult to read life in terms of an insult contest will be the person upon whom fall all the difficulties of the culturally unprovided for. The person who does not find it easy to humiliate a neighbor, nor to see humiliation in his own experience, who is genial and loving, may, of course, find some unstandardized way of achieving satisfactions in his society, but not in the major patterned responses that his culture requires of him. If he is born to play an important rôle in a family with many hereditary privileges, he can succeed only by doing violence to his whole personality. If he does not succeed, he has betrayed his culture; that is, he is abnormal.

I have spoken of individuals as having sets toward certain types of behavior, and of these sets as running sometimes counter to the types of behavior which are institutionalized in the culture to which they belong. From all that we know of contrasting cultures it seems clear that differences of temperament occur in every society. The matter has never been made the subject of investigation, but from the available material it would appear that these temperament types are very likely of universal recurrence. That is, there is an ascertainable range of human behavior that is found wherever a sufficiently large series of individuals is observed. But the proportion in which behavior types stand to one another in different societies is not universal. The vast majority of the individuals in any group are shaped to the fashion of that culture. In other words, most individuals are plastic to the moulding force of the society into which they are born. In a society that values trance, as in India, they will have supernormal experience. In a society that institutionalizes homosexual-

ity, they will be homosexual. In a society that sets the gathering of possessions as the chief human objective, they will amass property. The deviants, whatever the type of behavior the culture has institutionalized, will remain few in number, and there seems no more difficulty in moulding the vast malleable majority to the "normality" of what we consider an aberrant trait, such as delusions of reference, than to the normality of such accepted behavior patterns as acquisitiveness. The small proportion of the number of the deviants in any culture is not a function of the sure instinct with which that society has built itself upon the fundamental sanities, but of the universal fact that, happily, the majority of mankind quite readily take any shape that is presented to them.

The relativity of normality is not an academic issue. In the first place, it suggests that the apparent weakness of the aberrant is most often and in great measure illusory. It springs not from the fact that he is lacking in necessary vigor, but that he is an individual upon whom that culture has put more than the usual strain. His inability to adapt himself to society is a reflection of the fact that that adaptation involves a conflict in him that it does not in the so-called normal.

Therapeutically, it suggests that the inculcation of tolerance and appreciation in any society toward its less usual types is fundamentally important in successful mental hygiene. The complement of this tolerance, on the patients' side, is an education in self-reliance and honesty with himself. If he can be brought to realize that what has thrust him into his misery is despair at his lack of social backing he may be able to achieve a more independent and less tortured attitude and lay the foundation for an adequately functioning mode of existence. . . .

The relativity of normality is important in what may some day come to be a true social engineering. Our picture of our own civilization is no longer in this generation in terms of a changeless and divinely derived set of categorical imperatives. We must face the problems our changed perspective has put upon us. In this matter of mental ailments, we must face the fact that even our normality is man-made, and is of our own seeking. Just as we have been handicapped in dealing with ethical problems so long as we held to an absolute definition of morality, so too in dealing with the problems of abnormality we are handicapped so long as we identify our local normalities with the universal sanities. I have taken illustrations from different cultures, because the conclusions are most inescapable from the contrasts as they are presented in unlike social groups. But the major problem is not a consequence of the variability of the normal from culture to culture, but its variability from era to era. This variability in time we cannot escape if we would, and it is not beyond the bounds of possibility that we may be able to face this inevitable change with full understanding and deal with it rationally. No society has yet achieved self-conscious and critical analysis of its own normalities and attempted rationally to deal with its own social process of creating new normalities within its next generation. But the fact that it is unachieved is not therefore proof of its impossibility. It is a faint indication of how momentous it could be in human society.

There is another major factor in the cultural conditioning of abnormality. From the material that is available at the present time it seems a lesser factor than the one we have discussed. Nevertheless, disregard of its importance has led to many misconceptions. The particular forms of behavior to which unstable individuals of any group are liable are many of them matters of cultural patterning like any other behavior. It is for this obvious reason that the epidemic disorders of one continent or era are often rare or unreported from other parts of the world or other periods of history.

The baldest evidences of cultural patterning in the behavior of unstable individuals is in trance phenomena. The use to which such proclivities are put, the form their manifestations take, the things that are seen and felt in trance, are all culturally controlled. The tranced individual may come back with communications from the dead describing the minutiae of life in the hereafter, or he may visit the world of the unborn, or get information about lost objects in the camp, or experience cosmic unity, or acquire a life-long guardian spirit, or get information about coming events. Even in trance the individual holds strictly to the rules and expectations of his culture, and his experience is as locally patterned as a marriage rite or an economic exchange.

The conformity of trance experience to the expectations of waking life is well recognized. Now that we are no longer confused by the attempt to ascribe supernormal validity to the one or the other, and realize how trance experience bodies forth the preoccupations of the experiencing individual, the cultural patterning in ecstasy has become an accepted tenet.

But the matter does not end here. It is not only what is seen in trance experience that has clear-cut geographical and temporal distribution. It is equally true of forms of behavior which are affected by certain unstable individuals in any group. It is one of the prime difficulties in the use of such unprecise and casual information as we possess about the behavior of the unstable in different cultures, that the material does not correspond to data from our own society. It has even been thought that such definite types of instability as Arctic hysteria and the Malay running-amok were racial diseases. But we know at least, in spite of the lack of good psychiatric accounts, that these phenomena do not coincide with racial distributions. Moreover, the same problem is quite as striking in cases where there is no possibility of a racial correlation. Running amok has been described as alike in symptoms and alike in the treatment accorded it by the rest of the group from such different parts of the world as Melanesia and Tierra del Fuego.

The racial explanation is also ruled out of court in those instances of epidemic mania which are characteristic of our own cultural background. The dancing mania that filled the streets of Europe with compulsively dancing men, women, and children in mediaeval times is recognized as an extreme instance of suggestibility in our own racial group.

These behaviors are capable of controlled elaboration that is often carried to great lengths. Unstable individuals in one culture achieve characteristic forms that may be excessively rare or absent in another, and this is very marked where social value has been attached to one form or another. Thus when some form of borderline behavior has been associated in any society with the shaman and he is a person of authority and influence, it is this particular indicated seizure to which he will be liable at every demonstration. Among the Shasta of California, as we have seen, and among many other tribes in various parts of the world, some form of cataleptic seizure is the passport to shamanism and must constantly accompany its practice. In other regions it is automatic vision or audition. In other societies behavior is perhaps closest to what we cover by the term hystero-epilepsy. In Siberia all the familiar characteristics of our spiritualistic seances are required for every performance of the shaman. In all these cases the particular experience that is thus socially chosen receives considerable elaboration and is usually patterned in detail according to local standards. That is, each culture, though it chooses quite narrowly in the great field of borderline experiences, without difficulty imposes its selected type upon certain of its individuals. The particular behavior of an unstable individual in these instances is not the single and inevitable mode in which his abnormality could express itself. He has taken up a traditionally conditioned pattern of behavior in this as in any other field. Conversely, in every society, our own included, there are forms of instability that are out of fashion. They are not at the present time at least being presented for imitation to the enormously suggestible individuals who constitute in any society a considerable group of the abnormals. It seems clear that this is no matter of the nature of sanity, or even of a biological, inherited tendency in a local group, but quite simply an affair of social patterning.

The problem of understanding abnormal human behavior in any absolute sense independent of cultural factors is still far in the future. The categories of borderline behavior which we derive from the study of the neuroses and psychoses of our civilization are categories of prevailing local types of instability. They give much information about the stresses and strains of Western civilization, but no final picture of inevitable human behavior. Any conclusions about such behavior must await the collection by trained observers of psychiatric data from other cultures. Since no adequate work of the kind has been done at the present time, it is impossible to say what core of definition of abnormality may be found valid from the comparative material. It is as it is in ethics: all our local conventions of moral behavior and of immoral are without absolute validity, and yet it is quite possible that a modicum of what is considered right and what wrong could be disentangled that is shared by the whole human race. When data are available in psychiatry, this minimum definition of abnormal human tendencies will be probably quite unlike our culturally conditioned, highly elaborated psychoses such as those that are described, for instance, under the terms of schizophrenia and manic-depressive.

DISCUSSION QUESTIONS

1. Do you agree with Benedict's claim that morality is just a "convenient term for socially approved habits"? Why or why not?
2. If moral standards are only relative to the cultural group in which they are found, can anyone ever be mistaken in his or her moral beliefs? Why or why not?
3. Is Benedict's apparent acceptance of a "critical science of ethics" consistent with the rest of what she says about the cultural relativity of ethics? Explain.
4. What does Benedict mean by her distinction between "simpler peoples" and "higher cultures"? To what extent is this distinction an ethnocentric one?

42. Mary Midgley (b. 1919)
"Trying Out One's New Sword"

Mary Midgley is an internationally recognized British philosopher and a prolific writer on many aspects of moral philosophy over the past three decades or so. Until recently she was a senior lecturer at the University of Newcastle-upon-Tyne. In her work she has focused especially on human nature, including our natural moral capabilities and limitations as valuing creatures, and its effect on our chances of living life well or badly.

The selection is the fifth chapter from Midgley's 1981 book *Heart and Mind*, and in a roundabout way she is arguing for a position often referred to by philosophers as ethical (or moral) "universalism," or "objectivism." This position is in direct opposition to ethical relativism, of both the more moderate culture-specific type implied in Benedict's essay and the more extreme individualistic version that would make the truth of moral judgments simply a function of whatever an individual thinks, regardless of social norms. Generally, ethical universalism asserts that what is morally right or wrong, good or bad, is so for everyone in similar circumstances of choice, independently of what any particular person or group thinks about the matter. This position thus implies that some moral beliefs are more justified than others, whether or not we know which ones in specific cases, and that people can be mistaken in their moral judgments.

Midgley centers her analysis around a compelling example of a customary practice in one cultural context that would be seen as morally outrageous from a different cultural standpoint in order to show in the first place that ethical relativism doesn't really make any sense. She then goes on to argue that we rationally can, and should, engage in the critical evaluation of culturally scripted behaviors and character traits as they are found in our own as well as other cultures. To do so is both an appropriate concomitant of learning about and accurately understanding cultural life itself and part of a responsible and educated approach to decision making concerning how people ought to treat each other in this shared world.

QUESTIONS FOR CRITICAL READING

1. What is the position of "moral isolationism," what is Midgley's interpretation of its origins, and what is her assessment of its plausibility?
2. Regarding the problem of morally evaluating the Samurai custom Midgley uses as an illustration, what are the four questions she believes need to be addressed, and what are her answers to them?
3. How does Midgley characterize "immoralism," and how does she criticize it?
4. In Midgley's estimation, why is logical and practical consistency a major problem for the advocate of "moral isolationism"?

All of us are, more or less, in trouble today about trying to understand cultures strange to us. We hear constantly of alien customs. We see changes in our lifetime which would have astonished our parents. I want to discuss here one very short way of dealing with this difficulty, a drastic way which many people now theoretically favour. It consists in simply denying that we can ever understand any culture except our own well enough to make judgements about it. Those who recommend this hold that the world is sharply divided into separate societies, sealed units, each with its own system of thought. They feel that the respect and tolerance due from one system to another forbids us ever to take up a critical position to any other culture. Moral judgement, they suggest, is a kind of coinage valid only in its country of origin.

I shall call this position 'moral isolationism'. I shall suggest that it is certainly not forced upon us, and indeed that it makes no sense at all. People usually take it up because they think it is a respectful attitude to other cultures. In fact, however, it is not respectful. Nobody can respect what is entirely unintelligible to them. To respect someone, we have to know enough about him to make a *favourable* judgement, however general and tentative. And we do understand people in other cultures to this extent. Otherwise a great mass of our most valuable thinking would be paralysed.

To show this, I shall take a remote example, because we shall probably find it easier to think calmly about it than we should with a contemporary one, such as female circumcision in Africa or the Chinese Cultural Revolution. The principles involved will still be the same. My example is this. There is, it seems, a verb in classical Japanese which means 'to try out one's new sword on a chance wayfarer'. (The word is *tsujigiri*, literally 'crossroads-cut'.) A samurai sword had to be tried out because, if it was to work properly, it had to slice through someone at a single blow, from the shoulder to the opposite flank. Otherwise, the warrior bungled his stroke. This could injure his honour, offend his ancestors, and even let down his emperor. So tests were needed, and wayfarers had to be expended. Any wayfarer would do—provided, of course, that he was not another Samurai. Scientists will recognize a familiar problem about the rights of experimental subjects.

Now when we hear of a custom like this, we may well reflect that we simply do not understand it; and therefore are not qualified to criticize it at all, because we are not members of that culture. But we are not members of any other culture either, except our own. So we extend the principle to cover all extraneous cultures, and we seem therefore to be moral isolationists. But this is, as we shall see, an impossible position. Let us ask what it would involve.

We must ask first: Does the isolating barrier work both ways? Are people in other cultures equally unable to criticize *us*? This question struck me sharply when I read a remark in *The Guardian* by an anthropologist about a South American Indian who had been taken into a Brazilian town for an operation, which saved his life. When he came back to his village, he made several highly critical remarks about the white Brazilians' way of life. They may very well have been justified. But the interesting point was that the anthropologist called these remarks 'a damning indictment of Western civilization'. Now the Indian had been in that town about two weeks. Was he in a position to deliver a damning indictment? Would we ourselves be qualified to deliver such an indictment on the Samurai, provided we could spend two weeks in ancient Japan? What do we really think about this?

My own impression is that we believe that outsiders can, in principle, deliver perfectly good indictments—only, it usually takes more than two weeks to make them damning. Understanding has degrees. It is not a slapdash yes-or-no matter. Intelligent outsiders can progress in it, and in some ways will be at an advantage over the locals. But if this is so, it must clearly apply to ourselves as much as anybody else.

Our next question is this: Does the isolating barrier between cultures block praise as well as blame? If I want to say that the Samurai culture has many virtues, or to praise the South American Indians, am I prevented from doing *that* by my outside status? Now, we certainly do need to praise other societies in this way. But it is hardly possible that we could praise them effectively if we could not, in principle, criticize them. Our praise would be worthless if it rested on no definite grounds, if it did not flow from some understanding. Certainly we may need to praise things which we do not *fully* understand. We say 'there's something very good here, but I can't quite make out what it is yet'. This happens when we want to learn from strangers. And we can learn from strangers. But to do this we have to distinguish between those strangers who

are worth learning from and those who are not. Can we then judge which is which?

This brings us to our third question: What is involved in judging? Now plainly there is no question here of sitting on a bench in a red robe and sentencing people. Judging simply means forming an opinion, and expressing it if it is called for. Is there anything wrong about this? Naturally, we ought to avoid forming—and expressing—*crude* opinions, like that of a simple-minded missionary, who might dismiss the whole Samurai culture as entirely bad, because non-Christian. But this is a different objection. The trouble with crude opinions is that they are crude, whoever forms them, not that they are formed by the wrong people. Anthropologists, after all, are outsiders quite as much as missionaries. Moral isolationism forbids us to form *any* opinions on these matters. Its ground for doing so is that we don't understand them. But there is much that we don't understand in our own culture too. This brings us to our last question: If we can't judge other cultures, can we really judge our own? Our efforts to do so will be much damaged if we are really deprived of our opinions about other societies, because these provide the range of comparison, the spectrum of alternatives against which we set what we want to understand. We would have to stop using the mirror which anthropology so helpfully holds up to us.

In short, moral isolationism would lay down a general ban on moral reasoning. Essentially, this is the programme of immoralism, and it carries a distressing logical difficulty. Immoralists like Nietzsche are actually just a rather specialized sect of moralists. They can no more afford to put moralizing out of business than smugglers can afford to abolish customs regulations. The power of moral judgement is, in fact, not a luxury, not a perverse indulgence of the self-righteous. It is a necessity. When we judge something to be bad or good, better or worse than something else, we are taking it as an example to aim at or avoid. Without opinions of this sort, we would have no framework of comparison for our own policy, no chance of profiting by other people's insights or mistakes. In this vacuum, we could form no judgements on our own actions.

Now it would be odd if Homo sapiens had really got himself into a position as bad as this—a position where his main evolutionary asset, his brain, was so little use to him. None of us is going to accept this sceptical diagnosis. We cannot do so, because our involvement in moral isolationism does not flow from apathy, but from a rather acute concern about human hypocrisy and other forms of wickedness. But we polarize that concern around a few selected moral truths. We are rightly angry with those who despise, oppress or steamroll other cultures. We think that doing these things is actually *wrong*. But this is itself a moral judgement. We could not condemn oppression and insolence if we thought that all our condemnations were just a trivial local quirk of our own culture. We could still less do it if we tried to stop judging altogether.

Real moral scepticism, in fact, could lead only to inaction, to our losing all interest in moral questions, most of all in those which concern other societies. When we discuss these things, it becomes instantly clear how far we are from doing this. Suppose, for instance, that I criticize the bisecting Samurai, that I say his behaviour is brutal. What will usually happen next is that someone will protest, will say that I have no right to make criticisms like that of another culture. But it is most unlikely that he will use this move to end the discussion of the subject. Instead, he will justify the Samurai. He will try to fill in the background, to make me understand the custom, by explaining the exalted ideals of discipline and devotion which produced it. He will probably talk of the lower value which the ancient Japanese placed on individual life generally. He may well suggest that this is a healthier attitude than our own obsession with security. He may add, too, that the wayfarers did not seriously mind being bisected, that in principle they accepted the whole arrangement.

Now an objector who talks like this is implying that it *is* possible to understand alien customs. That is just what he is trying to make me do. And he implies, too, that if I do succeed in understanding them, I shall do something better than giving up judging them. He expects me to change my present judgement to a truer one—namely, one that is favourable. And the standards I must use to do this cannot just be Samurai standards. They have to be ones current in my own culture. Ideals like discipline and devotion will not move anybody unless he himself accepts them. As it happens, neither discipline nor devotion is very popular in the West at present. Anyone who appeals to them may well have to do some more arguing to make *them* acceptable, before he can use them to explain the Samurai. But if he does succeed here, he will have persuaded us, not just that there was something to be said for them in ancient Japan, but that there would be here as well.

Isolating barriers simply cannot arise here. If we accept something as a serious moral truth about one culture, we can't refuse to apply it—in however different an outward form—to other cultures as well, wherever circumstance admit it. If we refuse to do this, we just are not taking the other culture seriously. This becomes clear if we look at the last argument used by my objector—that of justification by consent of the victim. It is suggested that sudden bisection is quite in order, *provided* that it takes place between consenting adults. I cannot now discuss how conclusive this justification is. What I am pointing out is simply that it can only work if we believe that *consent* can make such a transaction respectable—and this is a thoroughly modern and Western idea. It would probably never occur to a Samurai; if it did, it would surprise him very much. It is *our* standard. In applying it, too, we are likely to make another typically Western demand. We shall ask for good factual evidence that the wayfarers actually do have this rather surprising taste—that they are really willing to be bisected. In applying Western standards in this way, we are not being confused or irrelevant. We are asking the questions which arise *from where we stand,* questions which we can see the sense of. We do this because asking questions which you can't see the sense of is humbug. Certainly we can extend our questioning by imaginative effort. We can come to understand other societies better. By doing so, we may make their questions our own, or we may see that they are really forms of the questions which we are asking already. This is not impossible. It is just very hard work. The obstacles which often prevent it are simply those of ordinary ignorance, laziness and prejudice.

If there were really an isolating barrier, of course, our own culture could never have been formed. It is no sealed box, but a fertile jungle of different influences—Greek, Jewish, Roman, Norse, Celtic and so forth, into which further influences are still pouring—American, Indian, Japanese, Jamaican, you name it. The moral isolationist's picture of separate, unmixable cultures is quite unreal. People who talk about British history usually stress the value of this fertilizing mix, no doubt rightly. But this is not just an odd fact about Britain. Except for the very smallest and most remote, all cultures are formed out of many streams. All have the problem of digesting and assimilating things which, at the start, they do not understand. All have the choice of learning something from this challenge, or, alternatively, of refusing to learn, and fighting it mindlessly instead.

This universal predicament has been obscured by the fact that anthropologists used to concentrate largely on very small and remote cultures, which did not seem to have this problem. These tiny societies, which had often forgotten their own history, made neat, self-contained subjects for study. No doubt it was valuable to emphasize their remoteness, their extreme strangeness, their independence of our cultural tradition. This emphasis was, I think, the root of moral isolationism. But, as the tribal studies themselves showed, even there the anthropologists were able to interpret what they saw and make judgements—often favourable—about the tribesmen. And the tribesmen, too, were quite equal to making judgements about the anthropologists—and about the tourists and Coca-Cola salesmen who followed them. Both

sets of judgements, no doubt, were somewhat hasty, both have been refined in the light of further experience. A similar transaction between us and the Samurai might take even longer. But that is no reason at all for deeming it impossible. Morally as well as physically, there is only one world, and we all have to live in it.

DISCUSSION QUESTIONS

1. Are critical analysis and respect for moral beliefs that are different from one's own compatible or incompatible? Explain.

2. Some people argue for a more extreme version of ethical relativism, which says that what is morally right or wrong, good or bad, is what any individual thinks it is, regardless of his or her cultural affiliation. How would you criticize or defend this position?

3. Is there a defensible distinction we can make between cultural practices that are appropriately susceptible to critical evaluation and those that are not? What would it be, and on what criteria would it be based?

4. How would you compare Benedict's and Midgley's positions on the justifiability of cross-cultural ethical judgments? Which position is more convincing to you? Why?

43. Mencius (c. 371–289 B.C.E.)
The Goodness of Human Nature

Also known as Meng-tzu, Mencius was a philosopher in ancient China who is still considered one of the most influential thinkers in all of Chinese intellectual history. He was a follower of Confucius, who lived a few centuries earlier (and about whom more will be said in reading 47), but he developed Confucian doctrines into a distinctive philosophical system of his own. Like Confucius, Mencius lived during a time of great political conflict and economic insecurity in China, and as a result he was interested primarily in moral and political issues in his philosophical study. As was typical of most Chinese philosophers in ancient times, Mencius also believed that the solutions to the fundamental human problems of what kind of person to be and how to treat

others were to be recommended especially to political rulers, with the hope of reestablishing peace, harmony, and security in society as a whole. Toward that end he spent many years of his life traveling around China offering moral advice to various heads of state, not only on how to improve their own moral characters but also on how this would result in improved lives for their subjects.

The reading consists of excerpts from the collection of his teachings, the *Book of Mencius,* or *Meng-tzu,* compiled by his students and followers. The translation and commentary is by Wing-Tsit Chan. Included is the formulation of the doctrine for which Mencius is most famous—that human nature is originally and essentially good, and the achievement of moral goodness in our lives is primarily a matter of actualizing (or, in many cases, "recovering") that original nature. This view of human nature had a major impact on all subsequent Confucian thought, as well as on Chinese culture generally, in the following millennium.

QUESTIONS FOR CRITICAL READING

1. How does Mencius argue for the position that human nature is essentially good, and how does he explain human evil?
2. How does Mencius criticize the position of Kao Tzu that essential human nature is neither good nor evil?
3. What does Mencius mean by the "Four Beginnings"?
4. How are we to achieve virtue, according to Mencius, and how does he explain the differences in moral character among humans?

TERMS TO NOTE

humanity: A common translation of *jen,* one of the central concepts in traditional Chinese moral philosophy. Sometimes it refers to the specific virtue of kindness, benevolence, or sympathy, and sometimes it refers to moral virtue generally; so the "morally good" person in the fullest sense is the person of *jen.*

heaven: The usual translation of *T'ien,* the traditional conception of the Supreme Being in Chinese cosmology. In the Confucian tradition with which Mencius is associated, Heaven is the impersonal though purposive source of the cosmos and its natural order.

The Book of Mencius[1]

Book Six, Part I

6A:1.   Kao Tzu[2] said, "Human nature is like the willow tree, and righteousness is like a cup or a bowl. To turn human nature into humanity and righteousness is like turning the willow into cups and bowls." Mencius said, "Sir, can you follow the nature of the willow tree and make the cups and bowls, or must you violate the nature of the willow tree before you can make the cups and bowls? If you are going to violate the nature of the willow tree in order to make cups and bowls, then must you also violate human nature in order to make it into humanity and righteousness? Your words, alas! would lead all people in the world to consider humanity and righteousness as calamity [because they required the violation of human nature]!"

6A:2.   Kao Tzu said, "Man's nature is like whirling water. If a breach in the pool is made to the east it will flow to the east. If a breach is made to the west it will flow to the west. Man's nature is indifferent to good and evil, just as water is indifferent to east and west." Mencius said, "Water, indeed, is indifferent to the east and west, but is it indifferent to high and low? Man's nature is naturally good just as water naturally flows downward. There is no man without this good nature; neither is there water that does not flow downward. Now you can strike water and cause it to splash upward over your forehead, and by damming and leading it, you can force it uphill. Is this the nature of water? It is the forced circumstance that makes it do so. Man can be made to do evil, for his nature can be treated in the same way."

6A:3.   Kao Tzu said, "What is inborn[3] is called nature." Mencius said, "When you say that what is inborn is called nature, is that like saying that white is white?" "Yes." "Then is the whiteness of the white feather the same as the whiteness of snow? Or, again,

---

the Mean as the "Four Books." From then on they ranked as Classics. These four books and Chu Hsi's commentaries on them were the basis of the civil service examinations from 1313 till 1905, replacing other Classics in importance and influence. For translations of the *Book of Mencius,* see Bibliography.

2. His dates are c.420–c.350 B.C., but otherwise nothing is known of him. Chao Ch'i (d. 201), in his *Meng Tzu chu* (Commentary on the *Book of Mencius*), says his name was Pu-hai. Chiao Hsün (1763–1820), in his *Meng Tzu cheng-i* (Correct Meanings of the *Book of Mencius*), thought Chao confused him with the Pu-hai who once studied under Mencius. The two different persons merely had the same private name.

3. According to Chu Hsi, *Meng Tzu chi-chu* (Collected Commentaries on the *Book of Mencius*), *sheng* refers not to man's inborn nature but to his consciousness and activities, and is comparable to the Buddhist theory that function is nature.

---

1. The *Book of Mencius, Meng Tzu* in Chinese, is divided into seven books, each subdivided into two parts. In all probability it was compiled by pupils of Mencius after his death. Chu Hsi (1130–1200) grouped it with the *Analects,* the *Great Learning,* and the *Doctrine of*

is the whiteness of snow the same as the whiteness of white jade?" "Yes." "Then is the nature of a dog the same as the nature of an ox, and is the nature of an ox the same as the nature of a man?"

6A:4. Kao Tzu said, "By nature we desire food and sex. Humanity is internal and not external, whereas righteousness is external and not internal." Mencius said, "Why do you say that humanity is internal and righteousness external?" "When I see an old man and respect him for his age, it is not that the oldness is within me, just as, when something is white and I call it white, I am merely observing its external appearance. I therefore say that righteousness is external." Mencius said, "There is no difference between our considering a white horse to be white and a white man to be white. But is there no difference between acknowledging the age of an old horse and the age of an old man? And what is it that we call righteousness, the fact that a man is old or the fact that we honor his old age?" Kao Tzu said, "I love my own younger brother but do not love the younger brother of, say, a man from the state of Ch'in. This is because I am the one to determine that pleasant feeling. I therefore say that humanity comes from within. On the other hand, I respect the old men of the state of Ch'u as well as my own elders. What determines my pleasant feeling is age itself. Therefore I say that righteousness is external." Mencius said, "We love the roast meat of Ch'in as much as we love our own. This is even so with respect to material things. Then are you going to say that our love of roast meat is also external?"

6A:5. Meng Chi Tzu[4] asked Kung-tu Tzu,[5] "What does it mean to say that righteousness is internal?" Kung-tu Tzu said, "We practice reverence, and therefore it is called internal." "Suppose a fellow villager is one year older than your older brother. Whom are you going to serve with reverence?" "I shall serve my brother with reverence." "In offering wine at a feast, to whom will you offer first?" "I shall offer wine to the villager first." Meng Chi Tzu said, "Now you show reverence to one but honor for age to the other. What determines your actions certainly lies without and not within." Kung-tu Tzu could not reply and told Men-

cius about it. Mencius said, "If you ask him whether he will serve with reverence his uncle or his younger brother, he will say that he will serve with reverence his uncle. Then you ask him, in case his younger brother is acting at a sacrifice as the representative of the deceased, then to whom is he going to serve with reverence? He will say he will serve the younger brother with reverence. Then you ask him 'Where is your reverence for your uncle?' He will then say, '[I show reverence to my younger brother] because he represents the ancestral spirit in an official capacity.' You can then likewise say, '[I show reverence to the villager] because of his position.' Ordinarily, the reverence is due the elder brother, but on special occasions it is due the villager." When Chi Tzu heard this, he said, "We show reverence to uncle when reverence is due him, and we show reverence to the younger brother when reverence is due him. Certainly what determines it lies without and does not come from within." Kung-tu Tzu said, "In the winter we drink things hot. In the summer we drink things cold. Does it mean that what determines eating and drinking also lies outside?"

6A:6. Kung-tu Tzu said, "Kao Tzu said that man's nature is neither good nor evil. Some say that man's nature may be made good or evil, therefore when King Wen and King Wu[6] were in power the people loved virtue, and when Kings Yu and Li[7] were in power people loved violence. Some say that some men's nature is good and some men's nature is evil. Therefore even under (sage-emperor) Yao[8] there was Hsiang [who daily plotted to kill his brother], and even with a bad father Ku-sou, there was [a most filial] Shun[9] (Hsiang's brother who succeeded Yao), and even with (wicked king) Chou[10] as uncle and ruler, there were Viscount Ch'i of Wei and Prince Pi-kan.[11] Now you say that human nature is good. Then are those people wrong?"

---

4. Chu Hsi thinks he was possibly a younger brother of Meng Chung Tzu, pupil of Mencius.
5. Mencius' pupil.

6. Sage-kings who founded the Chou dynasty (r. 1171–1122 B.C. and 1121–1116 B.C., respectively).
7. Wicked kings (r. 781–771 B.C. and 878–842 B.C., respectively).
8. Legendary ruler (3rd millennium B.C.).
9. Legendary ruler, successor of Yao.
10. King Chou (r. 1175–1112 B.C.) was responsible for the fall of the Shang dynasty (1751–1112 B.C.).
11. It is not sure whether they were King Chou's uncles. Their good advice to King Chou was rejected.

Mencius said, "If you let people follow their feelings (original nature),[12] they will be able to do good. This is what is meant by saying that human nature is good. If man does evil, it is not the fault of his natural endowment.[13] The feeling of commiseration is found in all men; the feeling of shame and dislike is found in all men; the feeling of respect and reverence is found in all men; and the feeling of right and wrong is found in all men. The feeling of commiseration is what we call humanity; the feeling of shame and dislike is what we called righteousness; the feeling of respect and reverence is what we called propriety (li);[14] and the feeling of right and wrong is what we called wisdom. Humanity, righteousness, propriety, and wisdom are not drilled into us from outside. We originally have them with us. Only we do not think [to find them]. Therefore it is said, 'Seek and you will find it, neglect and you will lose it.'[15] [Men differ in the development of their endowments], some twice as much as others, some five times, and some to an incalculable degree, because no one can develop his original endowment to the fullest extent. The *Book of Odes* says, 'Heaven produces the teeming multitude. As there are things there are their specific principles. When the people keep their normal nature they will love excellent virtue.'[16] Confucius said, 'The writer of this poem indeed knew the Way (Tao). Therefore as there are things, there must be their specific principles, and since people keep to their normal nature, therefore they love excellent virtue.'"

Comment. Mencius is the most important philosopher on the question of human nature, for he is the father of the theory of the original goodness of human nature. In spite of variations and modifications, this has remained the firm belief of the Chinese. Book Six, part 1, is almost entirely devoted to the subject. And of all the chapters, this is the most nearly central and the most comprehensive. It records the various theories on human nature in ancient China, except that of Hsün Tzu. It puts Mencius' own theory in direct and simple form. And it also points out that evil or failure is not original but due to the underdevelopment of one's original endowment. Later Confucianists, especially Neo-Confucianists, devoted much of their deliberations to these subjects, but they have never deviated from the general direction laid down by Mencius.

6A:7. Mencius said, "In good years most of the young people behave well.[17] In bad years most of them abandon themselves to evil.[18] This is not due to any difference in the natural capacity endowed by Heaven. The abandonment is due to the fact that the mind is allowed to fall into evil. Take for instance the growing of wheat. You sow the seeds and cover them with soil. The land is the same and the time of sowing is also the same. In time they all grow up luxuriantly. When the time of harvest comes, they are all ripe. Although there may be a difference between the different stalks of wheat, it is due to differences in the soil, as rich or poor, to the unequal nourishment obtained from the rain and the dew, and to differences in human effort. Therefore all things of the same kind are similar to one another. Why should there be any doubt about men? The sage and I are the same in kind. Therefore Lung Tzu[19] said, 'If a man makes shoes without knowing the size of people's feet, I know that he will at least not make them to be like baskets.' Shoes are alike because people's feet are alike. There is a common taste for flavor in our mouths. I-ya[20] was the first to know our common taste for food. Suppose one man's taste for flavor is different from that of others, as dogs and

---

12. Note that *ch'ing* here does not mean feelings which are sources of evil desires, as understood by later Confucianists, but feelings proper to the originally good nature of man. As Tai Chen has clearly pointed out in his *Meng Tzu tzu-i shu-cheng* (Commentary on the Meanings of Terms in the *Book of Mencius*), sec. 30, *ch'ing* is the original simple substance, not contrasted with the nature.
13. The word *ts'ai*, ordinarily meaning ability, is here interchangeable with *ts'ai* meaning raw material.
14. The word *li* here is not used in its narrow sense of rites and ceremonies but in the broad sense of principle of conduct and the sense of what is proper.
15. Probably an old saying.
16. Ode no. 260.

17. Juan Yüan (1764–1849) and Chao Ch'i understood *lai* to mean behaving well. Chiao Hsün, however, interpreted the term *lai* to mean "to become dependent or lazy." See Chiao, *Meng Tzu cheng-i.*
18. *Pao* is not to be understood in its ordinary meaning of violence, but evil, according to Chao Ch'i.
19. An ancient worthy.
20. An ancient famous gourmet, chef of Duke Huan (r. 685–643 B.C.) of Ch'i.

horses differ from us in belonging to different species, then why should the world follow I-ya in regard to flavor? Since in the matter of flavor the whole world regards I-ya as the standard, it shows that our tastes for flavor are alike. The same is true of our ears. Since in the matter of sounds the whole world regards Shih-k'uang[21] as the standard, it shows that our ears are alike. The same is true of our eyes. With regard to Tzu-tu,[22] none in the world did not know that he was handsome. Any one who did not recognize his handsomeness must have no eyes. Therefore I say there is a common taste for flavor in our mouths, a common sense for sound in our ears, and a common sense for beauty in our eyes. Can it be that in our minds alone we are not alike? What is it that we have in common in our minds? It is the sense of principle and righteousness (*i-li*, moral principles). The sage is the first to possess what is common in our minds. Therefore moral principles please our minds as beef and mutton and pork please our mouths."

> *Comment.* In saying that one is of the same kind as the sage, Mencius was pronouncing two principles of utmost significance. One is that every person can be perfect, and the other is that all people are basically equal.[23] Also, in pointing to the moral principle which is common in our minds, he is pointing to what amounts to the Natural Law. Belief in the Natural Law has been persistent in Chinese history. It is called Principle of Nature (*T'ien-li*) by Neo-Confucianists. It is essentially the same as Mencius' *i-li*.

6A:8. Mencius said, "The trees of the Niu Mountain[24] were once beautiful. But can the mountain be regarded any longer as beautiful since, being in the borders of a big state, the trees have been hewed down with axes and hatchets? Still with the rest given them by the days and nights and the nourishment provided them by the rains and the dew, they were not without buds and sprouts springing forth. But then the cattle and the sheep pastured upon them once and again. That is why the mountain looks so bald. When people see that it is so bald, they think that there was never any timber on the mountain. Is this the true nature of the mountain? Is there not [also] a heart of humanity and righteousness originally existing in man? The way in which he loses his originally good mind is like the way in which the trees are hewed down with axes and hatchets. As trees are cut down day after day, can a mountain retain its beauty? To be sure, the days and nights do the healing, and there is the nourishing air of the calm morning which keeps him normal in his likes and dislikes. But the effect is slight, and is disturbed and destroyed by what he does during the day. When there is repeated disturbance, the restorative influence of the night will not be sufficient to preserve (the proper goodness of the mind). When the influence of the night is not sufficient to preserve it, man becomes not much different from the beast. People see that he acts like an animal, and think that he never had the original endowment (for goodness). But is that his true character? Therefore with proper nourishment and care, everything grows, whereas without proper nourishment and care, everything decays. Confucius said, "Hold it fast and you preserve it. Let it go and you lose it. It comes in and goes out at no definite time and without anyone's knowing its direction.' He was talking about the human mind."

6A:9. Mencius said, "Don't suspect that the king[25] lacks wisdom. Even in the case of the things that grow most easily in the world, they would never grow up if they were exposed to sunshine for one day and then to cold for ten days. It is seldom that I have an audience with him, and when I leave, others who expose him to cold arrive. Even if what I say to him is taking root, what good does it do? Now chess playing is but a minor art. One cannot learn it unless he concentrates his mind and devotes his whole heart to it. Chess Expert Ch'iu is the best chess player in the whole country. Suppose he is teaching two men to play. One man will concentrate his mind and devote his whole heart to it, doing nothing but listening to Chess Expert Ch'iu's instructions. Although the other man listens to him,

---

21. An ancient expert on music, concert master for Duke P'ing (r. 557–532 B.C.) of Chin.
22. An ancient handsome man.
23. A similar idea is expressed in *Mencius*, 4B:28 and 32.
24. Outside the capital of the state of Ch'i.

25. Probably King Hsüan of Ch'i (r. 342–324 B.C.).

his whole mind is thinking that a wild goose is about to pass by and he wants to bend his bow, adjust the string to the arrow, and shoot it. Although he is learning along with the other man, he will never be equal to him. Is that because his intelligence is inferior? No, it is not."

6A:10.   Mencius said, "I like fish and I also like bear's paw. If I cannot have both of them, I shall give up the fish and choose the bear's paw. I like life and I also like righteousness. If I cannot have both of them, I shall give up life and choose righteousness. I love life, but there is something I love more than life, and therefore I will not do anything improper to have it. I also hate death, but there is something I hate more than death, and therefore there are occasions when I will not avoid danger. If there is nothing that man loves more than life, then why should he not employ every means to preserve it? And if there is nothing that man hates more than death, then why does he not do anything to avoid danger? There are cases when a man does not take the course even if by taking it he can preserve his life, and he does not do anything even if by doing it he can avoid danger.[26] Therefore there is something men love more than life and there is something men hate more than death. It is not only the worthies alone who have this moral sense. All men have it, but only the worthies have been able to preserve it.

Suppose here are a small basket of rice and a platter of soup. With them one will survive and without them one will die. If you offer them in a loud and angry voice, even an ordinary passer-by will not accept them, or if you first tread on them and then offer them, even a beggar will not stoop to take them. What good does a salary of ten thousand bushels do me if I accept them without any consideration of the principles of propriety and righteousness? Shall I take it because it gives me beautiful mansions, the service of a wife and concubines, and the chance gratitude of my needy acquaintances who receive my help? If formerly I refused to accept the offer (of rice and soup) in the face of death and now I accept for the sake of beautiful mansions, if formerly I refused the offer in the face of death and now I accept for the sake of the service of a wife

and concubines, if formerly I refused the offer and now accept for the sake of the gratitude of my needy acquaintances, is that not the limit? This is called casting the original mind away."[27]

6A:11.   Mencius said, "Humanity is man's mind and righteousness is man's path. Pity the man who abandons the path and does not follow it, and who has lost his heart and does not know how to recover it. When people's dogs and fowls are lost, they go to look for them, and yet, when they have lost their hearts, they do not go to look for them. The way of learning is none other than finding the lost mind.

6A:12.   Mencius said, "Suppose there is a man whose fourth finger is crooked and cannot stretch out straight. It is not painful and it does not interfere with his work. And yet if there were someone who could straighten out the finger for him, he would not mind going as far as to the states of Ch'in and Ch'u because his finger is not like those of others, yet he does not hate the fact that his mind is not like those of others. This is called ignorance of the relative importance of things."[28]

6A:13.   Mencius said, "Anybody who wishes to cultivate the *t'ung* and *tzu* trees, which may be grasped by one or both hands, knows how to nourish them. In the case of their own persons, men do not know how to nourish them. Do they love their persons less than the *t'ung* and *tzu* trees? Their lack of thought is extreme."

6A:14.   Mencius said, "There is not a part of the body that a man does not love. And because there is no part of the body that he does not love, there is not a part of it that he does not nourish. Because there is not an inch of his skin that he does not love, there is not an inch of his skin that he does not nourish. To determine whether his nourishing is good or not, there is no other way except to see the choice he makes for himself. Now, some parts of the body are noble and some are ignoble; some great and some small. We must not allow the ignoble to injure the noble, or the

---

26. Cf. *Analects*, 15:8.

---

27. According to Chu Hsi, this is the original mind of shame and dislike.
28. This interpretation is according to Sun Shih (962–1033), subcommentary on Chao Ch'i's commentary in the *Meng Tzu chu-shu* (Subcommentary and Commentary on the *Book of Mencius*) in the Thirteen Classics Series.

smaller to injure the greater. Those who nourish the smaller parts will become small men. Those who nourish the greater parts will become great men. A gardener who neglects his *t'ung* and *tzu* trees and cultivates thorns and bramble becomes a bad gardener. A man who takes good care of his finger and, without knowing it, neglects his back and shoulders, resembles a hurried wolf.[29] A man who only eats and drinks is looked down upon by others, because he nourishes the smaller parts of his body to the injury of the greater parts. If he eats and drinks but makes no mistake [of injuring the greater parts of his body], how should his mouth and belly be considered merely as so many inches of his body?"

6A:15.   Kung-tu Tzu asked, "We are all human beings. Why is it that some men become great and others become small?" Mencius said, "Those who follow the greater qualities in their nature become great men and those who follow the smaller qualities in their nature become small men." "But we are all human beings. Why is it that some follow their greater qualities and others follow their smaller qualities?" Mencius replied, "When our senses of sight and hearing are used without thought and are thereby obscured by material things, the material things act on the material senses and lead them astray. That is all. The function of the mind is to think. If we think, we will get them (the principles of things). If we do not think, we will not get them. This is what Heaven has given to us. If we first build up the nobler part of our nature, then the inferior part cannot overcome it. It is simply this that makes a man great."

> *Comment.* We shall find that the idea of building up the nobler part of our nature became an important tenet in the moral philosophy of Lu Hsiang-shan (Lu Chiu-yüan, 1139–1193), leader of the idealistic school of Neo-Confucianism.[30]

6A:16.   Mencius said, "There is nobility of Heaven and there is nobility of man. Humanity, righteousness, loyalty, faithfulness, and the love of the good without getting tired of it constitute the nobility of Heaven,

and to be a grand official, a great official, and a high official—this constitutes the nobility of man. The ancient people cultivated the nobility of Heaven, and the nobility of man naturally came to them. People today cultivate the nobility of Heaven in order to seek for the nobility of man, and once they have obtained the nobility of man, they forsake the nobility of Heaven. Therefore their delusion is extreme. At the end they will surely lose [the nobility of man] also."

6A:17.   Mencius said, "The desire to be honored is shared by the minds of all men. But all men have in themselves what is really honorable. Only they do not think of it. The honor conferred by men is not true honor. Whoever is made honorable by Chao Meng[31] can be made humble by him again. The *Book of Odes* says, 'I am drunk with wine, and I am satiated with virtue.'[32] It means that a man is satiated with humanity and righteousness, and therefore he does not wish for the flavor of fat meat and fine millet of men. A good reputation and far-reaching praise are heaped on him, and he does not desire the embroidered gowns of men."

6A:18.   Mencius said, "Humanity subdues inhumanity as water subdues fire. Nowadays those who practice humanity do so as if with one cup of water they could save a whole wagonload of fuel on fire. When the flames were not extinguished, they would say that water cannot subdue fire. This is as bad as those who are inhumane.[33] At the end they will surely lose [what little humanity they have]."

6A:19.   Mencius said, "The five kinds of grain are considered good plants, but if they are not ripe, they are worse than poor grains. So the value of humanity depends on its being brought to maturity."

6A:20.   Mencius said, "When Master I[34] taught people to shoot, he always told them to draw the bow to the full. The man who wants to learn [the way][35] must likewise draw his bow (his will) to the full. When a great carpenter teaches people, he always tells them to use squares and compasses. The man who wants to

---

29. The meaning of the phrase is obscure.
30. See below, ch. 33, secs. 8 and 24.

31. A high official of the Chin state.
32. Ode no. 247.
33. This is Chiao Hsün's interpretation. Chao Ch'i and Chu Hsi, however, interpret *yü* not as "the same as" but as "to help," that is, it greatly helps (encourages) the inhumane.
34. An ancient famous archer.
35. Insertion according to Chao Ch'i.

learn must likewise use squares and compasses (or moral standards)." ...

2A:3.   Mencius said, "A ruler who uses force to make a pretense at humanity is a despot. Such a despot requires a large kingdom. A ruler who practices humanity with virtue is a true king. To become a true king does not depend on a large kingdom. T'ang became so with only seventy *li*, and King Wen with only a hundred. When force is used to overcome people, they do not submit willingly but only because they have not sufficient strength to resist. But when virtue is used to overcome people, they are pleased in their hearts and sincerely submit, as the seventy disciples submitted to Confucius. The *Book of Odes* says:

> From the west, from the east,
> From the south, from the north,
> None wanted to resist.[36]

This is what is meant."

Comment. The foundation of Confucian political philosophy is "humane government," government of the true king, who rules through moral example.[37] His guiding principle is righteousness, whereas that of the despot is profit.[38] This contrast between kingliness and despotism has always remained sharp in the minds of Confucian political thinkers.

2A:5.   Mencius said, "If a ruler honors the worthy and employs the competent so that offices are occupied by the wisest, then scholars throughout the world will be delighted to stand in his court. If in the city he levies a rent but does not tax the goods, or enforces certain regulations but does not levy a rent, then traders throughout the world will be delighted to store goods in his city. If at his frontier passes there will be inspection but no tax, then travelers throughout the world will be delighted to travel on his highways. If farmers are required to give their mutual aid to cultivate the public field but not required to pay tax, then all farmers throughout the world will be delighted to farm in his land. If there is no fine for

the idler or the family that fails to meet a certain quota of cloth products, then all people throughout the world will be delighted to become his subjects. If a ruler can truly practice these five things, then the people in the neighboring states will look up to him as a parent. Ever since there has been mankind, none has succeeded in leading children to attack their parents. Thus such a ruler will have no enemy anywhere in the world, and having no enemy in the world, he will be an official appointed by Heaven. There has never been such a person who did not become the true king of the empire."

2A:6.   Mencius said, "All men have the mind which cannot bear [to see the suffering of][39] others. The ancient kings had this mind and therefore they had a government that could not bear to see the suffering of the people. When a government that cannot bear to see the suffering of the people is conducted from a mind that cannot bear to see the suffering of others, the government of the empire will be as easy as making something go round in the palm."

"When I say that all men have the mind which cannot bear to see the suffering of others, my meaning may be illustrated thus: Now, when men suddenly see a child about to fall into a well, they all have a feeling of alarm and distress, not to gain friendship with the child's parents, nor to seek the praise of their neighbors and friends, nor because they dislike the reputation [of lack of humanity if they did not rescue the child]. From such a case, we see that a man without the feeling of commiseration is not a man; a man without the feeling of shame and dislike is not a man; a man without the feeling of deference and compliance is not a man; and a man without the feeling of right and wrong is not a man. The feeling of commiseration is the beginning of humanity; the feeling of shame and dislike is the beginning of righteousness; the feeling of deference and compliance is the beginning of propriety; and the feeling of right and wrong is the beginning of wisdom. Men have these Four Beginnings just as they have their four limbs. Having these Four Beginnings, but saying that they cannot develop them is to destroy themselves. When they say that their ruler cannot develop them, they are destroying their ruler. If

---

36. Ode no. 244.
37. See above, Additional Selections, 1A:1, 5; and below, Additional Selections, 2A:5, 3A:3–4, 7A:13.
38. The contrast is strongly brought out in 1A:1.

39. According to Chao Ch'i, "cannot bear to do evil to others."

anyone with these Four Beginnings in him knows how to give them the fullest extension and development, the result will be like fire beginning to burn or a spring beginning to shoot forth. When they are fully developed, they will be sufficient to protect all people within the four seas (the world). If they are not developed, they will not be sufficient even to serve one's parents."

Comment. Practically all later Confucianists have accepted the Four Beginnings as the innate moral qualities. In K'ang Yu-wei's philosophy, the "mind that cannot bear" is the starting point.

DISCUSSION QUESTIONS

1. Do you agree with Mencius's view that human nature is essentially good? Why or why not?
2. Do you agree with Mencius's claim that all people are naturally constituted such that they "cannot bear to see the suffering of others"? Why or why not? How would he explain human cruelty?
3. Do you think the political implications of Mencius's moral philosophy (for example, his conception of a "true king") are applicable today in any societies? Why or why not?
4. How would you compare Mencius's theory of human nature with Sartre's existentialist account? Which view is more convincing? Why?

44. Thomas Hobbes (1588–1679)
Egoism and Human Relations

Thomas Hobbes was an English philosopher who is still viewed today as one of the major intellectual figures in the early modern period of European history. He knew Galileo and Descartes and was enthusiastic about both the emerging science of mechanics and the possibilities of applying methods of geometry to the explanation of all other dimensions of the natural world, including human society. Discovering certain "scientific" knowledge regarding the proper organization of political society seemed especially crucial to Hobbes because of the tumultuous times in which he lived. The monarchy and parliament in England were engaged in often violent conflict, and he saw the harmful consequences of the breakdown in social order resulting from the civil war of the 1640s.

Hobbes's subsequent influence on Western moral and political theory is due, in the first place, to his formulation of a version of "social contract theory," which says that a legitimate organized society is the product of a set of rational agreements between self-interested individuals. Secondly, he is remembered as one who systematically argued that a government (or sovereign) should have absolute power over its subjects once it has been chosen by the original creators of that state (thus making his social contract theory quite different from, for example, that of John Locke). Third, he advanced a the-

ory of human nature, which still is widely accepted in contemporary capitalist society, that all social relations are grounded in individual self-interest and conscious conduct is motivated by fear and greed.

The selection includes the sixth and thirteenth chapters of *Leviathan*, which was published in 1651 and remains Hobbes's most famous book. The focus is on both the makeup of the human individual and the social implications of this characterization of our natural capacities and motivations. Although his approach is for the most part empirical and descriptive, he does point to moral conclusions that can be derived from his account that, even if more or less positivistic, do not amount to a kind of relativism.

QUESTIONS FOR CRITICAL READING

1. How does Hobbes use the concept of motion to explain all aspects of individual human life?
2. How does Hobbes characterize good and evil, and when are there objective standards for their determination?
3. What does Hobbes mean by, and how does he argue for, the natural equality of all humans?
4. What is the "condition of Warre" that Hobbes describes, when does it come about, and why is it the result of human nature, in his account?

5. What does Hobbes mean by claiming that in the natural condition of war, "nothing can be Unjust"?

TERM TO NOTE

diffidence: In this context, distrust of others.

_____

Of the Interior Beginnings of Voluntary Motions; commonly called the Passions; and the Speeches by which they are expressed.

There be in animals, two sorts of "motions" peculiar to them: one called "vital;" begun in generation, and continued without interruption through their whole life; such as are the "course" of the "blood," the "pulse," the "breathing," the "concoction, nutrition, excretion," &c., to which motions there needs no help of imagination: the other is "animal motion," otherwise called "voluntary motion;" as to "go," to "speak," to "move" any of our limbs, in such manner as is first fancied in our minds. That sense is motion in the organs and interior parts of man's body, caused by the action of the things we see, hear, &c.; and that fancy is but the relics of the same motion, remaining after sense, has been already seen in the first and second chapters. And because "going," "speaking," and the like voluntary motions, depend always upon a precedent thought of "whither," "which way," and "what;" it is evident, that the imagination is the first internal beginning of all voluntary motion. And although unstudied men do not conceive any motion at all to be there, where the thing moved is invisible; or the space it is moved in is, for the shortness of it, insensible; yet that doth not hinder, but that such motions are. For let a space be never so little, that which is moved over a greater space, whereof that little one is part, must first be moved over that. These small beginnings of motion, within the body of man, before they appear in walking, speaking, striking, and other visible actions, are commonly called "endeavour."

This endeavour, when it is toward something which causes it, is called "appetite," or "desire;" the latter, being the general name; and the other oftentimes restrained to signify the desire of food, namely "hunger" and "thirst." And when the endeavour is fromward something, it is generally called "aversion." These words, "appetite" and "aversion," we have from the Latins; and they both of them signify the motions, one of approaching, the other of retiring. So also do the Greek words for the same, which are ὁρμὴ and ἀφορμὴ. For Nature itself does often press upon men those truths, which afterwards, when they look for somewhat beyond Nature, they stumble at. For the schools find in mere appetite to go, or move, no actual motion at all: but because some motion they must acknowledge, they call it metaphorical motion; which is but an absurd speech: for though words may be called metaphorical, bodies and motions cannot.

That which men desire, they are also said to "love:" and to "hate" those things for which they have aversion. So that desire and love are the same thing; save that by desire, we always signify the absence of the object: by love most commonly the presence of the same. So also by aversion, we signify the absence; and by hate, the presence of the object.

Of appetites and aversions, some are born with men; as appetite of food, appetite of excretion, and exoneration, which may also and more properly be called aversions, from somewhat they feel in their bodies; and some other appetites, not many. The rest, which are appetites of particular things, proceed from experience, and trial of their effects upon themselves or other men. For of things we know not at all, or believe not to be, we can have no further desire than to taste and try. But aversion we have for things, not only which we know have hurt us, but also that we do not know whether they will hurt us, or not.

Those things which we neither desire, nor hate, we are said to "contemn;" "contempt" being nothing else but an immobility, or contumacy of the heart, in resisting the action of certain things: and proceeding from that the heart is already moved otherwise, by other more potent objects; or from want of experience of them.

And because the constitution of a man's body is in continual mutation, it is impossible that all the same things should always cause in him the same appetites and aversions: much less can all men consent, in the desire of almost any one and the same object.

But whatsoever is the object of any man's appetite or desire, that is it which he for his part calleth "good:" and the object of his hate and aversion, "evil;" and of his contempt, "vile" and "inconsiderable." For these words of good, evil, and contemptible, are ever used with relation to the person that useth them: there being nothing simply and absolutely so; nor any common rule of good and evil, to be taken from the nature of the objects themselves; but from the person of the man, where there is no commonwealth; or, in a commonwealth, from the person that representeth it; or from an arbitrator or judge, whom men disagreeing shall by consent set up, and make his sentence the rule thereof.

The Latin tongue has two words, whose significations approach to those of good and evil; but are not precisely the same; and those are *pulchrum* and *turpe*. Whereof the former signifies that, which by some apparent signs promiseth good; and the latter, that which promiseth evil. But in our tongue we have not so general names to express them by. But for *pulchrum* we say in some things, "fair;" in others, "beautiful," or "handsome," or "gallant," or "honourable," or "comely," or "amiable;" and for *turpe*, "foul," "deformed," "ugly," "base," "nauseous," and the like, as the subject shall require; all which words, in their proper places, signify nothing else but the "mien," or countenance, that promiseth good and evil. So that of good there be three kinds; good in the promise, that is *pulchrum*; good in effect, as the end desired, which is called *jucundum*, "delightful;" and good as the means, which is called *utile*, "profitable;" and as many of evil: for "evil" in promise, is that they call *turpe*; evil in effect, and end, is *molestum*, "unpleasant," "troublesome;" and evil in the means, *inutile*, "unprofitable," "hurtful."

As, in sense, that which is really within us, is, as I have said before, only motion, caused by the action of external objects, but in apparence; to the sight, light and colour; to the ear, sound; to the nostril, odour, &c.: so, when the action of the same object is continued from the eyes, ears, and other organs to the heart, the real effect there is nothing but motion, or endeavour; which consisteth in appetite, or aversion, to or from the object moving. But the apparence, or sense of that motion, is that we either call "delight," or "trouble of mind."

This motion, which is called appetite, and for the apparence of it "delight," and "pleasure," seemeth to be a corroboration of vital motion, and a help thereunto; and therefore such things as caused delight, were not improperly called *jucunda, à juvando*, from helping or fortifying; and the contrary *molesta*, "offensive," from hindering, and troubling the motion vital.

"Pleasure" therefore, or "delight," is the apparence, or sense of good; and "molestation," or "displeasure," the apparence, or sense of evil. And consequently all appetite, desire, and love, is accompanied with some delight more or less; and all hatred and aversion, with more or less displeasure and offence.

Of pleasures or delights, some arise from the sense of an object present; and those may be called "pleasure of sense;" the word "sensual," as it is used by those only that condemn them, having no place till there be laws. Of this kind are all onerations and exonerations of the body; as also all that is pleasant, in the "sight," "hearing," "smell," "taste," or "touch." Others arise from the expectation, that proceeds from foresight of the end, or consequence of things; whether those things in the sense please or displease. And these are "pleasures of the mind" of him that draweth those consequences, and are generally called "joy." In the like manner, displeasures are some in the sense, and called "pain;" others in the expectation of consequences, and are called "grief."

These simple passions called "appetite," "desire," "love," "aversion," "hate," "joy," and "grief," have their names for divers considerations diversified. As first, when they one succeed another, they are diversely called from the opinion men have of the likelihood of attaining what they desire. Secondly, from the object loved or hated. Thirdly, from the consideration of many of them together. Fourthly, from the alteration or succession itself.

For "appetite," with an opinion of attaining, is called "hope."

The same, without such opinion, "despair."

"Aversion," with opinion of "hurt" from the object, "fear."

The same, with hope of avoiding that hurt by resistance, "courage."

Sudden "courage," "anger."

Constant "hope," "confidence" of ourselves.

Constant "despair," "diffidence" of ourselves.

"Anger" for great hurt done to another, when we conceive the same to be done by injury, "indignation."

"Desire" of good to another, "benevolence," "good will," "charity." If to man generally, "good-nature."

"Desire" of riches, "covetousness;" a name used always in signification of blame; because men contending for them, are displeased with one another attaining them; though the desire in itself, be to be blamed, or allowed, according to the means by which these riches are sought.

"Desire" of office, or precedence, "ambition:" a name used also in the worse sense, for the reason before mentioned.

"Desire" of things that conduce but a little to our ends, and fear of things that are but of little hindrance, "pusillanimity."

"Contempt" of little helps and hindrances, "magnanimity."

"Magnanimity," in danger of death or wounds, "valour," "fortitude."

"Magnanimity" in the use of riches, "liberality."

"Pusillanimity" in the same, "wretchedness," "miserableness," or "parsimony;" as it is liked or disliked.

"Love" of persons for society, "kindness."

"Love" of persons for pleasing the sense only, "natural lust."

"Love" of the same, acquired from rumination, that is, imagination of pleasure past, "luxury."

"Love" of one singularly, with desire to be singularly beloved, "the passion of love." The same, with fear that the love is not mutual, "jealousy."

"Desire," by doing hurt to another, to make him condemn some fact of his own, "revengefulness."

"Desire" to know why, and how, "curiosity;" such as is in no living creature but "man:" so that man is distinguished, not only by his reason, but also by this singular passion from other "animals;" in whom the appetite of food, and other pleasures of sense, by predominance, take away the care of knowing causes; which is a lust of the mind, that by a perseverance of delight in the continual and indefatigable generation of knowledge, exceedeth the short vehemence of any carnal pleasure.

"Fear" of power invisible, feigned by the mind, or imagined from tales publicly allowed, "religion;" not allowed "superstition." And when the power imagined, is truly such as we imagine, "true religion."

"Fear," without the apprehension of why, or what, "panic terror," called so from the fables that make Pan the author of them; whereas in truth, there is always in him that so feareth, first, some apprehension of the cause, though the rest run away by example, every one supposing his fellow to know why. And therefore this passion happens to none but in a throng, or multitude of people.

"Joy," from apprehension of novelty, "admiration;" proper to man, because it excites the appetite of knowing the cause.

"Joy," arising from imagination of a man's own power and ability, is that exultation of the mind which is called "glorying:" which if grounded upon the experience of his own former actions, is the same with "confidence:" but if grounded on the flattery of others, or only supposed by himself, for delight in the consequences of it, is called "vain-glory:" which name is properly given; because a well-grounded "confidence" begetteth attempt; whereas the supposing of power does not, and is therefore rightly called "vain."

"Grief," from opinion of want of power, is called "dejection" of mind.

The "vain-glory" which consisteth in the feigning or supposing of abilities in ourselves, which we know are not, is most incident to young men, and nourished by the histories or fictions of gallant persons; and is corrected oftentimes by age, and employment.

"Sudden glory," is the passion which maketh those "grimaces" called "laughter;" and is caused either by some sudden act of their own, that pleaseth them; or by the apprehension of some deformed thing in another, by comparison whereof they suddenly applaud themselves. And it is incident most to them, that are conscious of the fewest abilities in themselves; who are forced to keep themselves in their own favour, by observing the imperfections of other men. And therefore much laughter at the defects of others, is a sign of pusillanimity. For of great minds, one of the proper works is, to help and free others from scorn; and compare themselves only with the most able.

On the contrary, "sudden dejection," is the passion that causeth "weeping;" and is caused by such accidents, as suddenly take away some vehement hope, or some prop of their power: and they are most subject to it, that rely principally on helps external, such as are women and children. Therefore some weep for the loss of friends; others for their unkindness; others for the sudden stop made to their thoughts of revenge, by reconciliation. But in all cases, both laughter, and weeping, are sudden motions; custom taking them both away. For no man laughs at old jests; or weeps for an old calamity.

"Grief," for the discovery of some defect of ability, is "shame," or the passion that discovereth itself in "blushing:" and consisteth in the apprehension of something dishonourable; and in young men is a sign of the love of good reputation, and commendable: in old men it is a sign of the same; but because it comes too late, not commendable.

The "contempt" of good reputation is called "impudence."

"Grief," for the calamity of another, is "pity;" and ariseth from the imagination that the like calamity may befall himself; and therefore is called also "compassion," and in the phrase of this present time a "fellow-feeling:" and therefore for calamity arriving from great wickedness, the best men have the least pity; and for the same calamity, those hate pity, that think themselves least obnoxious to the same.

"Contempt," or little sense of the calamity of others, is that which men call "cruelty;" proceeding from security of their own fortune. For, that any man should take pleasure in other men's great harms, without other end of his own, I do not conceive it possible.

"Grief," for the success of a competitor in wealth, honour, or other good, if it be joined with endeavour to enforce our own abilities to equal or exceed him, is called "emulation;" but joined with endeavour to supplant, or hinder a competitor, "envy."

When in the mind of man, appetites, and aversions, hopes, and fears, concerning one and the same thing, arise alternately; and divers good and evil consequences of the doing, or omitting the thing propounded, come successively into our thoughts; so that sometimes we have an appetite to it; sometimes an aversion from it; sometimes hope to be able to do it; sometimes despair, or fear to attempt it; the whole sum of desires, aversions, hopes and fears continued till the thing be either done, or thought impossible, is that we call "deliberation."

Therefore of things past, there is no "deliberation;" because manifestly impossible to be changed: nor of things known to be impossible, or thought so; because men know, or think, such deliberation vain. But of things impossible, which we think possible, we may

deliberate; not knowing it is in vain. And it is called "deliberation;" because it is a putting an end to the "liberty" we had of doing or omitting according to our own appetite, or aversion.

This alternate succession of appetites, aversions, hopes and fears, is no less in other living creatures than in man: and therefore beasts also deliberate.

Every "deliberation" is then said to "end," when that whereof they deliberate, is either done or thought impossible; because till then we retain the liberty of doing or omitting, according to our appetite, or aversion.

In "deliberation," the last appetite, or aversion, immediately adhering to the action, or to the omission thereof, is that we call the "will;" the act, not the faculty, of "willing." And beasts that have "deliberation," must necessarily also have "will." The definition of the "will," given commonly by the schools, that it is a "rational appetite," is not good. For if it were, then could there be no voluntary act against reason. For a "voluntary act" is that which proceedeth from the "will," and no other. But if instead of a rational appetite, we shall say an appetite resulting from a precedent deliberation, then the definition is the same that I have given here. Will, therefore, is the last appetite in deliberating. And though we say in common discourse, a man had a will once to do a thing, that nevertheless he forbore to do; yet that is properly but an inclination, which makes no action voluntary; because the action depends not of it, but of the last inclination or appetite. For if the intervenient appetites, make any action voluntary; then by the same reason, all intervenient aversions should make the same action involuntary; and so one and the same action should be both voluntary and involuntary.

By this it is manifest, that not only actions that have their beginning from covetousness, ambition, lust, or other appetites to the thing propounded; but also those that have their beginning from aversion, or fear of those consequences that follow the omission, are "voluntary actions."

The forms of speech by which the passions are expressed, are partly the same, and partly different from those, by which we express our thoughts. And first, generally all passions may be expressed "indicatively;" as "I love," "I fear," "I joy," "I deliberate," "I will," "I command:" but some of them have particular expressions by themselves, which nevertheless are not affirmations, unless it be when they serve to make other inferences, besides that of the passion they proceed from. Deliberation is expressed "subjunctively;" which is a speech proper to signify suppositions, with their consequences: as, "if this be done, then this will follow;" and differs not from the language of reasoning, save that reasoning is in general words; but deliberation for the most part is of particulars. The language of desire, and aversion, is "imperative;" as "do this," "forbear that;" which when the party is obliged to do, or forbear, is "command;" otherwise "prayer;" or else "counsel." The language of vain-glory, of indignation, pity and revengefulness, "optative:" but of the desire to know, there is a peculiar expression, called "interrogative;" as, "what is it," "when shall it," "how is it done," and "why so?" other language of the passions I find none: for cursing, swearing, reviling, and the like, do not signify as speech; but as the actions of a tongue accustomed.

These forms of speech, I say, are expressions, or voluntary significations of our passions: but certain signs they be not; because they may be used arbitrarily, whether they that use them have such passions or not. The best signs of passions present, are either in the countenance, motions of the body, actions, and ends, or aims, which we otherwise know the man to have.

And because in deliberation, the appetites, and aversions, are raised by foresight of the good and evil consequences, and sequels of the action whereof we deliberate; the good or evil effect thereof dependeth on the foresight of a long chain of consequences, of which very seldom any man is able to see to the end. But for so far as a man seeth, if the good in those consequences be greater than the evil, the whole chain is that which writers call "apparent," or "seeming good." And contrarily, when the evil exceedeth the good, the whole is "apparent," or "seeming evil:" so that he who hath by experience, or reason, the greatest and surest prospect of consequences, deliberates best himself; and is able when he will, to give the best counsel unto others.

"Continual success" in obtaining those things which a man from time to time desireth, that is to say, continual prospering, is that men call "felicity;" I mean the felicity of this life. For there is no such thing

as perpetual tranquility of mind, while we live here; because life itself is but motion, and can never be without desire, nor without fear, no more than without sense. What kind of felicity God hath ordained to them that devoutly honour Him, a man shall no sooner know, than enjoy; being joys, that now are as incomprehensible as the word of school-men "beatifical vision" is unintelligible.

The form of speech whereby men signify their opinion of the goodness of anything, is "praise." That whereby they signify the power and greatness of anything, is "magnifying." And that whereby they signify the opinion they have of a man's felicity, is by the Greeks called μακαρισμός, for which we have no name in our tongue. And thus much is sufficient for the present purpose, to have been said of the "passions."

Of the Natural Condition of Mankind as concerning their Felicity and Misery.

Nature hath made men so equal, in the faculties of the body and mind; as that though there be found one man sometimes manifestly stronger in body, or of quicker mind than another, yet when all is reckoned together, the difference between man and man, is not so considerable, as that one man can thereupon claim to himself any benefit, to which another may not pretend, as well as he. For as to the strength of body, the weakest has strength enough to kill the strongest, either by secret machination, or by confederacy with others, that are in the same danger with himself.

And as to the faculties of the mind, setting aside the arts grounded upon words, and especially that skill of proceeding upon general and infallible rules, called science; which very few have, and but in few things; as being not a native faculty, born with us; nor attained, as prudence, while we look after somewhat else, I find yet a greater equality amongst men than that of strength. For prudence is but experience; which equal time, equally bestows on all men, in those things they equally apply themselves unto. That which may perhaps make such equality incredible, is but a vain conceit of one's own wisdom, which almost all men think they have in a greater degree than the vulgar; that is, than all men but themselves, and a few others, whom by fame or for concurring with themselves, they approve. For such is the nature of men, that howsoever they may acknowledge many others to be more witty, or more eloquent, or more learned; yet they will hardly believe there be many so wise as themselves; for they see their own wit at hand, and other men's at a distance. But this proveth rather that men are in that point equal, than unequal. For there is not ordinarily a greater sign of the equal distribution of anything, than that every man is contented with his share.

From this equality of ability, ariseth equality of hope in the attaining of our ends. And therefore if any two men desire the same thing, which nevertheless they cannot both enjoy, they become enemies; and in the way to their end, which is principally their own conservation, and sometimes their delectation only, endeavour to destroy or subdue one another. And from hence it comes to pass, that where an invader hath no more to fear than another man's single power; if one plant, sow, build, or possess a convenient seat, others may probably be expected to come prepared with forces united, to dispossess and deprive him, not only of the fruit of his labour, but also of his life or liberty. And the invader again is in the like danger of another.

And from this diffidence of one another, there is no way for any man to secure himself, so reasonable, as anticipation; that is, by force, or wiles, to master the persons of all men he can, so long, till he see no other power great enough to endanger him: and this is no more than his own conservation requireth, and is generally allowed. Also because there be some, that taking pleasure in contemplating their own power in the acts of conquest, which they pursue farther than their security requires; if others, that otherwise would be glad to be at ease within modest bounds, should not by invasion increase their power, they would not be able, long time, by standing only on their defence, to subsist. And by consequence, such augmentation of dominion over men being necessary to a man's conservation, it ought to be allowed him.

Again, men have no pleasure, but on the contrary a great deal of grief, in keeping company, where there is no power able to overawe them all. For every man looketh that his companion should value him, at the same rate he sets upon himself: and upon all signs of contempt, or undervaluing, naturally endeavours, as far as he dares, (which amongst them that have no common power to keep them in quiet, is far enough to make them destroy each other,) to extort a greater value from his contemners, by damage; and from others, by the example.

So that in the nature of man, we find three principal causes of quarrel. First, competition; secondly, diffidence; thirdly, glory.

The first, maketh men invade for gain; the second, for safety; and the third, for reputation. The first use violence, to make themselves masters of other men's persons, wives, children, and cattle; the second, to defend them; the third, for trifles, as a word, a smile, a different opinion, and any other sign of undervalue, either direct in their persons, or by reflection in their kindred, their friends, their nation, their profession, or their name.

Hereby it is manifest, that during the time men live without a common power to keep them all in awe, they are in that condition which is called war; and such a war, as is of every man, against every man. For "war" consisteth not in battle only, or the act of fighting; but in a tract of time, wherein the will to contend by battle is sufficiently known: and therefore the notion of "time" is to be considered in the nature of war, as it is in the nature of weather. For as the nature of foul weather lieth not in a shower or two of rain, but in an inclination thereto of many days together; so the nature of war consisteth not in actual fighting, but in the known disposition thereto during all the time there is no assurance to the contrary. All other time is "peace."

Whatsoever therefore is consequent to a time of war, where every man is enemy to every man, the same is consequent to the time wherein men live without other security than what their own strength and their own invention shall furnish them withal. In such condition there is no place for industry, because the fruit thereof is uncertain, and consequently no culture of the earth; no navigation, nor use of the commodities that may be imported by sea; no commodious building; no instruments of moving and removing such things as require much force; no knowledge of the face of the earth; no account of time; no arts; no letters; no society; and, which is worst of all, continual fear and danger of violent death; and the life of man, solitary, poor, nasty, brutish, and short.

It may seem strange to some man, that has not well weighed these things, that Nature should thus dissociate, and render men apt to invade and destroy one another; and he may therefore, not trusting to this inference, made from the passions, desire perhaps to have the same confirmed by experience. Let him therefore consider with himself, when taking a journey, he arms himself, and seeks to go well accompanied; when going to sleep, he locks his doors; when even in his house, he locks his chests; and this when he knows there be laws, and public officers, armed, to revenge all injuries shall be done him; what opinion he has of his fellow-subjects, when he rides armed; of his fellow-citizens, when he locks his doors; and of his children and servants, when he locks his chests. Does he not there as much accuse mankind by his actions as I do by my words? But neither of us accuse man's nature in it. The desires and other passions of man are in themselves no sin. No more are the actions that proceed from those passions, till they know a law that forbids them; which till laws be made they cannot know, nor can any law be made till they have agreed upon the person that shall make it.

It may peradventure be thought there was never such a time nor condition of war as this; and I believe it was never generally so, over all the world, but there are many places where they live so now. For the savage people in many places of America, except the government of small families, the concord whereof dependeth on natural lust, have no government at all, and live at this day in that brutish manner, as I said before. Howsoever, it may be perceived what manner of life there would be, where there were no common power to fear, by the manner of life which men that have formerly lived under a peaceful government, use to degenerate into in a civil war.

But though there had never been any time, wherein particular men were in a condition of war one against another; yet in all times, kings, and persons of sovereign authority, because of their independency, are in continual jealousies, and in the state and posture of gladiators; having their weapons pointing, and their eyes fixed on one another; that is, their forts, garrisons, and guns upon the frontiers of their kingdoms; and continual spies upon their neighbours; which is a posture of war. But because they uphold thereby the industry of their subjects; there does not follow from it that misery which accompanies the liberty of particular men.

To this war of every man, against every man, this also is consequent; that nothing can be unjust. The notions of right and wrong, justice and injustice, have there no place. Where there is no common power, there is no law: where no law, no injustice. Force and fraud, are in war the two cardinal virtues. Justice and injustice are none of the faculties neither of the body nor mind. If they were, they might be in a man that were alone in the world, as well as his senses, and passions. They are qualities that relate to men in society, not in solitude. It is consequent also to the same condition, that there be no propriety, no dominion, no "mine" and "thine" distinct; but only that to be every man's, that he can get; and for so long, as he can keep it. And thus much for the ill condition, which man by mere nature is actually placed in; though with a possibility to come out of it, consisting partly in the passions, partly in his reason.

The passions that incline men to peace, are fear of death; desire of such things as are necessary to commodious living; and a hope by their industry to obtain them. And reason suggesteth convenient articles of peace, upon which men may be drawn to agreement. These articles are they which otherwise are called the Laws of Nature: whereof I shall speak more particularly, in the two following chapters.

DISCUSSION QUESTIONS

1. Do you agree with Hobbes that all of our cognitive and emotive lives can be explained in terms of physical motion? Why or why not?

2. The implication of Hobbes's mechanistic account of human conduct and motivation is that a truly unselfish action is unnatural, if not mechanically impossible. Do you agree with this view of human nature? Why or why not?

3. Hobbes argues that people are only regularly sociable when forced to be so by a powerful sovereign who threatens them with punishment if they don't get along. Do you agree with this account of human interaction? Why or why not?

4. How would you compare Hobbes's account of human nature with that of Mencius? Which account do you find more convincing? Why?

45. Gunapala Dharmasiri
"Motivation in Buddhist Ethics"

Gunapala Dharmasiri is a Buddhist philosopher from Sri Lanka who has focused especially on issues within the Mahayana tradition (see reading 16 for the origins of Buddhism). This reading is from the second chapter of Dharmasiri's 1989 book *Fundamentals of Buddhist Ethics,* and among other things, it offers a helpful introduction to a number of central concepts in Buddhist metaphysical and moral theory.

Dharmasiri is addressing more specifically a set of questions that have arisen in many different moral traditions, having to do with what is often called moral agency. It is not obvious, upon reflection, just who (or what) counts as a "moral agent"—that is, a being capable of voluntary actions that can be evaluated ethically and thus to whom we can attribute moral responsibility as well as praise or condemnation. Are only adult human beings moral agents, or should some nonhumans be viewed similarly? Are only individual entities "actors" in this sense, or are collectivities such as business corporations or governments also morally responsible for "their" actions? Every ethical theory includes some kind of explicit or implicit answer to these foundational questions, and according to Dharmasiri the problem appears in Buddhist ethics particularly as a result of the standard metaphysical doctrine that the "self," "soul," or "person" ultimately is not real. If there really is no continuous identical thing called the self, but only a temporary, non-substantial combination of various "factors," it appears that we really can't say coherently who is morally responsible for actions and to whom any particular conduct or sentiments are owed. Dharmasiri attempts to show how this problem is resolved from a Buddhist perspective and what kind of moral life subsequently is to be recommended.

QUESTIONS FOR CRITICAL READING

1. According to Dharmasiri, what is the conceptual problem of personal moral responsibility in Buddhist thought, and how is it solved by the doctrine of karma?
2. What is the distinction between "conventional reality" and "absolute reality," and how is this relevant for explaining moral commitment, according to Dharmasiri?
3. What is the "theory of dependent origination" in Buddhist ethics, and what does it imply regarding our moral duty to others? Why is the egoism-altruism distinction dissolved in this theory?
4. Why does Buddhism include more than just a humanistic ethics?
5. In the Mahayana tradition, how does one become a Bodhisattva?

TERMS TO NOTE

salvific: Having to do with salvation.

Samsara: A Sanskrit term for the spatio-temporal world of birth, death, and rebirth governed by the law of karma.

Nirvana: A Sanskrit term literally meaning "cessation"; in Buddhism it refers to a state of release from all concerns of the individuated self, including the extinction of all craving, for those who have attained spiritual enlightenment.

There are some interesting issues that are specific to the Buddhist theory of ethics. These issues originate from the nature of the Buddhist theory of reality. A person does not have a self or a soul and is said to be made up of five factors. When these five factors come together, they constitute the person, just as a chariot is made up of the parts that constitute it. And, it is further said that these five factors are incessantly changing or are always in a state of flux. In this state of affairs, can one meaningfully speak of 'a person'? If there is no person, there are problems for moral discourse, because ethical discourse presupposes the notions of 'personal responsibility', 'personal identity', 'personal initiative' and 'moral commitment'.

One could imagine these problems easily solved if we were to accept the theory of a self. But for the

Buddha, the idea of a self could not be made meaningful in any way. The only way to make the idea of self meaningful is to verify it, and if we look at ourselves objectively in order to verify it, all we see is the above five factors. And if we introspect and subjectively look for a self, all we see is an ever changing series of thoughts and sensations. Therefore, if the idea of self or soul is not meaningful, we will have to explain things with the help of existing facts.

Although Buddhism does not accept the idea of a person as an enduring entity, it accepts the existence of a person as a composite of factors. Two criteria are used in determining the identity of a person. A person is made up of two types of groups of events, physical and mental. As all these groups are ever changing, the preceding events disappear, giving birth to succeeding events. Thus the succeeding events inherit the characteristics of the preceding events. This results in a causal sequence of events. In Buddhism, it is through this 'unbroken continuity or coherence of the series of events' (*avicchinna santati sāmaggi*—Buddhaghosa), that personal identity is traced. The person who lives at 9 a.m. this morning is a result of the person who lived at 7 a.m. this morning.

Doctrine of Karma

It is in this sense that the Buddhist doctrine of karma has to be interpreted. Though some assume that the doctrine of karma is a metaphysical doctrine, it is actually a psychological principle or a law based on the law of causation as applied to a series of mental events. If a person has a 'bad' thought now, this will generate further 'bad' thoughts, thus gradually leading to the formation of a karmic mental complex. This complex can generate various types of mental illnesses like anxiety and guilt, which gradually lead to further complications such as physical illnesses. The Buddha said that karma is a principle that can be verified in this life itself by looking into the causal relationships between mental phenomena and between mental and physical phenomena. A 'bad' thought leads to tension and anxiety, while a 'good' thought leads to calmness and relaxation. Thus, the problem of personal identity and moral responsibility is solved in terms of causal connectedness.

Another problem that arises within Buddhist ethics is how to justify altruistic or 'other-regarding' action. If real 'persons' do not exist, how can we make the idea of moral commitment to others meaningful? A difficult problem that comes up in the Buddhist teaching of egolessness is 'why should I do anything at all'?

Before we discuss acting or working for others, we must first be clear about what is meant by 'work'. Ordinarily, work is supposed to be physical. But Buddhism accepts two kinds of work: physical and spiritual. For example, a Brahmin farmer called Kasībhāradvāja accused the Buddha of leading an idle life, not doing any physical work or labor. The Buddha replied that he was also engaged in labor and that he was perhaps engaged in a task more important and arduous than what physical labor involves. Further, he said that if necessary, his work could also be easily described in the jargon of the physical labor of a farmer. The Buddha answers, "I also, O Brahmana, both plough and sow, and having ploughed and sown, I eat." Then the Brahmin retorts: "Thou professest to be a ploughman, and yet we do not see thy ploughing; asked about thy ploughing, tell us of it, that we may know thy ploughing." The Buddha answers, "Faith is the seed, penance the rain, understanding my yoke and plough, modesty the pole of the plough, mind the tie, thoughtfulness my ploughshare and goad . . . Exertion is my beast of burden; carrying me to *Nibbāna*, he goes without turning back to the place where, having gone, one does not grieve. So this ploughing is ploughed, it bears the fruit of immortality; having ploughed this ploughing, one is freed from all pain." Therefore, the Buddhist approach to asceticism should be properly understood. The Buddha recommended forests and lonely places only as ideal sites for training in meditation, but never for living, and he always advised monks that they "should travel around for the benefit and happiness of the multitude of human beings" (*Caratha bhikkhave cārikam bahu jana hitāya bahujana sukhāya*).

Conventional Reality and Absolute Reality

Buddhism also formulates another distinction we should be aware of, that between two levels of reality: conventional reality and absolute reality. Persons and morality exist in the conventional realm, while in the realm of absolute reality both these ideas do not make much sense. Ordinary moral theory presupposes the sense of 'a person'. Ordinary moral theory is valid and meaningful for one who believes that he is 'a person'. Once one realizes that there is no person, then he goes beyond this type of morality. However, it should be clearly noted that by going beyond morality one does not get permission to contravene ordinary moral values. In other words, the absolute dimension has no power or privilege to abrogate ordinary moral values. The Buddha shows this distinction by saying that an ordinary person, when he is moral, is conditioned by morality (*sīlamayo*), but an enlightened person is moral by "nature" (*sīlavā*), because the nature of Nirvana is moral perfection, *i.e.,* when viewed from the conventional standpoint. Therefore, when we discuss morality we must be aware of the conventional level of reality which is presupposed in our analysis.

"Other-Regarding" Actions

How does Buddhism recommend and justify 'other-regarding' actions? It has several grounds for doing so. One reason stems from the theory of dependent origination (*paṭicca-samuppāda*), which emphasizes that everything originates dependent on everything else. Therefore, everything owes its existence to everything else. Actually, it is the *Anatta* doctrine that involves one in altruistic actions. The doctrine of interdependence rules out the possibility of a separate soul, because nothing can be independent in a world where everything is interrelated. I cannot think of myself as separate from the rest of the universe because, for example, if I take my body, it is dependent on food (which means that my body is dependent on plants, animals, water, oxygen, *etc.*). My mind also exists dependently because the existence of thoughts is dependent on sense data derived from the external world of objects and persons.

A Buddha's altruistic commitment to others and other objects originates from this dependency. Because my existence is dependent on the rest of the universe, I naturally owe a debt and an obligation to the rest of the universe. Therefore, my attitude to others and other objects should be one of respect and gratitude. Thus, Buddhism advocates a sense of awe and respect towards living beings and nature. Here, it

is important to note that in Buddhism, the distinction between altruism and egoism breaks down as a meaningless distinction. The ideal moral attitude to other beings advocated by the Buddha is the "love a mother shows towards her one and only child" and the love relationship between mother and child cannot be characterized as egoistic or altruistic because it is a fluid mixture of both. Likewise, helping others is a way of helping oneself.

One has to understand that one is a part of a larger whole, and is not a separate person. That is why the ordinary unenlightened man is, in Buddhist terminology, called a 'Puthujjana' (*puthu* = separate; *jana* = people), or a person who believes that he is separate. The relationship between the part and whole is organic. In the way the whole creates the part, the part also creates the whole. Therefore one should realize that one can play a creative (in a cosmic sense) part in the cosmic order of events. In a way, the whole determines the part. But, the Buddhist point is that the part can also play a role in determining the whole. This is, of course, an inevitable implication of the principle of interrelatedness. Here, one can see that the Buddhist position highlights the nature of the problem of free will and determinism. One of the main teachings of the early Mahayana *Sutras* is that the nature of the ultimate reality is its paradoxicality. Free will being a part of the ultimate reality (as Kant also maintained), it may be that the principle of free will has to be inevitably understood as a paradoxical principle.

Hua-Yen Doctrine of Interdependence

The full implications of the Buddhist doctrine of interdependency were best explained by the Mahayana Buddhist school of thought called Hua-yen. . . .

What the doctrine of interdependence emphasizes is, from the fact that the rest of the universe is responsible for me, it follows that I too am responsible for the rest of the universe. In the *Sigālovāda Sutta*, the Buddha emphasizes that rights and duties imply each other. If the rights are not well reciprocated by the duties, a moral imbalance is bound to result. From the fact that nature treats us rightly, it follows that we should treat nature rightly. Buddhism strongly believes that morality is the best way to communicate with nature because morality is the nature of nature.

If we mishandle or mistreat nature we are bound to get back our due.

Love That Embraces All Beings

It is from the above considerations that an attitude of deepest love towards other beings and nature, which the Buddha advocates, is derived. It is important to note that Buddhism is much more than merely humanistic, because the Buddhist love embraces all types of beings. Whenever the Buddha talks about loving others, he always speaks of 'all beings' (*sabbe sattā*). The same love that prompts a mother to care for her one and only son should prompt persons to do their best to help the rest of the community. This attitude fosters virtues like sharing and sympathy.

Another reason why we should do anything at all is grounded on sympathy. A central theme in Buddhist ethics is that 'one should treat others in exactly the same way as one treats oneself' (*attānaṃ upamaṃ katvā*). In the *Anumāna Sutta,* the Buddha states that the basis of the 'other-regarding' principle is an inference from oneself to another. The inference works in two ways. The first is thinking of oneself in terms of others. According to the Buddha, the sense of the value of oneself or of one's own personality is derived from others. Therefore, 'personality' itself being a value concept, if one is to become a 'person' in the proper sense, it must necessarily be done in a social medium. For that reason, one should always be considerate of the value of others. Man's personality is largely a product and an item of the society around him. One becomes good or derives any value to one's personality only through the society, which is why one must consider and respect others. One does not become oneself without the help of others. Here, the so-called distinction between altruism and egoism breaks down. The Buddha states his inferential principle: "Therein, your reverences, self ought to be measured against self thus by a monk: 'That person who is of evil desires and who is in the thrall of evil desires, that person is displeasing and disagreeable to me; and similarly, if I were of evil desires and in the thrall of evil desires, I would be displeasing and disagreeable to other'." The dichotomy between egoism and altruism breaks down when he repeatedly emphasizes the necessity of 'other-regarding' virtues for one's development as a person,

not only on a social level, but even on the spiritual level where progress is impossible without cultivating 'other-regarding' virtues.

Referring to a prerequisite for meditation it is stated, "He dwells, having suffused the first quarter with a mind of friendliness, likewise the second, likewise the third, likewise the fourth; just so above, below, across; he dwells having suffused the whole world everywhere, in everyway, with a mind of friendliness that is far-reaching, widespread, immeasurable, without enmity, without malevolence. He dwells having suffused the first quarter with a mind of compassion . . . sympathetic joy . . . equanimity . . . that is far-reaching, widespread, immeasurable, without enmity, without malevolence." The Buddha preached that one's attitude towards other living beings should be similar to a mother's attitude towards her one and only son: "Just as a mother looks after her one and only son as her own life, one should look after all the living beings with an unlimited compassion." A mother's love for her child is neither egoistic nor altruistic.

The second way of inference is considering others in terms of oneself. "For a state that is not pleasant or delightful to me must be so to him also; and a state that is not pleasing or delightful to me: how could I inflict that upon another? As a result of such reflection, he himself abstains from taking the life of any creature and he encourages others so to abstain, and speaks in praise of so abstaining. Thus, as regards bodily conduct, he is utterly pure." (The Buddha goes on to elaborate that one should think similarly with regard to other moral principles also). Here he is suggesting the intrinsic value of other persons, in the only way that is possible to do it, through empathy or sympathetic feelings. It is an ultimate moral justification. Kant approximates the Buddhist ideal when he talks about the treatment of other persons as ends in themselves. But the Buddha goes much further when he advocates the treatment of all beings as ends in themselves. The Buddha maintains that life is the only ultimate, intrinsic and sacred value in this universe.

In the *Karaṇīya Metta Sutta* he says that, in spreading love, one must think of all possible types of beings: "Whatever living beings there may be: feeble or strong, long (or tall), stout, or medium, short, small, or large, seen or unseen, those dwelling far or near, those who are born and those who are yet to be born: may all beings, without exception, be happy-minded." We must respect all forms of life. What the Buddha believes is that whatever form it takes, life is life. As the Mahayanists say, all life forms are sacred because they all contain the seeds of Buddhahood or perfection. If one does not have this reverence towards life, one alienates oneself from life. Whether it is one's own or another's, life is treated as a commonly shared property. If one disrespects life that is manifested in any form, one deteriorates morally and spiritually because one becomes alienated from the most basic and intrinsic value of the world. Here, it is important to note the significant fact that the Buddha prohibited monks from harming trees and plants because "they are creatures with one sense-faculty (ekindriya), (i.e. touch)" and therefore, "people are of the opinion that there is life in trees." He also forbade monks to dig the earth because that would harm "tiny creatures living in earth" (But he did not enjoin these rules for laymen because of the practical difficulties).

Although a complete practice of Ahiṃsā (non-injury) is even theoretically impossible because the process of living itself automatically involves a process of killing or injuring many beings, perfect Ahiṃsā is always regarded as the ideal that one should always try to live up to as far as possible. What truly matters is this genuine desire or motive to respect life. The Buddha says that the ultimate and intrinsic value of life will be self-evident to any one who will care to look at one's own life. The Buddha's appeal to us is to realize that all other beings also think of themselves exactly in the same way one thinks about oneself. Therefore, in Buddhism, the sacredness of life is an ultimate ethical fact which is proved and made meaningful self-evidently, i.e., through empathy.

Morality and Salvific Power

Another important ground for moral commitment is the fact that morality has salvific power and potency. The four cardinal virtues of Buddhism are love, compassion, sympathetic joy and neutrality. The cultivation of these virtues, when coupled with wisdom, gradually leads one to Nirvana. The Buddha emphasizes that morality and wisdom are interrelated and

interactive: "From morality comes wisdom and from wisdom morality . . . Like washing one hand with another . . . so is morality washed round with wisdom and wisdom with morality." In the Buddhist tradition it is often said that since the attainment of insight is a comparatively difficult process, one should initially start with the practice of morality. Also, the establishment of oneself in morality is regarded as a kind of necessary prerequisite for the practice of insight. Buddhaghosa emphasizes this point when he quotes the famous verse: "After having established oneself in morality, one should train mind and wisdom" (Sīle patiṭṭhāya naro sapañño, cittaṃ paññaṃ ca bhāvayaṃ). Practicing morality is easier than the intellectual exercise of wisdom. The practice of morality leads one towards the understanding of the true nature of things. For example, the practice of Dāna (or charity) leads to empathy, the development of which leads one to the identification of oneself with others. What happens at that point is, one experiences the noble truth of Anatta or Soullessness with regard to oneself. On the other hand, a correct vision of reality as Anatta and interdependence prompts one to share with, give and be kind to others.

Thus, the Buddha once explained how the practice of morality gradually leads to the ultimate salvation: "So you see, Ananda, good conduct has freedom from remorse as object and profit; freedom from remorse has joy; joy has rapture; rapture has calm; calm has happiness; happiness has concentration; concentration has seeing things as they really are; seeing things as they really are has revulsion and fading of interest; revulsion and fading of interest have release by knowing and seeing as their object and profit. So you see, Ananda, good conduct gradually leads to the summit."

The Theory of Rebirth Supports Social Virtues

Another reason for moral and social commitment originates from the Buddhist theory of rebirth. According to this theory, we have been cycling in Samsara for an immeasurable period and during this period we have been relating ourselves to an infinite number of beings. Therefore, most of the beings that live in this cosmos have been, in one time or another, our close relatives, fathers or mothers, or close friends. Thus, this hypothesis or belief should be always in the back of our minds and prompt us to practice social virtues because this belief imposes a kind of moral obligation to reach out and help others.

In Buddhism, altruistic actions assume such a significant place that the ethics of the later school of Buddhism, Mahayana, devoted its dominant and exclusive emphasis on this when it developed the doctrine of the Bodhisattva. However, it should not be forgotten that the Bodhisattva ideal is equally central to early Buddhism, as it is emphasized in the *Jātakas* or the stories of the former lives of the Buddha. These *Jātaka* tales play a very active and important role in the minds of the Buddhists. Mahayana developed this concept in great detail to its logical extreme. A Bodhisattva is a person who postpones his ultimate attainment of Nirvana for the sake of all other beings. One becomes a Bodhisattva by taking the vow that he will not pass into Nirvana until he has helped the last blade of grass to attain Nirvana. Thus he vows to devote his whole life for the benefit of all sentient beings. Therefore, the

Bodhisattva concept portrays the ultimate stage of perfect altruism. Thus, from the point of view of the Bodhisattva ideal, the question would be, not "Why should I do anything at all?", but, "Why am I not doing everything possible to help others?"

DISCUSSION QUESTIONS

1. Do you agree with the Buddhist view that ultimately there is no self or soul? Why or why not?
2. Do you agree with the Buddhist position that the egoism-altruism dichotomy is a false one? Why or why not?
3. Do you agree with the Buddhist moral demand that we should treat all living things, not just humans, with love and respect? Why or why not?
4. How would you compare Dharmasiri's account of human nature and motivation with Hobbes's account? Who do you find more convincing? Why?

46. Laozi (c. sixth century B.C.E.)
From the *Dao De Jing*

In Chinese intellectual history Laozi (Lao Tzu in the Wade-Giles spelling) is generally thought to be the originator of the philosophical and spiritual school of thought known as Daoism (or Taoism). Especially in recent centuries there has been a fair amount of scholarly controversy surrounding his life and work because it is not certain just when he lived and died and whether he was the lone author of what became the classic text from which the excerpts in this reading are taken. However, the traditional account is that Laozi lived during the sixth century B.C.E., that he was a curator of the imperial archives in the capital of Chou, and that Confucius visited him for information on some ceremonies. When he retired, he headed to the western frontier where, upon the request of a gatekeeper, he wrote a book of around 5000 words, later divided into eighty-one short chapters and called the *Dao De Jing*, or the *Laozi*.

Along with Confucianism and eventually Buddhism, Daoism has been one of the major influences in the evolution of Chinese culture over the last 2500 years. Al-

though Daoism later also became an organized religion of sorts that included a priesthood, originally it was a "philosophy of life" that emphasized moral character and conduct as a product of a particular metaphysical vision of the world and the human place in it. This vision of reality was more mystical than that found in Confucian thought and yet at the same time fundamentally naturalistic and "this-worldly." In fact, Daoist principles can be most simply summed up as the recommendation to think, act, and live in harmony with Nature, which also means always allowing things to happen "naturally" without forcing them to be otherwise. In the passages included here, these principles are described and argued for using quite a bit of metaphorical and analogical language, and they are offered to humans generally and, once again, to political rulers in particular. The emphasis is on what kind of moral character traits to develop and avoid, as well as on the good and bad consequences for oneself and others that result from possessing these virtues and vices.

QUESTIONS FOR CRITICAL READING

1. According to Laozi, what is the ideal moral character for humans?
2. What are the characteristics of the ideal political ruler, according to Laozi?
3. What is the Tao (or Dao), what is its nature, and what is its relation to "Heaven" and "Earth"?
4. How does one live a life of "nonaction" (*wu-wei*), according to Laozi, and what are its consequences?
5. What are the criticisms of Confucianism found in these passages?

The Lao Tzu (Tao-Te Ching)[1]

1. The Tao (Way) that can be told of is not the eternal Tao;
The name that can be named is not the eternal name.
The Nameless is the origin of Heaven and Earth;
The Named is the mother of all things.
Therefore let there always be non-being so we may see their subtlety,[2]
And let there always be being[3] so we may see their outcome.
The two are the same,
But after they are produced, they have different names.[4]

They both may be called deep and profound (*hsüan*).[5]
Deeper and more profound,
The door of all subtleties!

Comment. While ancient Chinese philosophical schools differed in many respects, most of them insisted on the correspondence of names and actualities. They all accepted names as necessary and good. Lao Tzu, however, rejected names in favor of the nameless. This, among other things, shows the radical and unique character of Taoism. To Lao Tzu, Tao is nameless and is the simplicity without names, and when names arise, that is, when the simple oneness of Tao is split up into individual things with names, it is time to stop.[6]

2. When the people of the world all know beauty as beauty,
There arises the recognition of ugliness.
When they all know the good as good,
There arises the recognition of evil.
Therefore:
Being and non-being produce each other;
Difficult and easy complete each other;
Long and short contrast[7] each other;
High and low distinguish each other;
Sound and voice harmonize with each other;
Front and back follow each other.
Therefore the sage manages affairs without action (*wu-wei*)
And spreads doctrines without words.
All things arise, and he does not turn away from them.
He produces them, but does not take possession of them.
He acts, but does not rely on his own ability.[8]
He accomplishes his task, but does not claim credit for it.[9]
It is precisely because he does not claim credit that his accomplishment remains with him.

---

1. The *Lao Tzu* was originally not divided, but only later was it separated into two parts containing eighty-one chapters. There are many variations of a minor nature in words and order. The oldest and best text is that used by Wang Pi (226–249), the *Lao Tzu tao-te ching chu* (Commentary on the *Lao Tzu*). The text used by Ho-shang Kung (fl. 179–159 B.C.) in his *Lao Tzu chang-chü* (Commentary on the *Lao Tzu*) is supposed to be older, but its authenticity is doubted. For translations, see Bibliography. The following translation is also published separately with comments on all chapters and many more textual notes. See Chan, *The Way of Lao Tzu*, in Bibliography.
2. This translation of *miao* as "subtlety" rather than "mystery" is according to Wang Pi.
3. Ho-shang Kung and Wang Pi punctuated the sentences to mean "have desires" and "have no desires." This interrupts the thought of the chapter. Beginning with Wang An-shih's (1021–1086) *Lao Tzu chu* (Commentary), some scholars have punctuated the two sentences after *wu* (no) and *yu* (to be), thus making them to mean "There is always non-being" and "There is always being." The terms *yu* and *wu* appear in *Lao Tzu*, chs. 2, 11, and 40. I prefer Wang's punctuation.
4. Ch'en Ching-yüan (d. 1229), in his *Tao-te ching chu* (Commentary), punctuates the sentence after *t'ung* (the same) instead of *t'ung-ch'u* (produced from the same). This punctuation preserves the ancient rhyme of the verse.

5. The word *hsüan* means profound and mysterious. For a discussion of this term, see Appendix.
6. See *Lao Tzu*, chs. 37, 41, and 32, respectively.
7. Some texts substitute the character *chiao* for *hsing*, both of which mean to contrast. The former does not rhyme, while the latter appears in the older text.
8. Ho-shang Kung's interpretation: He does not expect any reward. These last two sentences also appear in *Lao Tzu*, chs. 10, 51, and 77.
9. This sentence is also found in *Lao Tzu*, ch. 77 with the variation of one word.

Comment. The idea of teachings without words anticipated the Buddhist tradition of silent transmission of the mystic doctrine, especially in the Zen School. This is diametrically opposed to the Confucian ideal, according to which a superior man acts and "becomes the model of the world"; he speaks, and "becomes the pattern for the world."[10] It is true that Confucianists say that a superior man "is truthful without any words,"[11] but they would never regard silence itself as virtue.

3. Do not exalt the worthy, so that the people shall not
    compete.
  Do not value rare treasures,[12] so that the people shall not
    steal.
  Do not display objects of desire, so that the people's
    hearts shall not be disturbed.
  Therefore in the government of the sage,
  He keeps their hearts vacuous (*hsü*),[13]
  Fills their bellies,
  Weakens their ambitions,
  And strengthens their bones,
  He always causes his people to be without knowledge
    (cunning) or desire,
  And the crafty to be afraid to act.
  By acting without action, all things will be in order.

4. Tao is empty (like a bowl),
  It may be used but its capacity is never exhausted.
  It is bottomless, perhaps the ancestor of all things.
  It blunts its sharpness,
  It unties its tangles.
  It softens its light.
  It becomes one with the dusty world.[14]
  Deep and still, it appears to exist forever.
  I do not know whose son it is.
  It seems[15] to have existed before the Lord.

Comment. This chapter shows clearly that, in Taoism, function is no less important than substance. Substance is further described in *Lao Tzu*, chs. 14 and 21, but here, as in *Lao Tzu*, chs. 11 and 45, function (*yung*, also meaning use) is regarded with equal respect. There is no deprecation of phenomenon as is the case with certain Buddhist schools.

5. Heaven and Earth are not humane (*jen*).[16]
  They regard all things as straw dogs.
  The sage is not humane.
  He regards all people as straw dogs.
  How Heaven and Earth are like a bellows!
  While vacuous, it is never exhausted.
  When active, it produces even more.
  Much talk will of course[17] come to a dead end.
  It is better to keep to the center (*chung*).[18]

Comment. The term "not humane" is of course extremely provocative. It may be suggested that this is Lao Tzu's emphatic way of opposing the Confucian doctrine of humanity and righteousness. Actually, the Taoist idea here is not negative but positive, for it means that Heaven and Earth are impartial, have no favorites, and are not humane in a deliberate or artificial way. This is the understanding of practically all commentators and is abundantly supported by the *Chuang Tzu*.[19] To translate it as unkind, as does Blakney, is grossly to misunderstand Taoist philosophy.

The two Taoist ideas, vacuity (*hsü*) and non-being (*wu*), later employed and elaborated by the Buddhists, were taboos to Confucianists. To them, these ideas are charged with a great danger of nihilism, even if Taoism is not. The Neo-Confucianist Chang Tsai (Chang Heng-ch'ü, 1020–1077) called Reality "Great Vacuity" (*T'ai-hsü*),[20] Chu Hsi (1130–1200) characterized man's nature as *hsü* and intelligent,[21] and Wang Yang-ming

---

10. *The Mean*, ch. 29.
11. *ibid.*, ch. 33.
12. These words also appear in *Lao Tzu*, ch. 64.
13. Literally "empty," *hsü* means absolute peace and purity of mind, freedom from worry and selfish desires. See Appendix for further comments on it.
14. These last four lines also appear in *Lao Tzu*, ch. 56.
15. The word *hsiang* here means "seems" and repeats the feeling expressed in the word "appear" two lines before. To interpret it as "image," as does Arthur Waley, would be to make the *Lao Tzu* more metaphysical than it really is. See his translation of the *Lao Tzu*.

16. Variously rendered as love, benevolence, human-heartedness, true manhood. For a discussion of this term, see Appendix.
17. The word *shu* means variously number, repeatedly, fate, truth, etc. According to the meaning of truth, the passage would read, "Much talk destroys truth." It seems better to adopt the meaning of repetition (always) here.
18. The word also means the mean or moderation, but here it means the center.
19. See below, ch. 8, n.35.
20. See below, ch. 30, B, 1, secs. 2–9, 16; and C, sec. 63.
21. In his *Ta-hsüeh chang-chü* (Commentary on the *Great Learning*), comment on the text.

(Wang Shou-jen, 1472–1529) described the original mind of man in the same terms.[22] But Chang's Vacuity is equivalent to material force (*ch'i*), which is real and active. To Chu and Wang, as to other Confucianists, vacuity means purity, being devoid of selfish desires, impartiality, and so forth. Even then, they used the term sparingly and with great care.

6. The spirit of the valley never dies.
>It is called the subtle and profound female.
>The gate of the subtle and profound female
>>Is the root of Heaven and Earth.
>It is continuous, and seems to be always existing.
>Use it and you will never wear it out.

7. Heaven is eternal and Earth everlasting.
>They can be eternal and everlasting because they do not exist for themselves,
>And for this reason can exist forever.
>Therefore the sage places himself in the background, but finds himself in the foreground.
>He puts himself away, and yet he always remains.
>Is it not because he has no personal interests?
>This is the reason why his personal interests are fulfilled.

8. The best (man) is like water.
>Water is good; it benefits all things and does not compete with them.
>It dwells in (lowly) places that all disdain.
>This is why it is so near to Tao.
>[The best man] in his dwelling loves the earth.
>In his heart, he loves what is profound.
>In his associations, he loves humanity.
>In his words, he loves faithfulness.
>In government, he loves order.
>In handling affairs, he loves competence.
>In his activities, he loves timeliness.
>It is because he does not compete that he is without reproach.

Comment. Water, the female, and the infant are Lao Tzu's famous symbols of Tao. The emphasis of the symbolism is ethical rather than metaphysical. It is interesting to note that while early Indians associated water with creation[23] and the Greeks looked upon it as a natural phenomenon, ancient Chinese philosophers,

whether Lao Tzu or Confucius,[24] preferred to learn moral lessons from it. Broadly speaking, these different approaches have characterized Indian, Western, and East Asian civilizations, respectively.

9. To hold and fill to overflowing
>Is not as good as to stop in time.
>Sharpen a sword-edge to its very sharpest,
>>And the (edge) will not last long.
>When gold and jade fill your hall,
>>You will not be able to keep them.
>To be proud with honor and wealth
>>Is to cause one's own downfall.
>Withdraw as soon as your work is done.
>Such is Heaven's Way.

. . .

16. Attain complete vacuity,
>Maintain steadfast quietude.
>All things come into being,
>And I see thereby their return.
>All things flourish,
>But each one returns to its root.
>This return to its root means tranquillity.
>It is called returning to its destiny.
>To return to destiny is called the eternal (Tao).
>To know the eternal is called enlightenment.
>Not to know the eternal is to act blindly to result in disaster.
>He who knows the eternal is all-embracing.
>Being all-embracing, he is impartial.
>Being impartial, he is kingly (universal).[25]
>Being kingly, he is one with Nature.[26]
>Being one with Nature, he is in accord with Tao.
>Being in accord with Tao, he is everlasting,
>And is free from danger throughout his lifetime.

Comment. In the philosophy of Lao Tzu, Tao is revealed most fully through tranquillity. The position of the Neo-Confucianists is just the opposite. They said

---

22. See below, ch. 35, B, sec. 32.
23. See *Rig Veda*, 10:129.

24. See *Analects*, 9:16.
25. Chiao Hung, *Lao Tzu i*, says that according to one tablet on which the *Lao Tzu* is inscribed, the word here is not *wang* (kingly) but *chou* (comprehension). Ma Hsü-lun, *Lao Tzu chiao-ku*, notes this approvingly but did not amend the text accordingly. Had he done so, it would not have made any improvement.
26. Ma thinks that the word *T'ien* (Nature) should have been *ta* (great).

that only through activity can the mind of Heaven and Earth be seen.

17. The best (rulers) are those whose existence is (merely)[27]
        known by the people.
    The next best are those who are loved and praised.
    The next are those who are feared.
    And the next are those who are despised.
    It is only when one does not have enough faith in
        others that others will have no faith in him.[28]
    [The great rulers] value their words highly.
    They accomplish their task; they complete their work.
    Nevertheless their people say that they simply follow
        Nature (*Tzu-jan*).[29]

18. When the great Tao declined,
    The doctrines of humanity (*jen*) and righteousness
        (*i*) arose.
    When knowledge and wisdom appeared,
    There emerged great hypocrisy.
    When the six family relationships[30] are not in harmony,
    There will be the advocacy of filial piety and deep love
        to children.[31]
    When a country is in disorder,
    There will be praise of loyal ministers.

19. Abandon sageliness and discard wisdom;
    Then the people will benefit a hundredfold.
    Abandon humanity and discard righteousness;
    Then the people will return to filial piety and deep love.[32]
    Abandon skill and discard profit;
    Then there will be no thieves or robbers.
    However, these three things are ornament (*wen*) and
        not adequate.

Therefore let people hold on to these:
    Mainfest plainness,
    Embrace simplicity,
    Reduce selfishness,
    Have few desires.

Comment. The sage as the ideal human being and the ideal ruler is mentioned thirty times in the book. And yet here sageliness is condemned. There is no contradiction, for sageliness here means a particular characteristic, that of broad and extensive learning, and is therefore mentioned along with wisdom, humanity, and righteousness. With regard to the sage, it is curious that while ancient kings were regarded as models by most ancient schools, and even by Chuang Tzu, they were ignored by Lao Tzu. It is not that Lao Tzu did not look to the past but rather that to him the sage transcended time.

20. Abandon learning and there will be no sorrow.[33]
    How much difference is there between "Yes, sir," and
        "Of course not"?
    How much difference is there between "good" and
        "evil"?
    What people dread, do not fail to dread.
    But, alas, how confused, and the end is not yet.
    The multitude are merry, as though feasting on a day of
        sacrifice,
    Or like ascending a tower at springtime.
    I alone am inert, showing no sign (of desires),
    Like an infant that has not yet smiled.
    Wearied, indeed, I seem to be without a home.
    The multitude all possess more than enough,
    I alone seem to have lost all.
    Mine is indeed the mind of an ignorant man,
    Indiscriminate and dull!
    Common folks are indeed brilliant;
    I alone seem to be in the dark.

Comment. A Confucianist would never say "Abandon learning." Also he would sharply distinguish between good and evil. The Neo-Confucianist, Ch'eng Hao

---

27. The word "not" does not appear either in the Wang Pi text or in the Ho-shang Kung text, but it appears here in the version used by Wu Ch'eng for his commentary, *Tao-te ching chu* (Commentary on the *Lao Tzu*), in the *Yung-lo ta-tien* (Great Library of the Yung-lo Period, 1403–1424), 1407, and also in the Japanese *Koitsu sōshō* (Collection of Missing Ancient Texts). This version has been accepted by many scholars, including Hu Shih, *Development of the Logical Method in Ancient China*, p. 16. The beginning phrase "the highest" is interpreted by most commentators as "the best ruler," by some as "the highest ruler," and by a few as "ruler of high antiquity."
28. This sentence is also found in ch. 23.
29. *Tzu-jan*, literally "self-so," means being natural or spontaneous.
30. Father, son, elder brother, younger brother, husband, and wife.
31. Some texts including the *Yung-lo ta-tien* read: "There will be filial sons" instead of "filial piety and deep love."
32. In some texts, including the *Yung-lo ta-tien*, this sentence precedes the first.

---

33. Some scholars have shifted this line to the beginning or the end of the last chapter. Rearranging the text of *Lao Tzu* has been undertaken by a number of modern scholars, especially Ma. Duyvendak has done so in his translation. But such rearrangements have no objective historical or textual foundation and add little to one's understanding of Taoist philosophy.

(Ch'eng Ming-tao, 1032–1085), has been severely criticized for his saying that "both good and evil in the world are both the Principle of Nature,"[34] and Wang Yang-ming was likewise widely attacked for teaching that "in the original substance of the mind there is no distinction between good and evil."[35]

> Common folks see differences and are clear-cut;
> I alone make no distinctions.
> I seem drifting as the sea;
> Like the wind blowing about, seemingly without
>   destination.
> The multitude all have a purpose;
> I alone seem to be stubborn and rustic.
> I alone differ from others,
> And value drawing sustenance from Mother (Tao).[36]

21. The all-embracing quality of the great virtue (*te*) follows
>   alone from the Tao.
> The thing that is called Tao is eluding and vague.
>   Vague and eluding, there is in it the form.
>   Eluding and vague, in it are things.
> Deep and obscure, in it is the essence.[37]
> The essence is very real; in it are evidences.
> From the time of old until now, its name
>   (manifestations) ever remains,
> By which we may see the beginning of all things.
> How do I know that the beginnings of all things are so?
> Through this (Tao).

Comment. Philosophically this is the most important chapter of the book. The sentence "The essence is very real" virtually formed the backbone of Chou Tun-i's (Chou Lien-hsi, 1017–1073) *Explanation of the Diagram of the Great Ultimate*, which centers on the "reality of the Non-Ultimate and the essence of yin and yang."[38] And Chou's work laid the foundation of the entire Neo-Confucian metaphysics. Of course Neo-Confucian metaphysics is more directly derived from the *Book of Changes*, but the concepts of reality in the *Book of Changes* and in this chapter are surprisingly similar.

22. To yield is to be preserved whole.
> To be bent is to become straight.
> To be empty is to be full.
> To be worn out is to be renewed.
> To have little is to possess.
> To have plenty is to be perplexed.
> Therefore the sage embraces the One
> And becomes the model of the world.
> He does not show himself; therefore he is luminous.
> He does not justify himself; therefore he becomes
>   prominent.
> He does not boast of himself; therefore he is given
>   credit.
> He does not brag; therefore he can endure for long.[39]
> It is precisely because he does not compete that the
>   world cannot compete with him.[40]
> Is the ancient saying, "To yield is to be preserved
>   whole," empty words?
> Truly he will be preserved and (prominence, etc.) will
>   come to him.

23. Nature says few words.[41]
> For the same reason a whirlwind does not last a whole
>   morning,
> Nor does a rainstorm last a whole day.
> What causes them?
> It is Heaven and Earth (Nature).
> If even Heaven and Earth cannot make them last long,
> How much less can man?
> Therefore he who follows Tao is identified with Tao.
> He who follows virtue is identified with virtue.
> He who abandons (Tao) is identified with the
>   abandonment (of Tao).
> He who is identified with Tao—Tao is also happy to
>   have him.
> He who is identified with virtue—virtue is also happy
>   to have him.
> And he who is identified with the abandonment (of
>   Tao)—the abandonment (of Tao) is also happy to
>   abandon him.
> It is only when one does not have enough faith in
>   others that others will have no faith in him.[42]

34. See below, ch. 31, sec. 8.
35. See below, ch. 35, sec. 315.
36. The term "mother" occurs also in *Lao Tzu*, chs. 1, 25, 52, 59. See below, n.97.
37. The word *ching* (essence) also means intelligence, spirit, life-force.
38. See below, ch. 28.

39. These last four lines are repeated with slight modification in *Lao Tzu*, ch. 24.
40. This sentence is also found in *Lao Tzu*, ch. 66.
41. Cf. *Analects*, 17:19.
42. Repeating the sentence in *Lao Tzu*, ch. 17.

24. He who stands on tiptoe is not steady.
    He who strides forward does not go.
    He who shows himself is not luminous.[43]
    He who justifies himself is not prominent.
    He who boasts of himself is not given credit.
    He who brags does not endure for long.[44]
    From the point of view of Tao, these are like remnants
        of food and tumors of action,
    Which all creatures detest.
    Therefore those who possess Tao turn away from them.

25. There was something undifferentiated and yet complete,
    Which existed before heaven and earth.
    Soundless and formless, it depends on nothing and
        does not change.
    It operates everywhere and is free from danger.
    It may be considered the mother of the universe.
    I do not know its name; I call it Tao.
    If forced to give it a name, I shall call it Great.
    Now being great means functioning everywhere.
    Functioning everywhere means far-reaching.
    Being far-reaching means returning to the original
        point.
    Therefore Tao is great.
    Heaven is great.
    Earth is great.
    And the king[45] is also great.
    There are four great things in the universe, and the king
        is one of them.
    Man models himself after Earth.
    Earth models itself after Heaven.
    Heaven models itself after Tao.
    And Tao models itself after Nature.

Comment. The doctrine of returning to the original is prominent in Lao Tzu. It has contributed in no small degree to the common Chinese cyclical concept, which teaches that both history and reality operate in cycles. . . .

32. Tao is eternal and has no name.
    Though its simplicity seems insignificant, none in the
        world can master it.

If kings and barons would hold on to it, all things would
    submit to them spontaneously.
Heaven and earth unite to drip sweet dew.
Without the command of men, it drips evenly over all.
As soon as there were regulations and institutions, there
    were names (differentiation of things).
As soon as there are names, know that it is time to stop.
It is by knowing when to stop that one can be free from
    danger.
Analogically, Tao in the world (where everything is
    embraced by it), may be compared to rivers and
    streams running into the sea.

33. He who knows others is wise;
    He who knows himself is enlightened.
    He who conquers others has physical strength.
    He who conquers himself is strong.
    He who is contented is rich.
    He who acts with vigor has will.
    He who does not lose his place (with Tao) will endure.
    He who dies but does not really perish enjoys long life.

Comment. What is it that dies but does not perish? Wang Pi said it was Tao on which human life depended, and Wu Ch'eng said it was the human mind. Other commentators have given different answers. Most of them, however, believe that Lao Tzu meant the immortality of virtue. Thus the Taoists conformed to the traditional belief which had already been expressed in the *Tso chuan* (Tso's Commentary on the *Spring and Autumn Annals*), namely, the immortality of virtue, achievement, and words,[46] and which has continued to be the typical Chinese idea of immortality.[47] It is to be noted that unlike Chuang Tzu, Lao Tzu showed no tendency to believe in earthly immortals (*hsien*, a fairy), although his exaltation of everlasting life undoubtedly contributed to the development of the belief. . . .

37. Tao invariably takes no action, and yet there is nothing
        left undone.

---

43. Cf. *The Mean,* chs. 26 and 33.
44. These last four lines virtually repeat *Lao Tzu,* ch. 22.
45. Both the Wang Pi and Ho-shang Kung texts read "king" instead of "man." The Fu I text and others have "man" instead. However, "king" is here understood as the representative of man.

46. See above, ch. 1, sec. 4.
47. Erkes thinks that death meant that a dead man still possessed power to influence the living and that perishing means that this power is gone as the body has been dissolved. Dubs rejects this interpretation and insists that Lao Tzu meant immortality of influence. (See Erkes, *Ssu erh pu-wang in Asia Major,* 3:2 [1952]. 156–159; note by Dubs, *ibid.,* 159–161; Erkes' reply, *ibid.,* 4:1 [1954], 149–150.) Most Chinese scholars would support Dubs.

If kings and barons can keep it, all things will transform
    spontaneously.
If, after transformation, they should desire to be active,
I would restrain them with simplicity, which has no
    name.
Simplicity, which has no name, is free of desires.
Being free of desires, it is tranquil.
And the world will be at peace of its own accord.

38. The man of superior virtue is not (conscious of) his virtue,
    And in this way he really possesses virtue.
    The man of inferior virtue never loses (sight of) his
        virtue,
    And in this way he loses his virtue.
    The man of superior virtue takes no action, but has no
        ulterior motive to do so.
    The man of inferior virtue takes action, and has an
        ulterior motive to do so.
    The man of superior humanity takes action, but has no
        ulterior motive to do so.
    The man of superior righteousness takes action, and
        has an ulterior motive to do so.
    The man of superior propriety[48] takes action,
    And when people do not respond to it, he will stretch
        his arms and force it on them.
    Therefore, only when Tao is lost does the doctrine of
        virtue arise.
    Only when virtue is lost does the doctrine of humanity
        arise.
    Only when humanity is lost does the doctrine of
        righteousness arise.
    Only when righteousness is lost does the doctrine of
        propriety arise.
    Now, propriety is a superficial expression of loyalty and
        faithfulness, and the beginning of disorder.
    Those who are the first to know have the flowers
        (appearance) of Tao but are the beginning of
        ignorance.
    For this reason the great man dwells in the thick
        (substantial), and does not rest with the thin
        (superficial).
    He dwells in the fruit (reality), and does not rest with
        the flower (appearance).
    Therefore he rejects the one, and accepts the other.

---

48. In a narrow sense, *li* means rites, ritual, ceremonies, etc., but in
a broad sense it means rules of behavior or principles of conduct.

Comment. Wang Pi, who wrote the best and most
philosophical commentary on the *Lao Tzu,* wrote the
longest of his comments on this chapter.[49] It is in this
commentary that the important Chinese concepts of
t'i-yung (substance and function) first appeared. Han
Fei Tzu, the first commentator on the *Lao Tzu,*[50] wrote
one of his longest and best comments on this chapter
also. . . .

76. When man is born, he is tender and weak.
    At death, he is stiff and hard.
    All things, the grass as well as trees, are tender and
        supple while alive.
    When dead, they are withered and dried.
    Therefore the stiff and the hard are companions of death.
    The tender and the weak are companions of life.
    Therefore if the army is strong, it will not win.
    If a tree is stiff, it will break.
    The strong and the great are inferior, while the tender
        and the weak are superior.

77. Heaven's Way is indeed like the bending of a bow.
    When (the string) is high, bring it down.
    When it is low, raise it up.
    When it is excessive, reduce it.
    When it is insufficient, supplement it.
    The Way of Heaven reduces whatever is excessive and
        supplements whatever is insufficient.
    The way of man is different.
    It reduces the insufficient to offer to the excessive.
    Who is able to have excess to offer to the world?
    Only the man of Tao.
    Therefore the sage acts, but does not rely on his own
        ability.[51]
    He accomplishes his task, but does not claim credit for it.[52]
    He has no desire to display his excellence.

78. There is nothing softer and weaker than water,
    And yet there is nothing better for attacking hard and
        strong things.
    For this reason there is no substitute for it.
    All the world knows that the weak overcomes the
        strong and the soft overcomes the hard.

---

49. See below, ch. 19, sec. 3.
50. For his elaboration on the concept of Tao, see below, ch. 12,
sec. 2.
51. This sentence is found also in *Lao Tzu,* chs. 2, 10, 51.
52. Repeating the sentence in ch. 2 with the variation of one word.

But none can practice it.
  Therefore the sage says:
  He who suffers disgrace for his country
  Is called the lord of the land.
  He who takes upon himself the country's misfortunes
  Becomes the king of the empire.
Straight words seem to be their opposite.

DISCUSSION QUESTIONS

1. Do you agree with Laozi's principles of the moral life? Why or why not?

2. How would you compare Laozi's characterization of the ideal political ruler with that of Mencius? Who do you find more convincing? Why?

3. Is the Dao real? Why or why not?

4. What Western writers have advocated a life of simplicity, humility, and nonaction in harmony with Nature? What other similarities or differences do you see between these thinkers and Laozi?

47. Confucius (551–479 B.C.E.)
From the *Analects*

According to Wing-Tsit Chan, the translator of these excerpts from the *Analects,* Confucius is the most influential and revered individual in all of Chinese history. In addition to being the source of the majority of philosophical systems in succeeding centuries, his teachings on social duty, propriety and etiquette, and moral character took hold in most dimensions of Chinese culture in a way unmatched before or since by any other doctrines. And yet, the evidence is ambiguous regarding his authorship of any written works. Even the *Analects,* generally accepted as the primary source of Confucius's actual teachings, is a compilation of his sayings and the sayings of some of his students, most likely collected by his students themselves, and their students, over many years. (See Chan's footnote at the beginning of the selection.)

The name Confucius is in fact a later Latinized form of his traditional title, K'ung Fu-Tzu (Wade-Giles spelling), meaning Grand Master K'ung. He grew up in the state of Lu, in a family that was part of the traditional nobility but that had become impoverished. Although he served in various minor governmental positions, almost all of his adult life was devoted to teaching, and some records indicate that by the time of his death at 73 he had 3000 pupils.

As in the selections from the *Dao De Jing,* these passages from the *Analects* include the commentaries by Chan, providing you with the illuminating interpretations of one of the major scholars of this and other classic Chinese texts working in the United States in the second half of the twentieth century. Both Chan's comments and his footnotes show how long-standing the debates have been concerning the meaning and philosophical implications of what Confucius actually said. Notice how this parallels some of the other scholarly traditions represented in this text, for example, those found in European and Indian history.

QUESTIONS FOR CRITICAL READING

1. How is the concept of the Tao (Dao) used in these excerpts, and how is it different from the Daoist use of the term?

2. What does Confucius mean by "humanity" (*jen*)?

3. What does Confucius mean by "propriety" (*li*)?

4. How does Confucius characterize the "superior man" and the "inferior man"?

5. What is the Confucian version of the "golden rule," according to Chan?

The Analects[1]

1:1. Confucius said, "Is it not a pleasure to learn and to repeat or practice from time to time what has been learned? Is it not delightful to have friends coming

---

1. The *Analects* is a collection of sayings by Confucius and his pupils pertaining to his teachings and deeds. It was probably put together

from afar? Is one not a superior man if he does not feel hurt even though he is not recognized?"

Comment. Interpretations of Confucian teachings have differed radically in the last 2,000 years. Generally speaking, Han (206 B.C.–A.D. 220) scholars, represented in Ho Yen (d. 249), *Lun-yü chi-chieh* (Collected Explanations of the *Analects*),[2] were inclined to be literal and interested in historical facts, whereas Neo-Confucianists, represented in Chu Hsi (1130–1200), *Lun-yü chi-chu* (Collected Commentaries on the *Analects*) were interpretative, philosophical, and often subjective. They almost invariably understand the Confucian Way (Tao) as principle (*li*), which is their cardinal concept, and frequently when they came to an undefined "this" or "it," they insisted that it meant principle. This divergency between the Han and Sung scholars has colored interpretations of this passage. To Wang Su (195–265), quoted in Ho, *hsi* (to learn) means to recite a lesson repeatedly. To Chu Hsi, however, *hsi* means to follow the examples of those who are first to understand, and therefore it does not mean recitation but practice. In revolt against both extremes, Ch'ing (1644–1912) scholars emphasized practical experience. In this case, *hsi* to them means both to repeat and to practice, as indicated in Liu Pao-nan (1791–1855), *Lun-yü cheng-i* (Correct

Meanings of the *Analects*). Thus Ho Yen, Chu Hsi, and Liu Pao-nan neatly represent the three different approaches in the three different periods. Generally speaking, the dominant spirit of Confucian teaching is the equal emphasis on knowledge and action. This dual emphasis will be encountered again and again.[3]

1:2. Yu Tzu[4] said, "Few of those who are filial sons and respectful brothers will show disrespect to superiors, and there has never been a man who is not disrespectful to superiors, and yet creates disorder. A superior man is devoted to the fundamentals (the root). When the root is firmly established, the moral law (Tao) will grow. Filial piety and brotherly respect are the root of humanity (*jen*)."

1:3. Confucius said, "A man with clever words and an ingratiating appearance is seldom a man of humanity."[5]

1:4. Tseng-Tzu[6] said, "Every day I examine myself on three points: whether in counseling others I have not been loyal; whether in intercourse with my friends I have not been faithful; and whether I have not repeated again and again and practiced the instructions of my teacher."[7]

1:6. Young men should be filial when at home and respectful to their elders when away from home. They should be earnest and faithful. They should love all extensively and be intimate with men of humanity. When they have any energy to spare after the performance of moral duties, they should use it to study literature and the arts (*wen*).[8]

---

by some of his pupils and their pupils. The name *Lun-yü* did not appear until the 2nd century B.C. At that time there were three versions of it, with some variations. Two of these have been lost. The surviving version is that of the state of Lu, where it circulated. It is divided into two parts, with ten books each. In the *Ching-tien shih-wen* (Explanation of Terms in the Classics) by Lu Te-ming (556–627), ch. 24, it is divided into 492 chapters. Chu Hsi combined and divided certain chapters, making a total of 482, one of which is divided into eighteen sections. In translations like Legge's *Confucian Analects,* and Waley's *The Analects of Confucius,* these divisions are taken as chapters, making 499. The same numbering is used in the following selections.

The material is unsystematic, in a few cases repetitive, and in some cases historically inaccurate. However, it is generally accepted as the most authentic and reliable source of Confucian teachings. Chu Hsi grouped it together with the *Book of Mencius,* the *Great Learning,* and the *Doctrine of the Mean* as the "Four Books." Thereupon they became Classics. From 1313 to 1905, they served as the basis for civil service examinations, replacing the earlier Classics in importance.
2. In the *Lun-yü chu-shu* (Commentary and Subcommentary on the *Analects*) in the Thirteen Classics Series.

3. See below, comment on *Analects,* 2:18.
4. Confucius' pupil whose private name was Jo (538–c.457 B.C.), thirteen years (some say thirty-three years) Confucius' junior. In the *Analects,* with minor exceptions, he and Tseng Ts'an are addressed as Tzu, an honorific for a scholar or gentleman, giving rise to the theory that the *Analects* was compiled by their pupils, who supplemented Confucius' sayings with theirs.
5. Cf. below, 13:27.
6. Tseng Ts'an (505–c.436 B.C.), pupil of Confucius, noted for filial piety, to whom are ascribed the *Great Learning* and the *Book of Filial Piety.*
7. Ho Yen's interpretation: Whether I have transmitted to others what I myself have not practiced. This interpretation has been accepted by many.
8. *Wen,* literally "patterns," is here extended to mean the embodiment of culture and the moral law (Tao)—that is, the Six Arts of ceremony, music, archery, carriage-driving, writing, and mathematics.

1:8. Confucius said, "If the superior man is not grave, he will not inspire awe, and his learning will not be on a firm foundation.[9] Hold loyalty and faithfulness to be fundamental. Have no friends who are not as good as yourself. When you have made mistakes, don't be afraid to correct them."

Comment. The teaching about friendship here is clearly inconsistent with *Analects,* 8:5, where Confucius exhorts us to learn from inferiors. It is difficult to believe that Confucius taught people to be selfish. According to Hsing Ping (932–1010),[10] Confucius meant people who are not equal to oneself in loyalty and faithfulness, assuming that one is or should be loyal and faithful; according to Hsü Kan (171–218), Confucius simply wanted us to be careful in choosing friends.[11]

1:11. Confucius said, "When a man's father is alive, look at the bent of his will. When his father is dead, look at his conduct. If for three years [of mourning] he does not change from the way of his father, he may be called filial."

Comment. Critics of Confucius have asserted that Confucian authoritarianism holds an oppressive weight on the son even after the father has passed away. Fan Tsu-yü (1041–1098) did understand the saying to mean that the son should observe the father's will and past conduct,[12] but he was almost alone in this. All prominent commentators, from K'ung An-kuo to Cheng Hsüan (127–200),[13] Chu Hsi, and Liu Pao-nan have interpreted the passage to mean that while one's father is alive, one's action is restricted, so that his *intention* should be the criterion by which his character is to be judged. After his father's death, however, when he is completely autonomous, he should be judged by his conduct. In this interpretation, the way of the father is of course the moral principle which has guided or should have guided the son's conduct.

1:12. Yu Tzu said, "Among the functions of propriety (*li*) the most valuable is that it establishes harmony. The excellence of the ways of ancient kings consists of this. It is the guiding principle of all things great and small. If things go amiss, and you, understanding harmony, try to achieve it without regulating it by the rules of propriety, they will still go amiss."

1:14. Confucius said, "The superior man does not seek fulfillment of his appetite nor comfort in his lodging. He is diligent in his duties and careful in his speech. He associates with men of moral principles and thereby realizes himself. Such a person may be said to love learning."

1:15. Tzu-kung[14] said, "What do you think of a man who is poor and yet does not flatter, and the rich man who is not proud?" Confucius replied, "They will do. But they are not as good as the poor man who is happy[15] and the rich man who loves the rules of propriety (*li*)." Tzu-kung said, "*The Book of Odes* says:

As a thing is cut and filed,
As a thing is carved and polished. . . .[16]

Does that not mean what you have just said?"

Confucius said, "Ah! Tz'u. Now I can begin to talk about the odes with you. When I have told you what has gone before, you know what is to follow."

1:16. Confucius said, "[A good man] does not worry about not being known by others but rather worries about not knowing them."[17]

2:1. Confucius said, "A ruler who governs his state by virtue is like the north polar star, which remains in its place while all the other stars revolve around it."

Comment. Two important principles are involved here. One is government by virtue, in

---

9. To K'ung An-kuo (fl. 130 B.C.), quoted by Ho Yen, *ku* means "obscure," not "firm." The sentence would read, "If he studies, he will not be ignorant."

10. *Lun-yü shu* (Subcommentary on the *Analects*). This is part of the *Lun-yü chu-shu.*

11. *Chung lun* (Treatise on the Mean), pt. 1, sec. 5, SPTK, 1:21b.

12. Quoted in Chu Hsi's *Lun-yü huo-wen* (Questions and Answers on the *Analects*), 1:20a, in *Chu Tzu i-shu* (Surviving Works of Chu Hsi).

13. *Lun-yü chu* (Commentary on the *Analects*).

14. Confucius' pupil, whose family name was Tuan-mu, private name Tz'u, and courtesy name Tzu-kung (520–c.450 B.C.). He was noted for eloquence and was thirty-one years younger than the Master. See *Analects,* 5:8 about him.

15. An old edition has "happy with the Way."

16. Ode no. 55. Describing the eloquence of a lover, but here taken by Tzu-kung to mean moral effort.

17. Similar ideas are found in *Analects,* 14:32; 15:18, 20.

which Confucianists stand directly opposed to the Legalists, who prefer law and force. The other is government through inaction, i.e., government in such excellent order that all things operate by themselves. This is the interpretation shared by Han and Sung Confucianists alike.[18] In both cases, Confucianism and Taoism are in agreement.[19]

2:2. Confucius said, "All three hundred odes can be covered by one of their sentences, and that is, 'Have no depraved thoughts.'"[20]

2:3. Confucius said, "Lead the people with governmental measures and regulate them by law and punishment, and they will avoid wrongdoing but will have no sense of honor and shame. Lead them with virtue and regulate them by the rules of propriety (li), and they will have a sense of shame and, moreover, set themselves right."[21]

2:4. Confucius said, "At fifteen my mind was set on learning. At thirty my character had been formed. At forty I had no more perplexities. At fifty I knew the Mandate of Heaven (T'ien-ming). At sixty I was at ease with whatever I heard. At seventy I could follow my heart's desire without transgressing moral principles."

Comment. What *T'ien-ming* is depends upon one's own philosophy. In general, Confucianists before the T'ang dynasty (618–907) understood it to mean either the decree of God, which determines the course of one's life, or the rise and fall of the moral order,[22] whereas Sung scholars, especially Chu Hsi, took it to mean "the operation of Nature which is endowed in things and makes things be as they are."[23] This

latter interpretation has prevailed. The concept of *T'ien-ming* which can mean Mandate of Heaven, decree of God, personal destiny, and course of order, is extremely important in the history of Chinese thought. In religion it generally means fate or personal order of God, but in philosophy it is practically always understood as moral destiny, natural endowment, or moral order.

2:5. Meng I Tzu[24] asked about filial piety. Confucius said: "Never disobey." [Later,] when Fan Ch'ih[25] was driving him, Confucius told him, "Meng-sun asked me about filial piety, and I answered him, 'Never disobey.'"[26] Fan Ch'ih said, "What does that mean?" Confucius said, "When parents are alive, serve them according to the rules of propriety. When they die, bury them according to the rules of propriety and sacrifice to them according to the rules of propriety."

2:6. Meng Wu-po[27] asked about filial piety. Confucius said, "Especially be anxious lest parents should be sick."[28]

2:7. Tzu-yu[29] asked about filial piety. Confucius said, "Filial piety nowadays means to be able to support one's parents. But we support even dogs and horses.[30] If there is no feeling of reverence, wherein lies the difference?"

2:11. Confucius said, "A man who reviews the old so as to find out the new is qualified to teach others."

2:12. Confucius said, "The superior man is not an implement (ch'i)."[31]

---

18. See Ho Yen's *Lun-yü chi-chieh* and Chu Hsi's *Lun-yü chi-chu.*
19. Cf. *Analects,* 15:4 and *Lao Tzu,* ch. 57.
20. *Odes,* ode no. 297. Actually there are 305 odes in the book. The word *ssu* means "Ah!" in the poem but Confucius used it in its sense of "thought." For discussion of the *Book of Odes,* see above, ch. 1, n.5.
21. The word *ko* means both to rectify (according to Ho Yen and most other commentators) and to arrive (according to Cheng Hsüan). In the latter sense, it can mean either "the people will arrive at goodness" or "the people will come to the ruler." See below, ch. 32, comment on sec. 44.
22. See Ch'eng Shu-te *Lun-yü chi-shih* (Collected Explanations of the *Analects*), 1943.
23. Chu Hsi, *Lun-yü chi-chu.*

24. A young noble, also styled Meng-sun, once studied ceremonies with Confucius.
25. Confucius' pupil, whose family name was Fan, private name Hsü, and courtesy name Tzu-ch'ih (b. 515 B.C.).
26. Not to disobey the principle of propriety, according to Hsing Ping; not to disobey moral principles, according to Chu Hsi; or not to obey parents, according to Huang K'an (448–545), *Lun-yü i-shu* (Commentary on the Meanings of the *Analects*).
27. Son of Meng I Tzu.
28. Another interpretation by Ma Jung (79–166), quoted by Ho Yen: A filial son does not do wrong. His parents' only worry is that he might become sick. About half of the commentators have followed him.
29. Confucius' pupil. His family name was Yen, private name Yen, and courtesy name Tzu-yu (b. 506 B.C.).
30. Alternative interpretations: (1) Even dogs and horses can support men; (2) Even dogs and horses can support their parents.
31. Literally "an implement or utensil," *ch'i* means narrow usefulness rather than the ability to grasp fundamentals.

Comment. A good and educated man should not be like an implement, which is intended only for a narrow and specific purpose. Instead, he should have broad vision, wide interests, and sufficient ability to do many things.[32]

2:13. Tzu-kung asked about the superior man. Confucius said, "He acts before he speaks and then speaks according to his action."[33]

2:14. Confucius said, "The superior man is broad-minded but not partisan; the inferior man is partisan but not broadminded."

2:15. Confucius said, "He who learns but does not think is lost; he who thinks but does not learn is in danger."

2:17. Confucius said, "Yu,[34] shall I teach you [the way to acquire] knowledge?[35] To say that you know when you do know and say that you do not know when you do not know—that is [the way to acquire] knowledge."

2:18. Tzu-chang[36] was learning with a view to official emolument. Confucius said, "Hear much and put aside what's doubtful while you speak cautiously of the rest. Then few will blame you. See much and put aside what seems perilous while you are cautious in carrying the rest into practice. Then you will have few occasions for regret. When one's words give few occasions for blame and his acts give few occasions for repentance—there lies his emolument."

Comment. The equal emphasis on words and deeds has been a strong tradition in Confucianism.[37] Eventually Wang Yang-ming identified them as one.[38]

2:24. Confucius said, "It is flattery to offer sacrifice to ancestral spirits other than one's own. To see what is right and not to do it is cowardice."

3:3. Confucius said, "If a man is not humane (*jen*), what has he to do with ceremonies (*li*)? If he is not humane, what has he to do with music?"

3:4. Lin Fang[39] asked about the foundation of ceremonies. Confucius said, "An important question indeed! In rituals or ceremonies, be thrifty rather than extravagant, and in funerals, be deeply sorrowful rather than shallow in sentiment."

3:12. When Confucius offered sacrifice to his ancestors, he felt as if his ancestral spirits were actually present. When he offered sacrifice to other spiritual beings, he felt as if they were actually present. He said, "If I do not participate in the sacrifice, it is as if I did not sacrifice at all."

3:13. Wang-sun Chia[40] asked, "What is meant by the common saying, 'It is better to be on good terms with the God of the Kitchen [who cooks our food] than with the spirits of the shrine (ancestors) at the southwest corner of the house'?" Confucius said, "It is not true. He who commits a sin against Heaven has no god to pray to."

3:17. Tzu-kung wanted to do away with the sacrificing of a lamb at the ceremony in which the beginning of each month is reported to ancestors. Confucius said, "Tz'u![41] You love the lamb but I love the ceremony."

3:19. Duke Ting[42] asked how the ruler should employ his ministers and how the ministers should serve their ruler. Confucius said, "A ruler should employ his ministers according to the principle of propriety, and ministers should serve their ruler with loyalty."

3:24. The guardian at I (a border post of the state of Wei) requested to be presented to Confucius, saying, "When gentlemen come here, I have never been prevented from seeing them." Confucius' followers introduced him. When he came out from the interview, he said, "Sirs, why are you disheartened by your master's loss of office? The Way has not prevailed in the world for a long time. Heaven is going to use your master as a wooden bell [to awaken the people]."

4:2. Confucius said, "One who is not a man of humanity cannot endure adversity for long, nor can he enjoy prosperity for long. The man of humanity is

---

32. Cf. below, 9:6.
33. Cf. below, 4:22, 24; 14:29.
34. Name of Confucius' pupil whose family name was Chung and courtesy name Tzu-lu (542–480 B.C.). He was only nine years younger than Confucius. He was noted for courage.
35. The sentence may also mean: "Do you know what I teach you?"
36. Courtesy name of Confucius' pupil, Chuan-sun Shih (503–c.450 B.C.).
37. See also *Analects,* 4:22, 24; 5:9; 13:3; 14:29; 15:5; 18:8; and *The Mean,* chs. 8, 13.
38. See below, ch. 35, B, sec. 5.

---

39. A native of Lu, most probably not a pupil of Confucius.
40. Great officer and commander-in-chief in the state of Wei.
41. Tzu-kung's private name.
42. Ruler of Confucius' native state of Lu (r. 509–495 B.C.).

naturally at ease with humanity. The man of wisdom cultivates humanity for its advantage."

4:3. Confucius said, "Only the man of humanity knows how to love people and hate people."[43]

4:4. Confucius said, "If you set your mind on humanity, you will be free from evil."[44]

4:5. Confucius said, "Wealth and honor are what every man desires. But if they have been obtained in violation of moral principles, they must not be kept. Poverty and humble station are what every man dislikes. But if they can be avoided only in violation of moral principles, they must not be avoided. If a superior man departs from humanity, how can he fulfill that name? A superior man never abandons humanity even for the lapse of a single meal. In moments of haste, he acts according to it. In times of difficulty or confusion, he acts according to it."

4:6. Confucius said, "I have never seen one who really loves humanity or one who really hates inhumanity. One who really loves humanity will not place anything above it.[45] One who really hates inhumanity will practice humanity in such a way that inhumanity will have no chance to get at him. Is there any one who has devoted his strength to humanity for as long as a single day? I have not seen any one without sufficient strength to do so. Perhaps there is such a case, but I have never seen it."

4:8. Confucius said, "In the morning, hear the Way; in the evening, die content!"

4:10. Confucius said, "A superior man in dealing with the world is not for anything or against anything. He follows righteousness as the standard."

Comment. This is a clear expression of both the flexibility and rigidity of Confucian ethics— flexibility in application but rigidity in standard. Here lies the basic idea of the Confucian doctrine of *ching-ch'üan,* or the standard and the exceptional, the absolute and the relative, or the permanent and the temporary.[46] This ex-

plains why Confucius was not obstinate,[47] had no predetermined course of action,[48] was ready to serve or to withdraw whenever it was proper to do so,[49] and, according to Mencius, was a sage who acted according to the circumstance of the time.[50]

The words *shih* and *mo* can be interpreted to mean being near to people and being distant from people, or opposing people and admiring people, respectively, and some commentators have adopted these interpretations.[51] But the majority follow Chu Hsi, as I have done here. Chu Hsi was thinking about the superior man's dealing with things. Chang Shih (Chang Nan-hsien, 1133–1180), on the other hand, thought Confucius was talking about the superior man's state of mind.[52] This difference reflects the opposition between the two wings of Neo-Confucianism, one inclining to activity, the other to the state of mind.[53]

4:11. Confucius said, "The superior man thinks of virtue; the inferior man thinks of possessions.[54] The superior man thinks of sanctions; the inferior man thinks of personal favors."

4:12. Confucius said, "If one's acts are motivated by profit, he will have many enemies."

4:15. Confucius said, "Ts'an,[55] there is one thread that runs through my doctrines." Tseng Tzu said, "Yes." After Confucius had left, the disciples asked him, "What did he mean?" Tseng Tzu replied, "The Way of our Master is none other than conscientiousness (*chung*) and altruism (*shu*)."

Comment. Confucian teachings may be summed up in the phrase "one thread" (*i-kuan*), but Confucianists have not agreed on what it means. Generally, Confucianists of Han

---

43. Hate here means dislike, without any connotation of ill will. See *Great Learning,* ch. 10, for an elaboration of the saying.
44. The word *e,* evil, can also be read *wu* to mean hate or dislike, but it is hardly ever done.
45. It is possible to interpret the phrase to mean "will not be surpassed by anyone," but few commentators chose it.
46. See below, ch. 3, comment on *Mencius,* Additional Selections, 4A:17.

47. *Analects,* 9:4.
48. *ibid.,* 18:8.
49. *Mencius,* 2A:2.
50. *ibid.,* 5B:1.
51. See Liu Pao-nan, *Lun-yü cheng-i.*
52. See Chu Hsi, *Lun-yü chi-chu,* and Chang Shih, *Lun-yü chieh* (Explanation of the *Analects*).
53. See Ch'eng Shu-te, *Lun-yü chi-shih,* on this point.
54. Literally "land," or one's shelter, food, etc.
55. Private name of Tseng Tzu.

and T'ang times adhered to the basic meaning of "thread" and understood it in the sense of a system or a body of doctrines. Chu Hsi, true to the spirit of Neo-Confucian speculative philosophy, took it to mean that there is one mind to respond to all things. In the Ch'ing period, in revolt against speculation, scholars preferred to interpret *kuan* as action and affairs, that is, there is only one moral principle for all actions.[56] All agree, however, on the meanings of *chung* and *shu,* which are best expressed by Chu Hsi, namely, *chung* means the full development of one's [originally good] mind and *shu* means the extension of that mind to others.[57] As Ch'eng I (Ch'eng I-ch'uan, 1033–1107) put it, *chung* is the Way of Heaven, whereas *shu* is the way of man; the former is substance, while the latter is function.[58] Liu Pao-nan is correct in equating *chung* with Confucius' saying, "Establish one's own character," and *shu* with "Also establish the character of others."[59] Here is the positive version of the Confucian golden rule. The negative version is only one side of it.[60]

4:16. Confucius said, "The superior man understands righteousness (*i*); the inferior man understands profit."

> *Comment.* Confucius contrasted the superior man and the inferior in many ways,[61] but this is the fundamental difference for Confucianism in general as well as for Confucius himself. Chu Hsi associated righteousness with the Principle of Nature (*T'ien-li*) and profit with the feelings of man, but later Neo-Confucianists strongly objected to his thus contrasting principle and feelings.

4:18. Confucius said, "In serving his parents, a son may gently remonstrate with them. When he sees that they are not inclined to listen to him, he should resume an attitude of reverence and not abandon his effort to serve them. He may feel worried, but does not complain."

4:19. Confucius said, "When his parents are alive, a son should not go far abroad; or if he does, he should let them know where he goes."

4:21. Confucius said, "A son should always keep in mind the age of his parents. It is an occasion for joy [that they are enjoying long life] and also an occasion for anxiety [that another year is gone]."

4:24. Confucius said, "The superior man wants to be slow in word but diligent in action."

5:11. Tzu-kung said, "What I do not want others to do to me, I do not want to do to them." Confucius said, "Ah Tz'u! That is beyond you."[62]

5:12. Tzu-kung said, "We can hear our Master's [views] on culture and its manifestation,[63] but we cannot hear his views on human nature[64] and the Way of Heaven [because these subjects are beyond the comprehension of most people]."

5:25. Yen Yüan[65] and Chi-lu[66] were in attendance. Confucius said, "Why don't you each tell me your ambition in life?" Tzu-lu said, "I wish to have a horse, a carriage, and a light fur coat[67] and share them with friends, and shall not regret if they are all worn out." Yen Yüan said, "I wish never to boast of my good qualities and never to brag about the trouble I have taken [for others]."[68] Tzu-lu said, "I wish to hear your ambition." Confucius said, "It is my ambition to comfort the old, to be faithful to friends, and to cherish the young."[69]

---

56. The Ch'ing viewpoint is best represented in Wang Nien-sun (1744–1832), *Kuang-ya shu-cheng* (Textual Commentary on the *Kuang-ya* Dictionary).
57. Chu Hsi, *Lun-yü chi-chu.* For discussion of *chung-shu,* see Appendix.
58. *I-shu* (Surviving Works), 21B:1b, in ECCS.
59. *Lun-yü cheng-i.* He is referring to *Analects,* 6:28.
60. See other positive versions in *Analects,* 14:45; *The Mean,* ch. 13; *Mencius,* 1A:7. The negative version is found in *Analects,* 5:11; 12:2; 15:23; in *The Mean,* ch. 13; and in the *Great Learning,* ch. 10.
61. See *Analects,* 2:14; 4:11, 16; 6:11; 7:36; 12:16; 13:23, 25, 26; 14:7, 24; 15:1, 20, 33; 17:4, 23.
62. Cf. *Great Learning,* ch. 10.
63. The term *wen-chang* can also mean literary heritage or simply the ancient Classics.
64. The word *hsing* (nature) is mentioned elsewhere in the *Analects* only once, in 17:2.
65. Confucius' favorite pupil, whose family name was Yen, private name Hui, and courtesy name Tzu-yüan (521–490 B.C.). He died at 32.
66. Tzu-lu.
67. The word "light" does not appear in the stone-engraved Classic of the T'ang dynasty and is probably a later addition.
68. Another interpretation: For his own moral effort.
69. This is Chu Hsi's interpretation. According to Hsing Ping, it would mean this: The old should be satisfied with me, friends should trust me, and the young should come to me.

5:27. Confucius said, "In every hamlet of ten families, there are always some people as loyal and faithful as myself, but none who love learning as much as I do."

6:5. Confucius said, "About Hui (Yen Yüan), for three months there would be nothing in his mind contrary to humanity. The others could (or can) attain to this for a day or a month at the most."[70]

Comment. On the basis of this saying alone, some philosophers have concluded that Yen Yüan was a mystic and that Confucius praised mysticism!

6:16. Confucius said, "When substance exceeds refinement (*wen*), one becomes rude. When refinement exceeds substance, one becomes urbane. It is only when one's substance and refinement are properly blended that he becomes a superior man."

6:17. Confucius said, "Man is born with uprightness. If one loses it he will be lucky if he escapes with his life."

Comment. Although the Confucian tradition in general holds that human nature is originally good, Confucius' own position is not clear. We have read that his doctrine of nature could not be heard,[71] and we shall read his statement that by nature men are alike.[72] But how they are alike is not clear. The saying here can be interpreted to mean that man can live throughout life because he is upright. This is the interpretation of Ma Jung (79–166),[73] which is followed by Wang Ch'ung (27–100?).[74] Most people followed Chu Hsi. He had the authority of Ch'eng Hao (Ch'eng Ming-tao, 1032–1085),[75] who echoed Cheng Hsüan's interpretation that Confucius said that man is *born* upright. This means that Confucius was not only the first one in Chinese philosophy to assume a definite position about human nature, but also the first to teach that human nature is *originally* good.

6:18. Confucius said, "To know it [learning or the Way] is not as good as to love it, and to love it is not as good as to take delight in it."

6:19. Confucius said, "To those who are above average, one may talk of the higher things, but may not do so to those who are below average."

6:20. Fan Ch'ih asked about wisdom. Confucius said, "Devote yourself earnestly to the duties due to men, and respect spiritual beings[76] but keep them at a distance. This may be called wisdom." Fan Ch'ih asked about humanity. Confucius said, "The man of humanity first of all considers what is difficult in the task and then thinks of success. Such a man may be called humane."

Comment. Many people have been puzzled by this passage, some even doubting the sincerity of Confucius' religious attitude—all quite unnecessarily. The passage means either "do not become improperly informal with spiritual beings,"[77] or "emphasize the way of man rather than the way of spirits."[78]

6:21. Confucius said, "The man of wisdom delights in water; the man of humanity delights in mountains. The man of wisdom is active; the man of humanity is tranquil. The man of wisdom enjoys happiness; the man of humanity enjoys long life."

Comment. In the Confucian ethical system, humanity and wisdom are like two wings, one supporting the other.[79] One is substance, the other is function. The dual emphasis has been maintained throughout history, especially in Tung Chung-shu (c. 179–c. 104 B.C.) and in a certain sense in K'ang Yu-wei (1858–1927).[80] Elsewhere, courage is added as the third virtue,[81] and Mencius grouped them with righteousness and propriety as the Four Beginnings.[82]

---

70. We don't know whether this was said before or after Yen Yüan's death.
71. *Analects,* 5:12.
72. *Analects,* 17:2.
73. Quoted by Ho Yen.
74. *Lun-heng* (Balanced Inquiries), ch. 5, SPPY, 2:2a. For English translation, see Forke, *Lun-heng,* vol. 1, p. 152.
75. See *Lun-yü chi-chu.*

---

76. Meaning especially ancestors.
77. According to *Lun-yü chi-chieh.*
78. According to Cheng Hsüan, Chu Hsi, and most commentators.
79. See also *Analects,* 4:2; 12:22; 15:32.
80. See below, ch. 14, E, sec. 3; ch. 39, sec. 3.
81. See *Analects,* 9:28; 14:30; *The Mean,* ch. 20.
82. *Mencius,* 2A:6; 6A:6.

6:23. Confucius said, "When a cornered vessel no longer has any corner, should it be called a cornered vessel? Should it?"

Comment. Name must correspond to actuality.[83]

6:25. Confucius said, "The superior man extensively studies literature (*wen*) and restrains himself with the rules of propriety. Thus he will not violate the Way."

6:26. When Confucius visited Nan-tzu (the wicked wife of Duke Ling of Wei, r. 533–490 B.C.) [in an attempt to influence her to persuade the duke to effect political reform], Tzu-lu was not pleased. Confucius swore an oath and said, "If I have said or done anything wrong, may Heaven forsake me! May Heaven forsake me!"[84]

6:28. Tzu-kung said, "If a ruler extensively confers benefit on the people and can bring salvation to all, what do you think of him? Would you call him a man of humanity?" Confucius said, "Why only a man of humanity? He is without doubt a sage. Even (sage-emperors) Yao and Shun fell short of it. A man of humanity, wishing to establish his own character, also establishes the character of others, and wishing to be prominent himself, also helps others to be prominent. To be able to judge others by what is near to ourselves may be called the method of realizing humanity."[85]

Comment. The Confucian golden rule in a nutshell.

7:1. Confucius said, "I transmit but do not create. I believe in and love the ancients. I venture to compare myself to our old P'eng."[86]

Comment. This is often cited to show that Confucius was not creative. We must not forget, however, that he "goes over the old so as to find out what is new."[87] Nor must we overlook the

fact that he was the first one to offer education to all.[88] Moreover, his concepts of the superior man and of Heaven were at least partly new.

7:2. Confucius said, "To remember silently [what I have learned], to learn untiringly, and to teach others without being wearied—that is just natural with me."

7:6. Confucius said, "Set your will on the Way. Have a firm grasp on virtue. Rely on humanity. Find recreation in the arts."

7:7. Confucius said, "There has never been anyone who came with as little a present as dried meat (for tuition)[89] that I have refused to teach him something."

7:8. Confucius said, "I do not enlighten those who are not eager to learn, nor arouse those who are not anxious to give an explanation themselves. If I have presented one corner of the square and they cannot come back to me with the other three, I should not go over the points again."

7:15. Confucius said, "With coarse rice to eat, with water to drink, and with a bent arm for a pillow, there is still joy. Wealth and honor obtained through unrighteousness are but floating clouds to me."

7:16. Confucius said, "Give me a few more years so that I can devote fifty years to study Change.[90] I may be free from great mistakes."

7:17. These were the things Confucius often[91] talked about—poetry, history, and the performance of the rules of propriety. All these were what he often talked about.

7:18. The Duke of She[92] asked Tzu-lu about Confucius, and Tzu-lu did not answer. Confucius said,

---

83. For the Confucian doctrine of the rectification of names, see below, comment on 13:3.
84. This episode took place when Confucius was 57.
85. See above comment on 4:15.
86. An official of the Shang dynasty (1751–1112 B.C.) who loved to recite old stories.
87. *Analects,* 2:11.

88. See Fung, *History of Chinese Philosophy,* vol. 1, pp. 46–49.
89. Cheng Hsüan's interpretation: From young men fifteen years old and upward. Cf. *Analects,* 15:38.
90. The traditional interpretation of the word *i* (change) is the *Book of Changes.* The ancient Lu version of the *Analects,* however, has *i* (then) instead of *i* (change). Some scholars have accepted this version, which reads ". . . to study, then I may be. . . ." Modern scholars prefer this reading because they do not believe that the *Book of Changes* existed at the time. However, the fact that Confucius was thinking of the *system* of Change instead of the *Book* should not be ruled out.
91. The word *ya* (often) was understood by Cheng Hsüan as standard, thus meaning that Confucius recited the Books of *Odes, History,* and *Rites* in correct pronunciation.
92. Magistrate of the district She in the state of Ch'u, who assumed the title of duke by usurpation.

"Why didn't you say that I am a person who for-gets his food when engaged in vigorous pursuit of something, is so happy as to forget his worries, and is not aware that old age is coming on?"[93]

7:19. Confucius said, "I am not one who was born with knowledge; I love ancient [teaching] and earnestly seek it."

7:20. Confucius never discussed strange phenomena, physical exploits, disorder, or spiritual beings.

7:22. Confucius said, "Heaven produced the virtue that is in me; what can Huan T'ui[94] do to me?"

7:24. Confucius taught four things: culture (*wen*), conduct, loyalty, and faithfulness.

7:26. Confucius fished with a line but not a net. While shooting he would not shoot a bird at rest.[95]

7:27. Confucius said, "There are those who act without knowing [what is right].[96] But I am not one of them. To hear much and select what is good and follow it, to see much and remember it, is the second type of knowledge (next to innate knowledge)."

---

93. According to *Shih chi* (Records of the Historian), PNP, 47:18a, Confucius was 62 when he made this remark. See Chavannes, trans., *Les mémoires historiques*, vol. 5, p. 361.
94. A military officer in the state of Sung who attempted to kill Confucius by felling a tree. Confucius was then 59 years old.
95. He would not take unfair advantage.
96. Other interpretations: Act without the necessity of knowledge; invent stories about history without real knowledge of it; write without knowledge.

7:29. Confucius said, "Is humanity far away? As soon as I want it, there it is right by me."

Comment. This is simply emphasizing the ever-present opportunity to do good. There is nothing mystical about it. The practice of humanity starts with oneself.

7:34. Confucius was very ill. Tzu-lu asked that prayer be offered. Confucius said, "Is there such a thing?" Tzu-lu replied, "There is. A Eulogy says, 'Pray to the spiritual beings above and below.'" Confucius said, "My prayer has been for a long time [that is, what counts is the life that one leads]."

7:37. Confucius is affable but dignified, austere but not harsh, polite but completely at ease.

Comment. The Confucian Mean in practice.

DISCUSSION QUESTIONS

1. What principles of good government can we derive from these teachings of Confucius?
2. How would you compare the Confucian version of the golden rule with the version found in the Judeo-Christian religious tradition?
3. How would you compare the Daoist and Confucian models of the morally virtuous individual? Which is more convincing to you? Why?
4. Do you agree with the Confucian emphasis on the duties of "filial piety" over almost all other duties? Why or why not?

48. Aristotle (384–322 B.C.E.)
Virtue and Happiness

After Plato, the Greek philosopher Aristotle is generally considered to have been the most influential individual in all of Western intellectual history. Born in ancient Chalcidice, he was the son of Nicomachus, the court physician to the king of Macedon. When he was about 17, Aristotle was sent to Athens to study at the school established by Plato, the Academy, and he stayed there for twenty years, until Plato's death in 347 B.C.E. After that he traveled to a variety of Mediterranean lands, until he accepted an appointment back in the Macedonian court to oversee the education of the king's

13-year-old son Alexander (one day to be known as Alexander the Great). He held that position for about three years and a few years later ended up in Athens again, where he started his own school, called the Lyceum.

Not surprisingly, Aristotle was very much influenced by twenty years of study with Plato, and like Plato, he wrote extensively on almost every topic that would have interested an intellectual of that era. Especially in his earlier career when, apparently, his views were Platonist in most respects, he also often used the dialogue form of written presentation. Although many of his writings have been lost over the ages, a huge body of his work has been preserved, variously edited, widely translated, and constantly argued about in one region of the world or another from the time of his death down to the present. The majority of Aristotle's writing shows a philosophical development away from Plato's "otherworldly" emphasis on the higher reality of the immaterial Forms and the corresponding unreality and devaluation of the material world. Aristotle arrived at a much more positive view of the things of "this world" and, in fact, created a philosophical system that relied quite a bit on an empirical investigative approach.

The reading consists of excerpts from his best-known work in moral philosophy, *Nicomachean Ethics* (presumably named after his father Nichomachus), in which Aristotle shares more assumptions with Plato concerning the moral life than is the case with their respective metaphysics and epistemologies. As was generally so in the ancient world, the relationship between moral character and right or wrong conduct is seen here as not only practically but also philosophically essential, and his analyses of human happiness, virtue, emotion, action, and community always function within this more holistic context.

QUESTIONS FOR CRITICAL READING

1. What is "happiness" for Aristotle, and how does he show that it is the "highest good" for humans?
2. What does Aristotle mean by, and how does he argue for, the conclusion that "the good of man is an activity of the soul in conformity with excellence or virtue"?
3. What is "virtue" and "vice" for humans, according to Aristotle, and what is the difference between "intellectual" and "moral" virtue?
4. In Aristotle's account, how do we become virtuous or vicious?
5. What does Aristotle mean by arguing that "virtue aims at the median"?

———

Let us return again to our investigation into the nature of the good which we are seeking. It is evidently something different in different actions and in each art: it is one thing in medicine, another in strategy, and another again in each of the other arts. What, then, is the good of each? Is it not that for the sake of which everything else is done? That means it is health in the case of medicine, victory in the case of strategy, a house in the case of building, a different thing in the case of different arts, and in all actions and choices it is the end. For it is for the sake of the end that all else is done. Thus, if there is some one end for all that we do, this would be the good attainable by action; if there are several ends, they will be the goods attainable by action.

Our argument has gradually progressed to the same point at which we were before, and we must try to clarify it still further. Since there are evidently several ends, and since we choose some of these—e.g., wealth, flutes, and instruments generally—as a means to something else, it is obvious that not all ends are final. The highest good, on the other hand, must be something final. Thus, if there is only one final end, this will be the good we are seeking; if there are several, it will be the most final and perfect of them. We call that which is pursued as an end in itself more final than an end which is pursued for the sake of something else; and what is never chosen as a means to something else we call more final than that which is chosen both as an end in itself and as a means to something else. What is always chosen as an end in itself and never as a means to something else is called final in an unqualified sense. This description seems to apply to happiness above all else: for we always choose happiness as an end in itself and never for the sake of something else. Honor, pleasure, intelligence, and all virtue we choose partly for themselves—for we would choose each of them even if no further advantage would accrue from them—but we also choose them partly for the sake of happiness, because we assume that it is through them that we will be happy. On the other hand, no one chooses happiness for the sake of honor, pleasure, and the like, nor as a means to anything at all.

We arrive at the same conclusion if we approach the question from the standpoint of self-sufficiency. For the final and perfect good seems to be self-sufficient. However, we define something as self-sufficient not by reference to the "self" alone. We do not mean a man who lives his life in isolation, but a man who also lives with parents, children, a wife, and friends and fellow citizens generally, since man is by nature a social and political being. But some limit must be set to these relationships; for if they are extended to include ancestors, descendants, and friends of friends, they will go on to infinity. However, this point must be reserved for investigation later. For the present we define as "self-sufficient" that which taken by itself makes life something desirable and deficient in nothing. It is happiness, in our opinion, which fits this description. Moreover, happiness is of all things the one most desirable, and it is not counted as one good thing among many others. But if it were counted as one among many others, it is obvious that the addition of even the least of the goods would make it more desirable; for the addition would produce an extra amount of good, and the greater amount of good is always more desirable than the lesser. We see then that happiness is something final and self-sufficient and the end of our actions.

To call happiness the highest good is perhaps a little trite, and a clearer account of what it is, is still required. Perhaps this is best done by first ascertaining the proper function of man. For just as the goodness and performance of a flute player, a sculptor, or any kind of expert, and generally of anyone who fulfills some function or performs some action, are thought to reside in his proper function, so the goodness and performance of man would seem to reside in whatever is his proper function. Is it then possible that while a carpenter and a shoemaker have their own proper functions and spheres of action, man as man has none, but was left by nature a good-for-nothing without a function? Should we not assume that just as the eye, the hand, the foot, and in general each part of the body clearly has its own proper function, so man too has some function over and above the functions of his parts? What can this function possibly be? Simply living? He shares that even with plants, but we are now looking for something peculiar to man. Accordingly, the life of nutrition and growth must be excluded. Next in line there is a life of sense perception. But this, too, man has in common with the horse, the ox, and every animal. There remains then an active life of the rational element. The rational element has two parts: one is rational in that it obeys the rule of reason, the other in that it possesses and conceives rational rules. Since the expression "life of the rational element" also

can be used in two senses, we must make it clear that we mean a life determined by the activity, as opposed to the mere possession, of the rational element. For the activity, it seems, has a greater claim to be the function of man.

The proper function of man, then, consists in an activity of the soul in conformity with a rational principle or, at least, not without it. In speaking of the proper function of a given individual we mean that it is the same in kind as the function of an individual who sets high standards for himself: the proper function of a harpist, for example, is the same as the function of a harpist who has set high standards for himself. The same applies to any and every group of individuals: the full attainment of excellence must be added to the mere function. In other words, the function of the harpist is to play the harp; the function of the harpist who has high standards is to play it well. On these assumptions, if we take the proper function of man to be a certain kind of life, and if this kind of life is an activity of the soul and consists in actions performed in conjunction with the rational element, and if a man of high standards is he who performs these actions well and properly, and if a function is well performed when it is performed in accordance with the excellence appropriate to it; we reach the conclusion that the good of man is an activity of the soul in conformity with excellence or virtue, and if there are several virtues, in conformity with the best and most complete.

But we must add "in a complete life." For one swallow does not make a spring, nor does one sunny day; similarly, one day or a short time does not make a man blessed and happy. . . .

The Psychological Foundations of the Virtues

Since happiness is a certain activity of the soul in conformity with perfect virtue, we must now examine what virtue or excellence is. For such an inquiry will perhaps better enable us to discover the nature of happiness. Moreover, the man who is truly concerned about politics seems to devote special attention to excellence, since it is his aim to make the citizens good and law-abiding. We have an example of this in the lawgivers of Crete and Sparta and in other great legislators. If an examination of virtue is part of politics, this question clearly fits into the pattern of our original plan.

There can be no doubt that the virtue which we have to study is human virtue. For the good which we have been seeking is a human good and the happiness a human happiness. By human virtue we do not mean the excellence of the body, but that of the soul, and we define happiness as an activity of the soul. If this is true, the student of politics must obviously have some knowledge of the workings of the soul, just as the man who is to heal eyes must know something about the whole body. In fact, knowledge is all the more important for the former, inasmuch as politics is better and more valuable than medicine, and cultivated physicians devote much time and trouble to gain knowledge about the body. Thus, the student of politics must study the soul, but he must do so with his own aim in view, and only to the extent that the objects of his inquiry demand: to go into it in greater detail would perhaps be more laborious than his purposes require.

Some things that are said about the soul in our less technical discussions are adequate enough to be used here, for instance, that the soul consists of two elements, one irrational and one rational. Whether these two elements are separate, like the parts of the body or any other divisible thing, or whether they are only logically separable though in reality indivisible, as convex and concave are in the circumference of a circle, is irrelevant for our present purposes.

Of the irrational element, again, one part seems to be common to all living things and vegetative in nature: I mean that part which is responsible for nurture and growth. We must assume that some such capacity of the soul exists in everything that takes nourishment, in the embryonic stage as well as when the organism is fully developed; for this makes more sense than to assume the existence of some different capacity at the latter stage. The excellence of this part of the soul is, therefore, shown to be common to all living things and is not exclusively human. This very part and this capacity seem to be most active in sleep. For in sleep the difference between a good man and a bad is least apparent—whence the saying that for half their lives the happy are no better off than the wretched. This is just what we would expect, for sleep is an inactivity of the soul in that it ceases to do things which cause it to be called good or bad. However, to a small extent some bodily movements do penetrate to the soul in sleep, and in this sense the dreams of honest men are better than those of average people. But enough of this subject: we may pass by the nutritive part, since it has no natural share in human excellence or virtue.

In addition to this, there seems to be another integral element of the soul which, though irrational, still does partake of reason in some way. In morally strong and morally weak men we praise the reason that guides them and the rational element of the soul, because it exhorts them to follow the right path and to do what is best. Yet we see in them also another natural strain different from the rational, which fights and resists the guidance of reason. The soul behaves in precisely the same manner as do the paralyzed limbs of the body. When we intend to move the limbs to the right, they turn to the left, and similarly, the impulses of morally weak persons turn in the direction opposite to that in which reason leads them. However, while the aberration of the body is visible, that of the soul is not. But perhaps we must accept it as a fact, nevertheless, that there is something in the soul besides the rational element, which opposes and reacts against it. In what way the two are distinct need not concern us here. But, as we have stated, it too seems to partake of reason; at any rate, in a morally strong man it accepts the leadership of reason, and is perhaps more obedient still in a self-controlled and courageous man, since in him everything is in harmony with the voice of reason.

Thus we see that the irrational element of the soul has two parts: the one is vegetative and has no share in reason at all, the other is the seat of the appetites and of desire in general and partakes of reason insofar as it complies with reason and accepts its leadership; it possesses reason in the sense that we say it is "reasonable" to accept the advice of a father and of friends, not in the sense that we have a "rational" understanding of mathematical propositions. That the irrational element can be persuaded by the rational is shown by the fact that admonition and all manner of rebuke and exhortation are possible. If it is correct to say that the appetitive part, too, has reason, it follows that the rational element of the soul has two subdivisions: the one possesses reason in the strict sense, contained within itself, and the other possesses reason in the sense that it listens to reason as one would listen to a father.

Virtue, too, is differentiated in line with this division of the soul. We call some virtues "intellectual" and others "moral": theoretical wisdom, understanding, and practical wisdom are intellectual virtues, generosity and self-control moral virtues. In speaking of a man's character, we do not describe him as wise or understanding, but as gentle or self-controlled; but we praise the wise man, too, for his characteristic, and praiseworthy characteristics are what we call virtues. . . .

1. Moral Virtue as the Result of Habits

Virtue, as we have seen, consists of two kinds, intellectual virtue and moral virtue. Intellectual virtue or excellence owes its origin and development chiefly to teaching, and for that reason requires experience and time. Moral virtue, on the other hand, is formed by habit, *ethos*, and its name, *ēthikē*, is therefore derived, by a slight variation, from *ethos*. This shows, too, that none of the moral virtues is implanted in us by nature, for nothing which exists by nature can be changed by habit. For example, it is impossible for a stone, which has a natural downward movement, to become habituated to moving upward, even if one should try ten thousand times to inculcate the habit by throwing it in the air; nor can fire be made to move downward, nor can the direction of any nature-given tendency be changed by habituation. Thus, the virtues are implanted in us neither by nature nor contrary to nature: we are by nature equipped with the ability to receive them, and habit brings this ability to completion and fulfillment.

Furthermore, of all the qualities with which we are endowed by nature, we are provided with the capacity first, and display the activity afterward. That this is true is shown by the senses: it is not by frequent seeing or frequent hearing that we acquired our senses, but on the contrary we first possess and then use them; we do not acquire them by use. The virtues, on the other hand, we acquire by first having put them into action, and the same is also true of the arts. For the things which we have to learn before we can do them we learn by doing: men become builders by building houses, and harpists by playing the harp. Similarly, we become just by the practice of just actions, self-controlled by exercising self-control, and courageous by performing acts of courage.

This is corroborated by what happens in states. Lawgivers make the citizens good by inculcating [good] habits in them, and this is the aim of every lawgiver; if he does not succeed in doing that, his legislation is a failure. It is in this that a good constitution differs from a bad one.

Moreover, the same causes and the same means that produce any excellence or virtue can also destroy it, and this is also true of every art. It is by playing the harp that men become both good and bad harpists, and correspondingly with builders and all the other craftsmen: a man who builds well will be a good builder, one who builds badly a bad one. For if this were not so, there would be no need for an instructor, but everybody would be born as a good or a bad craftsman. The same holds true of the virtues: in our transactions with other men it is by action that some become just and others unjust, and it is by acting in the face of danger and by developing the habit of feeling fear or confidence that some become brave men and others cowards. The same applies to the appetites and feelings of anger: by reacting in one way or in another to given circumstances some people become self-controlled and gentle, and others self-indulgent and short-tempered. In a word, characteristics develop from corresponding activities. For that reason, we must see to it that our activities are of a certain kind, since any variations in them will be reflected in our characteristics. Hence it is no small matter whether one habit or another is inculcated in us from early childhood; on the contrary, it makes a considerable difference, or, rather, all the difference.

2. Method in the Practical Sciences

The purpose of the present study is not, as it is in other inquiries, the attainment of theoretical knowledge: we are not conducting this inquiry in order to know what virtue is, but in order to become good, else there would be no advantage in studying it. For that reason, it becomes necessary to examine the problem of actions, and to ask how they are to be performed. For, as we have said, the actions determine what kind of characteristics are developed.

That we must act according to right reason is generally conceded and may be assumed as the basis of our discussion. We shall speak about it later and discuss what right reason is and examine its relation to the other virtues. But let us first agree that any discussion on matters of action cannot be more than an outline and is bound to lack precision; for as we stated at the outset, one can demand of a discussion only what the subject matter permits, and there are no fixed data in matters concerning action and questions of what is beneficial, any more than there are in matters of health. And if this is true of our general discussion, our treatment of particular problems will be even less precise, since these do not come under the head of any art which can be transmitted by precept, but the agent must consider on each different occasion what the situation demands, just as in medicine and in navigation. But although such is the kind of discussion in which we are engaged, we must do our best.

First of all, it must be observed that the nature of moral qualities is such that they are destroyed by defect and by excess. We see the same thing happen in the case of strength and of health, to illustrate, as we must, the invisible by means of visible examples: excess as well as deficiency of physical exercise destroys our strength, and similarly, too much and too little food and drink destroys our health; the proportionate amount, however, produces, increases, and preserves it. The same applies to self-control, courage, and the other virtues: the man who shuns and fears everything and never stands his ground becomes a coward, whereas a man who knows no fear at all and goes to meet every danger becomes reckless. Similarly, a man who revels in every pleasure and abstains from none becomes self-indulgent, while he who avoids every pleasure like a boor becomes what might be called insensitive. Thus we see that self-control and courage are destroyed by excess and by deficiency and are preserved by the mean.

Not only are the same actions which are responsible for and instrumental in the origin and development of the virtues also the causes and means of their destruction, but they will also be manifested in the active exercise of the virtues. We can see the truth of this in the case of other more visible qualities, e.g., strength. Strength is produced by consuming plenty of food and by enduring much hard work, and it is the strong man who is best able to do these things. The same is also true of the virtues: by abstaining from pleasures we become self-controlled, and once we are self-controlled we are best able to abstain from pleasures. So also with courage: by becoming habituated to despise and to endure terrors we become courageous, and once we have become courageous we will best be able to endure terror.

3. Pleasure and Pain as the Test of Virtue

An index to our characteristics is provided by the pleasure or pain which follows upon the tasks we have achieved. A man who abstains from bodily pleasures and enjoys doing so is self-controlled; if he finds abstinence troublesome, he is self-indulgent; a man who endures danger with joy, or at least without pain, is courageous; if he endures it with pain, he is a coward. For moral excellence is concerned with pleasure and pain; it is pleasure that makes us do base actions and pain that prevents us from doing noble actions. For that reason, as Plato says, men must be brought up from childhood to feel pleasure and pain at the proper things; for this is correct education.

Furthermore, since the virtues have to do with actions and emotions, and since pleasure and pain are a consequence of every emotion and of every action, it follows from this point of view, too, that virtue has to do with pleasure and pain. This is further indicated by the fact that punishment is inflicted by means of pain. For punishment is a kind of medical treatment and it is the nature of medical treatments to take effect through the introduction of the opposite of the disease. Again, as we said just now, every characteristic of the soul shows its true nature in its relation to and its concern with those factors which naturally make it better or worse. But it is through pleasures and pains that men are corrupted, i.e., through pursuing and avoiding pleasures and pains either of the wrong kind or at the wrong time or in the wrong manner, or by going wrong in some other definable respect. For that reason some people define the virtues as states of freedom from emotion and of quietude. However, they make the mistake of using these terms absolutely and without adding such qualifications as "in the right manner," "at the right or wrong time," and so forth. We may, therefore, assume as the basis of our discussion that virtue, being concerned with pleasure and pain in the way we have described, makes us act in the best way in matters involving pleasure and pain, and that vice does the opposite.

The following considerations may further illustrate that virtue is concerned with pleasure and pain. There are three factors that determine choice and three that determine avoidance: the noble, the beneficial, and the pleasurable, on the one hand, and on the other their opposites: the base, the harmful, and the painful. Now a good man will go right and a bad man will go wrong when any of these, and especially when pleasure is involved. For pleasure is not only common to man and the animals, but also accompanies all objects of choice: in fact, the noble and the beneficial seem pleasant to us. Moreover, a love of pleasure has grown up with all of us from infancy. Therefore, this emotion has come to be ingrained in our lives and is difficult to erase. Even in our actions we use, to a greater or smaller extent, pleasure and pain as a criterion. For this reason, this entire study is necessarily concerned with pleasure and pain; for it is not unimportant for our actions whether we feel joy and pain in the right or the wrong way. Again, it is harder to fight against pleasure than against anger, as Heraclitus says; and both virtue and art are always concerned with what is harder, for success is better when it is hard to achieve. Thus, for this reason also, every study both of virtue and of politics must deal with pleasures and pains, for if a man has the right attitude to them, he will be good; if the wrong attitude, he will be bad.

We have now established that virtue or excellence is concerned with pleasures and pains; that the actions which produce it also develop it and, if differently performed, destroy it; and that it actualizes itself fully in those activities to which it owes its origin.

4. Virtuous Action and Virtue

However, the question may be raised what we mean by saying that men become just by performing just actions and self-controlled by practicing self-control.

For if they perform just actions and exercise self-control, they are already just and self-controlled, in the same way as they are literate and musical if they write correctly and practice music.

But is this objection really valid, even as regards the arts? No, for it is possible for a man to write a piece correctly by chance or at the prompting of another: but he will be literate only if he produces a piece of writing in a literate way, and that means doing it in accordance with the skill of literate composition which he has in himself.

Moreover, the factors involved in the arts and in the virtues are not the same. In the arts, excellence lies in the result itself, so that it is sufficient if it is of a certain kind. But in the case of the virtues an act is not performed justly or with self-control if the act itself is of a certain kind, but only if in addition the agent has certain characteristics as he performs it: first of all, he must know what he is doing; secondly, he must choose to act the way he does, and he must choose it for its own sake; and in the third place, the act must spring from a firm and unchangeable character. With the exception of knowing what one is about, these considerations do not enter into the mastery of the arts; for the mastery of the virtues, however, knowledge is of little or no importance, whereas the other two conditions count not for a little but are all-decisive, since repeated acts of justice and self-control result in the possession of these virtues. In other words, acts are called just and self-controlled when they are the kind of acts which a just or self-controlled man would perform; but the just and self-controlled man is not he who performs these acts, but he who also performs them in the way just and self-controlled men do.

Thus our assertion that a man becomes just by performing just acts and self-controlled by performing acts of self-control is correct; without performing them, nobody could even be on the way to becoming good. Yet most men do not perform such acts, but by taking refuge in argument they think that they are engaged in philosophy and that they will become good in this way. In so doing, they act like sick men who listen attentively to what the doctor says, but fail to do any of the things he prescribes. That kind of philosophical activity will not bring health to the soul any more than this sort of treatment will produce a healthy body.

5. Virtue Defined: The Genus

The next point to consider is the definition of virtue or excellence. As there are three kinds of things found in the soul: (1) emotions, (2) capacities, and (3) characteristics, virtue must be one of these. By "emotions" I mean appetite, anger, fear, confidence, envy, joy, affection, hatred, longing, emulation, pity, and in general anything that is followed by pleasure or pain; by "capacities" I mean that by virtue of which we are said to be affected by these emotions, for example, the capacity which enables us to feel anger, pain, or pity; and by "characteristics" I mean the condition, either good or bad, in which we are, in relation to the emotions: for example, our condition in relation to anger is bad, if our anger is too violent or not violent enough, but if it is moderate, our condition is good; and similarly with our condition in relation to the other emotions.

Now the virtues and vices cannot be emotions, because we are not called good or bad on the basis of our emotions, but on the basis of our virtues and vices. Also, we are neither praised nor blamed for our emotions: a man does not receive praise for being frightened or angry, nor blame for being angry pure and simple, but for being angry in a certain way. Yet we are praised or blamed for our virtues and vices. Furthermore, no choice is involved when we experience anger or fear, while the virtues are some kind of choice or at least involve choice. Moreover, with regard to our emotions we are said to be "moved," but with regard to our virtues and vices we are not said to be "moved" but to be "disposed" in a certain way.

For the same reason, the virtues cannot be capacities, either, for we are neither called good or bad nor praised or blamed simply because we are capable of being affected. Further, our capacities have been given to us by nature, but we do not by nature develop into good or bad men. We have discussed this subject before. Thus, if the virtues are neither emotions nor capacities, the only remaining alternative is that they are characteristics. So much for the genus of virtue.

6. Virtue Defined: The Differentia

It is not sufficient, however, merely to define virtue in general terms as a characteristic: we must also specify what kind of characteristic it is. It must, then, be remarked that every virtue or excellence (1) renders good the thing itself of which it is the excellence, and (2) causes it to perform its function well. For example, the excellence of the eye makes both the eye and its function good, for good sight is due to the excellence of the eye. Likewise, the excellence of a horse makes it both good as a horse and good at running, at carrying its rider, and at facing the enemy. Now, if this is true of all things, the virtue or excellence of man, too, will be a characteristic which makes him a good man, and which causes him to perform his own function well. To some extent we have already stated how this will be true; the rest will become clear if we study what the nature of virtue is.

Of every continuous entity that is divisible into parts it is possible to take the larger, the smaller, or an equal part, and these parts may be larger, smaller, or equal either in relation to the entity itself, or in relation to us. The "equal" part is something median between excess and deficiency. By the median of an entity I understand a point equidistant from both extremes, and this point is one and the same for everybody. By the median relative to us I understand an amount neither too large nor too small, and this is neither one nor the same for everybody. To take an example: if ten is many and two is few, six is taken as the median in relation to the entity, for it exceeds and is exceeded by the same amount, and is thus the median in terms of arithmetical proportion. But the median relative to us cannot be determined in this manner: if ten pounds of food is much for a man to eat and two pounds little, it does not follow that the trainer will prescribe six pounds, for this may in turn be much or little for him to eat; it may be little for Milo and much for someone who has just begun to take up athletics. The same applies to running and wrestling. Thus we see that an expert in any field avoids excess and deficiency, but seeks the median and chooses it—not the median of the object but the median relative to us.

If this, then, is the way in which every science perfects its work, by looking to the median and by bringing its work up to that point—and this is the reason why it is usually said of a successful piece of work that it is impossible to detract from it or to add to it, the implication being that excess and deficiency destroy success while the mean safeguards it (good craftsmen, we say, look toward this standard in the performance of their work)—and if virtue, like nature, is more precise and better than any art, we must conclude that virtue aims at the median. I am referring to moral virtue: for it is moral virtue that is concerned with emotions and actions, and it is in emotions and actions that excess, deficiency, and the median are found. Thus we can experience fear, confidence, desire, anger, pity, and generally any kind of pleasure and pain either too much or too little, and in either case not properly. But to experience all this at the right time, toward the right objects, toward the right people, for the right reason, and in the right manner—that is the median and the best course, the course that is a mark of virtue.

Similarly, excess, deficiency, and the median can also be found in actions. Now virtue is concerned with emotions and actions; and in emotions and actions excess and deficiency miss the mark, whereas the median is praised and constitutes success. But both praise and success are signs of virtue or excellence. Consequently, virtue is a mean in the sense that it aims at the median. This is corroborated by the fact that there are many ways of going wrong, but only one way which is right—for evil belongs to the indeterminate, as the Pythagoreans imagined, but good to the determinate. This, by the way, is also the reason why the one is easy and the other hard: it is easy to miss the target but hard to hit it. Here, then, is an additional proof that excess and deficiency characterize vice, while the mean characterizes virtue: for "bad men have many ways, good men but one."

We may thus conclude that virtue or excellence is a characteristic involving choice, and that it consists in observing the mean relative to us, a mean which is defined by a rational principle, such as a man of practical wisdom would use to determine it. It is the mean by reference to two vices: the one of excess and the other of deficiency. It is, moreover, a mean because some vices exceed and others fall short of what is required in emotion and in action, whereas virtue finds and chooses the median. Hence, in respect of its essence and the definition of its essential nature virtue is

a mean, but in regard to goodness and excellence it is an extreme.

Not every action nor every emotion admits of a mean. There are some actions and emotions whose very names connote baseness, e.g., spite, shamelessness, envy; and among actions, adultery, theft, and murder. These and similar emotions and actions imply by their very names that they are bad; it is not their excess nor their deficiency which is called bad. It is, therefore, impossible ever to do right in performing them: to perform them is always to do wrong. In cases of this sort, let us say adultery, rightness and wrongness do not depend on committing it with the right woman at the right time and in the right manner, but the mere fact of committing such action at all is to do wrong. It would be just as absurd to suppose that there is a mean, an excess, and a deficiency in an unjust or a cowardly or a self-indulgent act. For if there were, we would have a mean of excess and a mean of deficiency, and an excess of excess and a deficiency of deficiency. Just as there cannot be an excess and a deficiency of self-control and courage—because the intermediate is, in a sense, an extreme—so there cannot be a mean, excess, and deficiency in their respective opposites: their opposites are wrong regardless of how they are performed; for, in general, there is no such thing as the mean of an excess or a deficiency, or the excess and deficiency of a mean.

DISCUSSION QUESTIONS

1. How do you define "happiness," and do you agree with Aristotle that it is the highest human good? Why or why not?

2. Aristotle identifies a number of specific moral virtues and vices. Do you think these character traits should still be considered important in contemporary society? Why or why not?

3. How would Aristotle explain virtuous people doing something immoral, and vicious ("bad") people sometimes doing the right thing?

4. How would Aristotle and Laozi be similar or different in their treatment of the role of reason in human character development? Which perspective makes more sense to you? Why?

49. Mary Wollstonecraft (1759–1797)
From *Vindication of the Rights of Woman*

Mary Wollstonecraft was an English philosopher born into a lower middle-class farming family. Her lack of access to formal academic study was partly due to lack of money and partly due to the customary exclusion of women from most educational opportunities in eighteenth-century Europe. She was as a result self-educated, and in her prolific writing during her short life she regularly returned to the theme of the need for radical change in the social support for and content of education for girls and women of all economic classes. She died at 38 from complications of giving birth to her second child, Mary, who herself would grow up to write the famous gothic novel *Frankenstein* and become the second wife of the poet Percy Bysshe Shelley.

The selection consists of excerpts from the book for which Wollstonecraft is most remembered today, and for which she was widely condemned and vilified in her own time. Contemporary readers may find it difficult to understand the hostility she generated when she published, in 1792, the opinion that rational consistency requires that the doctrine of human equality and equal rights be applied to the whole human species and not just half of it. But it was a radical and vigorously resisted idea at the time, even by many intellectuals who claimed to be enemies of all traditional, arbitrary authority and inequality and who saw, in the American and French revolutions, the dawning of a new age of rational social organization. In the excerpts here Wollstonecraft addresses one of the most often used traditional arguments against granting women equal rights in society—that they are by nature incapable of exercising such rights. Her emphasis on moral character, and the necessity of an educational system that would develop in males and females the human capacities for virtue, knowledge, and reason if society is to progress, is in direct response to this kind of defense of traditional gender hierarchy.

QUESTIONS FOR CRITICAL READING

1. How does Wollstonecraft characterize human "progress," and what does equal treatment of the sexes have to do with it?

2. In arguing for equal natural rights for women and men, how does Wollstonecraft refute the appeal to tradition?
3. According to Wollstonecraft, what is the relationship between virtue, knowledge, and reason, and the relationship between vice, ignorance, and oppression?
4. What religious reasoning does Wollstonecraft use to strengthen her case?
5. How does Wollstonecraft compare generally the moral character of the wealthy and of women in European society, and what are her recommendations for change in the moral education of both?

TERMS TO NOTE

witling: Someone who considers himself or herself to be witty.

sagacity: Wisdom or demonstrating insight.

brutes: Traditional European term for nonhuman animals, distinguished from humans by their assumed lack of reason and thus morality.

voluptuary: Here, someone devoted to sensual pleasure.

factitious: Artificial, forced, or unnatural.

sexual virtues: In this context, gender-specific virtues.

libertine: In this context, a person without moral restraint, especially in sexual relations.

dissenter: Here, one who is publicly nonconformist in matters of religion or politics.

To M. Talleyrand-Périgord, Late Bishop of Autun

SIR,—Having read with great pleasure a pamphlet which you have lately published, I dedicate this volume to you—the first dedication that I have ever written, to induce you to read it with attention; and, because I think that you will understand me, which I do not suppose many pert witlings will, who may ridicule the arguments they are unable to answer. But, sir,

I carry my respect for your understanding still farther; so far that I am confident you will not throw my work aside, and hastily conclude that I am in the wrong, because you did not view the subject in the same light yourself. And, pardon my frankness, but I must observe, that you treated it in too cursory a manner, contented to consider it as it had been considered formerly, when the rights of man, not to advert to woman, were trampled on as chimerical—I call upon you, therefore, now to weigh what I have advanced respecting the rights of woman and national education; and I call with the firm tone of humanity, for my arguments, sir, are dictated by a disinterested spirit—I plead for my sex, not for myself. Independence I have long considered as the grand blessing of life, the basis of every virtue; and independence I will ever secure by contracting my wants, though I were to live on a barren heath.

It is then an affection for the whole human race that makes my pen dart rapidly along to support what I believe to be the cause of virtue; and the same motive leads me earnestly to wish to see woman placed in a station in which she would advance, instead of retarding, the progress of those glorious principles that give a substance to morality. My opinion, indeed, respecting the rights and duties of woman seems to flow so naturally from these simple principles, that I think it scarcely possible but that some of the enlarged minds who formed your admirable constitution will coincide with me.

In France there is undoubtedly a more general diffusion of knowledge than in any part of the European world, and I attribute it, in a great measure, to the social intercourse which has long subsisted between the sexes. It is true—I utter my sentiments with freedom—that in France the very essence of sensuality has been extracted to regale the voluptuary, and a kind of sentimental lust has prevailed, which, together with the system of duplicity that the whole tenor of their political and civil government taught, have given a sinister sort of sagacity to the French character, properly termed *finesse*, from which naturally flow a polish of manners that injures the substance by hunting sincerity out of society. And modesty, the fairest garb of virtue! has been more grossly insulted in France than even in England, till their women have treated as *prudish* that attention to decency which brutes instinctively observe.

Manners and morals are so nearly allied that they have often been confounded; but, although the former should only be the natural reflection of the latter, yet, when various causes have produced factitious and corrupt manners, which are very early caught, morality becomes an empty name. The personal reserve, and sacred respect for cleanliness and delicacy in domestic life, which French women almost despise, are the graceful pillars of modesty; but, far from despising them, if the pure flame of patriotism have reached their bosoms, they should labour to improve the morals of their fellow-citizens, by teaching men, not only to respect modesty in women, but to acquire it themselves, as the only way to merit their esteem.

Contending for the rights of woman, my main argument is built on this simple principle, that if she be not prepared by education to become the companion of man, she will stop the progress of knowledge and virtue; for truth must be common to all, or it will be inefficacious with respect to its influence on general practice. And how can woman be expected to cooperate unless she knows why she ought to be virtuous? unless freedom strengthens her reason till she comprehends her duty, and see in what manner it is connected with her real good. If children are to be educated to understand the true principle of patriotism, their mother must be a patriot; and the love of mankind, from which an orderly train of virtues spring, can only be produced by considering the moral and civil interest of mankind; but the education and situation of woman at present shuts her out from such investigations.

In this work I have produced many arguments, which to me were conclusive, to prove that the prevailing notion respecting a sexual character was subversive of morality, and I have contended, that to render the human body and mind more perfect, chastity must more universally prevail, and that chastity will never be respected in the male world till the person of a woman is not, as it were, idolized, when little virtue or sense embellish it with the grand traces of mental beauty, or the interesting simplicity of affection.

Consider, sir, dispassionately these observations, for a glimpse of this truth seemed to open before you when you observed, 'that to see one-half of the human race excluded by the other from all participation of government was a political phenomenon that, according to abstract principles, it was impossible to explain'. If so, on what does your constitution rest? If the abstract rights of man will bear discussion and explanation, those of woman, by a parity of reasoning, will not shrink from the same test; though a different opinion prevails in this country, built on the very arguments which you use to justify the oppression of woman—prescription.

Consider—I address you as a legislator—whether, when men contend for their freedom, and to be allowed to judge for themselves respecting their own happiness, it be not inconsistent and unjust to subjugate women, even though you firmly believe that you are acting in the manner best calculated to promote their happiness? Who made man the exclusive judge, if woman partake with him of the gift of reason?

In this style argue tyrants of every denomination, from the weak king to the weak father of a family; they are all eager to crush reason, yet always assert that they usurp its throne only to be useful. Do you not act a similar part when you *force* all women, by denying them civil and political rights, to remain immured in their families groping in the dark? for surely, sir, you will not assert that a duty can be binding which is not founded on reason? If, indeed, this be their destination, arguments may be drawn from reason; and thus augustly supported, the more understanding women acquire, the more they will be attached to their duty—comprehending it—for unless they comprehend it, unless their morals be fixed on the same immutable principle as those of man, no authority can make them discharge it in a virtuous manner. They may be convenient slaves, but slavery will have its constant effect, degrading the master and the abject dependent.

But if women are to be excluded, without having a voice, from a participation of the natural rights of mankind, prove first, to ward off the charge of injustice and inconsistency, that they want reason, else this flaw in your NEW CONSTITUTION will ever show that man must, in some shape, act like a tyrant, and tyranny, in whatever part of society it rears its brazen front, will ever undermine morality.

I have repeatedly asserted, and produced what appeared to me irrefragable arguments drawn from matters of fact to prove my assertion, that women cannot by force be confined to domestic concerns; for

they will, however ignorant, intermeddle with more weighty affairs, neglecting private duties only to disturb, by cunning tricks, the orderly plans of reason which rise above their comprehension.

Besides, whilst they are only made to acquire personal accomplishments, men will seek for pleasure in variety, and faithless husbands will make faithless wives; such ignorant beings, indeed, will be very excusable when, not taught to respect public good, nor allowed any civil rights, they attempt to do themselves justice by retaliation.

The box of mischief thus opened in society, what is to preserve private virtue, the only security of public freedom and universal happiness?

Let there be then no coercion *established* in society, and the common law of gravity prevailing, the sexes will fall into their proper places. And now that more equitable laws are forming your citizens, marriage may become more sacred; your young men may choose wives from motives of affection, and your maidens allow love to root out vanity.

The father of a family will not then weaken his constitution and debase his sentiments by visiting the harlot, nor forget, in obeying the call of appetite, the purpose for which it was implanted. And the mother will not neglect her children to practise the arts of coquetry, when sense and modesty secure her the friendship of her husband.

But, till men become attentive to the duty of a father, it is vain to expect women to spend that time in their nursery which they, 'wise in their generation', choose to spend at their glass; for this exertion of cunning is only an instinct of nature to enable them to obtain indirectly a little of that power of which they are unjustly denied a share; for, if women are not permitted to enjoy legitimate rights, they will render both men and themselves vicious to obtain illicit privileges.

I wish, sir, to set some investigations of this kind afloat in France; and should they lead to a confirmation of my principles when your constitution is revised, the Rights of Woman may be respected, if it be fully proved that reason calls for this respect, and loudly demands JUSTICE for one-half of the human race.

I am, Sir,
Yours respectfully,
M.W.

. . .

I wish to sum up what I have said in a few words, for I here throw down my gauntlet, and deny the existence of sexual virtues, not excepting modesty. For man and woman, truth, if I understand the meaning of the word, must be the same; yet the fanciful female character, so prettily drawn by poets and novelists, demanding the sacrifice of truth and sincerity, virtue becomes a relative idea, having no other foundation than utility, and of that utility men pretend arbitrarily to judge, shaping it to their own convenience.

Women, I allow, may have different duties to fulfil; but they are *human* duties, and the principles that should regulate the discharge of them, I sturdily maintain, must be the same.

To become respectable, the exercise of their understanding is necessary, there is no other foundation for independence of character; I mean explicitly to say that they must only bow to the authority of reason, instead of being the *modest* slaves of opinion.

In the superior ranks of life how seldom do we meet with a man of superior abilities, or even common acquirements? The reason appears to me clear, the state they are born in was an unnatural one. The human character has ever been formed by the employments the individual, or class, pursues; and if the faculties are not sharpened by necessity, they must remain obtuse. The argument may fairly be extended to women; for, seldom occupied by serious business, the pursuit of pleasure gives that insignificancy to their character which renders the society of the *great* so insipid. The same want of firmness, produced by a similar cause, forces them both to fly from themselves to noisy pleasures, and artificial passions, till vanity takes place of every social affection, and the characteristics of humanity can scarcely be discerned. Such are the blessings of civil governments, as they are at present organized, that wealth and female softness equally tend to debase mankind, and are produced by the same cause; but allowing women to be rational creatures, they should be incited to acquire virtues which they may call their own, for how can a rational being be ennobled by anything that is not obtained by its *own* exertions? . . .

The stamen of immortality, if I may be allowed the phrase, is the perfectibility of human reason; for, were man created perfect, or did a flood of knowledge break in upon him, when he arrived at maturity, that precluded error, I should doubt whether his existence would be continued after the dissolution of the body. But, in the present state of things, every difficulty in morals that escapes from human discussion, and equally baffles the investigation of profound thinking, and the lightning glance of genius, is an argument on which I build my belief of the immortality of the soul. Reason is, consequentially, the simple power of improvement; or, more properly speaking, of discerning truth. Every individual is in this respect a world in itself. More or less may be conspicuous in one being than another; but the nature of reason must be the same in all, if it be an emanation of divinity, the tie that connects the creature with the Creator; for, can that soul be stamped with the heavenly image, that is not perfected by the exercise of its own reason?[1] Yet outwardly ornamented with elaborate care, and so adorned to delight man, 'that with honour he may love',[2] the soul of woman is not allowed to have this distinction, and man, ever placed between her and reason, she is always represented as only created to see through a gross medium, and to take things on trust. But dismissing these fanciful theories, and considering woman as a whole, let it be what it will, instead of a part of man, the inquiry is whether she have reason or not. If she have, which, for a moment, I will take for granted, she was not created merely to be the solace of man, and the sexual should not destroy the human character.

Into this error men have, probably, been led by viewing education in a false light; not considering it as the first step to form a being advancing gradually towards perfection[3]; but only as a preparation for life. On this sensual error, for I must call it so, has the false system of female manners been reared, which robs the whole sex of its dignity, and classes the brown and fair with the smiling flowers that only adorn the land. This has ever been the language of men, and the fear of departing from a supposed sexual character, has made even women of superior sense adopt the same

---

1. 'The brutes,' says Lord Monboddo, 'remain in the state in which nature has placed them, except in so far as their natural instinct is improved by the culture *we* bestow upon them.'
2. *Vide* Milton.
3. This word is not strictly just, but I cannot find a better.

sentiments.[4] Thus understanding, strictly speaking, has been denied to woman; and instinct, sublimated into wit and cunning, for the purposes of life, has been substituted in its stead.

The power of generalizing ideas, of drawing comprehensive conclusions from individual observations, is the only acquirement, for an immortal being, that really deserves the name of knowledge. Merely to observe, without endeavouring to account for anything, may (in a very incomplete manner) serve as the common sense of life; but where is the store laid up that is to clothe the soul when it leaves the body?

This power has not only been denied to women; but writers have insisted that it is inconsistent, with a few exceptions, with their sexual character. Let men prove this, and I shall grant that woman only exists for man. I must, however, previously remark, that the power of generalizing ideas, to any great extent, is not very common amongst men or women. But this exercise is the true cultivation of the understanding; and everything conspires to render the cultivation of the understanding more difficult in the female than the male world.

I am naturally led by this assertion to the main subject of the present chapter, and shall now attempt to point out some of the causes that degrade the sex, and prevent women from generalizing their observations.

I shall not go back to the remote annals of antiquity to trace the history of woman; it is sufficient to allow that she has always been either a slave or a despot, and to remark that each of these situations equally retards the progress of reason. The grand source of female folly and vice has ever appeared to me to arise from narrowness of mind; and the very constitution of civil governments has put almost insuperable obstacles in the way to prevent the cultivation of the female understanding; yet virtue can be built on no other foundation. The same obstacles are thrown in the way of the rich, and the same consequences ensue.

Necessity has been proverbially termed the mother of invention; the aphorism may be extended to virtue. It is an acquirement, and an acquirement to which pleasure must be sacrificed; and who sacrifices pleasure when it is within the grasp, whose mind has not been opened and strengthened by adversity, or the pursuit of knowledge goaded on by necessity? Happy is it when people have the cares of life to struggle with, for these struggles prevent their becoming a prey to enervating vices, merely from idleness. But if from their birth men and women be placed in a torrid zone, with the meridian sun of pleasure darting directly upon them, how can they sufficiently brace their minds to discharge the duties of life, or even to relish the affections that carry them out of themselves?

Pleasure is the business of woman's life, according to the present modification of society; and while it continues to be so, little can be expected from such weak beings. Inheriting in a lineal descent from the first fair defect in nature—the sovereignty of beauty—they have, to maintain their power, resigned the natural rights which the exercise of reason might have procured them, and chosen rather to be short-lived queens than labour to obtain the sober pleasures that arise from equality. Exalted by their inferiority (this sounds like a contradiction), they constantly demand homage as women, though experience should teach them that the men who pride themselves upon paying this arbitrary insolent respect to the sex, with the most scrupulous exactness, are most inclined to tyrannize over, and despise the very weakness they cherish. . . .

---

4.   'Pleasure's the portion of th' *inferior* kind;
         But glory, virtue, Heaven for *man* designed.'
      After writing these lines, how could Mrs Barbauld write the following ignoble comparison?

      'TO A LADY WITH SOME PAINTED FLOWERS

      'Flowers to the fair: to you these flowers I bring,
      And strive to greet you with an earlier spring.
      Flowers, SWEET, *and gay, and* DELICATE LIKE YOU;
      Emblems of innocence, and beauty too.
      With flowers the Graces bind their yellow hair
      And flowery wreaths consenting lovers wear.
      Flowers the sole luxury which Nature knew,
      In Eden's pure and guiltless garden grew.
      To loftier forms are rougher tasks assign'd;
      The sheltering oak resists the stormy wind,
      The tougher yew repels invading foes,
      And the tall pine for future navies grows;

      But this soft family, to cares unknown,
      Were born for pleasure and delights ALONE.
      Gay without toil, and lovely without art,
      They spring to CHEER *the sense, and* GLAD *the heart.*
      Nor blush, my fair, to own you copy these;
      Your BEST, *your* SWEETEST *empire is*—TO PLEASE.'

   So, the men tell us; but virtue, says reason, must be acquired by *rough* toils, and useful struggles with worldly *cares.*

It is not necessary to inform the sagacious reader, now I enter on my concluding reflections, that the discussion of this subject merely consists in opening a few simple principles, and clearing away the rubbish which obscured them. But, as all readers are not sagacious, I must be allowed to add some explanatory remarks to bring the subject home to reason—to that sluggish reason, which supinely takes opinions on trust, and obstinately supports them to spare itself the labour of thinking.

Moralists have unanimously agreed, that unless virtue be nursed by liberty, it will never attain due strength—and what they say of man I extend to mankind, insisting that in all cases morals must be fixed on immutable principles; and, that the being cannot be termed rational or virtuous, who obeys any authority, but that of reason.

To render women truly useful members of society, I argue that they should be led, by having their understandings cultivated on a large scale, to acquire a rational affection for their country, founded on knowledge, because it is obvious that we are little interested about what we do not understand. And to render this general knowledge of due importance, I have endeavoured to show that private duties are never properly fulfilled unless the understanding enlarges the heart; and that public virtue is only an aggregate of private. But, the distinctions established in society undermine both, by beating out the solid gold of virtue, till it becomes only the tinsel-covering of vice; for whilst wealth renders a man more respectable than virtue, wealth will be sought before virtue; and, whilst women's persons are caressed, when a childish simper shows an absence of mind—the mind will lie fallow. Yet, true voluptuousness must proceed from the mind—for what can equal the sensations produced by mutual affection, supported by mutual respect? What are the cold, or feverish caresses of appetite, but sin embracing death, compared with the modest overflowings of a pure heart and exalted imagination? Yes, let me tell the libertine of fancy when he despises understanding in woman—that the mind, which he disregards, gives life to the enthusiastic affection from which rapture, short-lived as it is, alone can blow! And, that, without virtue, a sexual attachment must expire, like a tallow candle in the socket, creating intolerable disgust. To prove this, I need only observe,

that men who have wasted a great part of their lives with women, and with whom they have sought for pleasure with eager thirst, entertain the meanest opinion of the sex. Virtue, true refiner of joy!—if foolish men were to fright thee from earth, in order to give loose to all their appetites without a check—some sensual weight of taste would scale the heavens to invite thee back, to give a zest to pleasure!

That women at present are by ignorance rendered foolish or vicious is, I think, not to be disputed; and, that the most salutary effects tending to improve mankind might be expected from a REVOLUTION in female manners, appears, at least, with a face of probability, to rise out of the observation. For as marriage has been termed the parent of those endearing charities which draw man from the brutal herd, the corrupting intercourse that wealth, idleness, and folly, produce between the sexes, is more universally injurious to morality than all the other vices of mankind collectively considered. To adulterous lust the most sacred duties are sacrificed, because before marriage, men, by a promiscuous intimacy with women, learned to consider love as a selfish gratification—learned to separate it not only from esteem, but from the affection merely built on habit, which mixes a little humanity with it. Justice and friendship are also set at defiance, and that purity of taste is vitiated which would naturally lead a man to relish an artless display of affection rather than affected airs. But that noble simplicity of affection, which dares to appear unadorned, has few attractions for the libertine, though it be the charm, which by cementing the matrimonial tie, secures to the pledges of a warmer passion the necessary parental attention; for children will never be properly educated till friendship subsists between parents. Virtue flies from a house divided against itself—and a whole legion of devils take up their residence there.

The affection of husbands and wives cannot be pure when they have so few sentiments in common, and when so little confidence is established at home, as must be the case when their pursuits are so different. That intimacy from which tenderness should flow, will not, cannot subsist between the vicious.

Contending, therefore, that the sexual distinction which men have so warmly insisted upon, is arbitrary, I have dwelt on an observation, that several sensible men, with whom I have conversed on the subject, allowed to be well founded; and it is simply this, that the little chastity to be found amongst men, and consequent disregard of modesty, tend to degrade both sexes; and further, that the modesty of women, characterized as such, will often be only the artful veil of wantonness instead of being the natural reflection of purity, till modesty be universally respected.

From the tyranny of man, I firmly believe, the greater number of female follies proceed; and the cunning, which I allow makes at present a part of their character, I likewise have repeatedly endeavoured to prove, is produced by oppression.

Were not dissenters, for instance, a class of people, with strict truth, characterized as cunning? And may I not lay some stress on this fact to prove, that when any power but reason curbs the free spirit of man, dissimulation is practised, and the various shifts of art are naturally called forth? Great attention to decorum, which was carried to a degree of scrupulosity, and all that puerile bustle about trifles and consequential solemnity, which Butler's caricature of a dissenter brings before the imagination, shaped their persons as well as their minds in the mould of prim littleness. I speak collectively, for I know how many ornaments in human nature have been enrolled amongst sectaries; yet, I assert, that the same narrow prejudice for their sect, which women have for their families, prevailed in the dissenting part of the community, however worthy in other respects; and also that the same timid prudence, or headstrong efforts, often disgraced the exertions of both. Oppression thus formed many of the features of their character perfectly to coincidence with that of the oppressed half of mankind; for is it not notorious that dissenters were, like women, fond of deliberating together, and asking advice of each other, till by a complication of little contrivances, some little end was brought about? A similar attention to preserve their reputation was conspicuous in the dissenting and female world, and was produced by a similar cause.

Asserting the rights which women in common with men ought to contend for, I have not attempted to extenuate their faults; but to prove them to be the natural consequence of their education and station in society. If so, it is reasonable to suppose that they will change their character, and correct their vices and follies, when they are allowed to be free in a physical, moral, and civil sense.[5]

Let woman share the rights, and she will emulate the virtues of man; for she must grow more perfect when emancipated, or justify the authority that chains such a weak being to her duty. If the latter, it will be expedient to open a fresh trade with Russia for whips: a present which a father should always make to his son-in-law on his wedding day, that a husband may keep his whole family in order by the same means; and without any violation of justice reign, wielding this sceptre, sole master of his house, because he is the only thing in it who has reason:—the divine, indefeasible earthly sovereignty breathed into man by the Master of the universe. Allowing this position, women have not any inherent rights to claim; and, by the same rule, their duties vanish, for rights and duties are inseparable.

Be just then, O ye men of understanding; and mark not more severely what women do amiss than the vicious tricks of the horse or the ass for whom ye provide provender—and allow her the privileges of ignorance, to whom ye deny the rights of reason, or ye will be worse than Egyptian task-masters, expecting virtue where Nature has not given understanding.

DISCUSSION QUESTIONS

1. Wollstonecraft is describing and critiquing gender relations in late eighteenth-century Europe. How relevant is her account for contemporary society? Explain.
2. Do you agree with Wollstonecraft's views on human progress and the essential role of moral character development as part of that progress? Why or why not?
3. Is it possible in a large, heterogeneous society to institutionalize an effective program of moral education that would enhance human equality and mutual respect? If so, how would it work? If not, why not?
4. How would you compare and contrast the views of Wollstonecraft and Confucius on the nature of virtuous and vicious persons and on the role of virtue in family life?

---

5. I had further enlarged on the advantages which might reasonably be expected to result from an improvement in female manners, towards the general reformation of society; but it appeared to me that such reflections would more properly close the last volume.

50. Jeremy Bentham (1748–1832)
On the Principle of Utility

Jeremy Bentham was an English philosopher, legal theorist, and political activist who was born in London and entered Oxford University when he was 12 and law school three years later, with the intention of being an attorney like his father. However, after his legal training Bentham never practiced as a lawyer, choosing instead to devote himself to reforming the English legal system itself. He became the acknowledged leader of a group of social reformers called the Philosophical Radicals and of a wider group of politicians and intellectuals referred to as the Benthamites. As part of this influential reformist movement, he was involved in the establishment of University College in London.

The reading consists of excerpts from Bentham's major philosophical work, *An Introduction to the Principles of Morals and Legislation.* First published in 1789, it is now considered one of the classic statements of modern utilitarianism—the normative ethical theory that recommends choosing the action that leads to the greatest net benefit for all concerned, when compared to the alternatives. Although versions of utilitarian ethics can be found in Western thought as far back as the ancient Greeks, Bentham's theoretical work and political advocacy served to make utilitarianism one of the dominant models of policy making and moral evaluation still followed today.

Especially in the philosophical field of ethics, many different utilitarian theories have been developed over the last 200 years, often as attempts to move away from Bentham's straightforward hedonistic approach that focused on the quantification of units of pleasure and pain likely to accrue from specific actions. And yet for many involved in the ongoing debate over which ethical standards of conduct are the most persuasive, Bentham's utilitarianism generated at least two essential principles that continue to exert a powerful influence: (1) We should always try to maximize benefit and minimize harm for as many people as possible who might be affected by our action, and (2) actions are to be evaluated as morally right or wrong solely on the basis of whether their consequences are good or bad for all relevant parties (the position often called consequentialism in contemporary ethical theory).

QUESTIONS FOR CRITICAL READING

1. What is the principle of utility, as Bentham characterizes it, and on what assumption about human nature is it based?
2. How does Bentham argue for this principle as the most important criterion of right and wrong action?
3. How should legislators, as well as private individuals, apply the principle of utility in their deliberations, in Bentham's view?
4. What seven factors need to be taken into account in deciding on the justifiability or unjustifiability of an action, according to Bentham?
5. In Bentham's account, what is the difference between a simple and complex pleasure or pain?

TERMS TO NOTE

despotical: Having to do with the arbitrary exercise of power or authority over others, not subject to law (from "despot").
propinquity: Nearness, proximity.
fecundity: fertility, fruitfulness.

Of the Principle of Utility

I. *Mankind governed by pain and pleasure.* Nature has placed mankind under the governance of two sovereign masters, *pain* and *pleasure.* It is for them alone to point out what we ought to do, as well as to determine what we shall do. On the one hand the standard of right and wrong, on the other the chain of causes and effects, are fastened to their throne. They govern us in all we do, in all we say, in all we think: every effort we can make to throw off our subjection, will serve but to demonstrate and confirm it. In words a man may pretend to abjure their empire: but in reality he will remain subject to it all the while. The *principle of utility* recognises this subjection, and assumes it for the foundation of that system, the object of which is to rear the fabric of felicity by the hands of reason and of law. Systems which attempt to question it, deal in sounds instead of sense, in caprice instead of reason, in darkness instead of light.

But enough of metaphor and declamation: it is not by such means that moral science is to be improved.

II. *Principle of utility, what.* The principle of utility is the foundation of the present work: it will be proper therefore at the outset to give an explicit and determinate account of what is meant by it. By the principle of utility is meant that principle which approves or disapproves of every action whatsoever, according to the tendency which it appears to have to augment or diminish the happiness of the party whose interest is in question: or, what is the same thing in other words, to promote or to oppose that happiness. I say of every action whatsoever; and therefore not only of every action of a private individual, but of every measure of government.

III. *Utility, what.* By utility is meant that property in any object, whereby it tends to produce benefit, advantage, pleasure, good, or happiness, (all this in the present case comes to the same thing) or (what comes again to the same thing) to prevent the happening of mischief, pain, evil, or unhappiness to the party whose interest is considered: if that party be the community in general, then the happiness of the community: if a particular individual, then the happiness of that individual.

IV. *Interest of the community, what.* The interest of the community is one of the most general expressions that can occur in the phraseology of morals: no wonder that the meaning of it is often lost. When it has a meaning, it is this. The community is a fictitious *body,* composed of the individual persons who are considered as constituting as it were its *members.* The interest of the community then is, what?—the sum of the interests of the several members who compose it.

V. It is in vain to talk of the interest of the community, without understanding what is the interest of the individual. A thing is said to promote the interest, or to be *for* the interest, of an individual, when it tends to add to the sum total of his pleasures: or, what comes to the same thing, to diminish the sum total of his pains.

VI. *An action conformable to the principle of utility, what.* An action then may be said to be conformable to the principle of utility, or, for shortness sake, to

utility, (meaning with respect to the community at large) when the tendency it has to augment the happiness of the community is greater than any it has to diminish it.

VII. *A measure of government conformable to the principle of utility, what.* A measure of government (which is but a particular kind of action, performed by a particular person or persons) may be said to be conformable to or dictated by the principle of utility, when in like manner the tendency which it has to augment the happiness of the community is greater than any which it has to diminish it.

VIII. *Laws or dictates of utility, what.* When an action, or in particular a measure of government, is supposed by a man to be conformable to the principle of utility, it may be convenient, for the purposes of discourse, to imagine a kind of law or dictate, called a law or dictate of utility: and to speak of the action in question, as being conformable to such law or dictate.

IX. *A partizan of the principle of utility, who.* A man may be said to be a partizan of the principle of utility, when the approbation or disapprobation he annexes to any action, or to any measure, is determined by and proportioned to the tendency which he conceives it to have to augment or to diminish the happiness of the community: or in other words, to its conformity or unconformity to the laws or dictates of utility.

X. *Ought, ought not, right and wrong, &c. how to be understood.* Of an action that is conformable to the principle of utility one may always say either that it is one that ought to be done, or at least that it is not one that ought not to be done. One may say also, that it is right it should be done; at least that it is not wrong it should be done: that it is a right action; at least that it is not a wrong action. When thus interpreted, the words *ought,* and *right* and *wrong,* and others of that stamp, have a meaning: when otherwise, they have none.

XI. *To prove the rectitude of this principle is at once unnecessary and impossible.* Has the rectitude of this principle been ever formally contested? It should seem that it had, by those who have not known what they have been meaning. Is it susceptible of any direct proof? it should seem not: for that which is used to prove every thing else, cannot itself be proved: a chain of proofs must have their commencement somewhere. To give such proof is as impossible as it is needless.

XII. *It has seldom, however, as yet been consistently pursued.* Not that there is or ever has been that human creature breathing, however stupid or perverse, who has not on many, perhaps on most occasions of his life, deferred to it. By the natural constitution of the human frame, on most occasions of their lives men in general embrace this principle, without thinking of it: if not for the ordering of their own actions, yet for the trying of their own actions, as well as of those of other men. There have been, at the same time, not many, perhaps, even of the most intelligent, who have been disposed to embrace it purely and without reserve. There are even few who have not taken some occasion or other to quarrel with it, either on account of their not understanding always how to apply it, or on account of some prejudice or other which they were afraid to examine into, or could not bear to part with. For such is the stuff that man is made of: in principle and in practice, in a right track and in a wrong one, the rarest of all human qualities is consistency.

XIII. *It can never be consistently combated.* When a man attempts to combat the principle of utility, it is with reasons drawn, without his being aware of it, from that very principle itself. His arguments, if they prove any thing, prove not that the principle is *wrong,* but that, according to the applications he supposes to be made of it, it is *misapplied.* Is it possible for a man to move the earth? Yes; but he must first find out another earth to stand upon.

XIV. *Course to be taken for surmounting prejudices that may have been entertained against it.* To disprove the propriety of it by arguments is impossible; but, from the causes that have been mentioned, or from some confused or partial view of it, a man may happen to be disposed not to relish it. Where this is the case, if he thinks the settling of his opinions on such a subject worth the trouble, let him take the following steps, and at length, perhaps, he may come to reconcile himself to it.

1. Let him settle with himself, whether he would wish to discard this principle altogether; if so, let him consider what it is that all his reasonings (in matters of politics especially) can amount to?

2. If he would, let him settle with himself, whether he would judge an act without any principle, or whether there is any other he would judge and act by?

3. If there be, let him examine and satisfy himself whether the principle he thinks he has found is really any separate intelligible principle; or whether it be not a mere principle in words, a kind of phrase, which at bottom expresses neither more nor less than the mere averment of his own unfounded sentiments; that is, what in another person he might be apt to call caprice?

4. If he is inclined to think that his own approbation or disapprobation, annexed to the idea of an act, without any regard to its consequences, is a sufficient foundation for him to judge and act upon, let him ask himself whether his sentiment is to be a standard of right and wrong, with respect to every other man, or whether every man's sentiment has the same privilege of being a standard to itself?

5. In the first case, let him ask himself whether his principle is not despotical, and hostile to all the rest of human race?

6. In the second case, whether it is not anarchial, and whether at this rate there are not as many different standards of right and wrong as there are men? and whether even to the same man, the same thing, which is right to-day, may not (without the least change in its nature) be wrong to-morrow? and whether the same thing is not right and wrong in the same place at the same time? and in either case, whether all argument is not at an end? and whether, when two men have said, 'I like this,' and 'I don't like it,' they can (upon such a principle) have any thing more to say?

7. If he should have said to himself, No: for that the sentiment which he proposes as a standard must be grounded on reflection, let him say on what particulars the reflection is to turn? if on particulars having relation to the utility of the act, then let him say whether this is not deserting his own principle, and borrowing assistance from that very one in opposition to which he sets it up: or if not on those particulars, on what other particulars?

8. If he should be for compounding the matter, and adopting his own principle in part, and the principle of utility in part, let him say how far he will adopt it?

9. When he has settled with himself where he will stop, then let him ask himself how he justifies to himself the adopting it so far? and why he will not adopt it any farther?

10. Admitting any other principle than the principle of utility to be a right principle, a principle that it

is right for a man to pursue; admitting (what is not true) that the word *right* can have a meaning without reference to utility, let him say whether there is any such thing as a *motive* that a man can have to pursue the dictates of it: if there is, let him say what that motive is, and how it is to be distinguished from those which enforce the dictates of utility: if not, then lastly let him say what it is this other principle can be good for? . . .

Value of a Lot of Pleasure or Pain, How to Be Measured

I. *Use of this chapter.* Pleasures then, and the avoidance of pains, are the *ends* which the legislator has in view: it behoves him therefore to understand their *value.* Pleasures and pains are the *instruments* he has to work with: it behoves him therefore to understand their force, which is again, in other words, their value.

II. *Circumstances to be taken into the account in estimating the value of a pleasure or pain considered with reference to a single person, and by itself.* To a person considered by *himself*, the value of a pleasure or pain considered by *itself*, will be greater or less, according to the four following circumstances:

1. Its *intensity.*
2. Its *duration.*
3. Its *certainty* or *uncertainty.*
4. Its *propinquity* or *remoteness.*

III. —*considered as connected with other pleasures or pains.* These are the circumstances which are to be considered in estimating a pleasure or a pain considered each of them by itself. But when the value of any pleasure or pain is considered for the purpose of estimating the tendency of any *act* by which it is produced, there are two other circumstances to be taken into the account; these are,

5. Its *fecundity,* or the chance it has of being followed by sensations of the *same* kind: that is, pleasures, if it be a pleasure: pains, if it be a pain.

6. Its *purity,* or the chance it has of *not* being followed by sensations of the *opposite* kind: that is, pains, if it be a pleasure: pleasures, if it be a pain.

These two last, however, are in strictness scarcely to be deemed properties of the pleasure or the pain itself; they are not, therefore, in strictness to be taken into the account of the value of that pleasure or that pain.

They are in strictness to be deemed properties only of the act, or other event, by which such pleasure or pain has been produced; and accordingly are only to be taken into the account of the tendency of such act or such event.

IV. —*considered with reference to a number of persons.* To a *number* of persons, with reference to each of whom the value of a pleasure or a pain is considered, it will be greater or less, according to seven circumstances: to wit, the six preceding ones; *viz.*

1. Its *intensity.*
2. Its *duration.*
3. Its *certainty* or *uncertainty.*
4. Its *propinquity* or *remoteness.*
5. Its *fecundity.*
6. Its *purity.*

And one other; to wit:

7. Its *extent;* that is, the number of persons to whom it *extends;* or (in other words) who are affected by it.

V. *Process for estimating the tendency of any act or event.* To take an exact account then of the general tendency of any act, by which the interests of a community are affected, proceed as follows. Begin with any one person of those whose interests seem most immediately to be affected by it: and take an account,

1. Of the value of each distinguishable *pleasure* which appears to be produced by it in the *first* instance.

2. Of the value of each *pain* which appears to be produced by it in the *first* instance.

3. Of the value of each pleasure which appears to be produced by it *after* the first. This constitutes the *fecundity* of the first *pleasure* and the *impurity* of the first *pain.*

4. Of the value of each *pain* which appears to be produced by it after the first. This constitutes the *fecundity* of the first *pain,* and the *impurity* of the first pleasure.

5. Sum up all the values of all the *pleasures* on the one side, and those of all the pains on the other. The balance, if it be on the side of pleasure, will give the *good* tendency of the act upon the whole, with respect to the interests of that *individual* person; if on the side of pain, the *bad* tendency of it upon the whole.

6. Take an account of the *number* of persons whose interests appear to be concerned; and repeat the above process with respect to each. *Sum up* the numbers ex-

pressive of the degrees of *good* tendency, which the act has, with respect to each individual, in regard to whom the tendency of it is *good* upon the whole: do this again with respect to each individual, in regard to whom the tendency of it is *good* upon the whole: do this again with respect to each individual, in regard to whom the tendency of it is *bad* upon the whole. Take the *balance;* which, if on the side of *pleasure,* will give the general *good tendency* of the act, with respect to the total number or community of individuals concerned; if on the side of pain, the general *evil tendency,* with respect to the same community.

VI. *Use of the foregoing process.* It is not to be expected that this process should be strictly pursued previously to every moral judgment, or to every legislative or judicial operation. It may, however, be always kept in view: and as near as the process actually pursued on these occasions approaches to it, so near will such process approach to the character of an exact one.

VII. *The same process applicable to good and evil, profit and mischief, and all other modifications of pleasure and pain.* The same process is alike applicable to pleasure and pain, in whatever shape they appear: and by whatever denomination they are distinguished: to pleasure, whether it be called *good* (which is properly the cause or instrument of pleasure) or *profit* (which is distant pleasure, or the cause or instrument of distant pleasure,) or *convenience,* or *advantage, benefit, emolument, happiness,* and so forth: to pain, whether it be called *evil,* (which corresponds to *good*) or *mischief,* or *inconvenience,* or *disadvantage,* or *loss,* or *unhappiness,* and so forth.

VIII. *Conformity of men's practice to this theory.* Nor is this a novel and unwarranted, any more than it is a useless theory. In all this there is nothing but what the practice of mankind, wheresoever they have a clear view of their own interest, is perfectly conformable to. An article of property, an estate in land, for instance, is valuable, on what account? On account of the pleasures of all kinds which it enables a man to produce, and what comes to the same thing the pains of all kinds which it enables him to avert. But the value of such an article of property is universally understood to rise or fall according to the length or shortness of the time which a man has in it: the certainty or uncertainty of its coming into possession: and the nearness or remoteness of the time at which, if at all, it is to

come into possession. As to the *intensity* of the pleasures which a man may derive from it, this is never thought of, because it depends upon the use which each particular person may come to make of it; which cannot be estimated till the particular pleasures he may come to derive from it, or the particular pains he may come to exclude by means of it, are brought to view. For the same reason, neither does he think of the *fecundity* or *purity* of those pleasures.

Thus much for pleasure and pain, happiness and unhappiness, in *general.* We come now to consider the several particular kinds of pain and pleasure. . . .

Pleasures and Pains, Their Kinds

I. *Pleasures and pains are either 1. Simple; or, 2. Complex.* Having represented what belongs to all sorts of pleasures and pains alike, we come now to exhibit, each by itself, the several sorts of pains and pleasures. Pains and pleasures may be called by one general word, interesting perceptions. Interesting perceptions are either simple or complex. The simple ones are those which cannot any one of them be resolved into more: complex are those which are resolvable into divers simple ones. A complex interesting perception may accordingly be composed either, 1. Of pleasures alone: 2. Of pains alone: or, 3. Of a pleasure or pleasures, and a pain or pains together. What determines a lot of pleasure, for example, to be regarded as one complex pleasure, rather than as divers simple ones, is the nature of the exciting cause. Whatever pleasures are excited all at once by the action of the same cause, are apt to be looked upon as constituting all together but one pleasure.

II. *The simple pleasures enumerated.* The several simple pleasures of which human nature is susceptible, seem to be as follows: 1. The pleasures of sense. 2. The pleasures of wealth. 3. The pleasures of skill. 4. The pleasures of amity. 5. The pleasures of a good name. 6. The pleasures of power. 7. The pleasures of piety. 8. The pleasures of benevolence. 9. The pleasures of malevolence. 10. The pleasures of memory. 11. The pleasures of imagination. 12. The pleasures of expectation. 13. The pleasures dependent on association. 14. The pleasures of relief.

III. *The simple pains enumerated.* The several simple pains seem to be as follows: 1. The pains of privation.

2. The pains of the senses. 3. The pains of awkwardness. 4. The pains of enmity. 5. The pains of an ill name. 6. The pains of piety. 7. The pains of benevolence. 8. The pains of malevolence. 9. The pains of the memory. 10. The pains of the imagination. 11. The pains of expectation. 12. The pains dependent on association.

IV. 1. *Pleasures of sense enumerated.* The pleasures of sense seem to be as follows: 1. The pleasures of the taste or palate; including whatever pleasures are experienced in satisfying the appetites of hunger and thirst. 2. The pleasure of intoxication. 3. The pleasures of the organ of smelling. 4. The pleasures of the touch. 5. The simple pleasures of the ear; independent of association. 6. The simple pleasures of the eye; independent of association. 7. The pleasure of the sexual sense. 8. The pleasure of health: or, the internal pleasureable feeling or flow of spirits (as it is called,) which accompanies a state of full health and vigour; especially at times of moderate bodily exertion. 9. The pleasures of novelty: or, the pleasures derived from the gratification of the appetite of curiosity, by the application of new objects to any of the senses.

V. 2. *Pleasures of wealth, which are either of acquisition or of possession.* By the pleasures of wealth may be meant those pleasures which a man is apt to derive from the consciousness of possessing any article or articles which stand in the list of instruments of enjoyment or security, and more particularly at the time of his first acquiring them; at which time the pleasure may be styled a pleasure of gain or a pleasure of acquisition: at other times a pleasure of possession.

3. *Pleasures of skill.* The pleasures of skill, as exercised upon particular objects, are those which accompany the application of such particular instruments of enjoyment to their uses, as cannot be so applied without a greater or less share of difficulty or exertion.

VI. 4. *Pleasures of amity.* The pleasures of amity, or self-recommendation, are the pleasures that may accompany the persuasion of a man's being in the acquisition or the possession of the good-will of such or such assignable person or persons in particular: or, as the phrase is, of being upon good terms with him or them: and as a fruit of it, of his being in a way to have the benefit of their spontaneous and gratuitous services.

VII. 5. *Pleasures of a good name.* The pleasures of a good name are the pleasures that accompany the per-

suasion of a man's being in the acquisition or the possession of the good-will of the world about him; that is, of such members of society as he is likely to have concerns with; and as a means of it, either their love or their esteem, or both: and as a fruit of it, of his being in the way to have the benefit of their spontaneous and gratuitous services. These may likewise be called the pleasures of good repute, the pleasures of honour, or the pleasures of the moral sanction.

VIII. 6. *Pleasures of power.* The pleasures of power are the pleasures that accompany the persuasion of a man's being in a condition to dispose people, by means of their hopes and fears, to give him the benefit of their services: that is, by the hope of some service, or by the fear of some disservice, that he may be in the way to render them.

IX. 7. *Pleasures of piety.* The pleasures of piety are the pleasures that accompany the belief of a man's being in the acquisition or in possession of the good-will or favour of the Supreme Being: and as a fruit of it, of his being in a way of enjoying pleasures to be received by God's special appointment, either in this life, or in a life to come. These may also be called the pleasures of religion, the pleasures of a religious disposition, or the pleasures of the religious sanction.

X. 8. *Pleasures of benevolence or good-will.* The pleasures of benevolence are the pleasures resulting from the view of any pleasures supposed to be possessed by the beings who may be the objects of benevolence; to wit, the sensitive beings we are acquainted with; under which are commonly included, 1. The Supreme Being. 2. Human beings. 3. Other animals. These may also be called the pleasures of good-will, the pleasures of sympathy, or the pleasures of the benevolent or social affections.

XI. 9. *Pleasures of malevolence or ill-will.* The pleasures of malevolence are the pleasures resulting from the view of any pain supposed to be suffered by the beings who may become the objects of malevolence; to wit, 1. Human beings. 2. Other animals. These may also be styled the pleasures of ill-will, the pleasures of the irascible appetite, the pleasures of antipathy, or the pleasures of the malevolent or dissocial affections.

XII. 10. *Pleasures of the memory.* The pleasures of the memory are the pleasures which, after having enjoyed such and such pleasures, or even in some case after having suffered such and such pains, a man will now and then experience, at recollecting them exactly in the order and in the circumstances in which they were actually enjoyed or suffered. These derivative pleasures may of course be distinguished into as many species as there are of original perceptions, from whence they may be copied. They may also be styled pleasures of simple recollection.

XIII. 11. *Pleasures of the imagination.* The pleasures of the imagination are the pleasures which may be derived from the contemplation of any such pleasures as may happen to be suggested by the memory, but in a different order, and accompanied by different groups of circumstances. These may accordingly be referred to any one of the three cardinal points of time, present, past, or future. It is evident they may admit of as many distinctions as those of the former class.

XIV. 12. *Pleasures of expectation.* The pleasures of expectation are the pleasures that result from the contemplation of any sort of pleasure, referred to time *future,* and accompanied with the sentiment of *belief.* These also may admit of the same distinctions.

XV. 13. *Pleasures depending on association.* The pleasures of association are the pleasures which certain objects or incidents may happen to afford, not of themselves, but merely in virtue of some association they have contracted in the mind with certain objects or incidents which are in themselves pleasurable. Such is the case, for instance, with the pleasure of skill, when afforded by such a set of incidents as compose a game of chess. This derives its pleasurable quality from its association partly with the pleasures of skill, as exercised in the production of incidents pleasurable of themselves: partly from its association with the pleasures of power. Such is the case also with the pleasure of good luck, when afforded by such incidents as compose the game of hazard, or any other game of chance, when played at for nothing. This derives its pleasurable quality from its association with one of the pleasures of wealth; to wit, with the pleasure of acquiring it.

XVI. 14. *Pleasures of relief.* Farther on we shall see pains grounded upon pleasures; in like manner may we now see pleasures grounded upon pains. To the catalogue of pleasures may accordingly be added the pleasures of *relief:* or, the pleasures which a man experiences when, after he has been enduring a pain of any kind for a certain time, it comes to cease, or to abate. These may of course be distinguished into as many species as there are of pains: and may give rise to so many pleasures of memory, of imagination, and of expectation.

XVII. 1. *Pains of privation.* Pains of privation are the pains that may result from the thought of not possessing in the time present any of the several kinds of pleasures. Pains of privation may accordingly be resolved into as many kinds as there are of pleasures to which they may correspond, and from the absence whereof they may be derived.

XVIII. *These include, 1. Pains of desire.* There are three sorts of pains which are only so many modifications of the several pains of privation. When the enjoyment of any particular pleasure happens to be particularly desired, but without any expectation approaching to assurance, the pain of privation which thereupon results takes a particular name, and is called the pain of *desire,* or of unsatisfied desire.

XIX. 2. *Pains of disappointment.* Where the enjoyment happens to have been looked for with a degree of expectation approaching to assurance, and that expectation is made suddenly to cease, it is called a pain of disappointment.

XX. 3. *Pains of regret.* A pain of privation takes the name of a pain of regret in two cases: 1. Where it is grounded on the memory of a pleasure, which having been once enjoyed, appears not likely to be enjoyed again: 2. Where it is grounded on the idea of a pleasure, which was never actually enjoyed, nor perhaps so much as expected, but which might have been enjoyed (it is supposed,) had such or such a contingency happened, which, in fact, did not happen.

XXI. 2. *Pains of the senses.* The several pains of the senses seem to be as follows: 1. The pains of hunger and thirst: or the disagreeable sensations produced by the want of suitable substances which need at times to be applied to the alimentary canal. 2. The pains of the taste: or the disagreeable sensations produced by the application of various substances to the palate, and other superior parts of the same canal. 3. The pains of the organ of smell: or the disagreeable sensations produced by the effluvia of various substances when applied to that organ. 4. The pains of the touch: or the disagreeable sensations produced by the application of various substances to the skin. 5. The simple pains of the hearing: or the disagreeable sensations excited in the organ of that sense by various kinds of sounds: independently (as before,) of association. 6. The simple pains of the sight: or the disagreeable sensations if any such there be, that may be excited in the organ of that sense by visible images, independent of the principle of association. 7. The pains resulting from excessive heat or cold, unless these be referable to the touch. 8. The pains of disease: or the acute and uneasy sensations resulting from the several diseases and indispositions to which human nature is liable. 9. The pain of exertion, whether bodily or mental: or the uneasy sensation which is apt to accompany any intense effort, whether of mind or body.

XXII. 3. *Pains of awkwardness.* The pains of awkwardness are the pains which sometimes result from the unsuccessful endeavour to apply any particular instruments of enjoyment or security to their uses, or from the difficulty a man experiences in applying them.

XXIII. 4. *Pains of enmity.* The pains of enmity are the pains that may accompany the persuasion of a man's being obnoxious to the ill-will of such or such an assignable person or persons in particular: or, as the phrase is, of being upon ill terms with him or them: and, in consequence, of being obnoxious to certain pains of some sort or other, of which he may be the cause.

XXIV. 5. *Pains of an ill-name.* The pains of an ill-name, are the pains that accompany the persuasion of a man's being obnoxious, or in a way to be obnoxious to the ill-will of the world about him. These may likewise be called the pains of ill-repute, the pains of dishonour, or the pains of the moral sanction.

XXV. 6. *Pains of piety.* The pains of piety are the pains that accompany the belief of a man's being obnoxious to the displeasure of the Supreme Being: and in consequence to certain pains to be inflicted by his especial appointment, either in this life or in a life to come. These may also be called the pains of religion; the pains of a religious disposition; or the pains of the religious sanction. When the belief is looked upon as well-grounded, these pains are commonly called religious terrors; when looked upon as ill-grounded, superstitious terrors.

XXVI. 7. *Pains of benevolence.* The pains of benevolence are the pains resulting from the view of any pains supposed to be endured by other beings. These may also be called the pains of good-will, of sympathy, or the pains of the benevolent or social affections.

XXVII. 8. *Pains of malevolence.* The pains of malevolence are the pains resulting from the view of any pleasures supposed to be enjoyed by any beings who happen to be the objects of a man's displeasure. These may also be styled the pains of ill-will, of antipathy, or the pains of the malevolent or dissocial affections.

XXVIII. 9. *Pains of the memory.* The pains of the memory may be grounded on every one of the above kinds, as well of pains of privation as of positive pains. These correspond exactly to the pleasures of the memory.

XXIX. 10. *Pains of the imagination.* The pains of the imagination may also be grounded on any one of the above kinds, as well of pains of privation as of positive pains: in other respects they correspond exactly to the pleasures of the imagination.

XXX. 11. *Pains of expectation.* The pains of expectation may be grounded on each one of the above kinds, as well of pains of privation as of positive pains. These may be also termed pains of apprehension.

XXXI. 12. *Pains of association.* The pains of association correspond exactly to the pleasures of association.

XXXII. *Pleasures and pains are either self-regarding or extra-regarding.* Of the above list there are certain pleasures and pains which suppose the existence of some pleasure or pain of some other person, to which the pleasure or pain of the person in question has regard: such pleasures and pains may be termed *extra-regarding.* Others do not suppose any such thing: these may be termed *self-regarding.* The only pleasures and pains of the extra-regarding class are those of benevolence and those of malevolence: all the rest are self-regarding.

XXXIII. *In what ways the law is concerned with the above pains and pleasures.* Of all these several sorts of pleasures and pains, there is scarce any one which is not liable, on more accounts than one, to come under the consideration of the law. Is an offence committed? It is the tendency which it has to destroy, in such or such persons, some of these pleasures, or to produce some of these pains, that constitutes the mischief of it, and the ground for punishing it. It is the prospect of some of these pleasures, or of security from some of these pains, that constitutes the motive or temptation, it is the attainment of them that constitutes the profit of the offence. Is the offender to be punished? It can be only by the production of one or more of these pains, that the punishment can be inflicted.

DISCUSSION QUESTIONS

1. Do you agree with Bentham's claims about human nature as fundamentally hedonistic? Why or why not?

2. Do you agree with Bentham that utilitarian calculations are inescapable in our everyday decision making? Why or why not?

3. Is Bentham's utilitarianism convincing to you as the best way to decide on the moral rightness or wrongness of an action? Why or why not?

4. Do you think lawmakers ought to follow Bentham's recommendations? Why or why not?

51. Immanuel Kant (1724–1804)
Nonconsequentialist Ethics

Immanuel Kant was a German philosopher, born into a tradesman's family in Königsberg in what was at the time East Prussia. He never traveled far from his home city, completing his education at the University of Königsberg and eventually spending almost all of his professional career as a professor at the same institution. In his earlier years as an academician, he became known for his writings on topics mainly in the physical sciences, but it is the more distinctively philosophical works produced in his later years for which he is remembered primarily today. His systematic analyses in metaphysics, epistemology, aesthetics, and ethics in many ways changed the orientation of European philosophy. It even has been argued that the contemporary postmodernist critique of modernism is traceable back to Kant and his demonstrations that knowledge and what we take to be reality are cognitively constructed rather than discovered as such in the external world.

This selection is from *Foundations of the Metaphysics of Morals,* his 1785 book on ethics, or "practical philosophy," and includes the discussion of several of his most influential ideas having to do with the criteria of moral evaluation of conduct in normative ethics. He argued that our makeup as rational beings allows us to recognize "the moral law" and thus the duties that are rationally binding on all of us, regardless of circumstances and independently of any concern for the consequences of our voluntary actions. In his analysis, these moral duties are grounded in the self-evident inherent worth of "persons" and what kind of treatment they subsequently are owed, which also implied for many later philosophers a strong support for universal human rights.

The Kantian approach to ethical theory in one form or another still predominates today in what is usually called nonconsequentialism, or deontological ethics (from the Greek word *deontos,* for "duty"). This position argues that the results of our actions are never the most important consideration in determining whether they are morally right or wrong. Contrast this with consequentialism, or teleological ethics (from the Greek *telos,* for "end" or "purpose"), of which utilitarianism is the representative still most widely accepted among contemporary philosophers. (See the previous reading on Bentham.)

QUESTIONS FOR CRITICAL READING

1. According to Kant, what is a "good will," how is it achieved, and how is it different from other human goods?

2. What is the nature of "duty," in Kant's analysis, and how is it different from "inclination" as a motive for action?

3. What does Kant mean by a "maxim," and what is its appropriate relation to "moral law"?

4. What is the difference between a "hypothetical" and a "categorical" imperative?

5. What are the two formulations of the "categorical imperative," and how are they to be applied in ethical decision making?

TERMS TO NOTE

axiom: In a theory or argument, a foundational assumption, or first premise, that is taken as self-evident and not itself argued for or proven.

apodictical: The quality of expressing necessary truth; absolutely certain.

contingent: That which is non-necessary, or non-absolute, or variable depending on circumstances.

Nothing in the world—indeed nothing even beyond the world—can possibly be conceived which could be called good without qualification except a *GOOD WILL*. Intelligence, wit, judgment, and other talents of the mind however they may be named, or courage, resoluteness, and perseverence as qualities of temperament, are doubtless in many respects good and desirable; but they can become extremely bad and harmful if the will, which is to make use of these gifts of nature and which in its special constitution is called character, is not good. It is the same with gifts of fortune. Power, riches, honor, even health, general well-being and the contentment with one's condition which is called happiness make for pride and even arrogance if there is not a good will to correct their influence on the mind and on its principle of action, so as to make it generally fitting to its entire end. It need hardly be mentioned that the sight of a being adorned with no feature of a pure and good will yet enjoying lasting good fortune can never give pleasure to an impartial rational observer. Thus the good will seems to constitute the indispensable condition even of worthiness to be happy.

Some qualities seem to be conducive to this good will and can facilitate its action, but in spite of that they have no intrinsic unconditional worth. They rather presuppose a good will, which limits the high esteem which one otherwise rightly has for them and prevents their being held to be absolutely good. Moderation in emotions and passions, self-control, and calm deliberation not only are good in many respects but seem even to constitute part of the inner worth of the person. But however unconditionally they were esteemed by the ancients, they are far from being good without qualification, for without the principles of a good will they can become extremely bad, and the coolness of a villain makes him not only far more dangerous but also more directly abominable in our eyes than he would have seemed without it.

The good will is not good because of what it effects or accomplishes or because of its competence to achieve some intended end; it is good only because of its willing (i.e., it is good in itself). And, regarded for itself, it is to be esteemed as incomparably higher than anything which could be brought about by it in favor of any inclination or even of the sum total of all inclinations. Even if it should happen that, by a particularly unfortunate fate or by the niggardly provision of a step-motherly nature, this will should be wholly lacking in power to accomplish its purpose, and if even the greatest effort should not avail it to achieve anything of its end, and if there remained only the good will—not as a mere wish, but as the summoning of all the means in our power—it would sparkle like a jewel all by itself, as something that had its full worth in itself. Usefulness or fruitlessness can neither diminish nor augment this worth. Its usefulness would be only its setting, as it were, so as to enable us to handle it more conveniently in commerce or to attract the attention of those who are not yet connoisseurs, but not to recommend it to those who are experts or to determine its worth.

But there is something so strange in this idea of the absolute worth of the will alone, in which no account is taken of any use, that, notwithstanding the agreement even of common sense, the suspicion must arise that perhaps only high-flown fancy is its hidden basis, and that we may have misunderstood the purpose of nature in appointing reason as the ruler of our will. We shall therefore examine this idea from this point of view.

In the natural constitution of an organized being (i.e., one suitably adapted to life), we assume as an axiom that no organ will be found for any purpose which is not the fittest and best adapted to that purpose. Now if its preservation, its welfare, in a word its happiness, were the real end of nature in a being having reason and will, then nature would have hit upon a very poor arrangement in appointing the reason of the creature to be the executor of this purpose. For all the actions which the creature has to perform with this intention of nature, and the entire rule of his conduct, would be dictated much more exactly by instinct, and the end would be far more certainly attained by instinct than it ever could be by reason. And if, over and above this, reason should have been granted to the favored creature, it would have served only to let him contemplate the happy constitution of his nature, to admire it, to rejoice in it, and to be grateful for it to its beneficent cause. But reason would not have been given in order that the being should subject his faculty of desire to that weak and delusive guidance and to meddle with the purpose of nature. In a word, nature would have taken care that reason did not break forth into practical use nor have the presumption, with its weak insight, to think out for itself the plan of happiness and the means of attaining it. Nature would have taken over the choice not only of ends but also of the means, and with wise foresight she would have entrusted both to instinct alone.

And, in fact, we find that the more a cultivated reason deliberately devotes itself to the enjoyment of life and happiness, the more the man falls short of true contentment. From this fact there arises in many persons, if only they are candid enough to admit it, a certain degree of misology, hatred of reason. This is particularly the case with those who are most experienced in its use. After counting all the advantages which they draw—I will not say from the invention of the arts of common luxury—from the sciences (which in the end seem to them to be also a luxury of the understanding), they nevertheless find that they have actually brought more trouble on their shoulders instead of gaining in happiness; they finally envy, rather than despise, the common run of men who are better guided by merely natural instinct and who do not permit their reason much influence on their conduct. And we must at least admit that a morose attitude or ingratitude to the goodness with which the world is governed is by no means found always among those who temper or refute the boasting eulogies which are given of the advantages of happiness and contentment with which reason is supposed to supply us. Rather, their judgment is based on the Idea of another and far more worthy purpose of their existence for which, instead of happiness, their reason is properly intended; this purpose, therefore, being the supreme condition to which the private purposes of men must, for the most part, defer.

Since reason is not competent to guide the will safely with regard to its objects and the satisfaction of all our needs (which it in part multiplies), to this end an innate instinct would have led with far more cer-

tainty. But reason is given to us as a practical faculty (i.e., one which is meant to have an influence on the will). As nature has elsewhere distributed capacities suitable to the functions they are to perform, reason's proper function must be to produce a will good in itself and not one good merely as a means, since for the former, reason is absolutely essential. This will need not be the sole and complete good, yet it must be the condition of all others, even of the desire for happiness. In this case it is entirely compatible with the wisdom of nature that the cultivation of reason, which is required for the former unconditional purpose, at least in this life restricts in many ways—indeed, can reduce to nothing—the achievement of the latter unconditional purpose, happiness. For one perceives that nature here does not proceed unsuitably to its purpose, because reason, which recognizes its highest practical vocation in the establishment of a good will, is capable of a contentment of its own kind (i.e., one that springs from the attainment of a purpose determined by reason), even though this injures the ends of inclination.

We have, then, to develop the concept of a will which is to be esteemed as good in itself without regard to anything else. It dwells already in the natural and sound understanding and does not need so much to be taught as only to be brought to light. In the estimation of the total worth of our actions it always takes first place and is the condition of everything else. In order to show this, we shall take the concept of duty. It contains the concept of a good will, though with certain subjective restrictions and hindrances, but these are far from concealing it and making it unrecognizable, for they rather bring it out by contrast and make it shine forth all the more brightly.

I here omit all actions which are recognized as opposed to duty, even though they may be useful in one respect or another, for with these the question does not arise as to whether they may be done *from* duty, since they conflict with it. I also pass over actions which are really in accord with duty and to which one has no direct inclination, rather doing them because impelled to do so by another inclination. For it is easily decided whether an action in accord with duty is done from duty or for some selfish purpose. It is far more difficult to note this difference when the action is in accord with duty and, in addition, the subject has a direct inclination to do it. For example, it is in accord with duty that a dealer should not overcharge an inexperienced customer, and whenever there is much trade the prudent merchant does not do so, but has a fixed price for everyone so that a child may buy from him as cheaply as any other. Thus the customer is honestly served, but this is far from sufficient to warrant the belief that the merchant has behaved in this way from duty and principles of honesty. His own advantage required this behavior, but it cannot be assumed that over and above that he had a direct inclination to his customers and that, out of love, as it were, he gave none an advantage in price over another. The action was done neither from duty nor from direct inclination but only for a selfish purpose.

On the other hand, it is a duty to preserve one's life, and moreover everyone has a direct inclination to do so. But for that reason, the often anxious care which most men take of it has no intrinsic worth, and the maxim of doing so has no moral import. They preserve their lives according to duty, but not from duty. But if adversities and hopeless sorrow completely take away the relish for life; if an unfortunate man, strong in soul, is indignant rather than despondent or dejected over his fate and wishes for death, and yet preserves his life without loving it and from neither inclination nor fear but from duty—then his maxim has moral merit.

To be kind where one can is a duty, and there are, moreover, many persons so sympathetically constituted that without any motive of vanity or selfishness they find an inner satisfaction in spreading joy and rejoice in the contentment of others which they have made possible. But I say that, however dutiful and however amiable it may be, that kind of action has no true moral worth. It is on a level with [actions done from] other inclinations, such as the inclination to honor, which, if fortunately directed to what in fact accords with duty and is generally useful and thus honorable, deserve praise and encouragement, but no esteem. For the maxim lacks the moral import of an action done not from inclination but from duty. But assume that the mind of that friend to mankind was clouded by a sorrow of his own which extinguished all sympathy with the lot of others, and though he still had the power to benefit others in distress their need left him untouched because he was preoccupied with his own. Now suppose him to tear himself, unsolicited

by inclination, out of his dead insensibility and to do this action only from duty and without any inclination—then for the first time his action has genuine moral worth. Furthermore, if nature has put little sympathy into the heart of a man, and if he, though an honest man, is by temperament cold and indifferent to the sufferings of others perhaps because he is provided with special gifts of patience and fortitude and expects and even requires that others should have them too—and such a man would certainly not be the meanest product of nature—would not he find in himself a source from which to give himself a far higher worth than he could have got by having a good-natured temperament? This is unquestionably true even though nature did not make him philanthropic, for it is just here that the worth of character is brought out, which is morally the incomparably highest of all: he is beneficent not from inclination, but from duty.

To secure one's own happiness is at least indirectly a duty, for discontent with one's condition under pressure from many cares and amid unsatisfied wants could easily become a great temptation to transgress against duties. But, without any view to duty, all men have the strongest and deepest inclination to happiness, because in this Idea all inclinations are summed up. But the precept of happiness is often so formulated that it definitely thwarts some inclinations, and men can make no definite and certain concept of the sum of satisfaction of all inclinations, which goes under the name of happiness. It is not to be wondered at, therefore, that a single inclination, definite as to what it promises and as to the time at which it can be satisfied, can outweigh a fluctuating idea and that, for example, a man with the gout can choose to enjoy what he likes and to suffer what he may, because according to his calculations at least on this occasion he has not sacrificed the enjoyment of the present moment to a perhaps groundless expectation of a happiness supposed to lie in health. But even in this case if the universal inclination to happiness did not determine his will, and if health were not at least for him a necessary factor in these calculations, there would still remain, as in all other cases, a law that he ought to promote his happiness not from inclination but from duty. Only from this law could his conduct have true moral worth.

It is in this way, undoubtedly, that we should understand those passages of Scripture which command us to love our neighbor and even our enemy, for love as an inclination cannot be commanded. But beneficence from duty, even when no inclination impels it and even when it is opposed by a natural and unconquerable aversion, is practical love, not pathological love; it resides in the will and not in the propensities of feeling, in principles of action and not in tender sympathy; and it alone can be commanded.

[Thus the first proposition of morality is that to have genuine moral worth, an action must be done from duty.] The second proposition is: An action done from duty does not have its moral worth in the purpose which is to be achieved through it but in the maxim whereby it is determined. Its moral value, therefore, does not depend upon the realization of the object of the action but merely on the principle of the volition by which the action is done irrespective of the objects of the faculty of desire. From the preceding discussion it is clear that the purposes we may have for our actions and their effects as ends and incentives of the will cannot give the actions any unconditional and moral worth. Wherein, then, can this worth lie, if it is not in the will in its relation to its hoped-for effect? It can lie nowhere else than in the principle of the will irrespective of the ends which can be realized by such action. For the will stands, as it were, at the crossroads halfway between its a priori principle which is formal and its posteriori incentive which is material. Since it must be determined by something, if it is done from duty it must be determined by the formal principle of volition as such, since every material principle has been withdrawn from it.

The third principle, as a consequence of the two preceding, I would express as follows: Duty is the necessity to do an action from respect for law. I can certainly have an inclination to an object as an effect of the proposed action, but I can never have respect for it precisely because it is a mere effect and not an activity of a will. Similarly, I can have no respect for any inclination whatsoever, whether my own or that of another; in the former case I can at most approve of it and in the latter I can even love it (i.e., see it as favorable to my own advantage). But that which is connected with my will merely as ground and not as consequence, that which does not serve my inclination but overpowers it or at least excludes it from being considered in making a choice—in a word, law itself—can be an object of respect and thus a command. Now

as an act from duty wholly excludes the influence of inclination and therewith every object of the will, nothing remains which can determine the will objectively except law and subjectively except pure respect for this practical law. This subjective element is the maxim* that I should follow such a law even if it thwarts all my inclinations.

Thus the moral worth of an action does not lie in the effect which is expected from it or in any principle of action which has to borrow its motive from this expected effect. For all these effects (agreeableness of my own condition, indeed even the promotion of the happiness of others) could be brought about through other causes and would not require the will of a rational being, while the highest and unconditional good can be found only in such a will. Therefore the preeminent good can consist only in the conception of law in itself (which can be present only in a rational being) so far as this conception and not the hoped-for effect is the determining ground of the will. This preeminent good, which we call moral, is already present in the person who acts according to this conception, and we do not have to look for it first in the result.†

---

* A maxim is the subjective principle of volition. The objective principle (i.e., that which would serve all rational beings also subjectively as a practical principle if reason had full power over the faculty of desire) is the practical law.

† It might be objected that I seek to take refuge in an obscure feeling behind the word "respect," instead of clearly resolving the question with a concept of reason. But though respect is a feeling, it is not one received through any [outer] influence but is self-wrought by a rational concept; thus it differs specifically from all feelings of the former kind which may be referred to inclination or fear. What I recognize directly as a law for myself I recognize with respect, which means merely the consciousness of the submission of my will to a law without the intervention of other influences on my mind. The direct determination of the will by law and the consciousness of this determination is respect; thus respect can be regarded as the effect of the law on the subject and not as the cause of the law. Respect is properly the conception of a worth which thwarts my self-love. Thus it is regarded as an object neither of inclination nor of fear, though it has something analogous to both. The only object of respect is law, and indeed only the law which we impose on ourselves and yet recognize as necessary in itself. As a law we are subject to it without consulting self-love; as imposed on us by ourselves, it is a consequence of our will. In the former respect it is analogous to fear and in the latter to inclination. All respect for a person is only respect for the law (of righteousness, etc.) of which the person provides an example. Because we see the improvement of our talents as a duty, we think of a person of talent as the example of a law, as it were (the law that we should by practice become like him in his talents), and that constitutes our respect. All so-called moral interest consists solely in respect for the law.

But what kind of law can that be, the conception of which must determine the will without reference to the expected result? Under this condition alone can the will be called absolutely good without qualification. Since I have robbed the will of all impulses which could come to it from obedience to any law, nothing remains to serve as a principle of the will except universal conformity to law as such. That is, I ought never to act in such a way that I could not also will that my maxim should be a universal law. Strict conformity to law as such (without assuming any particular law applicable to certain actions) serves as the principle of the will, and it must serve as such a principle if duty is not to be a vain delusion and chimerical concept. The common sense of mankind (*gemeine Menschenvernunft*) in its practical judgments is in perfect agreement with this and has this principle constantly in view.

Let the question, for example, be: May I, when in distress, make a promise with the intention not to keep it? I easily distinguish the two meanings which the question can have, viz., whether it is prudent to make a false promise, or whether it conforms to duty. The former can undoubtedly be often the case, though I do see clearly that it is not sufficient merely to escape from the present difficulty by this expedient, but that I must consider whether inconveniences much greater than the present one may not later spring from this lie. Even with all my supposed cunning, the consequences cannot be so easily foreseen. Loss of credit might be far more disadvantageous than the misfortune I am now seeking to avoid, and it is hard to tell whether it might not be more prudent to act according to a universal maxim and to make it a habit not to promise anything without intending to fulfill it. But it is soon clear to me that such a maxim is based only on an apprehensive concern with consequences.

To be truthful from duty, however, is an entirely different thing from being truthful out of fear of untoward consequences, for in the former case the concept of the action itself contains a law for me, while in the latter I must first look about to see what results for me may be connected with it. To deviate from the principle of duty is certainly bad, but to be unfaithful to my maxim of prudence can sometimes be very advantageous to me, though it is certainly safer to abide by it. The shortest but most infallible way to find the answer to the question as to whether a deceitful promise is consistent with duty is to ask myself: Would I be content that my maxim of extricating myself from difficulty by a false promise should hold as a universal law for myself as well as for others? And could I say to myself that everyone may make a false promise when he is in a difficulty from which he otherwise cannot escape? Immediately I see that I could will the lie but not a universal law to lie. For with such a law there would be no promises at all, inasmuch as it would be futile to make a pretense of my intention in regard to future actions to those who would not believe this pretense or—if they overhastily did so—would pay me back in my own coin. Thus my maxim would necessarily destroy itself as soon as it was made a universal law.

I do not, therefore, need any penetrating acuteness to discern what I have to do in order that my volition may be morally good. Inexperienced in the course of the world, incapable of being prepared for all its contingencies, I only ask myself: Can I will that my maxim become a universal law? If not, it must be rejected, not because of any disadvantage accruing to myself or even to others, but because it cannot enter as a principle into a possible enactment of universal law, and reason extorts from me an immediate respect for such legislation. I do not as yet discern on what it is grounded (this is a question the philosopher may investigate), but I at least understand that it is an estimation of a worth which far outweighs all the worth of whatever is recommended by the inclinations, and that the necessity that I act from pure respect for the practical law constitutes my duty. To duty every other motive must give place, because duty is the condition of a will good in itself, whose worth transcends everything. . . .

The conception of an objective principle, so far as it constrains a will, is a command (of reason), and the formula of this command is called an *imperative*.

All imperatives are expressed by an "ought" and thereby indicate the relation of an objective law of reason to a will which is not in its subjective constitution necessarily determined by this law. This relation is that of constraint. Imperatives say that it would be good to do or to refrain from doing something, but they say it to a will which does not always do something simply because the thing is presented to it as good to do. Practical good is what determines the will by means of the conception of reason and hence not by subjective causes but objectively, on grounds which are valid for every rational being as such. It is distinguished from the pleasant, as that which has an influence on the will only by means of a sensation from purely subjective causes, which hold for the senses only of this or that person and not as a principle of reason which holds for everyone.*

A perfectly good will, therefore, would be equally subject to objective laws of the good, but it could not be conceived as constrained by them to accord with them, because it can be determined to act by its own subjective constitution only through the conception of the good. Thus no imperatives hold for the divine will or, more generally, for a holy will. The "ought" here is out of place, for the volition of itself is necessarily in unison with the law. Therefore imperatives are only formulas expressing the relation of objective laws of volition in general to the subjective imperfection of the will of this or that rational being, for example, the human will.

All imperatives command either *hypothetically* or *categorically*. The former present the practical necessity of a possible action as a means to achieving something else which one desires (or which one may possibly desire). The categorical imperative would be one which presented an action as of itself objectively necessary, without regard to any other end.

Since every practical law presents a possible action as good and thus as necessary for a subject practically determinable by reason, all imperatives are formulas of the determination of action which is necessary by the principle of a will which is in any way good. If the action is good only as a means to something else, the imperative is hypothetical; but if it is thought of as good in itself, and hence as necessary in a will which of itself conforms to reason as the principle of this will, the imperative is categorical.

The imperative thus says what action possible for me would be good, and it presents the practical rule in relation to a will which does not forthwith perform an action simply because it is good, in part because the subject does not always know that the action is good, and in part (when he does know it) because his maxims can still be opposed to the objective principles of a practical reason.

The hypothetical imperative, therefore, says only that the action is good to some purpose, possible or actual. In the former case, it is a problematical, in the latter an assertorical, practical principle. The categorical imperative, which declares the action to be of itself objectively necessary without making any reference to any end in view (i.e., without having any other purpose), holds as an apodictical practical principle. . . .

Now, I say, man and, in general, every rational being exists as an end in himself and not merely as a means to be arbitrarily used by this or that will. In all his actions, whether they are directed toward himself or toward other rational beings, he must always be regarded at the same time as an end. All objects of inclination have only conditional worth, for if the inclinations and needs founded on them did not exist, their object would be worthless. The inclinations themselves as the sources of needs, however, are so lacking in absolute worth that the universal wish of every rational being must be indeed to free himself completely from them. Therefore, the worth of any objects to be obtained by our actions is at times conditional. Beings whose existence does not depend on our will but on nature, if they are not rational beings, have only relative worth as means, and are therefore called "things"; rational beings, on the other hand, are designated "persons" because their nature indicates that they are ends in themselves (i.e., things which may not be used merely as means). Such a being is thus an object of respect, and as such restricts all [arbitrary] choice. Such beings are not merely subjective ends whose existence as a result of our action has a worth

---

* The dependence of the faculty of desire on sensations is called inclination, and inclination always indicates a need. The dependence of a contingently determinable will on principles of reason, however, is called interest. An interest is present only in a dependent will which is not of itself always in accord with reason; in the divine will we cannot conceive of an interest. But even the human will can take an interest in something without thereby acting from interest. The former means the practical interest in the action; the latter, the pathological interest in the object of the action. The former indicates only the dependence of the will on principles of reason in themselves, while the latter indicates dependence on the principles of reason for the purpose of inclination, since reason gives only the practical rule by which the needs of inclination are to be aided. In the former case the action interests me, and in the latter the object of the action (so far as it is pleasant for me) interests me. In the First Section we have seen that, in the case of an action done from duty, no regard must be given to the interest in the object, but merely to the action itself and its principle in reason (i.e., the law).

for us, but are objective ends (i.e., beings whose existence is an end in itself). Such an end is one in the place of which no other end, to which these beings should serve merely as means, can be put. Without them, nothing of absolute worth could be found, and if all worth is conditional and thus contingent, no supreme practical principle for reason could be found anywhere.

Thus if there is to be a supreme practical principle and a categorical imperative for the human will, it must be one that forms an objective principle of the will from the conception of that which is necessarily an end for everyone because it is an end in itself. Hence this objective principle can serve as a universal law. The ground of this principle is: rational nature exists as an end in itself. Man necessarily thinks of his own existence in this way, and thus far it is a subjective principle of human actions. Also every other rational being thinks of his existence on the same rational ground which holds also for myself;* thus it is at the same time an objective principle from which, as a supreme practical ground, it must be possible to derive all laws of the will. The practical imperative, therefore, is the following: Act so that you treat humanity, whether in your own person or in that of another, always as an end and never as a means only. Let us now see whether this can be achieved. To return to our previous examples:

First, according to the concept of necessary duty to oneself, he who contemplates suicide will ask himself whether his action can be consistent with the idea of humanity as an end in itself. If in order to escape from burdensome circumstances he destroys himself, he uses a person merely as a means to maintain a tolerable condition up to the end of life. Man, however, is not a thing, and thus not something to be used merely as a means; he must always be regarded in all his actions as an end in himself. Therefore I cannot dispose of man in my own person so as to mutilate, corrupt, or kill him. (It belongs to ethics proper to define more accurately this basic principle so as to avoid all misunderstanding, e.g., as to amputating limbs in order to preserve myself, or to exposing my life to danger in order to save it; I must therefore omit them here.)

Second, as concerns necessary or obligatory duties to others, he who intends a deceitful promise to others sees immediately that he intends to use another man merely as a means, without the latter at the same time containing the end in himself. For he whom I want to use for my own purposes by means of such a promise cannot possibly assent to my mode of acting against him and thus share in the purpose of this action. This conflict with the principle of other men is even clearer if we cite examples of attacks on their freedom and property, for then it is clear that he who violates the rights of men intends to make use of the person of others merely as means, without considering that, as rational beings, they must always be esteemed at the same time as ends (i.e., only as beings who must be able to embody in themselves the purpose of the very same action).*

Thirdly, with regard to contingent (meritorious) duty to oneself, it is not sufficient that the action not conflict with humanity in our person as an end in itself; it must also harmonize with it. In humanity there are capacities for greater perfection which belong to the purpose of nature with respect to humanity in our own person, and to neglect these might perhaps be consistent with the preservation of humanity as an end in itself, but not with the furtherance of that end.

Fourthly, with regard to meritorious duty to others, the natural purpose that all men have is their own happiness. Humanity might indeed exist if no one contributed to the happiness of others, provided he did not intentionally detract from it, but this harmony with humanity as an end in itself is only negative, not positive, if everyone does not also endeavor, as far as he can, to further the purposes of others. For the ends

---

* Here I present this proposition as a postulate, but in the last Section grounds for it will be found.

* Let it not be thought that the banal "what you do not wish to be done to you . . ." could here serve as guide or principle, for it is only derived from the principle and is restricted by various limitations. It cannot be a universal law, because it contains the ground neither of duties to one's self nor of the benevolent duties to others (for many a man would gladly consent that others should not benefit him, provided only that he might be excused from showing benevolence to them). Nor does it contain the ground of obligatory duties to another, for the criminal would argue on this ground against the judge who sentences him. And so on.

of any person, who is an end in himself, must as far as possible be also my ends, if that conception of an end in itself is to have its full effect on me.

This principle of humanity, and in general of every rational creature an end in itself, is the supreme limiting condition on the freedom of action of each man. It is not borrowed from experience, first, because of its universality, since it applies to all rational beings generally, and experience does not suffice to determine anything about them; and secondly, because in experience humanity is not thought of (subjectively) as the purpose of men (i.e., as an object which we of ourselves really make our purpose). Rather it is thought of as the objective end which ought to constitute the supreme limiting condition of all subjective ends whatever they may be. Thus this principle must arise from pure reason. Objectively the ground of all practical legislation lies (according to the first principle) in the rule and form of universality, which makes it capable of being a law (at least a natural law); subjectively it lies in the end. But the subject of all ends is every rational being as an end in itself (by the second principle); from this there follows the third practical principle of the will as the supreme condition of its harmony with universal practical reason, viz., the Idea of the will of every rational being as making universal law.

By this principle all maxims are rejected which are not consistent with the will's giving universal law. The will is not only subject to the law, but subject in such a way that it must be conceived also as itself prescribing the law, of which reason can hold itself to be the author; it is on this ground alone that the will is regarded as subject to the law.

By the very fact that the imperatives are thought of as categorical, either way of conceiving them—as imperatives demanding the lawfulness of actions, resembling the lawfulness of the natural order; or as imperatives of the universal prerogative of the purposes of rational beings as such—excludes from their sovereign authority all admixture of any interest as an incentive to obedience. But we have been *assuming* the imperatives to be categorical, for that was necessary if we wished to explain the concept of duty; that there are practical propositions which command categorically could not of itself be proved independently, just

as little as it can be proved anywhere in this section. One thing, however could have been done: to indicate in the imperative itself, by some determination inherent in it, that in willing from duty the renunciation of all interest is the specific mark of the categorical imperative, distinguishing it from the hypothetical. And this is now done in the third formulation of the principle, viz., in the Idea of the will of every rational being as a will giving universal law. A will which is subject to laws can be bound to them by an interest, but a will giving the supreme law cannot possibly depend upon any interest, for such a dependent will would itself need still another law which would restrict the interest of its self-love to the condition that its [maxim] should be valid as a universal law.

Thus the principle of every human will as a will giving universal law in all its maxims is very well adapted to being a categorical imperative, provided it is otherwise correct. Because of the Idea of giving universal law, it is based on no interest; and thus of all possible imperatives, it alone can be unconditional. Or, better, converting the proposition: if there is a categorical imperative (a law for the will of every rational being), it can command only that everything be done from the maxim of its will as one which could have as its object only itself considered as giving universal law. For only in this case are the practical principle and the imperative which the will obeys unconditional, because the will can have no interest as its foundation.

DISCUSSION QUESTIONS

1. How would you compare Kant and Bentham on the role of pleasure and pain, or happiness, in ethical decision making? Who do you find more convincing? Why?

2. How would Kant criticize ethical relativism? Would you agree with his critique? Why or why not?

3. Do you agree with Kant's characterization of a "person" and his claim that only persons are "ends in themselves"? Why or why not?

4. In the determination of our moral duty in a particular case, how would Kant handle the problem of extenuating circumstances? Are there exceptions to the rule that his theory of duty could accommodate? Explain.

52. Carol Gilligan (b. 1936)
Care, Justice, and Gender

Carol Gilligan has been on the faculty of the Graduate School of Education at Harvard University for many years, where the majority of her research has centered around issues in human development and moral psychology, with special attention to gender differences in these domains. Although grounded in behavioral science, her investigations have been quite interdisciplinary and so also has been her influence. Her groundbreaking work on the relation of gender and moral development has brought responses from psychologists, educational theorists, and philosophers. Especially in the last few decades there has been an increasing interest, at least among Western academic philosophers, in the nature of a feminist ethics, and Gilligan's empirical findings have contributed significantly to the way theory construction generally has evolved in this area.

In this selection of excerpts from her book *In a Different Voice*, published in 1982, Gilligan is for the most part interpreting the results of three different sets of interviews with different groups of men and women. The questions in each case, as she puts it, are "about conceptions of self and morality, about experiences of conflict and choice" (p. 2). From the responses, she identifies two distinct moral perspectives that correlate roughly with the particular respondent being female or male. She talks about this distinction in terms of an "ethic of justice" (or of "equal rights"), on the one hand, and an "ethic of care" (or of "responsibility") on the other hand, with the former being much more often expressed by males and the latter being much more often expressed by females. It is this "care ethic" that constitutes the "different voice" to which Gilligan refers. Her study contrasts with prior studies of the stages of moral development that assumed the ethic of justice as the norm of maturity, in comparison with which all other types of moral reasoning were treated as immature or deficient.

QUESTIONS FOR CRITICAL READING

1. What does Gilligan mean by claiming that the different voice she describes is "characterized not by gender but theme"?

2. What is the ethic of care Gilligan describes, and how is it applied in dealing with moral dilemmas?

3. What is the ethic of justice Gilligan describes, and how is it applied in dealing with moral dilemmas?

4. In Gilligan's account, what is the difference between the ethical concepts of "equality" and "equity"?

5. What is Gilligan's conception of "moral maturity," and how does she argue for it as opposed to other theoretical models of human moral development?

TERMS TO NOTE

postconventional: A term originally used by Lawrence Kohlberg (1927–1987) in his studies in moral psychology. In contrast to "preconventional" and "conventional," it designates a more advanced, "mature" level of moral development. As Gilligan describes it in her book, "Postconventional judgment adopts a reflective perspective on societal values and constructs moral principles that are universal in application" (p. 73).

the Heinz dilemma: One of the hypothetical moral dilemmas Kohlberg asked his respondents to resolve, in which Heinz faces the choice of either stealing an exorbitantly priced medication that his desperately ill wife needs, but he can't afford, and risking legal punishment, or not getting the medication and risking her likely death.

Satyagraha: See Part V, reading 62, on Gandhi.

moral ideology: Here, a distinctive conceptual framework, or perspective, used in making sense out of life situations calling for ethical judgment.

Over the past ten years, I have been listening to people talking about morality and about themselves. Halfway through that time, I began to hear a distinction in these voices, two ways of speaking about moral problems, two modes of describing the relationship between other and self. Differences represented in the psychological literature as steps in a developmental progression suddenly appeared instead as a contrapuntal theme, woven into the cycle of life and recurring in varying forms in people's judgments, fantasies, and thoughts. The occasion for this observation was the selection of a sample of women for a study of the relation between judgment and action in a situation of moral conflict and choice. Against the background of the psychological descriptions of identity and moral development which I had read and taught for a number of years, the women's voices sounded distinct. It was then that I began to notice the recurrent problems in interpreting women's development and to connect these problems to the repeated exclusion of women from the critical theory-building studies of psychological research.

This book records different modes of thinking about relationships and the association of these modes with male and female voices in psychological and literary texts and in the data of my research. The disparity between women's experience and the representation of human development, noted throughout the psychological literature, has generally been seen to signify a problem in women's development. Instead, the failure of women to fit existing models of human growth may point to a problem in the representation, a limitation in the conception of human condition, an omission of certain truths about life.

The different voice I describe is characterized not by gender but theme. Its association with women is an empirical observation, and it is primarily through women's voices that I trace its development. But this association is not absolute, and the contrasts between male and female voices are presented here to highlight a distinction between two modes of thought and to focus a problem of interpretation rather than to represent a generalization about either sex. In tracing development, I point to the interplay of these voices within each sex and suggest that their convergence marks times of crisis and change. No claims are made about the origins of the differences described or their distribution in a wider population, across cultures, or

through time. Clearly, these differences arise in a social context where factors of social class and power combine with reproductive biology to shape the experience of males and females and the relations between the sexes. My interest lies in the interaction of experience and thought, in different voices and the dialogues to which they give rise, in the way we listen to ourselves and to others, in the stories we tell about our lives. . . .

The moral imperative that emerges repeatedly in interviews with women is an injunction to care, a responsibility to discern and alleviate the "real and recognizable trouble" of this world. For men, the moral imperative appears rather as an injunction to respect the rights of others and thus to protect from interference the rights to life and self-fulfillment. Women's insistence on care is at first self-critical rather than self-protective, while men initially conceive obligation to others negatively in terms of noninterference. Development for both sexes would therefore seem to entail an integration of rights and responsibilities through the discovery of the complementarity of these disparate views. For women, the integration of rights and responsibilities takes place through an understanding of the psychological logic of relationships. This understanding tempers the self-destructive potential of a self-critical morality by asserting the need of all persons for care. For men, recognition through experience of the need for more active responsibility in taking care corrects the potential indifference of a morality of noninterference and turns attention from the logic to the consequences of choice (Gilligan and Murphy, 1979; Gilligan, 1981). In the development of a postconventional ethical understanding, women come to see the violence inherent in inequality, while men come to see the limitations of a conception of justice blinded to the differences in human life.

Hypothetical dilemmas, in the abstraction of their presentation, divest moral actors from the history and psychology of their individual lives and separate the moral problem from the social contingencies of its possible occurrence. In doing so, these dilemmas are useful for the distillation and refinement of objective principles of justice and for measuring the formal logic of equality and reciprocity. However, the reconstruction of the dilemma in its contextual particularity allows the understanding of cause and consequence which engages the compassion and tolerance repeatedly noted to distinguish the moral judgments of women. Only when substance is given to the skeletal lives of hypothetical people is it possible to consider the social injustice that their moral problems may reflect and to imagine the individual suffering their occurrence may signify or their resolution engender.

The proclivity of women to reconstruct hypothetical dilemmas in terms of the real, to request or to supply missing information about the nature of the people and the places where they live, shifts their judgment away from the hierarchical ordering of principles and the formal procedures of decision making. This insistence on the particular signifies an orientation to the dilemma and to moral problems in general that differs from any current developmental stage descriptions. Consequently, though several of the women in the abortion study clearly articulate a postconventional metaethical position, none of them are considered principled in their normative moral judgments of Kohlberg's hypothetical dilemmas. Instead, the women's judgments point toward an identification of the violence inherent in the dilemma itself, which is seen to compromise the justice of any of its possible resolutions. This construction of the dilemma leads the women to recast the moral judgment from a consideration of the good to a choice between evils.

Ruth, the woman who spoke of her conflicting wishes to become a college president or to have another child, sees Heinz's dilemma as a choice between selfishness and sacrifice. For Heinz to steal the drug, given the circumstances of his life, which she infers from his inability to pay two thousand dollars, he would have "to do something which is not in his best interest, in that he is going to get sent away, and that is a supreme sacrifice, a sacrifice which I would say a person truly in love might be willing to make." However, not to steal the drug "would be selfish on his part. He would have to feel guilty about not allowing her a chance to live longer." Heinz's decision to steal is considered not in terms of the logical priority of life over property, which justifies its rightness, but rather in terms of the actual consequences that stealing would have for a man of limited means and little social power.

Considered in the light of its probable outcomes—his wife dead, or Heinz in jail, brutalized by the violence of that experience and his life compromised by a record of felony—the dilemma itself changes. Its resolution has less to do with the relative weights of life and property in an abstract moral conception than with the collision between two lives, formerly conjoined but now in opposition, where the continuation of one life can occur only at the expense of the other. This construction makes clear why judgment revolves around the issue of sacrifice and why guilt becomes the inevitable concomitant of either resolution.

Demonstrating the reticence noted in women's moral judgments, Ruth explains her reluctance to judge in terms of her belief:

> I think that everybody's existence is so different that I kind of say to myself, "That might be something that I wouldn't do," but I can't say that it is right or wrong for that person. I can only deal with what is appropriate for me to do when I am faced with specific problems.

Asked if she would apply to others her own injunction against hurting, she replies:

> I can't say that it is wrong. I can't say that it is right or that it's wrong, because I don't know what the person did that the other person did something to hurt him. So it is not right that the person got hurt, but it is right that the person who just lost the job has got the anger up and out. It doesn't put any bread on his table, but it is released. I don't mean to be copping out. I really am trying to see how to answer these questions for you.

Her difficulty in arriving at definitive answers to moral questions, her sense of strain with the construction of Heinz's problem, stems from the divergence between these questions and her own frame of reference:

> I don't even think I use the words *right* and *wrong* anymore, and I know I don't use the word *moral*, because I am not sure I know what it means. We are talking about an unjust society, we are talking about a whole lot of things that are not right, that are truly wrong—to use the word that I don't use very often—and I have no control to change that. If I could change it, I certainly would, but I can only

make my small contribution from day to day, and if I don't intentionally hurt somebody, that is my contribution to a better society. And so a chunk of that contribution is also not to pass judgment on other people, particularly when I don't know the circumstances of why they are doing certain things.

The reluctance to judge remains a reluctance to hurt, but one that stems not from a sense of personal vulnerability but rather from a recognition of the limitation of judgment itself. The deference of the conventional feminine perspective thus continues at the postconventional level, not as moral relativism but rather as part of a reconstructed moral understanding. Moral judgment is renounced in an awareness of the psychological and social determination of human behavior, at the same time that moral concern is reaffirmed in recognition of the reality of human pain and suffering:

> I have a real thing about hurting people and always have, and that gets a little complicated at times, because, for example, you don't want to hurt your child. I don't want to hurt my child, but if I don't hurt her sometimes, then that's hurting her more, you see, so that was a terrible dilemma for me.

Moral dilemmas are terrible in that they entail hurt. Ruth sees Heinz's decision as "the result of anguish: Who am I hurting? Why do I have to hurt them?" The morality of Heinz's theft is not in question, given the circumstances that necessitated it. What is at issue is his willingness to substitute himself for his wife and become, in her stead, the victim of exploitation by a society which breeds and legitimizes the druggist's irresponsibility and whose injustice is thus manifest in the very occurrence of the dilemma.

The same sense that the wrong questions are being asked is evident in the response of another woman who justifies Heinz's action on a similar basis, saying, "I don't think that exploitation should really be a right." When women begin to make direct moral statements, the issues they repeatedly address are those of exploitation and hurt. In doing so, they raise the issue of nonviolence in precisely the same psychological context that brings Erikson (1969) to pause in his con-

sideration of the truth of Gandhi's life. In the pivotal letter that he addresses to Gandhi and around which the judgment of his book turns, Erikson confronts the contradiction between the philosophy of nonviolence that informed Gandhi's dealing with the British and the psychological violence that marred his relationships with his family and with the children of the ashram. It was this contradiction, Erikson confesses, "which almost brought *me* to the point where I felt unable to continue writing *this* book because I seemed to sense the presence of a kind of untruth in the very protestation of truth; of something unclean when all the words spelled out an unreal purity; and, above all, of displaced violence where nonviolence was the professed issue" (pp. 230–231).

In an effort to untangle the relationship between the spiritual truth of Satyagraha and the truth of his own psychoanalytic understanding, Erikson reminds Gandhi that, "Truth, you once said, 'excludes the use of violence because man is not capable of knowing the absolute truth and therefore is not competent to punish'" (p. 241). The affinity between Satyagraha and psychoanalysis lies in their shared commitment to seeing life as an "experiment in truth," in their being "somehow joined in a universal 'therapeutics,' committed to the Hippocratic principle that one can test truth (or the healing power inherent in a sick situation) only by action which avoids harm—or better, by action which maximizes mutuality and minimizes the violence caused by unilateral coercion or threat" (p. 247). Thus Erikson takes Gandhi to task for his failure to acknowledge the relativity of truth. This failure is manifest in the coercion of his claim to exclusive possession of the truth, his "unwillingness to learn from *anybody anything* except what was approved by the 'inner voice'" (p. 236). This claim led Gandhi, in the guise of love, to impose his truth on others without awareness of or regard for the extent to which he thereby did violence to their integrity.

The moral dilemma, arising inevitably out of a conflict of truths, is by definition a "sick situation" in that its either/or formulation leaves no room for an outcome that does not do violence. The resolution of such dilemmas, however, lies not in the self-deception of rationalized violence: "I was" said Gandhi, "a cruelly kind husband. I regarded myself as her teacher and so harassed her out of my blind love for her" (p. 233).

The resolution lies rather in the replacement of the underlying antagonism with a mutuality of respect and care.

Gandhi, whom Kohlberg cites as exemplifying the sixth stage of moral judgment and whom Erikson initially sought as a model of an adult ethical sensibility, is criticized by a judgment that refuses to look away from or condone the infliction of harm. In denying the validity of his wife's reluctance to open her home to strangers and in blinding himself to the different reality of adolescent sexuality and temptation, Gandhi compromised in his everyday life the ethic of non-violence to which, in principle and in public, he steadfastly adhered.

The blind willingness to sacrifice people to truth, however, has always been the danger of an ethics abstracted from life. This willingness links Gandhi to the biblical Abraham, who prepared to sacrifice the life of his son in order to demonstrate the integrity and supremacy of his faith. Both men, in the limitations of their fatherhood, stand in implicit contrast to the woman who comes before Solomon and verifies her motherhood by relinquishing truth in order to save the life of her child. It is the ethics of an adulthood that has become principled at the expense of care that Erikson comes to criticize in his assessment of Gandhi's life.

This same criticism is dramatized explicitly as a contrast between the sexes in *The Merchant of Venice,* where Shakespeare goes through an extraordinary complication of sexual identity, dressing a male actor as a female character who in turn poses as a male judge, in order to bring into the masculine citadel of justice the feminine plea for mercy. The limitation of the contractual conception of justice is illustrated through the absurdity of its literal execution, while the need to "make exceptions all the time" is demonstrated contrapuntally in the matter of the rings. Portia, in calling for mercy, argues for that resolution in which no one is hurt, and as the men are forgiven for their failure to keep both their rings and their word, Antonio in turn forgoes his "right" to ruin Shylock.

The abortion study suggests that women impose a distinctive construction on moral problems, seeing moral dilemmas in terms of conflicting responsibilities. This construction was traced through a sequence of three perspectives, each perspective representing a more complex understanding of the relationship between self and other and each transition involving a critical reinterpretation of the conflict between selfishness and responsibility. The sequence of women's moral judgment proceeds from an initial concern with survival to a focus on goodness and finally to a reflective understanding of care as the most adequate guide to the resolution of conflicts in human relationships. The abortion study demonstrates the centrality of the concepts of responsibility and care in women's constructions of the moral domain, the close tie in women's thinking between conceptions of the self and of morality, and ultimately the need for an expanded developmental theory that includes, rather than rules out from consideration, the differences in the feminine voice. Such an inclusion seems essential, not only for explaining the development of women but also for understanding in both sexes the characteristics and precursors of an adult moral conception. . . .

Thus in the transition from adolescence to adulthood, the dilemma itself is the same for both sexes, a conflict between integrity and care. But approached from different perspectives, this dilemma generates the recognition of opposite truths. These different perspectives are reflected in two different moral ideologies, since separation is justified by an ethic of rights while attachment is supported by an ethic of care.

The morality of rights is predicated on equality and centered on the understanding of fairness, while the ethic of responsibility relies on the concept of equity, the recognition of differences in need. While the ethic of rights is a manifestation of equal respect, balancing the claims of other and self, the ethic of responsibility rests on an understanding that gives rise to compassion and care. Thus the counterpoint of identity and intimacy that marks the time between childhood and adulthood is articulated through two different moralities whose complementarity is the discovery of maturity.

The discovery of this complementarity is traced in the study by questions about personal experiences of moral conflict and choice. Two lawyers chosen from the sample illustrate how the divergence in judgment between the sexes is resolved through the discovery by each of the other's perspective and of the relationship between integrity and care.

The dilemma of responsibility and truth that McCarthy describes is reiterated by Hilary, a lawyer and the woman who said she found it too hard to describe herself at the end of what "really has been a rough week." She too, like McCarthy, considers self-sacrificing acts "courageous" and "praiseworthy," explaining that "if everyone on earth behaved in a way that showed care for others and courage, the world would be a much better place, you wouldn't have crime and you might not have poverty." However, this moral ideal of self-sacrifice and care ran into trouble not only in a relationship where the conflicting truths of each person's feelings made it impossible to avoid hurt, but also in court where, despite her concern for the client on the other side, she decided not to help her opponent win his case.

In both instances, she found the absolute injunction against hurting others to be an inadequate guide to resolving the actual dilemmas she faced. Her discovery of the disparity between intention and consequence and of the actual constraints of choice led her to realize that there is, in some situations, no way not to hurt. In confronting such dilemmas in both her personal and professional life, she does not abdicate responsibility for choice but rather claims the right to include herself among the people whom she considers it moral not to hurt. Her more inclusive morality now contains the injunction to be true to herself, leaving her with two principles of judgment whose integration she cannot yet clearly envision. What she does recognize is that both integrity and care must be included in a morality that can encompass the dilemmas of love and work that arise in adult life.

The move toward tolerance that accompanies the abandonment of absolutes is considered by William Perry (1968) to chart the course of intellectual and ethical development during the early adult years. Perry describes the changes in thinking that mark the transition from a belief that knowledge is absolute and answers clearly right or wrong to an understanding of the contextual relativity of both truth and choice. This transition and its impact on moral judgment can be discerned in the changes in moral understanding that occur in both men and women during the five years following college (Gilligan and Murphy, 1979; Murphy and Gilligan, 1980). Though both sexes move away from absolutes in this time, the absolutes themselves differ for each. In women's development, the absolute of care, defined initially as not hurting others, becomes complicated through a recognition of the need for personal integrity. This recognition gives rise to the claim for equality embodied in the concept of rights, which changes the understanding of relationships and transforms the definition of care. For men, the absolutes of truth and fairness, defined by the concepts of equality and reciprocity, are called into question by experiences that demonstrate the existence of differences between other and self. Then the awareness of multiple truths leads to a relativizing of equality in the direction of equity and gives rise to an ethic of generosity and care. For both sexes the existence of two contexts for moral decision makes judgment by definition contextually relative and leads to a new understanding of responsibility and choice.

The discovery of the reality of differences and thus of the contextual nature of morality and truth is described by Alex, a lawyer in the college student study, who began in law school "to realize that you really don't know everything" and "you don't ever know that there is any absolute. I don't think that you ever know that there is an absolute right. What you do know is you have to come down one way or the other. You have got to make a decision."

The awareness that he did not know everything arose more painfully in a relationship whose ending took him completely by surprise. In his belated discovery that the woman's experience had differed from his own, he realized how distant he had been in a relationship he considered close. Then the logical hierarchy of moral values, whose absolute truth he formerly proclaimed, came to seem a barrier to intimacy rather than a fortress of personal integrity. As his conception of morality began to change, his thinking focused on issues of relationship, and his concern with injustice was complicated by a new understanding of human attachment. Describing "the principle of attachment" that began to inform his way of looking at moral problems, Alex sees the need for morality to extend beyond considerations of fairness to concern with relationships:

> People have real emotional needs to be attached to something, and equality doesn't give you attachment. Equality fractures society and places on every person the burden of standing on his own two feet.

Although "equality is a crisp thing that you could hang onto," it alone cannot adequately resolve the dilemmas of choice that arise in life. Given his new awareness of responsibility and of the actual consequences of choice, Alex says: "You don't want to look at just equality. You want to look at how people are going to be able to handle their lives." Recognizing the need for two contexts for judgment, he nevertheless finds that their integration "is hard to work through," since sometimes "no matter which way you go, somebody is going to be hurt and somebody is going to be hurt forever." Then, he says, "you have reached the point where there is an irresolvable conflict," and choice becomes a matter of "choosing the victim" rather than enacting the good. With the recognition of the responsibility that such choices entail, his judgment becomes more attuned to the psychological and social consequences of action, to the reality of people's lives in an historical world.

Thus, starting from very different points, from the different ideologies of justice and care, the men and women in the study come, in the course of becoming adult, to a greater understanding of both points of view and thus to a greater convergence in judgment. Recognizing the dual contexts of justice and care, they realize that judgment depends on the way in which the problem is framed.

But in this light, the conception of development itself also depends on the context in which it is framed, and the vision of maturity can be seen to shift when adulthood is portrayed by women rather than men. When women construct the adult domain, the world of relationships emerges and becomes the focus of attention and concern. McClelland (1975), noting this shift in women's fantasies of power, observes that "women are more concerned than men with both sides of an interdependent relationship" and are "quicker to recognize their own interdependence" (pp. 85–86). This focus on interdependence is manifest in fantasies that equate power with giving and care. McClelland reports that while men represent powerful activity as assertion and aggression, women in contrast portray acts of nurturance as acts of strength. Considering his research on power to deal "in particular with the characteristics of maturity," he suggests that mature women and men may relate to the world in a different style.

That women differ in their orientation to power is also the theme of Jean Baker Miller's analysis. Focusing on relationships of dominance and subordination, she finds women's situation in these relationships to provide "a crucial key to understanding the psychological order." This order arises from the relationships of difference, between man and woman and parent and child, that create "the milieu—the family—in which the human mind as we know it has been formed" (1976, p. 1). Because these relationships of difference contain, in most instances, a factor of inequality, they assume a moral dimension pertaining to the way in which power is used. On this basis, Miller distinguishes between relationships of temporary and permanent inequality, the former representing the context of human development, the latter, the condition of oppression. In relationships of temporary inequality, such as parent and child or teacher and student, power ideally is used to foster the development that removes the initial disparity. In relationships of permanent inequality, power cements dominance and subordination, and oppression is rationalized by theories that "explain" the need for its continuation.

Miller, focusing in this way on the dimension of inequality in human life, identifies the distinctive psychology of women as arising from the combination of their positions in relationships of temporary and permanent inequality. Dominant in temporary relationships of nurturance that dissolve with the dissolution of inequality, women are subservient in relationships of permanently unequal social status and power. In addition, though subordinate in social position to men, women are at the same time centrally entwined with them in the intimate and intense relationships of adult sexuality and family life. Thus women's psychology reflects both sides of relationships of interdependence and the range of moral possibilities to which such relationships give rise. Women, therefore, are ideally situated to observe the potential in human connection both for care and for oppression.

This distinct observational perspective informs the work of Carol Stack (1975) and Lillian Rubin (1976) who, entering worlds previously known through men's eyes, return to give a different report. In the urban black ghetto, where others have seen social disorder and family disarray, Stack finds networks of domestic exchange that describe the organization of the black family in poverty. Rubin, observing the families of the white working class, dispels the myth of "the affluent and happy worker" by charting the "worlds of pain" that it costs to raise a family in conditions of social and economic disadvantage. Both women describe an adulthood of relationships that sustain the family functions of protection and care, but also a social system of relationships that sustain economic dependence and social subordination. Thus they indicate how class, race, and ethnicity are used to justify and rationalize the continuing inequality of an economic system that benefits some at others' expense.

In their separate spheres of analysis, these women find order where others saw chaos—in the psychology of women, the urban black family, and the reproduction of social class. These discoveries required new modes of analysis and a more ethnographic approach in order to derive constructs that could give order and meaning to the adult life they saw. Until Stack redefined "family" as "the smallest organized, durable network of kin and non-kin who interact daily, providing the domestic needs of children and assuring their survival," she could not find "families" in the world of "The Flats." Only the "culturally specific definitions of certain concepts such as family, kin, parent, and friend that emerged during this study made much of the subsequent analysis possible. . . . An arbitrary imposition of widely accepted definitions of the family. . . . blocks the way to understanding how people in The Flats describe and order the world in which they live" (p. 31).

Similarly, Miller calls for "a new psychology of women" that recognizes the different starting point for women's development, the fact that "women stay with, build on, and develop in a context of attachment and affiliation with others," that "women's sense of self becomes very much organized around being able to make, and then to maintain, affiliations and relationships," and that "eventually, for many women, the threat of disruption of an affiliation is perceived not just as a loss of a relationship but as something closer to a total loss of self." Although this psychic structuring is by now familiar from descriptions of women's psychopathology, it has not been recognized that "this psychic starting point contains the possibilities for an entirely different (and more advanced) approach to living and functioning . . . [in which] affiliation is valued as highly as, or more highly than, self-enhancement" (p. 83). Thus, Miller points to a psychology of adulthood which recognizes that develop-

ment does not displace the value of ongoing attachment and the continuing importance of care in relationships.

The limitations of previous standards of measurement and the need for a more contextual mode of interpretation are evident as well in Rubin's approach. Rubin dispels the illusion that family life is everywhere the same or that subcultural differences can be assessed independently of the socioeconomic realities of class. Thus, working-class families "reproduce themselves not because they are somehow deficient or their culture aberrant, but because there are no alternatives for most of their children," despite "the mobility myth we cherish so dearly" (pp. 210–211). The temporary inequality of the working-class child thus turns into the permanent inequality of the working-class adult, caught in an ebb-tide of social mobility that erodes the quality of family life.

Like the stories that delineate women's fantasies of power, women's descriptions of adulthood convey a different sense of its social reality. In their portrayal of relationships, women replace the bias of men toward separation with a representation of the interdependence of self and other, both in love and in work. By changing the lens of developmental observation from individual achievement to relationships of care, women depict ongoing attachment as the path that leads to maturity. Thus the parameters of development shift toward marking the progress of affiliative relationship.

The implications of this shift are evident in considering the situation of women at mid-life. Given the tendency to chart the unfamiliar waters of adult development with the familiar markers of adolescent separation and growth, the middle years of women's lives readily appear as a time of return to the unfinished business of adolescence. This interpretation has been particularly compelling since life-cycle descriptions, derived primarily from studies of men, have generated a perspective from which women, insofar as they differ, appear deficient in their development. The deviance of female development has been especially marked in the adolescent years when girls appear to confuse identity with intimacy by defining themselves through relationships with others. The legacy left from this mode of identity definition is considered to be a self that is vulnerable to the issues of separation that arise at mid-life.

But this construction reveals the limitation in an account which measures women's development against a male standard and ignores the possibility of a different truth. In this light, the observation that women's embeddedness in lives of relationship, their orientation to interdependence, their subordination of achievement to care, and their conflicts over competitive success leave them personally at risk in mid-life seems more a commentary on the society than a problem in women's development.

The construction of mid-life in adolescent terms, as a similar crisis of identity and separation, ignores the reality of what has happened in the years between and tears up the history of love and of work. For generativity to begin at mid-life, as Vaillant's data on men suggest, seems from a woman's perspective too late for both sexes, given that the bearing and raising of children take place primarily in the preceding years. Similarly, the image of women arriving at mid-life childlike and dependent on others is belied by the activity of their care in nurturing and sustaining family relationships. Thus the problem appears to be one of construction, an issue of judgment rather than truth.

In view of the evidence that women perceive and construe social reality differently from men and that these differences center around experiences of attachment and separation, life transitions that invariably engage these experiences can be expected to involve women in a distinctive way. And because women's sense of integrity appears to be entwined with an ethic of care, so that to see themselves as women is to see themselves in a relationship of connection, the major transitions in women's lives would seem to involve changes in the understanding and activities of care. Certainly the shift from childhood to adulthood witnesses a major redefinition of care. When the distinction between helping and pleasing frees the activity of taking care from the wish for approval by others, the ethic of responsibility can become a self-chosen anchor of personal integrity and strength.

In the same vein, however, the events of mid-life—the menopause and changes in family and work—can alter a woman's activities of care in ways that affect her sense of herself. If mid-life brings an end to relationships, to the sense of connection on which she relies, as well as to the activities of care through which she judges her worth, then the mourning that accompanies all life transitions can give way to the melancholia of self-deprecation and despair. The meaning of mid-life events for a woman thus reflects the interaction between the structures of her thought and the realities of her life.

When a distinction between neurotic and real conflict is made and the reluctance to choose is differentiated from the reality of having no choice, then it becomes possible to see more clearly how women's experience provides a key to understanding central truths of adult life. Rather than viewing her anatomy as destined to leave her with a scar of inferiority (Freud, 1931), one can see instead how it gives rise to experiences which illuminate a reality common to both of the sexes: the fact that in life you never see it all, that things unseen undergo change through time, that there is more than one path to gratification, and that the boundaries between self and other are less clear than they sometimes seem.

Thus women not only reach mid-life with a psychological history different from men's and face at that time a different social reality having different possibilities for love and for work, but they also make a different sense of experience, based on their knowledge of human relationships. Since the reality of connection is experienced by women as given rather than as freely contracted, they arrive at an understanding of life that reflects the limits of autonomy and control. As a result, women's development delineates the path not only to a less violent life but also to a maturity realized through interdependence and taking care.

In his studies of children's moral judgment, Piaget (1932/1965) describes a three-stage progression through which constraint turns into cooperation and cooperation into generosity. In doing so, he points out how long it takes before children in the same class at school, playing with each other every day, come to agree in their understanding of the rules of their games. This agreement, however, signals the completion of a major reorientation of action and thought through which the morality of constraint turns into the morality of cooperation. But he also notes how children's recognition of differences between others and themselves leads to a relativizing of equality in the direction of equity, signifying a fusion of justice and love.

There seems at present to be only partial agreement between men and women about the adulthood they commonly share. In the absence of mutual understanding, relationships between the sexes continue in varying degrees of constraint, manifesting the "paradox of egocentrism" which Piaget describes, a mystical respect for rules combined with everyone playing more or less as he pleases and paying no attention to his neighbor (p. 61). For a life-cycle understanding to address the development in adulthood of relationships characterized by cooperation, generosity, and care, that understanding must include the lives of women as well as of men.

Among the most pressing items on the agenda for research on adult development is the need to delineate *in women's own terms* the experience of their adult life. My own work in that direction indicates that the inclusion of women's experience brings to developmental understanding a new perspective on relationships that changes the basic constructs of interpretation. The concept of identity expands to include the experience of interconnection. The moral domain is similarly enlarged by the inclusion of responsibility and care in relationships. And the underlying epistemology correspondingly shifts from the Greek ideal of knowledge as a correspondence between mind and form to the Biblical conception of knowing as a process of human relationship.

Given the evidence of different perspectives in the representation of adulthood by women and men, there is a need for research that elucidates the effects of these differences in marriage, family, and work relationships. My research suggests that men and women may speak different languages that they assume are the same, using similar words to encode disparate experiences of self and social relationships. Because these languages share an overlapping moral vocabulary, they contain a propensity for systematic mistranslation, creating misunderstandings which impede communication and limit the potential for cooperation and care in relationships. At the same time, however, these languages articulate with one another in critical ways. Just as the language of responsibilities provides a weblike imagery of relationships to replace a hierarchical ordering that dissolves with the coming of equality, so the language of rights underlines the importance of including in the network of care not only the other but also the self.

As we have listened for centuries to the voices of men and the theories of development that their expe-

rience informs, so we have come more recently to notice not only the silence of women but the difficulty in hearing what they say when they speak. Yet in the different voice of women lies the truth of an ethic of care, the tie between relationship and responsibility, and the origins of aggression in the failure of connection. The failure to see the different reality of women's lives and to hear the differences in their voices stems in part from the assumption that there is a single mode of social experience and interpretation. By positing instead two different modes, we arrive at a more complex rendition of human experience which sees the truth of separation and attachment in the lives of women and men and recognizes how these truths are carried by different modes of language and thought.

To understand how the tension between responsibilities and rights sustains the dialectic of human development is to see the integrity of two disparate modes of experience that are in the end connected. While an ethic of justice proceeds from the premise of equality—that everyone should be treated the same—an ethic of care rests on the premise of nonviolence—that no one should be hurt. In the representation of maturity, both perspectives converge in the realization that just as inequality adversely affects both parties in an unequal relationship, so too violence is destructive for everyone involved. This dialogue between fairness and care not only provides a better understanding of relations between the sexes but also gives rise to a more comprehensive portrayal of adult work and family relationships.

As Freud and Piaget call our attention to the differences in children's feelings and thought, enabling us to respond to children with greater care and respect, so a recognition of the differences in women's experience and understanding expands our vision of maturity and points to the contextual nature of developmental truths. Through this expansion in perspective, we can begin to envision how a marriage between adult development as it is currently portrayed and women's development as it begins to be seen could lead to a changed understanding of human development and a more generative view of human life.

DISCUSSION QUESTIONS

1. Do you agree with Gilligan's conclusions regarding the gender differences in moral ideologies? Why or why not?

2. Do you agree with Gilligan's conception of moral maturity as a desirable outcome of moral development? Why or why not?

3. How might Gilligan critically evaluate both Kant's and Bentham's ethical standards of conduct?

4. Gilligan acknowledges that her empirical study of responses to moral dilemmas focuses on a fairly narrow cultural and socioeconomic context. How would a male or female from a culture other than that of European Americans assess her conclusions?

53. Riffat Hassan
On the Islamic View of Rights and Duties

Riffat Hassan has been on the faculty of the University of Louisville for a number of years, teaching courses on religion and writing extensively on various issues in Islamic theology and history. More recently she has focused on the problem of gender relations in Islam particularly and the monotheistic religious traditions generally.

This selection is an essay written as a contribution to an anthology on peace education, *Education for Peace,* edited by Haim Gordon and Leonard Grob and published in 1987. The title of Hassan's essay is "Peace Education: A Muslim Perspective," and in it she offers primarily a theological interpretation of the Qur'ān and other Islamic texts regarding the special value placed on both education and peace. As part of this investigation, she highlights the moral duties and respect for moral rights that Islamic doctrine recommends for the guidance of conduct.

Especially in the last few centuries in Western moral philosophy (religious and secular) there has evolved a strong emphasis on "rights" as providing at least one of the fundamental criteria for evaluating actions as ethically justified or not. That is, where a "right" is defined typically as a legitimate demand on others to be treated a certain way, many have argued that an action is morally wrong if it violates someone's rights and morally right or correct if it is in accordance with others' rights. And where there are moral rights at stake, they of course imply moral duties on the part of others to respect those rights. Hassan's account of the Islamic approach to rights and duties is generally consistent with this mainstream Western perspective, including her showing that there are other moral duties besides those correlated with people's rights. In addition, she identifies specific rights possessed by all people everywhere, which she and most others these days refer to as human rights.

QUESTIONS FOR CRITICAL READING

1. In Hassan's view, what are some of the problems in organized attempts at "dialogue" between Muslims and non-Muslims, and what are their causes?

2. According to Hassan, what duties regarding education are stated and implied in Islamic doctrine?

3. How does Hassan characterize "peace" based on her interpretation of Islamic teaching, and what moral duties does she believe are derived from the high value placed on peace?

4. How does Hassan define human rights, and how does she characterize the primary human rights we all possess?

TERMS TO NOTE

paradigm change: In general, the change from one structured worldview to another over historical time; more specifically, it often refers to the dramatic shift from one theoretical framework to a new one thought to be more adequate for making sense out of some dimension of experience.

apostasy: In this context, renouncing one's religious faith.

———

The concept of peace education is new in the world. Certainly not many Muslims have heard of it or have reflected on whether human beings can, or should, be educated for peace. So far as I am aware, there is no program or project—either academic or social, past or present—in any contemporary Muslim society. The few Muslims in the world who have been willing and able to participate in such an education have done so, almost exclusively, in non-Muslim settings under the guidance or sponsorship of non-Muslims. As one of these few Muslims I consider myself privileged to have had the opportunity to be an evaluator of a pioneer education for peace project at the Ben Gurion University in Beer Sheva, Israel, some years ago.

The fact that I was the only Muslim among all the evaluators and that the project, which involved Israeli Jewish and Arab Muslim students, was set in a far-from-neutral environment where an obvious inequality exists between Jews and Muslims, made my task a difficult and exacting one, not only intellectually but also emotionally and spiritually.[1] But I felt then, and feel now even more strongly, that the experience of observing and participating in the education for peace project at Ben Gurion University was one of the most worthwhile experiences of my life.

This experience, intense and bittersweet, taught me much. Most of all, it showed me that peace education was not a fantasy but an ideal that could be achieved even in conditions that appeared to be inimical to authentic dialogical interaction. More important still, it gave me a glimpse into what could be accomplished even by an experimental peace education project that was struggling continually to review its nature and goals as it moved gropingly from one phase to another in its three-year life span. I believe, both on the basis of my theoretical study as a theologian of Islam and my observation of pragmatic reality, that educating for peace is one of the most compelling religious/ethical imperatives for all persons who believe in the "transcendent" dimension of human life.

In this paper I will endeavor to show that Muslims are called upon by the Qur'ān and the example of the Prophet of Islam to strive for peace through all available means and that, therefore, peace education must have a high priority in Muslim societies and for Muslims generally. Inasmuch as, unfortunately, I have no empirical data relating to actual peace education projects initiated and developed by Muslims, my paper will focus on sources of "normative" Islam and will identify some important theological resources that could

be utilized for persuading Muslims not only to participate in peace education programs in non-Muslim societies but also, and more importantly, to establish such programs in their own societies.

As I see it, before one can argue convincingly that Muslims should be educated for peace it is necessary to demonstrate that education and peace are of pivotal significance to the Islamic worldview. This paper is, therefore, divided into two main sections, the first dealing with education and the second with peace, followed by a summation.

The Islamic View of Education

In education, attention must be drawn to an extremely important fact: the overwhelming majority of Muslims in the world are uneducated, the literacy rate of many Muslim countries being among the lowest in the world. Even among those who qualify as "literate," many can barely read or write.[2] Needless to say, the lack of education has an enormous impact upon all human activities in Muslim societies. It is painful—but necessary—to imagine the gap between those who have had the opportunity to develop what the Qur'ān regards as God's greatest gift to humanity—namely, the ability to conceptualize or to think,[3] which makes possible the miracles of our age—and those who have lived in darkness through the centuries, unaware of their own rich heritage, following the way of their forebears blindly, believing it to be the path of life, whereas, in truth, it is a path of death.

I consider it important to keep the general lack of education among Muslims in mind as one begins to reflect on the feasibility of peace education in the Islamic framework, because any scheme or proposal that ignores the facts of life is doomed to failure. Furthermore, it leads to the setting up of unreal expectations and false comparisons. All too often I have seen non-Muslim dialogue partners, including some of the most dedicated ones, throw up their hands in despair and exclaim: "Why are Muslims in general so hard to engage in dialogue?" Or "Why are Muslims who participate in dialogue so 'precritical'?"

What these dialogue participants need to realize is that the Muslim world has not gone through the paradigm changes that the Western Judeo-Christian world has, and that it is, therefore, not appropriate to compare either largely uneducated Muslim societies with much better educated Western societies or Muslims who have been educated in the pre-Enlightenment, perhaps even the pre-Reformation, mode, with Westerners who have been educated in the post-Enlightenment, perhaps even the postmodern, mode. It is a sign of insensitivity if not arrogance (or what is sometimes called "cultural imperialism" by Third World persons) to expect Muslims who have not had the opportunity to go through the process of becoming "critical" thinkers to engage in a dialogue that presupposes a "critical" mind-set defined in exclusively non-Muslim (often Western Christian) terms. Such an expectation tends to alienate even those Muslims who are willing to step outside their own "pre-critical" tradition and work toward evolving concepts and categories that are meaningful and acceptable to all dialogue partners. Such alienation can and must be avoided, not only because there are so few Muslims who are dialogue-oriented (out of the almost one billion Muslims in the world), but also because there are so many resources within Islam that can be used to eradicate the ignorance of Muslims as well as to irradiate the hearts and minds and spirits of those "others" who seek to understand Islam and Muslims from within.

The Attitude of "Normative" Islam toward Knowledge

The fact that there are so many illiterate and uneducated Muslims (particularly women) in the world constitutes not only a profound tragedy but also a profound irony in view of the tremendous stress that "normative" Islam puts on the importance of acquiring knowledge. This is clear from many quranic passages and prophetic *hadíth,* "tradition." It is of interest and importance to observe, for instance, that the Qur'ān refers 140 times to God as *alim:* one who has knowledge, and that the very first verse of the Qur'ān revealed to the Prophet Muhammad links to divine bounty the human ability to write and to know:

> Read in the name of thy Sustainer who has created—created man out of a germ-cell! Read— for thy Sustainer is the Most Bountiful One who has taught [man] the use of the pen— taught man what he did not know! [Surah 96.1].[4]

The Qur'ān describes the Prophet of Islam as one taught by God (Surah 4.113) and as an imparter of knowledge to others (Surah 2.151) but commands him, nevertheless, to pray: "O my Sustainer, cause me to grow in knowledge" (Surah 20.114).[5] Further, the Qur'ān exhorts believers not to pursue that of which they have no knowledge, because God will call them to account for actions that reflect a lack of knowledge:

> Pursue not that
> Of which thou hast
> No knowledge; for
> Every act of hearing,
> Or of seeing
> Or of [feeling in] the heart
> Will be enquired into
> [on the Day of Reckoning]
> [Surah 17.36].[6]

> Behold, ye rejected it
> on your tongues,
> And said out of your mouths
> Things of which ye had
> No knowledge; and ye thought
> It a light matter,
> While it was most serious
> In the sight of God
> [Surah 24.15].[7]

About those who have knowledge, the Qur'ān says:

> And whoever is given knowledge is given indeed great wealth [Surah 2.269].[8]
> God will exalt by [many] degrees those of you who have attained to faith and [above all] such as have been vouchsafed knowledge: for God is fully aware of all that you do [Surah 58.11].[9]

Sayings Attributed to Muhammad

Embodying the spirit of the Qur'ān are some famous sayings attributed to the Prophet of Islam: "The seeking of knowledge is obligatory upon every Muslim" (Baihaqi, *Mishkat);*[10] "Search for knowledge is compulsory for every Muslim male and Muslim female" (Ibn Majah);[11] "He who goes forth in search of knowledge is in the way of Allah till he returns" (Tirmidhi, Darimi);[12] "Search for knowledge though it be in China" (Baihaqi);[13] "Whoever searches after knowledge, it will be expiation for his past sins" (Tirmidhi).[14]

Further:

> If anyone travels on a road in search of knowledge, God will cause him to travel on one of the roads of paradise, the angels will lower their wings from good pleasure with one who seeks knowledge, and the inhabitants of the heavens and the earth and the fish in the depth of the water will ask forgiveness for him. The superiority of the learned man over the devout man is like that of the moon on the night when it is full over the rest of the stars. The learned are the heirs of the prophets who leave neither *dinar* nor *dirham* ["neither dollar nor dime"], leaving only knowledge, and he who accepts it accepts an abundant portion [Ahmad, Tirmidhi, Abu Dawud, Ibn Majah, Darimi, *Mishkat*].[15]

> Acquire knowledge, because he who acquires it in the way of the Lord performs an act of piety; who speaks of it, praises the Lord; who seeks it, adores God; who dispenses instruction in it, bestows alms; and who imparts it to its fitting objects, performs an act of devotion to God. Knowledge enables its possessor to distinguish what is forbidden from what is not; it lights the way to Heaven; it is our friend in the desert, our society in solitude, our companion when bereft of friend; it serves as an armor against our enemies. With knowledge, the servant of God rises to the heights of goodness and to a noble position, associates with sovereigns in this world, and attains to the perfection of happiness in the next [*Bihar-ul-Anwar, Mustatraf, Kashf uz-Zaman*].[16]

Although it is not possible to say whether any of the above-cited *ahadith* are authentic without a detailed scrutiny of their formal aspect (i.e., the *isnād*, "chain of transmission"), the fact that all of them conform in spirit to the ethos as well as specific teachings of the Qur'ān supports the assumption that they represent, if not the actual words of the Prophet, at least the general attitude of his companions and their successors. There is also historical evidence showing that the Prophet of Islam considered the education of his community a matter of high priority. For instance, Goldziher points out

> That Muhammad himself—partly, it may be, on utilitarian grounds—attached considerable importance to the acquisition of the most indispensable elements of knowledge, may be inferred from the conditions on which he released prisoners of war after his victory at Badr. He employed several Quraish captives to teach the boys of Medina to write, and this service counted as their ransom.[17]

Prophet Muhammad's attitude toward the acquisition of knowledge obviously had a strong impact upon the community in which he lived. As Seeman states: "In the realm of education, we may say, Muhammad instituted learning as an incumbent duty upon his people and this established a definite educational policy for Islam."[18] That the obligation to acquire knowledge was "a concept that possessed religious urgency and was ready to play a prominent role in a new religious movement" is testified to by Rosenthal.[19] Gulick expresses the belief that the knowledge-affirming *ahadith* which "have been widely accepted as authentic and . . . have exerted a wide and salutary influence . . . must assuredly have stimulated and encouraged the great thinkers of the golden age of Islamic civilization."[20]

The Content and Purpose of Knowledge According to "Normative" Islam

In Islam the seeking of knowledge includes formal education, but is not confined to such education, nor are academic credentials necessarily the measure of one's knowledge, though they may be regarded as instrumental to learning. To be educated, in Islamic terms, means to possess knowledge, which may be acquired through a variety of sources, particularly revelation, reason, empirical inquiry, history, and intuition. From the quranic perspective, knowledge is obviously not limited to what is learned through the reasoning mind or the senses. Acquisition of knowledge involves the total person in relationship with total reality. To become a "total" or "whole" person, integration of the diverse, often mutually conflicting, aspects of one's outer and inner self is required, as sages through the centuries have taught. To acquire knowledge of total reality, or to become educated ideally in Islamic terms, also requires a process of integration. By identifying and endorsing diverse sources of knowledge often considered to be mutually opposing (as revelation and reason, or reason and intuition), the Qur'ān points toward both the possibility of, and the need for, an integration or synthesis leading to a unity of knowledge that subsumes the multiplicity of the sources of knowledge. That the quranic vision has been internalized by at least some leaders of Muslim thought is clear from the following letter in which Muhammad Iqbāl, the philosopher-poet, describes his own philosophy of education:

> Modern India ought to focus on the discovery of man as a personality—as an independent "whole" in an all-embracing synthesis of life. But does our education today tend to awaken in us such a sense of inner wholeness? My answer is no. Our education does not recognise man as a problem, it impresses on us the visible fact of multiplicity without giving us an insight into the inner unity of life, and thus tends to make us more and more universal in our physical environment. The soul of man is left untouched and the result is a superficial knowledge with a mere illusion of culture and freedom. Amidst this predominantly intellectual culture which must accentuate separate centres within the "whole" the duty of higher minds in India is to reveal the inner synthesis of life.[21]

Although knowledge, defined in quranic terms, is the means "to awaken in man the higher consciousness of his manifold relations with God and the universe"[22] its ultimate purpose (as the existentialists would say) is not to see but to be. True believers in God seek to inculcate God's attributes in themselves. God is *alim*: one who has knowledge; hence the seeking of knowledge is obligatory upon all believers. However, the all-knowing God of the Qur'ān is not the Unmoved Mover, Logos, or Absolute of Greek thought, but the dynamic creator and commander of the universe. Hence a Muslim's "essential nature . . . consists in will, not intellect and understanding"[23] and Muslims identify with Ghazzali's statement: "I will, therefore I am," rather than with Descartes' statement: "I think, therefore I am." The will to act is an integral part of the quranic concept of knowledge.

The Qur'ān urges the seeking of knowledge so that through it both inner and outer reality may be transformed. It is of the essence of a river to flow and of the sun to give light. It is of the essence of an *alim* to translate knowledge into objective reality as did the Prophet of Islam and the Qur'ān calls those who know but do not act *jahilun* (ignorant ones) not *alimun* (knowledgeable ones). Understood in these terms, an *alim* is a *mujahid*—that is, one who engages in *jihād*, strives in the cause of God.

The Islamic View of Peace

It is profoundly ironic that stereotypes identify Islam with war and militancy, whereas the very term *islām* is derived from a root, one of whose basic meanings is "peace." Not only is the idea of peace of pivotal significance in the theological worldview of Islam, it also permeates the daily lives of Muslims. Each time two Muslims greet each other, they say *salam alaikum,* "peace be on you," and *alaikum assalam,* "peace be on you (too)." The regularity and fervor with which this greeting is exchanged shows that it is not a mechanical reiteration of words that have little or no meaning but a religious ritual of great importance. The ideal of being at peace with oneself, one's fellow human beings, the world of nature, and God, is deeply cherished by Muslims in general. But if that is the case, why is there such manifest lack of peace, and so much talk of violence, in the present-day world of Islam? In order to answer this question it is necessary to understand what "peace" means according to the perspective of "normative" Islam.

Many, including some who are committed to the ideal of peacemaking, tend, unfortunately, to define peace negatively, as "absence of war" (just as some tend to define "health" as "absence of sickness"). But, in quranic terms, peace is much more than mere absence of war. It is a positive state of safety or security in which one is free from anxiety or fear. It is this state that characterizes both *islām,*[24] self-surrender to God, and *īmān,*[25] true faith in God, and reference is made to it, directly or indirectly, on every page of the Qur'ān through the many derivatives of the roots "s-l-m" and "a-m-n" from which *islām* and *īmān* are derived, respectively. Peace is an integral part not only of the terms used for a believer, "muslim" (i.e., one who professes *islām*) and *mo'min* (i.e., one who possesses *īmān*), but also of God's names *As-Salām* and *Al-Mo'min* mentioned in the Qur'ān:

He is Allāh, beside whom there is no God; the King, the Holy, the Author of Peace [As-Salām], the Granter of Security [Al-Mo'min], Guardian over all, the Mighty, the Supreme, the Possessor of greatness [Surah 59.23].[26]

As pointed out by G. A. Parwez, *As-Salām* is the Being who is the source of peace and concord and who assures peaceful existence to all beings. *Al-Mo'min* is the Being who shelters and protects all and bestows peace in every sphere of life.[27]

That God "invites" humanity to *dār as-salām* (i.e., the abode of peace) is stated by the Qur'ān (Surah 10.25), which also promises the reward of peace to those who live in accordance with God's will:

God guides such as follow His pleasure into the ways of peace, and brings them out of darkness into light by His will, and guides them to the right path [Surah 5.16].[28]

And this is the path of thy Lord, straight. Indeed we have made the message clear for a people who mind. Theirs is the abode of peace with their Lord, and He is their Friend because of what they do [Surah 6.127–128].[29]

Can, then, he who knows that whatever has been bestowed from on high upon thee by thy Sustainer is the truth be deemed equal to one who is blind? Only they who are endowed with insight keep this in mind: they who are true to their bond with God and never break their covenant; and who keep together what God has bidden to be joined, and stand in awe of their Sustainer and fear the most evil reckoning (which awaits such as do not respond to Him); and who are patient in adversity out of a longing for their Sustainer's countenance, and are constantly in prayer, and spend on others, secretly and openly, out of what we provide for them as sustenance, and repel evil with good. It is these that shall find their fulfillment in the hereafter: gardens of perpetual bliss which they shall enter together with the righteous from

among their parents, their spouses, and their offspring: and the angels will come unto them from every gate (and will say): "Peace be upon you, because you have persevered!" [Surah 13.19–24].[30]

The verses cited above point the way a believer must follow in order to attain peace in the hereafter. But this way (i.e., of *islām*) is also the way of obtaining peace here and now. In other words, peace on earth (which is a precondition of peace in heaven) is the result of living in accordance with God's will and pleasure. Here it is important to note that Islam conceives of God as *Rabb Al-'Alamīn*: Creator and Sustainer of all the peoples and universes, whose purpose in creating (as stated in Surah 51.56) is that all creatures should engage in God's *ībādat*. This term, which is commonly understood as "worship," in fact has a much broader meaning and refers to "doing what God approves."[31] In Islam "doing what God approves" is not conceived in terms of seeking salvation from the burden of original sin through belief in redemption or a redeemer (none of these ideas/concepts being present in the Qur'ān) or through renunciation of the world (monasticism not being required by God, according to the Qur'ān).[32] Rather, it is conceived in terms of the fulfillment of *Haquq Allāh* (rights of God) and *Haquq al-'ibād* (rights of God's servants—namely, human beings). The Qur'ān considers the two kinds of "rights" to be inseparable as indicated by the constant conjunction of *salāt* (signifying remembrance of, and devotion to, God) and *zakāt* (signifying the sharing of one's possessions with those in need). In fact, as Surah 107 shows, the Qur'ān is severe in its criticism of those who offer their prayers to God but are deficient in performing acts of kindness to those in need:

Hast thou ever considered [the kind of person] who
   gives the lie to all moral law?
Behold, it is this [kind of person] who thrusts the
   orphan away,
and feels no urge to feed the needy.
Woe, then, unto those praying ones whose hearts from
   their prayers are remote—
those who want only to be seen and praised,
and, withal, deny all assistance [to their fellows].[33]

In quranic terms, then, peace is obtained in any human society when human beings, conscious of their duty to God, fulfill their duty to other human beings. In fulfilling this duty they honor what I call the "human rights" of others. These rights are those that all human beings *ought* to possess because they are rooted so deeply in our humanness that their denial or violation is tantamount to negation or degradation of that which makes us human. These rights came into existence when we did; they were created, as we were, by God in order that our human potential could be actualized. These rights not only provide us with an opportunity to develop all our inner resources, but they also hold before us a vision of what God would like us to be: what God wants us to strive for and live for and die for. Rights given by God are rights that ought to be exercised, because everything that God does is for "a just purpose" (Surah 15.85; 16.3; 44.39; 45.22; 46.3). Among these rights, there are some that have an important, perhaps even a crucial, bearing on whether or not a society can realize the ideal of peace; hence a brief account of them follows.

Right to Life

The sanctity and absolute value of human life is upheld by the Qur'ān, which states:

> And do not take any human being's life—
> which God has declared to be sacred—other-
> wise than in [the pursuit of] justice: this He has
> enjoined upon you so that you might use your
> reason [Surah 6.151].[34]

The Qur'ān also points out graphically in Surah 5.35 that in essence the life of each individual is comparable to the life of an entire community, and, therefore, should be treated with utmost care:

> We ordained
> For the Children of Israel
> That if any one slew
> A person—unless it be
> For murder or for spreading
> Mischief in the land—
> It would be as if
> He slew the whole people:
> And if anyone saved a life,
> It would be as if he saved
> The life of the whole people.[35]

Right to Respect

In Surah 17.70, the Qur'ān says: "Verily, we have honored every human being." Human beings are worthy of respect because they have been made "in the best of molds" (Surah 95.4), and possess the faculty of reason, which distinguishes them from all other creatures (Surah 2.30–34) and enables them to accept the "trust" of freedom of will, which no other creature is willing to accept (Surah 33.72). Human beings can acquire knowledge of good and evil, and strive to do the good and avoid the evil. Thus, they have the potential to be God's viceregents on earth. On account of the promise that is contained in being human, the humanness of all human beings is to be respected and regarded as an end in itself.

Right to Justice

In the Qur'ān, tremendous emphasis is put on the duty to do justice:

> O ye who believe, be maintainers of justice,
> bearers of witness for Allah, even though it be
> against your own selves or [your] parents or
> near relatives—whether he be rich or poor, Al-
> lah has the better right over them both. So fol-
> low not low desires, lest you deviate. And if you
> distort or turn away from [truth], surely Allah
> is ever aware of what you do [Surah 4.135].[36]
>
> O ye who believe, be upright for Allah, bear-
> ers of witness with justice; and let not hatred of
> a people incite you not to act equitably. Be just;
> that is nearer to observance of duty. And keep
> your duty to Allah. Surely Allah is aware of
> what you do [Surah 5.8].[37]

In the context of justice, the Qur'ān uses two concepts: *adl* and *ihsan*. Both are enjoined (Surah 16.91) and both are related to the idea of balance, but they are not identical in meaning. A. A. A. Fyzee, a well-known scholar of Islamic law, defined *adl* as "to be equal, neither more nor less," and stated: "in a court of justice the claims of the two parties must be considered evenly, without undue stress being laid upon one side or the other. Justice introduces balance in the form of scales that are evenly balanced."[38] Abu'l Kalam Azad, a noted Muslim scholar, described *adl* in similar terms: "What is justice but the avoiding of excess. There should be neither too much nor too little; hence the use of scales as the emblems of justice."[39] Lest anyone try to do too much or too little, the Qur'ān states that no human being can carry another's burden (Surah 53.38) or have anything without striving for it (ibid., 39).

It is important to note here that, according to the quranic perspective, justice is not to be interpreted as absolute equality of treatment, because human beings are not equal so far as their human potential or their human situation is concerned. Thus, though upholding the principle that the humanness of all human beings is to be respected, the Qur'ān maintains that the recognition of individual "merit" is also a fundamental human right. The Qur'ān teaches that merit is not determined by lineage, sex, wealth, success, or religion—but by righteousness. Righteousness consists not only of *īmān* (just belief) but also of *amal* (just action) as pointed out in the following passage:

> True piety does not consist in turning your faces towards the east or the west—but truly pious is he who believes in God, and the Last Day, and the angels, and revelation, and the prophets; and spends his substance—however much he himself may cherish it—upon his near of kin, and the orphans, and the needy, and the wayfarer, and the beggars, and for the freeing of human beings from bondage; and is constant in prayer, and renders the purifying dues; and [truly pious are] they who keep their promises whenever they promise, and are patient in misfortune and hardship and in time of peril: it is they who have proved themselves true, and it is they, they who are conscious of God.[40]

Surah 19.95 testifies to the higher merit of one who strives harder for the cause of God:

> Such of the believers as remain passive—other than the disabled—cannot be deemed equal to those who strive hard in God's cause with their possessions and their lives: God has exalted those who strive hard with their possessions and their lives far above those who remain passive.

> Although God has promised the ultimate good unto all [believers], yet has God exalted those who strive hard above those who remain passive by [promising them] a mighty reward—[many] degrees thereof—and forgiveness of sins, and His grace; for God is indeed much-forgiving, a dispenser of grace.[41]

Surah 49.13 affirms that "the most honored of you in the sight of God is the most righteous of you."

Just as it is in the spirit of *adl* that special merit be considered in the matter of rewards, so also special circumstances must be considered in the matter of punishments. In the case of punishment for crimes of "unchastity," for instance, the Qur'ān, being nonsexist, prescribes identical punishments for a man or a woman who is proved guilty (Surah 2.2), but it differentiates between different classes of women; for the same crime, a slave woman would receive half, and the Prophet's consort double, the punishment given to a "free" Muslim woman (Surah 4.25; 33.30). Making such a distinction shows compassion for the morally "disadvantaged," while upholding high moral standards for others, particularly those whose actions have a normative significance.

While constantly enjoining *adl*, the Qur'ān goes beyond this concept to *ihsan*, literally "restoring the balance by making up a loss or deficiency."[42] In order to understand this concept, it is necessary to understand the nature of the ideal community or society (*ummah*) envisaged by the Qur'ān. The word *ummah* comes from the term *umm* meaning "mother." The symbols of a mother and motherly love and compassion are also linked with the two attributes most characteristic of God, *Rahmān* and *Rahīm,* both of which are derived from the root r-h-m, meaning "womb." The ideal *ummah* cares about all its members as an ideal mother cares about all her children, knowing that all are not equal and that each has different needs. Although encouraging any one of her children to be parasitical would be injurious and unjust not only to her other children but also to the one who does not fulfill its human potential, she can, with justice, make up the deficiency of any child who, despite its best efforts, still cannot meet the requirements of life. *Ihsan* thus secures what even *adl* cannot; it shows the Qur'ān's sympathy for the downtrodden, oppressed, or weak classes of human beings (such as women, slaves, orphans, the poor, the infirm, minorities, etc.).

Right to Freedom

There is much in the Qur'ān that endorses J. J. Rousseau's famous statement: "Man is born free, and everywhere he is in chains." A large part of the Qur'ān's concern is to free human beings from the chains that bind them: traditionalism, authoritarianism (religious, political, economic), tribalism, racism, sexism, and slavery.

It is obvious that God alone is completely free and not subject to any constraints. The human condition necessitates that limits be set to what human beings may or may not do, so that liberty does not degenerate into license. Recognizing the human propensity toward dictatorship and despotism, the Qur'ān says with startling clarity and emphasis:

> It is not meet for a mortal that Allah should give him the Book and the judgment and the prophethood, then he should say to men: Be my servants besides Allah's; but [he would say]: Be worshippers of the Lord because you teach the Book and because you study [it] [Surah 3.78].[43]

The greatest guarantee of personal freedom for a Muslim lies in the quranic decree that no one other than God can limit human freedom (Surah 42.21) and in the statement that "judgment is only Allah's" (Surah 12.40).

Although it is beyond the scope of this paper to cite quranic pronouncements relating to human freedom in the diverse realms of life, it is important to mention that the Qur'ān abolished slavery (Surah 47.4); that it established the principle of *shura* or government by mutual consultation (Surah 3.159)[44] in order to eliminate the possibility of political authoritarianism; and that it prohibited coercion in matters of religious belief as is clearly stated in Surah 2.256:

> Let there be no compulsion
> In religion: truth stands out
> Clear from error: whoever
> Rejects evil and believes
> In God hath grasped
> The most trustworthy
> Hand-hold, that never breaks.[45]

The same is implied in Surah 18.29:

> The Truth is
> From your Lord:
> Let him who will
> Believe, and let him
> Who will, reject [it].[46]

It is noteworthy that in the matter of religious freedom, the Qur'ān is "liberal" to an amazing degree. Not only does it state quite clearly that the mission of the

Prophet (and Muslims) to non-Muslims consists only of a faithful transmission of the message of God and that the Prophet (and Muslims) ought not to feel responsible for the religious and moral choices made by other Muslims or by non-Muslims after they have received the message of God.[47] The Qur'ān also makes it clear that plurality of religions is part of God's plan for humanity:

> If it had been God's plan
> They would not have taken
> False gods: but we
> Made thee not one
> To watch over their doings,
> Nor art thou set
> Over them to dispose
> Of their affairs
> [Surah 6.107].[48]

> If it had been thy Lord's will
> They would have all believed,
> All who are on earth!
> Will thou then compel mankind,
> Against their will, to believe!
> [Surah 10.99].[49]

Going still further, the Qur'ān states:

> Those who believe [in the Qur'ān],
> And those who follow the Jewish [scriptures],
> And the Christians and the Sabians,
> Any who believe in God
> And the Last Day,
> And work righteousness,
> Shall have their reward
> With their Lord,
> Nor shall they grieve
> [Surah 2.62].[50]

In other words, not only does the Qur'ān uphold the right of human beings in general to religious freedom, it also recognizes the religious equality of all those who have "iman" and act righteously. Even to those beyond the pale of "right belief," the attitude of the Qur'ān is open-minded and more than merely tolerant, as may be seen from the following verses:

> But do not revile those whom they invoke instead of God, lest they revile God out of spite, and in ignorance: for, goodly indeed have we made their own doings appear unto every com-

munity. In time, however unto their Sustainer they must return: and then He will make them [truly] understand all that they were doing [Surah 6.108].[51]

And if any of those who ascribe divinity to aught beside God seeks thy protection, grant him protection, so that he might [be able to] hear the word of God [from thee]; and thereupon convey him to a place where he can feel secure: this, because they [may be] people who [sin only because they] do not know [the truth] [Surah 9.6].[52]

In the context of the human right to religious freedom, it is necessary to mention that, according to traditional Islam, the punishment for apostasy is death. There is, however, nothing in the Qur'ān that suggests any punishment at all, let alone the punishment of death. There is absolutely no reason why the quranic imperative that there must be no compulsion in religion should not apply also to the Muslims who wish to renounce Islam. (I believe that the death penalty was not originally for apostasy but for apostasy accompanied by "acts of war" against Muslims. Later, however, this distinction was obliterated by Muslim jurists in order to compel "wavering" Muslims to remain within the fold of Islam.)

Other Rights

Some other rights that may be mentioned in passing are: the right to be protected from defamation, sarcasm, offensive nicknames, and backbiting (Surah 49.11–12) as well as from being maligned on grounds of assumed guilt by scandal-mongers (Surah 24.16–19); the right to a secure place of residence (Surah 2.85); the right to a means of living (Surah 6.156; 11.6); the right to protection of one's personal property or possessions (Surah 2.29); the right to protection of one's covenants/contracts (Surah 3.177; 5.1; 17.34); the right to move freely (Surah 67.15); the right to seek asylum if one is living under oppression (Surah 4.97–100); the right to social and judicial autonomy for minorities (Surah 5.42–48); the right to protection of one's holy places (Surah 9.17); and the right to protection of one's home life from undue intrusion (Surah 24.27–28, 58; 33.53; 49.12).

It is essential in the context of human rights in Islam to mention that there is more quranic legislation pertaining to the regulation of man-woman relationships than on any other subject. The Qur'ān is fully cognizant of the fact that women have been among the most exploited and oppressed groups in the world, and aims, in multifarious ways, to establish their equality with men in terms of their humanness and to secure justice for them in domestic and public matters. An idea of tremendous importance implicit in many teachings of the Qur'ān is that if human beings can learn to order their homes justly so that the rights of all within its jurisdiction are safeguarded, then they can also order their society and the world at large justly. In other words, the Qur'ān regards the home as a microcosm of the *ummah* and the world community, and emphasizes the importance of making it "the abode of peace" through just living.

Even a brief reflection on the "human rights"[53] mentioned above gives one a good idea of the quranic concept of "the good life." This good life, which is made up of many elements and is characterized by peace, is possible only within a just environment. In other words, justice is a prerequisite for peace according to the Qur'ān, which does not understand peace to be a passive state of affairs, a mere absence of war. A peace generated by a thing such as the cold war would, in quranic terms, not only be "unholy" but also unreal because it does not guarantee the existence of the conditions that are required for the actualization of human potentialities or the fulfillment of the total human being who alone is capable of attaining the ideal of peace as the Qur'ān understands it. Without the elimination of the inequities, inequalities, and injustices that pervade the personal and collective lives of human beings, it is not possible to talk of peace in Islamic terms. Such talk makes sense only in a society in which ignorance and oppression have been eliminated, in which the means of sustaining and developing human life and capabilities are accessible to all, in which there is freedom from fear, uncertainty, and anxiety—in short, in a society where justice prevails in every way.

Summation

The central significance of both education and peace in "normative" Islam is clear from the foregoing discussion. There is no question at all that the Qur'ān would wholeheartedly support the idea of educating for peace provided its concepts of "education" and "peace" are properly understood. It is obvious that the quranic ideal is not easy to achieve in a world such as the one in which we live, because it entails not simply the desire to abolish violence and war as means of conflict-resolution but the commitment to "doing what God approves." However, from the quranic perspective, the securing of peace either here and now or in the hereafter is not meant to be easy, as the Qur'ān states in Surah 3.141:

> Did you think that ye
> Would enter al-jannah
> [i.e., "the garden": the abode of peace]
> Without God testing
> Those of you who fought hard
> (in His cause) and
> Remained steadfast?[54]

Peace is dependent upon justice and justice is dependent upon *jihād fi sabil Allāh*: striving in the cause of God. It is most unfortunate that *jihād,* which is the means whereby God's vision of a peaceful world can come to be, has become identified in the minds of many non-Muslims and—what is much worse—in the minds of many present-day Muslims, with mere destruction. According to the Qur'ān, Muslims have the right to defend themselves against injustice and the duty to protect the weak from injustice.[55] But they are reminded, over and over, that the "limits set by God" (*hudud Allāh*) are not to be transgressed at any time, and that justice must be done even to an enemy.[56] Furthermore, any initiative toward peace taken by an enemy must be accepted and responded to in good faith and with good will.[57]

The thought with which I should like to conclude this paper is that, in my judgment, the greatest *jihād* for Muslims today lies in the making of war not upon real or assumed enemies of Islam but upon the ignorance and narrowness of heart, mind, and spirit that prevent Muslims from becoming *mo'minum:* those who have attained peace through right knowledge leading to right action. The duty to seek learning even in the midst of war is where the quranic emphasis lies, as pointed out in Surah 9.122:

> With all this, it is not desirable that all of the believers take the field [in time of war]. From within every group in their midst, some shall

refrain from going forth to war, and shall devote themselves [instead] to acquiring a deeper knowledge of the faith, and [thus be able to] teach their home-coming brethren, so that these [too] might guard themselves against evil.[58]

Notes

1. Some of my reactions to the Education for Peace Project at the Ben Gurion University were recorded in "Response to 'Buberian Learning Groups: the Quest for Responsibility in Education for Peace,' by Haim Gordon and Jan Demarest," published in *Teachers College Record,* 84.2 (Fall 1982) 226–31, and in *Education for Peace and Disarmament: Toward a Living World,* Douglas Sloan, ed. (New York, Teachers College Press, 1983).

2. Pakistan is one of the most educated of Muslim countries in the world. The following citations from a government document entitled *Action Plan for Educational Development 1983–88,* published by the Ministry of Education, Islamabad (1984), give an indication of what this means—for it and for the other Muslim nations: "Literacy was estimated at 26.2% in 1981. Behind this unflattering figure, there are large disparities—in terms of rural/urban (17.3% against 47.1%) and male/female (35.1% against 16.0%). Rural female literacy is only 7.3%, the worst case being female literacy in Baluchistan, only 1.8%" (p. 43). "In 1981 the criterion [of literacy] became . . . 'the ability to read a newspaper and write a simple letter in any language'" (p. 43). "The inadequacy of our educational system leaves little scope for debate. . . . Yet, what is heartening is the widespread realization that today we stand at the edge of a precipice, and that our fall is being delayed only because of our tenuous links with the mere semblance of a system, which if precluded of its weaknesses might still prove to be viable. Pakistan as a nation is at the brink of complete educational chaos and disaster" (p. 13). "Today we stand at the crossroads of planning informed by the realization that no meaningful progress can be achieved in Pakistan without a breakthrough in the field of education. The task has forbidding magnitudes. . . . With a literacy rate of 26.2% we mark the borders of the bottom category of countries like Bhutan, Nepal, Afghanistan, Ethiopia, Sudan, Chad, Laos, and Zaire. . . . Of the microscopic minority that manage to get education, the quality is nowhere near the international standards. More and more young men are emerging from the high schools ready neither for college nor for work. The state of higher education is no different. The predicament becomes more acute as knowledge expands to new frontiers. Obviously, 'all is not well in the state of Denmark'" (p. 32).

3. See Surah 2.30–33.

4. Translation by Muhammad Asad, *The Message of the Qur'ān* (Gibraltar, Dar-Al-Andalus, 1980).

5. Ibid.

6. Translation by Abdullah Yusuf Ali, *The Holy Qur'ān* (Lahore, 1937–38).

7. Ibid.

8. Translation by Muhammad Ali, *A Manual of Hadith* (Lahore, Ahmadiyya Anjuman Ishaat-i-Islam, n.d.), p. 31.

9. Asad, *Message of the Qur'ān.*

10. Ali, *Manual of Hadith,* p. 39.

11. Nisar Ahmed, *The Fundamental Teachings of Qur'ān and Hadith* (Karachi, Jamiyatul Falah Publications, 1973), vol. 3, p. 111.

12. Abdallah al-Khatib at-Tabrizi, *Mishkat al-Masabih,* translated by James Robson (Lahore, Shaikh Muhammad Ashraf, 1975), vol. 1, p. 55.

13. Ahmed, *Fundamental Teachings,* vol. 3, p. 117.

14. Ibid., p. 111.

15. at-Tabrizi, *Mishkat al-Masabih,* vol. 1, p. 53.

16. Cited in *The Spirit of Islam* by Syed Ameer Ali (Karachi, Pakistan Publishing House, 1976), pp. 360–61.

17. I. Goldziher, "Education (Muslim)," in *Encyclopedia of Religion and Ethics,* J. Hastings, ed. (Edinburgh, 1967), vol. 5, p. 198, quoted in *Religious Education in Islam* by J. D. Kraan (Rawalpindi, Christian Study Centre, 1984), p. 14.

18. Seeman K., "Education in Islam, From the Jahiliyyah to Ibn Khaidun," *Muslim World,* 56/3 (1966) 188, quoted in Kraan, *Religious Education,* p. 15.

19. F. Rosenthal, *Knowledge Triumphant: The Concept of Knowledge in Medieval Islam* (Leiden, Brill, 1970), p. 23, quoted in Kraan, *Religious Education,* p. 13.

20. R. L. Gulick, *Muhammad the Educator* (Lahore, Institute of Islamic Culture, 1969), p. 45.

21. Letter dated Dec. 5, 1925, published in *The Indian Review,* Madras, 27/1 (Jan. 1926) 2.

22. Muhammad Iqbāl, *The Reconstruction of Religious Thought in Islam* (Lahore, 1944), pp. 8–9.

23. Vahid, S. A., ed., *Thoughts and Reflections of Iqbal* (Lahore, Shaikh Muhammad Ashraf, 1964), p. 35.

24. G. A. Parwez, *Lughat ul-Qur'ān* (Lahore, Idaru Tulu'-e-Islam, 1960), vol. 2, p. 894.

25. Ibid., vol. 1, p. 263.

26. Muhammad Ali, *The Holy Qur'ān* (Chicago, Specialty Promotions, 1973).

27. G. A. Parwez, *Islam: A Challenge to Religion* (Lahore, Idara Tulu'-e-Islam, 1968), p. 285.

28. M. Ali, *Holy Qur'ān.*

29. Ibid.

30. Asad, *Message of the Qur'ān.*

31. *Arabic-English Lexicon,* book 1, part 5, p. 1936.

32. See Surah 57.27.

33. Asad, *Message of the Qur'ān.*

34. Ibid.

35. A. Y. Ali, *Holy Qur'ān.*

36. M. Ali, *Holy Qur'ān.*

37. Ibid.

38. A. A. A. Fyzee, *A Modern Approach to Islam* (Lahore, Universal Books, 1978), p. 17.

39. Ibid.

40. Asad, *Message of the Qur'ān.*

41. Ibid.

42. G. A. Parwez, *Tabweeb ul-Qur'ān* (Lahore, Idara Tulu'-e-Islam, 1977), vol. 1, p. 78.

43. M. Ali, *Holy Qur'ān.*

44. Of relevance here is the following passage: "The Qur'ān gives to responsible dissent the status of a fundamental right. In exercise of their powers, therefore, neither the legislature nor the executive can demand unquestioning obedience. . . . The Prophet, even though he was the recipient of Divine revelation, was required to consult the Muslims in public affairs. Allah addressing the Prophet says: '. . . consult with them upon the conduct of affairs. And . . . when thou art resolved, then put thy trust in Allah (Surah 3.159)'" (K. Ishaque, "Islamic Law—Its Ideals and Principles," in *The Challenge of Islam,* A. Gauher, ed. [London, The Islamic Council of Europe, 1980], pp. 167–69).

45. A. Y. Ali, *Holy Qur'ān.*

46. Ibid.

47. See, e.g., Surah 6.107; 16:82; 42.48.

48. A. Y. Ali, *Holy Qur'ān.*

49. Ibid.

50. Ibid.

51. Asad, *Message of the Qur'ān.*

52. Ibid.

53. For a more detailed discussion of human rights in Islam, see my article, "On Human Rights and the Qur'anic Perspective," in *Human Rights in Religious Traditions,* A. Swidler, ed. (New York, Pilgrim Press, 1982), pp. 51–65; also in *Journal of Ecumenical Studies,* 19/3 (Summer 1982) 51–65.

54. A. Y. Ali, *Holy Qur'ān.*

55. See, e.g., Surah 2.190–93, 217; 4.75–78; 22.39–40, 60; 57.25.

56. See, e.g., Surah 5.8.

57. See, e.g., Surah 8.61.

58. Asad, *Message of the Qur'ān.*

DISCUSSION QUESTIONS

1. How is the image of Islam presented by Hassan different from or similar to the images typically presented by the Western mass media?

2. Do you agree with Hassan's account of human rights? Why or why not?

3. Hassan wrote this essay before the cold war was over. Are her arguments for widespread peace education still relevant today? Why or why not?

4. How would you compare the Islamic perspective on human rights presented here with the position on human rights found in some other religious tradition with which you are familiar?

54. Donald A. Grinde (b. 1946) and Bruce E. Johansen (b. 1950)
A Native American Perspective on Environmental Ethics

Donald Grinde Jr. is a member of the Yamasee tribe, a small indigenous group not recognized by the federal government but originally inhabiting the lower Savannah River valley in Georgia. Most recently he has been a member of the history faculty at California Polytechnic State University. Bruce Johansen is on the faculty at the University of Nebraska, Omaha, in the Departments of Communication and Native American Studies. Both authors have written extensively on Native American issues utilizing multidisciplinary resources and approaches.

The following essay is the concluding chapter of their 1995 coauthored work *Ecocide of Native America*. This book not only documents the environmental destruction of indigenous peoples' lands in various parts of North America but also offers a moral and political evaluation of those events and policies. The title of the essay itself is "Toward Liberation of the Natural World," which indicates the direction the authors take in arguing for a different, more ecologically justified orientation to the human use of the natural environment than has been the norm, especially since the emergence of industrialized society. More specifically, they make the case that a sound environmental ethics guiding individual conduct and social policy must be more thoroughly informed by the insights and values of traditional indigenous worldviews. As applied to North America then, the authors show how this approach to environmentalism will benefit all inhabitants more in the long run; but more particularly, they demonstrate the link between the liberation of nature and the liberation of Native Americans from the oppressive circumstances under which most of them have lived since the European invasion.

QUESTIONS FOR CRITICAL READING

1. According to Grinde and Johansen, what predictions about the situation of the human species, made by many different Native American thinkers during the last two centuries, seem to be coming true now?
2. How do the authors critically analyze the reduction of "nature" to "land"?
3. Regarding the relationship to the environment, what do the authors mean by claiming that "the Eurocentric thinker focuses on control while the native thinker focuses on harmony"?
4. How do the authors connect the liberation of people with the liberation of the natural environment, and what kind of "ethic" is implied here?

TERMS TO NOTE

ecocentric: A holistic way of understanding and morally evaluating experience and actions in terms of how they fit into the complex of natural relationships constituting an ecosystem, or the global biosphere as a totality.

omnipresent: Present everywhere at the same time; ubiquitous.

Although the destruction of American Indian peoples is well understood, the profound sorrow that American Indian people have for the resulting degradation of the environment and landscape is less well known. Three generations ago, an old Omaha voiced a profound sense of loss about environmental change in Nebraska:

When I was a youth the country was very beautiful. Along the rivers were belts of timberland, where grew cottonwood, maple, elm, ash, hickory, and walnut trees, and many other shrubs. And under these grew many good herbs and beautiful flowering plants. In both the woodland and the prairies I could see the trails of many animals and could hear the cheerful songs of many kinds of birds. When I walked abroad I could see many forms of life, beautiful living creatures which Wakanda had placed here; and these were, after their manner, walking, flying, leaping, running, playing all about.

But now the face of the land is all changed and sad. The living creatures are all gone. I see the land desolate and I suffer an unspeakable sadness. Sometimes I wake in the night and I feel as though I should suffocate from the pressure of this awful feeling of loneliness.[1]

This poignant statement preceded the environmental calamity of the Dust Bowl on the Great Plains in the 1930s. The Dust Bowl was not only created by overgrazing and intensive cereal crop agriculture but by the disappearance of the buffalo. As long as buffalo roamed the Great Plains, their enormous weight on their hooves turned the hard topsoil so that deeply rooted grasses like the buffalo grass could take hold and thus curb wind and water erosion on the Great Plains, especially in dry years.[2] Thus, plowing the Plains for agricultural use might have resulted in short-term economic benefits but profound long-term ecological consequences.

"Managing" the environment to increase productivity or even to maintain current environmental norms may have enormous future consequences. Although the complexity of creation is incomprehensible to the human mind, we can respect creation and its rhythms as native people have done for centuries. Perhaps this is the key to an environmental ethic for the future. In essence, as long as Western man feels that he is a demigod above creation and pretends to make environmental management decisions that allegedly preserve or "improve" the environment, then each generation will swap one set of environmental problems for another. But that is not all that happens; as time goes by a reductionist environmental problem (the disappearance of species and fragile environments) emerges that further limits a return to historical environments and confines our future environmental options.

Yet, many Native Americans understand that ultimately the Creator will reclaim the environment, and balance will be restored. It is only a question of how harsh this process will be in the resultant reclamation of creation. Indeed, Chief Smohalla, a Wanapum Indian, believed that

God . . . commanded that the lands and the fisheries should be common to all who lived upon them; that they were never to be marked off or divided, but that the people should enjoy the fruits that God planted in the land, and the animals that lived upon it, and the fishes in the water. God said he was the father and the earth was the mother of mankind; that nature was the law; that the animals, and fish, and plants obeyed nature, and that man only was sinful. This is the old law. . . . Those [people] who cut up the lands or sign papers for lands will be defrauded of their rights and be punished by God's anger.[3]

As human beings drift away from the processes of creation and develop a more indirect, engineered relationship with the environment, they will become increasingly vulnerable to the awesome powers of the natural world (fires, earthquakes, storms, drought, flooding, and climatic changes). Those human groups closer to nature experientially will adapt as best they can in order to survive, and those groups that suffer under the illusion of living outside or above nature will experience increasing difficulties in maintaining their economies and environments—if environmental degradation continues unimpeded. For traditional Native American medicine people like Bull Lodge (Sioux), "humbling [oneself] . . . with resignation to the will of [the] . . . Maker" will be the key to survival for both indigenous and industrial peoples.[4]

A few generations ago, statements lamenting environmental change and preparation for survival in an altered world were treated as the idealistic and unprogressive actions of "vanishing Americans," but today such statements resonate sympathetically with many non-native peoples. The attack on the environment is no longer just an attack on the indigenous peoples of the United States but also an assault on all the peoples of North America and the world. Environmental destruction and degradation can no longer be "contained" through technological fixes or shunted aside as the quaint musings of American Indian traditionalists.

Native Americans maintain this environmental "memory" of times past because their spirituality and philosophy reflect the centrality of nature in its orientation. Animals are to be venerated and respected as well as plants and all of creation. Often, American Indian spiritual communications are directed through the animal brothers, and the Creator often speaks to

American Indian people through visions and stories that involve animals. To many Native Americans, animals and the whole spectrum of life-forms in the natural environment give insights into the nature of the cosmic creative force. Through environmentally specific rites, Native Americans hand down to future generations the knowledge of their cultural realities. The environment is a mirror that reflects cultural values. The sweat lodge, the drum, thanksgiving ceremonies, pipe ceremonies, the Sun Dance, and many other rites reinforce the cyclical rhythms of creation and one's individual and collective connectedness to the immediate environment.[5]

In the Native American world, time becomes a continuum connected to place; linear time is viewed as an invention outside the reality of the processes of creation. The sacredness of time and place among Native Americans is reinforced through mythic realities. Experiencing local natural landmarks as a group and as individuals contributes to the identities of the people. Similarly, oral traditions of animal beings clarify, sanctify, and identify the myriad forms of the environment. Chief Oren Lyons (Onondaga Nation) summarizes this Native American valuing of the natural world and the living forms of creation in this way:

> We see it as our duty to speak as carektakers for the natural world . . . the principle being that all life is equal, including the four-legged and the winged things. The principle has been lost; the two-legged walks about thinking he is supreme with his manmade laws. But there are universal laws of all living things. We come here and we say they too have rights.[6]

Thus, each land form as well as the flora and fauna is an experience that places the group and the individual in a unique natural and mythic environment that sanctifies and imparts meaning to all facets of creation. By localizing meaning in places, Native Americans cannot conceive of themselves as being separate from the land and local environment. An old road man in the Native American Church summarized the concept succinctly when he said that "the white man thinks he owns the earth while the American Indian knows the earth owns him."[7]

In essence, those native societies and people that sanctify time and place, free humanity from the mundane, concrete, and profane manifestations of space and time. People that are constrained by the profaning of time and space often feel nostalgia for past historical environments or indulge in daydreams about outer space explorations. But such flights of fantasy cannot escape the limitations of time and space in the concrete world. Only the shaman can transcend time and space in a sacred manner and thus experience the world in its totality albeit fleetingly.[8]

The answer to the ecological crisis lies in ourselves. The capitalist restructuring of agriculture that began in the fifteenth century transformed the old subsistence agroecosystems throughout the world from a mosaic of forest lands, pasture lands, and intensive croplands into a landscape of intensive specialized croplands that produced commodities (tobacco, sugar, rice, wheat, maize, and so forth) for a market outside the place that it was produced. Old subsistence practices maintained much of the diversity and complexity of creation while maintaining social stability.[9] But while the old subsistence practices retained much of the wisdom of nature, capitalist land utilization practices became less responsible to the web of creation and more oriented to the price structure of the global market.

The capitalist mode of production commoditized goods and people. Plantation economies arose that sold not only cotton but people. In this new economic order, people like American Indians who did not fit were either killed or removed. Karl Marx's analysis of economic restructuring under capitalism largely ignores its environmental impact since he chose to emphasize the reconfiguration of human relations in industrial societies.[10]

And yet it is in agricultural capitalism that we see how clearly environmental degradation works. The most profound innovation of capitalism that changes the way human groups relate to nature is the selling of land. By creating a market for land, all the complex interactions of plants, animals, and minerals were reduced to one simple word, *land*. However, in reality, land is not a commodity (something produced by humans for sale in a market), but it was made to look as though it were a commodity. Once regarded as a commodity, it was traded without restraint. Traditional forms of meaning and identity that were invested in the land by native peoples were ridiculed as "savage" or suppressed so that the marketing of land could proceed. The results of this new mindset about land are not easily fathomed. Essentially, once nature was reduced to land it disappeared until the end of the nineteenth century when the American frontier closed and it was apparent that quantities of land as a commodity were quite fixed.[11] This realization has compelled some Americans to turn to science and economics to deal with the notion of a limited land base and its consequent consumption problems.

Native people such as Glen Morris (Shawnee) believe that faith in the abilities of science and technology to deliver us from ecological disaster will only result in variations of "fascism."[12] Morris asserts that the population of North America presently exceeds the carrying capacity by a factor of ten and that this human "overshoot" in population is presently sustained through the destruction of forests to create agricultural lands.[13]

As a result of the exploding population in the nineteenth century, vast areas of land were devoured to produce raw materials for the industrializing process. Energy consumption and the resulting toxic emissions were increased geometrically to maintain an ever-expanding industrial life support system. Indeed, the entire aquasystem of the North American continent was reoriented to support the burgeoning needs of the agricultural and industrial sectors of the new industrial economy.[14] The dominant society in North America saw this commoditization of land as a "civilizing" process for native peoples. In the ninteenth century, the powerful forces of capitalism felt that

> in integrating the native's resources (whether these be land or valuable ores or timber or water or labor) into an expanding industrial empire they were dragging native peoples from savagery into "higher" and "better" ways of life. Towards such worthy and constructive ends no measure of brutality was foreclosed.[15]

Essentially, Native American people have experienced the problems of reducing nature to a marketable item for a long time. The Haudenosaunee (Iroquois) summarized the resulting environmental problems at the end of the twentieth century in this way:

> In the beginning we were told that the human beings who walk about on the Earth have been provided with all the things necessary for life. We were instructed to carry a love for one another, and to show a great respect for all beings on this Earth. We were shown that our life exists with the tree of life, that our well-being depends on the well-being of the Vegetable Life, that we are close relatives of the four-legged beings.

> The original instructions direct that we who walk about on the Earth are to express a great respect, an affection and a gratitude toward all spirits which create and support Life. When people cease to respect and express gratitude for all these many things, then all life will be destroyed, and human life on this planet will come to an end.

> To this day the territories we still hold are filled with trees, animals, and the other gifts from the Creation. In these places we still receive our nourishment from our Mother Earth.

> The Indo-European people who have colonized our lands have shown very little respect for the things that create and support Life. We believe that these people ceased their respect for the world a long time ago. Many thousands of years ago, all the people of the world believed in the same Way of Life, that of harmony with the Universe. All lived according to the Natural Ways.

> Today the species of Man is facing a question of [its] very survival. The way of life known as Western Civilization is on a death path on which their own culture has no viable answers. When faced with the reality of their own destructiveness, they can only go forward into new areas of more efficient destruction.

> The air is foul, the waters poisoned, the trees dying, the animals are disappearing. We think even the systems of weather are changing. Our ancient teaching warned us that if Man interfered with the Natural laws, these things would come to be. When the last of the Natural Way of Life is gone, all hope for human survival will be gone with it. And our Way of Life is fast disappearing, a victim of the destructive process.

> The technologies and social systems which destroyed the animal and plant life are destroying the Native people. We know there are many people in the world who can quickly grasp the intent of our message. But our experience has

taught us that there are few who are willing to seek out a method for moving to any real change.

The majority of the world does not find its roots in Western culture or tradition. The majority of the world finds its roots in the Natural World, and it is the Natural World, and the traditions of the Natural World, which must prevail.

We all must consciously and continuously challenge every model, every program, and every process that the West tries to force upon us. The people who are living on this planet need to break with the narrow concept of human liberation, and begin to see liberation as something that needs to be extended to the whole of the Natural World. What is needed is the liberation of all things that support life— the air, the waters, the trees—all things which support the sacred web of Life.

The Native peoples of the Western Hemisphere can contribute to the survival potential of the human species. The majority of our peoples still live in accordance with the traditions which find their roots in the Mother Earth. But the Native people have need of a forum in which our voice can be heard. And we need alliances with the other people of the world to assist in our struggle to regain and maintain our ancestral lands and protect the Way of Life we follow.

The traditional Native people hold the key to the reversal of the processes of Western Civilization, which hold the promise of unimaginable future suffering and destruction. Spiritualism is the highest form of political consciousness. Our culture is among the world's surviving proprietors of that kind of consciousness. Our culture is among the most ancient continuously existing cultures in the world. We are the spiritual guardians of this place. We are here to impart that message.[16]

Land, and the culture that is connected with it, is what the Iroquois and other native peoples consider most important. It is central to understanding North American politics of the last five hundred years. Control of land, and the resources contained in it and on it, colors the course of the ecological juggernaut of post-1492 North America.

No discussion of American Indian ecology of the last five hundred years could end without the realization that resource development, land ownership, social control, and other configurations of European power are inextricably tied together to create an environmental ideology that is distinctly Eurocentric in its orientations. This makes substantive ecological change in North America decidedly difficult since decisions about the environment have been made by non-natives for so long a time. This Eurocentric theorizing about the North American environment assumes that European-developed theories about the environment are universal and that native peoples outside of Europe have little to teach the "civilized" world about environmental perspectives. Indeed, Calvin Martin has postulated that the American Indian cannot teach Europeans anything about the environment and that Native Americans were elevated intentionally and inappropriately to the high priesthood of the "ecology cult" in the late 1960s.[17] Martin believes that the conservationists needed a spiritual leader in the post-World War II era and that the American Indian served conveniently to flesh out the theology of environmentalism. Although he fails to make a convincing case concerning the idealization of Native Americans as the first ecologists, Martin nevertheless believes that

[t]he Indian still remains a misfit guru. Even if he were capable of leading us, we could never follow him. The Indian's was a profoundly different cosmic vision when it came to interpreting Nature—a vision Western man could never adjust to. There can be no salvation in the Indian's traditional conception of Nature for the troubled environmentalist. Some day, perhaps, he will realize that he must look to someone else other than the American Indian for realistic spiritual inspiration.[18]

From the Native American viewpoint, Martin's pessimistic and deterministic musings about the viability of American Indian environmental perspectives in today's world work against the liberation of native and non-native lands and peoples alike. In accepting the hegemony of European thought, he categorizes and isolates the wisdom of American Indian people as though it were unfathomable or at least inscrutable to European people. Martin's discussion of the commoditization of the fur trade in North America and his implication that Native American spiritualism was fractured by the ensuing market economy is a simplistic overgeneralization that cannot withstand scrutiny when factored into a complex and interrelated ecosystem.

Moreover, contemporary Native American intellectuals like Ward Churchill are diametrically opposed to Martin's opinion on American Indian environmentalism. In essence, Churchill charges that the Eurocentric intellectual isolation of American Indian environmental spirituality and thought is a form of monocultural orthodoxy that excludes Native American wisdom not for its message but because it fails to live up to European norms which involve assumptions about "savages" and other universalizing concepts inherent in the discourse of Eurocentric scholars.[19] Furthermore, Churchill maintains that the great majority of non-Indians in America have nothing to lose and a great deal to gain in returning American Indian lands to native peoples so that they can use the land in traditional ways. In fact, he states that liberation of the land must precede human liberation. Indeed, he maintains that most human liberation movements stand in the way of land liberation and thus implies that nothing can be accomplished until we restore the land (nature) to its rightful place as a central factor in human existence.[20]

The concept of liberation has been a very important part of the discourse of empire during the last two hundred years. As the problems of urban poverty arose as a by-product of industrialization in the nineteenth century, liberal caretakers evolved to "help" the poor; but control of the client people (like control of the land) remained a dominant force in poverty programs. But once the poor became increasingly restive under this control, many liberal caretakers switched to helping racial minorities, which also became vocal about the control exercised over them. Finally, the liberal caretakers focused on the environment, which did not talk back; but control rather than harmony was still the watchword. This emphasis on environmental control (such as the maintenance of "wilderness" and "recreation" areas) runs counter to an ethic of harmony and interrelatedness, and as such environmental control is as exclusive in its practices as any timber or railroad baron of olden times. In any discourse on environmentalism, the Eurocentric thinker focuses on control while the native thinker focuses on harmony.[21] This is an impasse that must be overcome so that the earth and its peoples can survive without excessive depletion of natural resources.

The Native American world of participative harmony is aptly summarized by the astronomer and anthropologist Anthony Aveni in the following passage on the intellectual life of the pre-Columbian Mayas:

> These people did not react to the flow of natural events by struggling to harness and control them. Nor did they conceive of themselves as totally passive observers in the essentially neutral world of nature. Instead, they believed that they were active participants and intermediaries in a great cosmic drama. The people had a stake in all temporal enactments. By participating in the rituals, they helped the gods of nature to carry their burdens along their arduous course, for they believed firmly that the rituals served formally to close time's cycles. Without their life's work the universe could not function properly. Here was an enviable balance, a harmony in the partnership between humanity and nature, each with a purposeful role to play.[22]

Another commentator elaborates on these spiritual and natural perceptions in a more comparative way:

> [Among the] . . . Andeans, . . . [t]he land surrounding one told the story of one's first ancestors as much as it told one's own story and the story of those yet to come. It was right that the familiar dead were seen walking through the fields they had once cultivated, thus sharing them with both the living and with the original ancestors who raised the first crops in the very same fields. Death was thus the great leveler not because, as in Christian thought, it reduced all human beings to equality in relation to each other and before God. Rather, death was a leveler because by means of it humans were reintegrated into a network of parents and offspring that embraced the entire natural order.[23]

In the Judeo-Christian world, soul is divorced from nature, and as a consequence humans place the existential maintenance of their individual souls above the collective maintenance of the environment. Scholars like Calvin Martin believe that such European philosophical differences from the holistic and participative views of Native Americans render the environmental ideas of American Indians useless to the Eurocentric peoples of North America. However, few North Americans go to Europe today for any length of time, and when they do they seem to achieve a profound sense of their identity as Americans. Indeed, Americans have an identity that involves something greater than Europe, one that has a Native American dimension to it. Perhaps that is why environmentalism is so deeply rooted in the American public discourse as the twentieth century ends. At the beginning of the twentieth century, it seems to have been mostly American Indians like the old Omaha who felt the "unspeakable sadness" and "loneliness" of environmental degradation. By the end of the twentieth century, it appears that many non-natives are experiencing the same spiritual malaise.

In the late twentieth century, it seems certain that multiple perspectives on the environmental dilemma are preferable to an exclusively Eurocentric approach. New and diverse ecological and spiritual views emerge to meet the demands of the human endeavor. These emerging worldviews and ways of life transform the human experience in the myriad environments that they function in. Such transformations help cultures (Native American, Eurocentric, and new syntheses) to deal with the changes that are encountered. And these changing paradigms (conservative or accommodating) seek to resolve the dilemmas of constancy and change through a process called "tradition."

Although we tend to learn about appropriate human behavior through example, we usually get most of our education about the environment from our local surroundings. In the modern world, we like to think that we get most of our knowledge from libraries, universities, and complex data bases. But how do we internalize such vast amounts of information into a meaningful whole? Unfortunately, the European mentality has abstracted today's natural world so much that many people are currently residing in an intellectually and artificially constructed universe that is self-threatening and self-defeating. In a world where people get their knowledge of birds, animals, and natural forces from the media, the natural world appears to be one of cuddly felines, comical coyotes, or cartoon ducks. Increasingly, people experience the animal forms of creation through zoos, domesticated animals that are dependent on us, and/or chance encounters with animals while driving along the freeway.

In the postmodern world configured and reconfigured through the electronic superhighway, the theoretical universe created by academic, corporate, and governmental authority in the past is crumbling. Abstract all-encompassing theories that explain and rationalize the *status quo* regardless of the realities of a given situation are giving way to electronic conversations, publications and information sharing that approach reality in a much more "tentative" and experiential way. Thus, the electronic information networks make knowledge more process oriented and less factual through the very technique through which they are distributed. Essentially in the Native American world, finding out what is going on is more important than "explaining" what happened. This "tentativeness" and process orientation in the information superhighway is more akin to Native American perceptions of the world and its workings. After several centuries of technologies that foster control and manipulation through military might, we may be entering into an era in which modern information technology liberates rather than controls situations. Of course, universal access remains a problem just as universal access to today's environment remains problematic. In the past, corporations, railroads, and governmental agencies sought to increase their control over the American people's access to the environment (that is, corporate and railroad development of the American West versus westward movement of squatters and frontiersmen). By making land a commodity at the beginning of the development of the United States, access to land and the fruits of the environment were controlled and distributed not so much on the basis of direct and obvious need for every member of the society, as it was in most indigenous societies, but rather on the basis of wealth and power that was vested in an elite. In essence, the very process of developing the environment industrially alienates the common people from the environment even before they are alienated from the factory work processes. This attentuation and alienation of the great mass of industrial humanity from the environment paves the way for those in power to attack the environment for short-term full employment goals and material profit.

In contrast to these attentuated industrially constructed experiences with creation, Native Americans perceived themselves as participating in a natural structure of life that deeply involved all other species. Since human beings were regarded as latecomers to creation, it was important to respect every other form of life so that we could learn lessons from animal beings necessary for survival and prosperity. Since it was recognized that they had detailed knowledge of the universe and how to live in it, the observation of animals was a very serious matter for American Indians. Clans and social systems were patterned after native perceptions of animal behavior with clan totems (bear, deer, turtle, and so forth) reflecting this process. Some American Indian nations even had a psychology of birds and animals that emphasized the parallels between human and animal behavioral traits; the accuracy of these psychological descriptions have surprised many European observers.

Technical skills could also be learned from animals to ensure continued prosperity. Native Americans could often determine the best materials for constructing houses in specific locales by observing bird nests, or learn the shortest routes over mountains through forests, or through deserts by observing game animals. Information about water sources and quality as well as edible plants could be obtained by observing beaver dams and by watching other animal brothers. Methods of gathering plants as well as hunting techniques were also gleaned from the habits of animals. For instance, a surplus rodent population might mean a declining coyote and/or cougar population. Watching animal behavior might also indicate the sites of medicinal plants useful to humans. As Native Americans collected such knowledge by observing the animals that inhabited the places they lived, they developed a pharmacology to treat animals as well as human maladies.

Observation of the natural process was also reflected in spiritual ceremonies and rituals. In the Hopi Snake Dance or Rain Dance the snake people were asked to bring water to the Hopis while, according to the Navajos, it was Coyote that brought fire to them.

Some rituals involved the sacrificing of an eagle or some other animal to ensure that the animal was incorporated into the process. In these rituals, the animals participated as partners in the process of living and dying.

For many Native Americans, the relationship with the animal kingdom was so close that it was thought that humans could take the shape of birds or animals after their death. Hence, the circling of a hawk, owl, or woodpecker over a village after the death of a loved one was not an uncommon site. Professor Grinde was personally visited by a bear shortly after the death of his brother-in-law. Such visitations in the native world are considered common and are to be taken literally not symbolically.

Many tribes classified birds and animals in order to explain complicated relationships. The Plains Indians made an important distinction between two-legged and four-legged animals. The two-legged animals were birds, bears, and humans. According to many native peoples, the knowledge of these creatures was concerned with healing, and it is the two-legged creatures that were responsible for putting the world back in harmony when it became unbalanced. In native societies certain animals and certain humans were often grouped together, and the animals often gave warnings of impending danger to the humans and to the environment in general. Thus, the disappearance or sufferings of a certain species might be a warning to human beings to restore harmony to the world. In today's world, many native peoples feel that they are the only ones who see the warning signs of an environment in trouble. Obviously, people lose their ability to sense subtle changes when their relation with the environment becomes attentuated and less direct, as it has in industrialized society.[24]

Thus, the means for comprehending the processes of creation, their meaning for human existence, and threats to such processes cannot be easily grasped in the abstract constructions of the European world. American society still has much to learn from the native peoples of America, just as the native peoples of the Americas have learned much from the Europeans. Today, ideas can mix freely between cultures and ethnic groups aided by modern communication and transportation. The notion of exclusivity in the pursuit of human awareness and knowledge narrows the diversity of our options and produces less joy in relating to the human and environmental condition. In the final analysis, the achievement of wisdom concerning environmental conditions should not be associated with any particular race or territory. Our feet all rest on the same earth.

As a result of the mass destruction of human life in World Wars I and II through the techniques of mechanized and nuclear war, the surviving European ideologies (democratic capitalism and Communism) turned away from the wholesale and physical destruction of people and instead developed policies that led to the wholesale exploitation and destruction of environments. From a pragmatic point of view, this decision produced some semblance of a lasting peace for a couple of generations since the physical environment neither reads nor comprehends the works of Karl Marx or Adam Smith. Unlike humanity, the environment could not register its disapproval of these policy decisions through rebellions and revolutions at the initial stages of its implementation. Since 1945, the world's populations enjoyed some material gains and respite from cataclysmic wars that destroyed people by the tens of millions. But the uneasy peace borne on accelerated environmental degradation is now coming to an end. Today, the environment is sending us a clear message that the partial shifting of exploitation from the masses of humanity to the physical environment in the quest for peace and stability cannot be sustained. Obviously, it would not be humane to return to the wholesale exploitation and destruction of human populations that occurred in the first half of the twentieth century. Conversely, we should not continue, willy nilly, to pursue policies that sacrifice our environment in the name of promoting economic stability and moderating international and national, as well as race, class, and gender tensions. What is to be feared is the path of least resistance—where the environment is allowed continually to deteriorate and the resulting mass destruction of populations will "appear" to be by the hand of "God." The Christian notion of the Apocalypse easily sanctifies this process as does Adam Smith's notion of the "invisible hand" (equivalent to the hand of God), when it really is a result of a lack of political courage, vision, and leadership. Such a destructive set of circumstances—if

allowed to work itself out—would represent a resurfacing of fascism in advanced industrialized societies, but this time around the destruction would appear to be done through the environment and not through human hands and war machines. Given the horrors of such a scenario, a positive and affirming spiritual path must evolve that explains and harmonizes the conflicting forces of environmental destruction, human "progress," and human freedom. In the framing and implementation of this new path, Native Americans and other indigenous peoples must play a crucial and central role—unfettered by the economic and intellectual tenets of empire and modernization.

At the same time that access to diverse modes of consciousness has become more widespread, the ecological crisis facing modern capitalist society has become more omnipresent, and more obvious. As we researched this book, we were consistently amazed at how far-reaching the environmental crisis has become—extending even to the most remote regions. At a time when PCBs are being found in mothers' milk above the Arctic Circle, the pervasiveness of the ecological crisis has spawned a search by many peoples, in many cultures, for alternative ways of thinking, living, and making a living. The popularity of Native American perspectives on the environment in the late twentieth century is no accident, but part of a species-wide search for modes of living that will address the number one problem everyone now faces: the survival of a sustaining earth.

More than a century and a half ago Chief Seal'th said, "We may be brothers after all"—at a time when most Euro-Americans looked at the bounty of America as free and nearly endless. Today, the perspective is much different, and there is widespread realization that time is short. More people of all cultures are realizing that the only way out of this dilemma is to think and act to sustain a viable earth. This is one issue that connects us all and on which our common survival has come to depend. Liberating "mother earth" from totally Eurocentric conceptions of the environment will allow for a wider range of choices and solutions that will hopefully serve a broader group of peoples and cultures in the future. Since most American Indian communities are ecocentric, liberation of the environment involves liberation of Native American people.

Notes

1. Quoted in Melvin R. Gilmore, *Prairie Smoke* (New York: Columbia University Press, 1929), 36.

2. For a good example of Plains Indian respect for the buffalo and admonitions to not overhunt the herds, see George Bird Grinnell, *Pawnee Hero Stories and Folk Tales* (New York: Forest and Stream Publishing Company, 1889), 132–44.

3. Chief Smohalla's speech in *Fourteenth Annual Report of the Bureau of American Ethnology* (Washington, D.C.: Government Printing Office, 1896), part 2, 220–21.

4. George Horse Capture, ed., *The Seven Visions of Bull Lodge* (Lincoln: University of Nebraska Press, 1980), 120.

5. Horse Capture, ed., *Visions of a Bull Lodge,* passim.

6. Quoted in Matthew Fox, *A Spirituality Named Compassion and the Healing of the Global Village, Humpty Dumpty and Us* (Minneapolis, Minn.: Winston Press, 1979), 164.

7. Conversation with Donald A. Grinde, Jr., and Elwood Koshiway (Otoe), April 4, 1983.

8. Joseph Epes Brown, *The Spiritual Legacy of the American Indian* (New York: Crossroad Publishing Co., 1982), 51–52.

9. See Ward Churchill and Elizabeth R. Lloyd, *Culture versus Economism: Essays on Marxism in the Multicultural Arena* (Denver, Colo.: Fourth World Center for the Study of Indigenous Law and Politics, 1989) for a fuller discussion of these issues.

10. Ibid.

11. For a more intensive discussion of these themes, see Donald Worster, "Transformations of the Earth: Toward an Agroecological Perspective in History," *Journal of American History* 76, no. 4 (March 1990): 1087–106.

12. Churchill and Lloyd, *Culture versus Economism*; see the introduction by Glen Morris, 4.

13. Ibid., 2. Morris gets his analysis in part from William Catton, *Overshoot: The Ecological Basis for Revolutionary Change* (Urbana: University of Illinois Press, 1980).

14. Churchill and Lloyd, *Culture versus Economism*, 3.

15. Ibid., 5.

16. Excerpted from Editors, *A Basic Call to Consciousness, Akwesasne Notes* (New York: Mohawk Nation via Rooseveltown, 1978).

17. Oddly enough, a survey of the environmental textbooks of the period Martin discusses contain little or no mention of American Indians as environmental gurus. In fact, mass-marketed texts such as Richard Wagner, *Environment and Man* (New York: W. W. Norton, 1974) contain no mention of American Indians at all.

18. Calvin Martin, *Keepers of the Game: Indian-Animal Relationships and the Fur Trade* (Berkeley: University of California Press, 1978), 188.

19. Churchill and Lloyd, *Culture versus Economism,* 29.

20. Ward Churchill, "The Earth Is Our Mother: Struggles for American Indian Land and Liberation in the Contemporary United States," in *The State of Native America*, ed. M. Annette Jaimes (Boston: South End Press, 1992), 177.

21. For some new approaches and perspectives with regard to environmental alliances between native peoples and environmentalists, see Al Gedicks, *The New Resource Wars: Native and Environmental Struggles Against Multinational Corporations* (Boston: South End Press, 1993).

22. Anthony Aveni, *Empires of Time* (New York: Basic Books, 1989), 252.

23. Sabine MacCormack, "Demons, Imagination and the Incas," *Representations* 33 (1991): 134.

24. Vine Deloria, Jr., *God Is Red* (New York: Dell Publishing Company, 1973), 73. See also Dennis Tedlock and Barbara Tedlock, eds., *Teachings from the American Earth* (New York: Liverwright, 1975) for a fuller discussion of the nature of American Indian spirituality and the environment.

DISCUSSION QUESTIONS

1. Do you agree with the authors' critique of the treatment of land as a commodity? Why or why not?

2. Grinde and Johansen argue that increasing access to information technology can have in its own way a positive, progressive impact on outgrowing historically destructive ways of relating to the natural environment. Why would you agree or disagree?

3. How would you criticize or defend the environmental ethics implied in the authors' analyses?

4. In arguing for a more ecocentric ethics, the authors stress the traditional indigenous focus on the expectations of a Supreme Being, or Creator. Can one argue cogently for a purely secular ecocentric environmental ethics? Why or why not?

PART V   Political Philosophy

IF ORGANIZED HUMAN communities are to remain viable over time, they not only need customary moral codes and some sort of social division of labor but also some acknowledged means of at least occasionally making decisions for the whole group. The issues of who is to exercise this decision-making authority, how it is to be carried out, and for what ends thus become possible sources of controversy in social life and, as a result, susceptible to philosophical analysis. Political philosophy, as another ancient branch of philosophical study, focuses on questions about the nature, purpose, and legitimacy of social authority, power, and coercion. Historically, these questions have most often been addressed with respect to the role of institutionalized government and the rights and obligations of those wielding governmental power.

Political philosophy is linked closely with the more general field of what is often called social philosophy, which itself is often treated as including the study of ethics as well. In any case, philosophical questions about the political in human affairs are for the most part normative rather than merely empirical, and as such, they are concerned with "good" and "bad" institutional arrangements and social goals and the evaluation of policies and laws as justified or unjustified. Over the centuries this orientation has led to extensive debate about the criteria of "better" or "worse" societies, states, and governments. Underlying this debate are fundamental value choices, for example, that the interests of the individual are more important than the interests of the group or vice versa. Because much of human suffering throughout history has been rationalized or condemned by appealing to various answers to these value questions, the critical analysis of our belief options in this domain once again can be seen to have practical worth well beyond its theoretical interest.

Readings 55 through 58 deal with issues that underlie the justification of this or that political organization or practice, especially the nature of human persons and their relation to the larger collectivity of which they are members. After all, whether a society is essentially just an aggregate of separate individuals, or whether instead individuals are who they are because of their relationship with others in a community, has a lot to do with what people can legitimately expect of each other and their regulatory institutions.

In readings 59 through 63, the focus is on political relations—that is, relations of power and control between groups within the larger social whole. The readings offer various perspectives on the problem of the appropriateness or inappropriateness of hierarchies of power and authority in society, as well as possible strategies for dealing with social conflict in a morally justifiable way.

Readings 64 through 68 give different answers to the age-old question of political philosophy: What is the best form of government? All of the different types of government recommended—including the anarchist position that all government should be abolished—still have their adherents today beyond the walls of academia.

55. Alison Jaggar (b. 1942)
"Political Philosophy and Human Nature"

Over the last few decades, Alison Jaggar has become one of the better-known feminist philosophers in the United States. Her extensive publications, widespread lecturing, and organizational work have helped guide the development of gender studies across disciplinary boundaries in North America, as well as within English-speaking academic philosophy itself. Currently she is on the faculty at the University of Colorado at Boulder.

This selection is the second chapter of her influential 1983 book, *Feminist Politics and Human Nature*. As a work of political philosophy, this book offers an account of four different approaches to feminist theory and practice, in effect, four different "feminisms." This taxonomy was current, especially among Western feminist thinkers, in the 1970s and 1980s and is still utilized today in the various modifications it has undergone. Jaggar identifies these four approaches as "liberal feminism," "traditional Marxism," "radical feminism," and "socialist feminism," and her book is largely an exploration of their differences and similarities regarding human nature and critical political analysis and advocacy. The chapter reprinted here serves to set the stage for her comparative investigations, and it focuses more generally on the inescapable relationship between assumptions about human nature and conclusions about what constitutes "the good society."

QUESTIONS FOR CRITICAL READING

1. According to Jaggar, what are the three aspects of political philosophy, and how are they interrelated?
2. In Jaggar's account, what is the relationship between political philosophy and science?
3. According to Jaggar, what elements typically are included in a "theory of human nature," and what does human nature have to do with visions of "the good society"?
4. In Jaggar's view, what role does, and should, gender play in political philosophy?

TERMS TO NOTE

heuristic: That which is useful for stimulating or guiding further inquiry.
ideological: In this context, having to do with a purportedly factual account of some aspect of social reality, which at the same time implies value judgments regarding appropriate responses to that reality and does so in accordance with some group's political interests. In this sense an "ideology" is a more accurate or more distorted, value-laden part of one's worldview (not simply identical to it).
prolegomenon: An introduction or prefatory remarks.

Three Aspects of Political Philosophy

The goal of political philosophy is to articulate a vision of the good society. Political philosophy is essentially a normative enterprise that seeks to determine the ideals and principles that should inform social organization.

This is not to deny that much political philosophy, especially contemporary political philosophy, appears on the surface to be concerned less with arguing in favor of such ideals as equality, democracy or community than with attempting to define them. Every theory, after all, must clarify its own key concepts and, in the case of political philosophy, many of the central concepts are controversial not so much as abstract ideals but rather in their interpretation. Even in their debates over the "meaning" of "freedom" or "individuality," "justice" or "equality" however, political philosophers are not really trying to discover how those terms are ordinarily used. Instead, although they often express their conclusions as claims about meaning, political philosophers in fact argue for their own stipulated *interpretation* of the disputed concepts. And in arguing for their own interpretation, political philosophers take into account not only traditional usage and conceptual clarity; they also employ explicitly normative arguments about the superiority of a society that instantiates this rather than that conception of democracy, freedom or justice. Thus, even the conceptual arguments of political philosophers have a normative dimension.

The normative nature of political philosophy is uncontroversial. Indeed, it is customary to distinguish political philosophy from political science precisely by claiming that political science, which is said to investigate how political systems in fact work, is empirical, while political philosophy, which tells us how they ought to work, is normative. Political science is seen as descriptive, political philosophy as prescriptive. Although I do not wish to deny the normative nature of political philosophy, I shall challenge this customary way of distinguishing political philosophy from political science by arguing that both, as they are commonly defined, include both normative and empirical elements. Interchangeably with "political philosophy," I shall also use the more ambiguous term "political theory," which is more generally recognized as including both claims in what is ordinarily called political science and also explicitly normative claims.[1]

Inseparable from a vision of the good society is a critique of the philosopher's own society. This critique may not be worked out in any detail but it is always at least implicit because a conception of justice is simultaneously a conception of injustice. Equality defines inequality; oppression defines liberation. How much emphasis a philosopher gives to the positive vision and how much to the negative critique depends on a number of things: on the philosopher's motives in writing, on her or his own situation (for some philosophers, an overt critique of their own society may be too dangerous to undertake) and also on the philosopher's conception of the nature and social function of political theory. Some philosophers may believe that their task is to provide a detailed blueprint for the future; others, like Marx, may have epistemological reasons for believing that the future society must be designed by its future inhabitants and that the immediate task is to struggle against specific forms of oppression. Thus Marx's philosophy, unlike Plato's, for instance, consists largely in a detailed critique of the capitalist future. Nevertheless, the vision of an alternative society, however indistinct, underlies every philosophical criticism of contemporary injustice or oppression, just as every philosophical theory of the good society contains an implicit condemnation of existing social evils.

A third aspect of political philosophy is a consideration of the means for traveling from here to there, a strategy for moving from the oppressive present to the liberated future. Many philosophers have failed to give explicit attention to the question of means. Some may have wished to avoid charges of subverting the status quo; others, however, have had an underlying epistemological rationale for ignoring the question of the means to social change. They have held an elevated conception of political philosophy as the articulation of universal ideals and have viewed the question of how to instantiate those ideals as being both logically secondary and non-universal. The Marxist tradition is one of the few that has given much weight to questions of means as well as of ends and this is because of the Marxist belief that theory is born from practice, that only in the process of struggling against oppression can people formulate new visions of liberation.

Whether or not one accepts this tenet of Marxist epistemology, there are other reasons for viewing questions of strategy as integral to political philosophy. One reason is that questions of means are not just questions of efficiency; they also involve normative issues about what means may be morally justifiable in achieving social change. Examples of such questions concern the justifiability as well as the effectiveness of propaganda, strikes, boycotts, restrictions on freedom of speech or movement, torture, sabotage, terrorism and war. Because questions of means have this normative aspect, they are related logically to questions of ends. So the basic principles of a political theory often seem to imply the propriety of some means to social change and to prohibit the use of other means. For instance, the liberal commitment to preserving individual rights seems to rule out censorship, let alone terrorism and assassination, as legitimate means to social change. On the other hand, a Marxist analysis of the state as an instrument of class domination undercuts the state's claims to political authority and justifies illegal and possibly violent forms of resistance to it on the part of the oppressed classes. For these reasons, as well as because political philosophy has an ultimately practical aim, I view a consideration of the appropriate strategies for social change as an integral part of political philosophy.

Political Philosophy and Scientific Knowledge

To acknowledge that political philosophy is concerned with means as well as with ends is to recognize that it must be practicable as well as practical; an adequate political theory must show how to translate its ideals into practice. To use a well-known if rather dated formula of analytic philosophy, "ought" implies "can." To know what can be, however, requires considerable information about what is. To know how certain political ideals can be instantiated, for instance, requires information about human motivation, in order to determine the circumstances in which people will cooperate; it requires information about the available technology, in order to determine the social possibility and social costs of satisfying certain human desires; and, in order to discover workable strategies, it requires information about the motors of social change. A political theory that is practicable as well as practical obviously depends heavily on scientific knowledge about the real world.

It is not only to discover the *means* of social change that political philosophers require scientific knowledge. In order to engage in a critique of contemporary society, a political philosopher must know what is going on in that society. Political ideals are designed to evaluate actual situations and actual situations must therefore be properly understood.

Finally, although it is obvious that the critical and the strategic aspects of political philosophy require a knowledge of the real world, it may be less obvious that to construct a positive vision of the good society also requires knowledge of the world. This is because abstract ideals need specific interpretations. For instance, the Marxist attack on the liberal conception of equality, a conception which defines that ideal primarily in terms of civil rights, draws on empirical data showing that individuals with more economic power in a society inevitably use that power to weaken or even eliminate the ability of those with less economic power to exercise their civil rights. It is partly on the basis of empirical considerations, therefore, that Marxists argue for an economic dimension to equality. To take an even more fundamental example, in order to make a general determination of what is socially desirable, it is necessary to be able to identify the basic human needs. For although "good" may not be defin-

able in terms of human need, as one form of philosophical naturalism claims, yet there is a conceptual connection between them such that, if something fulfills a basic human need, this constitutes a prima facie, although not an indefeasible, reason for calling it good.[2]

An intimate relation exists, then, between political philosophy, on the one hand, and, on the other hand, such sciences as psychology, economics, political science, sociology, anthropology and even biology and the various technologies. Some political philosophers recognize this explicitly. For instance, Rawls requires that those who formulate the principles of justice in his ideal society should know "whatever general facts affect the choice of those principles" and gives examples that include "political affairs and the principles of economic theory; . . . the basis of social organization and the laws of human psychology."[3] A knowledge of many sciences is necessary to give substance to the philosophical ideal of human well-being and fulfillment, to add trenchancy to philosophical critiques of oppression and to avoid idle speculation by setting limits to social and political possibility.

Science, Politics and Human Nature

The dependence of political philosophy on information about the world, particularly the sort of information that the human or life sciences are designed to provide, raises for political philosophers not only the problem of acquainting themselves with the findings of those sciences but the deeper problem of determining which of those findings they should accept as valid. Scientific claims to provide the information for which Rawls calls, that is, "the principles of economic theory," "the basis of social organization and the laws of human psychology," are all highly controversial. For instance, there are no generally accepted laws of psychology, and no prospect that any will be discovered soon.

One aspect of the intractability of the human sciences is that disputes within them often lack clear criteria of resolution. This is not to say that there are no relatively straightforward empirical questions about, for instance, the voting patterns or divorce rates of certain groups. But the more persistent disputes within the human sciences concern not facts, but the *interpretation* of facts; that is, they concern which theoretical models will best explain or make sense of these facts. To take a current example, the new "discipline" of sociobiology has developed a theoretical framework that attempts to explain instances of apparently altruistic behavior in both animals and humans in terms of an evolutionary strategy through which genes seek to maximize their chances of reproductive success. This theoretical framework is in sharp contrast, of course, to older theories about altruism which may interpret it as a triumph of the moral will over the selfish instincts or as a flowering of the human potential for self-actualization through cooperation.

I think it is illuminating to see many of the disputes in the various human sciences as grounded ultimately in competing conceptions of what it is to be human. Psychology provides perhaps the most convincing examples of this claim with its variety of theoretical models of the human mind: the behavioristic model, according to which people are complicated stimulus-response mechanisms; the "humanistic" model, which sees people in basically existential terms as agents who are capable of making an individual choice about their own destiny; the Marxian model, which views humans as self-creating only through social action; the Freudian model; the model of humans as computers, and so on. Conflicts between schools of economists, too, seem to involve competing conceptions of human nature: classical economics rests on a conception of humans as beings whose individual interests are constantly likely to conflict, whereas Marxist economics posits a fundamental identity of interest between members of the same class and ultimately, indeed, between all members of the human species. Within sociology, the structural-functionalist school conceives of human individuals simply as the bearers of roles, while other approaches ascribe more or less autonomy to human agents. And alternative models of human motivation may also be found to underlie competing analyses in political science. Making this point, Charles Taylor writes:

> For a given framework [of explanation] is
> linked to a given conception of the schedule of
> human needs, wants, and purposes, such that,
> if the schedule turns out to have been mistaken
> in some significant way, the framework itself

cannot be maintained. This is for the fairly obvious reason that human needs, wants, and purposes have an important bearing on the way people act, and that therefore one has to have a notion of the schedule which is not too wildly inaccurate if one is to establish the framework for any science of human behaviour, that of politics not excepted. A conception of human needs thus enters into a given political theory and cannot be considered something extraneous which we later add to the framework.[4]

To attribute the divisions within the human sciences to the lack of a generally accepted conception of what it is to be human is not to diagnose the problem, but to re-state it.[5] Yet I think that this restatement has heuristic value because it leads us to focus attention on the whole notion of a theory of human nature. What questions should a theory of human nature be designed to answer, what are the methods by which it might discover those answers and what are the criteria for determining the adequacy of the answers offered?

No single issue, of course, can be identified as "the" problem of human nature. Rather, there is a cluster of interrelated questions, many of which have been perennial objects of study for philosophy. These questions include ontological issues, such as whether human beings can be thought of as existing prior to or independently of society; and metaphysical or methodological issues, such as whether human beings are irreducibly different from the rest of nature or whether their activities can be understood in principle by the concepts and methods of natural sciences. Other questions include the basis, scope and limits of human knowledge, and the nature of human fulfillment and self-realization. In modern times, a skeptical issue has been raised: is it possible to identify any universal characteristics of human nature which all human beings have in common and which distinguish them from animals, or are persons living at different places and times, in different social contexts, so diverse that the only characteristics they may safely be assumed to share are biological? An attempt to provide a comprehensive and systematic answer to these and other questions may be called a theory of human nature.

Given the range and extent of these problems, it is obvious that a complete theory of human nature stretches beyond the findings of any single discipline, be it anthropology, sociology or psychology. Rather, each of these disciplines provides a partial contribution to a comprehensive theory of human nature. But, as well as contributing to the development of such a theory, there is a clear sense in which research in each of these disciplines also *presupposes* a certain model of human nature. Let us take as an example the problem of understanding human motivation. Empirical data are certainly required to develop an explanatory model but a systematic account of motivation is not simply derivable from empirical data. On the contrary, what are to count as data is determined by the conceptual framework set up to guide the project of research. Empirical observations do not simply discover what motivates human beings; they must also presuppose certain very general features of human motivation. For example, if psychologists believe that human behavior is governed by innate biological drives or instincts, then psychological research obviously will focus on attempts to identify those drives and will tend to ignore environmental stimuli and rational agency. If psychology is dominated by a conception of human motivation according to which persons are complicated stimulus-response mechanisms, then psychological research will attempt to explain behavior through the discovery of the stimuli to which the organism is responding and will tend to ignore biology and rational agency. And if psychology takes people to be essentially rational agents, then research will tend to ignore human biology and environmental stimuli and will be directed instead toward discovering the individual's reasons for action—the exact direction of the research being determined, of course, by the researcher's own conception of rational behavior. This example brings out the now familiar interdependence between theory and observation and it also illustrates the way in which questions, answers and methods are not independent aspects of a conception of human nature—or of any other theory. What count as appropriate methods and appropriate answers are determined by what one takes the questions to be and, conversely, what one takes to be significant questions is in part a function of one's preexisting theoretical and methodological commitments.

Theories of human nature do not differ from theories of non-human nature in their interdependence of question, answer and method, but in another respect they are generally taken to differ from such theories: in their normative element. A few philosophers of science deny the alleged contrast by arguing that all knowledge is pervaded by normative moral and political assumptions. Whether or not this is true for the physical sciences, it is certainly true for the theories that constitute the human sciences. For instance, to determine an individual's reasons for action requires an inevitably normative decision about what counts as rational behavior. More generally, the core of any theory of human nature must be a conception of human abilities, needs, wants and purposes; but there is no value-free method for identifying these. Obviously, a theory of human nature requires us to separate out the "real" or basic or ineliminable needs and wants from among the innumerable things that people in fact say they need and want, and there seems to be a strong conceptual connection between the notion of a basic need or want and the notion of human flourishing and well-being. What constitutes flourishing and well-being, however, is clearly a question of value, both with respect to the individual and with respect to the social group. It has been a commonplace for some time that the notion of mental health has overtly normative and ideological ingredients and philosophers are now beginning to argue the same for the notion of physical health. Even the standard of physical survival cannot be used as a value-free criterion for determining human needs, for it raises normative questions about how long and in what conditions humans can and should survive.

This discussion of human well-being brings out one way in which values are embedded in the human sciences. In later chapters, I shall give other examples of how valuational, including political, considerations influence the ways in which we conceptualize human nature. I shall argue that this is true even of our assumptions about what constitutes genuine knowledge. For the moment, however, I hope I have shown that the human sciences are grounded on conceptions of human nature that are not straightforwardly empirical, both because they presuppose certain very general features of what it is to be human and because they rest on certain normative assumptions. The presuppositions of the human sciences, in fact, constitute varying answers to what the western tradition has taken to be the central problems of philosophy. These include questions regarding the relations between human and non-human nature, between mind and body, and between individuals and other individuals, questions regarding the possibility and source of genuine human knowledge and questions regarding human well-being and fulfilment. The original object of this section thus has been turned on its head. I began by looking for standards of well-established scientific knowledge about human beings that could be used by political philosophers in constructing a theory of the good society. But now it seems that the human sciences themselves rest on a philosophical foundation. In part, moreover, this foundation consists precisely in answers to the central questions of political philosophy.

If this argument is sound, political philosophy and the human sciences, certainly including political science, are ultimately inseparable. None of them is "autonomous." Philosophy, science and politics are not distinct endeavors. The human sciences do not constitute a reservoir of factual knowledge, uncontaminated by values, on which political philosophers can draw; nor, since political philosophy depends on the findings of the human sciences, can the former be viewed simply as a prologomenon to the latter. Instead, a certain methodological approach to the human sciences is correlated with a basic perspective in political philosophy in such a way that each reinforces the other.[6] The unifying element in each case is a certain very general conception of human nature.

Human Nature and the Nature of Women

In developing its vision of the good society, every political theory gives at least some indication of women's and men's relative positions in that society—even if its view is indicated as much as by what it fails to say as by what it actually says. Consequently, since every political theory is grounded on a certain conception of human nature, each political theory incorporates some assumptions about the nature of women and of men. In the case of most classical theories, claims about women's nature were explicit, although definitely not accorded a central place in the total system.[7] In contemporary times, systematic political philoso-

phers, such as John Rawls and Robert Nozick, have rarely discussed women directly. Nevertheless, the very silence of contemporary philosophers on this topic is significant. Either it suggests that standard moral or political theories, such as natural rights theory, utilitarianism or even the theory of alienation, apply without modification to women, or it suggests that they do not apply to women at all. In other words, from contemporary philosophers' silence about women one might infer either that there are no differences between women and men that are relevant to political philosophy or that women are not part of the subject matter of political philosophy at all.

Feminists break this silence. Their critique of women's position in contemporary society demonstrates that every aspect of social life is governed by gender. In other words, it reminds us that all of social life is structured by rules that establish different types of behavior as appropriate to women and men.[8] Feminists subject these rules to critical scrutiny, arguing that, in many cases if not all, they are oppressive to women. To establish this critique, feminists are confronted inevitably by questions about women's nature, its potentialities and limitations. They are forced to reflect on the social and political significance of all the differences, including the biological differences, between the sexes. In other words, they are forced to develop a theory of human nature that includes an explicit account of the nature of women and men.

In Part II I shall trace the development of feminist theorizing about women and men's nature. I shall show how earlier feminists accepted, more or less uncritically, prevailing conceptions of human nature that took the male as paradigm, and concerned themselves primarily with demonstrating that women are as fully human as men. In making this argument, both liberal and Marxist feminists insisted on a sharp distinction between the biological attribute of sex and the cultural attribute of gender, and they argued that biological differences were, by and large, irrelevant to political theory. As contemporary feminism developed, however, it extended its critique to new areas of social life, including sexuality and childbearing. In those areas it was less plausible to assume the political irrelevance of biological differences between the sexes, and so some contemporary feminists have seen the need to reconsider the political and philosophical significance of biology. In some parts of the women's movement, this has led to a resurrection of biological determinism in the form of theories explaining gender as determined, at least in part, by sex. Other feminists have begun to look harder at the conceptual distinction between sex and gender, suggesting that the distinction itself may have what one feminist philosopher calls "a false clarity."[9] The result is a renewed series of attempts to conceptualize the nature of women and of men.

Although contemporary feminists focus mainly on women, their work has implications for political philosophy as a whole. One result of their work is that the adult white male can no longer be taken to represent all of humanity, nor the adult white male experience to encompass all that is important in human life. In examining four feminist theories of women's and men's nature, Part II of this book will show how contemporary feminism has come to challenge traditional androcentric paradigms of human nature and traditional androcentric definitions of political philosophy. If these feminist critiques are demonstrated to be valid, of course, they will necessitate a reconstruction not only of political philosophy, but of all the human sciences and perhaps of the physical sciences as well.

Materialist feminism is therefore an intellectual approach whose coming is crucial both for social movements, for the feminist struggle, and for knowledge. This project would not be—could not be, even if desired—limited to a single population, to the sole oppression of women. It will not leave untouched any aspect of reality, any domain of knowledge, any aspect of the world. As the feminist movement aims at revolution in social reality, the theoretical feminist point of view (and each is indispensable to each other) must also aim at a revolution in knowledge.[10]

Notes

1. Not everyone, of course, regards "political philosophy" and "political theory" as interchangeable. For instance, the political science department in my own university lodged a territorial objection when I proposed to teach a course in feminist political theory. The political scientists claimed that "theory" was their turf; I was qualified to teach only philosophy.

2. Charles Taylor, "Neutrality in Political Science," in Alan Ryan, ed., *The Philosophy of Social Explanation* (New York, Oxford: Oxford University Press, 1972), p. 161.

3. John Rawls, *A Theory of Justice* (Cambridge: Harvard University Press, 1971), p. 137.

4. Taylor, "Neutrality," p. 155.

5. That conceptions of rationality are inevitably normative will be argued in the next chapter.

6. One of the clearest examples of this correlation may be found in the historical and conceptual connections between the nineteenth-century idea of progress and the idea of organic evolution. Darwin's theory of evolution was inspired by a reading of Malthus, and Darwin's theory, in turn, provided scientific respectability for the ideology of "Social Darwinism." The general conception shared by all these theorists was the promise of progress at the cost of struggle. Underlying this conception was a view of human nature as "inert, sluggish and averse from labour, unless compelled by necessity." This quotation from Malthus and indeed the whole example is given by R. M. Young, "The Human Limits of Nature," in Jonathan Benthall, ed., *The Limits of Human Nature* (Frome and London: Allen Lane, 1973).

7. A fascinating collection of philosophers' views on women is Mary Briody Mahowald's *Philosophy of Woman: Classical to Current Concepts* (Indianapolis: Hackett Publishing Co., 1978).

8. A few societies are said to have more than two genders. For instance, Lila Leibowitz reports a four-gender system in traditional Navaho society (*Females, Males, Families* [North Scituate, Mass.: Duxbry Press, 1978], pp. 37–38). Contemporary feminism, however, focuses on modern industrial society, which has only two genders. Consequently, in this book I shall ordinarily assume the operation of a two-gender system, defining one standard of appropriate "masculine" behavior for males and a contrasting standard of appropriate "feminine" behavior for females.

9. Ann Palmeri, "Feminist Materialism: On the Possibilities and Power of the Nature/Culture Distinction," paper read to the mid-west division of the Society for Women in Philosophy, October 25, 1980.

10. Christine Delphy, "For a materialist feminism," *Proceedings of the Second Sex—Thirty Years Later: A Commemorative Conference on Feminist Theory,* September 27–29, 1979 (New York: New York Institute for the Humanities, 1979).

DISCUSSION QUESTIONS

1. Do you agree with Jaggar's arguments for the relevance of gender analysis in evaluating theories of human nature and "the good society"? Why or why not?

2. Which kind of study is more useful in contemporary society, political science or political philosophy? Justify your position.

3. Based on your views of human nature, what do you think the "ideal society" would look like?

4. Is radical social/political change for the better possible or likely in the contemporary world? Why or why not?

56. John Stuart Mill (1806–1873)

what are the 3 meanings of liberty that mill describes & which does he think is the most adequate?

From *On Liberty*

John Stuart Mill was a British philosopher whose wide-ranging writings on moral and political philosophy, logic, and economics made him, in the view of many, the most influential English-speaking thinker of the nineteenth century. He was born in London and provided with an extraordinarily rigorous education at home by his father, James Mill, who himself worked closely with Bentham as one of the leading Philosophical Radicals of that era. John Stuart Mill was in effect raised as a Benthamite, committed to utilitarianism and social reform, though his "day job" was for many years as a clerk and eventually administrator with the British East India Company, and he never held an academic position. After a personal crisis when he was 20, Mill felt compelled to reconstruct his approach to utilitarian ethics. He deemphasized the rational calculation of indiscriminate quantities of pleasure and pain associated with Bentham's version and made more room for the emotional and less calculable dimensions of personal experience, without the development of which individual and ultimately social life remains less well rounded, less complete, and thus less happy.

In addition to Mill's significant contribution to subsequent utilitarian ethical theory, his ideas continue to be a dominant theoretical influence in the political advocacy of maximum personal liberty over against government in particular and social forces in general. This selection is the introductory chapter from his major work on the subject of personal liberty, published in 1859 and now considered a classic statement of liberalism. A good deal of contemporary debate around the world regarding the protection of individual liberties still is shaped by the arguments Mill laid down in this book almost 150 years ago. Also, his warning that democratic government does not necessarily guarantee or even affirm personal liberty, given the dangers of the "tyranny of the majority" and the natural tendency toward intolerance in society, still constitutes a challenge to those who appeal to the "will of the people" to justify the repression of some individuals for the alleged benefit of everyone else. In addition, his treatment of society as an aggregate of separate individuals, each of whom knows best what is good for himself or herself and against whom the whole group stands as potential oppressor, still informs the dominant perspective in Western political discourse today.

QUESTIONS FOR CRITICAL READING

1. According to Mill, what are the differences between earlier history and his own "modern era" with respect to how the "struggle between liberty and authority" was manifested in society? How is the "tyranny of the majority" relevant here?
2. How does Mill argue for and illustrate his claim that intolerance of differences in belief and lifestyle has always come naturally to most people in society?
3. What is Mill's "one very simple principle" for deciding the appropriate limit of social interference in an individual's life, and how does he argue for it?
4. What categories of humans are to be excluded from this principle, in Mill's view, and how does he argue for this exclusion?
5. According to Mill, what are the three aspects of individual life where personal liberty should reign supreme?

TERMS TO NOTE

odium theologicum: A Latin phrase literally meaning "theological hatred."

indefeasible: That which cannot be annulled or taken away.

nonage: The condition of not yet being of legal or socially recognized age to exercise some responsibility or privilege; usually, being a "minor."

The subject of this essay is not the so-called liberty of the will, so unfortunately opposed to the misnamed doctrine of philosophical necessity; but civil, or social liberty: the nature and limits of the power which can be legitimately exercised by society over the individual. A question seldom stated and hardly ever discussed in general terms, but which profoundly influences the practical controversies of the age by its latent presence, and is likely soon to make itself recognized as the vital question of the future. It is so far from being new, that, in a certain sense, it has divided mankind almost from the remotest ages; but in the stage of progress into which the more civilized portions of the species have now entered, it presents itself under new conditions, and requires a different and more fundamental treatment.

The struggle between liberty and authority is the most conspicuous feature in the portions of history with which we are earliest familiar, particularly in that of Greece, Rome, and England. But in old times this contest was between subjects, or some classes of subjects, and the government. By liberty, was meant protection against the tyranny of the political rulers. The rulers were conceived (except in some of the popular governments of Greece) as in a necessarily antagonistic position to the people whom they ruled. They consisted of a governing One, or a governing tribe or caste, who derived their authority from inheritance or conquest, who, at all events, did not hold it at the pleasure of the governed, and whose supremacy men did not venture, perhaps did not desire, to contest, whatever precautions might be taken against its oppressive exercise. Their power was regarded as necessary, but also as highly dangerous; as a weapon which they would attempt to use against their subjects, no less than against external enemies. To prevent the weaker members of the community from being preyed upon by innumerable vultures, it was needful that there should be an animal of prey stronger than the rest, commissioned to keep them down. But as the king of the vultures would be no less bent upon preying on the flock than any of the minor harpies, it was indispensable to be in a perpetual attitude of defense against his beak and claws. The aim, therefore, of patriots was to set limits to the power which the ruler should be suffered to exercise over the community; and this limitation was what they meant by liberty. It was attempted in two ways. First, by obtaining a recognition of certain immunities, called political liberties or rights, which it was to be regarded as a breach of duty in the ruler to infringe, and which if he did

infringe, specific resistance, or general rebellion, was held to be justifiable. A second, and generally a later expedient, was the establishment of constitutional checks, by which the consent of the community, or of a body of some sort, supposed to represent its interests, was made a necessary condition to some of the more important acts of the governing power. To the first of these modes of limitation, the ruling power, in most European countries, was compelled, more or less, to submit. It was not so with the second; and, to attain this, or when already in some degree possessed, to attain it more completely, became everywhere the principal object of the lovers of liberty. And so long as mankind were content to combat one enemy by another, and to be ruled by a master, on condition of being guaranteed more or less efficaciously against his tyranny, they did not carry their aspirations beyond this point.

A time, however, came, in the progress of human affairs, when men ceased to think it a necessity of nature that their governors should be an independent power, opposed in interest to themselves. It appeared to them much better that the various magistrates of the State should be their tenants or delegates, revocable at their pleasure. In that way alone, it seemed, could they have complete security that the powers of government would never be abused to their disadvantage. By degrees this new demand for elective and temporary rulers became the prominent object of the exertions of the popular party, wherever any such party existed; and superseded, to a considerable extent, the previous efforts to limit the power of rulers. As the struggle proceeded for making the ruling power emanate from the periodical choice of the ruled, some persons began to think that too much importance had been attached to the limitation of the power itself. *That* (it might seem) was a resource against rulers whose interests were habitually opposed to those of the people. What was now wanted was, that the rulers should be identified with the people; that their interest and will should be the interest and will of the nation. The nation did not need to be protected against its own will. There was no fear of its tyrannizing over itself. Let the rulers be effectually responsible to it, promptly removable by it, and it could afford to trust them with power of which it could itself dictate the use to be made. Their power was but the nation's own power, concentrated, and in a form convenient for exercise. This mode of thought, or rather perhaps of feeling, was common among the last generation of European liberalism, in the Continental section of which it still apparently predominates. Those who admit any limit to what a government may do, except in the case of such governments as they think ought not to exist, stand out as brilliant exceptions among the political thinkers of the Continent. A similar tone of sentiment might by this time have been prevalent in our own country, if the circumstances which for a time encouraged it had continued unaltered.

But in political and philosophical theories, as well as in persons, success discloses faults and infirmities which failure might have concealed from observation. The notion that the people have no need to limit their power over themselves, might seem axiomatic when popular government was a thing only dreamed about, or read of as having existed at some distant period of the past. Neither was that notion necessarily disturbed by such temporary aberrations as those of the French Revolution, the worst of which were the work of a usurping few, and which, in any case, belonged not to the permanent working of popular institutions, but to a sudden and convulsive outbreak against monarchical and aristocratic despotism. In time, however, a democratic republic came to occupy a large portion of the earth's surface, and made itself felt as one of the most powerful members of the community of nations; and elective and responsible government became subject to the observations and criticisms which wait upon a great existing fact. It was now perceived that such phrases as 'self-government,' and 'the power of the people over themselves,' do not express the true state of the case. The 'people' who exercise the power are not always the same people with those over whom it is exercised; and the 'self-government' spoken of is not the government of each by himself, but of each by all the rest. The will of the people, moreover, practically means the will of the most numerous or the most active *part* of the people; the majority, or those who succeed in making themselves accepted as the majority: the people, consequently *may* desire to oppress a part of their number, and precautions are as much needed against this as against any other abuse of power. The limitation, therefore, of the power of government over individuals loses none of its impor-

tance when the holders of power are regularly accountable to the community, that is, to the strongest party therein. This view of things, recommending itself equally to the intelligence of thinkers and to the inclination of those important classes in European society to whose real or supposed interests democracy is adverse, has had no difficulty in establishing itself; and in political speculations 'the tyranny of the majority' is now generally included among the evils against which society requires to be on its guard.

Like other tyrannies, the tyranny of the majority was at first, and is still vulgarly, held in dread chiefly as operating through the acts of the public authorities. But reflecting persons perceived that when society is itself the tyrant—society collectively over the separate individuals who compose it—its means of tyrannizing are not restricted to the acts which it may do by the hands of its political functionaries. Society can and does execute its own mandates; and if it issues wrong mandates instead of right, or any mandates at all in things with which it ought not to meddle, it practices a social tyranny more formidable than many kinds of political oppression, since, though not usually upheld by such extreme penalties, it leaves fewer means of escape, penetrating much more deeply into the details of life, and enslaving the soul itself. Protection, therefore, against the tyranny of the magistrate is not enough: there needs protection also against the tyranny of the prevailing opinion and feeling; against the tendency of society to impose, by other means than civil penalties, its own ideas and practices as rules of conduct on those who dissent from them; to fetter the development, and, if possible, prevent the formation, of any individuality not in harmony with its ways, and compels all characters to fashion themselves upon the model of its own. There is a limit to the legitimate interference of collective opinion with individual independence; and to find that limit, and maintain it against encroachment, is as indispensable to a good condition of human affairs, as protection against political despotism.

But though this proposition is not likely to be contested in general terms, the practical question, where to place the limit—how to make the fitting adjustment between individual independence and social control—is a subject on which nearly everything remains to be done. All that makes existence valuable to anyone, depends on the enforcement of restraints upon the actions of other people. Some rules of conduct, therefore, must be imposed, by law in the first place, and by opinion on many things which are not fit subjects for the operation of law. What these rules should be is the principal question in human affairs; but if we except a few of the most obvious cases, it is one of those which least progress has been made in resolving. No two ages, and scarcely any two countries, have decided it alike; and the decision of one age or country is a wonder to another. Yet the people of any given age and country no more suspect any difficulty in it, than if it were a subject on which mankind had always been agreed. The rules which obtain among themselves appear to them self-evident and self-justifying. This all but universal illusion is one of the examples of the magical influence of custom, which is not only, as the proverb says, a second nature, but is continually mistaken for the first. The effect of custom, in preventing any misgiving respecting the rules of conduct which mankind impose on one another, is all the more complete because the subject is one on which it is not generally considered necessary that reasons should be given, either by one person to others or by each to himself. People are accustomed to believe, and have been encouraged in the belief by some who aspire to the character of philosophers, that their feelings, on subjects of this nature, are better than reasons, and render reasons unnecessary. The practical principle which guides them to their opinions on the regulation of human conduct, is the feeling in each person's mind that everybody should be required to act as he, and those with whom he sympathizes, would like them to act. No one, indeed, acknowledges to himself that his standard of judgment is his own liking; but an opinion on a point of conduct, not supported by reasons, can only count as one person's preference; and if the reasons, when given, are a mere appeal to a similar preference felt by other people, it is still only many people's liking instead of one. To an ordinary man, however, his own preference, thus supported, is not only a perfectly satisfactory reason, but the only one he generally has for any of his notions of morality, taste, or propriety, which are not expressly written in his religious creed; and his chief guide in the interpretation even of that. Men's opinions, accordingly, on what is laudable or blamable, are af-

fected by all the multifarious causes which influence their wishes in regard to the conduct of others, and which are as numerous as those which determine their wishes on any other subject. Sometimes their reason, at other times their prejudices or superstitions; often their social affections, not seldom their antisocial ones, their envy or jealousy, their arrogance or contemptuousness: but most commonly their desires or fears for themselves—their legitimate or illegitimate self-interest. Wherever there is an ascendant class, a large portion of the morality of the country emanates from its class interests, and its feelings of class superiority. The morality between Spartans and Helots, between planters and Negroes, between princes and subjects, between nobles and roturiers, between men and women, has been for the most part the creation of these class interests and feelings; and the sentiments thus generated react in turn upon the moral feelings of the members of the ascendant class, in their relations among themselves. Where, on the other hand, a class, formerly ascendant, has lost its ascendancy, or where its ascendancy is unpopular, the prevailing moral sentiments frequently bear the impress of an impatient dislike of superiority. Another grand determining principle of the rules of conduct, both in act and forbearance, which have been enforced by law or opinion, has been the servility of mankind towards the supposed preferences or aversions of their temporal masters or of their gods. This servility, though essentially selfish, is not hypocrisy; it gives rise to perfectly genuine sentiments of abhorrence; it made men burn magicians and heretics. Among so many baser influences, the general and obvious interests of society have of course had a share, and a large one, in the direction of the moral sentiments; less, however, as a matter of reason, and on their own account, than as a consequence of the sympathies and antipathies which grew out of them; and sympathies and antipathies which had little or nothing to do with the interests of society, have made themselves felt in the establishment of moralities with quite as great force.

The likings and dislikings of society, or of some powerful portion of it, are thus the main thing which has practically determined the rules laid down for general observance, under the penalties of law or opinion. And in general, those who have been in advance of society in thought and feeling, have left this condition of things unassailed in principle, however they may have come into conflict with it in some of its details. They have occupied themselves rather in inquiring what things society ought to like or dislike, than in questioning whether its likings or dislikings should be a law to individuals. They preferred endeavoring to alter the feelings of mankind on the particular points on which they were themselves heretical, rather than make common cause in defense of freedom, with heretics generally. The only case in which the higher ground has been taken on principle and maintained with consistency, by any but an individual here and there, is that of religious belief: a case instructive in many ways, and not least so as forming a most striking instance of the fallibility of what is called the moral sense; for the *odium theologicum,* in a sincere bigot, is one of the most unequivocal cases of moral feeling. Those who first broke the yoke of what called itself the Universal Church, were in general as little willing to permit difference of religious opinion as that church itself. But when the heat of the conflict was over, without giving a complete victory to any party, and each church or sect was reduced to limit its hopes to retaining possession of the ground it already occupied; minorities, seeing that they had no chance of becoming majorities, were under the necessity of pleading to those whom they could not convert, for permission to differ. It is accordingly on this battlefield, almost solely, that the rights of the individual against society have been asserted on broad grounds of principle, and the claim of society to exercise authority over dissentients openly controverted. The great writers to whom the world owes what religious liberty it possesses, have mostly asserted freedom of conscience as an indefeasible right, and denied absolutely that a human being is accountable to others for his religious belief. Yet so natural to mankind is intolerance in whatever they really care about, that religious freedom has hardly anywhere been practically realized, except where religious indifference, which dislikes to have its peace disturbed by theological quarrels, has added its weight to the scale. In the minds of almost all religious persons, even in the most tolerant countries, the duty of toleration is admitted with tacit reserves. One person will bear with dissent in matters of church government, but not of dogma; another can tolerate everybody,

short of a Papist or a Unitarian; another everyone who believes in revealed religion; a few extend their charity a little further, but stop at the belief in a God and in a future state. Wherever the sentiment of the majority is still genuine and intense, it is found to have abated little of its claim to be obeyed.

In England, from the peculiar circumstances of our political history, though the yoke of opinion is perhaps heavier, that of law is lighter, than in most other countries of Europe; and there is considerable jealousy of direct interference, by the legislative or the executive power, with private conduct; not so much from any just regard for the independence of the individual, as from the still subsisting habit of looking on the government as representing an opposite interest to the public. The majority have not yet learnt to feel the power of the government their power, or its opinions their opinions. When they do so, individual liberty will probably be as much exposed to invasion from the government, as it already is from public opinion. But, as yet, there is a considerable amount of feeling ready to be called forth against any attempt of the law to control individuals in things in which they have not hitherto been accustomed to be controlled by it; and this with very little discrimination as to whether the matter is, or is not, within the legitimate sphere of legal control; insomuch that the feeling, highly salutary on the whole, is perhaps quite as often misplaced as well grounded in the particular instances of its application. There is, in fact, no recognized principle by which the propriety or impropriety of government interference is customarily tested. People decide according to their personal preferences. Some, whenever they see any good to be done, or evil to be remedied, would willingly instigate the government to undertake the business; while others prefer to bear almost any amount of social evil, rather than add one to the departments of human interests amenable to governmental control. And men range themselves on one or the other side in any particular case, according to this general direction of their sentiments; or according to the degree of interest which they feel in the particular thing which it is proposed that the government should do, or according to the belief they entertain that the government would, or would not, do it in the manner they prefer; but very rarely on account of any opinion to which they consistently adhere, as to what things are fit to be done by a government. And it seems to me that in consequence of this absence of rule or principle, one side is at present as often wrong as the other: the interference of government is, with about equal frequency, improperly invoked and improperly condemned.

The object of this essay is to assert one very simple principle, as entitled to govern absolutely the dealings of society with the individual in the way of compulsion and control, whether the means used be physical force in the form of legal penalties, or the moral coercion of public opinion. That principle is, that the sole end for which mankind are warranted, individually or collectively, in interfering with the liberty of action of any of their number, is self-protection. That the only purpose for which power can be rightfully exercised over any member of a civilized community, against his will, is to prevent harm to others. His own good, either physical or moral, is not a sufficient warrant. He cannot rightfully be compelled to do or forbear because it will be better for him to do so, because it will make him happier, because, in the opinions of others, to do so would be wise, or even right. These are good reasons for remonstrating with him, or reasoning with him, or persuading him, or entreating him, but not for compelling him, or visiting him with any evil in case he do otherwise. To justify that, the conduct from which it is desired to deter him must be calculated to produce evil to someone else. The only part of the conduct of anyone, for which he is amenable to society, is that which concerns others. In the part which merely concerns himself, his independence is, of right, absolute. Over himself, over his own body and mind, the individual is sovereign.

It is perhaps hardly necessary to say that this doctrine is meant to apply only to human beings in the maturity of their faculties. We are not speaking of children, or of young persons below the age which the law may fix as that of manhood or womanhood. Those who are still in a state to require being taken care of by others, must be protected against their own actions as well as against external injury. For the same reason, we may leave out of consideration those backward states of society in which the race itself may be considered as in its nonage. The early difficulties in the way of spon-

taneous progress are so great, and there is seldom any choice of means for overcoming them; and a ruler full of the spirit of improvement is warranted in the use of any expedients that will attain an end, perhaps otherwise unattainable. Despotism is a legitimate mode of government in dealing with barbarians, provided the end be their improvement, and the means justified by actually effecting that end. Liberty, as a principle, has no application to any state of things anterior to the time when mankind have become capable of being improved by free and equal discussion. Until then, there is nothing for them but implicit obedience to an Akbar or a Charlemagne, if they are so fortunate as to find one. But as soon as mankind have attained the capacity of being guided to their own improvement by conviction or persuasion (a period long since reached in all nations with whom we need here concern ourselves), compulsion, either in the direct form or in that of pains and penalties for noncompliance, is no longer admissible as a means to their own good, and justifiable only for the security of others.

It is proper to state that I forego any advantage which could be derived to my argument from the idea of abstract right, as a thing independent of utility. I regard utility as the ultimate appeal on all ethical questions; but it must be utility in the largest sense, grounded on the permanent interests of a man as a progressive being. Those interests, I contend, authorized the subjection of individual spontaneity to external control, only in respect to those actions of each which concern the interest of other people. If anyone does an act hurtful to others, there is a *prima facie* case for punishing him, by law, or, where legal penalties are not safely applicable, by general disapprobation. There are also many positive acts for the benefit of others, which he may rightfully be compelled to perform: such as to give evidence in a court of justice; to bear his fair share in the common defense, or in any other joint work necessary to the interest of the society of which he enjoys the protection; and to perform certain acts of individual beneficence, such as saving a fellow-creature's life, or interposing to protect the defenseless against ill-usage, things which whenever it is obviously a man's duty to do, he may rightfully be made responsible to society for not doing. A person may cause evil to others not only by his actions but by his inaction, and in either case he is justly accountable to them for the injury. The latter case, it is true, requires a much more cautious exercise of compulsion than the former. To make anyone answerable for doing evil to others is the rule; to make him answerable for not preventing evil is, comparatively speaking, the exception. Yet there are many cases clear enough and grave enough to justify that exception. In all things which regard the external relations of the individual, he is *de jure* amenable to those whose interests are concerned, and, if need be, to society as their protector. There are often good reasons for not holding him to the responsibility; but these reasons must arise from the special expediencies of the case: either because it is a kind of case in which he is on the whole likely to act better, when left to his own discretion, than when controlled in any way in which society have it in their power to control him; or because the attempt to exercise control would produce other evils, greater than those which it would prevent. When such reasons as these preclude the enforcement of responsibility, the conscience of the agent himself should step into the vacant judgment seat, and protect those interests of others which have no external protection; judging himself all the more rigidly, because the case does not admit of his being made accountable to the judgment of his fellow-creatures.

But there is a sphere of action in which society, as distinguished from the individual, has, if any, only an indirect interest; comprehending all that portion of a person's life and conduct which affects only himself, or if it also affects others, only with their free, voluntary, and undeceived consent and participation. When I say only himself, I mean directly, and in the first instance; for whatever affects himself, may affect others through himself; and the objection which may be grounded on this contingency, will receive consideration in the sequel. This, then, is the appropriate region of human liberty. It comprises, *first*, the inward domain of consciousness; demanding liberty of conscience in the most comprehensive sense; liberty of thought and feeling; absolute freedom of opinion and sentiment on all subjects, practical or speculative, scientific, moral, or theological. The liberty of expressing and publishing opinions may seem to fall under a dif-

ferent principle, since it belongs to that part of the conduct of an individual which concerns other people; but, being almost of as much importance as the liberty of thought itself, and resting in great part on the same reasons, is practically inseparable from it. *Secondly,* the principle requires liberty of tastes and pursuits; of framing the plan of our life to suit our own character; of doing as we like, subject to such consequences as may follow: without impediment from our fellow-creatures, so long as what we do does not harm them, even though they should think our conduct foolish, perverse, or wrong. *Thirdly,* from this liberty of each individual, follows the liberty, within the same limits, of combination among individuals; freedom to unite, for any purpose not involving harm to others: the persons combining being supposed to be of full age, and not forced or deceived.

No society in which these liberties are not, on the whole, respected, is free, whatever may be its form of government; and none is completely free in which they do not exist absolute and unqualified. The only freedom which deserves the name, is that of pursuing our own good in our own way, so long as we do not attempt to deprive others of theirs, or impede their efforts to obtain it. Each is the proper guardian of his own health, whether bodily, or mental and spiritual. Mankind are greater gainers by suffering each other to live as seems good to themselves, than by compelling each to live as seems good to the rest.

Though this doctrine is anything but new, and, to some persons, may have the air of a truism, there is no doctrine which stands more directly opposed to the general tendency of existing opinion and practice. Society has expended fully as much effort in the attempt (according to its lights) to compel people to conform to its notions of personal as of social excellence. The ancient commonwealths thought themselves entitled to practice, and the ancient philosophers countenanced, the regulation of every part of private conduct by public authority, on the ground that the State had a deep interest in the whole bodily and mental discipline of every one of its citizens: a mode of thinking which may have been admissible in small republics surrounded by powerful enemies, in constant peril of being subverted by foreign attack or internal commotion, and to which even a short interval of relaxed energy and self-command might so easily be fatal that they could not afford to wait for the salutary permanent effects of freedom. In the modern world, the greater size of political communities, and, above all, the separation between spiritual and temporal authority (which placed the direction of men's consciences in other hands than those which controlled their worldly affairs), prevented so great an interference by law in the details of private life; but the engines of moral repression have been wielded more strenuously against divergence from the reigning opinion in self-regarding, than even in social matters; religion, the most powerful of the elements which have entered into the formation of moral feeling, having almost always been governed either by the ambition of a hierarchy, seeking control over every department of human conduct, or by the spirit of Puritanism. And some of those modern reformers who have placed themselves in strongest opposition to the religions of the past, have been no way behind either churches or sects in their assertion of the right of spiritual domination: M. Comte, in particular, whose social system, as unfolded in his *Système de Politique Positive,* aims at establishing (though by moral more than by legal appliances) a despotism of society over the individual, surpassing anything contemplated in the political ideal of the most rigid disciplinarian among the ancient philosophers.

Apart from the peculiar tenets of individual thinkers, there is also in the world at large an increasing inclination to stretch unduly the powers of society over the individual, both by the force of opinion and even by that of legislation; and as the tendency of all the changes taking place in the world is to strengthen society, and diminish the power of the individual, this encroachment is not one of the evils which tend spontaneously to disappear, but, on the contrary, to grow more and more formidable. The disposition of mankind, whether as rulers or as fellow-citizens, to impose their own opinions and inclinations as a rule of conduct on others, is so energetically supported by some of the best and by some of the worst feelings incident to human nature, that it is hardly ever kept under restraint by anything but want of power; and as the power is not declining, but growing, unless a strong barrier of moral conviction can be raised against the

mischief, we must expect, in the present circumstances of the world, to see it increase.

It will be convenient for the argument, if, instead of at once entering upon the general thesis, we confine ourselves in the first instance to a single branch of it, on which the principle here stated is, if not fully, yet to a certain point, recognized by the current opinions. This one branch is the *liberty of thought:* from which it is impossible to separate the cognate liberty of speaking and of writing. Although these liberties, to some considerable amount, form part of the political morality of all countries which profess religious toleration and free institutions, the grounds, both philosophical and practical, on which they rest, are perhaps not so familiar to the general mind, nor so thoroughly appreciated by many even of the leaders of opinion, as might have been expected. Those grounds, when rightly understood, are of much wider application than to only one division of the subject, and a thorough consideration of this part of the question will be found the best introduction to the remainder. Those to whom nothing which I am about to say will be new, may therefore, I hope, excuse me, if on a subject which for now three centuries has been so often discussed, I venture on one discussion more.

DISCUSSION QUESTIONS

1. Do you agree with Mill's arguments for the range of individual liberty in society? Why or why not? What seem to be his assumptions about the nature of the basic relationship between the individual and the group?

2. Do you agree with Mill's exclusion of "barbarians" and "backward" peoples from the right to liberty? Why or why not? Is his account irreparably ethnocentric or consistent? Why or why not?

3. Do you agree with Mill's position that social authorities can never legitimately force a rational, "mature adult" to do or not do something for his or her own good? Why or why not?

4. Do you think the tyranny of the majority, in the various forms it can take, is still a problem in society? Why or why not?

5. How might a non-European who lived under British colonial rule respond to Mill's arguments?

57. Lucas D. Introna (contemporary)

"Privacy and the Computer: Why We Need Privacy in the Information Society"

Lucas Introna received his undergraduate, M.B.A., and Ph.D. (Information Systems) degrees from the University of Pretoria, South Africa, and since 1995 has been Lecturer in the Department of Information Systems at the London School of Economics and Political Science. His work, which represents a fast-growing and wide-ranging trend affecting many academic disciplines as well as governmental and commercial policy making, focuses on the beneficial and detrimental social consequences of the continuing rapid developments in information and surveillance technology. In fact, since 1997 when the following essay was published in the journal *Metaphilosophy*, significant changes have occurred around the world along these lines, such as the further dramatic rise in Internet use and the increased capabilities for collecting personal genetic information.

In general, in this essay Introna is arguing for a proper balance in social life between what he considers the fundamental value of personal privacy, adequately defined, and what is called social "transparency." Although he recognizes that the concept of privacy has had no fixed, universal connotation, but instead has been understood differently in different cultural and historical contexts, he maintains that relevant common elements in the diversity of its characterizations can be identified. These elements more than ever need to be affirmed and protected, he believes, as the technological possibilities of "panoptic" social surveillance multiply. In these times then, this issue is a crucial one to address in getting at the nature of good and bad relations between individuals and their communities.

QUESTIONS FOR CRITICAL READING

1. According to Introna, what are the three current types of definitions of privacy, and what are the limits of each in his view?
2. How does Introna argue for privacy as a fundamental value in social life?
3. What is Introna's own view of the relationship between privacy and "transparency," and what does this have to do with moral and legal accountability for our actions?
4. How does the author apply his conclusions regarding the value of privacy to contemporary life in our "information society" and to the information systems field?

1. Introduction

There is very little doubt that many citizens in the emerging information society are explicitly or implicitly concerned over the rapid loss of their individual privacy. As far back as 1971, a survey by a Royal Commission on Privacy found that 93% of those surveyed saw a national official databank as the most disturbing example of intrusion on privacy and in fact 90% wanted it prohibited by law (Campbell & Connor 1987). The uneasy sense of being "watched," it seems, is more pervasive today than in any previous epoch of our history. The state administration and private corporations are collecting data on citizens and customers with the seemingly legitimate motive to more effectively serve them. The question that remains, however, is whether the application of these data is in the actual service of the people or whether it is in fact, more than anything else, just a means of more effective social control where the state or the corporation is the ultimate beneficiary. We have at least some evidence that it may be the latter as indicated by Kling and Iacono (1984) and Dunlop and Kling (1991) amongst others (see also Forester and Morrison 1994). With the emergence of new technological innovation in data collection and management come new forms of control such as computer matching (Shattuck 1984) and dataveillance (Clarke 1988). With practices such as these, information technology is fast becoming, as suggested by Zuboff and others, a virtual panopticon such as even Jeremy Bentham would not have been able to visualise in his wildest dreams.

There are some philosophers such as Wasserstrom and legal theorists such as Posner (1978) who argue that the loss of privacy and the move to a transparent society (as is, to a large degree, now technologically possible) will be to the ultimate benefit of society as a whole. After all, is the acknowledgement of the notion of privacy not merely creating a context in which both deceit and hypocrisy may flourish? Will it not create a society in which the guilty are protected against taking responsibility for their transgressions?—a society in which actions go unexposed to rigorous moral debate necessary for a moral and just society—a sort of secrecy that leaves society morally weak and exposed to exploitation? On the other hand, is there not something fundamental in the notion of privacy, something that made its eventual articulation inevitable as the modern information society evolved? What is it that the notion of privacy provides that makes it exemplary of debate and protection if at all? It seems to me, as projects such as the information superhighway leave the launchpad, the Internet explodes into a 30 million plus users network, and more and more individual communication becomes electronically mediated, that the discipline of information systems is in need of a fundamental rethinking of why we need to take the issue of individual privacy very seriously.

Because of the limitations of space and not wanting to risk the possibility of clouding the issue, I will focus primarily on the discussion of the privacy notion and limit my application to the information society and discipline to just a few examples. Hopefully these examples will show in a clear and distinct way the implication of the privacy notion for the information society and our discipline (in theory and practice). The in-depth analysis required for a proper assessment of the full spectrum of implications will be the topic of a next paper. I will structure the rest of the paper as follows: first, I will consider some definitions of privacy to create a sense of the notion involved; second, I will discuss the value of privacy as the essential context and as the foundation of human autonomy in social relationships; third, I will briefly discuss what I see as

the implications of this notion of privacy for the information society in general and for the discipline of information systems in particular.

2. Towards Defining Privacy

Privacy, intuitively, seems such a primordial notion. Some personal space, some area within which one is free from the gaze and judgment of others seems to be a basic need of most people. What is surprising, however, is that privacy did not get explicit attention from any of the great liberals. Liberal philosophers such as John Locke, Rousseau, Wilhelm van Humboldt and J. S. Mill did not spend as much as a page in their voluminous writings on the subject. Moreover, significant philosophical debate on the subject only emerged in the late 1960s. Why is this so? Could it be that privacy, as some suggest, is a modern, very suspect concept invented by Warren and Brandeis in 1890 in response to a personal situation?

The first explicit legal analysis of privacy by Brandeis and Warren was published in 1890 (Brandeis & Warren 1890) in the *Harvard Law Review*. This paper was apparently written in response to Warren's experience of intrusion by the press (the *Saturday Evening Gazette* in particular) on his family and social life. The press reported in detail the events and particulars of the elaborate social entertainments he and his wife held at their home. It was at the wedding of a daughter that he finally got so annoyed that he approached Brandeis to collaborate on writing the now seminal and celebrated paper (see Prosser 1960 for a more detailed and a well articulated legal critique of their concept of privacy). Nevertheless, if one works through philosophical and legal literature on the matter, it is clear that there is, even today, still a lot of controversy around the very notion of privacy. This fact emphasises that it is of increasing importance for the information-systems community to give it a fundamental rethinking and not to assume that the "why" is sorted out and all we have to do is work out the "how."

Privacy (or the lack thereof) for most at least is easy to identify when experienced but difficult to define. It seems that for every definition proposed by jurists and philosophers alike a counterexample can be found. This may be the reason for some of the severe critique raised against the very notion of privacy. Despite the fairly intense debate since the late 1960s, there is still no universally accepted definition of privacy. There have been various attempts to create a synthesis of existing literature such as the work by Parent (1983) and Schoeman (1984). What remains clear, however, is that there is no simple or elegant solution. It has been suggested that we will only make significant progress if we step down from the attempt to define privacy and instead further explore its actual functioning. Thus, we should move from the "what" question to the "how" question. This may be a good suggestion, since privacy as a moral category would continually leave one without an epistemological basis. Nonetheless, there might be advantages to starting the discussion with a review of some existing attempts at defining privacy. This will provide us with an indication of the complexity of the problem, as well as the issues or dimensions involved. It seems as if one could group the definition into three fairly distinct but not mutually exclusive categories, namely: (a) privacy as no access to the person or the personal realm; (b) privacy as control over personal information; and (c) privacy as freedom from judgment or scrutiny by others. I will elaborate somewhat on these groups of definitions.

2.1 Privacy as No Access to a Person or Personal Realm

Warren and Brandeis (1890, 205) defined privacy as "the right to be let alone." It is easy to see that there are various grounds upon which one can fault this definition. If I, for example, use an extremely strong telescope to watch your every move, I am in the strict sense of the word leaving you alone. However, one can hardly call this a condition of privacy. There are also certain institutions or individuals that have a legitimate right not to leave you alone, such as the tax service or your creditors. As is clear, this is a too limited definition that does not take enough cognisance of the subtle and complex social context where privacy is at stake. For Van Den Haag (1971, 149) "privacy is the exclusive access of a person to a realm of his own. The right to privacy entitles one to exclude others from (a) watching, (b) utilizing, (c) invading his private [personal] realm." In this (rather circular) definition,

the issue of a private or a personal realm comes to the fore. It implies that there is a certain realm, here expressed as personal, to which one may legitimately limit access. The obvious problem here is the definition of what is private or personal. For some cultures a bare torso or breasts are extremely personal. For some African tribes they are in the public domain. Most scholars agree that to a large extent the exact demarcation of the personal realm is culturally defined. There is no ontologically defined personal realm. Nevertheless, from a legal and communicative perspective, personal information can be defined as "those facts, communications or opinions which relate to the individual and which it would be reasonable to expect him to regard as intimate or confidential and therefore to want to withhold or at least to restrict their circulation" (Wacks 1980, 89). Gross (1967) is in agreement with this notion of privacy as "the condition of human life in which acquaintance with a person or with affairs of his life which are personal to him is limited." He also refers to "intellectual" access by using the word "acquaintance."

The above definitions, however, do not enable one to differentiate between the loss of privacy and the question of whether or not one's right to privacy has been violated. An individual may voluntarily give access to his personal realm to various other individuals intimately known or maybe unknown to him. In such a case, the person may be said to be less private, but no one has violated his right to privacy. This leads to the issue of control that is made explicit in the next group of definitions.

2.2 Privacy as Control over Personal Information

Fried (1968) defines privacy as "control over knowledge about oneself." This notion of control of personal information is also captured in the definition by Westin by defining privacy as "the claim of individuals, groups or institutions to determine for themselves when, how and to what extent information about them is communicated to others" (1967, 7, 42). Or in a more general sense by Parker (1974, 275) as the "control over when and whom the various parts of us can be sensed by others." This idea of control over the distribution of personal information (given that personal is culturally defined) is very powerful in situations where it is important to determine whether or not an individual's right to privacy has been violated. On the other hand someone can at his own discretion divulge personal information to whoever cares to listen thus, even though he has not lost control, he cannot be said to have any privacy. To take another example, you tap my phone and listen to all my conversations with my lover. We have, however, devised an elaborate coding system to exchange very intimate information. Because of this, you glean nothing from the tap. In this manner we have absolute control over the flow of personal information. Again you may have violated our right to privacy, but we have experienced no loss of privacy. Clearly, from a legal point of view, the violation of the right to privacy is very important. However, from a social relationship perspective it is the actual loss of privacy that is the issue at stake. Gavison (1980, 434) defines a loss of privacy occurring when "others obtain information about an individual, pay attention to him, or gain access to him." In this definition and the previous group the need for privacy is implicitly assumed. There is also no mention of the "other" in the relationship given that privacy is a relational notion. This is where the notion of judgment-by-others in the next group of definitions becomes explicit.

2.3 Privacy as Freedom from Judgment or Scrutiny by Others

The real issue of privacy according to Johnson (1989) is the judgment by others. He expresses it as follows:

> Privacy is a conventional concept. What is considered private is socially or culturally defined. It varies from context to context. It is dynamic, and it is quite possible that no single example can be found of something which is considered private in every culture. Nevertheless, all examples of privacy have a single common feature. They are aspects of a person's life which are culturally recognized as being immune from the judgment of others. (157)

It is the knowledge that others would judge us in a particular way, perhaps based on preconceived ideas and norms, that makes the individual's desire a personal or private space of immunity. Thus, it is the

inevitable loss of control over the decontextualization and recontextualization of the data obtained and subsequent judgment thereof that motivates the individual to "hide" it. It has been shown, quite convincingly, by the *Gestalt* psychologists that individuals will always recontextualise data back into an individually defined whole or context in order to interpret it. The person from whom the data originated does not, however, have any control over the particular whole or context (frame of reference, values, norms, etc.) within which the data will be recontextualized and interpreted.

This is exactly where the whole argument of Posner (1978) fails. Posner argues that personal information can be divided into discrediting or non-discrediting information. If the personal information is accurate and discrediting then we have a social incentive to make this information available to others who may have dealings with this person. To fail to do this is, according to Posner, the same as failing to reveal a fraudulent scheme. If the information is false or non-discrediting, there is no social value in such information and it could be kept privately. The begging question, of course, is what norms are used to make the judgment of discrediting or non-discrediting information. Posner assumes that there is a set of self-evident, universally accepted norms that can unequivocally separate discrediting information from non-discrediting information. The so called discrediting judgment is obviously also context dependent. For example, the fact that a person has a venereal disease may be discrediting for a potential sexual partner, but it should not necessarily be "discrediting" when applying for a job as a taxi driver. The whole point of Johnson is that the person may be unfairly judged as "not suitable" as a taxi driver as a result of his medical condition due to a personal moral value held by the owner of the cab company. Such very real possibilities surely create sufficient grounds to grant an individual some form of immunity within a personal realm or at least to refute Posner's reductionistic account of privacy as the creating of a context in which both deceit and hypocrisy may flourish. This judgment-by-others issue is well captured by DeCew (1986) in stating that "an interest in privacy is at stake when intrusion by others is not legitimate because it jeopardizes or prohibits protection of a realm free from scrutiny, judgment, and the pressure, distress, or losses they can cause" (171).

It is clear from the above discussion that there is no simple definition available to us. There are, however, certain aspects of the notion that one can summarise as follows:

a. Privacy is a relational concept. It comes to the fore in a community. Where people interact, the issue of privacy emerges.

b. Privacy is directed towards the personal domain. What is deemed personal is, to some extent at least, culturally defined. In general one may state that personal or private aspects of my life are those aspects that do not, or tend not to, affect the significant interests of others.

c. To claim privacy is to claim the right to limit access or control access to my personal or private domain.

d. An effective way to control access to my personal realm is to control the distribution of textual images or verbal information about it.

e. To claim privacy is to claim the right to a (personal) domain of immunity against the judgments of others.

f. Privacy is a relative concept. It is a continuum. Total privacy may be as undesirable as total transparency. It is a matter of appropriateness for the situation at hand. It is unfortunately (or fortunately) a matter of *judgment*.

Given this brief overview of some of the attempts at defining privacy, the question that must surely emerge very forcefully at this point is: Why ought we concern ourselves with privacy at all? What is the value of privacy? Or, differently stated, what would we lose if we abandoned the notion of privacy altogether? Is the need for privacy motivated by a frivolous sense of shame or embarrassment or is there something fundamental to it? The next section will present some arguments or at least outlines of arguments for the position that privacy is a fundamental notion that shapes society in a profound and indispensable way.

3. Why Privacy?

There are many ways to argue the case for privacy as a fundamental notion. This paper will present the de-

fence from four perspectives: (a) privacy as the context of social relationships; (b) privacy and intimate relationships; (c) privacy and social roles; and (d) privacy and self-constitution or autonomy.

3.1 Privacy as the Context of Social Relationships

Let us start with a thought experiment as an intellectual tool to assess in a general manner the role of privacy in social relationships. Imagine a world where there is a comprehensive and complete lack of privacy, complete and immediate access, complete and immediate knowledge, and complete and constant observation of every individual. There will be no private thoughts and no private places. Every thought and every act is completely transparent from motive right through to the actual thought or behaviour; body and mind immediately and completely transparent to each and every "other." I will call this world "the transparent world." Let us imagine the nature of social relationships in the transparent world. Would differentiated relationships be possible? How will your relationship with your wife or lover differ from your relationship with an official or your manager or your child? What is there to share since everything is already known? It seems that in the transparent world notions such as getting to know someone, or being intimate with someone, or sharing yourself with someone just fade into obscurity. In such a world, how would you differentiate yourself, how would you compete? Competitive advantage requires knowledge of a method, a technique or a way of doing that is not known to the other. Is creativity possible? How is it possible to say "this is my idea" or "this is what I think"? Does it make sense to talk of "my" or "me" at all, since original thought or original action would be impossible (or at least indeterminable)? It is clear that all social relationships, relationships of collaboration or of competition, require at least some level of privacy. Now one can protest against such a thought experiment by saying that the transparent world is a useless concept as total transparency is in anyway impossible. One can also say that surely the critics of privacy are not implying that the transparent world is a utopia. These protests are in order. It is, however, my contention that the issues that are very apparent in the transparent world as shown in the thought experiment above become issues in the everyday world long before we have reached total transparency. These are the issues brought into focus by total transparency that are at the heart of the privacy debate.

Given this introduction via the thought experiment, let us examine in more detail how privacy creates the context for most, if not all, social relationships.

3.2 Privacy and Intimate Relationships

Privacy and intimacy have been linked by many previous authors. One paper with considerable impact has been Charles Fried (1968). This paper in a way pioneered the investigation into the role of privacy and social relationships that emerged in the early 1970s. In his paper Fried argues that privacy provides the "moral capital" required by intimate relationships of love and friendship:

> Love and friendship, as analysed here, involve the initial respect for the rights of others which morality requires of everyone. They further involve the voluntary and spontaneous relinquishment of *something* between friend and friend, lover and lover. The title to information about oneself [one's beliefs, emotions, feelings, dreams, desires, etc.] conferred by privacy provides the necessary something. (483)

It is this possibility of exchanging personal information about oneself (within a context of caring) that creates the possibility for intimacy. Now one must refrain from a sort of "market economy" interpretation of what Fried is arguing. Reinman's (1976) critique on this point is fundamental to the argument. He argues that one may reveal information to one's psychoanalyst which one might even hesitate to reveal to a friend or lover. This hardly means that one has an intimate relationship with the analyst: "what matters is who cares about it and to whom I care to reveal it . . . what constitutes intimacy is not merely the sharing of otherwise withheld information, but the context of caring which makes the sharing of personal information significant" (31). Thus, the moral capital created by privacy is a necessary, but not sufficient, condition for intimacy. Intimacy also requires a context of caring and significant involvement as participant in the relationship as argued by Robert Gerstein (1984).

Gerstein argues that intimacy is an experience of a relationship in which one is deeply engrossed and in which one fully and wholly participates. It is a rela-

tionship where we relinquish our role as independent observer to lose ourselves in the experience. The key point is that we cannot *at the same time* be lost in an experience and be observers of it. We cannot continue to be immersed in the experience of intimacy if we begin to observe ourselves or other things around us. Thus, "when I have been involved in intimate communication and then am made suddenly aware that I am being observed [physically or electronically], I also am suddenly brought to an awareness of my own actions as object of observation . . . The temptation now to appraise the appearance I make, and to change my actions so that they will reflect to the observer what I would like them to, would certainly be very strong. To do this would be to kill the spontaneity which is essential to intimacy, to switch from participant to observer" (268). Thus, privacy creates the moral capital (the personal information) and the possibility to participate (share the information) in a relationship in which I am deeply and exclusively engrossed as participant. Without privacy such intimate relationships would not be possible, or at least they would be extremely difficult to maintain.

3.3 Privacy and Social Roles

It is a generally accepted fact that individuals maintain a variety of relationships by assuming or acting out different roles. This fact has been very well documented by the sociologist Erving Goffman (1959). It is in fact different patterns of behaviour or roles that to a large degree define the different relationships and make them what they are. James Rachels (1975) does an excellent job of articulating this very important idea. He argues that "the sort of relationship people have with one another involves a conception of how it is appropriate for them to behave with each other, and what is more, a conception of the kind and degree of knowledge concerning one another which it is appropriate to have" (328; see also Schoeman, 1984). Thus, it is our ability to control who has access to us, and who knows what about about us, that allows us to sustain a variety of relationships with others. Rachels uses a case of two friends to illustrate the point. I will cite the example *verbatim*:

> Consider what happens when two close friends are joined by a casual acquaintance. The character of the group changes; and one of the

changes is that conversation about intimate matters is now out of order [inappropriate]. Then suppose these friends could never be alone: suppose there were always third parties (let us say casual acquaintances or strangers) intruding. Then they could do either of two things. They could carry on as close friends do, sharing confidences, freely expressing their feelings about things [and themselves], and so on. But this would mean violating their sense of how it is appropriate to behave around casual acquaintances or strangers. Or, they could avoid doing or saying anything which they think inappropriate to do or say around a third party. But this would mean that they could no longer behave with one another in the way that friends do and further that, eventually, they would no longer *be* close friends. (328)

This example can easily be repeated for relationships such as husband and wife, mother and daughter, etc. Thus, each relationship has a repertoire of rules, rituals, gestures and language games that defines the exact nature of the interactions that are appropriate in the relationship. They are both the medium and the outcome of the relationship. They are for the most part culturally established. Nonetheless, they demarcate in a fairly distinct way how it is appropriate to behave and what kind and degree of knowledge concerning the other it is appropriate to have—thus, the degree of privacy or transparency that is appropriate.

In a similar but somewhat different fashion, Gavison (1984) argues that this repertoire of rules etc. that demarcates the private from the public for a given relationship enables individuals to continue relationships without denying one's inner thoughts, fears, doubts, or wishes that the other in the relationship may not or cannot accept. Privacy "permits individuals [in the reciprocal relationship] to do what they would not do without it for fear of an unpleasant or hostile reaction from others" (368). Some may argue that this role playing is fraudulent and deceitful, but, in fact, it is essential for the actual functioning of the diverse set of relationships that the average person will assume or act out every day. Imagine if the complexity (due to the intimacy and transparency) in the husband and wife relationship had to be repeated in even the

most casual relationship. Privacy, through the rules, rituals, etc. that demarcate the private/public domain for a specific class of relationships, creates simplified relational structures that allow the individual to cope with the complexity—also, to appropriately invest in a selected set of intimate relationships.

3.4 Privacy and Self-Constitution or Autonomy

One of the most common arguments for privacy is its role in the creation and preservation of individual autonomy. Simply put, the argument runs as follows: If a person is aware that he is being observed, the person becomes conscious of himself as an object of observation. As an object of observation the person will then not merely structure his action according to his own will or intention, but also in line with (or in realisation of) what he believes those who observe would expect to see. To a lesser or greater degree, the acts flowing from an observed person can never be conceived with any certainty (by himself or others) as his own. This almost automatic factoring-in of the other's gaze or expectations may be due to a desire to be accepted by, or maybe to influence, the observers in some desired way. Irrespective of the motive, the mere fact of becoming an object of observation forces the individual to act in a manner that he or she may not have chosen in a situation of privacy. Now some argue that such a condition of transparency may ultimately be good for society, since it will ensure that everybody acts in line with the moral guidelines of the specific society. After all, who would commit a murder or a theft, if it were known that every act is immediately known to all?

On the other hand, one may ask: what sort of person and what sort of society would we have if people merely acted in a moral manner out of fear of being observed in the act, rather than as a result of their own decision to freely accept and abide by the moral code of that particular society? Given privacy, the individual is entrusted with the moral decision to decide for himself. The problem with this view is, of course, that not all can be trusted. Is this, notwithstanding, sufficient grounds for a sort of moral blackmail through a transparent society? Will this transparent morality not merely create a conventional person, confirming to create an undifferentiated mass society? This is why Reinman (1976) argues that "privacy is a social ritual by means of which an individual's moral title to his existence is conferred. Privacy is an essential part of the complex social practice by means of which the social group recognizes and communicates to the individual that his existence is his own" (31).

Without privacy there would be no self. It would be difficult, even impossible, to separate the self from the other, since no act or thought could be said to be, in any significant way, original. Without privacy, a person would not be creator or originator, but merely a copier or enactor. As Reinman (1976) concludes: "privacy is necessary to the creation of *selves* out of human beings, since a self is at least in part a human being who regards his existence, his thoughts, his body, his actions as his *own*" (36). Or, as Kupfer (1987) argues: "Privacy contributes to the formation and persistence of autonomous individuals by providing them with control over whether or not their physical and psychological existence becomes part of another's experience. Just this sort of control is necessary for them to think of themselves as self-determining" (81–82).

There are many more issues here, which I have at this point deliberately left unchallenged. For example, from a post-modern perspective, Foucault (1980) argues that the subject, the individual, is not "some sort of elementary nucleus, a primitive atom, a multiple and inert material on which power comes to fasten or against which it happens to strike, and in so doing subdues or crushes individuals. In fact, it [the subject] is already one of the prime effects of power that certain bodies, certain gestures, certain discourses, certain desires, come to be identified and constituted as individuals. . . . The individual which power has constituted is at the same time its vehicle" (93). The notion of the subject as "free agent," as autonomous and sovereign subject must be abandoned as the subject is "already one of the prime effects of power." The transparency—the universal "gaze"—created by the panopticon effect (universal and continual surveillance) leads to the internalization of man. In his self-surveillance, man cultivates a self-consciousness. Thus, Foucault argues that our world is *de facto* transparent and that privacy is impossible, since ultimately we always observe ourselves. Nevertheless, without any privacy there is no possibility for any sort of authentic self to emerge (or be invented). In the transparent world the self is no more than the inscribing of the "outer" onto the "inner."

Another often held counter-argument is that "the disposition to act in accord with one's reflectively chosen principles might even be weakened by excessive privacy, since privacy affords no opportunity to face and resist the disapproval of others. Moral muscles can be weakened by disuse" (Andre 1986, 312). It seems that we need transparency to create an area for openness and feedback, and we need privacy for reflection and appropriation. Privacy and transparency in some way imply each other. The one cannot exist without the other as an absolute value. It is a matter of appropriate balance. It is a matter of judgment.

It is clear from the above that privacy plays a fundamental and crucial role in the shaping of everyday social relationships. In fact, it seems clear that without at least some level of privacy many social relationships will be extremely difficult, if not impossible, to establish and maintain. Since man is a social animal who, primarily, articulates his life in and through his social relationships, access to privacy seems to be an essential component of what it means to be an individual human being. If this is true, then all human beings, without any exception whatsoever, should have an inalienable and unalterable entitlement to an acceptable or appropriate level of privacy. Without the *prima facie* right to privacy, man will lose his worth as an individual. He will not be able to maintain his most important relationships, i.e., his intimate relationships. He will experience extreme ambiguity in coping with the variety of roles he must assume in everyday living; but most of all, he will lose his sense of meaning. Without a sense of meaning, man is but another animal species. Victor Frankl once wrote: "Man's concern about the meaning of life is the truest expression of the state of being human."

Does the right to privacy negate the importance of transparency and accountability? No, in fact the notion of accountability does not make any sense without privacy. We cannot talk of accountability without autonomy and trust. One would not expect a machine to be accountable. Someone can only be accountable if endowed with choice. Choice implies the ability to select from a set of options or alternatives. Accountability requires autonomy, the possibility to choose, also the possibility of making the wrong choice. Trust is the level of confidence held by society in one's ability to act in a moral way, i.e., to make the right choices. But, "there can be no trust where there is not a possibility of error. Constant surveillance [total transparency] negates the possibility of error and as such, the possibility of trust" (Fried 1968, 484). Thus, privacy creates the clearing from which autonomy, trust and accountability can emerge. Ultimately these notions are not the antipodes of privacy. They have privacy as a necessary condition. Privacy is the context of transparency, and transparency is the context of privacy. They are co-constitutive.

4. Privacy and the Computer

In this section I return to the implications of privacy, as discussed above, for the information society and for us in the information systems discipline. There are, of course, many implications that can be drawn. I will only highlight a few.

Let us consider first the concept of privacy (as discussed in section two on current definitions). Information technology, through electronically mediated communication, by removing time and space limitations, is rapidly multiplying interaction possibilities by orders of magnitude. This is simultaneously, in the same proportion, increasing privacy dilemmas that the typical inhabitant or co-habitant of cyberspace is faced with. Consider the following very mundane and practical example. In confined spaces such as public transport or public buildings, I am often forced to listen to very private conversations of people on their cellular telephones. I am drawn into their private space without having any choice in the matter. In fact, it has become increasingly difficult to separate the private from the public domain. With virtual offices that incorporate the home, traditionally clear physical demarcations are fading away. Now my virtual office is "entered" by many unsolicited electronic travellers. My ability to limit these cybertravellers is very limited. There seem to be only two alternatives: either I stay out of cyberspace (and risk the possibility of being isolated) or my activity enters the public domain. Not only this, but once I place some digital "print" into cyberspace, I lose control over it. It can be altered in some significant and potentially damaging way, and be distributed to many thousands of others in a matter of minutes. It can be decontextualized and recontextualized without a trace. I am not saying that this was not possible in the pre-electronic era. I am merely saying that it has now become so easy to do that the potential for privacy violation has become almost available on

demand. It is clear from these very brief comments that the issue of privacy is bound to become more acute as the information society expands.

The real issues, however, concern topics from the second part of this paper. As the technological infrastructure expands, the issues of social relationships, roles and autonomy will become more and more urgent. In the quotation above James Rachels argued that the sort of relationship people have with one another involves a conception of how it is *appropriate for them to behave* with each other, and what is more, a conception of the *kind and degree of knowledge concerning one another which it is appropriate to have.* Thus, it is our ability to control who has access to us, and who knows what about us, that allows us to sustain the variety of relationships we have with others. Electronic access is becoming more and more immediate and direct. It seems, therefore, that as more and more individuals get access to me via the electronic media, I will progressively lose control over my ability to clearly structure my diverse set of social roles. Inevitably, a host of role-ambiguous situations will develop, since electronic communication can jump through organizational levels, over organizational borders and socially constructed barriers. In many cases, one will find oneself dealing with a usercode— xyz@neon.abc.co—with whom one may or may not have had previous interaction. All the normal social cues such as physical setting, dress, titles, body language, etc. are missing. How did s/he get my e-mail address (how did s/he get access)? What may I request of (or supply to) this person or him to me? Can I trust him or her, etc.? In fact, the whole notion of trust, so important for social roles and relations, is becoming ambiguous. At present our social mechanisms for building relations of trust are physically bound for the most part (except maybe for something like personal recommendation). In most cases I would want to physically meet the person and talk to him or her. In cyberspace, however, it is easy to imagine the sort of role ambiguity that can develop. The appropriate demarcation of private and public (in terms of appropriate behaviour and knowledge) for a specific type of role now becomes very vague.

Thus, it seems that a whole new set of rules, rituals and gestures will have to evolve to deal with this new, more abstract set of electronically induced social roles.

Although this dimension of privacy in cyberspace is making the maintenance of social roles more complex and potentially much more ambiguous, it may be that all that is required is the articulation of a new set of protocols (not that this is at all a simple matter) that will enable us to cope with this new group of demands. It is, as I see it, in the area of individual autonomy that the more serious issues are located.

Reinman argued (cited above) that privacy is a social ritual by means of which an individual's moral title to his existence is conferred. Privacy is an essential part of the complex social practice by means of which the social group recognizes and communicates to individuals that their existence is their own. Thus, as information technology (cellular telephones, television, the Internet, groupware, etc.) progressively invades more and more private space (turning it into public space), individuals will be faced with fewer possibilities for making their existence their own. This is the essence of Foucault's argument that the modern society through its panoptic universal "gaze" is creating mechanisms of power that are far more subtle and encompassing than ever before. We see this for example in modern management theory. The current popular management paradigm is to decentralise management of the organization, to provide more autonomy through flatter structures and disperse decision-making and self control. This sounds very noble. However, the rationale held by many managers is that with information technology they can now decentralise "without losing control." Thus, they think (or make others believe) that they are giving more autonomy, but they are in fact just constructing more sophisticated methods of control. We can see this paradox (autonomy versus transparency or, in management theory terms, empowerment versus control) in the following quotation by Applegate:

Through the design of business information and communication models that simultaneously provide maximum stability of structure and flexibility of use, the *information infrastructure supported the design of management systems and structures that enabled both tight control [transparency] and continuous innovation [autonomy] in response to environmental change and organizational learning.* (75)

To be fair to Applegate, I would admit that I may be forcing the interpretation somewhat. What is interesting, however, is the way in which this paradoxical reasoning is embedded in most of our curent management theory language. By denying the employees lower down in the structure privacy (freedom from judgment), the conditions for autonomy and accountability are not met. This will merely mean that when individuals become aware that they are being observed (electronically), the temptation will be to appraise the appearance made, and to change their actions so that they will reflect to the observer what the observer would like them to be. This is not more autonomy, it is just more subtle control. As argued above, without the required privacy, there will be no self (autonomy). It would be difficult, if not impossible, to separate the self from the other, since no act or thought could be said to be, in any significant way, original. It is clear that there is a significant trade-off between creativity, autonomy and control.

Now one might object that the issue of creative self-actualization is not part of the mandate for a modern corporation. Is the possibility of autonomy just reserved for those at the "top"? Must subordinates be satisfied that they will always be subjected to control? Surely, even in the lowest ranks of the organization, there should be some domains of privacy: private areas where individuals can articulate their own ideas without fear of judgment. Only then would their actions in public become meaningful. Then, as argued above, can trust and accountability grow. The alternative is to turn our organizations into disciplinary societies where individuals are programmed through the electronic eye, the universal gaze.

It is for the ultimate good of society as a whole that privacy is preserved, even at the expense of legitimate social control. Without some preserved private spaces, society would lose its most valuable asset: the true *individual*. Without an appropriate environment the system would die. Without privacy, individuals would not mature into responsible managers, but would merely become managers controlled by "transparency blackmail." It is, as I see it, the information systems discipline that stands at the leading edge of information technology application (in the social space) that can play a major role in the preservation of the legitimate demand of humans for privacy (also in the context of the corporation). If we understand that privacy creates the "clearing" from which autonomy, trust and accountability can emerge, then privacy will become part of the design agenda, and not merely some annoying "nice to have" liberal value that may or may not be considered at a later stage. If I am wrong, this paper might be a "strawman" argument. If I am right, then privacy should become a much more prominent issue in the information systems' curriculum, systems design and systems implementation. Hopefully this paper will make a contribution towards that debate.

Department of Information Systems
London School of Economics and Political Science
Houghton Street
London WC2A 2AE
United Kingdom
4.Introna@lse.ac.uk

References

Andre, J. (1986). "Privacy as a Value and as a Right," *The Journal of Value Inquiry*, 20, 309–317.

Applegate, L. M. (1994). "Managing in the Information Age: Transforming the Organization for the 1990s." In R. Baskerville et al. (eds.) *Transforming Organizations with Information Technology*. Ann Arbor, Michigan: North-Holland, 10–35.

Bradeis, L. and Warren, S. D. (1890). "The Right to Privacy." *The Harvard Law Review*, 4, 5, 193–220.

Campbell, D. and Connor, S. (1987). "Surveillance. Computers and Privacy." In R. Finnegan et al. (eds.). *Information Technology: Social Issues*. London: Hodder & Stoughton, 134–144.

Clarke, R. C. (1988). "Information Technology and Dataveillance." *Communications of the ACM*, 31, 4, 498–512.

DeCew, J. W. (1986). "The Scope of Privacy in Law and Ethics." *Law and Philosophy*, 5, 145–173.

Dunlop, C. and Kling, R. (1991). *Computerization and Controversy*. Boston: Academic Press, 410–419.

Forester, T. and Morrison, P. (1994). *Computer Ethics: Cautionary Tales and Ethical Dilemmas in Computing*. Second Edition. Cambridge: The MIT Press.

Foucault, M. (1980). *The History of Sexuality* Volume I: *An Introduction*. R. Hurley (trans.). New York: Vintage Books.

Fried, C. (1968). "Privacy." *Yale Law Journal*, 77, 475–493.

Gavison, R. (1980). "Privacy and the Limits of the Law." *The Yale Law Journal*, 89, 3, 421–471.

Gavison, R. (1984). "Privacy and the Limits of the Law." In F. Schoeman (ed.). *Philosophical Dimensions of Privacy*. Cambridge: Cambridge University Press, 365–371.

Gerstein, R. S. (1984). "Intimacy and Privacy." In F. Schoeman (ed.). *Philosophical Dimensions of Privacy*. Cambridge: Cambridge University Press, 265–271.

Goffman, E. (1959). *The Presentation of Self in Everyday Life*. Garden City: Doubleday & Co.

Gross, H. (1967). "The Concept of Privacy." *New York University Law Review*, 42, 35–36.

Johnson, J. L. (1989). "Privacy and Judgement of Others." *The Journal of Value Inquiry*, 23, 157–168.

Kling, R. & Iacono, S. (1984). "Computing as an Occasion for the Social Control." *Journal of Social Issues*, 40, 3, 77–96.

Kupfer, J. (1987). "Privacy, Autonomy, and Self-Concept." *American Philosophical Quarterly*, 24, 1, 81–82.

Parent, W. A. (1983). "Recent Work on the Concept of Privacy." *American Philosophical Quarterly*, 20, 4, 341–355.

Parker, R. B. (1974). "A Definition of Privacy." *Rutgers Law Review*, 27, 1, 275–296.

Posner, R. (1978). "The Right to Privacy." *Georgia Law Review*, 12, 393–422.

Prosser, W. L. (1960). "Privacy." *The California Law Review*, 48, 383–422.

Rachels, J. (1975). "Why Privacy is Important." *Philosophy & Public Affairs*, 4, 4, 328.

Reiman, J. H. (1976). "Privacy, Intimacy, and Personhood." *Philosophy & Public Affairs*, 6, 1, 26–44.

Schoeman, F. (1984). "Privacy: Philosophical Dimensions." *American Philosophical Quarterly*, 21, 3, 199–213.

Schoeman, F. (1984). "Privacy and Intimate Information." In F. Schoeman (ed.). *Philosophical Dimensions of Privacy*. Cambridge: Cambridge University Press. 403–417.

Shattuck, J. (1984). "Computer Matching is a Serious Threat to Individual Rights." *Communications of the ACM*, 27, 6, 538–541.

Van Den Haag, E. (1971). "On Privacy." *Nomos*, 13, 147–153.

Wacks, R. (1980). "The Poverty of 'Privacy'." *The Law Quarterly Review*, 96, 73–95.

Westin, A. (1967). *Privacy and Freedom*. New York: Atheneum.

DISCUSSION QUESTIONS

1. Which of the various definitions of privacy discussed by Introna makes the most sense to you? Why?

2. As Introna points out, there are those who argue for more social transparency and less privacy. Do you agree with this position? Why or why not?

3. Do you agree with the author's own conclusions regarding the value of privacy in contemporary social life and the importance of emphasizing it as information systems technology develops? Why or why not?

4. Do you think the United Nations should become more involved in the protection of privacy rights worldwide? Why or why not?

58. Martin Luther King Jr. (1929–1968)
"Letter from Birmingham Jail"

Martin Luther King Jr. was a Baptist minister and theologian who became the most well known and influential African American leader of the civil rights movement in the United States during the 1950s and 1960s. He was born in Atlanta, Georgia, entered Morehouse College at 15, and when he graduated in 1948, he was also already ordained in the ministry. After divinity studies in Pennsylvania, he went on to earn a Ph.D. in theology at Boston University in 1955. Thereafter, he spent the rest of his life serving as pastor at parishes in Montgomery, Alabama, and Atlanta. At the same time, he was involved in political activism, primarily in the southern states, against the widespread official and unofficial racial segregation that kept blacks in a position of second-class citizenship in relation to whites. He is not only known for his direct involvement in organized public protests against racial and economic injustice, his gifted oratory, and his extensive writing, but he is also internationally recognized today as one of the major proponents in the twentieth century (along with Mohandas Gandhi) of the doctrine of nonviolent direct action as the most effective means of fighting oppression. For his work he was awarded the Nobel peace prize in 1964. He was assassinated on April 4, 1968, in Memphis, Tennessee, at the age of 39.

This selection, which has become King's most widely read essay, was written in 1963 while he was in jail for his antisegregation political activities in Birmingham, Alabama. He wrote it as a letter in response to Christian and Jewish clergy who had publicly criticized his organization's direct-action campaign in Birmingham. As part of his defense of his activist, confrontational approach to working for needed social and legal change, he deals with a variety of moral, religious, and political issues traditionally the concern of many philosophers. In this essay he also, once again, articulates the moral foundation and practical consequences of nonviolent active resistance to the social and legal forces of injustice, even in the face of violent retaliation. The principles he argues for here are inseparable, in his view, from an understanding of the basic interconnection between all people who together constitute a viable society.

QUESTIONS FOR CRITICAL READING

1. How does King argue for his claim that "injustice anywhere is a threat to justice everywhere"?
2. How does King describe and illustrate the "four basic steps" of a nonviolent action campaign?
3. How does King characterize and argue for the distinction between just and unjust laws?
4. In King's account, what is the difference between the civil disobedience he advocates and merely "evading or defying the law"?
5. How does King characterize the difference between "negative peace" and "positive peace"?
6. What are King's criticisms of "white moderates" and the "white church"?

TERMS TO NOTE

Zeitgeist: A German term meaning "the spirit of the times."

ekklesia: A Greek term meaning "church" but originally referring to an assembly of citizens in a city-state.

April 16, 1963

My Dear Fellow Clergymen:

While confined here in the Birmingham city jail, I came across your recent statement calling my present activities "unwise and untimely." Seldom do I pause to

---

Author's note: This response to a published statement by eight fellow clergymen from Alabama (Bishop C. C. J. Carpenter, Bishop Joseph A. Durick, Rabbi Hilton L. Grafman, Bishop Paul Hardin, Bishop Holan B. Harmon, the Reverend George M. Murray, the Reverend Edward V. Ramage and the Reverend Earl Stallings) was composed under somewhat constricting circumstances. Begun on the margins of the newspaper in which the statement appeared while I was in jail, the letter was continued on scraps of writing paper supplied by a friendly Negro trusty, and concluded on a pad my attorneys were eventually permitted to leave me. Although the text remains in substance unaltered, I have indulged in the author's prerogative of polishing it for publication.

answer criticism of my work and ideas. If I sought to answer all the criticisms that cross my desk, my secretaries would have little time for anything other than such correspondence in the course of the day, and I would have no time for constructive work. But since I feel that you are men of genuine good will and that your criticisms are sincerely set forth, I want to try to answer your statement in what I hope will be patient and reasonable terms.

I think I should indicate why I am here in Birmingham, since you have been influenced by the view which argues against "outsiders coming in." I have the honor of serving as president of the Southern Christian Leadership Conference, an organization operating in every southern state, with headquarters in Atlanta, Georgia. We have some eighty-five affiliated organizations across the South, and one of them is the Alabama Christian Movement for Human Rights. Frequently we share staff, educational and financial resources with our affiliates. Several months ago the affiliate here in Birmingham asked us to be on call to engage in a nonviolent direct-action program if such were deemed necessary. We readily consented, and when the hour came we lived up to our promise. So I, along with several members of my staff, am here because I was invited here. I am here because I have organizational ties here.

But more basically, I am in Birmingham because injustice is here. Just as the prophets of the eighth century B.C. left their villages and carried their "thus saith the Lord" far beyond the boundaries of their home towns, and just as the Apostle Paul left his village of Tarsus and carried the gospel of Jesus Christ to the far corners of the Greco-Roman world, so am I compelled to carry the gospel of freedom beyond my own home town. Like Paul, I must constantly respond to the Macedonian call for aid.

Moreover, I am cognizant of the interrelatedness of all communities and states. I cannot sit idly by in Atlanta and not be concerned about what happens in Birmingham. Injustice anywhere is a threat to justice everywhere. We are caught in an inescapable network of mutuality, tied in a single garment of destiny. Whatever affects one directly, affects all indirectly. Never again can we afford to live with the narrow, provincial "outside agitator" idea. Anyone who lives inside the United States can never be considered an outsider anywhere within its bounds.

You deplore the demonstrations taking place in Birmingham. But your statement, I am sorry to say, fails to express a similar concern for the conditions that brought about the demonstrations. I am sure that none of you would want to rest content with the superficial kind of social analysis that deals merely with effects and does not grapple with underlying causes. It is unfortunate that demonstrations are taking place in Birmingham, but it is even more unfortunate that the city's white power structure left the Negro community with no alternative.

In any nonviolent campaign there are four basic steps: collection of the facts to determine whether injustices exist; negotiation; self-purification; and direct action. We have gone through all these steps in Birmingham. There can be no gainsaying the fact that racial injustice engulfs this community. Birmingham is probably the most thoroughly segregated city in the United States. Its ugly record of brutality is widely known. Negroes have experienced grossly unjust treatment in the courts. There have been more unsolved bombings of Negro homes and churches in Birmingham than in any other city in the nation. These are the hard, brutal facts of the case. On the basis of these conditions, Negro leaders sought to negotiate with the city fathers. But the latter consistently refused to engage in good-faith negotiation.

Then, last September, came the opportunity to talk with leaders of Birmingham's economic community. In the course of the negotiations, certain promises were made by the merchants—for example, to remove the stores' humiliating racial signs. On the basis of these promises, the Reverend Fred Shuttlesworth and the leaders of the Alabama Christian Movement for Human Rights agreed to a moratorium on all demonstrations. As the weeks and months went by, we realized that we were the victims of a broken promise. A few signs, briefly removed, returned; the others remained.

As in so many past experiences, our hopes had been blasted, and the shadow of deep disappointment settled upon us. We had no alternative except to prepare for direct action, whereby we would present our very bodies as a means of laying our case before the conscience of the local and the national community. Mindful of the difficulties involved, we decided to undertake a process of self-purification. We began a series of workshops on nonviolence, and we repeatedly asked ourselves: "Are you able to accept blows without retaliating?" "Are you able to endure the ordeal of jail?" We decided to schedule our direct-action program for the Easter season, realizing that except for Christmas, this is the main shopping period of the year. Knowing that a strong economic-withdrawal program would be the by-product of direct action, we felt that this would be the best time to bring pressure to bear on the merchants for the needed change.

Then it occurred to us that Birmingham's mayoral election was coming up in March, and we speedily decided to postpone action until after election day. When we discovered that the Commissioner of Public Safety, Eugene "Bull" Connor, had piled up enough votes to be in the run-off, we decided again to postpone action until the day after the run-off so that the demonstrations could not be used to cloud the issues. Like many others, we waited to see Mr. Connor defeated, and to this end we endured postponement after postponement. Having aided in this community need, we felt that our direct-action program could be delayed no longer.

You may well ask: "Why direct action? Why sit-ins, marches and so forth? Isn't negotiation a better path?" You are quite right in calling for negotiation. Indeed, this is the very purpose of direct action. Nonviolent direct action seeks to create such a crisis and foster such a tension that a community which has constantly refused to negotiate is forced to confront the issue. It seeks so to dramatize the issue that it can no longer be ignored. My citing the creation of tension as part of the work of the nonviolent-resister may sound rather shocking. But I must confess that I am not afraid of the word "tension." I have earnestly opposed violent tension, but there is a type of constructive, nonviolent tension which is necessary for growth. Just as Socrates felt that it was necessary to create a tension in the mind so that individuals could rise from the bondage of myths and half-truths to the unfettered realm of creative analysis and objective appraisal, so must we see the need for nonviolent gadflies to create the kind of tension in society that will help men rise from the dark depths of prejudice and racism to the majestic heights of understanding and brotherhood.

The purpose of our direct-action program is to create a situation so crisis-packed that it will inevitably open the door to negotiation. I therefore concur with you in your call for negotiation. Too long has our beloved Southland been bogged down in a tragic effort to live in monologue rather than dialogue.

One of the basic points in your statement is that the action that I and my associates have taken in Birmingham is untimely. Some have asked: "Why didn't you give the new city administration time to act?" The only answer that I can give to this query is that the new Birmingham administration must be prodded about as much as the outgoing one, before it will act. We are sadly mistaken if we feel that the election of Albert Boutwell as mayor will bring the millennium to Birmingham. While Mr. Boutwell is a much more gentle person than Mr. Connor, they are both segregationists, dedicated to maintenance of the status quo. I have hope that Mr. Boutwell will be reasonable enough to see the futility of massive resistance to desegregation. But he will not see this without pressure from devotees of civil rights. My friends, I must say to you that we have not made a single gain in civil rights without determined legal and nonviolent pressure. Lamentably, it is an historical fact that privileged groups seldom give up their privileges voluntarily. Individuals may see the moral light and voluntarily give up their unjust posture; but, as Reinhold Niebuhr has reminded us, groups tend to be more immoral than individuals.

We know through painful experience that freedom is never voluntarily given by the oppressor; it must be demanded by the oppressed. Frankly, I have yet to engage in a direct-action campaign that was "well timed" in the view of those who have not suffered unduly from the disease of segregation. For years now I have heard the word "Wait!" It rings in the ear of every Negro with piercing familiarity. This "Wait" has almost always meant "Never." We must come to see, with one of our distinguished jurists, that "justice too long delayed is justice denied."

We have waited for more than 340 years for our constitutional and God-given rights. The nations of Asia and Africa are moving with jetlike speed toward gaining political independence, but we still creep at horse-and-buggy pace toward gaining a cup of coffee at a lunch counter. Perhaps it is easy for those who have never felt the stinging darts of segregation to say, "Wait." But when you have seen vicious mobs lynch your mothers and fathers at will and drown your sisters and brothers at whim; when you have seen hate-filled policemen curse, kick and even kill your black brothers and sisters; when you see the vast majority of your twenty million Negro brothers smothering in an airtight cage of poverty in the midst of an affluent society; when you suddenly find your tongue twisted and your speech stammering as you seek to explain to your six-year-old daughter why she can't go to the public amusement park that has just been advertised on television, and see tears welling up in her eyes when she is told that Funtown is closed to colored children, and see ominous clouds of inferiority beginning to form in her little mental sky, and see her beginning to distort her personality by developing an unconscious bitterness toward white people; when you have to concoct an answer for a five-year-old son who is asking: "Daddy, why do white people treat colored people so mean?"; when you take a cross-country drive and find it necessary to sleep night after night in the uncomfortable corners of your automobile because no motel will accept you; when you are humiliated day in and day out by nagging signs reading "white" and "colored"; when your first name becomes "nigger," your middle name becomes "boy" (however old you are) and your last name becomes "John," and your wife and mother are never given the respected title "Mrs."; when you are harried by day and haunted by night by the fact that you are a Negro, living constantly at tiptoe stance, never quite knowing what to expect next, and are plagued with inner fears and outer resentments; when you are forever fighting a degenerating sense of "nobodiness"—then you will understand why we find it difficult to wait. There comes a time when the cup of endurance runs over, and men are no longer willing to be plunged into the abyss of despair. I hope, sirs, you can understand our legitimate and unavoidable impatience.

You express a great deal of anxiety over our willingness to break laws. This is certainly a legitimate concern. Since we so diligently urge people to obey the Supreme Court's decision of 1954 outlawing segregation in the public schools, at first glance it may seem rather paradoxical for us consciously to break laws. One may well ask: "How can you advocate breaking some laws and obeying others?" The answer lies in the fact that there are two types of laws: just and unjust. I would be the first to advocate obeying just laws. One has not only a legal but a moral responsibility to obey just laws. Conversely, one has a moral responsibility to disobey unjust laws. I would agree with St. Augustine that "an unjust law is no law at all."

Now, what is the difference between the two? How does one determine whether a law is just or unjust? A just law is a man-made code that squares with the moral law or the law of God. An unjust law is a code that is out of harmony with the moral law. To put it in the terms of St. Thomas Aquinas: An unjust law is a human law that is not rooted in eternal law and natural law. Any law that uplifts human personality is just. Any law that degrades human personality is unjust. All segregation statutes are unjust because segregation distorts the soul and damages the personality. It gives the segregator a false sense of superiority and the segregated a false sense of inferiority. Segregation, to use the terminology of the Jewish philosopher Martin Buber, substitutes an "I-it" relationship for an "I-thou" relationship and ends up relegating persons to the status of things. Hence segregation is not only politically, economically and sociologically unsound, it is morally wrong and sinful. Paul Tillich has said that sin is separation. Is not segregation an existential expression of man's tragic separation, his awful estrangement, his terrible sinfulness? Thus it is that I can urge men to obey the 1954 decision of the Supreme Court, for it is morally right; and I can urge them to disobey segregation ordinances, for they are morally wrong.

Let us consider a more concrete example of just and unjust laws. An unjust law is a code that a numerical or power majority group compels a minority group to obey but does not make binding on itself. This is *difference* made legal. By the same token, a just law is a code that a majority compels a minority to follow and that it is willing to follow itself. This is *sameness* made legal.

Let me give another explanation. A law is unjust if it is inflicted on a minority that, as a result of being denied the right to vote, had no part in enacting or devising the law. Who can say that the legislature of Alabama which set up that state's segregation laws was democratically elected? Throughout Alabama all sorts of devious methods are used to prevent Negroes from becoming registered voters, and there are some counties in which, even though Negroes constitute a majority of the population, not a single Negro is registered. Can any law enacted under such circumstances be considered democratically structured?

Sometimes a law is just on its face and unjust in its application. For instance, I have been arrested on a charge of parading without a permit. Now, there is nothing wrong in having an ordinance which requires a permit for a parade. But such an ordinance becomes unjust when it is used to maintain segregation and to deny citizens the First-Amendment privilege of peaceful assembly and protest.

I hope you are able to see the distinction I am trying to point out. In no sense do I advocate evading or defying the law, as would the rabid segregationist. That would lead to anarchy. One who breaks an unjust law must do so openly, lovingly, and with a willingness to accept the penalty. I submit that an individual who breaks a law that conscience tells him is unjust, and who willingly accepts the penalty of imprisonment in order to arouse the conscience of the community over its injustice, is in reality expressing the highest respect for law.

Of course, there is nothing new about this kind of civil disobedience. It was evidenced sublimely in the refusal of Shadrach, Meshach and Abednego to obey the laws of Nebuchadnezzar, on the ground that a higher moral law was at stake. It was practiced superbly by the early Christians, who were willing to face hungry lions and the excruciating pain of chopping blocks rather than submit to certain unjust laws of the Roman Empire. To a degree, academic freedom is a reality today because Socrates practiced civil disobedience. In our own nation, the Boston Tea Party represented a massive act of civil disobedience.

We should never forget that everything Adolf Hitler did in Germany was "legal" and everything the Hungarian freedom fighters did in Hungary was "illegal." It was "illegal" to aid and comfort a Jew in Hitler's Germany. Even so, I am sure that, had I lived in Germany at the time, I would have aided and comforted my Jewish brothers. If today I lived in a Communist country where certain principles dear to the Christian faith are suppressed, I would openly advocate disobeying that country's antireligious laws.

I must make two honest confessions to you, my Christian and Jewish brothers. First, I must confess that over the past few years I have been gravely disappointed with the white moderate. I have almost reached the regrettable conclusion that the Negro's great stumbling block in his stride toward freedom is not the White Citizen's Counciler or the Ku Klux Klanner, but the white moderate, who is more devoted to "order" than to justice; who prefers a negative peace which is the absence of tension to a positive peace which is the presence of justice; who constantly says: "I agree with you in the goal you seek, but I cannot agree with your methods of direct action"; who paternalistically believes he can set the timetable for another man's freedom; who lives by a mythical concept of time and who constantly advises the Negro to wait for a "more convenient season." Shallow understanding from people of good will is more frustrating than absolute misunderstanding from people of ill will. Lukewarm acceptance is much more bewildering than outright rejection.

I had hoped that the white moderate would understand that law and order exist for the purpose of establishing justice and that when they fail in this purpose they become the dangerously structured dams that block the flow of social progress. I had hoped that the white moderate would understand that the present tension in the South is a necessary phase of the transition from an obnoxious negative peace, in which the Negro passively accepted his unjust plight, to a substantive and positive peace, in which all men will respect the dignity and worth of human personality. Actually, we who engage in nonviolent direct action are not the creators of tension. We merely bring to the surface the hidden tension that is already alive. We bring it out in the open, where it can be seen and dealt with. Like a boil that can never be cured so long as it is covered up but must be opened with all its ugliness to the natural medicines of air and light, injustice must be exposed, with all the tension its exposure creates, to the light of human conscience and the air of national opinion before it can be cured.

In your statement you assert that our actions, even though peaceful, must be condemned because they precipitate violence. But is this a logical assertion? Isn't this like condemning a robbed man because his possession of money precipitated the evil act of robbery? Isn't this like condemning Socrates because his unswerving commitment to truth and his philosophical inquiries precipitated the act by the misguided populace in which they made him drink hemlock? Isn't this like condemning Jesus because his unique God-consciousness and never-ceasing devotion to God's will precipitated the evil act of crucifixion? We must come to see that, as the federal courts have consistently affirmed, it is wrong to urge an individual to cease his efforts to gain his basic constitutional rights because the quest may precipitate violence. Society must protect the robbed and punish the robber.

I had also hoped that the white moderate would reject the myth concerning time in relation to the struggle for freedom. I have just received a letter from a white brother in Texas. He writes: "All Christians know that the colored people will receive equal rights eventually, but it is possible that you are in too great a religious hurry. It has taken Christianity almost two thousand years to accomplish what it has. The teachings of Christ take time to come to earth." Such an attitude stems from a tragic misconception of time, from the strangely irrational notion that there is something in the very flow of time that will inevitably cure all ills. Actually, time itself is neutral; it can be used either destructively or constructively. More and more I feel that the people of ill will have used time much more effectively than have the people of good will. We will have to repent in this generation not merely for the hateful words and actions of the bad people but for the appalling silence of the good people. Human progress never rolls in on wheels of inevitability; it comes through the tireless efforts of men willing to be co-workers with God, and without this hard work, time itself becomes an ally of the forces of social stagnation. We must use time creatively, in the knowledge that the time is always ripe to do right. Now is the time to make real the promise of democracy and transform our pending national elegy into a creative psalm of brotherhood. Now is the time to lift our national policy from the quicksand of racial injustice to the solid rock of human dignity.

You speak of our activity in Birmingham as extreme. At first I was rather disappointed that fellow clergymen would see my nonviolent efforts as those of an extremist. I began thinking about the fact that I stand in the middle of two opposing forces in the Negro community. One is a force of complacency, made up in part of Negroes who, as a result of long years of oppression, are so drained of self-respect and a sense of "somebodiness" that they have adjusted to segregation; and in part of a few middle-class Negroes who, because of a degree of academic and economic secu-rity and because in some ways they profit by segregation, have become insensitive to the problems of the masses. The other force is one of bitterness and hatred, and it comes perilously close to advocating violence. It is expressed in the various black nationalist groups that are springing up across the nation, the largest and best-known being Elijah Muhammad's Muslim movement. Nourished by the Negro's frustration over the continued existence of racial discrimination, this movement is made up of people who have lost faith in America, who have absolutely repudiated Christianity, and who have concluded that the white man is an incorrigible "devil."

I have tried to stand between these two forces, saying that we need emulate neither the "do-nothingism" of the complacent nor the hatred and despair of the black nationalist. For there is the more excellent way of love and nonviolent protest. I am grateful to God that, through the influence of the Negro church, the way of nonviolence became an integral part of our struggle.

If this philosophy had not emerged, by now many streets of the South would, I am convinced, be flowing with blood. And I am further convinced that if our white brothers dismiss as "rabble-rousers" and "outside agitators" those of us who employ nonviolent direct action, and if they refuse to support our nonviolent efforts, millions of Negroes will, out of frustration and despair, seek solace and security in black-nationalist ideologies—a development that would inevitably lead to a frightening racial nightmare.

Oppressed people cannot remain oppressed forever. The yearning for freedom eventually manifests itself, and that is what has happened to the American Negro. Something within has reminded him of his birthright of freedom, and something without has reminded him that it can be gained. Consciously or unconsciously, he has been caught up by the *Zeitgeist,* and with his black brothers of Africa and his brown and yellow brothers of Asia, South America and the Caribbean, the United States Negro is moving with a sense of great urgency toward the promised land of racial justice. If one recognizes this vital urge that has engulfed the Negro community, one should readily understand why public demonstrations are taking place. The Negro has many pent-up resentments and latent frustrations, and he must release them. So let him march; let him make prayer pilgrimages to the city hall; let him go on freedom rides—and try to understand why he must do so. If his repressed emotions are not released in nonviolent ways, they will seek expression through violence; this is not a threat but a fact of history. So I have not said to my people: "Get rid of your discontent." Rather, I have tried to say that this normal and healthy discontent can be channeled into the creative outlet of nonviolent direct action. And now this approach is being termed extremist.

But though I was initially disappointed at being categorized as an extremist, as I continued to think about the matter I gradually gained a measure of satisfaction from the label. Was not Jesus an extremist for love: "Love your enemies, bless them that curse you, do good to them that hate you, and pray for them which despitefully use you, and persecute you." Was not Amos an extremist for justice: "Let justice roll down like waters and righteousness like an ever-flowing stream." Was not Paul an extremist for the Christian gospel: "I bear in my body the marks of the Lord Jesus." Was not Martin Luther an extremist: "Here I stand; I cannot do otherwise, so help me God." And John Bunyan: "I will stay in jail to the end of my days before I make a butchery of my conscience." And Abraham Lincoln: "This nation cannot survive half slave and half free." And Thomas Jefferson: "We hold these truths to be self-evident, that all men are created equal . . ." So the question is not whether we will be extremists, but what kind of extremists we will be. Will we be extremists for hate or for love? Will we be extremists for the preservation of injustice or for the extension of justice? In that dramatic scene on Calvary's hill three men were crucified. We must never forget that all three were crucified for the same crime—the crime of extremism. Two were extremists for immorality, and thus fell below their environment. The other, Jesus Christ, was an extremist for love, truth and goodness, and thereby rose above his environment. Perhaps the South, the nation and the world are in dire need of creative extremists.

I had hoped that the white moderate would see this need. Perhaps I was too optimistic; perhaps I expected too much. I suppose I should have realized that few members of the oppressor race can understand the deep groans and passionate yearnings of the oppressed

race, and still fewer have the vision to see that injustice must be rooted out by strong, persistent and determined action. I am thankful, however, that some of our white brothers in the South have grasped the meaning of this social revolution and committed themselves to it. They are still all too few in quantity, but they are big in quality. Some—such as Ralph McGill, Lillian Smith, Harry Golden, James McBride Dabbs, Ann Braden and Sarah Patton Boyle—have written about our struggle in eloquent and prophetic terms. Others have marched with us down nameless streets of the South. They have languished in filthy, roach-infested jails, suffering the abuse and brutality of policemen who view them as "dirty nigger-lovers." Unlike so many of their moderate brothers and sisters, they have recognized the urgency of the moment and sensed the need for powerful "action" antidotes to combat the disease of segregation.

Let me take note of my other major disappointment. I have been so greatly disappointed with the white church and its leadership. Of course, there are some notable exceptions. I am not unmindful of the fact that each of you has taken some significant stands on this issue. I commend you, Reverend Stallings, for your Christian stand on this past Sunday, in welcoming Negroes to your worship service on a non-segregated basis. I commend the Catholic leaders of this state for integrating Spring Hill College several years ago.

But despite these notable exceptions, I must honestly reiterate that I have been disappointed with the church. I do not say this as one of those negative critics who can always find something wrong with the church. I say this as a minister of the gospel, who loves the church; who was nurtured in its bosom; who has been sustained by its spiritual blessings and who will remain true to it as long as the cord of life shall lengthen.

When I was suddenly catapulted into the leadership of the bus protest in Montgomery, Alabama, a few years ago, I felt we would be supported by the white church. I felt that the white ministers, priests and rabbis of the South would be among our strongest allies. Instead, some have been outright opponents, refusing to understand the freedom movement and misrepresenting its leaders; all too many others have been more cautious than courageous and have remained silent behind the anesthetizing security of stained-glass windows.

In spite of my shattered dreams, I came to Birmingham with the hope that the white religious leadership of this community would see the justice of our cause and, with deep moral concern, would serve as the channel through which our just grievances could reach the power structure. I had hoped that each of you would understand. But again I have been disappointed.

I have heard numerous southern religious leaders admonish their worshipers to comply with a desegregation decision because it is the law, but I have longed to hear white ministers declare: "Follow this decree because integration is morally right and because the Negro is your brother." In the midst of blatant injustices inflicted upon the Negro, I have watched white churchmen stand on the sideline and mouth pious irrelevancies and sanctimonious trivialities. In the midst of a mighty struggle to rid our nation of racial and economic injustice, I have heard many ministers say: "Those are social issues, with which the gospel has no real concern." And I have watched many churches commit themselves to a completely otherworldly religion which makes a strange, un-Biblical distinction between body and soul, between the sacred and the secular.

I have traveled the length and breadth of Alabama, Mississippi and all the other southern states. On sweltering summer days and crisp autumn mornings I have looked at the South's beautiful churches with their lofty spires pointing heavenward. I have beheld the impressive outlines of her massive religious-education buildings. Over and over I have found myself asking: "What kind of people worship here? Who is their God? Where were their voices when the lips of Governor Barnett dripped with words of interposition and nullification? Where were they when Governor Wallace gave a clarion call for defiance and hatred? Where were their voices of support when bruised and weary Negro men and women decided to rise from the dark dungeons of complacency to the bright hills of creative protest?"

Yes, these questions are still in my mind. In deep disappointment I have wept over the laxity of the church. But be assured that my tears have been tears of love. There can be no deep disappointment where there is not deep love. Yes, I love the church. How could I do otherwise? I am in the rather unique position of being the son, the grandson and the great-grandson of preachers. Yes, I see the church as the body of Christ. But, oh! How we have blemished and scarred that body through social neglect and through fear of being nonconformists.

There was a time when the church was very powerful—in the time when the early Christians rejoiced at being deemed worthy to suffer for what they believed. In those days the church was not merely a thermometer that recorded the ideas and principles of popular opinion; it was a thermostat that transformed the mores of society. Whenever the early Christians entered a town, the people in power became disturbed and immediately sought to convict the Christians for being "disturbers of the peace" and "outside agitators." But the Christians pressed on, in the conviction that they were "a colony of heaven," called to obey God rather than man. Small in number, they were big in commitment. They were too God-intoxicated to be "astronomically intimidated." By their effort and example they brought an end to such ancient evils as infanticide and gladiatorial contests.

Things are different now. So often the contemporary church is a weak, ineffectual voice with an uncertain sound. So often it is an archdefender of the status quo. Far from being disturbed by the presence of the church, the power structure of the average community is consoled by the church's silent—and often even vocal—sanction of things as they are.

But the judgment of God is upon the church as never before. If today's church does not recapture the sacrificial spirit of the early church, it will lose its authenticity, forfeit the loyalty of millions, and be dismissed as an irrelevant social club with no meaning for the twentieth century. Every day I meet young people whose disappointment with the church has turned into outright disgust.

Perhaps I have once again been too optimistic. Is organized religion too inextricably bound to the status quo to save our nation and the world? Perhaps I must turn my faith to the inner spiritual church, the church within the church, as the true *ekklesia* and the hope of the world. But again I am thankful to God that some noble souls from the ranks of organized religion have broken loose from the paralyzing chains of conformity and joined us as active partners in the struggle for freedom. They have left their secure congregations and walked the streets of Albany, Georgia, with us. They have gone down the highways of the South on tortuous rides for freedom. Yes, they have gone to jail with us. Some have been dismissed from their churches, have lost the support of their bishops and fellow ministers. But they have acted in the faith that right defeated is stronger than evil triumphant. Their witness has been the spiritual salt that has preserved the true meaning of the gospel in these troubled times. They have carved a tunnel of hope through the dark mountain of disappointment.

I hope the church as a whole will meet the challenge of this decisive hour. But even if the church does not come to the aid of justice, I have no despair about the future. I have no fear about the outcome of our struggle in Birmingham, even if our motives are at present misunderstood. We will reach the goal of freedom in Birmingham and all over the nation, because the goal of America is freedom. Abused and scorned though we may be, our destiny is tied up with America's destiny. Before the pilgrims landed at Plymouth, we were here. Before the pen of Jefferson etched the majestic words of the Declaration of Independence across the pages of history, we were here. For more than two centuries our forebears labored in this country without wages; they made cotton king; they built the homes of their masters while suffering gross injustice and shameful humiliation—and yet out of a bottomless vitality they continued to thrive and develop. If the inexpressible cruelties of slavery could not stop us, the opposition we now face will surely fail. We will win our freedom because the sacred heritage of our nation and the eternal will of God are embodied in our echoing demands.

Before closing I feel impelled to mention one other point in your statement that has troubled me profoundly. You warmly commended the Birmingham police force for keeping "order" and "preventing violence." I doubt that you would have so warmly commended the police force if you had seen its dogs sinking their teeth into unarmed, nonviolent Negroes. I doubt that you would so quickly commend the policemen if you were to observe their ugly and inhumane treatment of Negroes here in the city jail; if you were to watch them push and curse old Negro women

and young Negro girls; if you were to see them slap and kick old Negro men and young boys; if you were to observe them, as they did on two occasions, refuse to give us food because we wanted to sing our grace together. I cannot join you in your praise of the Birmingham police department.

It is true that the police have exercised a degree of discipline in handling the demonstrators. In this sense they have conducted themselves rather "nonviolently" in public. But for what purpose? To preserve the evil system of segregation. Over the past few years I have consistently preached that nonviolence demands that the means we use must be as pure as the ends we seek. I have tried to make clear that it is wrong to use immoral means to attain moral ends. But now I must affirm that it is just as wrong, or perhaps even more so, to use moral means to preserve immoral ends. Perhaps Mr. Connor and his policemen have been rather nonviolent in public, as was Chief Pritchett in Albany, Georgia, but they have used the moral means of nonviolence to maintain the immoral end of racial injustice. As T. S. Eliot has said: "The last temptation is the greatest treason: To do the right deed for the wrong reason."

I wish you had commended the Negro sit-inners and demonstrators of Birmingham for their sublime courage, their willingness to suffer and their amazing discipline in the midst of great provocation. One day the South will recognize its real heroes. They will be the James Merediths, with the noble sense of purpose that enables them to face jeering and hostile mobs, and with the agonizing loneliness that characterizes the life of the pioneer. They will be old, oppressed, battered Negro women, symbolized in a seventy-two-year-old woman in Montgomery, Alabama, who rose up with a sense of dignity and with her people decided not to ride segregated buses, and who responded with ungrammatical profundity to one who inquired about her weariness: "My feets is tired, but my soul is at rest." They will be the young high school and college students, the young ministers of the gospel and a host of their elders, courageously and nonviolently sitting in at lunch counters and willingly going to jail for conscience' sake. One day the South will know that when these disinherited children of God sat down at lunch counters, they were in reality standing up for what is best in the American dream and for the most sacred values in our

Judaeo-Christian heritage, thereby bringing our nation back to those great wells of democracy which were dug deep by the founding fathers in their formulation of the Constitution and the Declaration of Independence.

Never before have I written so long a letter. I'm afraid it is much too long to take your precious time. I can assure you that it would have been much shorter if I had been writing from a comfortable desk, but what else can one do when he is alone in a narrow jail cell, other than write long letters, think long thoughts and pray long prayers?

If I have said anything in this letter that overstates the truth and indicates an unreasonable impatience, I beg you to forgive me. If I have said anything that understates the truth and indicates my having a patience that allows me to settle for anything less than brotherhood, I beg God to forgive me.

I hope this letter finds you strong in the faith. I also hope that circumstances will soon make it possible for me to meet each of you, not as an integrationist or a civil-rights leader but as a fellow clergyman and a Christian brother. Let us all hope that the dark clouds of racial prejudice will soon pass away and the deep fog of misunderstanding will be lifted from our fear-drenched communities, and in some not too distant tomorrow the radiant stars of love and brotherhood will shine over our great nation with all their scintillating beauty.

Yours for the cause of Peace and Brotherhood,
Martin Luther King, Jr.

DISCUSSION QUESTIONS

1. Regarding the state of race relations in the United States today, are King's criticisms of white moderates and the white church still relevant? Why or why not?

2. Do you agree with King's belief in the moral interrelatedness of "all communities and states" in the United States and, by implication, in any country? Why or why not? Would this apply to the "global community" as well? Why or why not?

3. Is civil disobedience morally justified? Why or why not?

4. How would you compare the moral positions of King and Mill on civil rights?

59. Karl Marx (1818–1883) and Frederick Engels (1820–1895)
From the *Manifesto of the Communist Party*

Karl Marx and Frederick Engels were German revolutionary writers and political activists who were very influential in their own time in the workers' movement throughout Europe and North America. Their extensive social, economic, and political writings have been, and still are, used, critiqued, and defended not only by many philosophers and other academicians in a variety of fields but also by politicians and social movements around the world. Thus they are generally treated now as social philosophers, even though they tried to distance themselves from academic philosophy as it was usually practiced in nineteenth-century Europe and move toward what is often referred to today as critical social science.

Marx and Engels completed many works separately as well as some significant collaborative efforts, and Marx, especially, produced many volumes of economic analyses that weren't published until after his death. Together they are considered the founders of what was later called Marxism, the doctrine that became the dominant version of communist theory in the twentieth century. Ever since the latter half of the nineteenth century, Marxist principles have been interpreted and applied in widely divergent ways, often with significant historical consequences—for example, as seen in the rise and fall of the Soviet Union and the twentieth-century transformation of China.

The reading includes the majority of their most famous jointly written essay, which is widely viewed as a classic work of radical socialist/communist thought (in their time these two terms were often used interchangeably). The *Manifesto* came out in 1848, the same year a number of revolutionary uprisings by the European working classes occurred. Marx and Engels were invited to write a "platform" of theoretical and practical principles for the Communist League—at the time a clandestine German workers' organization—and the *Manifesto* was the product. It was almost immediately translated from German into many other languages and distributed widely to workers in Western capitalist societies. The essay provides in the first place a statement of the authors' general theory of human historical development, eventually called historical materialism, emphasizing the causal role of class conflict in social change. Secondly, it offers a critical analysis of the conditions of workers under capitalism at that time and of how European history had reached that point. Finally, it points to the possibilities of working people bringing about a radically better society for themselves after capitalism has been overcome and how this could be achieved.

QUESTIONS FOR CRITICAL READING

1. What do Marx and Engels mean by claiming that the "history of all hitherto existing society is the history of class struggle"? What is a "class" in this context?
2. According to Marx and Engels, what are the distinctive features of "bourgeois" (capitalist) society, in comparison to past forms of class society?
3. How do the authors explain the causes and effects of the situation of the proletariat (the "modern working class") under capitalism?
4. In this essay, what are the revolutionary goals of "the Communists," and how do the authors defend those goals against the usual criticisms? Why do they advocate an internationalist rather than a nationalist orientation for their movement?
5. How will social progress proceed after a successful revolutionary takeover of the government, and what specific policies do Marx and Engels envision generally being enacted?

TERMS TO NOTE

patrician: In this context, a member of the ancient Roman nobility; to be contrasted with a plebeian, one of the common people in ancient Rome (that is, not of noble birth).

sectarian: Having to do with the doctrines or aims of a political party, school of thought, or religious group that attempts to distinguish itself from other groups.

jurisprudence: The formal study of law.

———

A specter is haunting Europe—the specter of Communism. All the powers of old Europe have entered into a holy alliance to exorcise this specter: Pope and Czar, Metternich and Guizot, French Radicals and German police-spies.

Where is the party in opposition that has not been decried as communistic by its opponents in power? Where the Opposition that has not hurled back the branding reproach of Communism, against the more advanced opposition parties, as well as against its reactionary adversaries?

Two things result from this fact:

I. Communism is already acknowledged by all European powers to be itself a power.

II. It is high time that Communists should openly, in the face of the whole world, publish their views, their aims, their tendencies, and meet this nursery tale of the specter of Communism with a manifesto of the party itself.

To this end, Communists of various nationalities have assembled in London, and sketched the following manifesto, to be published in the English, French, German, Italian, Flemish, and Danish languages. . . .

I

Bourgeois and Proletarians

The history of all hitherto existing society is the history of class struggles.

Freeman and slave, patrician and plebeian, lord and serf, guild-master and journeyman, in a word, oppressor and oppressed, stood in constant opposition to one another, carried on an uninterrupted, now hidden, now open fight, a fight that each time ended, either in a revolutionary reconstitution of society at large, or in the common ruin of the contending classes.

In the earlier epochs of history, we find almost everywhere a complicated arrangement of society into various orders, a manifold gradation of social rank. In ancient Rome we have patricians, knights, plebeians, slaves; in the Middle Ages, feudal lords, vassals, guild-masters, journeymen, apprentices, serfs; in almost all of these classes, again, subordinate gradations.

The modern bourgeois society that has sprouted from the ruins of feudal society, has not done away with class antagonisms. It has but established new classes, new conditions of oppression, new forms of struggle in place of the old ones.

Our epoch, the epoch of the bourgeoisie, possesses, however, this distinctive feature: It has simplified the class antagonisms. Society as a whole is more and more splitting up into two great hostile camps, into two great classes directly facing each other—bourgeoisie and proletariat.

From the serfs of the Middle Ages sprang the chartered burghers of the earliest towns. From these burgesses the first elements of the bourgeoisie were developed.

The discovery of America, the rounding of the Cape, opened up fresh ground for the rising bourgeoisie. The East Indian and Chinese markets, the colonization of America, trade with the colonies, the increase in the means of exchange and in commodities generally, gave to commerce, to navigation, to industry, an impulse never before known, and thereby, to the revolutionary element in the tottering feudal society, a rapid development.

The feudal system of industry, in which industrial production was monopolized by closed guilds, now no longer sufficed for the growing wants of the new markets. The manufacturing system took its place. The guild-masters were pushed aside by the manufacturing middle class; division of labor between the different corporate guilds vanished in the face of division of labor in each single workshop.

Meantime the markets kept ever growing, the demand ever rising. Even manufacture no longer sufficed. Thereupon, steam and machinery revolutionized industrial production. The place of manufacture was taken by the giant, modern industry, the place of the industrial middle class, by industrial millionaires—the leaders of whole industrial armies, the modern bourgeois.

Modern industry has established the world market, for which the discovery of America paved the way. This market has given an immense development to commerce, to navigation, to communication by land. This development has, in its turn, reacted on the extension of industry; and in proportion as industry, commerce, navigation, railways extended, in the same proportion the bourgeoisie developed, increased its capital, and pushed into the background every class handed down from the Middle Ages.

We see, therefore, how the modern bourgeoisie is itself the product of a long course of development, of a series of revolutions in the modes of production and of exchange.

Each step in the development of the bourgeoisie was accompanied by a corresponding political advance of that class. An oppressed class under the sway of the feudal nobility, it became an armed and self-governing association in the medieval commune; here independent urban republic (as in Italy and Germany), there taxable "third estate" of the monarchy (as in France); afterwards, in the period of manufacture proper, serving either the semi-feudal or the absolute monarchy as a counterpoise against the nobility, and, in fact, cornerstone of the great monarchies in general—the bourgeoisie has at last, since the establishment of modern industry and of the world market, conquered for itself, in the modern representative state, exclusive political sway. The executive of the modern state is but a committee for managing the common affairs of the whole bourgeoisie.

The bourgeoisie has played a most revolutionary role in history.

The bourgeoisie, wherever it has got the upper hand, has put an end to all feudal, patriarchal, idyllic relations. It has pitilessly torn asunder the motley feudal ties that bound man to his "natural superiors," and has left no other bond between man and man than naked self-interest, than callous "cash payment." It has drowned the most heavenly ecstasies of religious fervor, of chivalrous enthusiasm, of philistine sentimentalism, in the icy water of egotistical calculation. It has resolved personal worth into exchange value, and in place of the numberless indefeasible chartered freedoms, has set up that single, unconscionable freedom—Free Trade. In one word, for exploitation, veiled by religious and political illusions, it has substituted naked, shameless, direct, brutal exploitation.

The bourgeoisie has stripped of its halo every occupation hitherto honored and looked up to with reverent awe. It has converted the physician, the lawyer, the priest, the poet, the man of science, into its paid wage-laborers.

The bourgeoisie has torn away from the family its sentimental veil, and has reduced the family relation to a mere money relation.

The bourgeoisie has disclosed how it came to pass that the brutal display of vigor in the Middle Ages, which reactionaries so much admire, found its fitting complement in the most slothful indolence. It has been the first to show what man's activity can bring about. It has accomplished wonders far surpassing Egyptian pyramids, Roman aqueducts, and Gothic cathedrals; it has conducted expeditions that put in the shade all former migrations of nations and crusades.

The bourgeoisie cannot exist without constantly revolutionizing the instruments of production, and thereby the relations of production, and with them the whole relations of society. Conservation of the old modes of production in unaltered form, was, on the contrary, the first condition of existence for all earlier industrial classes. Constant revolutionizing of production, uninterrupted disturbance of all social conditions, everlasting uncertainty and agitation distinguish the bourgeois epoch from all earlier ones. All fixed, fast-frozen relations, with their train of ancient and venerable prejudices and opinions, are swept away, all new-formed ones become antiquated before they can ossify. All that is solid melts into air, all that is holy is profaned, and man is at last compelled to face with sober senses his real conditions of life and his relations with his kind.

The need of a constantly expanding market for its products chases the bourgeoisie over the whole surface of the globe. It must nestle everywhere, settle everywhere, establish connections everywhere.

The bourgeoisie has through its exploitation of the world market given a cosmopolitan character to production and consumption in every country. To the great chagrin of reactionaries, it has drawn from under the feet of industry the national ground on which it stood. All old-established national industries have been destroyed or are daily being destroyed. They are dislodged by new industries, whose introduction becomes a life and death question for all civilized nations, by industries that no longer work up indigenous raw material, but raw material drawn from the remotest zones; industries whose products are consumed, not only at home, but in every quarter of the globe. In place of the old wants, satisfied by the production of the country, we find new wants, requiring for their satisfaction the products of distant lands and climes. In place of the old local and national seclusion and self-sufficiency, we have intercourse in every direction, universal inter-dependence of nations. And as in material, so also in intellectual production. The intellectual creations of individual nations become common property. National one-sidedness and narrow-mindedness become more and more impossible, and from the numerous national and local literatures there arises a world literature.

The bourgeoisie, by the rapid improvement of all instruments of production, by the immensely facilitated means of communication, draws all nations, even the most barbarian, into civilization. The cheap prices of its commodities are the heavy artillery with which it batters down all Chinese walls, with which it forces the barbarians' intensely obstinate hatred of foreigners to capitulate. It compels all nations, on pain of extinction, to adopt the bourgeois mode of production; it compels them to introduce what it calls civilization into their midst, i.e., to become bourgeois themselves. In a word, it creates a world after its own image.

The bourgeoisie has subjected the country to the rule of the towns. It has created enormous cities, has greatly increased the urban population as compared with the rural, and has thus rescued a considerable part of the population from the idiocy of rural life. Just as it has made the country dependent on the towns, so it has made barbarian and semi-barbarian countries dependent on the civilized ones, nations of peasants on nations of bourgeois, the East on the West.

More and more the bourgeoisie keeps doing away with the scattered state of the population, of the means of production, and of property. It has agglomerated population, centralized means of production, and has concentrated property in a few hands. The necessary consequence of this was political centralization. Independent, or but loosely connected provinces, with separate interests, laws, governments, and systems of taxation, became lumped together into one nation, with one government, one code of laws, one national class interest, one frontier, and one customs tariff.

The bourgeoisie, during its rule of scarce one hundred years, has created more massive and more colossal productive forces than have all preceding generations together. Subjection of nature's forces to man, machinery, application of chemistry to industry and agriculture, steam-navigation, railways, electric telegraphs, clearing of whole continents for cultivation, canalisation of rivers, whole populations conjured out of the ground—what earlier century had even a presentiment that such productive forces slumbered in the lap of social labour?

We see then that the means of production and of exchange, which served as the foundation for the growth of the bourgeoisie, were generated in feudal society. At a certain stage in the development of these means of production and of exchange, the conditions under which feudal society produced and exchanged, the feudal organisation of agriculture and manufacturing industry, in a word, the feudal relations of property became no longer compatible with the already developed productive forces; they became so many fetters. They had to be burst asunder; they were burst asunder.

Into their place stepped free competition, accompanied by a social and political constitution adapted to it, and by the economic and political sway of the bourgeois class.

A similar movement is going on before our own eyes. Modern bourgeois society with its relations of production, of exchange and of property, a society that has conjured up such gigantic means of production and of exchange, is like the sorcerer who is no longer able to control the powers of the nether world whom he has called up by his spells. For many a decade past the history of industry and commerce is but the history of the revolt of modern productive forces against modern conditions of production, against the property relations that are the conditions for the existence of the bourgeoisie and of its rule. It is enough to mention the commercial crises that by their periodical return put the existence of the entire bourgeois society on trial, each time more threateningly. In these crises a great part not only of the existing products, but also of the previously created productive forces, are periodically destroyed. In these crises there breaks out an epidemic that, in all earlier epochs, would have seemed an absurdity—the epidemic of over-production. Society suddenly finds itself put back into a state of momentary barbarism; it appears as if a famine, a universal war of devastation had cut off the supply of every means of subsistence; industry and commerce

seem to be destroyed. And why? Because there is too much civilization, too much means of subsistence, too much industry, too much commerce. The productive forces at the disposal of society no longer tend to further the development of the conditions of bourgeois property; on the contrary, they have become too powerful for these conditions, by which they are fettered, and no sooner do they overcome these fetters than they bring disorder into the whole of bourgeois society, endanger the existence of bourgeois property. The conditions of bourgeois society are too narrow to comprise the wealth created by them. And how does the bourgeoisie get over these crises? On the one hand, by enforced destruction of a mass of productive forces; on the other, by the conquest of new markets, and by the more thorough exploitation of the old ones. That is to say, by paving the way for more extensive and more destructive crises, and by diminishing the means whereby crises are prevented.

The weapons with which the bourgeoisie felled feudalism to the ground are now turned against the bourgeoisie itself.

But not only has the bourgeoisie forged the weapons that bring death to itself; it has also called into existence the men who are to wield those weapons—the modern working class—the proletarians.

In proportion as the bourgeoisie, i.e., capital, is developed, in the same proportion is the proletariat, the modern working class, developed—a class of laborers, who live only so long as they find work, and who find work only so long as their labor increases capital. These laborers, who must sell themselves piecemeal, are a commodity, like every other article of commerce, and are consequently exposed to all the vicissitudes of competition, to all the fluctuations of the market.

Owing to the extensive use of machinery and to division of labor, the work of the proletarians has lost all individual character, and, consequently, all charm for the workman. He becomes an appendage of the machine, and it is only the most simple, most monotonous, and most easily acquired knack, that is required of him. Hence, the cost of production of a workman is restricted, almost entirely, to the means of subsistence that he requires for his maintenance, and for the propagation of his race. But the price of a commodity, and therefore also of labor, is equal to its cost of production. In proportion, therefore, as the repulsiveness of the work increases, the wage decreases. Nay more, in proportion as the use of machinery and division of labor increases, in the same proportion the burden of toil also increases, whether by prolongation of the working hours, by increase of the work exacted in a given time, or by increased speed of the machinery, etc.

Modern industry has converted the little workshop of the patriarchal master into the great factory of the industrial capitalist. Masses of laborers, crowded into the factory, are organized like soldiers. As privates of the industrial army they are placed under the command of a perfect hierarchy of officers and sergeants. Not only are they slaves of the bourgeois class, and of the bourgeois state; they are daily and hourly enslaved by the machine, by the over-looker, and, above all, by the individual bourgeois manufacturer himself. The more openly this despotism proclaims gain to be its end and aim, the more petty, the more hateful and the more embittering it is.

The less the skill and exertion of strength implied in manual labor, in other words, the more modern industry develops, the more is the labor of men superseded by that of women. Differences of age and sex have no longer any distinctive social validity for the working class. All are instruments of labor, more or less expensive to use, according to their age and sex.

No sooner has the laborer received his wages in cash, for the moment escaping exploitation by the manufacturer, than he is set upon by the other portions of the bourgeoisie, the landlord, the shopkeeper, the pawnbroker, etc.

The lower strata of the middle class—the small tradespeople, shopkeepers, and retired tradesmen generally, the handicraftsmen and peasants—all these sink gradually into the proletariat, partly because their diminutive capital does not suffice for the scale on which modern industry is carried on, and is swamped in the competition with the large capitalists, partly because their specialized skill is rendered worthless by new methods of production. Thus the proletariat is recruited from all classes of the population.

The proletariat goes through various stages of development. With its birth begins its struggle with the bourgeoisie. At first the contest is carried on by individual laborers, then by the work people of a factory, then by the operatives of one trade, in one locality,

against the individual bourgeois who directly exploits them. They direct their attacks not against the bourgeois conditions of production, but against the instruments of production themselves; they destroy imported wares that compete with their labor, they smash machinery to pieces, they set factories ablaze, they seek to restore by force the vanished status of the workman of the Middle Ages.

At this stage the laborers still form an incoherent mass scattered over the whole country, and broken up by their mutual competition. If anywhere they unite to form more compact bodies, this is not yet the consequence of their own active union, but of the union of the bourgeoisie, which class, in order to attain its own political ends, is compelled to set the whole proletariat in motion, and is moreover still able to do so for a time. At this stage, therefore, the proletarians do not fight their enemies, but the enemies of their enemies, the remnants of absolute monarchy, the landowners, the nonindustrial bourgeois, the petty bourgeoisie. Thus the whole historical movement is concentrated in the hands of the bourgeoisie; every victory so obtained is a victory for the bourgeoisie.

But with the development of industry the proletariat not only increases in number; it becomes concentrated in greater masses, its strength grows, and it feels that strength more. The various interests and conditions of life within the ranks of the proletariat are more and more equalized, in proportion as machinery obliterates all distinctions of labor and nearly everywhere reduces wages to the same low level. The growing competition among the bourgeois, and the resulting commercial crises, make the wages of the workers ever more fluctuating. The unceasing improvement of machinery, ever more rapidly developing, makes their livelihood more and more precarious; the collisions between individual workmen and individual bourgeois take more and more the character of collisions between two classes. Thereupon the workers begin to form combinations (trade unions) against the bourgeoisie; they club together in order to keep up the rate of wages; they found permanent associations in order to make provision beforehand for these occasional revolts. Here and there the contest breaks out into riots.

Now and then the workers are victorious, but only for a time. The real fruit of their battles lies, not in the immediate result, but in the ever expanding union of the workers. This union is furthered by the improved means of communication which are created by modern industry, and which place the workers of different localities in contact with one another. It was just this contact that was needed to centralize the numerous local struggles, all of the same character, into one national struggle between classes. But every class struggle is a political struggle. And that union, to attain which the burghers of the Middle Ages, with their miserable highways, required centuries, the modern proletarians, thanks to railways, achieve in a few years.

This organization of the proletarians into a class, and consequently into a political party, is continually being upset again by the competition between the workers themselves. But it ever rises up again, stronger, firmer, mightier. It compels legislative recognition of particular interests of the workers, by taking advantage of the divisions among the bourgeoisie itself. Thus the ten-hour bill in England was carried.

Altogether, collisions between the classes of the old society further the course of development of the proletariat in many ways. The bourgeoisie finds itself involved in a constant battle. At first with the aristocracy; later on, with those portions of the bourgeoisie itself whose interests have become antagonistic to the progress of industry; at all times with the bourgeoisie of foreign countries. In all these battles it sees itself compelled to appeal to the proletariat, to ask for its help, and thus, to drag it into the political arena. The bourgeoisie itself, therefore, supplies the proletariat with its own elements of political and general education, in other words, it furnishes the proletariat with weapons for fighting the bourgeoisie.

Further, as we have already seen, entire sections of the ruling classes are, by the advance of industry, precipitated into the proletariat, or are at least threatened in their conditions of existence. These also supply the proletariat with fresh elements of enlightenment and progress.

Finally, in times when the class struggle nears the decisive hour, the process of dissolution going on within the ruling class, in fact within the whole range of old society, assumes such a violent, glaring character, that a small section of the ruling class cuts itself adrift, and joins the revolutionary class, the class that holds the future in its hands. Just as, therefore, at an earlier period, a section of the nobility went over to the bourgeoisie, so now a portion of the bourgeoisie goes over to the proletariat, and in particular, a portion of the bourgeois ideologists, who have raised themselves to the level of comprehending theoretically the historical movement as a whole.

Of all the classes that stand face to face with the bourgeoisie today, the proletariat alone is a really revolutionary class. The other classes decay and finally disappear in the face of modern industry; the proletariat is its special and essential product.

The lower middle class, the small manufacturer, the shopkeeper, the artisan, the peasant, all these fight against the bourgeoisie, to save from extinction their existence as fractions of the middle class. They are therefore not revolutionary, but conservative. Nay more, they are reactionary, for they try to roll back the wheel of history. If by chance they are revolutionary, they are so only in view of their impending transfer into the proletariat; they thus defend not their present, but their future interests; they desert their own standpoint to adopt that of the proletariat.

The "dangerous class," the social scum (*Lumpenproletariat*), that passively rotting mass thrown off by the lowest layers of old society, may, here and there, be swept into the movement by a proletarian revolution; its conditions of life, however, prepare it far more for the part of a bribed tool of reactionary intrigue.

The social conditions of the old society no longer exist for the proletariat. The proletarian is without property; his relation to his wife and children has no longer anything in common with bourgeois family relations; modern industrial labor, modern subjection to capital, the same in England as in France, in America as in Germany, has stripped him of every trace of national character. Law, morality, religion, are to him so many bourgeois prejudices, behind which lurk in ambush just as many bourgeois interests.

All the preceding classes that got the upper hand, sought to fortify their already acquired status by subjecting society at large to their conditions of appropriation. The proletarians cannot become masters of the productive forces of society, except by abolishing their own previous mode of appropriation, and thereby also every other previous mode of appropriation. They have nothing of their own to secure and to fortify; their mission is to destroy all previous securities for, and insurances of, individual property.

All previous historical movements were movements of minorities, or in the interest of minorities. The proletarian movement is the self-conscious, independent movement of the immense majority, in the interest of the immense majority. The proletariat, the lowest stratum of our present society, cannot stir, cannot raise itself up, without the whole superincumbent strata of official society being sprung into the air.

Though not in substance, yet in form, the struggle of the proletariat with the bourgeoisie is at first a national struggle. The proletariat of each country must, of course, first of all settle matters with its own bourgeoisie.

In depicting the most general phases of the development of the proletariat, we traced the more or less veiled civil war, raging within existing society, up to the point where that war breaks out into open revolution, and where the violent overthrow of the bourgeoisie lays the foundation for the sway of the proletariat.

Hitherto, every form of society has been based, as we have already seen, on the antagonism of oppressing and oppressed classes. But in order to oppress a class, certain conditions must be assured to it under which it can, at least, continue its slavish existence. The serf, in the period of serfdom, raised himself to membership in the commune, just as the petty bourgeois, under the yoke of feudal absolutism, managed to develop into a bourgeois. The modern laborer, on the contrary, instead of rising with the progress of industry, sinks deeper and deeper below the conditions of existence of his own class. He becomes a pauper, and pauperism develops more rapidly than population and wealth. And here it becomes evident, that the bourgeoisie is unfit any longer to be the ruling class in society, and to impose its conditions of existence upon society as an overriding law. It is unfit to rule because it is incompetent to assure an existence to its slave within his slavery, because it cannot help letting him sink into such a state, that it has to feed him, instead of being fed by him. Society can no longer live under this bourgeoisie, in other words, its existence is no longer compatible with society.

The essential condition for the existence and sway of the bourgeois class, is the formation and augmentation of capital; the condition for capital is wage-labor. Wage-labor rests exclusively on competition between the laborers. The advance of industry, whose involuntary promoter is the bourgeoisie, replaces the isolation of the laborers, due to competition, by their revolutionary combination, due to association. The development of modern industry, therefore, cuts from under its feet the very foundation on which the bourgeoisie produces and appropriates products. What the bourgeoisie therefore produces, above all, are its own grave-diggers. Its fall and the victory of the proletariat are equally inevitable.

II

Proletarians and Communists

In what relation do the Communists stand to the proletarians as a whole?

The Communists do not form a separate party opposed to other working-class parties.

They have no interests separate and apart from those of the proletariat as a whole.

They do not set up any sectarian principles of their own, by which to shape and mould the proletarian movement.

The Communists are distinguished from the other working-class parties by this only: 1. In the national struggles of the proletarians of the different countries, they point out and bring to the front the common interests of the entire proletariat, independently of all nationality. 2. In the various stages of development which the struggle of the working class against the bourgeoisie has to pass through, they always and everywhere represent the interests of the movement as a whole.

The Communists, therefore, are on the one hand, practically, the most advanced and resolute section of the working-class parties of every country, that section which pushes forward all others; on the other hand, theoretically, they have over the great mass of the proletariat the advantage of clearly understanding the line of march, the conditions, and the ultimate general results of the proletarian movement.

The immediate aim of the Communists is the same as that of all the other proletarian parties: Formation of the proletariat into a class, overthrow of bourgeois supremacy, conquest of political power by the proletariat.

The theoretical conclusions of the Communists are in no way based on ideas or principles that have been invented, or discovered, by this or that would-be universal reformer.

They merely express, in general terms, actual relations springing from an existing class struggle, from a historical movement going on under our very eyes. The abolition of existing property relations is not at all a distinctive feature of Communism.

All property relations in the past have continually been subject to historical change consequent upon the change in historical conditions.

The French Revolution, for example, abolished feudal property in favor of bourgeois property.

The distinguishing feature of Communism is not the abolition of property generally, but the abolition of bourgeois property. But modern bourgeois private property is the final and most complete expression of the system of producing and appropriating products that is based on class antagonisms, on the exploitation of the many by the few.

In this sense, the theory of the Communists may be summed up in the single sentence: Abolition of private property.

We Communists have been reproached with the desire of abolishing the right of personally acquiring property as the fruit of a man's own labor, which property is alleged to be the groundwork of all personal freedom, activity, and independence.

Hard-won, self-acquired, self-earned property! Do you mean the property of the petty artisan and of the small peasant, a form of property that preceded the bourgeois form? There is no need to abolish that; the development of industry has to a great extent already destroyed it, and is still destroying it daily.

Or do you mean modern bourgeois private property?

But does wage-labor create any property for the laborer? Not a bit. It creates capital, i.e., that kind of property which exploits wage-labor, and which cannot increase except upon condition of begetting a new supply of wage-labor for fresh exploitation. Property, in its present form, is based on the antagonism of capital and wage-labor. Let us examine both sides of this antagonism.

To be a capitalist, is to have not only a purely personal, but a social *status* in production. Capital is a collective product, and only by the united action of many members, nay, in the last resort, only by the united action of all members of society, can it be set in motion.

Capital is therefore not a personal, it is a social, power.

When, therefore, capital is converted into common property, into the property of all members of society, personal property is not thereby transformed into social property. It is only the social character of the property that is changed. It loses its class character.

Let us now take wage-labor.

The average price of wage-labor, is the minimum wage, i.e., that quantum of the means of subsistence which is absolutely requisite to keep the laborer in bare existence as a laborer. What, therefore, the wage-laborer appropriates by means of his labor, merely suffices to prolong and reproduce a bare existence. We by no means intend to abolish this personal appropriation of the products of labor, an appropriation that is made for the maintenance and reproduction of human life, and that leaves no surplus wherewith to command the labor of others. All that we want to do away with is the miserable character of this appropriation, under which the laborer lives merely to increase capital, and is allowed to live only insofar as the interest of the ruling class requires it.

In bourgeois society, living labor is but a means to increase accumulated labor. In Communist society, accumulated labor is but a means to widen, to enrich, to promote the existence of the laborer.

In bourgeois society, therefore, the past dominates the present; in Communist society, the present dominates the past. In bourgeois society capital is independent and has individuality, while the living person is dependent and has no individuality.

And the abolition of this state of things is called by the bourgeois, abolition of individuality and freedom! And rightly so. The abolition of bourgeois individuality, bourgeois independence, and bourgeois freedom is undoubtedly aimed at.

By freedom is meant, under the present bourgeois conditions of production, free trade, free selling and buying.

But if selling and buying disappears, free selling and buying disappears also. This talk about free selling and buying, and all the other "brave words" of our bourgeoisie about freedom in general, have a meaning, if any, only in contrast with restricted selling and buying, with the fettered traders of the Middle Ages, but have no meaning when opposed to the Communist abolition of buying and selling, of the bourgeois conditions of production, and of the bourgeoisie itself.

You are horrified at our intending to do away with private property. But in your existing society, private property is already done away with for nine-tenths of the population; its existence for the few is solely due to its non-existence in the hands of those nine-tenths. You reproach us, therefore, with intending to do away with a form of property, the necessary condition for whose existence is the nonexistence of any property for the immense majority of society.

In a word, you reproach us with intending to do away with your property. Precisely so; that is just what we intend.

From the moment when labor can no longer be converted into capital, money, or rent, into a social power capable of being monopolized, i.e., from the moment when individual property can no longer be transformed into bourgeois property, into capital, from that moment, you say, individuality vanishes.

You must, therefore, confess that by "individual" you mean no other person than the bourgeois, than the middle-class owner of property. This person must, indeed, be swept out of the way, and made impossible.

Communism deprives no man of the power to appropriate the products of society; all that it does is to deprive him of the power to subjugate the labor of others by means of such appropriation.

It has been objected, that upon the abolition of private property all work will cease, and universal laziness will overtake us.

According to this, bourgeois society ought long ago to have gone to the dogs through sheer idleness; for those of its members who work, acquire nothing, and those who acquire anything, do not work. The whole of this objection is but another expression of the tautology: There can no longer be any wage-labor when there is no longer any capital.

All objections urged against the Communist mode of producing and appropriating material products, have, in the same way, been urged against the Communist modes of producing and appropriating intellectual products. Just as, to the bourgeois, the

disappearance of class property is the disappearance of production itself, so the disappearance of class culture is to him identical with the disappearance of all culture.

That culture, the loss of which he laments, is, for the enormous majority, a mere training to act as a machine.

But don't wrangle with us so long as you apply, to our intended abolition of bourgeois property, the standard of your bourgeois notions of freedom, culture, law, etc. Your very ideas are but the outgrowth of the conditions of your bourgeois production and bourgeois property, just as your jurisprudence is but the will of your class made into a law for all, a will whose essential character and direction are determined by the economic conditions of existence of your class.

The selfish misconception that induces you to transform into eternal laws of nature and of reason, the social forms springing from your present mode of production and form of property—historical relations that rise and disappear in the progress of production—this misconception you share with every ruling class that has preceded you. What you see clearly in the case of ancient property, what you admit in the case of feudal property, you are of course forbidden to admit in the case of your own bourgeois form of property.

Abolition of the family! Even the most radical flare up at this infamous proposal of the Communists.

On what foundation is the present family, the bourgeois family, based? On capital, on private gain. In its completely developed form this family exists only among the bourgeoisie. But this state of things finds its complement in the practical absence of the family among the proletarians, and in public prostitution.

The bourgeois family will vanish as a matter of course when its complement vanishes, and both will vanish with the vanishing of capital.

Do you charge us with wanting to stop the exploitation of children by their parents? To this crime we plead guilty.

But, you will say, we destroy the most hallowed of relations, when we replace home education by social.

And your education! Is not that also social, and determined by the social conditions under which you educate, by the intervention of society, direct or indirect, by means of schools, etc.? The Communists have not invented the intervention of society in education; they do but seek to alter the character of that intervention, and to rescue education from the influence of the ruling class.

The bourgeois claptrap about the family and education, about the hallowed co-relation of parent and child, becomes all the more disgusting, the more, by the action of modern industry, all family ties among the proletarians are torn asunder, and their children transformed into simple articles of commerce and instruments of labor.

But you Communists would introduce community of women, screams the whole bourgeoisie in chorus.

The bourgeois sees in his wife a mere instrument of production. He hears that the instruments of production are to be exploited in common, and, naturally, can come to no other conclusion than that the lot of being common to all will likewise fall to the women.

He has not even a suspicion that the real point aimed at is to do away with the status of women as mere instruments of production.

For the rest, nothing is more ridiculous than the virtuous indignation of our bourgeois at the community of women which, they pretend, is to be openly and officially established by the Communists. The Communists have no need to introduce community of women; it has existed almost from time immemorial.

Our bourgeois, not content with having the wives and daughters of their proletarians at their disposal, not to speak of common prostitutes, take the greatest pleasure in seducing each other's wives.

Bourgeois marriage is in reality a system of wives in common and thus, at the most, what the Communists might possibly be reproached with is that they desire to introduce, in substitution for a hypocritically concealed, an openly legalized community of women. For the rest, it is self-evident, that the abolition of the present system of production must bring with it the abolition of the community of women springing from that system, i.e., of prostitution both public and private.

The Communists are further reproached with desiring to abolish countries and nationality.

The workingmen have no country. We cannot take from them what they have not got. Since the proletariat must first of all acquire political supremacy, must rise to be the leading class of the nation, must constitute itself *the* nation, it is, so far, itself national, though not in the bourgeois sense of the word.

National differences and antagonisms between peoples are vanishing gradually from day to day, owing to the development of the bourgeoisie, to freedom of commerce, to the world market, to uniformity in the mode of production and in the conditions of life corresponding thereto.

The supremacy of the proletariat will cause them to vanish still faster. United action, of the leading civilized countries at least, is one of the first conditions for the emancipation of the proletariat.

In proportion as the exploitation of one individual by another is put an end to, the exploitation of one nation by another will also be put an end to. In proportion as the antagonism between classes within the nation vanishes, the hostility of one nation to another will come to an end.

The charges against Communism made from a religious, a philosophical, and, generally, from an ideological standpoint, are not deserving of serious examination.

Does it require deep intuition to comprehend that man's ideas, views, and conceptions, in one word, man's consciousness, changes with every change in the conditions of his material existence, in his social relations and in his social life?

What else does the history of ideas prove, than that intellectual production changes its character in proportion as material production is changed? The ruling ideas of each age have ever been the ideas of its ruling class.

When people speak of ideas that revolutionize society, they do but express the fact that within the old society the elements of a new one have been created, and that the dissolution of the old ideas keeps even pace with the dissolution of the old conditions of existence.

When the ancient world was in its last throes, the ancient religions were overcome by Christianity. When Christian ideas succumbed in the 18th century to rationalist ideas, feudal society fought its death-battle with the then revolutionary bourgeoisie. The ideas of religious liberty and freedom of conscience, merely gave expression to the sway of free competition within the domain of knowledge.

"Undoubtedly," it will be said, "religion, moral, philosophical, and juridical ideas have been modified in the course of historical development. But religion, morality, philosophy, political science, and law, constantly survived this change.

"There are, besides, eternal truths, such as Freedom, Justice, etc., that are common to all states of society. But Communism abolishes eternal truths, it abolishes all religion, and all morality, instead of constituting them on a new basis; it therefore acts in contradiction to all past historical experience."

What does this accusation reduce itself to? The history of all past society has consisted in the development of class antagonisms, antagonisms that assumed different forms at different epochs.

But whatever form they may have taken, one fact is common to all past ages, viz., the exploitation of one part of society by the other. No wonder, then, that the social consciousness of past ages, despite all the multiplicity and variety it displays, moves within certain common forms, or general ideas, which cannot completely vanish except with the total disappearance of class antagonisms.

The Communist revolution is the most radical rupture with traditional property relations; no wonder that its development involves the most radical rupture with traditional ideas.

But let us have done with the bourgeois objections to Communism.

We have seen above, that the first step in the revolution by the working class, is to raise the proletariat to the position of ruling class, to establish democracy.

The proletariat will use its political supremacy to wrest, by degrees, all capital from the bourgeoisie, to centralize all instruments of production in the hands of the state, i.e., of the proletariat organized as the ruling class; and to increase the total of productive forces as rapidly as possible.

Of course, in the beginning, this cannot be effected except by means of despotic inroads on the rights of property, and on the conditions of bourgeois production; by means of measures, therefore, which appear economically insufficient and untenable, but which, in the course of the movement, outstrip themselves, necessitate further inroads upon the old social order, and are unavoidable as a means of entirely revolutionizing the mode of production.

These measures will of course be different in different countries.

Nevertheless in the most advanced countries, the following will be pretty generally applicable.

1. Abolition of property in land and application of all rents of land to public purposes.

2. A heavy progressive or graduated income tax.

3. Abolition of all right of inheritance.

4. Confiscation of the property of all emigrants and rebels.

5. Centralization of credit in the hands of the state, by means of a national bank with state capital and an exclusive monopoly.

6. Centralization of the means of communication and transport in the hands of the state.

7. Extension of factories and instruments of production owned by the state; the bringing into cultivation of waste lands, and the improvement of the soil generally in accordance with a common plan.

8. Equal obligation of all to work. Establishment of industrial armies, especially for agriculture.

9. Combination of agriculture with manufacturing industries; gradual abolition of the distinction between town and country, by a more equable distribution of the population over the country.

10. Free education for all children in public schools. Abolition of child factory labor in its present form. Combination of education with industrial production, etc.

When, in the course of development, class distinctions have disappeared, and all production has been concentrated in the hands of a vast association of the whole nation, the public power will lose its political character. Political power, properly so called, is merely the organized power of one class for oppressing another. If the proletariat during its contest with the bourgeoisie is compelled, by the force of circumstances, to organize itself as a class; if, by means of a revolution, it makes itself the ruling class, and, as such sweeps away by force the old conditions of production, then it will, along with these conditions, have swept away the conditions for the existence of class antagonisms, and of classes generally, and will thereby have abolished its own supremacy as a class.

In place of the old bourgeois society, with its classes and class antagonisms, we shall have an association, in which the free development of each is the condition for the free development of all.

DISCUSSION QUESTIONS

1. Do you agree with the view of Marx and Engels that recorded history in general is a history of "class struggle"? Why or why not?
2. Do you believe that a future classless society, with no centralized state, is possible or desirable for humans? Why or why not?
3. In the critique by Marx and Engels of capitalist society and their advocacy of a future communist society, what are the implications for gender relations?
4. Is this analysis of capitalism still relevant today, in terms of the dynamic relationship between the "forces" and "relations" of production, crises of "over-production," and the distribution of wealth and power nationally and internationally? Why or why not?

60. Nancy Hartsock (contemporary)

From *Money, Sex, and Power: Toward a Feminist Historical Materialism*

Nancy Hartsock is an American political philosopher at Johns Hopkins University. Like some of the other authors included in this anthology, she has focused on the development of and the controversies surrounding the nature and direction of feminist theory in recent decades in Western intellectual life. Her book *Money, Sex, and Power*, which came out in 1983, has had a significant impact on subsequent feminist thought. In it she formulates what is now generally called standpoint theory. This is a theoretical approach to analyzing the types and extent of social awareness individuals are likely to possess by virtue of their location in a stratified social system—that is, in a community structured by relations of dominance and subordination between diverse groups. Roughly, the theory holds that membership in groups lower in the social hierarchy—that is, having less power and more vulnerability to harm—generally provides one with a "standpoint" from which to more accurately understand the real nature of group relations in that society, along with the increased dangers that it entails for oneself. Conversely, the standpoint of groups with customarily the most power and control in such a society typically leads to the most distorted and superficial understanding of what's going on in that society, especially regarding the experience of the other groups over which they are dominant.

In these excerpts from her book, Hartsock is applying this theoretical orientation to structurally determined differences in social knowledge and experience to the "power relations" that exist in contemporary capitalist patriarchal society. Although she argues that race relations can also be analyzed in this light, she focuses primarily on the domination and exploitation of women by men and secondarily on the domination and exploitation of the working classes by the capitalist class. Her method of proceeding is to reconstruct the traditional Marxist analysis of the latter antagonistic relationship (the historical materialist theory) so that it can more adequately illuminate the former antagonistic relationship, as well as ways of overcoming it.

QUESTIONS FOR CRITICAL READING

1. According to Hartsock, what are the benefits for feminist theory and practice of critically analyzing "theories of power"?
2. How does Hartsock critique the traditional Marxist account of power relations in the capitalist form of class society?
3. How does Hartsock characterize and critique the nature and role of power in gender relations?
4. What does Hartsock mean by, and how does she argue for, the conception of social reality as being "three-tiered" rather than "bi-leveled," as in Marxist class analysis?
5. How does Hartsock explain the concept of "standpoint," and why is it valuable for analyzing group relations in hierarchically structured society?

TERMS TO NOTE

liberatory: Having to do with liberation from oppression and injustice.

apocryphal: Being of doubtful authorship or authenticity.

agonal: In this context, having to do with a contest or competition.

phallocratic: Having to do with the belief in the superiority of the male sex.

dramatis personae: A Latin phrase meaning "cast of characters."

solipsism: Either the ontological view that only one's own self exists or the epistemological view that one's own self and its experiences are all that one can know.

In recent decades, many of us have learned a great deal about the extent to which our society is structured by relations of domination and submission, relations constructed most importantly out of differences of race, sex, and class. Yet we lack theoretical clarity about *how* these relations of domination are constructed, how they operate, and how social theories and practices have both justified and obscured them. Due to the Marxian account of the ways capitalist domination is constructed and maintained, our understanding of class domination is the most advanced. But Marxian theory as such has had little to say about gender or racial domination; discussions of "the national question" and "the woman question" have proved unable to account for white and male supremacy. And to the extent that domination occurs along lines of race and sex, or that race and sex affect class domination, Marxian theory must be recognized as inadequate.

My particular concern here is with (1) how relations of domination along gender lines are constructed and maintained and (2) whether social understandings of domination itself have been distorted by men's domination of women. How can we develop a theory that can provide a more complete understanding both of relations of domination and of the transformations necessary to create a more egalitarian society? This book is an argument that an essential part of such a theory and practice is the critique of power relations—of the ways the exercise of power of some over others is constructed, legitimated, and reproduced.

Feminists have been more willing to focus attention on women's oppression than on the question of how men's dominance is constructed and maintained, and so over the last fifteen or so years, the subject of power has not received sustained feminist attention. Perhaps this is also a result of the effort feminists devoted to avoiding the exercise of power.[1] Feminist avoidance of exercising power took a variety of forms in the early 1970s. Most typically, it resulted in the adoption of a kind of personal, structureless politics; a widespread opposition to leadership; an insistence on working collectively; and an emphasis on process, often to the exclusion of getting things done. Implicit in these strategies was the view that power was "the ability to compel obedience" or was "control and domination," the view that power was something possessed, a property possessed by an actor that enabled him to alter the will or actions of others in ways that produce results in conformity with his own will.[2] The political practice of much of the contemporary feminist movement has indicated the tacit acceptance of the view that the exercise of power *is* the exercise of domination.[3] The effort to oppose domination, especially of course the domination of women, has taken the form of efforts to develop forms of organization (very amorphous forms) in which differences in personal attributes or differences in position within the group would not lead to differences in power—that is, small, structureless groups where there were no differences of sex, sexual preference, class, and so on.[4] The understanding of power as power over others was of course tacit and untheorized, that is, not recognized or discussed. And I do not mean to suggest that the effort to avoid power over others was necessarily wrong. I *do* mean to suggest that it is important for feminists to address questions of power more directly. There is, after all, a certain dangerous irony in the fact that both feminists and antifeminists agree that the exercise of power is a masculine activity and preoccupation, inappropriate to women or feminists, and not a subject to which attention should be directed.

Our opposition to relations of domination makes it essential for feminists to examine the exercise of power more directly. Is the exercise of power best understood as the ability to compel obedience? To what extent should power be understood as energy or ability? How should feminists understand the actions of individuals who compel others to behave in certain ways as opposed to the more impersonal force of circumstance that also compels people to particular actions? And if we look more closely at the exercise of power over others, can it really be connected with masculinity? If so, is there a way of exercising power that could be characterized as feminine or female? Are any exercises of power to be legitimate in the community we want? These are all questions a movement for social change must face if it is to succeed in transforming a society structured by domination.

A critique of theories that explain how power relations are constructed and how power is exercised can be an important resource for understanding what the construction of a more humane community would require. I argue that these theories of power can be helpful in several ways. First, theories of power are implicitly theories of community. To examine these theories of power is to involve oneself in the questions of how communities have been constructed, how they have been legitimized, and how they might be structured in more liberatory ways. Second, and related, because we live in a community structured by the domination of one gender and class, theories of power can be expected to carry both gender and class dimensions and thus provide a context in which to explore the impact of gender and class on the construction of communities.[5] Third, and perhaps most important, efforts to explain how power operates inevitably involve larger questions as well, and different theories of power rest on differing assumptions about both the content of existence and the ways we come to know it.[6] That is, different theories of power rest on differing ontologies and epistemologies, and a feminist rethinking of power requires attention to its epistemological grounding.

For this reason, both the critique of theories of power and the construction of a more adequate theory require attention to a series of questions that may at first seem only loosely related to issues of domination. These include questions such as the appropriate methods for social research, alternatives in epistemology and ontology, the relation of epistemology or theories of knowledge to human activity, historical tendencies in social development, and the relation between individual and collective capacities and actions. My focus on this set of concerns imposes a complicated logic on

the book, one that requires the simultaneous pursuit of two important lines of argument. One line of argument addresses issues of community, class, and gender; the other concerns the epistemological grounding of these issues.

Power and Community: Issues of Class and Gender

The fundamental questions posed for theorists of power are these: What are the legitimate bases on which a community of actors can be organized and maintained? What are the characteristics and limits of legitimate action within a community? To what extent can relations of domination legitimately structure the human community? And to what extent is it possible to construct a human community that does not fundamentally rest on relations of domination? These questions, as we shall see, recur with surprising consistency among theorists who answer them in profoundly different ways. My own understanding of the relation of power and community leads me to argue that the form taken by the exercise of power in a community structures human interaction within that community, and so, in a community where the exercise of power takes the form of structured and systematic domination of some over others, the community itself is formed by domination. It follows that to change the practice of power is to change the structure and nature of the community.

The class and gender content of power initially becomes evident in different areas, the one in the area of economics, the other in the area of sexuality.[7] Yet, as will be seen, there are deep interconnections and definite structured relations between the two.

Class

Economic activities (especially the economic activities characteristic of men's lives) have formed the contemporary context in which the class content of theorizations of power has been explored. I argue that one can distinguish capitalist and working-class theorizations of power on the basis of the specific economic activities each takes as paradigmatic for understanding/explaining power relations. Explanations whose class content Marx would label "bourgeois" tend to privilege activities having to do with money—using it to buy things, investing it in order to increase it, banking it. "Proletarian" explanations take the activity of production as the paradigm for power relations. This is the perspective from which I approach the arguments of contemporary social scientists that power is best understood on the model provided by the function of money in the market; that power, like money, is a means of getting others to act in ways they would not otherwise act. These social scientists focus explicitly on the conflict of interests characteristic of power relationships and often take the *personae* of the buyer and seller in the market as their point of reference. Power relations, conceived on this market-oriented model, are described as similar to the relation of a buyer and seller confronting each other with differential resources.

It may not be apparent that there is a conception of community implicit here. The significance of the market model can be somewhat clarified if one reminds oneself that despite their opposing interests, the buyer and seller not only *are* associated with each other but also that the association has a certain value for each. They have created a certain sort of community. True, the fundamental gulf between buyer and seller (and, in the analogy, between parties to a power relation) persists; participants have conflicting interests and therefore can be expected to distrust each other. In addition, the community established in this way can be only partial, since it is on the one hand constituted by the common interests of participants and on the other limited by their conflict. They are engaged in a contest to determine which of them will be the dominant party to an exchange; they need in principle have only enough in common to actually engage in a competition or exchange.

The class content of Marx's theorization of power is profoundly opposed to that carried by market theories. Marx held that power is best understood on the model provided by the workers' activity in production rather than the capitalists' activity in exchange. But here one must distinguish his view of the power relations operative in the capitalist production process from those he held would operate in a communist production process, and therefore in communist society. Thus, I argue that the Marxian account of the production of surplus value by workers and its appropriation by capitalists should be read as an explanation of the mechanisms by which class domination is substituted for the more encompassing human community potentially present in workers' cooperation in production. The Marxian account of class domination, then, can enable us to recognize the real existence of a fragile and deeply unsatisfactory human community in capitalist societies. But rather than conclude that human beings are by nature isolated and interest-driven, this theory holds instead that societies need not be structured by class domination. In their place, Marxian theory holds out a vision of both power and community rooted in production. This is most strikingly described by Marx in an extraordinary passage from the *1844 Manuscripts*:

> Supposing that we had produced in a human manner; each of us would in his production have doubly affirmed himself and his fellow men. I would have: (1) objectified in my production my individuality and its peculiarity and thus both in my activity enjoyed an individual expression of my life and also in looking at the object have had the individual pleasure of realizing that my personality was objective, visible to the senses and thus a power raised beyond all doubt. (2) In your enjoyment of use of my product I would have had the direct enjoyment of realizing that I had both satisfied a human need by my work and also objectified the human essence and therefore fashioned for another human being the object that met his need. (3) I would have been for you the mediator between you and the species and thus been acknowledged and felt by you as a completion of your own essence and a necessary part of your self and have thus realized that I am confirmed in both your thought and in your love. (4) In my expression of my life I would have fashioned your expression of life, and thus in my own activity have realized my own essence, my human, my communal essence.[8]

A Marxian critique of theories of power modeled on the market, coupled with the liberatory vision carried by his account of the possibilities for community available in unalienated production, can contribute importantly to our understanding of power. Yet Marx's account of class domination, like market theorists' accounts of power relations, operates with gender-blind and therefore gender-biased categories. By ignoring the genderedness of power relations he presents an incomplete account of relations of domination and of the possibilities for a more humane community.

Gender

Perhaps because issues of power are at the same time issues about the nature of legitimate community, power seems irreducibly to involve questions of *eros* or sexuality. Both the exchange of things and the erotic fusion of sexuality bring human beings together. Both represent important experiences of the ways one person can come into contact with another. The form of the interaction may vary: It may be nurturant, instrumental or rational; it may take the form of domination, force, persuasion, bargaining, or expression of love. In every case, however, what is at stake is the very existence of a relation with another, the existence of community.

In the literature on power, social scientists have frequently alluded to the links between virility and domination. For example, one scholar introduced a book on concepts of power, influence, and authority with the statement that the first is linked with notions of potency, virility, and masculinity and "appears much sexier than the other two."[9] Or consider philosopher Bertrand de Jouvenel's note that "a man feels himself more of a man when imposing himself and making others the instrument of his will."[10] And what are we to make of Robert Penn Warren's statement that "masculinity is closely tied to every form of power in our society,"[11] or Henry Kissinger's telling but perhaps apocryphal remark, "Power is the ultimate aphrodisiac"? One must conclude that the associative links between manliness, virility, power, and domination are very strong in Western culture.

Yet while it is not news that the exercise of power has links with masculine sexuality, the theoretical content and significance of these links remains to be explored. Despite their recognition of these links, social scientists and theorists have given little analytic attention to the erotic aspect of power relations. This failure to explore the gendered linkage between sexuality and power, despite the stated recognition of its existence, typifies a surprising range of theories of power. The lacuna is perhaps most surprising and most in need of remedy in the case of Marx, given his stress on the importance of sensuous material life. The failure is important because power structures the human community, and thus the current silence about the genderedness of power forms an obstacle to the construction of a society free from all forms of domination.

The gender carried by power has, however, been explored in a quite different context, one in which the central issue is the connection of sexuality with violence and even death. Activists in the contemporary feminist movement have contended that exercises of power and domination in Western culture are systematically confused with sexual acts. There is a growing literature which argues that rape is an act of domination, an act that has to do with power and even property rather than an act growing from sexual frustration.[12] And the feminist debate about whether pornography is erotic literature or represents violence against women represents a second locus in which the relation between (or fusion of) virility and domination has been pointed out. My reading of these and other analyses leads me to argue that sexuality in our society is defined almost exclusively in masculine terms, and moreover that hostility and domination are central to the construction of masculine sexuality.[13]

This dynamic of hostility and domination structures not just the "private" world of individual action and sexuality but has a larger significance as well. It is deeply implicated in ideals for public life. One can find what is perhaps its clearest expression in a society unencumbered with market ideology, in ancient Athenian political philosophy where the public world first took theoretical form. Masculine sexuality was central to the construction of an agonal community structured fundamentally by rivalry and competition. The Homeric warrior-hero, civic ideals for the Athenian citizen, and the nature of the communities they constructed bear the marks of a hostile and aggressive masculinity.

Feminists should not simply turn their backs on the agonal communities men have constructed and have justified in political theory. Like market theories, the theorization of an agonal politics, a politics based on struggle and competition, provides important resources for a feminist rethinking of power. Agonal communities should be critically understood as expressions of a specifically masculine social experience, a masculine attempt to solve the riddle of community. If these are the power relations that both construct and are reinforced by masculine sexuality, can one envisage alternative possibilities for community present in women's sexuality?[14] The beginnings of an answer to such a question will require attention to women's lives rather than men's to determine whether women's lives provide a ground for an alternative understanding of power and community.

Power and Epistemology: Exchange, Production, and Reproduction

Because alternative theories of power rest on different epistemologies, and because the adequacy of a given theory depends on the adequacy of its epistemological base, discussions of power can enable us to open the subject of a more encompassing feminist analysis. A more encompassing analysis would be able to account for the relation of theories of knowledge to human activity, and the relation of knowledge and domination in our society. It would be able to understand the forces involved in social change and would identify the areas of social life which hold the key to development of a more humane community.

In beginning to develop an encompassing theory, Marx's analysis of class domination in capitalist society provides both an important standard for a systematic feminist theory and a series of guidelines. The depth and profundity of Marx's analysis depended on the historical materialist approach he took toward these questions, and his success stands as an implicit suggestion that feminists should adopt a historical materialist approach to understanding male supremacy. At the outset I propose to take over two of Marx's important arguments about epistemology and ontology. (One should note that the two categories collapse into each other for Marx.) First, I critically adopt his insistence that conscious human activity, or practice, has both an ontological and epistemological status, that human feelings are not "merely anthropological phenomena" but are "truly ontological affirmations of being."[15] Thus, for Marx, each mode of producing subsistence, each form of the division of mental from

manual labor, can be expected to have consequences for human understanding. Thus, Marx argued that the practical activity—and therefore the world view—of capitalist and worker differed systematically because the activity of each was structured by the mental/manual division of labor. And because the activity of the ruling, or capitalist, class was structured by exchange, exchange structured not only the human community in capitalist society but also set limits to the modes in which this community could be understood. As Marx and Engels put it, the

> class which has the means of material production at its disposal, has control at the same time over the means of mental production, so that thereby, generally speaking, the ideas of those who lack the means of mental production are subject to it. The ruling ideas are nothing more than the ideal expression of the dominant material relationships, the dominant material relationships grasped as ideas; hence of the relationships which make the one class the ruling one, therefore, the ideas of its dominance.[16]

When we understand that economic categories are the theoretical expressions of the social relations of production, we recognize that data present themselves immediately, that is directly and obviously, in forms and categories that are part of capitalist society. To accept the data in this form as falling within eternal and unalterable categories is both to fail to see the underlying reality and to acquiesce in the reproduction of capitalist social relations.

Our society, however, is structured not simply by a ruling class dependent on the division of mental from manual labor but also by a ruling gender, defined by and dependent on the sexual division of labor. Control over the means of mental production belongs to this ruling gender as well as to the ruling class. Thus, one can expect that the categories in which experience is commonly presented are both capitalist and masculine. And to the extent that Marxian theory is grounded in men's activity in production and ignores women's activity in reproduction, one can expect that Marxian categories themselves will require critique.

The second point to be critically adopted is Marx's argument that the ruling ideas, because they are the ideas of the ruling class, give an incorrect account of reality, an account only of appearances. Thus, Marx argues,

> The final pattern of economic relations as seen on the surface, in their real existence and consequently in the conceptions by which the bearers and agents of these relations seek to understand them, is very much different from, and indeed quite the reverse of, their inner but concealed essential pattern and the conception corresponding to it.[17]

These inner but concealed patterns are visible from the point of view of the proletariat, those who embody, although involuntarily, the "negative result of society."[18] Only through a process of mediation, a process of uncovering the social relations and social consequences involved even in apparently simple things, can the authentic structure of phenomena be revealed.[19]

Marxian theory holds that accounts of power based at the level of circulation or exchange provide inadequate accounts of systematic domination and inequality. In contrast, Marx argues that the social relations of capitalism generate two epistemological systems, the one at the level of appearance, and rooted in the activity of exchange, the other at the level of real social relations, and rooted in the activity of production. Yet if the institutionalized structure of human activity generates an ontology and epistemology, and if the activity of women differs systematically from that of men, we must ask whether epistemology is structured by gender as well as class. If the reality of systematic class domination only becomes apparent at the epistemological level of production, what epistemological level can allow us to understand the systematic domination of women? I argue that the domination of one gender by the other can only be made visible at a still deeper level, an epistemological level defined by reproduction. Thus, rather than argue, with Marx, that reality must be understood as bi-leveled, I am suggesting that it must be understood as three-tiered. And if at the level of production, as Marx argues, one can not only see the real relations between human beings but also understand why theories at higher levels of abstraction fail, then at the level of reproduction we should ex-

pect to develop not only a more comprehensive account of the totality of social relations but as well understand why it is that neither the level of exchange nor the level of production provides an adequate and complete epistemological ground for the theorization of power.[20] The book, then, can be seen as a kind of Wittgensteinian ladder. But whereas he held that one could ascend and then discard the ladder, my own view is that the ladder should be seen as a means by which one gradually descends to the real material ground of human existence, a ground constituted by women's experience and life activity. . . .

[Notes]

1. I have argued elsewhere that this avoidance was progressive, constructive, and important at the time, but now must be redressed. See "Feminism, Power, and Change," in *Women Organizing*, ed. Bernice Cummings and Victoria Schuck (Metuchen, N.J.: Scarecrow Press, 1980); and "Difference and Domination in the Women's Movement: The Dialectic of Theory and Practice," in *The Scholar and the Feminist*, vol. 2; *Class, Race, and Sex: The Dynamics of Control*, ed. Amy Swerdlow and Hanna Lessinger (Boston: G. K. Hall, 1982). The staff of *Quest: a feminist quarterly* represented an important group exception to this, and are partially responsible for my own interest in the subject of power.

2. These definitions come, respectively, from Bertrand Russell, *Power: A New Social Analysis* (n.p., 1936), p. 35, cited by Anthony de Crespigny and Alan Wertheimer, *Contemporary Political Theory* (New York: Atherton Press, 1970), p. 22; and Talcott Parsons, "On the Concept of Political Power," in *Political Power*, ed. Roderick Bell, David B. Edwards, and R. Harrison Wagner (New York: Free Press, 1969), p. 256.

3. The definition of domination I propose to use provisionally is that put forward by Dorothy Emmet: "achievement of intended effects through coercing other people." See "The Concept of Power," *Proceedings of the Aristotelian Society* 54 (1954): 4. Later I hope to define domination as patterned and institutionally defined relations of domination.

4. Simply put, the feminist acceptance of the phallocratic understanding of power functioned as a justification for a series of separatist strategies. First, feminists responded to male domination by insisting that they could only work separately. The split between blacks and other minorities and whites was a similar response to a similar situation. When it became clear that heterosexual women were oppressing lesbians and trying to make them invisible within the women's movement, and that middle- and upper-class women were oppressing working-class women in the movement, the natural response was to split into smaller units. These units meant that no woman had to work with others who might

be in a position—whether through class, race, or heterosexual privilege—to exercise power over her.

5. To the extent that race is one of the fundamental structural lines along which domination is constructed, power should be expected to carry a racial dimension as well. My intent here, however, is to expose the genderedness of power, and to make use of the analysis of its class dimension to show what we should look for in terms of the genderedness of power. For an indication of one way to address the logic of the possible racial dimension of power, see note 7.

6. My point here is similar to W. B. Gallie's argument that power is an "essentially contested" concept. Power can be categorized as an "essentially contested" concept since it is appraisive, internally complex, open, and used both aggressively and defensively. Gallie, however, seems not to recognize the epistemological implications of his position. See W. B. Gallie, "Essentially Contested Concepts," *Proceedings of the Aristotelian Society* 56 (1955–56): 167–98.

7. There are some indications that the race carried by power may share the context in which power carries gender—the context of sexuality. Both the arguments of Susan Griffin and Charles Herbert Stember indicate that racial hostility is deeply connected with sexual excitement. Stember traces these connections through sociological and psychological data, to argue that sexual excitement is central to racial hostility, especially the racial hostility of white men toward black men. See *Sexual Racism* (New York: Harper & Row, 1976). Susan Griffin traces the similarities between pornography and anti-Semitism in *Pornography and Silence* (New York: Harper & Row, 1981).

8. Quoted in David McClellan, *Karl Marx* (New York: Viking, 1975), pp. 31–32.

9. David Bell, *Power, Influence, and Authority* (New York: Oxford University Press 1975), p. 8.

10. See Berenice Carroll, "Peace Research: The Cult of Power," *Journal of Conflict Resolution* 4 (1972): 588, citing Hanna Arendt, "Reflections on Violence," *Journal of International Affairs* 23, no. 1 (1969): 12. Arendt uses the same quotation in *On Violence* (New York: Harper & Row, 1969), p. 35, where she locates it as occurring in de Jouvenel's *Power: The Natural History of Its Growth* (London: n.p., 1952), p. 110.

11. Robert Penn Warren, *Who Speaks for the Negro* (New York: Vintage, 1966), p. 292.

12. See Susan Brownmiller, *Against Our Will* (New York: Simon and Schuster, 1975); Andrea Medea and Kathleen Thompson, *Against Rape* (New York: Farrar, Strauss, and Giroux, 1974): Susan Griffin, *Rape: The Power of Consciousness* (New York: Harper & Row, 1979); Heidi Hartmann and Ellen Ross, "Comment on 'On Writing the History of Rape,'" *Signs* 3, no. 4 (Summer 1978): 931–35.

13. I use the term "masculine" rather than "male" to indicate what I take to be the fundamentally social rather than biologically given nature of sexuality and, by implication, its susceptibility to change.

14. The subject of women's sexuality is one feminists are only beginning to explore. The difficulty, historic lack of discussion, is made apparent in the fact that the syntactic equivalent of masculine sexuality—feminine sexuality—seems to be a contradiction in terms, or else to imply passive receptiveness and perhaps masochism.

15. Karl Marx, *Economic and Philosophic Manuscripts of 1844*, ed. Dirk Stuik (New York: International Publishers, 1964), pp. 113, 165, 188.

16. Karl Marx and Frederick Engels, *The German Ideology*, ed. C. J. Arthur (New York: International Publishers, 1964), p. 64. See also Karl Marx, *Grundrisse,* trans. Martin Nicolaus (Middlesex, England: Penguin Books, 1973), p. 239.

17. Karl Marx, *Capital* (New York: International Publishers, 1967), 3: 209.

18. Karl Marx, "Introduction to a Critique of Hegel's Philosophy of Right," in *The Marx-Engels Reader,* ed. Robert Tucker (New York: Norton, 1973), p. 22.

19. Georg Lukács, *History and Class Consciousness* (Cambridge, Mass.: MIT Press, 1968), p. 162.

20. I should note here that my use of the category of reproduction to define an epistemological level of reality differs from several other uses, which have been rightly criticized. I am not, for example, discussing a "mode of reproduction" or a "sphere of reproduction." These expressions both indicate that there are different areas or realms of existence. They can even be used to impart a distinction between public (production) and private (reproduction) into feminist theory. In rough terms I intend the term "level of reproduction" to stand relative to the Marxian "level of production" as the "level of production" stands to the "level of circulation" or "exchange."

. . .

The different understandings of power put forward by women who have theorized about power implicitly pose the question of the extent to which gender is a world-view-structuring experience. In this chapter I explore some of the epistemological consequences of claiming that women's lives differ systematically and structurally from those of men. In particular, I suggest that, like the lives of proletarians according to Marxian theory, women's lives make available a particular and privileged vantage point on male supremacy, a vantage point that can ground a powerful critique of the phallocratic institutions and ideology that constitute the capitalist form of patriarchy. I argue that on the basis of the structures that define women's activity as contributors to subsistence and as mothers, the sexual division of labor, one could begin, though not complete, the construction of a feminist standpoint on which to ground a specifically feminist historical materialism. I hope to show how just as Marx's understanding of the world from the standpoint of the proletariat enabled him to go beneath bourgeois ideology, so a feminist standpoint can allow us to descend further into materiality to an epistemological level at which we can better understand both why patriarchal institutions and ideologies take such perverse and deadly forms and how both theory and practice can be redirected in more liberatory directions.

The reader will remember that the concept of a standpoint carries several specific contentions. Most important, it posits a series of levels of reality in which the deeper level both includes and explains the surface or appearance. Related to the positing of levels are several claims:

1. Material life (class position in Marxist theory) not only structures but sets limits on the understanding of social relations.

2. If material life is structured in fundamentally opposing ways for two different groups, one can expect that the vision of each will represent an inversion of the other, and in systems of domination the vision available to the rulers will be both partial and perverse.

3. The vision of the ruling class (or gender) structures the material relations in which all parties are forced to participate and therefore cannot be dismissed as simply false.

4. In consequence, the vision available to the oppressed group must be struggled for and represents an achievement that requires both science to see beneath the surface of the social relations in which all are forced to participate and the education that can only grow from struggle to change those relations.

5. As an engaged vision, the understanding of the oppressed, the adoption of a standpoint exposes the real relations among human beings as inhuman, points beyond the present, and carries a historically liberatory role.

Because of its achieved character and its liberatory potential, I use the term "feminist" rather than "women's standpoint." Like the experience of the proletariat, women's experience and activity as a dominated group contains both negative and positive aspects. A feminist standpoint picks out and amplifies the liberatory possibilities contained in that experience.

Women's work in every society differs systematically from men's. I intend to pursue the suggestion that this division of labor is the first, and in some societies the only, division of labor; moreover, it is central to the organization of social labor more generally.[1] On the basis of an account of the sexual division of labor, one should be able to begin to explore the oppositions and differences between women's and men's activity and their consequences for epistemology. While I cannot attempt a complete account, I put forward a schematic and simplified account of the sexual division of labor and its consequences for epistemology. I sketch out a kind of ideal type of the social relations and world view characteristic of men's and women's activity in order to explore the epistemology contained in the institutionalized sexual division of labor. In so doing, I do not mean to attribute this vision to individual women or men (any more than Marx or Lukács meant their theory of class consciousness to apply to any particular worker or group of workers). My focus is instead on institutionalized social practices and on the specific epistemology and ontology manifested by the institutionalized sexual division of labor. Individuals, as individuals, may change their activity in ways that move them outside the outlook embodied in these institutions, but such a move can be significant only when it occurs at the level of society as a whole.

I discuss the "sexual division of labor" rather than "gender division of labor" to stress, first, my desire not to separate the effects of "nature and nurture," or biology and culture, and my belief that the division of labor between women and men cannot be reduced to simply social dimensions. One must distinguish between what Sara Ruddick has termed "invariant and *nearly* unchangeable" features of human life, and those that, despite being "*nearly* universal," are "certainly changeable."[2] Thus the fact that women and not men *bear* children is not (yet) a social choice, but that women and not men rear children in a society structured by compulsory heterosexuality and male dominance is clearly a societal choice. A second reason to use the term "sexual division of labor" is to keep hold of the bodily aspect of existence, perhaps to grasp it overfirmly in an effort to keep it from evaporating altogether. There is some biological, bodily component to human existence. But its size and substantive content will remain unknown until at least the certainly changeable aspects of the sexual division of labor are altered.

On the basis of a schematic account of the sexual division of labor, I begin to fill in the specific content of the feminist standpoint and begin to specify how women's lives structure an understanding of social relations, that is, begin to follow out the epistemological consequences of the sexual division of labor. In addressing the institutionalized sexual division of labor, I propose to lay aside the important differences among women and instead to search for central commonalties across race and class boundaries. I take some justification from the fruitfulness of Marx's similar strategy in constructing a simplified, two-class, two-man model in which everything was exchanged at its value. Marx's schematic account in volume I of *Capital* left out of account such factors as imperialism; the differential wages, work, and working conditions of the Irish; the differences between women, men, and children; and so on. While all these factors are important to the analysis of contemporary capitalism, none changes either Marx's theories of surplus value or alienation, the two most fundamental features of the Marxian analysis of capitalism. My effort here takes a similar form, in an attempt to move toward a theory of the extraction and appropriation of women's activity and women themselves. Still, I adopt this strategy with some reluctance, since it contains the danger of making invisible the experience of lesbians or women of color.[3] At the same time, I recognize that the effort to uncover a feminist standpoint assumes that there are some things common to all women's lives in Western class societies.

The feminist standpoint that emerges through an examination of women's activities is related to the proletarian standpoint, but deeper-going. Women and workers inhabit a world in which the emphasis is on change rather than stasis, a world characterized by interaction with natural substances rather than separation from nature, a world in which quality is more important than quantity, a world in which the unification of mind and body is inherent in the activities performed. Yet there are some important differences, differences marked by the fact that the proletarian (if male) is immersed in this world only during the time

his labor power is being used by the capitalist. If, to paraphrase Marx, we follow the worker home from the factory, we can once again perceive a change in the *dramatis personae*. He who before followed behind as the worker, timid and holding back, with nothing to expect but a hiding, now strides in front, while a third person, not specifically present in Marx's account of the transactions between capitalist and worker (both of whom are male) follows timidly behind, carrying groceries, baby, and diapers.

Given what has been said about the life activity of the proletarian, one can see that, because the sexual division of labor means that much of the work involved in reproducing labor power is done by women, and because much of the male worker's contact with nature outside the factory is mediated by a woman, the vision of reality which grows from the female experience is deeper and more thoroughgoing than that available to the worker.

The Sexual Division of Labor

Women's activity as institutionalized has a double aspect: their contribution to subsistence and their contribution to childrearing. Whether or not all women do both, women as a sex are institutionally responsible for producing both goods and human beings, and all women are forced to become the kinds of persons who can do both. Although the nature of women's contribution to subsistence varies immensely over time and space, my primary focus here is on capitalism, with a secondary focus on the class societies that preceded it.[4] In capitalism, women contribute both production for wages and production of goods in the home, that is, they, like men, sell their labor power and produce both commodities and surplus value, and produce use values in the home. Unlike men, however, women's lives are institutionally defined by their production of use values in the home.[5] Here we begin to encounter the narrowness of Marx's concept of production. Women's production of use values in the home has not been well understood by socialists. It is no surprise to feminists that Engels, for example, simply asks how women can continue to do the work in the home and also work in production outside the home. Marx, too, takes for granted women's responsibility for household labor. He repeats, as if it were his own, the question of a

Belgian factory inspector: If a mother works for wages, "how will [the household's] internal economy be cared for; who will look after the young children; who will get ready the meals, do the washing and mending?"[6]

Let us trace both the outlines and the consequences of women's dual contribution to subsistence in capitalism. Women's labor, like that of the male worker, is contact with material necessity. Their contribution to subsistence, like that of the male worker, involves them in a world in which the relation to nature and to concrete human requirement is central, both in the form of interaction with natural substances whose quality, rather than quantity, is important to the production of meals, clothing, and so forth and in the form of close attention in a different way from men's. While repetition for both the wages and even more in household production involves a unification of mind and body for the purpose of transforming natural substances into socially defined goods. This, too, is true of the labor of the male worker.

There are, however, important differences. First, women as a group work more than men. We are all familiar with the phenomenon of the "double day," and with indications that women work many more hours per week than men.[7] Second, a larger proportion of women's labor time is devoted to the production of use values than men's. Only some of the goods women produce are commodities (however much they live in a society structured by commodity production and exchange). Third, women's production is structured by repetition in a different way from men's. While repetition for both the woman and the male worker may take the form of production of the same object, over and over—whether apple pies or brake linings—women's work in housekeeping involves a repetitious cleaning.[8]

Thus the man, in the process of production, is involved in contact with necessity and interchange with nature as well as with other human beings, but the process of production or work does not consume his whole life. The activity of a woman in the home as well as the work she does for wages keeps her continually in contact with a world of qualities and change. Her immersion in the world of use—in concrete, many-qualitied, changing material processes—is more complete than his. And if life itself consists of sensuous activity, the vantage point available to women on the basis of their contribution to subsistence represents an intensification and deepening of the materialist world view available to the producers of commodities in capitalism, an intensification of class consciousness. The availability of this outlook to even nonworking-class women has been strikingly formulated by a novelist: "Washing the toilet used by three males, and the floor and walls around it, is, Mira thought, coming face to face with necessity. And that is why women were saner than men, did not come up with the mad, absurd schemes men developed: they were in touch with necessity, they had to wash the toilet bowl and floor."[9]

The focus on women's subsistence activity rather than men's leads to a model in which the capitalist (male) lives a life structured completely by commodity exchange and not at all by production, and at the farthest distance from contact with concrete material life. The male worker marks a way station on the path to the other extreme—the constant contact with material necessity present in women's contribution to subsistence. There are of course important differences along the lines of race and class. For example, working-class men seem to do more domestic labor than men higher up in the class structure—car repairs, carpentry, and the like. And until very recently, the wage work done by most women of color replicated the housework required by their own households. Still, there are commonalties present in the institutionalized sexual division of labor that makes women responsible for both housework and wage work.

Women's contribution to subsistence, however, represents only a part of women's labor. Women also produce/reproduce men (and other women) on both a daily and a long-term basis. This aspect of women's "production" exposes the deep inadequacies of the concept of production as a description of women's activity. One does not (cannot) produce another human being in anything like the way one produces an object such as a chair. Much more is involved, activity that cannot easily be dichotomized into play or work. Helping another to develop, the gradual relinquishing of control, the experiencing of the human limits of one's actions—all these are important features of women's activity as mothers. Women, as mothers, even more than as workers, are institutionally involved in processes of change and growth, and more than workers, must understand the importance of avoiding excessive control in order to help others grow.[10] The activity involved is far more complex than instrumentally working with others to transform objects. (Interestingly, much of women's wage work—nursing, social work, and some secretarial jobs in particular—requires and depends on the relational and interpersonal skills women learned by being mothered by someone of the same sex.)

. . .

Clearly a number of large questions have been broached here. I have attempted to demonstrate that theorizations of power are cultural productions in the most complete sense of the word. Those which have been seen as most attractive show the impact of a number of features of the lives and world views of the ruling class and gender. An analysis that begins from the sexual division of labor, understood as the real, material activity of concrete human beings, could form the basis for an analysis of the real structures of women's oppression, an analysis that would not require that one sever biology from society, nature from culture, an analysis that would expose the ways women both participate in and oppose their own subordination. The elaboration of such an analysis cannot but be difficult. Women's lives, like men's, are structured by social relations that manifest the experience of the dominant gender and class. The ability to go beneath the surface of appearances to reveal the real but concealed social relations requires both theoretical and political activity. Feminist theorists must demand that feminist theorizing be grounded in women's material life activity and must as well be a part of the political struggle necessary to develop areas of social life modeled on this activity. The outcome could be the development of a political economy that fully included women's activity as well as men's. It could in addition be a step toward the restructuring of society as a whole in ways that will reflect a generalization of women's activity to all parts of the population. Thus, it could raise for the first time the possibility of a fully human community, a community structured by its variety of direct relations among people, rather than their separation and opposition.

My argument here opens a number of avenues for future work. Clearly, a systematic critique of Marx on the basis of a more fully developed understanding of the sexual division of labor is in order. And this is indeed being undertaken by a number of feminists. A second avenue for further investigation is the relation between the exchange abstraction and abstract masculinity. It may be that the solipsism of exchange is both an overlay on and a substitution for a deeper-going hostility, that the exchange of gifts is an alternative to war. We have seen that the need for recognizing and receiving recognition from another to take the form of a death struggle memorializes only the masculine experience of emerging as a person in a deeply phallocratic world. If the community created by exchange in turn rests on the more overtly and directly hostile death struggle of self and other, one might be able to argue that what lies beneath the exchange abstraction is abstract masculinity. One might then turn to the question whether capitalism rests on and is a consequence of male supremacy. Feminists might then be able to produce the analysis that could amend Marx to read: "Though class society appears to be the source, the cause of the oppression of women, it is rather its consequence." Thus, it is "only at the last culmination of the development of class society [that] this, its secret, appear(s) again, namely, that on the one hand it is the *product* of the oppression of women, and that on the other it is the *means* by which women participate in and create their own oppression."[25]

[Notes]

1. This is Iris Young's point. I am indebted to her persuasive arguments for taking what she terms the "gender differentiation of labor" as a central category of analysis. See Young, "Dual Systems Theory," *Socialist Review* 50, 51 (March–June 1980): 185. My use of this category, however, differs to some extent from hers. Young focuses on the societal aspects of the division of labor and chooses to use the term "gender division" to indicate that focus. I want to include the relation to the natural world as well. In addition, Young's analysis of women in capitalism does not seem to include marriage as a part of the division of labor. She is more concerned with the division of labor in capitalism in the productive sector.

2. See Sara Ruddick, "Maternal Thinking," *Feminist Studies* 6, no. 2 (Summer 1980): 364.

3. See, for a discussion of this danger, Adrienne Rich, "Disloyal of Civilization: Feminism, Racism, Gynephobia," in *On Lies, Secrets, and Silence* (New York: Norton, 1979),

pp. 275–310; Elly Bulkin, "Racism and Writing: Some Implications for White Lesbian Critics," *Sinister Wisdom,* no. 6 (Spring 1980); Bell Hooks, *Ain't I a Woman* (Boston: South End Press, 1981), p. 138.

4. Some cross-cultural evidence indicates that the status of women varies with the work they do. To the extent that women and men contribute equally to subsistence, women's status is higher than it would be if their subsistence work differed profoundly from that of men; that is, if they do none or almost all of the work of subsistence, their status remains low. See Peggy Sanday, "Female Status in the Public Domain," in *Woman, Culture and Society,* ed. Michelle Rosaldo and Louise Lamphere (Stanford: Stanford University Press, 1974), p. 199. See also Iris Young's account of the sexual division of labor in capitalism, mentioned in note 1.

5. It is irrelevant to my argument here that women's wage labor takes place under different circumstances than men's—that is, their lower wages, their confinement to only a few occupational categories, etc. I am concentrating instead on the formal, structural features of women's work. There has been much effort to argue that women's domestic labor is a source of surplus value, that is, to include it within the scope of Marx's value theory as productive labor, or to argue that since it does not produce surplus value it belongs to an entirely different mode of production, variously characterized as domestic or patriarchal. My strategy here is quite different from this. See, for the British debate, Mariarosa Dalla Costa and Selma James, *The Power of Women and the Subversion of the Community* (Bristol: Falling Wall Press, 1975); Wally Secombe, "The Housewife and Her Labor Under Capitalism," *New Left Review* 83 (January–February 1974); Jean Gardiner, "Women's Domestic Labour," *New Left Review* 89 (March 1975); and Paul Smith, "Domestic Labour and Marx's Theory of Value," in *Feminism and Materialism,* eds. Annette Kuhn and Ann Marie Wolpe (Boston: Routledge and Kegan Paul, 1978). A portion of the American debate can be found in Ira Gerstein, "Domestic Work and Capitalism," and Lisa Vogel, "The Earthly Family," *Radical America* 7, nos. 4/5 (July–October 1973); Ann Ferguson, "Women as a New Revolutionary Class," in *Between Labor and Capital,* ed. Pat Walker (Boston: South End Press, 1979).

6. Frederick Engels, *Origins of the Family, Private Property and the State* (New York: International Publishers 1942); Karl Marx, *Capital* (New York: International Publishers, 1967) 1: 671. Marx and Engels have also described the sexual division of labor as natural or spontaneous. See Mary O'Brien, "Reproducing Marxist Man," in *The Sexism of Social and Political Thought,* ed. Lorenne Clark and Lynda Lange (Toronto: University of Toronto Press, 1979).

7. For a discussion of women's work, see Elise Boulding, "Familial Constraints of Women's Work Roles," in *Women and the Workplace,* ed. Martha Blaxall and B. Reagan (Chicago: University of Chicago Press, 1976), esp. pp. 111, 113. An interesting historical note is provided by the fact that Nausicaa, the daughter of a Homeric king, did the household laundry. See M. I. Finley, *The World of Odysseus* (Middlesex, England: Penguin, 1979), p. 73. While aristocratic women were less involved in actual labor, the difference was one of degree. And as Aristotle remarked in the *Politics,* supervising slaves is not a particularly uplifting activity. The life of leisure and philosophy, so much the goal for aristocratic Athenian men, then, was almost unthinkable for any women.

8. Simone de Beauvoir holds that repetition has a deeper significance and that women's biological destiny itself is repetition. See *The Second Sex,* trans. H. M. Parshley (New York: Knopf, 1953), p. 59. But see also her discussion of housework in ibid., pp. 423 ff. There, her treatment of housework is strikingly negative. For her the transcendence of humanity is provided in the historical struggle of self with other and with the natural world. The oppositions she sees are not really stasis vs. change, but rather transcendence, escape from the muddy concreteness of daily life.

9. Marilyn French, *The Women's Room* (New York: Jove, 1978), p. 214.

10. Sara Ruddick, "Maternal Thinking," presents an interesting discussion of these and other aspects of the thought which emerges from the activity of mothering. Although I find it difficult to speak the language of interests and demands she uses, she brings out several valuable points. Her distinction between maternal and scientific thought is very intriguing and potentially useful (see esp. pp. 350–53).

. . .

25. Marx, *Economic and Philosophic Manuscripts of 1844,* ed. Dirk Stuik (New York: International Publishers, 1964), p. 117.

DISCUSSION QUESTIONS

1. Do you agree with Hartsock's critique of "exchange models" of social relations? Why or why not?

2. Do you agree with Hartsock's account of the typical roles of women and men in the division of labor in capitalist society? Why or why not?

3. Assuming that contemporary society is structured by "power relations" and thus inherent antagonisms, at least along the lines of gender, race, and class, do you think one of these forms of domination/subordination among social groups is more foundational than the others? Explain.

4. Do you agree with Hartsock's implied vision of a truly "humane," "good" society? Why or why not? Is it achievable? Why or why not?

5. How might a non-Western feminist such as Uma Narayan respond to Hartsock's analyses?

61. Kibujjo M. Kalumba
"The Political Philosophy of Nelson Mandela: A Primer"

Kibujjo Kalumba is on the philosophy faculty at Ball State University in Indiana, and in his research he has focused on issues within the growing field of study in African philosophy. The essay reprinted here was published in the *Journal of Social Philosophy* in 1995. In it Kalumba is primarily arguing for a certain interpretation of the political and ethical views of Nelson Mandela, one of the most well known and influential African leaders in the second half of the twentieth century.

Mandela was born in 1918 in South Africa, joined the African National Congress in 1944, and thereafter was in the forefront of the struggle against the minority white government of South Africa and its openly racist apartheid policies. Until his release in 1990, Mandela had been in prison for twenty-seven years as a result of his activism. In 1994, as apartheid finally was being dismantled, he became president in the country's first "non-racial" elections.

Although Mandela has articulated many of his philosophical beliefs in his various writings over the years, he has not (yet) composed them into a systematic theoretical statement. Kalumba is in effect giving the philosophical content of those beliefs an academic philosophical form, for the most part by locating them within traditional debates regarding the status of civil rights, the role of government in the overcoming of oppression and injustice in society, and the goals of indigenous liberation movements in a postcolonial world.

QUESTIONS FOR CRITICAL READING

1. What are "natural rights," what are the two "trends" in the natural rights tradition, and how does Kalumba locate Mandela within this tradition?
2. According to Kalumba, what is Mandela's position on nationalization?
3. How does Kalumba characterize the "nationalist-ideological" perspective in recent African philosophy, and what is Mandela's relation to this perspective?
4. What is the "historical-hermeneutical trend" in recent African philosophy, and how does Kalumba interpret Mandela's relation to this perspective?

TERMS TO NOTE

counterrevolutionary: After revolutionary change toward the egalitarian reorganization of society has been achieved, having to do with organized attempts to undo or destroy that achievement.

apartheid: The official policy of racial segregation and unequal civil rights in the Republic of South Africa, which after many decades was finally ended with that country's first nonracial elections in 1994.

reactionary: Having to do with the resistance to progressive (egalitarian) social change, motivated by the concern to preserve traditionally established hierarchical social relations.

Introduction

This paper is intended to be a brief introduction to Nelson Mandela's political philosophy; a philosophy embedded in a manifold of speeches, articles, declarations, and so on, spanning some five decades.[1]

My goal is twofold. First, I want to underscore what I think is the correct perspective for understanding Mandela's politics. This is important given the ongoing tradition of counterrevolutionary, redbaiting propaganda aimed at discrediting his views. It is no secret, for example, that the South African government has banned and imprisoned Mandela under the Suppression of Communism Act.[2] Not long ago, Oupa Gqozo, then president of the former Ciskei Bantustan, is reported to have urged that to capitulate to the demands of Mandela's African National Congress (ANC) is to have South Africa headed toward an "African socialist tyranny."[3] All this, despite the fact that

Mandela expresses admiration for democracy, and denies being a communist or a radical socialist.[4]

I want to contend that, contrary to the impression easily created by the counterrevolutionaries, Mandela's fundamental commitment is not to any of the conventional ideologies of capitalism, socialism, or communism. He is best seen, I argue, as belonging to the natural rights tradition of ethics and political philosophy. This commitment combined with apartheid's concrete realities, I urge, holds the key to the correct perspective on Mandela's views. In short, I want it emphasized that, to be correctly understood, Mandela's ideas must be viewed *in the framework of implementing the basic tenets of the natural rights tradition within the context of apartheid South Africa.*

I must admit that I am in basic agreement with Mandela's ideas, although any attempt to defend them in this paper would take us beyond its goal. I will settle for the hope that, read from the suggested perspective, and, thus, freed from reactionary distortions, Mandela's views will, on their own merit, win more cadres to the struggle for which he is the central leader. Practice, not theory, is the ultimate concern of this paper.

Second, I want to situate Mandela's views in the tradition of African liberation philosophy. How do they compare with those of Kwame Nkrumah and Julius Nyerere, for instance? Does he fit within the emerging historical-hermeneutical trend of African philosophy? These are some of the issues I will be addressing. I will now proceed with the natural rights tradition and Mandela's place within it.

I. Mandela and the Natural Rights Tradition

According to the natural rights tradition, certain rights (variably called human rights, natural rights, or basic rights) are at once natural and morally fundamental. They are said to be natural in the sense of having human nature as their sole basis. For this reason they are claimed to be possessed by all humans regardless of rank or position. They are taken to be morally fundamental in the sense of being the primordial grounding for all genuine moral claims and obligations. Ultimately, every valid moral justification is claimed to involve appeal to these rights.

There are two trends within the natural rights tradition: the negative rights trend (NRT) and the positive rights trend (PRT). To grasp their differences, one has to recall that to every right there corresponds a set of obligations, and that the nature of the corresponding obligations is the basis for distinguishing between two kinds of rights: positive rights and negative rights. Whereas positive rights entail obligations of provision, negative rights entail obligations of noninterference.[5]

For the NRT, the basic rights, normally taken to comprise life, liberty, and justly acquired property, are all negative, i.e., the obligations that correspond to them are those of noninterference. Thus, in this trend, the right to life merely entails the obligation not to kill others. It does not, for instance, entail the duty to provide anybody with the means of subsistence.

Those within the NRT who are concerned with defining the role of the political state tend to do so in negative terms. The tendency is to regard the state as a mere umpire whose job is limited to ensuring noninterference in people's peaceful enjoyment of their negative rights. This is the trend of John Locke, Robert Nozick, Judith J. Thomson, among others.[6]

For the PRT, negative rights don't exhaust the list of basic rights. For, in addition to the Lockean triad (life, liberty, and private property) mentioned above, this trend recognizes, as basic rights, certain claims that call for obligations of provision. The basic necessities of life such as food, shelter, and health care are the usual candidates for these basic positive rights. Norman Bowie and Robert Simon, two good representatives of the PRT, have given a persuasive argument for including the basic necessities of life in the list of basic rights. Their argument is that the ultimate reason for regarding life, liberty, and private property as basic rights is that doing so is necessary for people to pursue a dignified life. But, they continue, the basic necessities of life are as necessary for pursuit of a dignified life as the Lockean triad. "Where is dignity to a human life condemned to involuntary starvation?," they ask. And so, they conclude, the basic necessities should be regarded as basic rights as well.[7]

The state assumes a bigger role for the PRT than for the NRT. In addition to protecting basic negative rights, as in the NRT, the state's role for the PRT includes that of implementing basic positive rights as well, a role which may lead to its interference with some people's basic negative rights. Thus, implementing some citizens' basic positive rights to food may, for example, require state taxation of others' private property in the form of earned income.

As will soon be clear, Mandela's fundamental commitment puts him in the PRT. His "political loyalty," he has said in a declaration from apartheid's jails, "is owed primarily, if not exclusively" to the ANC, of which he sees himself as a "loyal and disciplined member."[8] Since 1956, the ANC has been building its struggle around the demands of the Freedom Charter (FC), which are, indeed, the organization's program.[9] It is, hence, appropriate to say that Mandela's fundamental commitment is to the demands of the FC.

Among the demands the FC puts before the apartheid regime, many, such as the call for universal suffrage, are, strictly speaking, not basic rights within the PRT framework; they are best seen as derived or conventional rights.[10] Except for including derived rights, however, the FC's package of demands does not differ substantially from the basic rights of the PRT. Thus, while, in a variety of ways, the FC poses the Lockean triad of negative rights, it does not hesitate to incorporate the basic necessities of life, as rights on a par. Hence, for the FC, being decently housed is not a privilege, but a right. So is the ability for all people "to bring up their families in comfort and security."[11] The lines that immediately follow spell out the contents of this general right: they are the provisions of food and medical care, among other things.

Time and again, the ANC has emphasized this same view. The organization has never been known to subordinate life's basic necessities to basic negative rights. Indeed, the ANC's National Executive Committee used the occasion of the organization's 81st anniversary to declare, once again, that "a better health system which caters for all is not a privilege, but a right which must be guaranteed." And, reiterating the Charter's perspective, the Committee continues that "all communities have a right to housing. . . ."[12]

Judging from the above discussion, Mandela's primary loyalty is to the basic rights of the PRT. This is why I am putting him in the PRT. As will soon be clear, this view is further corroborated by his position on the role of the postapartheid state.

But the FC calls for the nationalization of mines, banks, and "monopoly industry."[13] Doesn't this show that Mandela's commitment to nationalization is at least as profound as his commitment to the basic tenets of the PRT? If so, don't the communist charges carry some credibility? These are important questions. Fortunately, they are easy to answer, since Mandela's stance on the issue of nationalization is explicit and clear. It is to this issue that I am devoting the next section.

II. Mandela on Nationalization

Three things should be noted regarding Mandela's stance on the issue of nationalization. First, neither Mandela nor the FC calls for the wholesale nationalization of business firms, a fact which nullifies any accusation of thoroughgoing communism.[14] Second, nationalization is not pursued as an end, but as a *contextually indispensable means for realizing the demands of the FC.* Says Mandela, in his 1956 commentary on the FC:

> It is true that in demanding the nationalization of the banks, the gold mines, and the land, the Charter strikes a fatal blow at the financial and gold-mining monopolies and farming interests that have for centuries plundered the country and condemned its people to servitude. *But such a step is imperative because the realization of the Charter is inconceivable, in fact impossible, unless and until these monopolies are smashed and the national wealth of the country turned over to the people.*[15]

Mandela reiterates the same point in a more recent speech to a group of small-business-owners in Durban, South Africa, when he insists that the ANC

> has no ideological attachment to nationalization, but it's the only effective way to ensure there's an equal distribution of wealth. We say to the business community: if you have a better alternative tell us and if it's effective we'll abandon nationalization.[16]

At stake, in the above quotations, is Mandela's distinction between "a matter of principle" and a "tactical weapon of the struggle." While the former "must be applied invariably at all times and in all circumstances irrespective of the prevailing conditions," the latter is "to be employed if and when objective conditions permit. . . ."[17] Nowhere in Mandela's writings does he explicitly call anything a matter of principle. If anything can be said to qualify for this status, the basic rights (both positive and negative) surely do. What is clear from what has been said thus far is that nationalization is far from being a matter of principle for Mandela. It is best seen as a tactical weapon of the struggle in his program.

The third point is that the contextual and subordinate nature of nationalization in Mandela's program is evinced by the fact that his views on the subject have evolved since his 1956 article commenting on the FC. While the article, following the FC, earmarks specific kinds of firms for nationalization, Mandela has backed off from such specificity by 1990. Thus, by the time of his address to South African business executives, he is willing to subject the issue of the content and form of nationalization to the ongoing debate in the country. Says Mandela:

> The ANC has no blueprint that decrees that these or other assets will be nationalized, or that such nationalization would take this or the other form. But we do say that this option should also be part of the ongoing debate, subject to critical analysis as any other and viewed *in the context of the realities of South African society.*[18]

It should be clear from the above discussion that nationalization cannot be put on par with basic rights, in Mandela's world view. For him, the rights are the end to the implementation of which nationalization is subordinated as a necessary means, in the context of apartheid South Africa. It is a context of gross inequalities between the races, especially in the area of basic positive rights, as evinced by the three indicators in the following table:

	Whites	Asians	Africans
Infant mortality rate per 1,000 live births (1982)	14.9	25.3	94
Life expectancy at birth in years (1987)	71	67	59
Literacy (1990)	99%	69%	50%[19]

I have chosen the first indicator because, according to the United Nations Children's Fund (UNICEF), it is "the best single indicator" of a country's performance in the area of life's basic necessities. This is so because it "measures directly the health of mothers and children, and reflects other factors such as income and availability of food, access to drinkable water, effective sewage disposal, literacy levels, and social services."[20] The second indicator is chosen to add more weight to the data of the first one. For obvious reasons, life expectancy at birth "reflects" basically the same factors as those UNICEF attributes to infant mortality rate. The data for literacy is intended to corroborate the reliability of the first two indices.

Situated in the context of apartheid's gross inequalities, Mandela sees no effective way of ameliorating the situation of the disadvantaged majority short of tampering with private ownership of the means of production by the white minority.[21] Corroborating my view that he belongs to the PRT, Mandela sees the need for the postapartheid state to expropriate some of the privately owned business firms, if it is to acquire enough funds to begin implementing basic positive rights for the majority. This is the framework within which Mandela's call for nationalization has to be understood. And now for his place in the tradition of African liberation philosophy.

III. Mandela and African Liberation Philosophy

Nationalist-ideological philosophy is the third trend in Henry O. Oruka's fourfold classification of African philosophy.[22] It comprises the anticolonial, pro-independence literature of such thinkers as Kwame Nkrumah, Julius Nyerere, and Leopold Senghor. How does Mandela compare with the "ideological" trend?

There is no doubt that, from the very beginning, Mandela solidarized with the adherents of the ideological trend, and that he shared their dream of a liberated Africa.[23] However, his idea of liberation differs from theirs in one significant way. For the leading thinkers of this trend, liberation entailed forging a uniquely African political theory based on the idea of traditional African communalism, and for this they have been sharply criticized. Peter O. Bodunrin has, for instance, charged them with anachronism and backward-looking romanticism. The homogeneous societies within which communalism worked, he urges, have been largely replaced by heterogeneous ones. And besides, he contends, communalism did not work as smoothly as the ideologues suggest.[24]

There might have been "ideological" tendencies in youthful Mandela that made their way into the Manifesto of the ANC Youth League, which he helped to found in 1944.[25] Thus, in its "Statement of Policy," the Manifesto contrasts "the White man's" ideals with those of the African in terms reminiscent of the ideological trend. Whereas individualism is attributed to the White man, the African's vision is cast in a holistic, communitarian framework.

> The African . . . regards the Universe as one composite whole; an organic entity, progressively driving towards greater harmony and unity whose individual parts exist merely as interdependent aspects of one whole realising their fullest life in the corporate life where communal contentment is the absolute measure of values. His philosophy of life strives towards unity and aggregation; towards greater social responsibility.[26]

The important thing to observe here is that neither the Manifesto nor the Youth League nor Mandela ever prescribes this "African ideal" as part of the goal of the anti-apartheid struggle. On the contrary, that goal is always construed in the individualistic terms of extending the demands of the FC to every South African. In this regard, Mandela differs significantly from the ideological trend. He shows affinity, though, with the emerging historical-hermeneutical trend.

In the opening essay of *African Philosophy: The Essential Readings*, Tsenay Serequeberhan speaks of an emerging trend of African philosophy, the historical-hermeneutical trend.[27] As described by Serequeberhan, the trend exhibits at least three defining features:

> (1) The conviction that philosophy is always the contextual product of specific people engaged in specific purposive activities, and, hence, that it cannot be culture-neutral;
> (2) the belief that, in Africa, the overarching goal is liberation in its varied forms, and, therefore, that authentic African philosophy is the

contextual product of those engaged in the struggle to liberate the continent; and
> (3) emphasis on an ongoing dialectic between philosophy (theory) and practice.

Do Mandela's views fit this description?

The three features are essentially metaphilosophical. Consequently, it should not come as a surprise that their explicit articulation cannot be found in Mandela's writings. His concern is not professional philosophy. Nevertheless, one sees instances of adherence to the general spirit of these features in these same writings. I will elaborate.

As we have seen, Mandela treats nationalization as a tactical weapon whose form and content are "derived" from apartheid's concrete reality. In doing so, he follows the first two features in deriving a significant aspect of his political theory—his social structure—from the context. Let me explain.

Following convention, we can say that a country's social structure is determined by its predominant mode of ownership of the means of production. On this view, one can speak of two extreme kinds of social structures: "radical capitalism," in which all the means of production are privately owned, and "radical socialism," in which all of them are publicly owned. Obviously, these extremes constitute a continuum that leaves room for an infinity of possible social structures between them. Of much significance for the present discussion is the realization that the nature (form and content) of nationalization uniquely determines position on the continuum, i.e., to specify the nature of a country's nationalization is to specify its social structure. But for Mandela, as we have seen, the nature of nationalization is derived from South Africa's unique context. It follows that his social structure is ultimately derived from the very same context.

Dialectic between theory and practice (the third feature) is visible on at least two occasions in Mandela's works. First, there is the ANC's adoption of the *1949 Programme of Action* at the urging of Mandela, among others.[28] Before the adoption of this program, ANC policy was to bring about change through constitutional means: talks with the authorities, memoranda, resolutions, and so forth. But, as Mandela explains, practice proved constitutionalism wanting, and called for its supplementation with more militant (often unconstitutional) forms of mass action: strikes, stay-at-homes, civil disobedience, and so on.[29]

Second, there is the creation, in 1961, of *Umkhonto we Sizwe* (MK), the armed wing of the ANC, of which Mandela was a founding member and Commander-in-Chief. Until 1961, ANC policy was one of non-violent resistance. But, as the MK Manifesto explains, practice proved non-violence ineffective, since the state counteracted it with brutal violence. Henceforth, non-violence had to be augmented with calculated violence.[30]

In conclusion, this exposition of Mandela's views, hopefully, dispels any misconceptions easily created by counterrevolutionary propaganda. Mandela is neither a backward-looking romantic nor a fanatic ideologue, zealously pursuing nationalization as part of some utopian dream. We have seen that he advocates nationalization not as an independent end, but as a necessary means for extending basic rights to all South Africans, in the context of apartheid's gross inequalities. As a contextually dictated means, nationalization is subordinate and provisional in Mandela's program. Those who find the move unpalatable, Mandela challenges to propose an equally effective alternative. It is difficult to imagine an effective way of addressing apartheid's gross inequalities which leaves intact the current state of ownership of the means of production.[31]

Postscript

Much has changed in South Africa since January 1994 when I wrote the concluding remarks to this paper. The historic April 26–29, 1994, elections gave the ANC 62.6% of the total vote. Thus apartheid was dealt a fatal blow, and the ANC was given a decisive mandate to pursue its goal of building a united, nonracial, nonsexist, democratic South Africa. Since the elections, the Bantustans have been reincorporated into South Africa, an ANC-dominated Constituent Assembly has been sworn in, and Mandela has been installed as the country's first black president. The next general elections are scheduled for 1999, and the new Constituent Assembly has until then to write a new constitution for the republic. Meanwhile, Mandela and the ANC continue to push for implementation of the demands of the Freedom Charter. These demands are now articulated in a new package known as the *Reconstruction and Development Program*.

"We have at last achieved our political emancipation," said Mandela during his presidential inauguration. Given apartheid's legacy of extreme imbalances, many battles are still ahead in the struggle for complete emancipation.

Notes

1. Nelson Rolihlahla Mandela was born in 1918 into the ruling family of Tembuland, in the Transkei. He joined the African National Congress (ANC) in 1944 and helped to form its Youth League. For the next 46 years, leadership in the antiapartheid organization was to earn Mandela nothing but continued banishment and imprisonment. His last court appearance was in 1964 during the famous Rivonia Trial at the conclusion of which he was sentenced to life imprisonment. He was to languish behind bars for the next 27 years until his release in 1990. In 1994, in South Africa's first nonracial elections, Mandela led the ANC to a landslide victory and became the country's first black president. The bulk of Mandela's political philosophy is contained in his *The Struggle Is My Life*, 2nd ed. (New York: Pathfinder Press, 1990). More recently, Pathfinder Press has published a collection of Mandela's major speeches since his release from prison under the title of *Nelson Mandela Speaks: Forging a Democratic, Nonracial South Africa* (New York: Pathfinder Press, 1993).

2. Enacted in 1950, the Suppression of Communism Act was used to illegalize all organized demands for social change and to ban antiapartheid leaders. See Mandela, *The Struggle Is My Life*, p. 30.

3. Greg McCartan, "Struggle in South Africa Moves Forward: Mass Action Campaign Puts Revolutionary Movement in Stronger Position," *The Militant*, 13 November 1992, p. 8. McCartan gets this quotation from an unspecified issue of the British *Independent* magazine.

4. On this point see Mandela's statement of his political position during the Rivonia Trial (1963–1964), in Mandela, *The Struggle Is My Life*, pp. 173–180.

5. Some philosophers object to the distinction between positive and negative rights on the grounds that every right entails obligations of provision as well as those of noninterference. Personally, I don't think this objection challenges the validity of the distinction. If correct, the objection simply shows that there are no pure types in the realm of rights. But this leaves the distinction intact. On this issue, see, for example, Henry Shue, *Basic Rights: Subsistence, Affluence and U.S. Foreign Policy* (Princeton: Princeton University Press, 1980).

6. John Locke, *Second Treatise of Government*, 1690; Robert Nozick, *Anarchy, State and Utopia* (New York: Basic

Books, 1974); Judith Jarvis Thomson, *The Realm of Rights* (Cambridge: Harvard University Press, 1990).

7. Norman E. Bowie and Robert L. Simon, *The Individual and the Political Order: An Introduction to Social and Political Philosophy,* 2nd ed. (Englewood Cliffs: Prentice-Hall, 1986). The argument is developed in chapter 3 of this book. This chapter is also a clear description of the natural rights tradition.

8. See Mandela's July 1989 declaration to then South African president Pieter Botha in *The Militant,* 16 February 1990, p. 8.

9. The Freedom Charter was adopted in 1955 by a congress of nearly three thousand delegates, at Kliptown, near Johannesburg. The ANC officially adopted the Charter in early 1956. The entire text of the Charter is printed in Mandela, *The Struggle Is My Life,* pp. 50–54.

10. For this distinction, see Bowie and Simon, *The Individual and the Political Order,* chapter 3.

11. See the section titled "There shall be Houses, Security and Comfort," Mandela, *The Struggle Is My Life,* p. 53.

12. The entire text of the Executive Committee's statement is printed in *The Militant,* 29 January 1993, pp. 8–11.

13. Mandela, *The Struggle Is My Life,* p. 51.

14. Mandela makes it clear during the Rivonia Trial that postapartheid "nationalization would take place in an economy based on private enterprise." Mandela, *The Struggle Is My Life,* p. 173.

15. Mandela, *The Struggle Is My Life,* p. 55. Emphasis added.

16. Quoted by Greg McCartan, "Mandela: S. Africa Violence Caused by Apartheid Regime," *The Militant,* 1 November 1991, p. 11. If my interpretation of Mandela's views is correct, equal distribution of wealth is only an intermediate goal of nationalization in his program. Its ultimate goal is extension of basic rights to all South Africans.

17. See Mandela's 1958 article on political tactics, in *The Struggle Is My Life,* pp. 69–70.

18. Nelson Mandela, *Speeches 1990: Intensify the Struggle to Abolish Apartheid* (New York: Pathfinder Press, 1990), pp. 62–63. Emphasis added.

19. The data is from Mark S. Hoffman, ed., *The World Almanac and Book of Facts 1992,* (New York: Pharos Books, 1991), p. 801.

20. Quoted by Sara Lobman, "UNICEF Development Index Ranks Cuba First," in *The Militant,* 9 June 1989, p. 8.

21. The South African population estimation for 1990 is 39,550,000. Of these, 73% are black or African, 18% are white, 3% are coloured, and 3% are Asian. Hoffman, *The World Almanac and Book of Facts 1992,* p. 801.

22. Henry O. Oruka, "Four Trends in Current African Philosophy," *Philosophy in the Present Situation of Africa,* ed. Alwin Diemer (Wiesbaden: Franz Steiner Verlag, 1981).

23. On this point, see Mandela's article on American imperialism in *The Struggle Is My Life,* pp. 72–77.

24. Peter O. Bodunrin, "The Question of African Philosophy," in *African Philosophy: The Essential Readings,* ed. Tsenay Serequeberhan (New York: Paragon House, 1991), pp. 69–71.

25. The Manifesto is printed in Mandela, *The Struggle Is My Life,* pp. 11–20.

26. Mandela, *The Struggle Is My Life,* p. 12.

27. Tsenay Serequeberhan, "African Philosophy: The Point in Question" in *African Philosophy: The Essential Reading,* ed. Tsenay Serequeberhan, pp. 3–28. See also Serequeberhan editorial introduction to this anthology (xvii–xxii).

28. The text of the *1949 Programme of Action* is printed in Mandela, *The Struggle Is My Life,* pp. 28–30.

29. See Mandela's testimony during the Treason Trial (1956–1960) in Mandela, *The Struggle Is My Life,* p. 91.

30. The 1961 *Umkhonto we Sizwe* Manifesto is printed in Mandela, *The Struggle Is My Life,* pp. 122–123.

31. I am indebted to my colleague, Dr. Parker English. He read earlier versions of this paper and provided constructive suggestions.

DISCUSSION QUESTIONS

1. What assumptions about moral and civil rights do you think were implied in the former apartheid doctrine in South Africa, and how would this be similar to or different from the "natural rights tradition"?

2. What negative rights do you think all people have? What positive rights do you think all people have? Explain.

3. Where would you locate yourself on Kalumba's continuum between "radical capitalism" and "radical socialism"? Why?

4. How would you compare Mandela's beliefs regarding the struggle for racial equality, as characterized by Kalumba, with the beliefs of Martin Luther King Jr. on the same subject?

62. Mohandas K. Gandhi (1869–1948)
From *Nonviolent Resistance*

〰 Mohandas Gandhi was an Indian political activist and spiritual leader of the movement to liberate India from British colonial rule in the first half of the twentieth century. He was born in Porbandar, India, into a family belonging to the Vaishya caste (in traditional Hinduism, the merchant class, ranking third in social status of the four original castes). His formal education included law school in London, after which he returned to India to practice as an attorney. Soon finding the practice of law unsatisfactory, Gandhi went to South Africa in 1893, when it also was under British rule. There he found that the laws of the land were harshly discriminatory in the treatment of Indians as well as the other nonwhite peoples, and for the next twenty-one years he fought for Indian civil rights in South Africa.

Gandhi returned to India in 1915 and spent the rest of his life committed to that country's independence and establishment as a multiethnic, democratic state. This goal was achieved in 1947, but the partition into two nations of India and Pakistan mainly contributed to the already existing strife between Hindus and Muslims. As the recognized (though unofficial) leader of the country, Gandhi now found himself constantly working for peace between these two groups. At the age of 78, he was assassinated in New Delhi by a high-born Hindu opposed to Gandhi's program of social inclusiveness and mutual respect among all peoples and religions.

The selection consists of excerpts from *Nonviolent Resistance*, a collection of his writings spanning a number of decades. As was the case with Martin Luther King Jr., who was influenced significantly by his work, Gandhi provides a philosophical and spiritual foundation for the strategies of nonviolent direct action and civil disobedience he employed in the struggle against social oppression wherever he found it. Gandhi's legacy continues to be a powerful one internationally, especially with respect to the ongoing attempts not only to resolve conflicts in a truly peaceful manner around the world but also to change people's thinking about the assumed appropriateness of violence itself as a means of achieving individual or collective goals.

QUESTIONS FOR CRITICAL READING

1. According to Gandhi, what is "Satyagraha," and what is its goal?
2. How does Gandhi argue for the inseparability of means and ends in the struggle against injustice?
3. How does Gandhi characterize recorded "history," and what does that have to do with the success of Satyagraha in human life?
4. How does Gandhi argue against the position that people should always obey existing laws, whether they are good or bad laws?

TERM TO NOTE

"between Scylla and Charybdis": To be in a perilous situation between opposing dangers. In ancient Greek and Roman mythology, the monster Scylla inhabited a rock of the same name on the Italian coast and threatened those sailing by; Charybdis was a huge whirlpool opposite Scylla on the Sicilian coast.

———

3

*Satyagraha**

For the past thirty years I have been preaching and practising Satyagraha. The principles of Satyagraha, as I know it today, constitute a gradual evolution.

Satyagraha differs from Passive Resistance as the North Pole from the South. The latter has been conceived as a weapon of the weak and does not exclude the use of physical force or violence for the purpose of gaining one's end, whereas the former has been conceived as a weapon of the strongest and excludes the use of violence in any shape or form.

The term *Satyagraha* was coined by me in South Africa to express the force that the Indians there used for full eight years and it was coined in order to distin-

———

*Extract from a Statement by Gandhiji to the Hunter Committee.

guish it from the movement then going on in the United Kingdom and South Africa under the name of Passive Resistance.

Its root meaning is holding on to truth, hence truth-force. I have also called it Love-force or Soul-force. In the application of Satyagraha I discovered in the earliest stages that pursuit of truth did not admit of violence being inflicted on one's opponent but that he must be weaned from error by patience and sympathy. For what appears to be truth to the one may appear to be error to the other. And patience means self-suffering. So the doctrine came to mean vindication of truth not by infliction of suffering on the opponent but on one's self.

But on the political field the struggle on behalf of the people mostly consists in opposing error in the shape of unjust laws. When you have failed to bring the error home to the lawgiver by way of petitions and the like, the only remedy open to you, if you do not wish to submit to error, is to compel him by physical force to yield to you or by suffering in your own person by inviting the penalty for the breach of the law. Hence Satyagraha largely appears to the public as Civil Disobedience or Civil Resistance. It is civil in the sense that it is not criminal.

The lawbreaker breaks the law surreptitiously and tries to avoid the penalty, not so the civil resister. He ever obeys the laws of the State to which he belongs, not out of fear of the sanctions but because he considers them to be good for the welfare of society. But there come occasions, generally rare, when he considers certain laws to be so unjust as to render obedience to them a dishonour. He then openly and civilly breaks them and quietly suffers the penalty for their breach. And in order to register his protest against the action of the law givers, it is open to him to withdraw his co-operation from the State by disobeying such other laws whose breach does not involve moral turpitude.

In my opinion, the beauty and efficacy of Satyagraha are so great and the doctrine so simple that it can be preached even to children. It was preached by me to thousands of men, women and children commonly called indentured Indians with excellent results.

Rowlatt Bills

When the Rowlatt Bills were published I felt that they were so restrictive of human liberty that they must be resisted to the utmost. I observed too that the opposition to them was universal among Indians. I submit that no State however despotic has the right to enact laws which are repugnant to the whole body of the people, much less a Government guided by constitutional usage and precedent such as the Indian Government. I felt too that the oncoming agitation needed a definite direction if it was neither to collapse nor to run into violent channels.

The Sixth April

I ventured therefore to present Satyagraha to the country emphasizing its civil-resistance aspect. And as it is purely an inward and purifying movement I suggested the observance of fast, prayer and suspension of all work for one day—the 6th of April. There was a magnificent response throughout the length and breadth of India even in little villages although there was no organization and no great previous preparation. The idea was given to the public as soon as it was conceived. On the 6th April there was no violence used by the people and no collision with the police worth naming. The *hartal* was purely voluntary and spontaneous. I attach hereto the letter in which the idea was announced.

My Arrest

The observance of the 6th April was to be followed by Civil Disobedience. For the purpose the committee of the Satyagraha Sabha had selected certain political laws for disobedience. And we commenced the distribution of prohibited literature of a perfectly healthy type, e.g., a pamphlet written by me on Home Rule, a translation of Ruskin's *Unto This Last*, *The Defence and Death of Socrates*, etc.

Disorder

But there is no doubt that the 6th of April found India vitalized as never before. The people who were fear-stricken ceased to fear authority. Moreover, hitherto the masses had lain inert. The leaders had not really acted upon them. They were undisciplined. They had found a new force but they did not know what it was and how to use it.

At Delhi the leaders found it difficult to restrain the very large number of people who had remained un-moved before. At Amritsar, Dr Satyapal was anxious that I should go there and show to the people the peaceful nature of Satyagraha. Swami Shraddhanandji from Delhi and Dr Satyapal from Amritsar wrote to me asking me to go to their respective places for pacifying the people and for explaining to them the nature of Satyagraha. I had never been to Amritsar and for that matter to the Punjab before. These two messages were sent by the authorities and they knew that I was invited to both the places for peaceful purposes.

I left Bombay for Delhi and the Punjab on the 8th April and had telegraphed to Dr Satyapal whom I had never met before to meet me at Delhi. But after passing Mathura I was served with an order prohibiting me from entering the Province of Delhi. I felt that I was bound to disregard this order and I proceeded on my journey. At Palwal I was served with an order prohibiting me from entering the Punjab and confining me to the Bombay Presidency. And I was arrested by a party of Police and taken off the train at that station. The Superintendent of the Police who arrested me acted with every courtesy. I was taken to Mathura by the first available train and thence by goods train early in the morning to Siwai Madhupur, where I joined the Bombay Mail from Peshawar and was taken charge of by Superintendent Bowring. I was discharged at Bombay on the 10th April.

But the people of Ahmedabad and Viramgam and in Gujarat generally had heard of my arrest. They became furious, shops were closed, crowds gathered and murder, arson, pillage, wire-cutting and attempts at derailment followed.

Young India, 14-1-'20

4

Means and Ends

Reader: Why should we not obtain our goal, which is good, by any means whatsoever, even by using violence? Shall I think of the means when I have to deal with a thief in the house? My duty is to drive him out anyhow. You seem to admit that we have received nothing, and that we shall receive nothing by petitioning. Why, then, may we not do so by using brute force? And, to retain what we may receive we shall keep up the fear by using the same force to the extent that it

may be necessary. You will not find fault with a continuance of force to prevent a child from thrusting its foot into fire? Somehow or other we have to gain our end.

Editor: Your reasoning is plausible. It has deluded many. I have used similar arguments before now. But I think I know better now, and I shall endeavour to undeceive you. Let us first take the argument that we are justified in gaining our end by using brute force because the English gained theirs by using similar means. It is perfectly true that they used brute force and that it is possible for us to do likewise, but by using similar means we can get only the same thing that they got. You will admit that we do not want that. Your belief that there is no connection between the means and the end is a great mistake. Through that mistake even men who have been considered religious have committed grievous crimes. Your reasoning is the same as saying that we can get a rose through planting a noxious weed. If I want to cross the ocean, I can do so only by means of a vessel; if I were to use a cart for that purpose, both the cart and I would soon find the bottom. "As is the God, so is the votary", is a maxim worth considering. Its meaning has been distorted and men have gone astray. The means may be likened to a seed, the end to a tree; and there is just the same inviolable connection between the means and the end as there is between the seed and the tree. I am not likely to obtain the result flowing from the worship of God by laying myself prostrate before Satan. If, therefore, any one were to say: "I want to worship God; it does not matter that I do so by means of Satan," it would be set down as ignorant folly. We reap exactly as we sow. The English in 1833 obtained greater voting power by violence. Did they by using brute force better appreciate their duty? They wanted the right of voting, which they obtained by using physical force. But real rights are a result of performance of duty; these rights they have not obtained. We, therefore, have before us in England the force of everybody wanting and insisting on his rights, nobody thinking of his duty. And, where everybody wants rights, who shall give them to whom? I do not wish to imply that they do no duties. They don't perform the duties corresponding to those rights; and as they do not perform that particular duty, namely, acquire fitness, their rights have proved a burden to them. In other words, what they have obtained is an exact result of the means they adopted. They used the means corresponding to the end. If I want to deprive you of your watch, I shall certainly have to fight for it; if I want to buy your watch, I shall have to pay for it; and if I want a gift, I shall have to plead for it; and, according to the means I employ, the watch is stolen property, my own property, or a donation. Thus we see three different results from three different means. Will you still say that means do not matter?

Now we shall take the example given by you of the thief to be driven out. I do not agree with you that the thief may be driven out by any means. If it is my father who has come to steal I shall use one kind of means. If it is an acquaintance I shall use another; and in the case of a perfect stranger I shall use a third. If it is a white man, you will perhaps say you will use means different from those you will adopt with an Indian thief. If it is a weakling, the means will be different from those to be adopted for dealing with an equal in physical strength; and if the thief is armed from top to toe, I shall simply remain quiet. Thus we have a variety of means between the father and the armed man. Again, I fancy that I should pretend to be sleeping whether the thief was my father or that strong armed man. The reason for this is that my father would also be armed and I should succumb to the strength possessed by either and allow my things to be stolen. The strength of my father would make me weep with pity; the strength of the armed man would rouse in me anger and we should become enemies. Such is the curious situation. From these examples we may not be able to agree as to the means to be adopted in each case. I myself seem clearly to see what should be done in all these cases, but the remedy may frighten you. I therefore hesitate to place it before you. For the time being I will leave you to guess it, and if you cannot, it is clear you will have to adopt different means in each case. You will also have seen that any means will not avail to drive away the thief. You will have to adopt means to fit each case. Hence it follows that your duty is not to drive away the thief by any means you like.

Let us proceed a little further. That well-armed man has stolen your property; you have harboured the thought of his act; you are filled with anger; you argue that you want to punish that rogue, not for your own sake, but for the good of your neighbours; you have collected a number of armed men, you want to take

his house by assault; he is duly informed of it, he runs away; he too is incensed. He collects his brother robbers, and sends you a defiant message that he will commit robbery in broad daylight. You are strong, you do not fear him, you are prepared to receive him. Meanwhile, the robber pesters your neighbours. They complain before you. You reply that you are doing all for their sake, you do not mind that your own goods have been stolen. Your neighbours reply that the robber never pestered them before, and that he commenced his depredations only after you declared hostilities against him. You are between Scylla and Charybdis. You are full of pity for the poor men. What they say is true. What are you to do? You will be disgraced if you now leave the robber alone. You, therefore, tell the poor men: "Never mind. Come, my wealth is yours, I will give you arms, I will teach you how to use them; you should belabour the rogue; don't you leave him alone." And so the battle grows; the robbers increase in numbers; your neighbours have deliberately put themselves to inconvenience. Thus the result of wanting to take revenge upon the robber is that you have disturbed your own peace; you are in perpetual fear of being robbed and assaulted; your courage has given place to cowardice. If you will patiently examine the argument, you will see that I have not overdrawn the picture. This is one of the means. Now let us examine the other. You set this armed robber down as an ignorant brother; you intend to reason with him at a suitable opportunity; you argue that he is, after all, a fellow man; you do not know what prompted him to steal. You, therefore, decide that, when you can, you will destroy the man's motive for stealing. Whilst you are thus reasoning with yourself, the man comes again to steal. Instead of being angry with him you take pity on him. You think that this stealing habit must be a disease with him. Henceforth, you, therefore, keep your doors and windows open, you change your sleeping-place, and you keep your things in a manner most accessible to him. The robber comes again and is confused as all this is new to him; nevertheless, he takes away your things. But his mind is agitated. He inquires about you in the village, he comes to learn about your broad and loving heart, he repents, he begs your pardon, returns you your things, and leaves off the stealing habit. He becomes your servant, and you will find for him honourable employment.

This is the second method. Thus, you see, different means have brought about totally different results. I do not wish to deduce from this that robbers will act in the above manner or that all will have the same pity and love like you, but I only wish to show that fair means alone can produce fair results, and that, at least in the majority of cases, if not indeed in all, the force of love and pity is infinitely greater than the force of arms. There is harm in the exercise of brute force, never in that of pity.

Now we will take the question of petitioning. It is a fact beyond dispute that a petition, without the backing of force, is useless. However, the late Justice Ranade used to say that petitions served a useful purpose because they were a means of educating people. They give the latter an idea of their condition and warn the rulers. From this point of view, they are not altogether useless. A petition of an equal is a sign of courtesy; a petition from a slave is a symbol of his slavery. A petition backed by force is a petition from an equal and, when he transmits his demand in the form of a petition, it testifies to his nobility. Two kinds of force can back petitions. "We shall hurt you if you do not give this," is one kind of force; it is the force of arms, whose evil results we have already examined. The second kind of force can thus be stated: "If you do not concede our demand, we shall be no longer your petitioners. You can govern us only so long as we remain the governed; we shall no longer have any dealings with you." The force implied in this may be described as love-force, soul-force, or, more popularly but less accurately, passive resistance. This force is indestructible. He who uses it perfectly understands his position. We have an ancient proverb which literally means: "One negative cures thirty-six diseases." The force of arms is powerless when matched against the force of love or the soul.

Now we shall take your last illustration, that of the child thrusting its foot into fire. It will not avail you. What do you really do to the child? Supposing that it can exert so much physical force that it renders you powerless and rushes into fire, then you cannot prevent it. There are only two remedies open to you— either you must kill it in order to prevent it from perishing in the flames, or you must give your own life because you do not wish to see it perish before your very eyes. You will not kill it. If your heart is not quite full of pity, it is possible that you will not surrender yourself by preceding the child and going into the fire yourself. You, therefore, helplessly allow it to go to the flames. Thus, at any rate, you are not using physical force. I hope you will not consider that it is still physical force, though of a low order, when you would forcibly prevent the child from rushing towards the fire if you could. That force is of a different order and we have to understand what it is.

Remember that, in thus preventing the child, you are minding entirely its own interest, you are exercising authority for its sole benefit. Your example does not apply to the English. In using brute force against the English you consult entirely your own, that is the national, interest. There is no question here either of pity or of love. If you say that the actions of the English, being evil, represent fire, and that they proceed to their actions through ignorance, and that therefore they occupy the position of a child and that you want to protect such a child, then you will have to overtake every evil action of that kind by whomsoever committed and, as in the case of the evil child, you will have to sacrifice yourself. If you are capable of such immeasurable pity, I wish you well in its exercise.

Hind Swaraj or Indian Home Rule, chap. XVI

5

Satyagraha or Passive Resistance

Reader: Is there any historical evidence as to the success of what you have called soul-force or truth-force? No instance seems to have happened of any nation having risen through soul-force. I still think that the evil-doers will not cease doing evil without physical punishment.

Editor: The poet Tulsidas has said: "Of religion, pity, or love, is the root, as egotism of the body. Therefore, we should not abandon pity so long as we are alive." This appears to me to be a scientific truth. I believe in it as much as I believe in two and two being four. The force of love is the same as the force of the soul or truth. We have evidence of its working at every step. The universe would disappear without the existence of that force. But you ask for historical evidence. It is, therefore, necessary to know what history means. The Gujarati equivalent means: "It so happened". If that is the meaning of history, it is possible to give copious evidence. But, if it means the doings of kings and emperors, there can be no evidence of soul-force or passive resistance in such history. You cannot expect silver ore in a tin mine. History, as we know it, is a record of the wars of the world, and so there is a proverb among Englishmen that a nation which has no history, that is, no wars, is a happy nation. How kings played, how they became enemies of one another, how they murdered one another, is found accurately recorded in history, and if this were all that had happened in the world, it would have been ended long ago. If the story of the universe had commenced with wars, not a man would have been found alive today. Those people who have been warred against have disappeared as, for instance, the natives of Australia of whom hardly a man was left alive by the intruders. Mark, please, that these natives did not use soul-force in self-defence, and it does not require much foresight to know that the Australians will share the same fate as their victims. "Those that take the sword shall perish by the Sword." With us the proverb is that professional swimmers will find a watery grave.

The fact that there are so many men still alive in the world shows that it is based not on the force of arms but on the force of truth or love. Therefore, the greatest and most unimpeachable evidence of the success of this force is to be found in the fact that, in spite of the wars of the world, it still lives on.

Thousands, indeed tens of thousands, depend for their existence on a very active working of this force. Little quarrels of millions of families in their daily lives disappear before the exercise of this force. Hundreds of nations live in peace. History does not and cannot take note of this fact. History is really a record of every interruption of the even working of the force of love or of the soul. Two brothers quarrel; one of them repents and re-awakens the love that was lying dormant in him; the two again begin to live in peace; nobody takes note of this. But if the two brothers, through the intervention of solicitors or some other reason, take up arms or go to law—which is another form of the exhibition of brute force—their doing would be im-

mediately noticed in the press, they would be the talk of their neighbours and would probably go down to history. And what is true of families and communities is true of nations. There is no reason to believe that there is one law for families and another for nations. History, then, is a record of an interruption of the course of nature. Soul-force, being natural, is not noted in history.

Reader: According to what you say, it is plain that instances of this kind of passive resistance are not to be found in history. It is necessary to understand this passive resistance more fully. It will be better, therefore, if you enlarge upon it.

Editor: Passive resistance is a method of securing rights by personal suffering; it is the reverse of resistance by arms. When I refuse to do a thing that is repugnant to my conscience, I use soul-force. For instance, the Government of the day has passed a law which is applicable to me. I do not like it. If by using violence I force the Government to repeal the law, I am employing what may be termed body-force. If I do not obey the law and accept the penalty for its breach, I use soul-force. It involves sacrifice of self.

Everybody admits that sacrifice of self is infinitely superior to sacrifice of others. Moreover, if this kind of force is used in a cause that is unjust, only the person using it suffers. He does not make others suffer for his mistakes. Men have before now done many things which were subsequently found to have been wrong. No man can claim that he is absolutely in the right or that a particular thing is wrong because he thinks so, but it is wrong for him so long as that is his deliberate judgment. It is therefore meet that he should not do that which he knows to be wrong, and suffer the consequence whatever it may be. This is the key to the use of soul-force.

Reader: You would then disregard laws—this is rank disloyalty. We have always been considered a law-abiding nation. You seem to be going even beyond the extremists. They say that we must obey the laws that have been passed, but that if the laws be bad, we must drive out the law-givers even by force.

Editor: Whether I go beyond them or whether I do not is a matter of no consequence to either of us. We simply want to find out what is right and to act accordingly. The real meaning of the statement that we are a law-abiding nation is that we are passive resisters. When we do not like certain laws, we do not break the heads of law-givers but we suffer and do not submit to the laws. That we should obey laws whether good or bad is a newfangled notion. There was no such thing in former days. The people disregarded those laws they did not like and suffered the penalties for their breach. It is contrary to our manhood if we obey laws repugnant to our conscience. Such teaching is opposed to religion and means slavery. If the Government were to ask us to go about without any clothing, should we do so? If I were a passive resister, I would say to them that I would have nothing to do with their law. But we have so forgotten ourselves and become so compliant that we do not mind any degrading law.

A man who has realized his manhood, who fears only God, will fear no one else. Man-made laws are not necessarily binding on him. Even the Government does not expect any such thing from us. They do not say: "You must do such and such a thing," but they say: "If you do not do it, we will punish you." We are sunk so low that we fancy that it is our duty and our religion to do what the law lays down. If man will only realize that it is unmanly to obey laws that are unjust, no man's tyranny will enslave him. This is the key to self-rule or home-rule.

It is a superstition and ungodly thing to believe that an act of a majority binds a minority. Many examples can be given in which acts of majorities will be found to have been wrong and those of minorities to have been right. All reforms owe their origin to the initiation of minorities in opposition to majorities. If among a band of robbers a knowledge of robbing is obligatory, is a pious man to accept the obligation? So long as the superstition that men should obey unjust laws exists, so long will their slavery exist. And a passive resister alone can remove such a superstition.

To use brute-force, to use gunpowder, is contrary to passive resistance, for it means that we want our opponent to do by force that which we desire but he does not. And, if such a use of force is justifiable, surely he is entitled to do likewise by us. And so we should never come to an agreement. We may simply fancy, like the blind horse moving in a circle round a mill, that we are making progress. Those who believe that they are not bound to obey laws which are repugnant to their conscience have only the remedy of passive resistance open to them. Any other must lead to disaster.

Hind Swaraj or Indian Home Rule, chap. XVII

DISCUSSION QUESTIONS

1. Do you agree with Gandhi that Satyagraha, or "soul-force" (eventually, "truth-force"), is "natural" in human relations and thus much more common than violent conflict? Why or why not?

2. Do you agree with Gandhi that nonviolence is almost always more effective than violence in conflict resolution and resisting injustice or harm? Why or why not?

3. Do you agree with Gandhi that the nature of the means we use essentially affects the ends we seek? Why or why not? What are some examples that would strengthen or weaken his position here?

4. What are the similarities and differences between the social circumstances of Gandhi and King, the political struggles they were involved in, and the moral and spiritual principles they advocated?

63. Noam Chomsky (b. 1928)
"Democracy and the Media"

Noam Chomsky was born in Philadelphia, studied at Pennsylvania and Harvard universities, and eventually became professor of linguistics at the Massachusetts Institute of Technology, where he is currently Institute Professor in the Department of Linguistics and Philosophy. In the 1950s he developed a new theory of language called transformational generative grammar, which effectively transformed the whole field. In the last few decades he has become almost as well known internationally for his political writing and social activism and has published dozens of books on a variety of global and domestic issues. In all these works he has been a

strong advocate for human rights and increased democratization in social life, and a relentless critic of political
and economic power elites who try to maintain their position of domination and control regardless of the cost
to the majority of peoples affected.

The following selection is taken from the first chapter
of Chomsky's 1989 book *Necessary Illusions,* and in it he
examines the role of the mass media primarily in contemporary capitalist democracies. Especially regarding
the press in the United States, he shows that it is neither
"open" nor "free" except in the most formal, superficial,
and ultimately deceptive sense of those terms. As he
points out, this reality is contrary to the dominant images disseminated by those in the mass media business
to portray their profession; so it is unsurprising that
those (like himself) who expose the actual dynamics and
motivations underlying "news" gathering and presentation are either vilified or ignored as irrelevant in media-
controlled discussion of the media itself. In Chomsky's
view, the usually denied but actual role of the corporate
media in large affluent societies like the United States
involves narrowing the range of acceptable inquiry and
debate regarding the foreign and domestic policies of the
government and the large business interests (including
those of media conglomerates) that it serves. The effect
of this is to provide support for those policies, treating
them as unchallengeable at a more basic level even while
allowing for minor disagreements about details on the
surface. Such a constricting of information and public
discourse undermines the viability of a truly democratic
society.

QUESTIONS FOR CRITICAL READING

1. How does Chomsky critically analyze the mainstream claims about the so-called free market of
   ideas and its effect on the media in capitalist
   democracies?
2. What is the "propaganda model" of how the
   mass media function, and how does Chomsky
   argue for it?
3. According to Chomsky, what is the predominant
   conception of democracy in the United States,
   and how is it linked to John Jay's maxim, "The
   people who own the country ought to govern it"?
4. In Chomsky's account, what is "the manufacture
   of consent," and what is its impact on contemporary social life?

TERMS TO NOTE

desideratum: Something desired or needed.
jingoism: Nationalist chauvinism; aggressive patriotism.
rapporteur: A French term, in this context meaning
   the chairperson of a commission.

Under the heading "Brazilian bishops support plan to
democratize media," a church-based South American
journal describes a proposal being debated in the
constituent assembly that "would open up Brazil's powerful and highly concentrated media to citizen participation." "Brazil's Catholic bishops are among the
principal advocates [of this] . . . legislative proposal to
democratize the country's communications media,"
the report continues, noting that "Brazilian TV is in
the hands of five big networks [while] . . . eight huge
multinational corporations and various state enterprises account for the majority of all communications
advertising." The proposal "envisions the creation of a
National Communications Council made up of civil-
ian and government representatives [that] . . . would
develop a democratic communications policy and
grant licenses to radio and television operations." "The
Brazilian Conference of Catholic Bishops has repeatedly stressed the importance of the communications
media and pushed for grassroots participation. It has
chosen communications as the theme of its 1989
Lenten campaign," an annual "parish-level campaign
of reflection about some social issue" initiated by the
Bishops' Conference.[1]

The questions raised by the Brazilian bishops are
being seriously discussed in many parts of the world.
Projects exploring them are under way in several Latin
American countries and elsewhere. There has been
discussion of a "New World Information Order" that
would diversify media access and encourage alternatives to the global media system dominated by the
Western industrial powers. A UNESCO inquiry into
such possibilities elicited an extremely hostile reaction
in the United States.[2] The alleged concern was freedom of the press. Among the questions I would like to
raise as we proceed are: just how serious is this concern, and what is its substantive content? Further
questions that lie in the background have to do with a

democratic communications policy: what it might be, whether it is a desideratum, and if so, whether it is attainable. And, more generally, just what kind of democratic order is it to which we aspire?

The concept of "democratizing the media" has no real meaning within the terms of political discourse in the United States. In fact, the phrase has a paradoxical or even vaguely subversive ring to it. Citizen participation would be considered an infringement on freedom of the press, a blow struck against the independence of the media that would distort the mission they have undertaken to inform the public without fear or favor. The reaction merits some thought. Underlying it are beliefs about how the media do function and how they should function within our democratic systems, and also certain implicit conceptions of the nature of democracy. Let us consider these topics in turn.

The standard image of media performance, as expressed by Judge Gurfein in a decision rejecting government efforts to bar publication of the *Pentagon Papers,* is that we have "a cantankerous press, an obstinate press, a ubiquitous press," and that these tribunes of the people "must be suffered by those in authority in order to preserve the even greater values of freedom of expression and the right of the people to know." Commenting on this decision, Anthony Lewis of the *New York Times* observes that the media were not always as independent, vigilant, and defiant of authority as they are today, but in the Vietnam and Watergate eras they learned to exercise "the power to root about in our national life, exposing what they deem right for exposure," without regard to external pressures or the demands of state or private power. This too is a commonly held belief.[3]

There has been much debate over the media during this period, but it does not deal with the problem of "democratizing the media" and freeing them from the constraints of state and private power. Rather, the issue debated is whether the media have not exceeded proper bounds in escaping such constraints, even threatening the existence of democratic institutions in their contentious and irresponsible defiance of authority. A 1975 study on "governability of democracies" by the Trilateral Commission concluded that the media have become a "notable new source of national power," one aspect of an "excess of democracy" that contributes to "the reduction of governmental authority" at home and a consequent "decline in the influence of democracy abroad." This general "crisis of democracy," the commission held, resulted from the efforts of previously marginalized sectors of the population to organize and press their demands, thereby creating an overload that prevents the democratic process from functioning properly.

. . .

Two kinds of questions arise in connection with these vigorous debates about the media and democracy: questions of fact and questions of value. The basic question of fact is whether the media have indeed adopted an adversarial stance, perhaps with excessive zeal; whether, in particular, they undermine the defense of freedom in wartime and threaten free institutions by "flagellating ourselves" and those in power. If so, we may then ask whether it would be proper to impose some external constraints to ensure that they keep to the bounds of responsibility, or whether we should adopt the principle expressed by Justice Holmes, in a classic dissent, that "the best test of truth is the power of the thought to get itself accepted in the competition of the market" through "free trade in ideas."[4]

The question of fact is rarely argued; the case is assumed to have been proven. Some, however, have held that the factual premises are simply false. Beginning with the broadest claims, let us consider the functioning of the free market of ideas. In his study of the mobilization of popular opinion to promote state power, Benjamin Ginsberg maintains that

> western governments have used market mechanisms to regulate popular perspectives and sentiments. The "marketplace of ideas," built during the nineteenth and twentieth centuries, effectively disseminates the beliefs and ideas of the upper classes while subverting the ideological and cultural independence of the lower classes. Through the construction of this marketplace, western governments forged firm and enduring links between socioeconomic position and ideological power, permitting upper classes to use each to buttress the other . . . In the United States, in particular, the ability of the upper and upper-middle classes to dominate the marketplace of ideas has generally allowed these strata

to shape the entire society's perception of political reality and the range of realistic political and social possibilities. While westerners usually equate the marketplace with freedom of opinion, the hidden hand of the market can be almost as potent an instrument of control as the iron fist of the state.[5]

Ginsberg's conclusion has some initial plausibility, on assumptions about the functioning of a guided free market that are not particularly controversial. Those segments of the media that can reach a substantial audience are major corporations and are closely integrated with even larger conglomerates. Like other businesses, they sell a product to buyers. Their market is advertisers, and the "product" is audiences, with a bias towards more wealthy audiences, which improve advertising rates.[6] Over a century ago, British Liberals observed that the market would promote those journals "enjoying the preference of the advertising public"; and today, Paul Johnson, noting the demise of a new journal of the left, blandly comments that it deserved its fate: "The market pronounced an accurate verdict at the start by declining to subscribe all the issue capital," and surely no right-thinking person could doubt that the market represents the public will.[7]

In short, the major media—particularly, the elite media that set the agenda that others generally follow—are corporations "selling" privileged audiences to other businesses. It would hardly come as a surprise if the picture of the world they present were to reflect the perspectives and interests of the sellers, the buyers, and the product. Concentration of ownership of the media is high and increasing.[8] Furthermore, those who occupy managerial positions in the media, or gain status within them as commentators, belong to the same privileged elites, and might be expected to share the perceptions, aspirations, and attitudes of their associates, reflecting their own class interests as well. Journalists entering the system are unlikely to make their way unless they conform to these ideological pressures, generally by internalizing the values; it is not easy to say one thing and believe another, and those who fail to conform will tend to be weeded out by familiar mechanisms.

The influence of advertisers is sometimes far more direct. "Projects unsuitable for corporate sponsorship tend to die on the vine," the London *Economist* observes, noting that "stations have learned to be sympathetic to the most delicate sympathies of corporations." The journal cites the case of public TV station WNET, which "lost its corporate underwriting from Gulf+Western as a result of a documentary called 'Hunger for Profit,' about multinationals buying up huge tracts of land in the third world." These actions "had not been those of a friend," Gulf's chief executive wrote to the station, adding that the documentary was "virulently anti-business, if not anti-American." "Most people believe that WNET would not make the same mistake today," the *Economist* concludes.[9] Nor would others. The warning need only be implicit.

Many other factors induce the media to conform to the requirements of the state-corporate nexus.[10] To confront power is costly and difficult; high standards of evidence and argument are imposed, and critical analysis is naturally not welcomed by those who are in a position to react vigorously and to determine the array of rewards and punishments. Conformity to a "patriotic agenda," in contrast, imposes no such costs. Charges against official enemies barely require substantiation; they are, furthermore, protected from correction, which can be dismissed as apologetics for the criminals or as missing the forest for the trees. The system protects itself with indignation against a challenge to the right of deceit in the service of power, and the very idea of subjecting the ideological system to rational inquiry elicits incomprehension or outrage, though it is often masked in other terms. [11] One who attributes the best intentions to the U.S. government, while perhaps deploring failure and ineptitude, requires no evidence for this stance, as when we ask why "success has continued to elude us" in the Middle East and Central America, why "a nation of such vast wealth, power and good intentions [cannot] accomplish its purposes more promptly and more effectively" (Landrum Bolling).[12] Standards are radically different when we observe that "good intentions" are not properties of states, and that the United States, like every other state past and present, pursues policies that reflect the interests of those who control the state by virtue of their domestic power, truisms that are hardly expressible in the mainstream, surprising as this fact may be.

One needs no evidence to condemn the Soviet Union for aggression in Afghanistan and support for repression in Poland; it is quite a different matter when one turns to U.S. aggression in Indochina or its efforts to prevent a political settlement of the Arab-Israeli conflict over many years, readily documented, but unwelcome and therefore a non-fact. No argument is demanded for a condemnation of Iran or Libya for state-supported terrorism; discussion of the prominent—arguably dominant—role of the United States and its clients in organizing and conducting this plague of the modern era elicits only horror and contempt for this view point; supporting evidence, however compelling, is dismissed as irrelevant. As a matter of course, the media and intellectual journals either praise the U.S. government for dedicating itself to the struggle for democracy in Nicaragua or criticize it for the means it has employed to pursue this laudable objective, offering no evidence that this is indeed the goal of policy. A challenge to the underlying patriotic assumption is virtually unthinkable within the mainstream and, if permitted expression, would be dismissed as a variety of ideological fanaticism, an absurdity, even if backed by overwhelming evidence—not a difficult task in this case.

Case by case, we find that conformity is the easy way, and the path to privilege and prestige; dissidence carries personal costs that may be severe, even in a society that lacks such means of control as death squads, psychiatric prisons, or extermination camps. The very structure of the media is designed to induce conformity to established doctrine. In a three-minute stretch between commercials, or in seven hundred words, it is impossible to present unfamiliar thoughts or surprising conclusions with the argument and evidence required to afford them some credibility. Regurgitation of welcome pieties faces no such problem.

It is a natural expectation, on uncontroversial assumptions, that the major media and other ideological institutions will generally reflect the perspectives and interests of established power. That this expectation is fulfilled has been argued by a number of analysts. Edward Herman and I have published extensive documentation, separately and jointly, to support a conception of how the media function that differs sharply from the standard version.[13] According to this "propaganda model"—which has prior plausibility for such reasons as those just briefly reviewed—the media serve the interests of state and corporate power, which are closely interlinked, framing their reporting and analysis in a manner supportive of established privilege and limiting debate and discussion accordingly. We have studied a wide range of examples, including those that provide the most severe test for a propaganda model, namely, the cases that critics of alleged anti-establishment excesses of the media offer as their strongest ground: the coverage of the Indochina wars, the Watergate affair, and others drawn from the period when the media are said to have overcome the conformism of the past and taken on a crusading role. To subject the model to a fair test, we have systematically selected examples that are as closely paired as history allows: crimes attributable to official enemies versus those for which the United States and its clients bear responsibility; good deeds, specifically elections conducted by official enemies versus those in U.S. client states. Other methods have also been pursued, yielding further confirmation.

There are, by now, thousands of pages of documentation supporting the conclusions of the propaganda model. By the standards of the social sciences, it is very well confirmed, and its predictions are often considerably surpassed. If there is a serious challenge to this conclusion, I am unaware of it. The nature of the arguments presented against it, on the rare occasions when the topic can even be addressed in the mainstream, suggest that the model is indeed robust. The highly regarded Freedom House study, which is held to have provided the conclusive demonstration of the adversarial character of the media and its threat to democracy, collapses upon analysis, and when innumerable errors and misrepresentations are corrected, amounts to little more than a complaint that the media were too pessimistic in their pursuit of a righteous cause; I know of no other studies that fare better.[14]

There are, to be sure, other factors that influence the performance of social institutions as complex as the media, and one can find exceptions to the general pattern that the propaganda model predicts. Nevertheless, it has, I believe, been shown to provide a reasonably close first approximation, which captures essential properties of the media and the dominant intellectual culture more generally.

One prediction of the model is that it will be effectively excluded from discussion, for it questions a factual assumption that is most serviceable to the interests of established power: namely, that the media are adversarial and cantankerous, perhaps excessively so. However well-confirmed the model may be, then, it is inadmissible, and, the model predicts, should remain outside the spectrum of debate over the media. This conclusion too is empirically well-confirmed. Note that the model has a rather disconcerting feature. Plainly, it is either valid or invalid. If invalid, it may be dismissed; if valid, it *will* be dismissed. As in the case of eighteenth-century doctrine on seditious libel, truth is no defense; rather, it heightens the enormity of the crime of calling authority into disrepute.

If the conclusions drawn in the propaganda model are correct, then the criticisms of the media for their adversarial stance can only be understood as a demand that the media should not even reflect the range of debate over tactical questions among dominant elites, but should serve only those segments that happen to manage the state at a particular moment, and should do so with proper enthusiasm and optimism about the causes—noble by definition—in which state power is engaged. It would not have surprised George Orwell that this should be the import of the critique of the media by an organization that calls itself "Freedom House."[15]

Journalists often meet a high standard of professionalism in their work, exhibiting courage, integrity, and enterprise, including many of those who report for media that adhere closely to the predictions of the propaganda model. There is no contradiction here. What is at issue is not the honesty of the opinions expressed or the integrity of those who seek the facts but rather the choice of topics and highlighting of issues, the range of opinion permitted expression, the unquestioned premises that guide reporting and commentary, and the general framework imposed for the presentation of a certain view of the world. We need not, incidentally, tarry over such statements as the following, emblazoned on the cover of the *New Republic* during Israel's invasion of Lebanon: "Much of what you have read in the newspapers and newsmagazines about the war in Lebanon—and even more of what you have seen and heard on television—is simply not true."[16] Such performances can be consigned to the dismal archives of apologetics for the atrocities of other favored states.

I will present examples to illustrate the workings of the propaganda model, but will assume the basic case

to have been credibly established by the extensive material already in print. This work has elicited much outrage and falsification (some of which Herman and I review in *Manufacturing Consent,* some elsewhere), and also puzzlement and misunderstanding. But, to my knowledge, there is no serious effort to respond to these and other similar critiques. Rather, they are simply dismissed, in conformity to the predictions of the propaganda model.[17] Typically, debate over media performance within the mainstream includes criticism of the adversarial stance of the media and response by their defenders, but no critique of the media for adhering to the predictions of the propaganda model, or recognition that this might be a conceivable position. In the case of the Indochina wars, for example, U.S. public television presented a retrospective series in 1985 followed by a denunciation produced by the right-wing media-monitoring organization Accuracy in Media and a discussion limited to critics of the alleged adversarial excesses of the series and its defenders. No one argued that the series conforms to the expectations of the propaganda model—as it does. The study of media coverage of conflicts in the Third World mentioned earlier follows a similar pattern, which is quite consistent, though the public regards the media as too conformist.[18]

The media cheerfully publish condemnations of their "breathtaking lack of balance or even the appearance of fair-mindedness" and "the ills and dangers of today's wayward press."[19] But only when, as in this case, the critic is condemning the "media elite" for being "in thrall to liberal views of politics and human nature" and for the "evident difficulty most liberals have in using the word dictatorship to describe even the most flagrant dictatorships of the left"; surely one would never find Fidel Castro described as a dictator in the mainstream press, always so soft on Communism and given to self-flagellation.[20] Such diatribes are not expected to meet even minimal standards of evidence; this one contains exactly one reference to what conceivably might be a fact, a vague allusion to alleged juggling of statistics by the *New York Times* "to obscure the decline of interest rates during Ronald Reagan's first term," as though the matter had not been fully reported. Charges of this nature are often not unwelcome, first, because response is simple or superfluous; and second, because debate over this issue helps entrench the belief that the media are either independent and objective, with high standards of professional integrity and openness to all reasonable views, or, alternatively, that they are biased towards stylishly leftish flouting of authority. Either conclusion is quite acceptable to established power and privilege—even to the media elites themselves, who are not averse to the charge that they may have gone too far in pursuing their cantankerous and obstreperous ways in defiance of orthodoxy and power. The spectrum of discussion reflects what a propaganda model would predict: condemnation of "liberal bias" and defense against this charge, but not recognition of the possibility that "liberal bias" might simply be an expression of one variant of the narrow state-corporate ideology—as, demonstrably, it is—and a particularly useful variant, bearing the implicit message: thus far, and no further.

Returning to the proposals of the Brazilian bishops, one reason they would appear superfluous or wrongheaded if raised in our political context is that the media are assumed to be dedicated to service to the public good, if not too extreme in their independence of authority. They are thus performing their proper social role, as explained by Supreme Court Justice Powell in words quoted by Anthony Lewis in his defense of freedom of the press: "No individual can obtain for himself the information needed for the intelligent discharge of his political responsibilities . . . By enabling the public to assert meaningful control over the political process, the press performs a crucial function in effecting the societal purpose of the First Amendment."

An alternative view, which I believe is valid, is that the media indeed serve a "societal purpose," but quite a different one. It is the societal purpose served by state education as conceived by James Mill in the early days of the establishment of this system: to "train the minds of the people to a virtuous attachment to their government," and to the arrangements of the social, economic, and political order more generally.[21] Far from contributing to a "crisis of democracy" of the sort feared by the liberal establishment, the media are vigilant guardians protecting privilege from the threat of public understanding and participation. If these conclusions are correct, the first objection to democratizing the media is based on factual and analytic error.

A second basis for objection is more substantial, and not without warrant: the call for democratizing

the media could mask highly unwelcome efforts to limit intellectual independence through popular pressures, a variant of concerns familiar in political theory. The problem is not easily dismissed, but it is not an inherent property of democratization of the media.[22]

The basic issue seems to me to be a different one. Our political culture has a conception of democracy that differs from that of the Brazilian bishops. For them, democracy means that citizens should have the opportunity to inform themselves, to take part in inquiry and discussion and policy formation, and to advance their programs through political action. For us, democracy is more narrowly conceived: the citizen is a consumer, an observer but not a participant. The public has the right to ratify policies that originate elsewhere, but if these limits are exceeded, we have not democracy, but a "crisis of democracy," which must somehow be resolved.

This concept is based on doctrines laid down by the Founding Fathers. The Federalists, historian Joyce Appleby writes, expected "that the new American political institutions would continue to function within the old assumptions about a politically active elite and a deferential, compliant electorate," and "George Washington had hoped that his enormous prestige would bring that great, sober, commonsensical citizenry politicians are always addressing to see the dangers of self-created societies."[23] Despite their electoral defeat, their conception prevailed, though in a different form as industrial capitalism took shape. It was expressed by John Jay, the president of the Continental Congress and the first chief justice of the U.S. Supreme Court, in what his biographer calls one of his favorite maxims: "The people who own the country ought to govern it." And they need not be too gentle in the mode of governance. Alluding to rising disaffection, Gouverneur Morris wrote in a dispatch to John Jay in 1783 that although "it is probable that much of Convulsion will ensue," there need be no real concern: "The People are well prepared" for the government to assume "that Power without which Government is but a Name . . . Wearied with the War, their Acquiescence may be depended on with absolute Certainty, and you and I, my friend, know by Experience that when a few Men of sense and spirit get together and declare that they are the Authority, such few as are of a different opinion may easily be convinced of their Mistake by that powerful Argument the Halter." By "the People," constitutional historian Richard Morris observes, "he meant a small nationalist elite, whom he was too cautious to name"—the white propertied males for whom the constitutional order was established. The "vast exodus of Loyalists and blacks" to Canada and elsewhere reflected in part their insight into these realities.[24]

Elsewhere, Morris observes that in the post-revolutionary society, "what one had in effect was a political democracy manipulated by an elite," and in states where "egalitarian democracy" might appear to have prevailed (as in Virginia), in reality "dominance of the aristocracy was implicitly accepted." The same is true of the dominance of the rising business classes in later periods that are held to reflect the triumph of popular democracy.[25]

John Jay's maxim is, in fact, the principle on which the Republic was founded and maintained, and in its very nature capitalist democracy cannot stray far from this pattern for reasons that are readily perceived.[26]

At home, this principle requires that politics reduce, in effect, to interactions among groups of investors who compete for control of the state, in accordance with what Thomas Ferguson calls the "investment theory of politics," which, he argues plausibly, explains a large part of U.S. political history.[27] For our dependencies, the same basic principle entails that democracy is achieved when the society is under the control of local oligarchies, business-based elements linked to U.S. investors, the military under our control, and professionals who can be trusted to follow orders and serve the interests of U.S. power and privilege. If there is any popular challenge to their rule, the United States is entitled to resort to violence to "restore democracy"— to adopt the term conventionally used in reference to the Reagan Doctrine in Nicaragua. The media contrast the "democrats" with the "Communists," the former being those who serve the interests of U.S. power, the latter those afflicted with the disease called "ultranationalism" in secret planning documents, which explain, forthrightly, that the threat to our interests is "nationalistic regimes" that respond to domestic pressures for improvement of living standards and social reform, with insufficient regard for the needs of U.S. investors.

The media are only following the rules of the game when they contrast the "fledgling democracies" of Central America, under military and business control, with "Communist Nicaragua." And we can appreciate

why they suppressed the 1987 polls in El Salvador that revealed that a mere 10 percent of the population "believe that there is a process of democracy and freedom in the country at present." The benighted Salvadorans doubtless fail to comprehend our concept of democracy. And the same must be true of the editors of Honduras's leading journal *El Tiempo*. They see in their country a "democracy" that offers "unemployment and repression" in a caricature of the democratic process, and write that there can be no democracy in a country under "occupation of North American troops and contras," where "vital national interests are abandoned in order to serve the objectives of foreigners," while repression and illegal arrests continue, and the death squads of the military lurk ominously in the background.[28]

In accordance with the prevailing conceptions in the U.S., there is no infringement on democracy if a few corporations control the information system: in fact, that is the essence of democracy. In the *Annals of the American Academy of Political and Social Science*, the leading figure of the public relations industry, Edward Bernays, explains that "the very essence of the democratic process" is "the freedom to persuade and suggest," what he calls "the engineering of consent." "A leader," he continues, "frequently cannot wait for the people to arrive at even general understanding . . . Democratic leaders must play their part in . . . engineering . . . consent to socially constructive goals and values," applying "scientific principles and tried practices to the task of getting people to support ideas and programs"; and although it remains unsaid, it is evident enough that those who control resources will be in a position to judge what is "socially constructive," to engineer consent through the media, and to implement policy through the mechanisms of the state. If the freedom to persuade happens to be concentrated in a few hands, we must recognize that such is the nature of a free society. The public relations industry expends vast resources "educating the American people about the economic facts of life" to ensure a favorable climate for business. Its task is to control "the public mind," which is "the only serious danger confronting the company," an AT&T executive observed eighty years ago.[29]

Similar ideas are standard across the political spectrum. The dean of U.S. journalists, Walter Lippmann, described a "revolution" in "the practice of democracy" as "the manufacture of consent" has become "a self-conscious art and a regular organ of popular government." This is a natural development when "the common interests very largely elude public opinion entirely, and can be managed only by a specialized class whose personal interests reach beyond the locality." He was writing shortly after World War I, when the liberal intellectual community was much impressed with its success in serving as "the faithful and helpful interpreters of what seems to be one of the greatest enterprises ever undertaken by an American president" (*New Republic*). The enterprise was Woodrow Wilson's interpretation of his electoral mandate for "peace without victory" as the occasion for pursuing victory without peace, with the assistance of the liberal intellectuals, who later praised themselves for having "impose[d] their will upon a reluctant or indifferent majority," with the aid of propaganda fabrications about Hun atrocities and other such devices.

Fifteen years later, Harold Lasswell explained in the *Encyclopaedia of the Social Sciences* that we should not succumb to "democratic dogmatisms about men being the best judges of their own interests." They are not; the best judges are the elites, who must, therefore, be ensured the means to impose their will, for the common good. When social arrangements deny them the requisite force to compel obedience, it is necessary to turn to "a whole new technique of control, largely through propaganda" because of the "ignorance and superstition [of] . . . the masses." In the same years, Reinhold Niebuhr argued that "rationality belongs to the cool observers," while "the proletarian" follows not reason but faith, based upon a crucial element of "necessary illusion." Without such illusion, the ordinary person will descend to "inertia." Then in his Marxist phase, Niebuhr urged that those he addressed—presumably, the cool observers—recognize "the stupidity of the average man" and provide the "emotionally potent oversimplifications" required to keep the proletarian on course to create a new society; the basic conceptions underwent little change as Niebuhr became "the official establishment theologian" (Richard Rovere), offering counsel to those who "face the responsibilities of power."[30]

After World War II, as the ignorant public reverted to their slothful pacifism at a time when elites understood the need to mobilize for renewed global conflict,

historian Thomas Bailey observed that "because the masses are notoriously short-sighted and generally cannot see danger until it is at their throats, our statesmen are forced to deceive them into an awareness of their own long-run interests. Deception of the people may in fact become increasingly necessary, unless we are willing to give our leaders in Washington a freer hand." Commenting on the same problem as a renewed crusade was being launched in 1981, Samuel Huntington made the point that "you may have to sell [intervention or other military action] in such a way as to create the misimpression that it is the Soviet Union that you are fighting. That is what the United States has done ever since the Truman Doctrine"—an acute observation, which explains one essential function of the Cold War.[31]

At another point on the spectrum, the conservative contempt for democracy is succinctly articulated by Sir Lewis Namier, who writes that "there is no free will in the thinking and actions of the masses, any more than in the revolutions of planets, in the migrations of birds, and in the plunging of hordes of lemmings into the sea."[32] Only disaster would ensue if the masses were permitted to enter the arena of decision-making in a meaningful way.

Some are admirably forthright in their defense of the doctrine: for example, the Dutch Minister of Defense writes that "whoever turns against manufacture of consent resists any form of effective authority."[33] Any commisar would nod his head in appreciation and understanding.

At its root, the logic is that of the Grand Inquisitor, who bitterly assailed Christ for offering people freedom and thus condemning them to misery. The Church must correct the evil work of Christ by offering the miserable mass of humanity the gift they most desire and need: absolute submission. It must "vanquish freedom" so as "to make men happy" and provide the total "community of worship" that they avidly seek. In the modern secular age, this means worship of the state religion, which in the Western democracies incorporates the doctrine of submission to the masters of the system of public subsidy, private profit, called free enterprise. The people must be kept in ignorance, reduced to jingoist incantations, for their own good. And like the Grand Inquisitor, who employs the forces of miracle, mystery, and authority "to conquer and hold captive for ever the conscience of these impotent rebels for their happiness" and to deny them the freedom of choice they so fear and despise, so the "cool observers" must create the "necessary illusions" and "emotionally potent oversimplifications" that keep the ignorant and stupid masses disciplined and content.[34]

Despite the frank acknowledgment of the need to deceive the public, it would be an error to suppose that practitioners of the art are typically engaged in *conscious* deceit; few reach the level of sophistication of the Grand Inquisitor or maintain such insights for long. On the contrary, as the intellectuals pursue their grim and demanding vocation, they readily adopt beliefs that serve institutional needs; those who do not will have to seek employment elsewhere. The chairman of the board may sincerely believe that his every waking moment is dedicated to serving human needs. Were he to act on these delusions instead of pursuing profit and market share, he would no longer be chairman of the board. It is probable that the most inhuman monsters, even the Himmlers and the Mengeles, convince themselves that they are engaged in noble and courageous acts. The psychology of leaders is a topic of little interest. The institutional factors that constrain their actions and beliefs are what merit attention.

Across a broad spectrum of articulate opinion, the fact that the voice of the people is heard in democratic societies is considered a problem to be overcome by ensuring that the public voice speaks the right words. The general conception is that leaders control us, not that we control them. If the population is out of control and propaganda doesn't work, then the state is forced underground, to clandestine operations and secret wars; the scale of covert operations is often a good measure of popular dissidence, as it was during the Reagan period. Among this group of self-styled "conservatives," the commitment to untrammeled executive power and the contempt for democracy reached unusual heights. Accordingly, so did the resort to propaganda campaigns targeting the media and the general population: for example, the establishment of the State Department Office of Latin American Public Diplomacy dedicated to such projects as Operation Truth, which one high government official described as "a huge psychological operation of the kind the military conducts to influence a population in denied or enemy territory."[35] The terms express lucidly the attitude towards the errant public: enemy territory, which must be conquered and subdued.

In its dependencies, the United States must often turn to violence to "restore democracy." At home, more subtle means are required: the manufacture of consent, deceiving the stupid masses with "necessary illusions," covert operations that the media and Congress pretend not to see until it all becomes too obvious to be suppressed. We then shift to the phase of damage control to ensure that public attention is diverted to overzealous patriots or to the personality defects of leaders who have strayed from our noble commitments, but not to the institutional factors that determine the persistent and substantive content of these commitments. The task of the Free Press, in such circumstances, is to take the proceedings seriously and to describe them as a tribute to the soundness of our self-correcting institutions, which they carefully protect from public scrutiny.

More generally, the media and the educated classes must fulfill their "societal purpose," carrying out their necessary tasks in accord with the prevailing conception of democracy.

Notes

1. José Pedro S. Martins, *Latinamerica Press* (Lima), March 17, 1988.

2. See Philip Lee, ed., *Communication for All* (Orbis, 1985); William Preston, Edward S. Herman, and Herbert Schiller, *Hope and Folly: the United States and UNESCO, 1945–1985* (U. of Minnesota, forthcoming).

3. "Freedom of the Press—Anthony Lewis distinguishes between Britain and America," *London Review of Books,* Nov. 26, 1987.

4. Justice Holmes, dissenting in *Abrams v. United States,* 1919.

5. Benjamin Ginsberg, *The Captive Public* (Basic Books, 1986, 86, 89). Ginsberg's study is short on evidence and the logic is often weak: for example, his belief that there is a contradiction in holding both that Star Wars "could not protect the United States from a nuclear attack" and that it might "increase the probability that such an attack would occur," part of his argument that the advocacy of their causes by "liberal political forces" is motivated by "political interest"; but there is plainly no contradiction, whatever the merits of his conclusion about liberal political forces. He also believes that "student demonstrators and the like . . . have little difficulty securing favorable publicity for themselves and their causes," particularly anti-Vietnam War protestors, and accepts uncritically familiar claims about "the adversary

posture adopted by the media during the sixties and seventies," among other untenable assumptions.

6. Putting the point slightly differently, V. O. Key observes that "newspaper publishers are essentially people who sell white space on newsprint to advertisers." Cited by Jerome A. Barron, "Access to the Press—a New First Amendment Right," *Harvard Law Review,* vol. 80, 1967; from Key, *Public Opinion and American Democracy.*

7. Sir George Lewis, cited in James Curran and Jean Seaton, *Power without Responsibility* (Methuen, 1985, 31); Paul Johnson, *Spectator,* Nov. 28, 1987.

8. A panel of media critics organized annually by Carl Jensen, who select the "ten most censored stories" of the year, gave the first prize for 1987 to a study of these issues by Ben Bagdikian, referring of course not to literal state censorship but to media evasion or distortion of critical issues.

9. *Economist,* Dec. 5, 1987.

10. For more extensive study of these matters, see Edward S. Herman and Noam Chomsky, *Manufacturing Consent: The Political Economy of the Mass Media* (Pantheon, 1988), chapter 1.

11. For some discussion, see appendix I, section 1.

12. Bolling, *op. cit.,* 8.

13. Herman and Chomsky, *Manufacturing Consent;* Chomsky, *The Culture of Terrorism* (South End, 1988). See also our two-volume *Political Economy of Human Rights* (South End, 1979), an extension of an earlier study that was suppressed by the conglomerate that owned the publisher; see the author's preface for details. See also Herman, *The Real Terror Network* (South End, 1982); my *Pirates and Emperors* (Claremont, 1986; Amana, 1988); and much other work over the past twenty years. Also James Aronson, *The Press and the Cold War* (Beacon, 1970); Michael Parenti, *Inventing Reality* (St. Martin's, 1986).

14. For some further comments on these topics, discussed more extensively in the references of the preceding footnote, see appendix I, section 1.

15. On the role of Freedom House as a virtual propaganda arm of the government and international right wing, see Edward S. Herman and Frank Brodhead, *Demonstration Elections* (South End, 1984, appendix I), and *Manufacturing Consent.* According to a memo of NSC official Walter Raymond, Freedom House was one of the recipients of money raised by the Reagan administration propaganda apparatus (see note 35, below), a charge denied by Sussman, speaking for Freedom House. See Robert Parry and Peter Kornbluh, "Iran-Contra's Untold Story," *Foreign Policy,* Fall 1988; correspondence, Winter 1988–89. To demonstrate the impartiality and *bona fides* of Freedom House, Sussman states that "we cited the deplorable human rights record of the Sandinistas, as we publicize violators of human rights in many other countries, such as Chile and Paraguay." Nicaragua, Chile, and Paraguay are the three Latin American countries that the Reagan administration officially condemns for human rights violations, and, to the surprise of no one familiar with its record, Freedom House selects these three

examples. Sussman does not, however, select El Salvador and Guatemala, where human rights violations are vastly beyond anything attributable to the Sandinistas, but are not deplored by the Reagan administration, which bears much of the responsibility for them. The fact that Freedom House is taken seriously, in the light of its record, is startling.

16. Martin Peretz, *New Republic,* Aug. 2, 1982. See my *Fateful Triangle* (South End, 1983), for more on this curious document and others like it; and appendix I, section 2.

17. See appendix I, section 1, for some comment.

18. Bolling, *op. cit.* See appendix I, section 2, and *Manufacturing Consent* on the Vietnam War TV retrospective and others. On public attitudes towards the media as not critical enough of government and too readily influenced by power generally, see Mark Hertsgaard, *On Bended Knee* (Farrar Straus Giroux, 1988, 84–85).

19. Former *Time* senior editor Timothy Foote, who asserts that "any attentive reader" of that journal will know that its bias is sometimes "as obvious as the faces of Mount Rushmore" (Review of William Rusher, *The Coming Battle for the Media,* WP Weekly, June 27, 1988). Rusher condemns the "media elite" for distorting the news with their liberal bias. Press critic David Shaw of the *Los Angeles Times,* reviewing the same book in the *New York Times Book Review,* responds with the equally conventional view that "journalists love to challenge the status quo," and are "critics, nitpickers, malcontents" who "complain about everything."

20. For detailed analysis of media coverage of Cuba, see Tony Platt, ed., *Tropical Gulag* (Global Options, 1987). Wayne Smith, formerly head of the U.S. Interests Section in Havana and a leading Cuba specialist, describes the study as offering "devastating" confirmation of the "overwhelmingly negative" treatment of Cuba in the media, in conformity with "the Department of State's version," citing additional examples of "lack of balance" and refusal to cover significant evidence refuting Reaganite charges; *Social Justice,* Summer 1988. See also appendix I, section 1.

21. Cited by Ginsberg, *Captive Mind,* 34.

22. Distaste for democracy sometimes reaches such extremes that state control is taken to be the only imaginable alternative to domination by concentrated private wealth. It must be this tacit assumption that impels Nicholas Lemann (*New Republic,* Jan. 9, 1989) to assert that in our book *Manufacturing Consent,* Herman and I advocate "more state control" over the media, basing this claim on our statement that "In the long run, a democratic political order requires far wider control of and access to the media" on the part of the general public (p. 307). This quoted statement follows a review of some of the possible modalities, including the proliferation of public-access TV channels that "have weakened the power of the network oligopoly" and have "a potential for enhanced local-group access," "local nonprofit radio and television stations," ownership of radio stations by "community institutions" (a small cooperative in France is mentioned as an example), listener-supported radio in local

communities, and so on. Such options indeed challenge corporate oligopoly and the rule of the wealthy generally. Therefore, they can only be interpreted as "state control" by someone who regards it as unthinkable that the general public might, or should, gain access to the media as a step towards shaping their own affairs.

23. Appleby, *Capitalism and a New Social Order* (NYU, 1984, 73). On the absurd George Washington cult contrived as part of the effort "to cultivate the ideological loyalties of the citizenry" and thus create a sense of "viable nationhood," see Lawrence J. Friedman, *Inventors of the Promised Land* (Knopf, 1975, chapter 2). Washington was a "perfect man" of "unparalleled perfection," who was raised "above the level of mankind," and so on. This Kim Il Sung-ism persists among the intellectuals, for example, in the reverence for FDR and his "grandeur," "majesty," etc., in the *New York Review of Books* (see *Fateful Triangle*, 175, for some scarcely believable quotes), and in the Camelot cult. Sometimes a foreign leader ascends to the same semi-divinity, and may be described as "a Promethean figure" with "colossal external strength" and "colossal powers," as in the more ludicrous moments of the Stalin era, or in the accolade to Israeli Prime Minister Golda Meir by Martin Peretz from which the quotes just given are taken (*New Republic*, Aug. 10, 1987).

24. Frank Monaghan, *John Jay* (Bobbs-Merrill, 1935); Richard B. Morris, *The Forging of the Union* (Harper & Row, 1987, 46–47, 173, 12f.). See *Political Economy of Human Rights*, II, 41ff. on the flight of refugees after the American revolution, including boat people fleeing in terror from perhaps the richest country in the world to suffer and die in Nova Scotia in mid-winter; relative to the population, the numbers compare to the refugee flight from ravaged Vietnam. For a recent estimate, including 80,000–100,000 Loyalists, see Morris, 13, 17.

25. *The American Revolution Reconsidered* (Harper & Row, 1967, 57–58).

26. See Joshua Cohen and Joel Rogers, *On Democracy* (Penguin, 1983), for a perceptive analysis, and next chapter for some further comments.

27. For some discussion and further references, see *Turning the Tide*, 232f.

28. Editorials, *El Tiempo*, May 5, 10; translated in *Hondupress* (Managua), May 18, 1988, a journal of Honduran exiles who fear to return to the "fledgling democracy" because of the threat of assassination and disappearance. For more on the Salvadoran polls, see *Culture of Terrorism*, 102, and appendix IV, section 5. I found no reference in the media, though there is a regular chorus of praise for the progress of this noble experiment in democracy under U.S. tutelage.

29. Alex Carey, "Reshaping the Truth," *Meanjin Quarterly* (Australia), 35.4, 1976; Gabriel Kolko, *Main Currents in American History* (Pantheon, 1984, 284). For extensive discussion, see Alex Carey, "Managing Public Opinion: The Corporate Offensive," ms., U. of New South Wales, 1986.

30. For references, see my *Towards a New Cold War* (Pantheon, 1982, chapter 1). Niebuhr, *Moral Man and Immoral Society* (Scribners, 1952, 221–23, 21; reprint of 1932 edition); also Richard Fox, *Reinhold Niebuhr* (Pantheon, 1985, 138–39). For more on his ideas, and their reception, see my review of several books by and on Niebuhr in *Grand Street*, Winter 1987.

31. Bailey, cited by Jesse Lemisch, *On Active Service in War and Peace: Politics and Ideology in the American Historical Profession* (New Hogtown Press, Toronto, 1975). Huntington, *International Security*, Summer 1981.

32. *England in the Age of the American Revolution* (Macmillan, 1961, 40); cited by Francis Jennings, *Empire of Fortune* (Norton, 1988, 471).

33. Defense Minister Frits Bolkestein, *NRC Handelsblad*, Oct. 11, 1988. He is commenting (indignantly) on material I presented on this topic as a Huizinga lecture in Leiden in 1977, reprinted in *Towards a New Cold War*, chapter 1.

34. Fyodor Dostoyevsky, *The Brothers Karamazov* (Random House, 1950).

35. Alfonso Chardy, *Miami Herald*, July 19, 1987. The State Department Office of Public Diplomacy operated under CIA-NSC direction to organize support for the contras and to intimidate and manipulate the media and Congress. On its activities, condemned as illegal in September 1987 by the Comptroller General of the GAO, see Staff Report, *State Department and Intelligence Community Involvement in Domestic Activities Related to the Iran/Contra Affair*, Committee on Foreign Affairs, U.S. House of Representatives, Sept. 7, 1988; Parry and Kornbluh, *op. cit.* Also *Culture of Terrorism*, chapter 10, referring to Chardy's earlier exposures in two outstanding though generally neglected articles in the *Miami Herald*.

DISCUSSION QUESTIONS

1. In your view, if the strategy of "manufacturing consent" has been employed in the United States in recent years, how successful has it been?

2. Do you agree with Chomsky's propaganda model for explaining the role of the media in capitalist democracies? Why or why not?

3. Do you agree with John Jay's maxim, "The people who own the country ought to govern it"? Why or why not?

4. How do you think Marx and Engels would respond to Chomsky's account of the role of the corporate media in the contemporary United States?

5. Since 1989 when Chomsky published *Necessary Illusions*, what impact do you think the Internet and related communications technology have had on the social situation he describes?

64. Abul A'lā Maudūdi (1903–1979)
On the Islamic State

Born and raised in India, Abul A'lā Maudūdi became an influential Islamic scholar and political activist in the twentieth-century movement to establish Islamic states in that part of the world. He did a good deal of his writing while in prison for his political activities and, in his later life, moved to Pakistan, along with many other Muslims, after it was partitioned off from the rest of India and became a separate nation-state.

The selection includes excerpts from an essay Maudūdi composed in 1939, which is part of a collection of his writings first published in 1955 called *Islamic Law and Constitution*. This text was intended as a resource for the theological study of the doctrines and sacred writings of Islam as they are applicable to understanding human political affairs. Specifically, Maudūdi shows what Islamic doctrine requires of the Muslim community regarding the appropriate form of government to be created and the accompanying legal code to be established for the regulation of almost every aspect of individual and collective life. The political organization of society he advocates is a type of "theocracy," but as he explains, it is different from the theocracies that have appeared here and there in Western history.

QUESTIONS FOR CRITICAL READING

1. According to Maudūdi, what are the three main characteristics of an Islamic state that can be inferred from the Qur'an?
2. How does Maudūdi distinguish between an Islamic state and "western secular democracy," and how does he criticize the latter?
3. According to Maudūdi, what is the difference between Western "theocracy" and an Islamic "theo-democracy"?
4. How does Maudūdi characterize the purpose of the Islamic state?
5. What does Maudūdi mean by claiming that the Islamic state is "an ideological state"?

TERMS TO NOTE

suzerainty: The position or authority of a sovereign.
purdah: The custom of being kept hidden from men and strangers.

III

First Principle of Islamic Political Theory

The belief in the Unity and the sovereignty of Allah is the foundation of the social and moral system propounded by the Prophets. It is the very starting-point of the Islamic political philosophy. The basic principle of Islam is that human beings must, individually and collectively, surrender all rights of overlordship, legislation and exercising of authority over others. No one should be allowed to pass orders or make commands *in his own right* and no one ought to accept the obligation to carry out such commands and obey such orders. None is entitled to make laws on his own authority and none is obliged to abide by them. This right vests in Allah alone:

> "The Authority rests with none but Allah. He commands you not to surrender to any one save Him. This is the right way (of life)".[1]
> "They ask: 'have we also got some authority?' Say: 'all authority belongs to God alone'."[2]
> "Do not say wrongly with your tongues that this is lawful and that is unlawful."[3]
> "Whoso does not establish and decide by that which Allah hath revealed, such are disbelievers."[4]

According to this theory, sovereignty belongs to Allah. He alone is the law-giver. No man, even if he be a Prophet, has the right to order others *in his own right* to do or not to do certain things. The Prophet himself is subject to God's commands:

> "I do not follow anything except what is revealed to me".[5]

Other people are required to obey the Prophet because he enunciates not his own but God's commands:

1. *Al-Qur'an,* XII: 40.
2. *ibid.,* III: 154.
3. *ibid.,* XVI: 116.
4. *ibid.,* V: 44.
5. *ibid.,* VI: 50.

"We sent no messenger save that he should be obeyed *by Allah's leave.*"[6]

"They are the people unto whom We gave the Scripture and Command and Prophethood."[7]

"It is not (possible) for any human being unto whom Allah has given the Scripture and the Wisdom and the Prophethood that he should have thereafter said unto mankind: Become slaves of *me instead of Allah;* but (what he said was) be ye faithful servants of the Lord."[8]

Thus the main characteristics of an Islamic state that can be deduced from these express statements of the Holy Qur'an are as follows:—

(1) No person, class or group, not even the entire population of the state as a whole, can lay claim to sovereignty. God alone is the real sovereign; all others are merely His subjects;

(2) God is the real law-giver and the authority of absolute legislation vests in Him. The believers cannot resort to totally independent legislation nor can they modify any law which God has laid down, even if the desire to effect such legislation or change in Divine laws is unanimous;[9] and

(3) An Islamic state must, in all respects, be founded upon the law laid down by God through His Prophet. The government which runs such a state will be entitled to obedience in its capacity as a political agency set up to enforce the laws of God and only in so far as it acts in that capacity. If it disregards the law revealed by God, its commands will not be binding on the believers.

IV

The Islamic State: Its Nature and Characteristics

The preceding discussion makes it quite clear that Islam, speaking from the view-point of political phi-

losophy, is the very antithesis of secular Western democracy. The philosophical foundation of Western democracy is the sovereignty of the people. In it, this type of absolute powers of legislation—of the determination of values and of the norms of behaviour—rest in the hands of the people. Law-making is their prerogative and legislation must correspond to the mood and temper of their opinion. If a particular piece of legislation is desired by the masses, howsoever ill-conceived, it may be from religious and moral viewpoint, steps have to be taken to place it on the statute book; if the people dislike any law and demand its abrogation, howsoever just and rightful, it might be, it has to be expunged forthwith. This is not the case in Islam. On this count, Islam has no trace of Western democracy. Islam, as already explained, altogether repudiates the philosophy of popular sovereignty and rears its polity on the foundations of the sovereignty of God and the vice-regency (*Khilafat*) of man.[10]

A more apt name for the Islamic polity would be the "kingdom of God" which is described in English as a "theocracy." But Islamic theocracy is something altogether different from the theocracy of which Europe has had a bitter experience wherein a priestly class, sharply marked off from the rest of the population, exercises unchecked domination and enforces laws of its own making in the name of God, thus virtually imposing its own divinity and godhood upon the common people.[11] Such a system of government is satanic rather than divine. Contrary to this, the theocracy built up by Islam is not ruled by any particular religious class but by the whole community of Muslims including the rank and file. The entire Muslim population runs the state in accordance with the Book of God and the practice of His Prophet. If I were permitted to coin a new term, I would describe this

---

6. *Al-Qur'an,* IV: 64.
7. *ibid.,* VI: 90.
8. *ibid.,* III: 79.
9. Here the *absolute right of legislation* is being discussed. In the Islamic political theory this right vests in Allah alone. As to the scope and extent of human legislation provided by the *Shar'iah* itself please see Chapter II: 'Legislation and *Ijtihad* in Islam' and Chapter VI 'First Principles of Islamic State.'—*Editor.*

10. Here it must be clearly understood that democracy as a 'philosophy' and democracy as a 'form of organisation' are not the same thing. In the form of organisation, Islam has its own system of democracy as is explained in the following pages. But as a philosophy, the two i.e. Islam and Western democracy are basically different, rather opposed to each other.—*Editor.*
11. "Theocracy: a form of government in which God (or a deity) is recognised as the king or immediate ruler, and his laws are taken as the statute book of Kingdom, these laws being usually administered by a priestly order as his ministers and agents; hence (loosely) a system of government by a sacerdotal order claiming a divine commission. *The Shorter Oxford Dictionary,* Vol. II, Oxford, 1956, p. 2166.

system of government as a "theo-democracy", that is to say a divine democratic government, because under it the Muslims have been given a limited popular sovereignty under the suzerainty of God. The executive under this system of government is constituted by the general will of the Muslims who have also the right to depose it. All administrative matters and all questions about which no explicit injunction is to be found in the *shari'ah* are settled by the consensus of opinion among the Muslims. Every Muslim who is capable and qualified to give a sound opinion on matters of Islamic law, is entitled to interpret the law of God when such interpretation becomes necessary. In this sense the Islamic polity is a democracy. But, as has been explained above, it is a theocracy in the sense that where an explicit command of God or His Prophet already exists, no Muslim leader or legislature, or any religious scholar can form an independent judgment, not even all the Muslims of the world put together, have any right to make the least alteration in it.

Before proceeding further, I feel that I should put in a word of explanation as to why these limitations and restrictions have been placed upon popular sovereignty in Islam, and what is the nature of these limitations and restrictions. It may be said that God has, in this manner, taken away the liberty of human mind and intellect instead of safeguarding it as I was trying to prove. My reply is that God has retained the right of legislation in His own hand not in order to deprive man of his natural freedom but to safeguard that very freedom. His purpose is to save man from going astray and inviting his own ruin.

One can easily understand this point by attempting a little analysis of the so-called Western secular democracy. It is claimed that this democracy is founded on popular sovereignty. But everybody knows that the people who constitute a state do not all of them take part either in legislation or in its administration. They have to delegate their sovereignty to their elected representatives so that the latter may make and enforce laws on their behalf. For this purpose an electoral system is set up. But as a divorce has been effected between politics and religion, and as a result of this secularisation, the society and particularly its politically active elements have ceased to attach much or any importance to morality and ethics. And this is also a fact that only those persons generally come to the

top who can dupe the masses by their wealth, power, and deceptive propaganda. Although these representatives come into power by the votes of the common people, they soon set themselves up as an independent authority and assume the position of overlords (*ilahs*). They often make laws not in the best interest of the people who raised them to power but to further their own sectional and class interests. They impose their will on the people by virtue of the authority delegated to them by those over whom they rule. This is the situation which besets people in England, America and in all those countries which claim to be the haven of secular democracy.

Even if we overlook this aspect of the matter and admit that in these countries laws are made according to the wishes of the common people, it has been established by experience that the great mass of the common people are incapable of perceiving their own true interests. It is the natural weakness of man that in most of the affairs concerning his life he takes into consideration only some one aspect of reality and loses sight of other aspects. His judgments are usually one-sided and he is swayed by emotions and desires to such an extent that rarely, if ever, can he judge important matters with the impartiality and objectivity of scientific reason. Quite often he rejects the plea of reason simply because it conflicts with his passions and desires. I can cite many instances in support of this contention but to avoid prolixity I shall content myself with giving only one example: the Prohibition Law of America. It had been rationally and logically established that drinking is injurious to health, produces deleterious effects on mental and intellectual faculties and leads to disorder in human society. The American public accepted these facts and agreed to the enactment of the Prohibition Law. Accordingly the law was passed by the majority vote. But when it was put into effect, the very same people by whose vote it had been passed, revolted against it. The worst kinds of wine were illicitly manufactured and consumed, and their use and consumption became more widespread than before. Crimes increased in number. And eventually drinking was legalised by the vote of the same people who had previously voted for its prohibition. This sudden change in public opinion was not the result of any fresh scientific discovery or the revelation of new facts providing evidence against the advantages of prohibition, but because the people had been completely enslaved by their habit and could not forego the pleasures of self-indulgence. They delegated their own sovereignty to the evil spirit in them and set up their own desires and passions as their "*ilahs*" (gods) at whose call they all went in for the repeal of the very law they had passed after having been convinced of its rationality and correctness. There are many other similar instances which go to prove that man is not competent to become an absolute legislator. Even if he secures deliverance from the service of other *ilahs,* he becomes a slave to his own petty passions and exalts the devil in him to the position of a supreme Lord. Limitations on human freedom, provided they are appropriate and do not deprive him of all initiative, are absolutely necessary in the interest of man himself.[12]

That is why God has laid down those limits which, in Islamic phraseology, are termed 'divine limits' (*Hudud-Allah*). These limits consist of certain principles, checks and balances and specific injunctions in different spheres of life and activity, and they have been prescribed in order that man may be trained to lead a balanced and moderate life. They are intended to lay down the broad framework within which man is free to legislate, decide his own affairs and frame subsidiary laws and regulations for his conduct. These limits he is not permitted to overstep and if he does so, the whole scheme of his life will go awry.

Take for example man's economic life. In this sphere God has placed certain restrictions on human freedom. The right to private property has been recognised, but it is qualified by the obligation to pay *Zakat* (poor dues) and the prohibition of interest, gambling and speculation. A specific law of inheritance for the distribution of property among the largest number of surviving relations on the death of its owner has been laid down and certain forms of acquiring, accumulating and spending wealth have been declared unlawful. If people observe these just limits and regulate their

affairs within these boundary walls, on the one hand their personal liberty is adequately safeguarded and, on the other, the possibility of class war and domination of one class over another, which begins with capitalist oppression and ends in working-class dictatorship, is safely and conveniently eliminated.

Similarly in the sphere of family life, God has prohibited the unrestricted intermingling of the sexes and has prescribed *purdah,* recognised man's guardianship of woman, and clearly defined the rights and duties of husband, wife and children. The laws of divorce and separation have been clearly set forth, conditional polygamy has been permitted and penalties for fornication and false accusations of adultery have been prescribed. He has thus laid down limits which, if observed by man, would stabilise his family life and make it a haven of peace and happiness. There would remain neither that tyranny of male over female which makes family life an inferno of cruelty and oppression, nor that satanic flood of female liberty and licence which threatens to destroy human civilisation in the West.

In like manner, for the preservation of human culture and society God has, by formulating the law of *Qisas* (Retaliation), commanding to cut off the hands for theft, prohibiting wine-drinking, placing limitations on uncovering of one's private parts and by laying down a few similar permanent rules and regulations, closed the door of social disorder for ever. I have no time to present to you a complete list of all the divine limits and show in detail how essential each one of them is for maintaining equilibrium and poise in life. What I want to bring home to you here is that through these injunctions God has provided a permanent and immutable code of behaviour for man, and that it does not deprive him of any essential liberty nor does it dull the edge of his mental faculties. On the contrary, it sets a straight and clear path before him, so that he may not, owing to his ignorance and weaknesses which he inherently possesses, lose himself in the maze of destruction and instead of wasting his faculties in the pursuit of wrong ends, he may follow the road that leads to success and progress in this world and the hereafter. If you have ever happened to visit a mountainous region, you must have noticed that in the winding mountain paths which are bounded by deep caves on the one side and lofty rocks on the other, the border of the road is barricaded and

---

12. The question however is: Who is to impose these restrictions? According to the Islamic view it is only Allah, the Creator, the Nourisher, the All-Knowing Who is entitled to impose restrictions on human freedom and not *any man*. No man is entitled to do so. If any man arbitrarily imposes restrictions on human freedom, that is despotism pure and simple. In Islam there is no place for such despotism.—*Editor.*

protected in such a way as to prevent travellers from straying towards the abyss by mistake. Are these barricades intended to deprive the wayfarer of his liberty? No, as a matter of fact, they are meant to protect him from destruction; to warn him at every bend of the dangers ahead and to show him the path leading to his destination. That precisely is the purpose of the restrictions (*hudud*) which God has laid down in His revealed Code. These limits determine what direction man should take in life's journey and they guide him at every turn and pass and point out to him the path of safety which he should steadfastly follow.

As I have already stated, this code, enacted as it is by God, is unchangeable. You can, if you like, rebel against it, as some Muslim countries have done. But you cannot alter it. It will continue to be unalterable till the last day. It has its own avenues of growth and evolution, but no human being has any right to tamper with it. Whenever an Islamic State comes into existence, this code would form its fundamental law and will constitute the mainspring of all its legislation. Everyone who desires to remain a Muslim is under an obligation to follow the Qur'an and the *Sunnah* which must constitute the basic law of an Islamic State.

The Purpose of the Islamic State

The purpose of the state that may be formed on the basis of the Qur'an and *Sunnah* has also been laid down by God. The Qur'an says:

> "We verily sent Our messengers with clear proofs, and revealed with them the Scripture and the Balance, that mankind may observe right measure; and We revealed iron, wherein is mighty power and (many) uses for mankind."[13]

In this verse steel symbolises political power and the verse also makes it clear that the mission of the prophets is to create conditions in which the mass of people will be assured of social justice in accordance with the standards enunciated by God in His Book which gives explicit instructions for a well-disciplined mode of life. In another place God has said:—

> "(Muslims are) those who, if We give them power in the land, establish the system of *Salat*

(worship) and *Zakat* (poor dues) and enjoin virtue and forbid evil and inequity.[14]

"You are the best community sent forth unto mankind; ye enjoin the Right conduct and forbid the wrong; and ye believe in Allah."[15]

It will readily become manifest to anyone who reflects upon these verses that the purpose of the state visualised by the Holy Qur'an is not negative but positive. The object of the state is not merely to prevent people from exploiting each other, to safeguard their liberty and to protect its subjects from foreign invasion. It also aims at evolving and developing that well-balanced system of social justice which has been set forth by God in His Holy Book. Its object is to eradicate all forms of evil and to encourage all types of virtue and excellence expressly mentioned by God in the Holy Qur'an. For this purpose political power will be made use of as and when the occasion demands; all means of propaganda and peaceful persuasion will be employed; the moral education of the people will also be undertaken; and social influence as well as the force of public opinion will be harnessed to the task.

Islamic State Is Universal and All-Embracing

A state of this sort cannot evidently restrict the scope of its activities. Its approach is universal and all-embracing. Its sphere of activity is coextensive with the whole of human life. It seeks to mould every aspect of life and activity in consonance with its moral norms and programme of social reform. In such a state no one can regard any field of his affairs as personal and private. Considered from this aspect the Islamic state bears a kind of resemblance to the Fascist and Communist states. But you will find later on that, despite its all-inclusiveness, it is something vastly and basically different from the modern totalitarian and authoritarian states. Individual liberty is not suppressed under it nor is there any trace of dictatorship in it. It presents the middle course and embodies the best that the human society has ever evolved. The excellent balance and moderation that characterise the Islamic system of government and the precise distinctions made in it between right and wrong elicit from all men of hon-

---

13. *Al-Qur'an*, LVII: 25.

14. *Al-Qur'an*, XXII: 41.
15. *ibid.*, III: 110.

esty and intelligence the admiration and the admission that such a balanced system could not have been framed by anyone but the Omniscient and All-Wise God.

Islamic State Is an Ideological State

Another characteristic of the Islamic State is that it is an ideological state. It is clear from a careful consideration of the Qur'an and the *Sunnah* that the state in Islam is based on an ideology and its objective is to establish that ideology. State is an instrument of reform and must act likewise. It is a dictate of this very nature of the Islamic State that such a state should be run only by those who believe in the ideology on which it is based and in the Divine Law which it is assigned to administer. The administrators of the Islamic state must be those whose whole life is devoted to the observance and enforcement of this Law, who not only agree with its reformatory programme and fully believe in it but thoroughly comprehend its spirit and are acquainted with its details. Islam does not recognise any geographical, linguistic or colour bars in this respect. It puts forward its code of guidance and the scheme of its reform before all men. Whoever accepts this programme, no matter to what race, nation or country he may belong, can join the community that runs the Islamic state. But those who do not accept it are not entitled to have any hand in shaping the fundamental policy of the state. They can live within the confines of the State as non-Muslim citizens (*zimmis*). Specific rights and privileges have been accorded to them in the Islamic law. A *Zimmi's* life, property and honour will be fully protected, and if he is capable of any service, his services will also be made use of. He will not, however, be allowed to influence the basic policy of this ideological state. The Islamic state is based on a particular ideology and it is the community which believes in the Islamic ideology which pilots it. Here again, we notice some sort of resemblance between the Islamic and the Communist states. But the treatment meted out by the Communist states to persons holding creeds and ideologies other than its own bears no comparison with the attitude of the Islamic state. Unlike the Communist state, Islam does not impose its social principles on others by force, nor does it confiscate their properties or unleash a reign of terror by mass executions of the people and their transportation to the slave camps of Siberia. Islam does not want to eliminate its minorities, it wants to protect them and gives them the freedom to live according to their own culture. The generous and just treatment which Islam has accorded to non-Muslims in an Islamic State and the fine distinction drawn by it between justice and injustice and good and evil will convince all those who are not prejudiced against it, that the prophets sent by God accomplish their task in an altogether different manner—something radically different and diametrically opposed to the way of the false reformers who strut about here and there on the stage of history."[16]

DISCUSSION QUESTIONS

1. Do you agree with Maudūdi's criticisms of Western democracy? Why or why not?
2. Do you agree with Maudūdi's criticisms of any secular state? Why or why not?
3. How would you compare Maudūdi's vision of an Islamic state with the fundamentalist Christian advocacy of a Christian state?
4. What is Maudūdi's position on the legal protection of individual liberty? Is it consistent? Why or why not?

---

16. This paper was written in 1939 and in it the author has dealt with the theoretical aspect of the problem only. In his later articles he has discussed the practical aspects as well. In his article on the 'Rights of Non-Muslims in Islamic State' (see Chapter VIII) he writes:

"However, in regard to a parliament or a legislature of the modern conception, which is considerably different from *Shura* in its traditional sense, this rule could be relaxed to allow non-Muslims to become its members provided that it has been fully ensured in the Constitution that

(i) It would be *ultra vires* of the parliament or the legislature to enact any law which is repugnant to the Qur'an and the *Sunnah.*

(ii) The Qur'an and the *Sunnah* would be the chief source of the public law of the land.

(iii) The head of the state or the assenting authority would necessarily be a Muslim. With these provisions ensured, the sphere of influence of non-Muslims would be limited to matters relating to the general problems of the country or to the interests of minorities concerned and their participation would not damage the fundamental requirements of Islam."

The non-Muslims cannot occupy key-posts—posts from where the ideological policy of the state can be influenced—but they can occupy general administrative posts and can act in the services of the state. . . .

65. John Dewey (1859–1952)
On Democracy

John Dewey was an American pragmatist philosopher whose prolific writing and extensive lecturing in many different areas of philosophy, psychology, education, and current affairs, over a very long career, made him one of the most influential scholars in American history. After receiving his doctorate in philosophy from Johns Hopkins University in 1884, he taught at the University of Michigan until 1894, when he accepted an appointment at the University of Chicago. In 1904 he moved to Columbia University where he taught until his retirement in 1930. He continued his writing and public speaking thereafter, until his death at 93.

Given his pragmatist orientation (he apparently preferred the label "instrumentalism" for his own theoretical approach), Dewey was interested primarily in epistemological issues and how they intersected with other philosophical and practical problems. He focused especially on experience as the basis for knowledge acquisition, making him a kind of empiricist. But this experiencing was a naturally active, constructive, and goal-oriented process rather than merely passive, in his analysis. The dynamic of human experience, inquiry, and "knowing" could be seen in all aspects of life, he argued, and thus also could be tied into the basic goals of social and political organization. That is, in Dewey's view the cognitive and emotional self-actualization of individuals, in the context of mutually respectful and supportive social relations, was the fundamental value upon which collective problem solving and decision making should be based. This is why he emphasized throughout his career the importance of the rationally planned education of individuals who would contribute to their society as a result of being facilitated in their own self-development.

The selection consists of excerpts from an essay entitled "Democracy and Educational Administration," which Dewey read to a group of school administrators at a meeting of the National Education Association in 1937. In it he essentially argues for democracy as the best organizational means by which individuals can flourish in community with others. However, he not only describes and applauds the standard features of a democratic government and its presuppositions, but he also argues for democracy as a whole "way of life" that should permeate the economic, religious, family, and educational spheres of society as well. Further, at the time he wrote this piece, fascism, as an explicitly anti-democratic movement, had overthrown or undone democratic governments in several European countries and had attracted adherents in many other societies, including the United States. Dewey maintained that one of the major reasons for the continued vulnerability of "political democracy" to this sort of danger was the often undemocratic, authoritarian nature of those other domains of social activity where people simply accepted as a matter of custom relations of domination and subordination.

QUESTIONS FOR CRITICAL READING

1. What are the features of democratic government Dewey identifies, and what does he mean by claiming that they are only a means rather than an end in themselves?
2. What is a democratic "way of life," according to Dewey, and in what different dimensions of social life should it be manifested?
3. According to Dewey, what are the foundational assumptions and principles of the "democratic credo"?
4. In Dewey's estimation, what is the relationship between public "indifference," autocracy, and democracy?
5. In which societies is political democracy least secure, and why is this so, according to Dewey?

TERMS TO NOTE

universal suffrage: The legal right of every adult citizen to vote on matters of state where a vote is called for by the constitution.

autocracy: A form of government in which one person rules over everyone else with unrestricted power.

My experience in educational administration is limited. I should not venture to address a body of those widely experienced and continuously engaged in school administration about the details of the management of schools. But the topic suggested to me has to do with the relation of school administration to democratic ideals and methods and to the general subject of the relation of education and democracy I have given considerable thought over many years. The topic suggested concerns a special phase of this general subject. I shall begin, then, with some remarks on the broad theme of democratic aims and methods. Much of what I shall say on this subject is necessarily old and familiar. But it seems necessary to rehearse some old ideas in order to have a criterion for dealing with the special subject.

In the first place, democracy is much broader than a special political form, a method of conducting government, of making laws and carrying on governmental administration by means of popular suffrage and elected officers. It is that, of course. But it is something broader and deeper than that. The political and governmental phase of democracy is a means, the best means so far found, for realizing ends that lie in the wide domain of human relationships and the development of human personality. It is, as we often say, though perhaps without appreciating all that is involved in the saying, a way of life, social and individual. The key-note of democracy as a way of life may be expressed, it seems to me, as the necessity for the participation of every mature human being in formation of the values that regulate the living of men together: which is necessary from the standpoint of both the general social welfare and the full development of human beings as individuals.

Universal suffrage, recurring elections, responsibility of those who are in political power to the voters, and the other factors of democratic government are means that have been found expedient for realizing democracy as the truly human way of living. They are not a final end and a final value. They are to be judged on the basis of their contribution to end. It is a form of idolatry to erect means into the end which they serve. Democratic political forms are simply the best means that human wit has devised up to a special time

in history. But they rest back upon the idea that no man or limited set of men is wise enough or good enough to rule others without their consent; the positive meaning of this statement is that all those who are affected by social institutions must have a share in producing and managing them. The two facts that each one is influenced in what he does and enjoys and in what he becomes by the institutions under which he lives, and that therefore he shall have, in a democracy, a voice in shaping them, are the passive and active sides of the same fact.

The development of political democracy came about through substitution of the method of mutual consultation and voluntary agreement for the method of subordination of the many to the few enforced from above. Social arrangements which involve fixed subordination are maintained by coercion. The coercion need not be physical. There have existed, for short periods, benevolent despotisms. But coercion of some sort there has been; perhaps economic, certainly psychological and moral. The very fact of exclusion from participation is a subtle form of suppression. It gives individuals no opportunity to reflect and decide upon what is good for them. Others who are supposed to be wiser and who in any case have more power decide the question for them and also decide the methods and means by which subjects may arrive at the enjoyment of what is good for them. This form of coercion and suppression is more subtle and more effective than is overt intimidation and restraint. When it is habitual and embodied in social institutions, it seems the normal and natural state of affairs. The mass usually become unaware that they have a claim to a development of their own powers. Their experience is so restricted that they are not conscious of restriction. It is part of the democratic conception that they as individuals are not the only sufferers, but that the whole social body is deprived of the potential resources that should be at its service. The individuals of the submerged mass may not be very wise. But there is one thing they are wiser about than anybody else can be, and that is where the shoe pinches, the troubles they suffer from.

The foundation of democracy is faith in the capacities of human nature; faith in human intelligence and in the power of pooled and cooperative experience. It is not belief that these things are complete but that if given a show they will grow and be able to generate progressively the knowledge and wisdom needed to guide collective action. Every autocratic and authoritarian scheme of social action rests on a belief that the needed intelligence is confined to a superior few, who because of inherent natural gifts are endowed with the ability and the right to control the conduct of others; laying down principles and rules and directing the ways in which they are carried out. It would be foolish to deny that much can be said for this point of view. It is that which controlled human relations in social groups for much the greater part of human history. The democratic faith has emerged very, very recently in the history of mankind. Even where democracies now exist, men's minds and feelings are still permeated with ideas about leadership imposed from above, ideas that developed in the long early history of mankind. After democratic political institutions were nominally established, beliefs and ways of looking at life and of acting that originated when men and women were externally controlled and subjected to arbitrary power, persisted in the family, the church, business and the school, and experience shows that as long as they persist there, political democracy is not secure.

Belief in equality is an element of the democratic credo. It is not, however, belief in equality of natural endowments. Those who proclaimed the idea of equality did not suppose they were enunciating a psychological doctrine, but a legal and political one. All individuals are entitled to equality of treatment by law and in its administration. Each one is affected equally in quality if not in quantity by the institutions under which he lives and has an equal right to express his judgment, although the weight of his judgment may not be equal in amount when it enters into the pooled result to that of others. In short, each one is equally an individual and entitled to equal opportunity of development of his own capacities, be they large or small in range. Moreover, each has needs of his own, as significant to him as those of others are to them. The very fact of natural and psychological inequality is all the more reason for establishment by law of equality of opportunity, since otherwise the former becomes a means of oppression of the less gifted.

While what we call intelligence be distributed in unequal amounts, it is the democratic faith that it is sufficiently general so that each individual has something to contribute, whose value can be assessed only as enters into the final pooled intelligence constituted by the contributions of all. Every authoritarian scheme, on the contrary, assumes that its value may be assessed by some *prior* principle, if not of family and birth or race and color or possession of material wealth, then by the position and rank a person occupies in the existing social scheme. The democratic faith in equality is the faith that each individual shall have the chance and opportunity to contribute whatever he is capable of contributing and that the value of his contribution be decided by its place and function in the organized total of similar contributions, not on the basis of prior status of any kind whatever.

I have emphasized in what precedes the importance of the effective release of intelligence in connection with personal experience in the democratic way of living. I have done so purposely because democracy is so often and so naturally associated in our minds with freedom of *action*, forgetting the importance of freed intelligence which is necessary to direct and to warrant freedom of action. Unless freedom of individual action has intelligence and informed conviction back of it, its manifestation is almost sure to result in confusion and disorder. The democratic idea of freedom is not the right of each individual to *do* as he pleases, even if it be qualified by adding "provided he does not interfere with the same freedom on the part of others." While the idea is not always, not often enough, expressed in words, the basic freedom is that of freedom of *mind* and of whatever degree of freedom of action and experience is necessary to produce freedom of intelligence. The modes of freedom guaranteed in the Bill of Rights are all of this nature: Freedom of belief and conscience, of expression of opinion, of assembly for discussion and conference, of the press as an organ of communication. They are guaranteed because without them individuals are not free to develop and society is deprived of what they might contribute.

What, it may be asked, have these things to do with school administration? There is some kind of government, of control, wherever affairs that concern a number of persons who act together are engaged in. It is a superficial view that holds government is located in Washington and Albany. There is government in the family, in business, in the church, in every social group. There are regulations, due to custom if not to enactment, that settle how individuals in a group act in connection with one another.

It is a disputed question of theory and practice just how far a democratic political government should go in control of the conditions of action within special groups. At the present time, for example, there are those who think the federal and state governments leave too much freedom of independent action to industrial and financial groups, and there are others who think the government is going altogether too far at the present time. I do not need to discuss this phase of the problem, much less to try to settle it. But it must be pointed out that if the methods of regulation and administration in vogue in the conduct of secondary social groups are non-democratic, whether directly or indirectly or both, there is bound to be an unfavorable reaction back into the habits of feeling, thought and action of citizenship in the broadest sense of that word. The way in which any organized social interest is controlled necessarily plays an important part in forming the dispositions and tastes, the attitudes, interests, purposes and desires, of those engaged in carrying on the activities of the group. For illustration, I do not need to do more than point to the moral, emotional and intellectual effect upon both employers and laborers of the existing industrial system. Just what the effects specifically are is a matter about which we know very little. But I suppose that every one who reflects upon the subject admits that it is impossible that the ways in which activities are carried on for the greater part of the waking hours of the day; and the way in which the share of individuals are involved in the management of affairs in such a matter as gaining a livelihood and attaining material and social security, can not but be a highly important factor in shaping personal dispositions; in short, forming character and intelligence. . . .

Since, as I have already said, it is the problem I wish to present rather than to lay down the express ways in which it is to be solved, I might stop at this point. But there are certain corollaries which clarify the meaning of the issue. Absence of participation tends to produce lack of interest and concern on the part of those shut out. The result is a corresponding lack of effective responsibility. Automatically and unconsciously, if not consciously, the feeling develops, "This is none of our affair; it is the business of those at the top; let that particular set of Georges do what needs to be done." The countries in which autocratic government prevails are just those in which there is least public spirit and the greatest indifference to matters of general as distinct from personal concern. Can we expect a different kind of psychology to actuate teachers? Where there is little power, there is correspondingly little sense of positive responsibility. It is enough to do what one is told to do sufficiently well to escape flagrant unfavorable notice. About larger matters, a spirit of passivity is engendered. In some cases, indifference passes into evasion of duties when not directly under the eye of a supervisor; in other cases, a carping, rebellious spirit is engendered. A sort of game is instituted between teacher and supervisor like that which went on in the old-fashioned schools between teacher and pupil. Other teachers pass on, perhaps unconsciously, what they feel to be arbitrary treatment received by them to their pupils.

The argument that teachers are not prepared to assume the responsibility of participation deserves attention, with its accompanying belief that natural selection has operated to put those best prepared to carry the load in the positions of authority. Whatever the truth in this contention, it still is also true that incapacity to assume the responsibilities involved in having a voice in shaping policies is bred and increased by conditions in which that responsibility is denied. I suppose there has never been an autocrat, big or little, who did not justify his conduct on the ground of the unfitness of his subjects to take part in government. I would not compare administrators to political autocrats. Upon the whole, what exists in the schools is more a matter of habit and custom than it is of any deliberate autocracy. But, as was said earlier, habitual exclusion has the effect of reducing a sense of responsibility for what is done and its consequences. What the argument for democracy implies is that the best way to produce initiative and constructive power is to exercise it. Power, as well as interest, comes by use and practice. Moreover, the argument from incapacity proves too much. If it is so great as to be a permanent bar, then teachers can not be expected to have the intelligence and skill that are necessary to execute the directions given them. The delicate and difficult task of developing character and good judgment in the young needs every stimulus and inspiration possible. It is impossible that the work should not be better done when teachers have that understanding of what they are doing that comes from having shared in forming its guiding ideas.

Classroom teachers are those who are in continuous direct contact with those taught. The position of administrators is at best indirect by comparison. If there is any work in the world that requires the conservation of what is good in experience so that it may become an integral part of further experience, it is that of teaching. I often wonder how much waste there is in the traditional system. There is some loss even at the best of the potential capital acquired by successful teachers. It does not get freely transmitted to other teachers who might profit by it. Is not the waste very considerably increased when teachers are not called upon to communicate their successful methods and results in a form by which it would have organic effect upon general school policies? Add to this waste that results when teachers are called upon to give effect in the classroom to courses of study they do not understand the reasons for, and the total loss mounts up so that it is a fair estimate that the absence of democratic methods is the greatest single cause of educational waste.

I conclude by saying that the present subject is one of peculiar importance at the present time. The fundamental beliefs and practices of democracy are now challenged as they never have been before. In some nations they are more than challenged. They are ruthlessly and systematically destroyed. Everywhere there are waves of criticism and doubt as to whether democracy can meet pressing problems of order and security. The causes for the destruction of political democracy in countries where it was nominally established are complex. But of one thing I think we may be sure.

Wherever it has fallen it was too exclusively political in nature. It had not become part of the bone and blood of the people in daily conduct of its life. Democratic forms were limited to Parliament, elections and combats between parties. What is happening proves conclusively, I think, that unless democratic habits of thought and action are part of the fiber of a people, political democracy is insecure. It can not stand in isolation. It must be buttressed by the presence of democratic methods in all social relationships. The relations that exist in educational institutions are second only in importance in this respect to those which exist in industry and business, perhaps not even to them.

I recur then to the idea that the particular question discussed is one phase of a wide and deep problem. I can think of nothing so important in this country at present as a rethinking of the whole problem of democracy and its implications. Neither the rethinking nor the action it should produce can be brought into being in a day or year. The democratic idea itself demands that the thinking and activity proceed cooperatively. My utmost hope will be fulfilled if anything I have said plays any part, however small, in promoting cooperative inquiry and experimentation in this field of democratic administration of our schools.

DISCUSSION QUESTIONS

1. Do you agree with Dewey's evaluation of democratic government and its relationship to the rest of social life? Why or why not?

2. Should the other spheres of social life be more thoroughly democratized as well, as Dewey recommends? Why or why not?

3. Do you agree with Dewey's position on the role of institutionalized education in the development of a "democratic way of life"? Why or why not?

4. How would you compare Dewey's account of democracy and Maudūdi's position on an Islamic theocracy?

66. V. I. Lenin (1870–1924)
From *State and Revolution*

Vladimir Ilyich Ulyanov, who used different pen names in his earlier political writing until settling on "Lenin," was a Russian revolutionary theoretician and activist who is generally considered today to be one of the major political figures of the twentieth century. He was born in what was then Simbirsk and eventually obtained a law degree in 1891 from the University of Petersburg, after being kicked out of the University of Kazan for subversive activities and living under police surveillance for a few years. During the 1890s, Lenin did practice some law, but he devoted more and more of his time to revolutionary organization and writing against the czarist regime and the Russian economic system.

Lenin also studied the works of Marx and Engels during this time and became convinced that Marxist theory, appropriately updated, provided the intellectual means necessary for guiding the revolutionary transformation of Russia. After more time in prison and Siberian exile, Lenin left Russia in 1900 and lived abroad for most of the next seventeen years, until the successful Bolshevik revolution in October–November of 1917. As the charismatic leader of the Bolshevik party, Lenin was chosen to be the chairman of the new government, the Council of People's Commissars, and remained the de facto head of what became the Soviet Union until his death at 54.

This selection is the fifth chapter in the 1917 book *State and Revolution*. Thought by many to be his most important work in political theory, he wrote it while hiding from the Russian authorities in the months leading up to the October Revolution. The book takes the form of a commentary and application of some writings by Marx and Engels on the revolutionary transition from capitalism to communism, especially Marx's 1875 "Critique of the Gotha Programme," which was a response to a German Social Democratic Party program influenced by the ideas of Ferdinand Lassalle. As was always the case with Lenin, however, in his analyses he is thinking of the existing circumstances in Russia and the immediate action they require, rather than engaging in a purely theoretical study of hypothetical scenarios. As can be seen in this text as well as most of his other writing, Lenin's utilization of Marxist principles generated a revolutionary theory that was distinctively his, which ever since has been referred to as "Leninism," or "Marxism-Leninism." As an ideology, this theory has had a significant global impact in political and economic affairs ever since, undergoing many different permutations as it has been either embraced or excoriated in a variety of social conditions around the world.

QUESTIONS FOR CRITICAL READING

1. How does Lenin characterize democracy in capitalist society?
2. According to Lenin, what is the essential nature of any state, and what is its relation to human freedom?
3. How does Lenin characterize "socialism," and what is its relation to "democracy"?
4. How does Lenin characterize "communism," and what kind of regulatory organization will it include?
5. In Lenin's account, how does capitalism "give birth" to communism?

TERMS TO NOTE

Utopians: A name, usually used disparagingly, for a variety of eighteenth- and nineteenth-century communist visionaries whose "blueprints" for the ideal society didn't include any realistic strategies, based on accurate analyses of existing conditions, for achieving their goals on a large scale.

opportunists: Used by Lenin and other revolutionaries to refer to socialists who advocated working legally within the existing government in capitalist society, by winning parliamentary seats, for example, rather than working toward the revolutionary overthrow of that government.

the Commune: Here, the Paris Commune of 1871, a workers' government of Paris that resulted from a revolutionary uprising in September 1870 and lasted only a few months before being put down by imperial French forces.

soviet: Generally, a "revolutionary council," or "workers' council," the basic organizational unit of elected representatives in the former Soviet Union.

savant: A French term for "learned person" or "expert."

The Economic Base of the Withering Away of the State

A most detailed elucidation of this question is given by Marx in his *Critique of the Gotha Programme* (letter to Bracke, May 15, 1875, printed only in 1891 in the *Neue Zeit,* IX-1, and in a special Russian edition). The polemical part of this remarkable work, consisting of a criticism of Lassalleanism, has, so to speak, overshadowed its positive part, namely, the analysis of the connection between the development of Communism and the withering away of the state.

1. Formulation of the Question by Marx

From a superficial comparison of the letter of Marx to Bracke (May 15, 1875) with Engels' letter to Bebel (March 28, 1875), analysed above, it might appear that Marx was much more "pro-state" than Engels, and that the difference of opinion between the two writers on the question of the state is very considerable.

Engels suggests to Bebel that all the chatter about the state should be thrown overboard; that the word "state" should be eliminated from the programme and replaced by "community"; Engels even declares that the Commune was really no longer a state in the proper sense of the word. And Marx even speaks of the "future state in Communist society," *i.e.,* he is apparently recognising the necessity of a state even under Communism.

But such a view would be fundamentally incorrect. A closer examination shows that Marx's and Engels' views on the state and its withering away were completely identical, and that Marx's expression quoted above refers merely to this withering away of the state.

It is clear that there can be no question of defining the exact moment of the *future* withering away—the more so as it must obviously be a rather lengthy process. The apparent difference between Marx and Engels is due to the different subjects they dealt with, the different aims they were pursuing. Engels set out to show to Bebel, in a plain, bold and broad outline, all the absurdity of the current superstitions concerning the state, shared to no small degree by Lassalle himself. Marx, on the other hand, only touches upon *this* question in passing, being interested mainly in another subject—the *evolution* of Communist society.

The whole theory of Marx is an application of the theory of evolution—in its most consistent, complete, well considered and fruitful form—to modern capitalism. It was natural for Marx to raise the question of applying this theory both to the *coming* collapse of capitalism and to the *future* evolution of *future* Communism.

On the basis of what *data* can the future evolution of future Communism be considered?

On the basis of the fact that *it has its origin* in capitalism, that it develops historically from capitalism, that it is the result of the action of a social force to which capitalism *has given birth.* There is no shadow of an attempt on Marx's part to conjure up a Utopia, to make idle guesses about that which cannot be known. Marx treats the question of Communism in the same way as a naturalist would treat the question of the evolution of, say, a new biological species, if he knew that such and such was its origin, and such and such the direction in which it changed.

Marx, first of all, brushes aside the confusion the Gotha Programme brings into the question of the interrelation between state and society.

> "Contemporary society" is the capitalist society—he writes—which exists in all civilised countries, more or less free of mediaeval admixture, more or less modified by each country's particular historical development, more or less developed. In contrast with this, the "contemporary state" varies with every state boundary. It is different in the Prusso-German Empire from what it is in Switzerland, and different in England from what it is in the United States. The "contemporary state" is therefore a fiction.
>
> Nevertheless, in spite of the motley variety of their forms, the different states of the various civilised countries all have this in common: they are all based on modern bourgeois society,

only a little more or less capitalistically developed. Consequently, they also have certain essential characteristics in common. In this sense, it is possible to speak of the "contemporary state" in contrast to the future, when its present root, bourgeois society, will have perished.

Then the question arises: what transformation will the state undergo in a Communist society? In other words, what social functions analogous to the present functions of the state will then still survive? This question can only be answered scientifically, and however many thousand times the word people is combined with the word state, we get not a flea-jump closer to the problem. . . .

Having thus ridiculed all talk about a "people's state," Marx formulates the question and warns us, as it were, that to arrive at a scientific answer one must rely only on firmly established scientific data.

The first fact that has been established with complete exactness by the whole theory of evolution, by science as a whole—a fact which the Utopians forgot, and which is forgotten by the present-day opportunists who are afraid of the Socialist revolution—is that, historically, there must undoubtedly be a special stage or epoch of *transition* from capitalism to Communism.

2. Transition from Capitalism to Communism

Between capitalist and Communist society—Marx continues—lies the period of the revolutionary transformation of the former into the latter. To this also corresponds a political transition period, in which the state can be no other than *the revolutionary dictatorship of the proletariat.*

This conclusion Marx bases on an analysis of the role played by the proletariat in modern capitalist society, on the data concerning the evolution of this society, and on the irreconcilability of the opposing interests of the proletariat and the bourgeoisie.

Earlier the question was put thus: to attain its emancipation, the proletariat must overthrow the bourgeoisie, conquer political power and establish its own revolutionary dictatorship.

Now the question is put somewhat differently: the transition from capitalist society, developing towards Communism, towards a Communist society, is impossible without a "political transition period," and the state in this period can only be the revolutionary dictatorship of the proletariat.

What, then, is the relation of this dictatorship to democracy?

We have seen that the *Communist Manifesto* simply places side by side the two ideas: the "transformation of the proletariat into the ruling class" and the "establishment of democracy." On the basis of all that has been said above, one can define more exactly how democracy changes in the transition from capitalism to Communism.

In capitalist society, under the conditions most favourable to its development, we have more or less complete democracy in the democratic republic. But this democracy is always bound by the narrow framework of capitalist exploitation, and consequently always remains, in reality, a democracy for the minority, only for the possessing classes, only for the rich. Freedom in capitalist society always remains just about the same as it was in the ancient Greek republics: freedom for the slave-owners. The modern wage-slaves, owing to the conditions of capitalist exploitation, are so much crushed by want and poverty that "democracy is nothing to them," "politics is nothing to them"; that, in the ordinary peaceful course of events, the majority of the population is debarred from participating in social and political life.

The correctness of this statement is perhaps most clearly proved by Germany, just because in this state constitutional legality lasted and remained stable for a remarkably long time—for nearly half a century (1871–1914)—and because Social-Democracy in Germany during that time was able to achieve far more than in other countries in "utilising legality," and was able to organise into a political party a larger proportion of the working class than anywhere else in the world.

What, then, is this largest proportion of politically conscious and active wage-slaves that has so far been observed in capitalist society? One million members of the Social-Democratic Party—out of fifteen million wage-workers! Three million organised in trade unions—out of fifteen million!

Democracy for an insignificant minority, democracy for the rich—that is the democracy of capitalist society. If we look more closely into the mechanism of capitalist democracy, everywhere, both in the "petty" —so-called petty—details of the suffrage (residential qualification, exclusion of women, etc.), and in the technique of the representative institutions, in the actual obstacles to the right of assembly (public buildings are not for "beggars"!), in the purely capitalist organisation of the daily press, etc., etc.—on all sides we see restriction after restriction upon democracy. These restrictions, exceptions, exclusions, obstacles for the poor, seem slight, especially in the eyes of one who has himself never known want and has never been in close contact with the oppressed classes in their mass life (and nine-tenths, if not ninety-nine hundredths, of the bourgeois publicists and politicians are of this class), but in their sum total these restrictions exclude and squeeze out the poor from politics and from an active share in democracy.

Marx splendidly grasped this *essence* of capitalist democracy, when, in analysing the experience of the Commune, he said that the oppressed were allowed, once every few years, to decide which particular representatives of the oppressing class should be in parliament to represent and repress them!

But from this capitalist democracy—inevitably narrow, subtly rejecting the poor, and therefore hypocritical and false to the core—progress does not march onward, simply, smoothly and directly, to "greater and greater democracy," as the liberal professors and petty-bourgeois opportunists would have us believe. No, progress marches onward, *i.e.,* towards Communism, through the dictatorship of the proletariat; it cannot do otherwise, for there is no one else and no other way to *break the resistance* of the capitalist exploiters.

But the dictatorship of the proletariat—*i.e.,* the organisation of the vanguard of the oppressed as the ruling class for the purpose of crushing the oppressors—cannot produce merely an expansion of democracy. *Together* with an immense expansion of democracy which *for the first time* becomes democracy for the poor, democracy for the people, and not democracy for the rich folk, the dictatorship of the proletariat produces a series of restrictions of liberty in the case of the oppressors, the exploiters, the capitalists. We must crush them in order to free humanity from wage-slavery; their resistance must be broken by force; it is clear that where there is suppression there is also violence, there is no liberty, no democracy.

Engels expressed this splendidly in his letter to Bebel when he said, as the reader will remember, that "as long as the proletariat still *needs* the state, it needs it not in the interests of freedom, but for the purpose of crushing its antagonists; and as soon as it becomes possible to speak of freedom, then the state, as such, ceases to exist."

Democracy for the vast majority of the people, and suppression by force, *i.e.,* exclusion from democracy, of the exploiters and oppressors of the people—this is the modification of democracy during the *transition* from capitalism to Communism.

Only in Communist society, when the resistance of the capitalists has been completely broken, when the capitalists have disappeared, when there are no classes (*i.e.,* there is no difference between the members of society in their relation to the social means of production), *only then* "the state ceases to exist," and "*it becomes possible to speak of freedom.*" Only then a really full democracy, a democracy without any exceptions, will be possible and will be realised. And only then will democracy itself begin to *wither away* due to the simple fact that, freed from capitalist slavery, from the untold horrors, savagery, absurdities and infamies of capitalist exploitation, people will gradually *become accustomed* to the observance of the elementary rules of social life that have been known for centuries and repeated for thousands of years in all school books; they will become accustomed to observing them without force, without compulsion, without subordination, without the *special apparatus* for compulsion which is called the state.

The expression "the state *withers away,*" is very well chosen, for it indicates both the gradual and the elemental nature of the process. Only habit can, and undoubtedly will, have such an effect; for we see around us millions of times how readily people get accustomed to observe the necessary rules of life in common, if there is no exploitation, if there is nothing that causes indignation, that calls forth protest and revolt and has to be *suppressed*.

Thus, in capitalist society, we have a democracy that is curtailed, poor, false; a democracy only for the rich, for the minority. The dictatorship of the proletariat, the period of transition to Communism, will, for the first time, produce democracy for the people, for the majority, side by side with the necessary suppression of the minority—the exploiters. Communism alone is capable of giving a really complete democracy, and the more complete it is the more quickly will it become unnecessary and wither away of itself.

In other words: under capitalism we have a state in the proper sense of the word, that is, special machinery for the suppression of one class by another, and of the majority by the minority at that. Naturally, for the successful discharge of such a task as the systematic suppression by the exploiting minority of the exploited majority, the greatest ferocity and savagery of suppression are required, seas of blood are required, through which mankind is marching in slavery, serfdom, and wage-labour.

Again, during the *transition* from capitalism to Communism, suppression is *still* necessary; but it is the suppression of the minority of exploiters by the majority of exploited. A special apparatus, special machinery for suppression, the "state," is *still* necessary, but this is now a transitional state, no longer a state in the usual sense, for the suppression of the minority of exploiters, by the majority of the wage slaves of *yesterday,* is a matter comparatively so easy, simple and natural that it will cost far less bloodshed than the suppression of the risings of slaves, serfs or wage labourers, and will cost mankind far less. This is compatible with the diffusion of democracy among such an overwhelming majority of the population, that the need for *special machinery* of suppression will begin to disappear. The exploiters are, naturally, unable to suppress the people without a most complex machinery for performing this task; but *the people* can suppress the exploiters even with very simple "machinery," almost without any "machinery," without any special apparatus, by the simple *organisation of the armed masses* (such as the Soviets of Workers' and Soldiers' Deputies, we may remark, anticipating a little).

Finally, only Communism renders the state absolutely unnecessary, for there is *no one* to be suppressed—"no one" in the sense of a *class,* in the sense of a systematic struggle with a definite section of the population. We are not Utopians, and we do not in the least deny the possibility and inevitability of excesses on the part of *individual persons,* nor the need to suppress *such* excesses. But, in the first place, no special machinery, no special apparatus of repression is needed for this; this will be done by the armed people itself, as simply and as readily as any crowd of civilised people, even in modern society, parts a pair of combatants or does not allow a woman to be outraged. And, secondly, we know that the fundamental social cause of excesses which consist in violating the rules of social life is the exploitation of the masses, their want and their poverty. With the removal of this chief cause, excesses will inevitably begin to *"wither away."* We do not know how quickly and in what succession, but we know that they will wither away. With their withering away, the state will also *wither away.*

Without going into Utopias, Marx defined more fully what can *now* be defined regarding this future, namely, the difference between the lower and higher phases (degrees, stages) of Communist society.

3. First Phase of Communist Society

In the *Critique of the Gotha Programme,* Marx goes into some detail to disprove the Lassallean idea of the workers' receiving under Socialism the "undiminished" or "full product of their labour." Marx shows that out of the whole of the social labour of society, it is necessary to deduct a reserve fund, a fund for the expansion of production, for the replacement of worn-out machinery, and so on; then, also, out of the means of consumption must be deducted a fund for the expenses of management, for schools, hospitals, homes for the aged, and so on.

Instead of the hazy, obscure, general phrase of Lassalle's—"the full product of his labour for the worker"—Marx gives a sober estimate of exactly how a Socialist society will have to manage its affairs. Marx undertakes a *concrete* analysis of the conditions of life of a society in which there is no capitalism, and says:

> What we are dealing with here [analysing the programme of the party] is not a Communist society which has *developed* on its own foundations, but, on the contrary, one which is just *emerging* from capitalist society, and which therefore in all respects—economic, moral and intellectual—still bears the birthmarks of the old society from whose womb it sprung.

And it is this Communist society—a society which has just come into the world out of the womb of capitalism, and which, in all respects, bears the stamp of the old society—that Marx terms the "first," or lower, phase of Communist society.

The means of production are no longer the private property of individuals. The means of production belong to the whole of society. Every member of society, performing a certain part of socially-necessary work, receives a certificate from society to the effect that he has done such and such a quantity of work. According to this certificate, he receives from the public warehouses, where articles of consumption are stored, a corresponding quantity of products. Deducting that proportion of labour which goes to the public fund, every worker, therefore, receives from society as much as he has given it.

"Equality" seems to reign supreme.

But when Lassalle, having in view such a social order (generally called Socialism, but termed by Marx the first phase of Communism), speaks of this as "just distribution," and says that this is "the equal right of each to an equal product of labour," Lassalle is mistaken, and Marx exposes his error.

"Equal right," says Marx, we indeed have here; but it is *still* a "bourgeois right," which, like every right, *presupposes inequality.* Every right is an application of the *same* measure to *different* people who, in fact, are not the same and are not equal to one another; this is why "equal right" is really a violation of equality, and an injustice. In effect, every man having done as much social labour as every other, receives an equal share of the social products (with the above-mentioned deductions).

But different people are not alike: one is strong, another is weak; one is married, the other is not; one has more children, another has less, and so on.

> . . . With equal labour—Marx concludes—and therefore an equal share in the social consumption fund, one man in fact receives more than the other, one is richer than the other, and so forth. In order to avoid all these defects, rights, instead of being equal, must be unequal.

The first phase of Communism, therefore, still cannot produce justice and equality; differences, and unjust differences, in wealth will still exist, but the *exploita-* tion of man by man will have become impossible, because it will be impossible to seize as private property the *means of production,* the factories, machines, land, and so on. In tearing down Lassalle's petty-bourgeois, confused phrase about "equality" and "justice" *in general,* Marx shows the *course of development* of Communist society, which is forced at first to destroy *only* the "injustice" that consists in the means of production having been seized by private individuals, and which *is not capable* of destroying at once the further injustice consisting in the distribution of the articles of consumption "according to work performed" (and not according to need).

The vulgar economists, including the bourgeois professors and also "our" Tugan-Baranovsky, constantly reproach the Socialists with forgetting the inequality of people and with "dreaming" of destroying this inequality. Such a reproach, as we see, only proves the extreme ignorance of the gentlemen propounding bourgeois ideology.

Marx not only takes into account with the greatest accuracy the inevitable inequality of men; he also takes into account the fact that the mere conversion of the means of production into the common property of the whole of society ("Socialism" in the generally accepted sense of the word) *does not remove* the defects of distribution and the inequality of "bourgeois right" which *continue to rule* as long as the products are divided "according to work performed."

> But these defects—Marx continues—are unavoidable in the first phase of Communist society, when, after long travail, it first emerges from capitalist society. Justice can never rise superior to the economic conditions of society and the cultural development conditioned by them.

And so, in the first phase of Communist society (generally called Socialism) "bourgeois right" is *not* abolished in its entirety, but only in part, only in proportion to the economic transformation so far attained, *i.e.,* only in respect of the means of production. "Bourgeois right" recognises them as the private property of separate individuals. Socialism converts them into common property. *To that extent,* and to that extent alone, does "bourgeois right" disappear.

However, it continues to exist as far as its other part is concerned; it remains in the capacity of regulator (determining factor) distributing the products and allotting labour among the members of society. "He who does not work, shall not eat"—this Socialist principle is *already* realised; "for an equal quantity of labour, an equal quantity of products"—this Socialist principle is also *already* realised. However, this is not yet Communism, and this does not abolish "bourgeois right," which gives to unequal individuals, in return for an unequal (in reality unequal) amount of work, an equal quantity of products.

This is a "defect," says Marx, but it is unavoidable during the first phase of Communism; for, if we are not to fall into Utopianism, we cannot imagine that, having overthrown capitalism, people will at once learn to work for society *without any standards of right;* indeed, the abolition of capitalism *does not immediately lay* the economic foundations for *such* a change.

And there is no other standard yet than that of "bourgeois right." To this extent, therefore, a form of state is still necessary, which, while maintaining public ownership of the means of production, would preserve the equality of labour and equality in the distribution of products.

The state is withering away in so far as there are no longer any capitalists, any classes, and, consequently, no *class* can be suppressed.

But the state has not yet altogether withered away, since there still remains the protection of "bourgeois right" which sanctifies actual inequality. For the complete extinction of the state, complete Communism is necessary.

4. Higher Phase of Communist Society

Marx continues:

In a higher phase of Communist society, when the enslaving subordination of individuals in the division of labour has disappeared, and with it also the antagonism between mental and physical labour; when labour has become not only a means of living, but itself the first necessity of life; when, along with the all-round development of individuals, the productive forces too have grown, and all the springs of social wealth are flowing more freely—it is only at that stage that it will be possible to pass completely beyond the narrow horizon of bourgeois rights, and for society to inscribe on its banners: from each according to his ability; to each according to his needs!

Only now can we appreciate the full correctness of Engels' remarks in which he mercilessly ridiculed all the absurdity of combining the words "freedom" and "state." While the state exists there is no freedom. When there is freedom, there will be no state.

The economic basis for the complete withering away of the state is that high stage of development of Communism when the antagonism between mental and physical labour disappears, that is to say, when one of the principal sources of modern *social* inequality disappears—a source, moreover, which it is impossible to remove immediately by the mere conversion of the means of production into public property, by the mere expropriation of the capitalists.

This expropriation will make a gigantic development of the productive forces *possible*. And seeing how incredibly, even now, capitalism *retards* this development, how much progress could be made even on the basis of modern technique at the level it has reached, we have a right to say, with the fullest confidence, that the expropriation of the capitalists will inevitably result in a gigantic development of the productive forces of human society. But how rapidly this development will go forward, how soon it will reach the point of breaking away from the division of labour, of removing the antagonism between mental and physical labour, of transforming work into the "first necessity of life"—this we do not and *cannot* know.

Consequently, we have a right to speak solely of the inevitable withering away of the state, emphasising the protracted nature of this process and its dependence upon the rapidity of development of the *higher phase* of Communism; leaving quite open the question of lengths of time, or the concrete forms of withering away, since material for the solution of such questions is *not available*.

The state will be able to wither away completely when society has realised the rule: "From each according to his ability; to each according to his needs," *i.e.,* when people have become accustomed to observe the fundamental rules of social life, and their labour is so productive, that they voluntarily work *according to their ability.* "The narrow horizon of bourgeois rights," which compels one to calculate, with the hard-heartedness of a Shylock, whether he has not worked half an hour more than another, whether he is not getting less pay than another—this narrow horizon will then be left behind. There will then be no need for any exact calculation by society of the quantity of products to be distributed to each of its members; each will take freely "according to his needs."

From the bourgeois point of view, it is easy to declare such a social order "a pure Utopia," and to sneer at the Socialists for promising each the right to receive from society, without any control of the labour of the individual citizen, any quantity of truffles, automobiles, pianos, etc. Even now, most bourgeois "savants" deliver themselves of such sneers, thereby displaying at once their ignorance and their self-seeking defence of capitalism.

Ignorance—for it has never entered the head of any Socialist to "promise" that the highest phase of Communism will arrive; while the great Socialists, in *foreseeing* its arrival, presupposed both a productivity of labour unlike the present and a person not like the present man in the street, capable of spoiling, without reflection, like the seminary students in Pomyalovsky's book,* the stores of social wealth, and of demanding the impossible.

Until the "higher" phase of Communism arrives, the Socialists demand the *strictest* control, *by society and by the state,* of the quantity of labour and the quantity of consumption; only this control must *start* with the expropriation of the capitalists, with the control of the workers over the capitalists, and must be carried out, not by a state of bureaucrats, but by a state of *armed workers.*

Self-seeking defence of capitalism by the bourgeois ideologists (and their hangers-on like Tsereteli, Chernov and Co.) consists in that they *substitute* disputes and discussions about the distant future for the essential imperative questions of present-day policy: the expropriation of the capitalists, the conversion of *all* citizens into workers and employees of *one* huge "syndicate"—the whole state—and the complete subordination of the whole of the work of this syndicate to the really democratic state of the *Soviets of Workers' and Soldiers' Deputies.*

In reality, when a learned professor, and following him some philistine, and following the latter Messrs. Tsereteli and Chernov, talk of the unreasonable Utopias, of the demagogic promises of the Bolsheviks, of the impossibility of "introducing" Socialism, it is the higher stage or phase of Communism which they have in mind, and which no one has ever promised, or even thought of "introducing," for the reason that, generally speaking, it cannot be "introduced."

And here we come to that question of the scientific difference between Socialism and Communism, upon which Engels touched in his above-quoted discussion on the incorrectness of the name "Social-Democrat." The political difference between the first, or lower, and the higher phase of Communism will in time, no doubt, be tremendous; but it would be ridiculous to emphasise it now, under capitalism, and only, perhaps, some isolated Anarchist could invest it with primary importance (if there are still some people among the Anarchists who have learned nothing from the Plekhanov-like conversion of the Kropotkins, the Graveses, the Cornelissens, and other "leading lights" of Anarchism to social-chauvinism or Anarcho-*Jusquaubout*-ism,* as Ge, one of the few Anarchists still preserving honour and conscience, has expressed it).

But the scientific difference between Socialism and Communism is clear. What is generally called Socialism was termed by Marx the "first" or lower phase of Communist society. In so far as the means of production become *public* property, the word "Communism" is also applicable here, providing we do not forget that it is *not* full Communism. The great significance of Marx's elucidations consists in this: that here, too, he consistently applies materialist dialectics, the doctrine of evolution, looking upon Communism as something which evolves *out* of capitalism. Instead of artificial, "elaborate," scholastic definitions and profitless disquisitions on the meaning of words (what Socialism

---

*Pomyalovsky's *Seminary Sketches* depicted a group of student-ruffians who engaged in destroying things for the pleasure it gave them.—*Ed.*

Jusquaubout—combination of the French words meaning "until the end." Anarcho-*Jusquaubout*-ism—Anarcho-until-the-End-ism. —*Ed.*

is, what Communism is), Marx gives an analysis of what may be called stages in the economic ripeness of Communism.

In its first phase or first stage Communism *cannot* as yet be economically ripe and entirely free of all tradition and of all taint of capitalism. Hence the interesting phenomenon of Communism retaining, in its first phase, "the narrow horizon of bourgeois rights." Bourgeois rights, with respect to distribution of articles of *consumption,* inevitably presupposes, of course, the existence of the *bourgeois state,* for rights are nothing without an apparatus capable of *enforcing* the observance of the rights.

Consequently, for a certain time not only bourgeois rights, but even the bourgeois state remains under Communism, without the bourgeoisie!

This may look like a paradox, or simply a dialectical puzzle for which Marxism is often blamed by people who would not make the least effort to study its extraordinarily profound content.

But, as a matter of fact, the old surviving in the new confronts us in life at every step, in nature as well as in society. Marx did not smuggle a scrap of "bourgeois" rights into Communism of his own accord; he indicated what is economically and politically inevitable in a society issuing *from the womb* of capitalism.

Democracy is of great importance for the working class in its struggle for freedom against the capitalists. But democracy is by no means a limit one may not overstep; it is only one of the stages in the course of development from feudalism to capitalism, and from capitalism to Communism.

Democracy means equality. The great significance of the struggle of the proletariat for equality, and the significance of equality as a slogan, are apparent, if we correctly interpret it as meaning the abolition of *classes.* But democracy means only *formal* equality. Immediately after the attainment of equality for all members of society *in respect of* the ownership of the means of production, that is, of equality of labour and equality of wages, there will inevitably arise before humanity the question of going further from formal equality to real equality, *i.e.,* to realising the rule, "From each according to his ability; to each according to his needs." By what stages, by means of what practical measures humanity will proceed to this higher

aim—this we do not and cannot know. But it is important to realise how infinitely mendacious is the usual bourgeois presentation of Socialism as something lifeless, petrified, fixed once for all, whereas in reality, it is *only* with Socialism that there will commence a rapid, genuine, real mass advance, in which first the *majority* and then the whole of the population will take part—an advance in all domains of social and individual life.

Democracy is a form of the state—one of its varieties. Consequently, like every state, it consists in organised, systematic application of force against human beings. This on the one hand. On the other hand, however, it signifies the formal recognition of the equality of all citizens, the equal right of all to determine the structure and administration of the state. This, in turn, is connected with the fact that, at a certain stage in the development of democracy, it first rallies the proletariat as a revolutionary class against capitalism, and gives it an opportunity to crush, to smash to bits, to wipe off the face of the earth the bourgeois state machinery—even its republican variety: the standing army, the police, and bureaucracy; then it substitutes for all this a *more* democratic, but still a state machinery in the shape of armed masses of workers, which becomes transformed into universal participation of the people in the militia.

Here "quantity turns into quality": *such* a degree of democracy is bound up with the abandonment of the framework of bourgeois society, and the beginning of its Socialist reconstruction. If *every one* really takes part in the administration of the state, capitalism cannot retain its hold. In its turn, capitalism, as it develops, itself creates *prerequisites* for "every one" *to be able* really to take part in the administration of the state. Among such prerequisites are: universal literacy, already realised in most of the advanced capitalist countries, then the "training and disciplining" of millions of workers by the huge, complex, and socialised apparatus of the post-office, the railways, the big factories, large-scale commerce, banking, etc., etc.

With such *economic* prerequisites it is perfectly possible, immediately, within twenty-four hours after the overthrow of the capitalists and bureaucrats, to replace them, in the control of production and distribution, in the business of *control* of labour and products, by the armed workers, by the whole people in arms. (The question of control and accounting must not be confused with the question of the scientifically educated staff of engineers, agronomists and so on. These gentlemen work today, obeying the capitalists; they will work even better tomorrow, obeying the armed workers.)

Accounting and control—these are the *chief* things necessary for the organising and correct functioning of the *first phase* of Communist society. *All* citizens are here transformed into hired employees of the state, which is made up of the armed workers. *All* citizens become employees and workers of *one* national state "syndicate." All that is required is that they should work equally, should regularly do their share of work, and should receive equal pay. The accounting and control necessary for this have been *simplified* by capitalism to the utmost, till they have become the extraordinarily simple operations of watching, recording and issuing receipts, within the reach of anybody who can read and write and knows the first four rules of arithmetic.*

When the *majority* of the people begin everywhere to keep such accounts and maintain such control over the capitalists (now converted into employees) and over the intellectual gentry, who still retain capitalist habits, this control will really become universal, general, national; and there will be no way of getting away from it, there will be "nowhere to go."

The whole of society will have become one office and one factory, with equal work and equal pay.

But this "factory" discipline, which the proletariat will extend to the whole of society after the defeat of the capitalists and the overthrow of the exploiters, is by no means our ideal, or our final aim. It is but a *foothold* necessary for the radical cleansing of society of all the hideousness and foulness of capitalist exploitation, *in order to advance further.*

From the moment when all members of society, or even only the overwhelming majority, have learned how to govern the state *themselves,* have taken this business into their own hands, have "established" control over the insignificant minority of capitalists, over the gentry with capitalist leanings, and the workers thoroughly demoralised by capitalism—from this moment the need for any government begins to disappear. The more complete the democracy, the nearer the moment when it begins to be unnecessary. The more democratic the "state" consisting of armed workers, which is "no longer a state in the proper sense of the word," the more rapidly does *every* state begin to wither away.

For when *all* have learned to manage, and independently are actually managing by themselves social production, keeping accounts, controlling the idlers, the gentlefolk, the swindlers and similar "guardians of capitalist traditions," then the escape from this national accounting and control will inevitably become so increasingly difficult, such a rare exception, and will probably be accompanied by such swift and severe punishment (for the armed workers are men of practical life, not sentimental intellectuals, and they will scarcely allow any one to trifle with them), that very soon the *necessity* of observing the simple, fundamental rules of every-day social life in common will have become a *habit.*

The door will then be wide open for the transition from the first phase of Communist society to its higher phase, and along with it to the complete withering away of the state.

---

*When most of the functions of the state are reduced to this accounting and control by the workers themselves, then it ceases to be a "political state," and the "public functions will lose their political character and be transformed into simple administrative functions" . . .

DISCUSSION QUESTIONS

1. Do you agree with Lenin's analyses of political democracy in capitalist society? Why or why not?

2. Do you think it is possible for the state (national government) to eventually "wither away"? Why or why not? Is government only a means of enforcing dominant class interests? Why or why not?

3. In your estimation, what problems might arise in the "transitional" phase of communist society (also called socialism)?

4. In the "higher phase" of communist society, what social problems might appear?

67. Benito Mussolini (1883–1945)
"The Doctrine of Fascism"

Benito Mussolini was the fascist dictator of Italy from 1922 to 1943 and Adolph Hitler's main European ally from the 1930s through most of World War II. He was born in Dovia and completed his formal education at a teacher training school in Forlì. Although Mussolini taught elementary school on and off for a few years, he eventually became involved in journalism and socialist politics. He was expelled from the Italian Socialist Party in 1914 for publicly advocating that Italy enter the war against Germany, at a time when most of the socialist parties in Europe were trying to take a strong antiwar, antinationalism stand. After World War I, he formed the first "fascist" political group in Milan, and by 1922 his Fascist Party had grown strong enough for the Italian king to ask him to head the parliamentary government in Rome. Calling himself *Il Duce* ("the Leader"), Mussolini and his fascists soon dismantled the democratic state and created a totalitarian dictatorship that was widely popular for many years. But as World War II went badly for Italy, he was ousted by the Fascist Grand Council in 1943. In 1945 he was captured and executed in northern Italy by members of the underground.

The 1932 essay reprinted here is Mussolini's best-known attempt at a theoretical formulation of the principles of fascism. Other contemporaries had articulated most of these principles before the appearance of this work, but Mussolini was the one originally to call the doctrine "fascism." In many ways fascism is a political doctrine unique to the twentieth century, though most of the ideas and values associated with it, taken separately, can be traced to earlier epochs. It also is a somewhat amorphous doctrine, finding expression in many different versions among a variety of authors, political leaders, and parties, most notably Hitler and his National Socialists in Germany. This makes the task of labeling this or that government, group, or person as "fascist" unavoidably inexact, but Mussolini offers here a fairly thorough list of what fascists typically are for and against. On this basis we can still make judgments today regarding at least the fascist tendencies we can observe in many societies in an accurate, though noncategorical, manner.

QUESTIONS FOR CRITICAL READING

1. What does Mussolini mean by claiming that the fascist conception of life is a "spiritualized" and "ethical" one, and with what is he contrasting it?
2. How does Mussolini argue against individualism ("Liberalism") and for the supremacy of the state? What does this have to do with totalitarianism?
3. How does Mussolini argue against socialism/communism?
4. What are Mussolini's arguments against "Pacifism" and in favor of war?
5. In Mussolini's view, why does fascism affirm the "tendency to Empire"?
6. How does Mussolini argue against democracy?

TERMS TO NOTE

Jacobin: A member of a radical political group active during, and for a while after, the 1789 French Revolution.

syndicalism: A doctrine and political movement in the nineteenth and twentieth centuries advocating that control of the various industries as well as the government be in the hands of trade unions.

Lictors' rods: The reference here is to "fasces," the bundles of rods or sticks containing an ax with the blade protruding, carried by the attendants, or "lictors," of an official in ancient Rome as a sign of his authority and punitive power; from "fasces" we get the word "fascism."

sub specie aeternitatis: A Latin phrase meaning "under the form of eternity," it refers to the essential nature or form of something.

agnosticism: The position of refraining from judgment concerning the existence or nonexistence of God, due to lack of knowledge either way.

(i) Fundamental Ideas

1. Like every sound political conception, Fascism is both practice and thought; action in which a doctrine is immanent, and a doctrine which, arising out of a given system of historical forces, remains embedded in them and works there from within. Hence it has a form correlative to the contingencies of place and time, but it has also a content of thought which raises it to a formula of truth in the higher level of the history of thought. In the world one does not act spiritually as a human will dominating other wills without a conception of the transient and particular reality under which it is necessary to act, and of the permanent and universal reality in which the first has its being and its life. In order to know men it is necessary to know man; and in order to know man it is necessary to know reality and its laws. There is no concept of the State which is not fundamentally a concept of life: philosophy or intuition, a system of ideas which develops logically or is gathered up into a vision or into a faith, but which is always, at least virtually, an organic conception of the world.

2. Thus Fascism could not be understood in many of its practical manifestations as a party organization, as a system of education, as a discipline, if it were not always looked at in the light of its whole way of conceiving life, a spiritualized way. The world seen through Fascism is not this material world which appears on the surface, in which man is an individual separated from all others and standing by himself, and in which he is governed by a natural law that makes him instinctively live a life of selfish and momentary pleasure. The man of Fascism is an individual who is nation and fatherland, which is a moral law, binding together individuals and the generations into a tradition and a mission, suppressing the instinct for a life enclosed within the brief round of pleasure in order to restore within duty a higher life free from the limits of time and space: a life in which the individual, through the denial of himself, through the sacrifice of his own private interests, through death itself, realizes that completely spiritual existence in which his value as a man lies.

3. Therefore it is a spiritualized conception, itself the result of the general reaction of modern times against the flabby materialistic positivism of the nineteenth century. Anti-positivistic, but positive: not sceptical, nor agnostic, nor pessimistic, nor passively optimistic, as are, in general, the doctrines (all negative) that put the centre of life outside man, who with his free will can and must create his own world. Fascism desires an active man, one engaged in activity with all his energies: it desires a man virilely conscious of the difficulties that exist in action and ready to face them. It conceives of life as a struggle, considering that it behoves man to conquer for himself that life truly worthy of him, creating first of all in himself the instrument (physical, moral, intellectual) in order to construct it. Thus for the single individual, thus for the nation, thus for humanity. Hence the high value of culture in all its forms (art, religion, science), and the enormous importance of education. Hence also the essential value of work, with which man conquers nature and creates the human world (economic, political, moral, intellectual).

4. This positive conception of life is clearly an ethical conception. It covers the whole of reality, not merely the human activity which controls it. No action can be divorced from moral judgement; there is nothing in the world which can be deprived of the value which belongs to everything in its relation to moral ends. Life, therefore, as conceived by the Fascist, is serious, austere, religious: the whole of it is poised in a world supported by the moral and responsible forces of the spirit. The Fascist disdains the "comfortable" life.

5. Fascism is a religious conception in which man is seen in his immanent relationship with a superior law and with an objective Will that transcends the particular individual and raises him to conscious membership of a spiritual society. Whoever has seen in the religious politics of the Fascist regime nothing but mere opportunism has not understood that Fascism besides being a system of government is also, and above all, a system of thought.

6. Fascism is an historical conception, in which man is what he is only in so far as he works with the spiritual process in which he finds himself, in the family or social group, in the nation and in the history in which all nations collaborate. From this follows the great value of tradition, in memories, in language, in customs, in the standards of social life. Outside history

man is nothing. Consequently Fascism is opposed to all the individualistic abstractions of a materialistic nature like those of the eighteenth century; and it is opposed to all Jacobin utopias and innovations. It does not consider that "happiness" is possible upon earth, as it appeared to be in the desire of the economic literature of the eighteenth century, and hence it rejects all teleological theories according to which mankind would reach a definitive stabilized condition at a certain period in history. This implies putting oneself outside history and life, which is a continual change and coming to be. Politically, Fascism wishes to be a realistic doctrine; practically, it aspires to solve only the problems which arise historically of themselves and that of themselves find or suggest their own solution. To act among men, as to act in the natural world, it is necessary to enter into the process of reality and to master the already operating forces.

7. Against individualism, the Fascist conception is for the State; and it is for the individual in so far as he coincides with the State, which is the conscience and universal will of man in his historical existence. It is opposed to classical Liberalism, which arose from the necessity of reacting against absolutism, and which brought its historical purpose to an end when the State was transformed into the conscience and will of the people. Liberalism denied the State in the interests of the particular individual; Fascism reaffirms the State as the true reality of the individual. And if liberty is to be the attribute of the real man, and not of that abstract puppet envisaged by individualistic Liberalism, Fascism is for liberty. And for the only liberty which can be a real thing, the liberty of the State and of the individual within the State. Therefore, for the Fascist, everything is in the State, and nothing human or spiritual exists, much less has value, outside the State. In this sense Fascism is totalitarian, and the Fascist State, the synthesis and unity of all values, interprets, develops and gives strength to the whole life of the people.

8. Outside the State there can be neither individuals nor groups (political parties, associations, syndicates, classes). Therefore Fascism is opposed to Socialism, which confines the movement of history within the class struggle and ignores the unity of classes established in one economic and moral reality in the State; and analogously it is opposed to class syndicalism. Fascism recognizes the real exigencies for which the socialist and syndicalist movement arose, but while recognizing them wishes to bring them under the control of the State and give them a purpose within the corporative system of interests reconciled within the unity of the State.

9. Individuals form classes according to the similarity of their interests, they form syndicates according to differentiated economic activities within these interests; but they form first, and above all, the State, which is not to be thought of numerically as the sum-total of individuals forming the majority of a nation. And consequently Fascism is opposed to Democracy, which equates the nation to the majority, lowering it to the level of that majority; nevertheless it is the purest form of democracy if the nation is conceived, as it should be, qualitatively and not quantitatively, as the most powerful idea (most powerful because most moral, most coherent, most true) which acts within the nation as the conscience and the will of a few, even of One, which ideal tends to become active within the conscience and the will of all—that is to say, of all those who rightly constitute a nation by reason of nature, history or race, and have set out upon the same line of development and spiritual formation as one conscience and one sole will. Not a race,[1] nor a geographically determined region, but as a community historically perpetuating itself, a multitude unified by a single idea, which is the will to existence and to power: consciousness of itself, personality.

10. This higher personality is truly the nation in so far as it is the State. It is not the nation that generates the State, as according to the old naturalistic concept which served as the basis of the political theories of the national States of the nineteenth century. Rather the nation is created by the State, which gives to the people, conscious of its own moral unity, a will and therefore an effective existence. The right of a nation to independence derives not from a literary and ideal consciousness of its own being, still less from a more or less unconscious and inert acceptance of a *de facto* situation, but from an active consciousness, from a political will in action and ready to demonstrate its own rights: that is to say, from a state already coming

---

1. "Race; it is an emotion, not a reality; ninety-five per cent of it is emotion." Mussolini.

into being. The State, in fact, as the universal ethical will, is the creator of right.

11. The nation as the State is an ethical reality which exists and lives in so far as it develops. To arrest its development is to kill it. Therefore the State is not only the authority which governs and gives the form of laws and the value of spiritual life to the wills of individuals, but it is also a power that makes its will felt abroad, making it known and respected, in other words, demonstrating the fact of its universality in all the necessary directions of its development. It is consequently organization and expansion, at least virtually. Thus it can be likened to the human will which knows no limits to its development and realizes itself in testing its own limitlessness.

12. The Fascist State, the highest and most powerful form of personality, is a force, but a spiritual force, which takes over all the forms of the moral and intellectual life of man. It cannot therefore confine itself simply to the functions of order and supervision as Liberalism desired. It is not simply a mechanism which limits the sphere of the supposed liberties of the individual. It is the form, the inner standard and the discipline of the whole person; it saturates the will as well as the intelligence. Its principle, the central inspiration of the human personality living in the civil community, pierces into the depths and makes its home in the heart of the man of action as well as of the thinker, of the artist as well as of the scientist: it is the soul of the soul.

13. Fascism, in short, is not only the giver of laws and the founder of institutions, but the educator and promoter of spiritual life. It wants to remake, not the forms of human life, but its content, man, character, faith. And to this end it requires discipline and authority that can enter into the spirits of men and there govern unopposed. Its sign, therefore, is the Lictors' rods, the symbol of unity, of strength and justice.

(ii) Political and Social Doctrine

1. When in the now distant March of 1919 I summoned to Milan, through the columns of the *Popolo d'Italia,* my surviving supporters who had followed me since the constitution of the Fasces of Revolutionary Action, founded in January 1915, there was no specific doctrinal plan in my mind. I had known and lived through only one doctrine, that of the Socialism of 1903–4 up to the winter of 1914, almost ten years. My experience in this had been that of a follower and of a leader, but not that of a theoretician. My doctrine, even in that period, had been a doctrine of action. An unequivocal Socialism, universally accepted, did not exist after 1905, when the Revisionist Movement began in Germany under Bernstein and there was formed in opposition to that, in the see-saw of tendencies, an extreme revolutionary movement, which in Italy never emerged from the condition of mere words, whilst in Russian Socialism it was the prelude to Bolshevism. Reform, Revolution, Centralization—even the echoes of the terminology are now spent; whilst in the great river of Fascism are to be found the streams which had their source in Sorel, Peguy, in the Lagardelle of the *Mouvement Socialiste* and the groups of Italian Syndicalists, who between 1904 and 1914 brought a note of novelty into Italian Socialism, which by that time had been devitalized and drugged by fornication with Giolitti, in *Pagine Libere* of Olivetti, *La Lupa* of Orano and *Divenire Sociale* of Enrico Leone.

In 1919, at the end of the War, Socialism as a doctrine was already dead: it existed only as hatred, it had still only one possibility, especially in Italy, that of revenge against those who had wished for the War and who should be made to expiate it. The *Popolo d'Italia* expressed it in its sub-title—"The Newspaper of Combatants and Producers". The word "producers" was already the expression of a tendency. Fascism was not given out to the wet nurse of a doctrine elaborated beforehand round a table: it was born of the need for action; it was not a party, but in its first two years it was a movement against all parties. The name which I gave to the organization defined its characteristics. Nevertheless, whoever rereads, in the now crumpled pages of the time, the account of the constituent assembly of the *Fasci italiani di Combattimento* will not find a doctrine, but a series of suggestions, of anticipations, of admonitions, which when freed from the inevitable vein of contingency, were destined later, after a few years, to develop into a series of doctrinal attitudes which made of Fascism a self-sufficient political doctrine able to face all others, both past and present. "If the bourgeoisie", I said at that time, "thinks to find in us a lightning-conductor, it is mistaken. We must go forward in opposition to Labour. . . . We want to accustom the working classes to being under a leader, to convince them also that it is not easy to direct an industry or a commercial undertaking successfully. . . . We shall fight against technical and spiritual retrogression. . . . The successors of the present regime still being undecided, we must not be unwilling to fight for it. We must hasten; when the present regime is superseded, we must be the ones to take its place. The right of succession belongs to us because we pushed the country into the War and we lead it to victory. The present method of political representation cannot be sufficient for us, we wish for a direct representation of individual interests. . . . It might be said against this programme that it is a return to the corporations. It doesn't matter! . . . I should like, nevertheless, the Assembly to accept the claims of national syndicalism from the point of view of economics. . . ."

Is it not surprising that from the first day in the Piazza San Sepolcro there should resound the word "Corporation" which was destined in the course of the revolution to signify one of the legislative and social creations at the base of the regime?

2. The years preceding the March on Rome were years during which the necessity of action did not tolerate enquiries or complete elaborations of doctrine. Battles were being fought in the cities and villages. There were discussions, but—and this is more sacred and important—there were deaths. People knew how to die. The doctrine—beautiful, well-formed, divided into chapters and paragraphs and surrounded by a commentary—might be missing; but there was present something more decisive to supplant it—Faith. Nevertheless, he who recalls the past with the aid of books, articles, votes in Parliament, the major and the minor speeches, he who knows how to investigate and weigh evidence, will find that the foundations of the doctrine were laid while the battle was raging. It was precisely in these years that Fascist thought armed itself, refined itself, moving towards one organization of its own. The problems of the individual and the State; the problems of authority and liberty; political and social problems and those more specifically national; the struggle against liberal, democratic, socialist, Masonic, demagogic doctrines was carried on at the same time as the "punitive expeditions". But since the "system" was lacking, adversaries ingenuously denied that

Fascism had any power to make a doctrine of its own, while the doctrine rose up, even though tumultuously, at first under the aspect of a violent and dogmatic negation, as happens to all ideas that break new ground, then under the positive aspect of a constructive policy which, during the years 1926, 1927, 1928, was realized in the laws and institutions of the regime.

Fascism is to-day clearly defined not only as a regime but as a doctrine. And I mean by this that Fascism to-day, self-critical as well as critical of other movements, has an unequivocal point of view of its own, a criterion, and hence an aim, in face of all the material and intellectual problems which oppress the people of the world.

3. Above all, Fascism, in so far as it considers and observes the future and the development of humanity quite apart from the political considerations of the moment, believes neither in the possibility nor in the utility of perpetual peace. It thus repudiates the doctrine of Pacifism—born of a renunciation of the struggle and an act of cowardice in the face of sacrifice. War alone brings up to their highest tension all human energies and puts the stamp of nobility upon the peoples who have the courage to meet it. All other trials are substitutes, which never really put a man in front of himself in the alternative of life and death. A doctrine, therefore, which begins with a prejudice in favour of peace is foreign to Fascism; as are foreign to the spirit of Fascism, even though acceptable by reason of the utility which they might have in given political situations, all internationalistic and socialistic systems which, as history proves, can be blown to the winds when emotional, idealistic and practical movements storm the hearts of peoples. Fascism carries over this anti-pacifist spirit even into the lives of individuals. The proud motto of the *Squadrista*, "Me ne frego", written on the bandages of a wound is an act of philosophy which is not only stoical, it is the epitome of a doctrine that is not only political: it is education for combat, the acceptance of the risks which it brings; it is a new way of life for Italy. Thus the Fascist accepts and loves life, he knows nothing of suicide and despises it; he looks on life as duty, ascent, conquest: life which must be noble and full: lived for oneself, but above all for those others near and far away, present and future.

4. The "demographic" policy of the regime follows from these premises. Even the Fascist does in fact love his neighbour, but this "neighbour" is not for him a vague and ill-defined concept; love for one's neighbour does not exclude necessary educational severities, and still less differentiations and distances. Fascism rejects universal concord, and, since it lives in the community of civilized peoples, it keeps them vigilantly and suspiciously before its eyes, it follows their states of mind and the changes in their interests and it does not let itself be deceived by temporary and fallacious appearances.

5. Such a conception of life makes Fascism the precise negation of that doctrine which formed the basis of the so-called Scientific or Marxian Socialism: the doctrine of historical Materialism, according to which the history of human civilizations can be explained only as the struggle of interest between the different social groups and as arising out of change in the means and instruments of production. That economic improvements—discoveries of raw materials, new methods of work, scientific inventions—should have an importance of their own, no one denies, but that they should suffice to explain human history to the exclusion of all other factors is absurd: Fascism believes, now and always, in holiness and in heroism, that is in acts in which no economic motive—remote or immediate—plays a part. With this negation of historical materialism, according to which men would be only by-products of history, who appear and disappear on the surface of the waves while in the depths the real directive forces are at work, there is also denied the immutable and irreparable "class struggle" which is the natural product of this economic conception of history, and above all it is denied that the class struggle can be the primary agent of social changes. Socialism, being thus wounded in these two primary tenets of its doctrine, nothing of it is left save the sentimental aspiration—old as humanity—towards a social order in which the sufferings and the pains of the humblest folk could be alleviated. But here Fascism rejects the concept of an economic "happiness" which would be realized socialistically and almost automatically at a given moment of economic evolution by assuring to all a maximum prosperity. Fascism denies the possibility of the materialistic conception of "happiness" and leaves it to the economists of the first half of the eighteenth century; it denies, that is, the equation of prosperity with happiness, which would transform men into animals with one sole preoccupation: that of being well-fed and fat, degraded in consequence to a merely physical existence.

6. After Socialism, Fascism attacks the whole complex of democratic ideologies and rejects them both in their theoretical premises and in their applications or practical manifestations. Fascism denies that the majority, through the mere fact of being a majority, can rule human societies; it denies that this majority can govern by means of a periodical consultation; it affirms the irremediable, fruitful and beneficent inequality of men, who cannot be levelled by such a mechanical and extrinsic fact as universal suffrage. By democratic regimes we mean those in which from time to time the people is given the illusion of being sovereign, while true effective sovereignty lies in other, perhaps irresponsible and secret, forces. Democracy is a regime without a king, but with very many kings, perhaps more exclusive, tyrannical and violent than one king even though a tyrant. This explains why Fascism, although before 1922 for reasons of expediency it made a gesture of republicanism, renounced it before the March on Rome, convinced that the question of the political forms of a State is not pre-eminent today, and that studying past and present monarchies, past and present Republics it becomes clear that monarchy and republic are not to be judged *sub specie aeternitatis,* but represent forms in which the political evolution, the history, the tradition, the psychology of a given country are manifested. Now Fascism overcomes the antithesis between monarchy and republic which retarded the movements of democracy, burdening the former with every defect and defending the latter as the regime of perfection. Now it has been seen that there are inherently reactionary and absolutistic republics, and monarchies that welcome the most daring political and social innovations.

7. "Reason, Science", said Renan (who was inspired before Fascism existed) in one of his philosophical Meditations, "are products of humanity, but to expect reason directly from the people and through the people is a chimera. It is not necessary for the existence of reason that everybody should know it. In any case, if such an initiation should be made, it would not be made by means of base democracy, which apparently

must lead to the extinction of every difficult culture, and every higher discipline. The principle that society exists only for the prosperity and the liberty of the individuals who compose it does not seem to conform with the plans of nature, plans in which the species alone is taken into consideration and the individual seems to be sacrificed. It is strongly to be feared lest the last word of democracy thus understood (I hasten to say that it can also be understood in other ways) would be a social state in which a degenerate mass would have no other care than to enjoy the ignoble pleasures of vulgar men."

Thus far Renan. Fascism rejects in democracy the absurd conventional lie of political equalitarianism clothed in the dress of collective irresponsibility and the myth of happiness and indefinite progress. But if democracy can be understood in other ways, that is, if democracy means not to relegate the people to the periphery of the State, then Fascism could be defined as an "organized, centralized, authoritarian democracy".

8. In face of Liberal doctrines, Fascism takes up an attitude of absolute opposition both in the field of politics and in that of economics. It is not necessary to exaggerate—merely for the purpose of present controversies—the importance of Liberalism in the past century, and to make of that which was one of the numerous doctrines sketched in that century a religion of humanity for all times, present and future. Liberalism flourished for no more than some fifteen years. It was born in 1830, as a reaction against the Holy Alliance that wished to drag Europe back to what it had been before 1789, and it had its year of splendour in 1848 when even Pius IX was a Liberal. Immediately afterwards the decay set in. If 1848 was a year of light and of poetry, 1849 was a year of darkness and of tragedy. The Republic of Rome was destroyed by another Republic, that of France. In the same year Marx launched the gospel of the religion of Socialism with the famous *Communist Manifesto*. In 1851 Napoleon III carried out his unliberal *coup d'état* and ruled over France until 1870, when he was dethroned by a popular revolt, but as a consequence of a military defeat which ranks among the most resounding that history can relate. The victor was Bismarck, who never knew the home of the religion of liberty or who were its prophets. It is symptomatic that a people of high culture like the Germans should have been completely ignorant of the religion of liberty during the whole of the nineteenth century. It was, there, no more than a parenthesis, represented by what has been called the "ridiculous Parliament of Frankfort" which lasted only a season. Germany has achieved her national unity outside the doctrines of Liberalism, against Liberalism, a doctrine which seems foreign to the German soul, a soul essentially monarchical, whilst Liberalism is the historical and logical beginning of anarchism. The stages of German unity are the three wars of 1864, 1866 and 1870, conducted by "Liberals" like Moltke and Bismarck. As for Italian unity, Liberalism has had in it a part absolutely inferior to the share of Mazzini and of Garibaldi, who were not Liberals. Without the intervention of the unliberal Napoleon we should not have gained Lombardy, and without the help of the unliberal Bismarck at Sadowa and Sedan, very probably we should not have gained Venice in 1866; and in 1870 we should not have entered Rome. From 1870–1915 there occurs the period in which the very priests of the new creed had to confess the twilight of their religion: defeated as it was by decadence in literature, by activism in practice. Activism: that is to say, Nationalism, Futurism, Fascism. The "Liberal" century, after having accumulated an infinity of Gordian knots, tried to untie them by the hecatomb of the World War. Never before has any religion imposed such a cruel sacrifice. Were the gods of Liberalism thirsty for blood? Now Liberalism is about to close the doors of its deserted temples because the peoples feel that its agnosticism in economics, its indifferentism in politics and in morals, would lead, as they have led, the States to certain ruin. In this way one can understand why all the political experiences of the contemporary world are anti-Liberal, and it is supremely ridiculous to wish on that account to class them outside of history; as if history were a hunting ground reserved to Liberalism and its professors, as if Liberalism were the definitive and no longer surpassable message of civilization.

9. But the Fascist repudiations of Socialism, Democracy, Liberalism must not make one think that Fascism wishes to make the world return to what it was before 1789, the year which has been indicated as the year of the beginning of the liberal-democratic age. One does not go backwards. The Fascist doctrine has

not chosen De Maistre as its prophet. Monarchical absolutism is a thing of the past and so also is every theocracy. So also feudal privileges and division into impenetrable and isolated castes have had their day. The theory of Fascist authority has nothing to do with the police State. A party that governs a nation in a totalitarian way is a new fact in history. References and comparisons are not possible. Fascism takes over from the ruins of Liberal Socialistic democratic doctrines those elements which still have a living value. It preserves those that can be called the established facts of history, it rejects all the rest, that is to say the idea of a doctrine which holds good for all times and all peoples. If it is admitted that the nineteenth century has been the century of Socialism, Liberalism and Democracy, it does not follow that the twentieth must also be the century of Liberalism, Socialism and Democracy. Political doctrines pass; peoples remain. It is to be expected that this century may be that of authority, a century of the "Right", a Fascist century. If the nineteenth was the century of the individual (Liberalism means individualism) it may be expected that this one may be the century of "collectivism" and therefore the century of the State. That a new doctrine should use the still vital elements of other doctrines is perfectly logical. No doctrine is born quite new, shining, never before seen. No doctrine can boast of an absolute "originality". It is bound, even if only historically, to other doctrines that have been, and to develop into other doctrines that will be. Thus the scientific socialism of Marx is bound to the Utopian Socialism of the Fouriers, the Owens and the Saint-Simons; thus the Liberalism of the nineteenth century is connected with the whole "Enlightenment" of the eighteenth century. Thus the doctrines of democracy are bound to the *Encyclopédie*. Every doctrine tends to direct the activity of men towards a determined objective; but the activity of man reacts upon the doctrine, transforms it, adapts it to new necessities or transcends it. The doctrine itself, therefore, must be, not words, but an act of life. Hence, the pragmatic veins in Fascism, its will to power, its will to be, its attitude in the face of the fact of "violence" and of its own courage.

10. The keystone of Fascist doctrine is the conception of the State, of its essence, of its tasks, of its ends. For Fascism the State is an absolute before which individuals and groups are relative. Individuals and groups are "thinkable" in so far as they are within the State. The Liberal State does not direct the interplay and the material and spiritual development of the groups, but limits itself to registering the results; the Fascist State has a consciousness of its own, a will of its own, on this account it is called an "ethical" State. In 1929, at the first quinquennial assembly of the regime, I said: "For Fascism, the State is not the nightwatchman who is concerned only with the personal security of the citizens; nor is it an organization for purely material ends, such as that of guaranteeing a certain degree of prosperity and a relatively peaceful social order, to achieve which a council of administration would be sufficient, nor is it a creation of mere politics with no contact with the material and complex reality of the lives of individuals and the life of peoples. The State, as conceived by Fascism and as it acts, is a spiritual and moral fact because it makes concrete the political, juridical, economic organization of the nation and such an organization is, in its origin and in its development, a manifestation of the spirit. The State is the guarantor of internal and external security, but it is also the guardian and the transmitter of the spirit of the people as it has been elaborated through the centuries in language, custom, faith. The State is not only present, it is also past, and above all future. It is the State which, transcending the brief limit of individual lives, represents the immanent conscience of the nation. The forms in which States express themselves change, but the necessity of the State remains. It is the State which educates citizens for civic virtue, makes them conscious of their mission, calls them to unity; harmonizes their interests in justice; hands on the achievements of thought in the sciences, the arts, in law, in human solidarity; it carries men from the elementary life of the tribe to the highest human expression of power which is Empire; it entrusts to the ages the names of those who died for its integrity or in obedience to its laws; it puts forward as an example and recommends to the generations that are to come the leaders who increased its territory and the men of genius who gave it glory. When the sense of the State declines and the disintegrating and centrifugal tendencies of individuals and groups prevail, national societies move to their decline."

11. From 1929 up to the present day these doctrinal positions have been strengthened by the whole

economico-political evolution of the world. It is the State alone that grows in size, in power. It is the State alone that can solve the dramatic contradictions of capitalism. What is called the crisis cannot be overcome except by the State, within the State. Where are the shades of the Jules Simons who, at the dawn of liberalism, proclaimed that "the State must strive to render itself unnecessary and to prepare for its demise"; of the MacCullochs who, in the second half of the last century, affirmed that the State must abstain from too much governing? And faced with the continual, necessary and inevitable interventions of the State in economic affairs what would the Englishman Bentham now say, according to whom industry should have asked of the State only to be left in peace? Or the German Humboldt, according to whom the "idle" State must be considered the best? It is true that the second generation of liberal economists was less extremist than the first, and already Smith himself opened, even though cautiously, the door to State intervention in economics. But when one says liberalism, one says the individual; when one says Fascism, one says the State. But the Fascist State is unique; it is an original creation. It is not reactionary, but revolutionary in that it anticipates the solutions of certain universal problems. These problems are no longer seen in the same light: in the sphere of politics they are removed from party rivalries, from the supreme power of parliament, from the irresponsibility of assemblies; in the sphere of economics they are removed from the sphere of the syndicates' activities—activities that were ever widening their scope and increasing their power, both on the workers' side and on the employers'—removed from their struggles and their designs; in the moral sphere they are divorced from ideas of the need for order, discipline and obedience, and lifted into the plane of the moral commandments of the fatherland. Fascism desires the State to be strong, organic and at the same time founded on a wide popular basis. The Fascist State has also claimed for itself the field of economics and, through the corporative, social and educational institutions which it has created, the meaning of the State reaches out to and includes the farthest off-shoots; and within the State, framed in their respective organizations, there revolve all the political, economic and spiritual forces of the nation. A State founded on millions of individ-

uals who recognize it, feel it, are ready to serve it, is not the tyrannical State of the medieval lord. It has nothing in common with the absolutist States that existed either before or after 1789. In the Fascist State the individual is not suppressed, but rather multiplied, just as in a regiment a soldier is not weakened but multiplied by the number of his comrades. The Fascist State organizes the nation, but it leaves sufficient scope to individuals; it has limited useless or harmful liberties and has preserved those that are essential. It cannot be the individual who decides in this matter, but only the State.

12. The Fascist State does not remain indifferent to the fact of religion in general and to that particular positive religion which is Italian Catholicism. The State has no theology, but it has an ethic. In the Fascist State religion is looked upon as one of the deepest manifestations of the spirit; it is, therefore, not only respected, but defended and protected. The Fascist State does not create a "God" of its own, as Robespierre once, at the height of the Convention's foolishness, wished to do; nor does it vainly seek, like Bolshevism, to expel religion from the minds of men; Fascism respects the God of the ascetics, of the saints, of the heroes, and also God as seen and prayed to by the simple and primitive heart of the people.

13. The Fascist State is a will to power and to government. In it the tradition of Rome is an idea that has force. In the doctrine of Fascism Empire is not only a territorial, military or mercantile expression, but spiritual or moral. One can think of an empire, that is to say a nation that directly or indirectly leads other nations, without needing to conquer a single square kilometre of territory. For Fascism the tendency to Empire, that is to say, to the expansion of nations, is a manifestation of vitality; its opposite, staying at home, is a sign of decadence: peoples who rise or re-rise are imperialist, peoples who die are renunciatory. Fascism is the doctrine that is most fitted to represent the aims, the states of mind, of a people, like the Italian people, rising again after many centuries of abandonment or slavery to foreigners. But Empire calls for discipline, co-ordination of forces, duty and sacrifice; this explains many aspects of the practical working of the regime and the direction of many of the forces of the State and the necessary severity shown to those who would wish to oppose this spontaneous and destined

impulse of the Italy of the twentieth century, to oppose it in the name of the superseded ideologies of the nineteenth, repudiated wherever great experiments of political and social transformation have been courageously attempted: especially where, as now, peoples thirst for authority, for leadership, for order. If every age has its own doctrine, it is apparent from a thousand signs that the doctrine of the present age is Fascism. That it is a doctrine of life is shown by the fact that it has resuscitated a faith. That this faith has conquered minds is proved by the fact that Fascism has had its dead and its martyrs.

Fascism henceforward has in the world the universality of all those doctrines which, by fulfilling themselves, have significance in the history of the human spirit.

La Dottrina del Fascismo (1932)

DISCUSSION QUESTIONS

1. Do you agree with Mussolini's position on the proper relationship between the individual and the state? Why or why not?

2. Do you agree with Mussolini's views on international relations? Why or why not?

3. Do you agree with Mussolini's characterization of the role of religion in national life? Why or why not?

4. How would you compare Mussolini's and Lenin's views on the nature and function of the state? Which position do you find more convincing? Why?

5. How would you compare Mussolini's and Dewey's views on democracy? Which position do you find more convincing? Why?

68. Peter Kropotkin (1842–1921)
"Anarchism"

Peter Kropotkin was a Russian scientist and a well-known anarchist theoretician in the decades around the turn of the twentieth century. He was born into an aristocratic family in Moscow and completed his formal schooling at a prestigious military academy, where he graduated first in his class. His interest in geology, geography, and engineering led him to choose a military assignment in eastern Siberia, allowing him to do a great deal of exploration in Asiatic Russia. He soon became sufficiently disillusioned with the governmental and military authorities that he resigned from his position, thereafter spending most of his time in scientific study and travel until 1871. By then he had seen enough human suffering and deprivation caused by political and economic oppression that he could do nothing else morally than devote the rest of his life to the cause of revolutionary social change.

The essay reprinted here was written for inclusion in the eleventh edition of the *Encyclopaedia Britannica* of 1910. This probably accounts for the more descriptive, expository, and less polemical orientation of the piece, in contrast to some of his other extensive writings. Nonetheless, his own views do emerge regarding a number of the theoretical and strategic issues being not only debated but also acted on by different revolutionary groups all over the Western capitalist world at the time. Although the central theme of all anarchist doctrine is the rejection of any form of centralized government and legal authority (the "state," again), there was not much consensus beyond that point. Kropotkin highlights the major diverse strands of the anarchist movement as it was exerting its considerable influence at the beginning of the twentieth century, while being clear that he identified with the communist-anarchist faction. He and other similarly inclined anarchists thus agreed with the Marxist critique of capitalism and advocacy of a future classless, stateless, egalitarian society, but they strongly disagreed with the Marxist assertion of the need for a transitional state after a successful revolution, during the period of socialist social reconstruction toward that goal.

QUESTIONS FOR CRITICAL READING

1. According to Kropotkin, what are the general principles of anarchism, and how would social life be organized along anarchist lines?

2. How does Kropotkin defend the claim that anarchism (of the sort he advocated) was not utopian? What does history have to do with this, in his estimation?

3. What is socialist, or communist, anarchism, and how is it different from "individualist," or libertarian, anarchism?

4. How does Kropotkin critically evaluate the "mutualism" advocated by the anarchist Pierre-Joseph Proudhon?

TERM TO NOTE

enfranchisement: In this context, the liberation from oppression; often the term refers more narrowly to being granted the legal right to vote.

————

Anarchism (from the Gr. ἀν-, and ἀρχη, contrary to authority), is the name given to a principle or theory of life and conduct under which society is conceived without government—harmony in such a society being obtained, not by submission to law, or by obedience to any authority, but by free agreements concluded between the various groups, territorial and professional, freely constituted for the sake of production and consumption, as also for the satisfaction of the infinite variety of needs and aspirations of a civilized being.

In a society developed on these lines, the voluntary associations which already now begin to cover all the fields of human activity would take a still greater extension so as to substitute themselves for the State in all its functions. They would represent an interwoven network, composed of an infinite variety of groups and federations of all sizes and degrees, local, regional, national, and international—temporary or more or less permanent—for all possible purposes: production, consumption and exchange, communications, sanitary arrangements, education, mutual protection, defense of the territory, and so on; and, on the other side, for the satisfaction of an ever-increasing number of scientific, artistic, literary, and sociable needs.

Moreover, such a society would represent nothing immutable. On the contrary—as is seen in organic life

at large—harmony would (it is contended) result from an ever-changing adjustment and readjustment of equilibrium between the multitudes of forces and influences, and this adjustment would be the easier to obtain as none of the forces would enjoy a special protection from the State.

If, it is contended, society were organized on these principles, man would not be limited in the free exercise of his powers in productive work by a capitalist monopoly, maintained by the State; nor would he be limited in the exercise of his will by a fear of punishment, or by obedience towards individuals or metaphysical entities, which both lead to depression of initiative and servility of mind. He would be guided in his actions by his own understanding, which necessarily would bear the impression of a free action and reaction between his own self and the ethical conceptions of his surroundings. Man would thus be enabled to obtain the full development of all his faculties, intellectual, artistic, and moral, without being hampered by overwork for the monopolists, or by the servility and inertia of mind of the great number. He would thus be able to reach full *individualization*, which is not possible either under the present system of *individualism*, or under any system of State socialism in the so-called Volksstaat (popular State).

The anarchist writers consider, moreover, that their conception is not a Utopia, constructed on the *a priori* method, after a few desiderata have been taken as postulates. It is derived, they maintain, from an *analysis of tendencies* that are at work already, even though state socialism may find a temporary favor with the reformers. The progress of modern technics, which wonderfully simplifies the production of all the necessaries of life; the growing spirit of independence, and the rapid spread of free initiative and free understanding in all branches of activity—including those which formerly were considered as the proper attribution of church and State—are steadily reinforcing the no-government tendency.

As to their economical conceptions, the anarchists, in common with all socialists, of whom they constitute the left wing, maintain that the now prevailing system of private ownership in land, and our capitalist production for the sake of profits, represent a monopoly which runs against both the principles of justice and the dictates of utility. They are the main obstacle which prevents the successes of modern technics from being brought into the service of all, so as to produce general well-being. The anarchists consider the wage-system and capitalist production altogether as an obstacle to progress. But they point out also that the State was, and continues to be, the chief instrument for permitting the few to monopolize the land, and the capitalists to appropriate for themselves a quite disproportionate share of the yearly accumulated surplus of production. Consequently, while combating the present monopolization of land, and capitalism altogether, the anarchists combat with the same energy the State as the main support of that system. Not this or that special form, but the State altogether, whether it be a monarchy or even a republic governed by means of the *referendum.*

The State organization, having always been, both in ancient and modern history (Macedonian empire, Roman empire, modern European states grown up on the ruins of the autonomous cities), the instrument for establishing monopolies in favor of the ruling minorities, cannot be made to work for the destruction of these monopolies. The anarchists consider, therefore, that to hand over to the State all the main sources of economic life—the land, the mines, the railways, banking, insurance, and so on—as also the management of all the main branches of industry, in addition to all the functions already accumulated in its hands (education, State-supported religions, defense of the territory, etc.), would mean to create a new instrument of tyranny. State capitalism would only increase the powers of bureaucracy and capitalism. True progress lies in the direction of decentralization, both *territorial* and *functional,* in the development of the spirit of local and personal initiative, and of free federation from the simple to the compound, *in lieu* of the present hierarchy from the center to the periphery.

In common with most socialists, the anarchists recognize that, like all evolution in nature, the slow evolution of society is followed from time to time by periods of accelerated evolution which are called revolutions; and they think that the era of revolutions is not yet closed. Periods of rapid changes will follow the periods of slow evolution, and these periods must be taken advantage of—not for increasing and widening the powers of the State, but for reducing them, through the organization in every township or com-

mune of the local groups of producers and consumers, as also the regional, and eventually the international, federations of these groups.

In virtue of the above principles the anarchists refuse to be party to the present-State organization and to support it by infusing fresh blood into it. They do not seek to constitute, and invite the workingmen not to constitute, political parties in the parliaments. Accordingly, since the foundation of the International Working Men's Association in 1864–1866, they have endeavored to promote their ideas directly amongst the labor organizations and to induce those unions to a direct struggle against capital, without placing their faith in parliamentary legislation.

The Historical Development of Anarchism

The conception of society just sketched, and the tendency which is its dynamic expression, have always existed in mankind, in opposition to the governing hierarchic conception and tendency—now the one and now the other taking the upper hand at different periods of history. To the former tendency we owe the evolution, by the masses themselves, of those institutions—the clan, the village community, the guild, the free medieval city—by means of which the masses resisted the encroachments of the conquerors and the power-seeking minorities. The same tendency asserted itself with great energy in the great religious movements of medieval times, especially in the early movements of the reform and its forerunners. At the same time it evidently found its expression in the writings of some thinkers, since the times of Lao-tze, although, owing to its non-scholastic and popular origin, it obviously found less sympathy among the scholars than the opposed tendency.

As has been pointed out by Prof. Adler in his *Geschichte des Sozialismus und Kommunismus,* Aristippus (430 B.C.), one of the founders of the Cyrenaic school, already taught that the wise must not give up their liberty to the State, and in reply to a question by Socrates he said that he did not desire to belong either to the governing or the governed class. Such an attitude, however, seems to have been dictated merely by an Epicurean attitude towards the life of the masses.

The best exponent of anarchist philosophy in ancient Greece was Zeno (342–267 or 270 B.C.), from

Crete, the founder of the Stoic philosophy, who distinctly opposed his conception of a free community without government to the state-Utopia of Plato. He repudiated the omnipotence of the State, its intervention and regimentation, and proclaimed the sovereignty of the moral law of the individual—remarking already that, while the necessary instinct of self-preservation leads man to egoism, nature has supplied a corrective to it by providing man with another instinct—that of sociability. When men are reasonable enough to follow their natural instincts, they will unite across the frontiers and constitute the Cosmos. They will have no need of law-courts or police, will have no temples and no public worship, and use no money— free gifts taking the place of the exchanges. Unfortunately, the writings of Zeno have not reached us and are only known through fragmentary quotations. However, the fact that his very wording is similar to the wording now in use, shows how deeply is laid the tendency of human nature of which he was the mouth-piece.

In medieval times we find the same views on the State expressed by the illustrious bishop of Alba, Marco Girolamo Vida, in his first dialogue *De dignitate reipublicae* (Ferd. Cavalli, in *Men. dell' Istituto Vaento*, xiii.; Dr. E. Nys, *Researches in the History of Economics*). But it is especially in several early Christian movements, beginning with the ninth century in Armenia, and in the preachings of the early Hussites, particularly Chojecki, and the early Anabaptists, especially Hans Denk (cf. Keller, *Ein Apostel der Wiedertäufer*), that one finds the same ideas forcibly expressed—special stress being laid of course on their moral aspects.

Rabelais and Fénelon, in their Utopias, have also expressed similar ideas, and they were also current in the eighteenth century amongst the French Encyclopaedists, as may be concluded from separate expressions occasionally met with in the writings of Rousseau, from Diderot's Preface to the *Voyage* of Bougainville, and so on. However, in all probability such ideas could not be developed then, owing to the rigorous censorship of the Roman Catholic Church.

These ideas found their expression later during the great French Revolution. While the Jacobins did all in their power to centralize everything in the hands of the government, it appears now, from recently published documents, that the masses of the people, in their municipalities and "sections," accomplished a considerable constructive work. They appropriated for themselves the election of the judges, the organization of supplies and equipment for the army, as also for the large cities, work for the unemployed, the management of charities, and so on. They even tried to establish a direct correspondence between the 36,000 communes of France through the intermediary of a special board, outside the National Assembly (cf. Sigismund Lacroix, *Actes de la commune de Paris*).

It was Godwin, in his *Enquiry concerning Political Justice* (2 vols., 1973), who was the first to formulate the political and economical conceptions of anarchism, even though he did not give that name to the ideas developed in his remarkable work. Laws, he wrote, are not a product of the wisdom of our ancestors; they are the product of their passions, their timidity, their jealousies and their ambition. The remedy they offer is worse than the evils they pretend to cure. If and only if all laws and courts were abolished, and the decisions in the arising contests were left to reasonable men chosen for that purpose, real justice would gradually be evolved. As to the State, Godwin frankly claimed its abolition. A society, he wrote, can perfectly well exist without any government, only the communities should be small and perfectly autonomous. Speaking of property, he stated that the rights of every one "to every substance capable of contributing to the benefit of a human being" must be regulated by justice alone, the substance must go "to him who most wants it." His conclusion was communism. Godwin, however, had not the courage to maintain his opinions. He entirely rewrote later on his chapter on property and mitigated his communist views in the second edition of *Political Justice* (8 vols., 1796).

Proudhon was the first to use, in 1840 (*Qu'est-ce que la propriété?* first memoir), the name of anarchy with application to the no-government state of society. The name of "anarchists" had been freely applied during the French Revolution by the Girondists to those revolutionaries who did not consider that the task of the Revolution was accomplished with the overthrow of Louis XVI, and insisted upon a series of economical measures being taken (the abolition of feudal rights without redemption, the return to the village communities of the communal lands enclosed since 1669, the limitation of landed property to 120 acres, progressive income-tax, the national organization of exchanges on a just value basis, which already received a beginning of practical realization, and so on).

Now Proudhon advocated a society without government, and used the word anarchy to describe it. Proudhon repudiated, as is known, all schemes of communism, according to which mankind would be driven into communistic monasteries or barracks, as also all the schemes of state or state-aided socialism which were advocated by Louis Blanc and the collectivists. When he proclaimed in his first memoir on property that "Property is theft," he meant only property in its present, Roman-law, sense of "right of use and abuse;" in property-rights, on the other hand, understood in the limited sense of *possession,* he saw the best protection against the encroachments of the State. At the same time he did not want violently to dispossess the present owners of land, dwelling-houses, mines, factories, and so on. He preferred to attain the same end by rendering capital incapable of earning interest; and this he proposed to obtain by means of a national bank, based on the mutual confidence of all those who are engaged in production, who would agree to exchange among themselves their produces at cost-value, by means of labor checks representing the hours of labor required to produce every given commodity. Under such a system, which Proudhon described as "Mutuellisme," all the exchanges of services would be strictly equivalent. Besides, such a bank would be enabled to lend money without interest, levying only something like 1 per cent, or even less, for covering the cost of administration. Every one being thus enabled to borrow the money that would be required to buy a house, nobody would agree to pay any more a yearly rent for the use of it. A general "social liquidation" would thus be rendered easy, without expropriation. The same applied to mines, railways, factories, and so on.

In a society of this type the State would be useless. The chief relations between citizens would be based on free agreement and regulated by mere account keeping. The contests might be settled by arbitration. A penetrating criticism of the State and all possible forms of government and a deep insight into all economic problems, were well-known characteristics of Proudhon's work.

It is worth noticing that French mutualism had its precursor in England, in William Thompson, who be-

gan by mutualism before he became a communist, and in his followers John Gray (*A Lecture on Human Happiness,* 1825; *The Social System,* 1831) and J. F. Bray (*Labour's Wrongs and Labour's Remedy,* 1839). It had also its precursor in America. Josiah Warren, who was born in 1798 (cf. W. Bailie, *Josiah Warren, the First American Anarchist,* Boston, 1900), and belonged to Owen's "New Harmony," considered that the failure of this enterprise was chiefly due to the suppression of individuality and the lack of initiative and responsibility. These defects, he taught, were inherent to every scheme based upon authority and the community of goods. He advocated, therefore, complete individual liberty. In 1827 he opened in Cincinnati a little country store which was the first "Equity Store," and which the people called "Time Store," because it was based on labor being exchanged hour for hour in all sorts of produce. "Cost—the limit of price," and consequently "no interest," was the motto of his store, and later on of his "Equity Village," near New York, which was still in existence in 1865. Mr. Keith's "House of Equity" at Boston, founded in 1855, is also worthy of notice.

While the economic, and especially the mutual-banking, ideas of Proudhon found supporters and even a practical application in the United States, his political conception of anarchy found but little echo in France, where the christian socialism of Lamennais and the Fourierists, and the state socialism of Louis Blanc and the followers of Saint-Simon, were dominating. These ideas found, however, some temporary support among the left-wing Hegelians in Germany, Moses Hess in 1843, and Karl Grün in 1845, who advocated anarchism. Besides, the authoritarian communism of Wilhelm Weitling having given origin to opposition amongst the Swiss workingmen, Wilhelm Marr gave expression to it in the forties.

On the other side, individualist anarchism found, also in Germany, its fullest expression in Max Stirner (Kaspar Schmidt), whose remarkable works (*Der Einzige und sein Eigenthum* and articles contributed to the *Rheinische Zeitung*) remained quite overlooked until they were brought into prominence by John Henry Mackay.

Prof. V. Basch, in a very able introduction to his interesting book, *L'Individualisme anarchiste: Max Stirner* (1904), has shown how the development of the German philosophy from Kant to Hegel, and "the absolute" of Schelling and the *Geist* of Hegel, necessarily provoked, when the anti-Hegelian revolt began, the preaching of the same "absolute" in the camp of the rebels. This was done by Stirner, who advocated, not only a complete revolt against the State and against the servitude which authoritarian communism would impose upon men, but also the full liberation of the individual from all social and moral bonds—the rehabilitation of the "I," the supremacy of the individual, complete "a-moralism," and the "association of the egoists." The final conclusion of that sort of individual anarchism has been indicated by Prof. Basch. It maintains that the aim of all superior civilization is, not to permit *all* members of the community to develop in a normal way, but to permit certain better endowed individuals "fully to develop," even at the cost of the happiness and the very existence of the mass of mankind. It is thus a return towards the most common individualism, advocated by all the would-be superior minorities, to which indeed man owes in his history precisely the State and the rest, which these individualists combat. Their individualism goes so far as to end in a negation of their own starting-point,—to say nothing of the impossibility for the individual to attain a really full development in the conditions of oppression of the masses by the "beautiful aristocracies." His development would remain uni-lateral. This is why this direction of thought, notwithstanding its undoubtedly correct and useful advocacy of the full development of each individuality, finds a hearing only in limited artistic and literary circles.

Anarchism in the International Working Men's Association

A general depression in the propaganda of all fractions of socialism followed, as is known, after the defeat of the uprising of the Paris workingmen in June 1848 and the fall of the Republic. All the socialist press was gagged during the reaction period, which lasted fully twenty years. Nevertheless, even anarchist thought began to make some progress, namely in the writings of Bellegarrique (*Coeurderoy*), and especially Joseph Déjacque (*Les Lazaréennes, L'Humanisphère,* an anarchist-communist Utopia, lately discovered and reprinted). The socialist movement revived only after 1864, when some French workingmen, all "mutualists," meeting in London during the Universal Exhibition with English followers of Robert Owen, founded the International Working Men's Association. This association developed very rapidly and adopted a policy of direct economic struggle against capitalism, without interfering in the political parliamentary agitation, and this policy was followed until 1871. However, after the Franco-German War, when the International Association was prohibited in France after the uprising of the Commune, the German workingmen, who had received manhood suffrage for elections to the newly constituted imperial parliament, insisted upon modifying the tactics of the International, and began to build up a social-democratic political party. This soon led to a division in the Working Men's Association, and the Latin federations, Spanish, Italian, Belgian, and Jurassic (France could not be represented), constituted among themselves a federal union which broke entirely with the Marxist general council of the International. Within these federations developed now what may be described as *modern anarchism.* After the names of "federalists" and "anti-authoritarians" had been used for some time by these federations the name of "anarchists," which their adversaries insisted upon applying to them, prevailed, and finally it was revindicated.

Bakunin soon became the leading spirit among these Latin federations for the development of the principles of anarchism, which he did in a number of writings, pamphlets, and letters. He demanded the complete abolition of the State, which—he wrote—is a product of religion, belongs to a lower state of civilization, represents the negation of liberty, and spoils even that which it undertakes to do for the sake of general well-being. The State was an historically necessary evil, but its complete extinction will be, sooner or later, equally necessary. Repudiating all legislation, even when issuing from universal suffrage, Bakunin claimed for each nation, each region and each commune, full autonomy, so long as it is not a menace to its neighbors, and full independence for the individual, adding that one becomes really free only when, and in proportion as, all others are free. Free federations of the communes would constitute free nations.

As to his economic conceptions, Bakunin described himself, in common with his federalist comrades of the International, a "collectivist anarchist"—not in the sense of Vidal and Pecqueur in the forties, or of their modern social-democratic followers, but to express a state of things in which all necessaries for production are owned in common by the labor groups and the free communes, while the ways of retribution of labor, communist or otherwise, would be settled by each group for itself. Social revolution, the near approach of which was foretold at that time by all socialists, would be the means of bringing into life the new conditions.

The Jurassic, the Spanish, and the Italian federations and sections of the International Working Men's Association, as also the French, the German, and the American anarchist groups, were for the next years the chief centers of anarchist thought and propaganda. They refrained from any participation in parliamentary politics, and always kept in close contact with the labor organizations. However, in the second half of the eighties and the early nineties of the nineteenth century, when the influence of the anarchists began to be felt in strikes, in the first of May demonstrations, where they promoted the idea of a general strike for an eight hours' day, and in the anti-militarist propaganda in the army, violent prosecutions were directed against them, especially in the Latin countries (including physical torture in the Barcelona Castle) and the United States (the execution of five Chicago anarchists in 1887). Against these prosecutions the anarchists retaliated by acts of violence which in their turn were followed by more executions from above, and new acts of revenge from below. This created in the general public the impression that violence is the substance of anarchism, a view repudiated by its supporters, who hold that in reality violence is resorted to by all parties in proportion as their open action is obstructed by repression, and exceptional laws render them outlaws.

Anarchism continued to develop, partly in the direction of Proudhonian "Mutuellisme," but chiefly as communist-anarchism, to which a third direction, christian-anarchism, was added by Leo Tolstoy, and a fourth, which might be described as literary-anarchism, began amongst some prominent modern writers.

The ideas of Proudhon, especially as regards mutual banking, corresponding with those of Josiah Warren, found a considerable following in the United States, creating quite a school, of which the main writers are Stephen Pearl Andrews, William Greene, Lysander Spooner (who began to write in 1850, and whose unfinished work, *Natural Law*, was full of promise), and several others, whose names will be found in Dr. Nettlau's *Bibliographie de l'anarchie*.

A prominent position among the individualist anarchists in America has been occupied by Benjamin R. Tucker, whose journal *Liberty* was started in 1881 and whose conceptions are a combination of those of Proudhon with those of Herbert Spencer. Starting from the statement that anarchists are egoists, strictly speaking, and that every group of individuals, be it a secret league of a few persons, or the Congress of the United States, has the right to oppress all mankind, provided it has the power to do so, that equal liberty for all and absolute equality ought to be the law, and "mind every one your own business" is the unique moral law of anarchism, Tucker goes on to prove that a general and thorough application of these principles would be beneficial and would offer no danger, because the powers of every individual would be limited by the exercise of the equal rights of all others. He further indicated (following H. Spencer) the difference which exists between the encroachment on somebody's rights and resistance to such an encroachment; between domination and defense: the former being equally condemnable, whether it be encroachment of a criminal upon an individual, or the encroachment of one upon all others, or of all others upon one; while resistance to encroachment is defensible and necessary. For their self-defense, both the citizen and the group have the right to any violence, including capital punishment. Violence is also justified for enforcing the duty of keeping an agreement. Tucker thus follows Spencer, and, like him, opens (in the present writer's opinion) the way for reconstituting under the heading of "defense" all the functions of the State. His criticism of the present State is very searching, and his defense of the rights of the individual very powerful. As regards his economic views B. R. Tucker follows Proudhon.

The individualist anarchism of the American Proudhonians finds, however, but little sympathy amongst the working masses. Those who profess it— they are chiefly "intellectuals"—soon realize that the *individualization* they so highly praise is not attainable by individual efforts, and either abandon the ranks of the anarchists, and are driven into the liberal individualism of the classical economists, or they retire into a sort of Epicurean a-moralism, or super-man-theory, similar to that of Stirner and Nietzsche. The great bulk of the anarchist workingmen prefer the anarchist-communist ideas which have gradually evolved out of the anarchist collectivism of the International Working Men's Association. To this direction belong—to name only the better known exponents of anarchism —Élisée Reclus, Jean Grave, Sebastien Fauré, Emile Pouget in France; Enrico Malatesta and Covelli in Italy; R. Mella, A. Lorenzo, and the mostly unknown authors of many excellent manifestos in Spain; John Most amongst the Germans; Spies, Parsons, and their followers in the United States, and so on; while Domela Nieuwenhuis occupies an intermediate position in Holland. The chief anarchist papers which have been published since 1880 also belong to that direction; while a number of anarchists of this direction have joined the so-called syndicalist movement—the French name for the non-political labor movement, devoted to direct struggle with capitalism, which has lately become so prominent in Europe.

As one of the anarchist-communist direction, the present writer for many years endeavored to develop the following ideas: to show the intimate, logical connection which exists between the modern philosophy of natural sciences and anarchism; to put anarchism on a scientific basis by the study of the tendencies that are apparent now in society and may indicate its further evolution; and to work out the basis of anarchist ethics. As regards the substance of anarchism itself, it was Kropotkin's aim to prove that communism—at least partial—has more chances of being established than collectivism, especially in communes taking the lead, and that free, or anarchist-communism is the only form of communism that has any chance of being accepted in civilized societies; communism and anarchy are therefore two terms of evolution which complete each other, the one rendering the other possible and acceptable. He has tried, moreover, to indicate how, during a revolutionary period, a large city—if its inhabitants have accepted the idea—could organize itself on the lines of free communism; the city guaranteeing to every inhabitant dwelling, food, and clothing to an extent corresponding to the comfort now available to the middle classes only, in exchange for a half-day's, or a five-hours' work; and how all those things which would be considered as luxuries might be obtained by every one if he joins for the other half of the day all sorts of free associations pursuing all possible aims—educational, literary, scientific, artistic, sports, and so on. In order to prove the first of these assertions he has analyzed the possibilities of agriculture and industrial work, both being combined with brain work. And in order to elucidate the main factors of human evolution, he has analyzed the part played in history by the popular constructive agencies of mutual aid and the historical role of the State.

Without naming himself an anarchist, Leo Tolstoy, like his predecessors in the popular religious movements of the fifteenth and sixteenth centuries, Chojecki, Denk, and many others, took the anarchist position as regards the State and property rights, deducing his conclusions from the general spirit of the teachings of the Christ and from the necessary dictates of reason. With all the might of his talent he made (especially in *The Kingdom of God in Yourselves*) a powerful criticism of the church, the State, and law altogether, and especially of the present property laws. He describes the State as the domination of the wicked ones, supported by brutal force. Robbers, he says, are far less dangerous than a well-organized government. He makes a searching criticism of the prejudices which are current now concerning the benefits conferred upon men by the church, the State, and the existing distribution of property, and from the teachings of the Christ he deduces the rule of nonresistance and the absolute condemnation of all wars. His religious arguments are, however, so well combined with arguments borrowed from a dispassionate observation of the present evils, that the anarchist portions of his works appeal to the religious and the nonreligious reader alike.

It would be impossible to represent here, in a short sketch, the penetration, on the one hand, of anarchist ideas into modern literature, and the influence, on the other hand, which the libertarian ideas of the best contemporary writers have exercised upon the development of anarchism. One ought to consult the ten big volumes of the *Supplément littéraire* to the paper *La Révolte* and later the *Temps Nouveaux*, which contain reproductions from the works of hundreds of modern authors expressing anarchist ideas, in order to realize how closely anarchism is connected with all the intellectual movement of our own times. J. S. Mill's *Liberty*, Spencer's *Individual versus The State*, Marc Guyau's

Morality without Obligation or Sanction, and Fouillée's *La morale, l'art et la religion,* the works of Multatuli (E. Douwes Dekker), Richard Wagner's *Art and Revolution,* the works of Nietzsche, Emerson, W. Lloyd Garrison, Thoreau, Alexander Herzen, Edward Carpenter, and so on; and in the domain of fiction, the dramas of Ibsen, the poetry of Walt Whitman, Tolstoy's *War and Peace,* Zola's *Paris* and *Le Travail,* the latest works of Merezhkovsky, and an infinity of works of less known authors,—are full of ideas which show how closely anarchism is interwoven with the work that is going on in modern thought in the same direction of enfranchisement of man from the bonds of the State as well as from those of capitalism.

DISCUSSION QUESTIONS

1. Do you agree with Kropotkin's analysis of the state and the role it has always played in human affairs? Why or why not?

2. Given Kropotkin's characterizations of communist anarchism and libertarian anarchism, which theory is more convincing to you if applied to the contemporary world? Why?

3. How would you compare Kropotkin's and Lenin's views on revolution, the state, and a future communist society?

4. How would you compare Kropotkin's views on the state with those of Mussolini's?

PART VI Aesthetics

IN ALL CULTURES for which there is any historical record, there is evidence that people created things such as statues, embroidered clothing, or songs that were valued for their immediate sensory qualities as well as whatever other useful purposes they might have served. Accounts also can be found in most societies of at least some people's responses to the sensuous features of natural phenomena such as a sunrise, a heavy snow, or the calm at sea after a storm. These kinds of sensory experiences, along with the variety of emotions and meanings associated with them, have fascinated thinkers around the world for a very long time, and this domain of human concern became the focus of the area of academic philosophy called aesthetics.

The term "aesthetics" (or "esthetics") was invented relatively recently in Western philosophical history by the German Alexander Baumgarten in the eighteenth century. He derived it from an ancient Greek verb for sensory perception, *aisthanomai*. As the field has evolved, it now generally includes the philosophical study of the nature and functions of aesthetic experience and the nature and evaluation of art. It is usually treated as an area of "value theory" analogous to ethics and political philosophy, since our judgments of, say, a lakeshore as beautiful or ugly, a movie as meaningful or pointless, or a poem as insightful or trivial are value judgments. At the same time that philosophical debate continues regarding the proper boundaries of aesthetic inquiry, relevant questions in the field also have been addressed by artists themselves in most media, as well as by art critics, politicians, theologians, and social, behavioral, and natural scientists. The interdisciplinary and wide-ranging character of aesthetics thus is increasingly one of its most noticeable features, exemplifying the productive interconnections between philosophy and other types of intellectual pursuit.

Readings 69 through 74 address two general questions: What is aesthetic experience? and What is art? The authors dealing primarily with the first question focus on the defining characteristics as well as the psychological, existential, and epistemological causes and effects of the aesthetic encounter with both natural phenomena and works of art. The various answers offered to the second question illustrate the ongoing debate, especially (though not exclusively) among modern Western philosophers, regarding the construction of a justifiable definition of art generally, as well as its different genres, for example, painting, music, or poetry. This quest for a universal definition in turn has been challenged both by those who argue that the attempt to identify a fixed "essence" of art is misguided and those who argue that we can't adequately characterize the nature of art apart from its specific historical and cultural context.

In readings 75 through 78 the justifiability of judgments about "good" and "bad" art is more directly addressed. This kind of belief is logically distinct from judgments about whether an artifact is or is not "art" in the first place (the latter being a matter of definition, while the former involves an appraisal of value). The authors offer objectivist and relativist positions on aesthetic value judgments, as well as perspectives emphasizing the cultural context of such judgments, including the gender colorings historically affecting artistic production and community recognition.

69. Yuriko Saito (b. 1953)
"The Japanese Appreciation of Nature"

Yuriko Saito is a philosopher who has been on the faculty at the Rhode Island School of Design since 1981. Her extensive research and writing in the field of aesthetics ties in with her work on environmental issues and Asian spiritual traditions. As indicated in the title of this 1985 essay, the central theme is the human aesthetic response to natural phenomena as it typically appears in traditional Japanese culture.

Although the immediate aesthetic experience of a natural object or event is often distinguishable from an aesthetic encounter with a human-produced work of art, Saito illuminates the common Japanese attitudes toward nature primarily by focusing on artworks that express those attitudes and reinforce them on the part of the audience. This emphasizes the idea that in cognitive and emotive life there is no fundamental disconnection between nature and art, even if not all art is "about" nature. Her analyses also show that artistic creation is often a means by which individuals or peoples make intelligible to themselves their sense of place within the rest of the natural world. Her characterization of the differences between a traditional Japanese worldview and a traditional Western worldview is especially instructive on this point.

QUESTIONS FOR CRITICAL READING

1. What is the human experience of the "sublime," and why is it deemphasized in the aesthetic experience of nature in Japanese tradition, according to Saito?

2. How does Saito explain the "emotional identification" with nature that is typical of the Japanese worldview and expressed in traditional Japanese art?

3. According to Saito, how are the four seasons used as an "aesthetic organizing principle" in Japanese daily life and artistic creation?

4. How is the fundamental sense of unity with nature manifested in the Japanese aesthetic appreciation of the transient aspects of natural phenomena?

One of the characteristics of Japanese culture is often said to be the close and harmonious relationship between man and nature. Accordingly, the Japanese attitude towards nature is described as 'man in harmony with nature' or 'man in nature' while the Japanese appreciation of nature invokes such phrases as 'the Japanese traditional love of nature' or 'the great Japanese love of nature and sense of closeness to it'.[1]

Commentators on Japanese culture point to phenomena principally taken from the aesthetic realm as evidence for this unique attitude towards and appreciation of nature in Japan. There are important seasonal festivals that celebrate the beauty of nature (such as cherry blossom-viewing, moon-viewing, snow-viewing festivals); the Japanese often attempt to bring nature into the proximity of their daily lives by designing patterns in kimono fabric after natural objects and phenomena; they construct gardens even in confined spaces, or reduce nature into miniaturized presentations by arranging flowers in an alcove, cultivating a dwarfed pine tree (*bonsai*) or creating a miniature landscape on a tray (*bonkei*). Traditional Japanese architecture is designed to harmonize with, rather than dominate, its natural surroundings. The Japanese gardens are designed without references to the kind of abstract geometrical forms employed in European formal gardens. Various Japanese folk arts, crafts and even packaging often express the respect for the qualities inherent in the natural materials. Similarly, Japanese cooking is noted for preserving as much as possible the natural qualities (not only taste, but flavour, texture, colour, and shape) of the material. Perhaps most importantly, the subject-matter of Japanese art and literature is predominantly taken from natural objects and phenomena.[2]

Such a predominance of natural themes in art, cooking, literature and architecture appears to imply that the Japanese have a very intimate relationship with and a special love for nature. However, a precise analysis of the Japanese aesthetic appreciation of nature is needed to examine the ways in which the Japanese relationship between man and nature is considered to be harmonious, since there are several possible ways in which this is rendered harmonious. Man can conceive of nature as a contrasting force and still consider the relationship to be harmonious and unified through a balance of conflicting elements. Or man can consider nature as essentially identical with man and the relationship between the two to be harmonious because of their identity. In this essay, I shall show that the traditional Japanese love of nature is based upon the conceived identity between man and nature and this conception of nature forms an important basis for their aesthetic appreciation of nature.

1. The Lack of Sublime Objects in Japanese Appreciation of Nature

Many commentators have noted that the Japanese appreciation of nature is directed exclusively towards those objects and phenomena which are small, charming and tame. This characteristic becomes conspicuous especially when we compare it with the Western and other Oriental (such as Chinese and Korean) traditions which appreciate not only those small, tame objects of nature but also gigantic or frightful aspects of nature.

Citing various short ancient poems which are perhaps the best record of the traditional Japanese appreciation of nature, Hajime Nakamura points out that 'the love of nature, in the case of the Japanese, is tied up with their tendencies to cherish minute things and treasure delicate things'.[3] Even when a grand landscape is appreciated, it is not the grandeur or awesome scale of the scene but rather its composition compressed into a compact design that is praised.

Consider, for example, how mountains are described and appreciated by the Japanese. The following well-known poem from the eighth century illustrates that the poet's appreciation of Mount Fuji is due to its graphic, compositional aspect rather than its soaring height or voluminous mass.

> When going forth I look far from the Shore of Tago,
> How white and glittering is
> The lofty Peak of Fuji,
> Crowned with snow![4]

We do not find, in this kind of appreciation, the Chinese taste for the grandiose, 'a broad prospect from the top of a tall-peak . . . craggy mountains and the dim vastness of waters'.[5] Neither do we detect a sense of fright, mystery or darkness exuded by the mountain.

A graphic illustration of the Japanese appreciation of mountains as friendly and warm rather than hostile and formidable can be found in some of the wood block prints of the Edo period. Consider, for example, Andō Hiroshige's depiction of Mount Hakone from the *Fifty-Three Sceneries of Tōkaidō*. While successfully conveying the difficulty of passing this steep mountain by fantastically exaggerating its profile, this print does not give the viewer an impression that the mountain is hostile, or that it challenges us to conquer it. Moreover, despite its steep shape, the size of the mountain relative to the size of men in procession is rather reduced, avoiding the impression that the mountain is overbearing. In addition, the colour used for the men in procession and the mountain are almost indistinguishable, again avoiding a stark contrast between the two.

The same observation can be made of the Japanese depiction of the sea. When the Japanese appreciate the ocean, it is never 'great oceans' but 'bays where boats passed to and fro between islands'; never 'the mighty ocean over which the great ships to T'ang China sailed', but rather 'the sea . . . somewhere small used by tiny boats and pleasure craft'.[6] The following poems are representative of such appreciation of the ocean.

> As the tide flows into Waka Bay,
> The cranes, with the lagoons lost in flood,
> Go crying towards the reedy shore.
>
> As we row round the jutting beaches,
> Cranes call in flocks at every inlet
> Of the many-harboured lake of Omi.[7]

Even when a rough sea is depicted in visual art (which is not frequent), it never gives the impression of ferociousness. Take, for example, the famous wood block print by Katsushika Hokusai of a gigantic wave almost swallowing boats, with Mount Fuji seen at a distance. While the represented state of affairs might be horrifying, the work does not convey such a feeling at all. Although highly evocative of dynamic movement, because of a fairly contrived and calculated composition with a distant Mount Fuji as a static focal point, this print gives us a feeling which is neither insecure nor dreadful.

Likewise, creatures depicted by the Japanese are often small, harmless ones such as butterflies, warblers, copper pheasants, cuckoos. On the other hand, ferocious, life-endangering animals such as tigers are frequently objects of appreciation in other traditions. Indeed, in the Japanese tradition we do not find a praise for 'forests filled with wild beasts'; instead there is a constant appreciation of things which are 'small, gentle and intimate'.[8]

Some thinkers ascribe this conspicuous absence of the sublime in the Japanese appreciation of nature wholly to Japan's relatively tame landscape and mild climate.[9] Tall cliffs, unbounded landscapes and soaring mountains may indeed be lacking in Japanese topography. However, the lack of appreciation of the sublime in the Japanese tradition cannot be wholly accounted for by reference to this factor. The fierce and awful aspects of nature such as annual autumn typhoons, earthquakes and rough seas are fully experienced by the Japanese, perhaps most eloquently documented by a mediaeval Buddhist recluse, Kamo no Chōmei, in his *An Account of My Hut* (1212).

In spite of the frequent occurrences of devastating typhoons, however, it is noteworthy that the morning *after* a typhoon, not the typhoon itself, is praised for its aesthetic appeal in three major classics in the Japanese tradition, *The Pillow Book* (c. 1002), *The Tale of Genji* (c. 1004) and *Essays in Idleness* (c. 1340). For example, in *The Pillow Book,* a series of anecdotes and essays concerning the Heian period court life, Sei Shōnagon praises the beauty of the morning after the storm without describing her experience of the storm itself during the previous night. The only reference made to the storm is her amazement at recognizing the arrangement of leaves 'one by one through the chinks of the lattice-window' is the work of 'the same wind which yesterday raged so violently'.[10]

How do we then account for the fact that the grand and fearful aspects of nature, while experienced by the Japanese, are not acknowledged as objects of aesthetic appreciation in their tradition? It may be helpful here first to examine, as a point of comparison, the Western notion regarding the appreciation of the sublime. Per-

haps the most theoretical discussion of man's appreciation of the sublime in the West can be found in Kant's aesthetic theory. In his theory of the sublime, Kant proposes that man's appreciation of the sublime in nature (either vast or powerful parts of nature) is based upon the fundamental contrast between nature and man. The contrast is twofold. First, man is contrasted with nature because of his apparent inadequacy to grasp the magnitude of a vast part of nature or to have dominion over its powerful part. However, second, man is also contrasted with nature because of his ultimate dominion and superiority over nature. That is, in experiencing the vast parts of nature, the feeling of pleasure is generated because we recognize that our rational faculty is capable of *thinking of* infinity in spite of the inability of our sensible faculty to grasp it. Our appreciation of the powerful aspects of nature is brought about by a similar recognition. While the power of nature may have dominion over our physical being we have ultimate dominion over nature due to our super-sensible faculty of reason which is free from those causal laws governing the phenomenal world. Indeed, Kant describes the play of mental faculties (imagination and reason) involved in our experience of the sublime to be 'harmonious *through their very contrast*'.[11]

The lack of appreciation of the sublime in the Japanese appreciation of nature, then, is explained by the Japanese view of nature in its relation to man. Rather than conceiving the relationship between man and nature as contrasting, I shall argue that the Japanese appreciate nature primarily for its identity with man. As Masaharu Anesaki observes:

> Both Buddhism and Shintoism teach that the things of nature are not essentially unlike mankind, and that they are endowed with spirits similar to those of men. Accordingly awe and sublimity are almost unknown in Japanese painting and poetry, but beauty and grace and gentleness are visible in every work of art.[12]

In what way then is nature considered to be essentially the same as man in the Japanese tradition? There are two ways in which the Japanese have traditionally identified with nature. One may be called emotional identification and the other is identification based upon the transience of both man and nature.

2. Emotive Identification with Nature

There is a long tradition in Japanese literature of emotional expression in terms of natural objects or phenomena. Lament and love, two strong emotions which constitute the major subject-matters of Japanese literature, are often expressed not directly but in terms of or by reference to nature. This tradition goes as far back as the oldest anthology of Japanese poems, *Manyōshū*, compiled in the eighth century. Shūichi Katō explains that this anthology indicates 'the court poets of the *Manyōshū* expressed their profound feelings in terms of their daily natural surroundings'.[13]

Perhaps the most explicit expression of this tradition in Japanese literature is found in Ki no Tsurayuki's preface to *Kokinshū*, another anthology of poetry, compiled in 905. In this preface Tsurayuki explicitly defines the nature of poetry as expression of emotion *in terms of* nature. Its opening paragraph states:

> Japanese poetry has the hearts of men for its seeds, which grow into numerous leaves of words. People, as they experience various events in life, speak out their hearts *in terms of* what they see and hear. On hearing a warbler chirp in plum blossoms or a kajika frog sing on the water, what living thing is not moved to sing out a poem?[14]

This identification of man and nature through emotive affinity is developed into an important aesthetic concept by an Edo-period philologist and literary critic, Motoori Norinaga (1730–1801) in his theory of *mono no aware*. Variously translated as 'pathos of things' or 'sensitivity of things', and sometimes compared to the Latin notion of '*lacrimae rerum*' ('tears of things'), *mono no aware* refers to the essential experience of sympathetic identification with natural objects or situations.

The experience and appreciation of the identification with natural objects or situations occur in two ways. Sometimes we intuit the *kokoro* (essence, spirit) of the object or situation and sympathize with it: this results in an aesthetic experience of the object based upon *mono no aware*. Hence, with respect to situations (*koto*), Norinaga claims,

> What does it mean for one to be moved by knowing *mono no aware*? It is, for example,

when one is confronted by some situation which is supposed to be happy, one feels happy. One feels happy because one apprehends the *koto no kokoro* which is happiness in this case. By the same token, one feels sad when confronted with what is supposed to be sad; because one apprehends its *koto no kokoro*. Therefore, to know *mono no aware* is to apprehend the *koto no kokoro*, which is sometimes happy and sometimes sad, depending upon the situation in question.[15]

Regarding natural objects (*mono*), he makes a similar point:

> To see cherry blossoms in full bloom and to see them as beautiful flowers is to know *mono no kokoro*. To recognize their beauty and to be moved by feeling that they are deeply beautiful is to know *mono no aware*.[16]

Some other times, when we are possessed with a strong emotion, we experience an identification with natural objects and events by colouring these objects with our emotion. Norinaga claims that the aesthetic appeal of many classical Japanese literary works is derived from descriptions of this kind of emotional identification with nature. He agrees with Kino Tsurayuki that '*mono no aware*, which is so intense that any verbal expression seems inadequate, can be expressed in a profound manner if one expresses it by what one sees or hears' such as 'the sound of wind or crickets, . . . the colour of flowers or snow.'[17] Indeed, according to Norinaga, the most important aesthetic appeal of *The Tale of Genji*, the work he praises for its expression of *mono no aware*, is its description of nature which has affinity with the characters' emotive states.

Some natural objects and phenomena are associated with certain emotive content in Japanese literature so frequently that they have been established as symbols for expressing particular emotions. For example, cherry blossoms (especially when they are falling) are often associated with sorrow in classical Japanese literature because they epitomize the transience of beauty. The autumn evening is a favourite symbol among mediaeval poets for expressing desolation and loneliness.

Whether the emotive identification between man and nature is rendered primarily as a result of man's intuitive grasp of the essence of a natural object or as a result of the imposition of feeling onto the outward reality, this appreciation of nature for being emotionally charged constitutes an important aspect of the Japanese aesthetic appreciation of nature: the appreciation of nature for its expressive quality.

While the notion of expression relevant in the aesthetic sense has become a point of dispute, I believe that George Santayana's 'two-term' account of expression is generally correct. According to him, the aesthetic expression takes place when the following 'two terms' are united or fused together: 'the first is the object actually presented, the work, the image, the expressive thing; the second is the object suggested, the further thought, emotion, or image evoked, the thing expressed'.[18] Only when these two terms are 'fused' or 'confounded' in our experience is the object said to be expressive of the idea or emotion. Many instances of our aesthetic appreciation of nature are based upon this 'fusion' between the object's sensuous surface and various associated facts such as scientific facts, historical or literary associations, or practical values. For example, we may appreciate the tremendous geological age *manifested* by the weathered surface and many layers of a geological formation; the way in which the fierceness of a battle is *reflected* in a disfigured landscape with poor vegetation; or the manner in which the danger of an animal is perceptibly *realized* in its fierce appearance. The above are all *aesthetic* appreciation of these respective objects, distinct from mere appreciation of *the fact* that the landscape is aged, the battle took place on the site, or the animal is dangerous to us.

Emotion is also often associated with a natural object or phenomenon. Emotion can be said to be aesthetically expressed by a natural object when we can *see* the landscape as emotionally charged. If the emotive content remains distinct from the object and the viewer's experience is dominated by the emotion he experiences, then the aesthetic component in the appreciation diminishes. In other words, if the appreciation is directed merely towards the feeling of loneliness, the appreciation does not seem to be aesthetic; but if it is directed towards the way in which the feeling of loneliness is embodied by the actual landscape, then the appreciation is aesthetic. While this mode of appreciating nature as a mirror of one's emotion is not limited to the Japanese tradition, it constitutes an important aspect of the Japanese aesthetic appreciation of nature.

3. The Japanese Appreciation of the Transience of Nature

The Japanese appreciation of nature for its affinity rather than contrast with man has another basis. In addition to appreciating the relatively small and gentle objects and phenomena of nature, the Japanese are also known for their appreciation of the transitory aspects of nature. This fact is most significantly reflected in the traditional phrase by which the Japanese refer to nature as an object of appreciation—*kachōfūgetsu*, flower, bird, wind and moon. Flowers (most notably cherry blossoms) do not stay in bloom forever; the bird song is always changing and passing; wind is literally passing and transitory by definition; and the moon is constantly changing its appearance and location. Indeed these natural objects and phenomena form the favourite subjects for Japanese art. Other natural objects and phenomena frequently referred to in Japanese art are also short-lived: rain, dew, fog, insects, and various seasonal flowers.[19]

The Japanese preoccupation with the change of seasons should be understood in this regard. In many instances of appreciation of nature from the earliest record, the Japanese have been most sensitive to the characteristics of each season and the transition from one to the other. Consider the following examples. *The Pillow Book* begins with the famous description of the best of each season; the first six volumes of *Kokinshū* is organized according to the four seasons;[20] a famous passage in *Essays in Idleness* (a well-known series of essays by a fourteenth-century retired Buddhist monk, Yoshida Kenkō) also is directed towards appreciating the transition of seasons.[21]

The Japanese sensitivity towards seasonal change is even today manifested in the following aesthetic phenomena. Some natural objects or phenomena are celebrated for their symbolic presentation of their respective seasons. This symbolic import has been established throughout the long tradition of the required use of the season word, *kigo*, in haiku poetry and the celebration of the seasonal festivals mentioned at the beginning of this paper.[22]

The importance of seasons in the Japanese appreciation of nature is not limited to the symbolic import vested in various individual objects and phenomena. Just as emotion often organizes various components of nature into a unified expressive whole, seasons are also used as an aesthetic organizing principle. In other words, sometimes a composition made up of various natural objects and phenomena is praised for the 'fittingness' of the objects which creates a unified whole suggestive of a particular season. For example, one of the norms of flower arrangement is to suggest the mood of a season. Master Sennō advises: 'when there comes the season for autumn flowers like chrysanthemums and gentians, your work must suggest the desolation of a withered winter moor'.[23] Japanese cooking also reflects the Japanese appreciation of seasonal changes by its emphasis on seasonable dishes and the incorporation of appropriate materials for garnish and decoration. Accordingly, many contemporary Japanese cookbooks are arranged by season.

What is the basis for this Japanese appreciation of the transitory nature of natural objects and phenomena? There is an immediate aesthetic appeal of something which does not last for long. Psychologically we tend to cherish and appreciate objects or events more if we know that they will never be the same. Hence, commentators discussing the notion of Japanese wisdom point out that the Japanese appreciation of the flower, moon and snow is based upon 'regret for the transience of phenomena' which compels them to cherish 'those rare occurrences fitting to each season and time'.[24]

A contemporary Japanese painter, Higashiyama Kaii, indicates that his experience of viewing the full moon in the spring against the foreground of drooping cherry blossoms in full bloom in the Maruyama district of Kyoto is intensified by the recognition of the transitory and non-recurring nature of the phenomenon.

> Flowers look up at the moon. The moon looks at the flowers . . . This must be what is called an encounter. Flowers stay in their fullest bloom only for a short period of time and it is very difficult for them to encounter the moon. Moreover, the full moon is only for this one night. If cloudy or rainy, this view cannot be seen. Furthermore, I must be there to watch it . . .

> If flowers are in full bloom all the time and if we exist forever, we won't be moved by this encounter. Flowers exhibit their glow of life by falling to the ground.[25]

Higashiyama, therefore, recommends that we 'think of the encounter with a particular landscape occurring only once'.[26] Such advice would have us avoid the fatigue factor which is detrimental to the aesthetic experience of any object. It is not yet clear whether transitoriness itself directly contributes to the aesthetic quality of the object, but it is aesthetically relevant in the sense that it predisposes the viewer to attend very carefully to the object and fully savour whatever the object has to offer at the moment.

Another appeal of the transitoriness of natural objects and phenomena is also aesthetic. It is based upon the pleasure we derive from imagining the condition of the object before or after the present stage and comparing them. This aspect of the appeal of the transitory and changeable nature of natural objects and phenomena is discussed by Yoshida Kenkō. In a well-known passage in *Essays in Idleness* he claims that natural objects such as flowers or the moon are best appreciated before or after their full stage.[27] 'Branches about to blossom or gardens strewn with faded flowers are worthier of our admiration' than blossoms in full bloom. As in a love affair between a man and a woman, 'in all things, it is the beginnings and ends that are interesting' because such stages of the phenomena are more stimulating to one's imagination. In particular, we appreciate the exquisite contrast between the present condition and the imagined condition of the previous or following stage. Even when an object or phenomenon is at the peak of its beauty, the appreciation is deepened by pathos based upon the apparent contrast between its present appearance and what will become of it later on.

The Japanese taste for such natural objects as cherry blossoms and moon, therefore, can be explained from the aesthetic point of view: these objects most eloquently exhibit to one's senses the transience of nature in general. Cherry blossoms are more effective than other flowers for symbolizing transience because they look most fragile and delicate, they stay in full bloom for only a short period of time, and they drift down slowly petal by petal, giving an impression that they regret falling.[28] But why is such sensuous manifestation of transience so cherished and appreciated? Why not appreciate the (apparent) permanence and stability of a rock, for example? After all, isn't transience of everything, including ourselves, considered a primary source of man's suffering?

The Japanese traditional appreciation of the transient aspect of nature stems from a further metaphysical consideration. One of the most important ideas spread by the introduction of Buddhism in the sixth century was the impermanence of everything. Everything, both nature and man, will sooner or later change through modification, destruction or death. Transience of human life was often considered a source of people's suffering and an object of lament. Youth and beauty pass. Wealth and power do not last. And, of course, no one avoids death.

Lament over these facts is the subject-matter of major literary pieces in Japan. *An Account of My Hut*, for example, presents in the first chapter the following observation on the human condition.

> It might be imagined that the houses, great and small, which vie roof against proud roof in the capital remain unchanged from one generation to the next, but when we examine whether this is true, how few are the houses that were there of old. Some were burnt last year and only since rebuilt; great houses have crumbled into hovels and those who dwell in them have fallen no less. The city is the same, the people are as numerous as ever, but of those I used to know, a bare one or two in twenty remain. They die in the morning, they are born in the evening, like foam on the water. (197)

The same theme is expressed in the beginning paragraph of perhaps the most famous tale from the Japanese mediaeval period, *The Tale of the Heike:*

> Yes, pride must have its fall, for it is as unsubstantial as a dream on a spring night. The brave and violent man—he too must die away in the end, like a whirl of dust in the wind . . .[29]

What interests us here in these two passages is not merely their rather pessimistic outlook on man's life. What is noteworthy is that the description of the transience of human life is compared to the transience of natural phenomena. Kamo no Chōmei's passage is preceded by: 'The flow of the river is ceaseless and its water is never the same. The bubbles that float in the pools, now vanishing, now forming, are not of long duration: so in the world are man and his dwellings' (197). The passage from *The Tale of Heike* is also preceded by the famous beginning: 'The bell of the Gion Temple tolls into every man's heart to warn him that all is vanity and evanescence. The faded flowers of the sala trees by the Buddha's deathbed bear witness to the truth that all who flourish are destined to decay'.

This practice of comparing the transience of human life to the transience of natural phenomena abounds in Japanese literature. Consider, for example, a well-known poem by Ono no Komachi, a ninth-century poetess renowned for her beauty, in which she laments the passing of her youth and beauty by comparing them to the passing of flowers:

> The flowers withered,
> Their colour faded away,
> While meaninglessly
> I spent my days in the world
> And the long rains were falling.[30]

This frequent association between transience of nature and transience of human life stems from the conviction that nature and man are essentially the same, rooted in the same principle of existence. As Higashiyama remarks, referring to his discussion of viewing the full moon against the cherry blossoms at Maruyama,

> Nature is alive and always changing. At the same time, we ourselves, watching nature change, are also changing day by day. Both nature and ourselves are rooted in the same fated, ever-changing cycle of birth, growth, decline and death.[31]

This belief concerning the co-identity of man and nature is the ground of the Japanese appreciation of the evanescent aspects of nature. Grief experienced at the transience of human life is transformed to aesthetic pathos when it is compared to the transience of nature. By identifying human life with nature, the Japanese find a way to justify the transience of life. That is, since *everything* is in constant flux there is no escaping change and this recognition leads to resignation and finally to an acceptance of the sorrow of human existence.[32]

As a psychologist, Hiroshi Minami, commenting on Japanese psychological characteristics, suggests, this preoccupation with the co-identity of man and nature and the appreciation of the transient are based upon 'the perception of nature and life as one and the same, and the ascription of unhappiness and misfortune to the transiency and evanescence of nature and things impermanent'.[33] This identity between man and nature leads to resignation before the facts of life and then to acceptance of life, with all its sorrow and suffering. 'Unhappiness in life is expressed through the guise of nature; because of the evanescence of nature, man realizes that it is senseless to grieve and should become reconciled to fate'.[34]

Many contemporary thinkers, in particular those concerned with ecological matters, often praise the Japanese attitude of 'man in harmony with nature' for being ethically more desirable than the Western tradition of 'man over nature' or 'man against nature'. I believe that a further critical study is needed to determine whether their praise of the Japanese attitude towards nature for its ecological implication is justified. However, the preceding discussion does suggest that the Japanese regard man and nature as fundamentally identical and appreciate nature for its unity with man. The content of this unity and co-identity between man and nature should be understood in the sense that both man and nature share the most important principle of existence in common: transience.[35] The Japanese appreciation of the evanescent aspects of nature is rooted in the psychological benefit the Japanese derive from them: justification of the impermanence of human existence.

References

1. For discussion of the Japanese harmonious relationship to nature, see Ian McHarg, *Design with Nature* (New York: Doubleday/Natural History Press, 1971), pp. 27–8; Ian McHarg, 'The Place of Nature in the City of Man', in *Western Man and Environmental Ethics* (Reading: Addison-Wesley Publishing Company, 1973); Ian Barbour, 'Environment and Man: Western Thought', in *Encyclopedia of Bioethics*, ed. Warren Reich (New York: The Free Press, 1978), I: 336–73; Lynn White, 'The Historical Roots of Our Ecological Crisis', *Science*, 155 (March 1967): 1203–7; 'Towards an Ecological Ethic', Editorial, *New Scientist*, 48 (December 1970): 575. As for the Japanese appreciation of nature, the first phrase comes from Hajime Nakamura, *Ways of Thinking of Eastern People* (Honolulu: The University Press of Hawaii, 1981), p. 355. The second phrase comes from Edwin O. Reischauer, *The Japanese* (Cambridge, Mass.: Harvard University Press, 1982), p. 148.

2. In addition to various sources which discuss each specific item (such as Japanese architecture, kimono, or Japanese cooking), the above observation is presented in the following writings on the general characteristics of Japanese culture. Masaharu Anesaki, *Art, Life, and Nature in Japan* (Tokyo: Charles E. Tuttle, 1973), Chapter 1; Tatsusaburō Hayashiya, Tadao Umesao, Michitarō Tada and Hidetoshi Katō, *Nihonjin no Chie* (*The Japanese Wisdom*) (Tokyo: Chūōkōronsha, 1977); Hajime Nakamura, 'Environment and Man: Eastern Thought', in *Encyclopedia of Bioethics*; Hajime Nakamura, *Ways of Thinking*, Chapter 34; Masao Watanabe, 'The Conception of Nature in Japanese Culture', *Science*, 183 (January 1974): 279–82.

3. Nakamura, *Ways of Thinking*, p. 356.

4. By Yamabe no Akahito, included in *Manyōshū*. Translation is taken from Nakamura, *Ways of Thinking*, p. 356.

5. Sōkichi Tsuda, *An Inquiry into the Japanese Mind as Mirrored in Literature*, trans. Fukumatsu Matsuda (Tokyo: Japanese Society for the Promotion of Science, 1970), p. 282.

6. Shūichi Katō, *A History of Japanese Literature*, trans. David Chibbett (New York: Kodansha International, 1979), I; pp. 65–6.

7. The translation of the first poem is taken from Nakamura, *Ways of Thinking*, p. 356. The second poem is taken from Katō, *History*, p. 65.

8. Katō, *History*, p. 66. And Kamo no Chōmei explains that his appreciation of the mountain life with the hooting of the owl and various other elements is dependent upon the fact that 'it is not an awesome mountain' (209). *An Account of My Hut*, trans. Donald Keene, included in *Anthology of Japanese Literature*, ed. Donald Keene (New York: Grove Press, 1960). The page reference from this work will be indicated within parentheses.

9. Anesaki, *Art, Life, and Nature*, pp. 7–8.

10. *The Pillow Book of Sei Shōnagon*, trans. and ed. Ivan Morris (Harmondsworth: Penguin Books, 1982), p. 194. Another famous passage on the typhoon in *The Tale of Genji*, while describing the storm itself, does not express a sense of awe felt by being wholly overpowered by nature's brutal force. This is partly because the experience during the storm is narrated from a house, looking out to a small enclosed garden rather than in the midst of a vast moor or a thick forest where the effect of the storm is felt to the utmost degree. See the chapter entitled 'Typhoon' in *A Wreath of Cloud: Being the Third Part of 'The Tale of Genji'*, Trans. Arthur Waley (Boston: Houghton Mifflin Company, 1927). See also section 19 of *Essays in Idleness*, trans. Donald Keene (New York: Columbia University Press, 1967).

11. Kant, *Critique of Judgment*, trans. J. H. Bernard (New York: Hafner Press, 1974), section 27, p. 97, emphasis added.

12. Anesaki, *Art, Life, and Nature*, p. 10.

13. Katō, *History,* p. 66 (my translation). Chibbett's translation reads rather inaccurately: 'the court poets of the *Manyōshū* were profoundly influenced by nature and both their love poems and their elegies reflect this'.

14. Translation is taken from Makoto Ueda in *Literary and Art Theories in Japan* (Cleveland: The Press of Western Reserve University, 1967), p. 3. This practice of expressing one's emotion by reference to nature gives rise to the important aesthetic effects of 'constraint' and 'suggestion' in Japanese literature. See Donald Keene's discussion of these effects in *Japanese Literature: An Introduction for Western Readers* (New York: Grove Press, 1955), Chapter I 'Introduction'.

15. Motoori Norinaga, *Isonokami Sasamegoto (My Personal View of Poetry)* in *Complete Works* (Tokyo: Chikuma Shobō, 1968), II, pp. 99–100, my translation.

16. Motoori Norinaga, *Shibun Yōryō (The Essence of The Tale of Genji)* in *Complete Works,* IV, p. 57, my translation.

17. Norinaga, *Isonokami,* pp. 110–11.

18. George Santayana, *The Sense of Beauty* (New York: Dover Publications, 1955), p. 121.

19. Barbara Sandrisser points out that rain is often an aesthetically celebrated phenomenon in Japanese literature and visual art. She correctly attributes the Japanese finding attraction in rain to their preoccupation with impermanence: 'Rain is inspiring. Perhaps its impermanence encourages this feeling . . . Rain appears and disappears. The experience of rain, although similar, is never the same'. 'Fine Weather—the Japanese View of Rain', *Landscape,* 26 (1982), p. 47.

20. Volumes I and II of *Kokinshū* are devoted to spring poems, volume III to summer poems, volumes IV and V to autumn poems, and volume VI to winter poems. The rest (volumes VII–XX) is devoted to poems concerning love, travel, farewell, etc., but it is commonly regarded that the best poems are found in the first six volumes.

21. Sei Shōnagon further observes in section 245 that 'things which pass quickly' are 'boat with a hoisted sail, people's age, spring, summer, fall and winter'. Also see *Essays in Idleness,* section 19.

22. The bond between cherry blossoms and spring is so firm and entrenched in the Japanese mind that an Edo-period thinker felt it necessary to remind people that cherry blossoms blooming after the spring is over are also appreciable. (Referred to by Tsuda, *Inquiry,* p. 265.)

23. Translation is by Ueda in his *Literary and Art Theories,* p. 81.

24. Hayashiya, *et. al., Nihonjin,* pp. 60–1, my translation.

25. *Nihon no Bi o Motomete (In Search of Japanese Beauty)* (Tokyo: Kodansha, 1977), pp. 26–7, my translation. The same point is made by Yoshida Kenkō in *Essays in Idleness* in which he claims that 'if man were never to fade away like the dews of Adashino, never to vanish like the smoke over Toribeyama, but lingered on forever in the world, how things would lose their power to move us!', p. 7.

26. Ibid., p. 27.

27. Yoshida Kenkō, *Essays,* pp. 115–18.

28. This aspect of cherry blossoms can be contrasted with camellia flowers, for example, which Natsume Sōseki describes 'will live in perfect serenity for hundreds of years far from the eyes of man in the shadow of the mountains, flaring into blossom and falling to earth with equal suddenness'; they 'never drift down petal by petal, but drop from the branch intact'. *Kusamakura (Grass Pillow)* in *Complete Works* (Tokyo: Chikuma Shobō, 1971), II, p. 188, my translation.

29. *The Tale of Heike,* trans. Hiroshi Kitagawa and Bruce T. Tsuchida (Tokyo: University of Tokyo Press, 1975).

30. Translated by Donald Keene, included in Keene, *Anthology,* p. 81. Yoshida Kenkō similarly describes the changeableness of this world 'as unstable as the pools and shallows of Asuka River' (25) and transitoriness of people's affection 'like cherry blossoms scattering even before a wind blew' (27). Kenkō, *Essays.*

31. Higashiyama, *Nihon no Bi,* p. 27.

32. The Japanese tendency towards the absolute acceptance of the phenomenal world is thoroughly discussed by Nakamura in *Ways of Thinking,* Chapter 34.

33. Minami, *Psychology of the Japanese People,* trans. Albert R. Ikoma (Toronto: University of Toronto Press, 1971), p. 63.

34. Ibid., p. 60. I changed Ikoma's translation here because he translates the passage incorrectly as: 'because of the evanescence of nature, man should realize that it is senseless to grieve and should become reconciled to fate'.

35. I thank the editor for his helpful comments and advice on this paper.

DISCUSSION QUESTIONS

1. Based on Saito's analyses, how would you compare the traditional Japanese perspective and the traditional Western perspective on the relationship between humans and the rest of nature? How does this attitude affect the aesthetic experience of natural phenomena?

2. Are there differences in the aesthetic appreciation of nature if one approaches it with either a spiritual or a secular attitude? Why or why not?

3. How would you apply Saito's account here to your own aesthetic experience with natural phenomena?

4. What is the difference between aesthetic and nonaesthetic experience of nature?

70. Edward Bullough (1880–1934)
"'Psychical Distance' as a Factor in Art and as an Aesthetic Principle"

Edward Bullough was born in Switzerland but lived most of his life in England, where he was educated at Cambridge University and eventually served on the faculty there as well. As an academician he primarily taught languages and literature, especially German and Italian, and he became increasingly interested in the science of psychology as it was developing around the turn of the twentieth century. In particular, he thought psychology was useful to the study of aesthetics because it could get at the nature and causes of human "aesthetic consciousness" better than traditional philosophical approaches.

This selection is from what has become Bullough's most famous essay, published in *The British Journal of Psychology* in 1912 and titled "'Psychical Distance' as a Factor in Art and as an Aesthetic Principle." In it he explores the psychological dynamics involved in the aesthetic appreciation of both natural phenomena and works of art and how that kind of experience differs (and, he would say, *should* differ) from everyday practical experience even of the same thing. He develops the concept of "psychical distance" to account for this domain of human experience he believed was distinctive and which could be more or less cultivated by individuals. He uses this concept as a descriptive and explanatory notion and also as a normative principle recommended to guide spectators and artists whose goal is the generation of "truly" aesthetic experience.

QUESTIONS FOR CRITICAL READING

1. What does Bullough mean by the concept of "psychical distance"? What examples does he use to help explain it?
2. What does Bullough mean by "the antinomy of distance," and what does it imply regarding the proper psychological conditions for aesthetic appreciation?
3. What is the difference between "under-distancing" and "over-distancing," according to Bullough, and how is this relevant to the difference in perspective between artist and audience?
4. What does Bullough mean by saying that art is generally "anti-realistic," and how does his concept of "Distance" help explain this fact?

TERMS TO NOTE

Annahmen: A German term meaning "assumption" or "supposition."
Scheingefuhle: A German term translatable as "illusory feeling."
antinomy: An internal opposition in a concept, theory, or law.
mimesis: Having to do with imitation or copying.
pleinairism: Here, an approach to painting, popularized in France in the latter part of the nineteenth century, whereby artists used outdoor light rather than painting in a studio.

I

1. The conception of "Distance" suggests, in connection with Art, certain trains of thought by no means devoid of interest or of speculative importance. Perhaps the most obvious suggestion is that of *actual spatial* distance, i.e. the distance of a work of Art from the spectator, or that of *represented spatial* distance, i.e. the distance represented within the work. Less obvious, more metaphorical, is the meaning of *temporal* distance. The first was noticed already by Aristotle in his *Poetics;* the second has played a great part in the history of painting in the form of perspective; the distinction between these two kinds of distance assumes special importance theoretically in the differentiation between sculpture in the round, and relief-sculpture. Temporal distance, remoteness from us in point of time, though often a cause of misconceptions, has been declared to be a factor of considerable weight in our appreciation.

It is not, however, in any of these meanings that "Distance" is put forward here, though it will be clear in the course of this essay that the above mentioned kinds of distance are rather special forms of the conception of Distance as advocated here, and derive whatever *aesthetic* qualities they may possess from

Distance in its general connotation as "psychical distance."

A short illustration will explain what is meant by "Psychical Distance." Imagine a fog at sea: for most people it is an experience of acute unpleasantness. Apart from the physical annoyance and remoter forms of discomfort such as delays, it is apt to produce feelings of peculiar anxiety, fears of invisible dangers, strains of watching and listening for distant and un-localized signals. The listless movements of the ship and her warning calls soon tell upon the nerves of the passengers; and that special, expectant, tacit anxiety and nervousness, always associated with this experience, make a fog the dreaded terror of the sea (all the more terrifying because of its very silence and gentle-ness) for the expert seafarer no less than for the igno-rant landsman.

Nevertheless, a fog at sea can be a source of intense relish and enjoyment. Abstract from the experience of the sea fog, for the moment, its danger and practical unpleasantness, just as every one in the enjoyment of a mountain-climb disregards its physical labor and its danger (though, it is not denied, that these may in-cidentally enter into the enjoyment and enhance it); direct the attention to the features "objectively" con-stituting the phenomenon—the veil surrounding you with an opaqueness as of transparent milk, blurring the outline of things and distorting their shapes into weird grotesqueness; observe the carrying-power of the air, producing the impression as if you could touch some far-off siren by merely putting out your hand and letting it lose itself behind that white wall; note the curious creamy smoothness of the water, hypo-critically denying as it were any suggestion of danger; and, above all, the strange solitude and remoteness from the world, as it can be found only on the highest mountain-tops: and the experience may acquire, in its uncanny mingling of repose and terror, a flavor of such concentrated poignancy and delight as to con-trast sharply with the blind and distempered anxiety of its other aspects. This contrast, often emerging with startling suddenness, is like a momentary switching on of some new current, or the passing ray of a brighter light, illuminating the outlook upon perhaps the most ordinary and familiar objects—an impression which we experience sometimes in instants of direct extrem-ity, when our practical interest snaps like a wire from

sheer over-tension, and we watch the consummation of some impending catastrophe with the marveling unconcern of a mere spectator.

It is a difference of outlook, due—if such a meta-phor is permissible—to the insertion of Distance. This Distance appears to lie between our own self and its affections, using the latter term in its broadest sense as anything which affects our being, bodily or spiritually, e.g. as sensation, perception, emotional state or idea. Usually, though not always, it amounts to the same thing to say that the Distance lies between our own self and such objects as are the sources or vehicles of such affections.

Thus, in the fog, the transformation by Distance is produced in the first instance by putting the phenom-enon, so to speak, out of gear with our practical, actual self; by allowing it to stand outside the context of our personal needs and ends—in short, by looking at it "objectively," as it has often been called, by permitting only such reactions on our part as emphasize the "ob-jective" features of the experience, and by interpreting even our "subjective" affections not as modes of our being but rather as characteristics of the phenomenon.

The working of Distance is, accordingly, not sim-ple, but highly complex. It has a *negative*, inhibitory aspect—the cutting-out of the practical sides of things and of our practical attitude to them—and a *positive* side—the elaboration of the experience on the new basis created by the inhibitory action of distance.

2. Consequently, this distanced view of things is not, and cannot be, our normal outlook. As a rule, experiences constantly turn the same side towards us, namely, that which has the strongest practical force of appeal. We are not ordinarily aware of those aspects of things which do not touch us immediately and prac-tically, nor are we generally conscious of impressions apart from our own self which is impressed. The sud-den view of things from their reverse, usually un-noticed, side, comes upon us as a revelation, and such revelations are precisely those of Art. In this most gen-eral sense, Distance is a factor in all Art.

3. It is, for this very reason, also an aesthetic prin-ciple. The aesthetic contemplation and the aesthetic outlook have often been described as "objective." We speak of "objective" artists as Shakespeare or Velas-quez, of "objective" works or art-forms as Homer's *Iliad* or the drama. It is a term constantly occurring in

discussions and criticisms, though its sense, if pressed at all, becomes very questionable. For certain forms of Art, such as lyrical poetry, are said to be "subjective"; Shelley, for example, would usually be considered a "subjective" writer. On the other hand, no work of Art can be genuinely "objective" in the sense in which this term might be applied to work on history or to a scientific treatise; nor can it be "subjective" in the ordinary acceptance of that term, as a personal feeling, a direct statement of a wish or belief, or a cry of passion is subjective. "Objectivity" and "subjectivity" are a pair of opposites which in their mutual exclusiveness when applied to Art soon lead to confusion.

Nor are they the only pair of opposites. Art has with equal vigor been declared alternately "idealistic" and "realistic," "sensual" and "spiritual," "individualistic" and "typical." Between the defence of either terms of such antitheses most aesthetic theories have vacillated. It is one of the contentions of this essay that such opposites find their synthesis in the more fundamental conception of Distance.

Distance further provides the much needed criterion of the beautiful as distinct from the agreeable.

Again, it marks one of the most important steps in the process of artistic creation and serves as a distinguishing feature of what is commonly so loosely described as the "artistic temperament."

Finally, it may claim to be considered as one of the essential characteristics of the "aesthetic consciousness," if I may describe by this term that special mental attitude towards, and outlook upon, experience, which finds its most pregnant expression in the various forms of Art.

II

Distance, as I said before, is obtained by separating the object and its appeal from one's own self, by putting it out of gear with practical needs and ends. Thereby the "contemplation" of the object becomes alone possible. But it does not mean that the relation between the self and the object is broken to the extent of becoming "impersonal." Of the alternatives "personal" and "impersonal" the latter surely comes nearer to the truth; but here, as elsewhere, we meet the difficulty of having to express certain facts in terms coined for entirely different uses. To do so usually results in paradoxes, which are nowhere more inevitable than in discussions upon Art. "Personal" and "impersonal," "subjective" and "objective" are such terms, devised for purposes other than aesthetic speculation, and becoming loose and ambiguous as soon as applied outside the sphere of their special meanings. In giving preference therefore to the term "impersonal" to describe the relation between the spectator and a work of Art, it is to be noticed that it is not impersonal in the sense in which we speak of the "impersonal" character of Science, for instance. In order to obtain "objectively valid" results the scientist excludes the "personal factor," *i.e.* his personal wishes as to the validity of his results, his predilection for any particular system to be proved or disproved by his research. It goes without saying that all experiments and investigations are undertaken out of personal interest in the science, for the ultimate support of a definite assumption, and involve personal hopes of success but this does not affect the "dispassionate" attitude of the investigator, under pain of being accused of "manufacturing his evidence."

1. Distance does not imply an impersonal, purely intellectually interested relation of such a kind. On the contrary, it describes a *personal* relation, often highly emotionally colored, but of a *peculiar character*. Its peculiarity lies in that the personal character of the relation has been, so to speak, filtered. It has been cleared of the practical, concrete nature of its appeal, without, however, thereby losing its original constitution. One of the best-known examples is to be found in our attitude towards the events and characters of the drama: they appeal to us like persons and incidents of normal experience, except that that side of their appeal, which would usually affect us in a directly personal manner, is held in abeyance. This difference, so well known as to be almost trivial, is generally explained by reference to the knowledge that the characters and situations are "unreal," imaginary. In this sense Witasek operating with Meinong's theory of *Annahmen,* has described the emotions involved in witnessing a drama as *Scheingefuhle,* a term which has so frequently been misunderstood in discussions of his theories. But, as a matter of fact, the "assumption" upon which the imaginative emotional reaction is based is not necessarily the condition, but often the consequence, of Distance; that is to say, the converse of the reason

usually stated would then be true: *viz.* that Distance, by changing our relation to the characters, renders them seemingly fictitious, not that the fictitiousness of the characters alters our feelings toward them. It is, of course, to be granted that the actual and admitted unreality of the dramatic action reinforces the effect of Distance. But surely the proverbial unsophisticated yokel, whose chivalrous interference in the play on behalf of the hapless heroine can only be prevented by impressing upon him that "they are only pretending," is not the ideal type of theatrical audience. The proof of the seeming paradox that it is Distance which primarily gives to dramatic action the appearance of unreality and not *vice versa,* is the observation that the same filtration of our sentiments and the same seeming "unreality" of *actual* men and things occur, when at times, by a sudden change of inward perspective, we are overcome by the feeling that "all the world's a stage."

2. This personal, but "distanced" relation (as I will venture to call this nameless character of our view) directs attention to a strange fact which appears to be one of the fundamental paradoxes of Art: it is what I propose to call "the antinomy of Distance."

It will be readily admitted that a work of art has the more chance of appealing to us the better it finds us prepared for its particular kind of appeal. Indeed, without some degree of predisposition on our part, it must necessarily remain incomprehensible, and to that extent unappreciated. The success and intensity of its appeal would seem, therefore, to stand in direct proportion to the completeness with which it corresponds with our intellectual and emotional peculiarities and the idiosyncrasies of our experience. The absence of such a concordance between the characters of a work and of the spectator is, of course, the most general explanation for differences of "tastes."

At the same time, such a principle of concordance requires a qualification, which leads at once to the antinomy of distance.

Suppose a man, who believes that he has cause to be jealous about his wife, witnesses a performance of *Othello.* He will the more perfectly appreciate the situation, conduct and character of Othello, the more exactly the feelings and experiences of Othello coincide with his own—at least he ought to on the above principle of concordance. In point of fact, he will

probably do anything but appreciate the play. In reality, the concordance will merely render him acutely conscious of his own jealousy; by a sudden reversal of perspective he will no longer see Othello apparently betrayed by Desdemona, but himself in an analogous situation with his own wife. This reversal of perspective is the consequence of the loss of Distance.

If this be taken as a typical case, it follows that the qualification required is that the coincidence should be as complete as is compatible with maintaining Distance. The jealous spectator of *Othello* will indeed appreciate and enter into the play the more keenly, the greater the resemblance with his own experience—*provided* that he succeeds in keeping the Distance between the action of the play and his personal feelings: a very difficult performance in the circumstance. It is on account of the same difficulty that the expert and the professional critic make a bad audience, since their expertness and critical professionalism are *practical* activities, involving their concrete personality and constantly endangering their Distance. (It is, bye the way, one of the reasons why Criticism is an art, for it requires the constant interchange from the practical to the distanced attitude and *vice versa,* which is characteristic of artists.)

The same qualification applies to the artist. He will prove artistically most effective in the formulation of an intensely *personal* experience, but he can formulate it artistically only on condition of a detachment from the experience *qua personal.* Hence the statement of so many artists that artistic formulation was to them a kind of catharsis, a means of ridding themselves of feelings and ideas the acuteness of which they felt almost as a kind of obsession. Hence, on the other hand, the failure of the average man to convey to others at all adequately the impression of an overwhelming joy or sorrow. His personal implication in the event renders it impossible for him to formulate and present it in such a way as to make others, like himself, feel all the meaning and fullness which it possesses for him.

What is therefore, both in appreciation and production, most desirable is the *utmost decrease of Distance without its disappearance.*

3. Closely related, in fact a presupposition to the "antinomy," is the *variability of Distance.* Herein especially lies the advantage of Distance compared with such terms as "objectivity" and "detachment." Neither

of them implies a *personal* relaxation—indeed both actually preclude it; and the mere inflexibility and exclusiveness of their opposites render their application generally meaningless.

Distance, on the contrary, admits naturally of degrees, and differs not only according to the nature of the *object,* which may impose a greater or smaller degree of Distance, but varies also according to the *individual's capacity* for maintaining a greater or lesser degree. And here on my remark that not only do *persons differ from each other* in their habitual measure of Distance, but that the *same individual differs* in his ability to maintain it in the face of different objects and different arts.

There exist, therefore, two different sets of conditions affecting the degree of Distance in any given case: those offered by the object and those realized by the subject. In their interplay they afford one of the most extensive explanations for varieties of aesthetic experience, since loss of Distance, whether due to the one or the other, means loss of aesthetic appreciation.

In short, Distance may be said to be *variable both according to the distancing-power of the individual, and according to the character of the object.*

There are two ways of losing Distance: either to "under-distance" or to "over-distance." "Under-distancing" is the commonest failing of the *subject,* an excess of Distance is a frequent failing of Art, especially in the past. Historically it looks almost as if Art had attempted to meet the deficiency of Distance on the part of the subject and had overshot the mark in this endeavor. It will be seen later that this is actually true, for it appears that over-distanced Art is specially designed for a class of appreciation which has difficulty to rise spontaneously to any degree of Distance. The consequence of a loss of Distance through one or other cause is familiar: the verdict in the case of under-distancing is that the work is "crudely naturalistic," "harrowing," "repulsive in its realism." An excess of Distance produces the impression of improbability, artificiality, emptiness or absurdity.

The individual tends, as I just stated, to under-distance rather than to lose Distance by over-distancing. *Theoretically* there is no limit to the decrease of Distance. In theory, therefore, not only the usual subjects of Art, but even the most personal affections, whether ideas, percepts or emotions, can be sufficiently distanced to be aesthetically appreciable. Especially artists are gifted in this direction to a remarkable extent. The average individual, on the contrary, very rapidly reaches his limit of decreasing Distance, his "Distance-limit," *i.e.* that point at which Distance is lost and appreciation either disappears or changes its character.

In the *practice,* therefore, of the average person, a limit does exist which marks the minimum at which his appreciation can maintain itself in the aesthetic field, and this average minimum lies considerably higher than the Distance-limit of the artist. It is practically impossible to fix this average limit, in the absence of data, and on account of the wide fluctuations from person to person to which this limit is subject. But it is safe to infer that, in art practice, explicit references to organic affections, to the material existence of the body, especially to sexual matters, lie normally below the Distance-limit, and can be touched upon by Art only with special precautions. Allusions to social institutions of any degree of personal importance—in particular, allusions implying any doubt as to their validity—the questioning of some generally recognized ethical sanctions, references to topical subjects occupying public attention at the moment, and such like, are all dangerously near the average limit and may at any time fall below it, arousing, instead of aesthetic appreciation, concrete hostility or mere amusement.

This difference in the Distance-limit between artists and the public has been the source of much misunderstanding and injustice. Many an artist has seen his work condemned and himself ostracized for the sake of so-called "immoralities" which to him were *bona fide* aesthetic objects. His power of distancing, nay, the necessity of distancing feelings, sensations, situations which for the average person are too intimately bound up with his concrete existence to be regarded in that light, have often quite unjustly earned for him accusations of cynicism, sensualism, morbidness, or frivolity. The same misconception has arisen over many "problem plays" and "problem novels" in which the public have persisted in seeing nothing but a supposed "problem" of the moment, whereas the author may have been—and often has demonstrably been—able to distance the subject matter sufficiently to rise above its practical problematic import and to regard it simply as a dramatically and humanly interesting situation.

The variability of Distance in respect to Art, disregarding for the moment the subjective complication, appears both as a general feature in Art, and in the differences between the special arts.

It has been an old problem why the "arts of the eye and of the ear" should have reached the practically exclusive predominance over arts of other senses. Attempts to raise "culinary art" to the level of a Fine Art have failed in spite of all propaganda, as completely as the creation of scent or liqueur "symphonies." There is little doubt that, apart from other excellent reasons of a partly psycho-physical, partly technical nature, the actual, *spatial distance* separating objects of sight and hearing from the subject has contributed strongly to the development of this monopoly. In a similar manner *temporal remoteness* produces Distance, and objects removed from us in point of time are *ipso facto* distanced to an extent which was impossible for their contemporaries. Many pictures, plays and poems had, as a matter of fact, rather an expository or illustrative significance—as for instance much ecclesiastical Art—or the force of a direct practical appeal—as the invectives of many satires or comedies—which seem to us nowadays irreconcilable with their aesthetic claims. Such works have consequently profited greatly by lapse of time and have reached the level of Art only with the help of temporal distance, while others, on the contrary, often for the same reason have suffered a loss of Distance, through *over*-distancing.

Special mention must be made of a group of artistic conceptions which present excessive Distance in their form of appeal rather than in their actual presentation—a point illustrating the necessity of distinguishing between distancing an object and distancing the appeal of which it is the source. I mean here what is often rather loosely termed "idealistic Art," that is, Art springing from abstract conceptions, expressing allegorical meanings, or illustrating general truths. Generalizations and abstractions suffer under this disadvantage that they have too much applicability to invite a personal interest in them, and too little individual concreteness to prevent them applying to us in all their force. They appeal to everybody and therefore to none. An axiom of Euclid belongs to nobody, just because it compels everyone's assent; general conceptions like Patriotism, Friendship, Love, Hope, Life, Death, concern as much Dick, Tom, and Harry as myself, and I, therefore, either feel unable to get into any kind of personal relation to them, or, if I do so, they become at once, emphatically and concretely, *my* Patriotism, *my* Friendship, *my* Love, *my* Hope, *my* Life and Death. By mere force of generalization, a general truth or a universal ideal is so far distanced from myself that I fail to realize it concretely at all, or, when I do so, I can realize it only as part of my *practical actual being, i.e.* it falls below the Distance-limit altogether. "Idealistic Art" suffers consequently under the peculiar difficulty that its excess of Distance turns generally into an under-distance appeal—all the more easily, as it is the usual failing of the subject to *under*- rather than to *over*-distance.

The different special arts show at the present time very marked variations in the degree of Distance which they usually impose or require for their appreciation. Unfortunately here again the absence of data makes itself felt and indicates the necessity of conducting observations, possibly experiments, so as to place these suggestions upon a securer basis. In one single art, *viz.* the *theater,* a small amount of information is available, from an unexpected source, namely the proceedings of the censorship committee, which on closer examination might be made to yield evidence of interest to the psychologist. In fact, the whole censorship problem, as far as it does not turn upon purely economic questions, may be said to hinge upon Distance; if every member of the public could be trusted to keep it, there would be no sense whatever in the existence of a censor of plays. There is, of course, no doubt that, speaking generally theatrical performances *eo ipso* run a special risk of a loss of Distance owing to the material presentment of its subject-matter. The physical presence of living human beings as vehicles of dramatic art is a difficulty which no art has to face in the same way. A similar, in many ways even greater, risk confronts dancing: though attracting perhaps a less widely spread human interest, its animal spirits are frequently quite unrelieved by any glimmer of spirituality and consequently form a proportionately stronger lure to under-distancing. In the higher forms of dancing technical execution of the most wearing kind makes up a great deal for its intrinsic tendency towards a loss of Distance, and as a popular performance, at least in southern Europe, it has retained much of its ancient artistic glamour, producing a peculiarly subtle balancing of Distance between the pure delight of bodily movement and high technical accomplishment. In passing, it is interesting to observe (as bearing upon the development of Distance) that this art, once as much a fine art as music and considered by the Greeks as a particularly valuable educational exercise, should— except in sporadic cases—have fallen so low from the pedestal it once occupied. Next to the theater and dancing stands *sculpture*. Though not using a *living* bodily medium, yet the human form in its full spatial materiality constitutes a similar threat to Distance. Our northern habits of dress and ignorance of the human body have enormously increased the difficulty of distancing Sculpture, in part through the gross misconceptions to which it is exposed, in part owing to complete lack of standards of bodily perfection, and an inability to realize the distinction between sculptural form and bodily shape, which is the only but fundamental point distinguishing a statue from a cast taken from life. In *painting* it is apparently the form of its presentment and the usual reduction in scale which would explain why this art can venture to approach more closely than sculpture to the normal Distance-limit. As this matter will be discussed later in a special connection this simple reference may suffice here. *Music* and *architecture* have a curious position. These two most abstract of all arts show a remarkable fluctuation in their Distances. Certain kinds of music, especially "pure" music, or "classical" or "heavy" music, appear for many people over-distanced; light, "catchy" tunes, on the contrary, easily reach that degree of decreasing Distance below which they cease to be Art and become a pure amusement. In spite of its strange abstractness which to many philosophers has made it comparable to architecture and mathematics, music possesses a sensuous, frequently sensual, character: the undoubted physiological and muscular stimulus of its melodies and harmonies, no less than its rhythmic aspects, would seem to account for the occasional disappearance of Distance. To this might be added its strong tendency, especially in unmusical people, to stimulate trains of thought quite disconnected with itself, following channels of subjective inclinations— day-dreams of a more or less directly personal character. *Architecture* requires almost uniformly a very great Distance; that is to say, the majority of persons derive no aesthetic appreciation from architecture as

such, apart from the incidental impression of its decorative features and its associations. The causes are numerous, but prominent among them are the confusion of building with architecture and the predominance of utilitarian purposes, which overshadow the architectural claims upon the attention.

4. That all art requires a Distance-limit beyond which, and a Distance within which only, aesthetic appreciation becomes possible, is the *psychological formulation of a general characteristic of Art, viz.* its *anti-realistic nature*. Though seemingly paradoxical, this applies as much to "naturalistic" as to "idealistic" Art. The difference commonly expressed by these epithets is at bottom merely the difference in the degree of Distance; and this produces, so far as "naturalism" and "idealism" in Art are not meaningless labels, the usual result that what appears obnoxiously "naturalistic" to one person, may be "idealistic" to another. To say that Art is anti-realistic simply insists upon the fact that Art is not nature, never pretends to be nature and strongly resists any confusion with nature. It emphasizes the *art*-character of Art: "artistic" is synonymous with "anti-realistic"; it explains even sometimes a very marked degree of artificiality.

"Art is an imitation of nature," was the current art-conception in the eighteenth century. It is the fundamental axiom of the standard work of that time upon aesthetic theory by the Abbé Du Bos, *Reflexions critiques sur la poesie et la peinture*, 1719; the idea received strong support from the literal acceptance of Aristotle's theory of *mimesis* and produced echoes everywhere, in Lessing's *Laocoon* no less than in Burke's famous statement that "all Art is great as it Deceives." Though it may be assumed that since the time of Kant and of the Romanticists this notion has died out, it still lives in unsophisticated minds. Even when formally denied, it persists, for instance, in the belief that "Art idealized nature," which means after all only that Art copies nature with certain improvements and revisions. Artists themselves are unfortunately often responsible for the spreading of this conception. Whistler indeed said that to produce Art by imitating nature would be like trying to produce music by sitting upon the piano, but the selective, idealizing imitation of nature finds merely another support in such a saying. Naturalism, pleinairism, impressionism, even the guileless enthusiasm of the artist for the works of nature, her wealth of suggestion, her delicacy of workmanship, for the steadfastness of her guidance, only produce upon the public the impression that Art is, after all, an imitation of nature. Then how can it be anti-realistic?: The antithesis, Art *versus* nature, seems to break down. Yet if it does, what is the sense of Art?

Here the conception of Distance comes to the rescue. The solution of the dilemma lies in the "antinomy of Distance" with its demand: utmost decrease of distance without its disappearance. The simple observation that Art is the more effective, the more it falls into line with our predispositions which are inevitably moulded on general experience and nature, has always been the original motive for "naturalism." "Naturalism," "impressionism" is no new thing; it is only a new name for an innate leaning of Art, from the time of the Chaldeans and Egyptians down to the present day. Even the Apollo of Tenea apparently struck his contemporaries as so startlingly "naturalistic" that the subsequent legend attributed a superhuman genius to his creator. A constantly closer approach to nature, a perpetual refining of the limit of Distance, yet without overstepping the dividing line of art and nature, has always been the inborn bent of art. To deny this dividing line has occasionally been the failing of naturalism. But no theory of naturalism is complete which does not at the same time allow for the intrinsic idealism of Art: for both are merely degrees in that wide range lying beyond the Distance-limit. To imitate nature so as to trick the spectator into the deception that it is nature which he beholds, is to forsake Art, its anti-realism, its distanced spirituality, and to fall below the limit into sham, sensationalism or platitude.

DISCUSSION QUESTIONS

1. Do you agree with Bullough's distinction between objects of "amusement" and works of "art"? Why or why not?
2. Do you find convincing Bullough's explanation for why art usually has appealed to our sense of sight and hearing, but not to the other senses? Why or why not?
3. Is psychical distance necessary in order to have any aesthetic experience? Why or why not? Use examples to make your case.
4. How is Bullough's account of aesthetic experience of natural phenomena similar to or different from Saito's account of the same?

71. Leo Tolstoy (1828–1910)
From "What Is Art?"

Leo Nikolaevich Tolstoy (also spelled *Tolstoi*) was a Russian novelist, philosopher, and social and educational reformer, who is today considered one of the great writers in that country's history. He was born near Tula into an aristocratic family, but in his early adulthood Tolstoy found life among the members of the ruling class shallow and decadent and his university studies uninteresting, so he joined the military. His firsthand experiences of war were to influence significantly the development of his later pacifist, antiviolence views.

After leaving military service in 1856, he spent his time writing and running his family's country estate. A personal spiritual crisis during the 1870s caused him to give up his aristocratic title and wealth for a life of poverty, chastity, and simplicity among the local peasantry. All his writings thereafter were more thoroughly imbued with the moral and spiritual concerns about the meaning of life that precipitated his dramatic rejection of all social hierarchy, institutionalized religion, government, and material luxury. He did continue to write fiction, as well as nonfiction and some plays, for the rest of his life. He also corresponded for a while with Gandhi regarding the principles of nonviolent political struggle.

The selection consists of excerpts from an essay written in 1898. Tolstoy's overall goal in this work was to provide a moral basis for the social function of art, which he saw as a vehicle for the communication of feeling among people. As part of this aim he formulates a definition of art itself. This has since become a widely cited example in aesthetic theory of the attempt to identify the essential properties any human artifact must possess in order to be categorized as "art." Not surprisingly, his account of what art *is* also leads to his criteria for what makes one work of art *better* or *worse* than another work, and in both cases the key is the intention to "infect" an audience with emotions experienced by the artist.

QUESTIONS FOR CRITICAL READING

1. How does Tolstoy critique the other definitions of art that he identifies?
2. What is the "activity of art" according to Tolstoy, and how are intentions relevant?
3. According to Tolstoy, why is art a crucial part of human life?
4. What are the three qualities separating art from non-art, in Tolstoy's account, and how does he argue for them?
5. How are these three qualities also used by Tolstoy as the criteria for evaluating works of art as good or bad?

TERM TO NOTE

arabesque: In this context, a complex ornamental pattern especially found in the decoration of walls, ceilings, and Arabian Oriental rugs; also used to describe some musical passages.

———

What is art if we put aside the conception of beauty, which confuses the whole matter? The latest and most comprehensible definitions of art, apart from the conception of beauty, are the following:—(1) a, Art is an activity arising even in the animal kingdom, and springing from sexual desire and the propensity to play (Schiller, Darwin, Spencer), and b, accompanied by a pleasurable excitement of the nervous system (Grant Allen). This is the physiological-evolutionary definition. (2) Art is the external manifestation, by means of lines, colours, movements, sounds, or words, of emotions felt by man (Véron). This is the experimental definition. According to the very latest definition (Sully), (3) Art is 'the production of some permanent object or passing action which is fitted not only to supply an active enjoyment to the producer, but to convey a pleasurable impression to a number of spectators or listeners, quite apart from any personal advantage to be derived from it.'

Notwithstanding the superiority of these definitions to the metaphysical definitions which depended

on the conception of beauty, they are yet far from exact. The first, the physiological-evolutionary definition (1) a, is inexact, because instead of speaking about the artistic activity itself, which is the real matter in hand, it treats of the derivation of art. The modification of it, b, based on the physiological effects on the human organism, is inexact because within the limits of such definition many other human activities can be included, as has occurred in the neo-aesthetic theories which reckon as art the preparation of handsome clothes, pleasant scents, and even of victuals.

The experimental definition, (2), which makes art consist in the expression of emotions, is inexact because a man may express his emotions by means of lines, colours, sounds, or words and yet may not act on others by such expression—and then the manifestation of his emotions is not art.

The third definition (that of Sully) is inexact because in the production of objects or actions affording pleasure to the producer and a pleasant emotion to the spectators or hearers apart from personal advantage, may be included the showing of conjuring tricks or gymnastic exercises, and other activities which are not art. And further, many things the production of which does not afford pleasure to the producer and the sensation received from which is unpleasant, such as gloomy, heart-rending scenes in a poetic description or a play, may nevertheless be undoubted works of art.

The inaccuracy of all these definitions arises from the fact that in them all (as also in the metaphysical definitions) the object considered is the pleasure art may give, and not the purpose it may serve in the life of man and of humanity.

In order to define art correctly it is necessary first of all to cease to consider it as a means to pleasure, and to consider it as one of the conditions of human life. Viewing it in this way we cannot fail to observe that art is one of the means of intercourse between man and man.

Every work of art causes the receiver to enter into a certain kind of relationship both with him who produced or is producing the art, and with all those who, simultaneously, previously, or subsequently, receive the same artistic impression.

Speech transmitting the thoughts and experiences of men serves as a means of union among them, and art serves a similar purpose. The peculiarity of this latter means of intercourse, distinguishing it from intercourse by means of words, consists in this, that whereas by words a man transmits his thoughts to another, by art he transmits his feelings.

The activity of art is based on the fact that a man receiving through his sense of hearing or sight another man's expression of feeling, is capable of experiencing the emotion which moved the man who expressed it. To take the simplest example: one man laughs, and another who hears becomes merry, or a man weeps, and another who hears feels sorrow. A man is excited or irritated, and another man seeing him is brought to a similar state of mind. By his movements or by the sounds of his voice a man expresses courage and determination or sadness and calmness, and this state of mind passes on to others. A man suffers, manifesting his sufferings by groans and spasms, and this suffering transmits itself to other people; a man expresses his feelings of admiration, devotion, fear, respect, or love, to certain objects, persons, or phenomena, and others are infected by the same feelings of admiration, devotion, fear, respect, or love, to the same objects, persons, or phenomena.

And it is on this capacity of man to receive another man's expression of feeling and to experience those feelings himself, that the activity of art is based.

If a man infects another or others directly, immediately, by his appearance or by the sounds he gives vent to at the very time he experiences the feeling; if he causes another man to yawn when he himself cannot help yawning, or to laugh or cry when he himself is obliged to laugh or cry, or to suffer when he himself is suffering—that does not amount to art.

Art begins when one person with the object of joining another or others to himself in one and the same feeling, expresses that feeling by certain external indications. To take the simplest example: a boy having experienced, let us say, fear on encountering a wolf, relates that encounter, and in order to evoke in others the feeling he has experienced, describes himself, his condition before the encounter, the surroundings, the wood, his own lightheartedness, and then the wolf's appearance, its movements, the distance between himself and the wolf, and so forth. All this, if only the boy when telling the story again experiences the feelings he had lived through, and infects the hearers and compels them to feel what he had experienced—is art. Even if the boy had not seen a wolf but had frequently been afraid of one, and if wishing to evoke in others the fear he had felt, he invented an encounter with a wolf and recounted it so as to make his hearers share the feelings he experienced when he feared the wolf, that also would be art. And just in the same way it is art if a man, having experienced either the fear of suffering or the attraction of enjoyment (whether in reality or in imagination), expresses these feelings on canvas or in marble so that others are infected by them. And it is also art if a man feels, or imagines to himself, feelings of delight, gladness, sorrow, despair, courage, or despondency, and the transition from one to another of these feelings, and expresses them by sounds so that the hearers are infected by them and experience them as they were experienced by the composer.

The feelings with which the artist infects others may be most various—very strong or very weak, very important or very insignificant, very bad or very good: feelings of love of one's country, self-devotion and submission to fate or to God expressed in a drama, raptures of lovers described in a novel, feelings of voluptuousness expressed in a picture, courage expressed in a triumphal march, merriment evoked by a dance, humour evoked by a funny story, the feeling of quietness transmitted by an evening landscape or by a lullaby, or the feeling of admiration evoked by a beautiful arabesque—it is all art.

If only the spectators or auditors are infected by the feelings which the author has felt, it is art.

To evoke in oneself a feeling one has once experienced and having evoked it in oneself then by means of movements, lines, colours, sounds, or forms expressed in words, so to transmit that feeling that others experience the same feeling—this is the activity of art.

Art is a human activity consisting in this, that one man consciously by means of certain external signs, hands on to others feelings he has lived through, and that others are infected by these feelings and also experience them.

Art is not, as the metaphysicians say, the manifestation of some mysterious Idea of beauty or God; it is not, as the aesthetic physiologists say, a game in which man lets off his excess of stored-up energy; it is not the expression of man's emotions by external signs; it is not the production of pleasing objects; and, above all, it is not pleasure; but it is a means of union among men joining them together in the same feelings, and indispensable for the life and progress towards wellbeing of individuals and of humanity.

As every man, thanks to man's capacity to express thoughts by words, may know all that has been done for him in the realms of thought by all humanity before his day, and can in the present, thanks to this capacity to understand the thoughts of others, become a sharer in their activity and also himself hand on to his contemporaries and descendants the thoughts he has assimilated from others as well as those that have arisen in himself; so, thanks to man's capacity to be infected with the feelings of others by means of art, all that is being lived through by his contemporaries is accessible to him, as well as the feelings experienced by men thousands of years ago, and he has also the possibility of transmitting his own feelings to others.

If people lacked the capacity to receive the thoughts conceived by men who preceded them and to pass on to others their own thoughts, men would be like wild beasts, or like Kasper Hauser.[1]

And if men lacked this other capacity of being infected by art, people might be almost more savage still, and above all more separated from, and more hostile to, one another.

And therefore the activity of art is a most important one, as important as the activity of speech itself and as generally diffused.

As speech does not act on us only in sermons, orations, or books, but in all those remarks by which we interchange thoughts and experiences with one another, so also art in the wide sense of the word permeates our whole life, but it is only to some of its manifestations that we apply the term in the limited sense of the word.

We are accustomed to understand art to be only what we hear and see in theatres, concerts, and exhibitions; together with buildings, statues, poems, and novels. . . . But all this is but the smallest part of the art by which we communicate with one another in life. All human life is filled with works of art of every kind—from cradle-song, jest, mimicry, the ornamentation of houses, dress, and utensils, to church services, buildings, monuments, and triumphal processions. It is all artistic activity. So that by art, in the limited sense of the word, we do not mean all human activity transmitting feelings but only that part which we for some reason select from it and to which we attach special importance.

This special importance has always been given by men to that part of this activity which transmits feelings flowing from their religious perception, and this small part they have specifically called art, attaching to it the full meaning of the word.

That was how men of old—Socrates, Plato, and Aristotle—looked on art. Thus did the Hebrew prophets and the ancient Christians regard art. Thus it was, and still is, understood by the Mohammedans, and thus it still is understood by religious folk among our own peasantry.

Some teachers of mankind—such as Plato in his *Republic,* and people like the primitive Christians, the strict Mohammedans, and the Buddhists—have gone so far as to repudiate all art.

People viewing art in this way (in contradiction to the prevalent view of to-day which regards any art as good if only it affords pleasure) held and hold that art (as contrasted with speech, which need not be listened to) is so highly dangerous in its power to infect people against their wills, that mankind will lose far less by banishing all art than by tolerating each and every art.

Evidently such people were wrong in repudiating all art, for they denied what cannot be denied—one of the indispensable means of communication without which mankind could not exist. But not less wrong are the people of civilized European society of our class and day in favouring any art if it but serves beauty, that is, gives people pleasure.

Formerly people feared lest among works of art there might chance to be some causing corruption, and they prohibited art altogether. Now they only fear lest they should be deprived of any enjoyment art can afford, and they patronize any art. And I think the last error is much grosser than the first and that its consequences are far more harmful. . . .

Art in our society has become so perverted that not only has bad art come to be considered good, but even the very perception of what art really is has been lost. In order to be able to speak about the art of our society

---

1. 'The foundling of Nuremberg,' found in the marketplace of that town on 23rd May 1828, apparently some sixteen years old. He spoke little and was almost totally ignorant even of common objects. He subsequently explained that he had been brought up in confinement underground and visited by only one man, whom he saw but seldom.

it is, therefore, first of all necessary to distinguish art from counterfeit art.

There is one indubitable sign distinguishing real art from its counterfeit—namely, the infectiousness of art. If a man without exercising effort and without altering his standpoint, on reading, hearing, or seeing another man's work experiences a mental condition which unites him with that man and with others who are also affected by that work, then the object evoking that condition is a work of art. And however poetic, realistic, striking, or interesting, a work may be, it is not a work of art if it does not evoke that feeling (quite distinct from all other feelings) of joy and of spiritual union with another (the author) and with others (those who are also infected by it).

It is true that this indication is an *internal* one and that there are people who, having forgotten what the action of real art is, expect something else from art (in our society the great majority are in this state), and that therefore such people may mistake for this aesthetic feeling the feeling of diversion and a certain excitement which they receive from counterfeits of art. But though it is impossible to undeceive these people, just as it may be impossible to convince a man suffering from colour-blindness that green is not red, yet for all that, this indication remains perfectly definite to those whose feeling for art is neither perverted nor atrophied, and it clearly distinguishes the feeling produced by art from all other feelings.

The chief peculiarity of this feeling is that the recipient of a truly artistic impression is so united to the artist that he feels as if the work were his own and not some one else's—as if what it expresses were just what he had long been wishing to express. A real work of art destroys in the consciousness of the recipient the separation between himself and the artist, and not that alone, but also between himself and all whose minds receive this work of art. In this freeing of our personality from its separation and isolation, in this uniting of it with others, lies the chief characteristic and the great attractive force of art.

If a man is infected by the author's condition of soul, if he feels this emotion and this union with others, then the object which has effected this is art; but if there be no such infection, if there be not this union with the author and with others who are moved by the same work—then it is not art. And not only is infec-

tion a sure sign of art, but the degree of infectiousness is also the sole measure of excellence in art.

The stronger the infection the better is the art, as art, speaking of it now apart from its subject-matter—that is, not considering the value of the feelings it transmits.

And the degree of the infectiousness of art depends on three conditions:—

(1) On the greater or lesser individuality of the feeling transmitted; (2) on the greater or lesser clearness with which the feeling is transmitted; (3) on the sincerity of the artist, that is, on the greater or lesser force with which the artist himself feels the emotion he transmits.

The more individual the feeling transmitted the more strongly does it act on the recipient; the more individual the state of soul into which he is transferred the more pleasure does the recipient obtain and therefore the more readily and strongly does he join in it.

Clearness of expression assists infection because the recipient who mingles in consciousness with the author is the better satisfied the more clearly that feeling is transmitted which, as it seems to him, he has long known and felt and for which he has only now found expression.

But most of all is the degree of infectiousness of art increased by the degree of sincerity in the artist. As soon as the spectator, hearer, or reader, feels that the artist is infected by his own production and writes, sings, or plays, for himself, and not merely to act on others, this mental condition of the artist infects the recipient; and, on the contrary, as soon as the spectator, reader, or hearer, feels that the author is not writing, singing, or playing, for his own satisfaction—does not himself feel what he wishes to express, but is doing it for him, the recipient—resistance immediately springs up, and the most individual and the newest feelings and the cleverest technique not only fail to produce any infection but actually repel.

I have mentioned three conditions of contagion in art, but they may all be summed up into one, the last, sincerity; that is, that the artist should be impelled by an inner need to express his feeling. That condition includes the first; for if the artist is sincere he will express the feeling as he experienced it. And as each man is different from every one else, his feeling will be individual for every one else; and the more individual it is—the more the artist has drawn it from the depths of his nature—the more sympathetic and sincere will it be. And this same sincerity will impel the artist to find clear expression for the feeling which he wishes to transmit.

Therefore this third condition—sincerity—is the most important of the three. It is always complied with in peasant art, and this explains why such art always acts so powerfully; but it is a condition almost entirely absent from our upper-class art, which is continually produced by artists actuated by personal aims of covetousness or vanity.

Such are the three conditions which divide art from its counterfeits, and which also decide the quality of every work of art considered apart from its subject-matter.

The absence of any one of these conditions excludes a work from the category of art and relegates it to that of art's counterfeits. If the work does not transmit the artist's peculiarity of feeling and is therefore not individual, if it is unintelligibly expressed, or if it has not proceeded from the author's inner need for expression—it is not a work of art. If all these conditions are present even in the smallest degree, then the work even if a weak one is yet a work of art.

The presence in various degrees of these three conditions: individuality, clearness, and sincerity, decides the merit of a work of art as art, apart from subject-matter. All works of art take order of merit according to the degree in which they fulfil the first, the second, and the third, of these conditions. In one the individuality of the feeling transmitted may predominate; in another, clearness of expression; in a third, sincerity; while a fourth may have sincerity and individuality but be deficient in clearness; a fifth, individuality and clearness, but less sincerity; and so forth, in all possible degrees and combinations.

Thus is art divided from what is not art, and thus is the quality of art, as art, decided, independently of its subject-matter, that is to say, apart from whether the feelings it transmits are good or bad.

DISCUSSION QUESTIONS

1. Do you agree with Tolstoy's definition of art? Why or why not?
2. Why does Tolstoy seem to think that "beauty" is not an essential feature of good art? Do you agree with him? Why or why not?
3. What examples from the different arts might strengthen or weaken Tolstoy's position that the "degree of infectiousness" ought to be the general criterion of "better" or "worse" in the evaluation of art?
4. Tolstoy's account implies that there is no art without an audience. Do you agree? Why or why not?

72. Susanne Langer (1895–1985)
Art and Human Feeling

Susanne Langer was an American philosopher whose work in the areas of symbolic logic, philosophy of mind, and aesthetics has been very influential in the English-speaking academic world during the latter half of the twentieth century. She was born in New York and eventually received her doctorate in philosophy at Radcliffe, where she also taught for a number of years before moving on to positions at other institutions, including an appointment at Columbia University. She finished her teaching career at the Connecticut College for Women, thereafter continuing her prolific writing as an emeritus professor until her death.

The excerpts reprinted here are from the 1953 book *Feeling and Form,* usually considered her major contribution in aesthetic theory. This work was in fact meant to be a sequel to a book she had written a few years earlier entitled *Philosophy in a New Key,* in which she developed a theory of human symbol-use with special application to music. Langer maintained that her semantic theory could be applied to all the arts, not just music, and in this "sequel" she set about proving that claim. The result is a comprehensive account of the nature of art, in which she tries to show how any work of art in any genre can be understood as a complex, more or less abstract symbol of human feeling, or "sentient life."

QUESTIONS FOR CRITICAL READING

1. What is Langer's definition of art, and what does she mean by it?
2. How does Langer criticize the common view that the artistic image is supposed to represent, or copy, some "real object"?
3. What does Langer mean by claiming that a work of art is intended to present a "virtual" rather than an "actual" object?
4. What is the "vital import" of a work of art, in Langer's account, and how would it be different from the "meaning" found in ordinary language-use?

TERMS TO NOTE

demiurgic: Here, having to do with the capacity to create a material or sensory reality.

nondiscursive: Meaningful communication not intended to proceed in logical (deductive or inductive) sequence.

fata morgana: An illusory figure or perception.

nonrepresentative: Refers to art, or any created thing, that is not intended to directly represent, or imitate, anything else.

At this point I will make bold to offer a definition of art, which serves to distinguish a "work of art" from anything else in the world, and at the same time to show why, and how, a utilitarian object may be *also* a work of art; and how a work of so-called "pure" art may fail of its purpose and be simply bad, just as a shoe that cannot be worn is simply bad by failing of its purpose. It serves, moreover, to establish the relation of art to physical skill, or making, on the one hand, and to feeling and expression on the other. Here is the tentative definition, on which the following chapters are built: Art is the creation of forms symbolic of human feeling.

The word "creation" is introduced here with full awareness of its problematical character. There is a definite reason to say a craftsman *produces* goods, but *creates* a thing of beauty; a builder *erects* a house, but *creates* an edifice if the house is a real work of architecture, however modest. An artifact as such is merely a combination of material parts, or a modification of a natural object to suit human purposes. It is not a creation, but an arrangement of given factors. A work of art, on the other hand, is more than an "arrangement" of given things—even qualitative things. Something emerges from the arrangement of tones or colors, which was not there before, and this, rather than the arranged material, is the symbol of sentience.

The making of this expressive form is the creative process that enlists a man's utmost technical skill in the service of his utmost conceptual power, imagination. Not the invention of new original turns, nor the adoption of novel themes, merits the word "creative," but the making of any work symbolic of feeling, even in the most canonical context and manner. A thousand people may have used every device and convention of it before. A Greek vase was almost always a creation, although its form was traditional and its decoration deviated but little from that of its numberless forerunners. The creative principle, nonetheless, was probably active in it from the first throw of the clay.

To expound that principle, and develop it in each autonomous realm of art, is the only way to justify the definition, which really is a philosophical theory of art in miniature. . . .

It is a curious fact that people who spend their lives in closest contact with the arts—artists, to whom the appreciation of beauty is certainly a continual and "immediate" experience—do not assume and cultivate the "aesthetic attitude." To them, the artistic value of a work is its most obvious property. They see it naturally and constantly; they do not have to make themselves, first, unaware of the rest of the world. Practical awareness may be there, in a secondary position, as it is for anyone who is engrossed in interesting talk or happenings; if it becomes too insistent to be ignored, they may become quite furious. But normally, the lure of the object is greater than the distractions that compete with it. It is not the percipient who discounts the surroundings, but the work of art which, if it is successful, detaches itself from the rest of the world; he merely sees it as it is presented to him.

Every real work of art has a tendency to appear thus dissociated from its mundane environment. The most immediate impression it creates is one of "otherness" from reality—the impression of an illusion enfolding the thing, action, statement, or flow of sound that constitutes the work. Even where the element of representation is absent, where nothing is imitated or feigned—in a lovely textile, a pot, a building, a sonata—this air of illusion, of being a sheer image, exists as forcibly as in the most deceptive picture or the most plausible narrative. Where an expert in the particular art in question perceives immediately a "rightness and necessity" of forms, the unversed but sensitive spectator perceives only a peculiar air of "otherness," which has been variously described as "strangeness," "semblance," "illusion," "transparency," "autonomy," or "self-sufficiency."

This detachment from actuality, the "otherness" that gives even a bona fide product like a building or a vase some aura of illusion, is a crucial factor, indicative of the very nature of art. It is neither chance nor caprice that has led aestheticians again and again to take account of it (and in a period dominated by a psychologistic outlook, to seek the explanation in a state of mind). In the element of "unreality," which has alternately troubled and delighted them, lies the clue to a very deep and essential problem: the problem of creativity.

What is "created" in a work of art? More than people generally realize when they speak of "being creative," or refer to the characters in a novel as the author's "creations." More than a delightful combination of sensory elements; far more than any reflection or "interpretation" of objects, people, events—the figments that artists *use* in their demiurgic work, and that have made some aestheticians refer to such work as "re-creation" rather than genuine creation. But an object that already exists—a vase of flowers, a living person—cannot be re-created. It would have to be destroyed to be re-created. Besides, a picture is neither a person nor a vase of flowers. It is an image, created for the first time out of things that are not imaginal, but quite realistic—canvas or paper, and paints or carbon or ink.

It is natural enough, perhaps, for naive reflection to center first of all round the relationship between an image and its object; and equally natural to treat a picture, statue, or a graphic description as an imitation of reality. The surprising thing is that long after art theory had passed the naive stage, and every serious thinker realized that imitation was neither the aim nor the measure of artistic creation, the traffic of the image

with its model kept its central place among philosophical problems of art. It has figured as the question of form and content, of interpretation, of idealization, of belief and make-believe, and of impression and expression. Yet the idea of copying nature is not even applicable to all the arts. What does a building copy? On what given object does one model a melody?

A problem that will not die after philosophers have condemned it as irrelevant has still a gadfly mission in the intellectual world. Its significance merely is bigger, in fact, than any of its formulations. So here: the philosophical issue that is usually conceived in terms of image and object is really concerned with the nature of images as such and their essential difference from actualities. The difference is functional; consequently real objects, functioning in a way that is normal for images, may assume a purely imaginal status. That is why the character of an illusion may cling to works of art that do not represent anything. Imitation of other things is not the essential power of images, though it is a very important one by virtue of which the whole problem of fact and fiction originally came into the compass of our philosophical thought. But the true power of the image lies in the fact that it is an abstraction, a symbol, the bearer of an idea.

How can a work of art that does not represent anything—a building, a pot, a patterned textile—be called an image? It becomes an image when it presents itself purely to our vision, i.e. as a sheer visual form instead of a locally and practically related object. If we receive it as a completely visual thing, we abstract its appearance from its material existence. What we see in this way becomes simply a thing of vision—a form, an image. It detaches itself from its actual setting and acquires a different context.

An image in this sense, something that exists only for perception, abstracted from the physical and causal order, is the artist's creation. The image presented on a canvas is not a new "thing" among the things in the studio. The canvas was there, the paints were there; the painter has not added to them. Some excellent critics, and painters too, speak of his "arranging" forms and colors, and regard the resultant work primarily as an "arrangement." Whistler seems to have thought in these terms about his paintings. But even the forms are not phenomena in the order of actual things, as spots on a tablecloth are; the forms in a design—no matter how abstract—have a *life* that does not belong to mere spots. Something arises from the process of arranging colors on a surface, something that is created, not just gathered and set in a new order: that is the image. It emerges suddenly from the disposition of the pigments, and with its advent the very existence of the canvas and of the paint "arranged" on it seems to be abrogated; those actual objects become difficult to perceive in their own right. A new appearance has superseded their natural aspect.

An image is, indeed, a purely virtual "object." Its importance lies in the fact that we do not use it to guide us to something tangible and practical, but treat it as a complete entity with only visual attributes and relations. It has no others; its visible character is its entire being.

The most striking virtual objects in the natural world are optical—perfectly definite visible "things" that prove to be intangible, such as rainbows and mirages. Many people, therefore, regard an image or illusion as necessarily something visual. This conceptual limitation has even led some literary critics, who recognize the essentially imaginal character of poetry, to suppose that poets must be visual-minded people, and to judge that figures of speech which do not conjure up visual imagery are not truly poetic. F. C. Prescott, with consistency that borders on the heroic, regards "The quality of mercy is not strained" as unpoetic because it suggests nothing visible. But the poetic image is, in fact, not a painter's image at all. The exact difference, which is great and far-reaching, will be discussed in the following chapters; what concerns us right here is the broader meaning of "image" that accounts for the genuinely artistic character of non-visual arts without any reference to word painting, or other substitute for spreading pigments on a surface to make people see pictures.

The word "image" is almost inseparably wedded to the sense of sight because our stock example of it is the looking-glass world that gives us a visible copy of the things opposite the mirror without a tactual or other sensory replica of them. But some of the alternative words that have been used to denote the virtual character of so-called "aesthetic objects" escape this association. Carl Gustav Jung, for instance, speaks of it as "semblance." His exemplary case of illusion is not the reflected image, but the dream; and in a dream

there are sounds, smells, feelings, happenings, intentions, dangers—all sorts of invisible elements—as well as sights, and all are equally unreal by the measures of public fact. Dreams do not consist entirely of images, but everything in them is imaginary. The music heard in a dream comes from a virtual piano under the hands of an apparent musician; the whole experience is a semblance of events. It may be as vivid as any reality, yet it is what Schiller called "Schein."

Schiller was the first thinker who saw what really makes "Schein," or semblance, important for art: the fact that it liberates perception—and with it, the power of conception—from all practical purposes, and lets the mind dwell on the sheer appearance of things. The function of artistic illusion is not "make-believe," as many philosophers and psychologists assume, but the very opposite, disengagement from belief—the contemplation of sensory qualities without their usual meanings of "Here's that chair," "That's my telephone," "These figures ought to add up to the bank's statement," etc. The knowledge that what is before us has no practical significance in the world is what enables us to give attention to its appearance as such.

Everything has an aspect of appearance as well as of causal importance. Even so non-sensuous a thing as a fact or a possibility *appears* this way to one person and that way to another. That is its "semblance," whereby it may "resemble" other things, and—where the semblance is used to mislead judgment about its causal properties—is said to "dissemble" its nature. Where we know that an "object" consists entirely in its semblance, that apart from its appearance it has no cohesion and unity—like a rainbow, or a shadow—we call it a merely virtual object, or an illusion. In this literal sense a picture is an illusion; we see a face, a flower, a vista of sea or land, etc., and know that if we stretched out our hand to it we would touch a surface smeared with paint.

The object seen is given only to the sense of sight. That is the chief purpose of "imitation," or "objective" painting. To present things to sight which are known to be illusion is a ready (though by no means necessary) way to *abstract* visible forms from their usual context.

Normally, of course, semblance is not misleading; a thing is what it seems. But even where there is no deception, it may happen that an object—a vase, for instance, or a building—arrests one sense so exclusively that it seems to be given to that sense alone, and all its other properties become irrelevant. It is quite honestly there, but is *important* only for (say) its visual character. Then we are prone to accept it as a vision; there is such a concentration on appearance that one has a sense of seeing sheer appearances—that is, a sense of illusion.

Herein lies the "unreality" of art that tinges even perfectly real objects like pots, textiles, and temples. Whether we deal with actual illusions or with such quasi-illusions made by artistic emphasis, what is presented is, in either case, just what Schiller called "Schein"; and a pure semblance, or "Schein," among the husky substantial realities of the natural world, is a strange guest. Strangeness, separateness, otherness —call it what you will—is its obvious lot.

The semblance of a thing, thus thrown into relief, is its direct aesthetic quality. According to several eminent critics, this is what the artist tries to reveal for its own sake. But the emphasis on quality, or essence, is really only a stage in artistic conception. It is the making of a rarified element that serves, in its turn, for the making of something else—the imaginal art work itself. And this form is the nondiscursive but articulate symbol of feeling.

Here is, I believe, the clear statement of what Clive Bell dealt with rather confusedly in a passage that identified "significant form" (not, however, significant of anything) with "aesthetic quality." The setting forth of pure quality, or semblance, creates a new dimension, apart from the familiar world. That is its office. In this dimension, all artistic forms are conceived and presented. Since their substance is illusion or "Schein" they are, from the standpoint of practical reality, *mere* forms; they exist only for the sense or the imagination that perceives them—like the fata morgana, or the elaborate, improbable structure of events in our dreams. The function of "semblance" is to give forms a new embodiment in purely qualitative, unreal instances, setting them free from their normal embodiment in real things so that they may be recognized in their own right, and freely conceived and composed in the interest of the artist's ultimate aim—significance, or logical expression.

All forms in art, then, are abstracted forms; their content is only a semblance, a pure appearance, whose function is to make them, too, apparent—more freely and wholly apparent than they could be if they were exemplified in a context of real circumstance and anxious interest. It is in this elementary sense that all art is abstract. Its very substance, quality without practical significance, is an abstraction from material existence; and exemplification in this illusory or quasi-illusory medium makes the forms of things (not only shapes, but logical forms, e.g., proportions among degrees of importance in events, or among different speeds in motions) present themselves *in abstracto*. This fundamental abstractness belongs just as forcibly to the most illustrative murals and most realistic plays, provided they are good after their kind, as to the deliberate abstractions that are remote representations or entirely nonrepresentative designs.

But abstract form as such is not an artistic ideal. To carry abstraction as far as possible, and achieve pure form in only the barest conceptual medium, is a logician's business, not a painter's or poet's. In art forms are abstracted only to be made clearly apparent, and are freed from their common uses only to be put to new uses: to act as symbols, to become expressive of human feeling.

An artistic symbol is a much more intricate thing than what we usually think of as a form, because it involves *all* the relationships of its elements to one another, all similarities and differences of quality, not only geometric or other familiar relations. That is why qualities enter directly into the form itself, not as its contents, but as constitutive elements in it. Our scientific convention of abstracting mathematical forms, which do not involve quality, and fitting them to experience, always makes qualitative factors "content"; and as scientific conventions rule our academic thinking, it has usually been taken for granted that in understanding art, too, one should think of form as opposed to qualitative "content." But on this uncritical assumption the whole conception of form and content comes to grief, and analysis ends in the confused assertion that art is "formed content," form and content are one. The solution of that paradox is, that a work of art is a structure whose interrelated elements are often qualities, or properties of qualities such as their degrees of intensity; that qualities enter into the form and in this way are as much one with it as the relations which they, and they only, have; and that to speak of them as "content," from which the form could be abstracted logically, is nonsense. The form is built up out of relations peculiar to them; they are formal elements in the structure, not contents.

Yet forms are either empty abstractions, or they do have a content; and artistic forms have a very special one, namely their *import*. They are logically expressive, or significant, forms. They are symbols for the articulation of feeling, and convey the elusive and yet familiar pattern of sentience. And as essentially symbolic forms they lie in a different dimension from physical objects as such. They belong to the same category as language, though their logical form is a different one, and as myth and dream, though their function is not the same.

Herein lies the "strangeness" or "otherness" that characterizes an artistic object. The form is immediately given to perception, and yet it reaches beyond itself; it is semblance, but seems to be charged with reality. Like speech, that is physically nothing but little buzzing sounds, it is filled with its meaning, and its meaning is a reality. In an articulate symbol the symbolic import permeates the whole structure, because every articulation of that structure is an articulation of the idea it conveys; the meaning (or, to speak accurately of a nondiscursive symbol, the vital import) is the content of the symbolic form, given with it, as it were, to perception.

DISCUSSION QUESTIONS

1. Do you agree with Langer's definition of art? Why or why not? What examples might strengthen or weaken her position?
2. Do you agree with Langer's argument that works of art appropriately present a virtual reality rather than merely represent actual reality? Why or why not?
3. How would you compare Langer's definition of art with Tolstoy's definition? Which do you find more convincing? Why?

73. Morris Weitz (1916–1981)
A Nonessentialist Approach to Art

Morris Weitz was an American philosopher and member of the faculty at Ohio State University for many years. His primary area of study was aesthetics, which for him also included the analysis of issues in literary criticism. Although he wrote extensively, many philosophers are most familiar with this 1956 essay, "The Role of Theory in Aesthetics," which has had a major impact on the still lively debate among Anglo-American aestheticians regarding the defining properties of art.

The general position taken by Weitz in this essay is that the traditional philosophical interest in identifying the "necessary and sufficient conditions" for categorizing one thing rather than another as an art object is misguided. This attempt to fix the essential features of what is to count as art (sometimes called essentialism) always has failed in terms of finally resolving the issue, and it always will, according to Weitz, because it is pursuing the wrong questions. Consequently, he argues for what amounts to a "nonessentialist" approach to inquiry into how we use the concept of "art" and recommends refocusing in the direction of issues concerning what is *important* about art and what makes particular works more or less valuable.

QUESTIONS FOR CRITICAL READING

1. According to Weitz, what are the features of an aesthetic theory as traditionally constructed, and why do all such theories fail?
2. In Weitz's account, what is an "open concept," and why is the concept of "art" appropriately "open" rather than "closed"?
3. What does Weitz mean by claiming that the "primary task of aesthetics is not to seek a theory but to elucidate the concept of art"?
4. What does Weitz think is a more justified role for aesthetic theory, and how does he argue for it?

Theory has been central in aesthetics and is still the preoccupation of the philosophy of art. Its main avowed concern remains the determination of the nature of art which can be formulated into a definition of it. It construes definition as the statement of the necessary and sufficient properties of what is being defined, where the statement purports to be a true or false claim about the essence of art, what characterizes and distinguishes it from everything else. Each of the great theories of art—Formalism, Voluntarism, Emotionalism, Intellectualism, Intuitionism, Organicism—converges on the attempt to state the defining properties of art. Each claims that it is the true theory because it has formulated correctly into a real definition the nature of art; and that the others are false because they have left out some necessary or sufficient property. Many theorists contend that their enterprise is no mere intellectual exercise but an absolute necessity for any understanding of art and our proper evaluation of it. Unless we know what art is, they say, what are its necessary and sufficient properties, we cannot begin to respond to it adequately or to say why one work is good or better than another. Aesthetic theory, thus, is important not only in itself but for the foundations of both appreciation and criticism. Philosophers, critics, and even artists who have written on art, agree that what is primary in aesthetics is a theory about the nature of art.

Is aesthetic theory, in the sense of a true definition or set of necessary and sufficient properties of art, possible? If nothing else does, the history of aesthetics itself should give one enormous pause here. For, in spite of the many theories, we seem no nearer our goal today than we were in Plato's time. Each age, each art-movement, each philosophy of art, tries over and over again to establish the stated ideal only to be succeeded by a new or revised theory, rooted, at least in part, in the repudiation of preceding ones. Even today, almost everyone interested in aesthetic matters is still deeply wedded to the hope that the correct theory of art is forthcoming. We need only examine the numerous new books on art in which new definitions are proffered; or, in our own country especially, the basic textbooks and anthologies to recognize how strong the priority of a theory of art is.

In this essay I want to plead for the rejection of this problem. I want to show that theory—in the requisite classical sense—is *never* forthcoming in aesthetics, and that we would do much better as philosophers to supplant the question, "What is the nature of art?," by other questions, the answers to which will provide us with all the understanding of the arts there can be. I want to show that the inadequacies of the theories are not primarily occasioned by any legitimate difficulty such e.g., as the vast complexity of art, which might be corrected by further probing and research. Their basic inadequacies reside instead in a fundamental misconception of art. Aesthetic theory—all of it—is wrong in principle in thinking that a correct theory is possible because it radically misconstrues the logic of the concept of art. Its main contention that "art" is amenable to real or any kind of true definition is false. Its attempt to discover the necessary and sufficient properties of art is logically misbegotten for the very simple reason that such a set and, consequently, such a formula about it, is never forthcoming. Art, as the logic of the concept shows, has no set of necessary and sufficient properties, hence a theory of it is logically impossible and not merely factually difficult. Aesthetic theory tries to define what cannot be defined in its requisite sense. But in recommending the repudiation of aesthetic theory I shall not argue from this, as too many others have done, that its logical confusions render it meaningless or worthless. On the contrary, I wish to reassess its role and its contribution primarily in order to show that it is of the greatest importance to our understanding of the arts.

Let us now survey briefly some of the more famous extant aesthetic theories in order to see if they do incorporate correct and adequate statements about the nature of art. In each of these there is the assumption that it is the true enumeration of the defining properties of art, with the implication that previous theories have stressed wrong definitions. Thus, to begin with, consider a famous version of Formalist theory, that propounded by Bell and Fry. It is true that they speak mostly of painting in their writings but both assert that what they find in that art can be generalized for what is "art" in the others as well. The essence of painting, they maintain, are the plastic elements in relation. Its defining property is significant form, i.e., certain combinations of lines, colors, shapes, volumes—everything on the canvas except the representational elements—which evoke a unique response to such combinations. Painting is definable as plastic organization. The nature of art, what it *really* is, so their theory goes, is a unique combination of certain elements (the specifiable plastic ones) in their relations. Anything which is art is an instance of significant form; and anything which is not art has no such form.

To this the Emotionalist replies that the truly essential property of art has been left out. Tolstoy, Ducasse, or any of the advocates of this theory, find that the requisite defining property is not significant form but rather the expression of emotion in some sensuous public medium. Without projection of emotion into some piece of stone or words or sounds, etc., there can be no art. Art is really such embodiment. It is this that uniquely characterizes art, and any true, real definition of it, contained in some adequate theory of art, must so state it.

The Intuitionist disclaims both emotion and form as defining properties. In Croce's version, for example, art is identified not with some physical, public object but with a specific creative, cognitive and spiritual act. Art is really a first stage of knowledge in which certain human beings (artists) bring their images and intuitions into lyrical clarification or expression. As such, it is an awareness, nonconceptual in character, of the unique individuality of things; and since it exists below the level of conceptualization or action, it is without scientific or moral content. Croce singles out as the defining essence of art this first stage of spiritual life and advances its identification with art as a philosophically true theory or definition.

The Organicist says to all of this that art is really a class of organic wholes consisting of distinguishable, albeit inseparable, elements in their causally efficacious relations which are presented in some sensuous medium. In A. C. Bradley, in piece-meal versions of it in literary criticism, or in my own generalized adaptation of it in my *Philosophy of the Arts,* what is claimed is that anything which is a work of art is in its nature a unique complex of interrelated parts—in painting, for example, lines, colors, volumes, subjects, etc., all interacting upon one another on a paint surface of some sort. Certainly, at one time at least it seemed to

me that this organic theory constituted the one true and real definition of art.

My final example is the most interesting of all, logically speaking. This is the Voluntarist theory of Parker. In his writings on art, Parker persistently calls into question the traditional simple-minded definitions of aesthetics. "The assumption underlying every philosophy of art is the existence of some common nature present in all the arts."[1] "All the so popular brief definitions of art—'significant form,' 'expression,' 'intuition,' 'objectified pleasure'—are fallacious, either because, while true of art, they are also true of much that is not art, and hence fail to differentiate art from other things; or else because they neglect some essential aspect of art."[2] But instead of inveighing against the attempt at definition of art itself, Parker insists that what is needed is a complex definition rather than a simple one. "The definition of art must therefore be in terms of a complex of characteristics. Failure to recognize this has been the fault of all the well-known definitions."[3] His own version of Voluntarism is the theory that art is essentially three things: embodiment of wishes and desires imaginatively satisfied, language, which characterizes the public medium of art, and harmony, which unifies the language with the layers of imaginative projections. Thus, for Parker, it is a true definition to say of art that it is ". . . the provision of satisfaction through the imagination, social significance, and harmony. I am claiming that nothing except works of art possesses all three of these marks."[4]

Now, all of these sample theories are inadequate in many different ways. Each purports to be a complete statement about the defining features of all works of art and yet each of them leaves out something which the others take to be central. Some are circular, e.g., the Bell-Fry theory of art as significant form which is defined in part in terms of our response to significant form. Some of them, in their search for necessary and sufficient properties, emphasize too few properties, like (again) the Bell-Fry definition which leaves out subject-representation in painting, or the Croce theory which omits inclusion of the very important feature of the public, physical character, say, of architecture. Others are too general and cover objects that are not art as well as works of art. Organicism is surely such a view since it can be applied to *any* causal unity in the natural world as well as to art.[5] Still others rest on dubious principles, e.g., Parker's claim that art embodies imaginative satisfactions, rather than real ones; or Croce's assertion that there is nonconceptual knowledge. Consequently, even if art has one set of necessary and sufficient properties, none of the theories we have noted or, for that matter, no aesthetic theory yet proposed, has enumerated that set to the satisfaction of all concerned.

Then there is a different sort of difficulty. As real definitions, these theories are supposed to be factual reports on art. If they are, may we not ask, Are they empirical and open to verification or falsification? For example, what would confirm or disconfirm the theory that art is significant form or embodiment of emotion or creative synthesis of images? There does not even seem to be a hint of the kind of evidence which might be forthcoming to test these theories; and indeed one wonders if they are perhaps honorific definitions of "art," that is, proposed redefinitions in terms of some *chosen* conditions for applying the concept of art, and not true or false reports on the essential properties of art at all.

But all these criticisms of traditional aesthetic theories—that they are circular, incomplete, untestable, pseudo-factual, disguised proposals to change the meaning of concepts—have been made before. My intention is to go beyond these to make a much more fundamental criticism, namely, that aesthetic theory is a logically vain attempt to define what cannot be defined, to state the necessary and sufficient properties of that which has no necessary and sufficient properties, to conceive the concept of art as closed when its very use reveals and demands its openness.

The problem with which we must begin is not "What is art?," but "What sort of concept is 'art'?" Indeed, the root problem of philosophy itself is to explain the relation between the employment of certain kinds of concepts and the conditions under which they can be correctly applied. If I may paraphrase Wittgenstein, we must not ask, What is the nature of any philosophical *x*?, or even, according to the semanticist, What does "*x*" mean?, a transformation that leads to the disastrous interpretation of "art" as a name for some specifiable class of objects; but rather, What is the use or employment of "*x*"? What does "*x*" do in the language? This, I take it, is the initial question, the begin-all if not the end-all of any philosophical problem and solution. Thus, in aesthetics, our first problem is the elucidation of the actual employment of the concept of art, to give a logical description of the actual functioning of the concept, including a description of the conditions under which we correctly use it or its correlates.

My model in this type of logical description or philosophy derives from Wittgenstein. It is also he who, in his refutation of philosophical theorizing in the sense of constructing definitions of philosophical entities, has furnished contemporary aesthetics with a starting point for any future progress. In his new work, *Philosophical Investigations*,[6] Wittgenstein raises as an illustrative question, What is a game? The traditional philosophical, theoretical answer would be in terms of some exhaustive set of properties common to all games. To this Wittgenstein says, let us consider what we call "games":

> I mean board-games, card games, ball-games, Olympic games, and so on. What is common to them all?—Don't say: 'there *must* be something common, or they would not be called "games"' but *look* and see whether there is anything common to all.—For if you look at them you will not see something that is common to *all*, but similarities, relationships, and a whole series of them at that . . .

Card games are like board games in some respects but not in others. Not all games are amusing, nor is there always winning or losing or competition. Some games resemble others in some respects—that is all. What we find are no necessary and sufficient properties, only "a complicated network of similarities overlapping and crisscrossing," such that we can say of games that they form a family with family resemblances and no common trait. If one asks what a game is, we pick out sample games, describe these, and add, "This and *similar things* are called 'games'." This is all we need to say and indeed all any of us knows about games. Knowing what a game is not knowing some real definition or theory but being able to recognize and explain games and to decide which among imaginary and new examples would or would not be called "games."

The problem of the nature of art is like that of the nature of games, at least in these respects: If we actually look and see what it is that we call "art," we will also find no common properties—only strands of similarities. Knowing what art is is not apprehending some manifest or latent essence but being able to recognize, describe, and explain those things we call "art" in virtue of these similarities.

But the basic resemblance between these concepts is their open texture. In elucidating them, certain (paradigm) cases can be given, about which there can be no question as to their being correctly described as "art" or "game," but no exhaustive set of cases can be given. I can list some cases and some conditions under which I can apply correctly the concept of art but I cannot list all of them, for the all-important reason that unforeseeable or novel conditions are always forthcoming or envisageable.

A concept is open if its conditions of application are emendable and corrigible; i.e., if a situation or case can be imagined or secured which would call for some sort of *decision* on our part to extend the use of the concept to cover this, or to close the concept and invent a new one to deal with the new case and its new property. If necessary and sufficient conditions for the application of a concept can be stated, the concept is a closed one. But this can happen only in logic or mathematics where concepts are constructed and completely defined. It cannot occur with empirically-descriptive and normative concepts unless we arbitrarily close them by stimulating the ranges of their uses.

I can illustrate this open character of "art" best by examples drawn from its subconcepts. Consider questions like "Is Dos Passos' *U.S.A.* a novel?," "Is V. Woolf's *To the Lighthouse* a novel?," "Is Joyce's *Finnegan's Wake* a novel?" On the traditional view, these are construed as factual problems to be answered yes or no in accordance with the presence or absence of defining properties. But certainly this is not how any of these questions is answered. Once it arises, as it has many times in the development of the novel from Richardson to Joyce (e.g., "Is Gide's *The School for Wives* a novel or a diary?"), what is at stake is no factual analysis concerning necessary and sufficient properties but a decision as to whether the work under examination is similar in certain respects to other

works, already called "novels," and consequently warrants the extension of the concept to cover the new case. The new work is narrative, fictional, contains character delineation and dialogue but (say) it has no regular time-sequence in the plot or is interspersed with actual newspaper reports. It is like recognized novels, A, B, C, ... in some respects but not like them in others. But then neither were B and C like A in some respects when it was decided to extend the concept applied to A to B and C. Because work N + 1 (the brand new work) is like A, B, C . . . N in certain respects—has strands of similarity to them—the concept is extended and a new phase of the novel engendered. "Is N + 1 a novel?," then, is no factual, but rather a decision problem, where the verdict turns on whether or not we enlarge our set of conditions for applying the concept.

What is true of the novel is, I think, true of every subconcept of art: "tragedy," "comedy," "painting," "opera," etc., of "art" itself. No "Is X a novel, painting, opera, work of art, etc.?" question allows of a definitive answer in the sense of a factual yes or no report. "Is this *collage* a painting or not?" does not rest on any set of necessary and sufficient properties of painting but on whether we decide—as we did!—to extend "painting" to cover this case.

"Art," itself, is an open concept. New conditions (cases) have constantly arisen and will undoubtedly constantly arise; new art forms, new movements will emerge, which will demand decisions on the part of those interested, usually professional critics, as to whether the concept should be extended or not. Aestheticians may lay down similarity conditions but never necessary and sufficient ones for the correct application of the concept. With "art" its conditions of application can never be exhaustively enumerated since new cases can always be envisaged or created by artists, or even nature, which would call for a decision on someone's part to extend or to close the old or to invent a new concept. (E.g., "It's not a sculpture, it's a mobile.")

What I am arguing, then, is that the very expansive, adventurous character of art, its ever-present changes and novel creations, makes it logically impossible to ensure any set of defining properties. We can, of course, choose to close the concept. But to do this with "art" or "tragedy" or "portraiture," etc., is ludicrous since it forecloses on the very conditions of creativity in the arts.

Of course there are legitimate and serviceable closed concepts in art. But these are always those whose boundaries of conditions have been drawn for a *special* purpose. Consider the difference, for example, between "tragedy" and "(extant) Greek tragedy." The first is open and must remain so to allow for the possibility of new conditions, e.g., a play in which the hero is not noble or fallen or in which there is no hero but other elements that are like those of plays we already call "tragedy." The second is closed. The plays it can be applied to, the conditions under which it can be correctly used are all in, once the boundary, "Greek," is drawn. Here the critic can work out a theory or real definition in which he lists the common properties at least of the extant Greek tragedies. Aristotle's definition, false as it is as a theory of all the plays of Aeschylus, Sophocles, and Euripides, since it does not cover some of them,[7] properly called "tragedies," can be interpreted as a real (albeit incorrect) definition of this closed concept; although it can also be, as it unfortunately has been, conceived as a purported real definition of "tragedy," in which case it suffers from the logical mistake of trying to define what cannot be defined—of trying to squeeze what is an open concept into an honorific formula for a closed concept.

What is supremely important, if the critic is not to become muddled, is to get absolutely clear about the way in which he conceives his concepts; otherwise he goes from the problem of trying to define "tragedy," etc., to an arbitrary closing of the concept in terms of certain preferred conditions or characteristics which he sums up in some linguistic recommendation that he mistakenly thinks is a real definition of the open concept. Thus, many critics and aestheticians ask, "What is tragedy?," choose a class of samples for which they may give a true account of its common properties, and then go on to construe this account of the chosen closed class as a true definition or theory of the whole open class of tragedy. This, I think, is the logical mechanism of most of the so-called theories of the sub-concepts of art: "tragedy," "comedy," "novel," etc. In effect, this whole procedure, subtly deceptive as it is, amounts to a transformation of correct criteria for *recognizing* members of certain legitimately closed classes of works of art into recommended criteria for *evaluating* any putative member of the class.

The primary task of aesthetics is not to seek a theory but to elucidate the concept of art. Specifically, it is to describe the conditions under which we employ the concept correctly. Definition, reconstruction, patterns of analysis are out of place here since they distort and add nothing to our understanding of art. What, then, is the logic of "X is a work of art"?

As we actually use the concept, "Art" is both descriptive (like "chair") and evaluative (like "good"); i.e., we sometimes say, "This is a work of art," to describe something and we sometimes say it to evaluate something. Neither use surprises anyone.

What, first, is the logic of "X is a work of art," when it is a descriptive utterance? What are the conditions under which we would be making such an utterance correctly? There are no necessary and sufficient conditions but there are the strands of similarity conditions, i.e., bundles of properties, none of which need be present but most of which are, when we describe things as works of art. I shall call these the "criteria of recognition" of works of art. All of these have served as the defining criteria of the individual traditional theories of art; so we are already familiar with them. Thus, mostly, when we describe something as a work of art, we do so under the conditions of there being present some sort of artifact, made by human skill, ingenuity, and imagination, which embodies in its sensuous, public medium—stone, wood, sounds, words, etc.—certain distinguishable elements and relations. Special theorists would add conditions like satisfaction of wishes, objectification or expression of emotion, some act of empathy, and so on; but these latter conditions seem to be quite adventitious, present to some but not to other spectators when things are described as works of art. "X is a work of art and contains *no* emotion, expression, act of empathy, satisfaction, etc.," is perfectly good sense and may frequently be true. "X is a work of art and . . . was made by no one," or . . . "exists only in the mind and not in any publicly observable thing," or . . . "was made by accident when he spilled the paint on the canvas," in each case of which a normal condition is denied, are also sensible and capable of being true in certain circumstances. None of the criteria of recognition is a defining one, either necessary or sufficient, because we can sometimes assert of something that it is a work of art and go on to deny any one of these conditions, even the one which has traditionally been taken to be basic, namely, that of being an artifact: Consider, "This piece of driftwood is a lovely piece of sculpture." Thus, to say of anything that it is a work of art is to commit oneself to the presence of some of these conditions. One would scarcely describe X as a work of art if X were not an artifact, or a collection of elements sensuously presented in a medium, or a product of human skill, and so on. If none of the conditions were present, if there were no criteria present for recognizing something as a work of art, we would not describe it as one. But, even so, no one of these or any collection of them is either necessary or sufficient.

The elucidation of the descriptive use of "Art" creates little difficulty. But the elucidation of the evaluative use does. For many, especially theorists, "This is a work of art" does more than describe; it also praises. Its conditions of utterance, therefore, include certain preferred properties or characteristics of art. I shall call these "criteria of evaluation." Consider a typical example of this evaluative use, the view according to which to say of something that it is a work of art is to imply that it is a *successful* harmonization of elements. Many of the honorific definitions of art and its subconcepts are of this form. What is at stake here is that "Art" is construed as an evaluative term which is either identified with its criterion or justified in terms of it. "Art" is defined in terms of its evaluative property, e.g., successful harmonization. On such a view, to say "X is a work of art" is (1) to say something which is taken to mean "X is a successful harmonization" (e.g., "Art *is* significant form") or (2) to say something praiseworthy *on the basis* of its successful harmonization. Theorists are never clear whether it is (1) or (2) which is being put forward. Most of them, concerned as they are with this evaluative use, formulate (2), i.e., that feature of art that *makes* it art in the praise-sense, and then go on to state (1), i.e., the definition of "Art" in terms of its art-making feature. And this is clearly to confuse the conditions under which we say something evaluatively with the meaning of what we say. "This is a work of art," said evaluatively, cannot mean "This is a successful harmonization of elements"—except by

stipulation—but at most is said in virtue of the art-making property, which is taken as a (the) criterion of "Art," when "Art" is employed to assess. "This is a work of art," used evaluatively, serves to praise and not to affirm the reason why it is said.

The evaluative use of "Art," although distinct from the conditions of its use, relates in a very intimate way to these conditions. For, in every instance of "This is a work of art" (used to praise), what happens is that the criterion of evaluation (e.g., successful harmonization) for the employment of the concept of art is converted into a criterion of recognition. This is why, on its evaluative use, "This is a work of art" implies "This has P," where "P" is some chosen art-making property. Thus, if one chooses to employ "Art" evaluatively, as many do, so that "That is a work of art and not (aesthetically) good" makes no sense, he uses "Art" in such a way that he refuses to *call* anything a work of art unless it embodies his criterion of excellence.

There is nothing wrong with the evaluative use; in fact, there is good reason for using "Art" to praise. But what cannot be maintained is that theories of the evaluative use of "Art" are true and real definitions of the necessary and sufficient properties of art. Instead they are honorific definitions, pure and simple, in which "Art" has been redefined in terms of chosen criteria.

But what makes them—these honorific definitions—so supremely valuable is not their disguised linguistic recommendations; rather it is the *debates* over the reasons for changing the criteria of the concept of art which are built into the definitions. In each of the great theories of art, whether correctly understood as honorific definitions or incorrectly accepted as real definitions, what is of the utmost importance are the reasons proffered in the argument for the respective theory, that is, the reasons given for the chosen or preferred criterion of excellence and evaluation. It is this perennial debate over these criteria of evaluation which makes the history of aesthetic theory the important study it is. The value of each of the theories resides in its attempt to state and to justify certain criteria which are either neglected or distorted by previous theories. Look at the Bell-Fry theory again. Of course, "Art is significant form" cannot be accepted as a true, real definition of art; and most certainly it actually functions in their aesthetics as a redefinition of art in terms of the chosen condition of significant form. But what gives it its aesthetic importance is what lies behind the formula: In an age in which literary and representational elements have become paramount in painting, *return* to the plastic ones since these are indigenous to painting. Thus, the role of the theory is not to define anything but to use the definitional form, almost epigrammatically, to pin-point a crucial recommendation to turn our attention once again to the plastic elements in painting.

Once we, as philosophers, understand this distinction between the formula and what lies behind it, it behooves us to deal generously with the traditional theories of art; because incorporated in every one of them is a debate over and argument for emphasizing or centering upon some particular feature of art which has been neglected or perverted. If we take the aesthetic theories literally, as we have seen, they all fail; but if we reconstruct them, in terms of their function and point, as serious and argued-for recommendations to concentrate on certain criteria of excellence in art, we shall see that aesthetic theory is far from worthless. Indeed, it becomes as central as anything in aesthetics, in our understanding of art, for it teaches us what to look for and how to look at it in art. What is central and must be articulated in all the theories are their debates over the reasons for excellence in art—debates over emotional depth, profound truths, natural beauty, exactitude, freshness of treatment, and so on, as criteria of evaluation—the whole of which converges on the perennial problem of what makes a work of art good. To understand the role of aesthetic theory

is not to conceive it as definition, logically doomed to failure, but to read it as summaries of seriously made recommendations to attend in certain ways to certain features of art.

Notes

1. D. Parker, "The Nature of Art," reprinted in E. Vivas and M. Krieger, *The Problems of Aesthetics* (N.Y., 1953), p. 90.
2. *Ibid.*, pp. 93–94.
3. *Ibid.*, p. 94.
4. *Ibid.*, p. 104.
5. See M. Macdonald's review of my *Philosophy of the Arts, Mind*, Oct., 1951, pp. 561–564, for a brilliant discussion of this objection to the Organic theory.
6. L. Wittgenstein, *Philosophical Investigations* (Oxford, 1953), tr. by E. Anscombe; see esp. Part I, Sections 65–75. All quotations are from these sections.
7. See H. D. F. Kitto, *Greek Tragedy* (London, 1939), on this point.

DISCUSSION QUESTIONS

1. Do you agree with Weitz's position that all attempts to define art are doomed to failure? Why or why not?
2. Do you agree with Weitz's argument for treating the concept of art and its various "subconcepts" as "open concepts"? Why or why not?
3. How might Weitz evaluate the theories of art put forward by Tolstoy and Langer? Explain.
4. What do you think are the most important characteristics of "artworks" to which an audience should attend? Would your answer vary with respect to the different kinds of art? Why or why not?

74. Tomas Ybarra-Frausto (b. 1938)
"The Chicano Movement/The Movement of Chicano Art"

Tomas Ybarra-Frausto is an American aesthetician who in recent decades has written extensively on the nature and significance of the various forms of art produced within the Chicano, or Mexican American, community. In this reading he addresses that theme, focusing especially on the interrelations between aesthetic concerns and Chicano economic and political struggles since the mid-1960s. As part of this investigation he also

brings to light the diversity of production, particularly in the domain of visual art, and the ways in which mainstream standards of what counts as art in the dominant culture are challenged by these distinctively Chicano forms of aesthetic creation.

This essay originally was presented at a 1988 conference on the display of culturally diverse material in museums, hosted by the Smithsonian Institution and the

Rockefeller Foundation. Along with the other papers presented, Ybarra-Frausto's piece was published subsequently as part of an anthology entitled *Exhibiting Cultures: The Poetics and Politics of Museum Display.*

QUESTIONS FOR CRITICAL READING

1. How does Ybarra-Frausto characterize the mainstream cultural perspective on art in the United States, and how does he criticize it?
2. How does Ybarra-Frausto characterize Chicano art during its early phase ("Phase I"), and how did it challenge mainstream values and assumptions? What were its goals, according to the author?
3. What is *rasquachismo,* and how has it appeared in various forms of artistic production in the Chicano community?
4. How does Ybarra-Frausto characterize Chicano art during its second phase ("Phase II"), and what are its primary aims?

TERMS TO NOTE

rapprochement: A French term referring to the establishment of friendly relations.

campesino: A Spanish term for an agricultural worker, small farmer, or peasant.

totalizing: In this context, having to do with the intellectual attempt to account for as much experience and as many phenomena as possible from the standpoint of one comprehensive theory, one worldview, or one uniform set of evaluative principles.

––––––––––

Born in the tumultuous decade of the 1960s, Chicano art has been closely aligned with the political goals of Chicano struggles for self-determination. As an aesthetic credo, Chicano art seeks to link lived reality to the imagination. Going against mainstream cultural traditions of art as escape and commodity, Chicano art intends that viewers respond both to the aesthetic object and to the social reality reflected in it. A prevalent attitude toward the art object is that it should provide aesthetic pleasure while also serving to educate and edify. In its various modalities, Chicano art is

envisioned as a model for freedom, a call to both conscience and consciousness.[1]

Phase I, 1965–1975: Creation of the Project

Although struggles for social, political, and economic equality have been a central tenet of Chicano history since 1848, the efforts to unionize California farmworkers launched by Cesar Chavez in 1965 signaled a national mobilization, known as La Causa, among people of Mexican descent in the United States. The Chicano movement, or El Movimiento, was an ideological project closely aligned with the tactics, formulations, and beliefs of the civil-rights movement, the rise of Black Power, the political agenda of the New Left, the onset of an international student movement, and the struggles of liberation throughout the Third World. In retrospect, the Chicano movement was extremely heterogeneous, cutting across social class and regional and generational groupings.

Impelled by this mass political movement, Chicano artists, activists, and intellectuals united to articulate the goals of a collective cultural project that would meld social practice and cultural production. A primary aim of this project was to surmount strategies of containment by struggling to achieve self-determination on both the social and aesthetic planes. It was the Chicano movement—through various political fronts such as the farmworkers' cause in California, urban civil-rights activities, the rural-land-grant uprisings in New Mexico, the student and antiwar movements on college campuses, the labor struggles of undocumented workers, and the rise of feminism—that gave cogency to the cultural project.

Artists were integrated into the various political fronts of El Movimiento in unprecedented numbers and in significant ways. They organized, wrote the poems and songs of struggle, coined and printed the slogans, created the symbols, danced the ancient rituals, and painted ardent images that fortified and deepened understanding of the social issues being debated in Chicano communities.

An urgent first task was to repudiate external visions and destroy entrenched literary and visual representations that focused on Mexican Americans as receptors rather than active generators of culture. For the creative artist, whether painter, dancer, musician, or writer, this meant appropriation of his or her own self. Novelist Tomas Rivera further defines the enterprise:

> The invention of ourselves by ourselves is in actuality an extension of our will. Thus, as the Chicano invents himself he is complementing his will. Another complement. This is of great importance because these lives are trying to find form. This development is becoming a unifying consciousness. The thoughts of the Chicano are beginning to constantly gyrate over his own life, over his own development, over his identity, and as such over his own conservation. . . . Chicano literature has a triple mission: to represent, and to conserve that aspect of life that the Mexican American holds as his own and at the same time destroy the invention by others of his own life. That is—conservation, struggle and invention.[2]

This triad of conservation, struggle, and invention became a theme of Chicano literature. It served also as a core assumption in the production of energetic new forms of visual culture.

Sustained polemics by artists' groups throughout the country established the forms and content of Chicano art. Though few collective manifestos were issued, aesthetic guidelines can be gleaned from artists' statements, community-newspaper accounts, and oral interviews. Typical of this florescence of socially engaged artistic consciousness was the formation of the Mala Efe group (Mexican American Liberation Art Front) in the San Francisco Bay area. The artist Esteban Villa recalls:

> *Esto fue por eso del ano '68 . . . Era la época del* grape boycott *y del* Third World Strike *en* Berkeley. We would meet regularly to discuss the role and function of the artist in El Movimiento. At first our group was composed mainly of painters and we would bring our work and criticize it. Discussions were heated, especially the polemics on the form and content of revolutionary art and the relevance of murals and graphic art. Posters and other forms of graphics were especially discussed since many of us were creating *cartelones* as organizing tools for the various Chicano *mitotes* [spontaneous "happenings"] in the Bay Area.

> Our group kept growing and soon included local poets and intellectuals like Octavio Romano. In March of 1969, we decided to hold an exhibition in a big old frame house on 24th Street here in Oakland. The spacious but slightly *rasquache* house had been christened La Causa. The exhibition was called Nuevos Simbolos for La Nueva Raza and attempted to visually project images of *el hombre nuevo*: the Chicano who had emerged from the decolonization process.

> Opening night was *a todo dar* with *viejitos, wainitos,* and *vatos de la calle* walking in, checking it out and staying to rap. *Algunos poetas locales* read their work and there was music and *plática muy sabrosa.* We all sensed the beginning of an artistic rebirth. *Un nuevo arte del pueblo.*[3]

This "*nuevo arte del pueblo*" (a new art of the people) was to be created from shared experience and based on communal art traditions. Necessarily, a first step was to investigate, and give authority to, authentic expressive forms arising within the heterogeneous Chicano community. In opposition to the hierarchical dominant culture, which implicitly made a distinction between "fine art" and "folk art," attempts were made to eradicate boundaries and integrate categories. An initial recognition was that the practices of daily life and the lived environment were primary constituent elements of the new aesthetic.

In the everyday life of the barrio, art objects are embedded in a network of cultural sites, activities, and events. "The way folk art fits into this cultural constellation reveals time-tested aesthetic practices for accomplishing goals in social, religious and economic life. And these practices are on-going; they point not to an absolute standard or set of truths."[4] Inside the home, in the yard, and on the street corner—throughout the barrio environment—a visual culture of accumulation and bold display is enunciated. Handcrafted and store-bought items from the popular culture of Mexico and the mass culture of the United States mix freely and exuberantly in a milieu of inventive appropriation and recontextualization. The barrio environment is shaped in ways that express the community's sense of itself, the aesthetic display projecting a sort of visual biculturalism.

As communal customs, rituals, and traditions were appropriated by Movimiento artists, they yielded boundless sources of imagery. The aim was not simply to reclaim vernacular traditions but to reinterpret them in ways useful to the social urgency of the period.

Some Vernacular Sources of Chicano Art

ALMANAQUES *Almanaques* (calendars) are a common feature in Chicano households, given to favored customers each year by barrio businesses. *Almanaques* traditionally feature images from Mexican folklore. Favorite images include nostalgic rural landscapes, interpretations of indigenous myths or historical events, bullfighting and cockfighting scenes, and the full pantheon of Catholic saints. Two of the most common images from the *almanaque* tradition are the Virgin of Guadalupe and an Aztec warrior carrying a sleeping maiden, which is a representation of the ancient myth of Ixtacihuatl and Popocatepetl (two snow-covered volcanoes in the Valley of Mexico).

Almanaques are printed in the United States, but the lithographed or chromolithographed images are generally imported from Mexico because of the immense popularity of famous *almanaque* artists such as Jesus Helguera and Eduardo Catano.[5] Their pastel, romanticized versions of Mexican types and customs are saved from year to year and proudly displayed in homes.

In the *almanaque* tradition, many community centers began issuing *calendarios Chicanos* in the mid-1970s.

ESTAMPAS RELIGIOSAS In many Chicano households, images of Catholic saints, martyrs of the faith, and holy personages are mingled with family photographs and memorabilia and prominently displayed on home altars or used as wall decorations.

Dispensed at churches or purchased in religious-specialty stores, the *estampas religiosas* (religious images) vary from calling-card-size to poster-size. *Estampas* represent Catholic saints with their traditional symbols: for example, St. Peter with a set of two crossed keys, St. Clement with an anchor, or St. Catherine with a wheel. The images are folk religious narratives, depicting miracles, feats of martyrdom in defense of the faith, or significant stories from the lives of the saints. Parents refer to the *estampas* as they recount the heroic episodes depicted, both socializing their children and introducing them to the tenets of the Catholic church. The saints of the *estampas* become guides to proper behavior and are many a child's first encounter with traditional Christian symbols.

ALTARES Artists also focused on *altares* (home religious shrines) as expressive forms of cultural amalgamation. In their eclectic composition, they fuse traditional items of folk material culture with artifacts from mass culture. Typical constituents of an *altar* include crocheted doilies and embroidered cloths, *recuerdos* (such as flowers or favors saved from some dance or party), family photographs, personal mementos, *santos* (religious chromolithographs or statues) especially venerated by the family, and many other elements. The grouping of the various objects in a particular space—atop a television set, on a kitchen counter, atop a bedroom dresser, or in a specially constructed *nicho* (wall shelf)—appears to be random but usually responds to a conscious sensibility and aesthetic judgment of what things belong together and in what arrangement. *Altares* are organic and ever-changing. They are iconic representations of the power of relationships, the place of contact between the human and the divine. *Altares* are a sophisticated form of vernacular *bricolage,* and their constituent elements can be used in an infinite number of improvised combinations to generate new meanings. A number of Chicano artists, among them Amalia Mesa-Bains and Rene Yanez, became known as *altaristas* (makers of altars), experimenting with the *altar* form in innovative ways.

CARTELES Mexican *carteles* (theatrical posters) and the ubiquitous commercially designed advertisements for barrio social events, such as dances or artistic caravans of visiting Mexican entertainers, were also significant image sources.

EXPRESSIVE FORMS FROM YOUTH CULTURES Chicano youth cultures were acknowledged as guardians and generators of a style, stance, and visual discourse of pride and identity. Urban iconography melds customs, symbols, and forms of daily-life practices in the metropolis. *Placas* (graffiti), tattoos, customized *ranflas* (low-rider cars), gang regalia, and countless other expressive forms evoke and embody a contemporary barrio sensibility. It is a sense of being that is defiant, proud, and rooted in resistance. Gilbert Lujan, Willie Herron, John Valadez, Judith Baca, and Santos Martinez are among legions of artists who experiment with barrio symbology in their work.

Rasquachismo: *A Chicano Sensibility*

Beyond grounding themselves in vernacular art forms, Movimiento artists found strength from and recovered meaning sedimented in consistent group stances such as *rasquachismo*. *Rasquachismo*[6] is neither an idea nor a style, but more of a pervasive attitude or taste. Very generally, *rasquachismo* is an underdog perspective— a view from *los de abajo*. It is a stance rooted in resourcefulness and adaptability, yet ever mindful of aesthetics.

In an environment in which things are always on the edge of coming apart (the car, the job, the toilet), lives are held together with spit, grit, and *movidas*. *Movidas* are whatever coping strategies one uses to gain time, to make options, to retain hope. *Rasquachismo* is a compendium of all the *movidas* deployed in immediate, day-to-day living. Resilience and resourcefulness spring from making do with what is at hand (*hacer rendir las cosas*). This utilization of available resources makes for syncretism, juxtaposition, and integration. *Rasquachismo* is a sensibility attuned to mixtures and confluence. Communion is preferred over purity.

Pulling through and making do are not guarantors of security, so things that are *rasquache* possess an ephemeral quality, a sense of temporality and impermanence—here today and gone tomorrow. While things might be created using whatever is at hand, attention is always given to nuances and details. Appearance and form have precedence over function.

In the realm of taste, to be *rasquache* is to be unfettered and unrestrained, to favor the elaborate over the simple, the flamboyant over the severe. Bright colors (*chillantes*) are preferred to somber, high intensity to low, the shimmering and sparkling over the muted and subdued. The *rasquache* inclination piles pattern on pattern, filling all available space with bold display. Ornamentation and elaboration prevail and are joined with a delight in texture and sensuous surfaces. A work of art may be *rasquache* in multiple and complex ways. It can be sincere and pay homage to the sensibility by restating its premises, i.e., the underdog worldview actualized through language and behavior, as in the dramatic presentation *La Carpa de los Rasquaches,* by Luis Valdez. Another strategy is for the artwork to evoke a *rasquache* sensibility through self-conscious manipulation of materials or iconography. One thinks of the combination of found materials and the use of satiric wit in the sculptures of Ruben Trejo, or the manipulation of *rasquache* artifacts, codes, and sensibilities from both sides of the border in the performance pieces of Guillermo Gomez-Peña. Many Chicano artists continue to investigate and interpret facets of *rasquachismo* as a conceptual lifestyle or aesthetic strategy.

Fronts of Struggle, Forms of Art

The initial phase of the Chicano cultural project (circa the mid-1960s) was seminal in validating emancipatory communal practices and codifying the symbols and images that would be forcefully deployed in adversarial counterrepresentations. By that time, visual artists had been well integrated into the various political fronts of El Movimiento, within which they were gestating a Chicano art movement that was national in scope and developed outside the dominant museum, gallery, and arts-publication circuit. Fluid and tendentious, the art produced by this movement underscored public connection instead of private cognition.

Inscribed in multiple arenas of agitation, artists continued to evolve *un arte del pueblo* that aimed to close the gap between radical politics and community-based cultural practices. The rural farmworkers' cause and the urban student movement are prime examples of this rapprochement.

La Causa, the farmworkers' struggle, was a grassroots uprising that provided the infinitely complex human essence necessary for creating a true people's art. One of the early purveyors of *campesino* expression was the newspaper *El Malcriado* (The Ill-Bred). Established primarily as a tool for organizing, the periodical soon came to function as a vehicle that promoted unity by stressing a sense of class consciousness while building cultural and political awareness. In artistic terms, *El Malcriado* lived up to its name by focusing on art forms outside the "high-art" canon, such as caricature and cartoons. The pervasive aesthetic norm was *rasquachismo,* a bawdy, irreverent, satiric, and ironic worldview.

In California, among the first expressions of this *rasquache* art were the political drawings of Andy Zermano, which were reproduced in *El Malcriado* starting in 1965. With trenchant wit, Zermano created Don Sotaco, a symbolic representation of the underdog. Don Sotaco is the archetypal *rasquache,* the dirt-poor but cunning individual who derides authority and outsmarts officialdom. In his cuttingly satirical cartoons, Zermano created vivid vignettes that are a potent expression of *campesinos'* plight. His drawings clearly point out the inequalities existing in the world of the *patron* (the boss) and the agricultural worker. To a great extent, these graphic illustrations of social relations did much to awaken consciousness. With antecedents in the Mexican graphic tradition of Jose Guadalupe Posada and Jose Clemente Orozco, the vivid imagery of Andy Zermano documents the creation of art for a cause.

The farmworkers' journal *El Malcriado* was also significant in its efforts to introduce Chicanos to a full spectrum of Mexican popular art. Its pages were full of people's *corridos* (ballads), poems, and drawings. Its covers often reproduced images garnered from the various publications of the Taller de Grafica Popular (Workshop for Popular Graphic Art), an important source of Mexican political art. Through this journalistic forum, Chicano artists became acquainted with the notion that art of high aesthetic quality could substantially aid in furthering Chicano agrarian struggles.

As a primary impetus toward collaboration between workers and artists, *El Malcriado* planted the seed that would come to fruition in many other cooperative ventures between artists and workers. The creative capacities of artists were placed at the service of and welcomed by those struggling for justice and progress.

Simultaneously with the cultural expression of the farmworker's cause, a highly vocal and visible Chicano student movement emerged during the mid-1960s. Related to the worldwide radicalization of youth and inspired by international liberation movements, especially the Cuban revolution, the Black Power movement, and varied domestic struggles, the Chicano student movement developed strategies to overcome entrenched patterns of miseducation. Institutionalized racism was targeted as a key detriment, and cultural affirmation functioned as an important basis for political organization.

Chicano culture was affirmed as a creative, hybrid reality synthesizing elements from Mexican culture and the social dynamics of life experience in the United States. Scholars such as Octavio Romano published significant essays debunking orthodox views of Chicano life as monolithic and ahistorical. Contrary to these official notions, Chicano culture was affirmed as dynamic, historical, and anchored in working-class consciousness.

Within the student movement, art was assigned a key role as a maintainer of human signification and as a powerful medium that could rouse consciousness. Remaining outside the official cultural apparatus, the student groups originated alternative circuits for disseminating an outpouring of artistic production. As in the nineteenth century, when Spanish-language newspapers became major outlets for cultural expression in the Southwest, contemporary journals functioned as purveyors of cultural polemics and new representations. Although varying in emphasis and quality, most student-movement periodicals shared a conscious focus on the visual arts as essential ingredients in the formation of Chicano pride and identity. For many readers, it was a first encounter with the works of the Mexican muralists, the graphic mastery of Jose Guadalupe Posada, the Taller de Grafica Popular, and reproductions of pre-Columbian artifacts. Equally important, Movimiento newspapers such as *Bronze, El Machete, El Popo, Chicanismo,* and numerous others published interviews with local Chicano artists while encouraging and reproducing their work.

Knowledge about the Hispanic-Native American art forms of the Southwest came from neither academic nor scholarly sources, but rather from venues within the movement such as *El Grito del Norte,* a newspaper issued from Espanola, New Mexico, starting in 1968.

This journal had a grass-roots orientation and placed emphasis on preserving the culture of the rural agrarian class. Often, photographic essays focusing on local artisans or documenting traditional ways of life in the isolated *pueblitos* of northern New Mexico were featured. Cleofas Vigil, a practicing *santero* (carver of *santos*) from the region, traveled widely, speaking to groups of artists. The carvers Patrocinio Barela, Celso Gallegos, and Jorge Lopez, all master *santeros* who were collected, documented, and exhibited by Anglo patrons during the first part of the century, gained renewed influence within the budding associations of Chicano artists. Old and tattered exhibition catalogues, newspaper clippings, and barely legible magazine articles that documented their work were examined and passed from hand to hand to be eagerly scrutinized and savored. Primarily through oral tradition and the informal sharing of visual documentation, Chicano artists became aware of a major ancestral folk art tradition. And aside from the Movimiento press, literary and scholarly journals such as *El Grito* and *Revista Chicana Riqueña* often published portfolios of artists' works. All these alternative venues inserted art into life, propagating enabling visions of Chicano experience.

Asserting that Chicano art had a basic aim to document, denounce, and delight, individual artists and artists' groups resisted the formulation of a restricted aesthetic program to be followed uniformly. The Chicano community was heterogeneous, and the art forms it inspired were equally varied. Although representational modes became dominant, some artists opted for abstract and more personal expression. Artists in this group felt that internal and subjective views of reality were significant, and that formal and technical methods of presentation should remain varied.

Alternative Visions and Structures

By the early 1970s, Chicano artists had banded together to create networks of information, mutual support systems, and alternative art circuits. Regional artists' groups such as the Royal Chicano Air Force (R.C.A.F.) in Sacramento, the Raza Art and Media Collective in Ann Arbor, Michigan, the Movimiento Artistico Chicano (MARCH) in Chicago, the Con Safos group in San Antonio, Texas, and many others

persisted in the vital task of creating art forms that strengthened the will and fortified the cultural identity of the community.

With militant and provocative strategies, Chicano arts organizations developed and shared their art within a broad community context. They brought aesthetic pleasure to the sort of working people who walk or take the bus to work in the factories or in the service sector of the urban metropolis. In its collective character, in its sustained efforts to change the mode of participation between artists and their public, and, above all, as a vehicle for sensitizing communities to a pluralistic rather than a monolithic aesthetic, the Chicano alternative art circuit played a central and commanding role in nurturing a visual sensibility in the barrio.

POSTERS The combative phase of El Movimiento called for a militant art useful in the mobilization of large groups for political action. Posters were seen as accessible and expedient sources of visual information and indoctrination. Because they were inexpensive to reproduce and portable, they were well suited for mass distribution. Moreover, posters had historical antecedents in the Chicano community.[7] Many of the famous *planes* or political programs of the past had been issued as broadsides or posters to be affixed on walls, informing the populace and mustering them for political action.

The initial phase of Chicano poster production was directly influenced by both the work of Jose Guadalupe Posada and images from the Agustin Casasola photographic archives, which contained photos documenting the Mexican revolution.[8] Early Chicano poster makers appropriated images from these two primary sources and merely reproduced and massively distributed Posada and Casasola images embellished with slogans such as *Viva La Causa* and *Viva La Revolución*. Francisco "Pancho" Villa and Emiliano Zapata, iconic symbols of the Mexican Revolution, were among the first images that assaulted Chicano consciousness via the poster. Poster images of Villa and Zapata were attached to crude wooden planks and carried in picket lines and countless demonstrations. Quoting from Mexican antecedents was an important initial strategy of Chicano art. Having established a cultural and visual continuum across borders, Chicano artists could then move forward to forge a visual vocabulary and expressive forms corresponding to a complex bicultural reality.

Used to announce rallies, promote cultural events, or simply as visual statements, Chicano posters evolved as forms of communication with memorable imagery and pointed messages. The superb craftsmanship of artists such as Carlos Cortes, Amado Murillo Pena, Rupert Garcia, Malaquias Montoya, Ralph Maradiaga, Linda Lucero, Ester Hernandez, and a host of others elevated the poster from a mere purveyor of facts into visual statements that delighted as well as informed and stimulated. Formal elements such as color, composition, and lettering style echoed diverse graphic traditions: the powerful, socially conscious graphics of the Taller de Grafica Popular in Mexico, the colorful, psychedelic rock-poster art of the hippie counterculture, and the boldly assertive style of the Cuban *affiche*.

Such eclectic design sources taught graphic artists how to appeal and communicate with brevity, emphasis, and force. Chicano posters did not create a new visual vocabulary, but brilliantly united various stylistic influences into an emphatic hybrid expression. The two salient categories are political posters and event posters. The primary function of both forms was ideological mobilization through visual and verbal means.

Chicano posters generally were issued in hand-silk-screened editions of several hundred or lithographed runs of several thousand. They were posted on walls, distributed free at rallies, or sold for nominal prices. Within many sectors of the community, Chicano posters were avidly collected and displayed in personal spaces as a matter of pride and identification with their message. For a mass public unaccustomed and little inclined to visit museums and art galleries, the Chicano poster provided a direct connection to the pleasures of owning and responding to an art object. Chicano posters were valued both as records of historical events and as satisfying works of art.

MURALS The barrio mural movement is perhaps the most powerful and enduring contribution of the Chicano art movement nationwide. Created and nurtured by the humanist ideals of Chicano struggles for self-determination, murals functioned as a pictorial reflection of the social drama.

Reaching back to the goals and dicta of the Mexican muralists, especially the pronouncements of David Alfaro Siqueiros, in the mid-1960s Chicano artists called for an art that was public, monumental, and accessible to the common people. The generative force of Chicano muralism was also a mass social movement, but the artists as a whole did not have the same kind of formal training as the Mexican muralists, and they fostered mural programs through an alternative circuit independent of official sanction and patronage.

For their visual dialogue, muralists used themes, motifs, and iconography that gave ideological direction and visual coherence to the mural programs. In the main, the artistic vocabulary centered on the indigenous heritage (especially the Aztec and Mayan past), the Mexican Revolution and its epic heroes and heroines, renderings of both historical and contemporary Chicano social activism, and depictions of everyday life in the barrio. Internationalism entered the pictorial vocabulary of Chicano murals via iconographic references to liberation struggles in Vietnam, Africa, and Latin America and motifs from cultures in those areas. The muralists' efforts were persistently directed toward documentation and denunciation.

Finding a visual language adequate to depict the epic sweep of the Chicano movement was not simple. Some murals became stymied, offering romantic, archaicizing views of indigenous culture, uncritically depicting Chicano life, and portraying cultural and historical events without a clear political analysis. Successful mural programs, however, were most significant in reclaiming history. As the community read the visual chronicles, it internalized an awareness of the past and activated strategies for the future.

Apart from the aesthetic content, muralism was significant in actualizing a communal approach to the production and dissemination of art. Brigades of artists and residents worked with a director who solicited community input during the various stages of producing the mural. Through such collaborative actions, murals became a large-scale, comprehensive public-education system in the barrio.

In retrospect, it can be affirmed that Chicano art in the 1960s and 1970s encompassed both a political position and an aesthetic one. That art underscored a consciousness that helped define and shape fluid and integrative forms of visual culture. Artists functioned as visual educators, with the important task of refining and transmitting through plastic expression the ideology of a community striving for self-determination.

A Chicano national consciousness was asserted by a revival in all the arts. Aesthetic guidelines were not officially promulgated but arose within the actual arena of political practice. As opposed to mainstream art movements, where critical perspectives remain at the level of the work (art about itself and for itself), the Chicano art movement sought to extend meaning beyond the aesthetic object to include transformation of the material environment as well as of consciousness.

Phase II, 1975–1990: Neutralization and Recuperation of the Project

The late 1970s and the 1980s have been a dynamically complex juncture for the Chicano cultural project. Many of its postulates and aims have come to fruition during this time. Three of these aims are: (1) the creation of a core of visual signification, a bank of symbols and images that encode the deep structures of Chicano experience. Drawing from this core of commonly understood iconography, artists can create counterrepresentations that challenge the imposed "master narrative" of elite art practice; (2) the maintenance of alternative art structures, spaces, and forms. For more than two decades, Chicano arts organizations have persisted in the arduous task of creating a responsive working-class audience for art. A principal goal of these efforts has been to make art accessible, to deflect its rarefied, elitist aura, and especially to reclaim the art from its commodity status with the ideal of returning it to a critical role within the social practices of daily living; and (3) the continuation of mural programs. Although there has been a diminution in the number of public art forms such as murals and posters, what has been produced since 1975 is of deeper political complexity and superior aesthetic quality.

According to the muralist Judith Baca,

> Later works such as the Great Wall of Los Angeles developed a new genre of murals which have

close alliance with conceptual performance in that the overall mural is only one part of an overall plan to affect social change. Muralists such as ASCO [a performance group] began to use themselves as the art form, dressing themselves like murals and stepping down off walls to perform. Experiments with portable murals and new social content continue. There is a shift of interest from the process to the product. While fewer murals are being painted, they are of higher quality and the forms of image-making continue to be viewed as an educational process.[9]

Such accomplishments are especially praiseworthy, having transpired during a period of intense change and transformation in Chicano communities. The utopian buoyancy that sustained a national Chicano art movement has eroded. As the groundswell of collective political action has dispersed, as more Chicanos enter the professional class and are affected by its implied social mobility, and as public art forms have diminished in frequency, tracings of a new agenda of struggle have surfaced.

Given demographic data indicating that the number of people of Latin American descent in the United States is growing, and given sociological data indicating that Spanish-speaking groups remain definitely "other" for several generations, new cultural undercurrents among Chicanos call for an awareness of America as a continent and not a country. In the new typology an emergent axis of influence might lead from Los Angeles to Mexico City and from there to Bogotá, Lima, Buenos Aires, Managua, Barcelona, and back to the barrio. For the creative artists, such new political and aesthetic filiations expand the field with hallucinatory possibilities. As performance artist Guillermo Gomez-Peña points out:

> The strength and originality of Chicano-Latino contemporary art in the U.S. lies partially in the fact that it is often bicultural, bilingual and/or biconceptual. The fact that artists are able to go back and forth between two different landscapes of symbols, values, structures and styles, and/or operate within a "third landscape" that encompasses both. . . .[10]

To-ing and fro-ing between multiple aesthetic repertoires and venues including mainstream galleries, museums, and collectors as well as alternative infrastructures created by El Movimiento, Chicano artists question and subvert totalizing notions of cultural coherence, wholeness, and fixity. Contemporary revisions of identity and culture affirm that both concepts are open and offer the possibility of making and remaking oneself from within a living, changing tradition.

In contemporary Chicano art, no artistic current is dominant. Figuration and abstraction, political art and self-referential art, art of process, performance, and video all have adherents and advocates. The thread of unity is a sense of vitality and continual maturation. The mainstream art circuit continues to uphold rigid and stereotypical notions in its primitivistic and folkloristic categorizations of "ethnic art." This is an elite perspective that blithely relegates highly trained artists into a nether region in which Chicano art is inscribed in an imagined world that is a perpetual fiesta of bright colors and folk idioms—a world in which social content is interpreted as a cultural form unconnected to political and social sensibilities.

For the denizens of the arts establishment, Chicano art is uneasily accommodated within two viewpoints. It can be welcomed and celebrated under the rubric of pluralism, a classification that permissively allows a sort of supermarketlike array of choices among styles, techniques, and contents. While stemming from a democratic impulse to validate and recognize diversity, pluralism serves also to commodify art, disarm alternative representations, and deflect antagonisms. Impertinent and out-of-bounds ethnic visions are embraced as energetic new vistas to be rapidly processed and incorporated into peripheral spaces within the arts circuit, then promptly discarded in the yearly cycle of new models. What remains in place as eternal and canonical are the consecrated idioms of Euro-centered art. Seen from another perspective, the power structure of mainstream art journals, critics, galleries, and museums selectively chooses and validates what it projects, desires, and imposes as constituent elements of various alternative artistic discourses. For "Hispanic" art, this selective incorporation often foregrounds artwork deemed "colorful," "folkloric," "decorative," and

untainted with overt political content. While elements of these modalities might be present in the artistic production of "Hispanic" artists, they do not necessarily cohere into consistent and defining stylistic features.

Inscribed within multiple class-based and regional traditions, Chicanos in the United States have activated complex mechanisms of cultural negotiation, a dynamic process of analysis and the exchange of options between cultures. In an interconnected world system, traditions are lost and found, and angles of vision accommodate forms and styles from First and Third World modernist traditions as well as from evolving signifying practices in the barrio. What is vigorously defended is a choice of alternatives.

In the visual arts, this process of cultural negotiation occurs in different ways. At the level of iconography and symbolism, for example, the Chicano artist often creates a personal visual vocabulary freely blending and juxtaposing symbols and images culled from African American, Native American, European, and mestizo cultural sources. Resonating with the power ascribed to the symbols within each culture, the new combination emerges dense with multifarious meaning. Beyond symbols, artistic styles and art-historical movements are continually appropriated and recombined in a constant and richly nuanced interchange. Current Chicano art can be seen as a visual narration of cultural negotiation.

Presently in the United States, entrenched systems of control and domination affirm and uphold distinctions between "us" and "them." Dichotomies such as white/nonwhite, English-speaking/Spanish-speaking, the haves/the have-nots, etc., persist and are based on social reality. We should not dissemble on this fact, but neither should we maintain vicious and permanent divisions or permit dogmatic closure.

My own sense of the dialectic is that in the current struggle for cultural maintenance and parity within the Chicano community, there are two dominant strategies vying for ascendancy. On the one hand, there is an attempt to fracture mainstream consensus with a defiant "otherness." Impertinent representations counter the homogenizing desires, investments, and projections of the dominant culture and express what is manifestly different. On the other hand, there is the recognition of new interconnections and fil-iations, especially with other Latino groups in the United States. Confronting the dominant culture leads to a recognition that Anglos' visions of Chicanos and Chicanos' visions of themselves support and to an ex-tent reflect each other.

Rather than flowing from a monolithic aesthetic, Chicano art forms arise from tactical, strategic, and positional necessities. What Carlos Monsivais has called *la cultura de la necesidad* (the culture of necessity) leads to fluid multivocal exchanges among shifting cultural traditions. A consistent objective of Chicano art is to undermine imposed models of representation and to interrogate systems of aesthetic discourse, disclosing them as neither natural nor secure but conventional and historically determined.

Chicano art and artists are inscribed within multi-ple aesthetic traditions, both popular and elite. Their task is to recode themselves and move beyond dichot-omies in a fluid process of cultural negotiation. This negotiation usually reflects cultural change, variation by gender and region, and tensions within and among classes and groups of people, such as Mexican nation-als or other ethnic minorities in the United States.

In the dynamism of such a contemporary social reality, interests are culturally mediated, replaced, and created through what is collectively valued and worth struggling for. The task continues, and remains open.

Notes

1. This text is a reworking of my unpublished manu-script *Califas: California Chicano Art and Its Social Back-ground*. Sections have been excerpted in *Chicano Expressions: A New View in American Art* (New York: INTAR Latin Amer-ican Gallery, 1986) and *The Mural Primer* (Venice, Calif.: Social and Public Resource Center, 1987). My analysis par-allels ideas in James Clifford, *The Predicament of Culture: Twentieth-Century Ethnography, Literature and Art* (Cam-bridge: Harvard University Press, 1988).

2. Tomas Rivera, *Into the Labyrinth: The Chicano in Lit-erature* (Edinburg, Texas: Pan American University, 1971).

3. Esteban Villa, taped interview, 1979, in possession of the author.

4. Kay Turner and Pat Jasper, "La Causa, La Calle y La Esquina: A Look at Art Among Us," in *Art Among Us: Mexi-can American Folk Art of San Antonio* (San Antonio: San Antonio Museum Association, 1986).

5. See the catalog *Jesus Helguera: El Calendario Como Arte* (Mexico City: Subsecretaria de Cultura/Programa Cul-tural de Las Fronteras, 1987).

6. Tomas Ybarra-Frausto, "Rasquachismo: A Chicano Sensibility," in *Rasquachismo: Chicano Aesthetic* (Phoenix: Movimiento Artistico Del Rio Salado, 1988).

7. See Shifra M. Goldman, "A Public Voice: Fifteen Years of Chicano Posters," *Art Journal* 44, no. 1 (Spring, 1984).

8. Victor Sorell, "The Photograph as a Source for Visual Artists: Images From the Archivo Cassaola in the Works of Mexican and Chicano Artists," in *The World of Agustin Victor Casasola: Mexico 1900–1938* (Washington, D.C.: Fonda del Sol Visual Arts and Media Center, 1984).

9. Judith Baca, "Murals/Public Art," in *Chicano Expres-sions: A New View in American Art* (New York: INTAR Latin American Gallery, 1987), 37.

10. Guillermo Gomez-Peña, "A New Artistic Continent," *High Performance* 9, no. 3 (1986), 27.

DISCUSSION QUESTIONS

1. Do you agree with Ybarra-Frausto's critique of the mainstream art culture in the United States? Why or why not?

2. In Ybarra-Frausto's account, Chicano art in many ways challenges traditional Western as-sumptions concerning the distinction between "art" and "non-art." Is that distinction still use-ful in some way in our contemporary world? Why or why not?

3. According to the author, in Chicano art the aes-thetic and the political are often intertwined. Should art and political activism be kept sepa-rate? Why or why not? On the other hand, is all art inescapably "political," as some have claimed? Why or why not?

4. How would you compare Bullough's account of psychical distance in aesthetic experience with Ybarra-Frausto's account of the eclecticism and socially engaged, class-based character of Chi-cano art?

75. Curt Ducasse (1881–1969)
Aesthetic Liberalism

Curt Ducasse was an American philosopher known mostly for his work in the areas of aesthetics and the philosophy of mind. He was born in France but moved to the United States in 1900, eventually received his doctorate in philosophy from Harvard University, and thereafter spent most of his career first at the University of Washington and then at Brown University.

This selection is from his major work in aesthetics, published in 1929 and titled *The Philosophy of Art.* Part of his general aim in this text is to defend an "individualistic" relativism (which he often calls "liberalism") in the domain of aesthetic value judgment, particularly with respect to judgments of "immediate" rather than "instrumental" value. That is, in the case of either a work of art or a natural object, Ducasse argues that whether it is "beautiful" or "ugly," intrinsically valuable or not, is wholly dependent on whether any particular person thinks it is so. His position thus corresponds with the cliché often repeated today, "Beauty is in the eye of the beholder." Concerning the *nature* of art, Ducasse viewed it as essentially involving the "objectification of feeling"; but when it comes to the distinct question of the aesthetic *evaluation* of art, he maintained that there is no justifiable way to prove that somebody's judgment of immediate aesthetic value is right or wrong.

QUESTIONS FOR CRITICAL READING

1. How does Ducasse define "beauty" and "ugliness," and how does he apply these concepts to his theory of aesthetic judgment?
2. According to Ducasse, what is the difference between "judgments of immediate value" and "judgments of mediate value," and why are aesthetic judgments of the former rather than the latter type?
3. How does Ducasse criticize various arguments for "objective" standards of aesthetic taste?
4. What sorts of "provable" judgments can we make about works of art, in Ducasse's estimation?

TERMS TO NOTE

anomic: That which is aimless or directionless.
virtuoso: Here, someone who possesses great technical skill in an art.
savoir-faire: A French phrase meaning "knowing how to act."
nouveaux: French word for "new."
noematic: Here, having to do with accurate perception.
de gustibus non est disputandum: A Latin phrase meaning "there is no disputing taste."
argumentum ad baculum: A Latin phrase usually translated as "appeal to the stick"; it is the name traditionally given to a type of fallacious argument that tries to justify a conclusion by threatening those who might not accept it.

§10

Beauty is relative to the individual observer. Beauty, it will be recalled, was defined as the capacity of an object aesthetically contemplated to yield feelings that are pleasant. This definition cannot be characterized simply either as objective, or as subjective. According to it, "beautiful" is an adjective properly predicable only of objects, but what that adjective does predicate of an object is that the feelings of which it constitutes the aesthetic symbol for a contemplating observer, are pleasurable. Beauty being in this definite sense dependent upon the constitution of the individual observer, it will be as variable as that constitution. That is to say, an object which one person properly calls beautiful will, with equal propriety be not so judged by another, or indeed by the same person at a different time.

There is, then, no such thing as authoritative opinion concerning the beauty of a given object. There is only the opinion of this person or that; or the opinion of persons of some specified sort. When one has stated the opinion and mentioned the person or class of persons who hold it, one has gone as far as it is possible to go in the direction of a scientifically objective statement relating to the beauty of the object. When some matter (as that of beauty) is not of the sort which "is so," or "not so," in an *absolute* sense, the nearest approach that one can make to the wished-for absoluteness lies in furnishing, as fully as possible, the data to which the matter in question is *relative;* and this is what one does in the case of beauty when one indicates just who it happens to be, that judges the given object beautiful or the reverse.

All that was said above concerning aesthetic connoisseurship, i.e., concerning superior capacity for experiencing difference in aesthetic feeling in the presence of slight differences in the aesthetic object, applies equally here, where differences in the pleasantness of the feelings are particularly in question. There are connoisseurs of beauty, or, more often, of particular sorts of beauty; but their judgments of beauty are "binding" on no one. Indeed it is hard to see what could possibly be meant by "binding" in such a connection, unless it were an obligation on others to lie or dissemble concerning the aesthetic feelings which in fact they have or do not have on a given occasion. There is, of course, such a thing as good taste, and bad taste. But good taste, I submit, means either my taste, or the taste of people who are to my taste, or the taste of people to whose taste I want to be. There is no objective test of the goodness or badness of taste, in the sense in which there is an objective test of the goodness or badness of a person's judgment concerning, let us say, the fitness of a given tool to a given task.

§11

Why we have a natural inclination to think otherwise. What makes it so difficult for us to acknowledge that judgments of aesthetic value, i.e., of beauty and ugliness, which are truly judgments about objects, are not universally and necessarily valid, but on the contrary valid, except by chance, only for the individuals who make them, is that we are so constantly occupied otherwise with judgments concerning instrumental values. These have to do with relations of the object judged, *to other objects,* and such relations are socially observable, and the judgments concerning them socially valid. That a given railroad bridge is a good bridge can be proved or disproved by running over it such trains as we wished it to carry, and observing whether or not it does carry them. But there is no similar test by which the beauty of a landscape could be proved or disproved. Judgments of beauty (which is an immediate value) have to do with the relation of the object judged to the individual's own pleasure experience, of which he himself is the sole possible observer and judge. Judgments of beauty are therefore in this respect exactly on a par with judgments of the pleasantness of foods, wines, climates, amusements, companions, etc. Like these they are ultimately matters of the individual's own taste. It is of course quite possible that two persons, or two million, should have similar tastes, i.e., should happen alike to find pleasure in a given food or wine, or to obtain pleasurable feelings in contemplating aesthetically a given picture, melody, etc. But such community in the experience of pleasure, even then remains a bare matter of fact concerning just the persons who have it in common, and leaves wholly untouched the equally bare fact that other persons—whether many, few, or only one—find not pleasure but displeasure in the very same objects.

The fact that judgments of immediate value (such as judgments of aesthetic value) differ from judgments of mediate value in being incapable of proof, or disproof, and are therefore binding (except by accident) only on the individual who makes them, seems to be entirely overlooked by Professor Thomas Munro, in his recent interesting short book, *Scientific Method in Aesthetics.* Starting from the fact that the essence of science is verification,—"a constant checking up of results by various workers in the same subject,"—he goes on to say that, "carried over into aesthetics, this would suggest a systematic comparison of notes on the results of individual experiences in art. Its aim would be to discover more specifically how people agree and how they vary in aesthetic responses and critical appraisals" (p. 56). But supposing we should thus discover some widespread agreements and thereby be enabled to formulate some probable predictions, I then ask, what of it? What exactly will this prove concerning the aesthetic merits of the objects judged, and to whom will it prove it? And what is anybody going to do with information of that sort? Truly it is scientific, but it is information *not about laws of the objects studied* (as in chemistry, or mathematics), but *about the public* who looks at the objects. And art-creation is no manufacturing of spiritual candy, that the artist should need to inquire, and cater to, what the market happens to like. And supposing half-a-dozen people, or a hundred, agree that a certain melody is "gay and sprightly" (p. 58), what of it? If this is mere description, it is indeed either true or false, but is then no more criticism,—no more involves any "oughts" or "ought-nots,"—than, say, the assertion that a given animal is a dog. If on the other hand the assertion that the melody is "gay and sprightly" constitutes criticism,—implies praise or blame,—then the fact that a hundred people evaluate the melody alike has neither more nor less significance than the fact of a hundred people being similar in liking (or disliking), say, caviar, or tobacco. What Professor Munro regards as constituting scientific method in aesthetic criticism, seems to me, for these reasons, to be on the contrary the using of scientific method in the study of facts wholly irrelevant to aesthetic criticism, for the ultimate and sole foundation of aesthetic criticism is individual taste such as it happens to be, and whether shared or not.

Beside the fact that we are so constantly occupied with instrumental values, however, and tend unconsciously to carry the habits of thought acquired there into the realm of immediate values, there are other human traits which explain, or manifest themselves in, our persistent reaching for rules also in the domain of aesthetic values. Most of us, for instance, instinctively abhor anything that savors even remotely of anarchy, and refuse to consider the possibility that a realm of anomic values may exist where anarchy would be legitimate. We fear that if we should grant it the right to live even there, anarchy (or shall we say freedom?) would come forth a monster elsewhere and bite us. Again, whatever is individual is unpredictable and therefore likely to be upsetting; and we ourselves, hating and dreading the responsibility of being ourselves, cling for dear life,—or it may here be dear death—to any seeming ready rules that would promise to save us from the need. Were one to lean on modern slang for a contribution to the ancient game of differentiating the species *homo,* one could well say

that man is the animal that loves to "pass the buck" to a rule! But, like the fact or dislike it, there is a realm where each individual is absolute monarch, though of himself alone, and that is the realm of aesthetic values.

§12

Beauty cannot be proved by appeal to consensus, or to the "test of time," or to the type of person who experiences it in a given case. In the light of what precedes, it is obvious that the familiar attempts to prove the beauty of certain works of art by appeal to the consensus of opinion, or to the test of continued approval through long periods of time in the life either of society or of the individual, are, like the appeal to the connoisseur's verdict, entirely futile. Such tests cannot possibly prove the object's beauty to those who do not perceive any in it; and to those who do, they are needless. They prove nothing whatever, except that beauty is found in the object . . . by such as do find it there.

We might attempt to rank beauties on the basis of the particular aspect of human nature, or type of human being, that experiences aesthetic pleasure in given cases. This would lead to a classifying of beauties as, for instance, sentimental, intellectual, sexual, spiritual, utilitarian, sensuous, social, etc. We might well believe in some certain order of worth or dignity in the human faculties respectively concerned, but this would not lead to any aesthetically objective ranking of beauties. To suggest it would be as ludicrous as a proposal to rank the worth of various religions according to the average cost of the vestments of their priests. For a ranking of beauties, there are available only such principles as the relative intensity of the pleasure felt, its relative duration, relative volume, and relative freedom from admixture of pain. These principles, however, do not in the least release us from the need of relying upon the individual's judgment; on the contrary their application rests wholly upon it.

§13

Beauty cannot be proved by appeal to technical principles or canons. It may yet be thought, however, that there are certain narrower and more technical requirements in the various fields of art, without the fulfilling of which no work can be beautiful. Among such alleged canons of beauty may be mentioned the rules of so-called "harmony" in music; various precepts concerning literary composition; unity; truth to nature; such requirements as consistency, relevance, and unambiguity; and so on. There are indeed "rules" or "principles" of that sort, some of which are, I will freely declare, valid for me; so that when I find myself confronted by flagrant violations of them, I am apt to feel rather strongly, and to be impatient or sarcastic about "that sort of stuff." And indeed, on occasions when I have found myself inadvertently guilty of having drawn some line or written some sentence in violation of my own aesthetic canons, I have at times felt as ashamed of the line or the sentence as I should of having picked somebody's pocket. I admit having pronounced opinions about the beauty or ugliness of various things, and what is more, in many cases I am able to *give reasons* for my opinions.

But of what nature are those reasons? They are, ultimately, of the same nature as would be that offered by a man arguing that my pen had to fall when I let go of it a moment ago, *because of gravitation.* Gravitation is but the name we give to the general fact that unsupported objects *do* fall, and at a certain rate; but it is not a reason, or cause, or proof of that fact. To say that something always happens, is not to give any reason why it ever does. Therefore when I say that a certain design is ugly because it is against the "law of symmetry," I am not giving a reason why it *had* to give me aesthetic displeasure, but only mentioning the fact that it resembles in a stated respect certain others which as a bare matter of fact also do displease me. This character which displeases me and many persons, may, however, please others. And, what is more directly to the point, it not only may but it does,—jazzy or uncouth though I may call the taste of such persons. But what most obstinately drives me to the acquisition of a certain, at least abstract, sense of humor concerning the ravening intolerance and would-be-authoritativeness of my own pet canons of beauty, is the fact that they have changed in the past, and that I see no reason why they should not change again in the future. For all I can see to prevent it, I may well tomorrow, next year, or in some future incarnation,

burn what I aesthetically adore to-day, and adore what I now would burn. If this happens, I have no doubt at all that I shall then smugly label the change a progress and a development of my taste; whereas to-day I should no less smugly describe the possibility of a change of that sort in me, as a possibility that my taste may go to the devil. And, let it be noted, the sole foundation upon which either of the two descriptions would rest, would be the fact that the describer *actually* possesses at the time the sort of taste which he does. Tastes can be neither proved nor refuted, but only "called names," i.e., praised or reviled.

Certain limited and empirical generalizations have been found possible concerning factors upon which the aesthetic pleasure of most people, or of some kinds of people, appears to depend. Precarious generalizations of this sort may be found for instance in manuals of design and of pictorial composition, where they are often dignified by the name of "principles." People familiar with them may then be heard to say that a given picture, perhaps, is well composed and why; or that the tones, the masses, or the values are, as the case may be, well or ill balanced, and so on. Other statements that we may hear and which also imply "principles," would be that the color is clean, or else muddy; that the drawing is, perhaps, distorted; that the surfaces are well modelled; that the lines are rhythmical; that the color combinations are impossible; that the masses lack volume or solidity, etc. The words beauty and ugliness may not occur once, but it is nevertheless obvious that all such statements are not merely descriptive, but *critical.* They are not direct assertions of aesthetic value or disvalue, viz., of beauty or ugliness, but, taking it as an obvious fact, they attempt to trace it to certain definite sorts of features in the work. The more intelligent and better informed kind of art-criticism is of this analytical and diagnostic sort, and there is nothing beyond this that the art-critic could do.

All such comments, worded in the technical jargon of the particular craft, have the imposing sound of expert judgments based upon authoritative principles, and are likely to make the lay consumer of art feel very small and uninitiated. Therefore it cannot be too much emphasized here that a given picture is not ugly because the composition of it, or the color combinations in it, are against the rules; but that the rule against a given type of composition or of color combination is authoritative only because, or if, or for whom, or when, compositions or combinations of that type are *actually* found displeasing. All rules and canons and theories concerning what a painting or other work of art should or should not be, derive such authority as they have over you or me or anyone else, solely from the capacity of such canons to *predict to us* that we shall feel aesthetic pleasure here, and aesthetic pain there. If a given rule predicts this accurately for a given person, that person's *actual* feeling of aesthetic pleasure or displeasure then, proves that that rule *was* a valid one so far as *he* is concerned. That is, the feeling judges the rule, not the rule the feeling. The rule may not be valid for someone else, and it may at any time cease to be valid for the given person, since few things are so variable as pleasure. The *actual* experience of beauty or ugliness by somebody is the final test of the validity of all rules and theories of painting, music, etc., and that test absolutely determines how far, and when, and for whom any given rule or theory holds or does not hold.

The difference between the criticisms of the professionals, and those of the people who, having humbly premised that they "know nothing about art," find little more to say than that a given work is in their judgment beautiful, or as the case may be, ugly or indifferent;—the difference, I say, between the criticisms of professionals and of laymen is essentially that the former are able to trace the aesthetic pleasure or displeasure which they feel, to certain features of the object, while the latter are not able to do it. From this, however, it does not in the least follow that the evaluations of the professionals ultimately rest on any basis less subjective and less a matter of individual taste than do those of the layman. Indeed, so far as the non-professionals really judge at all, i.e., do not merely echo an opinion which they have somehow been bluffed into accepting as authoritative, their judgment is based on the fact that they actually feel something. The artists and professional critics, on the other hand, are exposed to a danger which does not threaten people who know nothing of the factors on which aesthetic pleasure or displeasure has in the past been found to depend for most people, or for some particular class of people,—the danger, namely, of erecting such empirical findings into fixed and rigid rules, and

of judging the work of art no longer by the aesthetic pleasure it actually gives them, but by that which they think it "ought" to give them according to such rules. This danger is really very great, especially for the artist, who, in the nature of the case, is constantly forced to give attention to the technical means by which the objective expression of his feeling is alone to be achieved. Having thus all the time to solve technical problems, it is fatally easy for him to become interested in them for their own sake, and, without knowing it, to be henceforth no longer an artist expressing what he feels, but a restless virtuoso searching for new stunts to perform. This may be the reason why so many of the pictures displayed in our exhibits, although well-enough painted, make one feel as though one were receiving a special-delivery, registered, extra-postage letter, . . . just to say, perhaps, that after Thursday comes Friday!

Listening to the comments of artists and of some critics on a picture will quickly convince one that, strange as it sounds, they are as often as not almost incapable of seeing the picture about which they speak. What they see instead is brush work, values, edges, dark against light, colored shadows, etc. They are thus often not more but less capable than the untrained public of giving the picture *aesthetic* attention, and of getting from it genuinely aesthetic enjoyment. The theory that *aesthetic* appreciation of the products of a given art is increased by cultivating an amateur's measure of proficiency in that art, is therefore true only so far as such cultivation results in more intimate and thoroughgoing *aesthetic* acquaintance with the products of that art. This is likely to be the case in an interpretative art like music (not music-composing). But in an art which, like painting, is not so largely interpretative, and is at the same time dependent on rather elaborate technical processes, the amateur practitioner's attention is from the very first emphatically directed to these processes; and, when it is directed to extant works of art it is directed to them as examples of a technique to be studied, not as aesthetic objects to be contemplated. The danger is then that such technical matters will come to monopolize his attention habitually, and that even in the face of nature he will forget to look at her, wondering instead whether the water or the sky be the brighter, or what color would have to be used to reproduce the appearance of a given shadow. Attention to technique is of course indispensable to the acquisition of it; and mastery of technique is in turn necessary to the production of art on any but the most humble scale. The risk is that the outcome of technical training will be not mastery of technique, but slavery to it. This risk disappears only when the technical apparatus has become as intimately a part of the artist as the hand is of the body for ordinary purposes, and is used without requiring attention. The attention can then turn from the means to the ends of art, viz., to the objective expression of feeling. But the stage at which technique has so become second-nature as to be forgotten, is not often fully reached. With most artists, what we may call their technical *savoir-faire* creaks more or less, as does the social *savoir-faire* of people who have become emilyposted but lately. Like the nouveaux gentlemen, such artists are too conscious of their technical manners, and forget what they are for.

§14

Beauty and accuracy of representation. Among the special criteria by which the merit of works of art—especially paintings—is judged by many, there is one about which something should be said here, namely, accuracy of representation. Accuracy of representation is important from the standpoint of aesthetic criticism only so far as beauty happens to be conditioned by it. Representation, in painting, is a relation between the perceptual varicolored canvas and the aesthetic object, when that aesthetic object is not simply a flat design as such, but contains imaginal and conceptual elements. Accuracy of representation of the intended aesthetic object, by the perceptual canvas is thus not in itself an aesthetic but a noematic merit. Nevertheless it is a merit which is indispensable since without it the intended aesthetic object (in the sort of cases considered), would be set up before the attention either not at all, or only in altered form.

Accuracy of representation of the aesthetic object is of course not at all the same thing as accuracy of representation of the model. An accurate representation of a model is, merely as such, not a work of art at all, but only a document,—a piece of reliable information about the appearance of an existing object. If it is ac-

curate, the copy will indeed have more or less the same aesthetic import and value as the model itself, but that copy as such will none the less be only a work of imitative skill. It will not be a work of art unless it also constitutes the conscious objective expression of a feeling experienced by the painter. Accuracy of representation of the aesthetic object, on the other hand, means only that the perceptual canvas sets up clearly before the ideational attention just the aesthetic object that embodies the feeling which it is intended should be obtained in contemplation.

Photographic accuracy of drawing, and faithfulness of representation of persons or things, provokes the pleasure of recognition, and admiration of the painter's capacity to act as a color camera. But this does not mean that his work is a work of art; nor even that he has created something beautiful, if the object which he has "photographed" happens not to be so. On the other hand, the fact that various elements are out of drawing in some pictures in which the artist is expressing himself in terms of represented objects, does not mean that they are necessarily ugly. What is important for beauty is *not truth but plausibility*. A dramatic entity represented may in fact be distorted, but it is not on this account ugly if it does not *look* distorted. Contrariwise, if something which in fact is photographically accurate looks distorted or unplausible, it will be disagreeable in aesthetic effect. The works of El Greco, who is famous for his distortions of drawing, illustrate this. Some people have thought that something was wrong with his eyes; but the true explanation of his distortions is much more probably his preoccupation with the design-aspect of his paintings. When his design needed a line or thing of a particular shape and size at a certain place, and the object represented at that place happened to be, say, a human leg incapable of the needed shape and size, then it was so much the worse for the leg. Either design or accuracy of representation had to be sacrificed, and in such cases El Greco did not hesitate to sacrifice the latter. Whether ugliness is produced thereby, however, depends on whether the sacrifice is obvious,—the inaccuracy flagrant. In many places it is not; and it does not there constitute an aesthetic fault. Where the distortion is not plausible, on the other hand, but thrusts itself upon our notice as distortion, it gives rise to ugliness and is therefore to that extent aesthetically bad, whatever aesthetic gains it may otherwise involve. Only the addicts of design, who are satisfied with but a half of what an aesthetically complete beholder demands, fail to see this. On the other hand, to the painter who justifies this or that bad part of his picture by insisting that "nature looked just like that," the answer is that even if she did, she ought not to have, so far as beauty was concerned. As often has been said, when truth is stranger than fiction, it does not make good fiction, but only news for the papers.

§15

Criticism of aesthetic objects in ethical terms. Instead of asking whether a work of art or other aesthetic object is beautiful or ugly, i.e., whether the feeling obtained in aesthetic contemplation of it is pleasant or unpleasant, we may on the contrary disregard this and ask whether the feeling so obtained by a person is or may become connected with the rest of his life, and in what manner it may affect it for good or ill. The ethical or the religious worth of the feelings obtained in aesthetic contemplation of works of art, it will be recalled, would have been made by Plato and by Tolstoi the ruling standard in terms of which to judge art as good or bad. It is worth noting, however, that standards of evaluation cannot themselves be evaluated, except in terms of some standard not itself in any way vindicated, but only dogmatically laid down. And any standard evaluated in this manner may itself equally well be laid down in turn as absolute, and be used to evaluate the standard which before was evaluating it. Arguments about the relative worth of various standards of worth are therefore wholly futile, inasmuch as, in the very nature of the logical situation, every such argument must to begin with beg as its premise the point essentially at issue. Ultimately, then, a given standard can only be sympathized with and adopted, or the reverse; and logic can come in only *after* this has occurred. Plato's and Tolstoi's choice of the ethical or religious nature of the aesthetic feelings imparted, as ruling standard for the evaluation of art, is legitimate, but it constitutes only a manifestation of their own ruling interest, and a different choice of ruling standard is equally legitimate by anyone else whose ruling interest happens to be different. With these remarks

concerning the permissibility, but the arbitrariness, of describing any one standard of worth as "supreme" or "ruling," we may leave the matter, and now simply consider the question raised, namely, whether the feelings obtained in aesthetic contemplation may affect the rest of one's life, and how.

The value other than aesthetic that aesthetic feelings may have depends upon the fact that if, when a feeling has been obtained through aesthetic contemplation, the aesthetic attitude is then given up and replaced by the practical, that which had up to that moment the status of aesthetic feeling now assumes that of impulse.

So long as our state is properly describable as aesthetic feeling, its value is immediate and intrinsic, and consists in the pleasantness or unpleasantness of the state. But when our state comes to be properly describable as impulse, then its value is as usual to be measured in terms of the eventual significance of the impulse. An impulse is a seed of conduct, and an aesthetic feeling is at least a potential seed of impulse; the terms in which we commonly appraise conduct are therefore potentially applicable to it.

The impulse or embryonic conduct resulting from the transmutation of an aesthetic feeling through a shift to the practical attitude, may be either a novel impulse in the life of the individual, or not. If it is an impulse of a sort already experienced and more or less established, with characteristic modes of manifestation in the life of the person concerned, then the reexperiencing of it as aftermath of aesthetic contemplation will not affect the individual's life qualitatively, but only quantitatively. It will be simply fuel to an engine already existing and functioning; it will add to the intensity of some aspect of life but will not alter it in kind, except perhaps indirectly if the changes of intensity involved are such as to upset an equilibrium previously existing, and thus force the recasting of life in a different qualitative pattern.

If however the impulse is a novel one in the life of the individual, then it constitutes directly the seed of a change in the kind of life that has been his. The evolution (whether towards good or evil) of the will-aspect of man's nature does not take place merely through increases in his knowledge of the facts and relations that constitute the field of action of his will, but also through the advent in him of qualitatively novel impulses. Indeed, it might well be argued that mere increase in the quantity as distinguished from the nature of one's knowledge and experience, only furnishes one with new means for the service of old ends, or makes one better aware of the ends to which one's hitherto blind impulses tended; but that, however such increase of knowledge may transform the manifestations of existing longings or impulses, it does not of itself alter their intrinsic nature. Transformation in the nature of the impulses themselves (apart from maturation) seems traceable to experiences of two sorts. One of them is awareness by the individual of the presence of a practically real situation novel in kind in his life. This may call forth in him an impulse hitherto foreign to him. The other is what we might call the surreptitious implantation of the impulse itself in him, through the transmutation which we are now considering of an aesthetic feeling into an impulse, by a shift to the practical attitude.

The aesthetic contemplation of nature and of various aspects of life is through such a shift of attitude, a source of germs of new impulses, and of food for old ones. Some persons are known to the writer, in whom the contemplation for the first time of the ocean, or of great mountains, seems to have produced feelings comparable in point of novelty and depth to those reported by the mystics, and the aftermath of impulse due to which gave to life a different pattern, somewhat as does a religious conversion. But art is capable of being as much more effective in the sowing of such seeds of novel impulse, as, for instance, the study of existing records is more effective than personal investigation in acquiring a knowledge of geography. For one thing, art is usually easier than nature to contemplate, being, we might almost say, made for that. Again, when nature was its model, art may be described as at least a drastic editing of nature, supplying what she forgot, omitting what was irrelevant, accenting her here or there into unambiguity. The work of art, being created specifically to give objective expression to a given feeling, is likely to have a pointedness of feeling-import which nature matches only by accident. The work of art, moreover, can be contemplated at length, and returned to again and again, whereas natural facts and the aspects they show us are mostly beyond our control. They come and go heedless of the conditions which alone would make it possible for us to contemplate them adequately. But lastly, art, although in some ways it falls short of nature, has in another way a range of resources far greater than nature's, for it has at its command the boundless resources of the imagination. What it cannot present it often can represent, and thus set up before our attention objects of contemplation never to be found in nature. It can lead us into new worlds, in the contemplation of which our feeling-selves spontaneously burgeon and bloom in all sorts of new ways. Some poems, some music, some statues and pictures, have had in an extraordinary degree this power to bring to birth in people qualities of feeling that had remained latent in them. One such work of art is Leonardo's Mona Lisa. Art theorists whose fundamental dogma is that the end of painting is the representation of plastic form, and who find that picture but indifferently successful in this respect, cannot understand why the theft of it a few years ago should have been deemed a world-calamity. Their only explanation is the aesthetic ineptitude of mankind at large. They cannot see that design and the representation of plastic form is not the whole of the art of painting, but is rather a means which may be used to the ends of art, *when it is important to those ends.* Not the aesthetic ineptitude of mankind, therefore, but the sophomoric character of the measuring-rod by which such theorists would judge Leonardo's picture, is the lesson of the effect produced by that famous theft. There are doubtless people who, in a similar way, would insist on characterizing Socrates essentially as a Greek who was not a "good provider."

§16

Liberalism in aesthetics. The principal standards in terms of which works of art and aesthetic objects may be criticized have been considered above, and the general nature of the conclusions reached concerning the significance and validity of such criticisms may now be summarily characterized.

Judgments of mediate or instrumental value are capable of being proved or disproved. Their truth or falsity is objective, in the sense that it is not conferred upon them by the individual's taste, but is a matter of connections in nature independent of the critic's taste. But the *relevance* or importance, if not the truth, of any judgment of mediate value, is a matter of the individual critic's taste or constitution, since for any such critic that relevance depends on a judgment of immediate value by him.

As regards judgments of immediate value, and in particular of beauty and ugliness, it seems to me that here as in other fields, ultimate analysis leads unavoidably to *the particular constitution of the individual critic* (no matter how he may have come by it), as the necessary and sufficient ground for all such judgments. The constitutions of numbers of individual critics may, of course, happen to be alike in some respects; or they can be made more or less alike by subjecting them to the sort of psychological pressure appropriate to the causation of such a result. If a number of critics are constituted alike in some respects, then any one of them will be able to formulate value judgments with which will agree as many of the other critics as are constituted like him in the respects needed for such agreement! I cannot see that "objective validity" in the case of a judgment of immediate value, means anything whatever but this; namely, several people judge alike because they are constituted alike. But whether a given taste be possessed by one person only, or by a thousand alike, the maxim that *de gustibus non est disputandum,* holds with regard to it.

Is there then no such thing as the refining and educating of taste? Certainly there is,—and there is also such a thing as perversion and depravation of taste. But the question in any given case is, which is which? No one so far as I know has yet pointed out any way of answering this question otherwise than arbitrarily and dogmatically, i.e., otherwise than in terms of the taste actually possessed by some person or other, usually oneself, *arbitrarily* taken as standard. That question, indeed, is hardly ever frankly faced. Those who have approached it at all seem always to have labored under the strange delusion that if only they succeeded in showing that the tastes of a large number or a majority of people were alike, the question was answered; whereas the truth is on the contrary, as just pointed out, that mere numbers have no bearing whatever on the question. Taking a vote is only a device for ascertaining in advance what would be the outcome of a fight between two groups of people, if every person were as strong as every other and strength alone counted. "Proof" by appeal to a vote is obviously but a civilized form of the *argumentum ad baculum.*

It may be asked, however, whether in the absence of any standard of immediate value objectively valid in any sense other than that described above, it is not possible at least to point to some respects in which the (immediate) value judgments of all people whatever, would agree. Nobody whatever, it may be urged, likes great hunger or thirst or cold, or cuts and burns, etc. Now it may be granted that certainly not many do. But after all there are masochists and ascetics and martyrs. It may be true because tautologous that nobody likes pain; but we must keep in mind that pain and pleasure are the predicates, not the subjects, of immediate-value-judgments. Their subjects are things, situations, experiences. The question is thus not whether painfulness is ever pleasurable, but whether there are any *situations* or *experiences* which everybody without exception finds, for instance, painful. And this is very doubtful. We can probably say only that with regard to some situations or experiences, the dissentients are very few. And as we have just seen, numbers mean nothing at all in such a matter.

This brings us to what may be called a dogmatico-liberalistic position. Neither I nor anyone can refute anyone else's judgments of immediate value—here, of beauty and ugliness; nor can anyone refute mine. This is the liberalistic aspect of the situation. The fullest insight into it, however, constitutes no reason whatever why any one should hold to his own immediate valuations any the less strongly. That our own opinion must in the nature of such matters be dogmatic is no reason why it should not be honest, vigorous, and unashamed.

DISCUSSION QUESTIONS

1. Do you agree with Ducasse's "dogmatico-liberalistic position" on judgments of beauty and ugliness? Why or why not?
2. Do you agree with Ducasse's definitions of "beauty" and "ugliness"? Why or why not?

3. How does Ducasse deal with the possibility of being "mistaken" in one's aesthetic judgment? Do you think anyone can ever be mistaken in the aesthetic judgment of art or natural phenomena? Use examples to show why or why not.

4. How would you compare the positions of Ducasse and Tolstoy on the standards of evaluating art as "better" or "worse"? Who do you find more convincing? Why?

76. Monroe Beardsley (1915–1981)
"Tastes Can Be Disputed"

Monroe Beardsley was an American philosopher known for his work in the areas of aesthetics and logic during the second half of the twentieth century. For many years he was on the philosophy faculty at Swarthmore College, and the essay reprinted here was published in that institution's alumni bulletin in 1958.

As indicated in the title, this article offers a critical response by the author to those who take the relativistic position on the evaluation of artworks, summarized in that ancient maxim *de gustibus non est disputandum* ("there is no disputing taste"). Beardsley takes what can be called an objectivist position on this issue, which argues that at least some of the time aesthetic judgments can be determined to be correct or incorrect, or at least more or less justified, on the basis of a rational assessment of the reasons that are put forward on their behalf. So, as applied categorically to value judgments of "good" or "bad" and "liking or "disliking" in response to art, he tries to show why that ancient maxim is false. Of course, this puts him in direct opposition to Ducasse's position in the previous reading, which essentially argues for the truth of the "no disputing" principle as applied to aesthetic evaluation.

QUESTIONS FOR CRITICAL READING

1. How does Beardsley analyze the concept of "taste" and its different uses?
2. How does Beardsley analyze the concept of a "dispute," and how is it used in the arts?
3. How does Beardsley characterize the position of the "Aesthetic Skeptic," and how does he criticize it?
4. How does Beardsley defend the position that judgments of aesthetic evaluation can be reasonably argued about and that people can be more or less justified in such judgments?

TERM TO NOTE

laissez-faire: A French term literally meaning "to let do"; it refers to a noninterventionist policy of leaving people free to do as they choose.

We are assured by an old and often-quoted maxim, whose authority is not diminished by its being cast in Latin, that there can be no disputing about tastes. The chief use of this maxim is in putting an end to disputes that last a long time and don't appear to be getting anywhere. And for this purpose it is very efficacious, for it has an air of profound finality, and it also seems to provide a democratic compromise of a deadlocked issue. If you can't convince someone that he is wrong, or bring yourself to admit that he is right, you can always say that neither of you is more wrong than the other, because nobody can be right.

Remarks that serve to close some people's debates, however, are quite often just the remarks to start a new one among philosophers. And this maxim is no exception. It has been given a great deal of thought, some of it very illuminating; yet there is still something to be learned from further reflection upon it. Nor is it of small importance to know, if we can, whether the maxim is true or false, for if it is true we won't waste time in futile discussion, and if it is false we won't waste opportunities for fruitful discussion.

The question whether tastes are disputable is one to be approached with wariness. The first thing is to be clear about what it really means. There are two key words in it that we should pay particular attention to.

The first is the word "taste." The maxim is perhaps most readily and least doubtfully applied to taste in its primary sensory meaning: some people like ripe olives, some green; some people like turnips, others cannot abide them; some people will go long distances for pizza pies, others can hardly choke them down. And there are no disputes about olives: we don't find two schools of thought, the Ripe Olive School and the Green Olive School, publishing quarterly journals or demanding equal time on television—probably because there simply isn't much you can say about the relative merits of these comestibles.

But we apply the word "taste," of course, more broadly. We speak of a person's taste in hats and neckties; we speak of his taste in poetry and painting and music. And it is here that the *non disputandum* maxim is most significantly applied. Some people like Auden and others Swinburne, some enjoy the paintings of Jackson Pollock and others avoid them when they can, some people are panting to hear Shostakovitch's latest symphony and others find no music since Haydn really satisfying. In these cases, unlike the olive case, people are generally not at a loss for words: there is plenty you can say about Shostakovitch, pro or con. They talk, all right; they may praise, deplore, threaten, cajole, wheedle, and scream—but, according to the maxim, they do not really dispute.

This brings us, then, to the second key word. What does it mean to say that we cannot *dispute* about tastes in literature, fine arts, and music, even though we can clearly make known our tastes? It certainly doesn't mean that we cannot disagree, or differ in taste: for obviously we do, and not only we but also the acknowledged or supposed experts in these fields. Consider James Gould Cozzens' novel, *By Love Possessed,* which appeared in August, 1957; consult the critics and reviewers to discover whether it is a good novel. Being a serious and ambitious work by a writer of standing, and also a best seller, it provoked unusually forthright judgments from a number of reviewers and critics—as may be seen in the accompanying quotations. "Masterpiece . . . brilliant . . . distinguished . . . high order . . . mediocre . . . bad;" that just about covers the spectrum of evaluation.

The International Council of the Museum of Modern Art recently took a large collection of American abstract expressionist paintings on tour in Europe. Its reception was reported in *Time.* In Spain some said,

"If this is art, what was it that Goya painted?" and others cheered its "furious vitality" and "renovating spirit." In Italy one newspaper remarked, "It is not painting," but "droppings of paint, sprayings, burstings, lumps, squirts, whirls, rubs and marks, erasures, scrawls, doodles and kaleidoscope backgrounds." In Switzerland it was an "artistic event" that spoke for the genius of American art. And of course all these judgments could be found in this country too.

Not a dispute? Well, what is a dispute? Let us take first the plainest case of a disagreement (no matter what it is about): two people who say, " 'Tis so!" and " 'Taint so!" Let them repeat these words as often as they like, and shout them from the housetops; they still haven't got a dispute going, but merely a contradiction, or perhaps an altercation. But let one person say, " 'Tis so!" and give a *reason* why 'tis so—let him say, "Jones is the best candidate for Senator because he is tactful, honest, and has had much experience in government." And let the other person say, " 'Taint so!" and give a reason why 'taint so—"Jones is not the best candidate, because he is too subservient to certain interests, indecisive and wishy-washy in his own views, and has no conception of the United States' international responsibilities." *Then* we have a dispute—that is, a disagreement in which the parties give reasons for their contentions. Of course this is not all there is to it; the dispute has just begun. But we see how it might continue, each side giving further reasons for its own view, and questioning whether the reasons given by the other are true, relevant, and compelling.

It is this kind of thing that counts as a dispute about the possibility of getting to the moon, about American intervention in the Middle East, about a Supreme Court decision, or anything else. And if we can dispute about these things, why not about art?

But here is where the *non disputandum* maxim would draw the line. We do not speak (or not without irony) about people's tastes in Senatorial candidates or missile policies (if the President replied to critics by saying, "Well, your taste is for speeding up the missile program and spending money, but that's not to my taste," we would feel he ought to back up his opinion more than that). Nor do we speak of tastes in international affairs, or laws, or constitutions. And that seems to be because we believe that judgments on these matters can be, and ought to be, based on good reasons—not that they always are, of course. To prefer a democratic to a totalitarian form of government is *not* just a matter of taste, though to like green olives better than ripe olives is a matter of taste, and we don't require the green olive man to rise and give his reasons, or even to *have* reasons. What kind of reasons could he have? "Green olives are better because they are green" would not look like much of a reason to the ripe olive devotee.

The question, then, is whether a preference for Picasso or Monteverdi is more like a preference for green olives or like a preference for a Senatorial candidate: is it *arguable*? can it be *reasoned*?

When we read what critics and reviewers have to say about the things they talk about, we cannot doubt that they do not merely praise or blame, but defend their judgments by giving reasons, or what they claim to be reasons. The judgments of *By Love Possessed,* here quoted out of context, are supplied with arguments, some of them with long arguments dealing in detail with the plot, style, characterization, structure, underlying philosophy, attitudes towards Catholics, Jews, and Negroes, and other aspects of the novel. Collect a number of these reviews together and it certainly *reads* like a dispute. Or here is one person who says, "Mozart's Quintet in E Flat Major for Piano and Winds (K. 452) is a greater piece of music than Beethoven's Quintet in E Flat Major for Piano and Winds (Op. 16) because it has greater melodic invention, subtlety of texture, a more characteristic scoring for the wind instruments, and a more expressive slow movement." And here is his friend, who replies, "The Beethoven quintet is greater because it has richer sonority, greater vigor and vitality, and a more powerful dynamic spirit." There's a dispute, or something that looks very much like one.

But according to the Aesthetic Skeptic—if I may choose this convenient name for the upholder of the "no disputing" doctrine—this is an illusion. The apparent reasons are not genuine reasons, or cannot be compelling reasons, like the ones we find in other fields. For in the last analysis they rest upon sheer liking or disliking, which is not susceptible of rational discussion. The defender of the Mozart Quintet, for example, seems to be trying to prove his point, but what he is actually doing (says the Skeptic) is better put this way: "*If* you like subtle texture and expressiveness in slow movements, *then* you (like me) will prefer the Mozart quintet." But what if his friend cares more for vigor and vitality? Then the so-called "argument" is bound to leave him cold. He can only reply, "*If* you like vigor and vitality, as I do, *then* you would prefer the Beethoven quintet." But this is no longer a dispute; they are talking completely at cross purposes, not even contradicting each other.

The Aesthetic Skeptic would analyze all apparent disputes among critics in these terms: the critic can point out features of the novel, the abstract expressionist painting, the quintet for winds, but when he does this he is taking for granted, what may not be true, that you happen to like these features. You can't, says the Skeptic, argue anybody into liking something he doesn't like, and that's why there's no disputing about tastes; all disputes are in the end useless.

Now this view, which I have here stated in a fairly rough way, can be worked out into a sophisticated and impressive position, and if it is mistaken, as I believe it is, its mistakes are not childish or simple-minded. Consequently, I cannot pretend to give here an adequate treatment of it. But I should like to consider briefly some of the difficulties in Aesthetic Skepticism, as I see it, and point out the possibility of an alternative theory.

The Skeptical theory takes people's likes and dislikes as ultimate and unappealable facts about them; when two people finally get down to saying "I like X" and "I don't like X" (be it the flavor of turnip or subtlety of texture in music), there the discussion has to end, there the dispute vanishes. But though it is true that you can't change a disliking into a liking by arguments, that doesn't imply that you can't change it at all, or that we cannot argue whether or not it *ought* to be changed. We don't expect such dramatic conversions as Lucy's successful appreciation of Bach's C Major fugue from *The Well-Tempered Clavier,* rendered by Schroeder in the *Peanuts* cartoon—assuming that Lucy is sincere, which, considering her character, is doubtful. Appreciation isn't something you do if you just decide to. But the fact remains that one person can give reasons to another why he would be better off if he *could* enjoy music or painting that he now abhors, and sometimes the other person can set about indirectly, by study and enlarged experience, to change his own tastes, or, as we say, to improve them. There is not just your taste and mine, but better and worse taste; and this doesn't mean just that I have a taste for my taste, but not yours—I might in fact have a distaste for the limitations of my own taste (though that is a queer way to put it). It is something like a person with deep-rooted prejudices, to which he has been conditioned from an early age; perhaps he cannot quite get rid of them, no matter how he tries, and yet he may acknowledge in them a weakness, a crippling feature of his personality, and he may resolve that he will help his children grow up free from them.

The Skeptic does not allow for the possibility that we might give reasons why a person would be better off if he liked or disliked *By Love Possessed* in the way, and to the degree, that it deserves to be liked or disliked. Sometimes, I think, he really holds that it would not be worth the trouble. After all, what does it matter whether people like green olives or ripe olives? We can obtain both in sufficient supply, and nothing much depends upon it as far as the fate of the world is concerned. That's another reason why we ordinarily don't speak of Senatorial candidates as a matter of taste—unless we want to be disparaging, as when people speak of the President's choice in Secretaries of State, to imply that he has no good reason for his choice. It does matter who is Senator, or Secretary of State—it matters a great deal. But what about music, painting, and literature? Why should it be "alarming," to quote the passage from Dwight Macdonald, if the critics and Book-of-the-Month Club members acclaim a novel that is (in his judgment) unworthy?

Now of course, if we are thinking of our two musical disputants about the relative merits of the two quintets, this is a dispute we may safely leave alone. Both quintets are of such a high order that it perhaps doesn't matter enormously which we decide to rank higher than the other, though there's no harm in trying to do this, if we wish. But the question about *By Love Possessed* is whether it is a "masterpiece" or "bad"; and the question about the paintings is whether they ought to be shown abroad at all. It may not matter so very much whether a person on the whole admires Mozart or Beethoven more, but what if he cannot make up his mind between Mozart and Strauss, or between Beethoven and Shostakovitch?

The fact is that the prevailing level of taste in the general public matters a great deal to me, for it has a great deal to do with determining what I shall have the chance to read, what movies will be filmed, shown, or censored, what music will be played most availably on the radio, what plays will be performed on television. And it has a great deal to do with what composers and painters and poets will do, or whether some of them will do anything at all. But more than that, even: if I am convinced that the kind of experiences that can only be obtained by access to the greatest works is an important ingredient of the richest and most fully-developed human life, then do I not owe it to others to try to put that experience within their reach, or them within its reach? It might be as important to them as good housing, good medical and dental care, or good government.

But here is another point at which the Skeptic feels uneasy. Isn't it undemocratic to go around telling other people that they have crude tastes—wouldn't it be more in keeping with our laissez-faire spirit of tolerance, and less reminiscent of totalitarian absolutism and compulsion, to let others like and enjoy what they like and enjoy? Isn't this their natural right?

There are too many confusions in this point of view to clear them all up briefly. But some of them are worth sorting out. Of course it is a person's right to hear the music he enjoys, provided it doesn't bother other people too much. But it is no invasion of his right, if he is willing to consider the problem, to try to convince him that he should try to like other things that appear to deserve it. When Schroeder makes Lucy uncomfortable because she doesn't appreciate classical music, this puts him one up on her, and in other moods she might retort that it gives her more time to spend pleasurably on trivial pursuits. But Schroeder, by admonishing her, is not denying any of her rights.

The distinction that many Skeptics find it hard to keep in mind is this: I may hold that there *is* a better and a worse in music and novels without at all claiming that *I know for certain* which are which. Those critics and reviewers who pronounced their judgments on *By Love Possessed* are not necessarily dogmatic because they deny that it's all a matter of taste (even though some of them were more positive than they had a right to be). They believe that some true and reasonable judgment of the novel is in principle possible, and that objective critics, given time and discussion, could in principle agree, or come close to agreeing, on it. But they do not have to claim infallibility—people can be mistaken about novels, as they can about anything else. Works of art are complicated. There need be nothing totalitarian about literary criticism, and there is nothing especially democratic in the view that nobody is wrong because there is no good or bad to be wrong about.

It would help us all, I think, to look at the problem of judging works of art in a more direct way. These judgments, as can easily be seen in any random collection of reviews, go off in so many directions that it sometimes seems that the reviewers are talking about different things. We must keep our eye on the object—the painting, the novel, the quintet. Because the composer's love affairs were in a sorry state at the time he was composing, people think that the value of the music must somehow be connected with this circumstance. Because the painter was regarding his model while he painted, people think that the value of the painting must depend on some relation to the way she really looked, or felt. Because the novelist is known to be an anarchist or a conservative, people think that the value of the novel must consist partly in its fidelity to these attitudes. Now, of course, when we approach a work of art, there are many kinds of interest that we can take in it, as well as in its creator. But when we are trying to judge it *as* a work of art, rather than as biography or social criticism or something else, there is a central interest that ought to be kept in view.

A work of art, whatever its species, is an object of some kind—something somebody made. And the question is whether it was worth making, what it is good for, what can be done with it. In this respect it is like a tool. Tools of course are production goods, instrumental to other instruments, whereas paintings and musical compositions and novels are consumption goods, directly instrumental to some sort of experience. And their own peculiar excellence consists, I believe, in their capacity to afford certain valuable kinds and degrees of aesthetic experience. Of course they do not yield this experience to those who cannot understand them, just as a tool is of no use to one who has not the skill to wield it. But we do not talk in the Skeptical way about tools: we do not say that the value

of a hammer is all a matter of taste, some people having a taste for hammering nails, some not. No, the value resides in its capability to drive the nail, given a hand and arm with the right skill, and if the need should arise. And this value it would have, though unrealized, even if the skill were temporarily lost.

So with works of art, it seems to me. Their value is what they can do to and for us, if we are capable of having it done. And for those who do not, or not yet, have this capacity, it is not a simple fact that they do not, but a misfortune, and the only question is whether, or to what extent, it can be remedied. It is because this question sometimes has a hopeful answer that we dispute, and must dispute, about tastes. When the political disputant gives his reasons for supporting one Senatorial candidate over another, he cites facts about that candidate that he knows, from past experience, justify the hope of a good performance—the hope that the candidate, once elected, will do what a Senator is supposed to do, well. When the critic gives his reasons for saying that a work of art is good or bad, he is not, as the Skeptic claims, trying to guess whom it will please or displease; he is pointing out those features of the work—its qualities, structure, style, and so on—that are evidence of the work's ability or inability to provide qualified readers, listeners, or viewers, with a deep aesthetic experience.

DISCUSSION QUESTIONS

1. Do you think disagreements about "good" and "bad" art are more like differences in preference for certain foods, or differences in preference for senatorial candidates (to use Beardsley's examples)? Explain.

2. How does Beardsley deal with the concept of being "mistaken" in one's aesthetic judgment?

3. How is the distinction between "immediate value" and "instrumental value" relevant for understanding Beardsley's position? Do you agree with his account of the nature of the value possessed by works of art? Why or why not?

4. How might Ducasse respond to Beardsley's critique of the "Aesthetic Skeptic's" position? Who do you find more convincing? Why?

77. Innocent C. Onyewuenyi (contemporary)
"Traditional African Aesthetics: A Philosophical Perspective"

Nigerian philosopher Innocent Onyewuenyi has been on the faculty at the University of Nsukka, Nigeria, for many years. His research over the last few decades has focused on issues in African philosophy particularly and comparative philosophy and cultural studies generally, especially involving the comparison between Western and African worldviews. The essay reprinted here, published in 1984 in the *International Philosophical Quarterly*, centers specifically around a comparison between traditional African standards of aesthetic evaluation and traditional Western standards.

In this article Onyewuenyi not only identifies the differences between criteria of "good" and "bad," or "successful" and "unsuccessful," art in European/American and African cultural contexts but also offers a critique of the traditional Western treatment of African art. In his analysis there has been a strong ethnocentric tendency among Western artists, art critics, art collectors, and others, to interpret and evaluate traditional African artworks according to Western standards and to fail thereby in their attempt to understand those works. Onyewuenyi thus affirms a qualified relativism concerning aesthetic judgment, based on differences in cultural worldviews rather than differences in "taste" among individual persons. But he also implies that once culturally specific standards of art evaluation/criticism are recognized, works of art produced within that cultural frame of reference and intended to satisfy those standards can be objectively evaluated in terms of whether they do so or not.

QUESTIONS FOR CRITICAL READING

1. How does Onyewuenyi characterize the prevailing standards of aesthetic evaluation and art criticism in Western culture?
2. How does Onyewuenyi argue for the claim that there is a distinctive "African aesthetics"?
3. In Onyewuenyi's account, what does metaphysics (and ontology) have to do with aesthetics, and how are Western aesthetics and African aesthetics different in this respect?
4. What does Onyewuenyi mean by claiming that "African art is functional, community-oriented, depersonalized, contextualized, and embedded"?

TERMS TO NOTE

évolués: A French African term referring to those who have received a European education.
physiognomy: Here, the characteristic facial features of a people or cultural group.

Ancient Greece supplies us with the first important contributions to aesthetic theory. Socrates is the first. We learn from Xenophon's account of him that he regarded the beautiful as coincident with the good. Every beautiful object is so called because it serves some rational end. Plato in his scheme for an ideal republic provided for the most inexorable censorship of poets and artists in general, so as to make art as far as possible an instrument of moral and political training.

Except for the very few dedicated aestheticians who have studied the history of aesthetics as it developed and progressed from Plato through medieval philosophers and then Kant and Hegel to its ramifications in the works of Benedetto Croce, Vico, Dewey etc., the general run of aestheticians conceives of the artist as a free agent bound by no societal conventions, at liberty and "condemned" to experimentation, whose productions must be judged in their individuality and uniqueness. "It has been argued by some people, that each work of art is unique and individual; that it is the essence of it. If you seek to explain the value of any work of art in terms of some general principles then you are destroying that value."[1]

Such a conception of the artist and his arts is so culturally natural to Europeans and Americans and

---

1. P. C. Chatterji, *Fundamental Questions in Aesthetics* (New Delhi: Indian Institute of Advanced Study, 1968), p. 13.

even évolués in Africa that to interpret art differently would be considered unacceptable and erroneous. It is this conception of art that influenced the colonial ambassadors in Africa—be they missionaries, administrators, merchants, educators—in their interpretation and evaluation of the arts in Africa. It explains the mistaken interpretation of African arts by otherwise outstanding European artists when they made the acquaintance of African visual arts. They even contradicted one another in their professional interpretation by extending their preference for one or another European school to African works of art accidentally resembling their favorite style and judged it accordingly. Jahnheinz Jahn comments:

> Gluck for example, praises the "baroquising element of form" in the mask of the Cameroons, the style of which "has understood so consciously how to master the grotesque," while Kiersmeier ascribes to the same masks "little artistic value," but predicates of the works of the Boula a "refined sensibility and technical delicacy" which lifts them far above the works of most African races'. Luschan praises the "great grace" of certain Benin heads, while Einstein places them in a "degenerate coastal tradition" which has recovered in the Cameroons in a late primitive rebirth."[2]

This paper is an attempt to think differently from western aestheticians. It will essay to show that African aesthetic standards are different from the "accepted" standards of uniqueness and individuality; that African works of art, be they visual, musical, kinetic, or poetic are created as an answer to a problem and serve some practical end. It will also delineate the philosophical foundation for such differences, and finally propose the theory of African works of art as the Africans see it.

Is There an African Aesthetics?

Before delving into the problem, we will first of all establish whether there is an African aesthetics or not.

By way of definitions, we are told that aesthetics is that branch of philosophy which has tried to answer such questions as "What is Art?" "What is Beauty?" Dagobert Runes defines aesthetics traditionally as the branch of philosophy dealing with beauty or the beautiful, especially in art, and with taste and standards of value in judging art.[3] Accepting the above definitions as universal, there is an intellectual temptation to take the position that it is unnecessary and even futile to ask such a question. If aesthetics is universal, it is as ridiculous to talk of African aesthetics as it is to talk of African physics or African chemistry. The question may even be regarded as racially and nationally loaded, indicating an attempt to narrow the discipline of aesthetics in order to satisfy some racial or national whim.

A similar problem arose in my paper "Is There an African Philosophy?" where I showed that philosophizing is a universal experience and that

> What is generally agreed about philosophy is that it seeks to establish order among the various phenomena of the surrounding world and it traces their unity by reducing them to their simplest elements . . . that while these phenomena are the same in all cultures and societies, each culture traces the unity of these, synthesizes, or organizes them into a totality *based* on each culture's concept of life. . . . Hence it is that the order or unity the people of a culture establish is their own order, relative to their own conception of life in which everything around them becomes meaningful.[4]

If the above is accepted as true, then we have the basis for calling a philosophy (and by extension, aesthetics) European, Indian, American, African. We can and should talk of African aesthetics because the African culture has its own "standards of value in judging art"; its own "general principles" in explaining the value of any work of art. Africa has its own view of life which Dilthey regarded as the starting point of philosophy. Georg Misch summarizes Dilthey thus:

2. Janheinz Jahn, *Muntu: An Outline of the New African Culture* (New York: Grove Press, 1961), p. 173.

3. Dagobert D. Runes, *Dictionary of Philosophy* (Totowa, NJ: Littlefield, Adams, 1966), p. 6.

4. Innocent C. Onyewuenyi, "Is There An African Philosophy?" *Journal of African Studies,* 3 (Winter 1976/77), 513–528.

Dilthey regarded life as the starting point of philosophy; life as actually lived and embodied or 'objectified' in the spiritual world we live in . . . Our knowledge of life is above all, contained in certain cultural and personal views of the world—which play a prominent part in philosophy as well as in religion and poetry.[5]

That philosophy of art is universal does not mean that all aestheticians should employ similar standards of value in judging art, similar general principles of explaining the value of any work of art. Neither does it mean that all the rationally warrantable or objectively granted principles or methods must be identical or that they must establish similar truths. Two separate aesthetic standards of value or general principles, both being rational, can be opposed to one another.

Hegel underscores the cultural and relative aspect of philosophy when he said:

But men do not at certain epochs merely philosophize in general. For there is a definite philosophy which arises among a people and the definite character which permeates all the other historical sides of the Spirit of the people, which is most intimately related to them, and which constitutes their foundation. The particular form of a philosophy is thus contemporaneous with a particular constitution of the people amongst whom it makes its appearance, with their institutions and forms of government; their morality, their social life and their capabilities, customs and enjoyments of the same.[6]

From the foregoing one may safely suggest that the general principles or standards of value of aesthetics, which is a branch of philosophy, are bound up intimately with a people's spirit and constitution, and are a factor in their life history, subject to the conditions of race, culture, and civilization.

One function of the arts is making explicit the images by which a society recognizes its own *values* and thus offering a means by which the members of a community may express and evaluate new elements in their lives. Furthermore, the arts afford a perspective on human experience as they are created to channel or express the powers of the super-human world on which men recognize their dependence. The Europeans/Americans and Africans evidently have different views of life here and hereafter; different conceptions of the powers of the super-human world to which they owe their existence, different ethical and moral values, different social institutions and forms of government—in short, different ideas of life and reality. Since the works of art, be they visual, musical, kinetic, or poetic are used "to convey the unfamiliar in the familiar, the abstract in the concrete, the discursive in the intuitive and the spiritual in the physical; in general to communicate the nonsensory through the sensory,"[7] it follows that the symbols must be culturally invested with the contents of their referents. Victor Uchendu may be quoted to round off these arguments in support of the issue of aesthetic relativity. He advised: "To know how a people view the world around them is to understand how they evaluate life, and a people's evaluation of life, both temporal and non-temporal, provides them with a 'charter' of action, a guide to behaviour."[8]

Metaphysics as the Foundation of Aesthetic Interpretation

The ultimate basis for cultural differences in interpreting and appreciating art works rests principally on differences in metaphysics, which is an integral vision of reality as such. Henry Alpern in his *March of Philosophy* highlighted the importance of metaphysics as the groundwork, the basis, the explanation of human behaviour:

Metaphysics by the very definition that it is the study of reality, of that which does not appear to our senses, of truth in the absolute sense, is the groundwork of any theory concerning all phases of human behaviour. David Hume, whom no one can charge of shutting his eyes to

---

5. Georg Misch, *The Dawn of Philosophy* (London, 1950), p. 47.
6. Georg Hegel, *Lectures on the History of Philosophy* (London, 1968), 1:53.

7. Arthur Berndtson, *Art Expression and Beauty* (New York: Holt, Rinehart and Winston, 1969), p. 36.
8. Victor Uchendu, *The Igbo of Southeast Nigeria* (New York: 1965), p. 12.

experience, said that metaphysics is necessary for art, morality, religion, economics, sociology; for the abstract sciences, as well as for every branch of human endeavour considered from the practical angle. It is the foundation upon which one builds one's career consciously and unconsciously; it is the guide; the author of human interests; upon its truth or falsity depends what type of man you may develop into.[9]

Researchers in African philosophy have amply shown that there is a difference between Western and African metaphysics and consequently a difference between the two cultures' "groundwork of any theory concerning all phases" of their behaviour vis-à-vis their art, morality, religion. Placide Tempels has clearly expressed the specific difference between the two:

> Christian thought in the West having adopted the terminology of Greek philosophy and perhaps under its influence, has defined the reality of all beings, or, as one should say, being as such: "the reality that is," "what is." Its metaphysics has most generally been based upon a fundamentally *static* conception of being.[10]

He goes on to add the crucial point, "Herein is to be seen the fundamental difference between Western thought and that of Bantu and other primitive peoples . . . we hold a *static* conception of 'being', they, a *dynamic*."[11]

If we accept what Henry Alpern and David Hume said about the importance of metaphysics as "the groundwork concerning all phases of human behaviour and necessary for art . . . as well as for every branch of human endeavour on the one hand," and the fundamental differences between Western and African ontology as suggested by Tempels on the other, it would follow that the aesthetic interpretation and appreciation of the works of art in the two cultures must necessarily be different. And indeed they are! "For philosophies of art and beauty are as various as the philosophies of human conduct, politics, science,

history and ultimate reality,"[12] claimed Albert Hofstadter and Richard Kuhns. They emphasized further the metaphysical dependence of all standards of value in judging art:

> In a philosophy of art or in philosophical aesthetics, more generally speaking, beauty and art are understood in terms of essential philosophical ideas . . . Thus the great philosophies of art have interpreted beauty and art in metaphysical terms. . . ."[13]

Influences of Metaphysics on Western Aesthetics

The concept of *staticity* which connotes the idea of separate beings, of substances, to use a scholastic term, which exist side by side, independent one of another, is a peculiarity of western ontology and explains the emphasis on individuality and uniqueness in the interpretation of works of art. This is what Mundy-Castle calls "'out-of-context' or modern art which is frequently without any specific social function. Its primary aim is to communicate personal experience and individualized intuition."[14] The work of art is often identified with the building, book, painting or status in its existence apart from human experience. I suggest that the dictatorship of the spectator, of the collector, even of the dealer over works of art in recent centuries in Europe and America is a function of individuality of interpretation and subjectivity of tastes and meaning. One can even go so far as to claim that the idea of museums which Nigeria's Uche Okeke describes as "a graveyard of human achievements"[15] in the great cities of Europe and other western countries is metaphysically influenced by the theory of uniqueness and individuality in aesthetics.

Much emphasis is placed on the "perfection" of art works, the prestige they possess because of a long history of unquestioned admiration. Descriptive terms such as "lively expression," "naturalistic," "disinterested

9. Henry Alpern, *The March of Philosophy* (New York, 1934), p. 99.
10. Placide Tempels, *Bantu Philosophy* (Paris: Présence Africaine, 1969), p. 19.
11. *Ibid.,* p. 50.

12. Albert Hofstadter and Richard Kuhns, *Philosophies of Art and Beauty* (Chicago: Univ. of Chicago Press, 1964), p. xiii.
13. *Ibid.,* p. xiv.
14. A. C. Mundy-Castle, "Art, Psychology and Social Change," *Black Orpheus,* 4, No. 1 (1981), p. 8.
15. Uche Okeke, "Towards a Rational Policy of Art Patronage in Nigeria," *Black Orpheus,* 4, No. 1 (1981), 64.

gratification," "ugly," "beautiful," etc. characterize European/American evaluation of designs and motifs of art works. Thus they are separated from conditions of history and origin and operation in experience. There is no interpenetration of one art work with another, not to mention their supposed function of making explicit the images by which a society recognizes its own values, of offering a means by which the members of a community may express and evaluate new elements in their lives, of affording a perspective on human experience as they are created to channel or express the powers of the super-human world on which human beings recognize their dependence.

John Dewey in his book *Art as Experience* criticizes the theory of individuality and uniqueness as standards of art evaluation by citing the example of the Parthenon, the great Athenian work of art which enjoys world-wide prestige because of a long history of unquestioned admiration. He maintains that the aesthetic standing is achieved only when one

> goes beyond personal enjoyment into the formation of a theory about that large republic of art of which the building is one member, and is willing at some point in his reflections to turn from it to the bustling, arguing, acutely sensitive Athenian citizens, with civic sense identified with a civic religion, of whose experience the temple was an expression and who built it not as a work art but as a civic commemoration.[16]

Dewey seems to be saying that until the function of an art work in relation to the members of a community is discovered and appreciated, the full aesthetic dimension cannot be achieved. John Dewey could hold this position because he was a great devotee of Hegel and Plato, who were absolute idealists and for whom sensory objects were moments of the Absolute.

A Brief Survey of African Ontology

An adequate understanding of African ontology, especially in its conception of the nature of "reality" or "being" as dynamic, is fundamentally important to our discussion of African art appreciation. The essence of anything is conceived by the African as force. "There is no idea among Bantu of 'being' divorced from the idea of 'force'. Without the element of 'force', 'being' cannot be conceived. Force is the nature of being; force is being; being is force."[17] The concept of force or dynamism cancels out the idea of separate beings or substances which exist side by side independent one of another and which we have shown in our discussion of Western ontology to be responsible for individuality and uniqueness as standards or essence of art. Existence-in-relation, communalism, being-for-self-and-others sum up the African conception of life and reality.

> The African thought holds that created beings preserve a bond one with another, an intimate ontological relationship. There is an interaction of being with being. . . . This is more so among rational beings, known as Muntu which includes the living and the dead, Orishas and God.[18]

Because of this ontological relationship among beings, the African knows and feels himself to be in intimate and personal relationship with other forces acting above and below him in the hierarchy of forces.

A corollary to this relationship is the traditional African view of the world as one of extraordinary harmony, which Adebayo Adesanya explains as

> not simply a coherence of fact and faith, nor of reason and traditional beliefs, nor of reason and contingent facts, but a coherence of compatibility among all disciplines. A medical theory, e.g., which contradicted a theological conclusion was rejected as absurd and viceversa. . . . Philosophy, theology, politics, social theory, landlaw, medicine, psychology, birth and burial, all find themselves logically concatenated in a system so tight that to subtract one item from the whole is to paralyse the structure of the whole.[19]

16. Hofstadter and Kuhns, *op. cit.*, p. 580.

17. Tempels, *op. cit.*, p. 37.
18. *Ibid.*, p. 104.
19. Jahn, *op. cit.*, p. 96.

Influences on African Aesthetics

Traditional African aesthetics, or interpretation, appreciation of works of art as a discipline in the body of African reality, cannot but fall in line with other theories and disciplines which "all find themselves logically concatenated" in the tight system of the African world-view; otherwise it would paralyze the whole structure of African life and being. Works of art, as expressions of ritual and religion, as clues to the temperament of the tribe and society, as language in a culture without writing, must do all these in service to the community whose ritual and religion they express, whose temperament they reveal, the being of whose ancestors they participate in. Its theory or standard of evaluation must conform to the theories of its sister disciplines and stem from identical metaphysical foundations. Hence African art is functional, community-oriented, depersonalized, contextualized, and embedded.

By functional and community-oriented we mean that African arts—visual, musical, kinetic or poetic—are designed to serve practical, meaningful purpose, beauty of appearance being secondary. All the same, "Functional beauty is also beauty,"[20] says Janheinz Jahn. A carving, for example, is aesthetically beautiful in the African standard if it functions well as stimulus in the worship of the deity, the community of worshippers being the judges. A mask, despite its "ugly" appearance, is judged beautiful and good if used correctly in the movement of the dance to depict the divine power with which it is imbued through the rhythmic incantations and sacrificial rites of the communal ceremonies. "Through his dance Efe has the power to please the witches and so turn their malevolent self-seeking power into a generous benevolence towards the community."[21]

If a sculpture of an ancestor for purposes of worship in an Igbo Society is scarified[22] and endowed with all the paraphernalia that combine to make a work aesthetically good, it would not be accepted by the Igbo and would have no aesthetic recognition simply because it is not true and meaningful. It does not fulfill the function which an Igbo society expects of it. For, the Igbos do not scarify their bodies, and the Muntu-face represented in such a sculpture cannot command their respect for a revered ancestor. Rather the same scarified Muntu-face may be aesthetically beautiful to the Yoruba or other tribes who culturally scarify their bodies.

> The various African peoples have coined various basic forms for the "Muntu-face" but they all express the Muntu-face. Within one people the Muntu face is constant, for it is derived from their common ancestor, that *muzimu* who formed the physiognomy of his people. Thus the artist is not free to think out a Muntu-face for himself, according to his own conception. The Muntu to be represented must belong to his own people.[23]

When we say that African art is depersonalized we mean that the artist's concern is not to depict his own individual whims and feelings. He works from a background diametrically opposed to the Nietzschean expressionist influence about which Benn writes: "Our background was Nietzsche: his drive to tear apart one's inner nature with words, to express oneself, to formulate, to dazzle, to sparkle at any risk and without regard for the results."[24] He performs rather in such a way as to fulfill the ritual and social purposes of his community for whom the arts are meant to regulate the spiritual, political, and social forces within the community.

Speaking specifically about African poets, Janheinz Jahn testifes that

> In reality, the neo-African poet is not primarily concerned about his own ego. He is Muntu man who speaks and through the word conquers the world of things. His word is the more powerful the more he speaks in the name of his people living as well as dead. As a poet he is the representative of all, and as a representative he is a poet.[25]

20. *Ibid.,* p. 174.
21. Peggy Harper, "The Inter-Relation of the Arts in the Performance of Masquerades as an Expression of Oral Tradition in Nigeria," *Black Orpheus*, 4, No. 1 (1981), 3.
22. To "scarify" means to adorn with indentations, scratches, or welts (on the skin).

23. *Ibid.,* p. 162.
24. *Ibid.,* p. 148. Ben Göttfried, Ch. 2, pp. 39ff.
25. *Ibid.,* p. 142.

Whether it is music, dancing, painting, poetry, etc., he cannot draw his own motifs, his themes, his obsessions from the very essence of his arts. The needs of the community determine the artist's production. His art is never "art for art's sake." He is responsible to his society. Hence the artists are "held in high esteem by the society because they supply those design needs as are vital to their spiritual and physical well-being. They are not as a rule separated or differentiated from the generality of their kindred people for whom they fashion tools and objects of belief."[26]

The foregoing emphasis on the depersonalization of the artist does not mean to rule out every professional freedom. While the artist is bound to adhere to the basic forms recognizable by the people, "the determinant of the first degree, the Muntu face for man, or the animal shape for beasts," he has some freedom with "the determinants of the second degree."[27] Thus he may indicate a chief by the coiffures, by the crown, or by the dress, or he may set the figure on a horse— or he may even use foreign European insignia and medals that are proper to kings.

Conclusion

An attempt has been made in this paper to show the philosophical foundation of traditional African aesthetics vis-à-vis Western aesthetics and thereby the culturally relative interpretation of works of art. It has been shown that uniqueness and individuality are not, and need not be, the only basis for theories of aesthetics; that African works of art are functional, community-oriented and depersonalized, unlike Western art which is arbitrary, representative of the values and emotions of the artist, without reference to the cultural environment and the historical reality of the people. I would suggest that the misinterpretation of African works of art by western scholars of aesthetics is due to an ignorance of the cultural differences.

In conclusion the words of Philip J. C. Dark are most appropriate and relevant:

> There is a strong tendency among those who write about primitive art, and particularly primitive symbolism, to attach descriptive terms deriving from their own culture to designs and motifs they observe, thus often giving the reader a false impression that such terms carry the meanings attached to them by the people themselves. It should be made clear that for the business of formal analysis of alien art forms such terms are purely tools for the purpose of analysis. The recognition of a design such as a snake, a bird, a part of the body and so on, by an observer does not necessarily mean that the particular design in question represents that for the members of a particular culture.[28]

DISCUSSION QUESTIONS

1. Do you agree with Onyewuenyi's critique of the typical Western understanding of African art? Use examples to show why or why not.
2. Is ethnocentrism inescapable in the interpretation and appreciation of art from cultures different from one's own? Why or why not?
3. Can the traditional African criteria for the aesthetic value of artworks, characterized by Onyewuenyi, be usefully employed by Westerners in the evaluation of art produced within a Western cultural context? Why or why not? Use examples to make your case.
4. How would you compare Onyewuenyi's account of a general African aesthetics with Tolstoy's account of the social character of art?

---

26. Uche Okeke, *op. cit.*, p. 62.
27. Jahn, *op. cit.*, p. 163.

28. Philip J. C. Dark, *Bush Negro Art* (London: Alec Tiranti, 1954), p. 49.

78. Linda Nochlin (b. 1931)
"Why Are There No Great Women Artists?"

Linda Nochlin, an American art historian, has been on the faculties of Vassar College and Yale University. She has written extensively on social and political issues having to do with the visual arts, including gender relations and the ways in which sexism has permeated the art world historically as much as any other cultural domain. The essay reprinted here deals specifically with the typical exclusion of women from the training necessary to become recognized professional painters and sculptors throughout a good deal of Western history. It was published as part of a 1971 anthology entitled *Women in Sexist Society.*

Nochlin's approach in this selection is to question the question itself, which serves as the essay's title, in order to illuminate some of the underlying assumptions and conventions in our male-dominant, patriarchal society regarding the proper places of women and men in the arts. She argues that ultimately it has been social and "institutional" factors rather than "private," personal characteristics that have most influenced who is to be supported in the development of their talents and thus who might become "good artists." In exposing these causal elements, often ignored in earlier studies of Western art history, and "contextualizing" attributions of artistic "genius" and "greatness," she reframed the questions and reoriented the investigation into the role of gender in the arts in a way that was fairly new in the academic world at the time but that continues to be productive today.

QUESTIONS FOR CRITICAL READING

1. How does Nochlin critically analyze the question itself, "Why are there no great women artists?", and the assumptions on which it is based?
2. How does Nochlin critically analyze the common portrayal of social conflicts in terms of this or that "problem," including "the woman problem"?
3. According to Nochlin, what institutional obstacles have been faced historically by aspiring female artists?
4. In Nochlin's account, how did social norms governing artists' use of nude models affect women artists?
5. What are Nochlin's recommendations for dealing with, and overcoming, the historical exclusion of women from the visual, or "plastic," arts?

TERMS TO NOTE

idées reçues: A French phrase meaning "customary ideas."

hagiography: Writing about the lives of saints.

Q.E.D.: An abbreviation for the Latin phrase *quod erat demonstrandum,* meaning "what was to be demonstrated"; traditionally written at the end of deductive proofs.

haute bourgeoisie: A French phrase usually referring to the "upper middle class."

metahistorical: Having to do with issues concerning the nature, aims, and methodology of historical inquiry itself.

chef d'école: A French phrase for "schoolmaster" or "head of the school."

daguerreotype: An early type of photograph, which was produced on a silvered metal plate made sensitive to light.

"Why are there no great women artists?" This question tolls reproachfully in the background of discussions of the so-called woman problem, causing men to shake their heads regretfully and women to grind their teeth in frustration. Like so many other questions involved in the red-hot feminist controversy, it falsifies the nature of the issue at the same time that it insidiously supplies its own answer: "There are no great women artists because women are incapable of greatness." The assumptions lying behind such a question are varied in range and sophistication, running anywhere from "scientifically" proven demonstrations of the inability of human beings with wombs rather than penises to create anything significant, to relatively open-minded wonderment that women, despite so many years of near-equality—and after all, a lot of men have had their disadvantages too—have still not achieved anything of major significance in the visual arts.

The feminist's first reaction is to swallow the bait, hook, line and sinker and to attempt to answer the question as it is put: that is, to dig up examples of worthy or insufficiently appreciated women artists throughout history; to rehabilitate rather modest, if interesting and productive careers; to rediscover forgotten flower painters or David-followers and make out a case for them; to demonstrate that Berthe Morisot was really less dependent upon Manet than one had been led to think—in other words, to engage in activity not too different from that of the average scholar, man or woman, making out a case for the importance of his own neglected or minor master. Whether undertaken from a feminist point of view, such attempts, like the ambitious article on women artists which appeared in the 1858 *Westminster Review*,[1] or more recent scholarly studies and reevaluations of individual woman artists like Angelica Kauffmann or Artemisia Gentileschi,[2] are certainly well worth the effort, adding to our knowledge both of women's achievement and of art history generally; and a great deal still remains to be done in this area. Unfortunately, such efforts, if written from an uncritically feminist viewpoint, do nothing to question the assumptions lying behind the question "Why are there no great women artists?"; on the contrary, by attempting to answer it and by doing so inadequately, they merely reinforce its negative implications.

At the same time that champions of women's equality may feel called upon to falsify the testimony of their own judgment by scraping up neglected female artistic geniuses or puffing up the endeavors of genuinely excellent but decidedly minor women painters and sculptors into major contributions, they may resort to the easily refuted ploy of accusing the questioner of using "male" standards as the criterion of greatness or excellence. This attempt to answer the question involves shifting the ground slightly; by asserting, as many contemporary feminists do, that there

is actually a different kind of greatness for women's art than for men's, one tacitly assumes the existence of a distinctive and recognizable feminine style, differing in both its formal and its expressive qualities from that of male artists and positing the unique character of women's situation and experience.

This, on the surface of it, seems reasonable enough: in general, women's experience and situation in society, and hence as artists, is different from men's; certainly, the art produced by a group of consciously united and purposefully articulate women intent on bodying forth a group consciousness of feminine experience might be stylistically identifiable as feminist, if not feminine art. Unfortunately, this remains within the realm of possibility; so far, it has not occurred. While the Danube School, Caravaggio's followers, the painters gathered around Gauguin at Pont Aven, the Blue Rider, or the Cubists may be recognized by certain clearly defined stylistic or expressive qualities, no such common qualities of femininity would seem to link the styles of women artists generally, any more than such qualities can be said to link all women writers—a case brilliantly argued, against the most devastating, and mutually contradictory, masculine critical clichés, by Mary Ellmann in her *Thinking About Women*.[3] No subtle essence of femininity would seem to link the work of Artemesia Gentileschi, Elisabeth Vigée-Lebrun, Angelica Kauffmann, Rosa Bonheur, Berthe Morisot, Suzanne Valadon, Käthe Kollwitz, Barbara Hepworth, Georgia O'Keefe, Sophie Taeuber-Arp, Helen Frankenthaler, Bridget Riley, Lee Bontecou, and Louise Nevelson, any more than one can find some essential similarity in the work of Sappho, Marie de France, Jane Austen, Emily Brontë, George Sand, George Eliot, Virginia Woolf, Gertrude Stein, Anaïs Nin, Emily Dickinson, Sylvia Plath, and Susan Sontag. In every instance women artists and writers would seem to be closer to other artists and writers of their own period and outlook than they are to each other.

Women artists are more inward-looking, more delicate and nuanced in their treatment of their medium, it may be asserted. But which of the women artists cited above is more inward turning than Redon, more subtle and nuanced in the handling of pigment than Corot at his best? Is Fragonard more or less feminine than Elisabeth Vigée-Lebrun? Or is it not more a question of the whole rococo style of eighteenth-century France being "feminine," if judged in terms of a two-valued scale of masculinity versus femininity? Certainly, though, if daintiness, delicacy, and preciousness are to be counted as earmarks of a feminine style, there is nothing very fragile about Rosa Bonheur's *Horse Fair,* or dainty and introverted about Helen Frankenthaler's giant canvases. If women have indeed at times turned to scenes of domestic life or of children, so did men painters like the Dutch Little Masters, Chardin, and the impressionists—Renoir and Monet as well as Berthe Morisot and Mary Cassatt. In any case, the mere choice of a certain realm of subject matter, or the restriction to certain subjects, is not to be equated with a style, much less with some sort of quintessentially feminine style.

The problem here lies not so much with the feminists' concept of what femininity is, but rather with their misconception of what art is:[4] with the naive idea that art is the direct, personal expression of individual emotional experience, a translation of personal life into visual terms. Art is almost never that, great art certainly never. The making of art involves a self-consistent language of form, more or less dependent upon, or free from, given temporally defined conventions, schemata, or systems of notation, which have to be learned or worked out, either through teaching, apprenticeship, or a long period of individual experimentation. The language of art is, more materially, embodied in paint and line on canvas or paper, in stone or clay or plastic or metal—it is neither a sob story nor a hoarse, confidential whisper. The fact of the matter is that there have been no great women artists, as far as we know—although there have been many interesting and good ones who have not been sufficiently investigated or appreciated—or any great Lithuanian jazz pianists, or Eskimo tennis players, no matter how much we might wish there had been. That this should be the case is regrettable, but no amount of manipulating the historical or critical evidence will alter the situation; neither will accusations of male-chauvinist distortions of history and obfuscation of actual achievements of women artists (or black physicists or Lithuanian jazz musicians). The fact is that there *are* no women equivalents for Michelangelo or Rembrandt, Delacroix or Cézanne, Picasso or Matisse,

or even, in very recent times, for de Kooning or Warhol, any more than there are any black American equivalents for the same. If there actually were large numbers of "hidden" great women artists, or if there really should be different standards for women's art as opposed to men's—and logically, one cannot have it both ways—then what would feminists be fighting for? If women have in fact achieved the same status as men in the arts, then the status quo is fine as it is.

But in actuality things as they are and as they have been in the arts, as in a hundred other areas, are stultifying, oppressive and discouraging to all who did not have the good fortune to be born white, preferably middle-class or above, males. The fault lies not in our stars, our hormones, our menstrual cycles, or our empty internal spaces, but in our institutions and our education—education understood to include everything that happens to us from the moment we enter, head first, into this world of meaningful symbols, signs, and signals. The miracle is, in fact, that given the overwhelming odds against women, so many have managed to achieve so much in bailiwicks of masculine prerogative like science, politics, or the arts. In some areas, indeed, women have achieved equality. While there may have been no great women composers, there have been great women singers; if no female Shakespeares, there have been Rachels, Bernhardts and Duses, to name only a few great women stage performers. Where there is a need there is a way, institutionally speaking: once the public and the authors themselves demanded more realism and range than boys in drag or piping castrati could offer, a way was found to include women in the institutional structure of the performing arts, even if in some cases they might have to do a little whoring on the side to keep their careers in order. In fact, in some of the performing arts like the ballet, women have exercised a virtual monopoly on greatness, though, it is true, they generally had to serve themselves up to Grand Dukes or aspiring bankers as an added professional obligation.

Under the institution of the British monarchy, weak women like Elizabeth I and Victoria were deemed fit to control the fate of entire nations and did so with noteworthy success. During World War II, the institutional structure of factory work found a way to transform fragile little women into stalwart Rosy the Riveters; after the war, when these jobs were needed by muscular males, the same riveters were found to be too frail to do anything more strenuous than checking out groceries at supermarkets, where they could stand on their feet lifting heavy packages all day long at much lower salaries—or housework and childcare, where they could cope with three or four children on a sixteen-hour shift at no salary at all. Wondrous are the works of man and the institutions he has established, or disestablished at his will!

When one really starts thinking about the implications of "Why are there no great women artists?" one begins to realize to what extent our very consciousness of how things are in the world has been conditioned—and too often falsified—by the way the most important questions are posed. We tend to take it for granted that there really are an East Asian problem, a poverty problem, a black problem—and a woman problem. But first we must ask ourselves who is formulating these "questions," and then, what purposes such formulations may serve; we may, of course, refresh our memories with the unspeakably sinister connotations of the Nazi's "Jewish problem." Obviously, for wolves, be they in sheep's clothing or in mufti, it is always best to refer to the lamb problem in the interests of public relations, as well as for the good of the lupine conscience. Indeed, in our time of instant communication, "problems" are rapidly formulated to rationalize the bad conscience of those with power. Thus, for example, what is in actuality the problem posed by the unwanted and unjustifiable presence of Americans in Vietnam and Cambodia is referred to by these intruding and destructive Americans as the East Asian problem, whereas East Asians may view it, more realistically, as the American problem; the so-called poverty problem might more directly and concretely be viewed as the wealth problem by the poor and hopeless denizens of urban ghettos or rural wastelands; the same not-so-foolish irony twists the white problem—what blacks are going to do to wrest their rights from a dominating, hypocritical, and often outright hostile white majority—into its opposite: a black problem; and the same inverse, but certainly not ineffective or unmotivated, logic turns up in the formulation of our own present state of affairs as the Woman Problem.

Now the women problem, like all human problems, so-called (and the very idea of calling anything to do with human beings a problem is, of course, a fairly recent one), and unlike mathematical or scientific ones, is not amenable to solution at all, since what human problems involve is an actual reinterpretation of the nature of the situation, or even a radical alteration of stance or program of action *on the part of the problems themselves,* recourses unavailable to mathematical symbols, molecules, or microbes. In other words, the "objects" involved in the solution to human problems are at the same time *subjects,* capable of turning on that other group of human beings who has decided that their fellows are problem-objects to be solved, and capable of refusing both the solution, and, at the same time, the status of being problematic at all. Thus, women and their situation in the arts, as in other realms of endeavor, are not a problem to be viewed through the eyes of the dominant male power elite, at whose will or whose whim their demands may possibly some day be answered, at masculine convenience, of course. Women must conceive of themselves as potentially—if not actually—equal subjects, willing to look the facts of their situation as an institutional and objective problem not merely as a personal and subjective one, full in the face, without self-pity or copouts. Yet at the same time, they must view their situation with that high degree of emotional and intellectual commitment necessary to create a world in which truly equal achievement will be not only made possible, but actively encouraged by social institutions.

It is certainly not realistic to hope, as some feminists optimistically do, that a majority of men in the arts or in any other field will soon see that it is actually in their own self-interest to grant complete equality to women or to maintain that men themselves will soon realize that they are diminished by denying themselves access to traditionally feminine realms and emotional reactions. After all, there are few areas that are really denied to men, if the level of operations demanded be transcendant, responsible, or rewarding enough: men who have a need for feminine involvement with babies or children can certainly fulfill their needs adequately, and gain status and a sense of achievement to boot, in the field of pediatrics or child psychology, with a female nurse to do the more routine work; those who feel the urge for creativity at the stove may gain fame as master chefs or restaurateurs; and of course, men who yearn to fulfill themselves through what are often termed feminine artistic interests can easily find themselves as painters or sculptors, rather than as volunteer museum aides or as part-time ceramicists, as their presumably more aesthetically oriented female counterparts so often end up. As far as scholarship is concerned, how many men would really be willing to exchange their roles as teachers and researchers for that of unpaid, part-time research assistants and typists as well as full-time nannies and domestic workers?

It is only the extraordinarily enlightened or altruistic man who can really want to grant—the term itself is revealing—equality to women, and he will certainly not offer to switch places with one under present circumstances; on the contrary, he realizes that true equality for women will certainly involve considerable sacrifice of comfort, convenience, not to speak of ego-support and "natural" prerogatives, even down to the assumption that "he" is the subject of every sentence unless otherwise stated. Such sacrifices are not made lightly. It is unlikely that the French aristocracy in the eighteenth century would willingly have changed places with the Third Estate, or even granted its members a shred more privilege than they already had, unless forced to do so by the French Revolution; the working classes did not convince their capitalist employers that it would actually be to the latters' advantage to grant them a living wage and a modicum of security until after a long and bloody struggle when unions could reinforce such modest demands; certainly, the slaveowners of the South were willing to go to war to preserve their way of life with its still viable social and economic advantages, conferred by the possession of black slaves. While some of the more enlightened slaveowners may have granted freedom to their slaves, certainly none of them in their right minds could have ever suggested in anything but a spirit of black humor that he might prefer the carefree, irresponsible, watermelon-eating, spiritual-singing life of the darky to his own burdensome superiority. "I've got plenty of nothin'" is the tag-line of bad faith, coined by the uneasy conscience that would metamorphose the powerless victim into the lucky devil. It is through such bad faith that the holders of power can avoid the sacrifices that a truly egalitarian society would demand of all holders of privilege. It is no wonder that those who have such privilege inevitably hold on to it, and hold tight, no matter how marginal the advantage involved, until compelled to bow to superior power of one sort or another.

Thus, the question of women's equality—in art as in any other realm—devolves not upon the relative benevolence or ill-will of individual men, or the self-confidence or abjectness of individual women, but rather on the very nature of our institutional structures themselves and the view of reality that they impose on the human beings who are part of them. As John Stuart Mill pointed out more than a century ago: "Everything which is usual appears natural. The subjection of women to men being a universal custom, any departure from it quite naturally appears unnatural."[5] Most men, despite lip service to equality, are reluctant to give up this natural order of things in which their advantages so far outweigh their disadvantages; for women the case is further complicated by the fact that, as Mill astutely pointed out, theirs is the only oppressed group or caste whose masters demand not only submission, but unqualified affection as well; thus, women are often weakened by the internalized demands of the male-dominated society itself, as well as by a plethora of material goods and comforts: the middle-class woman has a great deal more to lose than her chains.

This is not to say that the oppression of women does not, in some way, disadvantage the dominant male in our society: male supremacist attitudes may distort intellectual matters in the same way as any unquestioned assumptions about historical or social issues. Just as a very little power may corrupt one's actions, so a relatively minor degree of false consciousness may contaminate one's intellectual position. The question "Why are there no great women artists?" is simply the top tenth of an iceberg of misinterpretation and misconception revealed above the surface; beneath lies a vast dark bulk of shaky *idées reçues* about the nature of art and its situational concomitants, about the nature of human abilities in general and of human excellence in particular, and the role that the social order plays in all of this. While the woman problem as such may be a pseudoissue, the misconceptions involved in the question "Why are there no great women artists?" point to major areas of intellectual obfuscation beyond the specific political issues involved in the subjection of women and its ideological justifications.

Beneath the question lie naive, distorted, uncritical assumptions about the making of art in general, much less the making of great art. These assumptions, conscious or unconscious, link together such unlikely superstars as Michelangelo and Van Gogh, Raphael and Jackson Pollock under the rubric of Great Artist—an honorific attested to by the number of scholarly monographs devoted to the artist in question—and the Great Artist is conceived of as one who has genius; genius, in turn, is thought to be an atemporal and mysterious power somehow embedded in the person of the Great Artist.[6] Thus, the conceptual structure underlying the question "Why are there no great women artists?" rests upon unquestioned, often unconscious, metahistorical premises that make Hippolyte Taine's race-milieu-moment formulation of the dimensions of historical thought seem like a model of sophistication. Such, unfortunately, are the assumptions lying behind a great deal of art history writing. It is no accident that the whole crucial question of the conditions *generally* productive of great art has so rarely been investigated, or that attempts to investigate such general problems have, until fairly recently, been dismissed as unscholarly, too broad, or the province of some other discipline like sociology. To encourage such a dispassionate, impersonal, sociological, and institutionally oriented approach would reveal the entire romantic, elitist, individual-glorifying, and monograph-producing substructure upon which the profession of art history is based, and which has only recently been called into question by a group of younger dissidents within the discipline.

Underlying the question about woman as artist, then, we find the whole myth of the Great Artist—unique, godlike subject of a hundred monographs—bearing within his person since birth a mysterious essence, rather like the golden nugget in Mrs. Grass's chicken soup, called genius or talent, which must always out, no matter how unlikely or unpromising the circumstances.

The magical aura surrounding the representational arts and their creators has given birth to myths since earliest times. Interestingly enough, the same magical abilities attributed by Pliny to the Greek painter Lysippos in antiquity—the mysterious inner call in early youth, the lack of any teacher but nature herself—is repeated as late as the nineteenth century by Max

Buchon in his biography of the realist painter Courbet. The supernatural powers of the artist as imitator, his control of strong, possibly dangerous powers, have functioned historically to set him off from others as a godlike creator, one who creates being out of nothing like the demiurge. The fairy tale of the boy wonder, discovered by an older artist or discerning patron, usually in the guise of a lowly shepherd boy,[7] has been a stock in trade of artistic mythology ever since Vasari immortalized the young Giotto, whom the great Cimabue discovered drawing sheep on a stone, while the lad was guarding his flocks; Cimabue, overcome with admiration for the realism of the drawing, immediately invited the humble youth to be his pupil. Through some mysterious coincidence, later artists like Beccafumi, Andrea Sansovino, Andrea del Castagno, Mantegna, Zurbaran, and Goya were all discovered in similar pastoral circumstances. Even when the Great Artist was not fortunate enough to come equipped with a flock of sheep as a lad, his talent always seems to have manifested itself very early, independent of any external encouragement: Filippo Lippi, Poussin, Courbet, and Monet are all reported to have drawn caricatures in the margins of their schoolbooks, instead of studying the required subjects—we never, of course, hear about the myriad youths who neglected their studies and scribbled in the margins of their notebooks without ever becoming anything more elevated than department store clerks or shoe salesmen—and the great Michelangelo himself, according to his biographer and pupil, Vasari, did more drawing than studying as a child. So pronounced was the young Michelangelo's talent as an art student, reports Vasari, that when his master, Ghirlandaio, absented himself momentarily from his work in Santa Maria Novella and the young Michelangelo took the opportunity to draw "the scaffolding, trestles, pots of paint, brushes, and the apprentices at their tasks," he did so so skillfully that upon his return his master exclaimed: "This boy knows more than I do."

As is so often the case, such stories, which may indeed have a grain of truth in them, tend both to reflect and to perpetuate the attitudes they subsume. Despite the actual basis in fact of these myths about the early manifestations of genius, the tenor of the tales is itself misleading. It is no doubt true, for example, that the young Picasso passed all the examinations for entrance to the Barcelona, and later to the Madrid, Academy of Art at the age of fifteen in a single day, a feat of such difficulty that most candidates required a month of preparation; however, one would like to find out more about similar precocious qualifiers for art academies, who then went on to achieve nothing but mediocrity or failure—in whom, of course, art historians are uninterested—or to study in greater detail the role played by Picasso's art professor father in the pictorial precocity of his son. What if Picasso had been born a girl? Would Señor Ruiz have paid as much attention or stimulated as much ambition for achievement in a little Pablita?

What is stressed in all these stories is the apparently miraculous, nondetermined, and asocial nature of artistic achievement. [T]his gratuitous, semi-religious conception of the artist's role was elevated into a true hagiography in the nineteenth century, when both art historians, critics, and, not least, some of the artists themselves tended to erect the making of art into a substitute religion, the last bulwark of higher values in a materialistic world. The artist in the nineteenth-century Saints' Legend struggles onward against the most determined parental and social opposition, suffering the slings and arrows of social opprobrium like any Christian martyr, and ultimately succeeds against all odds—generally, alas, after his death—because from deep within himself radiates that mysterious, holy effulgence: genius. Here we have the mad Van Gogh, spinning out sunflowers despite epileptic seizures and near-starvation, or perhaps because of them; Cezanne, braving paternal rejection and public scorn in order to revolutionize painting; Gauguin, throwing away respectability and financial security with a single existential gesture to pursue his calling in the tropics, unrecognized by crass philistines on the home front; or Toulouse-Lautrec, dwarfed, crippled, and alcoholic, sacrificing his aristocratic birthright in favor of the squalid surroundings that provided him with inspiration.

Of course, no serious contemporary art historian ever takes such obvious fairy tales at their face value. Yet it is all too often this sort of mythology about artistic achievement and its concomitants that forms the unconscious or unquestioned assumptions of art scholars, no matter how many crumbs are thrown to social influences, ideas of the times, economic crises, and so on. Behind the most sophisticated investigations of great artists, more specifically, the art history monograph, which accepts the notion of the Great Artist as primary, and the social and institutional structures within which he lived and worked as mere secondary "influences" or "background," lurks the golden nugget theory of genius and the free enterprise conception of individual achievement. On this basis, women's lack of major achievement in art may be formulated as a syllogism: if women had the golden nugget of artistic genius, then it would reveal itself. But it has never revealed itself. Q.E.D. Women do not have the golden nugget of artistic genius. If Giotto, the obscure shepherd boy, and Van Gogh, the epileptic, could make it, why not women?

Yet as soon as one leaves behind the world of fairy tale and self-fulfilling prophecy and instead casts a dispassionate eye on the actual situations in which important art has been produced, in the total range of its social and institutional structures throughout history, one finds that the very questions that are fruitful or relevant for the historian to ask shape up rather differently. One would like to ask, for instance, from what social classes, from what castes and subgroups, artists were most likely to come at different periods of art history? What proportion of painters and sculptors, or more specifically, of major painters and sculptors, had fathers or other close relatives engaged in painting, sculpture, or related professions? As Nikolaus Pevsner points out in his discussion of the French Academy in the seventeenth and eighteenth centuries, the transmission of the artistic profession from father to son was considered a matter of course (as in fact it was with the Coypels, the Coustous, the Van Loos, and so forth); indeed, sons of academicians were exempted from the customary fees for lessons.[8] Despite the noteworthy and dramatically satisfying cases of the great father-rejecting révoltés of the nineteenth century, a large proportion of artists, great and not-so-great, had artist fathers. In the rank of major artists, the names of Holbein and Dürer, Raphael and Bernini immediately spring to mind; even in our more recent, rebellious times, one can cite the names of Picasso, Calder, Giacometti and Wyeth as members of artist families.

As far as the relationship of artistic occupation and social class is concerned, an interesting parallel to "why are there no great women artists?" might well be: "why have there been no great artists from the aristocracy?" One can scarcely think, before the anti-traditional nineteenth century at least, of any artist who sprang from the ranks of any more elevated class than the upper bourgeoisie; even in the nineteenth century, Degas came from the lower nobility—more like the *haute bourgeoisie,* in fact—and only Toulouse-Lautrec, metamorphosed into the ranks of the marginal by accidental deformity, could be said to have come from the loftier reaches of the upper classes. While the aristocracy has always provided the lion's share of the patronage and the audience for art—as indeed, the aristocracy of wealth does even in our more democratic days, it has rarely contributed anything but a few amateurish efforts to the actual creation of art itself, although aristocrats, like many women, have had far more than their share of educational advantage and leisure, and, indeed, like women, might often be encouraged to dabble in the arts or even develop into respectable amateurs. Napoleon III's cousin, the Princess Mathilde, exhibited at the official salons; Queen Victoria and Prince Albert studied art with no less a figure than Landseer himself. Could it be possible that the little golden nugget—genius—is as absent from the aristocratic make-up as from the feminine psyche? Or is it not rather that the demands and expectations placed on both aristocrats and women—the amount of time necessarily devoted to social functions, the very kinds of activities demanded—simply made total devotion to professional art production out of the question and unthinkable?

When the right questions are finally asked about the conditions for producing art (of which the production of great art is a subtopic), some discussion of the situational concomitants of intelligence and talent generally, not merely of artistic genius, has to be included. As Piaget and others have stressed in their studies of the development of reason and the unfolding of imagination in young children, intelligence—or, by implication, what we choose to call genius—is a dynamic activity, rather than a static essence, and an activity of a subject *in a situation.* As further investigations in the field of child development reveal, these abilities or this intelligence are built up minutely, step by step, from infancy onward, although the patterns of adaptation-accommodation may be established so

early within the subject-in-an-environment that they may indeed *appear* to be innate to the unsophisticated observer. Such investigations imply that, even aside from metahistorical reasons, scholars will have to abandon the notion, consciously articulated or not, of individual genius as innate and primary to the creation of art.[9]

The question "Why are there no great women artists?" has so far led to the conclusion that art is not a free, autonomous activity of a superendowed individual, "influenced" by previous artists, and, more vaguely and superficially, by "social forces," but rather, that art making, both in terms of the development of the art maker and the nature and quality of the work of art itself, occurs in a social situation, is an integral element of the social structure, and is mediated and determined by specific and definable social institutions, be they art academies, systems of patronage, mythologies of the divine creator and artist as he-man or social outcast.

The Question of the Nude

We can now approach our question from a more reasonable standpoint, since it seems probable that the answer to why there are no great women artists, or so few women artists at all, lies not in the nature of individual genius or the lack of it, but in the nature of given social institutions and what they forbid or encourage in various classes or groups of individuals. Let us first examine such a simple, but critical issue as availability of the nude model to aspiring women artists in the period extending from the Renaissance until near the end of the nineteenth century, a period in which careful and prolonged study of the nude model was essential to the training of every young artist, to the production of any work with pretensions to grandeur, and to the very essence of history painting, generally accepted as the highest category of art. Indeed, it was argued by defenders of traditional painting in the nineteenth century that there could be no great painting *with* clothed figures, since costume inevitably destroyed both the temporal universality and the classical idealization required by great art. Needless to say, central to the training programs of art academies since their inception late in the sixteenth and early in the seventeenth centuries, was life drawing from the nude, generally from the male, model. In addition, groups of artists and their pupils often met privately for life-drawing sessions from the nude model in their studios. In general, while individual artists and private academies employed the female model extensively, the female nude was forbidden in almost all public art schools as late as 1850 and after—a state of affairs which Pevsner rightly designates as "hardly believable."[10] Far more believeable, unfortunately, was the complete unavailability to the aspiring woman artist of *any* nude models at all, be they male or female. As late as 1893 "lady" students were not admitted to life drawing at the official academy in London; even when they were admitted after that date, the model had to be "partially draped."[11]

The very plethora of surviving "Academies"—detailed, painstaking studies from the nude studio model —in the youthful work of artists down through the time of Seurat and well into the twentieth century attests to the central importance of this branch of study in the pedagogy and development of the talented beginner. The formal academic program itself normally proceeded, as a matter of course, from copying from drawings and engravings, to drawing from casts of famous works of sculpture, to drawing from the living model. To be deprived of this ultimate stage of training meant, in effect, to be deprived of the possibility of creating major art works, unless one were a very ingenious lady indeed, or simply, as most of the few women aspiring to be painters ultimately did, restricted oneself to the "minor" and less highly regarded fields of portraiture, genre, landscape, or still life. It is rather as though a medical student were denied the opportunity to dissect or even examine the naked human body.

There exist, to my knowledge, no representations of artists drawing from the nude model that include women in any role but that of the nude model itself, an interesting commentary on rules of propriety: it is all right for a ("low," of course) woman to reveal herself naked-as-an-object for a group of men, but forbidden to a woman to participate in the active study and recording of naked-man-as-an-object, or even a fellow woman! An amusing example of this taboo on confronting a dressed lady with a naked man is embodied in Zoffany's group portrait of the members of the Royal Academy in London in 1772; all the distinguished members are gathered in the life room before two nude male models, with one noteworthy exception—the single female member, the renowned Angelica Kauffmann, who for propriety's sake, one assumes, is merely present in effigy, in the form of a portrait hanging on the wall. A slightly earlier drawing of *Ladies in the Studio* by the Polish artist Daniel Chodowiecki shows the ladies portraying a modestly dressed member of their own sex. In a lithograph dating from the relatively liberated epoch following the French Revolution, the lithographer Marlet has represented some women sketchers in a group of students working from the male model, but the model himself has been chastely provided with what appears to be a pair of bathing trunks, a garment hardly conducive to a sense of classical elevation; no doubt, such license was considered daring in its day, and the young ladies in question suspected of doubtful morals, but even this state of affairs seems to have lasted only a short while. In an English stereoscopic color view of the interior of a studio of about 1865, the standing, bearded male model is so heavily draped that not an iota of his anatomy escapes from the discreet toga, save for a single bare shoulder and arm: even so, he obviously had the grace to avert his eyes in the presence of the crinoline-clad young sketchers, who so clearly outnumber the men that one suspects this is a ladies' drawing class.

The women in the Women's Modeling Class at the Pennsylvania Academy were evidently not even allowed this modest privilege. A photograph by Thomas Eakins of about 1885 reveals these students modeling from a cow (bull? the nether regions are obscure in the photograph), a naked cow to be sure, perhaps a daring liberty when one considers that even piano legs might be concealed beneath pantalettes during this era; the idea of introducing a bovine model into the artist's studio stems directly from Courbet, who brought a living bull into his short-lived studio academy in the 1860s.

The question of the availability of the nude model is but a single aspect of the automatic, institutionally maintained discrimination against women. It reveals both the universality of the discrimination and its consequences, as well as the institutional rather than individual nature of but one facet of the necessary preparation and equipment for achieving mere proficiency, much less greatness, in the realm of art. One could equally well have examined other dimensions of the situation, such as the apprenticeship system, the academic educational pattern that, in France especially, was almost the only key to success; there was a regular progression and set competitions, crowned by the Prix de Rome, which enabled the young winner to work in the French Academy in that city; this was unthinkable for women, of course, and they were unable to compete for the prize until the end of the nineteenth century, when the whole academic system had lost its importance anyway. If one uses as an example nineteenth-century France—a country with the largest proportion of women artists—it seems clear that "women were not accepted as professional painters."[12] In the middle of the century, there were only a third as many women as men artists, but even this mildly encouraging statistic is deceptive, when we discover that even out of this relatively meager number, *none* had attended that major stepping stone to artistic success, the Ecole des Beaux-Arts; only 7 percent had received any official commission or had held any official office—and these might include the most menial sort of work—only 7 percent had ever received any salon medal; and *none* had ever received the Legion of Honor.[13] Deprived of encouragements, educational facilities, and rewards, it is almost incredible that a certain percentage of women, admittedly a small one, actually sought out a profession in the arts.

It also becomes apparent why women were able to compete on far more equal terms with men—and even become innovators—in the field of literature. While art making has traditionally demanded the learning of specific techniques and skills, in a certain sequence, in an institutional setting outside the home, as well as becoming familiar with a specific vocabulary of iconography and motifs; the same is by no means true for the poet or novelist. Anyone, even a woman, has to learn the language, can learn to read and write, and can commit personal experiences to paper in the privacy of the home. Naturally, this oversimplifies the very real difficulties and complexities involved in creating good or great literature, whether by man or woman, but it still gives a clue as to the possibility of the existence of an Emily Dickinson or a Virginia Woolf, and the lack of their counterparts, at least until quite recently, in the visual arts.

Then, of course, there were the "fringe" requirements for major artists, which were for the most part both psychically and socially closed to women, even if they hypothetically could have achieved the requisite grandeur in the performance of their craft. In the Renaissance and after, the great artist, aside from participating in the affairs of an academy, might well be intimate with members of humanist circles with whom he could exchange ideas, establish suitable relationships with patrons, travel widely and freely, perhaps politic and intrigue; in addition, he had to possess the sheer organizational acumen and ability required to run a major atelier-factory, like that of Rubens. An enormous amount of self-confidence and worldly knowledge-ability, as well as a natural sense of well-earned dominance and power, was needed by the great *chef d'école*, both in running the production end of painting and in controlling and instructing the numerous students and assistants who might flock to his studio.

The Lady's Accomplishment

In contrast to the single-mindedness and commitment demanded of a *chef d'ecole*, we might set the image of the "lady painter" established by nineteenth-century etiquette books and reinforced by the literature of the times. It is precisely the insistence upon a modest, proficient, self-demeaning level of amateurism, the looking upon art, like needlework or crocheting, as a suitable "accomplishment" for the well-brought up young woman, who naturally would want to direct her major attention toward the welfare of others—family and husband—that militated, and still militates today, against any real accomplishment on the part of women. It is this emphasis that transforms serious commitment to frivolous self-indulgence, busy work, or occupational therapy, and today, more than ever, in suburban bastions of the feminine mystique, tends to distort the whole notion of what art is and what kind of social role it plays. In Mrs. Ellis's widely read *The Family Monitor and Domestic Guide,* a book of advice popular both in the United States and in England, published before the middle of the nineteenth century, women were warned against the snare of trying too hard to excel in any one thing. Lest we are tempted to laugh, we may refresh ourselves with more recent samples of exactly the same advice cited in Betty Friedan's *Feminine Mystique* or in the pages of recent issues of popular women's magazines.

It must not be supposed that the writer is one who would advocate, as essential to woman, any very extraordinary degree of intellectual attainment, especially if confined to one particular branch of study. "I should like to excel in something" is a frequent, and, to some extent, laudable expression; but in what does it originate, and to what does it tend? *To be able to do a great many things tolerably well, is of infinitely more value to a woman, than to be able to excel in any one. By the former, she may render herself generally useful; by the latter, she may dazzle for an hour. By being apt, and tolerably well skilled in every thing, she may fall into any situation in life with dignity and ease—by devoting her time to excellence in one, she may remain incapable of every other.*

So far as cleverness, learning, and knowledge are conducive to woman's moral excellence, they are therefore desirable, and no further. *All that would occupy her mind to the exclusion of better things, all that would involve her in the mazes of flattery and admiration, all that would tend to draw away her thoughts from others and fix them on herself, ought to be avoided as an evil to her, however brilliant or attractive it may be in itself.*[14]

This sound bit of advice has a familiar ring: propped up by a bit of Freudianism and some taglines from the social sciences about the well-rounded personality, preparation for woman's chief career, marriage, and the unfemininity of deep involvement with work rather than sex, it is the very mainstay of the feminine mystique until this day. Such an outlook helps guard the male from unwanted competition in his "serious" professional activities and assures him of "well-rounded" assistance on the home front, so that he may have sex and family in addition to the fulfillment of his *own* specialized talent and excellence.

As far as painting specifically is concerned, Mrs. Ellis finds that it has one immediate advantage for the young lady over its rival branch of artistic activity, music—it is quiet and disturbs no one (this negative virtue, of course, would not be true of sculpture, but accomplishment with the hammer and chisel simply never occurs as a suitable accomplishment for the weaker sex); in addition, says Mrs. Ellis, "it [drawing] is an employment which beguiles the mind of many cares. . . . Drawing is of all other occupations, the one most calculated to keep the mind from brooding upon self, and to maintain that general cheerfulness which is a part of social and domestic duty. . . . It can also be laid down and resumed, as circumstance or inclination may direct, and that without any serious loss."[15] Again, lest we feel that we have made a great deal of progress in this area in the past hundred years, I might bring up the remark of a bright young doctor who, when the conversation turned to his wife and her friends "dabbling" in the arts, contemptuously snorted: "Well, at least it keeps them out of trouble!" Amateurism and lack of real commitment, as well as snobbery and emphasis on chic on the part of women in their artistic "hobbies," feeds the contempt of the successful, professionally committed man who is engaged in "real" work and can, with a certain justice, point to his wife's lack of seriousness in her artistic activities. For such men, the "real" work of women is only that which directly or indirectly serves themselves and their children: any other commitment falls under the rubric of diversion, selfishness, egomania, or, at the unspoken extreme, castration. The circle is a vicious one, in which philistinism and frivolity mutually reinforce each other, today as in the nineteenth century.

In literature, as in life, even if the woman's commitment to art was apparently a serious one, she was naturally expected to drop her career and give up this commitment at the behest of love and marriage: this lesson is still inculcated in young girls, directly or indirectly, from the moment they are born. Even the determined and successful heroine of Dinah Craik's mid-nineteenth century novel about feminine artistic success, *Olive,* a young woman who lives alone, strives for fame and independence, and actually supports herself through her art—such unfeminine behavior is, of course, at least partly excused by the fact that she is a cripple and automatically considers that marriage is denied to her—ultimately succumbs to the blandishments of love and its natural concomitant, marriage. To paraphrase the words of Patricia Thomson in *The Victorian Heroine*, Mrs. Craik, having shot her bolts in the course of her novel, is finally content to let her heroine, whose ultimate greatness the reader has never been able to doubt, sink gently into matrimony. "Of Olive, Mrs. Craik comments imperturbably that her husband's influence is to deprive the Scottish Academy of 'no one knew how many grand pictures.'"[16] Then, as so often is the case now, despite men's greater "tolerance," the choice for women seems always to be marriage *or* a career: solitude as the price of success *or* sex and companionship at the price of professional renunciation. If such were the alternatives presented to men, one wonders how many great artists, or even mediocre ones, would have opted for commitment to their art—especially if they had been constantly reminded from their earliest moments that their only true fulfillment *as* men could come from marriage and raising a family. That achievement in the arts, as in any field of endeavor, demands struggle and sacrifice, no one would deny; that this has certainly been true after the middle of the nineteenth century, when the traditional institutions of artistic support and patronage no longer fulfilled their customary obligations, is incontrovertible. One has only to think of Delacroix, Courbet, Degas, Van Gogh, and Toulouse-Lautrec, who all gave up the distractions and obligations of family life, at least in part, so that they could pursue their artistic careers more singlemindedly; yet none of them was automatically denied the pleasures of sex or companionship on account of this choice— on the contrary! Nor did they ever feel that they had sacrificed their manhood or their sexual role in order to achieve professional fulfillment. But if the artist in question happens to be a woman, a thousand years of guilt, self-doubt, and objecthood have been added to the undeniable difficulties of being an artist in the modern world.

An unconscious aura of titillation arises from a visual representation of an aspiring woman artist in the mid-nineteenth century. Emily Mary Osborne's heartfelt 1857 painting, *Nameless and Friendless*, a canvas representing a poor but lovely and respectable young girl at a London art dealers', nervously awaiting the verdict of the pompous proprietor on the worth of her canvases while two ogling "art lovers" look on, is really not too different in its underlying assumptions from an overtly salacious work like Bompard's *Debut of the Model*. The theme in both is innocence, delicious feminine innocence, exposed to the world. It is the charming *vulnerability* of the young woman artist, like that of the hesitating model, which is really the subject of Miss Osborne's painting, not the value of the young woman's work or her pride in it: the issue here is, as usual, sexual rather than serious. Always a model but never an artist might well have served as the motto of the seriously aspiring young woman in nineteenth-century art.

Successes

But what of the small band of heroic women, who, throughout the ages, despite obstacles, have achieved preeminence, if not the pinnacles of grandeur of a Michelangelo, a Rembrandt, or a Picasso? Are there any qualities that may be said to have characterized them as a group and as individuals? While such an investigation in depth is beyond the scope of this essay, we can point to a few striking characteristics of women artists generally: they all, almost without exception, were either the daughters of artist fathers, or generally later, in the nineteenth and twentieth centuries, had a close personal connection with a stronger or more dominant male artistic personality. Neither of these characteristics is, of course, unusual for men artists; it is simply true almost *without exception* for their feminine counterparts, at least until quite recently. From the legendary sculptor, Sabina von Steinbach, in the fifteenth century, who, according to local tradition, was responsible for the portal groups on the Cathedral of Strasbourg, down to Rosa Bonheur, the most renowned animal painter of the nineteenth century, and including such eminent women artists as Maria Robusti, daughter of Tintoretto, Lavinia Fontana, Artemisia Gentileschi, Elizabeth Chéron, Elisabeth Vigée-Lebrun, and Angelica Kauffmann—all without exception were the daughters of artists; in the nineteenth century, Berthe Morisot was closely associated with Manet, later marrying his brother, and Mary Cassatt based a good deal of her work on the style of her close friend, Degas. Precisely the same breaking of traditional bonds and discarding of time-honored practices that permitted men artists to strike out in directions quite different from those of their fathers in the second half of the nineteenth century enabled women, with additional difficulties, to be sure, to strike out on their own as well. Many of our more recent women artists, like Suzanne Valadon, Paula Modersohn-Becker, Käthe Kollwitz, or Louise Nevelson, have come from nonartistic backgrounds, although many contemporary and near-contemporary women artists have, of course, married fellow artists, a recourse impossible to their masculine contemporaries since there simply would not be enough women artists to go around.

It would be interesting to investigate the role of benign, if not outright encouraging, fathers in the formation of women professionals in the field: both Käthe Kollwitz and Barbara Hepworth, for example, recall the influence of unusually sympathetic and supportive fathers on their artistic pursuits. In the absence of any thoroughgoing investigation, though, one can only gather impressionistic data about the presence or absence of rebellion against parental authority in women artists, and about whether there may be more or less rebellion on the part of women, rather than men, artists. One thing, however, is clear: for a woman to opt for a career at all, much less for a career in art, has required a certain amount of unconventionality, both in the past and at present; whether or not the woman artist rebels against or finds strength in the attitude of her family, she must in any case have a good, strong streak of rebellion in her to make her way in the world of art at all, rather than conform to the socially approved role of wife and mother, the only role to which every social institution consigns her automatically, simply by virtue of her birth. It is only by adopting, however covertly, the "masculine" attributes of singlemindedness, concentration, tenaciousness, and absorption in ideas and craftsmanship for their own sake that women have succeeded and continue to succeed in the world of art.

Rosa Bonheur

It is instructive to examine in greater detail one of the most successful and accomplished women painters of all time, Rosa Bonheur (1822–1899), whose work, despite the ravages wrought upon its estimation by changes of taste and a certain admitted lack of variety, still stands as an impressive achievement to anyone interested in the art of the nineteenth century and in the history of taste generally. In Rosa Bonheur's career, partly because of the magnitude of her reputation, all the various conflicts, all the internal and external contradictions and struggles typical of her sex and profession, stand out in sharp relief.

The success of Rosa Bonheur firmly establishes the role of institutions and institutional change as a necessary, if not a sufficient, cause of achievement in art. We might say that Bonheur picked a fortunate time to become an artist if she was, at the same time, to have the disadvantage of being a woman: she came into her own in the middle of the nineteenth century, a time in which the struggle between traditional history painting and the less pretentious and more free-wheeling genre painting, landscape, and still life was won by the latter group hands down. A major change in the social and institutional support for art itself was well under way: with the rise of the bourgeoisie and the fall of the cultivated aristocracy, smaller paintings, generally of everyday subjects, rather than grandiose mythological or religious scenes, were much in demand. To cite H. C. and C. A. White: "Three hundred provincial museums there might be, government commissions for public works there might be, but the only possible paid destinations for the rising flood of canvases were the homes of the bourgeoisie. History painting had not and never would rest comfortably in the middle-class parlor. 'Lesser' forms of image art—genre, landscape, still life—did."[17] In mid-nineteenth-century France, as in seventeenth-century Holland, there was a tendency for artists to attempt to achieve some sort of security in a shaky market situation by specializing, that is, making a career out of a specific subject. Animal painting was a very popular field, and Rosa Bonheur was no doubt its most accomplished and successful practitioner, followed in popularity only by the Barbizon painter Troyon, who was at one time so pressed for his paintings of cows that he hired another artist to brush in the backgrounds. Rosa Bonheur's rise to fame accompanied that of the Barbizon landscapists, supported by those canny dealers, the Durand-Ruels, who later moved on to support the work of the impressionists. The Durand-Ruels were among the first dealers to tap this expanding market of movable decoration for the middle classes (to use the Whites' terminology), and Rosa Bonheur, who because of her sex would have almost certainly been unable to succeed so brilliantly as a history painter, climbed on board the bandwagon of burgeoning specialization. Her naturalism and ability to capture the individuality—even the unique "soul"—of each of her animal subjects again coincided with bourgeois taste at the time. The same combination of qualities, with a much stronger dose of sentimentality and pathetic fallacy, to be sure, likewise assured the success of her animalist contemporary, Landseer, in England.

Daughter of an impoverished drawing master, Rosa Bonheur showed her interest in art early; at the same time, she exhibited an independence of spirit and liberty of manner that immediately earned her the label of tomboy. According to her own later accounts, her "masculine protest" established itself early; to what extent *any* show of persistence, stubbornness, and overwhelming vigor would be counted as "masculine" in the first half of the nineteenth century is, of course, conjectural. Rosa Bonheur's attitude toward her father is somewhat ambiguous: while realizing that he had been influential in directing her toward her life's work, there is no doubt that she resented his thoughtless treatment of her beloved mother; in her reminiscences, she half affectionately makes fun of his bizarre form of social idealism. Raimond Bonheur had been an active member of the short-lived Saint-Simonian community, established in the third decade of the nineteenth century by "Le Pere" Enfantin at Menilmontant. Although in her later years Rosa Bonheur might have made fun of some of the more far fetched eccentricities of the members of the community and might have disapproved of the additional strain that her father's apostolate placed on her overburdened mother, it is obvious that the Saint-Simonian ideal of equality for women—they disapproved of marriage, their trousered feminine costume was a token of emancipation, and their spiritual leader, Le Pere Enfantin, made extraordinary efforts to find a woman Messiah to share his reign—made a strong impression on her as a child and may well have influenced her future course of behavior.

"Why shouldn't I be proud to be a woman?" she exclaimed to an interviewer. "My father, that enthusiastic apostle of humanity many times reiterated to me that woman's mission was to elevate the human race, that she was the Messiah of future centuries. It is to his doctrines that I owe the great, noble ambition I have conceived for the sex which I proudly affirm to be mine, and whose independence I will support to my dying day. . . ."[18] When she was still hardly more than a child, he instilled in her the ambition to surpass Elisabeth Vigée-Lebrun, certainly the most eminent model she could be expected to follow, and gave her early efforts every possible encouragement. At the same time, the spectacle of her uncomplaining mother's slow decline from sheer overwork and poverty might have been an even more realistic influence on her decision to control her own destiny and never to become the unpaid slave of a man and children through marriage. What is particularly interesting from the modern feminist viewpoint is Rosa Bonheur's ability to combine the most vigorous and unapologetic masculine protest with unabashedly self-contradictory assertions of "basic" femininity.

In those refreshingly straightforward pre-Freudian days, Rosa Bonheur could explain to her biographer that she had never wanted to marry for fear of losing her independence—too many young girls let themselves be led to the altar like lambs to the sacrifice, she maintained—without any awkward sexual overtones marring the ring of pure practicality. Yet at the same time that she rejected marriage for herself and implied an inevitable loss of selfhood for any woman who engaged in it, she, unlike the Saint-Simonians, considered marriage "a sacrament indispensable to the organization of society."

While remaining cool to offers of marriage, she joined in a seemingly cloudless, apparently completely platonic, lifelong union with a fellow woman artist, Nathalie Micas, who evidently provided her with the companionship and emotional warmth that she, like most human beings, needed. Obviously, the presence of this sympathetic friend did not demand the same sacrifice of genuine commitment to her profession which marriage would have entailed; in any case, the advantages of such an arrangement for women who wished to avoid the distraction of children in the days before reliable contraception are obvious.

Yet at the same time that she frankly rejected the conventional feminine role of her times, Rosa Bonheur still was drawn into what Betty Friedan has called the "frilly blouse syndrome," that innocuous version of the feminine protest which even today compels successful women psychiatrists or professors to adopt some ultrafeminine item of clothing or insist on proving their prowess as pie bakers.[19] Although she had early cropped her hair and adopted men's clothes as her habitual attire, following the example of George Sand, whose rural romanticism exerted a powerful influence over her artistic imagination, to her biographer she insisted, and no doubt sincerely believed, that she did so only because of the specific demands of her profession. Indignantly denying rumors to the effect that she had run about the streets of Paris dressed as a boy in her youth, she proudly provided her biographer with a daguerreotype of herself at sixteen years, dressed in perfectly conventional feminine fashion, except for her shorn head, which she excused as a practical measure taken after the death of her mother; "who would have taken care of my curls?" she demanded.[20]

As far as the question of masculine dress was concerned, she was quick to reject her interlocutor's suggestion that her trousers were a symbol of bold emancipation on her part. "I strongly blame women who renounce their customary attire in the desire to make themselves pass for men," she affirmed, thereby implicitly rejecting George Sand as a prototype:

> If I had found that trousers suited my sex, I would have completely gotten rid of my skirts, but this is not the case, nor have I ever advised my sisters of the palette to wear men's clothes in the ordinary course of life. If, then, you see me dressed as I am, it is not at all with the aim of making myself interesting, as all too many women have tried, but simply in order to facilitate my work. Remember that at a certain period I spent whole days in the slaughterhouses. Indeed, you have to love your art in order to live in pools of blood. . . . I was also fascinated with horses, and where better can one study these animals than at the fairs, surrounded by horsecopers? I had no alternative but to realize that the garments of my own sex were a total nuisance. That is why I decided to ask the prefect of Police for the authorization to wear masculine clothing.[21] But the costume I am wearing

is my working outfit, nothing else. The remarks of fools have never bothered me. Nathalie [her companion] makes fun of them as I do. It doesn't bother her at all to see me dressed as a man, but if you are even the slightest bit put off, I am completely prepared to put on a skirt, especially since all I have to do is to open a closet to find a whole assortment of feminine outfits.[22]

Yet at the same time, Rosa Bonheur is forced to admit: "My trousers have been my great protectors. . . . Many times I have congratulated myself for having dared to break with traditions which would have forced me to abstain from certain kinds of work, due to the obligation to drag my skirts everywhere. . . ." Yet the famous artist again feels obliged to qualify her honest admission with an ill-assumed "femininity": "Despite my metamorphoses of costume, there is not a daughter of Eve who appreciates the niceties more than I do; my brusque and even slightly unsociable nature has never prevented my heart from remaining completely feminine."[23]

It is somewhat pathetic that this highly successful artist, unsparing of herself in the painstaking study of animal anatomy, diligently pursuing her bovine or equine subjects in the most unpleasant surroundings, industriously producing popular canvases throughout the course of a lengthy career, firm, assured, and incontrovertibly masculine in her style, winner of a first medal in the Paris Salon, Officer of the French Legion of Honor, Commander of the Order of Isabella the Catholic and the Order of Leopold of Belgium, friend of Queen Victoria, should feel compelled late in life to justify and qualify her perfectly reasonable assumption of masculine ways, for any reason whatsoever, and should feel obliged to attack her less modest trouser-wearing sisters at the same time, in order to satisfy the demands of her own bad conscience. For her conscience, despite her supportive father, her unconventional behavior, and the accolade of worldly success, still condemned her for not being a "feminine" woman, since built in by the unconsciously incorporated prescriptions of society itself, it too was intractable to reasoned arguments of reality.

The difficulties imposed by these unconscious demands on the woman artist continue to add to their already difficult enterprise even today. The noted contemporary sculptor, Louise Nevelson, combines utter, "unfeminine" dedication to her work and conspicuously "feminine" false eyelashes; she openly admits that she got married at seventeen despite the certainty that she could not live without creating because "the world said you should get married."[24] Even in the case of these two outstanding artists—and whether we like *The Horsefair* or not, we still must admire Rosa Bonheur's achievement—the voice of the feminine mystique with its internalized ambivalent narcissism and guilt, subtly dilutes and subverts that total inner confidence, that absolute certitude and moral and aesthetic self-determination demanded by the highest and most innovative work in art.

Conclusion

We have tried to deal with one of the perennial questions used to challenge women's demand for true, rather than token, equality, by examining the whole erroneous intellectual substructure upon which the question "Why are there no great women artists?" is based; by questioning the validity of the formulation of so-called problems in general and the problem of women specifically; and by probing some of the limitations of the discipline of art history itself. By stressing the *institutional*—that is, the public—rather than the *individual* or private preconditions for achievement in the arts, we have provided a model for the investigation of other areas in the field. By examining in some detail a single instance of deprivation and disadvantage—the unavailability of nude models to women art students—we have suggested that it was made *institutionally* impossible for women to achieve artistic excellence or success on the same footing as men, *no matter what* the potency of their so-called talent or genius, or their lack of this mysterious ingredient. The existence of a tiny band of successful, if not great, women artists throughout history does nothing to gainsay this fact, any more than does the existence of a few superstars or token achievers among the members of any minority group. A brief glance at the inner conflicts—and real difficulties—experienced by two highly successful women artists confirms the obvious truth that while great achievement is rare and difficult at best, it is still rarer and more difficult if you

must wrestle with inner demons of self-doubt and guilt and outer monsters of ridicule or patronizing encouragement, none of which have any specific connection with the quality of the art work as such.

What is important is that women face up to the reality of their history and of their present situation, without making excuses or puffing mediocrity. Disadvantage may indeed be an excuse; it is not, however, an intellectual position. Rather, using their situation as underdogs in the realm of grandeur and outsiders in the realm of ideology as a vantage point, women can reveal institutional and intellectual weaknesses in general, and, at the same time that they destroy false consciousness, take part in the creation of institutions in which clear thought—and true greatness—are challenges open to anyone, man or woman, courageous enough to take the necessary risk, the leap into the unknown.

Notes

1. "Women Artists," Review of Ernest Guhl's *Die Frauen in die Kunstgeschichte* in *The Westminster Review* (American Edition) 70 (July 1858): 91–104. I am grateful to Elaine Showalter for having brought this review to my attention.

2. See, for example, Peter S. Walch's excellent studies of Angelica Kauffmann or his unpublished doctoral dissertation, "Angelica Kauffmann," Princeton University, 1968, on the subject; for Artemesia Gentileschi, see R. Ward Bissell, "Artemesia Gentileschi—A New Documented Chronology," *Art Bulletin* 50 (June 1968): 153–168.

3. Mary Ellmann, *Thinking about Women* (New York: Harcourt Brace, 1968).

4. A misconception they share with the public at large, it must be added.

5. John Stuart Mill, *The Subjection of Women* (1869) in *Three Essays by John Stuart Mill* (London: World's Classics Series, 1966), p. 441.

6. For the relatively recent genesis of the emphasis on the artist as the nexus of aesthetic experience, see M. H. Abrams, *The Mirror and the Lamp: Romantic Theory and the Critical Tradition* (New York: Oxford University Press 1953), and Maurice Z. Shroder, *Icarus: The Image of the Artist in French Romanticism* (Cambridge: Harvard University Press, 1961).

7. A comparison with the parallel myth for women, the Cinderella story, is revealing: Cinderella gains higher status on the basis of a passive, "sex-object" attribute—small feet (shades of fetishism and Chinese foot-binding!), whereas the boy wonder always proves himself through active accomplishment. For a thorough study of myths about artists, see Ernst Kris and Otto Kurz, *Die Legende vom Künstler: Ein Geschichtlicher Versuch* (Vienna: Krystall-Verlag, 1934).

8. Nikolaus Pevsner, *Academies of Art, Past and Present* (Cambridge, England: The University Press, 1940), p. 96f.

9. Contemporary directions in art itself—earthworks, conceptual art, art as information—certainly point away from emphasis on the individual genius and his saleable products; in art history, Harrison C. and Cynthia A. White's *Canvases and Careers: Institutional Change in the French Painting World* (New York: Wiley, 1965), opens up a fruitful new direction of investigation, as did Nikolaus Pevsner's pioneering *Academies of Art.* Ernst Gombrich and Pierre Francostel, in their very different ways, have always tended to view art and the artist as part of a total situation, rather than in lofty isolation.

10. Female models were introduced in the life class in Berlin in 1875, in Stockholm in 1839, in Naples in 1870, at the Royal College of Art in London after 1875. Pevsner, *op. cit.,* p. 231. Female models at the Pennsylvania Academy of the Fine Arts wore masks to hide their identity as late as about 1866—as attested to in a charcoal drawing by Thomas Eakins—if not later.

11. Pevsner, *op. cit.,* p. 231.

12. White and White, *op. cit.,* p. 51.

13. *Ibid.,* Table 5.

14. Mrs. Ellis, *The Daughters of England: Their Position in Society, Character, and Responsibilities* (1844) in *The Family Monitor* (New York, 1844), p. 35. My italics.

15. *Ibid.* pp. 38–39.

16. Patricia Thomson, *The Victorian Heroine: A Changing Ideal* (London: Oxford University Press, 1956), p. 77.

17. White and White, *op. cit.,* p. 91.

18. Anna Klumpke, *Rosa Bonheur: Sa vie, son oeuvre* (Paris, 1908), p. 311.

19. Betty Friedan, *The Feminine Mystique* (New York: Dell Publishing Co., 1963), p. 158.

20. Klumpke, *op. cit.,* p. 166.

21. Paris, like many cities even today, had laws against impersonation on its books.

22. Klumpke, *op. cit.,* pp. 308–309.

23. *Ibid.,* pp. 310–311.

24. Cited in Elizabeth Fisher, "The Woman as Artist," Louise Nevelson," *Aphra,* 1 (Spring 1970): p. 32.

DISCUSSION QUESTIONS

1. Do you agree with Nochlin's criticisms of some attempts by feminists to answer the question, "Why are there no great women artists?" Why or why not?

2. How would you compare Hartsock's analysis of how people understand gender relations (Part V, reading 60) with Nochlin's analysis of gender relations in the history of art?

3. This essay was published in 1971. Do you think things have changed substantially since then for women in the arts? Why or why not?

4. Are there typical features in artworks of any particular genre that can be justifiably identified as "feminine" or "masculine"? Why or why not? Without knowing the identity of the artist, can you ever tell if a particular artistic creation was done by a male or female? Use examples to explain.

Credits

READING 1: Plato, "The Apology," translated by F. M. Stawell in *Socratic Discourses by Plato and Xenophon,* London: J. M. Dent and Sons, Ltd., 1910, pp. 321–349. By permission of Everyman's Library, David Campbell Publishers Ltd.

READING 2: Boethius, *The Consolation of Philosophy,* translated by Richard Green, pp. 42–74. Copyright © 1962 Prentice-Hall, Inc. Reprinted by permission of the publisher.

READING 3: Sarvepalli Radhakrishnan and Charles Moore, eds., "General Introduction" in *A Sourcebook in Indian Philosophy,* Princeton University Press, pp. xx–xxix. Copyright © 1988 Princeton University Press. Reprinted by permission of the publisher.

READING 4: Nancy Tuana, "Epilogue" in *Woman and the History of Philosophy,* Paragon House, 1992, pp. 113–121, 133–135. Copyright © 1992 by Paragon House, St. Paul, MN. Reprinted with permission of the publisher.

READING 5: Leopoldo Zea, "The Actual Function of Philosophy in Latin America" in *Latin American Philosophy in the Twentieth Century,* Jorge J. E. Gracia, ed., Buffalo, NY: Prometheus Books, 1986, pp. 219–230. Reprinted with permission from the editor.

READING 6: Bertrand Russell, *The Problems of Philosophy,* London: Oxford University Press, 1912, pp. 153–161. Reprinted by permission of Oxford University Press.

READING 7: Tsenay Serequeberhan, "African Philosophy: The Point in Question" in *African Philosophy: The Essential Readings,* pp. 3–28, Paragon House, 1991. Reprinted with permission from the publisher.

READING 8: Satischandra Chatterjee, *The Nyaya Theory of Knowledge,* University of Calcutta Press, 1950, pp. 100–112.

READING 9: Friedrich Nietzsche, "On Truth and Lie in an Extra-Moral Sense" in *The Portable Nietzsche,* edited and translated by Walter Kaufmann, The Viking Press, 1968, pp. 42–47. Copyright © 1954 by The Viking Press, renewed © 1982 by Viking Penguin Inc. Used by permission of Viking Penguin, a division of Penguin Putnam Inc.

READING 11: Mao Zedong, "On Practice" in *Mao Tse-Tung: Selected Works,* Volume I, 1926–1936, International Publishers Co., Inc., 1954, pp. 282–297, 336. Reprinted with permission from the publisher.

READING 12: René Descartes, from *Meditations* (I and II) in *The Philosophical Works of Descartes,* edited and translated by Elizabeth S. Haldane and G.R.T. Ross, NY: Cambridge University Press, 1975, pp. 144–157. Used with permission of the publisher.

READING 14: Ernest Nagel, from *The Structure of Science,* Hackett Publishing Company, 1961, pp. 1–14. Reprinted by permission from Hackett Publishing Company. All rights reserved.

READING 15: John (Fire) Lame Deer and Richard Erdoes, *Lame Deer Seeker of Visions,* Simon and Schuster, Inc., 1972, pp. 11–16, 154–157. Copyright © 1972 John (Fire) Lame Deer and Richard Erdoes. Used with permission of the publisher.

READING 16: D. T. Suzuki, "The Meaning of Satori" in *The Field of Zen,* Harper and Row Publishers, 1970. Copyright © 1970 Buddhist Society. Used with permission.

READING 17: Uma Narayan, "The Project of Feminist Epistemology: Perspectives from a Nonwestern Feminist" from *Gender/Body/Knowledge,* edited by Alison M. Jaggar and Susan R. Bordo, Rutgers University Press, 1989, pp. 256–269. Copyright © 1989 by Rutgers, The State University. Reprinted by permission of Rutgers University Press.

READING 20: Lorraine Code, "Experience, Knowledge and Responsibility" in *Feminist Perspectives in Philosophy,* edited by Morwenna Griffiths and Margaret Whitford, Indiana University Press, pp. 187–204. Used with permission of the publisher.

READING 24: Sarvepalli Radhakrishnan and Charles Moore, eds., *A Sourcebook in Indian Philosophy.* Copyright © 1975 by Princeton University Press. Reprinted by permission of Princeton University Press.

READING 25: Thomas W. Overholt and J. Baird Callicott from *Clothed-in-Fur and Other Tales: An Introduction to an Ojibwa Worldview,* University Press of America, Inc., 1982, pp. xi–xii, 140–150, 160–161. Used with permission of the publisher.

READING 27: Kwame Gyekye, "The Concept of a Person" in *An Essay on African Philosophical Thought: The Akan Conceptual Scheme,* Cambridge University Press, 1987, pp. 85–103. Reprinted with permission from the author.

READING 28: Gilbert Ryle, from *The Concept of Mind,* Barnes and Noble, Inc., 1949, pp. 11–24.

READING 29: Sri Aurobindo, from *The Problem of Rebirth,* Pondicherry: Sri Aurobindo Ashram, 1952, pp. 20–27. Reprinted with permission from Sri Aurobindo Ashram Trust.

READING 30: B. F. Skinner, from *Walden Two: Freedom and the Science of Human Behavior,* Prentice-Hall, 1976, pp. 240–248, originally published by Macmillan Publishing Co., 1948. Courtesy of the B. F. Skinner Foundation.

READING 31: Walter T. Stace, *Religion and the Modern Mind,* pp. 248–258. Copyright © 1952 by Walter T. Stace. Reprinted by permission of HarperCollins Publishers, Inc.

READING 32: Jean-Paul Sartre, "Existentialism and Freedom," translated by Philip Mairet, from *Existentialism and Humanism,* London: Methuen and Co., Ltd., 1946. Used with permission of the publisher.

READING 33: From *Bhagavad-Gītā: Song of God,* translated by Swami Prabhavananda and Christopher Isherwood, Hollywood, CA: The Vedanta Society of Southern California, 1944, 1951, pp. 70–78, 97–105. Used with permission from the Vedanta Society of Southern California.

READING 34: Martin Buber, *I and Thou,* translated by Walter Kaufmann, Scribner, 1970. Copyright © 1970 by Charles Scribner's Sons. Reprinted with the permission of Scribner, a Division of Simon & Schuster.

READING 36: Thomas Aquinas, from *The Basic Writings of St. Thomas Aquinas,* Volume I, edited by Anton C. Pegis, 1997. Reprinted by permission of Hackett Publishing Company. All rights reserved.

READING 39: Carol P. Christ, "Why Women Need the Goddess: Phenomenological, Psychological, and Political Reflections." Used with permission of the author.

ical Quarterly, vol. 24, no. 3, September 1984, pp. 237–244. Reprinted by permission of the publisher.

READING 78: Linda Nochlin, "Why Are There No Great Women Artists?" from *Women in Sexist Society* by Vivian Gornick and Barbara K. Moran. Copyright © 1971 by Basic Books, Inc. Reprinted by permission of Basic Books, a member of Perseus Books Group, LLC.